Time Period	Important Philosophers	Political, Cultural, and Scientific Events of Period
A.D. 1600	Francis Bacon (1561–1626) Thomas Hobbes (1588–1679) Rene Descartes (1596–1650) Anne Conway (1631–1679) Baruch Spinoza (1632–1677) Nicolas de Malebranche (1638–1715) Gottfried Leibniz (1646–1716) William Paley (1743–1805)	Shakespeare (1564–1616) writes plays and poems Kepler (1571–1630) discovers laws of planetary motion Galileo (1564–1642) condemned by Inquisition (1633) Age of Enlightenment begins in Europe (c. 1641) Rembrandt (1606–1669) and Velasquez (1599–1660) paint Manchu Dynasty (1644–1911) rules in China Leibniz and Newton invent the calculus (c. 1670's) Newton (1642–1727) publishes *Principia* (1687)
A.D. 1700	John Locke (1632–1704) George Berkeley (1685–1753) Voltaire (1694–1778) David Hume (1711–1776) Immanuel Kant (1724–1804) Paul d'Holbach (1723–1789) Edmund Burke (1729–1797) Jeremy Bentham (1748–1832) Mary Wollstonecraft (1759–1797) William Paley (1743–1805)	Swift (1667–1745) publishes *Gulliver's Travels* (1726) Bach (1685–1750), Handel (1685–1759) compose music American Revolution (1775–1783) Smith (1723–1790) writes *Wealth of Nations* (1776) Industrial Revolution in England (1780) French Revolution (1789–1791) Mozart (1756–1791), Beethoven (1770–1827) compose symphonies Laplace (1749–1827) writes *Celestial Mechanics* (1799) Neoclassic art of David (1748–1825) and Ingres (1780–1867)
A.D. 1800	William Whewell (1794–1866) J. G. Fichte (1762–1814) F. Schleiermacher (1768–1834) G. W. F. Hegel (1770–1831) James Mill (1773–1835) Arthur Schopenhauer (1788–1860)	Jefferson (1743–1836) is president of U.S. (1801–1809) Friedrich (1774–1840), Blake (1757–1827) paint romantic art Goethe (1749–1832) publishes *Faust* (1808) Napoleon defeated at Waterloo (1815) Revolutions in Paris, Vienna, Venice, Berlin (1848) Mendel (1822–1884) publishes laws of heredity (1866)
A.D. 1850	Ludwig Feuerbach (1804–1872) John Stuart Mill (1806–1873) Soren Kierkegaard (1813–1855) Henry David Thoreau (1817–1862) Karl Marx (1818–1883) Friedrich Engels (1820–1895) Herbert Spencer (1820–1903)	Darwin (1809–1882) writes *Origin of Species* (1859) American Civil War (1861–1865) Lincoln issues Emancipation Proclamation (1863) Tolstoy (1828–1910) publishes *War and Peace* (1863) Huxley (1825–1895) publishes *Man's Place in Nature* (1864) Brahms (1833–1897) writes his symphonies Impressionist art of Manet (1832–1883), Degas (1834–1917), Monet (1840–1926), Renoir (1841–1919), Cassatt (1844–1926) Friedrich Nietzsche (1844–1900)
A.D. 1900	Charles S. Peirce (1839–1914) William James (1842–1910) Francis Bradley (1846–1924) Edmund Husserl (1854–1938) Henri Bergson (1859–1941) John Dewey (1859–1952) J. McTaggart (1866–1925) Mahatma Gandhi (1869–1948)	Freud (1856–1939) publishes *The Interpretation of Dreams* (1900) Wright brothers fly first successful airplane (1903) Einstein (1879–1955) discovers special relativity (1905) and general relativity (1915) Quantum theory developed by Planck (1858–1947), Heisenberg, (1901–1976), Bohr (1885–1962) World War I (1914–1917) October Revolution in Russia begins communist rule (1917)

PHILOSOPHY

A Text with Readings

TWELFTH EDITION

MANUEL VELASQUEZ

The Charles Dirksen Professor

Santa Clara University

Australia • Brazil • Japan • Korea • Mexico • Singapore • Spain • United Kingdom • United States

Philosophy: A Text with Readings, Twelfth Edition

Manuel Velasquez

Publisher: Clark Baxter

Senior Sponsoring Editor: Joann Kozyrev

Senior Development Editor: Sue Gleason Wade

Assistant Editor: Joshua Duncan

Editorial Assistant: Marri Straton

Content Project Manager: Jill Quinn

Art Director: Riezebos Holzbaur/Andrei Pasternak

Manufacturing Planner: Sandee Milewski

Rights Acquisition Specialist: Mandy Groszko

Production Service: S4Carlisle Publishing Services

Text and Cover Designer: Riezebos Holzbaur/Tim Heraldo

Cover Image: © Nikada

Compositor: S4Carlisle Publishing Services

© 2014, 2011, 2008 Wadsworth, Cengage Learning

ALL RIGHTS RESERVED. No part of this work covered by the copyright herein may be reproduced, transmitted, stored or used in any form or by any means graphic, electronic, or mechanical, including but not limited to photocopying, recording, scanning, digitizing, taping, Web distribution, information networks, or information storage and retrieval systems, except as permitted under Section 107 or 108 of the 1976 United States Copyright Act, without the prior written permission of the publisher.

For product information and technology assistance, contact us at **Cengage Learning Customer & Sales Support, 1-800-354-9706**

For permission to use material from this text or product, submit all requests online at **www.cengage.com/permissions.** Further permissions questions can be emailed to **permissionrequest@cengage.com.**

Library of Congress Control Number: 2012938983

ISBN-13: 978-1-133-93342-7
ISBN-10: 1-133-93342-4

Paper Edition:

ISBN-13: 978-1-133-61210-0
ISBN-10: 1-133-61210-5

Wadsworth
20 Channel Center Street
Boston, MA 02210
USA

Cengage Learning is a leading provider of customized learning solutions with office locations around the globe, including Singapore, the United Kingdom, Australia, Mexico, Brazil and Japan. Locate your local office at **international.cengage.com/region**

Cengage Learning products are represented in Canada by Nelson Education, Ltd.

For your course and learning solutions, visit **www.cengage.com.**

Purchase any of our products at your local college store or at our preferred online store www.cengagebrain.com.

Instructors: Please visit **login.cengage.com** and log in to access instructor-specific resources.

Printed in Canada
1 2 3 4 5 6 7 16 15 14 13 12

For Anita, Rebecca, and Lydia

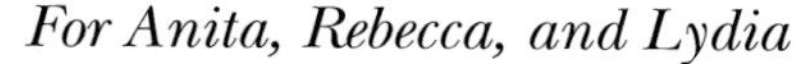

Contents

Preface *xv*

CHAPTER 1 The Nature of Philosophy 3

1.1 WHAT IS PHILOSOPHY? 4

Plato's Myth of the Cave 4

Plato's Parable and "Doing" Philosophy 6

THINKING CRITICALLY: Assumptions and Critical Thinking 8

The Diversity of Philosophy 9

THINKING CRITICALLY: Reasoning 10

1.2 THE TRADITIONAL DIVISIONS OF PHILOSOPHY 11

Epistemology: The Study of Knowledge 11

THINKING CRITICALLY: Avoiding Vague and Ambiguous Claims 12

Metaphysics: The Study of Reality or Existence 13

PHILOSOPHY AND LIFE: Philosophical Issues 15

THINKING CRITICALLY: Supporting Claims with Reasons and Arguments 15

Ethics: The Study of Values 16

Other Philosophical Inquiries 18

1.3 A PHILOSOPHER IN ACTION: SOCRATES 19

Euthyphro: Do We Know What Holiness Is? 20

THINKING CRITICALLY: Evaluating Arguments 24

The Republic: Is Justice What Benefits the Powerful? 24

The Apology: Socrates' Trial 27

Crito: Do We Have an Obligation to Obey the Law? 29

THINKING CRITICALLY: Identifying Premises, Conclusions, and Assumptions 31

PHILOSOPHY AND LIFE: Breaking the Law for the Sake of Justice 32

1.4 THE VALUE OF PHILOSOPHY 35

Achieving Freedom 35

Building Your View of Life 36

Cultivating Awareness 37

PHILOSOPHY AND LIFE: Albert Ellis and Rational Emotive Behavior Therapy 37

Learning to Think Critically 38

Does Philosophy Have a Male Bias? 38

The Theme of This Text 39

CHAPTER SUMMARY 40

1.5 READING 42
Voltaire's, "Story of a Good Brahman" 42
1.6 HISTORICAL SHOWCASE: THE FIRST PHILOSOPHERS 43
Pre-Socratic Western Philosophers 43
Eastern Philosophers 45

CHAPTER 2 Human Nature 49

2.1 WHY DOES YOUR VIEW OF HUMAN NATURE MATTER? 50
THINKING CRITICALLY: Deductive Arguments, Validity, and Soundness 52
The Importance of Understanding Human Nature 54
PHILOSOPHY AND LIFE: Is Selflessness Real? 55
2.2 WHAT IS HUMAN NATURE? 56
The Rationalistic Version of the Traditional Western View of Human Nature 57
PHILOSOPHY AND LIFE: Is Human Nature Irrational? 59
The Judeo-Christian Version of the Traditional Western View of Human Nature 62
The Darwinian Challenge 65
THINKING CRITICALLY: Inference to the Best Explanation 71
The Existentialist Challenge 74
The Feminist Challenge 77
2.3 THE MIND–BODY PROBLEM: HOW DO MIND AND BODY RELATE? 82
The Dualist View of Human Nature 83
THINKING CRITICALLY: EVALUATING AN ARGUMENT'S PREMISES 85
The Materialist View of Human Nature 87
The Mind/Brain Identity Theory of Human Nature 88
The Behaviorist View of Human Nature 90
The Functionalist View of Human Nature 91
Eliminative Materialism 94
The New Dualism 95
2.4 IS THERE AN ENDURING SELF? 96
The Soul as the Enduring Self 100
Memory as the Source of the Enduring Self 101
The No-Self View 102
2.5 ARE WE INDEPENDENT AND SELF-SUFFICIENT INDIVIDUALS? 106
The Atomistic Self 107
The Relational Self 109
Power and Hegel's View 111
Culture and Self-Identity 112
Search for the Real Self 113
CHAPTER SUMMARY 115

2.6 READINGS 117

Graham Greene, "The End of the Party" 118

Garrett I. DeWeese and J. P. Moreland, "The Self and Substance Dualism" 122

John R. Searle, "The Mind-Body Problem" 123

2.7 HISTORICAL SHOWCASE: PLATO, ARISTOTLE, AND CONFUCIUS 126

Plato 126

Aristotle 133

Confucius 138

CHAPTER 3 Reality and Being 143

3.1 WHAT IS REAL? 144

PHILOSOPHY AND LIFE: The Experience Machine, or Does Reality Matter? 146

Metaphysical Questions of Reality 146

The Search for Reality 147

3.2 REALITY: MATERIAL OR NONMATERIAL? 148

Materialism: Reality as Matter 148

Objections to Materialism 150

PHILOSOPHY AND LIFE: The Neutrino 153

Idealism: Reality as Nonmatter 154

PHILOSOPHY AND LIFE: Our Knowledge of the World 157

THINKING CRITICALLY: Conditional and Disjunctive Arguments 160

Objections to Idealism 163

3.3 REALITY IN PRAGMATISM 166

Pragmatism's Approach to Philosophy 166

The Pragmatic Method 167

Objections to Pragmatism 170

3.4 REALITY AND LOGICAL POSITIVISM 171

PHILOSOPHY AND LIFE: Parallel Universes 173

THINKING CRITICALLY: Categorical Syllogism Arguments 175

Objections to Logical Positivism 178

3.5 ANTIREALISM: THE HEIR OF PRAGMATISM AND IDEALISM 179

Proponents of Antirealism 181

Objections to Antirealism 183

3.6 ENCOUNTERING BEING: REALITY IN PHENOMENOLOGY AND EXISTENTIALISM 186

Phenomenology 187

Existentialism 194

Objections to Phenomenology and Existentialism 199

3.7 IS FREEDOM REAL? 202
Determinism 204
Libertarianism 206
PHILOSOPHY AND LIFE: Does Our Brain Make Our Decisions Before We Consciously Make Them? 208
Compatibilism 209

3.8 IS TIME REAL? 212
Time and Human Life 212
Augustine: Only the Present Moment Is Real 213
McTaggart: Subjective Time Is Not Real 215
Kant: Time Is a Mental Construct 216
Bergson: Only Subjective Time Is Real 218
CHAPTER SUMMARY 220

3.9 READINGS 222
Russell Maloney, "A Toast to Captain Jerk" 223
Robert Nozick, "Being More Real" 225

3.10 HISTORICAL SHOWCASE: HOBBES AND BERKELEY 226
Hobbes 227
Berkeley 231

CHAPTER 4 Philosophy, Religion, and God 237

4.1 THE SIGNIFICANCE OF RELIGION 238
Defining Religion 239
Religious Belief, Religious Experience, and Theology 240

4.2 DOES GOD EXIST? 241
The Ontological Argument 242
The Cosmological Argument 246
PHILOSOPHY AND LIFE: Religion and Science 250
The Design Argument 251
THINKING CRITICALLY: Arguments by Analogy 253

4.3 ATHEISM, AGNOSTICISM, AND THE PROBLEM OF EVIL 260
Atheism 260
PHILOSOPHY AND LIFE: God's Omniscience and Free Will 266
Agnosticism 267
THINKING CRITICALLY: Formal and Informal Fallacies 268

4.4 TRADITIONAL RELIGIOUS BELIEF AND EXPERIENCE 272
Religious Belief 272
"The Will to Believe" 272
Personal Experience of the Divine 275

4.5 NONTRADITIONAL RELIGIOUS EXPERIENCE 279
Radical Theology 279
Feminist Theology 283
Eastern Religious Traditions 286
CHAPTER SUMMARY 290

4.6 READINGS 291
Fyodor Dostoevsky, "Excerpt from *The Brothers Karamazov*" 292
William P. Alston, "The Inductive Argument from Evil and the Human Cognitive Condition" 294

4.7 HISTORICAL SHOWCASE: AQUINAS, DESCARTES, AND CONWAY 297
Aquinas 297
Descartes 302
Anne Conway 306

CHAPTER 5 The Sources of Knowledge 313

5.1 WHY IS KNOWLEDGE A PROBLEM? 314
Acquiring Reliable Knowledge: Reason and the Senses 317
The Place of Memory 318

5.2 IS REASON THE SOURCE OF OUR KNOWLEDGE? 319
Descartes: Doubt and Reason 321
Innate Ideas 326
PHILOSOPHY AND LIFE: Innate Ideas? 330

5.3 CAN THE SENSES ACCOUNT FOR ALL OUR KNOWLEDGE? 333
Locke and Empiricism 334
PHILOSOPHY AND LIFE: Science and the Attempt to Observe Reality 337
Berkeley and Subjectivism 340
Hume and Skepticism 343
THINKING CRITICALLY: Inductive Generalizations 346

5.4 KANT: DOES THE KNOWING MIND SHAPE THE WORLD? 351
Hume's Challenge 352
The Basic Issue 352
Space, Time, and Mathematics 353
PHILOSOPHY AND LIFE: Knowledge and Gestalt Psychology 354
Causality and the Unity of the Mind 356
Romantic Philosophers 359
Constructivist Theories and Recovered Memories 361

5.5 DOES SCIENCE GIVE US KNOWLEDGE? 363
Inductive Reasoning and Simplicity 364
PHILOSOPHY AND LIFE: Society and Truth 366
The Hypothetical Method and Falsifiability 367

Paradigms and Revolutions in Science 369
THINKING CRITICALLY: Distinguishing Science from Pseudoscience 372
Is the Theory of Recovered Memories Science or Pseudoscience? 373
CHAPTER SUMMARY 374

5.6 READINGS 376
Ambrose Bierce, "An Occurrence at Owl Creek Bridge" 377
Peter Ungera, "A Defense of Skepticism" 381
Thomas Nagel, "How Do We Know Anything?" 383

5.7 HISTORICAL SHOWCASE: HUME 385

CHAPTER 6 Truth 393

6.1 KNOWLEDGE, TRUTH, AND JUSTIFICATION 394
Knowledge as Justified True Belief 395
Justification 397

6.2 WHAT IS TRUTH? 401
Correspondence Theory 403
Coherence Theory 409
PHILOSOPHY AND LIFE: Truth and Paradox 410
PHILOSOPHY AND LIFE: Historical Facts 412
Pragmatic Theory 413
Does Truth Matter? 417
Reconciling the Theories of Truth 419
Deflating Truth 419

6.3 DOES SCIENCE GIVE US TRUTH? 421
The Instrumentalist View 423
The Realist View 424
The Conceptual Relativist View 425

6.4 CAN INTERPRETATIONS BE TRUE? 428
Symbolic Interpretation and Intention 430
Wittgenstein and the Ideal Clear Language 432
Gadamer and Prejudice 434
CHAPTER SUMMARY 436

6.5 READINGS 438
Ryunosuke Akutagawa, "In a Grove" 438
Hugh Tomlinson, "After Truth: Post-Modernism and the Rhetoric of Science" 442
John Searle, "Reality and Truth" 443

6.6 HISTORICAL SHOWCASE: KANT 444

CHAPTER 7 Ethics 455

7.1 WHAT IS ETHICS? 456

7.2 IS ETHICS RELATIVE? 458

7.3 DO CONSEQUENCES MAKE AN ACTION RIGHT? 463
Ethical Egoism 465
Utilitarianism 467
Some Implications of Utilitarianism 472

7.4 DO RULES DEFINE MORALITY? 474
Divine Command Theory 474
PHILOSOPHY AND LIFE: Embryonic Stem Cell Research 477
Implications of Divine Command Ethics 480
Kant's Categorical Imperative 483
Buddhist Ethics 491

7.5 IS ETHICS BASED ON CHARACTER? 495
Aristotle's Theory of Virtue 495
Love and Friendship 499
Male and Female Ethics? 503
Conclusions 506

7.6 CAN ETHICS RESOLVE MORAL QUANDARIES? 508
Abortion 509
Euthanasia 514
THINKING CRITICALLY: Moral Reasoning 518
CHAPTER SUMMARY 521

7.7 READINGS 522
Fyodor Dostoyevsky, "The Heavenly Christmas Tree" 522
Peter Singer, "Famine, Affluence, and Morality" 524

7.8 HISTORICAL SHOWCASE: NIETZSCHE AND WOLLSTONECRAFT 526
Nietzsche 526
Wollstonecraft 531

CHAPTER 8 Social and Political Philosophy 537

8.1 WHAT IS SOCIAL AND POLITICAL PHILOSOPHY? 538

8.2 WHAT JUSTIFIES THE STATE? 540
Hobbes and the War of All against All 541
Locke and Natural Moral Laws 543
Rousseau and the General Will 545
Contemporary Social Contract: Rawls 547
The Communitarian Critique 549
Social Contract and Women 553

8.3 WHAT IS JUSTICE? 558
PHILOSOPHY AND LIFE: The Purpose of Business 559
Justice as Merit 561
Justice as Equality 563
Justice as Social Utility 565
Justice Based on Need and Ability 567
Justice Based on Liberty 569
PHILOSOPHY AND LIFE: Welfare 570

8.4 LIMITS ON THE STATE 574
Unjust Laws and Civil Disobedience 575
Freedom 579
Human Rights 582
War and Terrorism 586
PHILOSOPHY AND LIFE: Society and the Bomb 595
CHAPTER SUMMARY 598

8.5 READINGS 600
Erich Maria Remarque, From "*All Quiet on the Western Front*" 600
Bertrand Russell, "The Ethics of War" 602

8.6 HISTORICAL SHOWCASE: MARX AND RAWLS 605
Marx 605
Rawls 611

CHAPTER 9 Postscript: The Meaning of Life 617

9.1 DOES LIFE HAVE MEANING? 618
What Does the Question Mean? 620

9.2 THE THEISTIC RESPONSE TO MEANING 621

9.3 MEANING AND HUMAN PROGRESS 623

9.4 THE NIHILIST REJECTION OF MEANING 626

9.5 MEANING AS A SELF-CHOSEN COMMITMENT 627
CHAPTER SUMMARY 631

Glossary *633*
Index *637*

Preface

Heraclitus, an early Greek philosopher, is reputed to have declared, *"Panta chorei!"* which is Greek for "Everything changes!" Heraclitus' words are certainly true of our social world today. And it is also true of the world of textbooks. So although *Philosophy: A Text with Readings* continues to excite readers about philosophy, changes in philosophy and in the world we inhabit necessitate revising the text. In my revisions, I tried to retain what users have said they like best about this book: that it provides depth and rigor yet is easy to read, fun to use, and manages to cover all the traditional issues with a unique combination of attention to the history of philosophy, regard for interesting contemporary concerns, and substantial selections from classical and contemporary texts. I have worked hard to explain the difficult concepts and texts of philosophy in a way that is technically rigorous and accurate, yet uses language and style that make it easy for a beginning college student with modest reading skills to understand them. I have also worked hard at making philosophy interesting and relevant to contemporary undergraduates by showing how it is directly related to their real-life concerns and preoccupations. In addition, by introducing a new series of critical thinking modules, I have tried to provide the tools that will enable students to develop their thinking and reasoning skills.

I should emphasize what a quick glance at the table of contents will confirm: this text is designed to cover more than most instructors would want to cover in a single course. Because the coverage is broad, the instructor can select those topics that he or she believes are most important and is not limited by the choice of topics that someone else might make. To make it easier for an instructor to choose what his or her course will cover, the chapters are largely independent of one another (with the exception of the new critical thinking modules) so that reading a later chapter will not require reading an earlier one. Moreover, the materials within each chapter are arranged so that the most basic or fundamental topics are at the beginning of the chapter, while later sections in the chapter address aspects of the topic that are less fundamental but that probe more deeply or more broadly into the topic. This arrangement gives the instructor the option of either having students study only the basic issues in a chapter by assigning only the early sections or pursuing the subject matter of the chapter more in depth by also assigning the later sections. Some instructors may want to cover the basics in class, and then assign students (or groups of students) the later sections as special projects. There are thus many different ways of teaching the materials in the book and many different courses that can be put together from these materials.

Changes in the Twelfth Edition

The most important change in this edition is one that affects almost all of the chapters. The text now includes an extended treatment of critical thinking that is spread out over sixteen new modules designed to develop the reader's critical thinking skills. These modules are entitled "Thinking Critically." Each "Thinking Critically" module not only teaches important reasoning skills, but also helps the reader apply these skills to the philosophical issues discussed in the text. Beginning with the introduction to critical thinking modules in Chapter 1, the aim of these sections is to teach students, step by step, how to critically evaluate their own philosophical thinking and reasoning, as well as the philosophical thoughts and arguments of others. Because critical thinking skills are so important to doing philosophy, most of the "Thinking Critically" modules occur in the earlier chapters of the book (most are in Chapters 1–4). Each "Thinking Critically" module is keyed with a special icon in the chapter-opening Learning Objectives and in the Chapter Summary. The ninth edition's "A Look at Logic" module is also still available separately for custom editions, although most of its content is now covered in the "Thinking Critically" modules.

The "Historical Showcases" have been moved to the very end of each chapter to facilitate briefer custom editions for instructors who want to exclude this coverage.

Seven new end-of-chapter Readings, some from works of fiction, have been added to the book, while numerous new excerpts from classical and contemporary texts have been added within the chapters. Blue icons in the margins indicate when the full texts from which excerpts have been taken are available online in Philosophy CourseMate, an online resource that contains content specific to the text as well as additional resources for students taking an Introduction to Philosophy course. Instructors who wish to do so can now package this text together with Philosophy CourseMate.

Aplia™ for Introduction to Philosophy is now also available with this text. Aplia™ will excite and engage your students with philosophy as never before.

In addition to numerous minor revisions, more substantive changes in specific chapters are as follows:

Chapter 1

- Six new "Thinking Critically" modules appear in this chapter (in sections 1.1, 1.2, 1.3, and 1.4); these introduce the topic of critical thinking, explain its importance in philosophy, and introduce the elements of an argument.
- Section 1.4 on the value of philosophy has been streamlined and revised.

Chapter 2

- Three new "Thinking Critically" sections have been added. These introduce the notions of deductive and inductive arguments, and validity and soundness (in section 2.1), explain what an inference to the best explanation is (in section 2.2), and show how the premises of an argument can be evaluated (in section 2.3).
- The discussion of Schlick in section 2.1 has been replaced with a discussion of the same issue (psychological egoism) by Mercer.
- The discussion of Darwin in section 2.2 now covers his own arguments for his theory.
- The discussions of eliminative materialism and property dualism in section 2.3 have been revised and expanded for greater clarity.
- New reading: Graham Greene, "The End of the Party."

Chapter 3

- Two new "Thinking Critically" sections have been added: one on evaluating the validity of conditional and disjunctive arguments (in section 3.2), and one on evaluating the validity of categorical syllogisms (in section 3.4).
- The discussions of pragmatism in section 3.3 have been revised, as well as the discussions of phenomenology and existentialism in section 3.6.

Chapter 4

- The chapter has been renamed "Philosophy, Religion, and God" to better indicate its contents.
- Two new "Thinking Critically" sections have been added: one on arguments by analogy (in section 4.2), and one on formal and informal fallacies (section 4.3).
- In section 4.2, the discussions of the ontological argument and the design argument have been revised and expanded, while the discussions of both Newton and the "Big Bang" theory have been expanded to highlight the changing relation between science and religion.
- The discussion of atheism in section 4.3 has been revised, and the discussion of the problem

of evil has been expanded to include discussions of its logical and evidential forms and the free-will defense.

- The discussion of religious experience in section 4.4 has been substantially expanded and revised.
- The discussion of the Hindu notions of Brahman and Atman in section 4.5 has been completely revised.
- New readings: Fyodor Dostoevsky, excerpt from *The Brothers Karamazov*, and William Alston, "The Inductive Argument from Evil and the Human Cognitive Condition."

Chapter 5

- Two new "Thinking Critically" sections have been added: one on inductive generalizations in section 5.3, and one on distinguishing science from pseudoscience in section 5.5.
- The discussion of Descartes in section 5.2 has been expanded and revised.
- The discussions of both Locke and Berkeley in section 5.3 have been revised.
- The treatment of Kant's transcendental idealism has been expanded.

Chapter 6

- The discussion of the correspondence theory of truth in section 6.2 has been simplified and shortened.
- New Readings: Ryunosuke Akutagawa, "In a Grove," and John R. Searle, "Reality and Truth."

Chapter 7

- A new "Thinking Critically" module on moral reasoning has been added to section 7.6.
- The discussion of moral relativism in section 7.2 has been substantially revised.
- The discussions of utilitarianism and of egoism in section 7.3 have also been substantially revised.
- In section 7.4, a discussion of the *Euthyphro* problem has been added, and the discussions of Kant and of Buddhist ethics have been revised.
- The discussion of feminist ethics in section 7.5 has been revised and streamlined.
- In section 7.6, the discussion of Dewey has been revised, and new excerpts from Mary Anne Warren and Don Marquis have been added to the discussion of abortion.
- New reading: Fyodor Dostoyevsky, "The Heavenly Christmas Tree."

Chapter 8

- Statistics on poverty in section 8.1 have been updated.
- The discussion of Nozick in section 8.3 has been expanded.
- The discussion of just war theory in section 8.4 has been updated to reflect current controversies over interrogation techniques involving torture.
- New reading: Bertrand Russell, "The Ethics of War."

Chapter 9

- The section entitled "What Is Art?" that was formerly part of this chapter is now available as a separate module, and instructors who wish to use it may have it custom-published with the text.

Organization

Self-discovery and autonomy remain the central notions around which this edition is organized (although these notions are critically discussed in Chapter 2). Each chapter repeatedly returns to these notions and links the materials discussed to the reader's growth in self-knowledge and intellectual autonomy. The ultimate aim of the text is to empower and encourage self-discovery and autonomy in the reader, in part by developing his or her critical thinking skills.

Although the text is organized by topics, the chapters have been arranged in a roughly historical order. The book opens with an introductory chapter on the nature of philosophy that focuses on Socrates as the exemplar of philosophy and includes substantial selections from the Socratic dialogues. Because of the book's focus on the self and the intrinsic importance of the topic, and because human nature was an important concern from the earliest time of philosophy, I turn immediately in Chapter 2 to the discussion of human nature, a discussion that raises several issues more fully treated in later chapters. Then, because Chapter 2 raises many metaphysical and religious issues, I turn to metaphysical issues in Chapter 3 and then to discussions of God and religion in Chapter 4. These issues, of course, were of passionate concern during the medieval and early modern periods of philosophy. Chapters 5 and 6 focus on questions of epistemology, interest in which historically followed the medieval and early modern interest in metaphysical issues. Chapters 7 and 8 are devoted respectively to ethics and social and political philosophy, topics that have preoccupied many philosophers during the late modern and contemporary periods. Chapter 9 focuses on the meaning of life, an issue that is particularly important for many of us today.

Yet no historical period has a monopoly on any of these topics. Consequently, each chapter moves back and forth from classic historical discussions of issues to contemporary discussions of the same or related issues. The chapter on metaphysics, for example, moves from the early modern controversy between materialism and idealism to current discussions of antirealism, some of which hark back to idealism.

Special Features

This text is unique in many ways and includes the following special features:

"Historical Showcases." Substantial summaries of the life and thought of major philosophers, including female and non-Western philosophers, are placed at the end of each chapter. These historical discussions feature large selections from the works of philosophers who have addressed the issues treated in the chapter. Arranged in chronological order, the "Historical Showcases" provide a clear and readable overview of the history of philosophy and enable students to see philosophy as a "great conversation" across centuries.

Readings by Philosophers. Near the end of each chapter are highly accessible readings examining a philosophical question raised in the text. These questions are as diverse as "Does the existence of evil prove God does not exist?" and "Is war morally justified?"

Literature Readings. At the end of many chapters is a short literature selection that addresses the issues discussed in the chapter. These readings provide a friendly entry into philosophy for readers who are unaccustomed to traditional philosophical style.

"Thinking Critically" Modules. A sequence of sixteen modules entitled "Thinking Critically," designed to develop the critical thinking and reasoning skills of the reader, is integrated into the text.

Marginal "Critical Thinking" Boxes. These boxes help the reader identify and criticize the underlying assumptions on which the arguments in the text depend. Several "Critical Thinking" boxes relate directly to the new "Thinking Critically" modules, described earlier.

Extended Selections from Primary Sources. Primary source material not only is included in all the "Historical Showcases" but also is liberally introduced in the main text, where it is always carefully explained. To make these materials accessible to beginning undergraduates, new and simplified translations of several texts (by Plato, Aristotle, Aquinas, and others) have been prepared, and several standard translations (such as Max Mueller's translation of Kant) have been simplified and edited.

Learning Objectives. The first page of each chapter outlines the chapter contents and describes the pedagogical objectives of each section of the chapter.

"Philosophy and Life" Boxes. These inserts throughout the text show the impact of philosophy on everyday life or its connections to current issues such as medical dilemmas, sociobiology, psychology, and science. Each box ends with a set of questions designed to spark further thought on the subject.

Marginal "Quick Reviews." These summaries, which appear alongside the text they summarize, help readers identify the main arguments of the chapter and give them an easy way to review the materials they have read.

Marginal References to CourseMate. Marginal references to primary sources at CourseMate provide students with further reading beyond the covers of this book.

"Philosophy at the Movies." At the end of each section of the text is a short paragraph that summarizes a film that addresses the topics treated in that section, along with questions that link the film to those topics.

End-of-Section Questions. To encourage students to think philosophically, questions and exercises are provided at the end of every section within a chapter.

"Chapter Summary." Each chapter ends with a summary of the main points that have been covered, organized according to the chapter's main headings and learning objectives (initially laid out at the chapter opening), making them particularly helpful as an overall review.

Color Illustrations. Color photos and art reproductions are used throughout the text to provide visual illustrations of the people and ideas discussed in the text and to stimulate student interest.

Glossary of Terms. Unfamiliar philosophical terminology is explained and defined in the text and highlighted in bold. These highlighted terms are defined again in an alphabetized glossary at the end of the book for easy reference.

Historical Timeline. Inside the front and back covers is a timeline that locates each philosopher in his or her historical context.

Ancillaries

***Aplia™ for Introduction to Philosophy with Velasquez's* Philosophy**

An online interactive learning solution that improves comprehension and outcomes by increasing student effort and engagement, Aplia™ provides innovative learning materials, animations, and automatically graded assignments that have detailed, immediate explanations for every question. The organization, core content, and exercises are consistent with many Introduction to Philosophy texts, making it an ideal complement to any Introduction to Philosophy text from Cengage Learning. Aplia's user-friendly grading and performance interface lets you track both individual and class-wide student performance quickly and easily, as well as generate and download detailed reports about students' work.

Telecourse The Examined Life

A series of videos for television has been produced to accompany Velasquez's *Philosophy: A Text with Readings.* Entitled *The Examined Life,* the 26 half-hour videos cover most (but not all) of the topics treated in this edition and move in sequence through each section of each chapter. Each video consists of interviews with contemporary philosophers, dramatizations, historical footage of well-known philosophers, discussions of classical philosophical texts, and visual interpretations of key philosophical concepts. Among the more than 100 philosophers specially interviewed for this video series are W. V. O. Quine, Hilary Putnam, John Searle, James Rachels, Martha Nussbaum, Marilyn Friedman, Hans Gadamer, Gary Watson, Susan Wolf, Peter Singer, Michael Sandel, Daniel Dennet, Ronald Dworkin, and many others.

CengageCompose. CengageCompose puts the power of the vast Cengage Learning library of learning content at your fingertips to create exactly the text you need. The all-new, web-based CengageCompose site lets you quickly scan contents and review materials to pick what you need for your text. Site tools let you easily assemble the modular learning units into the order you want and immediately provides you with an online copy for review. You can even choose from hundreds of vivid, art-rich, customizable, full color covers. The enrichment modules "A Look at Logic" and "What Is Art?" may be customized with any text.

CourseMate. Philosophy CourseMate contains content specific to the text as well as additional resources for students taking an Introduction to Philosophy Course. The site features quizzing, videos, note-taking guides for readings, web links, and movie screeners for each chapter's "Philosophy at the Movies." Discipline content includes guides to studying philosophy and researching and writing philosophy papers, biographies of major philosophers and excerpts from their most important works, and A Guide to Logic. Interactive activities include timelines and visual representations of fields of philosophy. This site also contains chapter-by-chapter links to a multimedia ebook that allows students to highlight text, take notes, and perform searches.

Instructor's Manual and Test Bank. This extensive manual contains many suggestions to help instructors highlight and promote further thought on philosophical issues. It also comes with a comprehensive Test Bank featuring multiple-choice, true/false, fill-in, and essay questions for each chapter, as well as ExamView® computerized testing.

WebTutor™ ToolBox. Offers basic online study tools, including learning objectives, flashcards, and practice quizzes.

Instructor's Companion Website. Upon adoption, instructors will have access to a variety of resources to aid learning and teaching, including chapter outlines and reviews, the instructor's manual, the test bank, flashcards, the glossary, web links, and chapter quizzes.

Acknowledgments

For their helpful comments and suggestions on the revision of this and earlier editions of the text, I offer sincere thanks to Cathryn Bailey, Minnesota State University; Teresa Cantrell, University of Louisville; A. Keith Carreiro, Bristol Community College atAttleboro; Michael Clifford, Mississippi State University; Christina Conroy, Morehead State University; Stephen Daniel, Texas A&M University; Janice Daurio, Moorpark College; Scott Davison, Morehead State University; Dennis Earl, Coastal Carolina University; Miguel Endara, Los Angeles Pierce College; Philip M. Fortier, Florida Community College at Jacksonville; Paul Gass, Coppin State University; Nathaniel Goldberg, Washington and Lee University; Khalil Habib, Salve Regina University; Randy Haney, Mount San Antonio College; William S. Jamison, University of Alaska Anchorage; Jonathan Katz, Kwantlen Polytechnic University; Stephen Kenzig, Cuyahoga Community College; Hye-Kyung Kim, University of Wisconsin–Green Bay; Emily Kulbacki, Green River Community College; Thi Lam, San Jacinto College Central; David Lane Mt. San Antonio College and California State University, Long Beach; Mary Latela, Sacred Heart University, Post University; Matthew Daude Laurents, Austin Community College; George J. Lujan, Mission College; Darryl Mehring, University of Colorado at Boulder; Scott Merlino, California State University Sacramento; Mark Michael, Austin Peay State University; Jonathan Miles, Quincy University; John C. Modschiedler, College of DuPage; Michael Monge, Long Beach City College; Jeremy Morris, Ohio University; Patrice Nango, Mesa Community College; Joseph Pak, Los Angeles City College; William Payne, Bellevue College; Steven Pena, San Jacinto College, Central Campus; Alexandra Perry, Bergen Community College; Michael Petri, South Coast College; James Petrik, Ohio University; Michael T. Prahl, Hawkeye Community College and University of Northern Iowa; Randy Ramal, Mt. San Antonio College; Matthew Schuh, Miami Dade College; Ted Shigematsu, Santa Ana College; Karen Sieben, Ocean County College; Paula J. Smithka, University of Southern Mississippi; Doran Smolkin, Kwantlen Polytechnic University; Tim Snead, East Los Angeles College; Mark Storey, Bellevue College; Matthew W. Turner, Francis Marion University; Frank Waters, Los Angeles Valley College; Diane S. Wilkinson, Alabama A&M; University; Holly L. Wilson, University of Louisiana at Monroe; and Paul Wilson, Texas State University–San Marcos.

PHILOSOPHY

A Text with Readings

C H A P T E R

1 The Nature of Philosophy

The feeling of wonder is the mark of the philosopher, for all philosophy has its origins in wonder.
PLATO

OUTLINE AND LEARNING OBJECTIVES

1.1 What Is Philosophy?

OBJECTIVE | When finished, you'll be able to:

- Explain how Plato's Myth of the Cave shows that philosophy is a freeing activity.
- **Show how philosophy is related to critically examining our most fundamental assumptions.**
- Explain the importance of the philosophical perspectives of women and non-Western cultures.
- **Define reasoning and its role in critical thinking.**

1.2 The Traditional Divisions of Philosophy

OBJECTIVE | When finished, you'll be able to:

- Define epistemology, metaphysics, and ethics, and explain the kinds of questions each asks.
- **Recognize and avoid vague or ambiguous claims.**
- **Identify an argument, its conclusion, and its supporting reasons.**

1.3 A Philosopher in Action: Socrates

OBJECTIVE | When finished, you'll be able to:

- Explain how Socrates' unrelenting questioning of conventional beliefs exemplifies the quest for philosophical wisdom.
- **Identify the main premises and conclusions of an argument, and its missing premises or assumptions.**

1.4 The Value of Philosophy

OBJECTIVE | When finished, you'll be able to:

- Compare Plato's and Buddha's claims that philosophical wisdom is related to freedom.

© Carmen Martínez Banús/iStockphoto.com

- **State how philosophy can help you build your outlook on life, be more mindful, and become a critical thinker.**
  - Explain the importance of examining our philosophical assumptions about men and women.

1.5 Reading: Voltaire, "Story of a Good Brahman"

1.6 Historical Showcase: The First Philosophers

1.1 What Is Philosophy?

QUICK REVIEW
Philosophy begins when we start to wonder about and question our basic beliefs.

Philosophy begins with wonder. Although many of us know very little about the jargon and history of philosophy, we have all been touched by the feeling of wonder with which philosophy begins. We wonder about why we are here; about who we really are; about whether God exists and what She or He is like; why pain, evil, sorrow, and separation exist; whether there is life after death; what true love and friendship are; what the proper balance is between serving others and serving ourselves; whether moral right and wrong are based on personal opinion or on some objective standard; and whether suicide, abortion, or euthanasia is ever justified.

This wondering and questioning begin early in our lives. Almost as soon as children learn to talk, they ask: Where did I come from? Where do people go when they die? How did the world start? Who made God? From the very beginning of our lives, we start to ask the questions that make up philosophy.

Indeed, the word *philosophy* comes from the Greek words *philein*, meaning "to love," and *sophia*, meaning "wisdom." Philosophy is thus the love of wisdom. It includes the pursuit of wisdom about what it means to be a human being, what the fundamental nature of reality is, what the sources and limits of our knowledge are, and what is good and right in our lives and in our societies.

Although philosophy begins with wonderment and questioning, it does not end there. Philosophy tries to go beyond the answers to these questions that we may have received when we were too young to seek our own answers. The goal of philosophy is to get us to answer these questions for ourselves—to make up our own minds about our self, life, knowledge, society, religion, and morality without simply depending on the authority of parents, peers, television, teachers, or society.

QUICK REVIEW
The goal of philosophy is to answer these questions for ourselves and achieve autonomy.

Many of our religious, political, and moral beliefs are beliefs that we accepted as children long before we could question them or understand the reasons behind them. Philosophy examines these beliefs. The aim is not to reject them but to learn why we hold them and to ask whether there are good reasons to continue holding them. In this way, our basic beliefs about reality and life become our own: We accept them because we have thought them through on our own, not because our parents, peers, and society have conditioned us to believe them. In this way, we gain a kind of independence and freedom, or what some modern philosophers call *autonomy*. The goal of philosophy, then, is **autonomy**: the freedom of being able to decide for yourself what you will believe in, by using your own reasoning abilities.

QUICK REVIEW
In Plato's Myth of the Cave, chained prisoners watch shadows cast on a cave wall by objects passing in front of a fire. They mistake the shadows for reality.

Plato's Myth of the Cave

Plato, one of the earliest and greatest Western philosophers, illustrated how philosophy aims at freedom with his famous parable called the Myth of the Cave. The Myth of the Cave is a story Plato tells in *The Republic*, his classic philosophical work on justice.

Here is an edited and simplified translation of the Myth of the Cave, which Plato wrote in his native Greek:

School of Athens, from the Stanza della Segnatura, 1510–1511 (fresco), Raphael (Raffaello Sanzio of Urbino) (1483–1520)/© Vatican Museums and Galleries, Vatican City, Italy, Giraudon/The Bridgeman Art Library International

Walking with his student Aristotle, Plato points upward: "And the climb upward out of the cave into the upper world is the ascent of the mind into the domain of true knowledge."

> Now let me describe the human situation in a parable about ignorance and learning. Imagine there are men living at the bottom of an underground cave whose entrance is a long passageway that rises through the ground to the light outside. They have been there since childhood and have their legs and necks chained so that they cannot move. The chains hold their heads so that they must sit facing the back wall of the cave and cannot turn their heads to look up through the entrance behind them. At some distance behind them, up nearer the entrance to the cave, a fire is burning. Objects pass in front of the fire so that they cast their shadows on the back wall where the prisoners see the moving shadows projected as if on a screen. All kinds of objects parade before the fire, including statues of men and animals whose shadows dance on the wall in front of the prisoners.
>
> Those prisoners are like ourselves. The prisoners see nothing of themselves or each other except the shadows each one's body casts on the back wall of the cave. Similarly, they see nothing of the objects behind them, except their shadows moving on the wall.
>
> Now imagine the prisoners could talk with each other. Suppose their voices echoed off the wall so that the voices seem to come from their own shadows. Then wouldn't they talk about these shadows as if the shadows were real? For the prisoners, reality would consist of nothing but the shadows.
>
> Next imagine that one prisoner was freed from his chains. Suppose he was suddenly forced to stand up and turn toward the entrance of the cave. Suppose he was forced to walk up toward the burning fire. The movement would be painful, and the glare from the fire would blind him so that he would not see clearly the real objects whose shadows he used to watch. What would he think if someone explained that everything he had seen before was an illusion, that now he was nearer to reality and that his vision was actually clearer?
>
> Imagine he was then shown the objects that had cast their shadows on the wall and he was asked to name each one—wouldn't he be at a complete loss? Wouldn't he think the shadows he saw before were truer than these objects?
>
> Next imagine he was forced to look straight at the burning light. His eyes would hurt. The pain would make him turn away and try to return to things he could see more easily. He would think that those things were more real than the new things they were showing him.
>
> But suppose that once more someone takes him and drags him up the steep and rugged ascent from the cave. Suppose someone forces him out into the full light of the sun. Won't he suffer greatly and be furious at being dragged upward? As he approaches the light his eyes will be dazzled and he won't be able to see any of this world we ourselves call reality. Little by little he will have to get used to looking at the upper world. At first he will see shadows on the ground best, next perhaps the reflections of men and other objects in water, and then maybe the objects themselves. After this, he would find it easier to gaze at the light of the moon

QUICK REVIEW
If a prisoner is freed and forced to see the fire and objects, he will have difficulty seeing and will think the shadows are more real than the objects.

QUICK REVIEW
If the prisoner were to be dragged out of the cave to the light of the sun, he would be blinded, and he would look first at shadows, then reflections, then objects, then the moon, and then the sun, which controls everything in the visible world.

and the stars in the night sky than to look at the daylight sun and its light. Last of all, he will be able to look at the sun and contemplate its nature. He will not just look at its reflection in water but will see it as it is in itself and in its own domain. He would come to the conclusion that the sun produces the seasons and the years and that it controls everything in the visible world. He will understand that it is, in a way, the cause of everything he and his fellow prisoners used to see.

Suppose the released prisoner now recalled the cave and what passed for wisdom among his fellows there. Wouldn't he be happy about his new situation and feel sorry for them? They might have been in the habit of honoring those among themselves who were quickest to make out the shadows and those who could remember which usually came before others so that they were best at predicting the course of the shadows. Would he care about such honors and glories or would he envy those who won them? Wouldn't he rather endure anything than go back to thinking and living like they did?

QUICK REVIEW
If he returns to the cave, he would be unable to see and would be laughed at.

Finally, imagine that the released prisoner was taken from the light and brought back into the cave to his old seat. His eyes would be full of darkness. Now he would have to compete in discerning the shadows with the prisoners who had never left the cave while his own eyes were still dim. Wouldn't he appear ridiculous? Men would say of him that he had gone up and had come back down with his eyesight ruined and that it was better not to even think of ascending. In fact, if they caught anyone trying to free them and lead them up to the light, they would try to kill him.

QUICK REVIEW
The climb out of the cave is the ascent of the mind to true knowledge.

I say, now, that the prison is the world we see with our eyes; the light of the fire is like the power of our sun. The climb upward out of the cave into the upper world is the ascent of the mind into the domain of true knowledge.[1]

Plato's Parable and "Doing" Philosophy

Plato wrote this intriguing parable more than two thousand years ago. The parable is important for us because it explains much about what philosophy is.

Philosophy as an Activity. First, in the parable, philosophy is the activity of journeying upward from the dark cave to the light. That is, philosophy is an activity. In this respect, it differs from other academic subjects. Unlike some other subjects, philosophy does not consist of a lot of information or theories. True, philosophers have developed many theories and views. However, philosophical theories are the *products* of philosophy, not philosophy itself. While studying philosophy, of course, you will be asked to study the theories of several important philosophers. But the point of studying them is not just to memorize them. You will study them, instead, as an aid to help you learn how to "do" philosophy. By seeing how the best philosophers have "done" philosophy and by considering their views and theories, you can better understand what philosophizing is. More importantly, you can use their insights to shed light on your own philosophical journey. It's the journey—the activity—that's important, not the products you bring back from your journey.

Philosophy Is Hard Work. Second, as Plato made clear in the parable, philosophy is a difficult activity. The journey upward is hard because it involves questioning and thinking through the most basic beliefs that each of us accepts about ourselves and the universe. This means, as the parable suggests, that your philosophical journey sometimes may lead your thinking in directions that society does not support. It may lead you toward views that others around you reject. Philosophy is also hard because it requires us to think critically, consistently, and carefully about our fundamental

1 Plato, *The Republic*, from bk. 7. This translation copyright © 1987 by Manuel Velasquez.

beliefs. We may rebel against being asked to systematically and logically question and criticize views that we have always accepted. Yet the journey out of the darkness of the cave requires intellectual discipline and the hard work of thinking things through as carefully and precisely as we can. That is why someone taking the first steps in philosophy can be helped by a teacher who, as Plato says, "drags him up the steep and rugged ascent from the cave and forces him out into the full light of the sun." The teacher does this by getting the learner to ask himself or herself the hard questions that the student is reluctant to ask on his or her own.

The Aim of Philosophy Is Freedom. Third, as Plato indicates and as we have already suggested, the aim of philosophy is freedom. Philosophy breaks the chains that imprison and hold us down, chains we often do not even know we are wearing. Like the prisoners in the cave, we uncritically accept the beliefs and opinions of those around us, and this leads us to see the world in narrow, rigid ways. Philosophy aims at breaking us free of the prejudices and unthinking assumptions we have long absorbed from those around us so we can move toward more reflective views that are truly our own.

> QUICK REVIEW
> The Myth of the Cave suggests philosophy is an activity that is difficult, has the aim of freedom, and examines the most basic assumptions of human existence.

Philosophy Examines Our Most Basic Assumptions. Fourth, Plato's parable suggests that the beliefs that philosophy examines are assumptions we have about the most basic aspects of human existence. These include many of the beliefs that we take for granted yet are not aware of even though they play a crucial role in our thinking and our actions. Like the prisoner who is led to look at the real objects whose shadows he always assumed were real, the person who does philosophy examines the most basic assumptions we make about the universe and our place in that universe. The word *philosophy* itself suggests this, for it means "the love of wisdom." To do philosophy is to love wisdom. Because wisdom is an understanding of the most fundamental aspects of human living, to love wisdom (to do philosophy) is to grapple with and seek to understand the fundamental assumptions we have about ourselves and our world.

The view of philosophy as the activity of examining our assumptions and beliefs about the most fundamental and significant aspects of our lives was perhaps most clearly expressed not by Plato, but by Perictione, a woman philosopher whom we think lived around the time of Plato:

> Humanity came into being and exists in order to contemplate the principle of the nature of the whole. The function of wisdom is to gain possession of this very thing, and to contemplate the purpose of the things that are. Geometry, of course, and arithmetic, and the other theoretical studies and sciences are also concerned with the things that are, but wisdom is concerned with the most basic of these. Wisdom is concerned with all that is, just as sight is concerned with all that is visible and hearing with all that is audible. . . . Therefore, whoever is able to analyze all the kinds of being by reference to one and the same basic principle, and, in turn, from this principle to synthesize and enumerate the different kinds, this person seems to be the wisest and most true and, moreover, to have discovered a noble height from which he will be able to catch sight of God and all the things separated from God in serial rank and order.[2]

> QUICK REVIEW
> Perictione suggests that philosophy is a search for the purpose of the universe.

Perictione is claiming that philosophy, the search for wisdom, is ultimately a search for an understanding of the ultimate truths about ourselves and our universe. It is a search for a kind of understanding that goes beyond mathematics and the other sciences. These—mathematics and the other sciences—look only at particular aspects

2 Quoted in A *History of Women Philosophers*, ed. Mary Ellen Waithe (Boston: Martinus Nijhoff, 1987), 56.

of our world. Philosophy, on the other hand, is the attempt to know the truth about the most basic assumptions we make about ourselves and the universe around us.

Philosophy examines the basic assumptions that underlie religion—for example, when it asks: Is there a God? Is there an afterlife? What truth is there in religious experience? It examines the basic assumptions that underlie science when it asks: Are the methods of science capable of uncovering what the physical universe is really like? Are scientific theories merely useful approximations, or do they impart real truths about the universe? Is there such a thing as truth? Philosophy examines the basic values that underlie our relations with one another when it asks: Is there really such a thing as justice? What, if anything, do we truly owe each other? Is true love really possible or are all our activities based on self-interest? And it examines the basic notions that underlie our views about reality when it asks: Do we really make the choices we think we make, or is everything we do determined by forces we do not control? Are the ordinary objects we experience all that reality contains, or does another kind of reality exist beyond the world that appears around us? To do philosophy, then, is to examine the basic and most important assumptions that underlie everything we do and believe. We can, in fact, define **philosophy**—the love and pursuit of wisdom—as the activity of critically and carefully examining the reasons behind our most fundamental assumptions about ourselves and the world around us.

thinking critically • Assumptions and Critical Thinking

Doing philosophy, then, will often involve trying to discover the assumptions we are making or that are being made by a philosopher we are discussing. Assumptions are beliefs of ours that we take for granted and that would have to be true if the other things we believe and say are true, or if what we do makes sense. For example, most of our religious beliefs assume that God exists. If it were not true that God exists, then most traditional religious beliefs could not be true and traditional religious activities would make little sense. In a similar way, most of us assume that what we perceive with our five senses is real. If it were not true that what we see is real, then most of our beliefs about what we know about reality would not be true. And most of us assume that what we are doing is worth doing, for otherwise it would make little sense for us to continue doing it.

QUICK REVIEW
Identifying assumptions—beliefs we take for granted and that have to be true if other beliefs are to be true and actions are to make sense—is part of critical thinking, which is essential to philosophy.

Doing this kind of thinking—trying to discover our own and others' assumptions—is an important part of what is called critical thinking. What is critical thinking? We are always thinking, of course, and we use our thinking any time we decide what we will do or what we will believe. But our thinking can be illogical, biased, close-minded, or based on mistaken assumptions, unsupported beliefs, false generalizations, and fallacious reasoning. Such thinking is bound to lead us astray. Critical thinking is the opposite of this kind of risky undisciplined thinking. **Critical thinking** is the kind of disciplined thinking we do when we base our beliefs and actions on unbiased and valid reasoning that uses well-founded evidence, that avoids false generalizations and unrecognized assumptions, and that considers opposing viewpoints.

Obviously, critical thinking is important in every aspect of life. But it is especially essential in philosophy because, as we have said, philosophy is the activity of thinking through the most basic beliefs we have accepted about ourselves and our world, and trying to form our own thoughtful views about these. If such philosophical thinking is not to go wrong, it has to be critical thinking.

Because critical thinking is so important in philosophy, this book contains several sections, like this one, entitled "Thinking Critically." Each of these sections explains some aspect of critical thinking and applies critical thinking to the philosophy discussed in the book. The aim of these sections is to enable you to learn, step by step, how to evaluate your own philosophical thinking, as well as the philosophical thinking of others. It is sometimes said that philosophy "Teaches you how to think." This is absolutely true. To learn philosophy is, at the same time, to learn to think critically.

An important part of critical thinking is identifying the assumptions we make but may not realize we make, just as the prisoners in the Myth of the Cave unthinkingly assumed the shadows they saw were real objects. As you read on through this book, we will often remind you to ask yourself what assumptions are being made by the various philosophers you encounter and whether those assumptions are true. To assist you, the "Critical Thinking" questions that appear in the margins will sometimes ask you about a particular assumption this or that philosopher may be making and what the significance of that assumption might be. An example of one of those "Critical Thinking" questions is in the margin next to this paragraph; read it and see what you think. Later we will look more closely at the process of identifying assumptions.

critical thinking

In the "Myth of the Cave," does Plato assume that it is better to know the truth and be unhappy than to be happy but ignorant? Is this assumption important for him?

The Diversity of Philosophy

Both Plato and Perictione are representatives of so-called Western philosophy. Western philosophy is a part of the cultural tradition that began in ancient Greece and then spread to the inhabitants of Europe, England, and the United States. Yet the search for wisdom has been a concern of all races and cultures. The study of Western philosophy is important for us, of course, because of its profound and direct influence on the social and political institutions that surround us and because it continues to influence and shape the thinking of each of us today. Yet other, non-Western cultural traditions have had equally profound impacts on the planet's civilizations and populations. Moreover, the nations of the world are now so interdependent that non-Western philosophical traditions influence what happens in our own society. Learning about those other philosophical traditions, therefore, is as vital as learning about the Western traditions that have directly shaped us and our society.

Consequently, although we will spend a good deal of time examining the views of Western philosophers, we cannot ignore the contributions of other cultures and races, such as those of Indian, African, and Asian philosophers. By looking at their contributions, you can expand your horizons. These perspectives provide new ways of looking at yourself and reality. By looking at worlds that are different from the one you live in, you can understand what your world is really like. More important, perhaps, you will envision ways of making it better.

We will also not ignore the contributions of a group of people who are sometimes overlooked in philosophy courses even though they make up 50 percent of the human race: women. For a number of historical reasons (including subtle and overt sexism), the major recognized contributors to Western philosophy have been males. Nevertheless, there are important women philosophers who, like Perictione, have made significant contributions to our philosophical traditions. Therefore, this book includes discussions of an approach to philosophy that tries to capture the special philosophical insights of female philosophers as well. This approach is what is generally referred to as "feminist philosophy." Feminist philosophy attempts to look at philosophical issues from the perspectives of women. The pages that follow, then, do not ignore the contributions of feminist philosophy, but instead include numerous discussions of the views of important feminist philosophers.

QUICK REVIEW
It is important to also look at philosophy from the perspective of non-Western cultures and of women.

thinking critically • Reasoning

We said earlier that philosophy "requires us to think critically" and that thinking critically requires "valid reasoning." In other words, reasoning is an essential component of philosophical thinking. Reasoning is the process of thinking by which we draw conclusions from the information, knowledge, or beliefs we have about something. We call the information from which we draw a conclusion the "reasons" or the "premises" or the "evidence" for the conclusion. We are reasoning, for example, when we use the information we have about the universe to try to figure out whether we should believe that God exists. We also use reasoning when we use our knowledge of a person to try to figure out whether we should marry that person, or when we use the information we have about a college to figure out whether we want to go to that college. In fact, reasoning pervades our whole life since we use reasoning every time we rely on the knowledge or information we have about something, to figure out what we should believe or do about it.

Although reasoning pervades our lives, it plays an especially important role in philosophy because when we philosophize we are always engaged in reasoning. In fact, so essential is reasoning in philosophy, that you could almost say that philosophizing *is* reasoning: it is reasoning about our most fundamental beliefs and assumptions.

But philosophers do not engage in just any kind of reasoning. Philosophers want their reasoning to be good reasoning. Good reasoning is reasoning in which the reasons we have for a conclusion provide sound and valid evidence for that conclusion. Consequently, a lot of the work of philosophizing involves trying to figure out or evaluate whether the reasons or evidence for a conclusion provide sound and valid support for that conclusion. Because we all use reasoning when we make important decisions in life, learning to evaluate reasoning will help you throughout all of your life. Good reasoning is not only a key to philosophy, it is also a key to success in getting whatever it is that you want out of life.

QUESTIONS

1. Ask six friends what they think philosophy is. Is there any agreement?
2. Would it be true to say that every profession has its own philosophy? What does this mean? How would you describe the educational philosophy of the school that you attend or have attended?
3. The text suggests that in Plato's Myth of the Cave, the climb from the cave represents the climb "from the dark cave of ignorance up into the light of knowledge." Can you suggest other reasonable interpretations of Plato's parable?
4. Suppose someone objected: "If philosophy is an ongoing process, what's the point of engaging in it? You'll never get any certain answers; your search will never end. Such a prospect is thoroughly depressing." How would you respond to this criticism?
5. Give an example of reasoning in which you used information about something important in your life to draw a conclusion about what you should do or believe about it.

PHILOSOPHY AT THE MOVIES

Watch *The Matrix* (1999) in which Neo, a computer hacker, is shown by a leader of a rebel group that the "reality" around him is actually a computer simulation—called the "Matrix." How is the "Matrix" like Plato's Cave, and how is Neo like Plato's released prisoner? How do they differ? Is your situation today in any way like that of the people in the "Matrix?" How do you know? While savoring a steak in a restaurant in the "Matrix," one of the rebels, Cypher, agrees to betray the rebels to Agent Smith and says, "Ignorance is bliss." What does he mean? Would Plato agree with Cypher? Why or why not? Would you agree? Why or why not?

Other movies with related themes: *The Animatrix* (2003); *Vanilla Sky* (2001); *Mulholland Dr.* (2001); some related older classics: *eXistenZ* (1999) and *The Thirteenth Floor* (1999).

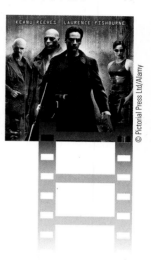

KEANU REEVES LAURENCE FISHBURNE

© Pictorial Press Ltd/Alamy

1.2 The Traditional Divisions of Philosophy

Another way of understanding what philosophy means is to look at the kinds of questions it has traditionally asked. Philosophy has been generally concerned with three broad questions: What is knowledge? What is real? What is right and good? Although these questions cannot be considered in isolation and although the distinction among them is sometimes blurred, philosophers have traditionally seen most philosophical questions as parts of these three inquiries.

These traditional concerns suggest the three categories under which philosophical topics are usually grouped: knowledge, reality, and values. Philosophers generally term the fields of philosophy that explore these topics *epistemology, metaphysics, and ethics.*

Epistemology: The Study of Knowledge

Epistemology literally means "the study of knowledge." Among the problems usually discussed as parts of epistemology are the structure, reliability, extent, and kinds of knowledge we have; the meaning of truth (including definitions of truth and validity); logic and a variety of strictly linguistic concerns (such as: How do words refer to reality? and What is meaning?); and the foundation of knowledge, including the question of whether real knowledge is even possible.

To get a fuller idea of what epistemology is, and its importance, consider the interesting views of Gail Stenstad, a contemporary feminist philosopher. Stenstad argues that male approaches to knowledge assume that there is only one truth—one correct theory—and that all other conflicting insights must be wrong. She contrasts this approach to knowledge, which she calls *theoretical thinking*, with a feminist approach to knowledge that she calls *anarchic thinking*. Feminist anarchic thinking, she says, recognizes that there is not just one "objective" truth but many different truths, none of which should be ruled out as "incorrect."

QUICK REVIEW
Epistemology looks at the extent and reliability of our knowledge, truth, and logic, and whether knowledge is possible.

> In some ways the difference between theoretical thinking and anarchic thinking is analogous to the difference between monotheism [belief in one God] and polytheism [belief in many gods]. Theoretical thinking and monotheism both tend toward "the one." Monotheism, obviously, is oriented toward one god; historically, many monotheistic religions have also been very concerned with oneness in doctrine, with arriving at doctrine that can be taken to be the only true or correct one. "One lord, one faith, one baptism." This sort of focus creates an in-group and an out-group: the saved and the damned. While none but the most rigid theorists

QUICK REVIEW
Stenstad claims that truth is many and that differing views can be accepted as equally valid and true.

> would go so far in demarcating an in-group and an out-group, accusations of "incorrectness" have been used to silence disagreement. Further, in its very structure, any claim to possess the truth, or the correct account of reality or the good, creates an out-group, whether we like it or not. The out-group is all those whose truth or reality or values are different from those posited in the theory. . . . [But] polytheism has room to include a monotheistic perspective (though the reverse is not the case). A belief in many gods, or in many possibilities or sacred manifestations, can allow for an individual's preference for any one (or more) of those manifestations. Likewise, anarchic thinking does not abandon or exclude or negate the insights achieved by theoretical thinking, but rather demotes "the theory" to a situational analysis, useful and accurate within limits clearly demarcated in each case. Other, very different analyses, based on other women's situations and experiences, are not ruled out.[3]

In this passage, Stenstad is comparing male or theoretical thinking with monotheism. **Monotheism** is the belief that there is just one God and is usually accompanied by the assertion that all beliefs in other gods should be rejected. In a similar way, she says, male "theoretical thinking" assumes that there is only one true view of reality and that any opposing ("different") views must be rejected as false. Her point appears to be that theoretical thinking, the male view of truth, assumes that if several views of reality conflict (are inconsistent), then only one can be true. We must reject such male approaches to knowledge and truth, she seems to imply. Instead, she is apparently saying we should embrace the feminist "anarchic" view that truth is many and that several opposing insights can be equally valid and equally true. This is a feminist approach to truth and knowledge that she believes will give us the power to break free of male theories that deny the equal validity of opposing views; it will also enable us to build communities that include individuals from different backgrounds and with different experiences, offering different insights and different truths.

Is truth many or one? Is there a male approach to knowledge and truth that is intolerant and exclusive? Should we embrace the view that truth is many and that there is no single correct truth about what the world is like? Are all truths, all knowledge, relative? Out of these kinds of puzzling questions arises the field of epistemology, the attempt to determine what knowledge and truth are. As this short discussion of Stenstad suggests, the answers to these questions may even influence how we relate to each other as male and female.

thinking critically • Avoiding Vague and Ambiguous Claims

The quotation of Stenstad above contains several claims. A claim is a statement or sentence or proposition that can be true or false. Stenstad makes the claim, for example, that there are two kinds of thinking: theoretical thinking and anarchic thinking. Earlier, we saw that Plato made the claim that the person who acquires "true knowledge" is like a prisoner who is freed from his chains. And Perictione made the claim that to have wisdom is to understand "the purpose of the things that are." The point is that philosophers proceed by making claims.

3 Gail Stenstad, "Anarchic Thinking: Breaking the Hold of Monotheistic Ideology on Feminist Philosophy," in *Women, Knowledge, and Reality: Explorations in Feminist Philosophy,* ed. Ann Garry and Marilyn Pearsall (Boston: Unwin Hyman, 1989), 333.

Like all claims, the claims of a philosopher can be clear or they can be vague or ambiguous. Vague claims are those that do not have a clear or precise meaning. Ambiguous claims are those that have several possible meanings. Some of Stenstad's claims about anarchic thinking, for example, seem unclear. She says that theoretical thinking holds that if one view about reality is "correct," then any "different" view has to be "incorrect," while anarchic thinking holds that if one view is correct, another view that is "very different" is "not ruled out." But what does she mean by a "different" view? Does her claim mean that in anarchic thinking views that *contradict* each other can both be true? Is she saying, for example, that if one person says God exists and another says God does not exist, anarchic thinking will accept both statements as true? Or does her claim just mean that anarchic thinking accepts views that are dissimilar but that do not contradict each other? For example, is she saying that if one person says God is loving and another says God is just, anarchic thinking can accept both views as true? The trouble is that we don't know exactly what her claim is because it is ambiguous: It could have at least two different meanings. There are, of course, times when vagueness or ambiguity is appropriate. If your wife asks you what you think of her mother, it may be best to be vague. But there is generally something wrong with philosophical claims when they are vague or ambiguous. Since we are not even sure what they mean, we cannot really reason about whether they are true or false.

One of the basic and most important ways of evaluating the claim of a philosopher (or anyone else), then, is by asking whether the meaning of his or her claim is clear, or whether the claim is too vague or ambiguous to allow us to figure out exactly what it means. Vague and ambiguous philosophical claims are defective and should be avoided. We will discuss numerous philosophical claims in the pages that follow. As you read and think about these claims, you should evaluate them by asking whether they have the most fundamental characteristic of an adequate claim: Is the meaning of the claim clear, or is the claim vague or ambiguous?

Metaphysics: The Study of Reality or Existence

Metaphysics, the second major area of philosophy, is the study of the most general or ultimate characteristics of reality or existence. Some issues that fall under metaphysics are the place of humans in the universe, the purpose and nature of reality, and the nature of mind, self, and consciousness. Also included are issues related to religion, such as the existence of God, the destiny of the universe, and the immortality of the soul.

One of the core questions of metaphysics—one that gives us an idea of what metaphysics is about—is this: Is everything in the universe determined by outside causes, or are we freely able to choose for ourselves? Again, looking at how some philosophers have treated this issue will give us a better understanding of metaphysics.

QUICK REVIEW
Metaphysics looks at ultimate characteristics of reality or existence.

One important theory in metaphysics is **determinism**, the claim that all things and all human beings are unfree because everything that occurs happens in accordance with some regular pattern or law. Paul Henri d'Holbach, who wrote in the eighteenth century, made such a claim:

> In whatever manner man is considered, he is connected to universal nature, and submitted to the necessary and immutable laws that she imposes on all beings she contains. . . . He is born without his own consent; his [physical and mental] organization does in no way depend on himself; his ideas come to him involuntarily; and his habits are in the power of those who cause him to have them. He is

QUICK REVIEW
D'Holbach claimed everything is determined by causes we do not control, so we are not free.

> unceasingly modified by causes, whether visible or concealed, over which he has no control and which necessarily regulate his existence, color his way of thinking, and determine his manner of acting. . . .
>
> In short, the actions of man are never free; they are always the necessary consequence of his temperament, of the ideas he has received, including his true or false notions of happiness, and of those opinions that are strengthened by example, by education, and by daily experience. . . . Man is not a free agent in any instant of his life.[4]

QUICK REVIEW
Frankl, in a Nazi prison, saw humans as being ultimately free.

Yet many other philosophers deny these deterministic claims about reality. One of them is Viktor Frankl, a twentieth-century Jewish psychologist and existentialist philosopher who lived through the Jewish persecutions during World War II. Frankl suffered terrible degradations while imprisoned by the Nazis after they murdered his entire family. There, in the terror-filled hellholes of the German prison camps, he was struck by how often people responded to their situation with generosity and selflessness. He said that his experiences proved to him that human beings are ultimately free and that each of us has the freedom to make of ourselves whatever kind of person we choose to be:

> Man is not fully conditioned and determined; he determines himself whether to give in to conditions or stand up to them. In other words, man is ultimately self-determining. Man does not simply exist, but always decides what his existence will be, what he will become in the next moment. By the same token, every human being has the freedom to change at any instant. . . .
>
> A human being is not one thing among others. *Things* determine each other, but man is ultimately self-determining. What he becomes—within the limits of endowment and environment—he has made out of himself. In the concentration camps, for example, in this living laboratory and on this testing ground, we watched and witnessed some of our comrades behave like swine while others behaved like saints. Man has both potentialities within himself. Which one is actualized depends on decisions but not on conditions.[5]

Some Eastern philosophers have turned to the Hindu idea of **karma** to claim that humans can be both free and determined. *Karma*, which literally means "action" or "deed," consists of the accumulation of a person's past deeds. For the Hindu, everything we have done in our past (possibly including past lives) determines our present situation—who and what we now are. Some Hindu philosophers have argued that although this seems to imply that we are not free, the idea of karma allows us to combine both determinism and freedom. Our past actions—our karma—they claim, determine the kind of being we have become, but we are still free to choose within the limits of what we have become. Freedom is choosing now within a situation that is determined by our past. As the Hindu philosopher Sarvepalli Radhakrishnan writes,

QUICK REVIEW
The Hindu idea of karma can combine determinism and freedom.

> Freedom is not caprice, nor is Karma necessity. . . . Freedom is not caprice since we carry our past with us. Our character, at any given point, is the condensation of our previous history. What we have been enters into the "me" which is now active and choosing. The range of one's natural freedom of action is limited. No man has the universal field of possibilities for himself. . . . Only the possible is the sphere of freedom. We have a good deal of present constraint and previous necessity in human life. But necessity is not to be mistaken for destiny which we can

4 Baron Paul Henri d'Holbach, *System of Nature* (London: Dearsley, 1797).
5 Viktor Frankl, *Man's Search for Meaning* (New York: Washington Square Press, 1963), 206, 213.

PHILOSOPHY AND LIFE

Philosophical Issues

Virtually every activity and every profession raises philosophical issues.

Science, psychology, the practice of law and medicine, and even taxation all involve questions that more or less directly force us to address philosophical issues.

Mark Woodhouse invites us to consider the following examples:

1. *A neurophysiologist, while establishing correlations between certain brain functions and the feeling of pain, begins to wonder whether the "mind" is distinct from the brain.*
2. *A nuclear physicist, having determined that matter is mostly empty space containing colorless energy transformations, begins to wonder to what extent the solid, extended, colored world we perceive corresponds to what actually exists and which world is more "real."*
3. *A behavioral psychologist, having increasing success in predicting human behavior, questions whether any human actions can be called "free."*
4. *Supreme Court justices, when framing a law to distinguish obscene and non-obscene art forms, are drawn into questions about the nature and function of art.*
5. *An IRS director, in determining which (religious) organizations should be exempted from tax, is forced to define what counts as a "religion" or "religious group."*

And, as Woodhouse also suggests, philosophical questions are continually raised in our everyday life and conversations. Consider, for example, the following statements, which all involve philosophical issues: Sociology is not a science. Drugs reveal new levels of reality. History never repeats itself. Every religion has the same core of truth. We should all be left free to do our own thing, as long as we don't hurt anyone else. All truth depends on your point of view. The most important thing you can do is find out who you are. This could all be a dream.

QUESTIONS

1. Identify other areas of life that involve philosophical issues and explain the issues they raise.
2. What are your views on the issues that Woodhouse lists? Can you give any good reasons to support your views on these issues, or is it all "just a matter of opinion"?

Source: From WOODHOUSE. *A Preface to Philosophy*, 8E. © 2007 Wadsworth, a part of Cengage Learning, Inc. Reproduced by permission. www.cengage.com/permissions

neither defy nor delude. Though the self is not free from the bonds of determination, it can subjugate the past to a certain extent and turn it into a new course. Choice is the assertion of freedom over necessity by which it converts necessity to its own use and thus frees itself from it.[6]

Which of these views is supported by the strongest reasons—the view that all reality (including ourselves) is causally determined, the view that humans, at least, are free to choose what we will do, or the view that we are determined but free to choose within the constraints set by our past? This is but one example of the fundamental questions that metaphysics asks.

thinking critically • Supporting Claims with Reasons and Arguments

Notice that the metaphysical claims of the philosophers we quoted earlier are not isolated statements. The philosophers accompany their claims with reasons in support of those claims. D'Holbach, for example, claims that humans are not free *because* every person "is unceasingly modified by causes . . . over which he has no control and which necessarily . . . determine his manner of action." On the other hand, Frankl claims that external conditions

6 Sarvepalli Radhakrishnan, *An Idealist View of Life* (London: George Allen & Unwin, 1932), 220–221.

do not determine what people do *because* in the concentration camps he saw some "comrades behave like swine while others behaved like saints" yet all of them were subject to the same external conditions.

As these examples suggest, in philosophy our claims should not only be clear, they should also be supported by reasons. Philosophy is not mere speculation. When we speculate we dream up grand ideas and visions about how things might be. We might speculate, for example, that "The world around us is a dream!" But philosophy is more than speculation. Philosophy has to prove its claims, so philosophers must give reasons for the claims they make. Without reasons, there is no philosophy, only speculation. Unsupported philosophical claims are inadequate because without reasons to back them up, we cannot know whether they are true or false, or whether we should accept or reject them.

QUICK REVIEW
Philosophical claims should be supported by reasons; a claim or conclusion together with its supporting reasons or premises is an argument.

A claim together with its supporting reasons is called an **argument**. An argument in philosophy is not a heated quarrel accompanied by shouting. Instead, an argument consists of a group of reasons or "premises" plus a claim or "conclusion" that the reasons are supposed to prove or support. Every argument has two parts, then: (1) a group of premises which provide reasons or evidence for a conclusion, and (2) a conclusion which is the claim that those premises are supposed to establish. In the argument d'Holbach gives, for example, the premises include the statement that every person "is unceasingly modified by causes . . . over which he has no control and which necessarily . . . determine his manner of action," and the conclusion is his claim that "the actions of man are never free." In the argument Frankl gives, the premises include the statement that in the concentration camps some "comrades behaved like swine while others behaved like saints" although all were subjected to the same external conditions, and his conclusion is the claim that "man is not fully . . . determined" by external conditions.

Once we know a philosopher's conclusion and the reasons or premises he gives to support his or her conclusion, we can move on to evaluate whether the premises provide adequate support for the conclusion. We can try to figure out whether d'Holbach's premises are true, for example. And if we find his premises are false, then we know that they do not give us a good reason to accept his claim. But the first step in this process of evaluating a philosopher's claim is crucial: We have to begin by identifying the philosopher's conclusion or main claim, and identifying the reasons or premises he gives to support his conclusion.

Ethics: The Study of Values

Ethics, the third major area of philosophy, refers to the study of morality. It is the attempt to understand and critically evaluate our moral values and moral principles and to see how these relate to our conduct and our social institutions. Ethics includes questions about the nature of moral virtue and moral obligation, what basic moral principles we should follow and what is morally good for human beings, the justice of social structures and political systems, and the morality of various kinds of behaviors, social policies, and social institutions.

QUICK REVIEW
Ethics, the study of morality, asks about our moral obligations and moral virtues, our moral principles, what is morally good, and the morality of behaviors, social policies, and social institutions.

The specific issues discussed in ethics vary widely and include questions such as these: Are abortion, suicide, and euthanasia ever morally right? Is capitalism or communism a better form of life? Should the law permit or prohibit adultery, pornography, capital punishment, or homosexuality? Again, some examples may make these inquiries a bit clearer. Consider the statement of Mahatma Gandhi, the great twentieth-century Indian statesman who successfully practiced nonviolent political resistance against the British rulers of India. Gandhi devoted his life to breaking down racial and religious forms of discrimination. He campaigned for equality of respect for all human beings. In doing this, he advocated and practiced *ahimsa*, or nonviolence. In Gandhi's view, we should harm no living thing. Nevertheless, we should resist evil. In his struggles against the British, therefore, he would simply stand in the path of their violence, letting their blows fall on him, and passively resist their oppressive policies. Gandhi lived the philosophy that service toward others is our primary moral duty:

QUICK REVIEW
Gandhi said that we should selflessly harm no living thing and passively resist evil without violence.

> To proceed a little further, sacrifice means laying down one's life so that others may live. Let us suffer so that others may be happy, and the highest service and the highest love is wherein man lays down his life for his fellow-men. That highest love is thus *Ahimsa* which is the highest service. . . . Learn to be generous towards each other. To be generous means having no hatred for those whom we consider to be at fault, and loving and serving them. It is not generosity or love, if we have goodwill for others only as long as they and we are united in thought and action. That should be called merely friendship or mutual affection.
>
> The application of the term "love" is wrong in such cases. "Love" means feeling friendship for the enemy.[7]

© India Images/Dinodia Images/Alamy

Gandhi: "The highest love is wherein man lays down his life for his fellow-men. That highest love is thus *Ahimsa*."

Yet not everyone agrees with such lofty sentiments. Many philosophers, in fact, have reasoned that ethics is a sham. For example, Harry Browne concludes that morality is really a kind of trap if we take it to mean that people should put the happiness of others ahead of their own. Selfishness, he holds, is and should be everyone's policy:

> Everyone is selfish; everyone is doing what he believes will make himself happier. The recognition of that can take most of the sting out of accusations that you're being "selfish." Why should you feel guilty for seeking your own happiness when that's what everyone else is doing, too? . . .
>
> To find constant, profound happiness requires that you be free to seek the gratification of your own desires.[8]

QUICK REVIEW
Browne says selfishness is and ought to be everyone's policy.

Browne's view that morality is a sham because humans always try to satisfy themselves—therefore, their actions are always selfish—is called **egoism**. The contemporary philosopher James Rachels strongly questions this view in the following passage:

> Why should we think that merely because someone derives satisfaction from helping others this makes him selfish? Isn't the unselfish man precisely the one who does derive satisfaction from helping others, while the selfish man does not? Similarly, it is nothing more than shabby sophistry to say, because Smith takes

QUICK REVIEW
Rachels claims that finding satisfaction in helping others is not selfishness.

7 Mahatma Gandhi, *Gita—My Mother,* quoted in *Beyond the Western Tradition*, ed. Daniel Bonevac, William Boon, and Stephen Phillips (Mountain View, CA: Mayfield, 1992), 243.

8 Harry Browne, *How I Found Freedom in an Unfree World* (New York: Macmillan, 1937).

> satisfaction in helping his friend, that he is behaving selfishly. If we say this rapidly, while thinking about something else, perhaps it will sound all right; but if we speak slowly, and pay attention to what we are saying, it sounds plain silly.[9]

Which of these views is correct—that morality is a sham or that we have a duty to love and serve even our enemies? These kinds of inquiries form the subject matter of ethics, the third major area of philosophy.

Other Philosophical Inquiries

Finally, there is a wide range of philosophical inquiries that we usually refer to as "the philosophy of . . ." or, simply, "philosophy and . . ." These include the philosophy of science, the philosophy of art, and philosophy and the meaning of life. Each of these areas of philosophy attempts to question and analyze the basic or fundamental assumptions of the subject. For example, the philosophy of science asks what the scientific method is, whether it is valid, and whether the theories it produces are merely useful mental constructs or objective descriptions of reality. The philosophy of art asks what art is, what its meaning is and what its point is, and whether we can judge art against objective standards or whether it is merely a matter of fads and personal tastes. An inquiry into philosophy and the meaning of life is an attempt to look carefully at the question of whether life has meaning and, if so, what that meaning might be.

The list of topics about which we can philosophize is in fact endless. Consider the titles of several books that have appeared mostly during the last few years: *Food and Philosophy, Beer and Philosophy, Philosophy Looks at Chess, Coffee and Philosophy, Green Lantern and Philosophy, The Philosophy of Tolkien, Running and Philosophy, South Park and Philosophy, The Daily Show and Philosophy, The Matrix and Philosophy, Physics and Philosophy, Batman and Philosophy, Bullshit and Philosophy, X-Men and Philosophy, iPod and Philosophy, The Beatles and Philosophy, The Philosophy of Martin Scorsese, Jimmy Buffett and Philosophy, The Philosophy of Science Fiction Film, Metallica and Philosophy, The Philosophy of Andy Warhol*, and even *The Philosophy of Philosophy*. In short, beyond the traditional areas of philosophy that are considered central—epistemology, metaphysics, and ethics—lies an entire universe of topics about which we can philosophize, or which raise interesting philosophical questions.

QUESTIONS

1. Read through the various passages quoted as examples of philosophical writings in epistemology, metaphysics, and ethics. What makes these philosophical writings? What reasons are provided in support of a philosophical position? How does philosophy differ from the natural sciences? The social sciences? Literature?
2. Think of as many philosophical questions as you can, and then place each in one or more of the three major philosophical categories.
3. List the philosophical concerns you wish to learn about during your introductory philosophy course. Try to be specific and avoid being vague or ambiguous.

9 James Rachels, "Egoism and Moral Skepticism," in *A New Introduction to Philosophy*, ed. Steven M. Cahn (New York: Harper & Row, 1971).

PHILOSOPHY AT THE MOVIES

Watch *Waking Life* (2001), in which the young man Wiley Wiggens floats from one intriguing conversation to another, all on philosophical issues and several with contemporary philosophers. Identify some of the questions of epistemology, metaphysics, and ethics that the movie raises in these conversations. Which of these questions interests you the most? Does the movie seem to give any answers to the questions? Have you arrived at any—perhaps tentative—answers to these questions? Are there any issues discussed in the movie that are not philosophical?

An older classic with related themes: *My Dinner with Andre* (1981).

1.3 A Philosopher in Action: Socrates

The best way to understand the nature of philosophy is to consider a philosopher in action. And the best place to begin is with the Greek thinker Socrates, who is sometimes called the father of Western philosophy. However, we should note that Socrates was not the first Western philosopher. A group of philosophers called the pre-Socratics preceded him. The **pre-Socratics** were the first thinkers in the West who questioned religious authority and tried to provide nonreligious explanations of nature. (For more information, see the Historical Showcase about the first philosophers at the end of this chapter.) Nevertheless, Socrates' life and views exemplify the meaning of philosophy, so we will look at his work.

Socrates was born in 469 BCE in Athens, Greece, a flourishing and remarkably vigorous city-state. The Greek theater had already produced the noted dramatist Aeschylus and would soon see the comedies of Aristophanes and the tragedies of Sophocles and Euripides. The Greek armies had defeated those of the much larger nation of Persia, and Athens was on the verge of attaining naval control of the Aegean Sea.

QUICK REVIEW
Socrates questioned the conventional beliefs of his fellow Athenians.

As he grew older, Socrates began to question the conventional beliefs held by his fellow Athenians. He would haunt the streets of Athens, buttonholing powerful men and asking them irreverent questions about their opinions. To those who pretended to know about justice, for example, he would ask, "What is justice? What does it mean? What do all just acts have in common?" Similarly, he would probe ideas about virtue, knowledge, morality, and religion. Through continual questioning, Socrates would plumb a person's system of beliefs, deflating cherished certainties and exposing their emptiness. Although Socrates' persistent questioning of traditional habits of thought left many people puzzled, many more reacted with anger.

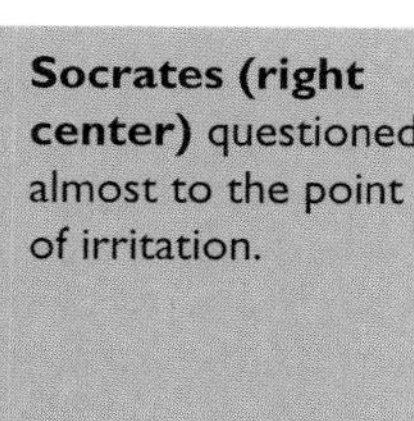

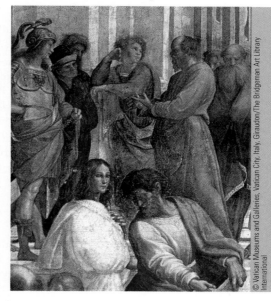

© Vatican Museums and Galleries, Vatican City, Italy, Giraudon/The Bridgeman Art Library International

Socrates (right center) questioned almost to the point of irritation.

Socrates saw Athens rise to glory under the great leader Pericles. During Pericles' reign, Athens enjoyed a splendid golden age of democracy, an age of great architectural, artistic, and literary advances. The golden age of Athens depended on the powerful military and economic forces that Athens commanded. But all this ended when Athens was defeated in war and then became embroiled in a disastrous 30-year civil war. Plague broke out, inflation struck the economy, and intense class struggles erupted between the rich old aristocratic families and their poorer fellow citizens. In the end, the defeated, desperate, and frustrated Athenians searched for scapegoats to blame. They determined that Socrates, with his habit of questioning everything, had weakened the traditional values and beliefs that had once made Athens strong. So they sentenced Socrates to death.

Because Socrates left no writings, most of what we know about him comes from the *Dialogues*, written by Socrates' disciple Plato. The *Dialogues* are short dramas in which the character of Socrates plays a major role. There is some controversy over how accurately Plato's *Dialogues* reflect the real conversations of Socrates. Nevertheless, most experts today agree that the first dialogues Plato wrote (for example, *Euthyphro, The Apology*, and *Crito*) are faithful to Socrates' views, although they may not contain Socrates' actual words.

Euthyphro: Do We Know What Holiness Is?

One of these early dialogues, *Euthyphro*, presents a marvelous example of how Socrates questioned people almost to the point of irritation. In fact, as you read through the dialogue, you will probably start feeling irritated yourself and begin asking why Socrates doesn't get past the questions and start giving answers. He gives no answers because he wants you to realize that you, too, do not have any good answers to his questions.

The dialogue takes place at the court of the king. Socrates is there to learn more about an indictment for "unholiness" brought against him for questioning traditional beliefs. He sees an old friend arrive, a priest named Euthyphro. Here, in a simplified and edited translation, is their dialogue as Plato wrote it:

QUICK REVIEW
In *Euthyphro*, Socrates questions a priest's knowledge of what holiness is.

To read more from Plato's *Euthyphro*, go to CourseMate for this text and browse by chapter or philosopher.

EUTHYPHRO: Socrates! What are you doing here at the court of the King?

SOCRATES: I am being charged, Euthyphro, by a young man I hardly know named Meletus. He accuses me of making up new gods and denying the existence of the old ones.

EUTHYPHRO: I am sure you will win your case, Socrates, just like I expect to win mine.

SOCRATES: But what is your case, Euthyphro?

EUTHYPHRO: I am charging my father with murder, Socrates. One of my slaves in a drunken fit killed a fellow slave. My father chained up the culprit and left him in a ditch unattended for several days to wait the judgment of a priest. But the cold, the hunger, and the chains killed him. So now I am charging my father with murder, against the ignorant wishes of my family who do not know what true holiness requires of a priest like me.

SOCRATES: Good heavens, Euthyphro! Do you have such a clear knowledge of what holiness is that you are not afraid you might be doing something unholy in charging your own father with murder?

EUTHYPHRO: My most valued possession, Socrates, is the exact knowledge I have of these matters.

SOCRATES: You are a rare friend, Euthyphro. I can do no better than take you as my teacher so that I can defend myself against Meletus who is accusing me of being unholy. Tell me, then, what is holiness and what is unholiness?

EUTHYPHRO: Holiness is doing what I am doing: prosecuting anyone who is guilty of murder, sacrilege, or of any similar crime—whether he is your father or mother, or whoever, it makes no difference—and not to prosecute them is unholiness.

SOCRATES: But wouldn't you say, Euthyphro, that there are many other holy acts?

EUTHYPHRO: There are.

SOCRATES: I was not asking you to give me examples of holiness, Euthyphro, but to identify the characteristic which makes all holy things holy. There must be some characteristic that all holy things have in common, and one which makes unholy things unholy. Tell me what this characteristic itself is, so that I can tell which actions are holy, and which unholy.

QUICK REVIEW
Socrates wants not examples, but the characteristic that all, and only, holy things have in common.

EUTHYPHRO: Well, then, holiness is what is loved by the gods and what is not loved by them is unholy.

QUICK REVIEW
Euthyphro says that whatever the gods love is holy.

SOCRATES: Very good, Euthyphro! Now you have given me the sort of answer I wanted. Let us examine it. A thing or a person that is loved by the gods is holy, and a thing or a person that the gods hate is unholy. And the holy is the opposite of the unholy. Does that summarize what you said?

EUTHYPHRO: It does.

SOCRATES: But you admit, Euthyphro, that the gods have disagreements. So some things are hated by some gods and loved by other gods.

QUICK REVIEW
But, Socrates replies, the gods can disagree.

EUTHYPHRO: True.

SOCRATES: Then upon your view the same things, Euthyphro, will be both holy and unholy.

EUTHYPHRO: Well, I suppose so.

SOCRATES: Then, my friend, you have not really answered my question. I did not ask you to tell me which actions were both holy and unholy; yet that is the outcome of your view. In punishing your father, Euthyphro, you might be doing what is loved by the god Zeus, but hateful to the god Cronos.

EUTHYPHRO: But, Socrates, surely none of the gods would disagree about the rightness of punishing an injustice.

SOCRATES: Both men and gods would certainly agree on the general point that unjust acts should be punished. But men and gods might disagree about whether this particular act is unjust. Is that not true?

EUTHYPHRO: Quite true.

SOCRATES: So tell me, my friend: How do you know that all the gods agree on this particular act: that it is just for a son to prosecute his father for chaining a slave who was guilty of murder and who died in chains before the religious authorities said what should be done with him? How do you know that all the gods love this act?

 critical thinking

Does Socrates assume you have to be able to define holiness in order to know what things are holy? If so, is this assumption correct?

EUTHYPHRO: I could make the matter quite clear to you, Socrates, although it would take me some time.

SOCRATES: Euthyphro, I will not insist on it. I will assume, if you like, that all the gods here agree. The point I really want to understand is this: Do the gods love what is holy because it is holy, or is it holy because they love it? What do you say, Euthyphro? On your definition whatever is holy is loved by all the gods, is it not?

QUICK REVIEW
Also, Socrates says, if the gods love what is holy because it is holy, then what makes things holy is not that they are loved by the gods.

EUTHYPHRO: Yes.

SOCRATES: Because it is holy? Or for some other reason?

EUTHYPHRO: No, that is the reason.

SOCRATES: Then what is holy is loved by the gods because it is holy? It is not holy because it is loved?

EUTHYPHRO: Yes.

SOCRATES: Then, Euthyphro, to be loved by the gods cannot be the same as to be holy. And to be holy cannot be the same as to be loved by the gods.

EUTHYPHRO: But why, Socrates?

SOCRATES: Because, Euthyphro, when I asked you for the essence of holiness, you gave me only a quality that accompanies holiness: the quality of being loved by the gods. But you have not yet told me what holiness itself is [that quality that leads the gods to love whatever has it]. So please, Euthyphro, do not hide your treasure from me. Start again from the beginning and tell me what holiness itself is.

EUTHYPHRO: I really do not know, Socrates, how to express what I mean. Somehow or other our arguments seem to turn around in circles and walk away from us.

SOCRATES: Then I will help you instruct me, Euthyphro. Tell me—is it not true that everything that is holy is also just?

EUTHYPHRO: Yes.

SOCRATES: Does it follow that everything that is just is also holy? Or is it rather the case that whatever is holy is just, but only some just things are holy while others are not? For justice is the larger notion of which holiness is only a part. Do you agree in that?

EUTHYPHRO: Yes, that, I think, is correct.

SOCRATES: Then, since holiness is a part of justice, let us ask what part.

EUTHYPHRO: I know, Socrates! Holiness is that part of justice which involves service to the gods, while the other part of justice involves service to our fellow men.

SOCRATES: Very good, Euthyphro. But there is still one small point on which I need your help: What do you mean by "service"? Is not service always designed to benefit or improve those who are served?

EUTHYPHRO: True.

SOCRATES: So does holiness, which is a kind of service, benefit or improve the gods? Would you say that when you do a holy act you make the gods better?

EUTHYPHRO: Good heavens, no!

QUICK REVIEW
Euthyphro next says that holiness is serving the gods with acts they love.

SOCRATES: Then what is this service to the gods that is called holiness?

EUTHYPHRO: It is the kind that slaves show their masters.

SOCRATES: I understand. A sort of ministering to the gods.

EUTHYPHRO: Exactly.

SOCRATES: And now tell me, my good friend, about this ministering to the gods: What activities does it involve?

EUTHYPHRO: It would be difficult to learn them all, Socrates. Let me simply say that holiness is learning how to please the gods by prayers and sacrifices.

SOCRATES: And sacrificing is giving to the gods, while prayer is asking of the gods?

EUTHYPHRO: Exactly, Socrates.

SOCRATES: But real giving involves giving them something they want from us, does it not? For surely it would be pointless to give someone what they do not want.

EUTHYPHRO: Very true, Socrates.

SOCRATES: But then tell me, what benefit comes to the gods from our gifts? Clearly they are the givers of every good thing we have. So it puzzles me how we can give them any good thing in return.

EUTHYPHRO: But Socrates, you do not imagine that the gods benefit from the gifts we give them?

SOCRATES: If not, Euthyphro, then what sort of gifts can these be?

EUTHYPHRO: What else but praise and honor and whatever is pleasing to them.

SOCRATES: Holiness, then, is doing what is pleasing to the gods and not what is beneficial to them?

EUTHYPHRO: I would say that holiness, above all, is doing what is loved by the gods.

SOCRATES: Does it surprise you our arguments go in circles? Surely you must remember that a few moments ago we concluded that to be holy is not the same as to be loved by the gods?

QUICK REVIEW
Socrates points out that this is the view they earlier decided was wrong.

EUTHYPHRO: I do.

SOCRATES: Then either we were wrong in that admission or we are wrong now.

EUTHYPHRO: Hmm. I suppose that is the case.

SOCRATES: Then we must begin again and ask, "What is holiness?" If any man knows, you must. For if you did not know the nature of holiness and unholiness I am sure you would never have charged your aged father with murder and run the risk of doing wrong in the sight of the gods. Speak, then, my dear Euthyphro, and do not hide your knowledge from me.

EUTHYPHRO: Perhaps some other time, Socrates. Right now I am in a hurry to be off somewhere.

SOCRATES: My friend! Will you leave me in despair? And here I had hoped that you could teach me what holiness itself is.[10]

In this dialogue, Socrates is doing the kind of critical questioning that characterizes philosophy. With careful, logical reasoning, and in a systematic manner, he probes the religious beliefs on which Euthyphro bases his life and actions.

Socrates brings logic and reason to bear on those issues that are most important both to Euthyphro and to himself, because Socrates himself is being accused of acting against religion.

Moreover, Socrates' method reveals that Euthyphro—and we ourselves—do not really understand the basic things we take for granted. Socrates questions Euthyphro's easy assumption that he knows what his religious duty is, that he knows what it means for something to be just, and that he knows what it is to serve the gods and why the gods want to be served through certain acts and not others. At every turn, Euthyphro finds that he does not really understand the conventional beliefs he has been brought up to hold. He does not even know what makes an action pleasing to the gods. All he can say is that he believes the gods approve of certain acts, but he has no idea why they approve of those acts and not others.

10 Plato, *Euthyphro*. This edited translation copyright © 1987 by Manuel Velasquez.

Euthyphro might be you or me. Are you so sure about your own most basic religious beliefs? Do those of us who believe in God really know why God approves and commands certain acts and not others? What makes an act right? As Socrates might ask, do you believe that actions are right because God (or society) approves of them, or do you believe that God (or society) approves of certain acts because they are right? Do you really know what right action is, or do you merely know one of its accompanying characteristics? If Socrates' method of questioning without arriving at answers seems frustrating, it is partly because it exposes our own lack of wisdom.

thinking critically • Evaluating Arguments

We said earlier that to evaluate a philosopher's claim we need to identify the premises and conclusion of his argument. So what is Socrates' argument in *Euthyphro*? Well, at the beginning of their dialogue Euthyphro brags to Socrates that he has an "exact knowledge" of what holiness is. Socrates then says that since Euthyphro knows exactly what holiness is, he must know what characteristic(s) a thing must have in order for it to qualify as something holy. But in the end Euthyphro cannot say what characteristics a thing must have in order for it to be holy.

QUICK REVIEW
The standard way of stating an argument is to put the premises and conclusion in a list with the conclusion at the bottom and the premises above it; the premises can then be evaluated.

Although Socrates does not explicitly say so, it is clear what his conclusion is: *Euthyphro does not know what holiness is.* And the reasons or premises that support this conclusion are also pretty clear: *If Euthyphro knew what holiness is, he would know what characteristics a thing must have in order for it to be holy, but Euthyphro does not know what characteristics a thing must have in order for it to be holy.* We can summarize Socrates' argument by putting the premises and conclusion in a numbered list, with the conclusion at the bottom, and the premises above it, like this:

1. If Euthyphro knew what holiness is, then he would know what characteristics a thing must have in order for it to be holy.
2. But Euthyphro does not know what characteristics a thing must have in order for it to be holy.
3. Therefore, Euthyphro does not know what holiness is.

Listing the premises and conclusion of an argument in this way is the standard way of stating an argument. Now that we know exactly what Socrates' argument is, we can begin to evaluate it by asking whether the premises are true. You will probably agree that premise (2) is true since in the dialogue Euthyphro clearly cannot say what characteristics qualify a thing as holy. But is premise (1) true? Is it true that if a person knows what something is, then he must know what characteristics a thing must have in order to be that kind of thing? Think about a specific example: Is it true that if you know what a dog is, then you must know what characteristics a thing must have in order for it to be a dog? Is it possible for a person to know what a dog is, without being able to say exactly what characteristics make it a dog? In other words, can you know what a thing is, even though you cannot define it?

The Republic: Is Justice What Benefits the Powerful?

QUICK REVIEW
Socrates' questioning gave him the reputation of an irritating "gadfly."

Perhaps it is not surprising to learn that Socrates' habit of showing people that they were ignorant of what they thought they knew angered many of them. In fact, Socrates quickly got a reputation for being a "gadfly," an irritating personality who picked away at people's confident assertions and who left them with nothing more than the embarrassing realization of their ignorance. Here, for example, in a selection from the *Republic,* we see Socrates using his questioning methods to show

Thrasymachus, a cynical teacher, that he does not know what he is talking about. We see, also, how Socrates used irony to poke fun at pretentiousness and how Socrates never pretended to know something he didn't. In this dialogue, Socrates has been asking people if they know what justice is. No one seems to have a good answer. Then Thrasymachus, who prides himself on his own knowledge as a teacher, and who is fed up with Socrates' methods, gets into the discussion:

THRASYMACHUS: What nonsense are you talking about, Socrates? Why does everyone always give in to you? If you really want to know what justice is, Socrates, then don't just keep asking your questions and showing that everyone else's answers are wrong. As you know, of course, it's easier to ask a lot of questions than to provide answers. So why don't you try giving us some answers yourself? Tell us what you think justice is, Socrates. And don't give us a simple-minded answer like "justice is what ought to be," or "justice is what benefits us," or "justice is what profits us," or "justice is what is useful to us." Tell us clearly and in detail what you think, and don't just give us some simplistic stupidity.

SOCRATES: Don't be so hard on us, Thrasymachus. If my friends and I have made a mistake in our discussions, I assure you we didn't do it on purpose. . . . We are searching for justice and that is more precious than gold. We don't want to spoil our chances of finding it by being easy on each other and not giving it our best efforts. As you see, we haven't been able to discover what it is. So a clever man like you shouldn't be angry with us. You should feel sorry for us.

THRASYMACHUS: Oh, God! That's a great example of your well-known irony, Socrates. I knew you would do this. In fact, I warned everyone here before you came that you wouldn't answer any questions yourself, but would pretend to be ignorant. I told them you'd do anything rather than answer someone else's questions.

SOCRATES: So you are very wise, Thrasymachus . . .

THRASYMACHUS: Well, what if I said that I'm willing to answer your question about justice anyway and that I can give you a better answer than anyone else has given? . . .

SOCRATES: Well, then, it would be best if an ignorant man like myself tried to learn from someone like you who has knowledge.

THRASYMACHUS: Oh, yes, of course! That way Socrates can again avoid giving any answers and can cross-examine others and refute them.

SOCRATES: But look, my friend, how can someone like myself answer a question if, to begin with, he doesn't know the answer and doesn't claim to know it? . . . Isn't it more reasonable for you to answer since you say you know and can tell us? Don't be so stubborn. Do us a favor by giving us your answer and stop being so selfish with your wisdom . . .

THRASYMACHUS: Listen up, then. I say that justice is nothing more than whatever is advantageous to the stronger. [Pause.] Well, why don't you praise me? But no, you'd never do that!

QUICK REVIEW
Thrasymachus claims justice is doing what benefits the strong.

SOCRATES: Well, first I have to understand what you mean, for I don't quite get your point yet. You say justice is whatever is advantageous to the stronger. What exactly do you mean by this?

QUICK REVIEW
And the strong are rulers who make the laws, so justice is following their laws.

THRASYMACHUS: As you must know, Socrates, some nations are ruled by tyrants, others are ruled by a democratic majority, and still others are ruled by a small aristocracy. . . . Whoever rules—the ruling party—is the stronger in each nation. . . . And in each nation, whoever rules passes laws that are to their own—the rulers'—advantage. After they pass these laws, they say that justice is obeying the law. Whoever fails to keep the law is punished as unjust and a lawbreaker. So that, my good man, is what I say justice is. Justice is the same in all nations: whatever is to the advantage of the ruling group. The ruling group, you must admit, is the stronger. So if one reasons correctly, one will conclude that everywhere justice is the same: It is whatever is advantageous to the stronger.

SOCRATES: Now I think I know what you mean. But now we have to figure out whether you are right or not. You say that justice is something advantageous, but you add that it is what is advantageous to the stronger.

THRASYMACHUS: Perhaps you think that's only a small point?

SOCRATES: That's not clear yet. We need to see whether what you say is true. For I too think that justice is something advantageous. But you say that it is what is advantageous to the stronger, while I don't claim to know this. So we need to inquire.

THRASYMACHUS: Inquire away.

SOCRATES: First tell me, do you admit that it is just for citizens to obey their rulers?

THRASYMACHUS: I do.

SOCRATES: But are the rulers of a nation absolutely infallible, or do they sometimes make mistakes?

THRASYMACHUS: Of course, they sometimes make mistakes.

SOCRATES: So when they pass laws, they sometimes pass the right laws, and sometimes they mistakenly pass the wrong laws?

THRASYMACHUS: True.

SOCRATES: When they pass the right laws, they pass laws that are advantageous to their own interests, but when they make mistakes they pass laws that are contrary to their own interests. Is this your view?

THRASYMACHUS: Yes.

SOCRATES: But whatever laws they pass must be obeyed by their subjects, and that is what you say justice is.

THRASYMACHUS: Of course.

QUICK REVIEW
Sometimes rulers mistakenly pass laws that do not benefit themselves; in such cases, if justice is following their laws, then justice would be following laws that do not benefit the rulers. But this contradicts what Thrasymachus said justice was.

SOCRATES: Then justice, according to you, is sometimes what is not in the interests of the stronger, but something contrary to the interests of the stronger?

THRASYMACHUS: What's that you just said?

SOCRATES: Didn't you just admit that the rulers might mistakenly pass laws that are not in their own interests, but that obeying such laws is still justice?

THRASYMACHUS: Why, yes, I think so.

SOCRATES: Then you must also acknowledge that justice is not what is in the interests of the stronger when the rulers unintentionally pass laws that are contrary to their own interests! . . .

THRASYMACHUS: Well, I hope that you have been completely entertained, Socrates, since today is a holiday for feasting.

SOCRATES: And it is you who furnished the feast for us, Thrasymachus.[11]

Thrasymachus is a cynical philosopher. His view is that might makes right. Justice is obeying the rules of society, and these rules, he claims, always favor the interests of whatever group happens to hold power in that society. For example, Thrasymachus might have said that in a society ruled by white people, right and wrong will be defined in terms of what benefits white people. But is this cynical view of justice true? Socrates shows easily that it leads to a contradiction, and in so doing, he makes Thrasymachus look foolish.

The Apology: Socrates' Trial

Socrates' relentless and, to some people, infuriating questioning of his fellow citizens eventually led to his death. Shortly after the scene described in *Euthyphro*, Meletus and others indicted Socrates and brought him to trial. In his brilliant work *The Apology*, Plato summarized the speech Socrates delivered in his defense. The speech is especially fascinating because it provides a summary of Socrates' life and of his devotion to philosophical questioning. Socrates is standing in court, facing the jury composed of five hundred Athenian citizens who have just heard the testimony of his accusers, who charge him with corrupting the youth of Athens and with not believing in the gods of the state, i.e., with being an atheist:

QUICK REVIEW
The Apology is Socrates' speech at his trial on charges of being an atheist and of corrupting youth.

> I do not know, my fellow Athenians, how you were affected by my accusers whom you just heard. But they spoke so persuasively they almost made me forget who I was. Yet they hardly uttered a word of truth.
>
> But many of you are thinking, "Then what is the origin of these accusations, Socrates?" That is a fair question. Let me explain their origins.
>
> Some of you know my good friend Chaerephon. Before he died he went to Delphi and asked the religious oracle there to tell him who the wisest man in the world is. The oracle answered that there was no man wiser than Socrates.
>
> When I learned this, I asked myself, "What can the god's oracle mean?" For I knew I had no wisdom. After thinking it over for a long time, I decided that I had to find a man wiser than myself so I could go back to the god's oracle with this evidence. So I went to see a politician who was famous for his wisdom. But when I questioned him, I realized he really was not wise, although many people—he especially—thought he was. So I tried to explain to him that although he thought himself wise, he really was not. But all that happened was that he came to hate me. And so did many of his supporters who overheard us. So I left him, thinking to myself as I left that although neither of us really knew anything about what is noble and good, still I was better off. For he knows nothing, and thinks that he knows, while I neither know nor think that I know. And in this I think I have a slight advantage.
>
> Then I went to another person who had even greater pretensions to wisdom. The result was exactly the same: I made another enemy. In this way I went to one man after another and made more and more enemies. I felt bad about this and it frightened me. But I was compelled to do it because I felt that investigating god's oracle came first. I said to myself, I must go to everyone who seems to be wise so I can find out what the oracle means.
>
> My hearers imagine that I myself possess the wisdom which I find lacking in others. But the truth is, Men of Athens, that only god is wise. And by his oracle he wanted to show us that the wisdom of men is worth little or nothing. It is as if he

QUICK REVIEW
Socrates says it was his mission to find if the oracle was right when it said he was the wisest man alive.

QUICK REVIEW
So he searched for a wiser man by questioning everyone's knowledge.

QUICK REVIEW
He made enemies but learned the wisest man is he who knows he does not know.

11 From *The Republic*, bk. I, lines 336c–339e, translated by Manuel Velasquez, © 1998 by Manuel Velasquez.

was telling us, "The wisest man is the one who, like Socrates, knows that his wisdom is in truth worth nothing." And so I go about the world obedient to god. I search and question the wisdom of anyone who seems to be wise. And if he is not wise, then to clarify the meaning of the oracle I show him that he is not wise. My occupation completely absorbs me and I have no time for anything else. My devotion to the god has reduced me to utter poverty.

QUICK REVIEW
His young followers did the same kind of questioning.

There is something more. Young men of the richer classes, who do not have much to do, follow me around of their own accord. They like to hear pretenders exposed. And sometimes they imitate me by examining others themselves. They quickly discover that there are plenty of people who think they know something but who really know nothing at all. Then those people also get angry at me. "This damnable Socrates is misleading our youth!" they say. And if somebody asks them, "How? What evil things does he do or teach them?" they cannot say. But in order not to appear at a loss, these people repeat the charges used against all philosophers: that we teach obscure things up in the clouds, that we teach atheism, and that we make the worst views appear to be the better. For people do not like to admit that their pretensions to knowledge have been exposed. And that, fellow Athenians, is the origin of the prejudices against me.

QUICK REVIEW
He must continue on his mission because it is better to obey god, not people.

But some of you will ask, "Don't you regret what you did since now it might mean your death?" To these I answer, "You are mistaken. A good man should not calculate his chances of living or dying. He should only ask himself whether he is doing right or wrong—whether his inner self is that of a good man or of an evil one."

QUICK REVIEW
If corruption is teaching the young to care more for their inner selves than anything else, then he does corrupt youth.

And if you say to me, "Socrates, we will let you go free but only on condition that you stop your questioning," then I will reply, "Men of Athens, I honor and love you. But I must obey god rather than you, and while I have life and strength I will never stop doing philosophy." For my aim is to persuade you all, young and old alike, not to think about your lives or your properties, but first and foremost to care about your inner self. I tell you that wealth does not make you good within, but that from inner goodness comes wealth and every other benefit to man. This is my teaching, and if it corrupts youth, then I suppose I am their corrupter.

QUICK REVIEW
Questioning is the greatest thing people can do because the unexamined life is not worth living.

Well, my fellow Athenians, you must now decide whether to acquit me or not. But whichever you do, understand that I will never change my ways, not even if I have to die many times. To talk daily about what makes us good, and to question myself and others, is the greatest thing man can do. For the unexamined life is not worth living.

[At this point, Socrates rested his case. The jury debated among themselves and then, in a split vote, they reached their final verdict.]

QUICK REVIEW
If death is a state of nothingness, dying is good; if there is an after-life, it is also good.

Men of Athens, you have condemned me to death. To those of you who are my friends and who voted to acquit me let me say that death may be a good thing. Either it is a state of nothingness and utter unconsciousness, or, as some people say, it is merely a migration from this world to another. If it is complete unconsciousness—like a sleep undisturbed even by dreams—then death will be an unspeakable gain. And if it is a journey to another world where all the dead live, then it will also be a great good. For then I can continue my search into true and false knowledge: In the next world, as in this one, I can continue questioning the great people of the past to find out who is wise and who merely pretends to be. So do not be saddened by death. No evil can happen to a good man either in this life or in death.

Well, the hour of departure has arrived, and we must each go our ways. I to die, and you to live. Which is better only god knows.[12]

Again, Socrates' speech provides a remarkable example of what philosophy is. Philosophy is the quest for wisdom: an unrelenting devotion to uncover the truth about what matters most in one's life. This quest is undertaken in the conviction

12 Plato, *The Apology*. This edited translation copyright © 1987 by Manuel Velasquez.

that a life based on an easy uncritical acceptance of conventional beliefs is an empty life. As Socrates puts it, "The unexamined life is not worth living." Philosophy is a quest that is difficult, not only because it requires hard thinking but also because it sometimes requires taking positions that are not shared by those around us. Taking such positions may offend others. In Socrates' case, his fellow citizens were so offended by what he said and did that they condemned him to death.

critical thinking

Socrates argues that death is either complete unconsciousness or a new life in a world like ours, and since both are great goods, death is a great good. Are the premises of this argument true?

Crito: Do We Have an Obligation to Obey the Law?

Socrates was jailed immediately after his trial. While awaiting his execution, he continued his avid questioning. But his questions then focused more on his own beliefs about right and wrong, good and evil. In one of his final conversations, recorded in the dialogue *Crito*, Socrates considered whether he had the courage to face death for his beliefs. The day before his execution, he awoke to find his close friend Crito sitting in his jail cell next to him:

To read more from Plato's *Crito*, go to CourseMate for this text and browse by chapter or philosopher.

SOCRATES: Crito! What are you doing here at this hour? It must be quite early.

CRITO: Yes, it is.

SOCRATES: What time is it?

CRITO: The dawn is breaking.

SOCRATES: I am surprised the jailer let you in. Did you just get here?

CRITO: No, I came some time ago.

SOCRATES: Then why did you sit and say nothing? Why have you come here this early?

CRITO: Oh my dear friend, Socrates! Let me beg you once again to take my advice and escape from here. If you die, I will not only lose a friend who can never be replaced, but people who do not know us will think that I could have saved you but was not willing to pay the necessary bribes. And you would be betraying your children since they surely will meet the unhappy fate of orphans.

QUICK REVIEW
In *Crito*, Socrates' friend urges him to escape from prison as "the many" would advise.

SOCRATES: Dear Crito, your zeal is invaluable, if it is right. But if wrong, the greater the zeal, the greater the evil. I have always been guided by reason. I cannot turn away now from the principles I have always tried to honor. So let us look carefully at the issues before us. Shall we begin with your views about what people will think? Tell me, were we right long ago when we said that not all the opinions of men should be valued? Consider the athlete: Should he follow the advice and opinions of every man? Or should he listen to one man only—his doctor or trainer?

CRITO: He should follow the one man's advice.

SOCRATES: He should train in the way that seems good to the one man who has understanding rather than listen to the opinions of the many?

CRITO: True.

SOCRATES: Doesn't the same principle hold, Crito, in the matter we are discussing: which course of action is right and good and which is wrong and evil? In this matter should we follow the opinions of the many or of the one who has understanding? If the athlete follows the advice of men who have no understanding, he will destroy his body, won't he?

CRITO: Yes.

SOCRATES: And is the body better than that inner part of ourselves—the soul—that is concerned with right and wrong, good and evil?!

QUICK REVIEW
Socrates replies that we should not listen to the opinions of the many but do what is truly right.

CRITO: Certainly not.

SOCRATES: Then, Crito, you are wrong to suggest that we should listen to the opinions of the many about right and wrong or good and evil. The values you bring up—money, loss of reputation, and educating children—are based on the opinions of the many. They do not concern the only real issue before us: Is it right or wrong for me to escape against the wishes of the Athenians? So follow me now in my questioning.

c.1650 (oil on canvas), Dufresnoy, Charles Alphonse (1611–68)/Galleria degli Uffizi, Florence, Italy/Alinari/The Bridgeman Art Library

The Death of Socrates

CRITO: I will do my best, Socrates.

SOCRATES: Is it true that we should never intentionally do wrong?

CRITO: It certainly is.

SOCRATES: And what about returning evil for evil—which is the morality of the many—is that right or not?

CRITO: It is not right.

SOCRATES: But in leaving this prison against the will of the Athenians, am I doing evil to anyone?

CRITO: I am not sure, Socrates.

SOCRATES: Well, imagine that just as I was about to escape, the laws of our government arrived and asked me, "Socrates, what are you trying to do? Do you want to destroy us? Won't government fall if its law has no power and if private citizens can set the law aside whenever they want?" How will I answer them, Crito? Perhaps I could respond, "Yes, but the government injured me: It sentenced me unjustly." Is that what I should say?

QUICK REVIEW
The government will collapse if its laws are not followed, so laws should be obeyed.

CRITO: Definitely, Socrates!

SOCRATES: Then what if the laws reply, "But didn't you agree to obey our judgments, Socrates?"

And if I show astonishment at this reply, the laws might add, "Do not be surprised, Socrates. You, who are always asking questions, answer us now. Long ago we gave you birth when your father married your mother by our aid and conceived you. Do you object to our marriage laws?"

"No," I would have to reply.

"Then do you object to the laws under which you were raised and which provided for your education?"

"They were fine," I would say.

"Well, then," they would conclude, "we gave you birth. And we raised and then educated you. Can you deny then that you are like our son and should obey us? Is it right to strike back at your father when he punishes you?

QUICK REVIEW
Moreover, citizens should obey their government because it is like a parent, because it gave them many benefits, and because they agreed to obey by freely choosing to stay. So it is wrong to escape the judgment of the government.

"Moreover, after we brought you into the world, and after we educated and provided you with many benefits, we proclaimed that you and all Athenians were free to leave us with all your goods when you came of age. But he who has experienced how we administer our society and freely chooses to stay, enters into an implied contract that he will obey us.

"So he who disobeys us, we maintain, does wrong in three ways: First, because in disobeying us he is disobeying his parents [since our marriage laws helped bring him into the world]; second, because in disobeying us he is disobeying those who gave him all the benefits involved with raising and educating him; third, because he agreed to obey us and now he neither obeys nor does he show us where we were wrong. But are we right in saying that you agreed to be governed by us?"

How shall I answer that question, Crito? Must I not agree?

CRITO: There is no other way, Socrates.

SOCRATES: Then the laws will say, "Then, Socrates, in escaping you are breaking the agreement you made with us. So listen to us and not to Crito. Think not of life and children first and of justice afterwards. Put justice first." This, Crito, is the voice I seem to hear quietly murmuring nearby, like a mystic who thinks he hears a flute playing in his ears. That voice is humming in my ears, and it prevents me from hearing any other. Still, if you have anything more to add, Crito, speak up.

CRITO: I have nothing more to say, Socrates.

SOCRATES: Then, Crito, let me do what I must, since it is the will of god.[13]

The next morning, after saying farewell to his family and friends, Socrates drank the poison hemlock and died.

Here again, then, on the evening of his death, we find Socrates doing philosophy. However, now he aims his philosophical questions at his own assumptions and his own life. He reasons that where morality is concerned, he should disregard the "opinions of the many"; that is, moral right and wrong do not depend on what most in our society believe. Instead, to determine what is right and wrong, we should rely on those who can reason correctly about these matters, i.e., reason correctly about whether one's actions inflict evil on others. Socrates therefore turns to the task of trying to reason correctly about whether escaping from prison as Crito suggests would inflict evil on anyone. Socrates' reasoning leads him to the conclusion that if he escaped, he would inflict evil on his government—the "laws"—because he has an obligation to obey it. He says he has this obligation, first, because his government is like a parent that gave him birth; second, because as he grew up the government bestowed important benefits on him; and third, because he tacitly agreed to obey the government. Other considerations, he claims, are irrelevant. What matters is that these three arguments prove that he has an obligation to obey the government. And so, Socrates concludes, it is wrong for him to escape.

critical thinking

In the Crito, *Socrates claims that he must obey the state. Does this claim contradict his claims in* The Apology, *where he says: "Men of Athens, I honor and love you. But I must obey god rather than you"?*

thinking critically • Identifying Premises, Conclusions, and Assumptions

How good are Socrates' arguments? To answer this question, we need first to figure out exactly what those arguments are. Let us focus on the three arguments he gives Crito at the very end of their conversation, since these state the fundamental reasons why

13 Plato, *Crito.* This translation copyright © 1987 by Manuel Velasquez.

PHILOSOPHY AND LIFE

Breaking the Law for the Sake of Justice

In 2011, huge crowds in the United States and other countries around the world broke the laws of their nations to protest against injustices. Hundreds of thousands of Arabs held illegal demonstrations in Tunisia, Lybia, Egypt, Yemen, Bahrain, Iran, Syria, and Morocco, protesting unjust government regimes. Protestors succeeded in overthrowing the governments of Tunisia, Lybia, and Egypt. In New York, "Occupy Wall Street" demonstrators illegally occupied a park near Wall Street to protest unjust economic inequalities that benefit the richest "1 percent" at the expense of the other "99 percent." Within days, the movement spread to Boston, Los Angeles, San Francisco, Washington, D.C., Salt Lake City, Philadelphia, Sacramento, Portland, Houston, Dallas, Tampa, New Orleans, Cleveland, Denver, Seattle, Berkeley, and more than a hundred other U.S. cities where demonstrators also illegally took over private property in protest of rising inequality. The movement also spread to dozens of cities in Europe, South America, and Australia where demonstrators used similar illegal tactics to protest the growing gap between the rich and the poor.

This was not the first time Americans deliberately broke the law to protest something they felt was morally wrong. During the 1960s, thousands of black people illegally sat in "white-only" sections of restaurants, theaters, buses, and other segregated businesses to protest unjust segregation laws, and thousands of blacks and whites engaged in civil disobedience to protest state laws that kept blacks from exercising their constitutional rights to vote and to attend the same public schools as whites. During the 1970s, tens of thousands of people broke the law to protest the U.S. war in Vietnam, occupying government property, refusing to pay taxes that would support the war, and trespassing on the private property of companies that made military weapons. In the 1990s, thousands broke the law to protest the Gulf War, and in 2003, thousands more did so to protest the war in Iraq. And during the past decade numerous groups have illegally occupied power plants, illegally blocked logging operations, illegally prevented construction workers from building new coal plants, and staged illegal sit-ins, all in protest of the ongoing destruction of the environment. When arrested, protesters have inevitably said that their actions are a matter of conscience and that they are obligated to obey their conscience rather than the law.

QUESTIONS

1. Is it morally wrong to break the law in the situations just described? Is it wrong when a demonstrator breaks only those specific laws the demonstrator believes are unjust? Explain your answers.
2. How would Socrates respond to the civil disobedience of these various groups of protesters? Who is right, Socrates or the demonstrators?

Socrates refuses to leave his prison. Socrates summarizes these arguments when he tells Crito that "the laws" (the government) will say:

> So he who disobeys us, we maintain, does wrong in three ways: First, because in disobeying us he is disobeying his parents [since our marriage laws helped bring him into the world]; second, because in disobeying us he is disobeying those who gave him all the benefits involved with raising and educating him; third, because he has agreed to obey us and now he neither obeys nor does he show us where we were wrong.

QUICK REVIEW
The conclusion of an argument is the basic claim the argument is trying to prove and is often indicated with the words: *so, therefore, consequently, hence, accordingly, which shows that, as a result, we may infer that, we may conclude that, which shows that.*

To figure out what Socrates' three arguments are, we need to identify the premises and the conclusion of each of the three arguments. The conclusion of an argument is the basic claim or assertion that the argument is trying to prove. Here the conclusion of the arguments is fairly easy to figure out since the three arguments are all supposed to prove that it is wrong to disobey "the laws." "The laws" here refers to the government. So the conclusion of the three arguments seems to be: "He who disobeys his government, does wrong," or, more simply: "It is wrong to disobey the government." How do we know that we have correctly identified the conclusion? When people state an argument, they often (but not always) use certain words to indicate what their conclusion is. Those words are: *so, therefore, consequently, hence, accordingly, which shows that, as a result, we may infer that, we may conclude that, which shows that.* Notice that in the earlier quote, Socrates uses the word "so": "*So* he who disobeys us, we maintain, does wrong in three ways." The use of the word "so" indicates that the sentence that follows is in fact the conclusion of the arguments.

So what are the premises of the arguments? The premises are the reasons or evidence given to support the conclusion. People tend to use certain words to indicate their premises. In particular, people often (but not always) use the following words to identify their premises: *because, inasmuch as, since, for, otherwise, in view of the fact that, for the reason that, on account of the fact that, in view of the fact that, considering that.* In the earlier quote, notice that Socrates uses the word "because" at the beginning of three sentences. That indicates that each of those sentences is the premise of an argument. So let's put each argument's premises and conclusion in a list, with the premises first and the conclusion last:

QUICK REVIEW
The premises of an argument consist of the reasons or evidence that support the conclusion and are often indicated with the words: *because, inasmuch as, since, for, otherwise, in view of the fact that, for the reason that, on account of the fact that, in view of the fact that, considering that.*

1st Argument: In disobeying the government, one is disobeying his parents [since the government's laws helped bring him into the world].
So: It is wrong to disobey the government.

2nd Argument: In disobeying the government, one is disobeying those who gave him all the benefits involved with raising and educating him.
So: It is wrong to disobey the government.

3rd Argument: One has agreed to obey the government and now he neither obeys nor does he show us where we went wrong.
So: It is wrong to disobey the government.

If you read over each of these arguments, you will notice that something seems to be missing in each: the arguments don't have a clear connection between what the premise says, and what the conclusion says. In each argument, the premise indicates what disobeying the government involves, but the premise does not say anything about the wrongness of this. Yet the conclusion jumps to a claim about the wrongness of disobeying. How does the argument move from a premise that says nothing about wrongness to a conclusion about wrongness? What is the connection between the premise and the conclusion?

Well, Socrates does not tell us what that connection is: It is an unstated assumption that he leaves for you to figure out. But this is not unusual. You will see a lot of arguments that jump from a premise to a conclusion without a clear connection between them. And when an argument does this, it is up to you to figure out what the unstated connection is, i.e., to figure out the unstated assumption that connects the premise to the conclusion.

Fortunately, in this case, the connecting assumptions are not hard to figure out. Let's take the first argument. The argument begins with the premise that disobeying the government is the same as disobeying a parent, and the argument concludes from this that disobeying the government is wrong. Obviously, the premise that disobeying the government is the same as disobeying a parent, proves that disobeying the government is wrong *only if it is wrong to disobey a parent.* So the argument as stated in (1) earlier is missing an unstated premise, i.e., a premise that is assumed but not stated and that is needed if the premises are to support or prove the conclusion. If we add the missing or assumed premise to the argument, and we get rid of unnecessary words, we can restate the complete argument like this:

QUICK REVIEW
To identify a missing premise or unstated assumption of an argument, we must identify the claim(s) that is needed if the premises are to support or prove the conclusion.

1st Argument: Disobeying one's government is the same as disobeying one's parents.
But disobeying one's parents is wrong.
Therefore, disobeying one's government is wrong.

The second argument is similar. The second argument begins with the premise that disobeying one's government is the same as disobeying someone who gives one the benefits of being raised and educated. How would this premise prove that disobeying one's government is wrong? Obviously, disobeying one's government would be wrong *only if it is wrong to disobey someone who gives one the benefits of being raised and educated.* So the second argument can be restated with the assumed premise like this:

> 2nd Argument: Disobeying one's government is the same as disobeying someone who gives one the benefits of being raised and educated.
> But disobeying someone who gives one the benefits of being raised and educated is wrong.
> Therefore, disobeying one's government is wrong.

The third argument begins with the premise that everyone makes an agreement to obey their government. Then it concludes that it is wrong to disobey the government. How can this premise and conclusion be connected? Well clearly, making an agreement to obey the government would make disobeying the government wrong, *only if not doing what you agree to do is wrong.* So inserting this assumed premise into the third argument leaves us with this:

> 3rd Argument: One makes an agreement to obey one's government.
> If one makes an agreement to obey one's government, then not obeying one's government is wrong.
> Therefore, not obeying (or disobeying) one's government is wrong.

Now that we have complete statements of Socrates' three arguments, we can see if they are acceptable. To do this, you need to ask whether the premises are true. Take the first argument: Is it true that the government is like a parent to you, and is it true that it is wrong to disobey a parent? Or take the second argument: Is it true that government has given you the benefits of helping to raise you and educate you, and is it true that if your government bestows such benefits on you, then you should repay it by obeying its laws? And take the third argument: Is it true, as Socrates suggests, that an adult who "has experienced how we administer our society and freely chooses to stay, enters into an implied contract that he will obey" the government? And is it true that if you make an agreement, then not doing what you agreed to do is wrong?

We will not answer these questions, but I think you will agree that their answers are significant, so we must return to them in a later chapter. At this point, what is important is the realization that stating arguments clearly and then pondering the questions they raise is crucial to philosophy. Socrates' own willingness to struggle with these questions even in the face of death gives us a priceless and still powerful example of what philosophy is.

QUESTIONS

1. Have you known bright people who weren't wise? Why weren't they wise? Make two lists, one containing the characteristics of intelligent people, the other the characteristics of wise people. How much overlap is there? What kind of wisdom would you like to possess?
2. Are actions right because your society believes they are right? When you are unsure whether an action is right, do you try to determine its rightness or wrongness by trying to find out what your society believes?
3. It is sometimes said that the admission of ignorance is the beginning of wisdom. Does Socrates' self-defense indicate this belief?
4. Do you have an obligation to obey the law? What is the basis of this obligation? How far does it extend? Could you ever have an obligation to disobey the law? What makes these questions philosophical questions?
5. What exactly is the meaning of Socrates' maxim "The unexamined life is not worth living"? How does this saying relate to philosophy?

6. Near the beginning of the *Crito*, Socrates claims that we should not listen to the opinions of the many about right and wrong or good and evil. What is the argument Socrates uses to support this claim?
7. At the end of the *Crito*, Socrates says: "For if you did not know the nature of holiness and unholiness I am sure you would never have charged your aged father with murder and run the risk of doing wrong in the sight of the gods." Supply the conclusion and the missing premise of the argument Socrates is suggesting here.
8. At the end of the *Apology*, Socrates claims that death is a good thing. What is the argument he uses to support this claim?
9. In his discussion with Thrasymachus (from the *Republic*), Socrates claims that justice is not merely following laws that benefit the rulers. What is the argument he gives for this claim?

PHILOSOPHY AT THE MOVIES

Watch *Hunger* (2009), a film about twenty-seven-year-old Bobby Sands who, in prison for his activities as a member of the PIRA (a paramilitary group battling against British rule of Northern Ireland), joins other PIRA prisoners who seek "prisoner of war" status and more humane treatment through protests such as refusing to wear prisoner garb, refusing to wash themselves, smearing their cells with excrement, and, finally, organizing a hunger strike in which Sands is the first to die. In what ways is Bobby Sands' commitment to what he believes is "right" similar to Socrates' commitment to what he believes is right? Is their commitment different in any important ways?

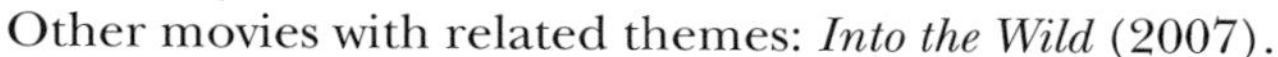

Other movies with related themes: *Into the Wild* (2007).

1.4 The Value of Philosophy

A person studying philosophy for the first time might ask a question: Why devote all this time and effort to study philosophy?

QUICK REVIEW
For Plato, philosophical knowledge makes us free.

Achieving Freedom

We have seen that Plato, in the Myth of the Cave, suggested an answer: The value of philosophy is that through it we achieve freedom—freedom from assumptions we have unquestioningly accepted from others, and freedom to decide for ourselves what we believe about ourselves and our place in the world around us.

Other philosophical traditions have also suggested that philosophical wisdom will lead to personal freedom, but to a different, more profound kind of freedom than Plato had in mind. For example, Buddhism holds that when we have dispelled our philosophical ignorance and have understood the true nature of the universe, we will be freed from the otherwise unending wheel of birth, suffering, death, and rebirth to which all living creatures are bound. In this view, each living thing, when it dies, is reincarnated in another living thing, its new condition determined by its past action, or karma. Yet by dispelling ignorance and acquiring wisdom we are each able to break out of the wheel. For example, Buddhist writings of the second century CE describe a vision experienced by the great Eastern sage, Buddha:

QUICK REVIEW
For Buddha, philosophical knowledge frees us from the cycle of birth, suffering, death, and rebirth.

> In the first watch of the night he recalled his previous births. He remembered thousands of births as if he was living them all over again. "There I was so and so and my name was such and such; I died and from there I came here." Upon recalling his many births and deaths in these lives, he was filled with compassion for all

> living things: "Again and again they tear themselves away from their family in one life, and must go on to live another. And they must do this endlessly. This world is truly helpless as it turns round and round like a wheel." Without flinching, he continued recalling his past and began to realize that this world of endless turning must be as insubstantial as the hollow core of a banana tree. In the second watch of the night . . . he saw the entire world as though reflected in a spotless mirror. He saw that the death and rebirth of each creature is determined by how inferior or superior its previous actions have been. This is the law of action. And his compassion grew even greater. He saw there was no resting place in the river of endless rebirth and death. . . . Then, as the third watch of that night approached, he meditated on the nature of this world: "How sad that living beings wear themselves out for nothing! Over and over again they are born, grow old, die, pass on, and are reborn! What is more, desire and illusion blind them so that they have no knowledge of how to end this suffering." . . . He looked at the processes by which one thing leads to another, and saw that it is ultimately because we lack knowledge that we end up subject to old age and death, and that ending this ignorance can lead to the end of rebirth, old age, death and suffering. The great seer realized that if our ignorance is overcome, then even the law of action will stop. At that moment he achieved a true knowledge of all there is to be known, and he stood out in the world as a Buddha. . . . For seven days he dwelt there. . . . He thought, "Here I have found freedom."[14]

In the Buddhist perspective, then, philosophy can lead to the ultimate freedom: an understanding of the universe that will allow us to escape from the endless cycles of birth, suffering, death, and rebirth to which we are condemned by our past. From this perspective, then, the value of philosophical wisdom is great indeed!

critical thinking

Philosophers assume that expanding our personal freedom, autonomy, and the alternatives open to us are all good. How important is this assumption to the claim that philosophy is also good?

Building Your View of Life

Still, the value that Plato and the Buddha attribute to philosophical wisdom may not be enough for you. Everyday tasks and social preoccupations crowd our lives and leave us little time for anything else. Why should we spend the time and effort to study philosophy when so many more practical needs are pressing in on us? For example, it is clear why we should spend time studying those subjects that will provide the knowledge and skills needed to get a job or succeed in a career. We each need a job or a career to get along, to earn our living and meet our basic needs. But why should we spend time studying philosophy?

Consider, first, that we all seek to make sense of the world we live in and to understand our place in that world. We seek to do this in a variety of ways: through allegiance to religious beliefs, adherence to political parties, commitments to causes. Such loyalties and behaviors reveal the human need to put order in our world and to make sense of things. One goal of philosophy is to develop a unified, coherent view of yourself and your life in the world. Studying philosophy will expose you to different ways of making sense of the world. It also will show you how various philosophers have conceived of the universe around us and of their place in that universe. Seeing all this will help you develop a view of life that can enable you, too, to make sense of yourself and your place in the world around you.

---

14 This translation is based in part on the translation in *Sacred Texts of the World*, ed. Ninian Smart and Richard D. Hecht (New York: Crossroad, 1982), 234–235, and in part on the translation of the same passages in E. H. Johnston, trans., *The Buddhacarita or Acts of the Buddha* (Delhi, India: Motilal Banarsidass, 1972), 203–204, 208–209, and 213. I have further edited the text to simplify and clarify it and to modernize the language.

What's more, philosophy will expose you to the history of thought. By portraying humanity's intellectual achievements, philosophy provides a perspective on the continuing development of human thought. As we confront the thoughts and views of various philosophers, we realize that there are many different ways of understanding the universe. A merit of this exposure is that it breeds humility. We realize that the way we have always thought about ourselves and our universe is but one way among many. As a result, we become more tolerant, more receptive, and more sympathetic to views that conflict with our own. We're less biased, provincial, ingrown; we're more open-minded and cosmopolitan.

Cultivating Awareness

Something else that makes philosophy worthwhile is the mindfulness or awareness that it can help us cultivate. Consider the importance of awareness. Personal freedom depends to a large extent on one's awareness of the self and how our actions and thoughts are being influenced by the world around us. To a large degree, we are free only to the extent that we are aware of these many significant influences. In helping us deepen our awareness of these, philosophy will give you the ability to deal with and perhaps throw off the blinders that keep you unaware and unfree.

PHILOSOPHY AND LIFE

Albert Ellis and Rational Emotive Behavior Therapy

Dr. Albert Ellis is a well-known clinical psychologist who has developed a form of therapy based on the idea that neurotic symptoms and psychological problems spring from an irrational philosophy: irrational beliefs that are the result of "philosophical conditioning." According to Ellis, our emotions and behaviors are the result of the beliefs and assumptions we have about ourselves, other people, and the world in general. It is what people *believe* about the situations they face—not the situations themselves—that determines how they feel and behave. According to Ellis, this idea was first stated by Epictetus, a Roman stoic philosopher who, in the first century CE, said that people are disturbed not by things but by the views they take of them. To eliminate the disturbance, we need merely change our views. In his book *The Essence of Rational Emotive Behavior Therapy* (1994), Ellis states that although many irrational philosophical beliefs exist, the three main ones that affect our happiness are:

1. *"I must do well and get approval, or I am worthless."*
2. *"You must treat me reasonably, considerately, and lovingly, or else you're no good."*
3. *"Life must be fair, easy, and hassle-free, or else it's awful."*

If a person is to be happy, he or she must change these irrational philosophical beliefs, which are the source of anxiety, depression, hopelessness, resentment, hostility, and violence. The person can change these irrational ideas by asking questions: "Is there any evidence for this belief?" "What is the evidence against this belief?" "What is the worst that can happen if I give up this belief?" "What is the best that can happen?" We can be happy only when the irrational beliefs that underlie our neuroses and other psychological problems are replaced by a more rational philosophy.

QUESTIONS

1. Do you agree that a person's philosophical assumptions can have the significant psychological impacts that Ellis' theory claims? If Ellis is right, what are the implications for philosophy?
2. Consider Ellis' three main irrational beliefs and determine whether they belong to the field of epistemology, metaphysics, or ethics.
3. Can you think of any other "philosophical beliefs" that can produce the kinds of psychological problems that Ellis describes?
4. What if Ellis' three beliefs are true? Could they be true? Explain.

Learning to Think Critically

QUICK REVIEW
Philosophy also helps us to build a view of life, to be more aware, and to think critically.

Finally, we should note that the study of philosophy will help you refine your ability to reason well, and this ability will help you get ahead in every area of your life and education. Philosophy can teach you to think critically, to reason, and to evaluate how adequate your own reasoning, or the reasoning of others, is. As we said earlier, such skills are the tools of philosophy. Pondering the great ideas and arguments of extraordinary thinkers will hone your powers of analysis and give you reasoning skills that you will be able to use in every area of your life: your job, your other classes, your close relationships, and your political and social activities.

In fact, the importance and value of good reasoning and critical thinking cannot be exaggerated. Every day we are bombarded by advertisements, political controversies, claims about climate change, arguments about the morality of abortion, assertions about the evils of immigration, and countless other claims and counterclaims, arguments and counterarguments. Politicians tell us what they think our country needs and try to convince us to vote for them. Companies try to persuade us to buy their products. News commentators, bloggers, and editorials try to influence our thinking. Every day we hear some people issue dire warnings about the future, while others argue that the warnings are exaggerated. Without the ability to think critically, to reason well, and to evaluate the reasoning of others, we are vulnerable to all these different interests and their constant clamor to have us do what they tell us to do, and think what they tell us to think. If we are to be able to defend ourselves against the countless attempts at persuasion that surround us every moment of every day, we must learn how to evaluate the many claims and arguments they hurl at us. Philosophy, with its ability to instill good reasoning skills, will be of invaluable help as you try to navigate your way through these numerous attempts to sway your thinking and your decisions.

Does Philosophy Have a Male Bias?

This is, perhaps, the place to consider an important objection to the value of philosophy. Recently, some feminist philosophers have questioned whether philosophy has any value to women. Philosophy, they have argued, is essentially a male activity because the basic ideas and methods of philosophy are biased against women and in favor of men.

The feminist philosopher Janice Moulton, for example, has pointed out that most philosophers use an "adversarial method" of inquiry. That is, most philosophers approach other philosophers as adversaries whose views they must attack and prove wrong. As she suggests, the adversarial method seems to leave no room for the kind of nonadversarial search for the truth that women favor. Instead, it may be rooted in male aggression.[15]

QUICK REVIEW
Feminists such as Moulton and Lloyd argue that philosophy has had a male bias.

Genevieve Lloyd, also a feminist philosopher, has pointed out in an insightful and masterful analysis of the history of philosophy that males have dominated philosophy from the beginning. These male philosophers have associated favorable traits with men and unfavorable ones with women. Lloyd notes that this approach has given philosophy a male bias that is unattractive to women:

> The equation of maleness with superiority goes back at least as far as the Pythagoreans. What is valued—whether it be odd as against even numbers, "aggressive" as against "nurturing" skills and capacities, or Reason as against emotion—has been readily identified with maleness. Within the context of this association of maleness

15 Janice Moulton, "A Paradigm of Philosophy: The Adversarial Method," in *Women, Knowledge, and Reality*, 5–20.

> with preferred traits, it is not just incidental to the feminine that female traits have been construed as inferior . . . to male norms of human excellence. The denigration of the "feminine" is to feminists, understandably, the most salient aspect of the maleness of the philosophical tradition.[16]

If Moulton and Lloyd are correct, if philosophy is at bottom a male activity with a male bias, it seems that women have little reason to consider philosophizing. Why engage in an activity that has produced such sexist views? Why should a woman engage in a man's game played by men's rules? Why should women philosophize? Lloyd answers these questions herself:

> Understanding the contribution of past thought to "male" and "female" consciousnesses, as we now have them, can help make available a diversity of intellectual styles and characters to men and women alike. It need not involve a denial of all difference. Contemporary consciousness, male or female, reflects past philosophical ideals as well as past differences in the social organization of the lives of men and women. Such differences do not have to be taken as norms; and understanding them can be a source of richness and diversity in a human life whose full range of possibilities and experience is freely accessible to both men and women.[17]

Lloyd suggests that the most important task—for women *and* men—is to understand and change the mistaken philosophical assumptions about men and women that past male philosophers have given us. Our world, our families, our friends, our music, our magazines, our movies, and our televisions all now repeat these assumptions.

If feminists such as Moulton and Lloyd are correct—and there is some reason to believe that they are—then philosophy has left us with sexist and distorted philosophical views of ourselves. We must all work together to change these. Women, no less than men, must engage in philosophical thought to correct these distortions. Women, especially, must create a new way of thinking about what it is to be a woman or a man in today's world. Moreover, unless women enter philosophy, male philosophers will continue to use methods of inquiry that are unpalatable to women and that result in distorted ideas. Women must philosophize, then, to reshape the philosophical assumptions that influence our thinking and to create more cooperative and inclusive methods of philosophizing. In short, if philosophy is the central problem, it is also the source of the fundamental solution.

QUICK REVIEW
Women must engage in philosophy to correct the male biases of previous philosophizing.

The Theme of This Text

In the pages ahead, as we consider many enduring philosophical questions and hone our reasoning skills, uppermost in each of our minds will be this question: Who and what am I? We could call this the unifying theme that draws together what may seem disparate philosophical concerns. We'll see that the study of philosophy can help us in answering this question, for ultimately a human being is many things: a real existing being; a moral, social, and political animal; a perceiver and knower; a scientist; a religionist; and a pilgrim in search of meaning. All these aspects of humanity and self are areas of intense philosophical concern and speculation. Therefore, our adventure into the world of philosophy is more than an encounter with great ideas, thinkers, systems, and movements. It's a voyage into ourselves, a quest for self-definition and understanding.

---

16 Genevieve Lloyd, *The Man of Reason: "Male" and "Female" in Western Philosophy* (Minneapolis: University of Minnesota Press, 1984), 103–104.
17 Ibid., 107.

QUESTIONS

1. Give an example of how increasing your awareness has made you freer.
2. What is the difference, if any, between approaching reality through poetry and approaching reality philosophically?
3. What is the difference, if any, between approaching reality through the methods of the natural sciences and approaching reality philosophically?
4. Is there anything that women can bring to philosophy that men cannot? Explain. Do you think that women philosophize in a different way or about different things than men do? Explain.

© Photos 12/Alamy

PHILOSOPHY AT THE MOVIES

Watch *Pleasantville* (1998) an older classic, about a young man, David, and his twin sister, Jennifer, who are sucked through their television into a 1950s black-and-white sitcom where it is always a pleasant 72 degrees, books have no words, there is no sex, and everyone accepts rigid conventional lives. Does the use of color in *Pleasantville* indicate enlightenment? What do black and white indicate? What role, if any, do you see autonomy, knowledge, rationality, freedom, and choice playing in the movie? What does the library represent?

Another movie with related themes: *Revolutionary Road* (2008); a related older classic: *A Clockwork Orange* (1971).

Chapter Summary

This opening chapter tries to communicate some of the interest and importance of philosophy and to show that philosophy is not to be feared but rather to be cultivated and relished. We began by observing that everyone philosophizes in daily life, and we saw how Plato pictured philosophy as a climb from darkness to light in the pursuit of wisdom. We cited the three main fields of philosophy and then turned to watch the philosopher Socrates at work. We saw the value of studying philosophy: Nevertheless, we noted that some feminists have charged that up to now philosophy has had a male bias.

The main points of this chapter are:

1.1 What Is Philosophy?

- Philosophy, which literally means the love of wisdom, begins with wonder about our most basic beliefs. Its goal is to help us achieve autonomy by making us more aware of our own beliefs and encouraging us to reason and think through issues for ourselves.
- The Myth of the Cave is one of the best-known passages in *The Republic*, a work of the Greek philosopher Plato. The myth describes the philosopher's climb from the dark cave of philosophical ignorance up into the light of philosophical wisdom.
- **Philosophy is the critical and rational examination of the most fundamental assumptions that underlie our lives, an activity of concern to men and women of all cultures and races.**
- **Reasoning is the process of thinking by which we draw a conclusion from the reasons or evidence that support or prove the conclusion. Critical thinking is disciplined thinking that bases beliefs and actions on well-founded evidence and unbiased and valid reasoning, that avoids false**

generalizations and unrecognized assumptions, and that considers opposing viewpoints.

1.2 The Traditional Divisions of Philosophy

- The three main fields of philosophy are epistemology, metaphysics, and ethics.
- Epistemology deals with questions of knowledge (including the structure, reliability, extent, and kinds of knowledge); truth, validity, and logic; and a variety of linguistic concerns. An example is the question of whether truth is relative.
- Metaphysics addresses questions of reality (including the meaning and nature of being); the nature of mind, self, and human freedom; and some topics that overlap with religion, such as the existence of God, the destiny of the universe, and the immortality of the soul. An example is the question of whether human behavior is free or determined.
- Ethics is the study of our values and moral principles and how they relate to human conduct and to our social and political institutions. For example, do we have a moral obligation to love and serve others, or is our only obligation to ourselves?
- Philosophy also includes several fields usually referred to as "the philosophy of . . .," including the philosophy of science, the philosophy of art, and the philosophical meaning of life. These fields of philosophy examine the basic assumptions underlying particular areas of human knowledge or activity.

Philosophical claims should be clear and neither vague nor ambiguous.

Philosophical claims, unlike speculation, must be supported by arguments. Arguments consist of (1) premises, which provide reasons or evidence for a conclusion, and (2) the conclusion, which is the claim that those premises support.

1.3 A Philosopher in Action: Socrates

- Socrates is usually considered the father of Western philosophy, although he was preceded by a group of earlier Greek philosophers, the pre-Socratics. Socrates was put to death for persistently examining the unquestioned assumptions of his fellow Athenians. Plato, a disciple of Socrates, preserved his views in dialogues, including *Euthyphro, The Republic, The Apology*, and *Crito*.
- *Euthyphro* shows Socrates questioning traditional religious beliefs; *The Republic* shows Socrates inquiring into the meaning of justice; *The Apology* shows Socrates at his trial explaining his lifelong commitment to philosophy; *Crito* shows Socrates awaiting death and questioning his own beliefs about the authority of the state.

To evaluate a philosopher's claims, like those of Socrates, we must identify the premises and conclusions of his or her arguments. Premises are reasons or evidence given to support a conclusion and are often indicated by words such as *because, inasmuch as, since, for, otherwise, in view of the fact that, for the reason that, on account of the fact that, in view of the fact that, considering that.* The conclusion is the main point or claim the argument is trying to prove or establish and is often indicated by words such as *because, inasmuch as, since, for, otherwise, in view of the fact that, for the reason that, on account of the fact that, in view of the fact that, considering that.*

- **Sometimes arguments, like some in the *Crito*, are missing an assumed premise. To identify the missing premise or unstated assumption of an argument, we must ask: What claim(s) is needed if the premises are to support or prove the conclusion? Once the premises and the conclusion of an argument are identified and organized into a list in which the premises are first and the conclusion is last, the argument can be assessed by figuring out whether the premises are true or false.**

1.4 The Value of Philosophy

- Both Plato and Buddha claim that philosophy can help us achieve freedom; philosophy can also make us more tolerant and enable us to think critically and reason well, skills that can help us in almost every area of our lives.
- Because philosophy has had many "male tendencies," it is especially important for women to philosophize now.

1.5 Reading

Why study philosophy? In his short story, the eighteenth-century French philosopher Voltaire suggests that even though an ignorant person may be much happier than a learned philosopher, we nevertheless "madly" prefer the despair of philosophy to the happy contentment of ignorance. Is this true? And if it is, why do we prefer knowledge to happiness?

VOLTAIRE

Story of a Good Brahman

I met on my travels an old Brahman, a very wise man, full of wit and very learned; moreover he was rich, and consequently even wiser; for, lacking nothing, he had no need to deceive anyone. His family was very well run by three beautiful wives who schooled themselves to please him; and when he was not entertaining himself with his wives, he was busy philosophizing.

Near his house, which was beautiful, well decorated, and surrounded by charming gardens, lived an old Indian woman, bigoted, imbecilic, and rather poor.

The Brahman said to me one day: "I wish I had never been born."

I asked him why. He replied:

"I have been studying for forty years, which is forty years wasted; I teach others, and I know nothing; this situation brings into my soul so much humiliation and disgust that life is unbearable to me. I was born, I live in time, and I do not know what time is; I find myself standing between two eternities, as our sages say, and I have no idea what eternity is. I am composed of matter; I think, and I have never been able to find out how it produces thought; I do not know whether my understanding is a simple faculty in me like that of walking or of digesting, and whether I think with my head, as I take with my hands. Not only is the source of my thinking unknown to me, but the source of my movements is equally hidden from me. I do not know why I exist. However, people every day ask me questions on all these points; I have to answer; I have nothing any good to say; I talk much, and I remain confounded and ashamed of myself after talking.

"It is much worse yet when they ask me whether Brahma was produced by Vishnu or whether they are both eternal. God is my witness that I don't know a thing about these, and it certainly shows in my answers. 'Ah! Reverend Father,' they say to me, 'teach us how it is that evil inundates the whole world.' I am as much at a loss as those who ask me that question; I sometimes tell them that everything that happens is for the best, but those who have been ruined and mutilated by war don't believe it, and neither do I; I retreat to my house overwhelmed with my curiosity and my ignorance. I read our ancient books, and they redouble the darkness I am in. I talk to my companions: some answer that we must enjoy life and laugh at men; the others think they know something, and lose themselves in absurd ideas; everything increases the painful feeling I endure. I am sometimes ready to fall into despair, when I think that after all my seeking I know neither where I come from, nor what I am, nor where I shall go, nor what shall become of me."

The state of this good man caused me real pain; no one was either more reasonable or more honest than he. I perceived that the greater the lights of his understanding and the sensibility of his heart, the more unhappy he was.

That same day I saw the old woman who lived nearby: I asked her whether she had ever been distressed not to know how her soul was made. She did not even understand my question: she had never reflected a single moment of her life over a single one of the points that tormented the Brahman; she believed with all her heart in the metamorphoses of Vishnu, and, provided she could sometimes have some water from the Ganges to wash in, she thought herself the happiest of women.

Struck by the happiness of this indigent creature, I returned to my philosopher and said to him:

"Aren't you ashamed to be unhappy at a time when right at your door there is an old automaton who thinks of nothing and who lives happily?"

"You are right," he answered; "I have told myself a hundred times that I would be happy if I was as stupid as my neighbor, and yet I would want no part of such a happiness."

This answer of my Brahman made a greater impression on me than all the rest. I examined myself and saw that indeed I would not have wanted to be happy on condition of being imbecilic.

I put the matter up to some philosophers, and they were of my opinion.

"There is, however," I said, "a stupendous contradiction in this way of thinking. For after all, what is at issue? Being happy. What does it matter whether one is witty or stupid? What is more, those who are content with their being are quite sure of being content; those who reason are not so sure of reasoning well.

"So it is clear," I said, "that we should not choose to have common sense, if common sense made us discontented."

Everyone was of my opinion, and yet I found no one who wanted to accept the bargain of becoming imbecilic in order to become content. From this I concluded that even if we value happiness, we value reason even more.

But, upon reflection, it appears that to prefer reason to happiness is to be mad. Then how can this contradiction be explained? Like all the others. There is much to be said about it.

"Story of a Good Brahman," from *Candide, Zadig and Selected Stories by Voltaire* by François Voltaire, translated by Donald M. Frame. Translation copyright 1961 by Donald M. Frame. Used by permission of Dutton Signet, a division of Penguin Putnam Inc.

1.6 HISTORICAL SHOWCASE

The First Philosophers

Because so much material is, and must be, covered in any introduction to philosophy, the overall treatment may lack focus and leave the student confused or with only a most superficial understanding. Although there is no easy solution to this problem, one useful device is to take a more in-depth look at important figures in the material being covered. This book will use this strategy. Because the purpose of this technique is to exhibit the writings and thoughts of philosophers, an appropriate term for it is *showcase*. Each showcase includes both an overview of the philosophy of important figures and edited selections from their writings so that you can read each philosopher's own words. Moreover, taken together, the showcases are intended to provide a feeling for the history of philosophy. Consequently, for the most part they are in historical order.

Because we are beginning philosophy, our first showcase spotlights the earliest Western and Eastern philosophers. Examining these will give us a better idea of the historical significance of philosophy. These first philosophers had a remarkable impact on how we view reality and ourselves today, an impact that philosophy continues to have through the ages.

Pre-Socratic Western Philosophers

THALES: EXPLAINING REALITY

Western philosophy began with a question the Greek thinker Thales asked around 585 BCE: What is the ultimate reality of which everything is made? Thales' answer will strike you as a bit funny and prosaic. He answered, "Everything ultimately is made of water!"

But the factual correctness of Thales' answer isn't really important. What is significant is that he was the first to take a radically new "philosophical" approach to reality. Thinkers before Thales were content to explain reality as the whimsical work of mythical gods. For example, the Greek poet Hesiod (circa 776 BCE) explains how the sky came to rain on the earth by describing the sky as a male god who was castrated by his son while sleeping with goddess Earth:

> Great Heaven came at night longing for love.
> He lay on Earth spreading himself full on her.
> Then from an ambush, his own son stretched out
> his left hand.
> And wielding a long sharp sickle in his right, He
> swiftly sliced and cut his father's genitals.
> Earth received the bloody drops that all gushed
> forth.
> And she gave birth to the great Furies and mighty
> giants.
> Now when chaste Heaven desires to penetrate the
> Earth,
> And Earth is filled with longing for this union,
> Rain falling from her lover, Heaven, impreg-
> nates her,
> And she brings forth wheat for men and pastures
> for their flocks.[1]

Thales departed in three ways from this mythological and poetic approach to reality. First, he had the idea that although reality is complex, it should be explainable in terms of one or a few basic elements. Second, he decided that reality should be explained in terms of natural, observable things (such as water) and not by poetic appeals to unobservable gods. Third, he rejected the idea that reality should be explained through the authority of religious myths from the past, which could neither be proved nor disproved. Instead, he tried to provide a literal and factual explanation that others could evaluate for themselves through reasoning and observation.

Thus, although Thales' theory—that water is the basic stuff out of which everything is made—seems naive, he was the first to break away from religious myth and strike out on a path that uses human reason and observation to explore the universe. His having taken this momentous and daring step marks him as a genius. In fact, today we continue to travel the road Thales showed us. Much of our basic scientific research is still devoted to finding the simplest elemental forces out of which everything in the universe is made, and we still proceed by proposing theories or *hypotheses* that can be proved or disproved through reason and observation. It took the genius of Thales to set Western civilization on this amazingly fruitful path of discovery.

But two other early Greek philosophers, Heraclitus (circa 554–484 BCE) and Parmenides (circa 480–430 BCE), proposed the most interesting and radical of the early philosophical views of reality. Both philosophers left the question of what things are made of and turned their attention to the problem of *change*—whether change is a basic reality or a mere illusion, real or merely appearance.

HERACLITUS: REALITY IS CHANGE

Heraclitus, in a remarkable series of sayings, proposed that change is the fundamental reality. He asserted that like a fire's flame, "All reality is changing." Like a flowing river, everything in the universe changes from moment to moment, so we can never touch or perceive the same thing in two different moments. The only enduring realities are the recurring patterns (like the seasons) of change itself:

> In the same rivers we step and yet we do not step; we ourselves are the same and yet we are not. You cannot step in the same river twice, for other waters are ever flowing on. The sun is new every day. The living and the dead, the waking and sleeping, the young and the old, these are changing into each other; the former are moved about and become the latter, the latter in turn become the former. Neither god nor man shaped this universe, but it ever was and ever shall be a living Fire that flames up and dies in measured patterns. There is a continual exchange: all things are exchanged for Fire and Fire for all things. Fire steers the universe. God changes like Fire.[2]

PARMENIDES AND ZENO: CHANGE IS AN ILLUSION

Parmenides, convinced that Heraclitus was completely mistaken, proposed a theory that was the exact opposite. Parmenides held that change is an illusion and that the universe in reality is a frozen, unchanging object: "We can speak and think only of

1 Hesiod, *The Theogony*, pt. 11, lines 177–185. This translation copyright © 1987 by Manuel Velasquez.

2 Diels-Kranz, *Fragments of the Presocratics*, Heraclitus, fragments 49, 12, 6, 88, 30, 90, 64, 67, trans. Manuel Velasquez.

what exists. And what exists is uncreated and imperishable, for it is whole and unchanging and complete. It was not nor shall be different since it is now, all at once, one and continuous."[3] How was Parmenides led to this view? He argued that nothingness or "nonbeing" cannot be real because we cannot even think of nothingness. Yet change requires nonbeing or nothingness. For if something changes, it must change into something that did not exist before: Something must come into being out of nonbeing. But nonbeing does not exist. So nothing can come from nonbeing. Therefore, change cannot exist; the universe has no beginning, and nothing in it changes:

> For what beginning of the universe could you search for? From what could it come? I will not let you say or think "From what was not" because you cannot even conceive of "what is not." Nor will true thinking allow that, besides what exists, new things could also arise from something that does not exist. How could what exists pass into what does not exist? And how can what does not exist come into existence? For if it came into existence, then it earlier was nothingness. And nothingness is unthinkable and unreal.[4]

Parmenides' strange view received support from one of his students, Zeno. Zeno argued that "a runner cannot move from one point to another. For to do so, he must first get to a point half-way across, and to do this, he must get half-way to the half-way point, and to do this he must get half-way to that point, and so on for an infinite number of spaces."[5] Because an infinite number of spaces cannot be crossed (at least not in a finite length of time), Zeno concluded that no object moves: Motion is an illusion of our senses!

CONTRIBUTIONS OF THE PRE-SOCRATIC PHILOSOPHERS

In spite of—or perhaps because of—their unusual views, the pre-Socratic philosophers made several crucial contributions to our thinking. They got us to rely on our reason and to search for new ways of looking at reality instead of relying on the authority of the past. They introduced us to the problem of the one and the many: Can the many things of our experience be explained in terms of one or a few fundamental constituents? They introduced the problem of appearance and reality: Does a more basic reality underlie the changing world that appears before us? Moreover, the views they proposed continue even today to have followers. Modern "process philosophers," for example, hold that change or "process" is the fundamental reality, and some modern British philosophers have held that change is an illusion.

Eastern Philosophers

THE VEDAS

But even before Thales, Parmenides, and Heraclitus had developed their fresh nonmythical approach to reality, the great visionaries of India had put Eastern philosophy (those systems of thought, belief, and action espoused by many peoples in the Near and Far East) on a similar road to reality. However, this road would take Eastern philosophy in a very different direction.

Between 1500 and 700 BCE, the first of a long line of Indian thinkers composed the Vedas, poetic hymns that contain the beginnings of Indian wisdom and that were meant to be chanted in religious ceremonies. The authors of many of these hymns are unknown, and many of the hymns describe "visions" of "seers." These writings, steeped in myth and symbolism, nevertheless also contain early attempts to find a new nonmythical understanding of the universe. Here is how one of the greatest of these hymns, the Rig Veda, describes the origin of the universe in the mythical terms of the seers, while at the same time wondering whether the seers' myths are adequate:

> Neither being nor non-being then existed
> There was no air or sky beyond it
> What was concealed? Where was it? What
>   sheltered it?
> And was there deep unfathomable water?
>
> There was neither death nor anything immortal,
> Nothing indicating it was day or night.
> By its own force, the breathless ONE breathed.
> Apart from that there was nothing.
>
> There was darkness hidden in darkness,
> All undifferentiated chaos.
> Everything was void and formless.
> Then by the power of heat that ONE was born.
>
> In that beginning there was love,
> The primal seed and source of spirit.
> Sages who searched with the wisdom of the heart
> Have seen the bond between being and
>   non-being.

3 Ibid., Parmenides, 7.
4 Ibid., 8.
5 Aristotle, *Physics*, 239b11, trans. Manuel Velasquez.

A crosswise line divided being and non-being.
What was above it and what was below?
There were fertile powers and mighty forces,
Pushing from below and pulling from above.

Who really knows and who here now can say
When the world was born and where it came from?
The gods were born after its creation,
So who can know its origin?

From where it came,
And whether he produced it,
Only He who sees it from the highest heaven knows
And maybe even He does not.[6]

Although the author of this hymn is still groping for a nonmythical way of understanding the universe, he nevertheless succeeds in expressing a great insight: There is a fundamental reality beyond all the distinctions and concepts we make in our language, and this reality is the ultimate source of the universe. This reality, which can only be pointed to as "That One," is neither "existence nor nonexistence," it is "neither the world nor the sky beyond," it is "undifferentiated," and it was there before even God or the gods existed. This great idea of the Vedas posed a basic question for Eastern philosophy: What is the nature of this ultimate reality?

THE UPANISHADS

In the Upanishads, writings later added to the Vedas, we find the first attempts of Indian thinkers to understand this ultimate reality in philosophical terms. The Upanishads refer to the ultimate reality as **Brahman** and describe it in negative terms:

> Invisible, incomprehensible, without genealogy, colorless, without eye or ear, without hands or feet, unending, pervading all and omnipresent, that is the unchangeable one whom the wise regard as the source of beings.[7]

Thus, Brahman cannot be seen, smelled, felt, or heard. It cannot be imagined, and words cannot describe it. But it is the ultimate reality that must be present behind everything in the universe, causing everything to be, while itself being unlimited and greater than any specific knowable thing.

At this point, the philosophers of the Upanishads took a momentous step that was destined to forever change the course of Eastern philosophy. Seeking to understand Brahman, the deepest reality that underlies the universe, they thought to ask, "What am I?" The self, after all, is part of reality. By understanding the self, one could perhaps also understand ultimate reality. The Upanishad philosophers thus turned to understand **atman**, or the deepest self.

The Upanishad philosophers argued that atman is the *me* that lies behind all my living, sensing, and thinking activities; it is the *me* that lies behind my waking experiences, my dreaming experiences, and my deep-sleeping experiences; it is the *me* that directs everything I do but that is not seen or heard or imagined. This deepest self, which can be known only by enlightened inner self-consciousness, the philosophers of the Upanishad concluded, is identical with Brahman, ultimate reality. This profound idea is the foundation of Indian philosophy.

These ideas—that one ultimate reality underlies everything in the universe and that the self is identical with this reality—are beautifully expressed in an Upanishad parable. The parable is about a proud young man, Svetaketu, who returns from the Hindu equivalent of college only to find that his father is wiser than all his teachers:

> Now, there was Svetaketu Aruneya. To him his father said: "Live the life of a student of sacred knowledge. Truly, my dear, from our family there is no one unlearned. . . ."
>
> He then, having become a pupil at the age of twelve, having studied all the Vedas, returned at the age of twenty-four, conceited, thinking himself learned, proud.
>
> Then his father said to him: "Svetaketu, my dear, since now you are conceited, think yourself learned, and are proud, did you also ask for that teaching whereby what has not been heard of becomes heard of, what has not been thought of becomes thought of, what has not been understood becomes understood?"
>
> "What, pray, sir, is that teaching?"
>
> "Just as, my dear, by one piece of clay everything made of clay may be known—the modification is merely a verbal distinction, a name; the reality is just 'clay'—
>
> "Just as, my dear, by one copper ornament everything made of copper may be known—the

6 Based on the translation of A. A. MacDonell, *Hymns from the Rigveda* (London: Oxford University Press, 1922), pp. 19–20.

7 Mundaka Upanishad, 1.1.6, in *Oriental Philosophies*, 28.

modification is merely a verbal distinction, a name; the reality is just 'copper'—

"Just as, my dear, by one nail-scissors everything made of iron may be known—the modification is merely a verbal distinction, a name; the reality is just 'iron'—so, my dear, is that teaching."

"Truly, those honored men did not know this; for if they had known it, why would they not have told me? But do, sir, tell me it."

"So be it, my dear," said he. . . .

"Understand that this [body] is a sprout which has sprung up. It cannot be without a root.

"Where else could its root be than in water? With water, my dear, as a sprout, look for heat as the root. With heat, my dear, as a sprout, look for Being as the root. All creatures here, my dear, have Being as their root, have Being as their abode, have Being as their support. . . .

"When a person here is deceasing, my dear, his voice goes into his mind; his mind, into his breath; his breath into heat; the heat into the highest divinity. That which is the finest essence—this whole world has that as its soul. That is Reality. That is Atman. That art thou, Svetaketu."[8]

Svetaketu's father is here explaining that everything in the universe arises out of the same ultimate reality. We say there are many different things in the universe, but the differences we see are of our own making: They are mere "verbal distinctions." Underlying the variety of objects is a single unified reality, Brahman. And Brahman is identical with atman—your deepest self. In short, you are the ultimate reality behind the universe!

8 Chandogya Upanishad, in Daniel Bonevac, William Boon, and Stephen Phillips, *Beyond the Western Tradition* (Mountain View, CA: Mayfield, 1992), 151.

The Upanishad philosophers did for the East what the pre-Socratics did for the West. Like the pre-Socratics, the Upanishad philosophers taught the need to inquire carefully into the nature of reality instead of merely accepting the authority of the past. And like the pre-Socratics, the Upanishad philosophers showed the need to look behind appearances to the one ultimate reality.

But the Upanishad philosophers took a further step that would forever distinguish the thought of the East from that of the West. The pre-Socratics taught the West that to find the ultimate constituents of reality, one must analyze the outer, physical world. The Upanishad philosophers, on the other hand, taught that the way to discover the ultimate reality of the universe is to look within ourselves.

QUESTIONS

1. Explain why Thales is so important to Western philosophy.
2. How would Heraclitus have responded to the following statement? "Heraclitus is wrong because the objects we see around us continue to endure through time; although a person, an animal, or a plant may change its superficial qualities, it still remains essentially the same person, animal, or plant throughout these changes. In fact, we recognize change only by contrasting it to the underlying permanence of things. So permanence, not change, is the essential reality."
3. How would you answer Zeno's proof that no object moves?
4. Are there any similarities between the views of Parmenides and those of the Upanishads? Are there essential differences? Explain.
5. In the Upanishads, Svetaketu's father says, "That art thou, Svetaketu." What does "that" refer to? What does "thou" refer to? Do you see any problem with saying that these two (what "that" refers to and what "thou" refers to) are identical—in other words, that they are exactly one and the same thing? Explain.

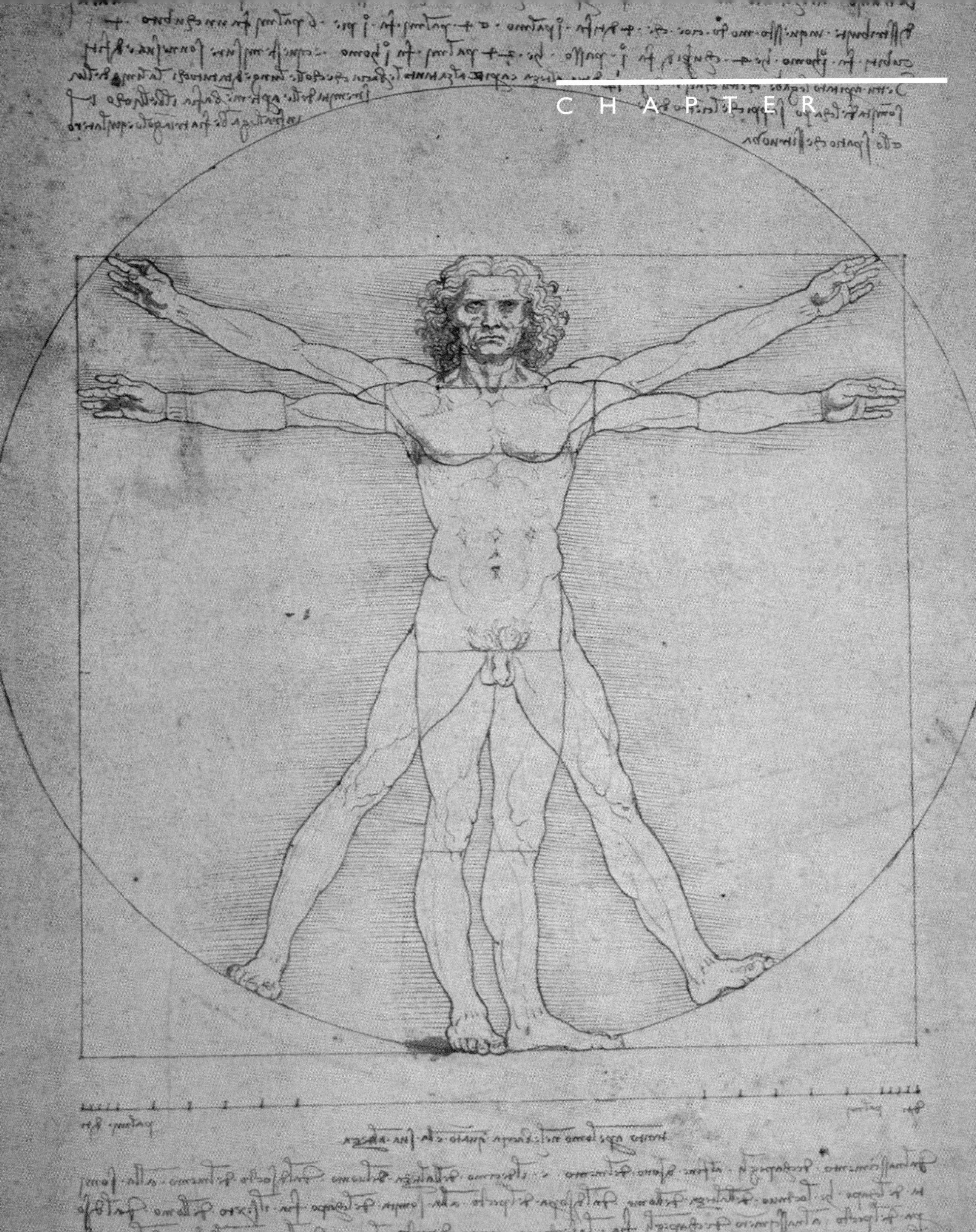
CHAPTER

2 Human Nature

Indeed it is of the essence of man . . . that he can lose himself in the jungle of his existence, within himself, and thanks to his sensation of being lost can react by setting energetically to work to find himself again.

JOSÉ ORTEGA Y GASSET

© Taxi/Getty Images

OUTLINE AND LEARNING OBJECTIVES

2.1 Why Does Your View of Human Nature Matter?

OBJECTIVES | When finished, you'll be able to:

- Define "human nature" and "psychological egoism."
- **Define what deductive and inductive (or probable) arguments are, explain what validity and soundness are, and apply these notions to arguments.**
- Explain how your views of human nature influence your relationships with other people, the universe, and your society.

2.2 What Is Human Nature?

OBJECTIVES | When finished, you'll be able to:

- Describe and critically evaluate the Greek rationalistic and Judeo-Christian versions of the Traditional Western view of human nature.
- Explain how Darwinism challenged these views.
- **Define what an inference to the best explanation is, explain what constitutes a "best explanation," and apply these notions to an argument.**
- Explain how existentialism and feminism have challenged the Traditional Western view of human nature.

2.3 The Mind–Body Problem: How Do Mind and Body Relate?

OBJECTIVES | When finished, you'll be able to:

- Explain why dualism is so influential a view of human nature, even though it leads to the mind–body problem.
- **Explain how to evaluate whether the premises of an argument are true.**
- Explain and critically evaluate the way materialism, identity theory, behaviorism, functionalism, the computer view of human nature, eliminative materialism, and property dualism each tries to solve the mind–body problem.

2.4 Is There an Enduring Self?

OBJECTIVES | When finished, you'll be able to:

- Explain the role an "enduring self" plays in human life and how it leads to the problem of personal identity.
- Explain and criticize attempts to solve the problem of personal identity by appealing to the body, the soul, the memory, and the no-self view.

2.5 Are We Independent and Self-Sufficient Individuals?

OBJECTIVES | When finished, you'll be able to:

- Describe the idea of an independent and self-sufficient self and explain the role it plays in our lives.
- Compare how Aristotle, Hegel, and Taylor challenge that idea.

Chapter Summary

2.6 Readings: Greene, "The End of the Party"

DeWeese and Moreland, "The Self and Substance Dualism"

Searle, "The Mind–Body Problem"

2.7 Historical Showcase: Plato, Aristotle, and Confucius

2.1 Why Does Your View of Human Nature Matter?

Imagine walking down the streets of a city on a wintry day and seeing an old unshaven man in ragged clothes sitting cross-legged on the sidewalk. In front of him is a sign that reads "I am blind and deaf. Please help me." Almost immediately you reach into your pocket for a couple of dollar bills, which you put into his cardboard box. Then, feeling good, you walk on.

Sigmund Freud: "Men are not gentle, friendly creatures wishing for love, but [possess] a powerful measure of desire for aggressiveness."

© Pictorial Press Ltd / Alamy

Why did you give him the money? You might respond with the easy answer that you wanted to help and relieve some of his obvious need. Yet was this your real motive for helping? Might it not be possible that your actual motive was self-interest? That you wanted the good feeling you knew you would get from helping him and wanted to avoid the guilt you would feel if you didn't? Are human beings, yourself included, moved ultimately and always by self-interested desires? Are all our actions, even those that seem to arise out of love for others, ultimately motivated by a desire for self-gratification and the avoidance of pain? Is self-interested action an inescapable and pervasive part of being human? Or do we at least sometimes act unselfishly?

The most basic question in philosophy is this: What kind of a being am I? Your answer to this question about **human nature**—what a human being is—will profoundly affect how you see yourself, how you see others, and how you live. To see how a view of human nature can affect us, let's look at what some psychologists and philosophers have said about human motivation.

Psychologists have long pondered the question of whether human nature is motivated solely by self-interest or whether unselfish considerations can also motivate human beings. Some psychologists have championed the view that humans are essentially not only selfish, but aggressively and cruelly so. As an illustration, consider the conclusion that the father of modern psychology, Sigmund Freud (1856–1939), presented in his work *Civilization and Its Discontents:*

> Men are not gentle, friendly creatures wishing for love, who simply defend themselves if they are attacked, but . . . a powerful measure of desire for aggressiveness has to be reckoned as part of their instinctual endowment. The result is that their neighbor is to them not only a possible helper or sexual object, but also a temptation to them to gratify their aggressiveness . . . to seize his possessions, to humiliate him, to cause him pain, to torture and to kill him.
>
> Anyone who calls to mind the atrocities of the early migrations, of the invasion of the Hun or the so-called Mongols under Genghis Khan and Tamerlane, of the sacks of Jerusalem by the pious crusaders, even indeed the horrors of the last world war, will have to bow his head humbly before the truth of this view of man.[1]

QUICK REVIEW
Psychologists such as Freud claimed humans are cruel, aggressive, and selfish.

Many philosophers have agreed with Freud that human beings are essentially selfish and aggressive. Long before Freud, the British philosopher Thomas Hobbes (1588–1679) argued for a view that we now call **psychological egoism**. This theory says that human beings are made so that they act only out of self-interest. Hobbes was a materialist who held that everything in "the Universe, that is the whole mass of things that are, is corporeal, that is to say body."[2] Humans, too, are material bodies, and we can explain their activities much like those of a biological machine. The mechanism of desire moves human beings to act. Consequently, whenever human beings do something, they are seeking satisfaction of their own mechanistic desires. In fact, Hobbes claimed, anticipating Freud, the antisocial desire for power over others is what mainly motivates human beings. "In the first place," he wrote, "I put for a general inclination of all mankind, a perpetual and restless desire of power after power, that ceaseth only in death."[3]

QUICK REVIEW
Hobbes claimed that humans act only out of self-interest and are material bodies.

Closer to our own time, the contemporary American philosopher Mark Mercer has argued that "behind any action whatever that an agent performs intentionally, ultimately there lies the agent's expectation of realizing one or more of her self-regarding ends, an expectation without which the agent would not have performed the action."[4] A "self-regarding end" is something that rewards or benefits one's own self, such as getting pleasure, being happy, avoiding pain, gaining power or possessions, having self-respect, being loved, feeling good about oneself, or having others think well of oneself. Mercer argues that when we look at our own intentional

QUICK REVIEW
Mark Mercer claims that when people act intentionally they always expect a self-regarding benefit or reward; introspection reveals this and we could not understand their actions as intentional unless we attributed such a motive to them.

---

1 Sigmund Freud, *Civilization and Its Discontents* (London: Hogarth, 1930), 85–86.
2 Thomas Hobbes, *Hobbes's Leviathan* (Oxford: Clarendon, 1909; original work published 1651), 524.
3 Ibid., 86.
4 Mark Mercer, "In Defense of Weak Psychological Egoism," *Erkenntnis*, vol. 55 (2001), no. 2, (pp. 217–237), p. 221.

actions (i.e., when we engage in "introspection"), we always see the presence of such self-regarding motives:

> Introspection reveals to me that whatever I decide to do, indeed I do expect that, should I meet with success in doing it, I will realize one of my self-regarding ends. Further, when I ask myself before acting on my decision to perform some particular action whether I would still do what I have decided to do were I to lack any expectation of realizing thereby a self-regarding end, I find that I answer no, I would not still do what I have decided to do. Were I not to expect to realize some self-regarding end in or through my action, I would find myself losing the desire to perform that action. I would, I think, cease to find important or attractive the goal I intend to achieve through that action . . . I now note that I am a typical agent in the world, not . . . different from other agents. This fact enables me to generalize from my own case to the case of all agents and actions. I conclude, then, that all actions are performed in expectation of reward.[5]

In fact, Mercer claims that when any person does something intentionally, we cannot fully understand what the person is doing until we understand what motivated him, and "without our perceiving a connection to an intention or an expectation of realizing some self-regarding end, we cannot see in any consideration we attribute to an agent, a motivation to act."[6] In short, Mercer claims that the only kind of human motivation we can understand is self-interest or, in his words, "the expectation of realizing some self-regarding end."

The views just briefly described, then, say that human nature is aggressive, selfish, and cruel (Freud); material, selfish, and desirous of power over others (Hobbes); and motivated always by self-interest (Mercer). Apart from their intrinsic interest, these views can have profound and highly personal implications for each of us. But before we look at those implications, let's look more closely at the reasons that support—or fail to support—these views.

thinking critically • Deductive Arguments, Validity, and Soundness

How good are the arguments given for the views about human nature that we have just seen? Take the views of the American philosopher Mercer, for example, who concludes that when people act intentionally they always expect to get a self-regarding end. Why does he reach this conclusion? The following seems to be his key argument:

1. I always expect a self-regarding end when I act intentionally.
2. If I always expect a self-regarding end when I act intentionally, then everyone always expects a self-regarding end when they act intentionally.
3. Therefore, everyone always expects a self-regarding end when they act intentionally.

Mercer says that we know premise (1) is true by "introspection" (i.e., by looking into ourselves), and we know premise (2) is true because we are each "not different from other agents." So Mercer also gives us reasons for each of his premises, which means you should be able to turn those reasons into arguments for each premise.

5 Ibid., pp. 229–230.
6 Ibid., p. 231.

Is Mercer's argument a good one? We saw in the last chapter that one requirement of a good argument is that the premises must be true. But true premises are not the only requirement of a good argument. In a good argument, the premises, if true, must prove or provide strong support for the conclusion. Assuming Mercer's premises are true, do they prove or strongly support his conclusion? To answer this question, we need to understand that there are two main kinds of arguments: deductive arguments and inductive (or probable) arguments. A **deductive argument** is one that is supposed to show that its conclusion *necessarily has to* be true if the premises are true, while an inductive **argument** is one that is supposed to show that its conclusion is *probably* true if its premises are true. We'll discuss inductive or probable arguments later because Mercer's argument is deductive. We know it is deductive because Mercer wants us to believe that if his premises are true then it *must* be true that everyone's actions are always motivated by self-regarding ends.

QUICK REVIEW
A deductive argument is meant to show its conclusion is necessarily true if its premises are true; an inductive or probable argument is meant to show its conclusion is probably but not necessarily true if its premises are true.

So, do the premises of Mercer's deductive argument prove or support his conclusion? The premises of a deductive argument prove or support the conclusion if in every situation in which the premises are true, the conclusion must also be true. We say a deductive argument is **valid** *when its conclusion must be true if the premises are true* (otherwise it is an "invalid" argument). Notice that the premises and conclusion of a valid argument do not have to be true. All that a valid deductive argument guarantees is that *if* its premises are true, the conclusion also has to be true.

QUICK REVIEW
A valid deductive argument is one whose conclusion must be true if its premises are true; in other words, one whose conclusion must be true in every situation in which its premises are true. We can evaluate whether an argument is valid by trying to imagine situations in which its premises are true but its conclusion is false.

Some examples might make this clearer. Here is a valid argument whose premises are true:

1. If Socrates is human, then he's a mammal.
2. Socrates is human.
3. Therefore, Socrates is a mammal.

Because this is a valid argument and its premises are true, we know its conclusion has to be true. That is, in every situation in which (1) and (2) are true, (3) must also be true. An argument that is both valid and has true premises like this is also called a **sound argument**.

Consider, next, this valid argument whose premises and conclusion are false:

1. If Arnold Schwarzenegger is President of the United States, he is ten years old.
2. Arnold Schwarzenegger is President of the United States.
3. Therefore, Arnold Schwarzenegger is ten years old.

In this valid argument, premise (1) and premise (2) are false, and so is the conclusion (3). But we said this argument is valid, so we know that *if there ever were* a situation in which premises (1) and (2) are true, then in that situation (3) would also have to be true. To test this, try to imagine a situation in which premises (1) and (2) are true, and see if in that situation (3) would also have to be true. Imagine, for example, this situation: Suppose the Constitution of the United States said the President *was required to be* exactly ten years old (remember this is an imaginary situation!) and suppose Arnold was elected President (use your imagination!). In that imaginary situation, premise (1) would be true, and premise (2) would be true. Could (3) be false in that specific situation? No, (3) would have to be true in that situation, because in that situation Arnold would be President and the President would be required to be ten years old! In fact, no matter how much you try, you will not be able to come up with a situation in which premises (1) and (2) are true and (3) is false. That is why we know that this argument is valid. But although the argument is valid, its premises are false. So the argument is not a *sound* argument.

How can we tell whether a deductive argument is valid? One answer to that question should now be clear: If we can think up an example—a situation—in which the premises of an argument are true and its conclusion false, then we know it is not valid. So read to the end of this next argument, and then stop reading and try to figure out whether this argument is valid. Figure out whether it's valid by asking yourself whether there is a way—a situation—in which the premises could be true, but the conclusion false:

1. If you get an "A" on the final, then you will get an "A" for the course.
2. You did not get an "A" on the final.
3. Therefore, you will not get an "A" for the course.

I'm sure you quickly figured out a bunch of ways in which (1) and (2) could be true and (3) false. For example, imagine you could get an "A" for the course either by getting an "A" or a "B" on the final, and you got a "B" on the final. In that situation, (1) and (2) would be true, but (3) would be false. So we now know the argument is not valid, and so even if it has true premises, it could not be sound.

So what about the argument that Mercer gives us to prove that when we act we are always motivated by a self-regarding end, i.e., by self-interest? His argument is complicated and uses complex abstract concepts, so it will be hard to think up situations in which its premises are true but the conclusion is false. But the main reason it will be hard for you to come up with such situations is because the argument is valid so there are no such situations.

Mercer's argument meets at least one of the two essential characteristics of a good argument: It is valid. But are the premises true? Take the first premise of the argument: Is it true that when you do something intentionally and look carefully at your own motives, you always find that there is some benefit or reward you expect to get from doing it? Or take the second premise: Is it true that if you are self-interested then everyone else must be self-interested? It's your job as a philosopher to try to figure out whether Mercer's premises are true.

The Importance of Understanding Human Nature

As we suggested, views of human nature—like Mercer's view that humans are always motivated by a kind of self-interest—can have a profound influence on what you believe and what you do. For example, if you accept that humans always act out of self-interest, this belief will shape your relationships with other people. If a person thinks that human beings are basically unselfish, won't that person instinctively relate to other people with trust and openness? Won't such a person accept the kind gestures of strangers as natural and not feel surprised that others help simply because they want to? But if a person believes that human beings are basically self-interested, won't that person mistrust others? Won't that person be suspicious of kindness and continually wonder what people are trying to get from her? Won't she feel that the only way to get help from others is by offering them something in return? Won't she believe that true altruism—actions that seek only the good of others—does not exist in this world?

Your views about human nature also influence your relationship to the universe. If a person believes that human beings are spiritual as well as material, won't that person be open to religious experience? Won't such a person see himself as having a spiritual aspect that makes him different from the purely material and biological universe? Won't such a person be willing to see his life in this material universe as a kind of preparation for a spiritual life in another world and universe? On the other hand, a person may feel that a human being is a purely physical creature. The person may feel that a human is a creature with a highly developed brain, to be sure, but not fundamentally different from other animals. For such a person, doesn't death have to be the end of existence? Won't such a

PHILOSOPHY AND LIFE

Is Selflessness Real?

Several contemporary biologists have argued that apparently selfless human behavior is actually a kind of selfish activity that our genes impel us to carry out. For example, Desmond Morris suggests that when a man rushes into a burning house to save his daughter—or if an old friend or even a complete stranger rescues the child—he is actually saving an organism that contains or, in the case of the friend or stranger, may contain his own genes. We have developed these protective behaviors so that our genes can survive and be passed on to future generations. Thus, helping behaviors are genetically selfish: They are mechanisms that our genes have evolved to ensure their own survival.

> The man who risks death to save his small daughter from a fire is in reality saving his own genes in their new body-package. And in saving his genes, his act becomes biologically selfish, rather than altruistic.
>
> But supposing the man leaping into the fire is trying to save, not his daughter, but an old friend? How can this be selfish? The answer here lies in the ancient history of mankind. For more than a million years, man was a simple tribal being. . . . [T]he chances were that every member of your own tribe was a relative of some kind. . . . [In saving your old friend] you would be helping copies of your own genes. . . . Again . . . genetic selfishness.
>
> [Moreover, when man] was tribal, . . . any inborn urge to help his fellow men would have meant automatically that he was helping gene-sharing relatives. . . . But with the urban explosion, man rapidly found himself in huge communities, surrounded by strangers, and with no time for his genetic constitution to alter to fit the startlingly new circumstances. So his altruism inevitably spread to include [complete strangers].

QUESTIONS

1. What do theories of evolution such as that proposed by Desmond Morris imply about our human nature?
2. Could all human behavior be explained in terms of genes?
3. If Morris is right, does it make sense to say that humans are or are not selfish?

Source: Desmond Morris, *Manwatching, A Field Guide to Human Behavior* (New York: Harry N. Abrams, 1977), 153–154.

person be convinced that this material universe is all there is and all that anyone can have?

Your perception of human nature determines even how you think we should set up our society. Ask yourself this, for example: Should our society be based on capitalism or socialism? Well, suppose that humans are essentially self-interested. Then, wouldn't the best way to get people to work be to allow every individual to keep whatever benefits he or she produces and to not support those who don't work? Won't self-interest then lead every person to work hard and to produce as much as he or she can? Isn't this the fundamental idea behind capitalist societies, with their free enterprise systems and ideas about individualism? If all people are basically self-interested, then shouldn't we spend more on police, prisons, the military, and other institutions we use to protect people from one another? On the other hand, what if humans are not basically self-interested, but cooperative and can act for purely unselfish motives? Then, wouldn't it make sense to inspire people to work for one another's good and to share whatever each produces? Aren't socialist institutions, such as welfare programs and redistributive taxes, based on the idea that human nature is basically social and that humans can and should share with one another? Isn't the huge sum of money that we spend on prisons, police, and the military a big waste that could be put to better use in helping meet human needs? Which of these two options is more realistic? How far should our

QUICK REVIEW
Beliefs about our nature influence our relationships, our view of our place in the universe, and our view of how society should be arranged.

society go in pursuing either one? Doesn't your answer depend on how you view human nature?

It is clear, then, that a lot hangs on how you answer the question "What is a human being? " In this chapter, you begin your philosophical journey by looking at how several philosophers have tried to answer this question. By examining what they say in support of their views, you will be in a better position to form your own answer and to make up your own mind, for example, about the extent to which we are unselfish and spiritual beings, or self-interested and material beings. The aim is not to convince you to accept any of the arguments about human nature presented here, but to help you use your own reasoning powers to decide for yourself what it means to be a human being.

QUESTIONS

1. Make a list of the fundamental properties that you think define a human being. Your list should enable you to distinguish humans from other kinds of creatures. How would you prove that these properties are essential to human beings?
2. Are there basic emotional and psychological differences between men and women? Are any such differences the result of their nature, or does society instill such differences through early training, education, and child-rearing practices?
3. In your judgment, are humans basically selfless or selfish? If there were no social restraints—such as laws and police—would humans tend to take advantage of one another, or would they tend to help one another? In your judgment, do our social institutions tend to corrupt a fundamentally good human nature, or do they tame a fundamentally evil human nature? Explain your answers.

© Archives du 7eme Art/Photos 12/Alamy

PHILOSOPHY AT THE MOVIES

Watch *Seven Pounds* (2008), in which Ben Thomas, an IRS agent driven by a secret that leads him to search for people worthy of a gift from him, finds seven recipients before he commits suicide. Is Ben's character consistent with your view of human nature? Was Ben selfless or selfish? Does the movie support or undermine the views, briefly summarized earlier, of Freud, Hobbes, and Mercer?

Older movies with related themes: *Schindler's List* (1993); *River's Edge* (1986).

2.2 What Is Human Nature?

Several years ago, a man who was revived after his heart stopped while he was in a hospital operating room described his experience as follows:

> I knew I was dying and that there was nothing I could do about it, because no one could hear me. . . . I was out of my body, there's no doubt about it, because I could see my own body there on the operating room table. My soul was out! All this made me feel very bad at first, but then, this really bright light came. It did seem that it was a little dim at first, but then it was this huge beam. It was just a tremendous amount of light, nothing like a big bright flashlight, it was just too much light. . . . It seemed that it covered everything, yet it didn't prevent me from seeing everything around me—the operating room, the doctors and nurses, everything. . . . The love which came from it is just unimaginable, indescribable.[7]

7 Raymond Moody Jr., *Life After Life* (New York: Bantam, 1979), 63–64.

This startling account is one of many similar stories told by people who have suffered near-death experiences. Frequently, people whose hearts have stopped and then started again report that at the moment of their "death" they left their body, hovered over the scene of their death, and encountered an "unimaginable, indescribable" bright white light that came for them. Convinced that they have experienced life after death, such people then lose all fear of death. They never again doubt that they have a soul that will survive. They are convinced that human life has a purpose: that humans have a destiny related to life after death.

QUICK REVIEW
The belief in life after death assumes that the self is conscious, has a purpose, and is distinct from its material body.

Notice that all these accounts of life after death ask us to make some fundamental assumptions about human nature. First, and most obviously, they ask us to believe that all human beings have a **self**: the ego or "I" that exists in a physical body and that is conscious and rational. That is, this self can think, reason, and perceive. Often tied to this is the idea that this thinking self can have a purpose: Its life can have a destiny. Second, they ask us to believe that this self is different from, but related to, the body. The body is a physical or material entity, whereas the self is a spiritual or immaterial entity (sometimes called a *soul*) that can survive the death of its body. Third, they ask us to believe that this self endures through time: Not only does the self remain the same self throughout its life, but it can also continue to be the same self after death. Finally, they ask us to believe that the self is an independent individual: It exists separate from other things and people, with an independent identity.

This complex view about human beings is prevalent among many of us today. It is also a view that many Western philosophers and thinkers have espoused. As we will see, it is a view with ancient roots. We call this view the Traditional Western view of human nature because it has influenced Western thinkers since ancient times. The Traditional view holds, then, that all humans have a rational spiritual self that is distinct from its body, has a purpose, endures over time, and exists as a separate individual.

Not everyone accepts the Traditional view. As we will see, many thinkers have rejected the view that humans have a rational nature that has a purpose. Others deny that the self is a kind of immaterial entity that is different from our physical body. Still others have rejected the assumption that humans have an enduring self. Still others quarrel with the idea that the self is an independent individual.

We continue our journey of self-exploration by looking more closely at the Western Traditional view of human nature. We consider two of the most influential versions of this Traditional view: first what we call the "rationalistic" view of human nature (which says that reason is our highest power), and then what we can call the "Judeo-Christian religious" view. We then look at several challenges to the Traditional Western view. By examining these views of ourselves, we can understand how the doctrines they espouse affect how we see ourselves, how we interact with others, and how we live our lives.

The Rationalistic Version of the Traditional Western View of Human Nature

Reason: Humanity's Highest Power. A highly influential version of the Traditional theory of human nature views the human primarily as a self capable of reasoning. This rationalistic view is well illustrated in the thoughts and writings of a man considered by some to be the greatest philosopher—Plato. Although Plato did not think that reason is the only constituent of human nature, he did hold that it was the most superior part of human nature. Conversing in *The Republic*, Socrates and Glaucon present Plato's view by discussing a question: What is the self? Notice in the following passage the use of the word *soul*, a common translation of Plato's term *psyche*. Because Plato did not intend all the theological meanings that we give the word *soul*, it would be wiser to substitute *inner self* for *soul*.

To read more from Plato's *Republic*, go to CourseMate for this text and browse by chapter or philosopher.

SOCRATES: Isn't it sometimes true that the thirsty person also, for some reason, may want not to drink?

GLAUCON: Yes, often.

SOCRATES: What can we say, then, if not that in his soul there is a part that desires drink and another part that restrains him? This latter part is distinct from desire and usually can control desire.

GLAUCON: I agree.

SOCRATES: And isn't it true in such cases such control originates in reason, while the urge to drink originates in something else?

GLAUCON: So it seems.

SOCRATES: Then we can conclude that there are in us two distinct parts. One is what we call "reason," and the other we call the nonrational "appetites." The latter hungers, thirsts, desires sex, and is subject to other desires.

GLAUCON: Yes, that is the logical conclusion.

SOCRATES: But what about our emotional or spirited element: the part in us that feels anger and indignation? . . . Anger sometimes opposes our appetites as if it is something distinct from them. . . . Yet this emotional part of ourselves is [also] distinct from reason.[8]

critical thinking

Plato assumes that the presence of two contrary desires in a person shows that there are at least two distinct parts in the person. Is this assumption correct?

To understand Plato's view, consider this illustration. Suppose that you are very thirsty. Before you is a glass of poisoned water. One part of yourself, what Plato called appetite (located in the abdomen), invites you to drink. By *appetite*, he meant thirst and hunger, as well as sexual and other physical desires. Yet a second part of yourself, reason, forbids you to drink. By *reason*, Plato meant the uniquely human capacity for thinking reflectively and drawing conclusions—the ability to follow relationships from one thought to another in an orderly and rational way. This rational part of the self, said Plato, has its center in the brain. In this illustration, a conflict arises between appetite and reason.

QUICK REVIEW
Plato claimed that reason often conflicts with our appetites or our aggressiveness, and our appetites can conflict with our aggressiveness.

But Plato claimed that conflict could arise in another way, as when our aggressive emotions flare up. Suppose that someone cuts you off on the highway. You become enraged; you begin to blow your horn and shake your fist at the other driver. You are even tempted to tailgate for a few miles just to vent your spleen. Yet your head tells you that would do no good. Besides, it would be dangerous. Plato would say that the conflict here is not between reason and appetite. The conflict is between reason and what he variously calls anger, "spirit," or the "spirited element." The spirited element is what we would probably call our aggressiveness or self-assertiveness. According to Plato, it resides in the chest and is displayed in war and anger. Whereas reason seeks what is good and right, aggression seeks to surpass others and assert itself. Plato described these conflicts among reason, appetite, and aggression in a striking image in which he compares reason to a charioteer pulled by the horses of desire and aggression:

> Let me speak briefly about the nature of the soul by using an image. Let the image have three parts: two winged horses and a charioteer. . . . One of the horses is of noble breed, the other ignoble. The charioteer controls them with great difficulty. . . . The vicious steed—when it has not been thoroughly trained—goes heavily, weighing down the charioteer to the earth . . .

8 Plato, *Republic*, from bk. 4. This edited translation copyright © 1987 by Manuel Velasquez.

PHILOSOPHY AND LIFE

Is Human Nature Irrational?

Many social psychologists who have studied the choices and behaviors of people have concluded that humans do not behave rationally. For example, Max Bazerman, in his book *Judgment in Managerial Decision Making,* cites numerous studies that show that humans rely on irrational beliefs and rules of thumb when making important decisions. For instance, people rely on a nonexistent "law of averages" that they believe influences the risks they take. People believe they can control purely chance events. People regularly underestimate the risk of dying in familiar but highly risky activities such as driving, smoking, or eating fried foods, and overestimate the risks of unlikely but memorable events such as dying in a plane crash or being attacked by a grizzly bear in a national park.

Robert Cialdini notes in his book *Influence* that he found people's choices can be manipulated by appealing to six nonrational norms or rules that we generally follow:

Reciprocity. I should do this for you because you did something for me.

Commitment and Consistency. I should do this because it is consistent with something I already committed myself to doing.

Liking. I should do this because I know and like you.

Authority. I should do this because an authority says I should.

Scarcity. I should do this because there's only a few chances left and I won't get a chance later.

QUESTIONS

1. Suppose that social psychologists are right in claiming that human beings behave irrationally. Does this show that human nature itself is not rational? Why or why not?
2. Can a psychological study of how people often—or even usually—behave disprove a philosophical theory of human nature? Why or why not?
3. Many advertisers, sellers, and promoters believe that Cialdini is right and that his theory provides the key for manipulating people into buying their products or doing what they want. Is there anything wrong with giving people the knowledge about human nature that will enable them to manipulate others?

> Above them, in the heaven above the heaven, . . . there abides the true reality with which real knowledge is concerned: the Forms which are visible only to the mind and have no color, shape, or hardness. The souls that are most like gods are carried up there by their charioteer, although troubled by their steeds and only with great difficulty beholding true being. . . . Other souls rise only to fall again, barely glimpsing it and then altogether failing to see because their steeds are too unruly.[9]

Notice Plato's use of the word *Forms.* For Plato, the forms are eternal and perfect ideals that exist in an unchanging perfect heaven. Things here on earth are but imperfect reflections of these ideals. The purpose or destiny of the soul is to be free of its body and ascend to heaven, where it will be united with these perfect forms. The soul can do this only if it controls its bodily desires and trains its aggressive impulses so that both obey reason.

QUICK REVIEW
Plato concluded that reason, appetite, and aggression are the three main parts of human nature.

Thus, in Plato's view, reason, appetite, and aggression are the three defining parts of human nature. Depending on which part dominates, we get three kinds of people, whose main desires are for knowledge, wealth, and power, respectively. Yet Plato leaves no doubt about which element can and should dominate: reason. True, each element plays a part, but appetite and aggression have no knowledge with which to order themselves and must be brought under the control of reason. Through reason we can discover the truth about how we ought to live, and when

QUICK REVIEW
Because reason can know how we ought to live, it should rule appetites and aggressions.

9 Plato, *Phaedrus,* selections from 246a–247e. This translation by Manuel Velasquez.

appetite and aggression are subordinate to reason, we live according to this truth. This truth, according to Plato, involves knowledge of ideals that exist in another dimension of reality that only reason can apprehend. After death, the person whose desires and aggressions are under the control of reason is freed of his or her body and can ascend to this dimension. (For a fuller discussion of Plato's view of human nature, see the Historical Showcase at the end of this chapter.)

QUICK REVIEW
If a person always gives in to his appetites or aggressive impulses, these will enslave him and reason can no longer rule them.

In Plato's rationalistic view, then, humans can control their appetites and their aggressive impulses by the use of their reason. They are not always motivated by self-interested desires, as Hobbes and Mercer seem to claim. However, Plato holds that reason's ability to control appetite and aggression depends on a person's past choices. If a person continually gives in to his aggressive impulses and appetites, he will lose the ability to control them. Such people become slaves of their appetites and aggressive impulses. When something arouses their anger, they give in to this impulse. When something arouses their desires, they cannot control themselves. But if, by practicing self-control, a person has learned to restrain and control his appetites and aggressive impulses, the person will gain the ability to do what reason says is best.

QUICK REVIEW
For Aristotle, reason is our highest power and what distinguishes human nature.

For Plato's student Aristotle (circa 384–322 BCE), reason is also the human's highest power. Although in many ways Aristotle's views differed from Plato's, he also held that human reason can discover the truth about human nature and how we ought to live. Still, Plato held that the truth about human nature involved knowledge of another world of reality. Aristotle, on the other hand, held that the truth about human nature required only knowledge of our own world. (For a fuller discussion of Aristotle's views, see the Historical Showcase at the end of this chapter.) However, Aristotle agreed that our ability to reason is the characteristic that sets the human self apart from all other creatures of nature.

The Human Purpose. Aristotle emphasized even more than Plato the idea that humans have a purpose. According to Aristotle, all living things have a purpose. For example, it is clear that the purpose of the eye is to see, and of the ears to hear. As he puts it:

QUICK REVIEW
For Aristotle, all living things have a purpose. The purpose of humans is to use their reason to think and to control desires and aggressions.

> Surely, just as each part of man—the eye, the hand, the foot—has a purpose, so also man as a whole must have a purpose. What is this purpose? Our biological functions we share in common even with plants. So these cannot be the purpose of man, since we are looking for something specific to man. The activities of our senses we also plainly share with other things: horses, cattle, and other animals. So there remain only the activities that belong to the rational part of man. . . . The specific purpose or function of man must involve the activities of that part of his soul that belongs to reason.[10]

critical thinking
Aristotle assumes that if each of the parts of an organism has a purpose, the whole must have a purpose. Evaluate this assumption.

Both Plato and Aristotle, then, stress reason as the most important feature of our human nature, certainly as more important than our desires and emotions. Reason is what is unique in humans—what makes us unique and different from all other animals. In addition, both see the exercise of reason as the purpose of human nature. That is, the purpose of human beings is to be rational: to use their reason well, both in thought and in action. And for both Plato and Aristotle, reason should control our desires and emotions. As Aristotle wrote in a work entitled *Nicomachean Ethics*, "human virtue consists of dealing with our feelings, [desires], and actions in such a way that we attain in them the kind of moderation that reason determines is right."

10 Aristotle, *Nicomachean Ethics*, bk. 1, ch. 7. This translation by Manuel Velasquez.

The Immaterial and Immortal Soul. Finally, Plato—but apparently not Aristotle—also claimed that human nature has a spiritual aspect. In one of his dialogues, *Phaedo,* Plato has Socrates argue that the self—the soul—is immaterial and so is immortal and survives our bodily death. Plato argues that our mental abilities provide the clearest evidence of the immaterial nature of the soul. That is, our ability to grasp perfect abstract ideals is evidence of our immaterial nature. When we think and reason, Plato held, we are engaged in activities that a physical body cannot carry on. In particular, our ability to think about ideals that do not exist in this material world provides evidence that we have an immaterial self—a soul. Notice in the following passage how Plato contrasts the changing physical objects around us with the unchanging nature of ideal concepts. He argues that the soul must be like these ideal immaterial concepts:

QUICK REVIEW
In *Phaedo*, Plato argues that the soul is immaterial and immortal because it can perceive nonmaterial ideals that do not exist in this world.

To read more from Plato's *Phaedo*, go to CourseMate for this text and browse by chapter or philosopher.

SOCRATES: Consider perfect equality or perfect beauty or any other ideal. Does each of these always remain the same perfect form, unchanging and not varying from moment to moment?

CEBES: They always have to be the same, Socrates.

SOCRATES: And what about the many individual [material] objects around us—people or horses or dresses or what have you. . . . Do these always remain the same or are they changing constantly and becoming something else?

CEBES: They are continually changing, Socrates.

SOCRATES: These changing [material] objects can be seen and touched and perceived with the senses [of the body]. But the unchanging Ideals can be known only with the mind and are not visible to the [body's] senses. . . . So there are two kinds of existing things: those which are visible and those which are not. . . . The visible are changing and the invisible are unchanging.

CEBES: That seems to be the case. . . .

SOCRATES: Now which of these two kinds of things is our body like?

CEBES: Clearly it is like the visible things. . . .

SOCRATES: And what do we say of the soul? Is it visible or not?

CEBES: It is not visible.

SOCRATES: Then the soul is more like the invisible and the body like the visible?

CEBES: That is most certain, Socrates.

SOCRATES: . . . [W]hen the soul turns within and reflects upon what lies in herself [knowledge of Ideals], she finds there the perfect, eternal, immortal, and unchanging realm that is most like herself. . . . That soul, I say, itself invisible, departs [at death] to the invisible world—to the divine and immortal and rational: arriving there, the soul is secure of bliss and is released from the error and folly of men, their fears and wild passions and all other human ills, and forever dwells, as they say of the initiated, in company with the gods.[11]

critical thinking
What is Plato assuming when he says that because the mind can think about immaterial objects, it must be immaterial?

In this classical rationalistic view of human nature, then, we are creatures of reason, appetite, and emotion. We are, however, distinct from the material world because our reason enables us to stand apart from our material environment and grasp immaterial Ideals. At death, if we have learned to control our passions and appetites,

11 Plato, *Phaedo.* This edited translation copyright © 1987 by Manuel Velasquez.

we can escape the confines of our material body and rise to the realm of perfect, eternal, and unchanging Ideals. We gain such self-mastery by learning to control our passions and appetites with our reason. To attain such self-mastery through the exercise of reason is the ultimate purpose of human beings.

QUICK REVIEW
Aristotle claimed that because barbarians were less rational than Greeks, they were less human and so could be ruled and enslaved by the Greeks.

Implications of the Traditional Rationalistic View. This view of human nature looks innocent and optimistic in the role it gives to reason. Yet is it? Consider one way that Aristotle used this theory. He claimed that if a group of people was less rational than the Greek people, they would be less human: They would be barbarians. Such "barbarians" could justifiably be enslaved by more rational, and therefore more human, people (e.g., the Greeks). As Aristotle wrote, "The lower sort are by nature slaves, and it is better for them as for all inferiors that they should be under the rule of a master." But if slavery can be justified by a view of human nature that says that full humans are only those who live up to its standards, then can't any form of exploitation be justified by such a view? Is it possible that all forms of racial and ethnic discrimination are ultimately justified by views of what true human nature is? That is, are racism and ethnic discrimination based on the idea that other races are not quite as human or as highly developed humans as one's own race?

Whatever its problems, the rationalistic view of human nature is one of the most influential theories in Western civilization. Many people still accept it, and it has deeply influenced a second important version of the Traditional view: the Judeo-Christian religious view of human nature.

The Judeo-Christian Version of the Traditional Western View of Human Nature

According to the Judeo-Christian tradition, humans are made in the image of God. They are like divine beings because they contain something of the ability to love and know that characterizes their Creator. For example, the Jewish scriptures portray God as saying, "And God said, let us make man in our image, after our likeness," while according to the Christian scriptures Jesus of Nazareth said "Love one another as I have loved you." The centrality of this notion of a loving God in whose image we are made and whose love we should emulate, introduces into the Judeo-Christian view of human nature some characteristics that separate it from the rationalistic view we just discussed. Nevertheless, a large part of the Greek rationalistic view of human nature has been incorporated into the Judeo-Christian view.

Plato, in particular, strongly influenced Christian thought through thinkers such as the early Christian Saint Augustine (354–430). Augustine was familiar with Platonist views and adapted many of Plato's doctrines to Christianity. For example, from Plato, Augustine took the doctrine that the human self is a rational self: a self that is conscious and can reason. The rational self, Augustine held, can with the help of God control its desires and rule over its passions.

Augustine also borrowed Plato's view that humans have an immaterial and immortal soul. Augustine used this idea to justify the Christian notion of an afterlife. Plato had said that after death the souls of those who love "perfect, eternal" ideals would rise to heaven. Augustine adopted this idea but modified it, arguing that the souls that will rise to heaven are those that know and love the perfect, eternal *God.*

QUICK REVIEW
Christians like Augustine adopted Plato's view that the self or soul is rational, immaterial, and immortal and not basically self-interested.

Unlike Plato, however, Augustine emphasized the notion of a will and not just that of reason. The will, Augustine held, is our ability to choose between good and evil. This ability is the seat of the most significant Christian virtue: love. For the Christian, as for the Jew, the fundamental religious duty is that of freely choosing to love and serve God. The human will, the power of choice over desire, allows human beings to make this choice. Still, the will is a two-edged sword. Whereas it enables us to choose the good, it also enables us to choose evil. We humans, Augustine held, are constantly attracted toward evil and away from God. He describes an event in his boyhood that illustrates this:

> Near our vineyard there was a pear tree, loaded with fruit. . . . I and some other wretched youths conceived the idea of shaking the pears off this tree and carrying them away. We set out late at night . . . and stole all the fruit we could carry. And this was not to feed ourselves. We may have tasted a few, but then we threw the rest to the pigs. Our real pleasure was simply in doing something that was forbidden. . . . I did evil for nothing, with no reason for the wrongdoing except the wrongdoing itself. . . . I loved the sin, not the thing for which I had committed the sin, but the sin itself.[12]

Here, Augustine is to a degree echoing Plato. Like Plato, Augustine held that humans have within them powerful desires that, like an unruly "steed," constantly "weigh" us down to the earth and away from "heaven above." And like Plato, Augustine held that human nature is capable of controlling its desires and mastering them with reason.Unlike Plato, however, Augustine held that we need God's help to overcome pride and lust, and only with God's help can our reason master our desires.The human being, then, has both reason and will: the ability to know the truth about God and the ability to choose and love that God. Thus, the Judeo-Christian view agrees with the classic rationalistic view, that human nature is not basically self-interested. Humans, with the help of God's grace, are capable of rising above their self-interested desires and genuinely loving both God and neighbor.

The Judeo-Christian tradition adopted and also modified another key part of the rationalistic tradition. Aristotle argues that like all living things, human beings have a purpose. The purpose of humans is to achieve happiness by using their reason. The Christian thinker Thomas Aquinas agreed that humans and all other creatures have a purpose. However, he said, the purpose of humans is to achieve happiness by using their reason to know God:

> The heavenly bodies cause the generation of all things here below. So the purpose of their motion is the generation of things below. Now [here below] . . . the simplest elements exist for the sake of compound minerals; these latter exist for the sake of living bodies, among which plants exist for animals, and animals for humans. So humans are the purpose of the whole order of generation. . . . Now humans naturally desire, as their ultimate purpose, to know the first cause of things. But the first cause of all things is God. So the ultimate purpose of humans is to know God.[13]

In many ways, both the classical rationalistic and the Judeo-Christian views of human nature are appealing. These two versions of the Traditional Western view of human nature seem to describe something that we all experience: the conflict between what our reason wants and what our desires pull us toward. It seems to provide an uplifting picture of human beings as fundamentally spiritual and capable of surviving death. Reason sets us off from other creatures, making us "unique" in the classical rationalistic version and "like God" in the Judeo-Christian version, while in both we humans are capable of choosing between good and evil.

---

12 Augustine, *The Confessions of St. Augustine*, trans. Rex Warner (New York: New American Library of World Literature, 1963), 45.

13 Aquinas, *Summa Contra Gentiles*, bk. III, ch. 22, paras. 5, 7, 8; ch. 25, para. 11. Translated by Manuel Velasquez.

Adam and Eve. In his idealized figures of the first man and woman being tempted by Satan, the fifteenth-century Christian artist Albrecht Dürer (1471–1528) attempted to portray humans as rational loving beings made in the image of God but capable of great good and evil.

© Galleria degli Uffizi, Florence, Italy/Alinari/The Bridgeman Art Library

© Galleria degli Uffizi, Florence, Italy/Alinari/The Bridgeman Art Library

All these are familiar ideas about ourselves: the idea that it is possible for us to survive bodily death because at death the soul can leave the confines of its body, the idea that we humans are special and different from other animals, the idea that it is reason that makes us different and that reason should rule over our passions, the idea that human beings have a purpose and that this purpose is related to the nonmaterial or spiritual dimension of the universe. As we noted, these views of ourselves have been among the most influential in Western civilization and beyond. Many of us today continue to look at ourselves in this manner.

Yet these views of ourselves have been challenged from several directions. Perhaps the most serious challenge to these ideas has come from science. As we will see, the theory of evolution, in particular, challenges key aspects of the Traditional Western views of what we are, and raises significant philosophical issues. In fact, numerous leading contemporary philosophers have recently written several book-length works addressing the philosophical implications that Darwin's theory of evolution has for human nature, including Daniel Dennet, Elliott Sober, Mary Midgley, Michael Ruse, Marjorie Grene, Richard Richards, Francisco Ayala, Alex Rosenberg, Janet Richards, Peter Singer, James Rachels, Alvin Plantinga, Jerry Fodor, and Stefan Linquist.[14] In addition, contemporary philosophers have written numerous articles on evolution and its philosophical implications, particularly in *Biology and Philosophy*, an entire journal devoted to the topic. This large and growing philosophical interest in the impact of evolutionary ideas on our contemporary views of human nature points to the major importance that Darwin and his theories have for us as we inquire into who and what we are.

---

14 Dennett, Daniel, *Darwin's Dangerous Idea: Evolution and the Meanings of Life* (London: Penguin Books, 1995); Elliott Sober, *Did Darwin Write the Origin Backwards: Philosophical Essays on Darwin's Theory* (New York: Prometheus Books, 2010); Mary Midgley, *The Solitary Self: Darwin and the Selfish Gene* (London: Acumen Publishers, Ltd., 2010); Michael Ruse, *The Philosophy of Human Evolution* (Cambridge: Cambridge University Press, 2012); Marjorie Grene, *The Philosophy of Biology: An Episodic History* (Cambridge: Cambridge University Press, 2004); Richard A. Richards, *The Species Problem: A Philosophical Analysis* (Cambridge: Cambridge University Press, 2010); Francisco J. Ayala, *Am I a Monkey? Six Big Questions About Evolution*, (Baltimore, MD: Johns Hopkins University Press, 2010); Alexander Rosenberg, *Darwinism in Philosophy, Social Science and Policy*, (Cambridge: Cambridge University Press, 2000); Janet Radcliffe Richards, *Human Nature After Darwin: A Philosophical Introduction* (London: Routledge, 2001); Peter Singer, *The Expanding Circle: Ethics, Evolution, and Moral Progress* (Princeton, NJ: Princeton University Press, 2011); James Rachels, *Created from Animals: The Moral Implications of Darwinism* (New York: Oxford University Press, 1999); Alvin Plantinga, *Where the Conflict Really Lies: Science, Religion, and Naturalism* (Oxford: Oxford University Press, 2011); Jerry Fodor and Massimo Piattelli-Palmarini, *What Darwin Got Wrong*, (New York: Farrar, Straus and Giroux, 2011); Stefan Linquist, *Philosophy of Evolutionary Biology* (London: Ashgate, 2010).

We will look closely now at the challenge evolutionary theory has posed for our Traditional Western view of human nature by looking at the ideas of Charles Darwin. It was Darwin who forced us to take the theory of evolution seriously and thereby significantly and forever affected our view of ourselves.

Charles Darwin (1809–82) (photo), Cameron, Julia Margaret (1815–79)/Private Collection/The Stapleton Collection/The Bridgeman Art Library International

Charles Darwin: "Natural selection is daily and hourly scrutinizing, throughout the world, the slightest variations; rejecting those that are bad, preserving and adding up all that are good; silently and insensibly working at the improvement of each organic being.

The Darwinian Challenge

Variation, the Struggle for Existence, and Natural Selection.

Darwin pro-posed three key ideas. The first is the idea that animals and plants are sometimes born with features that are different from those of their parents but that they can pass on to their own offspring. Darwin called these differences "variations." For example, a giraffe may be born with a longer neck than its parents. When mature, that giraffe can pass on this "variation" to its own offspring.

The second key idea Darwin advanced is that because living creatures produce more offspring than can survive, they are continuously caught in a great "struggle for existence"—that is, they must continuously compete with one another to stay alive:

> A struggle for existence inevitably follows from the high rate at which all organic beings tend to increase. Every being, which during its natural lifetime produces several eggs or seeds, must suffer destruction during some period of its life, and during some season or occasional year, otherwise, on the principle of geometrical increase, its numbers would quickly become so inordinately great that no country could support the product. Hence, as more individuals are produced than can possibly survive, there must in every case be a struggle for existence, either one individual with another of the same species, or with the individuals of distinct species, or with the physical conditions of life.[15]

A newborn bobcat, for example, starts life having to compete with its many brothers and sisters as they all struggle to suck from their mother's few nipples. Later, the bobcat has to compete with other bobcats for mates and food. Throughout its life, it struggles to keep away from wolves and other predators. Always it must struggle against heat and cold, sun and snow, droughts and storms.

The third key idea was "natural selection or survival of the fittest." Darwin pointed out that some variations give a creature an advantage over other members of its species in this great struggle for existence and thereby give it a better chance of surviving, having offspring, and passing the variation on to its descendants. A giraffe with a longer neck can feed itself better and so live longer, mate more often, and leave more offspring with longer necks than other giraffes can. The great struggle for existence, then, "selects" those organisms with advantageous variations and lets them survive and multiply. At the same time, the struggle for existence weeds out animals and plants that have less advantageous variations and lets them

15 Charles Darwin, *On the Origin of Species by Natural Selection* (London: John Murray, 1859), ch. 4.

die. After many generations, all the surviving members of the species will have the new advantageous variation, and those lacking the variation will have died out:

QUICK REVIEW
Darwin said that some creatures have variations that can be inherited by offspring, and those with advantageous variations can better survive and pass them on, while those with injurious variations are destroyed, a process he called "Natural Selection" or "Survival of the Fittest." Descendants of a species can be so different that they are a new species.

> [C]an we doubt (remembering that many more individuals are born than can possibly survive) that individuals having any advantage, however slight, over others, would have the best chance of surviving and of procreating their kind? On the other hand, we may feel sure that any variation in the least degree injurious would be rigidly destroyed. This preservation of favorable individual differences and variations, and the destruction of those which are injurious, I have called Natural Selection, or the Survival of the Fittest. . . .
>
> Let us take the case of a wolf, which preys on various animals, securing some by craft, some by strength, and some by fleetness; and let us suppose that the fleetest prey, a deer for instance, had from any change in the country increased in numbers, or that other prey had decreased in numbers, during that season of the year when the wolf was hardest pressed for food. Under such circumstances the swiftest and slimmest wolves would have the best chance of surviving and so be preserved or selected.[16]

After millions of years, so many advantageous variations can accumulate in the members of a species that they will be very different from what they were before. If they become sufficiently different, they will be a new species. A species of fish over millions of years may evolve into a species of amphibians that can take advantage of life on land; the amphibian species may evolve into a hardy dinosaur species that is better able to fight for its survival on land, and the dinosaur species may evolve into a bird species that has the advantages of flight:

> It may metaphorically be said that natural selection is daily and hourly scrutinizing, throughout the world, the slightest variations; rejecting those that are bad, preserving and adding up all that are good; silently and insensibly working, whenever and wherever opportunity offers, at the improvement of each organic being in relation to its organic and inorganic conditions of life. We see nothing of these slow changes in progress, until the hand of time has marked the lapse of ages, and then so imperfect is our view into long-past geological ages, that we see only that the forms of life are now different from what they formerly were.[17]

We are so used to the idea of evolution that it is hard for us to understand how incredible Darwin's theory was to people of his time. The idea that natural processes might make any species evolve into an entirely different species, was a disturbing new thought for many people. It meant that the living world around us had not been created as it was, but was the result of a still continuously changing nature.

Yet as disturbing as Darwin's ideas about the evolution of species were, his ideas were even more disturbing when he applied them to human beings. For humans are animals, and if Darwin's theory applied to animals, then humans also must have evolved from earlier non-human ancestors! Darwin himself made the point in *The Descent of Man*, a book that aroused a flurry of angry controversy:

QUICK REVIEW
Darwin's theory applies to humans. But if all human abilities evolved from lower animals, reason is not unique but just a more developed animal ability.

> Thus we can understand how it has come to pass that man and all other vertebrate animals have been constructed on the same general model, why they pass through the same early stages of development, and why they retain certain rudiments in common. Consequently we ought frankly to admit their community of descent: to take any other view, is to admit that our own structure, and that of all the animals

16 Ibid.
17 Ibid.

> around us, is a mere snare laid to entrap our judgment. . . . It is only our natural prejudice, and that arrogance which made our forefathers declare that they were descended from demigods, which leads us to demur to this conclusion.[18]

Implications for the Traditional View. Think of the implications of Darwin's theory for the Traditional view of human nature. Take, first, what the Traditional view says about the differences between humans and animals. The Traditional view says that although humans are animals, they have a characteristic that makes them unique. This is the ability to reason. Humans are rational animals, and our ability to reason and think are beyond the abilities of any other animal. Reason is not just a more developed and more powerful version of the same kinds of abilities that other animals have. Instead, the Traditional view says that our ability to reason is a completely different kind of ability than any of the abilities other animals have.

Darwin denied this. If humans evolved from nonhuman animals, then all human abilities evolved from the abilities that their earlier nonhuman predecessors had. If so, Darwin believed, then all human abilities, including reason, are merely more developed variations of the same kinds of abilities that nonhuman animals have. According to Darwin, "[T]here is no fundamental difference between man and the higher mammals in their mental faculties."[19] The Traditional view holds that the human power to reason is so unique, so different in kind from the powers of animals, that it could have come only from God. It is, in fact, what makes us like God. Yet in Darwin's view the human power to reason is not qualitatively unique but is merely a more developed version of the cognitive powers of nonhuman primates. Humans are made, not in the image of God, but in the image of the primates that preceded them.

Second, and even more important, the Traditional view holds that like all living things, human beings are obviously designed and so must have a purpose. Aristotle had noted that human organs, such as "the eye, the hand, and the foot," are like intricate instruments that have been put together to achieve a specific purpose: The eye is designed to see, the hand to grasp, and the foot to walk. Because each of our parts is obviously fashioned for a specific purpose, Aristotle argued, a human being as a whole must likewise have a purpose. Just as the purpose of the eye is to do what our other organs cannot do, the purpose of a human being must be to do what no other creature can do. Aristotle concluded that the purpose of humans is to exercise their reason since only humans have the ability to reason. Christian philosophers such as Augustine and Aquinas added to this that the purpose of humans is to use their reason to love God and neighbor.

Darwin's theory of evolution, however, undermined the idea that living things and their parts are designed for a purpose. Animal organs, such as the eye, the heart, and the foot, Darwin held, were not made to serve a specific purpose but developed bit by bit through the accumulation of countless tiny variations and the blind process of natural selection. It is true, as Aristotle and others had noted, that the eye and all our other organs seem to be specially designed to serve a specific purpose. But this apparent design and purpose are illusory: The eye is simply the accumulated outcome of numerous chance variations that have survived because each happened to confer a slight advantage to an animal. As the final outcome of this process of natural selection, the eye is adapted to seeing because that adaptation is an advantage in the great struggle for survival. The blind processes of natural selection, not purposeful design, resulted in the eye and each of its intricate parts. Neither did humans as a whole have a purpose. The evolution of a species, like the

> QUICK REVIEW
> Darwin's theory undermined the idea that living things and humans are designed for a purpose.

18 Charles Darwin, *The Descent of Man*, 2nd ed. (New York: A.L. Burt, 1874), ch. 1.
19 Ibid., ch. 3.

evolution of each of their organs, Darwin argued, is the result of blind natural selection, not of purposeful design.

Darwin's Evidence. Because Darwin's theory has such important implications for our view of human nature, we should look carefully at the arguments he gave in support of his theory. Darwin pointed to several kinds of phenomena as evidence for his theory, one of which was the way in which organisms today share similar characteristics. His theory that species had evolved from earlier species by the mechanisms of variation and natural selection meant that "probably all the organic beings which have ever lived on this earth have descended from some one primordial form." Variations would eventually have split an early species into several distinct species, some of which would have split into several more distinct species, some of which in turn would have split into other distinct species, much like an ever-branching tree that is continually growing new branches, which in turn develop new branches. This branching of species into other species that his theory implied, he argued, was the best explanation of the fact that all species can be classified into groups and subgroups of species that share common characteristics. According to his theory similar species (like monkeys and gorillas) shared common characteristics because they descended from a common ancestor. The fact that such species share common characteristics, Darwin added, could not be explained by the view that each species had been independently created and so was not organically related to any other species:

> It is a truly wonderful fact—the wonder of which we are apt to overlook from familiarity—that all animals and all plants throughout all time and space should be related to each other in groups subordinate to groups, in the manner which we everywhere behold—namely, varieties of the same species most closely related, species of the same genus less closely . . . related, . . . species of distinct genera much less closely related, . . . forming sub-families, families, orders, sub-classes, and classes. . . . If species had been independently created, no explanation would have been possible of this kind of classification; but it is explained through inheritance [from common ancestors] and the complex action of natural selection, entailing extinction and divergence of character.[20]

The way that species are geographically distributed over the face of the earth, Darwin argued, was also best explained by his theory, and not by the view that each species had been independently created. In his theory, each species would have originated in a single location and its members would then spread out from there, evolving into additional species as they moved, but being forced to stop wherever they met obstacles.This, he claimed, is what we see:

> We see the full meaning of the wonderful fact, which has struck every traveler, namely, that on the same continent, under the most diverse conditions, . . . most of the inhabitants within each great class are plainly related; for they are the descendants of the same progenitors. . . . We clearly see why species belonging to those groups of animals which cannot cross wide spaces of the ocean, as frogs and terrestrial mammals, do not inhabit oceanic islands; and why, on the other hand, new and peculiar species of bats, animals which can traverse the ocean, are often found on islands far distant from any continent. Such cases as the presence of peculiar species of bats on oceanic islands and the absence of all other terrestrial mammals are facts utterly inexplicable on the theory of independent acts of creation.[21]

---

20 *Origin of Species,* p. 104.
21 Ibid., pp. 418–419.

Moreover, Darwin argued, the bodies of different species of organisms living today also provide evidence that they descended from common ancestors and have attained their current structures and shapes by the gradual modifications produced by the accumulation of variations and natural selection. Bone structures, embryos, and useless rudimentary organs, he claimed, were best explained by his theory and not by the view that each species had been specially created:

> The similar framework of bones in the hand of a man, wing of a bat, fin of a porpoise, and leg of the horse; the same number of vertebrae forming the neck of the giraffe and of the elephant; and innumerable other such facts, at once explain themselves on the theory of descent [from a common ancestor] with slow and slight successive modifications. The similarity of pattern in the wing and in the leg of a bat, though used for such different purpose, in the jaws and legs of a crab, in the petals, stamens, and pistils of a flower is likewise, to a large extent, intelligible on the view of the gradual modification of parts or organs, which were originally alike in an early progenitor in each of these classes. On the principle of successive variations not . . . supervening at an early age, and being inherited at a corresponding [mature] . . . period of life, we clearly see why the embryos of mammals, birds, reptiles, and fishes [that descended from a common ancestor] should be so closely similar, and so unlike the adult forms. . . . [We can see how] disuse, aided sometimes by natural selection, will often have reduced organs when rendered useless under changed habits or conditions of life; and we can understand on this view the meaning of rudimentary organs [that remain but are useless]. . . . On the view of each organism with all its separate parts having been specially created, how utterly inexplicable is it that organs bearing the plain stamp of inutility, such as the teeth in the embryonic calf or the shriveled wings under the soldered wing-covers of many beetles, should so frequently occur. . . . It can hardly be supposed that a false theory would explain, in so satisfactory a manner as does the theory of natural selection, the several large classes of facts above specified.[22]

QUICK REVIEW
Darwin argued that his theory that "variations and natural selection" had caused species to evolve from earlier species explained numerous facts better than the view that each species was "independently created," including: the similarities between distinct species, their geographical distribution, the similar bones and embryos of different species, rudimentary organs, and the fossil record.

But the most important evidence to which Darwin pointed in support of his theory were the fossilized skeletons and other remains of ancient animals and plants found in layers of rocks under the earth. The oldest fossils found in the lowest layers of rock, he pointed out, were less like today's plants and animals than the more recent ones in higher layers of rock. Darwin claimed this fossil record was best explained by his theory that species living today had descended from different earlier species, which in turn had descended from yet earlier species, all by the gradual modifications his theory proposed:

> If we admit that the geological record is imperfect to an extreme degree, then the facts, which the record does give, strongly support the theory of descent with modification. . . . The fact of the fossil remains of each formation being in some degree intermediate in character between the fossils in the formations above and below is simply explained by their intermediate position in the chain of descent. The grand fact that all extinct beings can be classed with all recent beings naturally follows from the living and the extinct being the offspring of common parents.[23]

Darwin then pointed to a large number of facts as evidence for his theory. In every case, his argument came down to the same claim: His theory provided the best explanation for the facts, particularly when compared to the prevailing view that each species had been independently created.

22 Ibid., pp. 420–421.
23 Ibid., 417.

Responses to Darwin. In view of all the evidence that Darwin offered for his theory, is the Traditional view of human nature dead? Hardly. Supporters of the Traditional view have responded to Darwin's challenge, some by pointing to problems with the evidence he gave for his theory, others by arguing that Darwin was wrong in his belief that his theory disproved the idea that human nature has a purpose, and still others by claiming that, in spite of Darwin's claim, human reason is uniquely human.

QUICK REVIEW
Critics of Darwin claim that gaps in the fossil record disprove his theory, that a "theistic" view of evolution allows for purposeful design, and that reason does make us unique.

First, and most controversially, some have argued that fossils do not support Darwin's view that species gradually evolve into other species through natural selection. When we examine fossils, recent critics have claimed, we find that most new species seem to appear suddenly, without earlier, continuously different forms leading up to them, almost as if they were suddenly created. It is as if there were sudden jumps from one completely formed species in one layer of rock, to another completely formed species in a later layer of rock. Missing, in most cases, are the gradual changes and many intermediate steps that should be there if new species evolved slowly by gradual steps through natural selection as Darwin claimed. As the well-known biologist Stephen Jay Gould writes,

> The history of most fossil species includes two features inconsistent with [Darwinian] gradualism: 1. Stasis. Most species exhibit no directional change during their tenure on earth. They appear in the fossil record looking much the same as when they disappear. . . . 2. Sudden Appearance. In any local area, a species does not arise gradually by the steady transformation of its ancestors; it appears [in the fossil record] all at once and "fully formed."[24]

Gould, however, does not conclude that the large gaps in the fossil record disprove evolution. Gould claims that the gaps show only that evolution generally occurs by rapid "jumps" or "saltations" from one species to another that take place in such short time periods that they leave few if any fossils. Although some critics of Darwin insist that the gaps prove that Darwin was wrong, Gould argues that the "gaps" are either the result of the fact that we have not yet found all the fossils that would fill in the gaps or that evolution can work much faster than Darwin thought.

A second group of critics have argued that even if Darwin's theory is correct, it is a mistake to think that evolution proves that human nature is not designed for a purpose. For example, the contemporary philosopher George Mavrodes suggests that there are two ways of understanding evolution. A "naturalistic" understanding of evolution holds that evolution is "explicable entirely in terms of natural law without reference to a divine intention or intervention." But a "theistic" understanding of evolution holds that "there was a divine teleology in this process, a divine direction at each crucial stage in accordance with divine plan or intention."[25] In other words, a theistic understanding of evolution holds that although evolution occurred, God still directed evolution. On this view, Darwinian evolution is consistent with a belief that God, through evolution, produced human beings for a purpose. Other philosophers, such as Henri Bergson (1859–1941) and Pierre Teilhard de Chardin (1881–1955), have also argued that the process of evolution is not blind and random but directed and purposeful. More recently, Michael J. Behe, a biochemist who wrote *The Biochemical Challenge to Evolution* (1996), and William A. Dembski, a mathematician who authored *Intelligent Design: The Bridge between Science*

---

24 Stephen Jay Gould, *The Panda's Thumb* (New York: Norton, 1980), 182.
25 George Mavrodes, "Creation Science and Evolution," *Chronicle of Higher Education*, January 7, 1987, 43.

and Theology (1999), have argued that the complexity of living organisms, including human beings, cannot be explained by blind processes but requires the admission of "intelligent design" or purpose (we look at this argument more closely in Chapter 4).

A third group of critics attack Darwin's claim that there is no fundamental or qualitative difference between the cognitive abilities of many nonhuman animals and the reasoning ability of humans. Because the human ability to reason evolved from the mental abilities of our nonhuman ancestors, Darwin claimed, the difference between them is ultimately a difference of degree, not a fundamental difference in kind.

Yet critics of Darwin have argued that the human capacity to reason is unique in all of nature. The most telling difference between human mental capacities and the mental capacities of all other animals, critics have claimed, is our ability to use complex rule-governed languages in our reasoning processes. In fact, before Darwin was even born, Descartes had declared in the fifth part of his *Discourse on Method* that what distinguished humans from the "brutes" was the fact that humans can "arrange different words together, forming of them a statement by which they make known their thoughts; while, on the other hand, there is no other animal, however perfect and fortunately circumscribed it may be, which can do the same."[26] Although many animals can communicate by using simple signs and symbols, only humans seem to have the ability to communicate and think in languages that use complex syntactical rules capable of producing a potentially infinite number of new sentences expressing ideas that have never before been expressed. The human languages that we use to develop, express, and manipulate our complicated ideas, theories, technologies, cultural conceptions, religious beliefs, and imaginative artistry seem to be unique to human beings. Although numerous scientists have tried to show that nonhumans—including chimpanzees and gorillas—can be taught to "speak" and understand human languages, these attempts have proven frustratingly inconclusive. If human reason consists of the ability to think linguistically and the ability to create, understand, and engage in complex chains of reasoning about such linguistically embodied thoughts, then human reason may indeed be unique and qualitatively different from anything found in other animals.

thinking critically • Inference to the Best Explanation

Part of the reason why Darwin's theory is still looked at with suspicion by many people, is perhaps due to the kind of argument that he gave for his theory. Darwin argued, as we have seen, that his theory was true because it was the best explanation for the facts he described. This is not a deductive argument. Many different explanations can be given for any fact, including explanations that no one has yet thought of. So even if an explanation of a fact is the best one we currently have, there may be a better explanation that we have not yet discovered. Until the early seventeenth century, for example, the rising and setting of the sun were explained by the view that the sun rotates around the earth; only later in that century did people realize that those facts are better explained by the theory that the earth rotates while moving around the sun. So there is always at least a possibility that a theory is wrong even if it is the best explanation we have today. Darwin's argument, then, cannot show that if his evidence is correct, then his theory must be true;

26 René Descartes, *Discourse on Method*, pt. 5, in *Philosophical Works*, trans. E. Haldane and G. Ross (Cambridge: Cambridge University Press, 1911), vol. 1, pp. 116–117.

it can only conclude that his theory is probably true. His argument, then, is an inductive or probable argument.

Darwin's argument is a kind of argument called an "inference to the best explanation." An **inference to the best explanation** is an argument that assumes that the theory that best explains a large set of facts is probably true. For example, if we use the letters "p, q, r, s, . . ." as symbols for the many different kinds of facts a theory explains, and the letter "T" to symbolize the theory, then we can say that an inference to the best explanation has the following form:

1. Theory T is the best explanation we currently have for the facts p, q, r, s, . . .
2. If a theory is the best explanation for all the facts, then it is true.
3. Therefore, theory T is probably true.

Although this form of argument looks like it could be a deductive argument, it is not. Premise (1) says that Theory T is merely the best explanation we *currently* have, while premise (2) is talking about the absolutely best explanation there is, not just the best we currently have. As we've seen, the best explanation we currently have might be surpassed by a better one tomorrow. So it is possible that theory T may not be the absolutely best explanation there is and may actually be false.

We rely on this kind of argument every day. When you walk outdoors and find that the ground and vegetation are wet all over the neighborhood, you will conclude that it probably rained because that is the best explanation for all the wet things you see. Many, perhaps most, criminal trials rely on an inference to the best explanation: The fingerprints of the accused were found on the murder weapon, he had a motive for killing the victim, witnesses saw him fleeing the scene of the crime immediately after they heard a shot, and he has no alibi; although the accused says someone else did it, the jury concludes that the best explanation for all the facts is that the accused murdered the victim. Inferences to the best explanation are also common in science. We have already mentioned, for example, that during the seventeenth century, the view that the sun revolves around the earth was rejected in favor of the better explanation that the earth revolves as it moves around the sun. In fact, virtually all scientific theories are based on an inference to the best explanation, including the theory that light consists of waves, the theory of relativity, the theory of atoms, Newton's laws of motion, and so on.

QUICK REVIEW
Darwin's argument was an inference to the best explanation, which assumes the best explanation is probably true. The best explanation: is determined after considering all serious alternatives; harmonizes with well-established beliefs; accounts for more kinds of facts; provides more information about the causal mechanisms; and is simplest. However, we can't say why best explanations are probably true.

An inference to the best explanation, we said, is an inductive or probable argument. Good inductive or probable arguments are not said to be valid or invalid. Instead, we say they are either strong or weak. An inductive argument is strong when there's a high probability its conclusion is true, and weak when there's a low probability.

So when is an inference to the best explanation a strong argument? That is, what conditions does such an argument have to meet to be a strong argument? We can start to answer this question by looking first at premise (1) and asking when is it true? In other words, when is a theory the "best explanation" of a set of facts? To begin with, we say a theory "explains" a set of facts when we know that if the theory were true, then all the facts would turn out like they did.

Still, there are usually a lot of different theories that can explain a set of facts. For example, a lot of different theories could explain why all the vegetation we saw this morning was wet. So how do we decide which of these theories is the "best explanation" of the facts as premise (1) requires? Several criteria are used to determine whether a theory is the "best" explanation for a set of facts:

1. The theory that is the best explanation should be judged best only after all serious alternative theories have been considered. Obviously we don't have to consider preposterous theories, but it is not always easy to draw the line between a serious and a preposterous theory.

2. Other things being equal, the theory that is the best explanation should be consistent with our other well-established beliefs. The qualifier, "other things being equal" is important since many well-accepted theories overthrew beliefs we once thought were well-established. When the evidence for a theory is more convincing than the evidence we have for a "well-established" belief, however, we should be willing to change that belief.
3. The theory that is the best explanation should explain more *kinds* of facts (including predictions it makes that turn out to be true) than the competing theories do. That is, compared to the competing theories, the best explanation will explain more facts (including the accurate predictions it makes) about distinct phenomena that formerly seemed to be unrelated.
4. The theory that is the best explanation should provide more information about the underlying mechanisms that cause the phenomena than the competing theories do. That is, the best explanation will describe in greater detail how the phenomena are brought about and will identify the specific causes, conditions, processes, and relationships that bring the phenomena about.
5. Other things being equal, the theory that is the best explanation should be simpler than the alternative theories; that is, it will make fewer unsupported assumptions and refer to fewer unobservable entities (such as aliens or fairies or unseen agents). The qualifier "other things being equal" is important because we may be forced to accept a very complicated theory if no other theory can explain all the facts.

Premise (1) of an inference to the best explanation is true, then, to the extent that the theory T that it is talking about, meets these five requirements. The better it meets requirements 1–5, the stronger the case that it is the best explanation.

Now let us look at premise (2) of an inference to the best explanation: "If a theory is the best explanation for all the facts, then it is true." Is this premise true? In other words, does a theory that provides the best explanation for a set of facts have to be true? One answer to this question was suggested by Darwin himself who wrote: "It can hardly be supposed that a false theory would explain, in so satisfactory a manner as does the theory of natural selection, the several large classes of facts [I described]." Darwin's suggestion is similar to one made by the American philosopher Hilary Putnam who claimed that it would be "a miracle" if a theory was false yet was able to successfully explain all the facts (including the facts predicted by the theory). But critics have said that the suggestions of Darwin and Putnam are themselves based on an inference to the best explanation! Both are claiming that the best explanation of why theories that explain all the facts are true is because the best explanation of why they explain all the facts is that they are true! But then Darwin and Putnam are arguing in a circle: They rely on premise (2) to prove premise (2). The truth of the matter is that nobody has yet come up with an argument for premise (2) that everyone is willing to accept. We all must assume premise (2) is true, we use premise (2) every day of our lives, and our most basic scientific theories rely on premise (2). But we just don't know exactly why premise (2) is true.

Since we are forced to assume that premise (2) is true, the only premise that we should worry about in an inference to the best explanation is premise (1). So long as premise (1) meets the five requirements we just discussed, then conclusion (3) will follow. So the strength of an inference to the best explanation ultimately depends on how probable premise (1) is, and that, as we said, will depend on how well it meets the five requirements.

So, is Darwin's argument for his theory of evolution a strong one? That is, does Darwin's theory of evolution meet the five requirements of an inference to the best explanation? You must decide the answer to that large question yourself. However you answer that question, it is clear that your view of yourself, and of the kind of creature you are, ultimately depends on the answer you give.

The Existentialist Challenge

In the middle of the twentieth century, another very different view of human beings arose to challenge the Traditional Western view of human nature. This view, called **existentialism**, holds that there is no such thing as human nature because humans are whatever they make themselves. Existentialism denies any essential human nature in the traditional sense, insisting that individuals create their own nature through their free choices and actions.

QUICK REVIEW
Existentialists like Sartre say there is no God to determine our nature, so humans have no purpose or nature except the one they make themselves. We are free and fully responsible for what we are; knowing this causes anguish.

The chief exponent of existentialism is Jean-Paul Sartre (1905–1980). Sartre claimed that there are no true universal statements about what humans are, but he did make at least one general statement about the human condition: We are free. This freedom consists chiefly of our ability to envision additional possibilities for ourselves, to conceive of what is not the case, to suspend judgment, and to alter our condition. When we choose, nothing forces us to do what we do. We must therefore take full responsibility not only for our actions but also for our beliefs, feelings, and attitudes.

To illustrate, many people believe that we have little control over our emotions. If we feel depressed, we feel depressed, and there's little we can do about it. Sartre argued that if we're depressed, we've usually chosen to be. Emotions, he said, are not moods that come over us whether we want them or not, but are usually the result of how we freely choose to perceive the world and to participate in it.

The consciousness of this freedom and its accompanying responsibilities cause what Sartre refers to as "anguish." The most anguishing thought of all is that we alone are totally responsible for ourselves. We can escape this anguish by pretending we are not free. For example, we may pretend that our genes or our environment is the cause of what we are, or that we are spectators rather than participants, passive rather than active. When we so pretend, said Sartre, we act in "bad faith."

QUICK REVIEW
Bad faith is deceiving ourselves by pretending we are not free and so not responsible.

Self-deception, or bad faith, is the attempt to avoid anguish by pretending we are not free. We have many ways of doing this. We try to convince ourselves that outside influences have shaped our nature. Or that forces beyond our control or unconscious mental states have shaped us. One graphic example of self-deception provided by Sartre involves a young woman sitting with a man whom she knows is bent on seduction. He takes her hand. To avoid the painful necessity of making a decision to accept or reject the man, the woman pretends not to notice, leaving her hand in his. Isn't there bad faith in the woman's pretending to be a passive object, a being-in-itself, rather than what she

© Valentin Casarsa/iStockphoto.com

Jean-Paul Sartre: "The hand rests inert . . . neither consenting nor resisting—a thing."

really is, a conscious and, therefore, a free being? Here's Sartre's account of the incident, as he develops it in *Being and Nothingness:*

> Take the example of a woman who has consented to go out with a particular man for the first time. She knows very well the intentions which the man who is speaking to her cherishes regarding her. She knows also that it will be necessary sooner or later for her to make a decision. But she does not want to realize the urgency; she concerns herself only with what is respectful and discreet in the attitude of her companion. She does not apprehend this conduct as an attempt to achieve what we call "the first approach"; that is, she does not want to see possibilities of temporal development which his conduct presents. She restricts this behavior to what is in the present; she does not wish to read in the phrases which he addresses to her anything other than their explicit meaning. If he says to her, "I find you so attractive!" she disarms this phrase of its sexual background; she attaches to the conversation and to the behavior of the speaker, the immediate meanings, which she imagines as objective qualities. The man who is speaking to her appears to her sincere and respectful as the table is round or square, as the wall coloring is blue or gray. The qualities thus attached to the person she is listening to are in this way fixed in a permanence like that of things, which is no other than the projection of the strict present of the qualities into the temporal flux. This is because she does not quite know what she wants. She is profoundly aware of the desire which she inspires, but the desire cruel and naked would humiliate and horrify her. Yet she would find no charm in a respect which would be only respect. In order to satisfy her, there must be a feeling which is addressed wholly to her personality—i.e., to her full freedom—and which would be a recognition of her freedom. But at the same time this feeling must be wholly desire; that is, it must address itself to her body as object. This time then she refuses to apprehend the desire for what it is; she does not even give it a name; she recognizes it only to the extent that it transcends itself toward admiration, esteem, respect and that it is wholly absorbed in the more refined forms which it produces, to the extent of no longer figuring anymore as a sort of warmth and density. But then suppose he takes her hand. This act of her companion risks changing the situation by calling for an immediate decision. To leave the hand there is to consent in herself to flirt, to engage herself. To withdraw it is to break the troubled and unstable harmony which gives the hour its charm. The aim is to postpone the moment of decision as long as possible. We know what happens next; the young woman leaves her hand there, but she does not notice that she is leaving it. She does not notice because it happens by chance that she is at this moment all intellect. She draws her companion up to the most lofty regions of sentimental speculation; she speaks of Life, of her life, she shows herself in her essential aspect—a personality, a consciousness. And during this time the divorce of the body from the soul is accomplished; the hand rests inert between the warm hands of her companion—neither consenting nor resisting—a thing.
>
> We shall say that this woman is in bad faith, but we see immediately that she uses various procedures in order to maintain herself in this bad faith. She has disarmed the actions of her companion by reducing them to being only what they are.[27]

critical thinking

Does Sartre assume that we can discover the truth about our inner motivations by examining our own consciousness? Would you accept this assumption?

The self in Sartre's view is not necessarily rational, or material, or a creature of God. It is instead a "project" that possesses a subjective life; it is the sum, not of everything that happens to it, but of everything it ever does. In the end, we are what our choices make us; to be human means to create oneself.

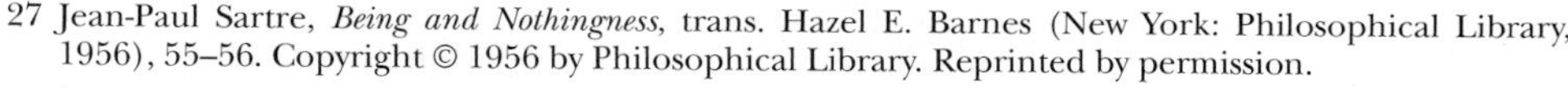

27 Jean-Paul Sartre, *Being and Nothingness*, trans. Hazel E. Barnes (New York: Philosophical Library, 1956), 55–56. Copyright © 1956 by Philosophical Library. Reprinted by permission.

QUICK REVIEW
The self has no rational nature but is the sum total of all its actions.

Yet can we have the kind of self-knowledge and control over ourselves that Sartre assumes people always have? Doesn't our unconscious mind—the unconscious motivations and desires that psychologists say operate without our knowledge—control much of what we do? For example, doesn't that unconscious mind heavily influence how the woman in Sartre's example reacts to the touch of the man or how a man might respond to that of a woman? Doesn't the kind of conditioning we have received in the past shape our external behavior in the present moment?

In *Existentialism and Humanism*, Sartre vigorously defends the existential view of human nature against such criticisms. He points out that when an artisan makes something, he knows ahead of time the nature of the object he will make. So its "essence"—its nature or what it is—is determined before it even exists. Similarly, if God is seen as an artisan that creates each person, then what a person is will be determined ahead of time by what God decides that person will be. But in the existentialist view of people, Sartre claims, a person's nature or "essence" is not determined ahead of time by God nor anything else. For "atheistic existentialism," this view is based on the fact that atheism denies God exists, but Sartre says earlier in his essay that the Christian existentialist also believes that human nature is not determined ahead of time. In the existentialist view of human beings, Sartre says, humans first begin to exist in the world, and only after they exist do they become what they are.The key to Sartre's view is the idea we mentioned earlier: humans, unlike things, are defined by their actions, so humans are nothing more than the sum total of what they have done and are doing: You are what you do. Since you have not yet done anything when you first come into the world, at that point you are not yet any kind of person. But as you mature, you begin to determine what you are—what your nature is—by the actions you choose. Sartre combines these ideas with a point we discussed earlier: that we are completely free. Since you are free to choose what you do, and because you define yourself by what you do, you alone are responsible for your own nature, i.e., for what you have become.

QUICK REVIEW
"Existence is prior to essence" means humans are first born (exist) and then define their nature (essence) by acting.

> If one considers an article of manufacture as, for example, a book or a paper-knife, one sees that it has been made by an artisan who had [in mind] a conception of [what it would be]. . . . Let us say, then, of the paper-knife that its essence . . . precedes its existence . . . When we think of God as the creator, we are thinking of him, most of the time, as a supernal artisan. . . . Thus, the conception of man in the mind of God is comparable to that of the paper-knife in the mind of the artisan: God makes man according to a procedure and a conception, exactly as the artisan manufactures a paper-knife, following a definition and a formula [he had in mind]. Thus each individual man is the realization of a certain conception that dwells in the divine understanding. . . . Here, then, the essence of man [would] precede that historic existence [of a man] which we confront in experience. Atheistic existentialism, of which I am a representative, declares . . . that if God does not exist there is at least one being whose existence comes before its essence, a being which exists before it can be defined by any conception of it. That being is man. . . . What do we mean by saying that existence precedes essence? We mean that man first of all exists, encounters himself, surges up in the world—and defines himself afterwards. If man as the existentialist sees him is not definable, it is because to begin with he is nothing. He will not be anything until later, and then he will be what he makes of himself. Thus, there is no human nature, because there is no God to have a conception of it. Man simply is. Not that he is simply what he conceives himself to be, but he is what he wills [himself to be]. . . .
> If, however, it is true that [for man] existence is prior to essence, [then] man is responsible for what he is. Thus, the first effect of existentialism is that it puts

> every man in possession of himself as he is, and places the entire responsibility for his existence squarely upon his own shoulders. . . . The doctrine I am presenting before you . . . declares that there is no reality except in action. It goes further, indeed, and adds, "Man is nothing else but what he proposes, he exists only in so far as he realizes himself, he is therefore nothing else but the sum of his actions, nothing else but what his life is." Hence we can well understand why some people are horrified by our teaching. For many have but one resource to sustain them in their misery, and that is to think, "Circumstances have been against me, I was worthy to be something much better than I have been. I admit I have never had a great love or a great friendship; but that is because I never met a man or a woman who were worthy of it; if I have not written any very good books, it is because I had not the leisure to do so; or, if I have had no children to whom I could devote myself it is because I did not find the man I could have lived with. So there remains within me a wide range of abilities, inclinations and potentialities, unused but perfectly viable, which endow me with a worthiness that could never be inferred from the mere history of my actions." But in reality and for the existentialist, there is no love apart from the deeds of love; no potentiality of love other than that which is manifested in loving; there is no genius other than that which is expressed in works of art. . . . In life, a man commits himself, draws his own portrait and there is nothing but that portrait.[28]

Clearly, existentialism provides a profound challenge to the Traditional view of human nature. If existentialism is correct, then there is no such thing as a universal human nature shared by all people. Instead, we each create our own nature. If Sartre is right, we cannot say that humans are defined by their rationality. Ahead of time, we cannot say what will define a person: Only his or her choices can determine this. Moreover, if Sartre is right, we cannot say that humans have a purpose. Humans are not made for anything. We simply exist, and each of us must decide for ourselves what purpose, if any, our existence will serve.

We are, therefore, according to Sartre, ultimately responsible for our own nature and purpose. Yet do we have the kind of absolute freedom to create our nature that Sartre attributes to us? Are we fully responsible for the nature we have? Are you wholly to blame for who and what you are today? If you deny that you are free and responsible, are you in fact using this very denial as an excuse to escape your responsibility? Is your denial of freedom always a form of bad faith?

QUICK REVIEW
Existentialism says there is no universal human nature, no rational human nature, no purpose for human nature.

The Feminist Challenge

The most troubling challenge to the Traditional picture of human nature is the criticism that it is fundamentally sexist—that is, it discriminates against women. This objection, raised by many—but not all—feminist philosophers, strikes at the very center of the Traditional picture, and to examine it, we must go back to Plato and Aristotle.

To understand the feminist criticism, recall that in the Traditional view of human nature, humans are rational beings whose reason should rule over the body and its desires and emotions. In the part of his dialogue *Phaedo* that follows the portion excerpted earlier in this chapter, Plato, putting his own views into the mouth of Socrates, explains the rationalistic view like this:

QUICK REVIEW
Some feminists claim that the Traditional view of human nature is sexist.

> SOCRATES: Yet once more consider the matter in another light: When the soul and the body are united, then nature orders the soul to rule and

28 Jean-Paul Sartre, *Existentialism and Humanism*, trans. Philip Mairet (London: Methuen, 1949), 85.

govern, and the body to obey and serve. . . . Does not the divine appear to you to be that which naturally orders and rules, and the mortal to be that which is subject and servant?

CEBES: True.

SOCRATES: And which does the soul resemble?

CEBES: The soul resembles the divine, and the body the mortal—there can be no doubt of that, Socrates.

SOCRATES: Then reflect, Cebes: of all which has been said is not this the conclusion?—that the soul is in the very likeness of the divine, and immortal, and intellectual, and uniform, and indissoluble, and unchangeable; and that the body is in the very likeness of the human, and mortal, and unintellectual, and multiform, and dissoluble, and changeable. Can this, my dear Cebes, be denied?

CEBES: It cannot. . .

SOCRATES: That soul, I say, itself invisible, departs [at death] to the invisible world—to the divine and immortal and rational: thither arriving, the soul is secure of bliss and is released from the error and folly of men, their fears and wild passions and all other human ills, and forever dwells, as they say of the initiated, in company with the gods. Is not this true, Cebes?

CEBES: Yes, beyond a doubt.

SOCRATES: But the soul which has been polluted, and is impure at the time of death, and is the companion and servant of the body always, and is in love with and fascinated by the body and by the desires and pleasures of the body, until it is led to believe that the truth only exists in a bodily form, which a man may touch and see and taste, and use for the purposes of his lusts—the soul, I mean, which is accustomed to hate and fear and avoids the intellectual principle, which to the bodily eye is dark and invisible, and can be attained only by philosophy;—do you suppose that such a soul will depart pure and unalloyed?

CEBES: Impossible.

SOCRATES: Such a soul is held fast by the corporeal, which the continual association and constant care of the body have wrought into its nature.

CEBES: Very true.

SOCRATES: And this corporeal element, my friend, is heavy and weighty and earthy, and is that element of sight by which a soul is depressed and dragged down again into the visible world, because it is afraid of the invisible and of the world below—prowling about tombs and sepulchres . . . and these must be the souls, not of the good, but of the evil, which are compelled to wander about such places in payment of the penalty of their former evil way of life.[29]

Plato associates the soul with reason and opposes these two to the body and its earthy desires. The "pure" soul is supposed to rule over the "impure" body and to turn away from the "desires and pleasures of the body." If the soul dominates the body and turns away from its desires and "wild passions" or emotions, it will be "good." At death, such a pure soul will rise to join the gods. But if the soul becomes the "companion and servant" of its body and bodily desires and pleasures, it will become "polluted" and "evil" and will be punished by being dragged down to wander among "tombs and sepulchres."

---

29 Plato, *Phaedo,in Dialogues of Plato,* trans. Benjamin Jowett and ed. Justin D. Kaplan (New York: Simon & Schuster, 1950), 103–106.

Is Reason "Male"? Some feminists have argued that here Plato inserted a critical assumption into the rationalistic view of human nature: The soul and reason are superior and should rule, whereas the body and its desires and emotions are inferior and should obey.

Although Plato thought men and women were more or less equal, his student Aristotle next made a move that would forever give the rationalistic view of human nature a sexist bias. Aristotle associated men with reason and claimed that women do not share fully in reason. Consequently, men should rule over women:

> QUICK REVIEW
> Plato said reason is superior to and should rule our desires and emotions; Aristotle then associated women with desires and emotions and men with rationality and concluded that men should rule over women.

> There are three elements of household rule, the first being the rule of the master over slaves, . . . the second that of the father over his children, and the third that of the husband over his wife. . . . His rule over his wife is like that of a magistrate in a free state, while his rule over his children is like that of a king. For the male is naturally more qualified to lead than the female, unless something unnatural happens, and the older and more complete adult is more qualified to rule than the younger and incomplete child. . . . For in the soul there is by nature an element that rules and also an element that is ruled; and in these elements we recognize different virtues, the virtue, to wit, of that which possesses reason, and the virtue of that which lacks reason [but which should obey reason]. It is clear, then, that the same rule holds good in other cases also, so that most things in the world by nature are rulers or are ruled. But it is in different ways that the free man rules the slave, the male rules the female, and the adult rules the child. Although in each of these there is present an appropriate share of soul, it is present in each in a different manner. For the slave, speaking generally, does not have a reasoning faculty; the woman has it but without the power to be effective; and the child has it, but in an incomplete degree.[30]

Aristotle claims that the reason that characterizes the essential nature of humans is fully operational only in males. Women, like children, are not fully rational, so, like our bodily appetites and emotions, they should obey males, who embody reason to the full degree.

From the very beginning of Western philosophy, several feminists have argued, this Traditional Western view of human nature has associated males with the superior traits that are supposed to set humans apart from all other beings. The rationalistic view associates men with rationality and reason and tends to associate women with the bodily appetites and emotions that must be controlled. Reason is male and should rule, whereas feelings and desires are female and must be ruled.

Centuries later, these feminists charge, the religious version of the Traditional Western view of human nature adopted this association of reason with men and of appetites and emotions with women. For example, in the *Confessions*, the Christian philosopher Saint Augustine wrote the following in a prayer to God:

> Then You took man's mind, which is subject to none but you and needs to imitate no human authority, and renewed it in Your own image and likeness. You made rational action subject to the rule of the intellect, as woman is subject to man.[31]

Somewhat earlier, the Jewish philosopher Philo also accepted the rationalistic view of human nature and brought it into Judaic thinking, but with the sexist bias:

> The male is more complete, more dominant than the female, closer akin to causal activity, for the female is incomplete and in subjection and belongs to the category

30 Aristotle, *Politics*, quoted in *Philosophy of Woman: Classical to Current Concepts*, ed. Mary Briody Mahowald (Indianapolis: Hackett, 1978), 68.

31 Augustine, *Confessions*, quoted in Genevieve Lloyd, "The Man of Reason," in *Women, Knowledge, and Reality: Explorations in Feminist Philosophy*, ed. Ann Garry and Marilyn Pearsall (Boston: Unwin Hyman, 1989), 111–128.

> of the passive rather than the active. So too with the two ingredients which constitute our life-principle, the rational and the irrational; the rational which belongs to mind and reason is of the masculine gender, the irrational, the province of sense, is of the feminine. Mind belongs to a genus wholly superior to sense as man is to woman.[32]

This brief look at the historical development of the rationalistic view of human nature clarifies the fundamental—but controversial—accusation of a number of feminist thinkers: The rationalistic view, and the Judeo-Christian religious view based on it, are sexist—they are biased against women. The rationalistic view holds that reason is the essential characteristic that sets humans off from the rest of creation. Yet, some feminists argue, the rationalistic view attributes full reason only to adult males: Reason and rationality are "male," whereas desire and feeling are "female." As a result, the rationalistic view allows only men to be fully human because only men are fully rational, while women are not fully rational but are driven by their emotions and desires which are "earthy," "impure," and "polluting." Moreover, these feminists argue, the rationalistic view asserts that reason must rule, and so it implies that men should rule over women. The rationalistic view thus justifies the oppression of women.

Many philosophers do not accept the arguments of the feminists who have put forward these objections to the rationalistic and religious views of human nature. And many others, both male and female, who have accepted the feminist arguments have looked for ways to get around their objections.

QUICK REVIEW
So, the rationalistic view implies that reason is good, is male, and should rule, whereas feelings and desires are bad, are female, and should be ruled. This is sexist.

Can We Think Differently? Are sexist views that assume the inferiority of women to men essential to the Traditional view of human nature? Can we talk about reason and emotion, body and spirit, truth and desire without covertly assuming sexist views? Although many people continue to think of rationality as a "male" trait and emotion as a "female" trait, some thinkers have asked: Can't we start to think differently? Granted, many people still feel that emotion is an obstacle to the attainment of the truth and knowledge that reason seeks. But can't we create new ways of thinking about truth, science, and knowledge? Granted, many people still believe that if we are to be moral and righteous, we should restrain our bodily appetites. But can't we start to think differently about the value of our body and its appetites? Finally, many religious people still feel that our bodily desires "pollute" us and prevent us from attaining eternal salvation. But can't we create new forms of religion and spirituality that look at our bodily desires from a different perspective? Is the rationalistic picture of human nature really such a deep part of our everyday way of thinking about ourselves that we can't change?

Consider a more radical proposal. Why don't we simply throw out the rationalistic view of human nature if it is sexist? Genevieve Lloyd, a feminist philosopher, argues that this is not as easy to do as it may first appear:

> It is a natural response to the discovery of unfair discrimination to affirm the positive value of what has been downgraded. But with the kind of bias we are confronting here the situation is complicated by the fact that femininity, as we have it, has been partly formed by relation to, and differentiation from, a male norm. We may, for example, want to insist against past philosophers that the sexes are equal in possession of Reason; and that women must now be admitted to full participation in its cultural manifestations. But . . . this approach is fraught with difficulty. . . . For it seems implicitly to accept the downgrading of the excluded character traits traditionally associated with femininity, and to endorse the assumption that the only human

32 Philo, *Special Laws*, in *Philo*, vol. 1, trans. F. H. Colson and G. H. Whitaker, Loeb Classical Library (London: Heinemann, 1929), 125.

> excellences and virtues which deserve to be taken seriously are those exemplified in the range of activities and concerns that have been associated with maleness.
>
> However, alternative responses are no less beset by conceptual complexities. For example, it may seem easy to affirm the value and strengths of distinctively "feminine" traits. . . . Thus, it is an understandable reaction . . . to stress . . . the warmth of feeling as against the chillingly abstract character of Reason. But . . . subtle accommodations have been incorporated into the social organization of sexual division which allow "feminine" traits and activities to be both preserved and downgraded. There has been no lack of male affirmation of the importance and attractiveness of "feminine" traits—in women—or of gallant acknowledgement of the impoverishment of male Reason. Making good the lacks in male consciousness, providing it with a necessary complementation by the "feminine," is a large part of what the suppression . . . of "womankind" has been all about.[33]

QUICK REVIEW
Insisting women are as rational as men still assumes that "male reason" is better than female desires and emotions; saying desires and emotions are as good as reason still allows that because males have reason they should rule females, who have emotions and desires.

Lloyd seems to be saying that one way of rejecting the rationalistic view is to simply insist that women have as much reason as men. Yet, as she points out, why would we insist on this unless we agree that reason—the "male" trait—is really as superior as the rationalistic view says it is? A second way of rejecting the rationalistic view, she suggests, is to insist that the "female" traits of feeling and emotion are as valuable as the "male" trait of reason. But males have always "gallantly" said that these "female" traits are valuable, Lloyd says. This implies that women should be content with their place in society: to serve as the companions of males who unfortunately are stuck with cold (but ruling!) reason.

Are the very notions used by the rationalistic view—reason and desire, body and mind, rationality and emotion—such an integral part of a centuries-old way of thinking that we can no longer rid ourselves of them? Do the very meanings of these words assume that women are inferior to men? When we use these notions, are we forced into seeing women as inferior to men? Is it possible for us to stop using the notions of reason and desire, body and mind, and rationality and emotion? In fact, is it possible for us to reject the rationalistic view of human nature, which seems to be built into our very notions of what men and women are?

QUESTIONS

1. What historical evidence indicates that we are rational animals? What evidence indicates that we are not?
2. Suppose that the theory of evolution is true. What implications would evolution have for how our societies should be arranged? What implications would evolution have for religion?
3. Sartre's existentialism leaves us with no moral rules or behavioral guidelines, yet it ultimately holds us responsible for all our choices. Do you find such a view appealing? Contradictory? Unsettling? Liberating? Explain. Do you experience your life as free as Sartre describes? Explain.
4. State and evaluate Aristotle's argument for the view that the purpose of human beings is to exercise their reason. State and evaluate Plato's view that the soul is not material like the body.
5. In your view, are there ways of looking at women that ordinarily are not seen as sexist but that when examined more closely turn out to be sexist? What are the consequences of sexist ways of looking at women and men?

33 Genevieve Lloyd, *The Man of Reason: "Male" and "Female" in Western Philosophy* (Minneapolis: University of Minnesota Press, 1984), 104.

PHILOSOPHY AT THE MOVIES

Watch *Control* (2004), in which Michael Copeland, a doctor doing research on a drug that is supposed to enable a person to control his anger, offers the drug to Lee Ray Oliver, a condemned murderer with an abusive childhood who is allowed to take part in his research program instead of being executed. In the end, is this movie consistent with the Traditional view of human nature, or is the character of Lee Ray Oliver in conflict with the Traditional view? What would Sartre say about the childhood influences on Lee Ray Oliver and the changes he undergoes after the drug? Is Sartre right?

2.3 The Mind–Body Problem: How Do Mind and Body Relate?

To most of us, it's obvious that we have a mind and a body. We spend much of our time fretting and fussing over our body and its properties. We exercise to keep it healthy, diet to keep its weight down, comb its hair and paint its face to make it more alluring, lift weights to inflate its muscles, jog to keep its stamina up, adorn it with clothes and jewelry to make it aesthetically pleasing, hire doctors to cure its illnesses. We know our body has weight and mass and is spread out in space. It has a definite color, size, shape. It can be seen and touched and measured. It is, in short, a material or physical entity with the properties that are characteristic of all physical bodies.

Your mind, too, gets its share of attention. We study and learn to increase its knowledge, we travel to expand its experiences, we read to keep it entertained, we spend many hours daydreaming to while its time away, we hire psychiatrists to cure it of its illnesses, and we sleep to keep it rested. The mind is the source of our creativity and deepest feelings. It is with the mind that we experience the ordinary and the unusual, feel desires and emotions, believe or doubt. It is with our mind that we feel hope, fear, love, hate, disgust, shame, pride, amusement. Strangely, and unlike the body, these features of the mind seem to have no observable color, size, or shape. It makes no sense, for example, to say that our mind's beliefs, desires, sensations, emotions, or ideas are colored, or that they are so many inches long, or shaped like a square or a sphere. In fact, the properties of the mind, and the mind itself, seem to lack the properties that all physical bodies have.

Most puzzling of all is the most characteristic feature of the mind: its consciousness. What is consciousness? Suppose you are sleeping, or sleepwalking, or anesthetized, or knocked out. Then, you are unconscious and have no consciousness. As you wake up in the morning, and as you gradually become aware of yourself and the world around you, as you become aware that you see your bedroom, become aware that you feel the wrinkled sheets beneath you, become aware that you smell the musty odors of your closed room, and become aware of the dry stale taste in your mouth, you are becoming conscious. Consciousness is this awareness you have of yourself and your sensing and thinking when you are awake.

Consciousness is subjective: I am directly in touch with and am directly aware of my own consciousness, and you with yours. But you are not directly aware of my consciousness, and neither can I be directly in touch with yours. Strangely, consciousness, like the other features of the mind, seems to lack all physical properties. Consciousness appears to have no weight, color, taste, mass, or physical dimensions. Your mind and its properties, then, seem to be completely different from your body and its properties.

QUICK REVIEW
To many, it is obvious that humans have both a mind and a body and that they are completely different from each other.

But although this all seems obvious and commonsensical, the view of human nature as consisting of a mind and body that are completely different from each other has given rise to profound problems. Philosophers, like each of us, have long pondered our nature. And the feature of human nature that has most troubled them is this apparent dual nature of human beings. Some have simply accepted the commonsense view and have agreed that humans consist of two different kinds of things: a physical body and a nonphysical or immaterial mind. But those who accept this view are faced with the problem of explaining how the mind—a nonphysical entity—can possibly interact with the physical body. Others, influenced by science, have recoiled from accepting this duality. Nothing exists beyond the physical, they have argued, and so somehow the conscious mind must be understood as a part of, or a property of, the physical body and its brain.

The Dualist View of Human Nature

The view that human beings are immaterial minds within material bodies is an ancient one. It is a view that many adherents of the Traditional view of human nature adopted, including Plato and Saint Augustine. Still, the view was most clearly expressed in the seventeenth century by the first philosophical figure of the modern European age, René Descartes (1596–1650). Notice that Descartes leaves no question that the human being has an immaterial mind. The essential nature of the mind is its conscious ability to think, which makes it very different from the body it inhabits:

QUICK REVIEW
Descartes said we can think of the self without a body, so it is not a body; we cannot think of the self without thinking, which is not a material act. So, the self must be a thinking, immaterial mind with a material body.

> And then, examining attentively that which I was, I saw that I could think that I had no body, and that there was no world nor place where I might be; but yet that I could not for all that think that I did not exist. On the contrary, I saw from the very fact that I thought of doubting the truth of other things, it very evidently and certainly followed that I existed. On the other hand, if I had only ceased from thinking, even if all the rest of what I had ever imagined had really existed, I should have no reason for thinking that I existed. From that I knew that I was a substance [a thing] the whole essence or nature of which is to think and that for its existence there is no need of any place, nor does it depend on any material thing; so that this "me," that is to say, the soul by which I am what I am, is entirely distinct from the body, and is even more easy to know than is the latter; and even if the body did not exist, the soul would not cease to be what it is.[34]

Descartes points out here that we can conceive of ourselves as existing without a body. He then makes a crucial assumption: If we can conceive of one thing without the other, then those two things are different; if we can't, then one must be an essential part of the other. Because we can conceive of the self as not having a body, he claims, the self is not a body—that is, it is not a physical thing. On the other hand, I cannot think of myself without thinking. So, thinking is necessary for the self; it is part of the **essence** (the defining characteristics that make something what it is) of my self. All humans, then, are selves that are immaterial, that are essentially conscious, and that can exist without the body, which is material and unconscious. But what is the body? Descartes describes the body thus:

> By the body I understand all that which can be defined by a specific shape: something which can be confined in a certain place, and which can fill a given space in

34 René Descartes, *Discourse on Method,* in *The Philosophical Works of Descartes,* vol. 1, trans. and ed. Elizabeth S. Haldane and G. R. T. Ross (Cambridge: Cambridge University Press, 1911), 101. I have replaced the word *conceive* with the word *think,* and in some places the word *is* with the word *exists* to make the meaning clearer.

 critical thinking

Descartes assumes that if it is possible to think of one thing without the other, then those two things are not identical. Do you accept this assumption? Why or why not.

such a way that every other body will be excluded from it; which can be perceived either by touch, or by sight, or by hearing, or by taste, or by smell: which can be moved in many ways not, in truth, by itself, but by something different, by which it is touched.[35]

The Traditional view of human nature, as Descartes explains it, says that a human is composed of two kinds of things: a material body and an immaterial mind, or "soul." Philosophers call this view **dualism** because it claims that humans are made up of dual (meaning "two") substances. To many people, traditional dualism seems obvious. Don't our bodies have physical characteristics (such as color, size, and shape) that our minds do not have? When people's bodies weaken, can't their minds remain strong? And can't the mind deteriorate even as the body remains vigorous? Don't these differences imply that the mind and the body are distinct entities? Isn't the separation of the mind from the body important for religions that say that after the body dies, the mind or soul can survive and live on in an afterlife?

QUICK REVIEW
But how can something that has no physical dimensions act on or be acted on by something that does?

Nevertheless, this dualist view—that the mind and body are two entities each made of a different kind of stuff—raises a hard problem. How can an immaterial mind move a physical body, and how can a body that consists of heavy, dense, spatial matter affect an immaterial mind? If the mind is immaterial, it is not part of the physical world. How can something like the mind reach into the physical world and affect it? If it did so, then the mind would somehow have to introduce new energy and force into the physical world. But scientists tell us that this is impossible because it would violate the principle of the conservation of matter and energy.

Descartes recognized the problems created by saying that we have an immaterial mind that somehow interacts with a material body. Nevertheless, he held that the mind and body obviously interact, so there must be some point of contact between the two. He suggested that perhaps the mind interacts with the body through the pineal gland, a tiny gland near the brain. Descartes apparently believed that this gland is so tiny and so sensitive that even the immaterial mind could move it. Yet Descartes' own contemporaries ridiculed the idea that the immaterial mind and the material body interact at the pineal gland. No matter how small and sensitive the pineal gland might be, it was still a physical entity, and the issue still remained: How can a nonphysical entity produce effects in the physical world?

QUICK REVIEW
Leibniz agreed that mind and body can't interact but said they run in parallel order like two synchronized clocks. Malebranche also agreed that mind and body can't interact, but he said that God obligingly moves the body for the mind and affects the mind for the body.

Descartes' theory of the mind and body convinced many philosophers of his day, prompting them to find a way of explaining how the mind can influence—indeed, control—the body. The philosopher Gottfried Leibniz (1646–1716) suggested that the mind and body don't really interact at all, but just seem to. Suppose, Leibniz said, that the mind and body run in parallel order, like two clocks that are synchronized so they seem to be connected yet operate independently. Then, whenever the mind issues a command, the body moves, and when the body is affected, the mind is affected also. Nevertheless, the two never really interact. Other philosophers said that this was as ridiculous as Descartes' pineal gland theory. For example, the philosopher Nicolas Malebranche (1683–1715) argued that the immaterial mind could not interact with a material body, and to that extent he agreed with Leibniz. Still, he refused to believe that by

35 René Descartes, *Meditations*, meditation ii, in *The Philosophical Works of Descartes*, vol. 1, trans. and ed. Elizabeth S. Haldane and G. R. T. Ross (Cambridge: Cambridge University Press, 1911), 151.

some incredible coincidence the mind and body were perfectly synchronized. What happens instead, he said, is that God steps in to synchronize the body and the mind. When something affects the body, God obligingly comes forward to cause a corresponding feeling in the mind. When the mind commands the body to move, God again obligingly steps forward to move the body for the mind.

Yet don't the contorted explanations of Descartes, Leibniz, and Malebranche show that dualism has gone wrong somewhere? Wouldn't it make more sense to reject dualism? This is the approach that many contemporary and several older philosophers have taken to the mind–body problem. Before we look at those philosophers' arguments, however, we'll look at some more critical thinking tools you can use to help you evaluate their arguments.

thinking critically • Evaluating an Argument's Premises

The arguments that Descartes, Leibniz, and Malebranche give us are interesting. But even if they are valid, are they sound? That is, are the premises or reasons they give for their conclusions true? We've said several times that "You will have to decide for yourself" whether this or that claim a philosopher makes in his or her argument is true. But how do you do this? Are there any rules or guidelines that can help you evaluate whether a philosopher's claims are true?

In a sense there are no step-by-step procedures that will always let us determine whether a claim is true. If there were such procedures, then we could use them to answer any question we had. But obviously, it takes a lot of investigation, thinking, ingenuity, and time to discover the truth about most important questions we have. For example, it took centuries to discover that genetic DNA controls how our cells and bodies function and that the heat of the sun is produced by atomic fusion. Nevertheless, there are some guidelines that can help guide our thinking when evaluating the premises of arguments. Before you use those guidelines, however, you should make sure you understand the claim you are trying to evaluate. To check your understanding of the claim, restate it in your own words or give examples of what it is talking about. Once you are sure you understand the claim, you can use the following guidelines to help you evaluate whether it is true.

First, ask yourself whether the claim fits with your own experience. Generally speaking, your own past experience is your best source of information about the world and is your best starting point when evaluating a claim someone makes. But there are two questions you need to ask when you rely on your own experience to evaluate a claim. First, your experience is not a reliable source of information if your memory of what you experienced is mistaken, or if your senses weren't working right when you had the experience, or if you weren't being sufficiently observant at the time. So when you rely on your experience to evaluate a claim, you should ask yourself: (1) Is there any reason for me to doubt the reliability of that particular experience? Second, your experience is not a reliable source of information if you are confusing *what you experienced*, with a *conclusion you drew* from what you experienced. For example, if I heard someone walking around in the bedroom next to mine, I may conclude that it was my brother, and afterward claim that I heard my brother walking around in his bedroom. But that claim about my brother would be a conclusion from what I experienced, because what I experienced were merely sounds and I did not actually see my brother in his bedroom. So when relying on your experience, you also need to ask: (2) Is this really what I experienced, or is this *a conclusion* I'm drawing from what I experienced? Both of these points raise important philosophical questions about our experience, such as whether experience is a reliable source of knowledge, and whether it is possible to completely separate what we experience from conclusions we draw about what we experience. We will examine these questions later. For now, and in

QUICK REVIEW
To evaluate a premise ask: (1) if it is consistent with your own experience and whether your experience is reliable; (2) if it is consistent with what you believe but learned from others and whether they are reliable sources of that information; (3) if it is a generalization and has counterexamples; (4) if it implies claims that are absurd, false, impossible, or inconsistent with other well-established claims; (5) if it can be supported by good arguments or undermined by good objections.

spite of these questions, your experience should always be your starting point when you ask whether a philosopher's premises are true.

Second, when evaluating a philosopher's claim you should ask whether the claim fits with all the information you accept and believe but that you acquired from someone else. Most of your information doesn't come from your own experience, but from others: from what friends and family tell you, from books and articles you read, from people you hear on radio or television, from what you find on the Internet. When the information you are using to evaluate a claim was acquired from someone else, however, you should ask: (1) Is the source of the information known to be trustworthy? (2) Is the source an expert on the subject? (3) Are the memory, senses, and powers of observation of the source reliable? (4) Does the source have any motive to mislead?"

Third, if the claim you are evaluating is a generalization, then you should ask whether there are any "counterexamples" to the generalization. Almost all claims philosophers make, and a large number of the claims everyone else makes, are generalizations. That is, they are claims about *ALL* the phenomena being discussed, or claims about what is *ALWAYS* the case. For example, we earlier saw that Aristotle claimed that *every* organ has a purpose. Generalizations are claims, then, that assert that all the members of some class of things have some characteristic. This means that the generalization is false if just one of those things do not have the characteristic, i.e., if there are exceptions to the generalization. So, one way to determine whether a generalization is false is by checking to see if there is an exception to the generalization. Such exceptions are called "counterexamples" to the generalization.

Fourth, when evaluating a philosophical claim or premise, you should ask if it implies or requires other claims that are absurd, false, impossible, or inconsistent with other well-established knowledge we have such as well-established scientific laws. For example, we have seen that Descartes claims that humans consist of a non-physical mind and a physical body. Descartes' claim implies that a non-physical entity can interact with a physical entity. But such interactions, some have argued, are impossible. Others have claimed that such interactions are inconsistent with the well-established scientific law of the conservation of matter and energy. Still others have claimed that such interactions would require an absurd theory to explain them, such as Descartes' own pineal gland theory, or Leibniz's parallelism of the mind and body theory, or Malebranche's theory that when the mind chooses to move its body, God obligingly steps in to move the body for the mind. If a claim implies other claims that are absurd, false, impossible, or inconsistent with other well-established claims, the claim usually should be rejected i.e., to "directly oppose what the generalization claimed".

Finally, when evaluating a philosophical premise or claim, you should ask whether there are any good arguments that support the claim, or whether there are any good objections to that claim (besides those you found by using the earlier guidelines). For example, we saw earlier that Mercer also provided arguments to support the premises of his main argument. And we've seen several objections that have been raised against the claims of the rationalistic view of human nature. But when a philosopher does not provide evidence to support the premises of his argument, or when someone does not give you ready-made objections to those premises, you will have to try to think up such evidence or objections on your own.

To evaluate the premise of an argument, then, begin by asking whether it is consistent with your own experience (and whether your experience is reliable). Second, ask whether it is consistent with information you believe but that you learned from others (and whether they are reliable sources of that information). Third, if the claim is a generalization, ask if it has counterexamples. Fourth, ask if the claim implies other claims that are absurd, false, impossible, or inconsistent with other well-established claims. And fifth, ask if the claim can be supported by good arguments or attacked by other good objections (besides those you found earlier).

We will now look at some of the arguments that philosophers have given in support of an alternative to Descartes' claim that humans are composed of an immaterial mind and a material body. The main alternative to dualism is the claim that only the material body exists and that what we call the mind is in some sense reducible to this material body. We will look at several philosophers who take this "materialist" approach, beginning with Thomas Hobbes who was one of the pioneers of this approach. As we look at his arguments and those of other philosophers, you should use the guidelines we just discussed to evaluate the premises of their arguments.

The Materialist View of Human Nature

The problem with Descartes' dualism, Hobbes said, is that it says there are two things in human nature. Instead, let us say there is only one: the material body that we observe with our senses. Let us agree, he argued, that only physical bodies exist. If so, then the activities we attribute to the mind are really activities of our material body, and we should be able to explain the operations of the mind in terms of the working of the body. Thomas Hobbes was a *materialist* who felt that we can explain all human activities, including our mental activities, as working much like those of a machine:

> For seeing life is but a motion of limbs, the beginning whereof is in some principal part within; why may we not say, that all *automata* (engines that move themselves by springs and wheels as does a watch) have an artificial life? For what is the *heart*, but a *spring*; and the *nerves*, but so many *strings*; and the *joints*, but so many *wheels*, giving motion to the whole body, such as was intended by the artificer?[36]

This kind of view—that processes such as thought and life are really nothing more than physical and chemical processes—is often called **reductionism**. Reductionism is the idea that we can completely understand or explain one kind of reality in terms of another kind, or that one kind of reality is actually a different kind of reality. Reductionists take what seems to be one thing and argue that it is really something else. Hobbes, in particular, argues that what seem to be immaterial mental processes, can be fully understood as physical processes. If so, then there is no need to postulate the existence of "immaterial substances." Instead, we must acknowledge that only material things exist.

What led Hobbes to embrace materialism? In part, Hobbes was led to reject the reality of immaterial substances because he thought he had shown that mental processes could be reduced to physical processes, and in part because he thought that the very idea of an "immaterial substance" was a contradiction since the very word "substance," he claimed, implied something material. But Hobbes was also motivated by the many advances that science was making at his time. Through careful observations and measurements of physical nature, Copernicus, Galileo, Kepler, and others had made gigantic strides in understanding the universe. Their scientific advances seemed to be based on what they could observe with their senses and measure quantitatively. Hobbes seems to have decided that a scientific view of the universe required accepting as real only what we can observe and measure. Because we can observe and measure only material or physical bodies, Hobbes came to his famous conclusion: "The Universe, that is the whole mass of things that are, is corporeal, that is to say body; and has the dimensions of magnitude, namely length, breadth, and depth . . . and that which is not body is no part of the Universe."

QUICK REVIEW
The materialist Hobbes said the mind could be reduced to the physical actions of a material body, so there is no need to believe that immaterial things exist. He was influenced by the science of his day.

36 Thomas Hobbes, *Hobbes's Leviathan* (Oxford: Clarendon, 1909; original work published 1651), 23.

Hobbes' theory failed to convince many of his contemporaries. Although he claimed that the operations of the mind could be explained in terms of the workings of the body, his explanations of mental activities in terms of physical processes were not persuasive. Neither was it clear, many objected, that this kind of reductionism was possible. How can a physical system, even a very complicated physical system, produce mental phenomena that seem to have no physical characteristics?

The Mind/Brain Identity Theory of Human Nature

critical thinking

Suppose that by restricting ourselves to studying only physical entities we were able to make great scientific strides. Would this show that only physical entities exist? Would it show that only the study of physical entities is worthwhile?

If materialist views like those of Hobbes are to be acceptable, then they must somehow explain exactly how the conscious mind is related to the material body. One kind of contemporary materialist view that attempts to provide such an explanation is what we now call the **identity theory** of the mind. The identity theory claims that states of consciousness are identical with states of the brain, which is a physical or material organ. When we have a mental experience such as a thought, this experience is nothing more than the material brain working. The same is true of any other conscious experience, such as dreaming, hoping, and feeling. Philosophers who accept the identity theory don't think that their theory is just a matter of definitions. In other words, they do not hold that words for mental states *mean the same* as words for brain states. Instead, they say, science will someday *discover* which mental states are identical to which brain states. The identity of mental states and brain states is thus a "contingent" relationship. For example, we now know that water and H_2O are identical. But science had to discover this. In the same way, we will someday know which brain states are identical to the mental states of desiring, seeing, feeling pain, being happy, and being sad. But science must discover this. We cannot know, just by thinking about the meanings of the words, what brain states are identical with "desiring," "seeing," "feeling pain," "being happy," and "being sad."

Yet the attempt to identify conscious experiences with brain states quickly ran into problems. Consider, for example, that whereas brain states are publicly observable, our conscious experiences are not. If a surgeon exposes the brain, she can observe its brain states, such as the reaction of a ganglion; she could pinpoint the brain state's precise location, describe its color and shape, and truthfully say that anyone can literally *see* it. On the other hand, because only you can have your conscious experiences, no one else can literally perceive or be directly aware of your experiences. Moreover, an experience such as thinking has no precise location, no color, and no shape. So, doesn't it seem that a brain state and a conscious experience are two different things, with very different qualities?

A prime proponent of identity theory, the contemporary Australian philosopher J. J. C. Smart (1920–), thinks not. Smart contends that future scientific discovery will show that all conscious experiences are identical to processes taking place in the brain. Smart defines materialism as the theory that "there is nothing in the world over and above those entities which are postulated by physics."[37] This means, he writes, that there are no "nonphysical entities and nonphysical laws." However, he asserts, energy is an entity postulated by physics, and so "energy counts as matter." What about our thoughts, feelings, perceptions, and other mental experiences? All of our conscious experiences, Smart claims, are nothing more than physical processes in our brains "involving millions of neurons."

Smart admits that when we have conscious experiences of things, we seem to be "aware of them as something different from" a brain process. When we experience a pain, for example, we do not seem to be experiencing a brain process; that is, pain does not seem to have the properties of a brain process. A pain in an arm hurts, for

---

37 J. J. C. Smart, "Materialism," *Journal of Philosophy*, October 24, 1963.

example, but we don't even feel the processes going on in our brain. Does this mean that the experience of a pain cannot be a brain process? Not at all, Smart asserts, since the properties of what we experience must not be confused with the properties of the brain processes that make up the experience. When we have the experience of seeing a green apple, for example, what we experience is green. But this does not mean that the brain processes that are involved are themselves green. Green is a property of what we experience, but it is not a property of the brain processes involved when we experience green. In other words, the *experience* is a brain process, but *what we experience* is not a brain process. So it would be a mistake to think that the properties of what we experience will be the same as the properties of the brain processes involved.

Why does Smart adopt this form of materialism? He writes that the fundamental reasoning supporting his theory of materialism, is based on the idea that a nonphysical property or nonphysical entity could not "suddenly arise in the course of animal evolution." Thus, Smart assumes that humans evolved from animals through the processes of evolution. Evolution, he notes, takes place through changes in the "complex molecules" that make up an organism's genes. What happens is that a change in the "complex molecules" of an animal's genes, will change the "biochemistry" of the animal's cells, and this, in turn will change the "shape or organization" of the offspring of the organism. So animals evolve when "chemical processes" change their genes, and they pass on these genetic changes to their offspring. All human properties, therefore, must be properties that evolved from our animal ancestors through these chemical processes. But chemical processes, he claims, cannot "lead to the springing into existence of something nonphysical." Chemical processes can only change one physical entity into another physical entity: they cannot create something nonphysical. All human capacities, then, are capacities that evolved from the physical capacities of our animal ancestors through chemical processes, and so human capacities all have to be physical.

QUICK REVIEW
The "identity theory of the mind" proposed by Smart says mental states, such as thinking, are contingently identical with states of the brain, a material organ.

In essence, Smart defends the position that states of consciousness are identical with states of the brain. Smart asserts that science will discover which particular brain states are identical with a particular mental state such as feeling a pain. As Smart puts it, the identity between a mental state and a brain state is "contingent" and not "necessary." If the identity were "necessary," we could deduce it from the meanings of the words. But because it is something that science must discover, it is "contingent."

Do all philosophers agree with Smart's analysis? American philosopher Norman Malcolm (1911–1990) pointed out two difficulties. Both of them depend on the fact that if two things are identical, then both must have exactly the same properties. For example, "George Washington" and "first president of the United States" are identical, so George Washington must have had exactly the same properties as the first president of the United States. Consequently, if mental phenomena are identical to brain phenomena, then, Malcolm asserts, "brain phenomena must have all the properties that mental phenomena have."[38] But mental phenomena have at least two kinds of properties that brain phenomena lack.

First, Malcolm points out, it makes no sense to "assign spatial locations to . . . mental phenomena," or thoughts. On the other hand, brain phenomena must have a specific spatial location. So, brain phenomena have a property (spatial location) that mental phenomena do not. It follows, Malcolm concludes, that mental phenomena like thoughts cannot be identical with brain phenomena.

Second, Malcolm argues, some thoughts require "a background" of social "practices, agreements, assumptions." Suppose, for example, that I think, "I promised you five dollars if Obama were re-elected." I cannot have such a thought unless money, elections, and promises exist and I am familiar with them. On the other

QUICK REVIEW
Malcolm objects that mental states have no location in space but that brain states do, and that thoughts require surroundings such as practices, agreements, and assumptions but that brain events don't, so mental states are not identical to brain states.

38 Norman Malcolm, "Scientific Materialism and the Identity Theory," *Journal of Philosophy*, October 24, 1963, 662–663.

hand, brain phenomena are all "explicable in terms of physics" and thus do not require a background of social practices, agreements, and assumptions. Again, therefore, mental phenomena have a property that brain phenomena do not, so one cannot be identical to the other.

However, such objections have not led materialists to abandon materialism. Many remain firmly convinced that dualism must be wrong. Objections to Smart's kind of materialism have therefore spurred efforts to find other, more defensible theories of materialism.

The Behaviorist View of Human Nature

One alternative kind of materialist view of human nature is behaviorism. **Behaviorism** began as a school of psychology that restricted the study of humans to what can be observed—namely, human behavior. Psychological behaviorists argued that they could not observe states of consciousness, so psychology should not be concerned with them. Some philosophers have agreed with this view. They have argued that when explaining human nature, we should restrict ourselves to what is publicly observable: the outward physical behavior of human beings. How, then, do we explain interior mental processes that are not physically observable, such as thinking, feeling, knowing, loving, hating, desiring, and imagining?

QUICK REVIEW
Behaviorists like Ryle say mental activities and states can be explained and defined in terms of our observable behaviors.

Behaviorist philosophers have argued that we can explain mental activities in terms of people's behaviors. For example, the British philosopher Gilbert Ryle claimed that we can explain mental activities and mental states in terms of the externally observable behaviors with which they are associated.[39] Ryle would argue, for example, that "John knows what chairs are" should be taken as meaning something like "When a chair is present, and given certain other conditions, John will engage in certain specific behaviors with the chair." In other words, to say that a person *knows* what a chair is, is to say that the person *behaves* in certain ways when a chair is present (sits on it, for example). Similarly, to say that a person *loves* someone is to say that she is *disposed to behave* in certain ways toward that person. For the behaviorist, then, the mind is nothing more than bodily behavior and dispositions to bodily behavior. If this were not so, behaviorists argue, how could children possibly learn the meaning of words that refer to mental states? If mental states and activities were totally private interior (perhaps nonphysical) phenomena, then we could never teach children the words that refer to these phenomena because we could never point to the phenomena to which the words refer. We can teach children what words such as *pain* and *fear* mean only if these words refer to exterior observable behaviors to which we can point when we teach children what these words mean.

QUICK REVIEW
But critics like Putnam say we can have an idea in mind without any externally observable behavior.

Still, are all interior thoughts reducible to exterior observable behavior? Can't you keep a certain very personal idea in your mind without ever betraying it in your exterior behavior? The contemporary philosopher Hilary Putnam has argued that it is very easy to come up with examples that show behaviorism is wrong. Imagine a "superactor" who is giving a perfect imitation of the behavior of someone in pain. Behaviorism says such a "superactor" is feeling pain, even if in fact the superactor is conscious of no pain whatsoever. Or imagine a "superspartan" who can endure pain without giving any external sign in his behavior of the pain he feels. Behaviorism says such a "superspartan" feels no pain even if the superspartan is conscious of excruciating pain.

In behaviorism, our consciousness seems to have disappeared. But there is something odd with the approach behaviorism takes. We seem to be directly aware of what is in our consciousness. We seem to know directly, in a way that others

39 See Gilbert Ryle, *The Concept of Mind* (London: Hutchinson, 1949).

cannot observe, what we are thinking, feeling, sensing. I know if something feels good to me in a way that you cannot know. Yet behaviorism says that all feelings are external behaviors that others can observe. So others who observe our behavior know just like I do—perhaps before I do—when something feels good to me. This seems wrong. In fact, behaviorism inspired a famous joke. Two behaviorist philosophers have just finished making love. So, the first behaviorist says to the second: "It was great for you. How was it for me?"

The problem, then, is that behaviorism, in reducing the mind to behaviors, leaves out anything about the mind that is not an outer behavior. In doing this, it seems to leave out the interior conscious states that characterize the mind and that are the actual cause of behavior.

The Functionalist View of Human Nature

Another contemporary materialist view, which does not try to reduce all mental activities to external behavior but which research in computers has inspired, is called *functionalism.* During the twentieth century, scientists and engineers made great strides in devising powerful computers that could calculate and manipulate bits of information at an amazing rate. When we give a computer certain "inputs," such as a mathematical problem, the computer calculates and provides an "output," such as the answer to the problem. Many philosophers began to think that perhaps the computer provided useful clues of how a behaviorist theory of the mind might be revised enough to avoid the problems that earlier behaviorists ran into.

Proposed by several philosophers, such as D. M. Armstrong,[40] **functionalism** holds that we should explain mental activities and mental states in terms of perceptual inputs and behavioral outputs. The inputs of the human mind are the stimulations that affect the nervous system—what we see, hear, taste, and feel. The outputs are the behaviors that result: running, walking, sitting, standing. Then, we can think of a mental concept such as *belief* as a connection the material brain makes between certain inputs and certain outputs. For example, suppose that when a certain man sees a dog (the input), he runs off (the output), and we explain this behavior by saying that he ran "because he believes that dogs bite people." Then, we can say that the man's *belief that dogs bite people* is just something in the body's brain that links his sensory input (seeing a dog) to his behavior (running away). Functionalists claim that all conscious mental states and activities are shorthand terms for the complex connections that the body and its brain make between sense inputs and behavioral outputs. Or, to use the language of functions, mental states and activities can be explained in terms of the functions they serve in the processes that connect our sensory inputs to our behavioral outputs.

QUICK REVIEW
Functionalists like Armstrong say mental states can be explained in terms of perceptual inputs and behavioral outputs; some mental states can be explained in terms of other mental states but ultimately must be connected to sense inputs and behavior outputs.

Unlike earlier forms of behaviorism, then, functionalism allows that interior mental states can explain other mental states; thus, it gives a role to mental states that earlier forms of behaviorism did not. For example, functionalists might agree that a person's intention (a mental state) can be explained in terms of the person's desires and beliefs (other mental states). For instance, when we see a man running to a bus stop after he sees a bus coming, we might say that he is doing so because he intends to catch the bus. We might then say that his intention to catch the bus is simply something that plays the role of linking his sensory stimulation (seeing the bus) to his desire to catch the bus and to his belief that by running he will catch the bus (mental states), and these to his behavior (running to the bus stop). Thus, some mental states (such as intentions) are to be explained in terms of other mental

40 See D. M. Armstrong, *A Materialist Theory of the Mind* (London: Routledge & Kegan Paul, 1968).

states (desires and beliefs). Yet, according to the functionalist, all mental states ultimately are to be explained in terms of the roles they play in linking our sensory stimulation to our external behavior. Thus, the terms *desire* and *belief* ultimately have to be explained in terms of the role (the function) they play in the network of connections that lead from a sensory input (such as seeing a bus) to a behavioral output (running for the bus).

For the functionalist, then, the mind is nothing more than a very complex set of functions within the body and its brain. That is, the mind consists of all those complex connections that the body makes when it receives sensory inputs and then produces external behaviors. In fact, the functionalist would say that any object—a machine, for example—that connects sensory inputs to behaviors in the way that our body does can be said to have a mind. And if any two objects (humans or machines) connect a group of sensory inputs to a group of behavioral outputs in exactly the same way, then those two objects can be said to have exactly the same mental states. Sameness of function implies sameness of mind.

QUICK REVIEW
Critics argue that if two people experience colors differently, they may link the same behavior outputs to the same sense inputs, yet they don't have the same mental states, as functionalism asserts.

But functionalism, too, seems to leave something out. Opponents argue that functionalism leaves out the inner conscious states we are directly aware of. These opponents argue as follows: imagine two people who experience colors differently. When one sees a red object, he has the kind of visual experience that the other person has when the other person sees a green object. The color red has the appearance to him that green has to the other person. And the color green has the appearance to him that red has to the other person. Otherwise, the two people are exactly the same. In fact, they don't even know that colors appear differently to them. How could they? Each can't get into the other's mind to see how colors appear. Now, suppose we ask them to look at some colored objects (the "input") and sort them into different piles (the "output"). Each person will sort colors exactly like the other: Green objects will go into one pile, red ones into another. Now, functionalism says that if two people have exactly the same inputs and give exactly the same outputs, those two people have exactly the same inner mental state. So, functionalism says that the inner conscious states of the two people must be exactly the same. But clearly this is wrong. Inside, what one person consciously experiences is different from what the other person consciously experiences. So, functionalism is mistaken. The problem is that functionalism wants to reduce mental states to inputs and outputs. But this seems to leave out what is most characteristic of our minds: our inner conscious states.

QUICK REVIEW
Turing said the mind is a computer following a program that generates certain outputs when given certain inputs. The "Turing Test" says that if the outputs a computer program gives to certain inputs cannot be distinguished from the outputs a human would make to the same inputs, the computer program is equivalent to the human mind.

Despite the difficulties of functionalism, it led some philosophers to the view that the human brain is a kind of computer that processes inputs (our sense observations) and generates outputs (our behaviors). Humans are sophisticated computers. Some functionalists, in fact, believe that very soon electronic computers will be able to imitate the input–output processing of the human brain. Some have argued that when computers can process inputs and outputs like the human brain does, they will have minds and be able to think. For example, Alan Turing suggested what we now call the "Turing Test."[41] Imagine that you are in a room where there are two computer keyboards and two printers. One keyboard and a printer are connected to a computer somewhere outside the room. The other keyboard and printer are connected to a human being who is also somewhere outside the room. You do not know which keyboard and printer are connected to the computer and which ones are connected to the human being. You can type questions on the keyboards, which the computer or human on the other end will respond to by printing out the answer on the printer. Your job is to figure out which answers are coming from the

41 A. M. Turing, "Computing Machinery and Intelligence," *Mind* LIX, no. 236 (1950).

computer and which are coming from the human being. According to Turing, when a computer is so powerful that we cannot tell the difference between its answers and the answers of a human being, that computer has a mind. That is, if the outputs a computer generates in response to the inputs it receives are the same as the outputs a human mind would generate in response to those same inputs, the computer is the equivalent of the human mind.

Many computer experts, including Turing himself, have predicted that it is only a matter of time before computers will match the abilities of the human mind and pass the Turing Test. Then, we can say that those computers think and have minds. We will then know that materialism is right. For if a machine, which is completely material, can have a mind, then the mind is not something nonphysical. It is a chunk of physical machinery.

Several philosophers hotly contest this computer theory of human nature. One of the most vociferous opponents of the theory is the American philosopher John Searle. Searle has pointed out that a computer is nothing more than a machine that follows the instructions in its program. But the instructions that a computer follows can also be followed by a human being. So, if following a program can produce mental states in a machine, then when a human being follows the same software program, the same mental states should be produced in the human being. However, says Searle, when a person follows a program that is supposed to let a computer have certain mental states, the person will not have those states.

Searle gives a simple example of what he means. Suppose a computer had a program that let it pass the Turing Test in Chinese. Then, supposedly, the computer could think in Chinese. Now suppose that a human being, such as yourself, followed the same program. Then, according to the Turing Test, you should now be able to think and understand Chinese. But in reality, says Searle, following a program will not put Chinese thoughts into your head:

> Suppose that we write a computer program to simulate the understanding of Chinese so that, for example, if the computer is asked questions in Chinese, the program enables it to give answers in Chinese; if asked to summarize stories in Chinese, it can give such summaries; if asked questions about the stories it has been given, it will answer such questions.
>
> Now suppose that I, who understand no Chinese at all and can't even distinguish Chinese symbols from some other kinds of symbols, am locked in a room with a number of cardboard boxes full of Chinese symbols. Suppose that I am given a book of rules in English that instruct me how to match these Chinese symbols with each other. The rules say such things as that the "squiggle-squiggle" sign is to be followed by the "squoggle-squoggle" sign. Suppose that people outside the room pass in more Chinese symbols and that following the instructions in the book I pass Chinese symbols back to them. Suppose that unknown to me the people who pass me the symbols call them "questions" and the book of instructions that I work from they call "the program." The symbols I give back to them they call "answers to the questions" and me they call "the computer." Suppose that after a while the programmers get so good at writing the programs and I get so good at manipulating the symbols that my answers are indistinguishable from those of native Chinese speakers. I can pass the Turing test for understanding Chinese. But all the same I still don't understand a word of Chinese. And neither does any other digital computer because all the computer has is what I have: a formal program that attaches no meaning, interpretation, or content to any of the symbols.[42]

QUICK REVIEW
Searle objects that a computer following a program is not conscious. His "Chinese Room" example is a person in a room who follows a program that outputs the right Chinese characters when given certain Chinese inputs. This passes the Turing Test, yet the person is not conscious of knowing Chinese.

---

42 John Searle, "The Myth of the Computer," *The New York Review of Books*, vol. 29, no. 7, April 29, 1982.

Searle claims that this argument shows there is something that human minds have that a computer following a program does not have. What does the computer lack? Consciousness. Consciousness, argues Searle, is essential to the human mind, and a computer following a program does not have consciousness.

Nevertheless, Searle is not a dualist, nor does he think that humans have immaterial minds that are somehow connected to physical bodies. Searle claims that humans are purely physical creatures in whom physical, chemical, and biological processes take place. These processes, he claims, cause or produce all our mental states or activities. These mental states or activities are not reducible to physical things, but a physical thing produces them—namely, our brain.

Eliminative Materialism

QUICK REVIEW
"Eliminative materialism" says that mental conscious states (desires, beliefs, intentions) don't exist; although our "folk psychology" refers to those states, it is mistaken and future science will let us eliminate all terms referring to such states.

Many philosophers today remain convinced that Hobbes was right: Only matter exists, so nonmaterial minds cannot exist. But the difficulties encountered by the identity theory, behaviorism, and functionalism have led philosophers to look for other ways of dealing with the problem of the mind. Some have adopted a view called "eliminative materialism." They claim that the ordinary commonsense views we have about the mind are wrong and that what we ordinarily talk about as the contents of our minds—desires, beliefs, fears, intentions—do not really exist. Paul Churchland, for example, refers to our ordinary views about human minds as "folk psychology." "Folk psychology," he argues, is really an antiquated "theory" of the mind.This antiquated theory uses terms like "desires, beliefs, fears, intentions, perceptions" and it incorporates several "laws," such as the "law" that if a person fears that something will happen, he will desire that it not happen, and if a person hopes that something will happen, then he will be pleased if it does happen. According to Churchland, this folk psychology theory "is a radically inadequate account of our internal activities, too confused and too defective to win survival through intertheoretic reduction . . . [and] will simply be displaced by a better theory of those activities."[43]

For the eliminative materialist, desires, beliefs, and intentions, are like demons. Folk theories about demon possession were once used to explain mental illness. But modern science has found other explanations for mental illness. Today's science-based theories of mental illness have eliminated the notion of demons, and most people today no longer believe that demons exist.

In the same way, advances of science, the eliminative materialist claims, will show desires, beliefs, and intentions also do not exist. When that happens, folk psychology will be replaced with a better scientific theory based on neuroscience, a theory that no longer refers to desires, beliefs, and intentions. In effect, the eliminative materialist is suggesting that consciousness as we ordinarily talk about it does not really exist, and that future science will allow us to eliminate such notions from our scientific theories.

QUICK REVIEW
Critics say that eliminative materialism denies the existence of what we all know we experience, and so gets rid of the very thing that has to be explained.

Yet eliminative materialism seems a bit extreme. It denies what we all seem to experience: that we have desires, beliefs, intentions, and other conscious states. Moreover, some critics of eliminative materialism have argued, if eliminative materialism were true, then it would be impossible for anyone to believe it is true. As one critic, Lynn Baker, says: "Obviously, if the common-sense conception [of belief] is eliminated, no one is justified in believing anything; indeed, no one believes anything, justifiably or not."[44] Other critics of eliminative materialism have argued that

43 Paul Churchland, "Eliminative Materialism and the Propositional Attitudes," *Journal of Philosophy*, vol. 78 (1981).

44 Lynne Rudder Baker, "Cognitive Suicide," in John Heil, ed., *Philosophy of Mind: A Guide and Anthology*, (Oxford: Oxford University Press, 2004), p. 402.

foundation of most Western thought. Westerners tend to believe that the private self is all-important and that individuality should be exalted. We are each taught that it is terribly important to become aware of "who we really are," and we each feel that our inner self is a unique being with immeasurable dignity and worth.

Yet not all people are convinced of the significance, or even the existence, of the self. Much of Eastern philosophy, in fact, is based on the notion that the individual self does not exist. Eastern philosophy holds that the delusion that the self exists is the source of all pain and suffering. When we speak of Eastern philosophy, we refer to those systems of thought, belief, and action espoused by many peoples in southwestern and eastern Asia. Because Eastern thought offers many views of human nature, it is impossible to mention them all.

QUICK REVIEW
The no-self view gets rid of the self altogether.

Buddhism. Here we briefly examine one Eastern philosophy, Buddhism, and its view of human nature. (Chapters 4 and 7 continue the discussion of Buddhism in more detail.) Our intention is not to exhaust the subject but to provide a transcultural perspective on our subject and show, as well, that our question has concerned and been discussed by people of other cultures.

Siddhartha Gautama (circa 563–483 BCE), the founder of Buddhism, was the son of a king or chief of a tribal kingdom in what is now Nepal. Tradition indicates that Prince Siddhartha was raised in great luxury and sensuality, completely shielded from the sight of suffering, old age, and death. But when, at twenty-nine, Siddhartha ventured out of his palace and saw an old man, he became upset when told that everyone grows old. He became more upset when he saw a diseased man and then a dead man and learned that these, too, are part of human life. The distraught Siddhartha now gave up his life of luxury to become an ascetic, hoping to overcome the suffering of old age, sickness, and death. After many years of great self-deprivation and meditation, Siddhartha realized that extreme asceticism would not achieve his goal. He became the leader of a small group of followers who practiced a "middle way" between extreme asceticism and an indulgent life of pleasure. As we saw in the last chapter, Siddhartha finally gained enlightenment and became the Buddha, when, meditating under a banana tree at Bihar, he understood the Wheel of Life and how to escape the cycle of birth, suffering, death, and rebirth. The Buddha is said to have devoted the rest of his life to teaching these truths to his followers. He died at the age of eighty in the fifth century BCE.

The Buddha: "It is simply the mind clouded over by impure desires and impervious to wisdom, that obstinately persists in thinking of 'me' and 'mine.'"

© Jeremy Edwards/iStockphoto.com

About a century after his death, the Buddha's growing group of followers split into two groups: a group of dissenters named the Mahasanghikas and the Theravada, who claimed to remain true to the original teachings of the Buddha's first followers. It is uncertain how many of the legends and sermons attributed to the Buddha by the Theravada are really his and how many are the later work of his followers. But for our purposes we can accept the doctrines of the Theravada as the core doctrines of Buddhism.

Central to Buddhist thought is the belief that all things are composite and transient, the key idea behind the Wheel of Life. All things are aggregates composed of elements that inevitably change and separate over time. Therefore, nothing abides permanently as an individual. Constant movement, change, and dissolution characterize everything, including the gods and all living things.

QUICK REVIEW
Buddhism holds that nothing in the universe, not even the self, remains the same from one moment to the next. Everything consists of aggregates of elements that are in constant flux.

The self, like everything else, is in a state of constant flux and disintegration. It, too, is nothing more than a fleeting momentary composite of constantly changing elements: our form and matter, our sensations, our perceptions, our psychic dispositions, and our conscious thoughts. But these are never the same from moment to moment and they are together only fleetingly. What we call the self, then, either considered as the body or considered as the mind, is utterly transient. It is a new aggregate from one moment to the next that cannot even control its own dissolving changes. As a permanently abiding individual entity, then, the self does not exist. In the Theravada writings, the Buddha argues that the idea of self is an illusory belief and that it is the source of suffering, one that produces harmful thoughts of "me," "mine," desire, vanity, egoism, and ill will:

> If the body were an ego-personality, it could do this and that as it would determine. [But] a king . . . becomes ill despite his intent and desire, he comes to old age unwillingly, and his fortune and his wishes often have little to do with each other.
>
> If the mind were an ego-personality it could do this and that as it would determine, but the mind often flies from what it knows is right and chases after evil unwillingly.
>
> If a man believes that such an impermanent thing [as the body], so changeable and replete with suffering, is the ego-personality, it is a serious mistake. The human mind is also impermanent and suffering; it has nothing that can be called an ego-personality.
>
> Therefore, both body and mind . . . are far apart from both the conceptions of "me" and "mine." It is simply the mind clouded over by impure desires and impervious to wisdom, that obstinately persists in thinking of "me" and "mine."[51]

Unless one grasps that everything, including the so-called self, is completely ephemeral, one cannot find salvation. If one resists the pervasive flux of phenomena and desires permanence and an enduring self when none exists, the inevitable result is the suffering that fills human life.

David Hume. Although the view that humans have no self is characteristic of Buddhist thought, some Western philosophers have put forward a very similar view. The Scottish philosopher David Hume (1711–1776) offered some strong reasons for rejecting the Traditional assumption that human beings have a self. In his book *A Treatise of Human Nature*, Hume argues that all real knowledge is based on what we can actually perceive with our senses: what we can see, hear, touch, smell, taste, and feel. Because genuine knowledge depends on prior sense experience, assertions that are not based on sense experience cannot be genuine knowledge. He then points out that we never actually perceive the self. Consequently, we have no real knowledge of a self and so have no justification for claiming that we have a self. What we perceive within ourselves is nothing more than a changing bundle

51 *The Teachings of Buddha* (Tokyo: Bukkyo Deudo Kyokai, 1976).

of disconnected sensations. The notion of a unified self is a fiction made up by Traditional philosophers:

> There are some philosophers who imagine we are every moment intimately conscious of what we call our SELF; that we feel its existence and its continuance in existence; and are certain, beyond the evidence of a demonstration, both of its perfect identity and simplicity. . . .
>
> Unluckily all these positive assertions are contrary to that very experience which is pleaded for them, nor have we any idea of *self*. . . . For from what impression could this idea be derived? . . . If any impression gives rise to the idea of self, that impression must continue invariably the same, through the whole course of our lives; since self is supposed to exist after that manner. But there is no impression constant and invariable. Pain and pleasure, grief and joy, passions and sensations succeed each other, and never all exist at the same time. It cannot, therefore, be from any of these impressions, or from any other, that the idea of self is derived; and consequently there is no such idea.
>
> For my part, when I enter most intimately into what I call *myself* I always stumble on some particular perception or other, of heat or cold, light or shade, love or hatred, pain or pleasure. I never can catch *myself* at any time without a perception, and never can observe anything but the perception. . . .
>
> [S]etting aside some metaphysicians . . . , I may venture to affirm of the rest of mankind, that they are nothing but a bundle or collection of different perceptions, which succeed each other with an inconceivable rapidity, and are in a perpetual flux and movement. . . . The mind is a kind of theatre, where several perceptions successively make their appearance, pass, re-pass, glide away, and mingle in an infinite variety of postures and situations.[52]

QUICK REVIEW
Hume also held that there is no self. He argues that only what we perceive exists. But we never perceive a self in the constant flow of changing sensations, so there is no self.

According to Hume, then, we never perceive among our sensations an object called an *inner self*. All we can say, Hume claims, is that we are "a bundle or collection of different perceptions." Not only is there no fixed nature in the Humean and Buddhist conceptions, but also, because everything is in flux, there is not even an enduring self.

Many similarities exist between Hume's views on the self and those of the Buddhist that distinguish them from other views we have seen. For both Hume and the Buddhist, our inner experience is one of pervasive flux and change without permanence. So, for both Hume and the Buddhist, the self has no fixed existence.

critical thinking
Does Hume assume that all our ideas must be derived from impressions? Are there other possible sources from which our idea of the self could be derived? If there are other alternatives, would this show that Hume's view of the self is mistaken?

Despite their similarities, Hume's view about how we should deal with the absence of the self differs in important ways from the Buddhist's. Buddhism believes that we can give up the idea that we have an individual self. Buddhism suggests, in fact, that salvation is achievable only by giving up the craving for self-identity and the striving for personal success and self-fulfillment. However, Hume did not believe that we can give up the idea of the self and its importance. Hume believed that, in the end, we will find it impossible to face the fact that there is no self.

We are left, then, with a mystery. We assume in virtually everything we do that we have an enduring self—in other words, that we remain the same person from day to day. So does everyone else. Every day, every hour, every moment we are engaged in making preparations for this individual self. Yet when we probe this ordinary assumption, it seems that there is little to support it. Neither the body, nor the soul, nor even memory seems to provide a sound basis for our belief that we endure through time. Yet giving up the idea of an enduring self is also profoundly unsatisfying. Perhaps we should look more closely at the idea of individuality.

QUICK REVIEW
But if there is no enduring self, then all the care we take for our future makes no sense.

52 David Hume, *A Treatise of Human Nature*, ed. L. A. Selby-Bigge (Oxford: Clarendon, 1896), 6.

QUESTIONS

1. Suppose that your soul could survive death. But suppose that at death your soul loses all memory of its past life, and all memories of who and what you were are completely erased from your soul. Suppose, also, that all personality traits, beliefs, desires, preferences, and all other conscious qualities are erased. Will you still exist after death? Explain why or why not.
2. Review the identity theory of human nature in the last section. Suppose that identity theory is true. Can you think of some ways you could still survive the death of your body even if the identity theory is true?
3. Suppose that the computer theory of human nature discussed in the section titled "The Functionalist View of Human Nature" earlier in this chapter is true. Can you think of some ways that you could still survive the death of your body even if the computer theory is true?
4. Contrast the Buddhist approach to human nature with the rational Western religious, scientific, and existentialist views.
5. Does the view of no self have anything to offer? What?

PHILOSOPHY AT THE MOVIES

Watch *Memento* (2000), parts of which use black and white to show a telephone conversation in chronological order, while the other parts use color to show in reverse chronological order the story of Leonard. Leonard is seeking his wife's murderer despite being unable to remember anything for more than a few minutes; he must keep track of events with photos, notes, and tattoos, and must see things much like the film's reverse chronology makes us see them. Do you think Leonard has an enduring self? Why or why not?

Other movies with related themes: *Total Recall* (1990); *The Bourne Identity* (2002); *Eternal Sunshine of the Spotless Mind* (2004); *50 First Dates* (2004).

2.5 Are We Independent and Self-Sufficient Individuals?

Isn't it obvious that parents should help their children achieve independence and self-sufficiency? Isn't it obvious that one of the worst things parents can do is to raise their children to become and remain dependent on others all of their lives? To ensure that children become independent individuals, parents teach them to value and cultivate self-reliance. Parents also try to teach their children how to think on their own, how to make judgments on their own, how to choose and explore on their own. They try to teach children independence of thought and action.

Or consider some things parents teach children to avoid. One is conformity. Most parents don't feel that it is good to teach a child to want to conform. They advise children not to follow their friends or peer groups blindly. They teach children that it is not good to always submit to the expectations of others. Parents advise children, instead, to think for themselves, to learn to judge and evaluate for themselves whether what others tell them is true.

Parents also teach their children to try to be true to themselves. Parents teach their children the importance of being in touch with their real individual nature and inner feelings and needs. They should not try to change themselves to please others.

Finally, think about some things we value that support these parental ideas. Take privacy, for example. Don't we feel that we should allow people to live their own lives? Don't we feel that something is wrong when society forces its values on private individuals? Or consider how we value creativity in people, or how we enjoy novelty, excitement, and challenge in life. Consider how much we prize freedom, being able to "do your own thing." How we praise individual achievement and ambition. How we cherish individual freedom. How we believe that choosing a path that is her own is all-important for a person, rather than choosing one that others impose on her.

The Atomistic Self

QUICK REVIEW
Many hold the view that the self is and should be independent of others and self-sufficient.

All these views about how we should raise children, and assumptions about what we should value, are part of a pattern. They are based on a certain view of the self: the view that the self is and should be independent of others and self-sufficient. This view has deep roots in our culture and in our ways of thinking and feeling. It is a view that some philosophers call the *atomistic view of the self.* On this view, the self is, like the atom, self-contained and independent of other atoms. The self is an autonomous individual with its own unique inner qualities. The things I go through, the people I meet, and the things I witness can touch me and move me. They can injure and hurt me. Yet the real me, the core of my self, can always rise above these and remain independent and different from all that it meets. The great American poet Walt Whitman perhaps expressed this idea best in his well-known poem "Song of Myself":

I celebrate myself, and sing myself. . . .
Trippers and askers surround me,
People I meet, the effect upon me of my early life or the ward and city I live in,
or the nation,
The latest dates, discoveries, inventions, societies, authors old and new,
My dinner, dress, associates, looks, compliments, dues,
The real or fancied indifference of some man or woman I love,
The sickness of one of my folks or of myself, or ill-doing or loss or lack of money,
or depressions or exaltations,
Battles, the horrors of fratricidal war, the fever of doubtful news, the fitful events;
These come to me days and nights and go from me again,
But they are not the Me myself.

Apart from the pulling and hauling stands what I am,
Stands amused, complacent, compassionating idle, unitary,
Looks down, is erect, or bends an arm on an impalpable certain rest,
Looking with side-curved head curious what will come next,
Both in and out of the game and watching and wondering at it.[53]

To see how powerful this atomistic view of the self is, think for a moment about your "real self." How do you get at the "real" you? Not the "you" that tries to live up to the expectations of others, not the face that the world sees, but the real and

53 Walt Whitman, "Song of Myself," in *The American Tradition in Literature,* 3rd ed., vol. 2, ed. S. Bradley, L. C. Beatty, and E. H. Long (New York: Grosset and Dunlap, 1967), 37, 39.

genuine "you." Don't you find this real you by withdrawing into yourself and contemplating the you that lies within?

This is what many philosophers have also thought. Consider the example of Descartes. He tells us that one day he resolved to understand himself better, so he withdrew from the company of others to discover within himself the truth about himself:

> After I had employed several years studying the book of the world and trying to acquire some experience, I one day formed the resolution of also making myself an object of study. . . . Winter detained me in a place where I found no society to divert me and no cares or passions to trouble me. I remained there the whole day shut up alone in a stove-heated room, where I had complete leisure to occupy myself with my own thoughts.[54]

Alone, apart from others, Descartes could search for his inner real self and could decide for himself what is true and what is false:

> I shall now close my eyes, I shall stop my ears, I shall call away all my senses, I shall efface even from my thoughts all the images of corporeal things, or at least (for that is hardly possible) I shall esteem them as vain and false; and thus holding converse only with myself and considering my own nature, I shall try little by little to reach a better knowledge of and a more familiar acquaintanceship with myself. I am a thing that thinks, that is to say, that doubts, affirms, denies, that knows a few things, that is ignorant of many, that loves, that hates, that wills, that desires, that also imagines and perceives. . . .
>
> In order to try to extend my knowledge further, I shall now look around more carefully and see whether I cannot still discover in myself some other things which I have not hitherto perceived. I am certain that I am a thing which thinks; but do I not then likewise know what is requisite to render me certain of a truth? Certainly in this first knowledge there is nothing that assures me of its truth, excepting the clear and distinct perception of that which I state. . . . And accordingly it seems to me that already I can establish as a general rule that all things which perceive very clearly and very distinctly are true.[55]

QUICK REVIEW
Descartes said the self exists and can be known independently of others and that only the self can judge the truth about what it is.

Notice what Descartes is saying. First, he says that the real me exists within myself. Second, he claims that this real me and its qualities—my desires, fears, hopes, loves, hatreds—exist there inside me independently of others. Third, he claims that I, by myself, can discover this real me by withdrawing or separating from others. Fourth, he claims that only I can be the judge of what the truth about myself is.

In short, Descartes gives us a picture of the independent and self-sufficient individual. I do not need others to be who I really am. Of course, I may need others to help me live. For example, I depend on others for food, housing, and the many other material things I need. Still, I do not need others to have the qualities that make me who I am: My desires, fears, hopes, loves, and hatreds are all there inside me, whether or not anyone is around to see them. These do not depend on others but come from within me: They are me. My real self is there, and it is independent of others. Moreover, a key aspect of the real me is my ability to decide for myself—that is, the ability to judge the truth of things for myself without relying on others.

Some philosophers have gone even further than Descartes in emphasizing the importance of this ability to judge things for oneself. For example, the German

54 Descartes, *Discourse on Method*, 87.
55 Descartes, *Meditations*, 157–158.

philosopher Immanuel Kant argued that the core of the real self is the ability to choose for oneself the moral laws and moral principles by which one will live one's life:

> The laws to which man is subject are only those that he himself makes. . . . [This is] the principle of autonomy of the will, that is, the principle of self-imposed law. . . . The will's autonomy consists in its capacity to be its own law, without being influenced by the objects it chooses. . . . The will is a causal power that living beings have if they are rational. We say such a causal power has freedom if its acts are not determined by causal influences other than itself.[56]

QUICK REVIEW
Kant argued that the core of the real self is the ability to choose for oneself.

Notice here how Kant claims that the real me is a being who can choose or will for himself. The real me can choose without having to conform to what external forces impose on him.

We see in Descartes and in Kant some sources of a view of the individual self that is very familiar to us: the view that who I am exists here inside me, independent of others and able to freely choose independently of others. As suggested earlier, we value this view of self. We try to raise our children to become independent individuals who will be true to their inner self, who will not merely conform to what external society demands, and who will exercise independent and free choice.

The Relational Self

Still, now let us ask ourselves this: Is there such a thing as the independent and self-sufficient individual we have been discussing? Is it possible for children, or adults, to be independent and self-sufficient? The twentieth-century Canadian philosopher Charles Taylor does not believe so:

> In the twentieth century, we may no longer believe, like Descartes, in the soul or mind as an inner space open to transparent introspection . . . but we retain the idea that self-understanding is getting a clear view of the desires, aversions, fears, hopes, aspirations that are within us. To know oneself is to get clear on what is within.
>
> This seems so normal and inescapable to us, that we can hardly imagine an alternative. But let us try. If I can only understand myself as part of a larger order; indeed, if man as the rational animal is just the one who is rationally aware of this order; then I only am really aware of myself, and understand myself, when I see myself against this background, fitting into this whole. I must acknowledge my belonging before I can understand myself. Engaged in an attempt to cut myself off, to consider myself quite on my own, autonomously, I should be in confusion, self-delusion, in the dark.[57]

QUICK REVIEW
Taylor objects that we depend on others for our very self because we need others to define for us who our real self is.

Taylor suggests that there is another way of understanding who the real me is besides that of getting in touch with what is within me apart from others. This other way is to see that who I am depends on my relationships to others.

We saw earlier that we depend on others for the material things we need to survive. Still, this is not what Taylor has in mind. Taylor suggests that we also depend on others for our very self: I need others to define for me who the real me is. Philosophers sometimes express this by saying that the self is relational because it is "constituted" by its relations to others.

---

56 Immanuel Kant, *Foundations of the Metaphysics of Reason*, quoted in M. Velasquez and C. Rostankowski, *Ethics: Theory and Practice* (Englewood Cliffs, NJ: Prentice Hall, 1985), 90–91.

57 Charles Taylor, "Legitimation Crisis?" in Charles Taylor, *Philosophy and the Human Sciences*, vol. 2 (New York: Cambridge University Press, 1985), 257.

Georg W. F. Hegel: "Each self is in a struggle to convince the other that he is a free being worthy of the other's respect and recognition. This struggle is the basis of the rise of masters and slaves. The slave gives up his attempt to be recognized as free. The master sees in the slave the very sign of his freedom."

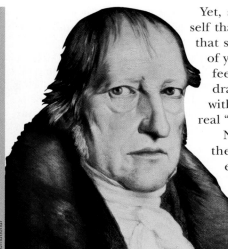

Portrait of Georg Wilhelm Friedrich Hegel (1770–1831), 1825, Jacob Schlesinger (1792–1855)/Nationalgalerie, Berlin, Germany/© The Bridgeman Art Library International

Yet, surprisingly, the traditional view of the self that most of us share is the atomistic view that says you are who you are independently of your relationships with other people. We feel that you can know yourself by withdrawing from others and looking deep within yourself to find the real you or your real "self."

Not all views of the self assume that the self is independent of others. For example, Aristotle declared that humans are "social animals" who are not self-sufficient:

> The individual, when isolated, is not self-sufficing; and therefore he is like a part in relation to the whole. But he who is unable to live in society, or who has no need because he is sufficient for himself, must be either a beast or a god. . . . social instinct is implanted in all men by nature.[58]

QUICK REVIEW
Aristotle argued that I depend on others not just to exist but to be the human that I am.

Aristotle is not just saying that we need others to survive. He is arguing that what a human being is, the person I am and the qualities I have, arise from my relationships with others. Without these relationships, which make me the human that I am, I would be an animal, or a god. The self is a relational self.

But it was the philosopher Hegel who most forcefully challenged the idea of the independent, self-sufficient individual and argued instead for the idea of a relational self. Hegel argued that my own identity—who I really am—depends on my relationships with others and that I cannot be who I am apart from my relationships with others:

> Every self wants to be united with and recognized by another self [as a free being]. Yet at the same time, each self remains an independent individual and so an alien object to the other. The life of the self thus becomes a struggle for recognition. . . . Each self is in a struggle to convince the other that he is [a free being] worthy of the other's respect and recognition. This mutual struggle for recognition by the other is mixed with feelings of mistrust and uncertainty. The struggle carries with it all the dangers and risks that the self faces when it dares to lay itself open to the other. This life-and-death struggle can degenerate into a bloody fight in which one of the combatants is killed. But then the whole issue of recognition will be missed. Recognition requires the survival of the other as a condition and sign of one's freedom.
>
> The struggle of the self is essentially a struggle for freedom. Historically, this struggle is the basis of the rise of masters and slaves. . . . Preferring survival to freedom, the slave gives up his attempt to be recognized as free. The master, on the other hand, is recognized as free. The master sees in the slave the very sign of his freedom.
>
> Independent masters and dependent slaves together form a community. To preserve and protect the life of his workers becomes the concern of the master. . . . The slave learns to work. He acquires habits and skills. At the same time he disciplines himself. In making objects [for the master] he also makes

58 Aristotle, *Politics*, bk. 1, ch. 2. This translation by Manuel Velasquez.

> himself. In working together with others he overcomes his isolation and is recognized for his excellence. In this process, the relation of dependence and independence is reversed. The independent master becomes dependent on the skills and virtues of the servant.[59]

Hegel claims that each of us can know we have certain human qualities only when others recognize those qualities in us. In particular, each of us can know that we are free and independent persons only if we see that others recognize us as free and independent persons. A free and independent person is one who is not a slave to his desires or to some external force. A free and independent person is one who is able to choose for himself what course his life will take. So Hegel is saying that we will not develop the capacity to choose for ourselves unless others develop this capacity in us by recognizing and affirming our freedom and self-mastery.

QUICK REVIEW
Hegel denied the independent self, arguing that who one is depends on one's relationships with others and that we can know we are free and independent only if others recognize us as such.

Power and Hegel's View

Moreover, Hegel claims that each of us is continually involved in a struggle to get the recognition from others that we need to exist as truly independent, free persons. We realize that to be free and competent, we need others to acknowledge that we are worthy of being respected as free and competent persons. So, we try to force others to respect us, even as they struggle to force us to respect them. In this struggle—a life-and-death struggle—some people emerge as dominant and others as submissive. The dominant ones are those who get the respect they demand, whereas the submissive ones are those who give up the struggle for respect and settle for merely being allowed to live. Thus are formed the two great social classes: masters and slaves—those who command and those who obey. Yet though the slave appears to have lost the battle to the master, eventually the tables are slowly turned. For as the slave serves the master, the master recognizes the capability of the slave. The slave then becomes more confident of himself. He sees himself as a capable competent supporter of the master. Meanwhile, the master gradually becomes dependent on the slave, and both recognize the master as incapable and incompetent.

QUICK REVIEW
Everyone struggles to get from others the recognition each needs to be independent and free. Some emerge as slaves, others as masters, yet the master becomes dependent on the slave, and the slave comes to see himself as more competent than the master.

QUICK REVIEW
Thus, the slave is slave because that is what others see him as being, and the master is master because others recognize him as such.

The key idea, then, is that who you are ultimately depends on your relationships to others. The slave who identifies himself as a slave is such because he defines himself through his relationship to the master. The master who sees himself as free and independent is such only to the extent that others will recognize him as this.

The implications of Hegel's idea are profound. In every society there are powerless and powerful people, strong and weak, dominant and submissive. Hegel is suggesting that these classifications are not there ahead of time. Instead, we create them by the qualities we are willing to recognize in others. The same is true of social classes. Some groups in society—perhaps some minority groups, for example—may exhibit submissive characteristics. Yet, to a large extent, we make them submissive by our failure to accord them the respect and recognition that alone can empower them to be assertive and independent. Charles Taylor is a leading authority on Hegel. He explains the importance of recognition:

QUICK REVIEW
Hegel implies that the powerful and powerless classes in society are created by the qualities we are willing to recognize in them.

> The thesis is that our identity is partly shaped by recognition or its absence, [or] by the misrecognition of others, and so a person or a group of people can suffer real damage, real distortion, if the people or society around them mirror back to them a confining or demeaning or contemptible picture of themselves. . . .

59 Wilhelm Hegel, *Encyclopedia of Philosophy*, trans. Gustav E. Mueller (New York: Philosophical Library, 1959), 215–217.

> Thus some feminists have argued that women in patriarchal societies have been induced to adopt a depreciatory image of themselves. They have internalized a picture of their own inferiority. . . . An analogous point has been made in relation to blacks: that white society has for generations projected a demeaning image of them, which some of them have been unable to resist adopting. Their own self-depreciation, on this view, becomes one of the most potent instruments of their own oppression.
>
> . . . Recently, a similar point has been made in relation to indigenous and colonized people in general. It is held that since 1492 Europeans have projected an image of such people as somehow inferior, "uncivilized," and through the force of conquest have often been able to impose this image on the conquered.[60]

QUICK REVIEW
Hegel also argues that a person gets through his culture the recognition that makes him free or enslaved.

Culture and Self-Identity

There is another important implication of Hegel's view. Consider that every person has a culture. A culture consists of the traditions and language; the arts, ideas, and outlooks; the practices and beliefs of a group of people. Hegel argues that a person's culture is the mirror through which society shows the person who and what she is. It is, in fact, through her culture that a person gets the recognition that makes her a free person. Recognition comes through culture.

What this means is that who I am, the qualities that define me, depends on my culture and on my relationships to the important people in my life. There is, then, no "real me" that I can find inside apart from others. Instead, I am who others tell me I am in the language that culture gives us. Again, Taylor expresses the idea best:

> In order to understand the close connection between identity and recognition, we have to take into account a crucial feature of the human condition. . . . This crucial feature of human life is its fundamentally dialogical character. We become full human agents, capable of understanding ourselves, and hence of defining our identity, through our acquisition of rich human languages of expression. For my purposes here, I want to take language in a broad sense, covering not only the words we speak, but also other modes of expression whereby we define ourselves, including the "languages" of art, of gesture, of love, and the like. But we learn these modes of expression through exchanges with others. People do not acquire the languages needed for self-definition on their own. Rather, we are introduced to them through interaction with others who matter to us. . . .
>
> Moreover, this is not just a fact about genesis, which can be ignored later on. We don't just learn the languages in dialogue and then go on to use them for our own purposes.
>
> . . . We define our identity always in dialogue with, sometimes in struggle against, the things our significant others want to see in us. Even after we outgrow some of these others—our parents, for instance—and they disappear from our lives, the conversation with them continues within us as long as we live. Thus, the contribution of significant others, even when it is provided at the beginning of our lives, continues indefinitely.[61]

---

60 Charles Taylor, "The Politics of Recognition," in *Multiculturalism and the Politics of Recognition*, ed. Amy Gutman (Princeton, NJ: Princeton University Press, 1992), 25.

61 Ibid., 32–33.

To understand what Taylor means, consider how you think of who you are, your self-identity. Don't you identify who you are by your relationships to others, particularly to the groups to which you belong? You identify yourself as the son or daughter of your parents. Your name identifies you in terms of the family to which you belong. You identify yourself as an American, a Canadian, a German, or a Mexican. You are a member of a racial or ethnic group: white or black, Indian or Asian. Consider the wants that make you who you are. The culture you were raised in determines the foods, the clothes, and the music you prefer. In short, all your wants are defined in terms of what your culture teaches you to want. From your culture you also draw all your ideas about the kind of person you might be. You use these ideas to understand yourself: lover, loner, kindly, coward, punk, stoner, preppy, hipster, jock, troll, beautiful, ugly, popular, unpopular, nerd, thug, jogger, drama queen, selfish, compassionate, animal, chick, rocket scientist, intellectual, creative, mother, father, son, daughter. Consider the most basic things you know: Each of them is the product of the investigations of all the humans who labored at discovering the nature of our world before you came along. Your religious ideas all come from the traditions of a church into which you have been socialized. The language you use to express your thoughts to yourself and others is a gift of your culture. Thus, we depend not only on the recognition of others to be who we are; we depend also on our culture to give us all the ideas we use to define who we are.

Search for the Real Self

Who is right, then? Is Descartes right when he claims that the real you is discovered within yourself and is independent of others? Or are Hegel and Taylor right when they claim that the real you is relational—in other words, is found only in relationship to others?

QUICK REVIEW
So, the self is not independent and self-sufficient, but depends on others for his or her existence as the kind of person he or she is.

Think about it. From childhood and from every side we hear the constant refrains: "Be true to yourself and not to what others expect you to be," "Think for yourself and don't just follow the crowd," and "Take responsibility for yourself and don't blame others for what you are." Yet, if Hegel and Taylor are right, then all these ideas are radically and deeply mistaken. The real me is not there inside, independent of others and waiting to be discovered. The real me is something that is created from my relationships with others and with my culture. The people I love and care for, the people who are important to me, the people whose opinions I trust, and the ideas and beliefs of my culture all make me who I am. It is to them I must turn to find myself. I cannot be true to myself unless I am what they and my culture make me. I cannot think for myself without using the ideas that they and my culture give me. I do not have responsibility for myself because in a very real way they have made me what I am.

Yet are Hegel and Taylor right? Perhaps not. If who and what you are depends on others, then you are not responsible for what you are. Neither are you responsible for what you do. But surely that is not right. Surely, in some way and to some extent, you are responsible for who you have become and what you do. As Sartre and others have argued, to some extent you make yourself who you are.

There is a deeper problem with the idea that who I am depends on my relationships with others. For my relationships with others are many. Are there many "me's"? For example, one "me" for each person to whom I am related? Hegel says that what I am depends on what others recognize in me. Still, suppose that different people recognize different things in me. This person recognizes me as loving, that one as mean, that other one as wise, and this one as stupid. Which is the real me?

Which of these different things go into making the real me? Are there many me's? The pragmatic philosopher William James was not afraid to accept this conclusion:

QUICK REVIEW
But if one has many relationships with others, does this mean one has many selves.

> Properly speaking, a man has as many social selves as there are individuals who recognize him . . . [but] we may practically say that he has as many social selves as there are distinct groups of persons about whose opinion he cares.[62]

Yet this seems an odd conclusion. How can I be many me's? Are we, without realizing it, multiple personalities? Do we turn a different face to each person depending on what that person sees in us? Perhaps we do. But which of these many faces would really be me?

QUICK REVIEW
And aren't many of our basic physical, mental, and personality traits independent of others.

Moreover, isn't it the case that many of the qualities you have do not depend on others? Take, for example, your basic physical qualities: your height, your weight, your hair color, your skin color, your facial features, your musculature, your health. Surely, these are a basic part of who you are and do not depend on your relationships with others. Or take your basic mental qualities, such as your I.Q. and your ability to feel pain, to hate, to love, to think. Even if *what* you feel, hate, love, or think depends on others, surely your *ability* to feel, hate, love, and think does not depend on others. Or take your basic personality traits, such as your tendency to feel cheerful or depressed, your willingness to take risks, and your disposition. We inherit many of these kinds of qualities, scientists tell us; they depend on the genes we are born with. And surely these personality traits are part of who you are.

We have, then, a dilemma. On the one hand, we seem to be only what others make us: what the significant people in our lives make us and what society through its culture makes us. On the other hand, we seem to be independent selves with basic qualities that we are born with, including perhaps the ability to choose freely the path our lives will take. Which are we? The choice between these is important. Clearly, if others make us, then we in turn make others. The way we raise our children, the money we spend on schools, the kinds of social environments we create, the respect or lack of respect we give others, the way our culture talks about different races—all these become tremendously important. For all these will ultimately make the young members of our society the kind of people they turn out to be: powerful or powerless, free or slave, capable or incapable, assertive or submissive. On the other hand, if we are independent selves with the ability to choose freely and in isolation from others, then these externals are not so important. More important is that we hold persons responsible for their choices, that people learn to look into themselves for their own inner power and resources, that people learn to rely on themselves and find in themselves who they really are.

The challenge for each of us, perhaps, is to find what comes from within and what comes from without—what comes from others and what comes from inside you. A great deal hangs on this.

QUESTIONS

1. Can you think of any qualities that you see in yourself that you do not need others to have?
2. If each self in society is what it is because other selves have made it that way, then is all responsibility ultimately group responsibility? That is, when an individual does something evil, must we say that everyone in society is responsible for the evil?

62 William James, *Psychology (Briefer Course)* (New York: Collier, 1962), 192.

3. Can you think of some of the implications that Hegel's views on the master–slave relationship have for workers in our society? Would Hegel explain the employer–employee or the boss–worker relationship as the outcome of the same processes of recognition that create the master–slave relationship? Explain your answer.

4. Compare the Buddhist–Hume no-self view with the view that the self is constituted by its relationships with others.

PHILOSOPHY AT THE MOVIES

Watch *The Long Walk Home* (1990), which takes place in the South during the 1955–1956 civil rights bus boycott led by Martin Luther King and tells of the relationship between Miriam Thompson, the rich white wife of a narrow-minded businessman, and Odessa Cotter, their black maid who is struggling to raise her family and whose participation in the boycott makes her arrive so late and tired that Miriam begins to drive her to work. Explain whether the movie supports or undermines Hegel's ideas about "recognition" and the origins of the master–slave relationship.

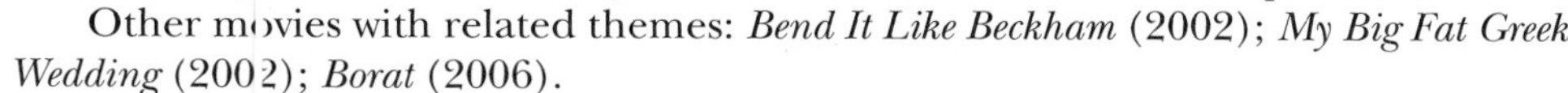

Other movies with related themes: *Bend It Like Beckham* (2002); *My Big Fat Greek Wedding* (2002); *Borat* (2006).

Chapter Summary

This chapter opens by raising the issue of human nature: What am I? How we see ourselves has been profoundly influenced by Traditional Western theories of human nature: the rationalistic view and the Western religious view. These Traditional views have been challenged on a number of fronts. Darwinian evolution challenges the ideas of uniqueness and purpose. Existentialism challenges the idea of a universal human nature. Feminists raise questions about the role of gender in forming our identities. The Traditional view also favors dualism. Dualism has in turn been challenged by various forms of materialism including identity theory, behaviorism, functionalism, and eliminative materialism. The Traditional view also assumes that humans are enduring selves and that humans can and should be independent and self-sufficient, and these, too, are contested.

The main points of this chapter are:

2.1 Why Does Your View of Human Nature Matter?

- *Human nature* refers to what a human is. An important issue about what humans are concerns whether humans are aggressive, material, and self-interested.
- **Arguments can be deductive or inductive; in a valid deductive argument the conclusion is necessarily true if the premises are true; that is, a valid deductive argument is one whose conclusion is true in every situation in which its premises are true. A valid deductive argument with true premises is sound.**

2.2 What Is Human Nature?

- Traditional Western views of human nature claim humans are rational selves, who are immaterial, have a purpose, endure through time, and exist independently of others.

- One important version of the Traditional Western view of human nature is the rationalistic view that sees humans as rational immaterial beings with a purpose, in whom reason should rule over passions and desires. The Judeo-Christian religious view claims that humans are made in the image of God, who has endowed them with reason and an ability to love; the self is immaterial and its purpose is to know and love God.
- Darwin argued that all living organisms evolved from earlier species through variations, a struggle for existence, and natural selection. Darwin's view has been taken to imply that humans have no purpose and are not unique.
- Existentialist views deny that there is a fixed human nature and claim that each human creates his or her own nature, and so human existence precedes essence. Existentialism asserts people are free and thus responsible for what they are: the sum total of their actions.
- Many feminists have argued that in the Traditional Western view of human nature, our concepts of reason, appetites, emotions, mind, and body are biased against women.
- **Darwin's argument claimed that his theory was the best explanation for many different phenomena, an argument called an inference to the best explanation. Criteria for "best explanation" include a consideration of all the alternatives, harmony with well-established beliefs, an ability to account for many different kinds of facts, information about causal mechanisms, and simplicity.**

2.3 The Mind–Body Problem: How Do Mind and Body Relate?

- Descartes' dualist view of human nature says that humans are immaterial thinking beings different from, but connected to, material bodies. It is unclear how immaterial minds can interact with material bodies.
- **To evaluate a premise, we should ask (1) if it is consistent with our experience and if our experience is reliable; (2) if it is consistent with what we believe but learned from others, and whether they are reliable sources of that information; (3) if it is a generalization and has counterexamples; (4) if it implies claims that are absurd, false, impossible, or inconsistent with other well-established claims; (5) if it can be supported by good arguments or undermined by good objections.**
- Materialist views say we are solely material bodies. Identity theory holds that conscious states are identical with the body's brain states. Behaviorism says that conscious mental states are bodily behaviors or dispositions. Functionalism says that mental states refer to the connections the body makes between sensory inputs and behavioral outputs. The computer view says that computers running programs can have minds, and the human mind is itself a computer; Searle uses the "Chinese Room" argument to show the mind is not a computer program. Eliminative materialism says beliefs, desires, and intentions are terms of a "folk psychology" and do not exist. Chalmers uses a "zombie argument" to support

property dualism, a view that claims mental properties are not physical properties.

2.4 Is There an Enduring Self?

- The Traditional view of human nature and our ordinary thinking assume that humans have a self that endures through time.
- Bodily continuity does not seem to be the basis of the enduring self. Descartes claims that the enduring self is a soul. Locke argues that memory is the basis of the enduring self. Buddhism and Hume suggest that there is no enduring self.

2.5 Are We Independent and Self-Sufficient Individuals?

- Many people believe that the human self can and should be independent of others, self-sufficient, and capable of thinking for itself, which is how Descartes seems to have conceived of human beings.
- Hegel argues that who we are depends on the recognition of others and on our culture.

2.6 Readings

In Graham Greene's haunting short story, British upper-class twin brothers, Peter and Francis, are invited to a party that Francis is fearful of attending because he dreads being forced to play hide and seek in the dark. Greene, a Christian, seems to portray the twin brothers, who communicate by mere thought without spoken words, as two conscious and nonmaterial minds within physical bodies; that is, Greene seems to assume the traditional Judeo-Christian view of human nature. As the story unfolds, Peter feels in his own consciousness the increasing terror that the darkness arouses in Francis' mind. And Peter seems to continue to experience Francis' terror even after he realizes what has happened to his brother.

In the second reading, philosophers Garrett J. DeWeese and J. P. Moreland defend substance dualism, a view of human nature that, like Descartes' view, says the mind is a nonmaterial substance distinct from its physical body. DeWeese and Moreland elsewhere say they are defending the traditional Judeo-Christian view of human nature. They give three arguments for this view: (1) we are directly aware of the self as distinct from the body, (2) the "self" we are directly aware of cannot be reduced to a physical thing, and (3) because we can conceive of the self, but not the body, as "disembodied," the self cannot be the same thing as the body. DeWeese and Moreland thus argue for the view of human nature that Graham Greene assumes in his short story.

In the third reading, philosopher John Searle argues that substance dualism is false because it is inconsistent with science. He proposes "biological naturalism," his own recently developed view of human nature that says brain processes "cause" our conscious states but one is not "ontologically" reducible to the other—that is, the two are not the same thing.

GRAHAM GREENE

The End of the Party

From: Graham Greene, *Collected Stories of Graham Greene* (New York: Penguin, 1929)

Peter Morton woke with a start to face the first light. Rain tapped against the glass. It was January the fifth.

He looked across a table on which a night-light [candle] had guttered [melted] into a pool of water, at the other bed. Francis Morton was still asleep, and Peter lay down again with his eyes on his brother. It amused him to imagine it was himself whom he watched, the same hair, the same eyes, the same lips and line of cheek. But the thought palled, and the mind went back to the fact which lent the day importance. It was the fifth of January. He could hardly believe a year had passed since Mrs. Henne-Falcon had given her last children's party.

Francis turned suddenly upon his back and threw an arm across his face, blocking his mouth. Peter's heart began to beat fast, not with pleasure now but with uneasiness. He sat up and called across the table, "Wake up." Francis's shoulders shook and he waved a clenched fist in the air, but his eyes remained closed. To Peter Morton the whole room seemed to darken, and he had the impression of a great bird swooping. He cried again, "Wake up," and once more there was silver light and the touch of rain on the windows.

Francis rubbed his eyes. "Did you call out?"' he asked.

"You are having a bad dream," Peter said. Already experience had taught him how far their minds reflected each other. But he was the elder, by a matter of minutes, and that brief extra interval of light, while his brother still struggled in pain and darkness, had given him self-reliance and an instinct of protection towards the other who was afraid of so many things.

"I dreamed that I was dead," Francis said.

"What was it like?"' Peter asked.

"I can't remember," Francis said.

"You dreamed of a big bird."

"Did I?"

The two lay silent in bed facing each other, the same green eyes, the same nose tilting at the tip, the same firm lips, and the same premature modeling of the chin. The fifth of January, Peter thought again, his mind drifting idly from the image of cakes to the prizes which might be won. Egg-and-spoon races, spearing apples in basins of water, blind man's bluff.

"I don't want to go," Francis said suddenly. "I suppose Joyce will be there . . . Mabel Warren." Hateful to him, the thought of a party shared with those two. They were older than he. Joyce was eleven and Mabel Warren thirteen. The long pigtails swung superciliously to a masculine stride. Their sex humiliated him, as they watched him fumble with his egg, from under lowered scornful lids. And last year . . . he turned his face away from Peter, his cheeks scarlet.

"What's the matter?" Peter asked.

"Oh, nothing. I don't think I'm well. I've got a cold. I oughtn't to go to the party."

Peter was puzzled. "But Francis, is it a bad cold?

"It will be a bad cold if I go to the party. Perhaps I shall die."

"Then you mustn't go," Peter said, prepared to solve all difficulties with one plain sentence, and Francis let his nerves relax, ready to leave everything to Peter. But though he was grateful, he did not turn his face towards his brother. His cheeks still bore the badge of a shameful memory, of the game of hide and seek last year in the darkened house, and of how he had screamed when Mabel Warren put her hand suddenly upon his arm. He had not heard her coming. Girls were like that. Their shoes never squeaked. No boards whined under the tread. They slunk like cats on padded claws.

When the nurse [maid] came in with hot water Francis lay tranquil leaving everything to Peter. Peter said, "Nurse, Francis has got a cold."

The tall starched woman laid the towels across the cans and said, without turning, "The washing won't be back till tomorrow. You must lend him some of your handkerchiefs."

"But, Nurse," Peter asked, "hadn't he better stay in bed?"

"We'll take him for a good walk this morning," the nurse said. "Wind'll blow away the germs. Get up now, both of you," and she closed the door behind her.

"I'm sorry," Peter said. "Why don't you just stay in bed? I'll tell mother you felt too ill to get up." But rebellion against destiny was not in Francis's power. If he stayed in bed they would come up and tap his chest and put a thermometer in his mouth and look at his tongue, and they would discover he was malingering. It was true he felt ill, a sick empty sensation in his stomach and a rapidly beating heart, but he knew the cause was only fear, fear of the party, fear of being made to hide by himself in the dark, uncompanioned by Peter and with no night-light to make a blessed breach.

"No, I'll get up," he said, and then with sudden desperation, "But I won't go to Mrs. Henne-Falcon's party. I swear on the Bible I won't." Now surely all would be well, he thought. God would not allow him to break so solemn an oath. He would show him a way. There was all the morning before him and all the afternoon until four o'clock. No need to worry when the grass was still crisp with the early frost. Anything might happen. He might cut himself or break his leg or really catch a bad cold. God would manage somehow.

He had such confidence in God that when at breakfast his mother said, "I hear you have a cold, Francis," he made light of it. "We should have heard more about it," his mother said with irony, "if there was not a party this evening," and Francis smiled, amazed and daunted by her ignorance of him.

His happiness would have lasted longer if, out for a walk that morning, he had not met Joyce. He was alone with his nurse, for Peter had leave to finish a rabbit hutch in the woodshed. If Peter had been there he would have cared less; the nurse was Peter's nurse also, but now it was as though she were employed only for his sake, because he could not be trusted to go for a walk alone. Joyce was only two years older and she was by herself.

She came striding towards them, pigtails flapping. She glanced scornfully at Francis and spoke with ostentation to the nurse. "Hello, Nurse. Are you bringing Francis to the party this evening? Mabel and I are coming." And she was off again down the street in the direction of Mabel Warren's home, consciously alone and self-sufficient in the long empty road.

"Such a nice girl," the nurse said. But Francis was silent, feeling again the jump-jump of his heart, realizing how soon the hour of the party would arrive. God had done nothing for him, and the minutes flew.

They flew too quickly to plan any evasion, or even to prepare his heart for the coming ordeal. Panic nearly overcame him when, all unready, he found himself standing on the doorstep, with coat-collar turned up against a cold wind, and the nurse's electric torch [flashlight] making a short trail through the darkness. Behind him were the lights of the hall and the sound of a servant laying the table for dinner, which his mother and father would eat alone. He was nearly overcome by the desire to run back into the house and call out to his mother that he would not go to the party, that he dared not go. They could not make him go. He could almost hear himself saying those final words, breaking down forever the barrier of ignorance which saved his mind from his parents' knowledge. "I'm afraid of going. I won't go. I daren't go. They'll make me hide in the dark, and I'm afraid of the dark. I'll scream and scream and scream."

He could see the expression of amazement on his mother's face, and then the cold confidence of a grown-up's retort. "Don't be silly. You must go. We've accepted Mrs. Henne-Falcon's invitation."

But they couldn't make him go; hesitating on the doorstep while the nurse's feet crunched across the frost-covered grass to the gate, he knew that. He would answer: "You can say I'm ill. I won't go. I'm afraid of the dark." And his mother: "Don't be silly. You know there's nothing to be afraid of in the dark." But he knew the falsity of that reasoning; he knew how they taught also that there was nothing to fear in death, and how fearfully they avoided the idea of it. But they couldn't make him go to the party. "I'll scream. I'll scream."

"Francis, come along." He heard the nurse's voice across the dimly phosphorescent lawn and saw the yellow circle of her torch wheel from tree to shrub. "I'm coming," he called with despair; he couldn't bring himself to lay bare his last secrets and end reserve between his mother and himself, for there was still in the last resort a further appeal possible to Mrs. Henne-Falcon. He comforted himself with that, as he advanced steadily across the hall, very small, towards her enormous bulk. His heart beat unevenly, but he had control now over his voice, as he said with meticulous accent, "Good evening, Mrs. Henne-Falcon. It was very good of you to ask me to your party." With his strained face lifted towards the curve of her breasts, and his polite set speech, he was like an old withered man. As a twin he was in many ways an only child. To address Peter was to speak to his own image in a mirror, an image a little altered by a flaw in the glass, so as to throw back less a likeness of what he was than of what he wished to be, what he would be without his unreasoning fear of darkness, footsteps of strangers, the flight of bats in dusk-filled gardens.

"Sweet child," said Mrs. Henne-Falcon absent-mindedly, before, with a wave of her arms, as though the children were a flock of chickens, she whirled them into her set program of entertainments: egg-and-spoon races, three-legged races, the spearing of apples, games which held for Francis nothing worse than humiliation. And in the frequent intervals when nothing was required of him and he could stand alone in corners as far removed as possible from Mabel Warren's scornful gaze, he was able to plan how he might avoid the approaching terror of the dark. He knew there was nothing to fear until after tea, and not until he was sitting down in a pool of yellow radiance cast by the ten candles on Colin Henne-Falcon's birthday cake did he become fully conscious of the imminence of what he feared. He heard Joyce's high voice down the table, "After tea we are going to play hide and seek in the dark."

"Oh, no," Peter said, watching Francis's troubled face, "don't let's. We play that every year."

"But it's in the program," cried Mabel Warren. "I saw it myself. I looked over Mrs. Henne-Falcon's shoulder. Five o'clock tea. A quarter to six to half past, hide and seek in the dark. It's all written down in the program."

Peter did not argue, for if hide and seek had been inserted in Mrs. Henne-Falcon's program, nothing which he could say would avert it. He asked for another piece of birthday cake and sipped his tea slowly. Perhaps it might be possible to delay the game for a quarter of an hour, allow Francis at least a few extra minutes to form a plan, but even in that Peter failed, for children were already leaving the table in twos and threes. It was his third failure, and again he saw a great bird darken his brother's face with its wings. But he upbraided himself silently for his folly, and finished his cake encouraged by the memory of that adult refrain, "There's nothing to fear in the dark." The last to leave the table, the brothers came together to the hall to meet the mustering and impatient eyes of Mrs. Henne-Falcon.

"And now," she said, "we will play hide and seek in the dark."

Peter watched his brother and saw the lips tighten. Francis, he knew, had feared this moment from the beginning of the party, had tried to meet it with courage and had abandoned the attempt. He must have prayed for cunning to evade the game, which was now welcomed with cries of excitement by all the other children. "Oh, do let's." "We must pick sides." "Is any of the house out of bounds?"' "Where shall home be?"'

"I think," said Francis Morton, approaching Mrs. Henne-Falcon, his eyes focused unwaveringly on her exuberant breasts, "it will be no use my playing. My nurse will be calling for me very soon."

"Oh, but your nurse can wait, Francis," said Mrs. Henne-Falcon, while she clapped her hands together to summon to her side a few children who were already straying up the wide staircase to upper floors. "Your mother will never mind."

That had been the limit of Francis's cunning. He had refused to believe that so well prepared an excuse could fail. All that he could say now, still in the precise tone which other children hated, thinking it a symbol of conceit, was, "I think I had better not play." He stood motionless, retaining, though afraid, unmoved features. But the knowledge of his terror, or the reflection of the terror itself, reached his brother's brain. For the moment, Peter Morton could have cried aloud with the fear of bright lights going out, leaving him alone in an island of dark surrounded by the gentle lapping of strange footsteps. Then he remembered that the fear was not his own, but his brother's. He said impulsively to Mrs. Henne-Falcon, "Please, I don't think Francis should play. The dark makes him jump so." They were the wrong words. Six children began to sing, "Cowardly, cowardly custard," turning torturing faces with the vacancy of wide sunflowers towards Francis Morton.

Without looking at his brother, Francis said, "Of course I'll play. I'm not afraid, I only thought . . ." But he was already forgotten by his human tormentors. The children scrambled round Mrs. Henne-Falcon, their shrill voices pecking at her with questions and suggestions.

"Yes, anywhere in the house. We will turn out all the lights. Yes, you can hide in the cupboards. You must stay hidden as long as you can. There will be no home."

Peter stood apart, ashamed of the clumsy manner in which he had tried to help his brother. Now he could feel, creeping in at the corners of his brain, all Francis's resentment of his championing. Several children ran upstairs, and the lights on the top floor went out. Darkness came down like the wings of a bat and settled on the landing. Others began to put out the lights at the edge of the hall, till the children were all gathered in the central radiance of the chandelier, while the bats squatted round on hooded wings and waited for that, too, to be extinguished.

"You and Francis are on the hiding side," a tall girl said, and then the light was gone, and the carpet wavered under his feet with the sibilance of footfalls, like small cold drafts, creeping away into corners.

"Where's Francis?"' he wondered. "If I join him he'll be less frightened of all these sounds." "These sounds" were the casing of silence: the squeak of a loose board, the cautious closing of a cupboard door, the whine of a finger drawn along polished wood.

Peter stood in the centre of the dark deserted floor, not listening but waiting for the idea of his brother's whereabouts to enter his brain. But Francis crouched with fingers on his ears, eyes uselessly closed, mind numbed against impressions, and only a sense of strain could cross the gap of dark. Then a voice called "Coming," and as though his brother's self-possession had been shattered by the sudden cry, Peter Morton jumped with his fear. But it was not his own fear. What in his brother was a burning panic was in him an altruistic emotion that left the reason unimpaired. "Where, if I were Francis, should I hide?"' And because he was, if not Francis himself, at least a mirror to him, the answer was immediate. "Between the oak bookcase on the left of the study door, and the leather settee." Between the twins there could be no jargon of telepathy. They had been together in the womb, and they could not be parted.

Peter Morton tiptoed towards Francis's hiding-place. Occasionally a board rattled, and because he feared to be caught by one of the soft questers through the dark, he bent and untied his laces. A tag struck the floor and the metallic sound set a host of cautious feet moving in his direction. But by that time he was in his stockings and would have laughed inwardly at the pursuit had not the noise of someone stumbling on his abandoned shoes made his heart trip. No more boards revealed Peter Morton's progress.

On stockinged feet he moved silently and unerringly towards his object. Instinct told him he was near the wall, and, extending a hand, he laid the fingers across his brother's face.

Francis did not cry out, but the leap of his own heart revealed to Peter a proportion of Francis's terror. "It's all right," he whispered, feeling down the squatting figure until he captured a clenched hand. "It's only me. I'll stay with you." And grasping the other tightly, he listened to the cascade of whispers his utterance had caused to fall. A hand touched the bookcase close to Peter's head and he was aware of how Francis's fear continued in spite of his presence. It was less intense, more bearable, he hoped, but it remained. He knew that it was his brother's fear and not his own that he experienced. The dark to him was only an absence of light; the groping hand that of a familiar child. Patiently he waited to be found.

He did not speak again, for between Francis and himself was the most intimate communion. By way of joined hands thought could flow more swiftly than lips could shape themselves round words. He could experience the whole progress of his brother's emotion, from the leap of panic at the unexpected contact to the steady pulse of fear, which now went on and on with the regularity of a heartbeat. Peter Morton thought with intensity, "I am here. You needn't be afraid. The lights will go on again soon. That rustle, that movement is nothing to fear. Only Joyce, only Mabel Warren." He bombarded the drooping form with thoughts of safety, but he was conscious that the fear continued. "They are beginning to whisper together. They are tired of looking for us. The lights will go on soon. We shall have won. Don't be afraid. That was someone on the stairs. I believe it's Mrs. Henne-Falcon. Listen. They are feeling for the lights." Feet moving on a carpet, hands brushing a wall, a curtain pulled apart, a clicking handle, the opening of a cupboard door. In the case above their heads a loose book shifted under a touch. "Only Joyce, only Mabel Warren, only Mrs. Henne-Falcon," a crescendo of reassuring thought before the chandelier burst, like a fruit-tree, into a bloom of light.

The voice of the children rose shrilly into the radiance. "Where's Peter?"' "Have you looked upstairs? "'Where's Francis?"' but they were silenced again by Mrs. Henne-Falcon's scream. But she was not the first to notice Francis Morton's stillness, where he had collapsed against the wall at the touch of his brother's hand. Peter continued to hold the clenched fingers in an arid and puzzled grief. It was not merely that his brother was dead. His brain, too young to realize the full paradox, wondered with an obscure self-pity why it was that the pulse of his brother's fear went on and on, when Francis was now where he had always been told there was no more terror and no more—darkness.

GARRETT J. DEWEESE AND J. P. MORELAND

The Self and Substance Dualism

In this section, we argue for substance dualism, namely, that the owner of consciousness—the soul or self—is immaterial. Substance dualists are also property dualists because substance dualists believe that both the ego and consciousness itself are immaterial. But one can be a mere property dualist without being a substance dualist if one accepts the immateriality of consciousness but holds that its owner is the body or, more likely, the brain. In contrast with mere property dualism, substance dualists hold that the brain is a physical thing which has physical properties and that the mind or soul is a mental substance which has mental properties. When I am in pain, my brain has certain physical properties (electrical, chemical), and my soul or self has certain mental properties (the conscious awareness of pain). The soul is the possessor of its experiences. It stands behind, over, and above them and remains the same throughout one's life. The soul and the brain can interact with each other, but they are different particulars with different properties.

We offer three arguments for some form of substance dualism.

Our basic awareness of the self. When we enter most deeply into ourselves, we become aware of a very basic fact: we are aware of our own self (ego, I, center of consciousness) as being distinct from our bodies and from any particular mental experience we have, and as being an uncomposed, spatially unextended center of consciousness. I simply have a basic direct awareness of the fact that I am not identical to my body or my mental events; rather I am the immaterial self that has a body and a conscious mental life.

An experiment may help convince you of this. Right now I am looking at a chair in my office. As I walk toward the chair, I experience a series of chair representations. That is, I have several different chair experiences that replace one another in rapid succession. As I approach the chair, my chair sensations vary. If I pay attention, I am also aware of two more things. First, I do not simply experience a series of sensory images of a chair. Rather, through self-awareness, I also experience the fact that it is I myself who has each chair experience. Each chair sensation produced at each angle of perspective has a perceiver who is I. An I accompanies each sensory experience to produce a series of awarenesses: *I am experiencing a chair sense image now.*

I am also aware of the basic fact that the same self that is currently having a fairly largechair experience (as my eyes come to within twelve inches of the chair) is the very same self as the one who had all of the other chair experiences preceding this current one. Through self-awareness, I am aware of the fact that I am an enduring I who was and am (and will be) present as the owner of all the experiences in the series.

These two facts—I am the owner of my experiences, and I am an enduring self—show that I am not identical to my experiences. I am the conscious thing that has them. I am also aware of myself as a simple, uncomposed, and spatially unextended center of consciousness. (I am "fully present" throughout my body; if my arm is cut off, I do not become four-fifths of a self.) In short, I am a mental substance.

Unity and the first-person perspective. A complete physicalist description of the world would be one in which everything would be exhaustively described from a third-person point of view in terms of objects, properties, processes, and their spatiotemporal locations. For example, a description of an apple in a room would go something like this: "There exists an object three feet from the south wall and two feet from the east wall, and that object has the property of being red, round, sweet, and so on."

The first-person point of view is the vantage point that I use to describe the world from my own perspective. Expressions of a first-person point of view utilize what are called *indexicals:* words like *I, here, now, there,* and *then.* Here and now are where and when I am; there and then are where and when I am not. Indexicals refer to me, myself. *I* is the most basic indexical, and it refers to my self that I know by acquaintance with my own self in acts of self-awareness. I am immediately aware of my own self, and I know to whom *I* refers when I use it: It refers to me as the self-conscious, self-reflexive owner of my body and mental states.

According to physicalism, there are no irreducible, privileged first-person perspectives. Everything can be exhaustively described in an object language from a third-person perspective. A physicalist description of me would say, "There exists a body at a certain location that is five feet eight inches tall, weighs 160 pounds," and so forth. The property dualist would add a description of the properties possessed by that body, such as "the body is feeling pain" or "the body is thinking about lunch."

But no amount of third-person descriptions captures my own subjective, first-person acquaintance of my own self in acts of self-awareness. In fact, for any third-person description of me, it would always be an open question as to whether the person described in third-person terms was the same person as I am. I do not know my self *because* I know some third-person description of a set of mental and physical properties and also know that a certain person satisfies that description. I know myself as a self immediately through being acquainted with my own self in an act of self-awareness. I can express that self-awareness by using the term I. *I* refers to my own substantial self. It does not refer to any conscious experience or bundle of such experiences I am having, nor does it refer to any body described from a third-person perspective.

The modal argument. Thought experiments have rightly been central to this debate in which two persons switch bodies, brains, or personality traits or in which a person exists disembodied. In these thought experiments, someone argues in the following way: Because some situation *S* (e.g., Smith's existing disembodied) is conceivable, this provides justification for thinking that *S* is metaphysically possible. Now if *S* is possible, then certain implications follow about what is or is not essential to personal identity (e.g., Smith is not essentially a body). We all use conceiving as a test for possibility/impossibility throughout our lives. I know that life on other planets is possible (even if I think it is highly unlikely or downright false) because I can conceive it to be so.

Let us apply these insights about conceivability and possibility to the modal argument for substance dualism. People know that disembodied life after death, even if false, is at least a possibility. When people hear of near-death experiences or ponder surviving the destruction of their bodies, they easily believe these things *could possibly* be so because they can conceive of them. But it is obvious that their brains and bodies could not survive in a disembodied state! Since something is true of them (they are disembodiable), not of their body/brain, they cannot be the same as their bodies/brains. The same is true of a person's mental life and character. A person could exist with a different set of memories and character traits, so a person is not the same thing as his or her memories or character. Rather a person is what has a body/brain and has a mental life and character.

A parallel argument can be advanced in which the notions of a body and disembodiment are replaced with the notions of physical objects in general. (It is not hard to conceive that one could exist even if the entire material world were destroyed.) So understood, the argument would imply the conclusion that one has good grounds for thinking that one is not identical to a physical object and that being physical is not essential to one's identity. A parallel argument can also be developed to show that possessing the ultimate capacities of sensation, thought, belief, desire, and volition are essential to one—that is, one is a substantial soul or mind.

Taken from *Philosophy Made Slightly Less Difficult: A Beginner's Guide to Life's Big Questions* by Garrett J. DeWeese and J. P. Moreland. Copyright © 2005 by Garrett J. DeWeese and J. P. Moreland. Used by permission of InterVarsity Press PO Box 1400 Downers Grove, IL 60515. www.ivpress.com.

JOHN R. SEARLE

The Mind–Body Problem

Troubles with Dualism

All forms of substance dualism inherit Descartes' problem of how to give a coherent account of the causal relations between the soul and the body, but recent versions have an additional problem. It seems impossible to make substance dualism consistent with modern physics. Physics says that the amount of matter/energy in the universe is constant; but substance dualism seems to imply that there is another kind of energy—mental energy or spiritual energy—that is not fixed by physics. So if substance dualism is true, then it seems that one of the most fundamental laws of physics, the law of conservation, must be false. Some substance dualists have attempted to cope with this problem by claiming that for each infusion of spiritual energy, there is a diminution of physical energy, thus preserving a constant amount of energy in the universe. Others have said that the mind rearranges the distribution of energy in the universe without adding to it or subtracting from it. Eccles says that the mind can affect the body by altering the probability of neuronal events without any energy input, and that quantum physics enables us to see how this can be done: "The hypothesis of mind-brain interaction is that mental events act by a quantal probability field to alter the probability of emission of vesicles from presynaptic vesicular grids." There is something ad hoc about these maneuvers, in the sense that the authors are convinced in advance of the truth of dualism and are trying to find some way, any way, that will make dualism consistent with physics.

It is important to understand what an extreme doctrine substance dualism is. According to substance dualism, our brains and bodies are not really conscious. Your body is just an unconscious machine like your car or your television set. Your body is alive in the way that plants are alive, but there is no consciousness to your body. Rather, your conscious soul is somehow attached to your body and remains attached to it until your body dies, at which time your soul departs. You are identical with your soul and only incidentally and temporarily inhabit this body.

The problem with this view is that, given what we know about how the world works, it is hard to take it seriously as a scientific hypothesis. We know that in humans consciousness cannot exist at all without certain sorts of physical processes going on in the brain. We might, in principle, be able to produce consciousness in some other physical substance, but right now we have no way of knowing how to do this. And the idea that consciousness might be produced apart from any physical substrate whatever, though conceivable, just seems out of the question as a scientific hypothesis.

There is a weaker version of dualism called "property dualism," and that view is fairly widespread. The idea is this: Though there are not two kinds of substances in the world, there are two kinds of properties. Most properties, such as having an electrical charge, or having a certain mass, are physical properties; but some properties, such as feeling a pain or thinking about Kansas City, are mental properties. It is characteristic of human beings that though they are not composed of two different kinds of substances, their physical bodies, and in particular their brains, have not only physical properties, but mental properties as well.

Property dualism does not force us to postulate the existence of a thing that is attached to the body but not really part of the body. But it still forces us to suppose that there are properties of the body, presumably properties of the brain, that are not ordinary physical properties like the rest of our biological makeup. And the problem with this is that we do not see how to fit an account of these properties into our overall conception of the universe and how it works. We really do not get out of the postulation of mental entities by calling them properties. We are still postulating nonmaterial mental things. It does not matter whether we say that my conscious pain is a mental property of my brain or that it is an event in my brain. Either way, we are stuck with the traditional difficulties of dualism.

The Solution to the Mind–Body Problem

My method in philosophy is to try to forget about the history of a problem and the traditional ways of thinking about it and just try to state the facts as far as we know them. Let us try this method with a fairly simple case. We will concentrate on consciousness. . . . Here goes: I now feel thirsty. Not a desperate thirst, just a conscious, medium-strength desire to drink some water. Such a feeling, like all conscious states, only exists as experienced by a human or animal subject, and in that sense it has a subjective or first-person ontology. In order for feelings like my thirst to exist they have to be experienced by a subject, by an "I" that is thirsty. But how do these subjective feelings of thirst fit into the rest of the world? The first thing we have to insist on is that my thirst is a real phenomenon, a part of the real world, and that it functions causally in my behavior. If I now drink, it is because I am thirsty. The next thing to notice is that my feelings of thirst are entirely caused by neurobiological processes in the brain. If I do not have enough water in my system, this shortage triggers a complex series of neurobiological phenomena and all of that causes my feelings of thirst. (There is, by the way, a strange reluctance to admit that our conscious states are caused by brain processes. Some authors fudge and say that the brain "gives rise" to consciousness; others say that the brain is the "seat" of consciousness. One who grants that consciousness is dependent on the brain says the relation is "not happily construed as causal.") But what are these feelings of thirst exactly? Where and how do they exist? They are conscious processes going on in the brain, and in that sense they are features of the brain, though at a level higher than that of neurons and synapses. The conscious feeling of thirst is a process going on in my brain system.

Just so it does not sound like I am vaguely talking about how things might be as opposed to how they are in fact, let me nail the whole issue down to reality by summarizing some of what we know about how brain processes cause feelings of thirst. Suppose an animal gets a shortage of water in its system. The shortage of water will cause "saline imbalances" in the system, because the ratio of salt to water is excessive in favor of salt. This triggers certain activities in the kidneys. The kidneys secrete rennin, and the rennin synthesizes a substance called angiotensin 2. This substance gets inside the hypothalamus and affects the rate of neuron firings. As far as we know, the differential rates of neuron firings cause the animal to feel thirsty. Now, of course, we do not know all of the details, and no doubt as we come to understand more this brief sketch I have given will seem quaint. But that is the sort of explanation of how the existence of conscious feelings of thirst fits into our overall world view. All forms of consciousness are caused by the behavior of neurons and are realized in the brain system, which is itself composed of neurons. What goes for thirst goes for all forms of our conscious life whatever, from wanting to throw up to wondering how to translate the poems of Stéphane Mallarmé into colloquial English. All conscious states are caused by lower-level neuronal processes in the brain. We have conscious thoughts and feelings; they are caused by neurobiological processes in the brain; and they exist as biological features of the brain system.

I believe that this brief account provides the germ of a solution to the "mind-body problem": I am suspicious of isms, but it is sometimes helpful to have a name, just to distinguish clearly between one view and another. I call my view "biological naturalism," because it provides a naturalistic solution to the traditional "mind–body problem," one that emphasizes the biological character of mental states, and avoids both materialism and dualism.

I will state biological naturalism about consciousness as a set of four theses:

1. Conscious states, with their subjective, first-person ontology, are real phenomena in the real world. We cannot do an eliminative reduction of consciousness, showing that it is just an illusion. Nor can we reduce consciousness to its neurobiological basis, because such a third-person reduction would leave out the first-person ontology of consciousness.
2. Conscious states are entirely caused by lower-level neurobiological processes in the brain. Conscious states are thus *causally reducible* to neurobiological processes. They have absolutely no life of their own, independent of the neurobiology. Causally speaking, they are not something "over and above" neurobiological processes.
3. Conscious states are realized in the brain as features of the brain system, and thus exist at a level higher than that of neurons and synapses. Individual neurons are not conscious, but portions of the brain system composed of neurons are conscious.
4. Because conscious states are real features of the real world, they function causally. My conscious thirst causes me to drink water, for example.

Can the solution to the famous "mind–body problem" really be that simple? If we can just get out of the traditional categories, I really think it is that simple. We know for a fact that all of our mental processes are caused by neurobiological processes, and we also know that they are going on in the brain and perhaps in the rest of the central nervous system. We know that they function causally, though they have no causal powers in addition to those of the underlying neurobiology, and we know that they are not ontologically reducible to third-person phenomena, because they have a first-person ontology. Why then does this apparently obvious solution encounter so much resistance? Many philosophers do not see how these apparently mysterious mental entities can exist at all, and if they do exist, how they can be caused by brute physical processes in the brain, and if they do exist and are caused by physical processes, how they can exist in the physical system of the brain. But notice that this way of posing the difficulties and questions already accepts the dualism of the mental and the physical. If we state the thesis without employing the traditional Cartesian vocabulary, it does not sound mysterious at all. My conscious feelings of thirst really do exist and function causally in my behavior. (Does anyone who has ever been thirsty really doubt their existence and causal power?) We know for a fact that they are caused by neuronal processes, and the feelings themselves are processes going on inside the brain.

From: John R. Searle, *Mind: A Brief Introduction* (New York: Oxford University Press, 2004), excerpts from pp. 29–32, 78–80. Reprinted by permission of Oxford University Press, Inc. Copyright © by Oxford University Press, Inc. All rights reserved. Address: Oxford University Press, Inc., 198 Madison Avenue, New York, New York 10016.

2.7 HISTORICAL SHOWCASE

Plato, Aristotle, and Confucius

The discussion of human nature was intended to provide an array of overviews of what it is to be human. Thus, it has certain pitfalls. One might conclude from the discussion that philosophy is merely a catalogue of diverse opinions, that when engaging an issue such as human nature, philosophy ultimately does little more than serve up a smorgasbord of opinions. Moreover, focusing on a single issue as we have just done inevitably dislodges the portion from the mosaic of interrelated pieces that, taken together, make up a full-scale philosophy. In fact, one cannot fully appreciate a position on an issue without understanding how it fits in with an entire outlook. To avoid these pitfalls and give the preceding material a sharper focus, we now take a more in-depth look at three philosophers: Plato, Aristotle, and Confucius.

Plato

Plato was born in 427 BCE into a wealthy family of the nobility of Athens, Greece. As a teenager, he met and became well acquainted with Socrates, eventually adopting him as an informal teacher. Plato admired Socrates deeply, feeling that Socrates' reliance on reason was the key to the solution of the many political and cultural problems that then plagued Athens. Since the death of the great Athenian statesman Pericles, Athens had been engaged in an unending series of wars that Pericles himself had initiated and that ended with the defeat of Athens at the hands of the city-state of Sparta. After peace was restored, the Athenians condemned Socrates to death, accusing him of undermining Athenian culture and thus being responsible for its many troubles. Shocked and disillusioned by Socrates' execution, Plato withdrew from public life and devoted himself to philosophy until his death in 347.

Plato: "If, as we say, perfect beauty and goodness and every ideal exist, then it is a necessary inference that just as these ideals exist, so our souls existed before we were born."

School of Athens, from the Stanza della Segnatura, 1510–1511 (fresco), Raphael (Raffaello Sanzio of Urbino) (1483–1520)/© Vatican Museums and Galleries, Vatican City, Italy, Giraudon/The Bridgeman Art Library International

In his philosophical theories, Plato fashioned a distinctive view of human nature, a view that has had a crucial formative influence on all subsequent theories of human nature. In fact, an important twentieth-century philosopher, Alfred North Whitehead, asserted that "all philosophy is nothing more than a footnote to Plato." Whitehead was referring to the fact that Plato was the first philosopher to develop philosophical notions of human nature, human knowledge, and metaphysics. He was also the first to pose the basic questions about these topics that all subsequent philosophers have continued to ask. Plato's views on human nature are important, then, not only for themselves but also because of their enduring influence.

Most of what we know about Plato's philosophy is based on the many dialogues he wrote in which the character of Socrates is the major speaker. In his early dialogues, Plato more or less faithfully reported Socrates' views. But as Plato grew older and his own theories began to develop, the character of Socrates increasingly became the mouthpiece for Plato's own views. In what are called the middle and late dialogues, in fact, the views expressed by the character Socrates are entirely those of Plato.

Plato's most fundamental contribution to philosophy was the distinction he drew between the changing physical objects we perceive with our senses and the unchanging ideals we can know with our minds. One of his clearest examples of this distinction is drawn from the science of geometry. Plato pointed out that we use our minds in geometry to discover unchanging truths about ideally perfect lines, squares, and circles. Yet the physical objects in the visible world are never perfectly straight, square, or circular, and they are continually changing.

At best, physical objects are imperfect replicas of the ideal objects we contemplate in geometry. As Plato put it, "Those who study geometry use visible figures and reason about them. But they are not thinking of these, but of the ideals which they resemble. They are thinking of a perfect square or a perfect line, and so on, and not of the imperfect figures they draw. . . . The visible figures they draw are merely replicas and what they are seeking is to understand the ideals which can be known only by the mind."[1]

Plato pointed out that this distinction between a perfect ideal and its imperfect replicas also applies to art and morality. With our minds we are able to think about the ideal of perfect beauty and perfect goodness. But the many physical objects we see with our senses are only imperfectly beautiful and imperfectly good. The following dialogue, in which Plato put his own ideas into the mouth of Socrates, expresses the matter in this way:

> SOCRATES: We say there are many objects that are beautiful and many objects that are good and similarly many objects that are instances of something specific.
>
> GLAUCON: Yes, indeed.
>
> SOCRATES: And, in addition, we say there is perfect beauty itself and perfect goodness itself. And a similar thing may be said about any definite ideal which has many instances. Each of the many instances is related to its perfect ideal insofar as each shares in that ideal and each gets its name from that ideal.
>
> GLAUCON: Very true.
>
> SOCRATES: The many objects are visible but they are not the objects we know [with our minds], while the ideals are the objects we know [with our minds] but they are not visible to the eye.[2]

As this passage suggests, Plato realized that his distinction between a perfect ideal and its many imperfect physical replicas actually extended to every class of things "of which there are many instances." The many human beings we see, the many oak trees, and the many tables are more or less imperfect replicas of what we think of as the ideal human being, the ideal oak tree, and the ideal table. Again, in Plato's words as expressed by Socrates in dialogue:

> SOCRATES: Don't we usually assume that when there are many things that have the same name, there is also an ideal that corresponds to them? You understand, don't you?
>
> GLAUCON: I do.
>
> SOCRATES: Consider any such group of many things. For example, there are many things we call beds and many tables.
>
> GLAUCON: Yes, there are.
>
> SOCRATES: And these have ideals corresponding to them. Two, in fact: one of the bed and one of the table.[3]

To these ideals, Plato gave the name *forms.* He came eventually to hold that a separate form exists for each kind of thing. For example, for things that are good, there is the form of goodness; for things that are human, there is the form of humanness; for things that are triangular, there is the form of triangle. The form of a certain class of objects consists of those characteristics that make those objects the kind of objects they are. For example, the form of horse consists of those characteristics that make each horse a horse.

The visible objects in our world never perfectly embody their forms: visible objects are only imperfect and changing reflections of the invisible, perfect, and unchanging forms. For example, each of the many horses in our world is an imperfect duplicate or copy of the one perfect form of horse, just as each human is a replica of the one perfect form of human being.

To a large extent, Plato's theory of forms was inspired by the questioning of his teacher Socrates. Socrates, you may recall, would ask his hearers for the characteristic that makes a thing what it is. For example, in the dialogue *Euthyphro,* Socrates says, "I was not asking you to give me *examples* of holiness, Euthyphro, but to identify the characteristic that makes all holy things holy. There must be some characteristic that all holy things have in common, and one which makes unholy things unholy. Tell me what this characteristic itself is." In a similar manner, Socrates searched

1 Plato, *Republic,* from bk.6. This translation copyright © 1987 by Manuel Velasquez.

2 Ibid.

3 Ibid., from bk. 10.

for the characteristic that makes a thing just and the characteristic that makes a thing beautiful. Plato believed that his forms were the characteristics for which Socrates had been searching because the form of a thing is what makes it what it is. Thus, Plato felt that in discovering the forms he had discovered the objects for which Socrates had searched all his life.

All sciences, Plato said, must be based on these ideals we know with our minds and not on their visible, changing, and imperfect replicas. As geometry is about ideal figures, and morality is about ideal goodness, so also each science is about the ideal forms that pertain to a certain class of things. For example, the science of medicine is based on the doctor's knowledge of the ideally perfect human body. Because visible objects are continually changing and imperfect, they cannot be what a science studies—for science, like geometry, tries to state laws and truths that are exact and do not change from moment to moment.

However, Plato's discovery that the mind knows perfect ideals that are not found in the visible world created a problem. Because they do not exist in the visible world, are those perfect ideals merely arbitrary creations of the mind? Are they mental figments that have no reality outside the mind? Plato saw that if the ideals that make up geometry, morality, and the sciences had no reality, then all of these sciences would be worthless, because they would be about unreal objects.

Plato had a passionate faith that our scientific and moral knowledge is concerned with reality, so he drew the only conclusion possible: The perfect ideals with which geometry, morality, and the sciences are concerned must be real. That is, these perfect ideals, or forms, really exist outside the mind. Because they do not exist in the visible world, they must exist in a world that is not visible to us. Plato concluded that there are two real worlds: the nonvisible world of unchanging perfect forms and the visible world that contains their many changing replicas. In fact, Plato held, the forms are *more* real than their replicas, for somehow (Plato suggested that God was responsible) the forms are the basic models according to which their imperfect replicas are made. As he put it, "These ideals are like patterns that are fixed into the nature of things. Each of the many things is made in the image of its ideal and is a likeness to it. The many replicas share in the ideal insofar as they are made in its image."[4]

4 Plato, *Parmenides*. This translation copyright © 1987 by Manuel Velasquez.

But how do we acquire our knowledge of the perfect ideals if they do not exist in the visible world? Plato's solution to this problem was ingenious. He argued that because we do not see the perfect ideals in our present world and because we obviously have knowledge of these ideals and investigate them in the sciences, we must have acquired this knowledge in a previous life. This shows, he held, that we have souls and that our souls must be immortal. Thus, Plato's theory of forms directly influenced his views on human nature, as Plato's own words, expressed by the character Socrates, reveal:

SOCRATES: Tell me, Simmias, do we think that there is such a thing as perfect justice?

SIMMIAS: We certainly do.

SOCRATES: And perfect beauty as well as perfect goodness?

SIMMIAS: Of course.

SOCRATES: Well, did you ever see these with your eyes?

SIMMIAS: Certainly not . . .

SOCRATES: And do we say there is such a thing as perfect equality? I do not mean the imperfect equality of two lengths of wood or two stones, but something more than that: absolute equality.

SIMMIAS: We most certainly say there is . . .

SOCRATES: But when did we come to think about perfect equality? Didn't we do so when we saw the imperfect equality of stones and pieces of wood and this brought to mind something else, namely perfect equality?

SIMMIAS: Certainly.

SOCRATES: Now when we see one thing and it brings to mind something else, that is what we call remembering, is it not?

SIMMIAS: Surely . . .

SOCRATES: Do we agree, then, that when someone sees something that he recognizes as an imperfect instance of some other thing he must have had previous knowledge of that other thing? . . .

SIMMIAS: We must agree . . .

SOCRATES: Then we must have had a previous knowledge of perfect equality before we first saw the imperfect equality of physical objects and recognized it fell short of perfect equality . . .

SIMMIAS: Yes.

SOCRATES: Then before we began to see or hear or use the other senses, we must somewhere have gained a knowledge of perfect equality . . .

SIMMIAS That follows necessarily from what we have said before, Socrates.

SOCRATES: And we saw and heard and had the other senses as soon as we were born?

SIMMIAS: Certainly.

SOCRATES: Then it appears that we must have acquired our knowledge of perfect equality before we were born.

SIMMIAS: It does.

SOCRATES: Now if we acquired that knowledge before we were born, and . . . lost it at birth, but afterwards by the use of our senses regained the knowledge which we had previously possessed, would not the process which we call learning really be recovering knowledge which we had? And shouldn't we call this recollection?

SIMMIAS: Assuredly.

SOCRATES: Then, Simmias, the soul existed previously, before it was in a human body. It existed apart from the body and had knowledge. . . . If, as we say, perfect beauty and goodness and every ideal exists, and if we compare to these whatever objects we see, then it is a necessary inference that just as these ideals exist, so our souls existed before we were born . . .

SIMMIAS: Yes, Socrates. You have convinced me that the soul existed before birth. . . . But perhaps Cebes here still has doubts . . .

SOCRATES: Well, these ideals of Forms, which are true reality, are they always the same? Consider perfect equality or perfect beauty or any other ideal. Does each of these always remain the same perfect form, unchanging and not varying from moment to moment?

CEBES: They always have to be the same, Socrates.

SOCRATES: And what about the many individual objects around us—people or horses or dresses or what have you—which we say are equal to each other or are beautiful? Do these always remain the same or are they changing constantly and becoming something else?

CEBES: They are continually changing, Socrates.

SOCRATES: These changing objects can be seen and touched and perceived with the senses. But the unchanging Forms can be known only with the mind and are not visible to the senses. . . . So there are two kinds of existing things: those which are visible and those which are not. . . . The visible are changing and the invisible are unchanging.

CEBES: That seems to be the case . . .

SOCRATES: Now which of these two kinds of things is our body like?

CEBES: Clearly it is like visible things . . .

SOCRATES: And what do we say of the soul? Is it visible or not?

CEBES: It is not visible.

SOCRATES: Then the soul is more like the invisible and the body like the visible?

CEBES: That is most certain, Socrates.

SOCRATES: Recall that we said long ago that when the soul relies on its bodily senses—like sight or hearing or the other senses—it is dragged by the body toward what is always changing. Then the soul goes astray and is confused as it staggers around drunkenly among these changing things.

CEBES: Very true.

SOCRATES: But when the soul turns within and reflects upon what lies in herself [knowledge of the Forms], she finds there the perfect, eternal, immortal, and unchanging realm that is most like herself. She would stay there forever if it were possible, resting from her confused wanderings. So long as she continues to reflect upon the unchanging [Forms], she herself is unchanging and has what we call wisdom.

CEBES: That is well and truly said, Socrates.

SOCRATES: So which kind of thing is the soul most like?

CEBES: The soul is infinitely more like what is unchanging . . .

SOCRATES: And the body is more like the changing?

CEBES: Yes.

SOCRATES: One more thing: When soul and body are united, it is the nature of the soul to rule and govern and of the body to obey and serve. Which of these two functions is like god and which is like a mortal? Is it not true that what rules is like god and what is ruled is like a mortal?

CEBES: True . . .

SOCRATES: Then, Cebes, does it not follow that the soul is most akin to what is divine, immortal, intellectual, perfect, indissoluble, and unchanging, while the body is most like what is mortal, unintellectual, indissoluble, and ever changing?

CEBES: That cannot be denied.[5]

Plato's view of human nature, then, is a direct consequence of his theory of forms. Because we know the forms, it follows that we have souls and that our souls existed apart from our bodies before we were born into this world. Whereas our bodies are visible, changing, and subject to decay, our souls are like the forms, so they are invisible, eternal, immortal, and godlike.

Having come to the conclusion that our souls—our inner selves—existed before we were born and will continue to exist after our deaths, Plato felt that it is imperative to care for our souls. He held that the soul consists of three parts that sometimes struggle against one another:

SOCRATES: But does our soul contain . . . three elements or not? . . . Do we gain knowledge with one part, feel anger with another, and with yet a third desire food, sex, drink, and so on? This is a difficult question.

GLAUCON: I quite agree.

SOCRATES: Let us approach the question in this way. It is clear that the same parts of a single thing cannot move in two opposing directions. So if we find that these three elements oppose each other, we shall know that they are distinct parts of ourselves.

GLAUCON: Very well . . .

SOCRATES: Now consider a thirsty man. Insofar as he is thirsty, his soul craves drink and seeks it.

GLAUCON: That is clear . . .

SOCRATES: Yet isn't it sometimes true that the thirsty person [who wants to drink] also, for some reason, may *not* want to drink?

GLAUCON: Yes, often.

SOCRATES: In his soul there is a part that desires drink and another part that restrains him. This latter part then is distinct from desire and usually can control desire. . . . Doesn't such control originate in reason, while the urge to drink originates in something else? . . .

GLAUCON: So it seems.

SOCRATES: Then we can conclude that there are in us two distinct parts. One is what we call "reason," and the other we call the nonrational "appetites." The latter hungers, thirsts, desires sex, and is subject to other desires . . .

GLAUCON: Yes, that is the logical conclusion.

SOCRATES: So there are at least two distinct elements in us. But what about our emotional or spirited part: the part in us that feels anger and indignation?

GLAUCON: Perhaps we should say that it is part of our appetites.

SOCRATES: Maybe. But think about this story which I think is true. Leontius was walking up from Piraeus one day when he noticed the bodies of some executed criminals on the ground. Part of him was overcome with a desire to run over and look at the bodies, while another part felt angry at himself and tried to turn away. He struggled with himself and shut his eyes, but at last

5 Plato, *Phaedo*. This edited translation copyright © 1987 by Manuel Velasquez.

the desire was too much for him. Running up to the bodies, he opened his eyes wide and cried, "There, damn you! Feast yourselves on that lovely sight!"

GLAUCON: I'm familiar with that story.

SOCRATES: The point of the story is that anger sometimes opposes our appetites as if it is something distinct from them. And we often find that when our appetites oppose our reason, we become angry at our appetites. In the struggle between appetite and reason, our anger sides with reason . . .

GLAUCON: That is true . . .

SOCRATES: Yet this emotional part of ourselves is distinct from reason. The poet Homer, for example, . . . describes people whose reason inclines them to choose the better course, contrary to the impulses of anger.

GLAUCON: I entirely agree.

SOCRATES: So . . . the soul has three distinct parts.[6]

Plato thought that his discovery of the three-part soul provided us with the key to happiness and virtue. Personal happiness and virtue, Plato held, can be achieved only when the three parts of our soul are in harmony with one another and are properly subordinated to one another. Happiness is possible only if reason rules the emotions and desires and both the emotions and desires have been trained to be led harmoniously by reason.

We become unhappy when the three parts of ourselves are constantly fighting against one another so that we lack inner harmony, and we fall victim to vice when we are ruled by our emotions or desires:

SOCRATES: A man is just when . . . each part within him does what is proper for it to do . . .

GLAUCON: Indeed.

SOCRATES: Isn't it proper for reason to rule since it can acquire knowledge and so can know how to care for the whole soul; and isn't it proper that the emotions should obey and support reason?

GLAUCON: Certainly . . .

SOCRATES: When reason and the emotions have been trained and each has learned its proper function, they should stand guard over the appetites . . . lest the appetites grow so strong that they try to enslave and overthrow them.

GLAUCON: Very true. . . .

SOCRATES: In truth, justice is present in a man . . . when each part in him plays its proper role. The just man does not allow one part of his soul to usurp the function proper to another. Indeed, the just man is one who sets his house in order, by self-mastery and discipline coming to be at peace with himself, and bringing these three parts into tune like the tones in a musical scale. . . . Only when he has linked these parts together in well-tempered harmony and has made himself one man instead of many will he be ready to go about whatever he may have to do, whether it be making money, satisfying his bodily needs, or engaging in affairs of state . . .

GLAUCON: That is perfectly true, Socrates . . .

SOCRATES: Next we must consider injustice. That must surely be a kind of war among the three elements, whereby they usurp and encroach upon one another's functions. . . . Such turmoil and aberration we shall, I think, identify with injustice, intemperance, cowardliness, or the other vices.

GLAUCON: Exactly . . .

SOCRATES: Virtue, then, seems to be a kind of health and beauty and strength of the soul, while vice is like a kind of disease and ugliness and weakness in the soul.[7]

To train the emotions and appetites so that they will readily obey reason was crucial for Plato. He likened our emotions and appetites to two winged steeds that can either drag our reason downward into the confusions and illusions of the visible changing world or help carry our reason upward to contemplate

6 Plato, *Republic*. This translation copyright © 1987 by Manuel Velasquez.

7 Ibid.

the world of unchanging perfect forms through the study of the sciences and the acquisition of wisdom. In a beautiful image, Plato compared the three-part soul to a chariot, with the charioteer driving a white-winged horse and a black-winged horse:

> Let me speak briefly about the nature of the soul by using an image. And let the image have three parts: a pair of winged horses and a charioteer. . . . One of the horses is of a noble breed, the other ignoble and the charioteer controls them with great difficulty. . . . The vicious steed goes heavily, weighing down the charioteer to the earth when it has not been thoroughly trained. . . . Above them . . . in the heaven above heaven . . . there abides the true reality with which real knowledge is concerned: the Forms which are visible only to the mind and have no color, shape, or hardness. . . . It is the place of true knowledge . . . where every soul which is rightly nourished feeds upon pure knowledge, rejoicing at once again beholding true reality. . . . There souls can behold perfect justice and temperance . . . not in things which change, but in themselves. The souls that are most like god are carried up there by their charioteer . . . , although troubled by their steeds and only with difficulty beholding true being. Other souls rise only to fall again, barely glimpsing it and then altogether failing to see because their two steeds are too unruly.[8]

As this passage suggests, Plato held that we can be completely virtuous only if our reason knows the forms. In particular, our reason must know the form of the good because only by grasping what goodness is can we know what the three parts of the soul must do to be good. Thus, for Plato, complete virtue can be achieved only by coming to have knowledge of the form of the good, which exists unchanging in a world of forms separate from ours.

Plato held that the best ruler, the perfect king, would be a person—male or female—whose soul was self-disciplined enough to enable him or her to contemplate true being in the perfect forms. Such a person, Plato wrote, would be a true *philosopher*, which in Greek means "lover of wisdom":

> SOCRATES: If a man believes there are many things which are beautiful but does not know beauty itself . . . is he awake or is his life nothing but a dream?
>
> GLAUCON: I would say he is dreaming.
>
> SOCRATES: And if a man knows beauty itself and can distinguish it from its many replicas, and does not confuse beautiful things with beauty itself . . . is he dreaming or awake?
>
> GLAUCON: He is awake . . .
>
> SOCRATES: If people look at the many visible things which are beautiful, but do not know beauty itself, . . . and similarly see things which are just but do not know justice itself, then they merely have opinions and do not have real knowledge of these things. . . . While those who know the real unchanging [Forms] have true knowledge . . . and are philosophers . . .
>
> GLAUCON: By all means.
>
> SOCRATES: Well, are those who have no knowledge of true being any better than blind men? They have no true models in their souls to illuminate things. They cannot fix their eyes on true reality nor can they refer to it when they lay down their laws regarding what is beautiful, just and good. . . . So should we make them rulers? Or should we establish as rulers those who know true reality and who are virtuous?
>
> GLAUCON: Obviously the latter.[9]

Thus, rulers, even more than ordinary citizens, must keep their minds fixed on the unchanging ideals or forms—especially the form of the good—and their emotions and appetites under the control of reason. Only in this way will they rule states in such a way that, like the virtuous individual, they will have harmony and happiness.

Plato's theory of forms, which he developed under the influence of Socrates' teaching, was the basis for his influential view of human nature. All future philosophers would struggle with Plato's problem: How can we account for the fact that our mind comprehends perfect ideals that this world only imperfectly duplicates? Many twentieth-century philosophers (such as Kurt Gödel, John McTaggart, Alfred North Whitehead, and Bertrand Russell) have agreed that only Plato's theory of forms can

8 Plato, *Phaedrus*. This edited translation copyright © 1987 by Manuel Velasquez.

9 Plato, *Republic*.

adequately account for our knowledge of certain ideals, especially mathematical ideals. And many philosophers who have rejected Plato's theory of forms have agreed, nevertheless, with Plato's claims concerning the soul and the body. Plato's philosophy remains very much alive today.

Aristotle

Although Aristotle was a student of Plato, his approach to human nature was very different. Son of a physician of a Macedonian king, Aristotle was born in 384 BCE at Stagira in northern Greece. When he was seventeen, his father sent him to Athens to study in Plato's Academy, the ancient equivalent of a modern-day university. There he found in Plato an inspiring teacher whom he later described as a man "whom bad men have not even the right to praise, and who showed in his life and teachings how to be happy and good at the same time." Aristotle stayed on as a teacher at the academy until Plato's death twenty years later. After leaving the academy, Aristotle was asked by King Philip II of Macedonia, the new conqueror of the Greeks, to tutor his young son, the future Alexander the Great. Three years later, when his pupil ascended the throne, Aristotle returned to Athens to set up his own school, the Lyceum. There he taught and wrote for twelve years until the death of Alexander, his protector, released a wave of pent-up anger the Greeks had long harbored toward their Macedonian conquerors and their friends. Under threat of death, Aristotle fled Athens and took refuge in a Macedonian fort, saying that he did not want the Athenians to "sin twice against philosophy" by killing him as they had killed Socrates. He died there one year later.

School of Athens, from the Stanza della Segnatura, 1510–1511 (fresco), Raphael (Raffaello Sanzio of Urbino) (1483–1520)/© Vatican Museums and Galleries, Vatican City, Italy, Giraudon/The Bridgeman Art Library International

Aristotle: "In all our activities there is an end which we seek for its own sake, and everything else is a means to this end.... Happiness is [this] ultimate end. It is the end we seek in all that we do."

As a young man, Aristotle seems to have been a close follower of Plato, but as he grew older, he came to have increasing doubts about Plato's views. Aristotle agreed that each class of things has certain essential characteristics—its form. But unlike Plato, Aristotle did not believe that forms exist in some separate world apart from the visible things around us. Instead, he held, the forms of visible things exist in the visible things themselves. How is this possible?

According to Aristotle, those characteristics that make a thing what it is and that all things of that kind have in common are the form of a thing. For example, the form of roundness consists of those characteristics that all round things have in common and that make a thing round. The form of a horse consists of those characteristics that all horses have in common and that make a thing a horse and not, say, a cow. Although we can distinguish *in our minds* between roundness and visible round things, this does not mean that, besides the visible round things around us, there also exists *in reality* a *separate* ideal object called roundness. Roundness exists only in round things, and horseness exists only in actual horses.

Once Aristotle realized that the world could be explained without a separate world of ideal forms, he began to develop a new view of reality that was much closer to common sense than Plato's. Aristotle explained the changing world by using his new concept of form together with three other kinds of causes: the material cause, or the stuff out of which things are made; the efficient cause, or the agent who brings about a change; and the final cause, or the purpose of the change.

Consider, for example, how a lump of marble can be changed into a statue of Socrates by a sculptor. If we ask *why* the marble changed as it did, we can give four kinds of explanations. First, we can explain why the marble statue came to have some of its characteristics by identifying its form, or *formal cause*: Because it has the form of a statue of Socrates, it came to be shaped like Socrates. Second, we can explain why the statue has other characteristics by identifying the matter out of which it is made, or the *material cause*: Because it is made out of marble, it is hard and white. Third, we can explain why the marble changed as it did by identifying the agent who made the statue, or the *efficient cause*: Because the artist chiseled the marble, it gradually came to be shaped like Socrates. And fourth, we can explain why the statue came to be by identifying the purpose for which it was made, or the *final cause*: The artist made the statue because he was trying to please a patron. Thus, things can be explained completely in terms of their causes in this world without having to theorize forms from some other world, as Plato did. Aristotle explained his four causes in these words:

> Next we must examine explanations or "causes," and state clearly the number and kinds of explanations there are. For we are seeking knowledge of things and we know a thing only when we can explain why it is as it is. And we explain something by identifying its basic causes. So, obviously, if our aim is to know the changing and perishing objects of nature, we will have to know their basic causes and use them to explain things.
>
> One kind of explanation [the material cause] is provided by identifying the material of which a thing is made and which remains present in the thing. For example, the bronze of which a statue is made or the silver of a bowl . . .
>
> A second kind of explanation [the formal cause] is provided by identifying the form or plan of a thing, that is, by stating the essential characteristics that define a thing . . .
>
> A third kind of explanation [the efficient cause] is provided by identifying the agent who produced or changed something. For example, an advisor is the efficient cause of the changes he advises, a father is the efficient cause of the children he produced, and generally whatever produces or changes anything is the efficient cause of what is produced or changed.
>
> Finally, a kind of explanation [the final cause] is also provided when we give the end or purpose of a thing. For example, health can explain taking a walk, as when we ask, "Why is he taking a walk?" and reply, "For the sake of his health" and thereby feel that we have given an explanation.[10]

Aristotle held, then, that everything in the universe has a certain form, is made out of a certain matter, is produced by certain efficient causes, and is made to serve a certain purpose or function. The purpose of science is to explain the many things in the universe by identifying their four causes. Science should study the individual things in *this* world to identify their various causes, Aristotle held, instead of spending time thinking about an invisible world of forms.

Besides rejecting Plato's views on a separate world of unchanging forms, Aristotle also rejected his views on the soul. Plato had argued that the soul can exist apart from the body and that in an earlier existence it had acquired knowledge of the forms, which it remembered in this life. Aristotle thought that here, too, we must adhere to the four causes, which involve our experience in this world only. Therefore, he noted, to say that something has a soul is to say that it is alive. Consequently, the human soul is nothing more than those characteristics that distinguish a living human from a dead one. This means that the soul cannot exist apart from the body and cannot survive death.[11] The soul is merely the form of a living human—those essential characteristics that make each of us a living human being—and like other forms, it cannot exist apart from the visible things in this world:

> Let us leave behind, then, the theories of the soul that have come down to us from our predecessors and let us make a fresh start by trying to define what the soul is. . . .
>
> As I have said, the individual things in the world are composed in part of the matter [out of which they are made] . . . , and in part of a form which makes them be the kind of thing that they are. . . .
>
> The most common individual things are physical bodies, especially the natural physical bodies from which everything else is made. Now some physical bodies have life, and some do not. . . . Every natural physical body that has life is an individual thing and so it, too, must be composed of matter and form. . . . Now a physical body itself, when it has life, cannot be a soul. For the body is what *has* attributes [such as life or soul] and is not itself an attribute. The body is rather the matter [of which the living being is made]. The soul, therefore, must be the form of a physical body that has the power of living. . . .
>
> It is as pointless, therefore, to ask whether the body and the soul are identical, as to ask whether the wax and its shape are identical, or,

10 Aristotle, *Physics*, bk. 2, ch. 3. This edited translation copyright © 1987 by Manuel Velasquez.

11 However, Aristotle may have thought that *part* of the soul—what he called the active intellect—survived death. In some passages he seems to hint at this, but scholars still debate his meaning.

5:12—Tsze-kung said, "The Master's personal displays of his principles and ordinary descriptions of them may be heard. His discourses about man's nature and the way of Heaven cannot be heard."

6:20—Fan Ch'ih asked what constituted wisdom. The Master said, "To give one's self earnestly to the duties due to men, and, while respecting spiritual beings, to keep aloof from them, may be called wisdom."

11:11—Chi Lu asked about serving the spirits of the dead. The Master said, "While you are not able to serve men, how can you serve their spirits? " Chi Lu added, "I venture to ask about death? " He was answered, "While you do not know life, how can you know about death?"[19]

Confucius' philosophy, then, turned away from supernatural matters and focused entirely on ethics and humanity. His philosophy, in fact, is often characterized as an "ethical humanism." That is, his ethics is not based on religion but on human nature. This basic idea is the unifying principle behind all his philosophy:

4:15—The Master said, "Shan, my doctrine is that of an all-pervading unity." The disciple Tsang replied, "Yes."

The Master went out, and the other disciples asked, saying, "What do his words mean?" Tsang said, "The doctrine of our master is to be true to the principles of our nature and the benevolent exercise of them to others,—this and nothing more."[20]

What are these "principles of our nature"? Confucius insisted that to develop our human nature, we must develop *jen*, or virtue. By virtue, Confucius meant those uniquely human qualities of benevolence and humanity that form the foundation for all human relationships. This sense of love for humanity is, Confucius claimed, the basis of all morality and the quality that distinguishes humans from animals. Without it, life is not worth living. Virtue, according to Confucius, should be our ultimate value, and we should forsake even riches or honor rather than act contrary to virtue:

4:5—The Master said, "Riches and honors are what men desire. If they cannot be obtained in the proper way, they should not be held. Poverty and meanness are what men dislike. If they cannot be obtained in the proper way, they should not be avoided.

"The superior man does not, even for the space of a single meal, act contrary to virtue. In moments of haste, he cleaves to it. In seasons of danger, he cleaves to it."[21]

But what, exactly, is virtue? For Confucius the heart of virtue is reciprocity, the firm resolve to treat others as you would like others to treat you:

12:2—Chung-kung asked about perfect virtue. The Master said, "It is, when you go abroad, to behave to everyone as if you were receiving a great guest; to employ the people as if you were assisting at a great sacrifice; not to do to others as you would not wish done to yourself; to have no murmuring against you in the country and none in the family." Chung-kung said, "Though I am deficient in intelligence and vigor, I will make it my business to practice this lesson."

15:23—Tsze-kung asked, saying, "Is there one word which may serve as a rule of practice for all one's life? " The Master said, "Is not RECIPROCITY such a word? What you do not want done to yourself, do not do to others."[22]

Such virtue, Confucius held, is the key to inner peace and tranquility. It is also the basis of true feelings toward others and the source of right behavior:

4:2—The Master said, "Those who are without virtue cannot abide long either in a condition of poverty and hardship, or in a condition of enjoyment. The virtuous rest in virtue; the wise desire virtue."

4:3—The Master said, "It is only the truly virtuous man who can love or who can hate others."

4:4—The Master said, "If the will be set on virtue, there will be no practice of wickedness."[23]

Achieving virtue is not an easy matter. Virtue requires self-restraint in the use of one's senses and in one's conduct. It requires that we channel our selfish impulses into civilized behavior. Such self-control, Confucius warned, is something that each individual must achieve for himself or herself; it is not something that others can do for one:

1:14—The Master said, "He who aims to be a man of complete virtue in his food does not seek to gratify his appetite, nor in his dwelling place does he seek the appliances of ease."

19 From Confucius, *The Analects*, in *The Chinese Classics*, vol. 1, ed. and trans. James Legge (Oxford: Clarendon, 1893), reprinted in Daniel Bonevac, William Boon, and Stephen Phillips, *Beyond the Western Tradition* (Mountain View, CA: Mayfield, 1992), 256, 257, 259. The numbers preceding the excerpts refer to the numbering of the paragraphs in the Oxford edition.

20 Ibid., 257.

21 Ibid., 256.

22 Ibid., 259.

23 Ibid., 256.

12:1—Yen Yuan asked about perfect virtue. The Master said, "To subdue one's self and return to propriety, is perfect virtue. If a man can for one day subdue himself and return to propriety, all under heaven will ascribe perfect virtue to him. Is the practice of perfect virtue then from a man himself or is it from others?"

Yen Yuan said, "I beg to ask the steps of that process." The Master replied, "Look not at what is contrary to propriety; listen not to what is contrary to propriety; speak not what is contrary to propriety; make no movement which is contrary to propriety." Yen Yuan then said, "Though I am deficient in intelligence and vigor, I will make it my business to practice this lesson."[24]

Although reciprocity in general should guide our actions, we need to know just what reciprocity requires in specific circumstances. Confucius held that *li*, the "rules of propriety" or the moral customs of one's society, provide this specific and concrete guidance. Reciprocity is attained, then, by restraining oneself in accordance with the moral customs of one's society, which spell out the proper behavior for specific situations:

2:5—The Master said, "Mang-sun asked me what filial piety was, and I answered him, "Not being disobedient.'"

Fan Ch'ih said, "What did you mean?" The Master replied, "That parents, when alive, should be served according to propriety; that, when dead, they should be buried according to propriety; and that they should be sacrificed to according to propriety."

6:25—The Master said, "The superior man, extensively studying all learning and keeping himself under the restraint of the rules of propriety, may thus likewise not overstep what is right."[25]

Confucius held that virtue should serve not only as the basis of personal behavior but also as the foundation of political authority. If the ruler exercised virtue, Confucius claimed, then citizens would eagerly follow his leadership. Moreover, if the ruler appointed virtuous ministers, social unrest would end. Thus, virtue is the foundation of a well-ordered society and the key to peace within the state:

2:1—The Master said, "He who exercises government by means of his virtue may be compared to the north polar star, which keeps its place and all the stars turn towards it."

24 Ibid., 255, 259.
25 Ibid., 255, 258.

2:19—The duke Ai asked, saying, "What should be done in order to secure the submission of the people?" Confucius replied, "Advance the upright and set aside the crooked, then the people will submit. Advance the crooked and set aside the upright, then the people will not submit."[26]

Confucius also believed that one of the functions of the ruler was to help make people virtuous. Government is not established merely to keep the peace or to raise taxes and fund public enterprises. The virtue of the ruler, Confucius held, affects the virtue of his subjects. For example, the ruler who attempted to instill order through laws and punishments would find that his subjects would be dependent upon external motivations and would not become virtuous. But the ruler who attempted to rule by setting a virtuous example and by enacting laws that were consistent with the rules of propriety would find that his subjects would be motivated by their own internal desire to do what is right and would in time become virtuous:

2:3—The Master said, "If the people be led by laws, and uniformity sought to be given them by punishments, they will try to avoid the punishment, but have no sense of shame.

"If they be led by virtue, and uniformity sought to be given them by the rules of propriety, they will have the sense of shame, and moreover will become good."

12:17—Chi K'ang asked Confucius about government. Confucius replied, "To govern means to rectify. If you lead on the people with correctness, who will dare not to be correct?"

13:6—The Master said, "When a prince's personal conduct is correct, his government is effective without the issuing of orders. If his personal conduct is not correct, he may issue orders, but they will not be followed."

13:13—The Master said, "If a minister make his own conduct correct, what difficulty will he have in assisting in government? If he cannot rectify himself, what has he to do with rectifying others?"[27]

Thus, for Confucius the key to overcoming the political strife and unrest that had held China in their grip for so many centuries was personal virtue. Virtue should not only be the primary concern of the individual; it should also be the basic concern of the ruler. When rulers and citizens behave virtuously

26 Ibid., 255, 256.
27 Ibid., 255, 259, 260.

in all their social relationships, political strife ends. These ideas are succinctly stated in *The Great Learning*, another work attributed to Confucius:

3. Things have their root and their branches. Affairs have their end and their beginning. To know what is first and what is last will lead near to what is taught in the Great Learning.
4. The ancients who wished to illustrate illustrious virtue throughout the kingdom, first ordered well their own states. Wishing to order well their states, they first regulated their families. Wishing to regulate their families, they first cultivated their persons. Wishing to cultivate their persons, they first rectified their hearts. Wishing to rectify their hearts, they first sought to be sincere in their thoughts. Wishing to be sincere in their thoughts, they first extended to the utmost their knowledge. Such extension of knowledge lay in the investigation of things.
5. Things being investigated, knowledge became complete. Their knowledge being complete, their thoughts were sincere. Their thoughts being sincere, their hearts were then rectified. Their hearts being rectified, their persons were cultivated. Their persons being cultivated, their families were regulated. Their families being regulated, their states were rightly governed. Their states being rightly governed, the whole kingdom was made tranquil and happy.
6. From the Son of Heaven [the ruler] down to the mass of the people, all must consider the cultivation of the person the root of everything besides.[28]

Confucius devoted his life to living and propagating these views. He spent numerous years traveling through China, teaching his views to more than three thousand disciples and students. Although during his lifetime most political rulers were uninterested in his views, his teachings eventually became part of the official philosophy of China.

QUESTIONS

1. Why is Plato's philosophy sometimes said to be poetic? Is this a good or bad quality for philosophy?

2. Mathematicians often make statements such as "There exist two primes between x and y." What kind of existence are they talking about? How does Plato explain this kind of existence?

3. What is the source of the ideas we have about ideals that are not encountered in our physical world (such as beauty, justice, goodness)?

4. "If each person derived her ideas of mathematics by generalizing from her personal experience, then the laws of mathematics would differ from person to person: for one person, 2 plus 2 would equal 4, and for another, it would not. If mathematical ideas were constructed by society, then the laws of mathematics would differ from society to society: in America, 2 plus 2 would equal 4, but in other societies, it might not. The fact that the laws of mathematics must be the same for every person and every society proves that numbers and their laws exist independently of any person or society. And this shows that Plato was right." Evaluate this argument.

5. Compare Plato's theory of the soul to Freud's view that the human psyche contains three parts—an irrational id, a conscious ego, and an unconscious superego, each of which can be distinguished from the others by the psychological conflicts that arise among them.

6. Do you agree with Plato's view that appetite and emotion (at least anger) must be subject to reason? Why or why not?

7. Does Aristotle's theory of abstraction account for the knowledge we have of mathematical laws, which must be the same for all persons and all societies? (See question 4.) Does Plato or Aristotle best account for our knowledge of mathematics and our knowledge of ideals such as beauty, goodness, and justice?

8. Do you agree with Aristotle's view that all moral virtue is a mean between the extremes of excess and deficiency? What about the virtues of honesty and love?

9. Does Aristotle's theory imply that only a virtuous person can be happy? Do you agree that happiness without virtue is impossible? Explain.

10. Is there any difference between doing what is morally right and doing what will make one happy?

11. Compare how Aristotle and Confucius each deal with virtue. In what ways are they similar, and in what ways do they differ?

12. What is reciprocity for Confucius? What role does reciprocity play in his philosophy?

13. Do you agree with Confucius' view that government should make people good? Explain your answer.

28 Ibid., 263

CHAPTER

3 Reality and Being

The true lover of knowledge is always striving after being. . . . He will not rest at those multitudinous phenomena whose existence is appearance only.

PLATO

©remi goc/iStockphoto.com

OUTLINE AND LEARNING OBJECTIVES

3.1 What Is Real?

OBJECTIVES | When finished, you'll be able to:

- State why our assumptions about what is real are vitally important.

3.2 Reality: Material or Nonmaterial?

OBJECTIVES | When finished, you'll be able to:

- Explain what materialism is and why consciousness is difficult for materialism to explain.
- Explain what idealism is and why some philosophers have objected to it.
- **Determine the validity of arguments using "if-then" and "either-or" by examining their logical forms.**

3.3 Reality in Pragmatism

OBJECTIVES | When finished, you'll be able to:

- Explain and critically evaluate pragmatism's approach to philosophy, its method for determining what reality is, and James' views on "sub-universes."

3.4 Reality and Logical Positivism

OBJECTIVES | When finished, you'll be able to:

- Explain why logical positivists such as Ayer hold that metaphysical claims about reality are meaningless.
- Explain why critics have said that the logical positivists are wrong.
- **Determine the validity of categorical syllogisms.**

3.5 Antirealism: The Heir of Pragmatism and Idealism

OBJECTIVES | When finished, you'll be able to:

- Explain what realism and antirealism are and why antirealists say that there is no reality independent of our language or concepts.
- Explain why feminists object to antirealism and how realists like Searle have tried to prove realism.

3.6 Encountering Being: Reality in Phenomenology and Existentialism

OBJECTIVES | When finished, you'll be able to:

- Describe what "bracketing the whole world" is and why this leads to the view that consciousness is ultimate reality.
- Describe what being is for Heidegger and for Sartre.
- Explain why critics have objected to phenomenology and existentialism.

3.7 Is Freedom Real?

OBJECTIVES | When finished, you'll be able to:

- Explain and evaluate determinism, libertarianism, and compatibilism.

3.8 Is Time Real?

OBJECTIVES | When finished, you'll be able to:

- Explain the difference between objective and subjective time and why some philosophers have argued that subjective time is not real and others argue that objective time is unreal.

Chapter Summary

3.9 Readings: Maloney, "A Toast to Captain Jerk"

Nozick, "Being More Real"

3.10 Historical Showcase: Hobbes and Berkeley

3.1 What Is Real?

One night you're awakened by a frightened scream. Even though you're groggy with sleep, you recognize your little brother's cry and quickly stumble out of bed. Apparently, your brother's cry did not awaken anyone else. You make your way through the darkness to his bedroom, where you find him shivering with his head hidden under his blanket. "What's the matter?" you ask.

"I'm scared."

"Of what?"

"I don't know. Something's here in my room."

"There's nothing here," you tell him as you flip on a small night-light: "See for yourself."

Your brother looks around the empty room but isn't convinced. "I *saw* them," he insists. "They're here. They're big, with big mouths and staring eyes. They were coming to get me."

"You were only dreaming," you assure him. "It wasn't real. What you saw was only a dream, and dreams aren't real."

"They're real!" he persists.

"No," you say. "If they were real, then why can't you see them now? Where did they go?"

"Sometimes you can see them and sometimes you can't," he replies. "They're here right now in the house, but you can't see them. They're spirits! They're waiting for the dark. They're waiting to get me alone again."

"Shush!" you say. "You're just scaring yourself. I'm going back to bed."

"Don't leave me alone!" he wails. "They'll get me!"

"Just tell yourself that they aren't real," you say as you turn off the light. You don't tell him, but for some reason you feel a little uneasy as you make your way back to your bed through the dark. You hear small creaking noises and faint rustling sounds behind you. So you tell yourself, "They aren't real. Spirits aren't real!" But how do you know? Recall the line in Shakespeare's *Hamlet:* "There are more things in heaven and earth, Horatio, / Than are dreamed of in your philosophy." Why *can't* spirits be real? Why does your philosophy reject the reality of spirits?

Metaphysics is the attempt to answer the question: What is real? A child trembling in the dark may be fearful because he believes that reality is more than the hard material objects around him: Reality for him also includes an unseen spiritual realm. You may defend yourself against these fears by insisting that such a realm cannot be a part of reality. Reality consists only of the hard enduring objects around you that can be seen, heard, touched, and smelled. But what grounds do you have for this belief? In fact, many intelligent and thoughtful people have concluded that reality includes more than material objects. And many people—perhaps even you—have suspected that spirits are very real. What reasons can you give for saying that they are wrong? Don't virtually all religions declare that reality is more than the material world around us? Can a person even claim to be religious without believing that there is more to reality than the material world around us? Doesn't God or "the gods" have to constitute a kind of reality that is utterly different from material reality?

QUICK REVIEW
For many, reality consists only of physical objects and excludes nonphysical entities. But then how real are God, economic forces, subatomic quarks, numbers, and laws?

But it isn't just spirits and gods that raise troubling metaphysical questions about what we admit to be real. For example, what are we to say about most of the things for which people are willing to live and die? Consider justice, or goodness, or liberty, or truth, or beauty, or love. Are these material? Can they be seen, touched, smelled, or heard? Do they have a size, a shape, or even a place? Are these real? Haven't millions of people died for these ideals? Don't millions of people devote their entire lives to the pursuit of ideals such as these? Doesn't such devotion imply that they are real?

Perhaps to a practical person these notions seem too soft-minded to be real. So, consider some tougher notions. Economists regularly discuss "inflationary pressures" and the "forces" of supply and demand. Has anyone ever heard, seen, or physically felt these pressures and forces? Yet surely they are real; indeed, their reality creates the wealth of the rich and the impoverishment of the poor. But in what sense are these pressures and forces real? What does it mean to say that these are real? And if these unseen entities are real, then why can't spirits be admitted into the realm of reality? Or consider the physicist's force fields, electrons, protons, neutrons, quarks, and other subatomic particles; the mathematician's numbers, formulas, roots, and equations; and the astronomer's laws, curved spaces, black holes, and compressed or stretched intervals of time. Do we admit these odd entities into our notion of "reality"? Yet none of these are like the hard, visible, colored objects that make up our material world. What, then, is reality? What does it include?

These questions are puzzling. But are they important? Let's see. Think about what you imply when you say that something is not part of reality. For example, consider what you imply when you tell your little brother that "spirits aren't real." Isn't the point of saying this to convince him that he should pay no attention to so-called spirits? Aren't you telling him that spirits can exert no causal influence on him? That they cannot act on him or on anything else and so can neither hurt nor harm (nor even help) him? That they do not matter and cannot matter? Aren't you saying that they have no importance, no power, no actuality, no significance? That they should be disregarded, paid no heed, dismissed?

PHILOSOPHY AND LIFE

The Experience Machine, or Does Reality Matter?

In his book *The Examined Life*, philosopher Robert Nozick suggests the following "thought experiment":

> Imagine a machine that could give you any experience (or sequence of experiences) you might desire. When connected to this experience machine, you can have the experience of writing a great poem or bringing about world peace or loving someone and being loved in return. You can experience the felt pleasures of these things, how they feel "from the inside." You can program your experiences for tomorrow, or this week, or this year, or even for the rest of your life. If your imagination is impoverished, you can use the library of suggestions extracted from biographies and enhanced by novelists and psychologists. You can live your fondest dreams "from the inside." Would you choose to do this for the rest of your life? If not, why not? . . . The question is not whether to try the machine temporarily, but whether to enter it for the rest of your life. Upon entering, you will not remember having done this; so no pleasures will get ruined by realizing they are machine produced.

Nozick suggests that at least the first instinctive impulse of most of us would be to choose not to enter the machine where we would live forever in a dream world that, unknown to us, was not real.

1. Would you enter the experience machine? Why or why not?
2. Nozick claims that the reason most of us would not enter the experience machine forever is because we don't just care about the feelings and sensations we experience but also want our lives to be based on reality and not on illusion. Do you agree? Is it enough to spend your life just thinking that you are accomplishing great things, are engaged in fulfilling and worthwhile activities, and are loved by, say, your children and a wonderful spouse? Or would these things have to be real to be worth devoting your life to them? Explain.
3. If a person in the experience machine thinks his experiences are real, then are they real? Is reality whatever you experience and think is real?

Source: Robert Nozick, *The Examined Life* (New York: Simon and Schuster, 1989), 104–105.

QUICK REVIEW
For many, what is real is important, significant, actual, makes a difference, matters, and must be attended to. For Nozick, what is real has "**value**, meaning, importance, and weight."

If these are some of the implications of saying something is unreal, then the implications of saying something is part of reality are great indeed. For in saying that something is part of reality, are we not saying that it has importance, significance, actuality, power? Are we not saying that it is something that should not be dismissed, something that can make a difference to our lives, something to which we need to be attentive? As the philosopher Robert Nozick has said, to say something is real is to say it has "value, meaning, importance, and weight."

Metaphysical Questions of Reality

Metaphysical questions about what reality is, then, are among the most significant questions we can ask because they are intimately linked to questions about what is important to us, what we need to pay attention to, what has significance, what matters. If ghosts are not real, then ghosts don't matter. If God is not real, then God doesn't matter. If the spiritual realm is not real, then it is something that can make no difference in our lives. If only the material exists, then only the material is important. Clearly, our beliefs about reality will profoundly affect what we do with our lives and what we strive for, what we respect and what we ridicule, what we dismiss and what we are willing to live and die for. Only what is real (in some sense) can matter.

In Chapter 2, we raised the question of whether human nature is material or spiritual. But we did not directly examine the more fundamental issue underlying this question: Is matter all there is, or is there another kind of reality besides matter? In this chapter, we focus directly on this question of what is ultimately real, what the essence of all being, including our own, is. The critical study of the nature of reality is called *metaphysics.*

Digital Image © The Museum of Modern Art/Licensed by SCALA/Art Resource, NY Copyright ARS, NY

The Persistence of Memory, Salvador Dali. The critical study of the nature of reality is called *metaphysics*. But perhaps we can never say what reality ultimately is; perhaps the question and any subsequent theories are meaningless.

The Search for Reality

QUICK REVIEW
Metaphysics is the study of the nature of reality.

Perhaps, however, we can never say definitely what reality is; perhaps both the question and the theoretical answers are meaningless. Perhaps the search for reality is meaningless. As we will see, some people believe that it is. If so, perhaps we cannot say with certainty what aspects of ourselves and of the universe around us are real. Perhaps we cannot say with certainty what must ultimately matter to us. We must wait and see.

We begin this chapter with what many still see as the most fundamental question in metaphysics: Is reality purely material, or does reality also include a nonmaterial element? We look first at the case for materialism and next consider its opposite, idealism.

QUESTIONS

1. In his book *The Examined Life,* the Harvard philosopher Robert Nozick writes the following: "The notion of reality has various aspects or dimensions. To be more intense and vivid is to be more real (holding other things equal), to be more valuable is to be more real, and so on." Can you provide examples of what he means? Do you agree? What are the implications of the claim that reality has these aspects?

2. Is it possible that nothing else exists in the universe besides you? Is it possible that the people and things you see around you are all products of your own mind, much like a dream? How could you show that other things exist in the universe besides you and your ideas?

PHILOSOPHY AT THE MOVIES

Watch *Buddy Boy* (1999) in which Francis, a reclusive, guilt-ridden young man who has suffered brutality and misfortune and who now cares for his abusive ill mother, spies obsessively on a beautiful young woman even after they become romantically involved, and eventually spirals into a bizarre world of suspicion, violence, and death. How much of what Francis sees is real? What distinguishes reality from unreality in this movie? How do you try to distinguish what could be real from what could not be real in this movie?

Other movies with related themes: *Mulholland Drive* (2001), *The Sixth Sense* (1999), *The Machinist* (2004).

3.2 Reality: Material or Nonmaterial?

Saint Augustine (354–430), one of the greatest of the early Christian theologians, did not find it difficult to believe that spirits are real. In fact, Augustine held that reality—the real existing universe—contains within itself every possible kind of being, from the "lowest" kind of inert matter to the "highest" kind of spirit. Because God is all-powerful and wanted to fill reality with goodness, Augustine reasoned, God placed in the universe every possible kind of creature that had within itself some degree of reality and so some degree of goodness:

QUICK REVIEW
For Augustine, reality contains every possible kind of being.

> So great is the variety of earthly things that we can conceive of nothing which belongs to the form of the earth in its full extent which God, the Creator of all things, has not already created. . . . There can exist in nature things which your reason is incapable of conceiving. It cannot be, however, that what you conceive with true reasoning cannot exist. You cannot conceive of anything better in creation which has escaped the Maker of the creation.[1]

Where are human beings in the order of Augustine's universe? Augustine placed us somewhere in the middle of his hierarchy of reality: Humans have material bodies, so we belong to the lower material world, but we also have spirits, or **souls**, making us part of the higher spiritual world. Humans are both matter and spirit: We straddle two realms of reality.

But can Augustine's view of reality make sense to a person in the modern world? Has modern science's success in explaining the universe in material terms made such beliefs impossible for us? Although much of the world continues to believe that spiritual beings inhabit the universe and that humans are partly spirit, does it make more sense now for us to believe that matter is all that exists in the universe? Many people today are in fact materialists, who deny that spirit can be real.

Materialism: Reality as Matter

Materialism, the view that matter is the ultimate constituent of reality, is as old as philosophy itself. Both Eastern and Western philosophers have argued for the view that only material things are real. A school of materialism flourished even in India, a land that has long celebrated spiritual values. In the West, many of the ancient Greeks thought that everything in the universe was made out of the four main physical substances: water, fire, air, and earth. Others, such as the Greek atomists, had more sophisticated theories but still held that the ultimate stuff of the universe was material.

Eastern Materialism: The Charvaka Philosophers of India. The "Charvaka" philosophers of India, who flourished around 600 BCE, ridiculed the spiritualism of their religious countrymen. The Charvaka philosophers were also known as "Lokyata," which means "those who go the worldly way" because of their view that we should seek our happiness in this material world and its physical pleasures, and turn away from religion and its delusions.

The views of the Charvaka philosophers were based on the idea that there is only one valid source of knowledge about the world around us: sense perception. Other possible sources of knowledge, such as inductive or deductive reasoning, they argued, are invalid. **Inductive reasoning** is generalizing about what we observe.

---

1 Saint Augustine, *On Free Choice of the Will*, trans. Anna S. Benjamin and L. H. Hackstaff (New York: Bobbs-Merrill, 1964), 96–97.

For example, after observing many cases of smoke accompanied by fire, we might generalize that "where there's smoke, there's always fire." The problem with such inductive reasoning, they argued, is that generalizations always go beyond what we observe. **Deductive reasoning** is also unreliable because deductive reasoning always appeals to general statements to reach its logical conclusions, so it ultimately depends on the generalizations that inductive reasoning produces. So, deductive reasoning can be no more reliable than the inductive reasoning on which it is based. Therefore, all reasoning—inductive or deductive—about what the world around us is like is unreliable. Our only reliable source of knowledge about the world, then, is what we can immediately see, hear, touch, smell, or taste with our senses.

Once the Charvaka philosophers had established that we can know only what we can perceive with our senses, it was easy for them to argue for materialism. Because all we know is what we can perceive with our senses, and because whatever we perceive with our senses is physical and material, it follows that all we can know is the material or physical world around us. Moreover, they argued, if we cannot know something, it is wrong to say it exists. Any "things" we cannot perceive with our senses—such as souls, god, or any other spiritual "realities"—cannot be said to exist at all. Beyond the material world, as far as we know, there is nothing. There is no god, so religious worship is a pointless waste and priests are charlatans. There is no soul that leaves the body after death, no heavenly rewards, no punishments of hell, no afterlife at all. Human life begins in this world and ends in this world, so people should try to get as much of the bodily pleasures of this life as they can, the Charvakas urged.

QUICK REVIEW
The Indian Charvaka philosophers said that only what the senses perceive is real, so only the physical material world is real.

Western Materialism. The Greek philosopher Democritus (460–360 BCE) also believed that reality could be explained in terms of matter. The smallest pieces of matter he called *atoms*; he described them as solid, indivisible, indestructible, eternal, and uncreated. Atoms were not qualitatively distinguishable from one another, and they constantly moved through space, where they combined to form the recognizable physical objects of the universe. According to Democritus, the universe consisted of atoms and empty space. He believed that even the soul, which he equated with **reason**, consisted of atoms. In this atomic universe, "all things happen by virtue of necessity, the vortex being the cause of the creation of all things."[2]

But Democritus' theory never became popular because people soon became disenchanted with philosophers' many attempts to explain the cosmos. Their interest turned to more personal concerns, such as how to lead a good and happy life. Although their interests reached much further than such questions, the Greek philosophers Socrates, Plato, and Aristotle also discussed questions about the good life. They argued that moral virtue was the road to a good and happy life. The rise of Christianity fanned this interest in personal moral conduct, which predominated throughout the Middle Ages. In particular, the idea of an afterlife and the soul, which included the concept of personal immortality, gave the view of reality a distinctly nonmaterial bias.

QUICK REVIEW
The ancient Greek philosopher Democritus said all real objects are made up of material atoms.

In the seventeenth century, however, a growing interest in the world and the rise of **scientific method** and scientific discovery turned minds once again to materialism. Awakened by the discoveries of Copernicus, Kepler, Galileo, and Newton, people watched science cultivate a full-blown materialism. Committed to the belief that the world could be quantified by scientists, several philosophers made the claim that all is matter.

2 Quoted in Diogenes Laërtius, *Lives and Opinions of Eminent Philosophers*, vol. 2, trans. R. D. Hicks (Cambridge, MA: Harvard University Press, 1925), 455.

According to Hobbes, "The universe, that is the whole mass of things that are, is corporeal, that is to say body." But according to Berkeley, "All of the choir of heaven and furniture of the earth, in a word all those bodies which compose the mighty frame of the world, have no substance without a mind. . . . [S]o long as they are not actually perceived . . . , they have no existence at all."

© Ewa Wysocka-Galka/iStockphoto.com

In the philosophy of Thomas Hobbes (1588–1679), whom we briefly mentioned in the previous chapter, for example, we see the Democritean belief that everything can be explained in terms of matter in motion presented as the view that everything can be explained in terms of measurable matter. Hobbes held that ultimately we can know nothing about the world other than its measurable aspects:

> Every object is either a part of the whole world, or an aggregate of parts. The greatest of all bodies, or sensible objects, is the world itself; which we behold when we look round about us from this point of the same which we call the earth. Concerning the world, as it is one aggregate of many parts, the things that fall under inquiry are but few; and those we can determine, none. Of the whole world we may inquire what is its magnitude, what its duration, and how many there be, but nothing else.[3]

critical thinking

Suppose that all reality could be explained in terms of matter. Would it follow that only matter exists?

QUICK REVIEW
Influenced by science, Hobbes held that we can know only the measurable aspects of objects, so we can say only that measurable material objects exist.

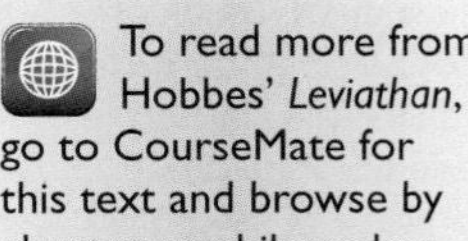
To read more from Hobbes' *Leviathan*, go to CourseMate for this text and browse by chapter or philosopher.

Hobbes concluded that measurable matter is all there is in the universe. Only matter is real:

> The universe, that is the whole mass of things that are, is corporeal, that is to say body; and has the dimensions of magnitude, namely, length, breadth, and depth. Also every part of body is likewise body, and has the like dimensions. And, consequently, every part of the Universe is body, and that which is not body is no part of the Universe. And because the Universe is all, that which is no part of it is nothing, and, consequently, nowhere.[4]

Anticipating many contemporary psychological theories, Hobbes postulated that our mental states (sensations, thoughts, and emotions) are states of our material brain and that a "general inclination of all mankind" is "a perpetual and restless desire of power after power." (For a fuller discussion of Hobbes' views, see the Historical Showcase at the end of this chapter.) In 1748, Julien Offray de La Mettrie carried Hobbesian psychology further when he published *Man a Machine*, a book that argues that humans are nothing more than complex machines. In de La Mettrie, materialism reached its logical conclusion.

What had happened to the religious doctrine of the soul? What remained of the creature supposedly made in the image of God and possessed of an eternal destiny? So much medieval superstition! declared the materialists.

But these early materialists' optimistic faith that humans could eventually explain the universe and themselves in terms of matter in motion has given way to doubt over the last century, as we shall see. Because the views of the ordinary person tend to lag behind the discoveries of science, many of us continue to believe in materialism unaware that modern science has created important difficulties for this theory.

Objections to Materialism

The fundamental objection to materialism is its difficulty in accounting for human consciousness—that is, for our conscious mental activities such as thinking,

3 Thomas Hobbes, "Elements of Philosophy," in *The English Works of Thomas Hobbes*, vol. 1, ed. Sir W. Molesworth (London: J. Bohn, 1839), chap. 1, sec. 8.
4 Thomas Hobbes, *Hobbes's Leviathan* (Oxford: Clarendon, 1909; original work published 1651), 524.

wishing, experiencing, hoping, dreaming, loving, and hating. Many people believe that these kinds of activities can be generated only by some kind of nonmaterial or spiritual entity: the human soul or a nonmaterial mind. But haven't many formerly widespread beliefs later turned out to be false, such as the belief that the earth is at the center of the universe? We must look more closely at why materialism is thought to have a difficult time accounting for human consciousness.

For traditional materialists such as Hobbes, a material thing is simply a physical object, moving or at rest in a specific location, that takes up space—has volume consisting of length, width, height—and has mass. So, materialists hold that human consciousness can be explained in terms of things that have these qualities. What do we mean by "consciousness"? Consciousness is the kind of awareness of things that we have when we are awake and that we do not have when we are sleeping. For example, when I am awake and thinking, I am aware of the thoughts I am thinking; when I perceive, I am aware of what I am perceiving; when I feel pain, I am aware of the pain I am feeling; and in general, when I am experiencing something, I am aware of what I am experiencing. This awareness is consciousness. An unusual aspect of consciousness is that the objects of which one is conscious need not exist. For example, I can think of a golden mountain or a unicorn, even though they do not exist. I can feel fear of things that aren't real. I can hallucinate and see or hear things that aren't there. Modern philosophers call this feature of consciousness its *intensionality*. Another peculiar aspect of consciousness is what we can call its *subjectivity*. This means that consciousness exists only to the extent that it is being experienced by someone. Because of this subjectivity, consciousness is sometimes said to have a "first-person" nature: Consciousness is something that one is directly aware of "from the inside" in a way that others cannot be aware of "from the outside." Finally, consciousness has no apparent location, no volume, no mass. Not surprisingly, many philosophers have felt that the qualities of consciousness are so different from those of matter that they must indicate the existence in the universe of two irreducibly different kinds of entities: material entities and conscious, nonmaterial entities.

QUICK REVIEW
The main problem with materialism is it cannot easily account for human consciousness. Matter has mass and spatial dimensions, but consciousness does not. Consciousness is the awareness of things that a person has when awake; it has intensionality and subjectivity, but no mass or spatial dimensions.

If materialists' views are to be acceptable, then mustn't they somehow reduce our supposedly unique human qualities, such as consciousness, to the material? For example, some materialists claim that states of consciousness are states of the brain, which is a physical or material organ. When we have a mental experience such as a thought, this experience is nothing more than the material brain functioning in a certain way. The same is true of any other conscious experience, such as dreaming, hoping, and feeling.

But doesn't the attempt to reduce conscious experience to brain states run into an almost insurmountable obstacle? Brain states can be seen, felt, and touched, whereas our conscious experiences cannot. For example, a brain surgeon can observe the state or condition of a ganglion in your brain and identify its location, color, and shape. Yet no one can know what your inner conscious experience is like. No one can know what it is like to consciously see and experience the world as you do. And your conscious experience has no location, color, or shape. Because they have such different qualities, mustn't we conclude that a brain state and a state of consciousness are two different things? The materialist doesn't seem to be able to account for these differences. To many people, in fact, the unique qualities that conscious experiences have, seem to imply that consciousness is a nonmaterial reality.

QUICK REVIEW
It is difficult to see how consciousness can be reduced to brain states, which, unlike consciousness, can be seen, felt, and touched.

The debate about the nature of consciousness has arisen in the midst of some startling discoveries in atomic physics. For a long time we have known that matter consists of molecules, of which there are a tremendous number of types. Molecules are composed of only a little more than 100 types of atoms. Before the twentieth century, no one believed that atoms could be split into smaller components. Today we know that several "subatomic" particles make up the atom—the electron, the proton, and the neutron—and these in turn can be broken down into yet more elementary particles. Physicists have discovered more than 200 of these so-called elementary particles. And these have turned out to be made up of still more elementary entities called *quarks.* The point is that modern scientists are showing reality to be ever more complex.

But, even more important, these elementary bits of stuff do not seem to be matter as traditionally conceived. They are more like energy, or fields, or, perhaps, probability waves. True, matter as it was traditionally conceived may depend on interactions of elementary particles, but the particles themselves do not seem to be composed of matter in the traditional sense—that is, a kind of hard, solid, perceptible stuff that occupies a definite volume of space and has a specific location. In his article "The Dematerialization of Matter," philosopher–scientist N. R. Hanson states the implications:

> Matter has been dematerialized, not just as a concept of the philosophically real, but now as an idea of modern physics. Matter can be analyzed down to the level of fundamental particles. But at that depth the direction of analysis changes, and this constitutes a major conceptual surprise in the history of science. The things which for Newton typified matter—e.g., an exactly determinable state, a point shape, absolute solidity—these are now the properties electrons do not, because theoretically they cannot, have . . .
>
> The dematerialization of matter . . . has rocked mechanics at its foundations. . . . The 20th century's dematerialization of matter has made it conceptually impossible to accept a Newtonian picture of the properties of matter and still do a consistent physics.[5]

Most materialists have been able to adjust to these new conceptions of elementary particles by expanding the traditional notion of matter. If matter is redefined to include anything that has scientifically observable effects, then the materialist can accommodate these new conceptions into his or her theory of the universe.

QUICK REVIEW
Hanson claims that Heisenberg's discovery that subatomic particles are like forces that do not have both determinate locations and velocities shows they are not material in the traditional sense.

Yet there is another aspect of these new discoveries that is not so easily accommodated by simply expanding the notion of matter. During the early 1930s, Werner Heisenberg found that we cannot say that a subatomic particle has a determinate (specific) location and momentum (momentum is the mass multiplied by the velocity) until it interacts with an observer. He called this the "principle of indeterminacy." This principle suggested that at its most fundamental level—the level of the subatomic—the world is intertwined with mind. This was because Heisenberg interpreted his principle of indeterminacy in a startling way: He claimed that at the subatomic level, things do not even exist at specific locations and are not moving with any specific momentum until they are observed. And even when they are observed, the more specific the location at which a particle exists, the less specific the momentum at which it is moving, and vice versa. Subatomic particles can no longer be thought of as tiny points of matter. Instead, they are areas or "waves" of probabilities—areas over which there is a greater or lesser probability that the subatomic particle, when observed, will pop into existence. And when it appears, the more definite its location is, the less definite its momentum; and the more definite its momentum, the less definite its location. As a result, many scientists, including Heisenberg, believe that we may live in an idealistic universe, one whose reality depends on the mind.

5 N. R. Hanson, "The Dematerialization of Matter," in *The Concept of Matter*, ed. Ernan McMillin (Notre Dame, IN: University of Notre Dame Press, 1963), 556–557.

PHILOSOPHY AND LIFE

The Neutrino

The neutrino is perhaps the most bewildering of all the elementary particles known to physics and among the most philosophically provocative. It has no physical properties—no mass, no electric charge, and no magnetic field. It is neither attracted nor repelled by the electric and magnetic fields of passing particles. Thus, a neutrino originating in the Milky Way or in some other galaxy and traveling at the speed of light can pass through the earth as if it were so much empty space. Can it be stopped? Only by a direct, head-on collision with another elementary particle. The chances of that are infinitesimally small. Fortunately, there are so many neutrinos that collisions do occur. Otherwise, physicists would never have detected them. Just think, even as you read this sentence, billions of neutrinos coming from the sun and other stars are passing through your skull and brain. And how would the universe appear to a neutrino? Eminent astronomer V. A. Firsoff provides a picture:

> *The universe as seen by a neutrino eye would wear a very unfamiliar look. Our earth and other planets simply would not be there, or might at best appear as thin patches of mist. The sun and other stars may be dimly visible, in as much as they emit some neutrinos. . . . A neutrino brain might suspect our existence from certain secondary effects, but would find it very difficult to prove, as we would elude the neutrino instruments at his disposal.*
>
> *Our universe is no truer than that of the neutrinos—they exist, but they exist in a different kind of space, governed by different laws. . . . The neutrino . . . is subject neither to gravitational nor to electromagnetic field. . . . It might be able to travel faster than light, which would make it relativistically recede in our time scale.*

QUESTIONS

1. What impact does the presence of neutrinos have on your view of reality?
2. Arthur Koestler writes: "To the unprejudiced mind, neutrinos have indeed a certain affinity with ghosts—which does not prevent them from existing." What does this mean?

Sources: V. A. Firsoff, *Life, Mind and Galaxies* (New York: W. A. Benjamin, 1967); Arthur Koestler, *The Roots of Coincidence* (New York: Random House, 1972), 63.

At its most fundamental level, the universe is made up of mind-dependent stuff! At the subatomic level, mind-independent reality seems to have disappeared, leaving only "probability fields" of potential entities that do not become real until they interact with a mind. To understand better what is meant by an idealistic universe, the opposite of a materialistic one, in the next section we consider various kinds of traditional forms of idealism as an explanation of ultimate reality.

QUESTIONS

1. Look up the meaning of *materialism* as it is ordinarily used. Do you detect any connection between its ordinary meaning and its philosophical meaning?
2. Some people claim that the persistence of a belief in the soul removes this belief from the realm of superstition or ignorance. Do you agree? Can you think of any beliefs that have so persisted? What about beliefs that lasted an extremely long time but are no longer widely held?
3. Our discussion so far has focused almost exclusively on the problem of self. How is this question relevant to the question of what is real?
4. Does research into the causes of human thought, consciousness, and behavior indicate a growing simplicity or a growing complexity of understanding?
5. Do you see the workings of the universe as orderly? Why or why not? (You might first define *orderliness* in terms of predictability.)

PHILOSOPHY AT THE MOVIES

Watch *Bicentennial Man* (1999) in which Andrew, a domestic robot purchased by the Martin family, gradually comes to display characteristics of a human being—such as creativity, compassion, love, and desire. He is eventually freed by the Martin family and many years later petitions to be legally recognized as a human being. Does this movie imply that Hobbes was right when he wrote: "The universe, that is the whole mass of things that are, is corporeal, that is to say body"? Do you think it is possible for a material creation like Andrew to really be conscious and "feel" compassion, love, and desire, or does Andrew merely act *as if* it experienced these? How would you tell the difference? Should Andrew be legally recognized as a human being?

Other movies with related themes: *A.I. Artificial Intelligence* (2001); *Blade Runner* (1982); *I, Robot* (2004).

Idealism: Reality as Nonmatter

Modern atomic theory has led some philosophers to claim that reality consists of more than matter. If we push the question of reality far enough, matter alone does not seem to account for everything; things are not just what they appear to be. In fact, some philosophers have held that if we push our investigation of nature far enough, we end up with only a mental world, a world of nonmaterial minds and ideas, not physical matter. Such philosophers are called idealists.

The Development of Western Idealism.

Although idealists differ, we can define **idealism** as the belief that reality is essentially composed of minds and their ideas rather than matter. Whether idealists believe that there is a single absolute mind or many minds, they invariably emphasize the mental or spiritual, not the material, presenting it as the creative force or active agent behind all things. This is the view that the great English playwright William Shakespeare expressed toward the end of his life in his final play, *The Tempest,* when he characterized the universe around us as "this vision" that exists only in our minds like a dream:

QUICK REVIEW
Idealists hold that reality consists of minds and their ideas.

Our revels now are ended. These our actors,
As I foretold you, were all spirits and
Are melted into air, into thin air:
And, like the baseless fabric of this vision,
The cloud-capp'd towers, the gorgeous palaces,
The solemn temples, that great globe itself,
Yea, all which it inherit, shall dissolve
And, like this insubstantial pageant [play] faded,
Leave not a rack behind. We are such stuff
As dreams are made on, and our little life
Is rounded with a sleep.

In the West, the belief that reality is ultimately idea is at least as old as the ancient Greek Pythagoras (about 600 BCE). However, Plato formalized one of the first versions of this belief. He held that the individual entities we perceive around us are merely shadows of reality, that behind each entity in our experience is a perfect form or ideal. This absolutely real form or ideal is what accounts for the lesser and derivative reality of the objects we see around us. Individual entities around us come and go, but the ideal forms are everlasting and indestructible.

Such thinking fit in well with the Christian thought developed by the Christian bishop, Saint Augustine. In *The City of God*, Augustine warned us to beware of the world and the flesh because they cannot last and so are not fully real. What is fully real is the enduring spiritual world, the world without matter. Although we are citizens of the physical world, we are ultimately destined to be citizens of the spiritual and fully real world of God.

But the founder of modern idealism is another Christian bishop, George Berkeley, who reacted against materialist philosophies like Hobbes'. Berkeley claimed that the conscious mind and its ideas or perceptions are the only reality. He did not deny the reality of the world we perceive. He denied only that this world is external to, and independent of, the mind. For Berkeley, only mind—only spirit—and its ideas can ultimately matter because only they are ultimately real.

Berkeley argued that all our experience of the external world consists of the sensations and perceptions that stream past our senses. We have no evidence for saying that reality is anything other than these sensations and perceptions. So, Berkeley concluded, all that exists are the sensations and ideas that we experience and the minds with which we experience them. (For a fuller explanation of Berkeley's views, see the Historical Showcase at the end of this chapter.)

To appreciate Berkeley's idealism, it's helpful to distinguish between two varieties of idealism: subjective and objective. Berkeley's version of idealism includes elements of both.[6]

Berkeley claimed that things are ultimately mental, or mind-dependent. This mind-dependency can be viewed as either dependent on my mind (subjective idealism) or dependent on some other mind such as God's (objective idealism). At least in its initial stages, Berkeley's idealism is subjective, or "me-dependent."

QUICK REVIEW
Subjective idealism says that reality consists of my mind (and perhaps other human minds) and its ideas; objective idealism says that, in addition, reality includes a supreme mind that produces an **objective** world of ideas that does not depend on my own mind, although it does depend on a mind—God's.

Berkeley said that we find out about the things of the world through perceptions conveyed through our senses. That is, we learn of trees, rocks, houses, cats, and dogs by using our senses of sight, touch, taste, smell, and hearing. When we use our senses, we see light or color; feel hardness or softness, smoothness or roughness; smell sweetness or decay. We have no other knowledge of things beyond these perceptions. So, Berkeley concludes, all the things that we perceive around us are nothing more than collections of perceptions. But perceptions are nothing more than mental states that have no existence outside the mind. So all the things we perceive around us are nothing more than mental states that have no existence outside the mind.

> By sight I have the ideas of light and colors. . . . By touch I perceive hard and soft, heat and cold, motion and resistance. . . . Smelling furnishes me with odors, the palate with tastes, and hearing conveys sounds. . . . As several of these are observed to accompany each other, they come to be marked by one name and so to be reputed as one thing. Thus, for example, a certain color, taste, smell, figure and consistency having been observed to go together, are accounted one distinct thing, signified by the name *apple*. Other collections of ideas constitute a stone, a tree, a book, and the like sensible things. . . .
>
> But besides all that endless variety of ideas or objects of knowledge, there is likewise something which knows or perceives them. . . . This perceiving, active being is what I call *mind, spirit, soul* or *myself*.
>
> It seems . . . evident that the various sensations or ideas imprinted on the sense, however blended or combined together (that is, whatever objects they compose), cannot exist otherwise than in a mind perceiving them. Their *esse* [being] is *percipi*

To read more from Berkeley's *Principles of Human Knowledge*, go to CourseMate for this text and browse by chapter or philosopher.

6 See Elmer Sprague, *Metaphysical Thinking* (New York: Oxford University Press, 1978), 93–103.

[to be perceived]. Nor is it possible they should have any existence out of the minds or thinking things which perceive them.

QUICK REVIEW
Berkeley argued that all objects are bundles of perceptions; because perceptions can exist only in a mind, all objects exist only in the mind, and there is no independent material reality outside the mind.

It is indeed an opinion strangely prevailing among men that houses, mountains, rivers, and, in a word, all sensible objects have an existence, natural or real, distinct from their being perceived by the understanding. But with how great an assurance and acquiescence soever this principle may be entertained in the world, yet whoever shall find in his heart to call it in question may, if I mistake not, perceive it to involve a manifest contradiction. For what are the forementioned objects but the things we perceive by sense? And what do we perceive besides our own ideas or sensations? And is it not plainly repugnant [contradictory] that any one of these or any combination of them should exist unperceived? . . .

All of the choir of heaven and furniture of the earth, in a word all those bodies which compose the mighty frame of the world, have no substance without a mind. Their being is to be perceived. Consequently, so long as they are not actually perceived by me or other created spirits, they must either have no existence at all or else exist in the mind of some eternal spirit.[7]

critical thinking

"We have no evidence for the existence of anything other than our sensations and perceptions, so only sensations, perceptions, and minds exist." Is this assumption correct?

Berkeley here seems to be arguing as follows: If we carefully examine the knowledge we have of the objects around us, we will see that our only knowledge of such objects consists of knowing the perceptions and sensations of them that we have in our minds. The objects we know, then, consist of nothing more than bundles of these perceptions and sensations in our minds. Because perceptions and sensations can exist only in the mind, it follows that every object must exist only in the mind. That is, every object that we think of as being in an external material world outside the mind is actually nothing more than a bundle of perceptions and sensations in the mind.

critical thinking

"We have no evidence for saying that reality is something other than our sensations and perceptions, so reality is not something other than our sensations and perceptions." What do you think of this assumption?

We may think that in addition to the perceptions and sensations we have in our mind, there also exists an external world of material objects that causes these mental perceptions and sensations. But the only basis we can have for claims about an external material world are our perceptual experiences, and these are entirely in the mind. However, because perceptions and sensations must exist in a mind, we know that in addition to perceptions and sensations, minds must exist. So, reality consists only of minds and their contents—their ideas, including perceptions and sensations.

QUICK REVIEW
Berkeley also argued that because our orderly perceptions of the world are not controlled by our minds, they must be produced by God's divine mind. This is an objective idealism.

Up to this point in his argument, Berkeley seems to be saying that everything I perceive is me-dependent. If we stop Berkeley's analysis right here, then, we would be left with **subjective idealism**, the position that the world consists only of my own mind and things that are dependent on my mind. But Berkeley went further and introduced an objective dimension.

critical thinking

Does Berkeley assume that if a perception is not under my voluntary control, it must be controlled by a divine mind? Is this assumption correct?

Berkeley pointed out that not all the contents of my mind are the same. There are two very different kinds of ideas in my mind. Some are short-lived, changeable, and within my control. For example, I can, if I choose, imagine a red horse with purple wings flying through a green sky and can easily control these imaginings. However, other ideas in my mind are more orderly, regular, enduring, and are not within my control. Consider, for instance, your usual route to class: You experience the same landmarks repeatedly—perhaps the library, the gym, and the student union—and when you get to class, you experience a comparable regularity, a steadiness about your perceptions. Unlike the imaginings of winged horses that you control, this latter collection of perceptions occurs in a way, in a sequence, and with a regularity that you do not control. But where does that collection of perceptions derive its uniformity, consistency, and continuity, if it is not from you? This can

7 George Berkeley, *Principles of Human Knowledge* (1710), part I, paras. 1–4, 6. Spelling and punctuation have been modernized.

PHILOSOPHY AND LIFE

Our Knowledge of the World

What kind of world do we live in? Physicists today generally describe it as a flux of energy that exists in different forms at different levels. Because of the limitations of our sense organs, our brains cannot know directly about all of the world's energy. Indeed, a relatively small part of the electromagnetic spectrum—that is, of the entire range of radiation—can stimulate our eyes. In other words, although we can hear or feel parts of it, we can't see a large portion of the spectrum. Electromagnetic energy covers a wide range of wavelengths, from extremely short gamma rays, having wavelengths of about a billionth of an inch, to the extremely long radio waves, which have wavelengths that are miles long. In fact, we can see very little of the electromagnetic spectrum.

Our ears also sense a limited range of the mechanical vibrations transmitted through the air. Similarly, although we can smell and taste certain chemical substances and feel the presence of some objects in contact with our skin, most of what occurs in our environment cannot be perceived by these senses either. In effect, the great flux of energy that physicists say exists is largely lost to our senses. We know about it only indirectly, through specially devised instruments that can detect radio waves, X-rays, infrared rays, and other energy forms that we can't directly experience.

What implications do these facts hold for our view of reality? If nothing else, they should make us wonder just how complete a picture of reality we have and how accurate our interpretation of it is. In *New Pathways in Science*, Sir Arthur Eddington addresses this issue:

> *As a conscious being I am involved in a story. The perceiving part of my mind tells me a story of a world around me. The story tells of familiar objects. It tells of colors, sounds, scents belonging to these objects; of boundless space in which they have their existence, and of an ever-rolling stream of time bringing change and incident. It tells of other life than mine busy about its own purposes.*
>
> *As a scientist I have become mistrustful of this story. In many instances it has become clear that things are not what they seem to be. According to the storyteller I have now in front of me a substantial desk; but I have learned from physics that the desk is not at all the continuous substance that it is supposed to be in the story. It is a host of tiny electric charges darting hither and thither with inconceivable velocity. Instead of being solid substance my desk is more like a swarm of gnats.*
>
> *So I have come to realize that I must not put overmuch confidence in the storyteller who lives in my mind.*

QUESTIONS

1. Undoubtedly, things are often not what they appear to be. But to say that is to imply another experience of things. Can we be sure that alternative experiences are any closer to how things are?
2. If a desk is indeed more like "a swarm of gnats" than a solid substance, what practical difference does that make in the way you live? Or is such a question irrelevant?

Source: Sir Arthur Eddington, *New Pathways in Science* (Ann Arbor: University of Michigan Press, 1959), 11.

only be explained as the work of another supreme mind: the mind of God. God produces in our minds the display of orderly perceptions that we call the external world, and it is God that gives this display its regularity and stability.

This second stage of Berkeley's idealism is an *objective* kind because it claims that the world of my perceptions does not depend on my mind, but on something external to my mind, i.e., on God. The advantages of **objective idealism** are that it accounts for the fact that the world I experience is not wholly in my control, and yet it allows the world to be viewed as an ultimately intelligible system because it is the product of mind.[8] It explains also why, for example, when I shut my eyes and open them again, the world I see before me is the same world that was there before I shut my eyes. It is the same world because God makes sure it is.

8 Sprague, *Metaphysical Thinking*, 97.

Many philosophers have agreed with the kind of idealist metaphysics that Berkeley put forward. Idealism, in fact, was the dominant philosophy in the English-speaking world during the early twentieth century, when it was championed by numerous philosophers including F. H. Bradley (1846–1924), J. M. E. McTaggart (1866–1925), Josiah Royce (1855–1916), and Bernard Bosanquet (1848–1923). In fact, idealism continues to have adherents today. The Canadian philosopher John Leslie (b. 1940), for example, proposes a kind of objective idealism when he claims that all the things in our universe are but thoughts in the mind of God:

> [T]he structures of galaxies, planets, and continents, of mice and of elephants, and of you and me, as well as of the houses, fields, and streams with which we interact, are nothing but the structures of various thoughts in the divine mind. The divine mind does not contemplate any universe that exists outside it. Its thinking about our universe is what our universe *is*.[9]

As you can no doubt guess, views like Berkeley's have been intensely controversial. But before we look at some of the objections his opponents raised, let's look briefly at other, non-Western versions of idealism.

Eastern Idealism. Idealism has not been confined to Western philosophy. Indian philosophy, in particular, has been home to a number of idealist philosophers. In fact, Vasubandhu, an Indian philosopher who lived in the fourth century CE, held views that were in some ways very similar to those of Berkeley. Vasubandhu is usually regarded as the greatest member of the "Yogacarin" or "Vijnanavada" school of Buddhist philosophy, one of the four great philosophical "schools" of India that interpreted the views of Buddha after his death. *Yogacarin* means truth through the practice of meditation, and *Vijnanavada* means the mind-only doctrine.

Like Berkeley, Vasubandhu argued that we do not directly perceive objects in the world around us. Instead, when we think that we are perceiving something, we are experiencing nothing more than a sensation in our minds. When we see colors, hear sounds, or smell odors, we infer from these sensations that there must be external objects that cause these sensations in us. But, Vasubandhu claimed, we are not justified in drawing such conclusions about the **existence** of external objects. All we ever perceive are sensations within us, so we have no basis for concluding that external objects cause these sensations.

QUICK REVIEW
The Indian philosopher Vasubandhu held that all our experiences of things consist of nothing more than sensations in our minds, which does not show that external objects exist. The apparent existence of an external world is an illusion as in a dream. When meditation "awakens" us, we will see that the "external world" is an illusion just as we know a dream is an illusion when we awaken from sleep.

To make his point, Vasubandhu draws attention to the way that many of us seem to see fine hairs regularly drifting across our vision or the way that we are sometimes afflicted with double vision. We do not conclude that these fine hairs exist in the air outside us or that things in the world have all suddenly doubled. Exactly the same can be said about all of our sensations, Vasubandhu argued. Just because we have sensations, we cannot conclude that there is anything outside of us that is causing these sensations: They are all in our mind. As Vasubandhu put it in one of his key works, *Twenty Verses and Their Commentary*, "When inner sensations arise, seemingly external objects appear. But this is like when persons having bad eyes see hairs that do not exist."[10]

But we can raise an important objection against Vasubandhu's view that the world is nothing but perceptions in our mind. The objection is this: If all the events we perceive are just sensations dancing in our mind, why does everything seem to happen in a specific position in space and at a specific point in time; that is, why

9 John Leslie, *Infinite Minds* (Oxford: Clarendon Press, 2001), 8.
10 Adapted from S. Radhakrishnan and C. Moore, eds., *A Source Book in Indian Philosophy* (Princeton, NJ: Princeton University Press, 1957), 328.

do events seem to occur in a spatial and temporal world outside of us? And why do the objects in that world physically affect us? Surely perceptions or sensations can exist only in the mind, not in a spatial and temporal world outside us. And surely our sensations or perceptions cannot physically affect us. In short, perceptions can exist only in the mind, yet the objects we perceive seem to exist in a world outside of our minds. And perceptions cannot have physical effects, yet the objects we perceive do physically affect us. So, we might object, the objects we perceive cannot be mere perceptions in our mind.

Vasubandhu had an answer to this objection. He pointed to what happens in our dreams:

> The place and time of objects we perceive is determined just like in a dream. . . . And dreams can physically affect us by, for example, sexually arousing us. . . .
>
> In a dream although there are no real objects, we nevertheless see things—like a village, a garden, a man or a woman—as if they exist in a specific place in the world. We do not see them as if they are in no specific place. And we see these things—a village, a garden, etc.—as if they exist at a specific time, not as if they exist at no specific time at all. . . . Again, although the objects we see in a dream are unreal, they nevertheless can have a physical effect on us, such as sexually arousing us.[11]

Vasubandhu is saying that just as in dreams, where we see, hear, feel, touch, and smell "things" that exist only in our minds, so also when we are awake we seem to see, hear, feel, touch, and smell things, yet these exist only in our minds. Just as the world that our dreams present to us is an orderly one where things happen in specific places and at specific times even though they exist only in our minds, so also the world we perceive when we are awake is one that is orderly yet exists only in our minds. And just as things in our dreams can physically affect us, so also the things in the world around us can affect us even though they exist only in our minds.

But you might raise another objection to Vasubandhu's view. Somehow, we can naturally tell that our dreams are not real. If the world we see is also not real, then why can't we just as naturally tell that the world we see around us is unreal? Vasubandhu's answer is quite simple: We can in fact tell that the world is unreal. Consider, he says, that we know a dream is unreal only after we have awakened from the dream. During the time of the dream, we think the dream is real. In the same way, most of us think the world we perceive around us is real because we live out our lives in a kind of dream. While we are in this illusory dream world, we think it is real. But by practicing meditation, we can awaken our mind from its slumber and attain a true, pure, and enlightened understanding of reality. When we have thus awakened, we will understand perfectly that the external world we thought was so real was, in truth, nothing more than a dream:

> It may be asked: if, when we are awake as well as when we are dreaming, perceptions may arise although there are no real objects, then, just as everyone naturally knows that dream objects are non-existent, why is the same not naturally known of the objects we perceive when we are awake? I reply: Before we have awakened we cannot know that what is seen in the dream does not exist. In the same way it is only afterwards, when the purified knowledge of the world is obtained, that this knowledge will take precedence. Then we can know according to the truth and clearly understand that those objects we perceived were unreal. The principle is the same.[12]

11 Ibid., 328–329.
12 Ibid., 329.

Vasubandhu concluded in a famous statement that "only mind exists." But he did more. Vasubandhu also tried to point his followers in the direction of a method by which they could come to understand directly for themselves that the seemingly hard and unyielding world around us is nothing more than a dream world existing only in our minds. This method is the method of meditation and ethical living. Meditation and an ethical life, he claimed, are the keys to waking up from our dream and seeing reality as it actually is.

thinking critically • Conditional and Disjunctive Arguments

Here is one of the arguments Berkeley uses to support his objective idealism:

> If we have perceptions of things whose uniformity, consistency, and continuity do not come from us (p), then they must come from a supreme mind (m).
> We have perceptions of things whose uniformity, consistency, and continuity do not come from us.
> So they must come from a supreme mind.

Is this argument valid? We explained earlier that to determine the validity of a deductive argument we see if we can imagine a situation in which its premises are true and its conclusion false. We could use that method to evaluate Berkeley's argument. But this method is time consuming, so we'll now look at a shorter way to determine the validity of deductive arguments, one that uses the notion of a "logical form."

> QUICK REVIEW
> The logical form of a claim with the connectives "either-or," "if-then," and "not" is the result of replacing its sentences with lowercase letters. The logical form of an argument is the result of translating all its claims into their logical forms.

To explain what the logical form of an argument is, we begin by noticing that most arguments contain compound claims. A compound claim consists of sentences joined together by connectives like "either-or," and "if-then." For example:

Either Tom went ***or*** Susan went.	***If*** the ground is wet, ***then*** Tom went.
Either it's raining ***or*** Susan went.	***If*** it's raining, ***then*** the ground is wet.

Claims that use these connectives—"either-or," and "if-then"—can be "translated" into their "logical form" by replacing their sentences with letters (lowercase) that we assign to represent those sentences. For example, we can assign letters to represent the sentences of the compound claims above in this way:

t: Tom went.	r: It's raining.
s: Susan went.	w: The ground is wet.

Then if we use these assignments to translate the compound claims above into their logical forms, we get:

Either t or s	If w then t
Either r or s	If r then w

Arguments can also contain negative claims like "Tom did not go" or "It's not raining." To translate negative claims into their logical form, we attach "Not-" in front of the letter assigned to the *positive version* of the claim:

"Not-t" is the logical form of "Tom did not go."

"Not-r" is the logical form of "It's not raining."

Whole arguments, like their claims, also have a logical form. The logical form of an argument is what we get when we translate all of its claims into their proper logical forms. For example, here are two arguments, (1) and (2):

(1) If it's raining, then the ground is wet.	(2) If it's raining, then the ground is wet.
It's not raining.	The ground is not wet
So the ground is not wet	So it's not raining.

If we translate the claims of these arguments into their logical form, using the letters we assigned earlier, then the logical form of argument (1) is (1*), and the logical form of argument (2) is (2*):

(1*) If r then w	(2*) If r then w
Not-r	Not-w
So: Not-w	So: Not-r

Notice that when you write down the logical form of an argument, you need to keep using the same letter to represent the same sentence through the whole argument. Of course, you don't have to use "r" and "w". We could have used "p" and "q" by making these assignments:

p: It's raining. q: The ground is wet.

And then we would have written the logical forms of (1) and (2) like this:

(1**) If p then q	(2**) If p then q
Not-p	Not-q
So Not-q	So Not-p

Although they use different letters, (1*) and (1**) are exactly the same logical form, and (2*) and (2**) are also the same logical form. It doesn't matter which letters you use to write down a logical form; if the connectives of two logical forms are the same and both the connectives and letters are arranged in the same way, then the two forms are the same regardless of the letters you used.

Now we can explain the shorter method of figuring out if an argument is valid. Here is the basic idea: If an argument is valid, then every other argument with the *same logical form* is also valid; if an argument is invalid, then every other argument with the *same logical form* is also invalid. So you don't need to test the validity of every new argument that comes along. All you need to do is, first, translate the new argument into its logical form. Then, if you earlier found that another argument with the same form was *valid (or invalid)*, you know without having to test the new one, that it, too, is *valid (or invalid)*.

For example, take argument (1). To test whether it is valid, try to imagine a situation in which its premises are true, but its conclusion is false. Here is one such situation: Suppose it's true that when it rains the ground gets wet, but today the ground got wet because the sprinklers were on although it was not raining. In that situation, the first two premises of argument (1) are true, but the conclusion is false. So argument (1) is invalid. But the logical form of argument (1) is (1*). So any argument with logical form (1*) will also be invalid. For example, these arguments have the same logical form, so they are invalid:

If it's raining, then John went.	If the ground is wet, then Susan went.
It's not raining.	The ground is not wet.
So John did not go.	So Susan did not go.

QUICK REVIEW
If an argument is valid, then any argument with the same logical form is also valid; if an argument is invalid, then any argument with the same logical form is also invalid. So to determine a new argument's validity, translate it into its logical form; if its logical form is that of a valid argument, then the new argument is valid; if its logical form is that of an invalid argument, it is invalid.

Next, take argument (2). No matter how much you try, you will not be able to come up with a situation in which the premises of (2) are true but its conclusion is false. Argument (2) is valid. But (2*) is the logical form of argument (2). So any other argument with logical form (2*) is also valid. For example, these arguments have the same logical form, so they are valid:

If it's raining, then Susan went.	If the ground is wet, then John went.
Susan did not go.	John did not go.
So it's not raining.	So the ground is not wet.

QUICK REVIEW
The logical forms of the most common *valid* "if-then" arguments are: "If p then q; p; So q," and "If p then q; Not-q, So Not-p." The logical forms of the most common *invalid* "if-then" arguments are: "If p then q; q; So p" and "If p then q; Not-p; So Not-q." The logical forms of the most common *valid* "either-or" arguments are: "Either p or q; Not-p; So q," "Either p or q; Not-q; so p," and "Either p or q; If p then r; If q then r; So r."

Being able to use an argument's logical form to evaluate its validity is extremely useful, especially if you have memorized the logical forms of the most common type of valid arguments and of the most common types of invalid arguments. Here, then, are the logical forms of the most common kind of *VALID* arguments that use the "if-then" connective in their premises. You should memorize these logical forms so that you can use them to quickly check whether an "if-then" argument is valid. *Any argument with one of these forms has to be VALID.* The first of these two forms of *VALID* arguments is called "Affirming the Antecedent" and the second is "Denying the Consequent."

If p then q	If p then q
p	Not-q
So q	So Not-p

And here are the logical forms of the two most common *INVALID* arguments that use the "if-then" connective. *Any argument that has one of these forms has to be INVALID.* The first of these two forms of *INVALID* arguments is called "Affirming the Consequent" and the second is "Denying the Antecedent."

If p then q	If p then q
q	Not-p
So p	So Not-q

Here are the most commonly used *FORMS* of *VALID* arguments that use the "either-or" connective in the premises. Notice that the third form also uses the "If-then" connective in its premises:

Either p or q	Either p or q	Either p or q
Not p	Not-q	If p then r
So q	So p	If q then r
		So r

The main difficulty you will have when using these logical forms to evaluate arguments will be trying to translate the premises and conclusions of English arguments into their proper logical forms. To help you, here are some of the kinds of English expressions that students often have trouble translating into their proper logical form. The letters we assign to each sentence are in parentheses, and the troublesome expressions are underlined; the correct logical form of each statement is at the right in bold:

John gets to school (s) <u>only if</u> his alarm rings (r): **If s then r**

John gets to school (s) <u>only when</u> his alarm rings (r): **If s then r**

You'll die (d) <u>unless</u> you jump (j): **If not-j then d**

<u>Unless</u> you jump (j), you'll die (d): **If not-j then d**

We're now ready to use an argument's logical form to evaluate Berkeley's argument for objective idealism; the letters we assign to each sentence are in parentheses:

If we have perceptions of things whose uniformity, consistency, and continuity do not come from us (p), then they must come from a supreme mind (m).
We have perceptions of things whose uniformity, consistency, and continuity do not come from us (p).
So they must come from a supreme mind (m).

The logical form of this argument is:

If p then m

p

So m

A quick glance at our list of the forms of valid arguments shows that this form is on that list, so Berkeley's argument is valid. You, of course, will have to decide for yourself whether its premises are true. To help you we'll look at some objections to Berkeley's idealism next.

Objections to Idealism

An important problem for idealists is this: Don't idealists commit the fallacy of **anthropomorphism**? That is, don't they project a human faculty—the mind and its contents—onto the nonhuman universe as a whole when they claim the universe is like the human mind and its contents? It is one thing to speak of people as having minds with ideas, but can we speak of the objects in the universe as being made up of ideas within a human-like mind? Doesn't this come down to the claim that the universe is made up of the same kind of "mind-stuff" that human minds are made of?

Consider, also, whether you or anyone else has ever experienced mind, idea, or spirit independent of a material biological system. All the minds and ideas we know about seem to require the wet hardware of the living brain, for once the brain dies then the mind and its ideas seem to vanish. These thoughts suggest further problems, which require a closer look at subjective and objective idealism.

QUICK REVIEW
Critics of idealism claim that idealists wrongly project human characteristics onto nonhuman parts of the universe.

Objections to Subjective Idealism. Subjective idealism claims that whatever I perceive is merely one of my perceptions or a collection of perceptions. But this is at least puzzling and suggests that subjective idealism is based on a mistake: the mistake of failing to distinguish between my *perception* of a thing and the *thing* that I perceive. If I'm looking at a tree, for example, isn't there a difference between my *seeing* a tree and *the tree* that I see? Can subjective idealism make such a distinction? In saying that all we perceive are our own perceptions, isn't Berkeley mistakenly saying that there is no difference between my perception of a tree and the tree that I perceive?

On the other hand, if I say that there is more to the tree than my perception of the tree, can't subjective idealists ask me how this "more" is to be found out? Can't the subjective idealist say that there is no way to find out about trees other than by examining my perception of the tree? Thus, if I claim that there's more to the tree than my perception of it, I am postulating the existence of something that I cannot know. But am I justified in claiming that something is real when I can't even know it?

"But," as philosopher Elmer Sprague points out, "it still seems odd to say that I perceive my perceptions, and not that I perceive something out there to be perceived. It seems odd to say that to perceive the [tree] is but to perceive my own mind. It is all very well for the Subjective Immaterialist to say 'That's just the way it is.' Less hardy mortals still wonder if we might not say something else instead."[13] Sprague concedes that what subjective idealists say cannot be disproved experimentally because their theories cannot be falsified. But we can still ask them how they know that their claim is true. Ultimately, the claim seems to hinge on the assumption that perceptible *things* are mere collections of perceptions of them. But why this

QUICK REVIEW
Critics of subjective idealism propose that it mistakenly claims that our perceptions are what we perceive.

13 Sprague, *Metaphysical Thinking*, 98.

assumption? Why not the more commonsensical distinction between perceptions and the objects of perception?

Related to this mistaken assumption is subjective idealism's insistence that things are collections of perceptible qualities. This belief also follows only if we don't make a sharp distinction between the things we perceive and our perceptions of them. But can we say how things really and objectively are without making such a distinction? Subjective idealism does not really answer the question of what things are like independent of us—rather it seems to dissolve the question. In saying that what I perceive are my own perceptions, subjective idealism is saying that things are exactly as I perceive them because they are nothing but my perceptions. But doesn't this rule out the possibility of objective knowledge of things? Doesn't it rule out the possibility of being mistaken about what we perceive?

Objections to Objective Idealism. As for objective idealism, we observed two apparent strengths: It explains why perceptible things seem to be independent of the mind, and why the universe seems to have an ultimately intelligible and rational order. However, Sprague believes that neither of these aspects is as strong as it may appear.

Recall your classroom experience. You perceive the classroom anew each day exactly as it was the day before because some other mind, call it God, perceives it all the time, thus holding the classroom in place each time you happen to perceive it. But do we really need such an explanation? Won't a materialistic explanation account for the composition of the classroom and of the things that you pass en route to it? And should they one day disappear, can't materialism also account for that eventuality—they fell down, were torn down, or were blown up? Why do you need to involve the mind of God?

Objective idealists are seeking some ultimate explanation of the order and permanence of the world. Thus, "God does it" is the ultimate explanation of the objective idealist. But what does that tell us? If the classroom stands, God does it. When it lies in ruins, it does so because God does it. What does "God does it" add to a commonsensical account of the classroom or of its destruction?

Objective idealists also claim that the world is intelligible because it's a product of God's mind or of some sort of cosmic intelligence. But simply because our own mind may be intelligible, does that mean God's is? How are we to know God's mind? How can we distinguish between our own perceptions, which by strict idealistic principles we can never get beyond, and God's perceptions? Shouldn't idealism answer these questions before it can be considered a compelling explanation of ultimate reality?

QUICK REVIEW
Critics of objective idealism say that materialism, not God, provides the best explanation of the order and permanence of the world we perceive.

But what is the alternative to idealism? Many philosophers believe that materialism is just as inadequate. Is perhaps the most viable option to admit that the universe contains both nonmaterial spirit and physical matter? As we saw in Chapter 2, this is the view of dualism. Dualism holds that reality contains two irreducibly different kinds of things: immaterial spirits and material objects. Yet, as we saw in our earlier discussion of dualism, this view raises an almost insoluble question: How can an immaterial spirit or mind interact with a material universe? If a nonphysical entity moved or affected an object in the physical universe, it would violate the most basic law of science. Science is based on the law of the conservation of energy (sometimes called the first law of thermodynamics) discovered by James Joule and

Lord Kelvin in the nineteenth century. This law states that the total energy contained in a closed physical system can change its forms, but can neither increase nor decrease in total quantity. For example, energy in the form of motion may be changed into heat, which is another form of energy (for example, when you rub your hands together quickly to heat them). But the total amount of energy in the physical universe can neither increase nor decrease. Yet if an immaterial spirit somehow changed or altered some physical object in the slightest way, this would introduce additional energy into the physical universe. This would violate the basic law of the conservation of energy. Similarly, if a physical object somehow moved or changed an immaterial spirit, this would in effect dissipate energy out of the physical universe, again violating the law of the conservation of energy. If nonmaterial spirits coexist with material objects, then neither should be able to affect each other in the slightest way. Neither should even be able to perceive the existence of the other!

So, dualism seems as improbable as materialism and idealism. What, then, is left? Perhaps a different approach is needed. Pragmatism offers another approach to reality, one that rejects the entire materialism/idealism debate.

QUESTIONS

1. Some people argue that a universal law is at work in the universe, giving everything design and purpose and ordering our experiences. Do you see such a principle or law? If so, what would its source have to be like?
2. Read, again, the quotation from Shakespeare's *Tempest* at the beginning of this section. How do the views Shakespeare expresses in this passage differ from Berkeley's views? How are they similar? What similarities and differences are there between the views of Shakespeare and the views of the Indian philosopher Vasubandhu? What similarities and differences are there between the views of Berkeley and those of Vasubandhu?
3. In what sense is it true that we have no access to reality other than the perceptions we have in our mind?
4. Is it true or false that our perceptions are what we perceive? Explain your view.
5. It has often been said that idealism encourages a withdrawal from the world, a retreat from secular problems, and an immersion in otherworldly concerns. As a result, the idealist neglects real and pressing social concerns. Explain why you think this charge is justified or not justified.

PHILOSOPHY AT THE MOVIES

Watch *The Thirteenth Floor* (1999) in which Douglas Hall, accused of murdering a friend who invented a virtual reality simulation of 1937 Los Angeles, enters the simulation and there is almost killed by an angry man who has discovered he is only an artificial simulation, leading Hall to quickly exit the simulation and return to our own world—only to discover that our world, too, is a simulation. According to this movie, how many worlds are there? According to idealism, is our world "real" in this movie? Does this movie imply an acceptance or rejection of idealism? Explain. Does the movie imply there is no reality? Is this possible?

Other movies with related themes: *eXistenZ* (1999), *Matrix* (1999), *Matrix Reloaded* (2003), *Matrix Revolutions* (2003), *Vanilla Sky* (2001), and *Total Recall* (1990).

3.3 Reality in Pragmatism

To many people, the debate between materialism and idealism seems to be a pointless philosophical exercise. Nothing will change, they claim, if we decide that all reality is ultimately matter. For example, people who believe in an afterlife will continue to believe in an afterlife, but the afterlife will be in a material world. And similarly, they insist, nothing will change if we decide that all reality is ultimately immaterial. The things around us will still feel hard, will still smell, will still have shapes, colors, positions, and motions, even if we decide that they are made up of something we term "immaterial reality." Because the outcome of the debate between materialism and idealism seems to have no important consequences, such people have concluded that it is pointless to debate whether reality is material or spiritual.

Underlying their conclusion is the assumption that our beliefs about reality are meaningful only to the extent that they have important consequences. This assumption is the cornerstone of a particularly American approach to reality called *pragmatism.*

Pragmatism as a philosophical movement has grown in the United States during the last hundred years through the writings of Charles S. Peirce (1839–1914), William James (1842–1910), and John Dewey (1859–1952). James defines **pragmatism** as "the attitude of looking away from first things, principles, 'categories,' supposed necessities; and of looking towards last things, fruits, consequences, facts."[14] Pragmatism is also a reaction to traditional systems of philosophy, such as materialism and idealism. These systems, claim the pragmatists, have erred in looking for absolutes. Reality is hardly a single thing: It is pluralistic. And we are part of it. Using intelligence and reason, we can understand and exercise some control over nature; we can help create it.

QUICK REVIEW
James held that philosophy should not lose its connection to personal and social problems.

To grasp the metaphysical content of pragmatism, it is essential to understand its general approach to philosophy and the social climate out of which it arose.[15]

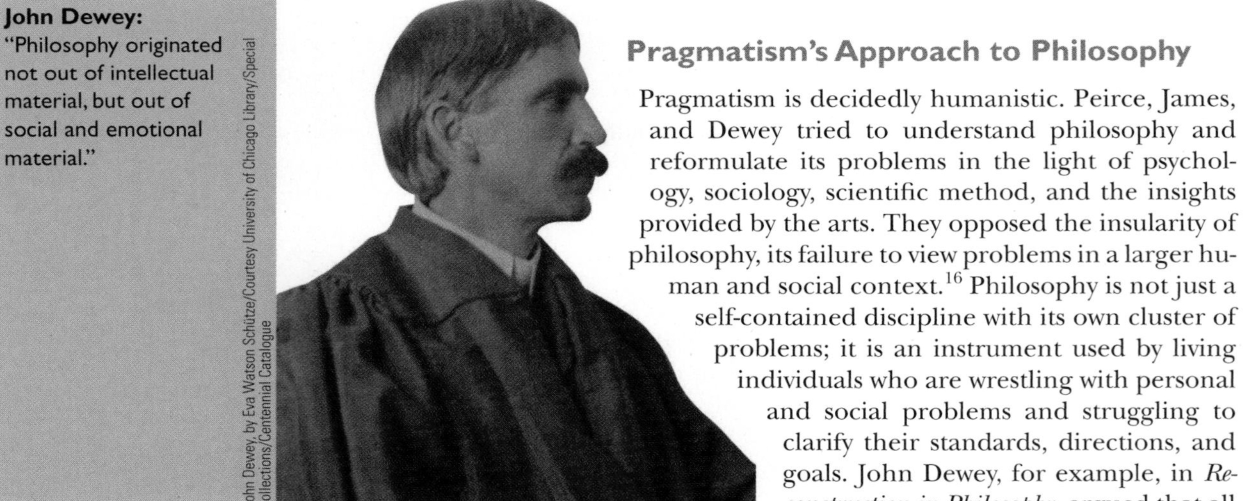

John Dewey: "Philosophy originated not out of intellectual material, but out of social and emotional material."

John Dewey, by Eva Watson Schütze/Courtesy University of Chicago Library/Special Collections/Centennial Catalogue

Pragmatism's Approach to Philosophy

Pragmatism is decidedly humanistic. Peirce, James, and Dewey tried to understand philosophy and reformulate its problems in the light of psychology, sociology, scientific method, and the insights provided by the arts. They opposed the insularity of philosophy, its failure to view problems in a larger human and social context.[16] Philosophy is not just a self-contained discipline with its own cluster of problems; it is an instrument used by living individuals who are wrestling with personal and social problems and struggling to clarify their standards, directions, and goals. John Dewey, for example, in *Reconstruction in Philosophy*, argued that all

14 William James, *Pragmatism: A New Name for Some Old Ways of Thinking* (New York: Longmans, Green, 1907), 54–55.

15 The following discussion is indebted to Charles Frankel, *The Golden Age of American Philosophy* (New York: George Braziller, 1960), 1–17.

16 Quoted in Frankel, *Golden Age*, 3.

philosophy arises out of people's continual struggles to deal with social and moral problems:

> This is the trait which, in my opinion, has affected most deeply the classic notion about the nature of philosophy. Philosophy has arrogated to itself the office of demonstrating the existence of a transcendent, absolute or inner reality and of revealing to man the nature and features of this ultimate and higher reality. It has therefore claimed that it was in possession of a higher organ of knowledge than is employed by positive science and ordinary practical experience, and that it is marked by a superior dignity and importance—a claim which is undeniable *if* philosophy leads man to proof and intuition of a Reality beyond that open to day-by-day life and the special sciences.
>
> Various philosophers have of course, denied this claim at various times. But for the most part these denials have been agnostic and skeptical. They have contented themselves with asserting that absolute and ultimate reality is beyond human ken. . . . Only comparatively recently has another conception of the proper office of philosophy arisen. This course of lectures will be devoted to setting forth this different conception of philosophy. . . . At this point, it can be referred to only by anticipation and in cursory fashion . . .
>
> If this lecture succeeds in leaving in your minds as a reasonable hypothesis the idea that philosophy originated not out of intellectual material, but out of social and emotional material, it will also succeed in leaving with you a changed attitude toward traditional philosophies. They will be viewed from a new angle and placed in a new light. New questions about them will be aroused and new standards for judging them will be suggested.[17]

critical thinking
Suppose that no one feels that materialism and idealism are meaningful, stimulating, or interesting views. Does it follow that they are false?

QUICK REVIEW
According to Dewey, philosophy arises out of social and emotional material.

Underlying Dewey's "conception" that philosophy arises out of our "social and emotional" lives, is the view that all thinking—not just philosophical thinking—exists to defend interests and conscious or unconscious human wishes. All thinking strengthens or secures some human interest. Rather than compromising human ideals, this notion shows that ideals have a natural home in the world. We discover new ways of thinking to realize these ideals more effectively.

critical thinking
Suppose it is proven that a philosophical view originated out of the social and emotional influences operating on a philosopher. Does it follow that the view should be rejected?

Pragmatism denies sharp distinctions between matter and mind, science and morals, and experience and reason. For pragmatists, we must examine human ideas and ideals from the biological and social points of view and treat them as instruments for making sense of experience. We must judge any idea or ideal in terms of its context. Its value depends on its problem-solving capacity. These ideas lie at the heart of the pragmatic method.

The Pragmatic Method

The *pragmatic method* is a way to discover what our ideas mean by studying their consequences in actual experience. Any inferences about the world drawn from metaphysical inquiries must have premises that refer to facts in the world and not to human reasoning alone. We cannot base judgments on their connectedness to some presupposed transcendent or ultimate reality. Any judgment must be rooted in experiences that are meaningful to humans. Thus, any view of reality is tied to the values inherent in social traditions. In effect, there are no ultimate principles, no self-evident values, and no irreducible sense data. In fact, pragmatism allows few certainties. Ultimately, the test of an idea or ideal is its capacity to solve the particular

To read a variety of James's works, go to CourseMate for this text and browse by chapter or philosopher.

17 John Dewey, *Reconstruction in Philosophy* (New York: Henry Holt, 1920), 406–407.

William James: "Pragmatism is the attitude of looking away from first things, principles, 'categories,' supposed necessities; and of looking towards last things, fruits, consequences, facts."

© Bettmann/CORBIS

problems that it addresses. Both materialism and idealism fail this test. Here is how William James expresses the point in his important work *Pragmatism* (1907):

> The pragmatic method is primarily a method of settling metaphysical disputes that otherwise might be interminable. Is the world one or many? Fated or free? Material or spiritual? Here are notions either of which may or may not hold good of the world; and disputes over such notions are unending. The pragmatic method in such cases is to try to interpret each notion by tracing its respective practical consequences. What difference would it practically make to anyone if this notion rather than that notion were true? If no practical difference whatever can be traced, then the alternatives mean practically the same thing, and all dispute is idle. Whenever a dispute is serious, we ought to be able to show some practical difference that must follow from one side or the other's being right.[18]

QUICK REVIEW
For James, the pragmatic method interprets an idea in terms of its practical consequences and asks what difference it would make if it were true.

Pragmatists differ—understandably, for pragmatism is not a monolithic system of thought. For example, Charles S. Peirce was concerned with the logical implications of ideas, not their psychological effects. He focused on the scientific function of ideas—their role in fostering reasoned consensus. In contrast, James, a physiologist and psychologist, was interested in ideas as events in personal experience, as instruments of will and desire. Dewey was neither a student of logic and science nor a psychologist. His main interest was social criticism. He used the pragmatic method to reassess the functions of education, logic, the arts, and philosophy in human civilization. Nonetheless, the observations about pragmatism presented here underlay the thought of each of these highly influential American philosophers, and the pragmatic method guided their thoughts. We will focus, however, on the writings of William James.

Applied to metaphysical questions, the pragmatic method indicates certain criteria for determining what's real. Many materialists rely on sense observation and scientific method; some idealists (although not Berkeley) rely primarily on reason. In contrast, James accepted neither of these as the final determinant of reality. According to James, we determine whether an object is real by its relation to "our emotional and active life." In particular, he wrote, "whatever excites and stimulates our interest is real." Because it is possible that different systems of ideas or objects might excite our interest, he argued, people can recognize a number of different "sub-universes" or real worlds. Among them are the worlds of sense experience; of scientific knowledge; of belief and opinion; and of the transcendent, the religious, or the supernatural. According to James, each of us selects the world or worlds that are most personally meaningful to us, and these, for us, are "reality":

> Really there are more than two sub-universes of which we take account, some of us of this one, and others of that. . . . The most important sub-universes commonly

18 William James, *Pragmatism*, 46.

discriminated from each other and recognized by most of us as existing, each with its own special and separate style of existence, are the following:

1. The world of sense, or of physical "things" as we instinctively apprehend them, with such qualities as heat, color, and sound, and such "forces" as life, chemical affinity, gravity, electricity, all existing as such within or on the surface of the things.
2. The world of science, or of physical things as the learned conceive them, with secondary qualities and "forces" (in the popular sense) excluded, and nothing real but solids and fluids and their "laws" (i.e., customs) of motion.
3. The world of ideal relations, or abstract truths believed or believable by all, and expressed in logical, mathematical, metaphysical, ethical, or aesthetic propositions.
4. The world of "idols of the tribe," illusions or prejudices common to the race. All educated people recognize these as forming one sub-universe. The motion of the sky round the earth, for example, belongs to this world . . .
5. The various supernatural worlds, the Christian heaven and hell, the world of the Hindoo mythology. . . . The various worlds of deliberate fable may be ranked with these worlds of faith—the world of the Iliad, that of King Lear, of the Pickwick Papers, etc.
6. The various worlds of individual opinion, as numerous as men are.
7. The worlds of sheer madness and vagary, also indefinitely numerous.

QUICK REVIEW
James said, "whatever excites and stimulates our interest is real"; because there are many different interests, there are many different real worlds or "sub-universes."

Every object we think of gets at last referred to one world or another of this or of some similar list. It settles into our belief as a common-sense object, a scientific object, an abstract object, a mythological object, an object of some one's mistaken conception, or a madman's object; and it reaches this state sometimes immediately, but often only after being hustled and bandied about amongst other objects until it finds some which will tolerate its presence and stand in relations to it which nothing contradicts. The molecules and ether-waves of the scientific world, for example, simply kick the object's warmth and color out, they refuse to have any relations with them. But the world of "idols of the tribe" stands ready to take them in. . . . Each world while it is attended to is real after its own fashion; only the reality lapses with the attention. . . . Each thinker, however, has dominant habits of attention; and these practically elect from among the various worlds some one to be for him the world of ultimate realities. . . . For most men, as we shall immediately see, the "things of sense" hold this prerogative. . . . [But in] the sense in which we contrast reality with simple unreality, and in which one thing is said to have more reality than another, and to be more believed, reality means simply relation to our emotional and active life. . . . In this sense, whatever excites and stimulates our interest is real; whenever an object so appeals to us that we turn to it, accept it, fill our mind with it, or practically take account of it, so far it is real for us, and we believe it. Whenever, on the contrary, we ignore it, fail to consider it or act upon it, despise it, reject it, forget it, so far it is unreal for us and disbelieved.[19]

In effect, we choose our own ultimate reality by the criterion of its meaningful relation to our emotions and actions. Although some metaphysicians may speak of one world—for example, the world of "matter" or the world of "mind"—as having more reality than another, James interpreted their views as indicating merely one of many possible worlds that can be real because of their relation to our

19 William James, "The Perception of Reality," in *The Principles of Psychology* (New York: Henry Holt, 1890), selections from pp. 291–294.

emotional and active lives. Simply put, reality is what stimulates and interests us, and these interests ultimately determine what is real. A newly perceived object becomes part of one of our "real worlds" when it can be brought into a consistent relationship with the other objects that are already in that particular real world. In this way, we gradually build up and increase the contents we recognize as part of our reality.

Although rejecting the scientific method as the exclusive determinant of reality, William James was willing to employ it to learn the secrets of one particular reality and the self that was part of that reality. But he did not look for cosmic mind or reason, as some idealists would.

Objections to Pragmatism

Is pragmatism an acceptable way of getting beyond the disputes between materialism and idealism? Or is it muddled thinking? Does pragmatism give us a clear notion of what it understands to be real? Some pragmatists claimed to know only their experiences, which critics argue is a claim of idealism. Peirce, in fact, eventually adopted a version of idealism. But if we know only our experiences, how can we maintain the pragmatic belief in an objective physical reality?

Are pragmatists correct, also, in holding that the mind and its ideas are only instruments for the pursuit of interests? Don't people create disinterested mathematical theories, try to understand the universe in a dispassionate way, and attempt to investigate philosophical questions in an objective way that is not distorted by our interests and emotions? The mind and its ideas, say the pragmatists, exist to fulfill desires. Then how to explain the commitment to dispassionate scientific inquiry? Why do we place such a stress on impartiality when seeking truth and not more reliance on the subjective impulses of the mind?

Consider, finally, whether pragmatism erases the distinction between the mind and the universe, between our knowledge of facts and the existence of facts apart from our knowledge.[20] When pragmatism emphasizes that multiple realities exist because of the mind's capacity to have multiple interests, does this imply that there is no reality apart from the mind? Does it mean that there is no configuration of things aside from what we may think or desire? This seems close to the version of pragmatism that is being proposed by James and Dewey. Of course, pragmatists do not completely deny the existence of a world independent of the presence of human beings, yet they do deny that anything counts as "real" unless it is related to human interests and emotions. We later explore some of the implications of these ideas when, subsequently, we turn to discussing the ideas of recent "pragmatic idealists."

QUESTIONS

1. What are the assumptions of materialism and idealism that pragmatism ignores?
2. In what respects does pragmatism incorporate materialism and idealism?
3. If you were a pragmatist, how would you reconcile your belief that you can know only your experiences with your belief that an objective reality exists?
4. Compare and contrast the everyday and philosophical meanings of *pragmatist*.

---

20 See Frankel, *Golden Age*, 7.

PHILOSOPHY AT THE MOVIES

© Archives du 7eme Art/Photos 12/Alamy

Watch *Hilary and Jackie* (1998), the true story of a brilliant musician, Jacqueline du Pré, who gives up everything to pursue her career only to succumb to a fatal disease, and her sister, Hilary, who pursues a domestic life with husband and children and witnesses her sister's decline. The movie is divided into three parts: The first, labeled "Hilary and Jackie" shows reality from the point of view of both Hilary and Jackie; the second, marked "Hilary," shows reality from Hilary's point of view; and the third, marked "Jackie" shows much of the same reality as "Hilary," but now from the point of view of Jackie. At three points these realities diverge: when Kifer first visits the du Pré home, when Hilary tells Jackie in a darkened bedroom that she is engaged to Kifer, and when Kifer has sex with Jackie. To what extent does this movie illustrate the pragmatic view of what reality is?

3.4 Reality and Logical Positivism

We saw that pragmatism attempts to understand reality in terms of pragmatic consequences. However, another influential modern philosophy ends by rejecting all metaphysical attempts to understand reality. This is the outlook of **logical positivism**, which concentrates on language and meaning.

Like pragmatism, logical positivism is a reaction to the disputes between idealists and materialists. Pragmatism reacts by objecting that these disputes are pointless because they do not focus on "fruits, consequences, facts." Logical positivists react by objecting that idealists and materialists never stop to look carefully at the meaning of the language they use. In fact, positivist philosophers have claimed, the trouble with all metaphysical approaches to reality, including those of the pragmatists, is that the language they use is essentially meaningless. All metaphysics, logical positivists claim, is literally nonsense.

One of the most influential of the logical positivists was Alfred J. Ayer (1910–1989), a British philosopher. According to Ayer, philosophers have to be extremely careful to ensure that they are not speaking nonsense, and almost all metaphysics is mere nonsense. To clarify his point, Ayer offered "a criterion by which it can be determined whether or not a sentence is literally meaningful":

critical thinking

Is Ayer's assumption correct that all meaningful statements are tautologies or statements of fact? Are there other possibilities?

> I divide all genuine [meaningful] propositions into two classes: those which, in this terminology, concern "relations of ideas," and those which concern "matters of fact." The former class comprises the *a priori* propositions of logic and pure mathematics, and these I allow to be necessary and certain only because they are analytic. That is, I maintain that the reason why these propositions cannot be confuted in experience is that they do not make any assertion about the empirical world, but simply record our determination to use symbols in a certain fashion. Propositions concerning empirical matters of fact, on the other hand, I hold to be hypotheses, which can be probable but never certain. . . . I require of an empirical hypothesis . . . that some possible sense-experience should be relevant to the determination of its truth or falsehood. If a putative proposition fails to satisfy this principle, and is not a tautology, then I hold that it . . . is neither true nor false, but literally senseless.[21]

QUICK REVIEW
Ayer's "criterion of meaning" says a statement is meaningful only if it is a tautology (true by definition) or an empirically verifiable statement (verifiable in principle by observation). Because metaphysical statements are neither tautologies nor empirically verifiable, Ayer says they are meaningless.

Ayer's point is that there can only be two kinds of meaningful statements: (1) tautologies, or "relations of ideas," and (2) empirical hypotheses, or "statements

21 Alfred J. Ayer, *Language, Truth, and Logic*, 2nd ed. (New York: Dover, 1952), 31.

of fact." Tautologies are statements that are true by definition, such as "All bachelors are unmarried," "His sister is a female," and "Triangles have three sides." Tautologies, sometimes called *analytic propositions,* are propositions in which the meaning of the predicate is part of the meaning of the subject. Tautologies do not give us any real information about the world but only about the meanings of words. Statements of fact, on the other hand, are those that can, at least in theory, be verified by some imaginable observation of the world around us. Examples are "It's raining," "California is about three thousand miles from New York," and "A spirochete causes syphilis." Statements of fact, which are sometimes called *synthetic* or *empirical statements,* do give us information about the world. They tell us that the world is one way rather than another. We cannot know whether such statements are true without making some observations of the world.

critical thinking

Does Ayer assume that statements of fact—that is, statements about what the real universe around us is like—must be based on what we observe? Is this assumption correct? What else might statements of fact be based on?

critical thinking

Suppose I didn't know what observations would lead me to accept a proposition as true or reject it as false. Would it necessarily follow that I do not understand it?

If a statement is neither a tautology nor a statement of fact, Ayer argued, then it is meaningless; it is nonsensical. Because metaphysical statements are neither tautologies nor statements of fact, he concluded, they are meaningless. Look at how he argues for this point:

> The criterion which we [will] use to test the genuineness of apparent statements of fact [such as those of metaphysics] is the criterion of verifiability. We say that a sentence is factually significant to any given person if, and only if, he knows how to verify the proposition which it purports to express—that is, if he knows what observations would lead him, . . . to accept the proposition as being true, or reject it as being false. If, on the other hand, the putative proposition is of such a character that the assumption of its truth, or falsehood, is consistent with any assumption whatsoever concerning the nature of his future experience, then, as far as he is concerned, it is, if not a tautology, a mere pseudo proposition. The sentence expressing it may be emotionally significant to him; but it is not literally significant. . . .
>
> In the first place, it is necessary to draw a distinction between practical verifiability and verifiability in principle. Plainly we all understand, in many cases believe, propositions which we have not in fact taken steps to verify. Many of these are propositions which we could verify if we took enough trouble. But there remain a number of significant propositions concerning matters of fact which we could not verify even if we chose, simply because we lack the practical means of placing ourselves in the situation where the relevant observations could be made. A simple and familiar example of such a proposition [in 1936] is the proposition that there are mountains on the further side of the moon. No rocket has yet [in 1936] been invented which would enable me to go and look at the further side of the moon, so that I am unable to decide the matter by actual observation. But I do know what observations would decide it for me, if, as is theoretically conceivable, I were once in a position to make them. And therefore I say that the proposition is verifiable in principle, if not in practice, and is accordingly significant. On the other hand, such a metaphysical pseudoproposition as "the Absolute enters into, but is itself incapable of, evolution and progress," is not even in principle verifiable. For one cannot conceive of an observation which would enable one to determine whether the Absolute did, or did not, enter into evolution and progress. Of course it is possible that the author of such a remark is using English words in a way in which they are not commonly used by English-speaking people, and that he does, in fact, intend to assert something which could be empirically verified. But until he makes us understand how the proposition that he wishes to express would be verified, he fails to communicate anything to us. And if he admits, as I think the author of the remark in question would have admitted, that his words were not intended to express either a

PHILOSOPHY AND LIFE

Parallel Universes

Max Tegmark, a physicist/astronomer highly respected as an international expert on the nature of the universe, has argued that there must be parallel universes: other areas of space that are about the size of the universe that is visible to us and that are exact replicas of own visible universe. (The "visible universe" consists of a sphere around us whose farthest point is the longest distance from us that light has been able to travel during the 14 billion years since the Big Bang began everything.) Such a replica of our visible universe would have to contain "a person who is not you but who lives on a planet called earth, with misty mountains, fertile fields and sprawling cities. . . . The life of this person has been identical to yours in every respect."

The idea that there must be another area of space that is an exact copy of our visible universe—and that contains an exact copy of you—is required by the fact that astronomers have concluded that the entire cosmos—that is, everything that extends beyond our visible universe—is infinite and is uniformly filled with galaxies, stars, and planets like our own visible universe. A volume of space the size of own visible universe, if it were fully packed with matter, could contain only up to 10^{118} protons. In a different volume of space the same size, each of these protons may or may not, in fact, be present. Hence there are, at most, only 2 to the 10^{118} different possible arrangements of protons in a volume of space the size of our own visible universe. That means that, in a volume of space larger than 2 to the 10^{118} times the volume of our own visible universe, the arrangements of protons would have to start repeating. Beyond that huge volume, then, there would have to be a volume of space the size of our own visible universe that was, proton for proton, an exact copy of our own visible universe. Because observations of the cosmos indicate that it is infinite in volume, this means that somewhere in that infinite volume there must be an area of space the size of our own visible universe that is an exact replica of the volume of space we call our "visible universe" and that therefore includes an exact replica of you.

QUESTIONS

1. Tegmark makes assumptions about what lies beyond the visible universe (the part of the universe that we cannot perceive with even the most powerful telescopes or any other instruments we could possibly invent). In what sense do you think such parallel universes are "real"?
2. What would a materialist, an idealist, a pragmatist, a phenomenologist, or a logical positivist probably have to say about the reality of these parallel universes?
3. Tegmark says his parallel universes are not part of the "domain of metaphysics" but belong to the "frontiers of physics." What do you think he means by this? Do you agree?

Source: Max Tegmark, "Parallel Universes," *Scientific American*, April 14, 2003; see also Joel Achenbach, "The Multiuniverse," *National Geographic*, August 2003.

tautology or a proposition which was capable, at least in principle, of being verified, then it follows that he has made an utterance which has no literal significance even for himself.[22]

Logical positivists such as Ayer would view not only metaphysical statements as meaningless but most ethical and religious claims as well, because most of them are neither tautologies nor statements of fact that can be verified by observation. Thus, they would consider the following statements nonsensical: "God exists," "God doesn't exist," "Lying is wrong," "Lying is right," "A moral law operates in the universe," and "The best form of government is the one that governs least." The fact that very few people consider such statements meaningless raises a question: How

22 Ibid., 33–36.

can such statements be rejected as meaningless when so many people believe that they are filled with meaning?

Logical positivists have replied that although metaphysical statements are not literally meaningful, they nevertheless carry another, non-literal kind of meaning: They express emotion. Much as lyrical poets use words to express feelings, metaphysicians—and philosophers in general, they claim—use words to express feelings and not to represent facts about the world. Here is how the point is put by Rudolf Carnap (1891–1970), another analyst of the logical positivist school:

> Now many linguistic utterances are analogous to laughing in that they have only an expressive function, no representative function. Examples of this are cries like "Oh, Oh" or, on a higher level, lyrical verses. The aim of a lyrical poem in which occur the words "sunshine" and "clouds" is not to inform us of certain meteorological facts, but to express certain feelings of the poet and to excite similar feelings in us. A lyrical poem has no assertive sense, no theoretical sense, it does not contain knowledge.
>
> The meaning of our anti-metaphysical thesis may now be more clearly explained. This thesis asserts that metaphysical statements—like lyrical verses—have only an expressive function, but no representative function. Metaphysical statements are neither true nor false, because they assert nothing, they contain neither knowledge nor error, they lie completely outside the field of knowledge, of theory, outside the discussion of truth or falsehood. But they are like laughing, lyrics, and music, expressive. They express not so much temporary feelings as permanent emotional or volitional dispositions. Thus, for instance, a metaphysical system of **monism** [the view that reality is only one kind of thing—either matter or spirit, but not both] may be an expression of an even and harmonious mode of life, a dualistic system [the view that reality is made up of two kinds of things, matter and spirit] may be an expression of the emotional state of someone who takes life as an eternal struggle. . . . Realism [materialism] is often a symptom of the type of constitution called by psychologists extroverted, which is characterized by easily forming connections with men and things; idealism, of an opposite constitution, the so-called introverted type, which has a tendency to withdraw from the unfriendly world and to live within its own thoughts and fancies.
>
> Thus we find a great similarity between metaphysics and lyrics. But there is one decisive difference between them. Both have no representative function, no theoretical content. A metaphysical statement, however—as distinguished from a lyrical verse—seems to have such a content, and by this not only is the reader deceived, but the metaphysician himself. He believes that in his metaphysical treatise he has asserted something, and is led by this into argument and polemics against the statements of some other metaphysician. A poet, however, does not assert that the verses of another are wrong or erroneous; he usually contents himself with calling them bad.
>
> The non-theoretical character of metaphysics would not be in itself a defect; all arts have this non-theoretical character without thereby losing their high value for personal as well as for social life. The danger lies in the *deceptive* character of metaphysics; it gives the illusion of knowledge without actually giving any knowledge. This is the reason why we reject it.[23]

QUICK REVIEW
Carnap argued that meaningless metaphysical statements express emotions.

Metaphysical statements about reality, then, are meaningless. They serve only to express our feelings about reality.

23 Rudolph Carnap, "The Rejection of Metaphysics" (1935), in *Twentieth-Century Philosophy: The Analytic Tradition*, ed. Morris Weitz (New York: Free Press, 1966), 215–216.

thinking critically • Categorical Syllogism Arguments

The key argument Ayer earlier makes is this:

> All meaningful statements are tautologies or empirically verifiable.
> Metaphysical statements are not tautologies or empirically verifiable.
> Therefore, metaphysical statements are not meaningful.

This is an interesting argument but it does not fit into any of the logical forms we studied earlier, so we don't yet have a way of testing whether it is valid or not. Ayer's argument is what we call a "categorical argument," and we'll turn now to explaining how to determine whether a categorical argument is valid.

Categorical arguments are made up of categorical claims. A **categorical claim** is a claim that has a subject and a predicate and that uses the connectives "all," "some," "no," "not," "is," and "are." For example: "All dogs are small mammals" and "Some of the apples in this box are not edible." A categorical claim says that all or some of a general category of things (like "dogs") is included in another general category of things (like "small mammals"), or that some or all of a general category of things (like "apples in this box") is excluded from another general category of things (like "edible things"). Categorical claims always have exactly two terms, one for the subject and one for the predicate. The following statements are all categorical claims; in parentheses are explanations of how the claim should be interpreted:

(1) *All religious statements are meaningful.* (The whole category of religious statements is a part of the category of meaningful statements.)
(2) *No religious statements are meaningful.* (The whole category of religious statements is excluded from the whole category of meaningful statements.)
(3) *Some religious statements are meaningful.* (A part of the category of religious statements is a part of the category of meaningful statements.)
(4) *Some religious statements are not meaningful.* (A part of the category of religious statements is excluded from the whole category of meaningful statements.)

There are only four kinds of categorical claims, and the preceding four statements are examples of those four. If we use capital letters in place of the terms of the four statements mentioned (R for "religious statements" and M for "meaningful statements"), we can see that these four kinds of categorical claims have the following four logical forms:

QUICK REVIEW
The logical form of a categorical claim is the result of replacing both of its terms with capital letters. There are four kinds of categorical claims and they have these four logical forms: "All R are M," "No R are M," "Some R are M," and "Some R are not M."

(1*) All *R* are *M*. (The whole category of R is a part of the category of M.)
(2*) No *R* are *M*. (The whole category of R is excluded from the whole category of M.)
(3*) Some *R* are *M*. (A part of the category of R is a part of the category of M.)
(4*) Some *R* are not *M*. (A part of the category of R is excluded from the whole category of M.)

Notice that the explanations in parentheses indicate whether the terms refer to a whole category or to only part of a category. This is important, as we'll see in a moment.

QUICK REVIEW
A categorical syllogism has two premises and a conclusion that are a combination of the four categorical claims, and that contain three terms.

Now we can explain what a "categorical argument" is. A categorical argument is one that consists entirely of some combination of the four categorical claims. The most important kind of categorical argument is called the **categorical syllogism**. The categorical syllogism contains exactly *two premises* and *a conclusion*. In addition, a categorical syllogism contains only *three terms*. For example, here is a categorical syllogism that is based on Berkeley's argument for idealism:

(5) All ideas exist in the mind.
(6) All of the things we perceive are ideas.
(7) Therefore, all of the things we perceive exist in the mind.

Suppose we assign the following letters to represent the three terms of this syllogism:

I = ideas

M = things that exist in the mind

P = things we perceive

Then this syllogism has the following form:

(5*) All *I* are *M*. (The whole category of I is a part of the category of M.)
(6*) All *P* are *I*. (The whole category of P is a part of the category of I.)
(7*) Therefore, all *P* are *M*. (The whole category of P is a part of the category of M.)

As we will see, a syllogism with this form is valid. Notice that one of the terms, *I*, occurs in both of the premises but not in the conclusion. This term is called the "middle term" because it relates the other two terms to each other. In the categorical form mentioned earlier, premise (5*) relates M to I and premise (6*) relates I to P, so the conclusion (7*) says M must be related to P.

How can we figure out whether a categorical syllogism is invalid? One way is to use the method we've seen before: Try to imagine a situation in which the premises are true, but the conclusion is false. But this method, as we've seen, has some drawbacks.

QUICK REVIEW
Categorical claims can be negative or positive, and their terms can refer to a whole category or to a part of a category. A term that occurs immediately after "all," or a term that occurs anywhere in a claim after "no" or "not" refers to a whole category.

Fortunately, logicians have developed four rules for determining whether or not a categorical syllogism is valid. But to understand the rules, you need to keep two things in mind. First, categorical claims can be affirmative or negative; that is, they can say that one category *is* included in another, or that it is *not* (i.e., that it is *excluded* from the other). For example: "All *A* are *B*" (e.g., "all abortions are bad") is affirmative, and "No *A* are *B*" (e.g., "no abortions are bad") is negative. Second, as we mentioned earlier, the *terms* in a categorical statement can refer to a whole category of things or to a part of the category. When we say "All X," we are referring to the whole category of X. When we say "No X is Y" we are saying that the whole category of X is excluded from the whole category of Y, so both X and Y refer to a whole category. When we say "Some X are not Y," we are saying that a part of the category of X is excluded from the whole category of Y's, so only the Y term refers to a whole category. And when we say "Some X are Y," we are saying that a part of the category of X is a part of the category of Y, so neither X nor Y refer to a whole category. *As a rule, a term that occurs immediately after "all," or a term that occurs anywhere in a claim after "no" or "not" refers to a whole category.* In the following summary, the terms that refer to a whole category are in underlined bold italics:

QUICK REVIEW
A categorical argument is valid when and only when: (1) the middle term refers to a whole category in a premise; (2) If a term in the conclusion refers to a whole category, it also refers to the whole category in a premise; (3) Both premises are not negative; (4) If a premise is negative, the conclusion must be negative.

All ***<u>A</u>*** are B	Some A are B
No ***<u>A</u>*** are ***<u>B</u>***	Some A are not ***<u>B</u>***

Now here are the four rules that a valid categorical syllogism must follow; if a categorical syllogism breaks one or more of these rules, it is invalid:

1. The middle term (the term that is present in both premises but absent from the conclusion) must refer to a whole category in at least one premise.
2. If a term in the conclusion refers to a whole category, it must also refer to the whole category in one of the premises.
3. Both premises must not be negative.
4. If one of the premises is negative, then the conclusion must be negative.

You can see more clearly why syllogisms that break these rules are invalid by testing each rule. Just find an argument that breaks the rule and then imagine a situation in which the premises are true and the conclusion is false. Here, for example, is an argument that breaks rule 1:

Some Men in this town are Barbers.
Some Men in this town are Tall.
Therefore, some Barbers in this town are Tall.

Now imagine a situation in which all the barbers in town are short men, and all non-barbers are tall men. Then the premises would be true, but the conclusion false; so the argument, which breaks rule 1, is not valid. You should test the other rules on your own.

One more thing: As with other kinds of arguments, if you know a certain categorical argument is valid (or invalid), then any other argument *with the same logical form* will also be valid (or invalid). So if you memorize the logical forms of the common kinds of categorical arguments, and know which are valid and which are invalid, then you can easily tell whether other arguments with the same form are valid or not.

Now let's return to Ayer's argument:

All meaningful statements are tautologies or empirically verifiable.
Metaphysical statements are not tautologies or empirically verifiable.
Therefore, metaphysical statements are not meaningful statements.

Let's assign these letters to the three terms of Ayer's argument:

M: Meaningful statements
T: Statements that are tautologies or empirically verifiable
E: Metaphysical statements.

Here is the logical form of Ayer's categorical syllogism:

All M is T
No E are T
So: No E are M

You should now be able to check whether this argument is valid by using the four preceding rules.

Categorical arguments are combinations of the four main forms of categorical claims: "All A are B," "No A are B," "Some A are B," and "Some A are not B." It is not always easy to translate the claims of an ordinary English argument into one of these four forms. So here are some suggestions to help you.

First, when translating English sentences into their logical forms, keep in mind that terms have to refer to *categories of things*. This means that when an English sentence consists of a subject and a verb, both the subject and the verb have to be interpreted as categories of things. You can do this by adding "things that are . . ." or "things that . . ." to the subject and verb. For example, you should interpret "All wolves run in a pack" as meaning "All things that are wolves are things that run in a pack," and interpret "Some of the sheep hid from the wolf" as meaning "Some of the things that are sheep are things that hid from the wolf."

Second, here are some English expressions you should translate as "All X are Y":

Every X is Y	Only Y's are X's
Whatever is X is Y	Nothing is X without being Y
If something is X then it is Y	Nothing is X unless it is Y

Here are some English expressions that should be translated as "No X are Y":

X's are not Y's	Not a single X is Y
Each X is not Y	Not any X is Y
Whatever is X is not Y	If something is X, then it isn't Y

These English expressions should be translated as "Some X are Y":

One or more X's are Y's	X's are sometimes Y's
There are X's that are Y's	A few X's are Y's

And here are some English expressions you should translate as "Some X's are not Y's":

One or more X's are not Y's	Sometimes X's are not Y's
There are X's that are not Y's	Not all X's are Y's

Now that we've seen what kind of argument Ayer has given us, and how to figure out whether this kind of argument is valid, let's examine some objections to the premises of Ayer's argument.

Objections to Logical Positivism

Although many contemporary philosophers, especially in the United States and England, have embraced the views of the positivists, others continue to feel that they are mistaken. One of the fundamental objections to the views of the logical positivists in particular is that their basic "criterion of meaning" is an unproved assumption. As we've seen, logical positivists like Ayer argue in this way:

All meaningful statements are tautologies or empirically verifiable.

Metaphysical statements are not tautologies or empirically verifiable.

Therefore, metaphysical statements are not meaningful statements.

QUICK REVIEW
Critics of logical positivism say that its criterion of meaning is unprovable and that if it is applied to itself, it implies that it is itself meaningless.

But, say critics, the first premise in this argument is not proved by the analysts and can never be proved. Perhaps utterances other than those that are tautologies or empirically verifiable *can* transmit meaning and truth. Moreover, critics contend, if we apply the logical positivists' criterion of meaning to **positivism** itself, it would turn out to be meaningless. The criterion of meaning states that "all *meaningful statements* are either tautologies or empirically verifiable." But this statement is not a tautology because the dictionary does not define *meaningful statements* as "either tautologies or empirically verifiable." Neither is this statement empirically verifiable because we cannot verify it by observing the world around us. So, critics say, by its own standards the criterion of meaning is meaningless and just the analysts' own "expression of emotion."

Other critics have argued that in refusing to discuss metaphysical questions about reality merely because they do not meet their own unproved assumptions about meaning, the analysts have in effect pretended that our real human questions and problems do not exist. By taking this approach, logical positivists have avoided the many hard questions raised by materialists, idealists, and pragmatists. But that is playing ostrich. The problems, critics contend, are still there, and people still continue to think about them. But in failing to deal with these problems, logical positivists have turned away from dealing with some of the most profound and significant issues that human beings face. This, critics claim, is one of the most disappointing aspects of logical positivism: its failure to discuss questions that really matter.

Many philosophers who were once sympathetic to logical positivism have noticed this failure and have come to recognize as legitimate not just one or two but many modes of meaning, including those dealing with the questions posed by metaphysics. Ultimately, they may agree with the critics of logical positivism, who defend the philosopher's right and need to discuss questions not only of language but also of metaphysics, morality, religion, politics, and education. Certainly, any inquiry into ourselves, any search for what we are, that ignores these aspects of our experience seems incomplete.

QUESTIONS

1. In what sense do the logical positivists apply the adjective *meaningless* to nonsensical statements? Can something be intellectually meaningless but emotionally meaningful? Can you give an example?
2. What is your reaction to the following claims of Alfred J. Ayer?

   > It is impossible to find a criterion for determining the validity of ethical judgment[s] . . . because they have no objective validity whatsoever. If a sentence makes no statement at all, there is obviously no sense in asking whether what it says is true or false. . . . They are pure expressions of feeling . . . unverifiable for the same reason as a cry of pain or a word of command is unverifiable—because they do not express genuine propositions.[24]

   What is the logical form of the categorical argument Ayer is proposing here? Is his argument valid? Is it sound?
3. How valid do you consider the criticism that the logical positivist's definition of what is meaningful makes a sham of the things that we take seriously? Express this criticism in the form of a valid argument. How could a logical positivist respond to your argument?
4. Some people charge that the logical positivist's position is inconsistent and self-contradictory. Why do they say this? Do you agree?
5. What would you say is the primary contribution of logical positivism to philosophy?

PHILOSOPHY AT THE MOVIES

Watch *Contact* (1997) in which scientist Ellie Arroway discovers a radio signal coming from the star Vega that has to have been transmitted by nonterrestrial intelligent beings and that when deciphered includes plans for a machine to transport a human to Vega, a journey that Ellie undertakes although few later believe she did so. To what extent are Ellie's beliefs and outlook on the world consistent with the logical positivist view of what is real; to what extent do they diverge? In what ways does the logical positivist view of reality conflict with Palmer Joss's view of reality? How would a logical positivist respond to the events Ellie experiences on her "journey"? How would a logical positivist respond to Ellie's views at the very end of the movie?

3.5 Antirealism: The Heir of Pragmatism and Idealism

Throughout much of the last century, the "new" philosophies of pragmatism and logical positivism overshadowed the earlier debates between idealists and materialists. Recently, however, some philosophers, including a number of feminists, have begun to espouse views that are in many ways a return to traditional idealism's rejection of the existence of an independent external reality, as well as a return to pragmatism's view that there are many "realities." These views, as we will see, are

24 Ayer, *Language, Truth, and Logic*, 107–109.

"postmodern" in the sense that they reject the "modern" belief in a single reality. We must examine these "new" views about reality because, as will become apparent, they have critically important implications about the relations between men and women. These new approaches to reality have been labeled *antirealist* by many contemporary philosophers to indicate that, like Berkeley, they reject the view that an external reality exists that is independent of our minds. There are many different kinds of antirealist views, such as views that deny the existence of mental phenomena or of supernatural phenomena or of mathematical objects. But here we focus on the kind of antirealism that denies the existence of an external physical world that is independent of the mind or its products. (In Chapter 6, we look at a kind of antirealism in science.) The opposite of antirealism is realism, which claims that some realm of objects exists. The kind of realism we are interested in discussing here is the kind that claims that there is an external world that is independent of our minds.

QUICK REVIEW
Contemporary antirealists who are characterizable as the heirs of pragmatism and idealism claim that (1) reality depends on the mind or its products, and (2) there are many distinct external realities. Views that assert claim 2 are "postmodern."

More precisely, **realism** is the view that a real world exists independent of our language, our thoughts, our perceptions, and our beliefs—that is, independent of the mind.[25] The realist holds that the features of this world around us would have been exactly the same as they are now even if no one had ever existed who could perceive them, think about them, or describe them with language. And these features will continue to be the same long after each of us is gone. Take, for example, the object in our sky that we refer to as the moon and describe as the largest satellite orbiting the earth. The realist holds that the moon would exist and continue to be the largest object orbiting the earth whether or not we or anyone else ever described it, perceived it, or thought of it in this or any other way.

QUICK REVIEW
Many contemporary antirealists argue that the features of reality depend on the language or system of concepts we use to describe or think about reality. Because there are different languages, there are different realities, each dependent on the mind and its system of concepts.

The realist holds, then, that an external world exists, a world whose existence and features don't depend on how, or even whether, anyone describes it, perceives it, or thinks about it. The antirealist, on the other hand, denies that such a world exists. **Antirealism**, as we use the term here, claims that the world or worlds we inhabit and everything in them depend completely or partially on how they are described, perceived, and thought about.

Unlike Berkeley, modern antirealists do not argue that all we know are our own sensations or ideas. Instead, the new antirealists base their views on language, arguing, in effect, that all we know are our own linguistic creations. These antirealists argue that when we think about or talk about reality, we must use a particular language with its own special way of describing things. Different languages describe the same reality in different ways, and each of these different descriptions describes the world as having different features. So, antirealists conclude, we cannot say that reality has features that are independent of our language. The features of reality depend on the language or system of concepts we use to describe or think about reality. For us, as an example,

"If a tree falls in the forest and no one is around to hear it, does it make a sound?"

© westphalia/iStockphoto.com

25 My account here follows the discussion of realism by philosopher John Searle in his unpublished paper "Is There a Problem About Realism?" presented on February 28, 1992, at Santa Clara University.

the moon exists because our language and way of thinking mark off a part of the sky as the moon, and in our language it is the largest satellite orbiting the earth. But our language did not have to mark off the sky in this particular way. In fact, if our language had partitioned the sky in a different way, we might not have counted the moon as the largest satellite orbiting the earth.

Proponents of Antirealism

For the antirealist, then, no reality is completely independent of the particular language or system of concepts we use. Moreover, our different languages and systems of concepts create different realities. Many contemporary philosophers have held this antirealist view, including Paul Feyerabend, Richard Rorty, Jacques Derrida, Liz Stanley, Sue Wise, Ruth Hubbard, Nelson Goodman, Hilary Putnam, and Dale Spender. Here, we concentrate on the arguments of Goodman, Putnam, and Spender.

Nelson Goodman was one of the first contemporary philosophers to argue that there is no independent real world: All reality depends on the way we humans have chosen to describe the world. Goodman asserts that we "make" reality or "worlds" by choosing a particular way of describing, or drawing boundaries around things:

> Now as we thus make constellations by picking out and putting together certain stars rather than others, so we make stars by drawing certain boundaries rather than others. Nothing dictates whether the sky shall be marked off into constellations or other objects. We have to make what we find, be it the Great Dipper, Sirius, food, fuel, or a stereo system.[26]

QUICK REVIEW
Goodman argues "we make what we find" in reality by "drawing certain boundaries rather than others" around things. By using different languages and systems of thought, we construct many realities, each dependent on the mind.

QUICK REVIEW
Putnam argues that just as different systems of counting indicate that different numbers of objects are in a container, what reality is depends on the system our minds use to describe it.

Goodman suggests, further, that we humans in fact construct and live in a multitude of different real worlds, each created by different and overlapping languages and systems of thought. Not only do artists, poets, and novelists create new and pleasing worlds by fashioning new languages and ways of thinking, but many others of us also create our own more or less pleasing, more or less successful worlds, each of them as "real" as the others. Goodman's theories, like those of other antirealists, echo those that, as we saw, the pragmatic philosopher William James once expressed.

Hilary Putnam, another prominent antirealist—one who has said that he accepts some of the claims of pragmatism—makes a similar argument.[27] Consider, he suggests, objects such as in Figure 3.1. Our ordinary system of counting would say there are three objects in Figure 3.1. But certain nonstandard systems of counting would say there are seven objects. In addition to the three objects A, B, and C, these nonstandard systems would "see" the object that consists of A and B together, the object that consists of B and C together, the object that consists

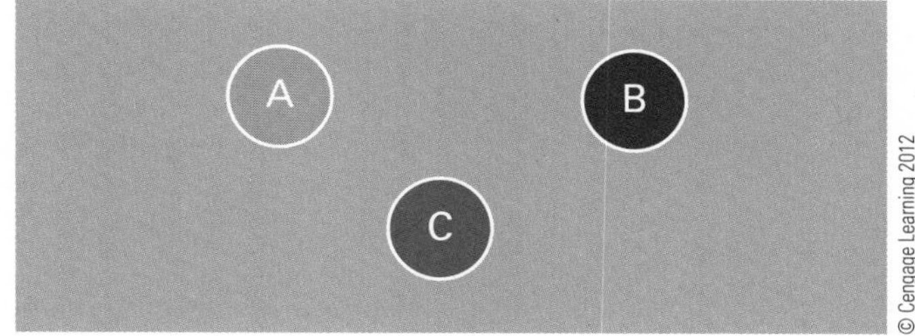

© Cengage Learning 2012

Figure 3.1 Hilary Putnam's circles—how many objects do *you* count?

26 Nelson Goodman, *Of Mind and Other Matters* (Cambridge, MA: Harvard University Press, 1984), 36.

27 Hilary Putnam discusses how his views are related to the "inheritance of pragmatism" in his book *Words and Life* (Cambridge, MA: Harvard University Press, 1994), see especially p. 152 where he summarizes the "theses" of pragmatism that he accepts. Putnam gives his counting argument in several places, including his book *The Many Faces of Realism* (LaSalle, IL: Open Court Publishing, 1987), 18–20.

of A and C together, and the object that consists of A, B, and C together. There is, Putnam concludes, no single correct answer to this question: How many objects are there in reality in the figure? What reality is depends on the system we use to describe it.

The antirealist position has been especially important to several feminist philosophers. For example, Dale Spender has also argued that there is no reality independent of our language:

> Language is not neutral. It is not merely a vehicle which carries ideas. It is itself a shaper of ideas, it is the programme for mental activity. In this context it is nothing short of ludicrous to conceive of human beings as capable of grasping things as they really are, of being impartial recorders of their world. For they themselves, or some of them, at least, have created or constructed that world and they have reflected themselves within it.
>
> Human beings cannot impartially describe the universe because in order to describe it they must first have a classification system. But, paradoxically, once they have that classification system, once they have a language, *they can see only certain arbitrary things.*[28]

QUICK REVIEW
Spender argues that we cannot know "things as they really are" because the classification system of the language we use "shapes" the reality we see. By creating our language, men have shaped our reality "to suit their own ends." But there are many other equally true realities and not just one true "objective" male reality.

The importance of the antirealist view for feminists such as Dale Spender is that it explains why the world that women ordinarily are forced to accept is so sexist. Often the words we use to describe women are demeaning; male experiences are taken as the norm for thinking about and describing the experiences of women. Women, for example, have long been referred to by the supposedly generic word *man.* If language creates reality, then it is not surprising that our common reality is focused on males:

> Given that language is such an influential force in shaping our world, it is obvious that those who have the power to make the symbols and their meanings are in a privileged and highly advantageous position. They have, at least, the potential to order the world to suit their own ends, the potential to construct a language, a reality, a body of knowledge in which they are the central figures, the potential to legitimate their own primacy and to create a system of beliefs which is beyond challenge . . .
>
> In the patriarchal order this potential has been realized.
>
> Males, as the dominant group, have produced language, thought and reality. Historically it has been the structures, the categories and the meanings which have been invented by males—though not of course by all males—and they have been validated by reference to other males. In this process women have played little or no part.[29]

Like Nelson Goodman, Dale Spender suggests that we must recognize that there are different female worlds or realities that are just as real as the male world that women are usually forced to inhabit:

> Most women within the women's movement are developing their skills at handling more than one reality. The pluralism of the movement is itself both a source and a manifestation of the ability to function in a multidimensional frame of reference. There are numerous "truths" available within feminism and it is falling into male defined (and false) patterns to try and insist that only one is correct. Accepting the validity of multidimensional reality predisposes women

28 Dale Spender, *Man Made Language*, 2nd ed. (Boston: Routledge & Kegan Paul, 1985), 139.
29 Ibid., 142–143.

> to accept multiple meanings and explanations without feeling that something is fundamentally wrong . . .
>
> The concept of multidimensional reality is necessary, for it allows sufficient flexibility to accommodate the concept of equality. Multiple reality is a necessary condition for the acceptance of the experience of all individuals as equally valuable and viable. Only within a multidimensional framework is it possible for the analysis and explanation of everyone to avoid the pitfalls of being rejected, of being classified as wrong.[30]

The new antirealists, then, do more than deny that there is one external real world independent of our thought and language. For the new antirealists, there are many different real worlds, each created by different, but perhaps overlapping, languages and ways of thinking. Moreover, each of these worlds is as real and valid as the others.

The views of such antirealists are sometimes described as "postmodern" views. **Postmodernism** is a late-twentieth-century movement that rejects the view—popular from the eighteenth to the early twentieth century—that there is only one reality and that through rational inquiry we are progressing toward an ever fuller unified scientific understanding of that one reality. Whereas the "modern" world of the eighteenth to the early twentieth century believed in this unified account of a single reality, our own "postmodern" world recognizes a Babel of different and contradictory accounts of many distinct and equally valid realities created by people from many different cultures and subcultures and from many different times and places. Postmodernism, then, is the view that there are many realities and that these realities are constructed by the many languages of the cultures and subcultures that now swirl around us.

Objections to Antirealism

Not everyone has been convinced by the postmodern arguments of the antirealists. In particular, several feminists have voiced concern over the implications of some antirealist claims, and we must consider their objections.

The antirealist claims that the worlds created by different languages and ways of thinking are equally real and valid and that there is no reality apart from our language and thought. But if all worlds are equally valid, then isn't the oppressive world created by sexist male language as valid a reality as any other? Moreover, if most men do not see women as oppressed so that in most men's reality women are not oppressed, don't we have to admit that this reality is entirely valid? And if men's reality is every bit as valid as women's reality, then shouldn't we stop criticizing men? As the feminist philosopher Jean Grimshaw writes,

> This highlights what is perhaps the most central problem of all in the theory of "multiple realities," all of which are equally "valid." Theories, ideas and ideologies are not only ways of "making sense" of the world. They may also be means by which one group of people may dominate or exercise control over another. And the fact that one group has power over or exploits another, cannot be reduced to anyone's belief that this is so; nor does the fact that someone does not understand their own experience in terms of oppression or exploitation necessarily mean that they are *not* oppressed or exploited. . . . [T]he assumption of multiple female "realities," all of which are "valid" and none of which have any claim to be

30 Ibid., 102–103.

> regarded as more adequate than any other, cannot provide a way of conceptualizing things such as oppression, exploitation, the domination of one social group by another.[31]

Grimshaw is pointing to a fundamental problem in antirealism. For the antirealist, something is real if and only if it is part of someone's language or way of thinking; otherwise, it is not real. But this means that if women do not believe they are being exploited, oppressed, or dominated, then in reality they are not being exploited, oppressed, or dominated. And if women speak and think in a male language that sees them as inferior, weak, and contemptible, then in reality they are inferior, weak, and contemptible. And if men think and speak as if nothing they do is domineering and oppressive, then this too is as real and as valid as the view that some male actions are oppressive and domineering.

QUICK REVIEW
Critics of Spender point out that if language created multiple realities that were all equally true, then the supposedly sexist reality created by sexist male language would be as true and acceptable as any other; sexism would not be an objective reality because there would be no one true objective reality.

Antirealism seems to imply, then, that sexism or oppression cannot be an objective reality because there is no objective reality. Sexism and the oppression of women cannot be real if men think otherwise in their world. And if men or women believe there is no sexism, then this belief is as valid and real as the feminist belief that sexism exists, and the matter is closed. Antirealism, then, does not allow the feminist to say that sexism is objectively real or that in reality all women suffer oppression, as long as men or women think and speak otherwise. It allows the feminist to say merely that sexism and oppression exist in her own world. Thus, antirealism seems to counter some of the basic claims of feminism.

Many other contemporary philosophers have argued that antirealism is mistaken. Philosopher John Searle is an example. He agrees that there are many different languages or systems for describing or "seeing" reality. But he claims that although the descriptions we give of reality depend on our language, the reality we are describing does not. Searle argues that Putnam and Goodman confuse our descriptions of reality (which depend on language) with the reality we are describing (which does not depend on language):

> From the fact that the *description* of any fact can only be made relative to a set of categories, it does not follow that the facts themselves only *exist* relative to a set of categories. . . . What counts as a correct application of the term "cat" . . . is up to us to decide and is to that extent arbitrary. But once we have fixed the meaning of such terms in our vocabulary by arbitrary definitions, it is no longer a matter of any kind of relativism or arbitrariness whether actual features of the world satisfy those definitions. We arbitrarily define the word "cat" in such and such a way; and only relative to such definitions can we say, "That's a cat." But once we have made the definitions and once we have applied the concepts relative to the system of definitions, whether or not something satisfies our definition is no longer arbitrary or relative.[32]

To understand Searle's point, let us return to Putnam's example of the three objects. In our ordinary system of counting objects, Figure 3.1 must be described as showing three objects. And in the proposed nonstandard system of counting objects, the figure must be described as seven objects. But in either case the objects—the reality—in the figure remain the same and do not change. Thus, our *description* of the figure depends on the system of concepts we use, but the *reality* of

---

31 Jean Grimshaw, *Philosophy and Feminist Thinking* (Minneapolis: University of Minnesota Press, 1986), 100, 102.

32 Searle, "Is There a Problem About Realism?" 10.

the figure does not depend on either system because it remains unchanged whichever system we use.

Is it possible to *prove* that the real world exists, as the realist says it does? Searle believes that a kind of proof is possible. To understand his argument, it will help if we first consider a point that Searle makes about Berkeley's idealism. Searle points out that "Berkeley saw that it was a problem for his account that if each person refers only to his own ideas when he speaks, then there is a question about how we succeed in communicating with other people." Searle's point is this: If idealists like Berkeley were correct, then each of us would know only his or her own particular ideas. If so, people could never talk to one another about the same thing; each of us could know and talk only about our own personal ideas, which no one else could know! Because people would never be talking about the same thing, they could never really communicate with and understand one another. But we do sometimes succeed in communicating with and understanding one another. So, Berkeley's idealism must be wrong: Sometimes, at least, we must be talking about the same external reality.

Searle makes a similar argument against the new antirealism of Putnam, Goodman, and Spender. If we believe that people at least sometimes understand one another's language, Searle claims, then we must believe that they are referring to an independent reality. For two people to understand each other's statements, their statements must mean the same thing to both of them. But for a statement to mean the same thing to two people, both must see their statements as having the same "conditions of satisfaction." That is, both people must take the same facts as making their statement true. This means that the two people must take their statements as expressing the same facts about the same reality. Thus, if people understand one another, they must assume the existence of an independent reality—an external world—that they are all talking about:

> The person who denies metaphysical realism presupposes the existence of a public language, a language in which he or she communicates with other people. But what are the conditions of possibility of communication in a public language? What do I have to assume when I ask a question or make a claim that is supposed to be understood by others? At least this much: if we are using words to talk about something, in a way that we expect to be understood by others, then there must be at least the possibility of something those words can be used to talk about. Consider any claim, from particular statements such as "my dog has fleas," to theoretical claims such as "water is made of hydrogen and oxygen," to grand theories such as evolution or relativity, and you will see that they presuppose for their intelligibility that we are taking metaphysical realism for granted.
>
> I am not claiming that one can prove metaphysical realism to be true from some standpoint that exists apart from our human linguistic practices. What I am arguing, rather, is that those practices themselves presuppose metaphysical realism. So one cannot within those practices intelligibly deny metaphysical realism, because the meaningfulness of our public utterances already presupposes an independently existing reality to which expressions in those utterances can refer.[33]

QUICK REVIEW
Searle argues that if people successfully communicate, they must assume there is one independent external reality because for people to understand each other's statements, they must be talking about the same independent external reality. So, our ability to communicate implies that antirealism is false.

Notice that Searle assumes that, sometimes at least, we understand and communicate with one another. But is it possible that we never really succeed in understanding one another? That we never really know what others are talking about

33 John Searle, "The Storm over the University," *New York Review of Books*, December 6, 1990, 40.

because we live in different worlds created by our different ways of thinking and speaking? For example, do men and women live in different worlds and therefore always misunderstand one another? Are all worlds equally real and valid, even those that deny the reality of sexism and oppression? Or is there only one real world in which we all live and about which we all talk and think? Is it possible to say that sexism, for example, is an objective reality for all women, even those who believe otherwise?

The debate between the realists and the antirealists has intensified during these last few years and has not yet been resolved. However, it is clear that a great deal hangs on this debate's resolution.

QUESTIONS

1. Compare the views of the new antirealists with the views of Berkeley. On what points do they agree? On what points do they differ?
2. Some people have claimed that if you are an antirealist, you cannot really care about changing or reforming the world. Can you explain what this claim means and how people who have made this claim would probably argue for it? Do you agree with their claim?
3. Putnam says that the same reality can be described as three objects or as seven objects. Is he assuming that reality is there to be described even before we describe it? If he is, then is he also assuming that reality exists independently of our descriptions and our language, just as the realist says it does?
4. Is it possible that each of us lives in a different world, as some antirealists have suggested? If so, can we ever really understand one another? Is each of us ultimately alone, locked in a private world that no one else can ever know or understand?

PHILOSOPHY AT THE MOVIES

Watch *He Said, She Said* (1991) in which Dan and Lorie are journalists who write columns with opposing views on issues and who eventually launch a TV program in which they do the same, and in which key events in their lives are replayed twice, once from Dan's perspective and once from Lorie's. Does this movie accept or reject the antirealist views of Goodman, Putnam, and Spender? Does it confirm or disconfirm Searle's argument against antirealism? Do men and women live in the kind of different worlds this movie suggests? Is there a "real" reality according to this movie?

3.6 Encountering Being: Reality in Phenomenology and Existentialism

Many people believe that the approaches to reality that we have examined are too distant from human reality. In trying to understand existence, traditional philosophies have reduced it to abstractions having little to do with our concrete existence and concerns. But there is nothing abstract about existing, or *being*. Existence, or *being*, is what is real. And existence or being involves the human individual who exists. We find this emphasis on human existence in existentialism and its predecessor, phenomenology.

Of course, we cannot hope, in a few pages, to achieve a full understanding of phenomenology and existentialism. Phenomenological and existentialist philosophers have written hundreds of books and thousands of articles about these approaches to reality. No summary can possibly do justice to these. All we can hope to accomplish in these few pages is to understand a few of the ideas about reality that these approaches have given us.

Phenomenology and existentialism share a number of outlooks on reality. For example, many phenomenologists and existentialists focus on the human condition as a key to what reality is. In particular, existentialists point out that we endure all kinds of pain: physical, emotional, and psychological. We feel anxious, uncertain, and indecisive. We know what it is to dread, to feel despair, and to suffer. Daily, we face the reality of death. True, we are not always conscious of death's imminence, but it is always with us. Anxiety, uncertainty, dread, suffering, and death all reveal something about reality, such as how contingent, fortuitous, and limited it is.

Building on such insights into the human condition, phenomenologists and existentialists claim that we shall never understand reality as long as we attempt to explain life and people merely objectively—from the outside, as it were. Materialism in particular has been guilty of this failure. In reducing individuals to material entities, materialism in effect turns people into objects.

The phenomenologist and the existentialist try to approach reality from the inside, by focusing on reality as it is subjectively revealed to our consciousness in its human condition. And they attempt to approach reality not by relying on theoretical presuppositions but by trying to examine and describe reality as it presents itself to our unprejudiced view. Truth about our human existence cannot be grasped and repeated by means of neat, objective statements. We experience truth, like everything else, through being; the truth is within, not without. Despite these general similarities, various points distinguish phenomenology and existentialism.

QUICK REVIEW
Phenomenology and existentialism approach reality as it is subjectively revealed in our human consciousness and human condition.

Phenomenology

To understand phenomenology, look at the term itself. *Phenomenology* consists of the Greek root *phenomenon*, meaning "what appears," and the suffix–*logy*, meaning "the study of." Without becoming enmeshed in the historical development of the term, we can say that as a method of investigation, *phenomenology* means the study of what appears to consciousness.

In his *Phenomenology of Perception*, Maurice Merleau-Ponty (1907–1961) says, "The aim of phenomenology is described as the study of experiences with a view to bringing out their 'essences,' their underlying reason."[34] As a philosophy, then, **phenomenology** has come to be regarded as the philosophical school that contends that being is the underlying reality that appears to our consciousness, which itself is being.

Husserl. The founder of phenomenology, Edmund Husserl (1859–1938), was born the same year that Dewey, the pragmatist, was born. For Husserl, the overriding issue is the reality that discloses itself to consciousness and that discloses itself as consciousness. You can think away everything, but you cannot think away thinking itself, which is consciousness. Reality, to the extent that it means anything to us, must be what is revealed to our consciousness, and, Husserl argued, the most fundamental reality that is revealed to us is our consciousness itself.

34 Quoted in Edo Pivcevic, *Husserl and Phenomenology* (London: Hutchinson University Library, 1970), 11.

To understand what Husserl is saying, it's helpful to know more about him.[35] An entry in his diary from 1906 provides a good look at what concerned him: "I have been through enough torment from lack of clarity and from doubt that goes back and forth. Only one need absorbs me: I must win clarity else I cannot live; I cannot bear life unless I can believe that I shall achieve it."[36] His intense desire for clarity and certainty was intensified by the **relativism** of the age, the widespread belief that there is no absolute truth but that all truth is relative to groups or persons, acculturation or personal bias. This relativism he saw as encouraged by the belief that scientific method is the only reliable way of knowing anything. In Husserl's view, however, relativism is self-contradictory. Anyone who denied the possibility of absolute certainty was involved in a contradiction, for to deny that possibility was to logically disallow the existence of "an objectively valid science."

Husserl attacked relativism not only because he viewed it as inconsistent but also because he felt that it generated undesirable social consequences. Writing in 1935, when the Nazis held power in Germany, Husserl viewed the European crisis as fundamentally attributable to the gradual erosion of the belief in rational certainty.

In Husserl's view, Europe had inherited rational certainty from the Greeks. The attitude of the Greek philosophers Plato and Aristotle was that of the disinterested spectator, the overseer of the world. With this attitude, they were led to a distinction between the presented and the real world, and ultimately to a universally valid truth—to truth in itself. Dewey, and pragmatism generally, condemned the Greek attitude for locking people into ultimate principles, self-evident views, and a hierarchy of absolute values. Dewey wanted philosophy to adopt the methods of natural science instead and to turn to the practical problems that beset individuals and society. In contrast, Husserl attributed the "crisis of European man" to a blind allegiance to the methods of natural science. His prescription was to revive the disinterested attitude and to return to rationality in the original Greek sense.

Specifically, Husserl objected to the application of the methods of natural science to the mental life, to treating mental phenomena as if they were material objects. Such thinking leads to a caricature of reality. What's more, he saw psychology as compounding this error. Having distinguished between minds and bodies, psychologists treated minds as if they were like bodies. Husserl proposed a radically different investigative method to avoid these errors, a method, he believed, that could ultimately be applied to all the sciences.

In his early works, Husserl developed the idea that to properly understand something philosophically we have to trace it back to the experience in which we first become directly aware or conscious of that thing, and then carefully describe what our awareness or consciousness of that thing is like. This was, he felt, a new kind of philosophical method, one that he described as a "phenomenological" method—that is, a method that studies how things appear to our consciousness.

With this phenomenological method, Husserl tried to explain the fundamental things we encounter—such as the physical world around us or the human world in which we live—by describing the kinds of consciousness through which we become aware of them. We become conscious of the physical world, for example, through the experience of perception, and we become conscious of the human world through the experience of empathy, and careful descriptions of these forms of consciousness—of perceiving and of empathizing—will produce, he felt, a deep philosophical understanding of the things these forms of consciousness reveal.

35 See W. T. Jones, *From Kant to Wittgenstein and Sartre* (New York: Harcourt Brace, 1969), 385–399.

36 Quoted in H. S. Spiegelberg, *The Phenomenological Movement* (The Hague: Martinus Nijhoff, 1965), 82.

The perfection of this phenomenological method, he felt, would demonstrate that the quest for certainty was not futile or frivolous. The phenomenological method itself would provide clarity and certainty and thereby establish a firm foundation for the sciences.

Vital to understanding Husserl's method is understanding his phenomenological stance, which he explained by contrasting it with what he called "the natural standpoint":

> Our first outlook upon life is that of natural human beings, imagining, judging, feeling, willing, "*from the natural standpoint.*" Let us make clear to ourselves what this means in the form of simple meditations which we can best carry on in the first person.
>
> I am aware of a world, spread out in space endlessly, and in time becoming and become, without end. I am aware of it, that means, first of all, I discover it immediately, intuitively, I experience it. Through sight, touch, hearing, etc., in the different ways of sensory perception, corporeal things, somehow spatially distributed, are *for me simply there*, in verbal or figurative sense "present," whether or not I pay them special attention by busying myself with them, considering, thinking, feeling, willing [them] . . .
>
> As it is with the world in its ordered being as a spatial present—the aspect I have so far been considering—so likewise it is with the world in respect to its *ordered being in the succession of time.* This world now present to me, and in every waking "now" obviously so, has its temporal horizon, infinite in both directions. . .
>
> [Moreover,] this world is not there for me as a mere *world of facts and affairs*, but, with the same immediacy, as a *world of values*, a *world of goods*, a *practical world*. . . . I find the things before me furnished not only with the qualities that befit their positive nature, but with value-characters such as beautiful or ugly, agreeable or disagreeable, pleasant or unpleasant, and so forth . . .
>
> We emphasize a most important point once again in the sentences that follow: I find continually present and standing over against me the one spatiotemporal fact-world to which I myself belong, as do all other men found in it. . . . This "fact-world," as the word already tells us, I find to *be out there*, and also *take it just as it gives itself to me as something that exists out there.* All doubting and rejecting of the data of the natural world leaves standing the *general thesis of the natural standpoint.* "The" world is as fact-world always there; at the most it is at odd points "other" than I supposed, this or that under such names as "illusion," "hallucination," and the like, must be struck *out of it*, so to speak; but the "it" remains ever . . . a world that has its being out there.[37]

QUICK REVIEW
For Husserl, the "natural standpoint" is our normal awareness of the world spread out in space and time, with value characteristics and as something that exists "out there."

People usually assume the natural standpoint toward the world. This consists of being aware of a world around us that is "simply there," whether or not we pay any special attention to it. This "fact-world," as Husserl calls it, we take to be "out there," and we experience it as a world in space and time. Occasionally, this fact-world differs from what we supposed: We experience illusions or hallucinations and what we thought was out there turns out not to be there. But even then we assume a world that has its being out there remains. Thus, although we may suspect or even reject parts of our experience, we most often unquestioningly accept the world as it presents itself to us, as something that always exists and remains out there. Indeed, this natural standpoint seems a most reasonable position, and Husserl calls our assumption that the world exists out there the "thesis" of the natural standpoint. Yet Husserl

---

37 Edmund Husserl, *Ideas: General Introduction to Pure Phenomenology*, trans. W. R. Boyce-Gibson (New York: Macmillan, 1962), sec. 27, 30. Copyright © 1962 by Macmillan Publishing Group. Reprinted with permission of Scribner, an imprint of Simon & Schuster Adult Publishing Group.

asks us to set it aside—to suspend judgment about the world out there and to focus, instead, on the nature of our consciousness or awareness of that world—that is, on how that world appears to us within our consciousness.

> Now instead of remaining at this [natural] standpoint, we propose to alter it radically. . . . The General Thesis according to which the real world about me is at all times known as a fact-world that has its being out there, does not consist of course in an explicit act, i.e., in an express judgement about [its] existence. Nevertheless, we can treat this potential and unexpressed thesis exactly like the thesis of an explicit judgement.
>
> We do not abandon this general thesis which we have adopted [in our everyday life], and we will make no changes in our convictions about it. . . . Yet we will make the thesis undergo a modification. While it remains what it is in itself, we will set it as it were "out of action." We "disconnect it" [from our considerations and] "bracket it." . . . We put out of action the general thesis which belongs to the essence of the natural standpoint, we place in brackets whatever it includes respecting the nature of its being: this entire natural world, therefore, which is continually "there for us" and "present at hand," and will always remain there, is still a "fact world" of which we continue to be conscious, even though we have chosen to put it in brackets.
>
> If I do this . . . I do not then [actually] deny this world, . . . [and] I do not [actually] come to doubt that it is there. . . . Instead, I use the "phenomenological" epoche which completely bars me from using any judgment that concerns spatio-temporal existence.[38]

QUICK REVIEW
Husserl asks us to "bracket" the natural standpoint by suspending judgment about whether the spatiotemporal world we experience really exists "out there."

Husserl does not want us to deny the thesis of the natural standpoint—that the fact-world has its being out there—but he asks us to set it aside, to suspend making any judgment about it. He asks us to "set it as it were out of action," to "disconnect it, bracket it." The natural standpoint remains, but we simply make no use of it. We suspend all judgments based on the natural standpoint. Husserl calls this suspension of judgment an "epoche." Although we continue to be conscious of the entire natural world, we phenomenologically bracket it, an act that "completely bars us from using any judgment that concerns spatio-temporal existence." By setting aside any judgments about the natural spatiotemporal world out there, we are able to concentrate our attention on our inner consciousness of this world. Husserl uses the example of dice to clarify what he means. Suppose that you are looking at a single die in the palm of your hand. What do you experience? From the natural standpoint, the die is a cube of a certain color and size and it exists in a certain space and time. There are dots on each side, from one to six of them. When you bracket this experience, as Husserl suggests, you do not doubt that you have the experience of seeing a die in your hand, but you do not assume that you actually have a die in your hand. After all, you may be dreaming,

Husserl asks you not to assume that a die has being in the mode of existence "out there."

© bahadir derici/iStockphoto.com

38 Ibid., sec. 33.

hallucinating, or imagining, and your hand may actually be empty. Husserl asks you not to assume that the die has being in the mode of existence "out there." This is what he means when he says that the phenomenological stance brackets all judgments about the world out there.

Husserl suggests, then, that we suspend the truth claims of our everyday cognitive processes about the natural world. Because in our ordinary lives we assume the natural standpoint, this suspension seems unnatural for most of us. Why should I not assume that I actually have a die in my hand when I can feel and see it? Husserl insists that bracketing, far from leaving us in a state of ignorance and skepticism, will present important truths that would otherwise elude us. He believes that these truths are important because whatever remains after bracketing is absolutely certain.

critical thinking

Does Husserl assume that people have the ability to bracket? Is this assumption correct?

The obvious question is this: What remains after bracketing? In general, Husserl believes that what survives is our consciousness and that ultimate reality consists of this consciousness:

> We have learnt to understand the meaning of the phenomenological epoche. But we are still quite in the dark as to its usefulness. . . . For what can remain over when the whole world is bracketed, including ourselves and our thinking? . . .
>
> Consciousness in itself has a being of its own which in its absolute uniqueness of nature remains unaffected by the phenomenologic disconnection. It therefore remains over as a "phenomenological residue," as a region of Being which is in principle unique, and that can become in fact the field of a new science—the science of Phenomenology. . . . Thus the "phenomenological epoche" is the necessary operation which renders "pure" consciousness accessible to us, and subsequently the whole phenomenological region.[39]

By *consciousness*, Husserl means that which involves both an act of intending (the experience of *being conscious of* something) and the intended object *(that of which* one is conscious). For example, when you look at the palm of your hand, you may be conscious of a die, on one of whose faces are three dots. Husserl points out that from the natural standpoint we hardly ever doubt this kind of fact. But, says Husserl, you can doubt that there was in fact a die on your palm. However, you cannot doubt you had the experience of seeing and feeling a die in the palm of your hand. Moreover, within this experience, it is possible to distinguish what you experienced—the die's sight and feel—(the intentional object) from your act of intending it (your experience of seeing and feeling). When you bracket by making no judgment about whether the die really exists, you are still certain that you are experiencing (seeing and feeling) what appears as a die. That is, bracketing the existence of what you experience still leaves both your consciousness of the die in the palm of your hand and what you are conscious of: the sight and feel of a die. Even when we try to bracket everything, we can still be certain of both our consciousness and what we are conscious of.

QUICK REVIEW
After bracketing, what remains is our consciousness, which involves both being *conscious of* something and *that of which* one is conscious. Analyzing this consciousness reveals *being.*

Further thought about how objects are present to consciousness persuaded Husserl to emphasize acts of consciousness more than the objects we are conscious of. Bracketing revealed to him deeper and deeper levels of consciousness that are impossible to understand without profound phenomenological training. Suffice it to say that when all is bracketed, including ourselves, Husserl contends that consciousness remains, so this is the most fundamental being, the ultimate reality of which we can be absolutely certain. When we bracket our whole outer world and

critical thinking

Does Husserl assume that if something remains after you make yourself think that nothing around you has existence, that thing is part of "ultimate reality"? Is this assumption correct?

39 Ibid.

focus on our inner consciousness, we tap our own essence and realize that something precedes our experiences—namely, the unique being of consciousness itself: "It therefore remains as a region of Being which is in principle unique."[40]

For Husserl, phenomenology was a new science of being. It revealed a sphere of being—consciousness—that is ultimate, in the sense that it presents itself with complete certainty and clarity within our experience even when we bracket everything out. Studying being is not, for Husserl, investigating another reality. It is delving deeper and deeper into the reality, the being, that is our own consciousness.

Heidegger. Profoundly influenced by Husserl's phenomenology, Martin Heidegger (1889–1976) made the question of being his primary approach to reality: What does it mean to say of something that it *is*, that it *exists*? Yet, although Heidegger used Husserl's phenomenological approach, he did not focus it on the study of pure consciousness as Husserl did. Instead, Heidegger focused on understanding our own human being or existence in the world. For Heidegger, the nature of reality is revealed by studying the nature of human beings, the way that humans exist in their ordinary day-to-day world. The problem with traditional thinking, claimed Heidegger, is that it is confused about being. Being does not consist of any of the qualities or properties of the individual—that is, being is not *what* an individual is. Neither is being a particular being, like a chair or a blade of grass. Neither is being a group of beings. Instead, being is the "is-ing" of things. This, wrote Heidegger, is a difficult notion to understand, but understanding being is the basic task of philosophy:

> Can something like being be imagined? If we try to do this, doesn't our head start to swim? Indeed, at first we are baffled and find ourselves clutching at thin air. A being—that's something, a table, a chair, a tree, the sky, a body, some words, an action. A being, yes, indeed—but being? . . . On the other hand, it is just as certain that we are constantly thinking being. We think being just as often as, daily, on innumerable occasions, whether aloud or silently, we say "This *is* such and such," "That other is *not* so," "That *was*," "It *will be*." In each use of a verb we have already thought, and have always in some way understood, being. We understand immediately "Today is Saturday; the sun is up." We understand the "is" we use in speaking, although we do not comprehend it conceptually. The meaning of this "is" remains closed to us. . . . [W]hat Aristotle says on one of his most important investigations in the *Metaphysics* has been completely forgotten. "That which has been sought for from of old and now and in the future and constantly, and that on which inquiry founders over and over again, is the problem What is being?" If philosophy is the science of being, then the first and last and basic problem of philosophy must be, What does being signify?[41]

Being is a difficult concept to understand because it is not a thing, although we may identify it with things. But this identification makes it all the more elusive, for we end up identifying the thing with being. One way to try to comprehend being is to think of it as that which remains when all the qualities and properties of the individual are set aside, leaving only the very act of existing: It is the "isness" of things as opposed to the "whatness" of things.

To try to get at the mysterious notion of being that Heidegger is attempting to get us to understand, you might try to meditate on what being is. For example, go

---

40 Quoted in Pivcevic, *Husserl and Phenomenology*, 11

41 Martin Heidegger, "Introduction," *The Basic Problems of Phenomenology* (Indiana University Press, 1975; original work published 1954), 13–14.

sit down in some quiet place, perhaps outdoors, and pick up something and put it in the palm of your hand: a blade of grass, a pebble, a pencil. Now try to get an appreciation of the miraculous fact that this little object actually exists, that it might never have existed and might never have been this thing here in your hand, that it might have been nothing. Try to get a sense of the huge gap between the nothingness that might have been and the sheer actuality of this little existing object in your hand. What is the actuality, the "isness," the existence that distinguishes this little object from the nonexistence it might have had? Can you reach the point of astonishment about existence that led Heidegger, in his essay "What Is Metaphysics?" to say: "Let the sweep of suspense take its full course, so that it swings back into the basic question of metaphysics which the nothing itself compels: Why are there beings at all, and why not rather nothing?"

How does one get at being in Heidegger's sense? What kind of method does one use to study being? As a student of Husserl, Heidegger believed that phenomenology, which lets the phenomenon "show itself . . . in the very way in which it shows itself," was the only appropriate method by which to study being.

Heidegger also felt that to understand being, one must begin by understanding the human kind of being, which he called "Dasein." *Dasein* is a German word that means "being there"; for Heidegger, being human is "being there" in this world into which we have been "thrown" by no choice of our own. Unlike "things" in this world, we humans can "question" or try to understand our own being. By becoming conscious of our own being, our Dasein, or how we exist within our world, we may better understand not only our own being, but the being that underlies everything:

> On what path can we advance toward the meaning of being in general? . . . Comportment toward beings belongs, on its part, to a definite being, the being which we ourselves are, the human Dasein. It is to the human Dasein that there belongs the understanding of being which first of all makes possible every comportment toward beings. The understanding of being has itself the mode of being of the human Dasein. . . . The analysis of the understanding of being in regard to what is specific to this understanding and what is understood in it or its intelligibility presupposes an analytic of the Dasein ordered to that end. This analytic has the task of exhibiting the basic constitution of the human Dasein and of characterising the meaning of the Dasein's being. In this ontological analytic of the Dasein, the original constitution of the Dasein's being is revealed to be temporality.[42]

QUICK REVIEW
For Heidegger, the job of philosophy is to study being, which is the individual's very act of existing within the human world. To understand reality, we must understand our own individual being in our world, or Dasein.

In his greatest work, *Being and Time*, Heidegger embarked on a phenomenological study of Dasein. He began by studying the ways Dasein appears to us in our "average everyday" lives. Heidegger concludes from this phenomenological study that Dasein is essentially finite and temporal: Our being is a temporal process of becoming the unique person we are through our personal decisions until our being ends with a death that is possible at any moment. We can also fail to become our real selves by conforming with the habits and conventions of our society and becoming an "anonymous one," an object for the use of others. If we are "authentic," we feel "anxiety" at the ever-present but unpredictable possibility of a death that ends everything it was still possible for us to become. But we also can be "inauthentic." We are inauthentic when we make ourselves feel an "indifferent tranquility" toward death and try to escape our responsibility for making ourselves who we are. We do this by telling ourselves that death lies in a distant future, so we have time to pursue all the possibilities that still lie before us and need not decide on them now. Doing

QUICK REVIEW
Dasein is temporal and finite—that is, bounded by death. If we are authentic, we respond with anxiety and face our responsibility for who we are; if inauthentic, we deny the present possibility of death and flee our responsibility for ourselves.

42 Ibid., 15–16.

this is inauthentic, says Heidegger, because we are denying the very real possibility of dying right now, and so avoiding our anxiety-filled responsibility for deciding who we will be while we yet live.

QUICK REVIEW
For Heidegger, reality, or being, is temporal and finite.

Thus, for Heidegger, reality, as revealed in his phenomenological study of our own human being in the world—our Dasein—is essentially a temporal and finite process of becoming who we are. To be real is to be temporal—embedded in time—and finite.

This emphasis on reality as being underlies the view of the human as an existential being. Interestingly, it is similar to some Buddhist views. Although Heidegger is undoubtedly a Western thinker, his thought has enough similarities to some Eastern ideas that he remarked, on reading the work of Zen scholar D. T. Suzuki, "If I understand this man correctly, this is what I have been trying to say in all my writings."[43] A Buddhist thinker such as Suzuki is generally more concerned with our inner being than with an objective, empirically verifiable reality. The world of the senses is short-lived and illusory. Because it is such, Eastern thinkers like Suzuki are preoccupied not with the reality of the outer world as it appears to us but rather with the reality that consists of our deepest inner being.[44] Heidegger was similarly preoccupied in his focus on human Dasein in *Being and Time.*

But it is to the ideas of the Western existentialist philosopher Søren Kierkegaard (1813–1855) that Heidegger's own views were most similar. It was from Kierkegaard, in fact, that Heidegger drew much of the inspiration for his views on "anxiety" and on "authentic" and "inauthentic" responses to the human condition. We must turn next, then, to look at Kierkegaard and at existentialism, an approach to being that he originated.

Existentialism

The emphasis that phenomenology, particularly in the hands of Heidegger, has given to consciousness and being takes a more concrete form in the philosophy of existentialism. Along with phenomenology, existentialism can be viewed partially as a reaction to the idea that an objective knowledge of the human can be attained by applying the scientific method to sociology and psychology. Like phenomenology, existentialism is unsympathetic to science as a cognitive enterprise, suspicious of scientism, and wary of applying the scientific method to the solution of our human problems. What interests existentialists is the subjectivity of the human individual and the individual's responsibility for who he or she is. But whereas phenomenologists might suggest that we become truly a self in the classical contemplation of the human condition, existentialists find self-definition in the passionate commitment to action. Also common to much existentialist thinking is the idea that the human condition gives rise to "angst," or anxiety. Some existentialists link anxiety to an awareness of our finitude and impending death, others to the meaninglessness or emptiness of life, and others to the extent to which we alone are responsible for what we have made of ourselves. These characteristics must be remembered to understand existentialism's metaphysical leanings.

Kierkegaard. In sketching the thought of Husserl, the section began by quoting from his diary. We glimpsed the energizing force behind his philosophy: the need

43 D. T. Suzuki, *Zen Buddhism*, ed. William Barrett (Garden City, NY: Doubleday Anchor Books, 1956), xi–xii.
44 Alan Watts, *The Way of Zen* (New York: Pantheon, 1957), 120–121.

for certainty. It is useful to compare this with an entry from the journals of the founder of modern existentialism, Søren Kierkegaard:

> What I really lack is to be clear in my mind what I am to do, not what I am to know, except insofar as a certain understanding must precede every action. The thing is to understand myself, to see what God really wishes me to do; the thing is to find a truth which is true *for me*, to find *the idea for which I can live and die*. What would be the use of discovering so-called objective truth, of working through all the systems of philosophy and of being able if required, to review them all and show up the inconsistencies within each system;—what good would it do me to be able to develop a theory of the state and combine all the details into a single whole, and so construct a world in which I did not live, but only held up to the view of others;—what good would it do me to be able to explain the meaning of Christianity if it had no deeper significance *for me* and *for my life*;—what good would it do me if truth stood before me, cold and naked, not caring whether I recognized her or not, and producing in me a shudder of fear rather than a trusting devotion? I certainly do not deny that I still recognize an *imperative of understanding* and that through it one can work upon men, *but it must be taken up into my life*, and that is what I now recognize as the most important thing.[45]

QUICK REVIEW
Kierkegaard's philosophy is focused on (1) getting clarity about what to do, (2) understanding reality through subjectivity, and (3) overcoming the gap between God and humanity.

Several themes are worth noting in this entry. First, Kierkegaard, like Husserl, is desperately seeking clarity. But unlike Husserl, who sought the clarity of an objective abstract knowledge, Kierkegaard wants clarity about action, about what he is to do. This emphasis on action and doing recurs in all existentialist thinking. It constitutes a lens through which existentialists view all philosophical questions, including metaphysical questions about what is real. Second, notice the emphasis Kierkegaard gives to the subjective, to what is "true *for me*" and has "significance *for me* and *for my life*." This is a recurring theme in existential philosophy and literature. Reality must be understood from the subjective perspective of the self who chooses and acts. Third, notice Kierkegaard's intense focus on decision and commitment, on what "I can live and die" for and what I "take up into my life." For the existentialists, as for Kierkegaard, our reality is an outcome of our choices and commitments. Through our decisions we create the reality of the self. Finally, observe Kierkegaard's religiosity, an aspect of his thought that is not shared by all existentialists. Kierkegaard was deeply religious, and the central issue of his life and thought was what it means to be a Christian.

Like Heidegger, Kierkegaard claimed that we experience "anxiety" because of our human finitude. Kierkegaard's words, in fact, read almost like they could have been written by Heidegger:

> Anxiety is being "afraid" when there is nothing to fear. We struggle with something in the dark, but we don't know what it is. From somewhere and yet nowhere seeps out a vague feeling of threat. Floating around in our body, unsettling our stomach, a generalized sense of menace possesses our whole being. This uneasiness has no identifiable cause. Our anxiety is seldom an object of consciousness that we can focus on; rather, it seems to be a deep, inner state of our being, which makes itself felt without the aid of conceptual thought—indeed against our fervent wish to be free of anxiety. In *angst* we confront the fundamental precariousness of existence; our being is disclosed as unspeakably fragile and tenuous. And when it bursts thru the protective shell in which we try to encapsulate it, our anxious dread renders us helpless.[46]

---

45 Søren Kierkegaard, *The Journals of Kierkegaard*, trans. A. Dru (London: Collins, 1958), 44. Reprinted by permission of Alexander Dru.

46 Søren Kierkegaard, *The Concept of Anxiety*, trans. Reidar Thomte (Princeton, NJ: Princeton University Press, 1980; original work published 1844), 41.

QUICK REVIEW
Anxiety is a response to our freedom to choose to "leap" into the unknown future or nothingness that attracts and repels us, especially the "leap of faith."

However, unlike Heidegger, for Kierkegaard anxiety is most closely connected with our freedom to choose: with the free "leap of faith" into nothingness that we must make when we make significant choices in the absence of clear knowledge that we are choosing correctly. In such moments, we are both attracted and repelled by a future that is unknown, and we feel anxiety at our freedom to make a "leap of faith" into the "nothingness" of an unknown future. For example, when we look over the edge of a cliff, we feel anxiety, we feel repelled by the thought of falling over, and at the same time we almost have an urge to jump into the "nothingness." Our anxiety arises from our realization that we are free to do it. For Kierkegaard, this was particularly true of the "leap of faith" in which we are free to choose to trust in God yet have no intellectual proof that God exists. We must often, perhaps always, make our important life choices without full intellectual knowledge of what our choices will bring, and so feel both repelled and attracted by the leap into a nonexistent and unknown future. We experience anxiety at our freedom to "leap" into the nothingness.

Kierkegaard argued that for us humans, to exist is to make such free, anxiety-filled choices. *What* we choose in those crucial moments is not as important as *how* we choose. When making a significant choice—such as choosing whether to marry or not, or choosing whether to do what is morally right or morally wrong, or choosing whether to become a serious Christian or not—we must choose passionately, with energy and while conscious of the significant consequences our choices will have:

QUICK REVIEW
How we choose is more important than what we choose. Through our choices we become the persons we are: Our free choices bring us into existence.

> If you will understand me aright. I should like to say that in making a choice it is not so much a question of choosing the right as of the energy, the earnestness, the pathos with which one chooses. Thereby the personality announces its inner infinity, and thereby, in turn, the personality is consolidated. Therefore, even if a man were to choose the wrong, he will nevertheless discover, precisely by reason of the energy with which he chose, that he had chosen the wrong. For the choice being made with the whole inwardness of his personality, his nature is purified and he himself brought into immediate relation with the eternal Power whose omnipresence interpenetrates the whole of existence.[47]

In choosing, as Kierkegaard indicates, "the personality is consolidated." That is, through our choices we come to be the person we are. That is, we come to exist; we become real. For Kierkegaard, to exist, and to become who I am, are identical. To choose and thereby to exist is *to become* a self. Kierkegaard does not say there are no right and wrong choices. But he believed that if people choose earnestly and passionately, they will know when they have made a wrong choice and will be able to get back on the right track.

Even this brief sketch of Kierkegaard's thought shows that for him the freely choosing self is the fundamental reality—not the self as thinker, but as passionate doer and actor, as free decision maker. "It is impossible to exist without passion," he wrote, "unless we understand the word 'exist' in the loose sense of a so-called 'existence.'" Kierkegaard's metaphysical concerns focus on the reality of the human being we create through our own choices; consequently, he is preoccupied with the predicament and anxiety of our freedom to choose. What is *really* real? Reality is the becoming of a self whose anxiety-filled free choices bring her into existence and make her who she is. Kierkegaard wants people to take their decisions seriously, to choose passionately, and in those choices become real.

47 Søren Kierkegaard, *Either/Or—A Fragment of Life*, trans. David F. Swenson and Lillian Marvin Swenson (Princeton, NJ: Princeton University Press, 1949), vol. 2, p. 141.

This Kierkegaardian idea—that we make ourselves through our choices and thereby come to truly exist, that is, to be real—becomes a fundamental notion for all future existentialist thinkers. We have seen it already in Heidegger's philosophy. It is an idea that also lies at the core of the philosophy of Jean-Paul Sartre, an existentialist who, unlike Kierkegaard, did not believe in God.

Sartre. Although Kierkegaard first propounded existentialism, its chief proponent has been Jean-Paul Sartre (1905–1980), whom we first encountered in Chapter 2. Kierkegaard believed in God, though he felt that authentic belief required a "leap of faith." However, Sartre felt that belief in God was no longer possible. For Sartre, this idea that God does not exist was a deeply disturbing thought and a source of much anguish. In his essay "Existentialism and Human Emotions," he wrote the following: "The existentialist thinks it very distressing that God does not exist." In Sartre's view, because there is no God to define us, there is no fixed human nature, so we can be only what we choose to be. If God existed, then he would have conceived a nature for humans, and his conception of human nature would have fixed what humans are. But without a fixed human nature, all the responsibility for what we are rests with ourselves. There is nothing we ought to do because there is nothing we ought to be. There are no absolutes, no norms of right behavior; we are on our own. We exist; whatever is uniquely ours, whatever explains each of us as an individual—our *essence*—is ours for the making. We do not discover who we are so much as we *make* ourselves.

QUICK REVIEW
Sartre believes there is no God and so no fixed human nature; we make ourselves by our choices so that we are completely responsible for what we are.

What kind of creatures are we who have no fixed nature? What are we to do who find ourselves living in a world without a compass? How is it that we are able to make ourselves? These are some of Sartre's central concerns that cannot be answered by Kierkegaard's "leap" of faith. Indeed, for Sartre the leap of faith is a cowardly act because through it one enters into a world of unfreedom, a world where choices are made for us, and so a world of illusion and false hope.

In contrast, Sartre's prescription for some of these dilemmas is related to his view of reality. Like phenomenologists, Sartre believes that reality is revealed in our conscious experience. Sartre argues that a phenomenological study of our conscious experience reveals two kinds of being in our conscious experiences, and so reveals that there are two kinds of reality. First, there is our consciousness itself; second, there are the objects of which we are conscious. He terms the being of the first kind of reality (consciousness) being that is *for-itself*, and the being of the latter kind of reality (the objects of consciousness) being that is *in-itself*.

QUICK REVIEW
A phenomenological study of our conscious experience reveals two kinds of reality: consciousness, or *being-for-itself*, and the objects of which we are conscious, or *being-in-itself*.

To grasp this distinction, consider a table that stands across the room from you. Clearly, there are innumerable ways in which you can be conscious of the table—you can think about it, remember it, and imagine it. The table, of course, cannot perform any of these operations of our conscious mind. It has no consciousness. For Sartre, the table that we can think about, remember, and imagine, is an in-itself. On the other hand, you, the one who is doing the thinking, remembering, and imagining, are a for-itself. The in-itself consists of the hard, impersonal, unconscious world that presents itself all around us as nonconscious objects. The for-itself consists of any thinking, hoping, loving, hating, seeing, imagining, conscious beings, including ourselves.

QUICK REVIEW
Being-for-itself is nothing until it acts, and then the reality it becomes is whatever it chooses to do. This is why humans, who are being-for-itself, make themselves through their choices. *Being-in-itself* is not conscious and cannot make itself other than what it is.

As a consciousness, being-for-itself is nothing until, through its conscious activities, it makes itself be something; on the other hand, an in-itself cannot choose and so cannot make itself into anything other than what it already is. This distinction between an in-itself that is not conscious and a for-itself that is conscious and so able to choose and thereby create itself is the basis of Sartre's argument that humans, each of whom is a for-itself, *are* only insofar as they act. That is, unlike the hard impersonal world of objects around us, each of us is a free consciousness that can change and

Jean-Paul Sartre: "Thus human reality does not exist first in order to act later; but for human reality, to be is to act, and to cease to act is to cease to be."

Lipnitzki/Roger Viollet/Getty Images

form itself by its own free choices. We can choose what we will do, and our actions then define who and what we are. Our action may be trivial or momentous. We may sit on a chair, or we may risk our lives for a cause. This is of no matter to Sartre. What counts is that we choose and act—in other words, that we freely adopt a "project." When we do, we are truly human beings because we are in the mode of a for-itself. Failing to act, we are in the mode of an in-itself. Sartre expresses this point in *Being and Nothingness*, a definitive statement of his philosophy:

> A first glance at human reality informs us that for it being is reduced to doing. . . . Thus we find no *given* in human reality in the sense that temperament, character, passions, principles of reason would be acquired or innate *data* existing in the manner of things. . . . Thus human reality does not exist first in order to act later; but for human reality, to be is to act, and to cease to act is to cease to be. . . .
>
> Furthermore, . . . the act . . . must be defined by an *intention*. No matter how this intention is considered, it can be only a surpassing of the given toward a result to be obtained. This given . . . cannot provide the reason for a phenomenon which derives all its meaning from a result to be attained; that is, from a non-existent.
>
> Since the intention is a choice of the end and since the world reveals itself across our conduct, it is the intentional choice of the end which reveals the world, and the world is revealed as this or that (in this or that order) according to the end chosen. The end, illuminating the world, is a state *of the* world to be obtained and not yet existing. . . . Thus my *end* can be a good meal if I am hungry. . . . This meal which [is] beyond the dusty road on which I am travelling is projected as the *meaning of this* road . . .
>
> Thus the intention by a single unitary upsurge posits the end, chooses itself, and appreciates the given in terms of something which does not yet exist; it is in the light of non-being that being-in-itself is illuminated . . .
>
> This characteristic of the for-itself implies that it is the being which finds *no help, no pillar of support* in what it *was*. But on the other hand, the for-itself is free and can cause there to be a world because the for-itself is *the being which has to be what it was in the light of what it will be*. Therefore the freedom of the for-itself appears as its *being*. . . . We shall never apprehend ourselves except as a choice in the making. But freedom is simply the fact that this choice is always unconditioned.
>
> Such a choice made without base of support and dictating its own causes to itself . . . is absurd.[48]

critical thinking

Does Sartre assume that we can act or choose without reliance on our past, our temperament, our character, or our learning? Is it true that this kind of freedom is possible?

Sartre suggests a rather unconventional view of human behavior here. Because of the influence of social science, such as psychological behaviorism, many people assume that we are what we are because of our environment, so we are not responsible for what we have become. They might say that a man cheats and robs because he's a thief, and he's a thief because of the conditions under which he grew up. Sartre rejects this notion. He would argue that a man is a free consciousness, so what he is

48 Jean-Paul Sartre, *Being and Nothingness*, trans. Hazel E. Barnes (New York: Philosophical Library, 1956), 476–479. Copyright © 1956 by Philosophical Library. Reprinted by permission.

is the sum total of the free choices he makes. If he is a thief, it is because he has chosen to act as a thief, and he is himself completely responsible for those choices. As a free consciousness, he could choose to act as an honest man. He could choose, in effect, a new project rather than the one he has adopted. Furthermore, he may do this at any point in time. In other words, nothing about a thief's past makes his future inevitable. In fact, there's no telling how many different projects he could undertake in defining who he will be.

For Sartre, then, as we saw in Chapter 2, we first *exist*—we are born. But *what* we are, our *essence*, is not yet determined. Rather, what we are—our reality—depends on whether and how we will choose to act. And then the sum total of our conscious actions—our history—will define what we become. Our reality—who we really are—is what we each create through our free conscious choices, and we ourselves are fully responsible for the reality that we become. Sartre succinctly expresses this seminal core of his metaphysics in his statement "Existence precedes essence."

QUICK REVIEW
Simone de Beauvoir argued that men and women both define women in terms of their relation to men, and thereby become mere things for men and fail to make use of their freedom to make themselves.

Simone de Beauvoir (1908–1986), perhaps the greatest female existentialist philosopher and a companion of Sartre, agreed that humans are not determined and must accept ultimate responsibility for what they are. She focused on the implications for women in particular. Women, de Beauvoir argued, are subject to social influences that attempt to rob them of an awareness of their own freedom, and they must overcome these constraints through courageous self-assertion. In *The Second Sex*, de Beauvoir argues that in our male-dominated society, men define women wholly in terms of men's own nature: A woman is simply "the other," the nonmale one who relates to the male. Moreover, women accept this role and thereby forgo their freedom to define and make themselves: They become mere things for men. Women must reject the male myths that define what they are; they must instead collectively create woman as a free and independent being. This will require, she suggests, overcoming the social and economic institutions through which men keep women effectively enslaved. Social and economic liberation is the key to freedom and self-determination for women.

Even this brief exposition should suggest that existentialism could encompass an extremely diverse group of philosophers. Among the best-known existentialists are Kierkegaard, the Jewish scholar Martin Buber (1878–1965), the Protestant theologian Paul Tillich (1886–1965), the atheists Friedrich Nietzsche (1844–1900) and Sartre, the novelist Albert Camus (1913–1960), and many other thinkers, writers, and artists. Although their views often differ radically, they share a concern for conscious experience, for the importance of personal freedom and responsibility, and for the idea that in our choices we become who we are and thereby come to exist. In our treatment of phenomenology and existentialism, of course, we have been able to touch only on a few topics of metaphysical importance. Even here we have had to be sketchy. These important thinkers have had many ideas of merit that the serious student of philosophy will want to explore farther.

Objections to Phenomenology and Existentialism

Because phenomenological thought and existential thought have so many nuances, let's confine our critical remarks to Husserl and Sartre. As Husserl became more skilled in bracketing, he uncovered more and more activities of the ego at increasingly deeper levels. For Husserl, these activities do not underlie experience but are within it, waiting to be disclosed by bracketing. But, critics have asked, what of those less adept at bracketing than Husserl? What about people who are unable to uncover these activities? It seems that if such people are not to doubt the entire method, they must view these activities as lying entirely outside of the field of phenomenon.

QUICK REVIEW
What one sees when one brackets as Husserl recommended depends on one's assumptions, values, language, and so forth. So, bracketing cannot reveal the same thing to everyone.

Critics have also asked whether things are "self-given" when we bracket. To illustrate, suppose that you had bracketed and reported that you did not find anything that was self-given, anything that presented itself with absolute certainty within experience. Husserl might accuse you of having bracketed unsuccessfully, but you could reply that bracketing itself is a frame within which Husserl insists on viewing things. In other words, you could argue that all seeing is relative to the frame through which one chooses to view things—relative, that is, to our assumptions, presuppositions, and values. If you were of a different philosophical bent from Husserl, you could go on and associate these frames with language. Husserl would counter that his is a special kind of seeing that's free of language when we bracket correctly. Thus, we see what is the case, and then we hunt around for the right words to describe it. But is this so? Much of twentieth-century philosophy argues that all philosophy, including phenomenology, is linguistic. In other words, all thinking and seeing are related to certain preconceptions that are inherent in language. Thus, bracketing is also a kind of frame, though admittedly subtler than most. Thus, what for Husserl seems certain might be better described as his own projection of the quest for certainty.

Turning to Sartre, recall that he insists that to be human is to make ourselves by adopting a project. For example, suppose that you find that you are a Christian. Perhaps you didn't *choose* to become one; you simply followed a script or line or direction that, for a number of reasons, was laid out for you. Sartre would say that you're caught in a logical contradiction: You're a person who is not a person, a for-itself whose being is in the mode of an in-itself. For Sartre, this evaluation is not just a bias or even a value judgment. It's an assertion of an ontological truth. But is it?

Even if you were a Christian who did not *choose* Christianity, you wouldn't be a Christian in the way that a desk is a desk or a rock is a rock. You wouldn't have being in the mode of the in-itself in the way that those things do. In fact, Sartre would agree that as humans, we can't have being simply in the mode of the in-itself. Like it or not, we're condemned to be free.

QUICK REVIEW
Critics say one can be in the mode of being-for-itself by freely choosing to be committed to a group where one gives up his freedom. But this contradicts Sartre's view that to be a being-for-itself one must always remain free to choose.

If we can't be simply in the mode of the in-itself, then we're always in the mode of the for-itself. But is it any more possible to be in the mode of the for-itself? Suppose that you don't drift or slip into being a Christian, but you *choose* it. This fact doesn't seem to make any real difference to Sartre because once you become a Christian, you accept a set of values, ways of looking at things, and a course of conduct. Christianity becomes your "taken for granted," and, evidently, you now have being in the mode of the for-itself.

Obviously, this problem doesn't exist only for Christians. People who adopt **nihilism** as their project slip just as easily from freedom to playing the role of nihilist. Even those who adopt existential freedom as their project can slide from freedom while playing the role of existentialist. True, some projects are more likely to invite slippage into bad faith than others. But is any project immune? Professor of philosophy W. T. Jones captures this paradox:

> One of the difficulties for a man who is committed to "commitment" is that in order to get things done in this world he must combine forces with other men—not only join a movement but institutionalize (even bureaucratize) it. And this, it would seem, means surrendering one's freedom and hence becoming a thing. This is the paradox Sartre encountered in his own life; it helps to explain his on-again, off-again relationship with the Communist Party.[49]

49 Jones, *From Kant*, 444.

Sartre's account of the for-itself, then, seems to commit him to holding freedom as an all-or-nothing proposition. But many people see it as one of degree. The same is true of responsibility. In the Holocaust, for example, the German Nazi regime attempted to exterminate the Jewish race by murdering them in prison camps. Who was responsible? Some people might reply that the individual Nazi soldiers who committed the murders were responsible. But those individuals all claimed that they were merely "following orders." Were the military officers who ordered the murders responsible? What about Nazi politicians who designed the plans that the military followed? Or the German citizens who supported the Nazi regime, or those who knew about the camps and did nothing to stop them? What about the English and Americans who were aware of the camps and also did nothing? Are these parties each responsible but to different degrees?

The idea of degrees of responsibility doesn't seem to fit with Sartre's view of morality. Sartre says humans are totally responsible because they are totally free. Because all of us could have made a world that excluded the Nazi massacre, we are all equally responsible. It's true that in *Being and Nothingness* Sartre relaxes this view by speaking of the social restraints on individual freedom, but then one wonders whether this modification is consistent, or even needs to be, with his existential phenomenology.

Despite their differences, existentialists, phenomenologists, and many of their critics agree at least on one point: Statements about ultimate reality and being are meaningful. Whether reality is matter, idea, a combination, being, or consciousness, all the views we have discussed so far—except for the logical positivists—agree that we can sensibly talk about metaphysical issues.

QUESTIONS

1. What would an existentialist mean if he said, "It's clear that, for you, *what or who* I am is more important than *that* I am"? Why would this matter to him?
2. What is the difference between being and being human?
3. In what sense are you both being and *a* being?
4. Show how a failure to distinguish between being as a thing and the being of a thing leads to "thingifying" everything, including people.
5. Do existentialism, phenomenology, and pragmatism share any beliefs?
6. In what sense would you call Kierkegaard a rationalist?
7. Sartre claims that Kierkegaard's leap of faith to God is cowardly and not in the true existential spirit. Why would he say this? Do you agree?
8. What does Sartre mean when he says, "Existence precedes essence"?
9. How would you describe what Heidegger calls your being?
10. If someone said, "If everything is being, then everything is nothing," what would she mean?
11. Is it possible to maintain a concept of individual difference if everything has being in common?
12. Sartre claims that in making a choice for self, we are really making a choice for other. Is this statement consistent with a denial of any kind of universal human nature? If it is, why did Sartre make such a claim?

PHILOSOPHY AT THE MOVIES

Watch *Leaving Las Vegas* (1995) in which screenwriter Ben Anderson has been drinking heavily since losing his wife and son and, when fired from his job, decides to drive to Las Vegas where he plans to drink himself to death and where he meets Sera, a prostitute who chooses to take him in, accepts him as he is, and cares for him until he kills himself by drinking. To what extent do Ben and Sera exemplify the philosophies of Sartre, Kierkegaard, and Heidegger? Does this film support or contradict Sartre's claim that "for human reality, to be is to act" as well as Kierkegaard's view that to be real is to choose passionately? Are Sera and Ben authentic? What role do the ideas of freedom and responsibility play in the movie?

3.7 Is Freedom Real?

No other metaphysical issue is as debated as the question of freedom. It has given rise to a controversy that still rages in our society. Consider the case of Leopold and Loeb.

Nathan Leopold and Richard Loeb, both eighteen-year-olds, were wealthy and brilliant. They had just graduated from college when they brutally murdered a fourteen-year-old boy in a rented automobile in Chicago's south side on May 21, 1924. During college, the two had been addicted to reading crime magazines and novels. They had experimented in petty theft and arson. Then, together they came up with the idea of committing the "perfect crime." The challenge of planning, executing, and getting away with a murder intrigued and fascinated them. For what they later described as the "intellectual thrill" of it, they kidnapped young Bobbie Franks. They beat him on the head with a chisel, suffocated him by stuffing a gag in his mouth, and then phoned his wealthy parents to demand $10,000 in ransom. The family alerted police investigators, who soon found the boy's bloody body half-buried in a railway culvert. Lying next to the body were Leopold's eyeglasses. When confronted, the two quickly confessed and were subsequently tried for murder, punishable by death.

Nathan Leopold (left), and Richard Loeb, who were convicted for the kidnapping and murder of Loeb's distant cousin, fourteen-year-old Bobby Franks.

© Hulton Archive/Getty Images

Their lawyer was the famous defense attorney Clarence Darrow. At trial before Judge John R. Caverly, for thirty-three days in July and August 1924, Darrow argued that the boys, who had already pleaded guilty, should not be executed. Science has proved, Darrow suggested, that everything in the universe is governed by rigid laws of causality. These laws ensure that everything that happens has to happen. Therefore, no one is responsible for his or her actions. The real causes of our actions lie outside us, in the events and conditions that caused us to act as we did and in the laws that govern our acts. In particular, Darrow claimed, Leopold and Loeb's murderous act was caused by their heredity and the way they were raised. Speaking in defense of "Dickie" Loeb, Darrow said this at the trial:

> I do not claim to know how it happened. I know that something or some combination of things is responsible for this mad act. I know that there are not accidents in nature. I know that effect follows cause. What had this boy to do with it? He was not his own father. All this was handed to him. He did not make himself. . . . Do you mean to tell me that Dickie Loeb had any more to do with his making than any other product of heredity that is born upon the earth? . . . And yet there are men who seriously say that for what nature has done, for what life has done, for what training has done, you should hang these boys. . . . [But] to believe that any boy is responsible for himself or his early training is an absurdity that no lawyer or judge should be guilty of today. . . . I know that if this boy had been understood and properly trained . . . he would not be in this courtroom today with the noose above his head. If there is responsibility anywhere, it is back of him; somewhere in the infinite number of his ancestors, or in his surroundings, or in both. And I submit, your Honor, that under every principle of natural justice, under every principle of conscience, of right, and of law, he should not be made responsible for the acts of someone else . . .[50]

QUICK REVIEW
Darrow argued that their heredity and upbringing together with the laws of causality made Leopold and Loeb do what they did, so they were not morally responsible for killing Bobbie Franks.

In the end, Judge Caverly agreed with Darrow and refused to impose the death penalty. Instead, he sentenced the two boys to life in prison, the only other option available to him. His decision raised a public outcry. Darrow was simply wrong, the public claimed. Leopold and Loeb acted freely and deliberately. They were fully responsible for what they did and deserved the maximum penalty.

Although the case of Leopold and Loeb is an old one, the issues it raised are still argued in courtrooms today. For example, in December 2002, Thomas Koskovich was put on trial for a murder that he and a friend had committed in 1997 when they lured two pizza delivery men into driving to a deserted rural house to bring them a pizza they had ordered as a ruse. When the two delivery men drove up with their order, Koskovich and his friend came up to the car, pulled out pistols, and shot both of them dead through the car windows. Eleven days before, they had stolen the guns and practiced to prepare for the killings. Earlier, Koskovich had told a girlfriend he was planning a murder so that he could see "what it felt like" to kill someone. After emptying the pockets of their victims, the leader, Koskovich, hugged his friend excitedly, thrilled with what they had just done. "I love you, man," his friend said. Returning home, the two changed out of their bloody clothing and went to church. The following day, Koskovich said to a friend who stopped by the house, "How does it feel to shake the hand of a killer?"

During Koskovich's trial, his defense lawyers argued that the crime was caused by his environment: Koskovich had grown up neglected and unloved in a household that was plagued by violence, drugs, alcoholism, abuse, abandonment, and suicide attempts. A local newspaper reporter wrote the following:

> Citing her client's "horrific, depraved, tragic" family life, a lawyer asked a jury Thursday to spare the life of convicted killer Thomas Koskovich, but the prosecution demanded the ultimate penalty for "murder done for the thrill of it." . . . [Koskovich's lawyer] said defense witnesses will show that the murder . . . was the product of mitigating factors—immaturity, drug use, stunted emotional development, mental and psychological disorders, family abandonment and rejection, and a home life rife with infidelity, gambling, psychological abuse, and criminal activity.[51]

QUICK REVIEW
Darrow's view often shows up in murder trials today.

50 Clarence Darrow, "Leopold and Loeb," quoted in G. L. Bowie, M. W. Michaels, and R. C. Solomon, *Twenty Questions: An Introduction to Philosophy* (New York: Harcourt Brace, 1988), 688, 691.

51 John Cichowski, "New Penalty Trial Opens in Thrill Killing," *The Record* (Bergen County, NJ), November 1, 2002.

During the trial, witnesses stated that his father abandoned his mother and went to live with another woman when Koskovich was nine, telling the boy as he walked away that he "loved him the least" of any of the children. The house became a noisy, chaotic place where stray cats, dogs, and a goat wandered freely and where his mother took on lovers, his brother became a hardened criminal hooked on drugs and alcohol, his sister several times attempted suicide, and an assortment of cousins, nieces, nephews, an uncle who was in and out of jail, and several acquaintances slept on the floors and the couches of the small littered house. In the sometimes violent, chaotic household, Koskovich was neglected; nobody cared if he didn't get to school, and neither did anyone notice if he failed to come home. His addicted uncle sometimes had Koskovich cut up lines of cocaine for him. When Koskovich was twelve, his mother abandoned him to go live with a boyfriend. She took his younger brother with her but left him in the house with his grandmother, Bertha Lippincott, a woman who had been raped by her father, was a convicted robber and drug abuser, and was now living with her lesbian lover because her husband had left her for her aunt. Like his parents, his grandmother neglected him emotionally, and Koskovich became a depressed, barbiturate-addicted teenager.

On December 5, 2002, the jury found that the criminal activity of his family, abandonment by his parents during his adolescence, family infidelity, domestic violence, substance abuse, gambling, criminal activity, and suicide attempts were so pervasive in his household that they "mitigated" his responsibility for the killings, so Koskovich should not be sentenced to die. Thomas Koskovich, instead, was sentenced to life in prison.

Koskovich's lawyers obviously felt that his crime was the predictable outcome of the violent life that had preceded it, so he should not be held fully morally responsible for his acts. It was right that he not receive the death penalty. Others, like one of the victims' sister, strongly disagreed. People are morally responsible for what they do. No matter how we are brought up, we have the power to choose what we will do. Believing that Koskovich freely chose to kill and so should have received a fitting punishment, the one victim's sister reacted bitterly after hearing Koskovich had avoided the death penalty. "Is this justice?" she asked. "No. This is not justice."

Determinism

There is, perhaps, no more controversial question in metaphysics than the one raised in the preceding cases: Is what happens in the universe, including human actions, determined by the laws of nature? Many philosophers have thought so. Everything that happens, including every human action, is determined by previous events and the biological and psychological laws that govern human nature. There can be no freedom.

The view that human actions are completely determined by prior events is called *determinism.* Stated in another and perhaps more accurate way, **determinism** is the view that every event has prior conditions that cause it, so each event is at least theoretically predictable if we know all its prior conditions and the laws governing those conditions. Determinists argue that human actions are part of this causal chain of nature and so are also determined. Stated in another way, determinists hold that there is only one path leading from the past through the present and into the future. It is not possible for the future to take any path other than the one that prior events and the laws of nature force it to take.

QUICK REVIEW
Determinists argue that previous events and the laws of nature cause all human acts, so humans are not free or responsible for their acts.

Materialism and determinism have been close allies. Materialism holds that mental events—our decisions and choices—are caused by the brain or are events in the brain. But these brain processes are physical processes. As such, they have to be caused by antecedent physical events that are governed by scientific laws, like any other physical process.

This materialist view received important support in the seventeenth century from the theories of the great British scientist Sir Isaac Newton (1642–1727). Newton argued that all material bodies in the universe, from the smallest atoms to the largest planets and stars, move in accordance with the universal laws of nature that he described in *Principia Mathematica Philosophia Naturalis.* These laws include the law of inertia, which states that all bodies continue moving in a straight line unless acted on by an external force, and the law of universal gravitation, which states that all bodies in the universe attract all other bodies with a force proportional to their masses and their distances from one another. If the locations, masses, and velocities of any set of bodies are known for any moment in the past, then one can determine their exact locations and velocities at any moment in the future by using Newton's laws. Materialists quickly saw that if the brain is made up of small bodies such as atoms, then the motions and activities of the atoms that make up the brain must also follow Newton's universal laws. The activities of the human brain, then, are as enmeshed in the mechanical workings of the universe as are atoms, clocks, and planets. Because human actions and choices are the outcome of the activities of the brain, they, too, are subject to the universal laws of nature.

These ideas were brilliantly expressed by the French mathematician Pierre Simon, Marquis de LaPlace, who wrote the following in 1812:

> Present events have a connection with previous ones that is based on the self-evident principle that a thing cannot come into existence without a cause that produces it. This axiom . . . extends even to actions which people regard as [free]. . . . We must regard the present state of the universe as the effect of its preceding state and as the cause of the one which is to follow. An intelligence which in a single instant could know all the forces which animate the natural world, and the respective situations of all the beings that made it up, could, provided it was vast enough to make an analysis of all the data so supplied, be able to produce a single formula which specified all the movements in the universe from those of the largest bodies in the universe to those of the lightest atom.[52]

QUICK REVIEW
Encouraged by Newton's laws of motion, LaPlace argued that human actions are determined.

It may seem to us that we are free. But, in actuality, this freedom is just a result of our ignorance of the laws that govern us. Eventually, LaPlace thought, we will discover the laws that govern human actions. Then we will see clearly that freedom is nothing but an illusion.

In our own time, determinism has been encouraged by psychological theories, such as those of Sigmund Freud. Although Freud did not explicitly espouse a determinist position, some of his followers used his theories to argue that unconscious psychological desires are the real causes of actions that people think they have freely chosen. Psychological mechanisms place human actions squarely within the causal chain of nature. For example, the contemporary philosopher John Hospers holds that "the unconscious is the master of every fate and the captain of every soul":

> A man is faced by a choice: shall he kill another person or not? Moralists would say, here is a "free" choice—the result of deliberation, an action consciously entered into. And yet, though the agent himself does not know it, and has no awareness of the forces that are at work within him, his choice is already determined for him: his conscious will is only an instrument, a slave, in the hands of a deep

QUICK REVIEW
Hospers argues that unconscious motivations such as Freud described determine all our actions.

52 Pierre Simon de LaPlace, *Essai Philosophique sur les Probabilités* (1812), trans. John Cottingham. Quoted in *Western Philosophy, an Anthology*, ed. John Cottingham (Oxford, UK: Blackwell, 1996), 227.

> unconscious motivation which determines his action. If he has a great deal of what the analyst calls "free-floating guilt," he will not; but if the guilt is such as to demand immediate absorption in the form of self-damaging behavior, this accumulated guilt will have to be discharged in some criminal action. The man himself does not know what the inner clockwork is; he is like the hands on the clock, thinking they move freely over the face of the clock.[53]

Determinists don't just hold that everything is determined. They also assume that determinism rules out human freedom and responsibility. Freedom is the ability to choose among alternatives. If humans cannot help but do what they do, then they are not free to act otherwise. In this sense, they lack freedom. They also lack responsibility. We are responsible for an action only if we are in control of the action or its causes. But we do not control our actions if determinism is right. Instead, the events and forces that led us to act control what we do. Determinism is therefore inconsistent with the idea that we are each personally responsible for our actions. The determinist view of reality, then, is summarized in the following argument (you should try to determine the argument's logical form and its validity):

QUICK REVIEW
Determinism holds that (1) human acts are causally determined, (2) such determination rules out freedom and responsibility, so (3) humans are neither free nor responsible.

1. All events and actions are causally determined by previous events and the laws of nature.
2. Causal determinism rules out human freedom and personal responsibility.
3. So, humans are not free, and neither are they personally responsible for what they do.

The implications of determinism are disturbing. If determinism is true, then punishment, at least in the traditional sense, makes little sense. More broadly, if determinism is true, then it makes no sense to hold individuals responsible for their actions, whether for good or evil. The saint should no more be praised than the criminal should be punished. For neither is ultimately responsible for what he did. Regret would also become incomprehensible because one cannot regret doing what one could not help but do.

But is determinism correct? Perhaps events in the natural world are determined, but should human actions be assimilated to natural events? When we act, don't we directly experience our freedom? Aren't we sometimes directly aware that we have control over our actions and so are morally responsible at that moment for the actions we choose? Some philosophers have argued that unlike objects in nature, which are determined, human beings are free.

Libertarianism

Many people have argued that determinism is wrong because it denies the freedom that we all directly experience when we choose. But how can we be outside the causal chain of nature? No philosopher has argued so vigorously in favor of freedom as Jean-Paul Sartre. We have seen how Sartre's existentialism analyzes our consciousness of reality. Based on this experience of ourselves as conscious, Sartre argues that we are indeed free.

QUICK REVIEW
Sartre argues that human consciousness can withdraw itself from any existing situation to seek a future that does not exist, so humans are not determined by any existing situation but are free and responsible.

Sartre's argument for freedom depends on an interesting view he has of how humans choose. When humans act, he points out, they intend to do something they have not yet done, or to get something they do not yet have. In short, they think about going from a present that exists to a future that does not yet exist. In this way,

53 John Hospers, "What Means This Freedom?" in *Determinism and Freedom in the Age of Modern Science*, ed. Sidney Hook (New York: New York University Press, 1958).

argues Sartre, humans can stand apart from the world as it is at present and can conceive and be moved by a future that does not yet exist. Sartre calls this ability—to conceive and be moved by what is not—the ability to apprehend "negativity" or "non-being." Past or present existence, says Sartre, cannot determine a person's conception of what does not exist. In this power to conceive what is not lies our freedom:

> It is strange that philosophers have been able to argue endlessly about determinism and free-will, to cite examples in favor of one or the other thesis without ever attempting first to make explicit the structures contained in the very idea of action. We should first observe that an action is on principle intentional. . . . But if this is the case, we establish that an action necessarily implies as its condition the recognition of a "desideratum" [something desired], that is, of an objective lack or negativity. The [emperor Constantine's] intention of [building a Christian city to] rival Rome could come to him only through the apprehension of an objective lack: . . . a Christian city at the moment is missing.
>
> This means that from the moment of the first conception of the act, consciousness has been able to withdraw itself from the full world of which it is conscious and leave the level of being [what exists] to approach that of non-being [what does not yet exist]. Consciousness . . . cannot find in being any motive for revealing nonbeing.
>
> Two important consequences result. (1) No factual state whatever it may be (the political and economic structure of society, the psychological state, etc.) is capable by itself of motivating any act whatsoever. For an act is a projection of the for-itself [the human being] toward what is not, and what is can in no way determine by itself what is not. (2) No factual state can determine consciousness to apprehend it as a negativity or as a lack. . . .
>
> Human-reality is free because . . . it is perpetually wrenched away from itself and because it has been separated by a nothingness from what it is and from what it will be. . . . Freedom is precisely the nothingness which is made to be at the heart of man and which forces human reality to make itself instead of to simply be.[54]

Sartre utterly rejects determinism. Instead, Sartre holds a form of what is sometimes called **libertarianism**. A libertarian holds that people have control over what they do and are free to choose to act other than the way they do. We are, in Sartre's view, radically free. Our ability to conceive of what is not allows us to form plans that are not determined by the past or the present. They cannot be determined because what is cannot determine what is not. Being cannot determine nonbeing. By this ability to pursue what is not, we make ourselves whatever we choose to be regardless of the influences of our environment or our heredity. We can tell ourselves that other forces make us do what we do, but this is a form of "bad faith." It is a deliberate attempt to deceive ourselves, a way of trying to avoid our radical responsibility. We choose whether we give in to our emotions and desires; we choose whether we allow our environment to influence us; we choose whether we follow the promptings of our hereditary makeup. Because we are ultimately free, Sartre holds that we are fully responsible for our behavior and actions.

The future, then, is not fixed according to Sartre. There is not just one possible path leading from the past into the future, as the determinist says. Instead, the libertarian holds that the future branches off into many possible paths. Of course, only one of those futures will be chosen. But we could have chosen one of the other paths. We are free because we could have acted other than the way we did.

---

54 Jean-Paul Sartre, *L'Etre et le Neant*, trans. H. E. Barnes (London: Methuen, 1957; original work published 1943), 433–437.

PHILOSOPHY AND LIFE

Does Our Brain Make Our Decisions Before We Consciously Make Them?

Four scientists found that your brain appears to determine what you will do about seven seconds before you "freely" decide to do it. In their study, the four scientists found that brain activity indicating which hand participants would use to press a button near each hand was present in the brain seven seconds before the participants consciously decided which hand to use. They wrote:

> The impression that we are able to freely choose between different possible courses of action is fundamental to our mental life. However, it has been suggested that this subjective experience of freedom is no more than an illusion and that our actions are initiated by unconscious mental processes long before we become aware of our intention to act. . . . We directly investigated which regions of the brain predetermine conscious intentions and the time at which they start shaping a motor decision. [Our] subjects carried out a freely paced motor-decision task while their brain activity was measured using functional magnetic resonance imaging [fMRI] machines. [fMRI machines produce images of the brain that show what parts of the brain are active when the image is made]. Subjects were asked . . . to freely decide between [pressing] one of two buttons [and to indicate] when their motor decision was consciously made. . . . We found . . . brain regions encoded [indicated] with high accuracy whether the subject was about to choose the left or right response prior to the conscious decision. . . . [One] region was in [the] frontopolar cortex. . . . The predictive information in the fMRI signals from this brain region was already present 7 seconds before the subject's [conscious] motor decision. . . . [T]his prior activity is not an unspecific preparation of a response. Instead, it specifically encodes how the subject is going to decide. . . . [T]he lead times are too long to be explained by any timing inaccuracies in reporting the onset of awareness.

Some scientists have concluded from experiments like these that if our unconscious brain determines our decisions before we have even consciously made a decision, then our feeling that we consciously and freely make our decisions is an illusion: Our unconscious brain, not our conscious mind, makes our decisions.

QUESTIONS

1. Explain why the experiment is supposed to indicate that free will is "an illusion."
2. Do you see any way of arguing that even if the experiment is correct, free will is not an illusion?
3. Some people have suggested that choosing which hand to use to press a button is not the kind of complex decision in which we humans express our freedom, such as a decision to marry or to choose a certain career. These complex human decisions indicate that we have free choice, so the experiment does not really show that we are not free. Do you agree with this suggestion?

Source: Chun Siong Soon, Marcel Brass, Hans-Jochen Heinze, and John-Dylan Haynes, "Unconscious Determinants of Free Decisions in the Human Brain," *Nature Neuroscience*, April 13, 2008.

QUICK REVIEW
Libertarians hold that (1) humans are free and responsible, (2) determinism rules out such freedom and responsibility, and (3) human acts are not causally determined.

Although the libertarian rejects the determinist's claim that all human actions are caused by antecedent events, he agrees with the determinist on one important point. The libertarian agrees with the determinist that determinism would rule out freedom and responsibility. We can summarize the view of the libertarian, then, in the following argument (again, figure out its logical form and compare it to the logical form of the determinist's argument):

1. Humans are free and are personally responsible for what they do.
2. Human freedom and personal responsibility rule out causal determinism.
3. So, human actions are not causally determined by previous events and the laws of nature.

Yet do we have the kind of absolute freedom that Sartre attributes to us? Is the criminal wholly to blame for his crimes? Do environment and heredity play no role in what we do? Are you wholly to blame for who and what you are today? And if you deny that you are free and responsible, are you really using this very denial as an excuse to escape your responsibility? Is the denial of freedom always a form of bad faith?

Other nondeterminists have argued that new scientific theories, in particular quantum theory, also imply that the future is not causally determined by the past. Quantum theory holds that at least at the subatomic level, it is not possible to simultaneously determine both the position and the velocity of a particle, so it is not possible to predict its position at a future moment. At the subatomic level, therefore, the future is indeterministic.

But not everyone accepts these arguments. Determinists have claimed that Sartre makes human choices mysterious and unexplainable, and that Sartre's views also fly in the face of what we know about human psychology and the extent to which we are shaped by our past. Moreover, determinists have argued that the appeals to quantum theory are beside the point because what is at stake is human behavior at the level of ordinary objects, not the behavior of subatomic particles.

Compatibilism

But perhaps libertarianism is not the only way of saving freedom and responsibility. In an effort to reconcile our notions of freedom and moral responsibility with determinism, some philosophers have advanced a view called compatibilism. **Compatibilism** rejects the view that determinism rules out freedom and responsibility. Instead, compatibilists argue, causal determinism is compatible with freedom. How is this possible?

Compatibilism saves freedom by redefining it. According to the compatibilist, to say that a person is free is to say that the person is not impeded by external restraints or confinements. A person wearing handcuffs or in prison is not free. But a person who is free to do what her own desires or character move her to do is free. Still, because a person's desires and character are molded by her heredity and upbringing, they are causally determined by external factors. Ultimately, then, a person's actions are determined by the antecedent causes that formed her desires and character.

One of the first philosophers to propose a compatibilist view was the British materialist Thomas Hobbes:

> LIBERTY, or freedom, signifies properly the absence of opposition; by [this], I mean [the absence of] external impediments to motion. . . . [When] living creatures . . . are imprisoned, or restrained with walls or chains . . . we . . . say they are not at liberty. . . . [When] man . . . finds no[thing to] stop [him from] doing what he has the will, desire, or inclination to do [he is at liberty]. . . . Liberty and necessity are consistent. . . . [Like] the water that has not only liberty, but a necessity of descending by the channel; so, likewise . . . the actions which men voluntarily do . . . because they proceed [from] their will, proceed from liberty, and yet because every act of man's will and every desire and inclination proceeds from some cause, and that from another cause, in a continual chain . . . [all actions also] proceed from necessity. So that to him that could see the connexion of those causes, the necessity of all men's voluntary actions would appear manifest.[55]

QUICK REVIEW
Hobbes argued that freedom is the absence of physical restraints, so when restraints are absent, our acts are free and responsible even though they are causally determined.

55 Thomas Hobbes, *Leviathan*, in *Hobbes Selections*, ed. Fredrick J. E. Woodbridge (New York: Scribner's, 1930), ch. 21, 369–371.

Compatibilists are also able to recognize moral responsibility. To say that a person is responsible for an action is to say that the action flowed from inside the person, from what he is. So, when a person's actions are caused by his inner desires and his character, they flow from the person and from what he is, making him responsible for those actions.

The compatibilist, then, can agree with the determinist that human actions are predetermined. But he rejects the idea that determinism rules out freedom or responsibility. The compatibilist argues like this (find the logical form of this argument and compare it to those of the determinists and the libertarian):

QUICK REVIEW
Compatibilists hold that (1) human acts are causally determined, but (2) determinism does not rule out freedom and responsibility, so (3) humans are predetermined yet can be free and responsible.

1. Human actions are causally determined by previous events and the laws of nature.
2. Causal determinism does not rule out freedom and personal responsibility.
3. So, humans are predetermined and can also be free and personally responsible for what they do.

QUICK REVIEW
Critics say compatibilism ignores the real issue: Are we unfree in the sense that our acts are causally determined.

But whereas compatibilism appears to wed freedom with determinism, doesn't it leave the key question unanswered? If we are not free to act against our desires, then isn't there still a clear sense in which we are not free? Maybe we are "free" in the sense that we are not chained down and physically restrained from acting. But aren't we unfree in the more important sense that we do not ultimately control what we do? If a person is not free to choose her desires, and these desires determine her actions, then isn't she ultimately unfree? How can we hold a person responsible for the actions that flow from her desires when she does not control her desires?

Is it clear, then, that compatibilism has really reconciled freedom and determinism? Yet the other views on determinism that we have examined seem to be equally problematic. Because it denies freedom and moral responsibility, determinism does not accord with how we generally experience our own actions. Libertarianism seemingly preserves freedom and responsibility at the expense of scientific respectability. Compatibilism, which tries to reconcile freedom and responsibility with determinism, apparently leaves the issue unresolved in some ultimate sense. Which view of reality makes the most sense?

Some philosophers have agreed that perhaps we are both free and determined, as Hobbes suggests. But they add that we do not need to redefine *freedom* to make this point. Perhaps, they suggest, we are simply stuck with two different ways of looking at human reality. Perhaps we have to see ourselves as both free and determined. This is the view of Immanuel Kant:

> Is it possible that we take one point of view when we think of ourselves as free causes, and another point of view when we see ourselves as determined effects?
>
> . . . Insofar as he knows himself through his senses, man must see himself as part of the world of sense. But insofar as he assumes he has a conscious active self, he must regard himself as part of the world of understanding. . . .
>
> So a rational being has two points of view from which he can regard himself. . . . First, to the extent that he belongs to the world of sense, he sees himself as subject to the laws of nature. Second, to the extent that he belongs to the world of understanding, he sees himself as subject only to moral rules that are based on reason. . . . As a rational being that belongs to the world of understanding, man must think of his will as free . . .[56]

56 Immanuel Kant, *Foundations of the Metaphysics of Morals*, sec. 3. Translated by Manuel Velasquez.

Here Kant is suggesting that we have two ways of understanding ourselves and our world. First, we can think of ourselves as part of the world that we observe when we use our senses, the world that science tries to explain through scientific laws. When we think of ourselves in this way, we are looking at ourselves as an object in the world. We feel that objects in this world have to be determined, and our own actions, as part of this world, must be determined as well. But Kant also suggests that we can think of ourselves as conscious beings who act in the world. When we think of ourselves in this way, we have to think of ourselves as free. We have to think of ourselves as free because if we thought other forces were determining our acts, we would not feel that we ourselves were really acting. If I am to see myself as really acting, I must believe that what I am doing comes out of my own choices and is not caused by forces external to me.

QUICK REVIEW
Kant says when we act, we have to assume we are free, and when we try to explain our acts scientifically, we have to assume we are determined. Both viewpoints are necessary.

Kant does not see any way of escaping these two very different ways of looking at ourselves. We sometimes have to look at ourselves as physical objects, particularly when we try to explain our actions in terms of the laws of science, such as psychology. But we sometimes also have to look at ourselves as free conscious beings, particularly when we try to understand ourselves as beings who act in the world. Determinism, then, is not a feature of the world. It is a feature of one way of looking at ourselves and our actions. **Indeterminism** is also not a feature of the world. Rather, it is a feature of another way of looking at ourselves and our actions. But both are inescapable.

Many people today agree with Kant. The philosopher/psychologist Steven Pinker, for example, writes the following:

> Science and morality are separate spheres of reasoning. Only by recognizing them as separate can we have them both. . . . A human being is simultaneously a machine and a sentient free agent, depending on the purposes of the discussion. . . . The mechanistic stance allows us to understand what makes us tick and how we fit into the physical universe. When those discussions wind down for the day, we go back to talking about each other as free and dignified human beings.[57]

Here Pinker is agreeing with Kant. When we are "playing the morality game," he says, we have to think of ourselves as free. When we are "playing the science game," we have to think of ourselves as deterministic machines. Unfortunately, he argues, we need to play both of these "games," so we must see ourselves as free agents when we are discussing morality and as determined machines when discussing science.

So, are we free or determined? Are we responsible agents or passive victims? Was Darrow right? Or was Sartre right? Or were both right, as Kant and Pinker suggest? What do you think?

QUESTIONS

1. Think about a situation in which you felt intense desire. Did you feel you were free to choose whether to give in to your desire?
2. Suppose that an airplane crashes. After a lengthy inquiry, investigators announce that they have ruled out every possible cause of the crash. They have concluded that the crash actually had no cause at all. It was uncaused. Would you find this conclusion acceptable? Explain why.

---

57 Steven Pinker, *How the Mind Works* (New York: Norton, 1997), 56.

3. A determinist says that when a person deliberately does anything, she must have wanted to do it. Otherwise, why did she do it? But if so, the determinist concludes, desires cause everything we do. Is this argument correct? Why or why not?

4. Explain how you think that Sartre would explain addiction, such as an addiction to hard drugs or to smoking. Do addictions prove that Sartre is wrong? Explain why.

5. The philosopher John Searle, author of the book *The Rediscovery of the Mind*, once said the following in conversation: "You can't think away your own freedom. Just think what it would be like. You go into a restaurant and they confront you with a menu. Now you can't say, 'Well, look, I'm a determinist, so I'll just wait and see what I order' or 'I'll just wait and see what happens.' You have to make up your mind. . . . I can't sit back and wait for the choice to happen. . . . You have to act, and this is the way Kant put it, you have to act on the presupposition of freedom." What does Searle's statement imply about determinism and indeterminism? How close is Searle's view to Kant's? Is Searle right?

PHILOSOPHY AT THE MOVIES

Watch *Gattaca* (1997) in which Vincent Freeman, living in a future when government uses a person's genes to determine his role in society, wants to become an astronaut, but because his DNA limits him to menial jobs, he must pay a disabled athlete with good genes for the blood, tissue, and urine samples that let him pass the gene tests for astronaut training in which he does well until he is discovered. Is the world of Gattaca free or determined? Is it both? Explain.

3.8 Is Time Real?

There is something that the discussions of determinism and freedom have assumed we understand. Both the determinist and the indeterminist assume we know what it is for one event or action to cause another. But causality involves time: the movement from an earlier cause toward its later effect. So they assume that we understand what time is. But do we? Let us see.

QUICK REVIEW
Time is an intimate aspect of who we are and the lives we live, yet difficult to understand.

Time and Human Life

Time seems to be the most familiar of all realities. To every action, appointment, event, experience, happening, phenomenon, circumstance, situation, sensation, incident, adventure, occasion, quest, affair, occurrence, and climax we assign a time. We continuously talk about what happened "yesterday," what we are doing "today," and what we plan to do "tomorrow." We use the notion of time as easily as our lungs take in air. We have no trouble understanding the meaning of "past," "present," "future," "then,"

Sometimes time seems like an unstoppable river continuously flowing past a bank on which we stand.

© Suzanne Tucker/iStockphoto.com

"now," "before," "after," "when," "whenever," "later," "earlier," "always," "never," "soon." Yet what is time? When we ask the question, the reality that seemed so familiar slips away. As Saint Augustine wrote, "If no one asks me, I know what time is; if someone asks and I want to explain it, I do not know."[58]

Yet time is an intimate aspect of who we are and how we feel. Time, in fact, makes us who we are. To find out who I am, I need to look into my memory of my past and see what I've done and where I've been, how I've acted and responded to the needs and demands of others and to the events of my life. The same is true of other people. My understanding of who they are is based on how I have experienced them in the past: what I have seen them do and how I have seen them act. For example, have I seen them act with integrity and courage, or with expedience and cowardliness? Many of our feelings, too, depend on time. Take regret, for example. I feel regret about what is in the past that I wish I had not done. I feel regret because I cannot change the past.

Time seems especially mysterious because it seems to flow or move ever onward past us or with us. Sometimes it seems like an unstoppable river continuously flowing past a bank on which we stand. An event we look forward to in the future comes nearer to us carried in the river of time; it approaches, it is finally here, and then it passes us and recedes into the past. Sometimes it seems as if we ourselves are in the river, carried along by the river of time whether we want to be or not. It moves us inexorably forward no matter what we do, sweeping us past events lying along its banks. We grow, mature, and age. Our bodies move on from the immaturity of childhood, through the bloom of youth, into the maturity of adulthood, and on into the gradual decay of age. We go places and do things; then our actions, pleasures, and enjoyments become vivid memories; they grow dim, and finally are forgotten. All the while death, that final end of time for us, approaches ever closer. The flow of time seems to carry us inexorably toward death, like swimmers caught in a current being swept onward toward a waterfall.

Augustine: Only the Present Moment Is Real

What is this time, whose flow seems so familiar, so ordinary, so threatening? To many philosophers, it has seemed that the flow of time we experience is so strange that in some sense it must be unreal. For example, Saint Augustine after puzzling long and hard over the nature of time, came to the conclusion that time in a sense does not exist:

> A day contains 24 hours; during the first of these hours the rest do not yet exist; during the last of these hours the first no longer exist. . . . A single hour contains minutes that vanish as they pass. Whatever minutes have passed no longer exist, and whatever still remain do not yet exist. If we can conceive of an instant of time that cannot be divided into yet shorter moments, that is the only point of time that can exist at present. And that point flies at such lightning speed from being future to being past, that it can have no duration at all. . . . Time passes from that which does not yet exist, through that which does not endure, into that which no longer exists.[59]

QUICK REVIEW
Augustine argued that only the present instant of time really exists because the past no longer exists and the future does not yet exist.

So, the present instant is the only part of time that is real according to Augustine. The rest—everything in our lives that is past and everything that is future—does not

58 Augustine, *Confessions*, bk. 11, ch. 14. Translated by Manuel Velasquez.
59 Ibid., bk. 11, chs. 15, 18, 20, 21.

exist. The past and the future have only a shadowy mental existence in our mind. Memory preserves past instants, and by anticipation we can think about the future. But outside the mind, in reality, there exists only the changing point-like instant of time that makes up the present.

However, Augustine suggested an important distinction between time from the point of view of God and time as we experience it. Think of it like this: God is outside time. From God's point of view, time is like a line of events that lies stretched out before Him. Every event and every moment of our lives lies on the line, earlier ones to the left and later ones to the right. This time line of events does not flow. In fact, nothing on the line ever changes. Everything on it is fixed. This is time from God's point of view. Notice that although nothing on the line of time changes from being future to being past, events still lie "before" or "after" each other. Time from God's point of view has "before" and "after" but no "future," "present," or "past." On the other hand, time from our point of view is very different. We are in time. We experience time as a movement along the time line of events. For us, time is experienced as flowing by, one instant at a time. Time that was future becomes present and moves on to become the past. Moreover, we experience the past as frozen while the future is not yet fixed.

QUICK REVIEW
Augustine distinguished subjective from objective time. Subjective time is time as we experience it—that is, as flowing from future to present to past. Objective time is time as God might see it: a fixed line of events that are before and after each other but not future or present or past.

We have, then, two very different ways to think about the time in which we live. The first is time as a fixed series of events, or a line containing all events, each located before, after, or at the same time as other events on the line, the whole line being viewed as if from someplace outside time. The second is time as we experience it from within, as a flow from the future, through the present, and into the past. Let us call time as a fixed line of events—time as God views it, according to Augustine—the *objective* view of time. Let us call time as we experience it the *subjective* view of time. Philosophers today generally refer to subjective time as the "A series" and objective time as the "B series." (The philosopher McTaggart, whom we discuss later, invented the terms "A series" and "B series.")

Why should these two views of time matter? Some people have felt that peace of mind can be found only in taking the objective view of time. The subjective view of time is the source of all our pain and sorrow. It is in subjective time that we endure separations from loved ones and from everything else that we treasure. As time flows onward, those we love will all age, their youth will dissipate, middle age will end, and eventually they will die. Our bodies weaken and waste away in subjective time. Childhood is present momentarily, then departs and is gone; adolescence is briefly there then vanishes. Things we buy or make always decay, wear out, fall apart, and are lost to us. Saint Augustine put it like this:

> My life is a distraction and dispersal [in time]. . . . I am wasted and scattered on things which are to come and which pass away. . . . Time is spent in grieving. . . . I am spilled and scattered among times whose order I do not know. My thoughts, the innermost bowels of my soul, are torn apart with the crowding tumults of change, and so it will be until I die.[60]

On the other hand, if we can adopt the view of time as objective, then perhaps we will not feel the pain and sorrow of separation and loss as intensely. We can see that from outside time nothing changes: Everything that happens is still there, fixed in objective time, never lost. We can, perhaps, see that from God's point of view, nothing is lost but always remains and endures. Loss and separation exist only from our point of view in subjective time, not in objective time.

---

60 Ibid., bk. 11, ch. 29.

We can, perhaps, understand why many philosophers have argued that subjective time is not real and that only objective time exists. For example, the existentialist philosopher Merleau-Ponty argued that the flow of time as we experience it cannot be real. We experience time as changing and moving toward the future because of the way our mind relates to real objective time. However, real time does not change. The flow of time we feel is an illusion produced because we experience objective time one moment at a time.

McTaggart: Subjective Time Is Not Real

However, the philosopher who argued most vigorously that the flow of time as we experience it is unreal is the idealist British philosopher J. M. E. McTaggart (1886–1925). McTaggart pointed out that we can think of time as a fixed series of moments, each one "before" or "after" the others. This is objective time, or what he called the "B series." We can also think of time as a sequence of flowing moments, each of which changes from being "future" to "present" to "past." This is subjective time, or what he referred to as the "A series." McTaggart argued that if time did flow as it was supposed to flow in the A series, then the same moment would first be "future," then it would be "present," and then it would be "past." But "past," "present," and "future" are incompatible with one another: The past excludes both future and present; the present excludes both past and future; the future excludes both past and present. Because "past," "present," and "future" are necessarily incompatible with one another, it is impossible for the same thing—the same moment—to be future, present, and past. Yet if time did flow, then every moment would have to be future, and then present, and then past. The A series, our subjective idea of time, then, is inherently contradictory and so cannot be real:

> Past, present and future are incompatible determinations. Every event must be one or the other, but no event can be more than one. If I say that any event is past, that implies that it is neither present nor future, and so with the others. And this exclusiveness is essential to change, and therefore to time. For the only change we can get [if time changes as in the A series] is from future to present, and from present to past.
>
> The characteristics [past, present, and future], therefore, are incompatible. But every event has them all [in the A series]. If *M* is past, it has been present and future. If it is future, it will be present and past. If it is present, it has been future and will be past. Thus all the three characteristics belong to each event. How is this consistent with their being incompatible? . . .
>
> I believe that nothing that exists can be temporal, and that therefore time [as the A series] is unreal.[61]

QUICK REVIEW
McTaggart argues that only subjective time is really time because the very idea of subjective time with moments that are future, present, and past is contradictory, so time is not real.

Moreover, McTaggart claimed, only the A series is really time. For time requires change, and the events or moments in objective time—the B series—do not change. Time, in the B series, is an unchanging, fixed series of events frozen onto the line that makes up the series. This is not really time. Only the A series could really count as time. And because the A series is impossible, time cannot be real.

Many philosophers have agreed with McTaggart's view that the subjective view of time—the A series—is unreal. But they have rejected McTaggart's claim that the B series—objective time—is not really time at all. The B series, or objective time,

61 J. M. E. McTaggart, *The Nature of Existence,* (Cambridge: Cambridge University Press, 1927), vol. 2, bk. 5, ch. 33, p. 20.

they argue, is really a kind of time; in fact, it is the only kind of time that is real. For these philosophers, then, objective time is real, and subjective time is not.

The Australian philosopher J. J. C. Smart agrees with McTaggart's view that our experience of time as passing is an illusion. If we wanted to, he argued, we could get rid of words like *past*, *future*, and *now*, and talk only about where things happen in objective time. For example, instead of saying the Industrial Revolution was in "the past," we could say the Industrial Revolution lies in objective time at a point *t* that is before the year 1900. Once we give up talking about past, present, and future, we will see that events don't move from being future to being past. They are all fixed in objective time and don't change at all. So, the flow of time we think we experience is really an illusion. It is not real. Objective time, however, is real.

In some ways, the denial of subjective time is comforting. Perhaps nothing ends, nothing dies, nothing changes. Everything is there, fixed in the frozen vastness of objective time. Yet are the arguments of these philosophers correct? Suppose that Smart is right, and we can stop using words that refer to past, present, and future. Will this get rid of our experience of time as flowing past us and as carrying us on through youth, old age, and death? Just because we do not talk about something, does this mean that it is no longer there?

QUICK REVIEW
Critics respond that because reality is consistent and has a past, present, and future, these notions must also be consistent.

Or let us look at McTaggart's argument. McTaggart argues that because the past, present, and future are inconsistent notions, and because reality is consistent, reality can't have a past, present, and future. But can't McTaggart's argument be turned on its head? Can't we say that because reality is consistent, and because reality has a past, present, and future, these notions must be consistent notions?

Kant: Time Is a Mental Construct

Is it really possible for us to dismiss the flow of time? Aren't we like an ostrich with its head in the ground when we try to tell ourselves that subjective time—the time of anticipation and loss, of birth, growth, and decay—is not real? Yet some philosophers have gone even further. Some philosophers have argued that all time is unreal.

Immanuel Kant (1774–1804), for example, claimed that time—whether subjective or objective—is simply a construct of the human mind. He argued for this view by asking us to consider our sense experiences. The sensations that flow into us through our senses, he argued, come into us as a parade of colors, shapes, sounds, tastes, feels, and smells. These ever-changing sensations are in themselves a mere jumble of meaningless sense impressions, but the mind immediately imposes order and meaning on them.

QUICK REVIEW
Kant claimed that time is a mental construct.

To get a sense for what Kant means, imagine that you had been born blind and had lived your whole life with absolutely no idea of what seeing even was. Then, suppose an operation was found that cured your blindness so that one day, as you sat on your hospital bed, the bandages were removed from your eyes and you suddenly started seeing flashing lights, flowing colors, and changing shapes. These first visual experiences of yours would be an incomprehensible and meaningless jumble of ever-changing sensations. You would see lights, colors, and changing shapes but would have no idea of what these were. To you in these first moments, your visual sensations would be an example of what Kant means when he says that the sensations that flow into us from our senses are in themselves a mere meaningless jumble. Undoubtedly, as you lay there on your hospital bed, your mind would begin trying to put these sensations into some sort of order, to organize them into stable patterns and regularities. You would have to do this to make sense of what you were seeing.

Kant claimed, in fact, that we could not understand or comprehend the many sensations that flood into us unless our mind first imposes some kind of order and regularity onto them.

According to Kant, space and time are the two basic systems that the mind uses to organize this flow of changing sensations. What happens is that the mind organizes its sensations by putting each sensation at a specific point in space and in time, generally by assigning the sensation to some object located at a specific place in time and space. Thus, space and time are mental maps that the mind uses to organize its sensations by locating them in a spatial and temporal "grid." As a sensation flows into the mind, the mind assigns it to some object that it locates in the spatial and temporal maps we carry around inside our heads, or simply assigns it to a specific point in time or space. We might say, for example, that "Red is the surface color of that apple right there" or "That heat I feel is coming from this boiling pot" or "That sound is coming from over here" or "That crashing noise yesterday came from over there near that rock." Every sensation is thus assigned a location in these mental grids of space and time. The most basic mental map we use is our time map because we assign every single sensation to a specific point in time, but some sensations (such as sounds) might not have a specific location in space. Kant calls our mental time map a "representation":

> Time is a necessary representation, lying at the foundation of all our perceptions. With regard to phenomena in general, we cannot think away time from them, and represent them to ourselves as out of and unconnected with time. But we can quite easily represent to ourselves time empty of any phenomena. Time is therefore given *a priori*. In it alone is all reality of phenomena possible.[62]

Here Kant is pointing out that we necessarily have to think of each of our sensations as occurring at a particular time: Sensations depend on time because we cannot even have a sensation unless it occurs at a specific time. On the other hand, we can easily imagine time continuing in our minds even without any sensations occurring in that time. Time, then, does not depend on the sensations we experience, and we can have the time map in our heads without any sensations in it. Time is something that is already in our mind before we experience any sensations. So, the mind must construct time before it has any sensations as a means of ordering its sensations as they come into the mind through the senses. The mind does this by locating each sensation at some point on the time map. The mind next goes on, Kant argues, to group these sensations together into objects located in its mental map of space. (We might think, for example, "This crunchy hardness, sweetness, and reddish color all belong to this apple right here.") Kant argues, in fact, that the mind puts together everything in the world we see around us by grouping its sensations into objects. But the key point is that time is nothing more than a construct of the mind. Even objective time is not a feature of things as they really exist in themselves, apart from our minds. Time, then, is not real but is a mere mental construct. (You can find a much fuller explanation of Kant's philosophy in the Historical Showcase at the end of Chapter 6.)

However, many scientists have claimed that time really exists "out there" in objects. Still, for science, they claim, the time that is really "out there" is objective time, not subjective time. Subjective time, as we experience it, flows from the future into the past. Moreover, the past, as we experience it, cannot change, whereas the future

---

62 Immanuel Kant, *Critique of Pure Reason, Transcendental Aesthetic,* quoted in *Great Treasury of Western Thought,* ed. Mortimer J. Adler and Charles Van Doren (New York: R. R. Bowker, 1977), 1247.

is indeterminate and can still change. So, in time as we experience it, the fixed past is radically different from the indeterminate future. For science, however, there is no difference between past time and future time. In a scientific formula, scientists claim, we can calculate the future exactly as we can the past. For science, subjective time is not real. As Einstein himself said, "You have to accept the idea that subjective time with its emphasis on the 'now' has no objective meaning . . . the distinction between past, present and future is only an illusion, however persistent."[63] Only objective time, Einstein felt, can be real.

Bergson: Only Subjective Time Is Real

But don't all the attempts to convince us that the flow of time is unreal seem wrong? Isn't the flow of time something we directly and undeniably experience? When we wish that a future event were here (such as the end of school, or a celebration, or a vacation), don't we feel ourselves stuck in the present and powerless to make time move faster? When we are sorry that a past event has ended that we wish had gone on (such as a pleasurable event, or time spent with a friend, or even a person's life), don't we feel the inexorable movement of time carrying us away from the past into the future? Doesn't the mind gradually fill with memories of the past, and only of the past? Don't we experience the flow of time that carries us past birth, through childhood, into adulthood, and on to the slow decline of age? Surely, all of this must be real.

The French philosopher Henri Bergson (1859–1941) agrees. Bergson argues that the scientist's objective time is just a conceptual abstraction, a construct of the mind. The image of time as a line is just that: an image. The concept of objective time is just that: a concept. Neither images nor concepts, he argues, can get at the reality. Only what we directly experience—what we "intuit"—is real. What we directly experience or "intuit" within ourselves is the flow of time. We directly experience ourselves as changing and as flowing through time. Bergson calls this experience the "intuition of duration":

> If I search in the depth of my being . . . I find . . . a continuous flux which is not comparable to any flux I have ever seen. There is a succession of states, each of which announces that which follows and contains that which precedes it. They can, properly speaking, only be said to form multiple states when I have already passed them and turn back to observe their track. In reality no one of them begins or ends, but all extend into each other . . .
>
> The unrolling of our duration resembles in some of its aspects the unity of an advancing movement and in others the multiplicity of expanding states; and, clearly, no metaphor can express one of these two aspects without sacrificing the other. If I use the comparison of the spectrum with its thousand shades, I have before me a thing already made, while duration is continually in the making. If I think of an elastic which is being stretched, or of a spring which is extended or relaxed, I forget the richness of color, characteristic of duration that is lived, and see only the simple movement by which consciousness passes from one shade to another. The inner life is all this at once: variety of qualities, continuity of progress, and unity of direction. It cannot be represented by images.
>
> But it is even less possible to represent it by concepts, that is, by abstract, general or simple ideas. . . . If a man does not himself have the intuition of the

QUICK REVIEW
Bergson argued that objective time is a mental construct, whereas the duration of subjective time that we experience is real.

63 Quoted in Paul Davies, "Time," in *The Experience of Philosophy*, ed. Daniel Kolak and Raymond Martin (Belmont, CA: Wadsworth, 1993), 88.

> constitutive duration of his own being, nothing will ever give it to him, concepts no more than images.
>
> We easily persuade ourselves that by setting concept beside concept we can reconstruct the whole of the object with its parts, thus obtaining, so to speak, its intellectual equivalent. In this way we believe that we can form a faithful representation of duration by setting in line the concepts of unity, multiplicity, continuity, finite or infinite divisibility, etc. There precisely is the illusion. . . . For . . . these concepts, laid side by side, never actually give us more than an artificial reconstruction of the object, and they can only symbolize certain general aspects. It is therefore useless to believe that with them we can seize a reality of which they present to us the shadow alone . . .
>
> However much I manipulate the concepts . . . I never obtain anything which resembles the simple intuition that I have of duration.[64]

Real time, then, for Bergson, is subjective time, the time flow that I experience as moving from future, through present, and into the past. I directly intuit this time. On the other hand, objective time is an intellectual reconstruction and thus is an illusion.

Yet is Bergson correct? Do we really have this so-called **intuition** of flowing time? Many people have argued that they do not have such an intuition. Others have claimed that even if they have this intuition, it is nothing more than an illusion. Real time has to be objective time.

Who is right? Is subjective time real, or is only objective time real? Do things end? Do we and our loved ones die and vanish into nothing? Or is every life and event really fixed eternally in objective time? Perhaps it depends on your point of view. Perhaps we cannot get by with only one of these two ways of approaching time. Both may be necessary, and maybe we should reject neither as unreal. When we do science and perhaps when we think about God, we may have no choice but to use the idea of objective time. When we think of ourselves and our human lives, we may have no choice but to use the idea of subjective time. Perhaps both are real. Or are they?

QUESTIONS

1. Describe as carefully as you can how you experience the sensation of the flow of time. What are its qualities?
2. Suppose that you were convinced that only objective time is real. Would this reduce your anxieties about aging, dying, or losing what you love? Why or why not?
3. Suppose that subjective time is not real. What would this imply about the "obviousness" of the experience of time as flowing? Are there other areas where what seems obvious turns out on examination to be wrong?
4. Suppose that the flow of time is an illusion. Can you think of ways in which this illusion might be caused? The physicist Paul Davies has suggested that the feeling of the flow of time is an illusion exactly like the dizzy feeling we sometimes have (perhaps after having too much to drink) that the universe is spinning, which is obviously an illusion. Is this a good comparison? Why or why not?

---

64 Henri Bergson, *An Introduction to Metaphysics*, trans. T. E. Hulme (London: Macmillan, 1913), selections from pp. 9, 10, 13, 15, 16, 20.

PHILOSOPHY AT THE MOVIES

Watch *Terminator II: Judgment Day* (1991) or *Terminator III: Rise of the Machines* (2003), in both of which computers in the future are fighting a losing war against the few humans who have survived their initial attack. The computers send a "cyborg" robot into the past to kill John Connor, the person destined to become the leader of the humans, while the humans send back a robot to protect John Connor. Several time loops and paradoxes occur in these films. Which concept or concepts of time does the action of these films presuppose? Explain.

Chapter Summary

This chapter opens by noting that what we ultimately consider real reflects and influences how we see ourselves. Questions of reality, which fall in the realm of metaphysics, tell us what ultimately matters. We discussed a number of metaphysical views, including the materialism–idealism debate; the responses of pragmatism, existentialism, and analytic philosophy; and the revival of a kind of idealism in the postmodern versions of antirealism. The main points made in the chapter are:

3.1 What Is Real?

- Metaphysics is the branch of philosophy that asks what reality and being are, and questions what can ultimately matter.

3.2 Reality: Material or Nonmaterial?

- Materialism is the position that reality is ultimately matter. Hobbes, an early materialist, argued that only physical objects are real.
- Idealism is the position that reality is nonmatter: idea, mind, or spirit, for example. Berkeley, an idealist, argued that because all we perceive are our own ideas, only minds and their ideas are real.
- **Arguments with "if-then" and "either-or" connectives are valid when their logical form is that of a valid argument, otherwise they are invalid.**

3.3 Reality in Pragmatism

- Pragmatism, as developed in the United States by Peirce, James, and Dewey, rejects all absolutistic assumptions about reality, admits the pluralistic nature of reality, and refuses to consider any claims but those focused on "fruits, consequences, facts."

3.4 Reality and Logical Positivism

- Logical positivists, who base their views on how language works, have generally held that metaphysics is based on linguistic confusions. Logical positivists such as Alfred J. Ayer and Rudolph Carnap argue that metaphysical statements about reality are meaningless expressions of emotion and not statements of fact.
- **A categorical syllogism is valid when (1) the middle term refers to a whole category in a premise; (2) A term in the conclusion that refers to a whole category also refers to the whole category in a premise; (3) Both premises are not negative; (4) the conclusion is negative if a premise is negative.**

3.5 Antirealism: The Heir of Pragmatism and Idealism

- Postmodern antirealists say no reality exists independent of our language, our thoughts, our perceptions, and our beliefs. Different languages, thoughts, perceptions, and beliefs create different realities.

3.6 Encountering Being: Reality in Phenomenology and Existentialism

- The concept of human existence and being plays an important part in phenomenology and existentialism, which arose out of disillusionment with past philosophies.
- Husserl's phenomenology emphasizes that only reality as it appears to consciousness can have any meaning to us. Heidegger's phenomenology stresses being. What is ultimately real for the phenomenologist is pure consciousness, which itself has being. Existentialism stresses personal freedom, the lack of an essential human nature, and the lack of behavioral guidelines.

3.7 Is Freedom Real?

- Determinism has significant implications for our views on punishment and responsibility.
- Determinists hold that all human actions are caused by previous events and the laws of nature; indeterminists hold that human actions are free and so determinism is false; compatibilists hold that determinism and human freedom are compatible.
- Kant claimed that determinism and indeterminism arise from two different but inescapable ways of thinking about our actions.

3.8 Is Time Real?

- Time may be thought of as objective time, which does not flow from the future into the past, or as subjective time, which we experience as flowing from the future into the past.
- Many philosophers and scientists have agreed that real time is objective time, whereas subjective time is an illusion that does not exist. Henri Bergson has argued that subjective time is real, whereas objective time is an abstraction and not real.

Despite the diversity of metaphysical views, most metaphysicians agree on some important issues. These points of agreement and disagreement suggest insights into ourselves.

To begin with, most metaphysicians agree that reality has an order that our reason can discover. True, materialism may hold that the order is strictly mechanistic; idealism, that it is spiritual; existentialism and phenomenology, that it is being; analytic philosophy, that it what is empirically verifiable; and antirealism, that it depends on the system of concepts that we use to describe our experience. But members within each school hold that some order exists and that we can understand it. Most important, each of us is part of that order, whatever its nature. To know the self is at least partially to know that order and how we fit into it, a point that phenomenology and existentialists emphasize.

At the same time, fundamental differences among these metaphysical outlooks reflect and reinforce different views of human nature and of self. For the materialist, we are part of the matter that composes the universe and are subject to the same laws. When we speak of mind, we really mean brain; when we refer to mental states, we are really talking about brain states.

For many idealists, in contrast, the individual is part of a cosmic mind or spirit that is conscious of itself. Only the individual can be aware of his or her own consciousness. In the last analysis, this personal awareness makes each of us unique. For some idealists, the order in the universe is a divine dimension; it is the order of God's mind. In understanding this cosmic order or plan, we understand our position in it and thus the self.

The pragmatist views the self as neither primarily matter nor primarily idea. Pragmatists see the self as consisting of many dimensions and existing in many worlds. Our philosophical views arise out of our emotional and social needs. We shall not find personal meaning and purpose in the cosmos because it possesses none. For personal meaning, we must turn to the consequences of our actions, judging them according to the results that they produce.

Existentialism shares pragmatism's skepticism of absolutistic doctrines. But more than any of the other outlooks, it stresses personal freedom. The self is essentially a reality in the making that is not finished until the individual dies. The reality of the self is whatever we choose to make it. We are ultimately free to think, choose, and act however we wish. Such freedom without guidelines is frightening, leading to uncertainty, anxiety, and despair. But this, say the existentialists, is the human condition.

For many phenomenologists, our reality is our existence. The fundamental self is not its characteristics, properties, or the other objective qualities, but being. The self is not our idea of what we are but the immediate concrete reality of being ourselves. We move furthest from a knowledge of the self when we separate self from subjective reality, as we do when we view it as some object to be studied, quantified, and known. We are closest to the self when we strip from consciousness the experiences of objects that occupy it. Then, we realize that the self is what precedes its experiences—that is, pure being.

And for the postmodern antirealists, the self is a constructed self. The many languages and systems of concepts that we use contain within them the elements out of which we construct the concept of the self. This construct is all there is to the self. Outside of our language there is no objective "real" self.

So, although members of different metaphysical schools share some beliefs, they vary in their approach to the issue of self. Their views have dramatically different implications for the self and its place in the world.

3.9 Readings

We began this chapter by describing some of the interesting and new metaphysical ideas about reality put forth by the late Robert Nozick, an unusually innovative and creative philosopher who taught at Harvard until 2001. In these readings. we return to Nozick's ideas, particularly around the questions, "What is real? and "Are there degrees of reality?" Is being a soldier fighting a war, for example, more or less real than, say, working as an actor? Nozick's questions are at the heart of the first reading, a short story by Russell Maloney entitled "A Toast to Captain Jerk." In the story—which takes place as Britain enters World War II—a young British actor apparently living in New York tries to convince his American girlfriend that his decision to return home and fight in the war is right because war is "real" while he, she, and their lives are "make believe"; his girlfriend counters that she is real, that what they were planning to do as actors would have been real, and that he's a "jerk" to risk his life in a war he can avoid. You might ask yourself: What do the young man and his girlfriend believe reality is? Do you agree with either? Of the views about reality that we have seen in this chapter, which ones make the views of the young actor or his girlfriend most understandable? What does the last sentence in the story mean: "He looked as if he might never know what was real, even if he died trying to find out"?

In the second reading, philosopher Robert Nozick reflects on exactly the same issues that underlie the argument between the young man and his girlfriend. Nozick thought deeply about what "reality" signifies and came to some highly unorthodox conclusions. In this reading, Nozick tries to show that there are degrees of reality and that a person doing one thing can be more or less real than another person who does something else. To explain this, Nozick tries to identify exactly what characteristics make one person, activity, or work of art more or less real than another. Is Nozick's argument persuasive to you? With whom does Nozick ultimately side: the young actor or his girlfriend? In what way are Nozick's views similar to those of Heidegger or the existentialists? Do you see any similarities between Nozick's views and those of the pragmatists? If you apply to yourself Nozick's "dimensions" of degrees of reality, what would you say is your degree of reality? What would you say has been the degree of reality of your life until now?

RUSSELL MALONEY

A Toast to Captain Jerk

Saturday night is the night the actors sit up late, getting drunk and boasting. Oreste's, the Italian restaurant near Eighth Avenue which is the semi-official clearing house for forty-dollar Equity minimum salary checks, was almost filled by eleven-thirty. There was a surge of words in the little smoky room, properly sustained on a column of breath, pushed forward by well-exercised, perfectly controlled diaphragms, sharply audible: *Orson definitely told me but no casting till week after next from hunger what does he think Skowhegan who else could they get for that money little bitch left my pictures three months on the Coast fake the dancing but they cut half my lines Chamberlain Brown Sardi's out of town but his secretary said they say Crosby Gaige but I can't see Zelda in one of those grass skirts from hunger.*

Only one girl in Oreste's was eating alone. She was a slender, long-boned girl, attractive in a manner that represented a definite choice. The candid wideness of her eyes was the result of spaced eyebrows and eye shadow on the outer corners of the lids. Her hair was brushed away from her brow to make her face naked and without guile. Girls of this candid type can be becomingly greedy, and this one was eating a plate of spaghetti, winding up neat forkfuls with precise motions of her narrow brown hands, stopping now and then to drink from a tumbler of red wine. She glanced at the doorway every few minutes, raising her chin and turning her head with unconscious theatrical emphasis.

The man she was waiting for arrived a little before midnight, running lithely down the three steps that led from the street and striding straight to her table. He wore a blue serge suit, white shirt, starched collar, plain tie, and black shoes with only a dull polish. "I'm late," he said, sitting down. He had a lean, brownish head and wide shoulders.

"That's all right," the girl said. "It must have taken you three hours to dress. You eaten?"

"Yes, hours ago." The man looked over his shoulder, caught the waiter's eye, and called, "Whiskey soda."

The waiter crossed the room and stood at the man's shoulder. "Rye whiskey or Scotch?" he said.

"Oh, for God's sake," the man said. *"Scotch."*

"The idea, Joe! Only Americans drink rye," Mona said to the waiter. "Filthy stuff, rye," she added to the man, speaking in an approximation of his own clipped accent.

"Mona," the man said, "let's not—"

"Tracy," she said, "Let's." Looking at him calmly, she searched her patent-leather handbag for cigarettes and matches. "Very interesting," she said, taking out a cigarette and tapping it on a scarlet thumbnail. "Your clothes, I mean." She tapped the cigarette once more, and put the wrong end in her mouth. "The last time I saw you in those particular clothes, Tracy, was two summers ago, when we did 'the End of the Story.' Detective Inspector Harrod of Scotland Yard." She lit the cigarette and flicked the match across the room. "Veddy stiff, veddy British. 'I'm afraid this is murder. No one must leave the house.' So on and so on.... Joe!" she called suddenly to the waiter. "Joe, I'd like another glass of this lovely red ink. Ink-and-soda, eh, Tracy?"

"I hoped we wouldn't get drunk," Tracy said. "Tonight."

"Well, I decided we would, so shut up," she said. "As I was saying, I note with interest that we have combed our wardrobe. I know your wardrobe as well as you do—do you mind? We decided against the brown tweeds, and gray jacket with flannels, and the double-breasted pin stripe and the single-breasted herring-bone. And, of course, the dinner jacket, and the tails. No, we wanted something solid and respectable, because we were mousing around in banks and steamship offices, and maybe even in the British Ambassador's office."

"The Consulate," Tracy said. "For God's sake."

"And all because we've decided that our wardrobe isn't quite complete. We want a nice little uniform, too. Journey's End.' Captain Stanhope."

"That's not the way to take it," Tracy said. "I'm going to do it, and you might as well make up your mind."

"My mind's made up, all right," she said. "And you're not going to do it."

"Yes."

"No. For one thing, they won't let you. With your first papers and all."

"It'll be a little irregular," he said. "But don't tell me you don't think people are getting over there. And there's Canada."

"Listen," the girl said, a note of urgency in her voice. "We won't be in it. Stay here, and you won't be in it. Why do you think you have to be in it? I bet they can have a dandy war without you."

"It's no use, Mona."

"Well, aren't actors supposed to keep on being actors in a war? In canteens and so on? They did before."

"My God, the war's *real*," the man said. "It's got nothing to do with all this we've had over here."

"And *I'm* not real? And it isn't real that we were both getting screen tests this fall, or that Gordon talked to you about that thing he's doing?"

"No, not a bit real," Tracy said, "Everything I've done here is silly make-believe. You're a nice bit of make-believe, but the rest of it isn't so nice—all the cheap hotel rooms and the bit parts, and making believe that I or you or Brooks Atkinson or anybody else on earth cares whether I'm any good at pretending to be Detective Inspector Harrod. Over there, it'll be real, at least."

The girl settled back in her chair. "I've lent you money for some damn silly things, but you won't get it for this," she said.

"I won't have to. I borrowed some tonight from some friends of Mother's uptown, and besides, I haven't paid my room rent for the past month, I've kept that."

"So that's what's really real, is it?" she said. "All that over there?"

"It is now, for me."

"Captain Stanhope," the girl said. "Captain Jerk, the unknown fall guy. You know what I'm going to do, when this is all over? I'm going to find where they've buried you, and put a special little epitaph over you. I'll say 'He skipped his bill at the Trafton Hotel. He was in arrears with his Equity dues. He owed Oreste twelve dollars for drinks. He behaved just as badly as everybody else in the world today.'" She sat up straight in her chair, in the smoke and the noise of the laughter around her. "And if you think I'm going to apologize tomorrow for saying this, you're wrong. Because it's what I think. You're just skipping your hotel bill."

"It'll be real, at least," he said again, but there was no certainty in his face. He looked as if he might never know what was real, even if he died trying to find out.

Reprinted from *The New Yorker* by permission. Copyright © 1939 The New Yorker Magazine, Inc.

ROBERT NOZICK

Being More Real

At some times a person feels more real to himself or herself. Stop, now, to ask, and answer this question: When do you feel most real? (Stop, now, to actually think about it. What is *your* answer?)

Someone may think the question is confused. At all the times when a person exists, he does exist then and so must be real then. Nevertheless, though we may not be able yet to state what notion of reality is involved, we do seem to be able to distinguish degrees of reality.

First, consider literary characters. Some literary characters are more real than others. Think of Hamlet, Sherlock Holmes, Lear, Antigone, Don Quixote, Raskolnikov. Even though none of them exist, they seem more real even than some people we know who do exist. It is not that these literary characters are real because they are "true to life," people we could meet believably. The reality of these characters consists in their vividness, their sharpness of detail, the integrated way in which they function toward or are tortured over a goal. Even when their own focus is not completely clear, they are intent on focusing or are presented (as Flaubert presents Madame Bovary) in clear focus. These characters are "realer than life," more sharply etched, with few extraneous details that do not fit. In the characteristics they exhibit they are more concentrated centers of psychological organization. Such literary characters become bywords, paradigms, models, epitomes. They are intensely concentrated portions of reality.

The same features that make some literary characters more real than others, clicking them into paradigmatic focus, apply outside the literary realm also. Works of art, paintings or music or poems, often seem intensely real; their sharply etched features make them stand out against the usual background of blurry and vague objects. In a mode of organization more tight and coherent, or at least having a more evident mode of organization and a more interesting one, they constitute more integrated wholes. The beauty of works of art or of natural scenes, the dynamic balance of the array, makes it more vivid, more real than the usual jumble we encounter. . . .

Just as some literary characters are more real, so are some people. Socrates, Buddha, Moses, Gandhi, Jesus—these figures capture our imagination and attention by their greater reality. They are more vivid, concentrated focused, delineated, integrated, inwardly beautiful. Compared to us, they are more real.

We, too, however, are more real at some times than at others, more real in some modes than in others. People often say they feel most real when they are working with intense concentration and focus, with skills and capacities effectively brought into play; they feel most real when they feel most creative. Some say during sexual excitement, some say when they are alert and learning new things. We are more real when all our energies are focused, our attention riveted, when we are alert, functioning completely, utilizing our (valuable) powers. Focusing intensely brings us into sharper focus. . . .

This increase in (awareness of) integration of previously isolated parts enables one to act with more power and a wider band of intense focus, and thus to feel more real.

The realm of reality, what has reality to more than a certain degree, is not the same as what exists. Literary characters can be real though they do not exist; existing things may have only that minimal degree of reality requisite for existing. It seems plausible to locate reality's lower bound at existence; nothing *less* vivid and focused than what exists will count as real. Reality comes in degrees, though, and the reality that especially interests us here lies above this minimal lower boundary.

According to this notion, reality has many aspects; there are various dimensions that can contribute to a higher degree of reality. To have a higher position or score along one of these dimensions (holding constant the position on the other relevant dimensions) is to have a higher degree of reality. These other dimensions may be connected with clarity of focus and vividness or organization, but they are not simply an instance of it. We have already mentioned beauty in discussing works of art; the more beautiful something is, the more reality it has. Another dimension of reality, I think, is (greater) value. The greater something's intrinsic value, the more reality it has. Greater depth also brings greater reality, as do greater perfection and greater expressiveness. . . .

I want to say that you are your reality. Our identity consists of those features, aspects, and activities that don't just exist but also are (more) real. The greater the reality a feature has, the more weight it has in our identity. Our reality consists partly in the values we pursue and live by, the vividness, intensity, and integration with which we embody them. Our values alone, even our value, is not the whole of our reality, however; the notion of reality in general includes dimensions other than value. In saying that we are constituted by our reality, I mean that the substance of the self is the reality it manages to achieve. One view of immortality might be that what survives our death is our reality, whatever reality we manage to realize. . . .

Is "reality" the most fundamental evaluative category, or is there another even more fundamental one to use in understanding and evaluating it? The most basic category, as I see it, is that of reality. This category has various subdimensions. Along these dimensions (all other things being equal) a higher position makes something more real. Consider, now, the question of whether it is more valuable to be more real. As one of the component dimensions of reality, being more valuable is *one* way of being more real. It does not follow, however, that whenever something is more real it is more valuable. It may possess its high degree of reality because of its high place along another dimension of reality, one different than value. Value is a particular dimension which, although of great inclusiveness, does not encompass everything good. To seek only value is like seeking only beauty in a work of art while caring nothing for power of statement, depth of insight, surprise, energy, or wit.

Reality is a general notion that encompasses value, beauty, vividness, focus, integration. To say of any one of these—for example, beauty—that it yields greater reality is not merely to say repetitiously that more beauty brings more beauty. There is a general notion of reality that includes beauty as one strand; seeing beauty as a way of being more real places it within the pattern of this general notion, alongside the other strands, to their mutual illumination. But why think these various dimensions all are aspects of one thing and not simply separate; isn't it arbitrary to group them together as dimensions under one broader notion and call that reality? These dimensions do not constitute an unconnected list, though. As we shall see, they intertwine in an intricate structure of cross-connections that bind them together in a family, as dimensional aspects of one broader notion.

Can we really distinguish reality from actuality, though; is not something real precisely when it exists, when it is actual? Nevertheless, despite our temptation to make this objection, reality does lend itself to being spoken of in terms of *degrees*; while one thing does not exist more than another (which also exists) and is not more actual than another, one thing can be more real than another. We speak of someone as "a real friend," not simply in contrast to a false friend, for there are intermediate cases also of friends who are less than real friends. We speak also of someone's being a real ballplayer, a real poet, a real man, and in each case the term *real* is used as a grading notion that compares and admits of degrees. . . .

Religious views, too, sometimes speak of God as "more real" than we are, and mystics say their experiences are more real than ordinary experiences—*of* something more real and also more real themselves. One reason the mystic gives his experience such credence, and maintains it to be so valuable, is because it is (or seems) so very real. My point now is not to endorse any of these particular claims, but rather to notice that (the notion of) reality does lend itself to being structured this way, in degrees or levels; it can comfortably be used to grade or rank things, to evaluate them comparatively.

Robert Nozick, *The Examined Life: Philosophical Meditations* (New York: Simon & Schuster, 1989), selections taken from pp. 129, 130, 131, 132, 137. Copyright © 1989 by Robert Nozick.

3.10 HISTORICAL SHOWCASE

Hobbes and Berkeley

We have suggested throughout this chapter that people's metaphysical views influence their views of human nature. Two seventeenth-century philosophers—Thomas Hobbes and George Berkeley—illustrate the profound impact a metaphysical view can have on one's view of human nature.

Hobbes, as was briefly mentioned earlier, proposed the metaphysical view that everything in the universe is material. The view led him to propose a materialistic view of human nature. Hobbes believed that humans are, in effect, complicated machines. Berkeley, on the other hand, advanced the metaphysical claim that everything in the universe is spiritual or nonmaterial. This claim then led him to hold a thoroughly spiritualistic view of human nature: To be human is to be a kind spirit.

Examining the views of Hobbes and Berkeley in some detail will help us see how metaphysics is related to the positions we take on other philosophical issues, in particular on the issue of human nature. It will become clear, also, how metaphysics can influence our views of God and society.

HOBBES

Thomas Hobbes was a thoroughgoing materialist: He held that only material objects exist. In this respect he differed considerably from his contemporary, René Descartes (whom we showcase in the next chapter). Descartes carried over from medieval philosophers like Aquinas the view that reality consists of both material and immaterial (or "spiritual") entities. Hobbes rejected this dualistic view. The recent astronomical discoveries of Copernicus, Kepler, and Galileo had all been based on the observation of moving bodies. Influenced by their approach to reality, Hobbes reasoned that perhaps all reality could be explained in terms of the motions of bodies in space.

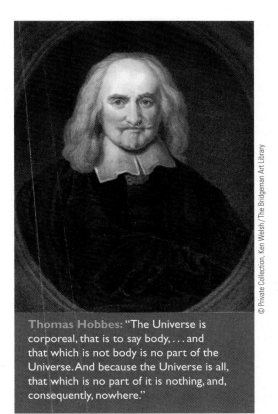

Thomas Hobbes: "The Universe is corporeal, that is to say body, . . . and that which is not body is no part of the Universe. And because the Universe is all, that which is no part of it is nothing, and, consequently, nowhere."

© Private Collection, Ken Welsh / The Bridgeman Art Library

Born prematurely in 1588 when his mother, overcome with fear at the approach of the invading Spanish navy, went into early labor, Hobbes throughout his youth had a melancholy personality that earned him the nickname of the Crow. The son of a clergyman, Hobbes was sent at the age of fourteen to study at Oxford, where he tells us he learned to hate philosophy. However, he apparently learned enough so that when he graduated in 1608 he was hired by the wealthy and aristocratic Cavendish family as a tutor for their sons. He later remarked that the job left him more than enough time to read and study while his young charges were "making visits" in town. Traveling with the Cavendish family gave Hobbes the opportunity to see much of Europe and to become acquainted with the great thinkers of the period, especially the Italian astronomer Galileo, who at this time was busily tracing the motions of the heavenly bodies with the aid of geometry. At about the age of forty, probably under Galileo's influence, Hobbes came to the conclusion that everything in the universe could be explained in terms of the motions of material bodies and that geometry could provide the basic laws of their motions. He attempted to work out the details of this philosophy in a remarkable series of writings that included his masterpiece *Leviathan* and a trilogy bearing the titles *De Corpore (On Material Bodies), De Homine (On Man)*, and *De Cive (On the Citizen).* Hobbes' final years were relatively happy. He died in 1679, famous for his materialistic philosophy and the political theories that grew out of it.

Hobbes was unequivocal in claiming that matter is all there is in the universe:

> The Universe, that is the whole mass of things that are, is corporeal, that is to say body; and has the dimensions of magnitude, namely, length, breadth, and depth. Also every part of body is likewise body, and has the like dimensions. And, consequently, every part of the Universe is body, and that which is not body is no part of the Universe. And because the Universe is all, that which is no part of it is nothing, and, consequently, nowhere.[1]

(Hobbes' archaic spelling has been modernized in this and following quotations.)

---

1 Thomas Hobbes, *Hobbes's Leviathan* (Oxford: Clarendon, 1909; original work published 1651), 524.

In Hobbes' view, the characteristics and activities of all objects, including human beings, can be explained in purely mechanical terms:

> For seeing life is but a motion of limbs, the beginning whereof is in some principal part within; why may we not say, that all *automata* (engines that move themselves by springs and wheels as does a watch) have an artificial life? For what is the *heart*, but a *spring*; and the *nerves*, but so many *strings*; and the *joints*, but so many *wheels*, giving motion to the whole body, such as was intended by the artificer?[2]

Hobbes attempted to apply this **mechanism** to explain the mental activities of human beings. Many philosophers, Descartes in particular, believed that the mental activities of perceiving, thinking, and willing were evidence that human minds are spiritual or nonmaterial. Mental activities (thinking) and mental contents (thoughts) seem to have no physical characteristics (that is, they have no color, size, or position and seem to be nonbodily). Hobbes was particularly concerned with showing that even mental activities could be entirely explained in terms of the motions of material bodies. He begins this task by first arguing that all of our thoughts originate in our sensations (or, as he writes, in "sense"). And sensations, he claims, are nothing more than motions in us that are caused by external objects. These motions in us travel through our nerves to our brains:

> Concerning the thoughts of man, I will consider them first singly, and afterwards in train or dependence upon one another . . .
>
> The origin of them all, is that which we call SENSE [sensation], for there is no conception in a man's mind, which has not at first, totally, or by parts, been begotten upon the organs of sense . . .
>
> The cause of sense is the external body, or object, which presses the organ proper to each sense . . . , which pressure, by the mediation of the nerves, and other strings and membranes of the body, continues inwards to the brain and heart, causes there a resistance, or counter-pressure, or endeavor [movement] of the heart . . . , which endeavor [movement], because [it is] *outward*, seems [to us] to be some matter without. And this *seeming* or *fancy*, is that which men call *sense*. [Sense] consists, as to the eye in *light*, or *color* . . . ; to the ear, in a *sound*; to the nostril, in an *odor*; to the tongue . . . , in a *savor*; and to the rest of the body, in *heat*, *cold*, *hardness*, *softness*, and such other qualities as we discern by *feeling*.
>
> All [these] qualities . . . are, in the object that causes them, but so many . . . motions of the matter, by which it presses our organs. Neither in us, that are pressed, are they anything else, but . . . motions; for motion produces nothing but motion. . . . [Just] as pressing, rubbing, or striking the eye makes us fancy a light, and pressing the ear produces a din, so do the bodies we see, or hear, produce the same [sensations] by their . . . action.[3]

Once the motion created in our senses has traveled to the brain, the brain retains this motion, much like water continues moving after the wind stops. This "decaying" motion in our brain is the residual image that we retain in our memory. Thus, our memory of an object is nothing more than the residual motion the object leaves impressed on our brain:

> When a body is once in motion, it moves, unless something else hinders it, eternally; and whatever hinders it, cannot in an instance, but [only] in time, and by degrees, quite extinguish it. And as we see in the water, though the wind cease, the waves [continue] . . . rolling for a long time after, so also it happens in that motion which is made in the internal parts of man . . .
>
> This decaying sense, when we would express the thing itself, . . . we call *imagination*. . . . But when we would express the decay, and signify that the sense is fading, old, and past, it is called *memory*. So that imagination and memory are but one thing.[4]

But what does all of this have to do with thinking? Hobbes held that when we are thinking, we are merely linking together the decaying images (or motions) that we have retained in our memory. Our thinking activities are thus nothing more than a sequence of motions linked together, usually as they are linked together when we first experienced them as sensations. Sometimes our thinking is "un-guided," as when we daydream, and sometimes it is "regulated," as when we are trying to solve some problems:

> *By consequence* or TRAIN of thoughts, I understand that succession of one thought to another, which is called, to distinguish it from discourse in words, *mental discourse*.

2 Ibid., 8.

3 Ibid., 12.
4 Ibid., 13–14.

> When a man thinks on anything whatsoever, his next thought after is not altogether . . . casual. . . . The reason . . . is this. All fancies [images] are motions within us, relics of those made in the sense. And those motions that immediately succeeded one another in the sense, continue also together after sense. . . .
>
> This train of thoughts, or mental discourse, is of two sorts. The first is *unguided, without design,* and inconstant, wherein there is not passionate thought, to govern and direct those that follow to itself, [such] as the end and scope of some desire, or other passion, in which case the thoughts are said to wander and seem impertinent one to another, as in a dream. . . .
>
> The second is more constant, as being *regulated* by some desire and design. . . . From desire arises the thought of some means we have seen produce the like of that which we aim at; and from the thought of that, the thought of means to that mean; and so continually, till we come to some beginning within our own power. . . . The train of regulated thoughts is of two kinds: one, when an effect imagined we seek the causes, or means that produce it. . . . The other is, when imagining anything whatsoever, we seek all the possible effects that can by it be produced.[5]

But "trains of thoughts" are not the only things produced by the motions that begin in our senses and end in the imaginations of our brains. The motions of our imaginations also produce motions in our organs of appetite (which Hobbes thought were located mainly in the heart); these are called *desires.* The motions called desires, in turn, are what lead us to engage in "voluntary actions":

> There be in animals, two sorts of *motions* peculiar to them. One [is] called *vital* . . . such as the *course* of the *blood,* the *pulse,* the *breathing,* the *concoction, nutrition, excretion, etc.* . . . The other is . . . *voluntary motion,* as to *go,* to *speak,* to *move* any of our limbs, in such manner as is first fancied in our minds. . . . And because *going, speaking,* and the like voluntary motions, depend always upon a precedent thought . . . it is evident that the imagination is the first internal beginning of all voluntary motion. . . . These small beginnings of motion, within the body of man, before they appear in walking, speaking, striking, and other visible actions, are commonly called ENDEAVOR.
>
> This endeavor, when it is toward something which causes it, is called APPETITE, or DESIRE. . . . And when the endeavor is from something, it is generally called AVERSION. . . . That which men desire, they are also said to LOVE, and to HATE those things for which they have aversion. . . . But whatsoever is the object of any man's appetite or desire, that . . . he . . . calls *good,* and the object of his hate and aversion, *evil.* . . .
>
> As, in sense, that which is really within us is, as I have said before, only motion, caused by the action of external objects. . . . So, when the action of the same object is continued from the eyes, ears, and other organs to the heart, the real effect there is nothing but motion or endeavor, which consists in appetite or aversion, to or from the object moving [us].
>
> When in the mind of man, appetites, and aversions, hopes, and fears, concerning one and the same thing, arise alternately; and divers good and evil consequences of the doing, or omitting the thing propounded come successively into our thoughts; so that sometimes we have an appetite to it; sometimes an aversion from it; sometimes hope to be able to do it; sometimes despair, or fear to attempt it; the whole sum of desires, aversions, hopes and fears continued till the thing be either done, or thought impossible, is that we call DELIBERATION. . . .
>
> In *deliberation,* the last appetite, or aversion, immediately adhering to the action, or to the omission thereof, is what we call the WILL. . . . *Will,* therefore, is *the last appetite in deliberating.*[6]

Thus, Hobbes concluded, not only can a materialist philosophy fully account for all our obviously physical characteristics, but it can also account for all of those inner mental activities that other philosophers take as evidence of a spiritual or nonmaterial mind: sensing, remembering, thinking, desiring, loving, hating, and willing. These mental activities do not require us to say that some kind of nonmaterial reality exists in addition to the material objects in the world. There is no such thing as a nonmaterial reality: Everything consists of matter and its motions.

Hobbes felt that his materialistic philosophy also provided the foundations for a social philosophy. By examining the basic material characteristics of human individuals, he felt he could explain why our societies are structured as they are. Hobbes began by maintaining that the central desires that affect the

5 Ibid., 18–20.

6 Ibid., 39, 41, 46, 47.

relations between individuals inevitably lead them to quarrel with one another:

> So that in the nature of man, we find three principal causes of quarrel. First, competition; secondly, diffidence; thirdly, glory.
>
> The first makes men invade for gain; the second, for safety; and the third, for reputation. The first use violence, to make themselves masters of other men's persons, wives, children, and cattle; the second, to defend them; the third, for trifles, as a word, a smile, a different opinion, and any other sign of undervalue, either direct in their persons, or by reflection in their kindred, their friends, their nation, their profession, or their name.[7]

Because of these antagonistic drives, individuals would inevitably strive "to destroy or subdue one another" if it were not for the restraints that the "common power" of government is able to impose on them. If people were in a "state of nature"—that is, if they were in the situation they were in before any government restrained them from harming one another—they would be constantly at war, and life would be miserable:

> Hereby it is manifest, that during the time men live without a common power to keep them all in awe, they are in that condition which is called war, and such a war as is of every man against every man. . . . In such condition, there is no place for industry, because the fruit thereof is uncertain: and consequently no culture of the earth; no navigation, nor use of the commodities that may be imported by sea; no commodious building; no instruments of moving, and removing, such things as require much force; no knowledge of the face of the earth; no account of time; no arts; no letters; no society; and which is worst of all, continual fear, and danger of violent death; and the life of man, solitary, poor, nasty, brutish, and short.[8]

To escape the brutal state of nature into which their passions continually push them, people at last decide to form a government (or, as Hobbes calls it, a Leviathan). This government is meant to set up a "common power" possessing enough force to establish law and order and thereby put an end to fighting. We set up a government by entering into a "social contract" with one another. That is, we make an agreement (or "covenant") with one another to hand over all power to a person or a group. That person or group then becomes the "sovereign" ruler and has the authority to use the power or force of the citizens themselves to enforce the law (which the sovereign makes) and to establish peace and order. We thus emerge from the dreadful state of nature by becoming "subjects" and taking on the constraints of life in a civil society:

> The final cause, end, or design of men, who naturally love liberty and dominion over others, in the introduction of that restraint upon themselves, in which we see them live in commonwealths, is the foresight of their own preservation, and of a more contented life thereby; that is to say, of getting themselves out from that miserable condition of war, which is necessarily consequent, as has been shown, to the natural passions of men, when there is no visible power to keep them in awe, and tie them by fear of punishment to the performance of their covenants . . .
>
> The only way to erect such a common power, as may be able to defend them from the invasion of foreigners, and the injuries of one another, and thereby to secure them in such sort, as that by their own industry, and by the fruits of the earth, they may nourish themselves and live contentedly; is, to confer all their power and strength upon one man, or upon one assembly of men, that may reduce all their wills, by plurality of voices, unto one will: which is as much to say, to appoint one man, or assembly of men, to bear their person; and every one to own, and acknowledge himself to be the author of whatsoever he that so bears their person, shall act, or cause to be acted, in those things which concern the common peace and safety; and therein to submit their wills, every one to his will, and their judgments, to his judgment. This is more than consent or concord; it is real unity of them all, in one and the same person, made by covenant of every man with every man, in such manner, as if every man should say to every man, *I authorize and give up my right of governing myself, to this man, or to this assembly of men, on this condition, that you give up your right to him, and authorize all his actions in like manner.* . . . [T]his is the generation of the great LEVIATHAN. . . . And he that carries this person, is called SOVEREIGN, and said to have *sovereign power*, and everyone besides, his SUBJECT.[9]

Thus, the materialist philosophy that Hobbes created also gave him the basic concepts he needed to explain the formation of governments. Governments are simply the outcome of the motions we

7 Ibid., 234–296.
8 Ibid.

9 Ibid., 128, 131–132.

call "desires." Desires lead people to fight with one another (for their material possessions), and this results in a continual "war of all against all." A further desire or motion, the desire for peace, then leads people to form governments.

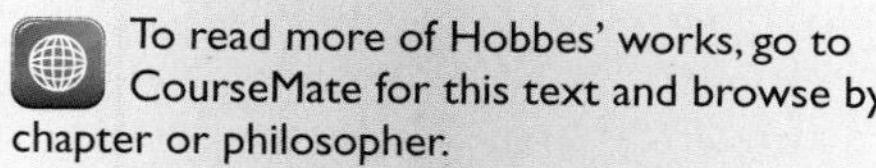
To read more of Hobbes' works, go to CourseMate for this text and browse by chapter or philosopher.

BERKELEY

George Berkeley is perhaps the most famous of all those idealist philosophers who hold that reality is primarily spiritual and not material. To some extent, Berkeley was reacting to the philosophy of materialists such as Hobbes, whose views were becoming popular in the wake of the growing influence of the new sciences. Such materialist philosophies, Berkeley felt, left no room for God and thus were inimical to religion. What better way to combat atheism than to prove that materialism was false and that all reality is spiritual!

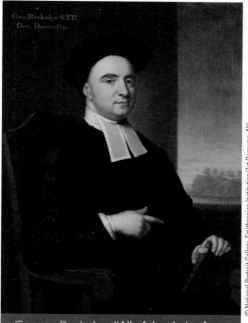

George Berkeley: "All of the choir of heaven and furniture of the earth, in a word all those bodies which compose the mighty frame of the world, have no substance without a mind. Their being is to be perceived. Consequently, so long as they are not actually perceived by me or other created spirits, they must either have no existence at all or else exist in the mind of some eternal spirit."

© National Portrait Gallery, Smithsonian Institution/Art Resource, NY

Berkeley was born in 1685 in Kilkenney, Ireland. As a teenager, he was sent to Trinity College in Dublin, where he graduated with a master's degree in 1707. Berkeley stayed on at Trinity College as a teacher for six years. There, at the age of twenty-four, he finished writing what was to become the classic exposition of an idealist philosophy, *A Treatise Concerning the Principles of Human Knowledge.* In 1713, Berkeley left Trinity College. He was by now an ordained Protestant minister, and in 1729 he and his recent bride traveled as missionaries to Newport, Rhode Island, where he planned to organize a college that would eventually be established in Bermuda. But funding for the college never materialized, and in 1731 he returned to England. In 1734, Berkeley became a bishop in the Church of England and was assigned to the diocese of Cloyne in Ireland. Sixteen years later, at the age of sixty-five, he retired to Oxford with his wife and family. There he died in 1753.

Berkeley held the view that all we know or perceive of the world around us are the sensations we have: the colors, sights, sounds, and tastes we experience. We commonly attribute these sensations to material objects outside us. When our eyes see a small round patch of red, for example, we might infer that outside us there exists a material object that we call an apple and that light coming from this material object causes our eyes to have the sensation of red color. However, Berkeley questioned this inference. He pointed out that we really have no reason to say that in addition to the sensations we experience within our minds, there *also* exists outside us (or, in his words, "without us") some kind of material objects. We do not even have any idea what these so-called material objects would be like, for all we perceive are our sensations, and these sensations are clearly not material objects because our sensations exist entirely in our minds (or, in Berkeley's words, "our spirits"). All that exists besides our minds, or "spirits," Berkeley concluded, are the sensations we perceive in our minds and the mental images we voluntarily form in them. Berkeley used the term *ideas* to refer to the contents of our minds, including both the sensations we have and the mental images we form. Thus, for Berkeley, the world consists entirely of minds ("spirits") and ideas.

Berkeley summarized his view in the Latin slogan *esse est percipi*, which means "to exist is to be perceived": The only things that exist, besides minds, are the ideas perceived within minds. As he flamboyantly asserted, "All the Choir of Heaven and the furniture of earth, in a word all those bodies which compose the mighty frame of the world, have no substance without a mind."[10] Thus, Berkeley was a complete idealist: He held the view that reality consists of nothing more than the ideas in our minds.

Berkeley's views are most clearly expounded in the short work he titled *A Treatise Concerning the Principles of Human Knowledge.* He opens the treatise with a remark expressing what many newcomers to philosophy feel: that philosophy seems to create more "doubts and difficulties" than it resolves:

> Philosophy being nothing else but the study of wisdom and truth, it may with reason be expected that those who have spent most time and pains in it should enjoy a greater calm and serenity of mind, a greater clearness and evidence of knowledge, and be less disturbed with doubts and difficulties than other men. Yet so it is, we see the illiterate bulk of mankind that walk the high road of plain common sense, and are governed by the dictates of nature, for the most part easy and undisturbed. To them nothing that is familiar appears unaccountable or difficult to comprehend. They complain not of any want of evidence in their sense, and are out of all danger of becoming skeptics. But no sooner do we depart from sense and instinct to follow the light of a superior principle, to reason, meditate, and reflect on the nature of things, but a thousand scruples spring up in our minds concerning those things which before we seemed fully to comprehend. Prejudices and errors of sense do from all parts discover themselves to our view; and, endeavoring to correct these by reason, we are insensibly drawn into uncouth paradoxes, difficulties, and inconsistencies, which multiply and grow upon us as we advance in speculation, till at length, having wandered through many intricate mazes, we find ourselves just where we were, or, which is worse, sit down in a forlorn skepticism.[11]

To resolve the "uncouth paradoxes, difficulties, and inconsistencies" that give philosophy a bad name, Berkeley undertakes to examine "the first principles of human knowledge"—that is, the primary sources from which we draw all our knowledge.

He begins by pointing out that if we look into our minds, we will see that everything we know consists either of sensations ("ideas imprinted on the senses or perceived by attending to the passions") or mental images ("ideas formed by help of memory and imagination"). Consequently, each object we know in the world around us (such as an "apple, a stone, a tree, a book and the like") is really nothing more than a collection of ideas (sensations of color, touch, smell, taste, or hearing). In addition to ideas, he notes, there are also "active beings" or "minds." In fact, ideas can exist only in minds. Because all objects consist of ideas and because ideas can exist only in the mind, it follows that the objects in the world exist only in the mind! Berkeley argues for this startling conclusion in the following passages:

> It is evident to anyone who takes a survey of the *objects* of human knowledge that they are either ideas actually imprinted on the senses, or else such as are perceived by attending to the passions and operations of the mind, or lastly, ideas formed by help of memory and imagination—either compounding, dividing, or barely representing those originally perceived in the aforesaid ways. By sight I have the ideas of light and colors, with their several degrees and variations. By touch I perceive, for example, hard and soft, heat and cold, motion and resistance, and of all these more and less either as to quantity or degree. Smelling furnishes me with odors, the palate with tastes, and hearing conveys sounds to the mind in all their variety of tone and composition. As several of these are observed to accompany each other, they come to be marked by one name, and so to be reputed as one thing. Thus, for example, a certain color, taste, smell, figure, and consistency having been observed to go together are accounted one distinct thing signified by the name "apple"; other collections of ideas constitute a stone, a tree, a book, and the like sensible things—which as they are pleasing or disagreeable excite the passions of love, hatred, joy, grief, and so forth.
>
> But, besides all that endless variety of ideas or objects of knowledge, there is likewise something which knows or perceives them and exercises diverse operations, as willing, imagining, remembering, about them. This perceiving, active being is what I call "mind," "spirit," "soul," or "myself." By which words I do not denote any one of my ideas, but a thing entirely distinct from them, wherein they exist or, which is the same thing, whereby they are perceived—for the existence of an idea consists in being perceived.

---

10 George Berkeley, *A Treatise Concerning the Principles of Human Knowledge*, in *The Works of George Berkeley*, vol. 1, ed. George Sampson (London: George Bell & Sons, 1897), 181–182.

11 Ibid., 161.

That neither our thoughts, nor passions, nor ideas formed by the imagination exist without the mind is what everybody will allow. And it seems no less evident that the various sensations or ideas imprinted on the sense, however blended or combined together (that is, whatever objects they compose), cannot exist otherwise than in a mind perceiving them.—I think an intuitive knowledge may be obtained of this by anyone that shall attend to what is meant by the term "exist" when applied to sensible things. The table I write on I say exists, that is, I see and feel it; and if I were out of my study I should say it existed—meaning thereby that if I was in my study I might perceive it, or that some other spirit actually does perceive it. There was an odor, that is, it was smelled; there was a sound, that is to say, it was heard; a color or figure, and it was perceived by sight or touch. This is all that I can understand by these and the like expressions. For as to what is said of the absolute existence of unthinking things without any relation to their being perceived, that seems perfectly unintelligible. Their *esse* is *percipi*, nor is it possible they should have any existence out of the minds or thinking things which perceive them.

It is indeed an opinion strangely prevailing amongst men that houses, mountains, rivers, and, in a word, all sensible objects have an existence, natural or real, distinct from their being perceived by the understanding. But with how great an assurance and acquiescence soever this principle may be entertained in the world, yet whoever shall find in his heart to call it in question may, if I mistake not, perceive it to involve a manifest contradiction. For what are the forementioned objects but the things we perceive by sense? And what do we perceive besides our own ideas or sensations? And is it not plainly repugnant that any one of these, or any combination of them, should exist unperceived? . . .

But, say you, though the ideas themselves do not exist without the mind, yet there may be things like them, whereof they are copies or resemblances, which things exist without the mind in an unthinking [material] substance. I answer, an idea can be like nothing but an idea; a color or figure can be like nothing but another color or figure. If we look ever so little into our thoughts, we shall find it impossible for us to conceive a likeness except only between our ideas. Again, I ask whether those supposed originals or external things, of which our ideas are the pictures or representations, be themselves perceivable or not? If they are, then they are ideas and we have gained our point; but if you say they are not, I appeal to anyone whether it be sense to assert a color is like something which is invisible; hard or soft, like something which is intangible; and so of the rest. . . .

But, [suppose] it were possible that solid, figured, movable substances may exist without the mind, corresponding to the ideas we have of bodies, yet how is it possible for us to know this? Either we must know it by sense or by reason. As for our senses, by them we have the knowledge only of our sensations, ideas, or those things that are immediately perceived by sense, call them what you will; but they do not inform us that things exist without the mind, or unperceived, like to those which are perceived. This the materialists themselves acknowledge. It remains, therefore, that if we have any knowledge at all of external things, it must be by reason, inferring their existence from what is immediately perceived by sense. But what reason can induce us to believe the existence of bodies without the mind, from what we perceive, since the very patrons of matter themselves do not pretend there is any necessary connection betwixt them and our ideas? I say it is granted on all hands (and what happens in dreams, frenzies, and the like, puts it beyond dispute) that it is possible we might be affected with all the ideas we have now, though no bodies existed without resembling them. Hence it is evident the supposition of external bodies is not necessary for the producing of our ideas; since it is granted they are produced sometimes, and might possibly be produced always in the same order we see them in at present, without their concurrence . . .

But, say you, surely there is nothing easier than to imagine trees, for instance, in a park, or books existing in a closet, and nobody by to perceive them. I answer you may so, there is no difficulty in it; but what is all this, I beseech you, more than framing in your mind certain ideas which you call books and trees, and at the same time omitting to frame the idea of anyone that may perceive them? But do you yourself perceive or think of them all the while? This therefore is nothing to the purpose; it only shows you have the power of imagining or forming ideas in your mind; but it does not show that you can conceive it possible the objects of your thought may exist without the mind. To make out this, it is necessary that you conceive them existing unconceived or unthought of, which is a manifest repugnancy. When we do our utmost to conceive the existence of external bodies, we are all the while only contemplating our own ideas. But the mind, taking no notice of itself, is deluded to think it can and does conceive bodies existing

> unthought of or without the mind, though at the same time they are apprehended by or exist in itself. A little attention will discover to anyone the truth and evidence of what is here said, and make it unnecessary to insist on any other proofs against the existence *of material substance.*[12]

Berkeley's views were naturally accused of leading to skepticism, the view that we cannot know anything about reality. For Berkeley's views are but a short step away from the view that because the ideas in our minds might be false and because all we know are the ideas in our minds, we can never know anything for sure about the real world. However, Berkeley did not intend his idealist philosophy to encourage skepticism. On the contrary, he felt that "the grounds of Skepticism, Atheism and Irreligion" lay in materialism. Those who hold that only matter exists, he felt, were inevitably led to the view that God does not exist because God is a nonmaterial spirit. The best way to combat atheism, then, is to prove that matter does not exist and that, on the contrary, only spirits and their ideas exist. If spirits and ideas are the only reality, in knowing these we know all the reality there is. Thus, skepticism, like atheism, is false.

Berkeley, in fact, took great pains in his attempt to show that God exists. God is a crucial part of his universe and plays an essential role as the source of the world we see displayed before our senses. If we examine the ideas in our minds, he argues, we will see that some of them require the existence of another "spirit" to produce them, and this is God. God produces in us the sensations that we perceive as reality and ensures that we perceive an orderly reality in which we can plan our lives and look easily toward the future. Berkeley concludes that the "surprising magnificence, beauty, and perfection" of the orderly display that God creates in our minds and that we call the world should fill us with admiration:

> I find I can excite [some] ideas in my mind at pleasure, and vary and shift the scene as oft as I think fit. It is no more than willing, and straightway this or that idea arises in my fancy [imagination]; and by the same power it is obliterated and makes way for another . . .
>
> But whatever power I may have over my own thoughts, I find the ideas actually perceived by sense have not a like dependence on my will. When in broad daylight I open my eyes, it is not in my power to choose whether I shall see or no, or to determine what particular objects shall present themselves to my view; and so likewise as to the hearing and other senses; the ideas imprinted on them are not creatures of my will. There is therefore some *other* will or spirit that produces them.
>
> The ideas of sense are more strong, lively, and distinct than those of the imagination; they have likewise a steadiness, order, and coherence, and are not excited at random, as those which are the effects of human wills often are, but in a regular train or series, the admirable connection whereof sufficiently testifies to the wisdom and benevolence of its Author. Now the set rules or established methods wherein the mind we depend on excites in us the ideas of sense are called "the laws of nature"; and these we learn by experience which teaches us that such and such ideas are attended with such and such other ideas in the ordinary course of things.
>
> This gives us a sort of foresight which enables us to regulate our actions for the benefit of life. And without this we should be eternally at a loss; we could not know how to act on anything that might procure us the least pleasure or remove the least pain of sense. That food nourishes, sleep refreshes, and fire warms us; that to sow in the seedtime is the way to reap in the harvest; and in general to obtain such or such ends, such or such means are conducive—all this we know, not by discovering any necessary connection between our ideas, but only by the observation of the settled laws of nature, without which we should all be in uncertainty and confusion, and a grown man no more knows how to manage himself in the affairs of life than an infant just born . . .
>
> But if we attentively consider the constant regularity, order, and concatenation of natural things, the surprising magnificence, beauty, and perfection of the larger, and the exquisite contrivance of the smaller parts of the creation, together with the exact harmony and correspondence of the whole, but above all the never-enough-admired laws of pain and pleasure, and the instincts or natural inclinations, appetites, and passions of animals; I say if we consider all these things, and at the same time attend to the meaning and import of the attributes: one, eternal, infinitely wise, good, and perfect, we shall clearly perceive that they belong to the aforesaid spirit, "who works all in all," and "by whom all things consist." . . .
>
> It is therefore plain that nothing can be more evident to anyone that is capable of the least reflection than the existence of God, or a spirit who is intimately present to our minds, producing in them all that variety of ideas or sensations which continually affect us, on whom we have an absolute and entire dependence, in short "in whom we live, and move, and have

12 Ibid., 179, 180–182, 186–187, 189.

> our being." That the discovery of this great truth, which lies so near and obvious to the mind, should be attained to by the reason of so very few, is a sad instance of the stupidity and inattention of men who, though they are surrounded with such clear manifestations of the Deity, are yet so little affected by them that they seem, as it were, blinded with excess of light.[13]

Berkeley's idealist philosophy, then, provided him with what he thought was an irrefutable proof of the existence of spiritual reality, including God, and of the nonexistence of the material world on which Hobbes and other materialists insisted.

To read more of Berkeley's works, go to CourseMate for this text and browse by chapter or philosopher.

QUESTIONS

1. Carl Sagan said that "each human being is a superbly constructed astonishingly compact, self-ambulatory computer." In what respects is this similar to Hobbes' view? In what respects does it differ?

2. As the contemporary philosopher J. J. C. Smart writes, "By 'materialism' I mean the theory that there is nothing in the world over and above those entities which are postulated by physics. Thus I do not hold materialism to be wedded to the billiard-ball physics of the nineteenth century. The less visualizable particles of modern physics count as matter [for me]." In what respects is Smart's materialism similar to Hobbes'? In what respects does it differ? Does Smart's materialism have any philosophical implications that are radically different from Hobbes'?

3. Hobbes claims that you are nothing more than your physical body (or your brain). If this is true, then *you* are exactly the same as *your body* (or your brain), so whatever is true of *you* must be true of *your body*. But consider the following objection to Hobbes: "Although *you* can be morally blameworthy or praiseworthy, can we say that *your body* or *your brain* is morally blameworthy or praiseworthy? Although *you* can have wishes (for example, to do math) or thoughts (for example, about philosophy), does it make sense to say that *your body* or *your brain* has these wishes or thoughts? Although *you* can love God, isn't it absurd to say *your body* or *your brain* loves God? Although it makes sense to say that *you* have a body, does it make sense to say that *your body* has a body?" Evaluate these criticisms.

4. Do you think Hobbes' description of the quarrelsomeness of human nature is an accurate description of your own self? Of others? Is Hobbes correct in claiming that without the restraints of government, you would involve yourself in a continual "war against every man" and that your life would be "solitary, poor, nasty, brutish, and short"?

5. Must a materialist philosophy like Hobbes' take a pessimistic view of human beings?

6. Do you agree with Berkeley's criticism that philosophy inevitably draws us "into uncouth paradoxes, difficulties, and inconsistencies, which multiply and grow as we advance, till, at length, . . . we find ourselves just as we were, or, which is worse, sit down in a forlorn skepticism"? What assumptions about the purpose and nature of philosophy does Berkeley make? How does this compare to Plato's conception of philosophy?

7. Do you think this is an adequate summary of Berkeley's main argument: "All the objects we perceive are only ideas; ideas exist only in minds; therefore, all the objects we perceive exist only in minds"? Do you think that any parts of this argument are false? Explain.

8. The English writer Dr. Samuel Johnson once said something like the following as he kicked a rock: "There! I thus refute Berkeley!" Would this show that Berkeley's idealism is false? Why?

9. To what extent do the following two verses (of unknown authorship) correctly express the role God plays in Berkeley's philosophy?

   I have always thought that God
   Must find it exceedingly odd
   To think that his tree
   Won't continue to be
   When there's no one about in the quad.

   Dear Sir:
   Your astonishment's odd.
   For I am always about in the quad.
   And so my tree will continue to be,
   Since observed by
   Yours faithfully,
   God.

10. Berkeley's idealism is very different from the way we usually think of the world, but does it make any *practical* difference? Would anything be different for you if Berkeley is correct? Should you do anything differently?

13 Ibid., 191–192, 247–248.

C H A P T E R

4 Philosophy, Religion, and God

The highest that man can attain in these matters is wonder.
GOETHE

© angelo gilardelli/iStockphoto.com

OUTLINE AND LEARNING OBJECTIVES

4.1 The Significance of Religion

OBJECTIVES | When finished you will be able to:

- Explain the importance of the choice between belief and unbelief.
- Define religion and distinguish it from religious belief, religious experience, and theology.

4.2 Does God Exist?

OBJECTIVES | When finished you will be able to:

- Explain and critically evaluate the ontological, cosmological, and design arguments for the existence of God.
- **Identify and evaluate an argument from analogy**

4.3 Atheism, Agnosticism, and the Problem of Evil

OBJECTIVES | When finished you will be able to:

- Explain the difference between atheism and agnosticism.
- Define the Problem of Evil and critically evaluate the claim that evil shows that God does not exist.
- **Understand how formal and informal fallacies can affect discussions of religion and God.**

4.4 Traditional Religious Belief and Experience

OBJECTIVES | When finished you will be able to:

- State and critically evaluate James' view that our passional nature should determine what to believe when an option is living, forced, and momentous.
- Define what a numinous religious experience is and evaluate the claim that such an experience provides reasonable grounds for belief in God.

4.5 Nontraditional Religious Experience

OBJECTIVES | When finished you will be able to:

- Explain and evaluate Kierkegaard's view that only subjective thinking can know the truth about God, and Tillich's view that God cannot be proved but only experienced as one's ultimate concern.
- Explicate and evaluate the feminist claim that traditional religious concepts of God are sexist.
- Describe some of the central claims of Hinduism and Buddhism and how these differ from traditional Western approaches to religion.

Chapter Summary

4.6 Readings: Fyodor Dostoevsky, excerpt from *The Brothers Karamazov*

William P. Alston, "The Inductive Argument from Evil and the Human Cognitive Condition"

4.7 Historical Showcase: Aquinas, Descartes, and Conway

4.1 The Significance of Religion

Perhaps no other area of life is as important yet contains such excruciating uncertainties as religion. Consider "The Road," a very brief "parable" told by John Hick:

> Two men are traveling together along a road. One of them believes that it leads to the Celestial City, the other that it leads nowhere. But since this is the only road there is, both must travel it. Neither has been this way before, therefore neither is able to say what they will find around each corner. During their journey they meet with moments of refreshment and delight, and with moments of hardship and danger. All the time one of them thinks of his journey as a pilgrimage to the Celestial City. He interprets the pleasant parts as encouragements and the obstacles as trials of his purpose and lessons in endurance, prepared by the king of that city and designed to make him a worthy citizen of the place when at last he arrives. The other, however, believes none of this, and sees their journey as an unavoidable and aimless ramble. Since he has no choice in the matter, he enjoys the good and endures the bad. For him there is no Celestial City to be reached, no all-encompassing purpose ordaining their journey; there is only the road itself and the luck of the road in good weather and in bad.
>
> They do not entertain different expectations about the coming details of the road but only about its ultimate destination. Yet, when they turn the last corner, it will be apparent that one of them has been right all the time and the other wrong. . . . [T]he choice between theism [belief in God] and atheism [belief in no god] is a real and not merely an empty or verbal choice.[1]

QUICK REVIEW
The choice between belief and unbelief influences one's view of oneself and much more.

So much depends on the choice between belief and unbelief! There is perhaps no greater influence on one's view of oneself and one's destiny than the choice between belief and unbelief. For example, the Judaic and Christian religious traditions share the belief that humans are creatures who stand midway between nature and

1 J. H. Hick, *Philosophy of Religion* (Englewood Cliffs, NJ: Prentice Hall, 1973), 91.

spirit. We are on the one hand finite, bound to earth, and capable of sin. On the other, we are able to transcend nature and to achieve infinite possibilities because we possess the divine (Godlike) qualities of consciousness and the ability to love. Primarily because of Christianity, we view ourselves as beings with a supernatural destiny. Both Judaism and Christianity affirm that we are made "in the image of God," a likeness which many have said is based on our ability to apprehend the world around us. Shakespeare expressed this view: "What a piece of work is a man! How noble in reason! How infinite in faculty! In form, in moving, how express and admirable! In action how like an angel! In apprehension how like a god!" *(Hamlet,* II, ii, 317).

On the other hand, those who reject all religious belief do not see themselves as transcending nature; in fact, nature is all there is. For those who reject religion, humans are certainly not immortal, and neither do they have any kind of spiritual nature. Those who reject religion do not see human life as having a supernatural destiny, or any destiny at all beyond death. Shakespeare also expressed this sentiment when he wrote these lines, late in his life: "Life's but a walking shadow, a poor player that struts and frets his hour upon the stage, and then is heard no more; it is a tale told by an idiot, full of sound and fury, signifying nothing" *(Macbeth,* V, v, 17).

Obviously, the choice to accept or to reject religion can deeply influence our view of ourselves and of our destiny. In fact, as the example of Shakespeare suggests, our religious choices can change as we travel on our journey through life, and this in turn can transform profoundly how we look at ourselves and our final destiny. Yet, as Hick's parable of the Road implies, the choice to accept or reject religious belief will not be definitively validated or refuted until the end of our journey—if then. Which, then, should we choose? Which choice—to accept or reject religious belief—is more reasonable during the journey? That is the basic question we address in this chapter: How reasonable is religion?

Defining Religion

Before we turn to address this question directly, however, we should briefly look at a more basic issue: What exactly is religion? Although religion is extremely difficult to define, we should attempt to get a clearer idea of what it is before we continue.

When you hear the word *religion*, what do you think of? A church? A synagogue? A mosque? Belief in God? For many people, the word *religion* refers to a belief in God that is institutionalized and incorporated in the teachings of some group such as Catholicism, Judaism, or Islam. Yet some religions do not seem to have a belief in God. Buddhism, for example, although usually considered a religion, contains no belief in a personal God like the God of the Judaic and Christian traditions. Other "noncreedal" religions have few or no official beliefs, such as the Unitarian Universalist Church, for example, which asserts that its members are not bound by any belief or creed and have "no requirement to believe in a god of any sort."[2] Some religions, such as the Episcopal Church, have highly institutionalized rituals. Others, like the Quaker Church, have little ritual. Many religions stress personal commitment based on a meaningful relationship with the sacred, which is often a Supreme Being. Other religions, like animistic religions, seem to place little importance on personal commitment. It is easier, perhaps, to note common features of religion than to define it, and that is the approach we will take, although qualifications may still be necessary.

QUICK REVIEW
Religion is difficult to define because some religions do not believe in God, some have no official beliefs, some are not institutionalized, and some do not value personal commitment.

2 See the Unitarian Universalist Church Association of Congregations website at http://uua.org/index.shtml.

QUICK REVIEW
Smart says all religions have some or all of six dimensions: (1) doctrine, (2) experience, (3) myth, (4) ritual, (5) morality, and (6) organization.

Professor Ninian Smart suggests that religion has six dimensions.[3] Although not all six dimensions are found in all religions, every religion shares in most of these to some degree: (1) doctrine, or a set of beliefs about the universe and its relation to the supernatural, such as the belief that there is a single God who created the universe or the belief that the universe is controlled by the law of karma; (2) experience of, or an emphasis on, events in which the believer feels immediately and strikingly the presence of God or of a supernatural dimension; (3) myth, or a set of stories that convey sacred or special meaning, such as the story of Adam and Eve or the story of the illumination of the Buddha; (4) ritual, or acts of worship, prayer, sacraments, and readings of sacred scriptures; (5) morality, or a set of rules and precepts that believers are enjoined to follow; and (6) organization, or an organized social group that preserves and perpetuates the religion.

Although religion frequently finds expression through institutionalized ritual and orthodox belief, religion is not just an institution, a collection of doctrines, or a stylized ritual. Morality, feeling, and emotion are also important features of religion. In fact, many people today feel that the emphasis on a symbolic object of devotion, ritualized through an organizational structure, has blurred religion's real import: a deep and personal experience with the object of one's chief loyalty. Many religious leaders have spoken in terms of personal commitment, experience, and need. In so doing, they have recognized one of the roots from which religion springs: our unending search for meaning and fulfillment.

In our investigation of religion, however, we will set aside many of these prominent dimensions of religion in order to concentrate on two: religious doctrine and religious experience. Our aim, as suggested earlier, is to look closely at the issue that should be critical for the person considering the kind of fundamental choice between belief and unbelief that Hick's parable suggests: Is religion reasonable? So, we look most closely at how reasonable it is to believe what religion asks us to believe, and how reasonable it is to trust the experiences of religion.

Religious Belief, Religious Experience, and Theology

In this chapter, we will have numerous occasions to speak of **religious belief**, a term we use in its most general sense: the doctrines of a religion about the universe and religion's relation to the supernatural. On the other hand, when we use the term *religious experience*, we refer to an experience of this supernatural dimension. Having experienced this dimension, a person may feel an intense personal relationship with the rest of creation, perhaps even with a Creator. In this respect, possibly, we all seek a religious experience; we all search for an internal peace resulting from a harmonious personal relationship with all other living things. Religious belief and experience continue to be of intense philosophical interest. They are also intimately joined with the issue of self.

QUICK REVIEW
Religious belief refers to doctrines held about a supernatural dimension; *religious experience* refers to experience of this supernatural dimension.

Where do we find religious experience today? Some find it in the existence of a personal God. Therefore, we begin by examining the most basic religious belief; we will look at whether it is reasonable to believe that God exists. We then look more closely at what religious belief itself is and whether it is possible to believe even without good reasons to believe. However, many people relate to the divine without relating to a Supreme Being. They claim that religious experience is an intimately personal encounter with the basis of all being, with the source of all reality. Therefore, we turn next to discussing religious experience to develop a clearer

3 Ninian Smart, *Worldviews* (New York: Charles Scribner's Sons, 1983).

understanding of what it is and whether it makes sense. Finally, there are many Westerners who turn to Eastern thought—Hinduism and Buddhism, for example—in their search for a belief that is reasonable. We therefore look briefly at some major themes in Eastern religious traditions.

It is important not to confuse the philosophy of religion with theology. Literally speaking, **theology** means simply the rational study of God. In practice, however, the term is usually reserved for the rational study of religious beliefs by scholars committed to those beliefs. Theologians study God and the religious beliefs of a community with the assumption that God exists and that those religious beliefs are true. By contrast, philosophers approach God and religious beliefs without these assumptions: For the philosopher, these assumptions must themselves be proved.

QUICK REVIEW
Theology, the study of religious beliefs, assumes that God exists and the beliefs are true; the philosophy of religion studies religious beliefs but does not assume that they are true or that God exists.

QUESTIONS

1. Explain the difference between religious belief and theology.
2. Evaluate this statement: "For many people, belief in science has achieved the status of a religion." Can science be a religion? Explain.
3. What kinds of beliefs or behavior would someone have to adopt before you would be willing to say that the person is "religious"? What does the term mean to you?

PHILOSOPHY AT THE MOVIES

Watch *Water* (2005) which takes place in India and in which Chuyia, a little girl married to an old man who has died, must, according to Hindu Scriptures, live out her life with other widows in an "ashram" (Hindu monastery). There she is befriended by Kalyani, a beautiful young widow who must work as a prostitute to support the ashram and who falls in love with a man whom Hindu Scriptures forbid her to marry. How does religion in this film affect who and what each character thinks he or she is, i.e., affect their self-understanding? In what sense are the beliefs that force the widows to live in the ashram and that prevent Kalyani from marrying, "religious" beliefs? In what sense are they not "religious" beliefs?

4.2 Does God Exist?

The most common way for people of a Judeo-Christian culture to find their place in the scheme of things is through a relationship with a personal God. **Theism** is belief in a personal God who is creator of the world. *Monotheism* is the belief that there is only one God. Most of us have been raised to believe that the God of monotheism is an individual loving Being who, having created the universe, cares for each individual, actively participates in the life of each person, and listens to and answers the prayers of individuals.

This theistic concept has perhaps never been under greater attack than it is today. We live in a period that has often pitted traditional religious concepts against the growing weight of scientific discovery. Can we, *should* we, believe in the God of theism, or must we modify this belief, perhaps even abandon it in light of what science has found? Even theologians are asking whether the believer can any longer believe in a traditional God. They are questioning an idea that has centuries of tradition behind it, that is a cornerstone of the lives of many people today, and that forms the basis not only for our religious beliefs and experiences but also for our conception of ourselves and our place in the universe.

critical thinking

"I believe in God because the Bible says that God exists." Is anything wrong with this claim?

QUICK REVIEW
Scientific discoveries and theories today challenge religious belief, although for some, science strengthens belief.

 critical thinking

Suppose psychologists prove that belief in God originates when people are taught to believe in God from an early age. Would this show that the belief must be wrong?

QUICK REVIEW
For some people, proof of God's existence is not needed, but for others, proof strengthens religious belief.

Consider, for example, a scientific discovery that still amazes, yet has been accepted fact since 1995 when the Hubble telescope was used to count the galaxies: the visible universe around us contains about 125 billion galaxies with billions of stars in each, many—perhaps most—of which have worlds rotating around them like the planet earth rotates around our own star, the sun. And beyond the visible universe there are undoubtedly hundreds of billions—perhaps approaching an infinity—more galaxies. Can we even comprehend an individual divine person who could rule over such an immense multitude of worlds? And how are we to believe that such a God is personally concerned with each person's daily life and immortal destiny on our own tiny planet? All our traditional ideas of God suddenly shrink in the great vastness of the universe that science has uncovered.

Science has brought many of us to ask today not only if we accept the traditional concept of God, but also if there is any God at all. Nevertheless, despite the rise of science and the decay of many traditional religious forms, religion thrives in this country. Although science might shake the beliefs of many people, just as many continue to hold fast to their belief in a personal caring God, and this belief continues to be their way of locating themselves in the scheme of things. Others, as we will see, even find in science a new basis for religious belief. In fact, the relationship between science and religion has never been one of complete opposition nor complete harmony. Science has often called the claims of religion into question, but at other times the claims of science have been used to support religious claims.

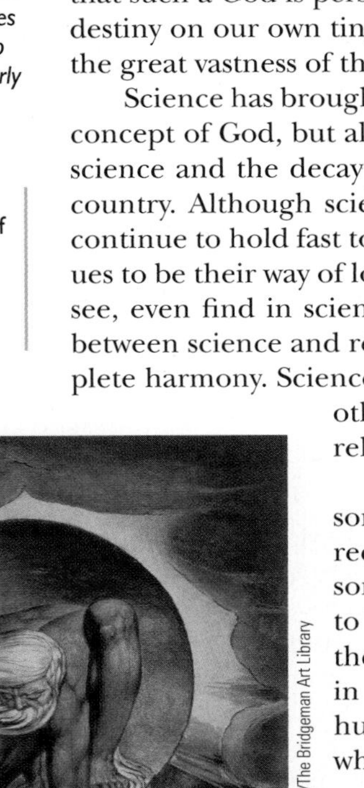

© Whitworth Art Gallery, The University of Manchester, UK/The Bridgeman Art Library

The Ancient of Days.

We begin our overview of philosophy and religion with some of the arguments for the existence of God. It is vital to recognize the purpose of these arguments: to advance the personal quest to know God. Knowledge of God was and continues to be one of the most significant topics occupying thinkers. And the arguments advanced for God's existence are one element in the centuries-long attempt to determine the extent to which humans can have rational knowledge of God and the extent to which science has a bearing on our knowledge of God.

We present the arguments for the existence of God as illustrations of a traditional way by which people have fortified their religious convictions, strengthened their relationship with a personal God, and discovered something about that God. In reading these arguments, notice their reliance on reason and sense experience, and keep in mind the contrasting approach, which we will also examine, which is essentially to believe on a non-rational basis. We examine how this latter approach has been attempted and how for many people today it serves as the basis for religious belief and experience. In reading this chapter, then, you will begin to mine two rich veins in the development of religious thought, the rational and the non-rational.

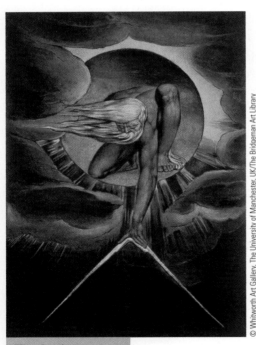

The Ontological Argument

Earlier theologians had propounded arguments that God's existence is self-evident, but Saint Anselm (1033–1109) was the first to assert this kind of argument in a formal, self-conscious manner. Anselm, who was the archbishop of Canterbury, argued that if we merely think about what God is, we will see that God has to exist. Anselm's argument, now known as the ontological argument, relied on reason alone. Later arguments for God's existence (like the "cosmological arguments" we discuss next) would be based on what we discover about the world when we look around us.

But Anselm held that the mind, by merely reasoning about its own ideas, could arrive at the realization that God exists.

The **ontological argument** is an argument that deduces the existence of God from the mere idea we have of God. God, Anselm reasoned, is "that than which nothing greater can be conceived." Since we understand this idea of God (i.e., we understand the meaning of these words), this idea of God exists in our minds. Now, what if we believed that God was just an idea in our minds and that God did not exist in the real world? If so, we could easily conceive of something greater: a real God who exists in the real world. For the real thing is greater than the mere idea of that thing. Therefore, Anselm concluded, if God is "that than which nothing greater can be conceived," then God must exist.

To read more from Anselm's *Proslogion*, go to the CourseMate for this text and browse by chapter or philosopher.

This is about as distilled a version of Anselm's ontological argument as one is likely to get. To appreciate Anselm's argument fully, however, you must follow its development in his most important philosophical work, the *Proslogion*. While reading the following passage, keep in mind the impulse behind it, which, in the words of Anselm is: "*Credo ut intelligam*"—"I believe in order that I may understand." Thus, without belief, one can have no understanding of God:

QUICK REVIEW
Anselm's ontological proof says (1) God is that than which nothing greater can be conceived, (2) that than which nothing greater can be conceived must exist in reality and not merely in the mind, (3) so God exists in reality.

> Truly there is a God, although the fool hath said in his heart, there is no God.
>
> And so, Lord, do thou, who dost give understanding to faith, allow me . . . to understand that thou exists and that thou art that which we believe thou art. And, indeed, we believe that thou art a being than which nothing greater can be conceived. But perhaps such a being does not exist, for hasn't the fool said in his heart, there is no God (Psalms xiv.1)? But, at any rate, this very fool, when he hears of this being of which I speak—a being than which nothing greater can be conceived—understands what he hears, and what he understands is in his understanding; although he does not believe it exists.
>
> For, it is one thing for an object to be in one's understanding, and another to understand that the object exists. When a painter first conceives of a painting he will later create, he has the painting in his understanding, but he does not yet believe it exists, since he has not yet painted it. But after he has produced the painting, he will both have it in his understanding, and he will also believe that it exists, because he has made it.
>
> Hence, even the fool [who denies that God exists] must agree that he has in his understanding, at least, the idea of that than which nothing greater can be conceived. For, when he hears this idea, he understands it. And whatever he understands, exists in his understanding. But assuredly that than which nothing greater can be conceived, cannot merely exist in his understanding. For, suppose he believed it existed only in his understanding. Then he could conceive of this being also existing in reality, which would be greater.
>
> Therefore, if that, than which nothing greater can be conceived, existed only in the understanding, it would be that than which something greater could be conceived. But obviously this is an impossible [contradiction]. Hence, there is no doubt that there is a being, than which nothing greater can be conceived, and this being exists both in the understanding and in reality. . . . There is, then, so truly a being than which nothing greater can be conceived to exist, that it cannot even be conceived not to exist; and this being thou art, O Lord, our God.[4]

critical thinking

Does Anselm assume that if it is impossible to think of something with the human mind, then it is impossible for that to be real? Is this assumption correct?

A key term in this argument is the word "greater." What does Anselm mean by "greater" when he says that God is that than which nothing "greater" can be conceived, and when he says something that exists in reality is "greater" than something that merely exists in the mind? In Section 3.1 of Chapter 3, we saw that the

4 Saint Anselm, *Saint Anselm: Basic Writings*, trans. S. N. Deane (La Salle, IL: Open Court Publishing, 1962).

***Saint Anselm, Archbishop** of Canterbury after Unknown artist.* Line engraving, late sixteenth century, 7 5/8 in. × 5 1/2 in. (195 mm × 141 mm) paper size. Given by the daughter of compiler William Fleming MD, Mary Elizabeth Stopford, 1931. Reference Collection. Sitter: Saint Anselm (1033–1109), Archbishop of Canterbury. Sitter associated with three portraits. Artist: Unknown artist. Artist associated with 6,523 portraits. Portrait Set. Fleming Collection: Granger Fleming (volume 1).

© National Portrait Gallery, London

philosopher Robert Nozick suggests that to say something is real is to say that it has importance, weight, and power. Anselm's word "greater" can be understood in terms of this notion of reality. Within Anselm's argument, we can understand "greater" to mean something like "more potent" or "more powerful."[5] Anselm assumes that if a thing exists in reality it has more power than if it just exists in the mind. Anselm, therefore, seems to be arguing as follows: God is "that than which nothing greater can be conceived." Since we understand this idea of God, the idea of God exists in our minds. But we can conceive of something greater than a God that exists only in our minds, namely a God who exists in reality. A God that exists in reality is greater than a God that exists only in our minds, because a God that exists in reality is more powerful than a God that exists only in our minds. So if God is that than which nothing greater can be conceived, we must conceive of Him as existing in reality and not just in our minds. Therefore, we must agree that God exists in reality.

Objections to Anselm. Anselm has had his supporters over the years. But many more philosophers seem to have attacked the ontological argument than have supported it. The eighteenth-century German philosopher Immanuel Kant, many people feel, identified the fundamental problem with the ontological argument when he wrote:

> Existence is not a real predicate, that is, it is not a kind of concept that can be added to the concept of a thing. Existence is merely the positing of a thing [in the real world]. . . . Now, if I take the subject (God) with all its predicates (omnipotence, etc.), and say: God exists, or, There is a God, I add no new predicate to the concept of God, I merely affirm the existence of God with all His predicates . . . However many predicates—even all the predicates that completely determine what it is—I may think belong to a thing, I do not in the least add anything at all to its concept when I add the statement: This thing exists. . . . Even if I think of a being as the highest reality, without defect or imperfection, the question will still remain, Does this being exist or not?[6]

Kant is claiming that there is a fundamental difference between the *concept* or *idea* of a thing, and its *existence,* i.e., the fact that it exists. But in his argument Anselm

---

5 See Stephen T. Davis, *God, Reason and Theistic Proofs* (Grand Rapids, MI: WM. B. Eerdmans Publishing Company, 1997), 19; Davis says we should "read greatness as *power, ability, freedom of action*"; in Chapter V of his *Proslogium,* Anselm equates "that than which nothing greater can be conceived" as including that "which exists through itself and creates all other things from nothing" (i.e., as what is omnipotent so "more powerful" than anything else), and as also including being "just, truthful, blessed, and whatever it is better to be than not to be." From this one can also infer that for Anselm, one thing is "greater" than another when it is, to a greater degree, "whatever it is better to be than not to be."

6 Immanuel Kant, *Critique of Pure Reason,* trans. Norman Kemp Smith (New York: St. Martin's, 1929; original work published 1781), 504–505.

wrongly assumes that existence can be part of the concept or definition of a thing. In particular, his ontological argument says that the idea of God with existence is "greater" than the idea of God without existence. But in saying this, the argument is in effect saying that existence can be part of the idea or concept of God. This, according to Kant, mixes together two utterly different categories of things. Kant expresses this criticism with the now famous slogan that "existence is not a real predicate." He means that *what* a thing is, i.e., the predicates or qualities that make up our idea or definition of what a thing is, is utterly different from *whether* a thing with those qualities exists. Once we fully describe what a thing is—by listing all its predicates or qualities—we do not add any more to *what* it is when we say it exists. Existence, then, is not one of the qualities or predicates that define a thing, so the ontological argument goes wrong when it assumes that existence can be a quality or predicate of God, i.e., when it assumes that existence can be part of our definition or concept of God.

But although many have agreed with Kant's objection to Anselm's argument, others have questioned whether Kant is right. The key issue is Kant's claim that "existence is not a predicate." Kant does not give a full argument for this claim, which has led some philosophers to ask: "Why should we think it is wrong to claim that existence is a predicate?"[7] If we understand the notion of "greater" in terms of being more powerful, and agree that if something exists in reality it has more power than if it is only in our minds, then we are in effect agreeing that existence is a predicate. For if we say existence renders a thing more powerful, then we are saying that existence is a predicate that includes the idea of having power. So while many philosophers agree with Kant's criticism of the ontological argument, others believe that Kant is wrong: existence is a predicate and so it can be part of the concept of God.

QUICK REVIEW
Kant claimed that Anselm wrongly assumed existence is a real property (or "predicate") that can be part of the concept of a thing—of the concept "that than which nothing greater can be conceived." But some philosophers argue that it is Kant that was wrong because existence can be a property.

Another objection to Anselm's argument, however, is that it seems to allow us to magically prove that many bizarre things exist. One of Anselm's own acquaintances, a monk named Gaunilo, made this objection. If Anselm was right, Gaunilo argued, then someone could prove that a perfect island that is "the island greater than which none can be conceived" would have to exist. For if such an island existed only in the mind, it would not be "the island greater than which none can be conceived." In this way, we could prove that the island—or any other "perfect" kind of thing we want such as the perfect flea or the perfect cow—has to exist in reality. But if he accepted that proof for the existence of an island, Gaunilo said, then he was "a greater fool" than the person who made up the proof.

QUICK REVIEW
Gaunilo argued that if Anselm was right then one could "foolishly" prove that any bizarre thing, x, existed by defining it as "the x than which nothing greater can be conceived." Anselm replied that his argument worked only with an infinitely perfect being, and only God was infinitely perfect.

Anselm agreed that only a "fool" would try to use his argument to prove that there exists an island "greater than which none can be conceived." The reason his argument works when it is applied to God, but not when it is applied to a finite thing like an island is because unlike an island, God and only God, is infinitely perfect. Unlike any finite thing, God has all perfections—such as omnipotence—to an infinite degree and so is indeed greater than anything else we can conceive, and so has to exist in reality. But a finite thing like an Island cannot have all perfections to an infinite degree otherwise it would be God. So a finite thing cannot be a thing "greater than which none can be conceived" and so it does not have to exist in reality.

Since Saint Anselm of Canterbury proposed his ontological argument in the twelfth century, many other philosophers have offered somewhat different versions of the argument including, in the seventeenth century, René Descartes, Gottfried Leibniz, and Baruch Spinoza, and, in the twentieth century, Charles Hartshorne,

---

7 For example, B. Miller, "In Defense of the Predicate 'Exists,'" *Mind*, vol. 84 (1975), 338–354; J. Hintikka, "Kant, Existence, Predication and the Ontological Argument," in S. Knuttila and J. Hintikka, eds., *The Logic of Being* (Dordrecht: Reidel, 1986) 249–268; J. Shaffer, "Existence, Predication, and the Ontological Argument," *Mind*, vol. 71 (1962), 307–325.

Norman Malcolm, Alvin Plantinga, and Kurt Gödel. In spite of their ingenious efforts, however, philosophers to this day still debate whether the ontological argument is correct or not.

The Cosmological Argument

To read works by Saint Thomas Aquinas, go to CourseMate for this text and browse by chapter or philosopher.

Aquinas and the Chain of Motion. After Anselm, the next important attempt to justify God's existence was made by the greatest of all the rational theologians, the thirteenth-century Christian philosopher Saint Thomas Aquinas (1225–1274). His arguments are systematically organized and borrow many ideas from Aristotle. In his monumental works *Summa Theologica* and *Summa Contra Gentiles*, Aquinas offers a total of five proofs. The two proofs we examine here begin with an observation about the physical universe. Thus, they are said to be a kind of **cosmological argument** because they result from a study of the cosmos. (For the other proofs and a fuller discussion of Aquinas' philosophy, see the Historical Showcase at the end of this chapter.)

Aquinas' version of the cosmological argument—which he borrowed from Aristotle—begins with the observation that things in the universe "are moving":

> It is evident that some things in the world around us are moving. Now if something is moving, it must have been moved by something else. But if that which moves the things we see around us is itself moving, then it too must have been moved by something else, and that by something else again. But this cannot go on to infinity because then there would be no first mover. So there must be a first mover that is not itself moved, and this is God.[8]

Aquinas' point is that if any object in our universe is moving, it must have been moved by something else that was also moving, and this second moving object must have been moved by something else that was also moving, and this must have been moved by a fourth moving object, and so on. But a chain of moving objects in which the motion of each depends on the motion of an earlier moving object has to derive its original motion from somewhere. Aquinas argues that this chain of motion cannot be just an infinite chain that never had an originating mover. For if there were nothing that first started things moving, then they would never have begun to move. So, he concludes, there must be a "First Mover"—that is, a being in whom all the motions of our universe originate. This being, of course, would have to be very different from the beings we see around us. For unlike the beings in our own experience, this being must be able to initiate motion without itself being moved. For if it were moved as other things in our universe are moved, then it would have to be moved by something else and would not be the "First Mover."

QUICK REVIEW
Aquinas' first cosmological proof says (1) Some things move. (2) What moves must be moved by another moving thing, which must be moved by another moving thing, and so on. (3) This series of moving movers cannot be infinite, for then their motion would have no origin. (4) The origin of their motion cannot be moving, for then it would have to be moved by another.
(5) This unmoving origin of motion is God.

It is important to understand what Aquinas is getting at here. He is saying that in our universe, any moving thing has to derive its motion from some other moving thing. This is the nature of motion as we experience it in our universe: The motion of one thing is dependent on the motion of some other thing. The existence of this dependent motion in our universe then leads us inexorably back to the existence of a being whose motion could not depend on something else, and so a being that has to be unlike anything we know in our own universe! And this, Aquinas notes, is what we mean by God. Is Aquinas' argument correct? Before we discuss that

8 Thomas Aquinas, *Summa Contra Gentiles*, bk. 1, ch. 13, translated by Manuel Velasquez.

question, let's look at a second, more sophisticated kind of cosmological argument that Aquinas also presents.

Aquinas' second kind of cosmological argument starts by noting that things in this universe are caused: Their existence is caused by other things. In fact, the existence of anything in this universe must be caused by something else because nothing in this universe can cause itself to exist. Aquinas then reasons that these observed effects are the last in a chain of such effects. However, this chain must not go back endlessly because then it would have no beginning to its existence, so nothing would now exist. The chain of dependent existents, like the chain of dependent motions, must start somewhere. According to this cosmological argument, the chain of causes must start with a being whose existence is uncaused. This being, Aquinas notes, is what we mean by God. Later, Aquinas explains that this being, whose existence is uncaused, has to be very different from the beings we know in this universe because the existence of a being in this universe is always caused by some other being. That is, the fact that any existent in our universe always depends on some other existent, inexorably leads us to a being that, utterly unlike anything in our universe, is the uncaused, non-dependent origin of all other existents.

critical thinking

Does Aquinas assume that cause–effect relations really exist between things outside the mind? Could cause–effect relations be nothing more than mental constructs we make up to connect things we experience and to make predictions? If they were mental constructs, then would Aquinas' argument still stand up?

Aquinas' second cosmological argument is elaborated in the following passage from his *Summa Theologica*:

> [Another] way [of proving God's existence] is based on the nature of efficient causes. In the world we see around us, there are ordered lines of efficient causes [in which each member of the line produces the next member]. But nothing can be its own efficient cause, since then it would have to exist prior to itself and this is impossible. Now it is not possible for a line of efficient causes to extend to infinity. For in any line of efficient causes, the first is the cause of the intermediate ones, and the intermediate ones cause the last one. Now if we remove any of the causes, we remove all the remaining effects. So if there were no first cause then there would be no last cause nor any intermediate ones. But if a line of efficient causes extended back to infinity, then we would find no first cause. Consequently, if the line of causes extended back to infinity, there would be no intermediate causes nor any last causes in existence in the universe. But we know this is false. So it is necessary to admit that there is a first efficient cause. And this we call God.[9]

QUICK REVIEW
Aquinas' second cosmological proof says: (1) Some things are caused to exist by other things. (2) What is caused to exist must be caused by another thing, for nothing can cause itself to exist. (3) The series of causes cannot extend back infinitely, for then there would be no beginning to the existence of the series of causes, so no causes would exist at all. (4) So, there is a first cause of existence, and this is God.

Objections to Aquinas. Scientists and philosophers have raised several objections to Aquinas' cosmological arguments. A first objection to Aquinas' cosmological arguments—in particular to his first argument from motion—arose out of the scientific revolution of the seventeenth century when Sir Isaac Newton discovered the three laws of motion and universal gravitation. These laws are still regarded today as the foundations of our scientific understanding of the motions of ordinary objects under everyday conditions. Newton's first law of motion showed that a moving object continues moving forever on its own without needing anything to keep it moving, so long as an external force does not interfere with its motion. So, critics conclude, God is not needed to explain why the objects we see all around us are moving as they are. But defenders of Aquinas have responded to this objection by saying that his argument should be interpreted as applying to the initiation of motions or, more simply, to acceleration. For an object to accelerate or begin moving, even according to Newton's laws, it must be acted on by an outside force. Something, therefore, is needed to explain how all of the motion we see in the universe ultimately began, and this "something" is God.

QUICK REVIEW
Some critics say that Aquinas' views on motion were disproved by the scientific laws of motion Newton discovered, but supporters of Aquinas argue that his views can be reconciled with Newtonian science.

9 Saint Thomas Aquinas, *Summa Theologica*, I, q.2, a.3. This edited translation is by Manuel Velasquez.

A second and more perplexing group of philosophical objections to Aquinas' cosmological arguments concerns Aquinas' contention that there can be no **infinite regress** in the causal sequences that produced the universe we now see around us. But why not? Isn't it possible that the universe has simply existed forever and that things in it have simply been moving forever? Isn't it possible that the universe has always been around and that both motion and causality have always operated within it?

QUICK REVIEW
Aquinas also held that even if the universe existed forever, the existence of the entire perpetual chain of motions and causes still needs a cause to explain its source and that is God. Hume responded that in an infinite chain of causes and motions stretching back in time, each individual motion or cause will have a previous motion or cause that explains it, and once each individual motion or cause is explained, the whole chain needs no additional cause.

Aquinas was aware, of course, of the possibility that the universe may have existed forever and that the chain of motions causing motions, and effects causing effects, might stretch back in time infinitely. Consequently, he argued that even if we assume that the universe has existed forever and that the chain of motions and causes stretches back in an infinite regress, a First Cause is still necessary. Aquinas reasoned that an infinite regress of causes would allow each individual link in the causal chain to be accounted for by a previous link, but the existence of the entire chain itself would still need to be explained. Similarly, in an infinite regress of motions, the motion of each moving thing can be accounted for by the motion of a prior moving thing, but the question still arises: What is the origin of the motion of the entire chain? To explain how the entire chain of causes, or the entire chain of motions, came into existence, he claimed, we must posit a God who ultimately created it all.

The eighteenth-century philosopher David Hume, however, questioned Aquinas' claim that if there was an infinite regress of motions and causes, an explanation of each link in the chain would still require an explanation of the whole chain. Hume wrote:

> Did I show you the particular causes of each individual in a collection of twenty particles of matter, I should think it very unreasonable, should you afterwards ask me, what was the cause of the whole twenty. For this is sufficiently explained in explaining the cause of the parts.[10]

Hume is arguing that if each of the individual links in the causal chain can be explained, no additional explanation of the whole is needed. The explanation of each part is itself a sufficient explanation of the whole. The same kind of logic can be applied either to motions or to efficient causes. In other words, if Hume's argument has merit, there is no need or any logical justification for positing a first mover or a first cause of existence.

Yet is it clear that Hume is right? Notice that Hume's objection relies on the assumption that the whole is not greater than the sum of its parts. Critics of Hume say that this assumption is false. If so, then an explanation is required for both the parts and the whole. And then, perhaps, we might want to conclude that Aquinas is right after all.

QUICK REVIEW
Defenders of Aquinas say that the discovery of the "Big Bang" shows the series of motions and causes in the universe had a beginning and is not infinite, so an infinite regress is not possible anyway.

Supporters of the cosmological argument, moreover, have claimed that the idea that the universe might have existed forever is no longer tenable anyway. They base this claim on the discovery by astronomers during the twentieth century that the universe began with a "Big Bang" about 13.75 billion years ago. The discovery of the Big Bang is an important example of a scientific discovery that had a major impact on religion, this time in an apparently positive way. As we mentioned earlier, the universe we see around us consists of billions of galaxies, each of which is a cluster of billions of stars, each star somewhat like our own sun, perhaps also with planets

10 David Hume, *Dialogues Concerning Natural Religion*, ed. N. Kemp Smith (Edinburgh: Nelson, 1947), 18.

revolving around it. During the early decades of the twentieth century, American astronomer Edwin Hubble discovered that the universe around us is expanding. All the galaxies in the universe are being hurled outward and away from each another, as if still moving after being propelled apart by a terrific explosion that suddenly expanded the universe a very long time ago. But if the universe is expanding, then sometime in the past it would have been smaller than now, and before that smaller yet. Astronomers have concluded that about 13.75 billion years ago, the universe began as a an incredibly tiny and very hot mass that exploded suddenly into a huge inflating expanse of matter and space and that has continued inflating outward to form the gigantic and still expanding universe we see around us. This theory was given substantial support in 1963 when two scientists, Arno Penzias and Robert Wilson, discovered the whole universe is suffused with a microwave radiation that could only be explained as the left-over heat from the big bang. That explosive expansion—the Big Bang—marked the beginning of the universe and set everything in the universe moving and changing as it is still doing today. Until the Big Bang occurred, the universe as we know it did not exist: There would have been no time, no space, and no objects other than an incredibly small mass into which the whole universe was densely packed. With the Big Bang, matter, space, and time all came into existence.

Many philosophers have asserted that the Big Bang is exactly the kind of starting point of the universe that the cosmological argument points toward. If the Big Bang theory is correct, then the universe has not existed forever. There could then be no infinite chain of motions and causes stretching backward in time forever. Instead, we are forced to conclude that the universe has existed for only a few billion years and that it had a definite beginning. And, supporters of the cosmological arguments claim, only an infinitely powerful being—God—can account for the big bang beginning of the universe.

Yet even if the Big Bang theory is correct, does it really prove there is a God that created the universe? Could something other than God have caused our universe to come into existence? Some cosmologists have speculated, for example, that the universe we know was caused by events in some other unknown universe, which in turn was caused by some other unknown universe, and so on to infinity. In short, even if the universe as we know it had a beginning, can we be sure that ours is not one of an infinite series of universes that goes back forever? Critics of such speculations, however, have pointed out that there is little scientific evidence supporting these speculations. In the absence of any evidence for such infinite regresses, they conclude, we should accept the evidence we have that our universe in fact had a beginning, and that God initiated that beginning.

critical thinking

Suppose we can explain all phenomena by assuming that no supernatural beings exist. Would this show that supernatural beings do not exist?

A third important set of objections to the cosmological argument argue that its conclusion contradicts its premise. To illustrate, critics say that Aquinas insists that everything must have a cause. But if this is so, then shouldn't we ask what caused God? The notion of an uncaused cause seems to contradict the premise that everything has a cause. The nineteenth-century German philosopher Arthur Schopenhauer (1788–1860) expresses this objection succinctly when he writes that the law of universal causation "is not so accommodating as to let itself be used like a cab for hire, which we dismiss when we have reached our destination."[11]

QUICK REVIEW
Critics say if "everything has a cause," then God should have a cause, so Aquinas' starting premise is in conflict with his conclusion. But Aquinas says only that *in our universe* everything has a cause and that this requires a being who, unlike anything in the universe, is uncaused.

Yet Aquinas has a response to those who object that he contradicts himself when he supposedly says everything has a cause yet God has no cause. Aquinas would respond that he claims only that everything *in our universe*—the world of finite objects

11 Quoted in C. J. Ducasse, *A Philosophical Scrutiny of Religion* (New York: Ronald Press, 1953), 335.

PHILOSOPHY AND LIFE

Religion and Science

The highly respected scientific journal *Nature* regularly publishes articles on the relationship between religion and science. An article published in 2004, for example, asserts that science and faith have collided with "explosive force" over the issues of "nanotechnology, artificial intelligence, cloning, creationism and genetic modification." According to the authors of the article, stem cell research, in particular, has strained the relationship between faith and science because it involves a clash between the "religion-based belief in the sanctity of human life even . . . of an embryo," and the "desire to alleviate suffering and cure disease" which are the aims of stem cell research. Dr. Francis Collins, a Christian scientist who heads up the National Human Genome Research Institute, is quoted as saying he is "intensely conflicted" about stem-cell research. This conflict between the "religion-based" value of embryonic life, and stem cell research which destroys human embryos, the article claims, lay behind the decision of President George W. Bush—who is himself an evangelical Christian—to forbid the use of federal funds to pay for any stem cell research that destroyed more embryos. (This Bush policy ended with President Barack Obama.) Not all scientists feel that religion and science are opposed. The National Academy of Sciences, the most distinguished group of scientists in the United States, declares on its website that "Scientists and theologians have written eloquently about their awe and wonder at the history of the universe and of life on this planet, explaining that they see no conflict between their faith in God and the evidence for evolution." On the website of the BioLogos Foundation, Francis Collins (the Christian scientist quoted earlier) defends "the compatibility of Christian faith with what science has discovered about the origins of life and the universe." Collins argues that many scientific findings, such as the Big Bang and the universal effectiveness of our mathematics, "point" to a God, and that scientific theories such as evolution can be reconciled with faith.

QUESTIONS

1. Are there any aspects of science that make you more inclined to religious belief? Less inclined?
2. Should the sincere religious beliefs of those in public office (such as the president) influence policies regarding scientific research that they put in place?
3. Are the National Academy of Sciences and Dr. Dennis Collins right, or do some scientific theories contradict faith?

Sources: Tony Reichhardt, David Cyranoski, and Quirin Schiermeier, "Religion and Science," *Nature*, December 9, 2004; 432:666; National Academy of Sciences website at http://www.nationalacademies.org/evolution/Compatibility.html; Dennis Collins on BioLogos Foundation website at http://biologos.org/about.

we experience—has a cause because everything in our universe is a limited, dependent being. Such dependent beings require the existence of a being that is utterly different from them, an infinite being that is not dependent on anything, a being who is not another object in our universe but on whom the whole universe depends. Why would we think that it should be otherwise? Why would we think that God would just be like any other object in the world around us? How could our universe of dependent objects be explained by some other dependent object within our universe? The whole point of his arguments, Aquinas might say, is to show that the finite, dependent, and contingent nature of our world requires a being who is neither finite nor dependent, nor contingent—an "unmoved" mover of everything and an "uncaused" cause of everything that exists.

A number of contemporary theologians who generally agree with Aquinas have interpreted his first-cause argument in a way that brings out some important implications. These theologians claim that the endless series that the argument tries to dismiss should not be understood as a mere regress of events in time but as a regress of explanations for the universe. John Hick (b. 1922), who teaches at Cambridge University, for example, suggests that the argument is saying that some facts in the universe are "rendered intelligible" by other facts, and these facts are made intelligible by yet other facts, and these, in turn, are rendered intelligible by other facts. At the end of such a series of explanations, he claims, there must be a reality which is "self-explanatory" and "whose existence constitutes the ultimate explanation of the whole." If there is no such ultimate reality, he claims, then the universe is "a mere unintelligible brute fact."[12]

Hick's point is that Aquinas' cosmological argument can be seen as setting a choice before us. We can choose to see the universe around us as an ultimately intelligible home that makes sense and can be explained in a rational way; that choice is the choice to accept the basic rightness of the cosmological argument. Or we can see the universe as something that is just an unexplainable, unintelligible, ultimately "absurd" place into which we have been cast for no reason at all; to make that choice is to reject the cosmological argument.

QUICK REVIEW
Some of his defenders say Aquinas may be interpreted as believing that an endless series of explanations in which one thing is explained by some other thing ends up being no explanation at all.

Hick appears to leave us with a dilemma: Either a first cause exists, or the universe makes no sense. But can't the universe make sense as something that is simply there, or is Hick right in his claim that without an ultimate explanation, in the final analysis the universe is literally senseless? But how can we be sure that the universe is not "a mere unintelligible brute fact"? Is it possible that in the last analysis the universe just doesn't make sense? Yet to take the route that the universe does not make sense seems to contradict the foundations of science itself since science is based on the idea that the universe is intelligible. Are we willing to abandon so much?

A final problem with the cosmological argument that we should consider is the objection that it does not seem to prove that a loving personal God exists; it shows only that there is some powerful force that is the source of all the motions and causes we see operating in the cosmos. Aquinas would probably acknowledge this problem, but he would point out that this does not mean his arguments are wrong, only that they have a limited purpose. The cosmological arguments by themselves are intended only to show that there is a creator. Much more analysis of the implications of this, as well as other arguments for God's existence, would be needed to show that the being that created the universe is a loving, all-knowing, and all-powerful person.

QUICK REVIEW
Critics object that the cosmological argument does not prove a loving and personal God exists. Aquinas might respond that this objection does not show his argument is wrong, only that it has a limited purpose.

One of the arguments that Aquinas thought could provide insight into what God is like, is what we now call the "design argument." The design argument is based, in his words, on the idea that although they lack intelligence, "natural creatures act for an end" and could not do so "unless they are directed toward that end by some being that has knowledge and intelligence, much like an archer directs an arrow toward its target." The most well-known version of the argument from design is the version that was crafted not by Aquinas, however, but by William Paley.

The Design Argument

The design argument is certainly the most popular of the arguments for God's existence. Simply put, the **design argument**, or the **argument from design**, states that the order and purpose manifest in the works of nature indicate that they were designed by an intelligent Being. As we will see, the design argument has turned out to be the battleground where much of the skirmishing between religion and science is now being waged. Discussing the design argument, therefore, will reveal much about the relation between religion and science, both how science has been used to support religion and how it has been used to discredit it.

The "Divine Watchmaker." Traditionally a prominent argument for God's existence, the design proof is still accepted today by many scientists, such as biologist

12 Hick, *Philosophy of Religion*, 21.

Edmund W. Sinnot and physicist and cosmologist Paul Davies, as well as by many theologians and philosophers, such as Robert E. D. Clark, Richard Swinburne, Alvin Plantinga, and Michael A. Corey. In 1802, theologian William Paley presented what is now the classic exposition of the design argument. Comparing natural organisms to the mechanism of a watch, Paley argued that just as the design of a watch implies the existence of an intelligent watchmaker, so the design found in natural organisms implies the existence of an intelligent "Divine Agency":

QUICK REVIEW
Paley's argument from design says: (1) If we find an artifact, like a watch, that is designed to achieve a purpose, we can conclude it was made by an intelligent being. (2) But things we find in nature, especially living things and their parts, are designed to achieve a purpose. (3) So, by **analogy**, we can conclude they were made by an intelligent being, and this is God.

> In crossing a heath, suppose I pitched my foot against a *stone*, and were asked how the stone came to be there. I might possibly answer, that for anything I knew to the contrary, it had lain there for ever: nor would it perhaps be very easy to show the absurdity of this answer. But suppose I had found a *watch* upon the ground, and it should be inquired how the watch happened to be in that place; I should hardly think of the answer which I had before given, that for anything I knew the watch might have always been there. Yet why should not this answer serve for the watch as well as for the stone? Why is it not as admissible in the second case as in the first? For this reason, and for no other, viz. that when we come to inspect the watch, we perceive (what we could not discover in the stone) that its several parts are framed and put together for a purpose, e.g., that they are so formed and adjusted as to produce motion, and that motion so regulated as to point out the hour of the day; that if the different parts had been differently shaped from what they are, of a different size from what they are, or placed after any other manner, or in any other order, than that in which they are placed, either no motion at all would have been carried on in the machine, or none which would have answered the use that is now served by it. . . . This mechanism being observed . . . the inference, we think, is inevitable, that the watch must have had a maker; that there must have existed, at some time, and at some place or other, an artificer or artificers, who formed it for the purpose which we find it actually to answer; who comprehended its construction and designed its use. . . .
>
> [E]very indication of contrivance, every manifestation of design, which existed in the watch, exists in the works of nature; with the difference, on the side of nature, of being greater and more, and that in a degree which exceeds all computation. I mean, that the contrivances of nature surpass the contrivances of art, in the complexity, subtlety, and curiosity, of the mechanism; and still more, if possible, do they go beyond them in number and variety; yet, in a multitude of cases, are not less evidently mechanical, not less evidently contrivances, not less evidently accommodated to their end, or suited to their office, than are the most perfect productions of human ingenuity. . . .
>
> Every observation which was made [above] concerning the watch, may be repeated with strict propriety concerning the eye, concerning animals, concerning plants, concerning, indeed, all the organized parts of the works of nature . . . .
>
> Were there no example in the world of contrivance, except that of the *eye*, it would be alone sufficient to support the conclusion which we draw from it, as to the necessity of an intelligent Creator. . . . If there were but one watch in the world, it would not be less certain that it had a maker. . . . So it is with the evidences of a Divine agency.[13]

As was the custom of religious thinkers of his day, Paley called on a long list of examples from the sciences (especially biology) to demonstrate his argument. The migration of birds, the instincts of animals, the adaptability of species to various environments, and the human ability to base forecasts on probable causation, all suggested a plan and a planner. But for Paley, the most impressive example of a

13 William Paley, "Natural Theology," in *The Works of William Paley* (Philadelphia: Crissy & Markley, 1857), 387–485.

natural creation that was obviously made by an intelligent designer was the eye. "As far as the examination of the instrument goes," he wrote, "there is precisely the same proof that the eye was made for vision, as there is that the telescope was made for assisting it." To drive his point home, Paley presented a detailed description of the eye and its parts that, he felt, showed that the eye had to have been produced by an intelligent creator who carefully designed it, then selected and assembled its complex parts so that together they would serve the purpose of sight. The eye, he pointed out, was exactly shaped so that its lens focused light on its sensitive interior exactly in accordance with the laws of optics; the skull was hollowed out into a socket exactly sized to enclose and protect the eye; the exterior skin was shaped into an eyelid that carefully protected the eye, wiped it, and closed it in sleep; a gland was provided to produce tears that continuously washed the eye; a tube from the eye to the nose was placed precisely so that it would drain the tears that washed the eyes. "Are there in any work of art whatever," Paley asked, "purposes more evident than those which this organ fulfills?"

thinking critically • Arguments by Analogy

Paley's argument is usually described as an "argument by analogy." An "analogy" is a comparison between two similar things. An **argument by analogy** claims that since two things are alike in certain respects, they are probably alike in another related respect. A scientist, for example, might argue that since rats and humans are biologically similar in many ways, a drug that cures a disease in rats, will probably cure the same disease in humans. In other words, since rats and humans have certain biological similarities, they will probably share a characteristic that is related to those similarities.

An argument by analogy like Paley's is not a deductive argument. Since its conclusion is only probable, it is an inductive argument. The conclusion of an argument by analogy is only probable because although two things may share many similarities, they may also differ in other relevant ways. For example, they may differ in ways that prevent one from having the characteristic that the other has. So an argument by analogy will not hold up if we know there are significant relevant differences between the two things that are being compared.

QUICK REVIEW
An argument by analogy is a probabilistic argument that claims that since two things are alike in certain respects, they are probably alike in another related respect, provided they do not differ in any relevant way.

An argument by analogy, then, requires that two things, say x and y, have the same characteristics, say F; it requires that one of those things, say x, has another characteristic, K, that is related to F; and it requires that we know of no relevant differences between x and y. All this may be clearer if we express it in terms of the basic form that any argument by analogy will have:

1. x and y both have characteristics F.
2. x also has characteristic K (which is related to F).
3. There are no known relevant differences between x and y.
4. So y probably also has characteristic K.

For example, in 2009 Novavax, a drug company, developed a vaccine against the H1N1 flu virus which was spreading over the entire world at that time. To test whether the vaccine worked, they gave it to ferrets which can also be infected by the H1N1 flu virus and which have many biological similarities to humans. Novavax found that the ferrets became immune to the H1N1 virus when they received the vaccine. So Novavax concluded that the vaccine would also make humans immune to the virus. They (correctly) reasoned:

1. Ferrets and humans can both be infected by the H1N1 virus and they have many of the same biological characteristics.
2. Ferrets become immune to H1N1 when given the new vaccine (such immunity is related to an animal's biological characteristics).

3. Humans are not different from ferrets in any known relevant way.
4. So humans probably will become immune to H1N1 when given the new vaccine.

Since Paley's argument is an argument by design, it too will have the form mentioned earlier. If we put Paley's argument into the form of an argument from analogy, we have:

1. Watches and living organisms both have parts precisely adjusted to achieve a purpose.
2. A watch is made by an intelligent agent (who produces the precise adjustment of its parts so they will achieve its purpose).
3. Watches and living organisms do not differ in any known relevant way.
4. So living organisms are (probably) made by an intelligent agent.

QUICK REVIEW
An argument by analogy is a good or strong argument if its premises are true, the two things being compared share many of the same characteristics, the shared characteristics are related to the additional characteristic that one thing has and the other is claimed to have, and there are no relevant differences between the two things.

Is Paley's argument by analogy a good argument? From our brief discussion it should already be clear that whether an argument by analogy is a good argument—and how good of an argument it is—depends on four things:

1. The premises must all be true.
2. The greater the number of characteristics shared by the two things being compared, the better the argument is.
3. The characteristics the two things share should be related to the additional characteristic, K, that one thing has and that the conclusion claims the other one has. (Here, one characteristic is "related" to a second characteristic, K, when having the one characteristic increases the probability of having the second characteristic, K. Sometimes we can't explain why two characteristics are related, we just know from past experience that they are.)
4. There should be no relevant differences between x and y. A "relevant" difference is one that decreases (perhaps to zero) the probability that y will also have the characteristic K that x has.

If we evaluate Paley's argument using these four requirements of an argument by analogy, does his turn out to be a good argument? This is an evaluation you should be able to make on your own, by asking whether his argument meets the four requirements just mentioned.

We'll look next at what other philosophers have said about the argument by design.

Objections to the Design Argument. Even before Paley published his design argument, the British philosopher David Hume had already pointed out a fundamental problem with any argument from design. We have the experience of people making and designing watches, he pointed out, so we know that the orderly design we see in the mechanism of the watch was put there by an intelligent agent. But we have never experienced how an animal, or an eye, or a universe is made. So for all we know, the order we see in an animal, or an eye, or the entire universe may not have been produced in the same way that the order we see in a watch was produced.

QUICK REVIEW
Hume objected that although we know how artifacts like watches are made, we have no knowledge of how nature and living things are made, so for all we know nature and living things are produced by a non-intelligent mechanism.

Hume was questioning a key assumption in the argument from design (you might ask yourself which of Paley's four premises Hume was questioning). The argument from design assumes that an intelligent agent must produce the complex order found in any object. But this assumption is unproved, Hume argues. Perhaps the order found in some things is produced by a mechanism that is not intelligent. For all we know, Hume argued, the order in the universe might have been produced by random processes through an incredibly long—perhaps infinite—period of development. We know from past experience that the order of a watch was produced by an intelligent watchmaker, but we have no experience of how a universe comes to be, so we cannot assume to know how its order originated.

But the most powerful objection to Paley was the theory of evolution that Charles Darwin proposed. Darwin provided exactly what Hume could only suggest: a mechanism that could produce order and the appearance of design but one that was not intelligent. This mechanism was natural selection: a non-intelligent mechanical process that over millions of years could produce organisms that were perfectly adapted to do what they do.

As we saw in Section 2.2 of Chapter 2 (which we can only briefly summarize here), Charles Darwin claimed that the life around us developed through a series of inheritable "variations" that were gradually selected in the "struggle for survival"—variations that gave an advantage to their possessors so that they survived as they competed with those that lacked the variation and who perished in this struggle. Through the process of natural selection, those organisms whose variations allow them to adapt survive and the rest die, until all surviving organisms end up being perfectly adapted to their environment. They—and each of their parts—give every appearance of having been carefully designed for a purpose: the whole organism seems to have been designed to survive in its environment, and its organs appear to have been designed to carry out the functions that enable the whole organism to survive. But the appearance of purpose is an illusion since both the organism and its organs were the result of the blind processes of natural selection. Taking direct aim at Paley's favorite example, Darwin argued that even the apparent "design" of the eye can be the product of a long but non-intelligent evolutionary process:

QUICK REVIEW
Darwin argued that the nonintelligent mechanism of evolution through natural selection, working over millions of years, can produce living things whose parts seem designed to achieve some purpose.

> To suppose that the eye, with all its inimitable contrivances for adjusting the focus to different distances, for admitting different amounts of light, and for the correction of spherical and chromatic aberration, could have been formed by natural selection, seems, I freely confess, absurd in the highest possible degree. Yet reason tells me, that if numerous gradations from a perfect and complex eye to one very imperfect and simple, each grade being useful to its predecessor, can be shown to exist . . . then the difficulty of believing that a perfect and complex eye could be formed by natural selection, though insuperable by our imagination, can hardly be considered real. . . . In living bodies, variation will cause the slight alterations, generation will multiply them almost infinitely, and natural selection will pick out with unerring skill each improvement. Let this process go on for millions on millions of years; and enduring each year on millions of individuals of many kinds; and may we not believe that a living optical instrument might thus be formed as superior to one of glass, as the works of the Creator are to those of man?[14]

critical thinking
Scientists say evolution and natural selection explain why the parts of living creatures seem so perfectly adapted to their functions. Does this mean the design argument has to be mistaken?

Despite the challenges posed by Darwin's theory of evolution, many believers continue to embrace the argument from design and to feel that a Designer's hand is revealed in the intricate complexities of nature. Some have argued that although Darwin showed that living organisms evolved through natural selection, this merely means that natural selection is the instrument God used to design and produce life. The philosopher George Mavrodes, as we saw in Chapter 2, suggests that a theistic understanding of evolution holds that "there was a divine **teleology** in this process, a divine direction at each crucial stage in accordance with divine plan or intention." For the believer who accepts this theistic understanding of evolution, the complex order we see in organisms was put there by God through natural selection;

QUICK REVIEW
Defenders of the argument from design argue that even if evolution is a fact, the believer can still hold that evolution is the means by which God produces living things and their parts.

14 Charles Darwin, *On the Origin of Species by Natural Selection* (London: John Murray, 1859), 186–189.

thus, they are evidence of God's intelligent design. This approach, in other words, accepts the theory of evolution, but adds to it the idea that evolution is directed.

However, critics charge that the claim that God directs evolution conflicts with the fact that natural selection is based on random variations and mechanical processes. These processes are often cruel (natural selection requires that the weak be killed by the strong, for example) and produce creatures with useless or harmful characteristics. Such cruelty and useless "vestigial organs," together with the random and mechanical nature of evolution, indicate that the evolutionary process is not "intelligently directed," critics argue. Evolutionary processes, therefore, should be interpreted not as signs of an intelligent purposeful Creator, but merely as the complex products of random, blind, unconscious forces.

critical thinking

Suppose that scientists proved that life could arise from a "primeval soup" of nonliving chemicals. Would this show that life on earth was not created by God?

QUICK REVIEW
Dembski, a proponent of intelligent design, argues that the "specified complexity" (their improbability and their susceptibility to being independently defined) of the arrangement of molecules in genes implies they were produced by an intelligence and not by chance or by natural laws.

Paley's Defenders: Intelligent Design. Contemporary proponents of "intelligent design" have countered that these critics of Paley are wrong. William A. Dembski, for example, has argued in *Intelligent Design: The Bridge between Science and Theology* that the complexity of living organisms cannot be explained by random processes but requires the admission of "intelligent design" or purpose:

> Intelligent design is the field of study that investigates *signs of intelligence.* It identifies those features of objects that reliably signal the action of an intelligent cause. . . . Designed objects like Mount Rushmore exhibit . . . features or patterns [that] constitute signs of intelligence. Proponents of intelligent design, known as *design theorists,* purport to study such signs formally, rigorously, and scientifically. In particular, they claim that a type of information, known as *specified complexity,* is a key sign of intelligence. . . . What is specified complexity? Recall the novel *Contact* by Carl Sagan (1985). In that novel, radio astronomers discover a long sequence of prime numbers from outer space. Because the sequence is long, it is *complex.* Moreover, because the sequence is mathematically significant, it can be characterized independently of the physical processes that bring it about. As a consequence, it is also *specified.* Thus, when the radio astronomers in *Contact* observe specified complexity in this sequence of numbers, they have convincing evidence of extraterrestrial intelligence. . . . [M]any special sciences already employ specified complexity as a sign of intelligence—notably forensic science, cryptography, random number generation, archeology, and the search for extraterrestrial intelligence. Design theorists take these methods and apply them to naturally occurring systems.[15]

Dembski claims that the genes that direct how every living organism is formed and how it operates provide evidence of intelligent design because they have "specified complexity." Genes consist of complex sequences of hundreds of protein molecules, so their arrangement exhibits "complexity." The arrangement of these molecules, moreover, is not just any random arrangement, but the one that will achieve a certain goal, i.e., produce a working, living organism and direct its life functions so that the organism flourishes. So this arrangement has "specificity" since the arrangement can be specified (defined) as the arrangement that will achieve that specific goal, and such a specification can be made independently of the arrangement itself (unlike a random arrangement which could only be defined by listing each molecule in the arrangement).

Dembski argues that the "specified complexity" of genes cannot be produced by chance, nor by natural law, but require intelligence. He argues, first, that it is impossible for hundreds of protein molecules to have come together by chance in exactly

15 William Dembski, "In Defense of Intelligent Design," in *Oxford Handbook of Religion and Science,* ed. Philip Clayton (New York: Oxford University Press, 2006).

the right complex sequences required to produce a working, living animal or plant and to make it flourish. The probability that something of such complexity would occur by chance is so tiny that it would take longer than the universe has been in existence. Second, he claims, the specific protein sequences of genes could not have been produced by natural laws. The protein molecules in the gene have to be brought together in a specific sequence that can achieve a specific goal: produce a living, working organism and then direct its life functions so that the organism will flourish. There are no physical laws, he claims, that bring proteins together according to whether the pattern they form will produce a living organism and direct its life functions. Third, Dembski argues, the specified complexity of genes is itself also evidence that they are the product of intelligent design. It requires intelligence, he claims, to produce such specified complexity because it requires selecting a specific arrangement of proteins whose complexity is so great that it is improbable that that specific arrangement would ever be selected without the intervention of an intelligent agent.

© Christian Anthony/iStockphoto.com

DNA double helix chromosome conceptual three-dimensional rendering with blue, green, and brown luminescent highlights.

Notice that Dembski is no longer using an argument by analogy as Paley did. He has turned to using an inference to the best explanation. He is claiming that the best explanation for what he calls "specified complexity" is that an intelligent being produced it. Not surprisingly, critics have attacked this fundamental premise of his argument, claiming that there are mechanical non-intelligent forces that can produce specified complexity. In fact, they argue, that is precisely what the non-intelligent processes of evolution through natural selection do. Other critics have attacked the concept of "specified complexity" itself and have argued that Dembski's claims about specified complexity do not hold up when examined closely.

Paley's Defenders: The "Fine Tuning" Argument. Recently, some philosophers have resurrected the argument from design in a form that is related to the inductive arguments of intelligent design proponents, but that appeals to what has come to be called the "fine tuning" exhibited by the universe (this argument, as we will see, is also an inference to the best explanation). Paley, and some of his defenders like Dembski, appealed to biological organisms as evidence of design, but such appeals were vulnerable to the objection that evolution can explain such "design." For evidence of design, the new "fine tuning" argument appeals to the physical laws and physical constants of the physical universe, where evolution does not operate. In his book *The Mind of God*, for example, physicist Paul Davies points out that the physical laws of the universe seem to have been designed specifically to make sure that our universe would have those qualities that are necessary for human life to develop and flourish. If the force of gravity had been stronger by a tiny degree or weaker by a tiny amount, then galaxies, stars, and planets could not have formed. If the density of matter in the early universe had been higher by a minuscule amount, everything would have collapsed into black holes; if it had been just minutely lower, galaxies and stars could never have formed. If the universe were expanding a tiny bit faster, then

QUICK REVIEW
Others argue that if the features of the universe that make human life possible were slightly different, human life could not exist. It is so improbable that a universe would have these features out of an infinite range of other possible features it could have that they had to be deliberately selected by an intelligent Being to make human life possible. This is the "Fine Tuning" argument for God.

galaxies would not have formed; if it were expanding a tiny fraction more slowly, then galaxies would have collapsed into black holes. Atomic particles have exactly the numerical properties needed to allow them to form into the elements needed for life, such as carbon and oxygen. If any of these numerical properties of atomic particles had been a tiny fraction higher or lower, life could never have developed in our universe. Davies points out that all of these laws, forces, expansion rates, and atomic properties could have had any of an infinite range of different values. The probability that out of this almost infinite range of values our universe would have the specific ones needed to support life is one chance out of "a one followed by a thousand billion billion zeroes, at least."[16] So it seems extremely improbable that our universe could have turned out like it did unless all of these laws, forces, and numerical properties were deliberately picked so as to allow humans to exist here. The best explanation of the fact that the physical laws and numerical constants that govern the material universe are "finely tuned" to produce the highly improbable conditions that enable us to live and flourish is that those laws and constants were deliberately selected by an intelligent designer of the universe.

QUICK REVIEW
Critics of this new argument say that for all we know, some physical process, not God, selected the "improbable" features that make life possible. Other critics suggest that an infinite number of universes exist and that it is to be expected that in such a "multiverse," at least one universe would have the features that make life possible. Critics of multiverse theories argue the theories are scientifically unprovable.

Many scientists have accepted this new "fine tuning" version of the argument from design, including George Ellis (author of *Before the Beginning*), J. C. Polkinghorne (author of *One World: The Interaction of Science and Theology*), and Holmes Rolston (author of *Science and Religion*). But many others believe the new arguments from design have the same weakness that Paley's old argument had: They assume that the order we see in the universe must have been produced by an intelligent being. Hume, as we saw, objected that for all we know some non-intelligent mechanism might be capable of producing the patterns we see in the universe. Many critics of the new version of the argument from design have repeated Hume's objection. Some argue that perhaps there exist an infinite number of other universes each with different laws and numerical properties. If there are an infinite number of other universes, then it was not improbable but very likely that at least one of them would turn out to have the conditions necessary to support life.

Some scientists have proposed theories that might explain how there could be an infinite number of other universes with different laws and numerical properties.[17] The "oscillating universe" theory says that perhaps the universe has been exploding and then contracting an infinite number of times and each time the "new" universe gets different laws and numerical properties. The "many worlds" theory of quantum physics suggests that each time an atomic or subatomic event occurs that could turn out in two or more ways, the universe splits into two or more universes in each of which one of those ways actually turns out to be the way the event occurred. Since trillions upon trillions of such events are continuously occurring throughout the universe, there would be trillions upon trillions of universes continuously coming into existence, and each of those universes would continuously give rise to trillions upon trillions of additional universes. The "eternal inflation" theory says our universe has inflated or is inflating to an infinite size and so could contain an infinite number of distinct regions of space, each with different laws and numerical properties, and each constituting in effect a different "universe."

But supporters of the fine-tuning argument respond that these "multiverse" scenarios are bizarre and farfetched speculations supported by little or no real scientific evidence. George F. R. Ellis, for example, one of the world's leading scientists and cosmologists (and not a proponent of the fine-tuning argument), has argued

16 Paul Davies, *Other Worlds* (London: Dent, 1980), 56.

17 George F. R. Ellis, "Does the Multiverse Really Exist?" *Scientific American*, Vol. 305 (2011), Issue 2 (August), 38–43.

that "the case for the multiverse is inconclusive" because other universes "remain beyond our capacity to see, now or ever" and so "we have no information about these regions and never will"; multiverse theories, he concludes, lack the "empirical testing [that] is the core of science."[18] Supporters of the fine-tuning argument claim that since their critics don't have a well-supported alternative explanation for our finely tuned improbable universe, they resort to unprovable hypotheses, and offer them as if they were real scientific explanations.

Debate about the argument from design, then, lives on in this latest confrontation between science and religion. After Darwin, many philosophers and theologians thought science had fatally wounded the argument and most abandoned it for dead. But the surprising new evidence of fine-tuning that science itself discovered has resurrected it from the dead so that now it is the most vigorous and dynamic of all the arguments. At its heart lies a key assumption: unusual or improbable design demands a conscious designer. You must decide for yourself whether this assumption makes sense of the world as you know it. If you accept it, the argument from design can lead you to feel awe and reverence for the universe because you see it as the handiwork of an intelligent being. Or, if you reject it, it can leave you feeling that in the end the universe must be accepted as a beautiful, intricate, and amazing product of nothing more than the blind workings of physical processes.

QUESTIONS

1. Anselm argues that a perfect being must exist because the lack of existence is an imperfection. Could you argue that, on the contrary, a perfect being must not exist because existence is an imperfection? Explain.
2. Do you agree that if there is no first cause, the universe makes no sense? Is an infinite regress nonsensical?
3. Some people have claimed that the order we attribute to the universe is only apparent. We crave order and so see things as having an order even when they do not. How would these claims affect the argument from design?
4. Scientists who study thermodynamics claim that the universe as a whole is gradually becoming more and more disordered (i.e., entropy is increasing). How would this claim, if true, affect the argument from design?
5. Do you believe there is a God? If so, do any of the proofs of God's existence seem to express more or less the reasons why you believe?

PHILOSOPHY AT THE MOVIES

Watch *The Exorcism of Emily Rose* (2005), based on a true story, in which a young woman, Emily Rose, believing she is possessed by the devil, asks a priest to perform an exorcism during which she dies, leading to the priest's arrest for negligent homicide and a trial at which the jurors must decide whether Emily died of natural or supernatural causes. Should belief or disbelief in the existence of God affect a juror's decision? Why? Do the proofs for God's existence affect what you think might have been going on in Emily's death?

Globe Photos/ZUMApress.com

The Exorcism of Emily Rose.

18 See Max Tegmark, "Parallel Universes," *Scientific American*, vol. 288 (2003), Issue 5 (May), 40–51.

4.3 Atheism, Agnosticism, and the Problem of Evil

As we've just seen, various philosophers have pointed out what they consider to be obvious flaws in each of the traditional proofs for God's existence. These and other objections to the arguments for the existence of God have led many people to the conclusion that the existence of God is uncertain. Whereas agnostics have concluded that they just don't know whether or not God exists, atheists go a step further and decide that they know that God does not exist. Let's look first at atheism.

Atheism

Atheism denies the major claims of all varieties of theism. In the words of Ernest Nagel (1901–1985), an atheist himself, "Atheism denies the existence . . . of a self-consistent, omnipotent, omniscient, righteous and benevolent being who is distinct from and independent of what has been created."[19]

Religious people sometimes portray atheists as evil curmudgeons. But, as Nagel points out, philosophical atheists tend to share a number of respectable characteristics. First, many agree with the idea that sense observation and public verification are instrumental to truth and that scientific method is the best approach to gain reliable knowledge of the material world around us. This idea is, in fact, a fundamental belief of many atheists. As Nagel states, "It is indeed this commitment to the use of an empirical method which is the final basis of the atheistic critique of theism."

Second, and as a consequence of believing that sense observation and public verification provide the only reliable basis of knowledge, atheists also tend to be materialists. As Nagel bluntly puts it: "An atheistic view of things is a form of materialism."

QUICK REVIEW
Atheists believe there are good reasons to think there is no God. Many atheists base their atheism on the ability of science and the scientific method to explain the material world, and so focus their concerns on the world here and now.

Third, as a result of the view that nothing more exists beyond our material world, many thoughtful atheists have focused their moral and social concerns on the world here and now. They have taken firm stands against authoritarianism, oppression, and war while stressing the importance and value of the individual. For example, the philosopher Bertrand Russell was an anti-war activist, who opposed British imperialism, and condemned totalitarian governments. Because atheists cannot fortify their moral positions with promises of haven or threats of hell, they must rely on what Nagel calls "a vigorous call to intelligent activity—activity for the sake of realizing human potentialities and for eliminating whatever stands in the way of such realization."

But the fourth and most central characteristic of atheists is the belief that there are good reasons to believe that God does not exist. What can such reasons look like? We have seen several objections to the arguments for the existence of God. But even if these objections were correct, all they would show is that we don't have a good proof that God exists. For all we know, God might exist even though we can't prove He exists. So is it possible, instead, to prove that God does not exist? Here we consider perhaps the major argument against the existence of God, the problem

19 Quoted in *Encounter: An Introduction to Philosophy*, ed. Ramona Cormier, Ewing Chinn, and Richard Lineback (Glenview, IL: Scott Foresman, 1970), 224.

of evil. More than any other consideration, the problem of evil has led many to atheism.

The Problem of Evil. Clearly, humans and other living things continue to be beset by all kinds of evils: sickness, pain, suffering, and death. Here are but a few examples taken from the pages of recent editions of the news:[20]

> PHILADELPHIA - Police said that a 3-year old boy died after being tortured by the adults responsible for his care. . . . Police say that he was kicked, punched and had his hands, feet and rear end burned with a blowtorch. . . . 22-year old Nadera Batson was arrested and charged with murder. . . . [H]er boyfriend, Marcus King, has also been implicated in the boy's death.
>
> PAYNESVILLE, MIN. - Fire burned through a barn at one of Minnesota's largest rabbit farms early Wednesday morning, killing hundreds of the animals. . . . The rabbits were literally burned alive in their cages . . . "There were roughly 100 moms in there," said Scott, "and they all had eight to nine babies with them at the time."
>
> TOKYO - A ferocious tsunami spawned by one of the largest earthquakes ever recorded slammed Japan's eastern coast Friday, killing hundreds of people as it swept away boats, cars and homes while widespread fires burned out of control.
>
> HENRYVILLE, IND. - A string of violent storms demolished small towns in Indiana and cut off rural communities in Kentucky as an early season tornado outbreak killed more than 30 people, and the death toll rose as daylight broke on Saturday's search for survivors.

Are these kinds of events compatible with the claim that there exists an all-good, all-knowing, all-powerful Creator? A Creator, in other words, who is benevolent, omniscient, and omnipotent? Is this belief in a benevolent God not at least paradoxical in the face of such events? If God is benevolent, He would surely not want people and other living things to suffer. If God is omniscient, He surely knows when people and other living things are suffering. If God is omnipotent, surely God could prevent any suffering He wants to prevent. Yet the evil of suffering obviously exists. Is God perhaps not all-powerful or not all-knowing? Or is it that God does not want to prevent suffering? But if God does not want to prevent suffering, then God seems to have evil intentions, which certainly aren't consistent with the nature of a benevolent God.

In his *Dialogues Concerning Natural Religion*, a three-person discussion of the chief arguments for God's existence, Hume considers the question of evil. His conclusion, in the words of one of his characters, Philo, is that our experience of the world argues against the existence of an all-good, all-powerful being:

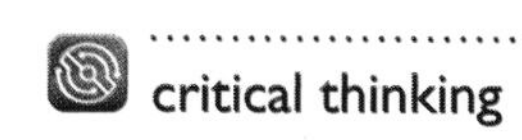

Does Hume assume that if a good God could prevent evil, God would? Is this assumption correct?

> My sentiments, replied Philo, are not worth being made a mystery of; and, therefore, without any ceremony, I shall deliver what occurs to me with regard to the

20 The four stories are, respectively, from: "3-Year Old Boy Dies After Being Tortured, Burned by Baby Sitters," *Salem-News*, Jul 16, 2011, accessed March 10, 2012 from http://www.salem-news.com/articles/july162011/child-burned-dies.php; Mark Saxenmeyer, "Hundreds of Rabbits Die in Stearns County Barn Fire," *KSAX.com*, February 22, 2012, accessed March 10, 2012 from http://ksax.com/article/stories/S2508647.shtml?cat=10230; Jay Alabaster, Mari Yamaguchi, Tomoko A. Hosaka, and Yuri Kageyama, "Japan Earthquake: 8.9 Magnitude Earthquake Hits, 30-Foot Tsunami Triggered," *Huffington Post*, March 11, 2011, accessed March 10, 2012 from http://www.huffingtonpost.com/2011/03/11/japan-earthquake-tsunami_n_834380.html; Associated Press, "Storms Demolish Small Towns in Ind., Kr.; 37 Dead," *The Augusta Chronicle*, March 2, 2012, accessed March 10, 2012 from http://chronicle.augusta.com/latest-news/2012-03-02/storms-kill-15-3-states.

> present subject. It must, I think, be allowed that, if a very limited intelligence whom we shall suppose utterly unacquainted with the universe were assured that it were the production of a very good, wise, and powerful being, however finite, he would, from his conjectures, form *beforehand* a different notion of it from what we find it to be by experience; nor would he ever imagine, merely from these attributes of the cause of which he is informed, that the effect could be so full of vice and misery and disorder, as it appears in this life. Supposing now that this person were brought into the world, still assured that it was the workmanship of such a sublime and benevolent being, he might, perhaps, be surprised at the disappointment, but would never retract his former belief if founded on any very solid argument, since such a limited intelligence must be sensible of his own blindness and ignorance, and must allow that there may be many solutions of those phenomena which will forever escape his comprehension. But supposing, which is the real case with regard to man, that this creature is not antecedently convinced of a supreme intelligence, benevolent, and powerful, but is left to gather such a belief from the appearances of things—this entirely alters the case, nor will he ever find any reason for such a conclusion. He may be fully convinced of the narrow limits of his understanding, but this will not help him in forming an inference concerning the goodness of superior powers, since he must form that inference from what he knows, not from what he is ignorant of. The more you exaggerate his weakness and ignorance, the more diffident you render him, and give him the greater suspicion that such subjects are beyond the reach of his faculties. You are obliged, therefore, to reason with him merely from the known phenomena, and to drop every arbitrary supposition or conjecture.[21]

QUICK REVIEW
Many atheists argue, like Hume did, that if a benevolent, omniscient, omnipotent God existed, there would be no evil. But there is evil. So, a benevolent, omniscient, omnipotent God does not exist.

Hume is saying that if we believe that the Creator of the universe is "a very good, wise, and powerful being," our natural conclusion should be that the universe He created would have no "vice and misery and disorder." But the universe we experience has a great deal of "vice and misery and disorder." So if we want to remain committed to the belief that the Creator is "good, wise, and powerful" we will have to rationalize away this evil, perhaps as something beyond our ability to comprehend. But suppose we were not already committed to the belief that the Creator is "good, wise, and powerful." Suppose that, instead, we are willing to accept whatever conclusion the evidence around us suggests. Then our experience of the world could not support the claim that it was created by "a very good, wise, and powerful being" but would, instead, argue against the existence of such a being.

QUICK REVIEW
The "logical problem of evil" is a deductive argument based on the premise that it is a contradiction to claim (1) God is omnipotent, omniscient, and benevolent, and (2) evil exists. The "evidential problem of evil" is a probabilistic argument based on the premise that the best explanation for evil is that an omnipotent, omniscient, and benevolent God does not exist.

There are two ways of understanding what Hume is saying. First, Hume may be suggesting a *deductive* argument that proves definitively that a benevolent, omniscient, and omnipotent God necessarily does not exist. He would be suggesting what we now call the "logical problem of evil" which is this kind of argument:

1. If a benevolent, omniscient, and omnipotent God exists, then there could be no evil in our world.
2. But there is evil in our world.
3. Therefore, a benevolent, omniscient, and omnipotent God does not exist.

In this "logical problem of evil," premise (1) is supposed to express the idea that it is a logical contradiction to say both that (A) "A benevolent, omniscient, and omnipotent God exists" and that (B) "There is evil in our world." In other words, it is impossible for both (A) and (B) to be true together. Or, to express this in terms we used when we explained logical validity: premise (1) says it is impossible to imagine a situation in which both (A) and (B) are true.

21 Hume, *Dialogues Concerning Natural Religion*, pt. XI.

On the other hand, Hume may be suggesting an *inductive or probable* argument that claims only that the evidence supports the conclusion that God *probably* does not exist. In this case, he would be suggesting what we now call the "evidential problem of evil," which is an argument like this:

1. There is evil in our world.
2. The best explanation of the evil in our world is that there is no benevolent, omniscient, and omnipotent God.
3. Therefore, there probably is no benevolent, omniscient, and omnipotent God.

This argument or "evidential problem of evil" is an inference to the best explanation. The reason why the conclusion is only probable is because in an inference to the best explanation, it is always possible that there is a better explanation but we just haven't found it yet.

For many philosophers, the problem of evil is the "logical problem of evil." J. L. Mackie, for example, says: "In its simplest form the problem is this: God is omnipotent; God is wholly good; and yet evil exists. There seems to be some contradiction between these three propositions, so that if any two of them were true, the third would be false."[22] The reason why Mackie believes that it is a contradiction to say (A) "God is omnipotent [and omniscient] and wholly good" and (B) "Evil exists" is because, as he puts it: "good is opposed to evil, in such a way that a good thing always eliminates evil as far as it can, and there are no limits to what an omnipotent thing can do."[23] But is Mackie right? As we have seen, to say that (A) and (B) are contradictions, is to say that it is impossible to imagine a situation in which both (A) and (B) are true. So the challenge to the believer is to come up with a situation—even an imaginary situation would do the job—in which both (A) and (B) could both be true. Do you think it is possible to meet this challenge?

For some philosophers, however, the problem of evil is the "evidential problem of evil." The philosopher William L. Rowe, for example, grants that it may be possible for the theist to explain a lot of the evil we see by the theory that a benevolent, omniscient, omnipotent God exists.[24] For example, believers might say God permits suffering because that is the only way that humans can become morally virtuous, and this greater good outweighs the evil of suffering. Or believers might say God permits suffering because that is the only way to prevent a greater evil, like people sinking into vice. But surely, Rowe claims, not all evil is like this. For example, the suffering of an innocent baby that is tortured and then killed, or of an animal that is caught in a fire and dies after many days of intense pain, cannot be needed to achieve a greater good or prevent a greater evil. Such examples of intense suffering that do not achieve a greater good nor prevent a greater evil, Rowe concludes, cannot be explained by the theory that a benevolent, omniscient, omnipotent God exists. A few years later the philosopher Paul Draper added a key claim to this kind of argument.[25] Such "gratuitous" (i.e., pointless) evils, Draper claimed, are much better explained by the hypothesis that if there are supernatural beings, they just don't care about the gratuitous suffering we experience in this world. In short, there most likely is no benevolent, omniscient, omnipotent God.

---

22 J. L. Mackie, "Evil and Omnipotence," in Marilyn McCord Adams and Robert Merrihew Adams (eds.), *The Problem of Evil* (Oxford, 1990), 25.

23 Ibid., 26.

24 William L. Rowe, "The Problem of Evil and Some Varieties of Atheism," *American Philosophical Quarterly*, vol. 16, (1979), 335–341.

25 Paul Draper, "Pain and Pleasure: An Evidential Problem for Theists," *Nous*, vol. 23, no. 3, 331–350.

Are the "evidential" arguments of Rowe and Draper right? Is it true that at least some terrible evils are pointless, and that the best explanation of such evils is that either there is no God or God does not care?

QUICK REVIEW
Augustine argued that God produces what is good and only what is good. Because evil is the absence of good, God does not produce evil. Moreover, what God creates must be finite and lack some good. So, if God is to create a finite world, and thereby bring at least some goodness into existence, it has to contain some evil.

Theistic Responses to the Problem of Evil. Several theists have responded to the evidential problem of evil (the kind of argument Rowe and Draper advance) by attempting to show that the best (or as good as any other) explanation of the existence of evil is that an all-powerful, omniscient, benevolent God created the world. One approach argues that although God created the world, he did not create evil in the world. This does not mean there is no evil, but that our understanding of evil as something God produces and could prevent is wrong. The early Christian theologian Saint Augustine (354–430), for one, argued that evil is a negative thing—that is, evil is the absence of something good. Sickness, for example, is the lack of health; pain is the lack of bodily integrity; suffering is the absence of peace. Only God, he claims, can be perfectly and completely good. So, anything that is not God must necessarily lack some good. Therefore, God's creation, being something other than God, must be finite and limited, and so must contain incomplete goodness—that is, evil. Moreover, because God produces only what is good, He does not produce that part of the world where goodness is absent, so He does not produce evil. Moreover, God had reason to create this finite and limited universe because thereby He created something good—a finite and limited good, of course, but still a true good. It is a mistake, then, to argue that the best explanation for evil is that an all-good and all-powerful God does not exist. Instead, a better explanation for evil is that the world had to contain some evil or lack of goodness if it was to be distinct from the all-good God. God *could not* prevent evil in our universe, unless he were to have created another God like himself. The evil in the universe is not evidence that God is uncaring or lacks benevolence. Instead we can explain evil as an aspect of the world that a good and benevolent God did not produce and could not prevent.

But many critics of Augustine claim that his argument seems to dodge the issue. Call sickness lack of health, if you wish, and suffering lack of peace—the fact remains that people experience pain and suffering, which they commonly regard as evil. Why does an all-powerful God allow such tremendous and painful "absences of good"? Surely a benevolent omnipotent God could have created a world that contained much less evil than ours does, or one that lacked the amount of seemingly gratuitous suffering we see all around us.

QUICK REVIEW
Some believers argue that evil is necessary for good, in particular the good of human free will. Critics say an omnipotent God could produce good without evil, in particular that God could have left humans free but made them incapable of inflicting so much evil on each other. Moreover, this "free will" defense of God's existence would explain only "moral evil," it would not explain "natural evils."

But the most common attempt to escape the problem of evil (both the evidential and the logical problem of evil) is to claim that God has to allow evil in order to achieve an important good. One approach is to claim that human freedom is the cause of evil. According to proponents of this view, God made us free. Because we are free, we are free to do evil as well as good. Even an omnipotent God could not make us free in all other respects but not free to do evil, for this would be contradictory. Here is how Richard Swinburne states this argument:

> The free-will defense claims that it is a great good that humans have a certain sort of free will, which I will call free and responsible choice, but that, if they do, then necessarily there will be the natural possibility of moral evil. (By the "natural possibility" I mean that it will not be determined in advance whether or not the evil will occur.) A God who gives humans such free will necessarily brings about the possibility, and puts outside his own control, whether or not that evil occurs. It is not logically possible—that is, it would be self-contradictory to suppose—that God could give us such free will and yet ensure that we always use it in the right way. . . . Free and responsible choice is . . . free will . . . to make significant choices between good and evil, which make a big difference to the agent, to others, and to the

world. . . . It is good that the free choices of humans should include genuine responsibility for other humans, and that involves the opportunity to benefit or harm them.[26]

© Sandra O'Claire/iStockphoto.com

A house in the Lower Ninth Ward in New Orleans, Louisiana. This house was approximately one-quarter mile from the break in the levy. A river of water hit it. Stoops lay empty with no houses behind them. This photo was taken about nine months after Hurricane Katrina. Natural evils like this pose a problem for the "free will defense."

However, critics of this kind of "free will defense" claim there are several problems with the argument. First, and most importantly, the argument does not explain all kinds of evil. Philosophers usually distinguish "moral evils" from "natural evils." A moral evil is one that is intentionally produced by a human being or that a human being could have prevented but intentionally did not. Examples of moral evils would include the pain and suffering people cause by murders, beatings, stabbings, torturing, and so on. A natural evil, on the other hand, is one that is produced by natural processes and whose production does not require the intentional actions or omissions of humans. Examples would include pain and suffering caused by earthquakes, lightning strikes, hurricanes, tornadoes, and floods, as well as the pain and suffering that animals and other non-humans can cause each other. The problem with the free will defense is that while it perhaps gives a satisfactory account of moral evils, it ignores natural evils. Humans apparently exercise no control over these. So, the argument can pertain only to moral evils—that is, those perpetrated by humans on other creatures: war, murder, and torture, for example.

The second problem with the free will defense is that it is not clear that it even gives a good account of moral evils. Perhaps God does leave us free to do evil, but why does an all-powerful God enable us to inflict such horrendous evils? After all, if God is all-powerful, God could have made us capable of inflicting only a limited amount of suffering. Already we are vulnerable, limited creatures. Why not make us unable to inflict the tremendous kind of suffering that we are able to inflict?

John Hick, whom we encountered earlier in this chapter, has provided a different explanation of why God had to allow evil. In his *Philosophy of Religion*, Hick suggests that a world without suffering would be unsatisfactory. Consistent with the thinking of early Hellenistic fathers of the Christian church, such as Irenaeus, Hick argues that although humans are made in the image of God, they have not yet been become free and responsible agents in the finite likeness of God as revealed in Christ. The world, then, "with all its rough edges," must be the sphere in which this stage of the creative process takes place, a role that the world could not serve if God did not allow evil.

To support his claim, Hick asks us to imagine what the world would be like if God did not allow any evils in it. Imagine the world was a "paradise from which all . . . pain and suffering" were excluded.[27] In such a world, people could not injure each other. A murderer's knife might turn to paper, or his bullets might melt into thin air. When thieves robbed a bank, the money they took would miraculously return to the bank. All "fraud, deceit, conspiracy and treason" would no longer have any harmful effects on society. People would no longer be injured in accidents. A child, for example, who fell from a tall building, would somehow float safely down to the ground. Reckless driving would never result in death or injury. People would not

26 Richard Swinburne, *Is There a God?* (New York: Oxford University Press, 1996), 98–99.
27 Hick, *Philosophy of Religion*, 45–46.

PHILOSOPHY AND LIFE

God's Omniscience and Free Will

According to the traditional Western concept of God, God is **omniscient**—that is, God is all-knowing. But does God's knowledge leave any room for **free will**? Many people believe it does not. If God is all-knowing, they claim, then humans cannot be free. Here is how they argue:

1. Suppose God is all-knowing.
2. If God is all-knowing, then God knows what I will do in the future.
3. God cannot be wrong, so if God knows what I will do in the future, then it has to happen.
4. So what I will do in the future has to happen.
5. But if what I will do in the future has to happen, then I am not free to do anything else.
6. So I am not free—I am not able to do anything other than what God now knows I will do.

But this conclusion is distressing to believers. For if our actions are not free, then we cannot be held responsible for them. That is, I cannot be blamed for doing something if I was not able to do anything else. But if we can't be blamed for anything we do, then what of traditional doctrines of heaven and hell? How can we be punished for something if we couldn't do anything else? How can we "repent" if we never had the ability to avoid any sinful action? How can I be blamed for what I had no power to change?

To avoid these conclusions, believers have rejected one or more of the premises of the preceding argument. Some reject point 1 and say God is not all-knowing—his knowledge is limited. Others reject point 2 and say God does not know now what I will do in the future because I have not yet decided what I will do and God leaves me free to decide what I will do. Others reject point 3 and say that God can be wrong because God is a fallible God. But, obviously, none of these options is very attractive to the believer.

QUESTIONS

1. If you are a believer, do you agree with the preceding argument? If you don't agree with it, which premise do you think you should reject?
2. Suppose that instead of "God," the preceding argument was about a supercomputer that knew everything that would happen in the future and was infallible. Assuming such a supercomputer is possible, would the argument still work?

have to work because they would not suffer any harm if they refused to work. Most importantly, we would not have to be concerned about each other because none of us would ever face any "real needs or dangers."

How would this kind of world work? Hick suggests that nature would no longer operate through general laws that each of us would have to learn and respect if we wanted to avoid pain and death. Instead, nature would work through "special providences." Gravity, for example, would usually operate, but would be suspended when allowing it to operate would end in someone being injured. Objects would sometimes be hard and solid, but would become soft when necessary to avoid an injury. Science would become useless since the world would no longer operate by fixed unchanging laws. Our lives would become like a kind of aimless dream in which "we would float and drift at ease."

QUICK REVIEW
Hick argues that evil is necessary, for "in a paradise" without pains, harms, injuries, needs, suffering, dangers, or difficulties, ethical concepts would be meaningless and people could not develop into virtuous beings.

In such a "hedonistic paradise," Hick claims, our ethical concepts "would have no meaning." If doing wrong, for example, essentially involves harming someone, then there could be no wrongdoing in such a world. Nor could any actions be right as distinct from wrong. A moral virtue like courage would have no point in a world in which there are no dangers. Generosity and kindness would likewise be pointless since no one would have unmet needs or require the help of others. Prudence also would not be possible in a world without a stable environment.

A world without evil, then, would be one that might promote pleasure, but it would not be one in which people could develop "the moral qualities of human personality." In that respect, such a world would, Hicks claims, be the worst of all possible worlds. If our world is to be one in which we can become morally good people, then, it must be a world very much like the world in which we actually live. That is, it must operate by regular laws. It must, Hick concludes, be a world with real dangers, one in which people have problems and must overcome obstacles, a world in which pain, failure, sadness, frustration, and defeat are all real possibilities. In short, it must be a world with some evils. And if it did not contain the evils our world contains, then it would have to contain others instead.

Persons of faith may be largely indifferent to evil as an issue because they "know" their God in a manner that is beyond rationality and can easily say that we can't begin to fathom God's mystery. For such people, evil just isn't a problem.

Not so, however, for the atheist. For the atheist, the problem of evil is a plain and unanswerable reason for concluding that God does not exist. Yet many people charge atheism with abandoning humankind to its own devices and with ignoring the persistent belief in a force superior to humankind, a force that often leaves us with hope, confidence, faith, and love in the face of apparently insurmountable troubles. To strip us of these qualities is to leave us both ill equipped to cope with life and, possibly, morally bankrupt. But are such sentiments truly evidence that the atheist is wrong?

Finally, consider this observation about atheism, which is more of an insight than a criticism. Atheism involves a "commitment"—a term used by Ernest Nagel, the self-proclaimed atheist we met earlier—in much the same way that theism or monotheism does. In other words, empirically minded atheists erect their position as much on a commitment of faith as those who hold religious positions. All the characteristics of atheism that Nagel cites are founded as much on a categorical commitment as are the characteristics of the religionist. The commitments obviously differ: The religionist's commitment is to remaining open to the possibility of a nonempirical access to a spiritual reality; the atheist's is to empiricism as a method of knowing a material world. If this is so, we might ask the atheist for empirical-rational reasons for committing oneself to empirical-rational standards and subsequently to atheism. Lacking these reasons, by what criterion can we judge the empiricist-atheistic commitment of faith more sound than the theistic commitment?

critical thinking

Suppose that all of the arguments for the existence of God are mistaken and that it is impossible to prove that God exists. Does this show that God does not exist? Suppose that there is no way of showing that God does not exist. Is this a good reason to believe that God does exist?

Agnosticism

Having studied the arguments for and against the existence of God, many thinkers claim that neither side is convincing. As a result, they say they just don't know whether God exists—a position known as **agnosticism**.

QUICK REVIEW
Some argue that atheism requires a "commitment" to certain beliefs just like theism does.

The nineteenth-century English scientist Thomas Huxley was a well-known agnostic. For Huxley, agnosticism expressed absolute faith in the validity of the principle that "it is wrong for a man to say that he is certain of the objective truth of any proposition unless he can produce evidence which logically justifies that certainty."[28] So Huxley suspended **judgment**, about the existence of God, just as he did on the real nature of such ultimates as matter and mind. As Huxley put it:

critical thinking

Does agnosticism assume that suspension of belief is possible? Is this assumption correct?

> We have not the slightest objection to believe anything you like, if you will give us good grounds for belief; but, if you cannot, we must respectfully refuse, even if that refusal should wreck morality and insure our damnation several times over. We are quite content to leave the decision to the future. The course of the past has impressed us with the firm conviction that no good ever comes of falsehood, and we feel warranted in refusing even to experiment in that direction.[29]

QUICK REVIEW
Huxley, an agnostic, held "it is wrong" to believe unless one has evidence that "logically justifies" belief, so he "suspended judgment."

28 Quoted in *Encounter: An Introduction to Philosophy*, ed. Ramona Cormier, Ewing Chinn, and Richard Lineback, 227.
29 Ibid., 230.

Why We Believe: Freud's View. But if it is unclear whether or not God exists, as the agnostic claims, why then do so many of us continue to believe? In his short work *The Future of an Illusion,* Sigmund Freud suggested an influential answer to that question. Freud, who was the founder of modern psychoanalysis, was hostile to religious belief. He suggested that our belief in God is an "illusion" that has its origins in "infantile" needs. Despite having no good reason to believe in God, he claimed, people continue to believe because they have an "infantile" need to feel that someone is protecting and watching out for them. This need leads them to believe that there is a being that watches out for them, and they imagine that this being is like the father who looked after them when they were children. In a later work, *New Introductory Lectures in Psychoanalysis,* Freud wrote the following:

QUICK REVIEW
Freud claimed that people believe because they have an "infantile" need to believe someone like a "father" is still watching over them.

> The God-Creator is openly called Father. Psychoanalysis has concluded that he really is the father, clothed in the grandeur in which he first appeared to the small child. The religious man's picture of the creation of the universe is the same as his picture of his own creation. . . . He therefore looks back on the memory-image of the overrated father of his childhood, exalts it into a Deity, and brings it into the present and into reality. The emotional strength of this memory-image and the lasting nature of his need for protection are the two supports of his belief in God.[30]

Freud's suggestion is intriguing. And many people today accept it. But is it true? Is there any way of proving that it is true? Perhaps not. Freud offers even less in the way of proof than traditional believers have offered for their own belief in God. Moreover, even if Freud is correct, and our belief in God originates in our own childhood needs, does this show that belief in God is an "illusion"?

QUICK REVIEW
Fallacies are defective arguments that present inadequate evidence or no evidence at all for their conclusions. Formal fallacies are arguments with an invalid form; informal fallacies are arguments that are bad because of their content. The most common formal fallacies are *denying the consequent* and *affirming the antecedent.* Common informal fallacies include *appeal to emotion, inappropriate appeal to authority, ad hominem, argument from ignorance, begging the question, hasty generalization, biased statistics, genetic fallacy, forgetful induction,* and *post hoc ergo propter hoc.*

thinking critically • Formal and Informal Fallacies

No other subject matter raises the intense kinds of arguments that discussions of religion and God do. Unfortunately these discussions are often rife with fallacies, that is, with bad arguments, and Freud's argument may perhaps be an example. It will be useful, then, for us to consider the topic of fallacies here, and see how they can affect discussions of religion and God.

A fallacy is a defective argument, a case of bad or faulty reasoning. Fallacies present inadequate evidence, or, more often, no evidence at all, for the conclusion they are supposed to support. They are, in short, bad arguments, sometimes so bad that they hardly deserve to be called arguments at all. Nevertheless, we are often taken in by fallacies, and to avoid this it will help if you know what they are. There are two broad groups of fallacies: formal fallacies and informal fallacies.

Formal fallacies are arguments that are offered as sound logical arguments when in fact they have an invalid form. We have already seen some formal fallacies and here it is enough to remind ourselves of the two most common formal fallacies, the fallacy of *denying the antecedent* and the fallacy of *affirming the consequent*:

If p, then q	If p then q
Not-p	q
So Not-q	So p

Arguments of either of these forms are always bad arguments. Nevertheless, we frequently make such fallacious arguments, and just as frequently they fool us. Here is an example of

30 From Sigmund Freud, *New Introductory Lectures in Psychoanalysis* (W. W. Norton & Company: New York, 1965).

the fallacy of denying the antecedent: "If you could prove God exists, then religion would be justified, but you can't prove God exists, so religion is not justified." And here is an example of affirming the consequent: "If God is good, then he would create a world in which we could enjoy ourselves; but God has created a world in which we can enjoy ourselves, so God must be good." Both of these are invalid, and so bad arguments, although to some people—maybe even to you—they look like good ones. Don't be fooled!

While formal fallacies are bad arguments because they have an invalid form, *informal fallacies* are bad arguments because of their content, i.e., because the content of the claims they make do not provide real support for their conclusions. There are many kinds of informal fallacies, but here are some of the most important ones:

Appeal to emotion. This common fallacy is the attempt to establish a claim not by providing good reasons for the claim but by appealing to the passions or prejudices of the audience. Here's an example: "If you don't accept that God exists, you're going to Hell!" Emotional appeals may persuade people to accept a claim, but they do not provide any evidence that the claim is true.

Inappropriate appeal to authority. Another common fallacy is the attempt to establish a conclusion by appealing to an "authority" who is not an expert on the subject of the claim, or who has a motive to mislead, or who is known to be unreliable, or whose claim is highly improbable on its face. A few years ago, for example, a journalist working for the tabloid *Weekly World News* wrote that "scientists have determined" that heaven is "a mind-boggling 3-billion light years from earth" because the Hubble telescope sighted "a shining white city" suspended in space "roughly 3 billion light-years away." Relying on the tabloid's journalist to prove a claim about heaven's location would be an inappropriate appeal to authority.

Ad hominem argument. This is an argument that attacks the person making an argument instead of addressing the argument itself. I use an *ad hominem* argument, for example, when someone argues that God does not exist and I reject his argument because "He's an evil person." The moral character of the person who makes a claim is irrelevant to whether the claim is true or false.

Argument from ignorance. This kind of argument claims that because there is no evidence that something is false, it must be true. For example, I am arguing from ignorance if I say that because you cannot prove that God does not exist, God must exist. But the lack of evidence against a claim is not in itself evidence in favor of a claim.

Begging the question. This fallacy is also called a circular argument. It is an argument in which the premises or reasons used to prove a conclusion already assume that the conclusion is true. For example, I am begging the question if I argue, "What the bible says must be true because the bible says it is the word of God."

Hasty Generalization This type of fallacy occurs when an inductive generalization is not based on a sufficiently large sample. For example: "All of my friends who are religious are really happy people, so all religious people must be really happy persons." The few religious people who happen to be my friends, do not form a sufficiently large sample to base on it a conclusion about millions of others.

Biased Statistics An inductive generalization makes this fallacy when it relies on a sample that's not representative. When surveys dealing with religious issues poll people from only one social class or from only one region of the U.S. and draw conclusions about everyone in the U.S., they generally make the fallacy of biased statistics.

Genetic Fallacy This fallacy occurs when a person argues that the causal origin of a belief or claim is evidence that it is false or that it is true. For example, the geneticist Dean Hammer claimed in his book, *The God Gene: How Faith is Hardwired into Our Genes*, that a human gene called $VMAT_2$ causes spiritual feelings including feelings of the presence of God. Some people then argued that genes must cause us to believe in God, so the belief that God exists must be false. But this argument is fallacious since even if our genes cause our belief in God, the belief might still be true, since whether a belief is true does not depend on where the belief came from. The *cause* of a belief is not *evidence* for or against the truth of the belief.

Forgetful Induction This is the fallacy of failing to take into account all the evidence that might affect one's conclusion and, in particular, ignoring evidence that would disprove one's conclusion or shed doubt on one's conclusion. A person, for example, might argue that astrology is a true theory on the basis of astrology predictions that turned out to be correct, while ignoring astrology's many predictions of things that didn't happen.

Post Hoc Ergo Propter Hoc This Latin phrase, which means "after it, therefore caused by it," refers to the fallacy of arguing that since a first event occurred *before* a second one, the first must have *caused* the second. This is also sometimes called the fallacy of *false cause*. An example of a *post hoc ergo propter hoc* fallacious argument is when a person claims that since she prayed before she recovered from an illness, her prayer must have caused her recovery.

There are many kinds of fallacies, then, and you should be able to recognize and point them out when people try to use them to get you to accept their claims. Any of them has the power to ensnare a person who is not careful. In fact, as we mentioned earlier, Freud's argument that belief in God is an "illusion," might be a fallacy. But we leave it to you to determine whether his argument or other arguments in this chapter are fallacies.

Why We Believe: Kant's View. The philosopher Immanuel Kant proposed an explanation of why we believe in God even though we cannot prove that God exists that, unlike Freud's explanation, did not conclude that belief in God is "an illusion." Kant agreed that there is evil and injustice in this world. Morally good people often suffer and end up unhappy, while many bad people prosper and live happy lives. But the fact that sometimes good people unjustly suffer while evil people unjustly prosper should not lead us to reject God. On the contrary, Kant argued, the fact that this world is unjust obliges us to pursue a world that is perfectly just, and this in turn obliges us to believe in a God who alone can bring about a perfectly just world:

QUICK REVIEW
Kant argued that our morality forces us to believe in the possibility of a just world where evil is punished and good is rewarded, and this is possible only if there is a God and an afterlife. So, we have to believe in a God and an afterlife.

> We ought to strive to bring about the supreme good [perfect justice]. Because we ought to bring about this supreme good, it must be possible for it to exist. . . . But the supreme good is possible in the world only if there exists a Supreme Being who can bring about a world in which happiness is correlated with moral goodness. Now a being that is capable of bringing about a just world as the moral law requires, is an intelligence (a rational being). And a being that acts according to the requirements of the moral law, has a will. Therefore, the supreme creator of the world, whose existence must be supposed if the *sumum bonum* is possible, is a Being who causes the world by His intelligence and will . . . that is, God.[31]

Kant is arguing that we feel an obligation to work for a world in which, we might say, "Justice prevails." This would be a world in which moral goodness is rewarded with happiness. But, claims Kant, if we have an obligation to do something, then it must be possible to do it. For we cannot have a moral obligation to do something that is impossible. So, because we have an obligation to work for a world in which justice prevails, we must believe it is possible for such a world to exist. In other words, we must believe that it is possible for a world to exist in which good people are always

31 Immanuel Kant, *Critique of Practical Reason*, trans. T. K. Abbot (London: Longmans Green, 1927), pt. 1, bk. 2, ch. 2, para. 5, pp. 220–222.

rewarded with happiness and in which evil people likewise get what they deserve. Such a world is possible only if there is a God who will eventually punish evil and reward the good, perhaps in some afterlife. So, because our obligation to pursue a just world forces us to believe that a just world is possible, we are also forced to believe that there exists a God who can make such a world possible.

Kant's suggestion, like Freud's, is an intriguing response to our inability to either prove or disprove that God exists. It is an alternative to agnosticism. But, again, we must ask this: Is it reasonable? Unlike Freud, of course, Kant does not claim that belief in God is an illusion. Kant claims only that even if God's existence cannot be proved, and even if evil in the world casts doubt on God's existence, we are still forced to believe that God exists. We are forced to believe in God—that is, if we feel that we have an obligation to make this a better, more just world. However, Kant's argument leaves open the question of whether God exists. Although we must *believe* that God exists, we cannot *know* that God exists.

Perhaps, then, the existence or nonexistence of a theistic God cannot be proved. But lack of certain evidence does not make the question any less important. Even if we feel we lack sufficient evidence, we still must live our lives as if we believe or disbelieve. If we disbelieve, we will not join a church, pray, or worship. We will not feel the presence of God as we walk through a hushed forest of tall trees. If we believe, however, we will not only do these things, but we will also see ourselves as having a spiritual dimension, perhaps one that survives after death. In short, if we lack belief, then we will live our lives in one way, and if we believe, we will live in another way. The question is this: Is it possible to be an agnostic in practice? In the end, mustn't the agnostic choose to live either as a believer or as a nonbeliever?

QUESTIONS

1. In your view, is atheism more or less rational than agnosticism? Is atheism more or less virtuous than agnosticism?
2. Explain the following statement: "The existence of evil can show only that God is either not all-knowing or not omnipotent; it cannot show that God does not exist." Is this statement correct?
3. Theists sometimes claim that God could not have denied human beings free will and still made them morally responsible for their actions and so deserving of heaven or hell in an afterlife. Explain this claim and evaluate it.
4. A playwright once wrote, "If God is good, He is not God; if God is God, He is not good." Explain.
5. The seventeenth-century French philosopher Blaise Pascal suggested that atheism is not a good bet: "Let us weigh the gain and loss in betting that God exists: if you win, you win everything; if you lose, you lose nothing. You should unhesitatingly bet that He exists!" Do you agree?

© Savoy Pictures/Everett Collection

PHILOSOPHY AT THE MOVIES

Watch *Shadowlands* (1993), the true story of C. S. Lewis, a teacher at Oxford who meets, befriends, and eventually marries Joy Gresham, an American woman who then discovers she has terminal cancer and whom Lewis comes to love deeply before she dies. Early in the film, how does C. S. Lewis view the problem of evil? What are his views on the problem of evil toward the end of the film? Is Lewis at any point in the film an agnostic? Does he at any point consider atheism?

4.4 Traditional Religious Belief and Experience

Religious Belief

For many believers, the arguments for and against the existence of God are inconclusive, yet this hardly matters to them. For their belief does not depend on rational proofs. Instead, they believe because belief seems to cohere—to fit—with what they have experienced in their lives, and with who they are. In short, they choose to believe "for reasons of the heart" even though they do not have conclusive evidence that the beliefs they have chosen to adopt are true beliefs.

"The Will to Believe"

Is it legitimate to base belief on a personal decision made with the heart instead of the head? Are we justified in choosing to believe in the absence of irrefutable reasons for believing? In a classic address titled "The Will to Believe," American philosopher William James confronted these issues. (After delivering the speech, he wrote that he wished he had titled it "The Right to Believe.") The thrust of James' views is captured in the following excerpt from his essay "The Will to Believe":

> Let us give the name of hypothesis to anything that may be proposed to our belief. . . . Next, let us call the decision between two hypotheses an option. Options may be of several kinds. They may be: (1) living or dead; (2) forced or avoidable; (3) momentous or trivial; and for our purpose we may call an option a genuine option when it is of the forced, living, and momentous kind:
>
> 1. A living option is one in which both hypotheses are live ones. If I say to you: "Be a theosophist or be a Mohammedan," it is probably a dead option, because for you neither hypothesis is likely to be alive. But if I say: "Be an agnostic or be Christian," it is otherwise: trained as you are, each hypothesis makes some appeal, however small, to your belief.
> 2. Next, if I say to you: "Choose between going out with your umbrella or without it," I do not offer you a genuine option, for it is not forced. You can easily avoid it by not going out at all. . . . But if I say, "Either accept this truth or go without it," I put on you a forced option, for there is no standing place outside of the alternative. Every dilemma based on a complete logical disjunction, with no possibility of not choosing, is an option of this forced kind.
> 3. Finally, if I were [the arctic explorer] Dr. Nansen and proposed to you to join my North Pole expedition, your option would be momentous; for this would probably be your only similar opportunity, and your choice now would either exclude you from the North Pole sort of immortality altogether or put at least the chance of it into your hands. . . . [On the other hand,] an option is trivial when the opportunity is not unique, when the stake is insignificant, or when the decision is reversible if it later prove unwise. . . .
>
> The thesis I defend is, briefly stated, this: Our passional nature not only lawfully may, but must, decide an option between propositions, whenever it is a genuine option that cannot by its nature be decided on intellectual grounds; for to say, under such circumstances, "Do not decide, but leave the question open," is itself a passional decision,—just like deciding yes or no,—and is attended with the same risk of losing the truth.[32]

QUICK REVIEW
James held that when an option is a "genuine"—a "living, momentous, and forced"—option that "by its nature cannot be decided on intellectual grounds," it is legitimate (not wrong) to choose on the basis of our "passional nature," even without sufficient evidence in support of the option we choose.

---

32 William James, *The Will to Believe, and Other Essays in Popular Philosophy* (Longmans, Green and Co.: New York, 1898), 2–4, and 11.

James is claiming that under certain conditions it is both rationally and morally permissible to believe something without adequate intellectual evidence for the belief. In particular, he is saying, when we are faced with a "momentous, living, and forced option" where to "not decide . . . is itself a decision" and when the option is one that "cannot by its nature be decided on intellectual grounds," it is then legitimate to follow "our passional nature" and choose to believe even though we lack sufficient intellectual evidence for the belief. Without understanding his terms as James understands them, we can easily misconstrue what he is saying.

First, consider James' statement that "we may call an option a genuine option when it is of the forced, living, and momentous kind." What does this mean? By the word *option* James means a choice among beliefs or "hypotheses" that may be proposed to us, such as whether or not to believe in God. Some options are what James calls "genuine" options—that is, they are choices we have to make and they will affect our lives in a significant way. James explains that these options are "living, forced, and momentous." An option is *living* when it proposes a belief that we can take seriously. For example, the option of choosing whether to believe in the gods of the ancient Greeks—such as Zeus, Hera, Apollo—is no longer a living option for us, although it was for the ancient Greeks. Second, an option is *forced* when it's a choice you cannot escape by deciding not to choose. For example, if someone proposes, "Either vote for me or vote for my opponent," you could avoid the decision by choosing not to vote at all. On the other hand, if someone says, "Either come follow me or don't come," you would be forced to make a choice. Even by choosing not to choose you would be making a choice: the choice not to follow. Finally, an option is *momentous* when the opportunity is unique, the stakes are important, and the decision is irreversible. If a depressed man, for example, is choosing whether or not to leap over a cliff to his death, his option is momentous.

Next, consider James' view that we are sometimes faced with an option "that cannot by its nature be decided on intellectual grounds." By this, he means that the intellectual evidence for either alternative is inadequate, or the intellectual reasons supporting the alternatives are balanced—the reasons in favor of one choice are as good or as bad as the reasons favoring the other choice. For example, the question that asks whether you will still be alive ten years from now is one that "cannot by its nature be decided on intellectual grounds."

According to James, when faced with an option that is living, forced, and momentous, and that by its nature cannot be decided on intellectual grounds, we can rationally and morally rely on our "passional nature" to make the decision. What is our "passional nature"? For James, our "passional nature" consists of all our nonintellectual interests, emotions, desires, hopes, fears, commitments, and so forth. They are the nonintellectual part of who we are. So, his point is that when we are faced with a "genuine" option that by its nature can't be decided on intellectual grounds, it is legitimate for us to decide what we will believe by relying on the nonintellectual emotions, desires, hopes, and so on, that are part of who we are.

James does not mean that one should simply rely on one's emotions to believe in anything for which there is no good evidence. When options are not living, forced, and momentous, James claims that we should save ourselves from falling into error by deciding to not make up our minds until all the evidence is in. This approach would apply to most of the scientific questions and human issues that we are likely to face. In other words, in most real choices the need to act is not forced on us nor is the choice momentous, so if the evidence is lacking, we should wait for more evidence before making up our minds. It is only when faced with those "living, forced, and momentous" choices that "by their nature cannot be decided on intellectual grounds" that we should and must rely on our passional nature. In such cases, we cannot ("as men who may be interested at least as much in positively gaining truth as in merely escaping dupery") sit back and wait to make our decision; instead, we have to choose since waiting to choose is itself a choice. When such choices arise, we are intellectually and morally justified to choose on the basis of our nonintellectual interests, emotions, desires, and so forth. James believes that there are several areas of our lives where such choices inevitably arise. These include situations where we are faced with important moral decisions, situations where we are faced with questions about whether to trust in the reality of a personal relationship such as a love relationship or one of friendship, and, of course, situations where we are faced with questions of religious belief.

critical thinking

Does James assume that if belief in something has significant benefits, then the belief must be true? Is this assumption correct?

Granted, for some people religious belief is not a living option. But for most it is. To these people, James says that religious belief is also a momentous option. They stand to gain much by their belief and to lose much by their nonbelief. It is also a forced option. If they choose to wait to avoid error, they risk losing the chance of attaining the good that religious belief promises. If the ice cream stand closes while you are debating your choice, the result will be the same as if you had chosen to have no ice cream. For many, religious belief is also an option "that cannot by its nature be decided on intellectual grounds." James himself argues that the intellectual evidence in favor of belief balances the intellectual evidence against it, and there is no intellectual evidence that is absolutely persuasive on either side. Because the choice whether to believe in God or a religious dimension to life is a living, momentous, and forced question that by its nature cannot be decided on intellectual grounds, James concludes that we not only can but *should* allow our "passional nature" to decide it.

Critics of James' View. James' view obviously goes counter to the views of those who claim that we should not believe unless we have sufficient and strong evidence in favor of belief. One critic of James' view, and, in fact, the person against whom he was writing, is W. K. Clifford, who in an earlier essay "The Ethics of Belief" asserted that "it is wrong always, everywhere and for anyone, to believe anything upon insufficient evidence." Against Clifford, James argued that with respect to questions of belief, we have two options: We can choose to protect ourselves from ever believing something false by strictly withholding our belief when the evidence is insufficient, or we can choose to protect ourselves from missing out on the truth by choosing to believe even when evidence is insufficient. Which is the better option? James wrote:

QUICK REVIEW
James answers critics who claim it is always wrong to believe without sufficient evidence by arguing that this claim itself has no sufficient evidence, so those who believe this claim believe it on the basis of their passional nature; the claim that it is legitimate to believe when faced with a genuine option that cannot be decided on intellectual grounds is also a claim that must be chosen or rejected on the basis of our passional nature.

> We may regard the chase for truth as paramount, and the avoidance of error as secondary; or we may, on the other hand, treat the avoidance of error as more imperative, and let truth take its chance. Clifford, in the instructive passage which I have quoted, exhorts us to the latter course. Believe nothing, he tells us, keep your mind in suspense forever, rather than by closing it on insufficient evidence incur the awful risk of believing lies. You, on the other hand, may think that the risk of being in error is a very small matter when compared with the blessings of real knowledge, and be ready to be duped many times in your investigation rather than postpone indefinitely the chance of guessing true. I myself find it impossible to go with Clifford. We must remember that these feelings of our duty about either truth or error are in any case only expressions of our passional life. Biologically considered, our minds are as ready to grind out falsehood as veracity, and he who says, "Better go without belief forever than believe a lie!" merely shows his own preponderant private horror of becoming a dupe. He may be critical of many of his desires and fears, but this fear he slavishly obeys. He can not imagine any one questioning its binding force. For my own part, I have also a horror of being duped; but I can believe that worse things than being duped may happen to a man

> in this world: so Clifford's exhortation has to my ears a thoroughly fantastic sound. It is like a general informing his soldiers that it is better to keep out of battle forever than to risk a single wound. Not so are victories either over enemies or over nature gained.[33]

James' point here is that when we are faced with a "genuine"—momentous, living, and forced—option, there is a cost to be paid if we adopt the policy of withholding our belief until we have sufficient evidence. The cost is that by adopting this policy and withholding our belief, we may miss out on the truth. On the other hand, there is also a cost to be paid when we adopt the policy of choosing to believe when faced with a "genuine" option, despite having insufficient evidence. The cost is that this policy might lead us to believe a falsehood. Which policy should we adopt? In the end, James subtly implies, the choice between these policies is itself a "genuine option" that cannot be decided on intellectual grounds. So we have to choose between these two policies on the basis of our passional nature! James points out that even Clifford had to choose on the basis of his own passional nature. He chose to withhold belief because of his "horror" of falling into error, a "fear he slavishly obeys." He, too, chose on the basis of emotion. We are in the same boat insofar as we, too, must choose between these two policies on the basis of our passional nature.

James' argument has relevance not only for those who believe in a personal God but also for those who sense a divine dimension at work in the cosmos, but not necessarily a Supreme Being. Because he relies on the importance of personal feeling and emotion in religious belief, James provides a philosophical basis for belief in a personal encounter with the sacred, whatever we may perceive that to be. Just what constitutes a personal experience of the divine is a complex question, but individuals often use it as their source of or justification for religious belief.

Personal Experience of the Divine

Many believers, maybe most, do not need any rational proof for their religious belief. Many people who believe in God do so, they claim, because they have actually experienced God or experienced a religious dimension of reality—an experience, in fact—that was deeper and more real than their sensory experiences.

For many people, such religious experiences are simply quiet moments in which they have "felt" a divine presence. Consider this report of a 17-year-old boy:

> QUICK REVIEW
> Many believe in God not on the basis of rational proofs but because of a direct personal experience of the divine.

> Sometimes as I go to church, I sit down, join in the service, and before I go out I feel as if God was with me, right side of me, singing and reading the Psalms with me . . . And then again I feel as if I could sit beside him, and put my arms around him, kiss him, etc. When I am taking Holy Communion at the altar, I try to get with him and generally feel his presence.[34]

Other people claim to have had a more vivid direct experience of God or of a divinity. Here is how St. Teresa described one of her religious experiences:

> One day when I was at prayer . . . I saw Christ at my side—or, to put it better, I was conscious of Him, for I saw nothing with the eyes of the body or the eyes of the soul. He seemed quite close to me and I saw that it was He. As I thought, He was speaking to me. Being completely ignorant that such visions were possible, I was

33 Ibid., 18–19.
34 William James, *The Variety of Religious Experience* (New York: The Modern Library, 1936), 71.

> very much afraid at first, and could do nothing but weep, though as soon as He spoke His first word of assurance to me, I regained my usual calm and became cheerful and free from fear. All the time Jesus Christ seemed to be at my side.[35]

And here is how the Old Testament prophet Isaiah described his encounter with God:

> In the year that King Ussiah died, I saw the Lord sitting on a throne, high and lofty . . . Seraphs were in attendance above him; each had six wings; with two they covered their faces, and with two they covered their feet, and with two they flew. And one called to another and said: "Holy, Holy, Holy is the Lord of hosts; the whole earth is full of his glory" . . . And I said: "Woe is me! I am lost, for I am a man of unclean lips, and I live among a people of unclean lips; yet my eyes have seen the King, the Lord of Hosts.[36]

QUICK REVIEW
James claims that religious experiences of the divine are ineffable and noetic. Rudolf Otto called the direct experience of a religious reality a "numinous experience" and claimed it involves terror, fascination, difference, unworthiness, mystery, and bliss.

What are such experiences like? In his *Varieties of Religious Experience*, James suggests that such experiences have two common characteristics. One is *ineffability*—that is, the experience cannot be adequately described in words. The other is a noetic quality—that is, to the individual the experience is a source of knowledge, often illuminations full of meaning, truth, and importance.

Rudolf Otto, a German theologian who wrote *The Idea of the Holy*, a classic study of religious experience, used the term "numinous experience" to describe an experience in which the power or presence of a divinity or supernatural reality was felt or perceived. Based on his study of such experiences, Otto claimed that a numinous experience had several characteristic qualities. First, the experience is accompanied by a kind of amazement, fear, even terror, at the power and awesome nature of what is being experienced. Second, what is experienced attracts, fascinates, and draws one in with an almost irresistible force. Third, what is experienced is wholly unlike anything that one has encountered before. Fourth, the person having the numinous experience feels unworthy and insignificant in the presence of a sacred reality. Fifth, the experience is suffused with a sense of mystery. And sixth, the experience is accompanied by bliss, a feeling of fulfillment, of contentment and satisfaction. Of course, not all of these qualities are present in all religious experiences of the divine, and in some cases they may be extremely attenuated. The characteristics Otto identifies, however, communicate well what a numinous experience is like.

QUICK REVIEW
Davis argues that many people claim to have experiences of God, that such experiences are probably veridical, so probably God exists. Swinburne supports the claim that numinous experiences are probably real experiences of God with his principle of credulity, which states that in the absence of special considerations, "if it seems (epistemically) to a subject that x is present, then probably x is present."

The point, however, is that many people approach religion through such numinous experiences because such experiences of God or of a supernatural dimension of reality convince them that God or a supernatural dimension of reality exists. But should such experiences be trusted? Is it rational to believe that God or a supernatural dimension of reality exists on the basis of such experiences? How can we be sure the experience is not an illusion or a hallucination? The philosopher Stephen T. Davis offers the following argument in support of the claim that religious experiences can legitimately serve as the basis for belief in God:

1. Throughout human history, and in very many human societies and cultures, people claim to have experiences of God or of some Godlike being.
2. The claim that those experiences are veridical is more probable than the claim that they are delusive.
3. Therefore, probably God or some Godlike being exists.[37]

---

35 St. Teresa of Avila, *The Life of St. Teresa of Avila by Herself*, quoted in Davis, op. cit., p. 124.
36 Isaiah, 6: 1-4.
37 Davis, op. cit., p. 128.

Davis' first premise is clearly true and uncontroversial. The term "veridical" in the second premise of Davis' argument means "real" or "genuine." The second premise means, therefore, that when a person claims to have experienced God through a numinous experience, the claim is probably true. And if it is true that a person really experienced God, of course, it follows that God really exists.

The Ecstasy of Saint Teresa (close-up). Gian Lorenzo Bernini (1598–1680). Location: S. Maria della Vittoria, Rome, Italy.

© Scala/Art Resource, NY

But what can be said in favor of premise (2), i.e., in support of the claim that numinous experiences are probably real experiences of God (or of a supernatural reality)? Davis claims that one reason for accepting (2) is the "principle of credulity" proposed by philosopher Richard Swinburne. Swinburne explains the principle of credulity in this way:

> I suggest that it is a principle of rationality that (in the absence of special considerations), if it seems (epistemically) to a subject that x is present, then probably x is present; what one seems to perceive is probably so. How things seem to be is good grounds for a belief about how things are. . . . [Therefore] in the absence of special considerations, all religious experiences ought to be taken by their subjects as genuine, and hence as substantial grounds for belief in the existence of their apparent object—God, or Mary, or Ultimate Reality, or [the Greek god] Poseidon.[38]

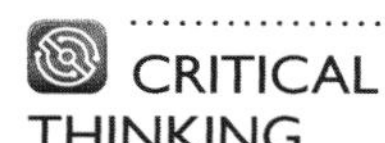

CRITICAL THINKING

Does Swinburne assume that if one feels deeply that something is real, then it must be real?

QUICK REVIEW

Critics argue that Swinburne's principle of credulity should not be applied to numinous experiences because the unusual nature of such experiences should count as a "special consideration" against accepting those experiences as veridical. Swinburne replies that numinous experiences are not unusual and the only reason for claiming that no numinous experiences should be taken as veridical is if one assumes God does not exist, but that is what has to be proven.

By "seems (epistemically) to a subject that x is present" Swinburne means that one's perception of x is the basis of one's belief that x is present. So the principle of credulity basically says that we are justified to rely on our perceptions, unless we have a special reason not to trust a particular perception. Such "special considerations" might include things like: I was dreaming when I had the perception; I was diagnosed with schizophrenia at the time; I had just taken LSD; I have well-supported knowledge that the perception is unreal like the perception of a man carrying his head under his arm.

But why should we accept the principle of credulity? According to Swinburne, we already accept the principle and have no choice but to continue doing so. For we must rely on our perceptions virtually every moment we are awake. If we were not justified in relying on our perceptions of the world, then everything we think or believe about the world would be unjustified. We must rely on our perceptions even to get information from others since we have to perceive what they say or what they write. Moreover, precisely because the principle of credulity is so fundamental, there is no way to prove it (or disprove it). For in order to prove it I would have to rely on at least some perceptions, so any proof would depend on the principle and thus would be circular.

Nevertheless, critics may object that even if we must accept the principle of credulity for ordinary perceptions, it is not acceptable to apply it to perceptions during

38 Richard Swinburne, *The Existence of God* (Oxford: Oxford University Press, 1979), 254.

a "numinous experience." A numinous experience is so unusual that its unusualness should count as a "special consideration" against relying on one's perceptions during such an experience. But Swinburne replies that, first, numinous experiences are not unusual, but extremely common. He cites surveys which show that millions and millions of people today have such experiences. Second, Swinburne claims, even if some numinous experiences are false, this does not mean that all of them are. The only reason we can have for thinking that all numinous experiences are false, is the claim that they all must be false because God does not exist. But such a "reason" assumes to know the very thing that has to be proven: whether God exists.

If we accept Swinburne's principle of credulity, then we seem to have good grounds for accepting the second premise of Davis' argument. Assuming his first premise is true, it would follow that our religious experiences provide reliable grounds for thinking that God probably exists. Why "probably"? Undoubtedly because Davis believes that although some religious experiences are "veridical," it is at least possible that none of them are. We may someday discover, for example, that all religious experiences are the product of a brain misfunction. Davis apparently believes that would be unlikely; nevertheless, it is still a possibility. And since that possibility remains, his argument must be a probabilistic one.

QUICK REVIEW
However, one can question whether people really have direct experiences of the divine, a possibility that seems beyond the capacity of our human ability to perceive things.

Yet the claim that people have direct experiences of the divine can still be questioned. How can a finite human being experience an infinite God? If we experience something, then mustn't we experience it through the senses that we have? And if so, then won't it have to have sensory qualities such as colors, sounds, feelings, and shapes? But certainly God does not have these sensory qualities. So how can what we experience be God?

Despite these difficulties, we see in many people a continuing and intense search for a direct experience of a divine dimension. Many people feel a need to locate themselves in the cosmic scheme of things. Often, they reject traditional religious prescriptions and instead follow their own vague but pressing sense of what they personally need to find. This pursuit takes many forms—among them the New Age movement, self-healing, consciousness expansion, the human potential movement—but all reject some or all of traditional religion.

In the following section, we introduce three nontraditional religious movements—radical theology, feminist theology, and the study of Eastern religious traditions. Although quite different in content and methodology, they are similar in their attempts to gain religious understanding through a nontraditional transformation of consciousness.

QUESTIONS

1. Can you give some examples from your own life of what James means by "a live hypothesis"?
2. Have you ever had what you call a personal religious experience? What made it religious and different from other, more ordinary experiences? Could a person have religious experiences without believing in God? Explain. How would you distinguish a real from a false religious experience?
3. Some numinous experiences emphasize feelings at the expense of reason. Is there any reason to accept feelings when they conflict with reason? Is this question self-contradictory?
4. Evaluate this statement by the seventeenth-century French philosopher Blaise Pascal: "If we submit everything to reason, our religion will have nothing in it mysterious or supernatural. If we violate the principles of reason, our religion will be absurd and ridiculous." Are we forced to accept this dilemma?

PHILOSOPHY AT THE MOVIES

Watch *The Apostle* (1997) in which Eulis "Sonny" Dewey, a foot-stomping, shouting, charismatic Texas preacher, becomes so enraged when he finds his wife Jessie (also a minister) is sleeping with the youth minister that he hits the younger man in the head with a baseball bat, which sends the man into a coma and forces Sonny to flee to Louisiana where he starts preaching in a renovated country church using the alias "Apostle E.F." Do you think Sonny believes on intellectual grounds? How would William James and W. K. Clifford view Sonny's grounds of belief? Who is right? Which, if any, of the religious experiences many people in this film seem to have are "numinous experiences."

4.5 Nontraditional Religious Experience

Radical Theology

Some philosophers have responded to nagging questions about the existence and nature of a Supreme Being by developing a school of theology that deviates in radical ways from traditional theism. The radical theologians, as these thinkers are often termed, perceive God not as a being among other beings but as an aspect of reality. As a result, they feel that our relationship with God is more experiential than rational. The modern roots of this view can be traced to such thinkers as the Danish philosopher Søren Kierkegaard (1813–1855).

Kierkegaard. The northern European society into which Kierkegaard was born was thoroughly Christian but had adopted a stylized formal kind of religious life that, Kierkegaard believed, lacked a passion that should be at the heart of religion. Where the Christians around him should have felt fear, they were complacent; where they should have shown intensity, they were secure. To put it bluntly, Kierkegaard was revolted by these self-professed pillars of the Christian community. Appropriately enough, then, in works such as *Philosophical Fragments and Concluding Unscientific Postscript,* Kierkegaard expounded a view of Christianity and of being a Christian that was at once new and yet very old.

Danish philosopher Søren Aabye Kierkegaard (1813–1855), the founder of existentialism.

© Hulton Archive / Getty Images

Central to Kierkegaard's religious thought is his distinction between the objective and subjective thinker, which is essentially a distinction between reason and faith. The objective thinker strikes an intellectual, dispassionate, scientific posture toward life. In effect, the objective thinker adopts the view of an observer. In contrast, the subjective thinker is passionately and intensely involved with truth. Truth for the subjective thinker is not just a matter of accumulating evidence to establish a viewpoint, but something of profound personal concern. Questions of life and death, of the meaning of one's existence, of one's ultimate destiny, preoccupy the subjective thinker.

Although Kierkegaard is primarily concerned with subjective thinking, he never denies that objective thinking has its place. He simply asserts that not all of life's concerns are open to objective analysis. Indeed, from Kierkegaard's view, it would be fair to say that life's most important questions defy objective analysis. Religious belief in particular, says Kierkegaard, is not open to objective thinking because it involves a relationship with God. Stated more exactly, religion and religious belief are a confrontation with the unknown, not something knowable. In the following passage from *Philosophical Fragments*, Kierkegaard demonstrates what he means:

critical thinking

"If God exists, it would be folly to attempt to prove it." Is this true?

> But what is this unknown something with which the Reason collides when inspired by its paradoxical passion, with the result of unsettling even man's knowledge of himself? It is the Unknown. It is not a human being, in so far as we know what man is; nor is it any other known thing. So let us call this unknown something: *the God.* It is nothing more than a name we assign to it. The idea of demonstrating that this unknown something (the God) exists, could scarcely suggest itself to the Reason. For if the God does not exist it would of course be impossible to prove it; and if he does exist it would be folly to attempt it. For at the very outset, in beginning my proof, I would have presupposed it, not as doubtful but as certain (a presupposition is never doubtful, for the very reason that it is a presupposition), since otherwise I would not begin, readily understanding that the whole would be impossible if he did not exist. But if when I speak of proving the God's existence I mean that I propose to prove that the Unknown, which exists, is the God, then I express myself unfortunately. For in that case I do not prove anything, least of all an existence, but merely develop the content of a conception. . . .
>
> The works from which I would deduce God's existence are not directly and immediately given. The wisdom in nature, the goodness, the wisdom in the governance of the world—are all these manifest, perhaps, upon the very face of things? Are we not here confronted with the most terrible temptations to doubt, and is it not impossible finally to dispose of all these doubts? But from such an order of things I will surely not attempt to prove God's existence; and even if I began I would never finish, and would in addition have to live constantly in suspense, lest something so terrible should suddenly happen that my bit of proof would be demolished. From what works then do I propose to derive the proof? From the works as apprehended through an ideal interpretation, i.e., such as they do not immediately reveal themselves. But in that case it is not from the works that I make the proof; I merely develop the ideality I have presupposed, and because of my confidence in *this* I make so bold as to defy all objections, even those that have not yet been made. In beginning my proof I presuppose the ideal interpretation, and also that I will be successful in carrying it through; but what else is this but to presuppose that the God exists, so that I really begin by virtue of confidence in him?[39]

critical thinking

"If I cannot find out whether or not a certain thing exists, but its existence is critically important for me, then I should simply make a leap of faith that it exists." Evaluate this argument?

QUICK REVIEW
Kierkegaard distinguishes objective (dispassionate, scientific) from subjective (passionate, involved) thinking. Religious belief is not open to objective thinking, and it is useless to try to prove God's existence. This causes "anguish."

From this passage it is clear that Kierkegaard condemns the attempt to "prove" God's existence, as well as all other intellectual attempts to define God. The reason is that by Kierkegaard's account, God cannot be known; God is not subject to rational, objective analysis. But if the point of religion and religious faith is not to know God, then just what is their point? To *feel*, rather than to know.

In the end, rational thinking, which is the religious expression of objective thinkers, points to the existence of God but gives individuals little on which to erect

39 Søren Kierkegaard, *Philosophical Fragments*, trans. David Swenson (Princeton, NJ: Princeton University Press, 1936). Copyright © 1936, 1962 by Princeton University Press.

a relationship with God. "I contemplate the order of nature," says Kierkegaard, "in the hope of finding God, and I see omnipotence and wisdom; but I also see much else that disturbs my mind and excites anxiety. The sum of all this is objective uncertainty."

Faced with objective uncertainty, with the inconclusiveness of objective analysis and rational debate and "proofs," we are anguished. This anguish, this suffering, is compounded by the anticipation of our own death and our feeling of smallness and insignificance in the face of the eternal order of things. The debates go on; our lives ebb away. We must make a decision.

Kierkegaard calls this decision the "leap of faith"; it consists of a commitment to a relationship with God that defies objective analysis. Of course, we may choose not to make the leap of faith; we may, instead, try to minimize our suffering through rational understanding and knowledge, through objective analysis. But for this alternative, Kierkegaard has only sarcasm. *"The two ways,"* he says: "one is to suffer; the other is to become a professor of the fact that another suffered."

QUICK REVIEW
Religion and God must be approached through a "leap of faith," a commitment that defies objective analysis.

Tillich. The chief exponent of radical theology in modern time has been Protestant theologian Paul Tillich (1886–1965). Tillich, an existentialist, contends that traditional theism has erred in viewing God as *a* being and not as *being itself.* He believes that the proofs for God's existence, discussed earlier, have fostered this error. As a result, we have bound God to our subject–object structure of reality. *He*—notice the sexualization—is an object for us as subjects, becoming the target for our prayers, worship, and supplications. "He" becomes almost some *thing* to which we direct our lives. At other times we make ourselves an object for God as subject. Because theism posits an all-knowing, all-powerful God, and because we are neither, the relationship must therefore be one of superior (God) to inferior (us), controller to controlled, subject to object. An antagonistic tension results. As Tillich says, "He deprives me of my subjectivity because he is all-powerful and all-knowing. I revolt and try to make him into an object, but the revolt fails and becomes desperate. God appears as an invincible tyrant, the being in contrast with whom all other things are without freedom and subjectivity."[40] This image of God as "invincible tyrant," he feels, is a much more telling refutation of theological theism than all the objections to the traditional proofs for God's existence. Tillich believes that his criticism is justified, for God as tyrant is "the deepest root of the Existentialist despair and the widespread anxiety of meaninglessness in our period."

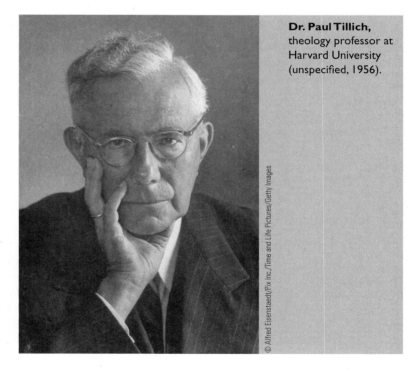

Dr. Paul Tillich, theology professor at Harvard University (unspecified, 1956).

© Alfred Eisenstaedt/Pix Inc./Time and Life Pictures/Getty Images

40 This and all other Tillich quotations are from Paul Tillich, *The Courage to Be* (New Haven, CT: Yale University Press, 1952).

QUICK REVIEW
Tillich claimed that traditional concepts of God objectified God and turned God into an "invincible tyrant."

If Tillich and other radical theologians reject the theistic concept of God, what do they offer as a substitute? What kind of God do they believe in? For Tillich, God is not one being among other beings; instead, God is "the ground of being," that is, the foundation and source of all existence. This God transcends the God of theism and so dissipates the anxiety of doubt and meaninglessness. This ground of being is not provable because it cannot be. It is neither an object nor a subject. It is present, although hidden, in every divine–human encounter.

That God is the "ground of being" is only one of Tillich's many difficult concepts. "Depth" is another difficult concept that is central to his thought. "Depth is what the word God means," he writes, realizing that for many the word may have no meaning. "If the word has not much meaning for you, translate it," advises Tillich, "and speak of the depths of your life, of the source of your being, of your ultimate concern, of what you take seriously without reservation." Tillich writes:

QUICK REVIEW
For Tillich, God is "the source of your ultimate concern" and "of what you take seriously without reservation." So, anyone who has an ultimate concern believes in God.

> What does the metaphor *depth* mean? It means that the religious aspect points to that which is ultimate, infinite, unconditional in man's spiritual life. Religion, in the largest and most basic sense of the word, is ultimate concern. And ultimate concern is manifest in all creative functions of the human spirit. It is manifest in the moral sphere as the unconditional seriousness of the moral demand. Therefore, if someone rejects religion in the name of the moral function of the human spirit, he rejects religion in the name of religion. Ultimate concern is manifest in the realm of knowledge as the passionate longing for ultimate reality. Therefore, if anyone rejects religion in the name of the cognitive function of the human spirit, he rejects religion in the name of religion. Ultimate concern is manifest in the aesthetic function of the human spirit as the infinite desire to express ultimate meaning. Therefore, if anyone rejects religion in the name of the aesthetic function of the human spirit, he rejects religion in the name of religion. You cannot reject religion with ultimate seriousness, because ultimate seriousness, or the state of being ultimately concerned, is itself religion. Religion is the substance, the ground, and the depth of man's spiritual life. This is the religious aspect of the human spirit.[41]

For Tillich, to be religious is to have an ultimate concern. If there is something about which you deeply and truly care, then you are religious; you have a religion. And the object of your ultimate concern is the way that God is manifested to you.

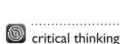

critical thinking
"Everyone has an ultimate concern, so everyone believes in God." Evaluate the assumptions of this argument.

An atheist might say, "I do not believe in God." But Tillich would say that this is virtually impossible, for a genuine atheist would have to be someone who does not believe that there is anything that is worth caring about deeply. Anyone who has an "ultimate concern" believes in God. The only people who can rightly call themselves atheists are those who can say, "Life has no depth. Life is shallow. Being itself is surface only." Writes Tillich, "If you could say this in complete seriousness, you would be an atheist; but otherwise you are not. He who knows the depth knows about God."

Like many existentialists, Tillich is not easy to understand. But clearly he believes that traditional theism, and its attempts to "prove" God exists, have erred in making God an object:

QUICK REVIEW
Tillich claimed that traditional proofs of God turn God into an object and ultimately lead to a loss of faith.

> If you start with the question whether God does or does not exist, you can never reach Him; and if you assert that He does exist, you can reach Him even less than if you assert that He does not exist. A God about whose existence or non-existence you can argue is a thing beside others within the universe of existing things. And the question is quite justified whether such a thing does exist, and the answer is equally justified that it does not exist.[42]

41 Paul Tillich, *Theology of Culture*, ed. Robert C. Kimball (London: Oxford University Press, 1964), 6–7.
42 Ibid., 4–5.

God cannot be proved, as if God were an object for which one was searching. Such "objectification" not only limits the deity but also raises the very kinds of inconsistencies that lead to a loss of faith. Therefore, Tillich's God defies traditional definitions and proofs. Tillich is no escapist, no dodger of doubt. On the contrary, he faces the concrete world of finite values and meanings and uses all its imperfections, skepticism, and meaninglessness to confront what is ultimately real: being. And in this ground of all being he experiences God. Everyone does "who knows the depth."

Besides having many elusive concepts, Tillich's theology provokes other objections. By saying that God is the object of a person's ultimate concern, he seems to be doing away with what we have always recognized as God. Even the atheist who is ultimately concerned about something, Tillich claims, can be said to believe in God. But what could this possibly mean? How can someone who does not believe in that which we call God possibly be said to nevertheless believe in God if, say, he or she is deeply committed to atheism itself as the ultimate concern? What does "God" mean here? Related to this is another objection: that Tillich's statements about God amount to nothing but tautologies. In logic, a statement whose predicate repeats its subject is called a **tautology**. When Tillich says, "He who knows the depth knows about God," is he actually saying, "He who knows about God knows about God"? When he argues, "If one is ultimately concerned or has the courage to be, then one knows God," isn't he saying, "If one knows God or knows God, then one knows God"?

QUICK REVIEW
But it is unclear what Tillich means by "God," and statements he makes about what "God" is seem to be mere tautologies.

Tillich also claims to have had an experience of divine presence, of a merging with some fundamental reality, and this experience became the foundation of many of his views. Of course, no one may question Tillich's experience; it is as personal as a headache or a hunger pang. But his interpretation of his experience can be questioned. We can and should, it seems, ask for verification when he interprets that experience as resulting from contact with the ground of all being. Tillich must verify the reality of the ground of all being and establish it as the cause of his transcendent experiences.

Tillich would probably reply that knowledge about the God he describes—the ground of all being—is a completely different kind of knowledge from the intellectual kind of knowledge we have about other ordinary things. He would argue that his knowledge transcends empirical data and defies scientific verification. It is knowledge whose source is much closer to mystical intuition than to senses or reason. This knowledge, he might say, is rooted in personal experience induced through prayer and meditation.

Feminist Theology

Many feminists have also challenged the traditional Western concept of God and religion. Their most important objections are that God is portrayed as male and is associated with religious beliefs and practices that are oppressive to women.

For example, God has traditionally been said to have no sex, and many philosophers have been careful to emphasize this point. Yet these same philosophers, as well as the majority of people, continue to use male pronouns—*He and Him*—to refer to God. Both Christianity and Judaism have traditionally characterized "Him" in male roles, particularly as a male parent, a "Father." The result is that in Western people's real, practical, and lived religious experience, God is thought of as a male despite the denials of philosophers and theologians. In her groundbreaking book *Beyond God the Father*, the feminist philosopher and theologian Mary Daly has argued that this male conception of God has had a profoundly oppressive impact on women:

> If God in "his" heaven is a father ruling his people then it is in the "nature" of things and according to divine plan and the order of the universe that society be male dominated. Within this context, a *mystification of roles* takes place: The husband dominating his wife represents God "himself." The images and values of a given society have been projected into the realm of dogmas and "Articles of Faith" and these in turn justify the social structures which have given rise to them and which sustain their plausibility.[43]

Moreover, in a surprising reversal of biological fact, Christianity and Judaism have suggested that the woman is born from the man's body and not the man from the woman's. The Old Testament story that Eve, the first female, was made out of Adam's rib implies that males are prior to females and are their source. The Judeo-Christian Bible also implies that sin and evil originated with a woman—Eve—who tempted the man—Adam—into the "Fall." Subsequently, Christianity went on to hold that salvation has to come from a male person—Jesus Christ, who is the "Son of God" and whom God sent forth to be crucified as a sacrifice to save us all from sin and evil. Christianity has also given mostly to males—priests and pastors—the authority to lead Christians in their daily lives, and many of the major Christian religions—such as Roman Catholicism—still refuse to ordain women as priests or allow them to become bishops. The most orthodox segments of Judaism have also similarly allowed only males—rabbis—to play leadership roles.

Daly, perhaps the most articulate feminist critic of traditional religious beliefs, summarizes her criticisms of religion in general, and Christianity in particular, in these propositions:

> There exists a planetary sexual caste system [patriarchy], essentially the same in Saudi Arabia and in New York, differing only in degree.
>
> This system is masked by sex role segregation, by the dual identity of women, by ideologies and myths. . . .
>
> All of the major world religions function to legitimate patriarchy. This is true also of the popular cults such as the Krishna movement and the Jesus Freaks.
>
> The myths and symbols of Christianity are essentially sexist. Since "God" is male, the male is God. . . .
>
> The myth of feminine evil, expressed in the story of the Fall, is reinforced by the myth of salvation/redemption by a single human being of the male sex [Jesus Christ]. The idea of a unique divine incarnation in a male, the God-man of the "hypostatic union," is inherently sexist and oppressive. Christolatry is idolatry.[44]

QUICK REVIEW
Feminist theologian Daly holds that the traditional concept of God is male, sexist, oppressive to women, and legitimates patriarchy—the rule of men over women. We must reject it, especially in its Christian form, and replace it with "the Goddess."

Daly argues that by making God male, males have been able to use God to justify and maintain their power and authority over women: It is right for males to rule because the highest "Lord"—God—and the "savior"—Jesus Christ—are male. Moreover, because women are the source of evil and had their origins in man (Adam's rib), it is appropriate that they be ruled by men. Thus, the traditional male concept of God has played and continues to play a major role in keeping women oppressed and dominated by men.

Daly and other feminist thinkers have suggested that the male concept of God cannot be reformed because it has too many masculine connotations that make

---

43 Mary Daly, *Beyond God the Father* (Boston: Beacon, 1974), 206.

44 Mary Daly, "The Qualitative Leap Beyond Patriarchal Religion," *Quest* 1, no. 4 (Spring 1975), 20.

it oppressive to women. Maleness is an essential part of the traditional Western concept of God and cannot be separated from it. Instead, the concept must be abandoned, allowed to wither and die, and replaced with new religious symbols and concepts associated with "the Goddess":

> For some feminists concerned with the spiritual depth of the movement, the word "God" is becoming increasingly problematic, however. This by no means indicates a movement in the direction of "atheism" or "agnosticism." . . . Some reluctantly still use the word "God" while earnestly trying to divest the term of its patriarchal associations, attempting to think perhaps of the "God of the philosophers" rather than the overtly masculist and oppressive "God of the theologians." But the problem becomes increasingly troublesome, the more the "God" of the various Western philosophers is subjected to feminist analysis. "He"—"Jahweh"—still often hovers behind the abstractions, stunting our own thought, giving us a sense of contrived doublethink. The word "God" just may be inherently oppressive . . . .
>
> For an increasing minority of women—and even for some men—"Goddess" is becoming more functional, meaningful, and loaded with healing associations. . . . The use of the expression, "The Goddess," is a way . . . of exorcising the male "God," and of affirming a different myth/reality.[45]

A significant and growing number of women, Daly holds, are breaking away from the Judeo-Christian concept of God, which "legitimates patriarchy—the prevailing power structure and prevailing world view." Efforts to reform these Western religions, she claims, are useless and will "eventually come to be recognized as comparable to a Black person's trying to reform the Ku Klux Klan." Instead, feminists who seek a religious dimension in their lives should find meaning in "the Goddess." Many are already creating a revolutionary and powerful new community, a new "sisterhood," that rejects the prevailing male view that power must be understood as power *over* people. In the consciousness of this new sisterhood, power is experienced as "power of presence to ourselves and to each other." This new movement is not hierarchical—that is, unlike male organizations, it is not based on leaders who have "power" over their followers. Thus, the notion of "the Goddess" will not lead to an oppressive female-dominated society like the male-dominated society that the notion of a male God produced.[46]

Daly is perhaps the harshest and most extreme critic of traditional religious concepts, and it is certainly difficult for men not to feel put off by her strong language and unrelenting attacks on everything that is male. Nevertheless, many of her criticisms of religion are incisive and telling blows against the often oppressive maleness of the traditional Western concept of God and the sexism that affects much of traditional Western religious thought and practice. It cannot be denied that these traditions have been used to justify the so-called right of men to rule over women. Thus, although one might argue with this or that element of the feminist perspective represented by Daly, much of what she says rings absolutely true.

Nevertheless, many feminists, while agreeing with much of Daly's critique, have objected to several facets of her thinking. In particular, some feminist theologians have questioned whether the male features of the traditional Western concepts of God and religion are really as necessary and essential to these as Daly claims they are. For example, as the feminist theologian Pamela Dickey Young writes, "Although for Christians it is in Jesus that they see God's presence, God's love and

45 Ibid., 33.
46 Ibid., 28.

care exemplified, that this decisive revelation has taken place in a man is, in a very real sense, accidental."[47] Young argues that the male qualities attached to the concept of God and to Christianity are not necessary to either. Male qualities are "accidental" or non-essential elements that got attached to God and to Christianity when these were introduced into human societies that were already sexist and dominated by males. Young argues that it is the task of the feminist to identify the sexist, oppressive, and male elements that have infected religious thinking and to work for reform.

It is not clear whether feminists such as Young can succeed in purging the Western concepts of God and religion of their sexist leanings. Daly may be correct when she writes that "dressing up old symbols just will not work for women who are conscious of sexist religiosity." Both Daly and Young are inviting us to come with them on different journeys toward an understanding of God and religion that is neither sexist nor oppressive. But where either of those journeys will lead—or even whether they will succeed in going anywhere—is still unclear. What is clear is that each one of us has to make his or her own journey toward an understanding—or rejection—of God and religion as they are today, with all their faults and blemishes.

QUICK REVIEW
Hinduism views Brahman as the only reality and all else is illusion; atman is the deepest consciousness within each person and distinct from the ordinary self which is an illusion.

Eastern Religious Traditions

Eastern religious traditions are many and varied. It is neither our intention nor within our capabilities to mention all of them, let alone discuss them adequately. But we outline some of the central beliefs of two related Eastern religions to which many Westerners are turning for meaningful religious experience: Hinduism and Buddhism.

Boltin Picture Library/The Bridgeman Art Library

Dharmachakra, Wheel of Transmigratory Existence (paper).

Hinduism. One of the oldest Eastern traditions is Hinduism, which has been practiced by hundreds of millions of people for about five thousand years. Hinduism has many divisions and subdivisions, and no leader or belief is accepted by every Hindu sect. In fact, Hinduism is so diversified that it is very difficult to describe as a whole. Any attempt at description is bound to be an oversimplification. A further complication is that our language has no precise equivalents for certain Indian terms and concepts.

With awareness of these limitations, let us begin with the literary source of Hindu teaching. Although many texts form the body of Hindu scripture, one has influenced Hindu thought more than any other: the Bhagavad-Gita, the Song of the Lord, which is part of the great epic Mahabharata. Reading the Gita will introduce you to the principal concepts of Hinduism, as well as to beautiful poetry.

One concept common to all expressions of Hinduism is the idea that there is a fundamental reality that underlies all the distinctions we make when we talk about the things around us. This underlying reality is the one ultimate source of the whole universe, and cannot be described since words would attribute distinctions to it that it does not have; one can only point to it. This ultimate reality is the absolute, or *Brahman*, a reality that is present behind everything, that causes

47 Pamela Dickey Young, *Feminist Theology/Christian Theology* (Minneapolis: Fortress Press, 1990), 97, 98, 99, 101.

whatever there is, and that is unlimited, incomprehensible, all-pervasive, omnipresent, and unchangeable. All of the objects we see around us are illusions: they are the illusory manifestations of Brahman.

A correlative idea is the concept of *atman,* the deepest *consciousness* that lies within each of us, beneath all our living, sensing, and thinking activities and beneath all our dreaming and waking experiences. Atman is not the ordinary individual we commonly call "I"; that individual self that we are aware of and refer to as "me," is also an illusion. Beneath the illusionary individual self that I am aware of, however, lies atman. Atman is the *profound inner consciousness* of which I am not aware, a *consciousness* within myself that is not seen, sensed, or imagined but that directs everything I do. Yet, I can come to know the atman within through meditation that achieves an enlightened inner self-consciousness that sees beyond the many differentiated illusionary things we ordinarily perceive.

When, through mediation, I am able to contact the atman-consciousness within, I will see that my inner deep consciousness is identical with Brahman. When we truly and profoundly realize our unity with Brahman, we can understand that the ultimate reality that underlies everything in the universe is identical with the deep consciousness that lies within ourselves. Our deepest inner consciousness is the ultimate reality that is the source of all the illusory universe we see around us.

In Hindu thought, the highest spiritual value is enlightenment, by which one is illuminated and liberated and, most importantly, finds release from the wheel of existence. Repeated existence is the destiny of those who do not achieve enlightenment.

QUICK REVIEW
Hindu thought affirms enlightenment as the key to liberation from the great wheel of existence. The destiny of each is the enlightened realization that Brahman, the ultimate reality that underlies all the differentiated things in the universe, is identical with atman, the profound consciousness within each of us that underlies the illusorily self. When enlightened, we at last can be freed from the wheel of existence.

To understand enlightenment, you must understand the law of karma, the law of sowing and reaping. All of us, through what we do or do not do, supposedly determine our destiny. If we are particularly evil, we may find ourselves reborn as something less than human. If we are noble, we may be reborn as especially favored humans. This wheel of existence turns unless and until we achieve enlightenment, which can enable us to be released from the series of rebirths and from the endless striving to cling to material things.

Buddhism. Another major Eastern tradition is Buddhism, contained in the teachings of its founder, Siddhartha Gautama, or the Buddha. Because Gautama found no evidence for belief in a personal God, his teachings are a diagnosis of and a prescription for the "disease" of living.

The Buddha preached the Four Noble Truths. As we saw in Chapter 2, he held that nothing in the universe endures. To try to cling to what is impermanent inevitably leads to loss and suffering. Everything that lives dies and is then forced to rise, repeat life again, and then fall again into death in a ceaseless round of loss and suffering. Our cravings keep us returning to this passing world through successive "rebirths." Release from this suffering, he preached, could be gained only by putting an end to our craving for pleasure, for continued life, and for power. And the key to ending this craving is following the Noble Eightfold Path:

> And this is the Noble Truth of Sorrow. Birth is sorrow, age is sorrow, disease is sorrow, death is sorrow; contact with the unpleasant is sorrow, separation from the pleasant is sorrow, every wish unfulfilled is sorrow—in short, all the five components of individuality are sorrow.
>
> And this is the Noble Truth of the Arising of Sorrow. It arises from craving, which leads to rebirth, which brings delight and passion, and seeks pleasure now here, now there—the craving for sensual pleasure, the craving for continued life, the craving for power.

QUICK REVIEW
Buddhism emphasizes the four noble truths: All life is sorrow, sorrow arises from craving, stopping craving will stop sorrow, and the Noble Eightfold Path will stop craving; it requires right views, right resolve, right speech, right conduct, right livelihood, right effort, right mindfulness, and right concentration.

> And this is the Noble Truth of the Stopping of Sorrow. It is the complete stopping of that craving, so that no passion remains, leaving it, being emancipated from it, being released from it, giving no place to it.
>
> And this is the Noble Truth of the Way which leads to the Stopping of Sorrow. It is the Noble Eightfold Path—[having] Right Views, Right Resolve, Right Speech, Right Conduct, Right Livelihood, Right Effort, Right Mindfulness, and Right Concentration.[49]

The First Noble Truth is concerned with the suffering that we experience in living within an impermanent universe. The Second identifies the cause of this suffering: the clinging or grasping of what cannot last, which is based on **avidya**—ignorance and unawareness of the illusory nature of the things around us. The person who lacks awareness is committed to the world of things and illusion, **maya**, unaware of any deeper fundamental reality behind the world of illusion. The unaware person tries to control himself and his environment. These attempts are futile; the result is frustration and the viciously circular pattern of life called **samsara**, the cycle of births and deaths. The Third Noble Truth concerns the ending of samsara, called **nirvana**—release or liberation. We achieve nirvana when we stop grasping and clinging and become aware of the profound reality that underlies all things; we are released from the cycle of births and deaths when we at last enter a state in which all difference between oneself and fundamental reality is obliterated, a state that defies definition. The Fourth Noble Truth describes the Eightfold Path of the Buddha's **dharma**—that is, the moral doctrine about what we must do to end the grasping and clinging that leads to self-frustration and that is an obstacle to finding nirvana. We examine this concept more carefully in Chapter 7.

Differences between East and West. Obviously, there is much more to Hinduism and Buddhism than we have outlined. Nevertheless, these sketches already suggest some of the major differences between Eastern and Western religious thought. Let's consider some of these differences more closely.

QUICK REVIEW
Broadly speaking, these forms of Eastern thought reject the Western concept of an all-powerful, all-knowing personal God and of the moral law as something God commands.

First, the East rejects the West's "objectified" God. There is no claim of a personal, all-knowing, all-good, all-powerful, and all-loving divine individual as there is in the Western tradition. Consequently, Eastern thinkers have generally not been as preoccupied with debating God's existence as Western thinkers have. As a corollary, Buddhism does not share the Western view that there is a moral law, enjoined by God, that we must obey or suffer eternal damnation. In short, our tradition presents a God who expects us to behave in a certain way. In contrast:

> the Buddha's precepts of conduct—abstinence from taking life, taking what is not given, exploitation of the passions, lying, and intoxication—are voluntarily assumed rules of expedience, the intent of which is to remove the hindrances to clarity of awareness. Failure to observe the precepts produces bad *"karma"* not because *karma* is a law or moral retribution, but because all motivated and purposeful actions, whether conventionally good or bad, are *karma* insofar as they are directed to the grasping of life. Generally speaking, the conventionally "bad" actions are rather more grasping than the "good."[50]

---

48 Sarvepalli Radhakrishnan and Charles A. Moore, eds., *A Source Book in Indian Philosophy* (Princeton, NJ: Princeton University Press, 1957), xx–xxvi.
49 William Theodore de Bary, *Sources of Indian Tradition*, vol. 1, from Samyutta Nikaya (New York: Columbia University Press, 1958), 99.
50 Alan Watts, *The Way of Zen* (New York: Pantheon, 1957), 61.

Moreover, whereas the traditional thrust of Western religion has been to align us with the divine Creator, Eastern thought aims to ground us in an ultimate reality. To do so, Eastern thought generally prescribes discipline, self-control, moderation, and detachment. Although these values are frequently observed in Western religious practice, they are usually practiced as a means to an end: salvation and reward. They are ways of attaining wisdom and truth, but they are also ways of avoiding damnation.

Perhaps these differences explain why there has been a growing interest in the United States in Eastern thinking and religions. Many people are turning away from traditional faiths in favor of Buddhism, yoga, Transcendental Meditation, Vedanta, and so on. Obviously, converts to Eastern religions have not stopped asking about their place in the scheme of things. On the contrary, they are asking perhaps more intensely than ever before. Apparently, the traditional Western concepts of self, subject–object distinction, Judeo-Christian dogma, the emphasis on one's personal relationship with God, are no longer meaningful for them. Many features of Eastern thought allow people to explore in new directions: the emphasis on the workings of consciousness and inner growth; the importance of discipline, practice, and method; a distrust of doctrines and dogmas; and hope for integrating body and intellect, feelings and reason, through a personal philosophy. But a central feature seems to be the reevaluation and redefinition of one's concept of the divine and one's relationship to it.

The many differences between Eastern thought and Western outlook should not be ignored. In the end, those differences raise the fundamental question that the Westerner must ask about Eastern religion: Is it too alien to be truly understood by us? Is it too alien to meet our standards of what is reasonable? Is it too alien to be ultimately meaningful for us?

QUESTIONS

1. In your own words, what is Tillich's objection to traditional or theological theism? Are you sympathetic to Tillich's objections? Why or why not?
2. Anselm's ontological argument claims that existence is a necessary part of the meaning of a perfect being. Is Tillich similarly claiming that God is a necessary part of the meaning of "ultimately concerned"? Is he defining God into existence?
3. Some people claim that the mere fact that Tillich interprets his own knowledge of the "depth" as an experience of God does not make it so. Neither does it guarantee the existence of God. Are such critics distinguishing between belief and knowledge? How?
4. Would you say that James' two characteristics of a mystical experience would also apply to a drug-induced state of consciousness?
5. Do you agree that the Western concept of God is sexist? If not, how do you respond to Daly's criticisms? If you agree that our idea of God is sexist, then do you believe it can be changed?
6. What would you say are the main sources of attraction for Westerners in Eastern thought?

PHILOSOPHY AT THE MOVIES

Watch *Spring, Summer, Winter, Fall and Spring* (2003) which tells the story of a Buddhist monk and his very young apprentice as they move through the cycles of life, desire, attachment, loss, search, redemption, and death. The story takes place on a small floating monastery that is drifting on a lake in a mountainous forest where the monk teaches the boy prayer and meditation and respect for life, until the boy enters adolescence and falls in love with a girl whom he follows away from the monastery, only to return many years later after the monk has died and after he has changed considerably. What aspects of Buddhist thought do you see in this movie? Are Tillich's claims about people's "ultimate concern" supported in this film? Do Mary Daly's criticisms apply to the Buddhism you see in this movie?

Chapter Summary

All religions speak of personal commitment and of our need to find our place in the cosmic scheme of things. Traditionally in the West, these phenomena have been sought through a relationship to a personal, theistic God, and many arguments have been assembled for God's existence. Seeing weaknesses in the theistic position, however, many people have adopted atheism or agnosticism.

Whether or not the arguments for God are sound, the question of religious belief persists and affects our lives. For many people, belief arises from their personal religious experience. In this connection, we examined whether it was reasonable to believe on the basis of religious experience, and then looked at movements that reject the traditional Western approach to religion, such as radical theology, feminism, and Eastern religious thought. The main points of this chapter are:

4.1 The Significance of Religion

- Religions differ profoundly: some do not believe in God, some have no official beliefs, some are not institutionalized.
- Six dimensions characterize most religions: (1) doctrine, (2) experience, (3) myth, (4) ritual, (5) morality, and (6) organization.

4.2 Does God Exist?

- Anselm's ontological argument claims that God, as "that than which nothing greater can be conceived," must exist.
- The cosmological argument of Aquinas' argues that the motions and effects we see in the world demand an origin in an unmoved mover and an uncaused cause.
- William Paley's design argument claims the order we see in nature implies that it was produced by an intelligent deity; a contemporary version says the improbability of the fine-tuning in the universe requires a God, and critics reply that if we live in a "multiverse" such fine-tuning is not improbable.
- **An argument by analogy claims that since two things are alike in certain respects, they are probably alike in another related respect.**

4.3 Atheism, Agnosticism, and the Problem of Evil

- Atheism and agnosticism are responses to the difficulties in the traditional arguments for a theistic God.

- Atheism claims that we know that God does not exist, arguing particularly that the existence of evil implies there is no God. Theists argue that evil is necessary for good, in particular the good of human free will.
- Agnostics claim that we do not know whether or not God exists.
- Freud and Kant argued that people cannot help but believe in a God.
- **Fallacies, which often intrude into discussions of religion and God, are defective forms of reasoning, and include both formal and informal fallacies.**

4.4 Traditional Religious Belief and Experience

- William James held that a "living, momentous, and forced" option that "cannot be decided on intellectual grounds," must be decided on the basis of our "passional nature," even without sufficient evidence in support of the option we choose; such was the case with religious belief.
- Many people believe in God not because of rational proofs but because of a direct personal experience of the divine. Davis and Swinburne argue such experiences are veridical.

4.5 Nontraditional Religious Experience

- Radical theology, as presented by Søren Kierkegaard and Paul Tillich, rejects traditional rational proofs of God. Kierkegaard sees religion as a "leap of faith"; Tillich sees religion in terms of one's "ultimate concern."
- Feminist theology has argued that much in the Western concept of God and religion is sexist and that these sexist notions have been used to oppress women.
- Eastern religious views, such as Hinduism and Buddhism, reject the Western traditional view of God, and both advocate the search for enlightenment.

Clearly, the philosophy of religion has had a long and illustrious history that continues to unfold. The concept of religious experience is inextricably linked with who we are, for religious experience is one way that we can integrate our personalities and lives and thereby achieve wholeness.

The potential for what we have been calling religious experience, then, is staggering. In the future, areas of conscious awareness that we hardly dream of today may open up. This awareness will no doubt be accompanied by a deep and reverent sensitivity to the profound mystery of life and our wondrous part in it.

4.6 Readings

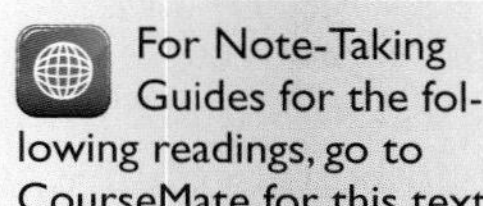
For Note-Taking Guides for the following readings, go to CourseMate for this text.

The following two readings are both concerned with the Problem of Evil. The first is drawn from the classic Russian novel, *The Brothers Karamazov*, by Fyodor Dostoevsky. In the reading, one of the brothers, Ivan, is speaking to his younger brother, Alyosha, who has entered a monastery and is now a novice monk preparing to take the vows by which he will forever renounce marriage and possessions and devote himself to prayer and service to God. Alyosha is a gentle young man with a simple faith, a genuine love for all humanity, and a wisdom beyond his years. Ivan, a university student, is a brilliant and logical thinker who searches for a rational explanation for everything and who is tortured by religious doubts due to his inability to reconcile a loving God with the existence of suffering. The conversation described in the reading, which is central to Dostoevsky's novel, shows Ivan explaining the reasons for his doubts to Alyosha. In the second reading, the American philosopher William P. Alston argues against a key premise that is assumed to be true by probable (or "inductive") arguments that say evil is evidence that God probably does not exist (including the argument Ivan makes in the first reading). All arguments that say evil is evidence that a good God probably does not exist assume that a good God could and would have prevented at least some of the evils in our world. (Alston uses Rowe's version of that assumption as an example.) Alston argues that we humans just do not have the mental abilities to know whether that assumption is true or not. Notice that Alston is, in effect, trying to answer the argument that Ivan explains to Alyosha, in Dostoevsky's *The Brothers Karamazov.* Who is right, Alston or Ivan?

FYODOR DOSTOEVSKY

Excerpt from *The Brothers Karamazov*

From: Fyodor Dostoyevsky, *The Brothers Karamazov*, Constance Garnett, translator, (New York: The Lowell Press, 1912).

"I must make one confession," Ivan began. "I could never understand how one can love one's neighbours. It's just one's neighbours, to my mind, that one can't love, though one might love those at a distance . . . For anyone to love a man, he must be hidden, for as soon as he shows his face, love is gone."

"Father Zossima has talked of that more than once," observed Alyosha. "He, too, said that the face of a man often hinders many people not practised in love, from loving him. But yet there's a great deal of love in mankind, and almost Christ-like love. I know that myself, Ivan."

"Well, I know nothing of it so far, and can't understand it, and the innumerable mass of mankind are with me there. . . . But enough of that. I simply wanted to show you my point of view. I meant to speak of the suffering of mankind generally, but we had better confine ourselves to the sufferings of the children. . . . Children can be loved even at close quarters, even when they are dirty. . . . Are you fond of children, Alyosha? I know you are, and you will understand why I prefer to speak of them. If they, too, suffer horribly on earth, they must suffer for their fathers' sins, . . . but that reasoning is of the other world and is incomprehensible for the heart of man here on earth. The innocent must not suffer for another's sins, and especially such innocents! . . . You don't know why I am telling you all this, Alyosha? My head aches and I am sad."

"You speak with a strange air," observed Alyosha uneasily, "as though you were not quite yourself."

"By the way, a Bulgarian I met lately in Moscow," Ivan went on, seeming not to hear his brother's words, "told me about the crimes committed by Turks and Circassians in all parts of Bulgaria . . . . They burn villages, murder, outrage women and children. . . . These Turks took a pleasure in torturing children, too; cutting the unborn child from the mother's womb, and tossing babies up in the air and catching them on the points of their bayonets before their mothers' eyes. Doing it before the mothers' eyes was what gave zest to the amusement." . . .

"Brother, what are you driving at?" asked Alyosha. . . .

"You see, I am fond of collecting certain facts, and, would you believe, I even copy anecdotes of a certain sort from newspapers and books, and I've already got a fine collection. . . . I've collected a great, great deal about Russian children, Alyosha. There was a little girl of five who was hated by her father and mother, 'most worthy and respectable people, of good education and breeding.' . . . This poor child of five was subjected to every possible torture by those cultivated parents. They beat her, thrashed her, kicked her for no reason till her body was one bruise. Then, they went to greater refinements of cruelty—shut her up all night in the cold and frost in a privy, and because she didn't ask to be taken up at night (as though a child of five sleeping its angelic, sound sleep could be trained to wake and ask), they smeared her face and filled her mouth with excrement, and it was her mother, her mother did this. And that mother could sleep, hearing the poor child's groans! Can you understand why a little creature, who can't even understand what's done to her, should beat her little aching heart with her tiny fist in the dark and the cold, and weep her meek unresentful tears to dear, kind God to protect her? Do you understand that, friend and brother, you—pious and humble novice? Do you understand why this infamy must be and is permitted? Without it, I am told, man could not have existed on earth, for he could not have known good and evil. Why should he know that diabolical good and evil when it costs so much? Why, the whole world of knowledge is not worth that child's prayer to dear, kind God! . . . I am making you suffer, Alyosha. I'll leave off if you like."

"Never mind. I want to suffer, too," muttered Alyosha.

"One picture, only one more, because it's so curious, so characteristic . . . It was in the darkest days of serfdom at the beginning of the century . . . There was in those days a general of aristocratic connections, the owner of great estates. . . . One day a serf-boy, a little child of eight, threw a stone in play and hurt the paw of the general's favourite hound. 'Why is my favourite dog lame?' He is told that the boy threw a stone that hurt the dog's paw. 'So you did it.' The general looked the child up and down. 'Take him.' He was taken—taken from his mother and kept shut up all night. Early that morning the general comes out on horseback, with the hounds, his dependents, dog-boys, and huntsmen, all mounted around him in full hunting parade. The servants are summoned for their edification, and in front of them all stands the mother of the child. The child is brought from the lock-up. It's a gloomy, cold, foggy, autumn day, a capital day for hunting. The general orders the child to be undressed; the child is stripped naked. He shivers, numb with terror, not daring to cry . . . 'Make him run,' commands the general. 'Run! run!' shout the dog-boys. The boy runs . . .'At him!' yells the general, and he sets the whole pack of hounds on the child. The hounds catch him, and tear him to pieces before his mother's eyes! . . . Well—what did he deserve? To be shot? To be shot for the satisfaction of our moral feelings? Speak, Alyosha!"

"To be shot," murmured Alyosha, lifting his eyes to Ivan with a pale, twisted smile.

"Bravo!" cried Ivan delighted. "You're a pretty monk! So there is a little devil sitting in your heart, Alyosha Karamazov!" . . .

Ivan for a minute was silent, his face became all at once very sad. . . .

"I must have justice, or I will destroy myself. . . . I want to see it, and if I am dead by then, let me rise again, for if it all happens without me, it will be too unfair. . . . I want to see with my own eyes [that harmony when] the hind lies down with the lion and the victim rises up and embraces his murderer. I want to be there when everyone suddenly understands what it has all been for. . . . But then there are the children, and what am I to do about them? That's a question I can't answer. . . . Listen! If all must suffer to pay for the eternal harmony, what have children to do with it, tell me, please? It's beyond all comprehension why they should suffer, and why they should pay for the harmony. . . . Some jester will say, perhaps, that the child would have grown up and have sinned, but you see he didn't grow up, he was torn to pieces by the dogs, at eight years old. Oh, Alyosha, I am not blaspheming! I understand, of course, what an upheaval of the universe it will be when everything in heaven and earth blends in one hymn of praise and everything that lives and has lived cries aloud: 'Thou art just, O Lord, for Thy ways are revealed.' When the mother embraces the fiend who threw her child to the dogs, and all three cry aloud with tears, 'Thou art just, O Lord!' then, of course, the crown of knowledge will be reached and all will be made clear. But what pulls me up here is that I can't accept that harmony. . . . It's not worth the tears of that one tortured child who beat itself on the breast with its little fist and prayed in its stinking outhouse, with its unexpiated tears to 'dear, kind God'! It's not worth it, because those tears are unatoned for. They must be atoned for, or there can be no harmony. But how? How are you going to atone for them? Is it possible? By their being avenged? But what do I care for avenging them? What do I care for a hell for oppressors? What good can hell do, since those children have already been tortured? . . . And if the sufferings of children go to swell the sum of sufferings that was necessary to pay for truth, then I protest that the truth is not worth such a price. I don't want the mother to embrace the oppressor who threw her son to the dogs! . . . I don't want harmony. . . . Besides, too high a price is asked for harmony. . . . And so I hasten to give back my entrance ticket, and if I am an honest man I am bound to give it back as soon as possible. And that I am doing. It's not God that I don't accept, Alyosha, only I most respectfully return him the ticket."

"That's rebellion," murmured Alyosha, looking down.

"Rebellion? I am sorry you call it that," said Ivan earnestly. . . . "Tell me yourself, I challenge your answer. Imagine that you are creating a fabric of human destiny with the object of making men happy in the end, giving them peace and rest at last, but that it was essential and inevitable to torture to death only one tiny creature—that baby beating its breast with its fist, for instance—and to found that edifice on its unavenged tears, would you consent to be the architect on those conditions? Tell me, and tell the truth."

"No, I wouldn't consent," said Alyosha softly.

WILLIAM P. ALSTON

"The Inductive Argument from Evil and the Human Cognitive Condition"

From: William P. Alston, "The Inductive Argument from Evil and the Human Cognitive Condition," *Philosophical Perspectives*, vol. 5 (1991), pp. 29, 54, 55, 59, 60.

William Rowe [a critic who argues that evil is evidence that God probably does not exist, claims (as all such critics claim)]:

> (1) There exist instances of intense suffering which an omnipotent, omniscient being could have prevented without thereby losing some greater good or permitting some evil equally bad or worse.

. . . [I will argue we do not have the ability to know whether (1) is true or not. First, can the critic claim that there are particular cases of suffering that God has no good reason to allow and that God could miraculously prevent by intervening in the natural order? To claim this] . . . we would have to be justified in supposing that God would have a sufficient reason to make, in this case, an exception to the general [laws of Nature]. And how could we be justified in supposing that? We would need an adequate grasp of the full range of cases from which God would have to choose whatever exceptions He is going to make, if any, to the general policy of letting nature take its course. Without that we would not be in a position to judge that . . . a [particular] evil is among the n% of the cases most worthy of being miraculously prevented. And it is abundantly clear that we have and can have no such grasp of this territory as a whole. We are quite unable, by our natural powers, of determining just what cases, or even what kinds of cases, of suffering there would be throughout the history of the universe if nature took its course. We just don't know enough about the constituents of the universe even at present, much less throughout the past and future, to make any such catalogue. And we could not make good that deficiency without an enormous enlargement of our cognitive capacities. Hence we are in no position to judge that God does not have sufficient reason for refraining from interfering in [a particular] case.

[Second, can the critic claim] that God could have instituted a quite different natural order, one that would not involve human and animal suffering, or at least much less of it? Why couldn't there be a natural order in which there are no viruses and bacteria the natural operation of which results in human and animal disease, a natural order in which rainfall is evenly distributed, in which earthquakes do not occur, in which forests are not subject to massive fires? To be sure, even God could not bring into being just the creatures we presently have while subjecting their behavior to different laws. For the fact that a tiger's natural operations and tendencies are what they are is an essential part of what makes it the kind of thing it is. But why couldn't God have created a world with different constituents so as to avoid subjecting any sentient creatures to disease and natural disasters? Let's agree that this is possible for God. But then the critic must also show that at least one of the ways in which God could have done this would have produced a world that is better on the whole than the actual world. For even if God could have instituted a natural order without disease and natural disasters, that by itself doesn't show that He would have done so if He existed. For if that world had other undesirable features and/or lacked desirable features in such a way as to be worse, or at least no better than, the actual world, it still doesn't follow that God would have chosen the former over the latter. It all depends on the overall comparative worth of the two systems. . . .I merely want to show that the critic is not justified in supposing that some alternative natural order open to God that does not involve suffering (to the extent that we have it) is better on the whole.

There are two points I want to make about this. . . . First, it is by no means clear what possibilities are open to God. Here it is important to remember that we are concerned with metaphysical possibilities (necessities . . .), not merely with conceptual or logical possibilities in a narrow sense of 'logical'. The critic typically points out that we can consistently and intelligibly conceive a world in which there are no diseases, no earthquakes, floods, or tornadoes, no predators in the animal kingdom, while all or most of the goods we actually enjoy are still present. He takes this to show that it is possible for God to bring about such a world. But, as many thinkers have recently argued, consistent conceivability (conceptual possibility) is by no means sufficient for metaphysical possibility, for what is possible given the metaphysical structure of reality. To use a well worn example, it may be meta-physically necessary that the chemical composition of water is H_2O since that is what water essentially is, even though, given the ordinary concept of water, we can without contradiction or unintelligibility, think of water as made up of carbon and chlorine. Roughly speaking, what is conceptually or logically (in a narrow sense of 'logical') possible depends on the composition of the concepts, or the meanings of the terms, we use to cognize reality, while metaphysical possibility depends on what things are like in themselves, their essential natures, regardless of how they are represented in our thought and language.

It is much more difficult to determine what is metaphysically possible or necessary than to determine what is conceptually possible or necessary. The latter requires only careful reflection on our concepts. The former requires—well, it's not clear what will do the trick, but it's not something we can bring off just by reflecting on what we mean by what we say, or on what we are committing ourselves to by applying a certain concept. To know what is metaphysically possible in the way of alternative systems of natural order, we would have to have as firm a grasp of this subject matter as we have of the chemical constitution of familiar substances like water and salt. It is clear that we have no such grasp. We don't have a clue as to what essential natures are within God's creative repertoire, and still less do we have a clue as to which combinations of these into total lawful systems are doable. We know that you can't have water without hydrogen and oxygen and that you can't have salt without sodium and chlorine. But can there be life without hydrocarbons? Who knows? Can there be conscious, intelligent organisms with free will that are not susceptible to pain? That is, just what is metaphysically required for a creature to have the essential nature of a conscious, intelligent, free agent? Who can say? Since we don't have even the beginnings of a canvass of the possibilities here, we are in no position to make a sufficiently informed judgment as to what God could or could not create by way of a natural order that contains the goods of this order (or equal goods of other sorts) without its disadvantages.

One particular aspect of this disability is our inability to determine what consequences would ensue, with metaphysical necessity, on a certain alteration in the natural order. Suppose that predators were turned into vegetarians. Or rather, if predatory tendencies are part of the essential natures of lions, tigers, and the like, suppose that they were replaced with vegetarians as much like them as possible. How much like them is that? What other features are linked to predatory tendencies by metaphysical necessity? We may know something of what is linked to predation by natural necessity, e.g., by the structure and dispositional properties of genes. But to what extent does metaphysical possibility go beyond natural possibility here? To what extent could God institute a different system of heredity such that what is inseparable from predation in the actual genetic code is separable from it instead? Who can say? To take another example, suppose we think of the constitution of the earth altered so that the subterranean tensions and collisions involved in earthquakes are ruled out. What would also have to be ruled out, by metaphysical necessity? (Again, we know something of what goes along with this by natural necessity, but that's not the question.) Could the earth still contain soil suitable for edible crops? Would there still be mountains? A system of flowing streams? We are, if anything, still more at a loss when we think of eradicating all the major sources of suffering from the natural order. What metaphysical possibilities are there for what we could be left with? It boggles the (human) mind to contemplate the question.

The second main point is this. Even if we could, at least in outline, determine what alternative systems of natural order are open to God, we would still be faced with the staggering job of comparative evaluation. How can we hold together in our minds the salient features of two such total systems sufficiently to make a considered judgment of their relative merits? *Perhaps* we are capable of making a considered evaluation of each feature of the systems (or many of them), and even capable of judicious comparisons of features two-by-two. For example, we might be justified in holding that the reduction in the possibilities of disease is worth more than the greater variety of forms of life that goes along with susceptibility to disease. But it is another matter altogether to get the kind of overall grasp of each system to the extent required to provide a comprehensive ranking of those systems. We find it difficult enough, if not impossible, to arrive at a definitive comparative evaluation of cultures, social systems, or educational policies. It is far from clear that even if I devoted my life to the study of two primitive cultures, I would thereby be in a position to make an authoritative pronouncement as to which is better on the whole. How much less are we capable of making a comparative evaluation of two alternative natural orders, with all the indefinitely complex ramification of the differences between the two . . .

I have drawn on various limits to our cognitive powers, opportunities, and achievements in arguing that we are not in a position to deny that God could have [a sufficient] reason for various cases of suffering. In conclusion it may be useful to list the cognitive limits that have formed the backbone of my argument.

1. *Lack of data.* This includes, inter alia, the secrets of the human heart, the detailed constitution and structure of the universe, and the remote past and future, including the afterlife if any.
2. *Complexity greater than we can handle.* Most notably there is the difficulty of holding enormous complexes of fact—different possible worlds or different systems of natural law—together in the mind sufficiently for comparative evaluation.
3. *Difficulty of determining what is metaphysically possible or necessary.* Once we move beyond conceptual or semantic modalities (and even that is no piece of cake) it is notoriously difficult to find any sufficient basis for claims as to what is metaphysically possible, given the essential natures of things, the exact character of which is often obscure to us and virtually always controversial. This difficulty is many times multiplied when we are dealing with total possible worlds or total systems of natural order.
4. *Ignorance of the full range of possibilities.* This is always crippling when we are trying to establish negative conclusions. If we don't know whether or not there are possibilities beyond the ones we have thought of, we are in a very bad position to show that there can be no divine reasons for permitting evil.
5. *Ignorance of the full range of values.* When it's a question of whether some good is related to [an evil] in such a way as to justify God in permitting [that evil], we are, for the reason mentioned in question 4., in a very poor position to answer the question if we don't know the extent to which there are modes of value beyond those of which we are aware. For in that case, so far as we can know, [the evil] may be justified by virtue of its relation to one of those unknown goods.
6. *Limits to our capacity to make well considered value judgments.* The chief example of this we have noted is the difficulty in making comparative evaluations of large complex wholes.

. . . The point is that the critic is engaged in attempting to support a particularly difficult claim, a claim that there isn't something in a certain territory, while having a very sketchy idea of what is in that territory, and having no sufficient basis for an estimate of how much of the territory falls outside his knowledge. This is very different from our more usual situation in which we are forming judgments and drawing conclusions about matters concerning which we antecedently know quite a lot, and the boundaries and parameters of which we have pretty well settled.

4.7 HISTORICAL SHOWCASE

Aquinas, Descartes, and Conway

In this chapter, we have examined a broad range of philosophical issues raised by belief in God. But we have tended to treat these issues in isolation from other philosophical questions. By contrast, most major philosophers have felt that questions about God are deeply related to other important philosophical issues. For this reason, philosophers' views on God have profoundly influenced their positions on other philosophical questions.

Here we showcase three philosophers whose views about God determine their views on other important philosophical issues: Thomas Aquinas, René Descartes, and Anne Conway. By examining their work, we get an idea of how these three philosophers incorporate God into a large philosophical system. Moreover, in becoming acquainted with them, we will see how a person's position on one philosophical issue can dramatically affect and interact with that person's views on other issues in philosophy.

National Trust Photographic Library/The Bridgeman Art Library

Saint Thomas Aquinas (oil on silvered copper).

AQUINAS

No period of history has been more preoccupied with religion than the medieval era, and the greatest of the medieval thinkers was Thomas Aquinas. Although Aquinas was influenced by the writings of Aristotle, he was also deeply affected by the events of the fifteen centuries (322 BCE to 1225 CE) that separated him from Aristotle, Plato, and the other Greek philosophers. Those centuries saw the Roman Empire (circa 300 BCE to circa 500 CE) rise and spread over Europe and also witnessed the birth of Christianity at the very height of the empire's power. They also saw the collapse of civilization, as barbarian tribes repeatedly invaded the empire until, after centuries of battering, it was destroyed and Europe descended into the Dark Ages. During the Dark Ages, Christianity spread gradually, but most philosophy ceased while men and women concentrated on surviving in the barbaric world that Europe had become.

It was not until Aquinas' times that conditions in Europe once again became conducive to philosophical activities and that new centers of learning—the first universities—were established. But the Europe that emerged from the Dark Ages had become completely Christianized; consequently, philosophy tended to focus on religious concerns. It was only natural that Thomas Aquinas' thinking should focus on the philosophical problems raised by the religion that now dominated Europe.

Born in 1225 to a wealthy family of the Italian nobility, Saint Thomas Aquinas was raised to hold high office in the Roman Catholic Church, a position that his family hoped would prove advantageous to their political fortunes. In preparation for this career, the family sent him at the age of five to study in a Benedictine monastery, where he remained until he entered the University of Naples at the age of 14. At Naples, Thomas came into contact with the Dominicans, an inspiring order of monks dedicated to poverty and to service through teaching. Despite vigorous opposition from his family, Thomas entered the Dominican Order in 1241, dashing his family's hopes for his ecclesiastical career. Four years later, the order sent him to the new University of Paris to study under Albert the

Great, a scholar of towering intellect already famous for his knowledge of Aristotle's doctrines. Under Albert's influence, Thomas began to draw heavily on Aristotle's teachings, gradually producing a brilliant synthesis of Christian theology and Aristotelian philosophy. Aquinas remained a dedicated Christian scholar and teacher throughout his life, churning out a prodigious number of writings until his death in 1274. In his two greatest works, the *Summa Contra Gentiles* and the *Summa Theologica*, Thomas addresses virtually every philosophical issue raised by Christianity and resolves them in a way that many feel is philosophically sound yet true to the Christian faith. Aquinas' philosophy, in fact, has often been called the Christian philosophy and is still held by a large number of Christians.

Aquinas did not confuse religious faith with philosophy. With great care he distinguished among truths that are known by faith, truths that are known by reason, and truths that are known by both faith and reason. Philosophy, he held, consists of truths that our unaided reason can discover by reflecting on our natural experience in the world. Theology, on the other hand, begins with truths that have been revealed by God through Scripture and accepted by faith, and from these revealed truths draws further religious truths. There is some overlap between philosophy and theology, however, because some truths that can be discovered by our unaided reason have also been revealed by God:

> Some truths about God exceed the capacity of our human reason. An example of this is the truth that God is three persons in one. But there are some truths that reason by its very nature is also able to discover. Examples of these are the truths that God exists, that there is only one God, and similar truths. In fact, these truths about God have been proved by several philosophers who have relied completely on the light of their natural reason.[1]

Aquinas' Five Proofs. Central to Aquinas' philosophy are his famous five proofs for the existence of God (one of which is the cosmological proof), some of which were influenced by Aristotle's views on causes. Each of the proofs begins by pointing to some aspect of the world we experience: its motion, its causality, its contingency, its imperfection, or its unthinking order. Each proof then argues that this aspect of the world cannot account for itself: Each aspect depends for its existence on something—a Divine Being—that is utterly different from the objects we experience. The motion of objects demands the existence of an unmoved mover, the causality we see at work demands the existence of something that is uncaused, the contingency of objects demands the existence of something that is noncontingent, the existence of imperfect objects demands the existence of something that is perfect, and the existence of order among objects that do not think demands the existence of something that thinks and that produces that order:

> That God exists can be proved in five ways.
>
> The first and clearest way is the argument from motion. It is certain and evident to our senses that some things in the world are in motion. Now if something is moved, it must be moved by something else. . . . For nothing can change from being potentially in motion to being in a state of actual movement unless something else that is in actual movement acts on it. . . . So whatever is moving must be moved by something else. Now if that by which it is moved is itself moving, then it, too, must be moved by something else, and that by something else again. But this cannot go on to infinity because then there would be no first mover. And if there were no first mover, then nothing would move since each subsequent mover will move only to the extent that it is moved by the motion imparted by the first mover. The [other] parts of a staff, for example, will move only to the extent that the [top of the] staff is moved by the hand. Therefore, there must be a first mover that is not moved. And this first unmoved mover is what we mean by God.
>
> The second way is based on the nature of efficient causes. In the world we see around us, there are ordered lines of efficient causes [in which each member of the line produces the next member]. But nothing can be its own efficient cause, since then it would have to exist prior to itself and this is impossible. Now it is not possible for a line of efficient causes to extend to infinity. For in any line of efficient causes, the first is the cause of the intermediate ones, and the intermediate ones cause the last one. Now if we remove any of the causes, we remove all the remaining effects. So if there were no first cause then there would be no last cause nor any intermediate ones. But if a line of efficient causes extended back to infinity, then we would find no first cause. Consequently, if the line of causes extended back to infinity,

1 Saint Thomas Aquinas, *Summa Contra Gentiles*, I, q.3, a.2. This edited translation is by Manuel Velasquez.

there would be no intermediate causes nor any last causes in existence in the universe. But we know this is false. So it is necessary to admit that there is a first efficient cause. And this we call God.

The third way is based on contingency and necessity. It proceeds as follows. We find in nature things that are contingent. These are things that are generated and that can corrupt, and which therefore can exist or can cease to exist. Now it is impossible for such contingent things to exist forever. For if it is possible for something to cease existing, then eventually a moment will come when it will cease to exist. Therefore, if everything were contingent, then eventually everything would have ceased existing. If this happened, then even now nothing would exist, because something can start to exist only through the action of something that already exists. It follows that not everything is contingent, that is, some things must exist necessarily, that is, forever. Now every necessary thing is caused to exist forever either by something else or not by anything else. But as we proved above, it is impossible for a line of causes to be infinite. So there must exist something which derives its necessary existence from itself and not from something else, and which causes the existence of all other necessary beings. This is what we all mean by God.

The fourth way is based on the degrees of perfection that we find in things. Among the objects in our world some are more and some less good, true, noble, and the like. But to say that a thing has more or less of a certain perfection is to say that it resembles to a greater or lesser degree something which perfectly exemplifies that perfection. . . . So there must be something which is most perfectly true, most perfectly good, most perfectly noble, and, consequently, which most perfectly exists (since, as Aristotle shows, those things that are perfectly true also exist perfectly). Now that which most perfectly exemplifies some quality, also causes other things to have that quality to a greater or lesser degree. Fire, for example, which most perfectly exemplifies the quality of heat, is the cause of the heat in hot things. Therefore, there must be something which is the cause of the being, goodness, and every other perfection in things. And this we call God.

The fifth way of proving God's existence is based on the order in the universe. We see that things which lack knowledge, such as natural objects, act for an end. That is, their activity is always or nearly always aimed at achieving the best result. It is clear, therefore, that their activity is not produced by chance but by design. Now things which lack knowledge cannot move unerringly toward an end unless they are directed toward that end by some being that has knowledge and intelligence much like an arrow is directed toward its target by an archer. Therefore there must exist an intelligent Being Who directs all natural things toward their respective ends. This Being we call God.[2]

Aquinas says that each of the five proofs for the existence of God tells us something about God. The first proof implies that unlike anything in the universe, God imparts motion to everything without moving and therefore without being in time or being material. The second implies that unlike anything we know, God is the uncreated creator that causes everything to exist. The third tells us that—again unlike anything in our experience—God cannot cease existing because God's existence does not depend on anything else. The fourth tells us that unlike anything in the universe, God is perfect goodness, perfect truth, perfect nobility, and perfect existence. And the fifth tells us that God is the supremely wise intelligence in whom all the order in the universe originates.

Nevertheless, Aquinas cautions, there is such a vast gulf between ourselves and God that the knowledge of God that we can glean from the five proofs is very imperfect. Each proof merely tells us that some aspect of the universe we experience requires the existence of something else that is *unlike* anything in that universe and therefore *unlike* anything in our experience. Aquinas expresses this idea by asserting that although the proofs show us *that* God is, they do not tell us *what* God is. The proofs give us what Aquinas calls a "negative way" of knowing God. They do not give us a positive conception of God but lead us to *remove* certain ideas from our conception of God: God is *not* in motion, God is *not* created, God is *not* dependent, God is *not* imperfectly good, God is *not* a blind unintelligent force.

Analogical Knowledge of God. But does this *via negativa*—this negative approach—provide us with the only knowledge we have of God? Are we doomed to know only what God is *not* and never to

---

2 Saint Thomas Aquinas, *Summa Theologica*, I, q.2, a.3. This translation copyright © 1978 by Manuel Velasquez.

have any positive knowledge of God? At first sight, it would seem that we could never have any positive knowledge of God because all our positive knowledge is based on our experience of the universe, and God is unlike anything in our experience. However, Aquinas identifies an imperfect kind of positive knowledge of God that is open to us. He calls this "knowledge by analogy" or "analogical knowledge" of God.

Aquinas explains analogical knowledge as follows: He points out that there are certain words—such as *good, wise,* and *loving*—that we apply both to God, whom we do not experience, and to human creatures, whom we do experience. We say, for example, that God is good, wise, and loving, and we say that this or that person of our experience is good, wise, or loving. We could conceivably be applying such words to both God and humans in any of three ways.

First, the words could have a *univocal* meaning—that is, they could have exactly the same meaning when applied to God, whom we do not experience, as when applied to the humans we do experience. But this is impossible because God and humans are so unlike that the goodness, wisdom, and love of God must be different from the goodness, wisdom, and love we experience in humans:

> It is impossible for a word to be applied univocally to both God and the creatures he produces. For when an effect is not equal to the power of the cause that produced it, the effect receives only an imperfect likeness of the cause: that is, the effect will be like the cause only to an imperfect degree. . . . Thus, when the word "wise" is applied to human beings, the word in a way comprehends and includes in its meaning the thing to which it refers [i.e., imperfect wisdom as we experience it and as God produced it]. But this is not so when the word is applied to God. For when the word "wise" is applied to God it refers to something [perfect wisdom] that exceeds the meaning of the word and which is not comprehended.[3]

Second, then, words applied to both God and creatures could have an *equivocal* meaning: They could mean something totally different when applied to each. But this, too, is inadequate, Aquinas insists. If the words we use changed their meaning when we applied them to God, then we could not say anything at all about God. For we would never know what our words meant when we applied them to God because their meaning derives entirely from our experience of creatures:

> Neither can we say that words that are applied to God and creatures have a purely equivocal sense, although some thinkers have held this view. If words that applied to both God and creatures were purely equivocal, then our experience of creatures would not allow us to know anything about God nor to prove anything about God. For the words we used in our reasoning would always be exposed to the fallacy of equivocation. [They would have one meaning in part of our reasoning and another meaning in another part.] Now this is contrary to the procedure of some philosophers, such as Aristotle, who managed to prove many things about God. It also contradicts scripture which says "The invisible things of God are clearly seen, being understood from the things that He created."[4]

Humans, then, must reflect God's nature to some degree because they are God's creation: The goodness, wisdom, and love of humans that we experience must reflect imperfectly the perfect goodness, wisdom, and love of God, in whom they originate. So, Aquinas concludes, the third and correct way in which we apply to God certain words whose meaning is based on our experience of humans is *by analogy*. Words such as *wise, good,* and *loving* are applied both to God and humans with an *analogical* meaning. The words do not have a completely different meaning when applied to each, but their meaning is also not exactly the same:

> We have to conclude that these words are applied to both God and creatures in an *analogous* sense, that is, with a meaning that is based on a relationship. . . . For example, the word "healthy" can be applied to a medicine as well as to an animal because of the relationship the medicine has to the health of the animal: the medicine is the cause of the animal's health. In a similar way, words can be applied to both creatures and to God in an analogous and not in a purely univocal nor in a purely equivocal sense. Consider that we can apply to God only words whose meanings we draw from our experience of creatures. Consequently, when we apply a word to both God and creatures, its meaning

---

3 Ibid., I, q.13, a.5.

4 Ibid.

> has to be based on the relationship that creatures have to God: they are related to God as to their origin and their cause in whom all their perfections pre-exist in a way that excels their existence in creatures. Now this kind of common possession of perfections is the basis of a kind of meaning that is midway between pure univocation and pure equivocation. When a word is applied analogically in this way to two different beings its meaning does not remain completely identical as with univocal uses, nor does it have completely different meanings as in equivocal uses.[5]

Our experience of humans, then, gives us an imperfect but positive knowledge of attributes that exist in God in a perfect way. We can never fully comprehend God's own unique and perfect goodness, wisdom, and love, which are quite different from our imperfect and partial goodness, wisdom, and love. So *good, wise,* and *loving* do not have exactly the same meaning when applied to God and humans. Nevertheless, we do experience the partial goodness, wisdom, and love of humans and know that it reflects the perfect goodness, wisdom, and love of God from whom they derive. This knowledge allows us to say that there is some similarity of meaning among *good, wise,* and *loving* when used to describe both God and humans.

The Law of God. The universe that God created, Aquinas holds, is governed by laws that are imposed by God. Aquinas calls these laws the *eternal law,* and he likens God to a ruler or a craftsman who fashions the laws of the universe:

> Before any craftsman makes something, he must have in his mind an idea of what he will make. Similarly, before a ruler governs his subjects, he must have in his mind some idea of what his subjects are to do. The craftsman's idea of what he will make constitutes a plan of the object to be made (it is also part of what we call his skill). And the ruler's idea of what his subjects are to do constitutes a kind of law. . . . Now since God is the wise creator of the universe, He is like a craftsman who makes something. And He is also like the ruler since He governs every act and motion of every single creature. Consequently, the idea in God's wise mind, according to which everything was created, can be called a plan (or an ideal model, or even a part of God's skill); and since everything is also governed according to this same idea, it can also be called a law. So the eternal law is nothing more than a plan in God's mind, in accordance with which every act and motion of the universe is directed.[6]

The laws that order the universe govern creatures through the natural forces and inclinations that were made part of their natures when they were created. As part of that universe, human beings are also subject to the eternal law of God through the natural inclinations within us that move us toward our own ends and activities. Unlike other creatures, however, human beings use their reason to direct themselves toward their ends:

> It is clear from the preceding article that the eternal law is the guide and standard for everything that is subject to God's provident direction. Clearly, therefore, the activities of all creatures are equally determined by the eternal law. Their activities are determined by the natural forces and inclinations that were made part of their natures when they were created [by God]. These natural forces and inclinations cause creatures to engage in their appropriate activities and attain their appropriate ends.
>
> Now rational creatures [such as humans] are also subject to God's provident direction, but in a way that makes them more like God than all other creatures. For God directs rational creatures by instilling in them certain natural inclinations and [reasoning] abilities that enable them to direct themselves as well as other creatures. Thus human beings also are subject to the eternal law and they too derive from that law certain natural inclinations to seek their proper ends and proper activities. These inclinations of our nature constitute what we call the "natural law" and they are the effects of the eternal law imprinted in our nature.
>
> Thus, even scripture suggests that our natural ability to reason (by which we distinguish right from wrong) in which the natural law resides, is nothing more than the image of God's own reason imprinted on us. For Psalm Four asks, "Who will show us what is right?" and it answers, "The light of Thy Mind, O Lord, which has been imprinted upon us."[7]

5 Ibid.

6 Ibid., I–IIae, q.93, a.1.

7 Ibid., I–IIae, q.91, a.2.

Aquinas argued that morality is based on these "natural inclinations" or this "natural law" that God instilled within us. Our reason perceives as good those things toward which we are naturally inclined and perceives as evil whatever is destructive of those goods. It is morally right to pursue the goods toward which we are naturally inclined and morally wrong to pursue what is destructive of those goods. Thus, natural law is the basis of morality:

> A thing is good if it is an end that we have a natural inclination to desire; it is evil if it is destructive of what our nature is inclined to desire. Consequently, those kinds of things that our nature is inclined to desire are perceived by our reason as good for our human nature. And our reason will conclude that those kinds of things ought to be pursued in our actions. But if our reason sees a certain type of thing as destructive of what human nature is inclined to desire, it will conclude that that type of thing ought to be avoided.
>
> We can therefore list the basic [moral] precepts of the natural law by listing the kinds of things that we naturally desire. First, like every other nature, human nature is inclined to desire its own survival. Consequently it is a natural [moral] law that we ought to preserve human life and avoid whatever is destructive of life. Secondly, like other animals, human nature is inclined to desire those things that nature teaches all animals to desire by instinct. For example, all animals have an instinctive desire to come together in a union of male and female, and an instinctive desire to care for their young. [So it is morally right to pursue these things.] Thirdly, human nature is inclined to desire those goods that satisfy our intellects. This aspect of our nature is proper to human beings. Thus, human nature is inclined to desire knowledge (for example, to know the truth about God) and to desire an orderly social life. Consequently, it is a natural [moral] law that we ought to dispel ignorance and avoid harming those among whom we live.[8]

Thus, for Aquinas, the God whose existence is implied by an imperfect universe is also the God who creates the moral laws that we come to know by reflecting on our basic human inclinations. God is not only the foundation of the existence of the universe but also the foundation of morality.

8 Ibid., I–IIae, q.94, a.2.

To read more of Aquinas' works, go to CourseMate for this text and browse by chapter or philosopher.

DESCARTES

The role that God plays in the philosophy of Descartes is different from the role that God plays in other philosophies, such as that of Aquinas. For Aquinas as well as for other philosophers, God's existence is a conclusion we reach by coming to know the world around us. For Descartes, however, God is the One who guarantees that we can come to know the world around us. For Descartes, God is not a Being whom we come to know *after* we know the world around us; instead, God is a Being whom we must know about *before* we can know anything for certain about the world around us. God does not come at the end of knowledge but at the beginning.

There are many other differences between Descartes and Aquinas. Some of these differences undoubtedly reflect the changes that had taken place in Europe during the 350 years between them. Europe was no longer dominated by a single religion: Protestantism had appeared to compete

Louvre, Paris, France/Lauros/Giraudon/The Bridgeman Art Library

Portrait of Rene Descartes (1596–1650) c. 1649 (oil on canvas) (detail of 32939). This painting is after the lost original that was painted in 1649. Artist: Frans Hals (1582/83–1666).

with Catholicism. The physical sciences were emerging under the impetus of the new discoveries and theories of Galileo and Copernicus. Many of the new modern nations of Europe had already established themselves with their own particular languages, governments, and cultures. The New World of the Americas was being explored. And everywhere fresh minds were bubbling with new ideas and disputing the old medieval views—including those of Aquinas—that had so long dominated European intellectual life.

René Descartes was born in 1596 in Touraine, the son of a councillor of the Parliament of Brittany. A brilliant young man, he was sent in 1604 to study in the Jesuit college of La Fleche, where, although he was impressed by the precision of mathematics, he was deeply distressed by the disputes and doubts that surrounded all other realms of knowledge, especially philosophy. The end of school, in 1612, left him feeling unsettled and dissatisfied. As he later wrote in his *Discourse on Method*, a short philosophical work in which he described how he came to formulate his own philosophy:

> As soon as I had completed the entire course of study at the close of which one is usually received into the ranks of the learned, . . . I found myself embarrassed with so many doubts and errors that it seemed to me that the effort to instruct myself had no effect other than the increasing discovery of my own ignorance. And yet I was studying at one of the most celebrated Schools in Europe. . . . I was delighted with Mathematics because of the certainty of its demonstrations and the evidence of its reasoning. . . . On the other hand, . . . I shall not say anything about Philosophy, but that, [although] it has been cultivated for many centuries by the best minds that have ever lived, . . . nevertheless no single thing is to be found in it which is not subject to dispute, and in consequence which is not dubious. . . . [A]s to the other sciences, inasmuch as they derive their principles from Philosophy, I judged that one could have built nothing solid on foundations so far from firm.[9]

Disillusioned, Descartes joined the army at the age of 17 and began to travel, hoping that by studying "the great book of the world" he would find more truth than he had found in school:

> This is why, as soon as age permitted me to emerge from the control of my tutors, I entirely quitted the study of letters. And resolving to seek no other knowledge than that which could be found in myself, or at least in the great book of the world, I employed the rest of my youth in travel, in seeing courts and armies, in speaking with men of diverse temperaments and conditions, in collecting varied experiences, in proving myself in the various predicaments in which I was placed by fortune, and under all circumstances bringing my mind to bear on the things which came before it, so that I might derive some profit from my experience.[10]

But the young Descartes found himself as dissatisfied by the many conflicting opinions he encountered on his travels with the army as he had been by his formal studies in school. This led him one fateful winter day to resolve to see whether he could reach the truth by studying his own inner being:

> [During the time] I only considered the manners of other men I found in them nothing to give me settled convictions; and I remarked in them almost as much diversity as I had formerly seen in the opinions of philosophers. . . . But after I had employed several years in thus studying the book of the world and trying to acquire some experience, I one day formed the resolution of also making myself an object of study and of employing all the strength of my mind in choosing the road I should follow. . . . I was then in Germany, . . . returning from the coronation of the Emperor to rejoin the army, [when] the setting in of winter detained me in a quarter where, since I found no society to divert me, while fortunately I had also no cares or passions to trouble me, I remained the whole day shut up alone in a stove-heated room where I had complete leisure to occupy myself with my own thoughts.[11]

There in his quiet little "stove-heated room," Descartes thought back to the careful method of reasoning that he had admired in mathematics. This method, Descartes felt, begins with "simple" truths that are so "clearly and distinctly perceived" that they cannot be doubted and proceed to the

9 René Descartes, *Discourse on Method*, in *The Philosophical Works of Descartes*, vol. 1, trans. and ed. Elizabeth S. Haldane and G. R. T. Ross (Cambridge: Cambridge University Press, 1911), 83, 85, 87.

10 Ibid., 86.

11 Ibid., 87.

more complex truths that rest on the simple truths. Perhaps this method of reasoning could be used in other fields to establish all truth with certitude:

> Those long chains of reasoning, simple and easy as they are, of which geometricians make use in order to arrive at the most difficult demonstrations, had caused me to imagine that all those things which fall under the cognizance of man might very likely be mutually related in the same fashion; and that, provided only that we abstain from receiving anything as true which is not so, and always retain the order which is necessary in order to deduce the one conclusion from the other, there can be nothing so remote that we cannot reach to it, nor so recondite that we cannot discover it. . . . Considering also that of all those who have hitherto sought for the truth in the Sciences, it has been the mathematicians alone who have been able to succeed in . . . producing reasons which are evident and certain, I did not doubt that it had been by means of a similar method that they carried on their investigations.[12]

Convinced that in mathematics he had found an instance of the only reliable method for discovering truth, Descartes summarized his new method in four rules:

> The first of these was to accept nothing as true which I did not clearly recognize to be so: that is to say, carefully to avoid precipitation and prejudice in judgments, and to accept in them nothing more than what was presented to my mind so clearly and distinctly that I could have no occasion to doubt it.
>
> The second was to divide up each of the difficulties which I examined into as many parts as possible, and as seemed requisite in order that it might be resolved in the best manner possible.
>
> The third was to carry on my reflections in due order, commencing with objects that were the most simple and easy to understand, in order to rise little by little, or by degrees, to knowledge of the most complex. . . .
>
> The last was in all cases to make enumerations so complete and reviews so general that I should be certain of having omitted nothing.[13]

12 Ibid., 91–92.
13 Ibid., 92.

Believing that he now had a method for pursuing the truth, Descartes left his little room and again took up his travels. Nine years passed before he felt ready to apply his method to philosophical issues:

> Inasmuch as I hoped to be able to reach my end more successfully in converse with man than in living longer shut up in the warm room where these reflections had come to me, I hardly awaited the end of winter before I once more set myself to travel. And in all the nine following years I did nothing but roam hither and thither. . . . Nine years thus passed away before I had taken any definite part in regard to the difficulties as to which the learned are in the habit of disputing, or had commenced to seek the foundation of any philosophy. . . . [Then I] resolved to remove myself from all places where any acquaintances were possible, and to retire to this country [Holland, where] . . . I can live as solitary and retired as in deserts the most remote.[14]

Here, in solitude, Descartes began writing a long series of "meditations." Slowly, he built a philosophy that, he was convinced, was as solid and certain as mathematics because it relied on the same method. He began by putting his first rule into practice by "rooting out of my mind" all opinions that were the least bit doubtful. Through this "method of doubt," Descartes came upon the basic truth that was to serve as the "simple" principle from which he would "rise to the most complex":

> I do not know that I ought to tell you of the first meditations there made by me, for they are so metaphysical and so unusual that they may perhaps not be acceptable to everyone. . . . Because I wished to give myself entirely to the search after Truth, I thought that it was necessary for me to take an apparently opposite course, and to reject as absolutely false everything as to which I could imagine the least ground of doubt, in order to see if afterwards there remained anything in my belief that was entirely certain. Thus, because our senses sometimes deceive us, I wished to suppose that nothing is just as they cause us to imagine it to be; and because there are men who deceive themselves in their reasoning and fall into fallacies, even concerning the simplest matters of geometry, and judging that I was as subject

14 Ibid., 98–100.

> to error as was any other, I rejected as false all the reasons formerly accepted by me as demonstrations. And since all the same thoughts and conceptions which we have while awake may also come to us in sleep without any of them being at that time true, I resolved to assume that everything that ever entered into my mind was no more true than the illusions of my dreams.
>
> But immediately afterwards I noticed that while I thus wished to think all things false, it was absolutely essential that the "I" who thought this should be something, and remarking that this truth, "I think, therefore I am" was so certain and so assured that all the most extravagant suppositions brought forward by the skeptics were incapable of shaking it, I came to the conclusion that I could receive it without scruple as the first principle of the Philosophy which I was seeking.
>
> And then, examining attentively that which I was, I saw that I could conceive that I had no body, and that there was no world nor place where I might be; but yet that I could not for all that conceive that I was not. On the contrary, I saw from the very fact that I thought of doubting the truth of other things, it very evidently and certainly followed that I was. On the other hand if I had only ceased from thinking, even if all the rest of what I had ever imagined had really existed, I should have no reason for thinking that I had existed. From that I knew that I was a substance the whole essence or nature of which is to think, and that for its existence there is no need of any place, nor does it depend on any material thing; so that this "me," that is to say, the soul by which I am what I am, is entirely distinct from body, and is even more easy to know than is the latter; and even if body were not, the soul would not cease to be what it is.
>
> After this I considered generally what in a proposition is requisite in order to be true and certain; for since I had just discovered one which I knew to be such, I thought that I ought also to know in what this certainty consisted. And having remarked that there was nothing at all in the statement, "I think, therefore I am" which assures me of having thereby made a true assertion, excepting that I see very clearly that to think it is necessary to be, I came to the conclusion that I might assume, as a general rule, that the things which we conceive very clearly and distinctively are all true—remembering, however, that there is some difficulty in ascertaining which are those that we distinctly conceive.
>
> Following upon this, and reflecting on the fact that I doubted, and that consequently my existence was not quite perfect (for I saw clearly that it was a greater perfection to know than to doubt), I resolved to inquire whence I had learnt to think of Something more perfect than I myself was. And I recognized very clearly that this conception must proceed from some Nature which was really more perfect. As to the thoughts which I had of many other things outside of me, like the heavens, the earth, light, heat, and a thousand others, I had not so much difficulty in knowing whence they came, because, remarking nothing in them which seemed to render them superior to me, I could believe that, if they were true, they were dependencies upon my nature, in so far as it possessed some perfection; and if they were not true, that I held them from nothing, that is to say, that they were in me because I had something lacking in my nature. But this could not apply to the idea of a Being more perfect than my own, for to hold it came from nought would be manifestly impossible; and because it is no less contradictory to say of the more perfect that it is what results from and depends on the less perfect, than to say that there is something which proceeds from nothing, it was equally impossible that I should hold it from myself. In this way it could not but follow that it had been placed in me by a Nature which was really more perfect than mine could be, and which even had within itself all the perfections of which I could form any idea—that is to say, to put it in a word, which was God. To which I added that since I knew some perfections which I did not possess, I was not the only being in existence; but there was necessarily some other more perfect Being on which I depended, or from which I acquired all that I had.[15]

Thus, Descartes was led by his method to realize that he existed, that he had a soul, and, most important, that God existed, for, as Descartes reasoned, God is the foundation of all truth. God is not a deceiver, and God ensures that whatever we "clearly and distinctly" understand is true. Error arises only when we pass judgment on matters that are not clearly and distinctly understood:

> For, first of all, I recognize it to be impossible that He should ever deceive me; for in all fraud and deception some imperfection is

15 Ibid., 100–102.

> to be found, and although it may appear that the power of deception is a mark of subtlety or power, yet the desire to deceive without doubt testifies to malice or feebleness, and accordingly cannot be found in God. . . .
>
> Whence, then, come my errors? They come from the sole fact that since the will is much wider in its range and compass than the understanding, I do not restrain it within the same bounds, but extend it also to things which I do not understand . . . .
>
> But if I abstain from giving my judgment on anything when I do not perceive it with sufficient clearness and distinctness, it is plain that I will act rightly and will not be deceived. But if I decide to deny or affirm [what is not clear and distinct], then I no longer make use as I should of my free will. . . .
>
> So long as I restrain my will within the limits of my knowledge so that it forms no judgment except on matters which are clearly and distinctly represented to it by the understanding, I can never be deceived. For every clear and distinct perception is without doubt something and hence cannot derive its origin from what is nothing, but must of necessity have God as its author—God, I say, who, being supremely perfect, cannot be the cause of any error; and consequently we must conclude that such a perception is true.[16]

Having found the source of truth and knowledge, Descartes turned to the final major philosophical question that confronted him: Did the material world around him really exist, or was it merely a figment of his imagination?

> Now that I have noted what must be done to arrive at a knowledge of the truth, my principal task is to endeavor to emerge from the state of doubt into which I have these last days fallen, and to see whether nothing certain can be known regarding material things. . . . Nothing further remains, then, but to inquire whether material things exist. . . . I find that . . . there is in me a certain passive faculty of perception, that is, of receiving and recognizing the ideas of material things. . . . But, since God is no deceiver, it is very manifest that He does not communicate to me these ideas directly and by Himself, nor yet by the intervention of some creature [different from the material objects I think I perceive]. For since He has given me no faculty to recognize that this is the case, but, on the other hand, a very great inclination to believe that they are conveyed to me by material objects, I do not see how He could be defended from the accusation of deceit if these ideas were produced by causes other than material objects. Hence we must allow that material things exist.[17]

Thus, the existence of a perfect God is our only guarantee that our knowledge about the world is accurate. If it were not for God, we could never be sure that any of our so-called knowledge of external reality is true. For earlier philosophers, God is primarily the foundation of reality, what accounts for the existence of the objects in the universe. But for Descartes, God is primarily the foundation of our knowledge, what accounts for the fact that we can know the objects in our universe.

Descartes' philosophy made him famous, and within a short time at least two of the crowned heads of Europe were asking his advice. In 1649, Descartes received an invitation from Queen Christina of Sweden, who requested him to instruct her in the mysteries of philosophy. Being eager to please her, Descartes traveled north to Sweden and there began tutoring the busy queen at the only hour she had free: five o'clock in the morning. The bitter cold and the early hour combined to weaken Descartes' health, and within a few months he caught pneumonia. On February 11, 1650, Descartes died.

ANNE CONWAY

Whereas both Aquinas and Descartes give God a very prominent position in their philosophies, Anne Conway more thoroughly developed a philosophy based wholly on the nature of God. She was truly obsessed by the idea of a God who is perfect in every way, and her fascinating and visionary philosophy is an attempt to describe the consequences of this idea. Unfortunately, because Conway was a woman in a male-dominated society, her work was largely ignored, and when male philosophers took over her ideas, they failed to attribute them to her.

Conway was born on December 14, 1631, into a wealthy, energetic, and intellectually talented English family headed by Elizabeth and Heneage Finch,

16 René Descartes, *Meditations on First Philosophy*, in *Philosophical Works*, 172, 175–176, 178.

17 Ibid., 179, 185, 191.

a lawyer. Tragically, her father died just a week before her birth. Virtually nothing is known of Anne's childhood other than that she received a remarkably full education. In 1651, she married Edward Conway, a wealthy landowner with some connections to the court of Charles II. Several philosophers, including Henry More and Ralph Cudworth, were frequent guests at their house; through them, especially More, Anne came in contact with some of the major philosophical currents of the age.

Throughout her life, Conway was plagued by migraine headaches. These may have been partially responsible for her death in 1679 at the age of forty-eight. Conway died while her husband was away in Ireland, and his friends, wanting to let him see her before she was buried, had her body pickled in wine and stored in a vat in his library until he returned to bury her.

Toward the end of her life, Conway wrote a short work called *The Principles of the Most Ancient and Modern Philosophy*, which was published after her death. In that work she traced the fundamentals of her philosophical views.

Conway begins her philosophy focused on God, the most perfect of all beings. From this simple beginning, she deduces in a rationalist manner the main characteristics of the universe as she sees it. Although she does not attempt to prove that God exists, she goes to great lengths to explain what God has to be like. Because God is perfect, he must possess all perfections, including unlimited ("infinite") wisdom, goodness, justice, omniscience, and omnipotence. God is also a "spirit"—that is, a being capable of thinking and awareness. Although God has no physical body (and so no shape), he is the creator of the life, the bodies, and all other goods that creatures have:

> God is a Spirit, Light, and Life, infinitely Wise, Good, Just, Mighty, Omniscient, Omnipresent, Omnipotent, Creator and Maker of all things visible and invisible. . . . He hath no manner of darkness or corporiety [physical body] in him, and so consequently no kind of Form of Figure whatsoever. . . . He is in a true and proper sense a creator of all things, who doth not only give them their Form and figure, but also being, life, body, and whatsoever else of good they have.[18]

18 Anne Conway, *The Principles of the Most Ancient and Modern Philosophy*, ed. Peter Loptson (Boston: Martinus Nijhoff, 1982; original work published 1692), 149.

God, Conway holds, cannot change because he is already perfect. If he were to change, he would then have to become either more perfect or less perfect. But he cannot become more perfect, for he is already fully perfect, and neither can he become less perfect, for then he would not be God.

Moreover, Conway argues, because God is unchanging, he is outside of time. To see what she means, it may help to consider that, when we say that time is passing, we mean that certain changes have occurred: The hands of a clock have moved across its face, or the sun above us has moved across the sky. But imagine that everything in our universe came to a complete stop so that nothing changed in any way: Absolutely nothing moved, and everything remained completely fixed in a frozen state. In such a completely frozen universe, nothing would distinguish one moment from another. Time would then be meaningless. Time requires change; without change, there is no time. Thus, Conway claimed, time itself is nothing but change. Because God is unchanging, God is not in time: He exists outside of the universe of time and change in a timeless state called "eternity," where the whole history of the universe appears before him as if in a single present, unchanging moment. By contrast, all creatures change and so are subject to time:

> In God there is neither time nor Change, nor Composition, nor Division of parts: He is wholly and universally one in himself and of himself, without any manner of variety or mixture. . . . For . . . Times . . . are nothing else but successive Motions and operations of created beings. . . . The eternity of God himself hath no times in it; nothing therein can be said to be past, or to come, but the whole is always present. . . . And the reason hereof is manifest; because time is nothing else but the successive motion or operation of creatures; which motion or operation, if it should cease, time would also cease, and the creatures themselves would cease with time. Wherefore such is the nature of every creature, that it is in motion, or hath a certain motion, by means of which it advances forward, and grows to a farther perfection. And seeing in God there is no successive motion or operation to a farther perfection; because he is most absolutely perfect. Hence there are not times in God or his eternity.[19]

19 Ibid., 149, 154, 155.

Conway argues that although God is completely free to create whatever he chooses to create, he had to create us. God is free, yet he has to do what he does. How is this possible? How can God be both free and unfree? Conway explains that there is nothing greater than God that can force him to do anything: There is no external force that can make him do one thing rather than another. So, God is completely free from any *external* forces. But God is perfectly good, so he cannot be "indifferent" (unconcerned) about doing good; that is, his own inner goodness forces him to do what is good. So, whatever God does, he does it because it is a good thing to do. Therefore, although God is free from external forces, he is also unfree because his own inner goodness forces him to do whatever is good. Because it is good to create good things, God is forced to create good creatures:

> Although the Will of God be most free, so that whatsoever he doth in the behalf of his creatures, he doth freely without any external violence, compulsion, or any cause coming from them—whatsoever he doth, he doth of his own accord—Yet that indifference of acting, or not acting, can by no means be said to be in God. . . . Seeing his infinite wisdom, goodness, and justice is a law unto him, which he cannot transgress. . . . Hence therefore it evidently follows that it was not indifferent to God, whether he would give being to his creatures or no; but he made them out of a certain internal impulse of his divine wisdom and goodness, and so he created the world or creatures as soon as he could.[20]

In fact, Conway argues, because God has to create anything that is good, and because there are infinite numbers of good things that an all-powerful God can create, God must create infinite numbers of creatures inhabiting infinite numbers of worlds:

> These attributes duly considered, it follows that creatures were created in infinite numbers, or that there is an infinity of worlds or creatures made of God: for seeing God is infinitely powerful, there can be no number of creatures so great, that he cannot always make more: and because, as is already proved, he doth whatsoever he can do [that is good]; certainly his will, goodness, and bounty is as large and extensive as his power; whence it manifestly follows that creatures are infinite, and created in infinite manners, so that they cannot be limited or bounded with any number or measure.[21]

Not only are there infinite numbers of worlds in the universe around us, but there are also infinite numbers of worlds within each of us, and within each of these worlds in us is another infinity of worlds, and within each of these worlds another infinity of worlds, and so on. For God can create ever-smaller good things or "monads" within each good thing he creates, and, after all, God must create whatever is good:

> Also by the like reason is proved, that not only the whole body or system of creatures considered together is infinite, or contains in itself a kind of infinity; but also that every creature even the least that we can discern with our eyes, or conceive in our minds, hath therein such an infinity of parts, or rather entire creatures, that they cannot be numbered; even as it cannot be denied that God can place one creature within another, so he can place two as well as one, and four as well as two, so also eight as well as four, so that he could multiply them without end, always placing the less within the greater. . . . This being sufficient to demonstrate that in every creature, whether the same be a spirit or a body, there is an infinity of creatures, each whereof contains an infinity and again each of these, and so *ad infinitum.*[22]

Thus, for Conway, creativity is one of God's essential attributes: For God to be God, he must create. And, Conway holds, this creativity is from all eternity, so for an infinite length of time an infinity of creatures have existed. The universe is infinite in time as it is infinite in creatures.

According to Conway, the essential difference between God and the infinite creatures he creates is changeability. God, as we have seen, does not change and is outside of time. However, the creatures he creates all change in time. Whereas God is perfect and cannot become better or worse, creatures are imperfect and so can change for the better or for the worse. But their changes into better or worse creatures are governed by God's justice.

At this point, Conway reaches a breathtaking conclusion. She argues that God's justice demands that over time each creature change into a higher or lower kind of creature. Consider, Conway suggests,

20 Ibid., 157, 158.

21 Ibid., 158–159.

22 Ibid., 159–160.

that all creatures have a soul or a spirit. Now what is to become of this spirit at death?

> Now I demand, unto what higher perfection and degree of goodness, the being or essence of a horse doth or may attain after he hath done good service for his master, and so performed his duty, and what is proper for such a creature? Is a horse then a mere fabrick or dead matter? Or hath he a spirit in him, having knowledge, sense, and love, and divers other faculties and properties of a spirit? If he hath, which cannot be denied, what becomes of this spirit when the horse dies?[23]

Conway's answer is simple. If a creature has done good deeds in its life, she proposes, then justice demands that at death it be changed into a better creature. On the other hand, if a creature has done evil in its life, then at death justice demands it change into a lower creature. Thus, Conway argues, because God is just, his justice requires a kind of transmigration of spirits. Men and any other creatures who do evil are changed at death by God's justice into worse creatures, whereas creatures who do good are changed by God's justice into better ones:

> Now we see how gloriously the justice of God appears in this transmutation of things out of one species into another; and that there is a certain justice which operates not only in men and angels, but in all creatures, is most certain; and he that doth not observe the same may be said to be utterly blind: for this justice appears as well in the ascension of creatures as in their descension; that is, when they are changed into the better and when into the worse; when into the better, this justice distributes to them the reward and fruit of their good deeds; when into the worse, the same punishes them with due punishments, according to the nature and degree of the transgression. . . .
>
> For example: is it not just and equitable, if a man on earth liveth a pure and holy life, like unto the heavenly angels, that he should be exalted to an angelical dignity after death, and be like unto them . . .? But if a man here on earth lives so wickedly and perversely that he is more like a devil raised from hell than any other creature, if he dies in such a state without repentance . . . shall not such deservedly become like devils . . .? But if a man hath neither lived an angelical or diabolical, but a brutish, or at leastwise an animal or sensual life on earth; so that his spirit is more like the spirit of a beast than any other thing: shall the same justice most justly cause that as he is become a brut, as to his spirit . . . that he also (at least as to his external form in bodily figure) should be changed into that species of beasts, to whom he was inwardly most like . . .?[24]

But Conway's greatest contribution to philosophy lies in her method of bringing the body and the spirit together. The philosopher Descartes, before her, had claimed that humans have both a body and a spirit. But the body, Descartes claimed, is utterly different from and distinct from the spirit: They are two different and separate things. So different are they that it seems that the body and the spirit cannot possibly affect each other. That set the basic problem for philosophy after Descartes: How is the body related to the spirit when they are two different and separate things?

Conway avoids Descartes' problem by proposing that body and spirit are not two different things, but rather that they are merely aspects or qualities of the same thing. Every creature, Conway claims, exhibits both bodily qualities and spiritual qualities. Even the "lowest" physical creatures such as rocks and plants have some rudimentary spiritual consciousness, some minimal levels of awareness, life, and thinking. On the other hand, even the "highest" spiritual creatures, such as angels, have some residual bodily qualities, some minimal degree of physical qualities. Everything in the universe, then, is both bodily and spiritual. So, body and spirit are not to be thought of as *things*. Instead, they are merely two different kinds of qualities that all creatures possess to a greater or lesser degree.

Conway provides several arguments in support of her view that every creature—even something like a rock—has both physical and spiritual qualities. For example, she argues that whatever God creates has to have some of his qualities: God communicates something of himself to each thing he creates. Because God is a spirit, everything he creates has to have some spiritual qualities. Moreover, God creates creatures so that they can share eternal life with him. But how can they do this unless they have spiritual qualities?

---

23 Ibid., 180–181.

24 Ibid., 184, 185.

> For seeing God is infinitely good and communicates his goodness in finite ways to his creatures; so that there is no creature which doth not receive something of his goodness, and that very largely: and seeing the goodness of God is a living goodness, which hath life, power, love, and knowledge in it, which he communicates to his creatures, how can it be that any dead thing should proceed from him or be created by him? . . . Has not God created all his creatures of this end, that in him they might be blessed and enjoy his divine goodness, in their several states and conditions? But how can this be without life or sense?[25]

Thus, the universe as conceived by Conway is much richer and more dynamic and orderly than other philosophers had ever suggested. Not only are there an infinity of worlds within worlds in her vision of the universe, but these infinite numbers of creatures are all living, thinking, and feeling creatures as well. Everything in the universe is alive and has some degree of awareness, from the simplest grain of dust to the highest angel. Moreover, although there is a constant churn of change as creatures continuously mutate into higher or lower creatures, this change is all regulated by God's justice, which ensures that each creature at death will be reborn into the kind of creature it deserves to be.

Perhaps because Conway was a woman, and so condemned to be ignored by a world thoroughly dominated by males, her thought had very little direct impact on philosophy. However, after her death, the German philosopher Gottfried Leibniz (1646–1716) studied her work and based his own famous views on those of Conway. Leibniz took from Conway the idea that God creates infinitely many "monads" (without, of course, giving her credit for the idea). Leibniz also took from her the idea that God's goodness compels him to create good things, as well as the idea that because God is perfectly good, the universe of creatures he creates also has to be perfectly good. Thus, through Leibniz and other male philosophers, many of the major ideas of Conway entered the mainstream of philosophy, although the men who took over her ideas relegated her name to obscurity.

Conway's philosophy is notable not only for its unwavering focus on God, but also because of the view that it provides of human beings. Conway's views on God's justice and the transmigration of creatures, in fact, are very similar to the Hindu religious view of karma and rebirth. Hindu religious thought has traditionally held that at death all living creatures are reborn as new living creatures. The kind of creature one becomes after death depends on one's karma—that is, the totality of good or evil deeds one has performed during one's past. If one's deeds were good, then one is reborn into a higher creature; if one's deeds were evil, then one is reborn into a lower animal. Conway's philosophy comes to exactly the same conclusions, but on the basis of a conception of God that is much more familiar to Westerners.

QUESTIONS

1. Evaluate each of Aquinas' proofs for the existence of God. Why do you think a believer like Aquinas would be concerned with proving God's existence? Does it make sense to believe without proof? Why or why not?
2. Does Aquinas' theory of analogy really explain how it is possible for religious believers to speak about God? Contemporary theories of language hold that words mean whatever we, the speakers of the language, *intend* them to mean. How can we intend words to have a meaning that we do not understand when applied to God? Does Aquinas' theory imply that God must be *like* the world that God creates?
3. Compare the interests and approaches of Descartes and Aquinas. What accounts for these differences? Which seem to be more "modern"? Why?
4. How useful are Descartes' four rules for discovering the truth? Could you use them, for example, as the basis for discovering the truth about God for yourself? Explain.
5. Descartes criticized all philosophy prior to his because "no single thing is to be found in it which is not subject to dispute, and in consequence which is not dubious." Explain whether this criticism applies to Descartes' own philosophy and to his own views about God. Why would Descartes have felt that his philosophy was immune from his criticism?
6. Is Descartes correct in claiming that "if I abstain from giving my judgment on anything when I do not perceive it with sufficient clearness and distinctness, it is plain that I will act rightly and will not be deceived"? Do you decide of your own free will to believe what you believe?

25 Ibid., 196.

you grew up in, of the friends and experiences you have had—constitute your understanding of who you now are. Yet how do you know whether your memories are true? Consider the following account recently written by a young college student:

> Jana never calls. I live a long way away and she is my only sibling, but she never calls. . . .
>
> Suddenly, out of the blue, she was calling me, talking to me, sharing her life with me. . . . [But] the circumstances that finally broke down the barriers between us were catastrophic, unspeakable. Our parents, my dear sister told me, had repeatedly abused her when she had been very young.
>
> I was stunned. "This abuse was . . . sexual?"
>
> "Yes, sexual."
>
> "And they both were involved?"
>
> "Yes, they and others."
>
> "Are you sure?"
>
> "YES, OF COURSE I AM!"
>
> I was furious with my parents. I had left home a few years back under the cloud of ongoing arguments with them and, since then, I had been slowly trying to patch things up. This revelation shattered the reconciliations, shattered even the desire to make the effort. With each of the many collect phone calls I accepted from Jana, my parents became more and more strangers, less the people I remembered knowing as a child. When I commented on this fact, Jana taught me about repressed memories. I was frightened beyond description. My entire life was nothing more than my memories of it. If suddenly those are taken away, if suddenly they are found to be fiction, then what am I? I too am fiction. I am the man with amnesia who knows not even his name. I am a 24-year-old adult with no memories of what really happened to him as a child. It was in the midst of that horror of no longer knowing who the hell I was that I began to search desperately for answers. . . . Jana called every other day or so to tell me new stories of abuse that had gurgled up from the black well-spring of repressed memories in her unconscious mind. Abuse by groups. Abuse with guns. Abuse with various crude medical instruments. Abuse by physical and psychological torture.
>
> It was in this atmosphere of dread and disgust that I discovered I too had been sexually abused as a kid. . . . I discovered my own personal experiences with the help of a psychiatric social worker. . . . The therapist suggested that it would be odd if I had been left alone while my sister had been so harmed. . . . No wonder I couldn't remember anything about my childhood! It was too horrible to remember! Over the next couple sessions she walked me through what she called "relaxation therapy." Whatever I should see, assuming it wasn't too happy, I was to consider truth. . . .
>
> The clarity of the new memories was striking, photographic. So much better than my old memories, those fake cover-up daydreams I'd used to help me suppress the truth; they had all been cloudy. I was beginning to feel like a survivor, like I was on to the truth and it was just a matter of time until I could feel whole again. The trouble was, the closer I came to being "whole," the worse I felt. I was flunking my college classes. I was calling in to work sick. I was smoking a lot. I didn't shave. I didn't eat well. And I didn't care. . . .
>
> Dr. Michael Fane, a psychiatrist . . . was my lucky break. He ran the clinic where my therapist worked, and part of the deal was that I had to have one diagnostic session with him before treatment proceeded. I explained to him my situation, my recent discovery of abuse, and the things I believed had been done to me. . . . [But during the diagnostic session Dr. Fane explained how such memories can be fabricated by one's own mind and how "recovered memories" may not be true at all.] By the next morning I would wake up to find my faith in my new memories shattered. . . . I had never heard of False Memory Syndrome at this point in my life, but I knew that I had it.[1]

---

1 Eleanor Goldstein and Kevin Farmer, *True Stories of False Memories* (Boca Raton, FL: Social Issues Resources Series, 1993), 117, 118, 199, 120, 125. Used by permission of the publisher.

Working with Dr. Fane during numerous sessions, the college student who wrote this account eventually decided that his "recovered" memories of sexual abuse were false memories. However, his sister, Jana, remains convinced that her memories are true. She has broken off all contact with her parents, whom she now sees as monsters who turned her into a dysfunctional person. She believes that her brother, who refuses to accept her knowledge that their parents sexually abused them, is "in denial" of the truth.

Jana and her brother are not the only people who fear that the most fundamental things they thought they knew about themselves might be completely false. Today, tens of thousands of men and women believe they have recalled formerly repressed memories of being sexually abused as children by parents, siblings, relatives, and family friends. Before entering therapy, they claimed, they had no knowledge of the acts but suffered from a variety of "symptoms," including depression, anxiety, eating disorders, sexual problems, and difficulty with intimacy. Sometimes the recovered memories include terrifying details of torture, participation in satanic rituals, animal sacrifices, and even murder.

The theory of "recovered memories" has stirred fierce controversy. Supporters of the theory cite studies based on clinical practice. For example, Judie Alpert, a professor of applied psychology at New York University, asserts the following:

> There is absolutely no question that some people have repressed some memories of early abuse that are just too painful to remember. In their 20s and 30s some event triggers early memories, and slowly they return. The event has been so overwhelming that the little girl who is being abused can't tolerate to be there in the moment, so she leaves her body, dissociates, as if she is up on a bookshelf looking down on the little girl who is being abused. Over time, she pushes it deep down because she can't integrate the experience.[2]

Other psychologists flatly deny that these theories are scientifically valid. Professor Elizabeth Loftus is professor of psychology at the University of Washington. She asserts that the theory that people can repress memories of repeated traumatic experiences in childhood and recall them decades later is false:

> If repression is the avoidance in your conscious awareness of unpleasant experiences that come back to you, yes, I believe in repression. But if it is a blocking out of an endless stream of traumas that occur over and over that leave a person with absolutely no awareness that these things happened, that make them behave in destructive ways and re-emerge decades later in some reliable form, I don't see any evidence for it. It flies in the face of everything we know about memory.[3]

The controversy over repressed and recovered memories is a dramatic illustration of some profound issues raised by our views of what knowledge is, how we acquire knowledge, how we establish truth, and whether science gives us the truth. It shows how important it is to be clear about these issues. As Jana's brother says, if a person accepts the view that recovered memories are the basis of true knowledge, then his past identity was but a mere "fiction" and the parents he thought he knew are really "strangers." If, as a society, we accept that recovered memories provide true knowledge of past crimes, then countless people who are unjustly living

---

2 Quoted in Leon Jaroff, "Lies of the Mind," *Time*, November 29, 1993, 52; for a more recent review of the literature on the controversy over recovered memories, see Elizabeth F. Loftus and Deborah Davis, "Recovered Memories," *Annual Review of Clinical Psychology*, vol. 2 (2006), pp. 469–98.

3 Ibid.

comfortable lives should be stripped of their respectability and cast into the deepest prisons. If we accept that the studies used to establish the theory of recovered memory are valid science, then we should accept that recovered memories provide true knowledge of past crimes.

Yet are recovered memories a source of true knowledge, and is the theory of recovered memories valid science? Many critics of recovered memories remind us of the seventeenth-century Salem witch trials. During these trials, many women were condemned to death because men "knew" they were witches because of their supposedly witchlike behavior and then-accepted theories of witchcraft. Indeed, how often have entire societies found themselves deluded about the valid sources of knowledge and truth? For several hundred years, European society and science believed that the earth was flat and that it lay at the center of the universe. Everyone believed that the sun, planets, and stars revolved around the earth. When Copernicus, Galileo, and others suggested that this was a mistake, they were condemned and persecuted by church authorities. Church authorities believed that Scripture is the only source of true knowledge. According to Scripture, they claimed, the earth lies at the center of the universe. Today, biologists who believe in the theory of evolution are sometimes attacked by "creationists," who believe that the Bible account of how God created the world is literally true. During the Nazi era, German society claimed that it was a "scientific fact" that the Germanic races were superior to all others, and on this basis, they rounded up Jews and Gypsies, imprisoned them, tortured them, and eventually murdered millions. Here in the United States several researchers once claimed that scientific research shows that the white race is genetically superior to the black race and concluded that race-based public policies are justified. And in the recent past, reputable scientists claimed that women were inferior to men and that society should treat them as such.

QUICK REVIEW
The controversy on recovered memories, and court cases based on them, raise urgent questions about how we acquire knowledge, how we know the truth, and whether science gives us truth.

All these events demonstrate the critical importance—both to us personally and as a society—of looking carefully at the issues of truth and knowledge. What is knowledge? What is truth? How do you tell the difference between true scientific knowledge and bogus theories of pseudoscience? What are valid sources of knowledge and truth?

In this chapter, we examine the question of how reliable knowledge is acquired. We ask what distinguishes the way in which reliable knowledge is acquired from the way in which unreliable beliefs are acquired. In the next chapter, we examine what true knowledge *is* instead of looking at how it is *acquired.*

Acquiring Reliable Knowledge: Reason and the Senses

How do we acquire reliable knowledge? What is the source or basis of our knowledge? Philosophers have given considerable attention to questions about the sources of knowledge. One popular way of approaching the subject, though by no means the only way, is to begin by examining two very important views about the sources of our knowledge: rationalism and empiricism. **Rationalism** is the view that knowledge can be obtained by relying on reason without the aid of the senses. In this view, reason is a key source of the knowledge we have about the universe. For example, what distinguishes real knowledge from mere opinion, in the rationalist view, is that real knowledge is based on the logic, the laws, and the methods that reason develops. The best example of real knowledge, many rationalists hold, is mathematics, a realm of knowledge that is obtained entirely by reason and that we use to understand the universe.

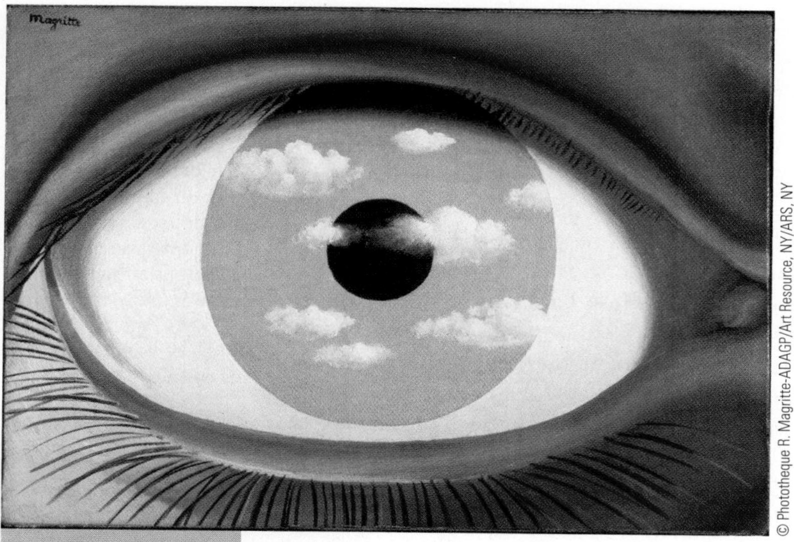

© Phototheque R. Magritte-ADAGP/Art Resource, NY/ARS, NY

The False Mirror, René Magritte. Are there different kinds of knowledge? If there are, how can each be obtained? What are their sources? What are their limits? Rationalists endorse reason, arguing that only rational knowledge is certain. Empiricists contend that reason can only relate the facts that are presented by the senses.

Empiricism, on the other hand, is the view that knowledge can be attained only through sense experience: Sense experience is the source of all our knowledge of the world that surrounds us. According to the empiricist, real knowledge is based on what our sight, hearing, smell, and other senses tell us is really out there, not what people discover in their heads.

In this chapter, we look more closely at these two seminal theories of the sources of our knowledge and consider an influential alternative, *transcendental idealism*, which attempts to integrate the insights of empiricism and rationalism. We will then discuss how these theories relate to the knowledge generated by the sciences, and whether scientific knowledge can be distinguished from pseudoscience.

The Place of Memory

Before we turn to these tasks, however, you might be asking a question: So where does memory fit into all this? After all, in the cases of repressed and recovered memories discussed earlier, the key issue is whether people's "recovered" memories of past traumatic events give us real knowledge of those events. So shouldn't we discuss memory as a source of knowledge in addition to sense experience and reason?

QUICK REVIEW
The two main views on the sources of our knowledge are rationalism, which says that reason is one source of knowledge, and empiricism, which says that sense experience is the only source of knowledge.

To answer this question, let us first look a bit more closely at what memory is. Memory is, basically, the ability to bring facts or our past experiences into our present consciousness or activities. However, there are different kinds of memory. Some philosophers have argued that we have at least three kinds of memory: habit memory, personal memory, and factual memory. *Habit memory* is our ability to remember how to do something that we learned in the past, such as how to ride a bicycle or how to ski. Habit memory is essentially our ability to bring into our present activities the skills whose learning we experienced in the past. *Personal memory*, on the other hand, is our ability to bring into our present consciousness a representation of events that we personally and directly experienced in the past. I use personal memory, for example, when I directly remember personally talking with you yesterday or directly remember personally playing with my cousin many years ago. Finally, *factual memory* is our memory of all the facts that make up our knowledge of the world. For example, I remember that George Washington was the first president of the United States. Although I personally acquired the facts that make up my factual memories, I did not personally experience those facts; for example, I didn't personally experience Washington's presidency.

Memory is obviously a critically important aspect of knowledge, as the cases of recovered memories demonstrate. Without memory of my past, I wouldn't have any knowledge of who I am, I wouldn't retain any knowledge of the world around me, and I would lack the knowledge that I need to relate to the people I love and the things that matter to me. In fact, without memory, I would retain no knowledge whatsoever.

PHILOSOPHY AT THE MOVIES

Watch *The Crucible* (1996), which is based on the play by Arthur Miller and portrays the Salem, Massachusetts, witch trials of 1692 where several men and women accused of witchcraft were jailed, tortured, and executed when a group of teenage girls testified against them. Analyze each of the main characters—John Proctor, his wife Elizabeth, the Reverend Parris, the Reverend Hale, and Judge Danforth—and explain what each assumes are valid and reliable sources of knowledge. In what ways does this movie show the importance of having a correct understanding of what real knowledge is, what the valid sources of knowledge are, and how "knowledge" should be tested and evaluated to ensure it really is knowledge?

But is memory a *source* of the fundamental knowledge we have? Apparently not. Any knowledge that I now remember I must have acquired earlier, through some other more fundamental source. For example, my personal memories consist of things that I experienced through my senses—what I directly saw, heard, touched, tasted, or felt. My "habit memories" or skills I also acquired by working with my senses and learning through the experience of practicing. And my factual memories I acquired through reading or hearing, or through using my reason to think things out for myself. In every case, then, memory does not bring any new knowledge to me but merely preserves knowledge that I acquired through some other source. If we are to study the source of the knowledge we have in our memories, then, we should not study memory itself, but the sources from which our memories were acquired. And the two basic sources of all of our knowledge and memories, most philosophers agree, are sense perception and reason. For these reasons, then, in the sections that follow we will discuss sense perception and reason as sources of knowledge, but we will not directly discuss memory as a source of knowledge.

QUICK REVIEW
Memory is not an independent source of knowledge because any knowledge we have in memory had to be acquired from some other source, such as sense experience or reason.

5.2 Is Reason the Source of Our Knowledge?

By rationalism, we mean the belief that reason, without the aid of sensory perception, is capable of arriving at some knowledge, some undeniable truths about the world. **Perception** refers to the processes of seeing, hearing, smelling, touching, and tasting by which we become aware of or apprehend ordinary objects such as chairs, tables, rocks, and trees. When rationalists claim that at least some of our knowledge is based on reason rather than perception, they mean that we do not rely on sensory experience for all of the fundamental knowledge we have.

In effect, rationalists contend that some of our knowledge is not a product of experience but depends solely on our mental processes. They hold that we can acquire accurate knowledge about the world around us by simply looking into our minds without observing the world.

At first sight, this contention may strike you as an astonishingly stupid view: How can we know anything about the world without first observing it? But before you brush aside this view of knowledge, think a little about how mathematicians work and how their work differs from that of other scientists. Scientists such as chemists and physicists work in laboratories, where they conduct experiments and observe the results. Astronomers use giant telescopes to observe the stars. Biologists use microscopes to determine what living organisms are like. In short, these scientists need to observe the external world to check whether their theories are true. Not so the mathematician. The mathematician typically works huddled over her desk, perhaps with the shades drawn. Nevertheless, the mathematician can discover new

QUICK REVIEW
Rationalists claim that not all knowledge of the world around us is acquired through sense observation. For example, mathematical knowledge is acquired by reasoning alone without observation of the world, yet it tells us how the world works.

mathematical theorems in her windowless office by using nothing more than pencil, paper, and reason. The mathematician does not need to observe the external world to see whether her theories and theorems are true. Yet the mathematical theories that the mathematician discovers by simply reasoning in her mind can accurately describe the vast reaches of the universe outside her little office.

Because such knowledge does not depend on sense experience, rationalists term it **a priori**, knowledge that is known independently of sense perception and that is necessarily true and indubitable. Moreover, the rationalist holds, this knowledge that reason discovers without making experiments or relying on the findings of sense experience underlies our understanding of the universe. When astronomers investigate black holes and stars in galaxies billions of miles away, they use the theories that the mathematician reasoned out in isolation. When physicists explore the intricacies of subatomic particles or when biologists examine the chemistry of DNA, they also use the mathematical theories that the mathematician simply thought up. Perhaps the greatest scientist ever, Albert Einstein, who thought it was astonishing that the mathematician's theories described the world so precisely, once asked: "How is it possible that mathematics, a product of human thought that is independent of experience, fits so excellently the objects of physical reality?" In fact, mathematics can tell us facts about the world that scientific observation has not yet discovered. In 1867, for example, James Maxwell expressed all that was known about electromagnetic fields in four mathematical equations. The mathematics of the equations showed that radio waves—unknown at the time—existed, but it took 20 years to detect them. Similar points may be made about the laws of logic. The laws of logic (such as "At least one of any two contradictory propositions must be false" and "No proposition can both be and not be true at the same time") are also not established by observation. Yet they underlie all our reasoning processes. So, reason, without relying on sense experience, apparently gives us knowledge of truths about the world that are so basic that all our other knowledge depends on our prior knowledge of these truths.

QUICK REVIEW
Knowledge acquired by reasoning alone is a priori: It is not acquired through sense experience, and it is necessarily true and indubitable. Examples are mathematical truths and the laws of logic.

Rationalists do not necessarily believe that all knowledge is acquired through reason alone. Many of them agree that some of our knowledge—for example, whether the sun is shining, whether giraffes have spots, whether dinosaurs existed—is derived from what we observe with our senses. However, the rationalist characteristically holds that *some* of our knowledge—particularly our most fundamental knowledge—about reality is acquired without sense experience. Just as we discover mathematical truths about the universe by reasoning inside our minds, we can discover other basic laws of the universe without ever having to observe the universe.

Rationalists also insist that some of the knowledge we acquire by using reason alone is knowledge about the world around us. We obviously have knowledge that is not about the world and that is not based on sensory experience, such as the knowledge that all bachelors are unmarried. But such knowledge is true by definition and thus does not give us any information about the world. However, the rationalist claims that some of our knowledge about the world is acquired by the use of reason alone, without sense experience. For example, some rationalists have held that the laws of logic and of mathematics tell us what the world has to be like and that these laws are established solely by reason. Other rationalists have claimed that our knowledge that "every event has a cause," that "the shortest distance between two points on a plane surface is a straight line," that "the universe follows the same laws in all of its parts," and that "the processes of the universe are regular and can be explained in terms of consistent laws" are all examples of fundamental knowledge about the world around us that cannot be established by using our senses.

Eastern philosophy has given birth to some interesting views that can be classified as rationalist. For example, although every traditional school of Indian philosophy agrees that sense perception is a source of knowledge, several Indian philosophers hold that sense perception is ultimately erroneous and that we must rely on other sources of knowledge to know what is ultimately real. A good example is the great Indian philosopher Shankara (788–822), a charismatic mystic, saint, and poet who founded the Advaita Vedanta school of philosophy before he died at the young age of thirty-two. Shankara's philosophy can be summed up in this statement: "Brahman [Ultimate Reality] is real, the world is false, and the self is not different from Brahman." A basic idea that Shankara developed is the idea of "sublation." Sublation is the process of correcting an error about reality when it is contradicted by a different but more correct understanding of reality. For example, a thirsty man in a desert might run to a mirage of water he sees in the distance. But when he gets there and finds nothing but sand, he realizes and corrects his error.

QUICK REVIEW
The Indian philosopher Shankara was a rationalist who held that our knowledge of ultimate reality is not acquired through our senses but through reasoning and meditation.

According to Shankara, hallucinations, dreams, mirages, and other illusions give rise to errors that we "sublate" when we see that they are contradicted by other things our senses show us in the world around us. Moreover, Shankara argues, everything in the world around us that we perceive with our senses can also be sublated. It is sublated when through study of the Hindu Scriptures, through reasoning, and through meditation we come to know the ultimate reality, which he called Brahman and which Westerners might mistakenly call "God." When we come to know Brahman, the ultimate reality that underlies everything, we realize that the world we perceive with our senses—the world of many different objects separate from us—is an illusion in relation to the absolute reality of Brahman. Thus, just as a dream has its own reality yet is an illusion in comparison to the world our senses reveal, so also the world our senses reveal has its own reality yet is an erroneous illusion in comparison to Brahman. Moreover, argues Shankara, when we meditate and come to experience our own deepest self—that pure inner consciousness where we realize there is absolutely no difference between our self and other selves nor between our self and all other things—then we also recognize that this pure self is Brahman. We then realize who and what we really are and attain bliss as ignorance disappears.

What is important to notice about Shankara's philosophy is his key idea that the senses are not a source of knowledge of ultimate reality. Instead, thinking (study, reasoning, and meditating) is the key to knowing the ultimate reality—the Self that is identical with Brahman—and reveals the illusory nature of the world that our senses perceive.

The history of Western philosophy also records the thinking of many other outstanding rationalists, including Plato (circa 428–348 BCE), Saint Augustine (354–430), Benedict Spinoza (1632–1677), Anne Conway (1631–1679), Gottfried Wilhelm Leibniz (1646–1716), and Georg Hegel (1770–1831). Three important rationalists living today include Noam Chomsky, Laurence Bonjour, and Peter Carruthers. The most noteworthy rationalist, however, is René Descartes, the seventeenth-century scientific giant who not only invented analytic geometry but also advanced a view of knowledge that greatly influenced philosophy. We begin with Descartes because his ideas have been so influential in Western thought.

Descartes: Doubt and Reason

Curiously, many of us today can identify with Descartes' methodological point of departure—an attitude of doubt or **skepticism** toward what we think we know. Today, we might call his frame of mind *disillusionment.* Some would say that Descartes suffered an epistemological "credibility gap" of sorts. He seriously wondered about what he could believe, what he could be certain of. He was driven to this point by the many intellectual, scientific, and religious upheavals that his world was undergoing.

Only a few decades before Descartes was born, Martin Luther had launched the great Protestant revolution. That revolution eventually engulfed all of Europe and gave birth to the religious wars that rocked the continent for decades. Church doctrines that everyone had accepted as unchangeable dogmas were suddenly cast into doubt. At the same time, scientists such as Copernicus and Galileo challenged views that had been accepted for more than two thousand years. Copernicus rejected the ancient view that the earth was at the center of the universe and that the sun revolved around it. In place of this old theory, Copernicus proposed the startling new idea that the earth and the planets revolve around the sun. Peering through the newly invented telescope, Galileo discovered that the moon has mountains, that there are spots on the sun, and that the Milky Way is composed of countless stars. All this was contrary to the ancient belief that the moon, sun, and stars are perfect crystalline bodies. Galileo also rejected ideas about motion that dated back to the ancient Greeks, such as that heavy bodies fall faster than light ones or that moving bodies eventually must come to rest. Instead, Galileo's experiments proved all bodies fall to earth at the same rate, and moving bodies continue in motion unless stopped by friction or another external force.

We live in an age much like that of Descartes. Ours is an era of rapid change and new discoveries, of constant sensory input, and of an information explosion. Cell phones, computers, the Internet, television, blogs, Facebook pages, Twitter, iPads, and countless other forms of electronic communication have unleashed a flood of instantaneous news and globally distributed information. Stock prices fall in Japan, and minutes later they drag down the stock market in New York. Television programs aired in Los Angeles instantaneously create a stir in Europe. The flow of new discoveries in science, medicine, and technology is so fast and so massive that no one can keep up. Advances in medicine extend life in ways that create troubling new questions about when life ends. Genetic engineering raises questions about the wisdom of manipulating life and even creating it. Rather than adding stability to life, a fast-paced, continuous flow of new knowledge and information can leave us unsteadily wobbling between old beliefs and new discoveries.

QUICK REVIEW
In Descartes' time, new scientific discoveries overturned established views, creating uncertainty about what truths were valid. He turned to mathematics as a model of reasoning that leads from basic indubitable truths to new indubitable truths.

Just as new discoveries and technological advances in our own time leave us uncertain and disoriented, the people of the seventeenth century were racked with uncertainty about how to reconcile the new ideas of Copernicus and Galileo with their old religious, philosophical, and scientific beliefs. Indeed, the age of Descartes was marked by a profound questioning of established religious doctrines and time-honored scientific opinions. Amid this dizzying and destabilizing questioning, Descartes searched for something firm to believe in, some fixed foundation on which he could stand. Impressed by the sureness and confidence with which mathematicians seemed to attain undeniable truth, Descartes dared to hope that mathematical methods of reasoning could help him find the stable foundations of knowledge that his skeptical age needed:

To read more from Descartes' Discourse, *go to CourseMate for this text and browse by chapter or philosopher?*

> The long chains of simple and easy reasonings by means of which geometers are accustomed to reach the conclusions of their most difficult demonstrations, had led me to imagine that all things, to the knowledge of which man is competent, are mutually connected in the same way, and that there is nothing so far removed from us as to be beyond our reach, or so hidden that we cannot discover it, provided only we abstain from accepting the false for the true, and always preserve in our thoughts the order necessary for the deduction of one truth from another.[4]

4 René Descartes, *Discourse on the Method of Rightly Conducting the Reason, and Seeking Truth in the Sciences*, in *The Philosophical Works of Descartes*, vol. 1, trans. and ed. Elizabeth S. Haldane and G. R. T. Ross (Cambridge, England: Cambridge University Press, 1911).

Filled with the kind of doubt, uncertainty, and anxiety that many of us experience today, Descartes believed that the step-by-step methods by which mathematical reasoning derives new truths from more foundational, self-evident, and axiomatic truths might help him discover some firm truths about the universe. Hoping to discover some foundational knowledge that he could hold on to as unshakable truth and from which he could derive other truths, Descartes examined each of his beliefs, asking himself whether it could be accepted as undeniably true:

> All that up to the present time I have accepted as most true and certain I have learned either from the senses or through the senses; but it is sometimes proved to me that these senses are deceptive, and it is wiser not to trust entirely to any thing by which we have once been deceived. . . .
>
> At the same time I must remember that I am a man, and that consequently I am in the habit of sleeping, and in my dreams representing to myself the same things or sometimes even less probable things, than do those who are insane in their waking moments. How often has it happened to me that in the night I dreamt that I found myself in this particular place, that I was dressed and seated near the fire, whilst in reality I was lying undressed in bed! At this moment it does indeed seem to me that it is with eyes awake that I am looking at this paper; that this head which I move is not asleep, that it is deliberately and of set purpose that I extend my hand and perceive it; what happens in sleep does not appear so clear nor so distinct as does all this. But in thinking over this I remind myself that on many occasions I have in sleep been deceived by similar illusions, and in dwelling carefully on this reflection I see so manifestly that there are no certain indications by which we may clearly distinguish wakefulness from sleep that I am lost in astonishment. And my astonishment is such that it is almost capable of persuading me that I now dream. . . .
>
> I have long had fixed in my mind the belief that an all-powerful God existed by whom I have been created such as I am. But how do I know that He has not brought it to pass that there is no earth, no heaven, no extended body, no magnitude, no place, and that nevertheless [I possess the perceptions of all these things and that] they seem to me to exist just exactly as I now see them? And, besides, as I sometimes imagine that others deceive themselves in the things which they think they know best, how do I know that I am not deceived every time that I add two and three, or count the sides of a square, or judge of things yet simpler, if anything simpler can be imagined? But possibly God has not desired that I should be thus deceived, for He is said to be supremely good. If, however, it is contrary to His goodness to have made me such that I constantly deceive myself, it would also appear to be contrary to His goodness to permit me to be sometimes deceived, and nevertheless I cannot doubt that He does permit this.
>
> I shall then suppose, not that God who is supremely good and the fountain of truth, but some evil genius not less powerful than deceitful, has employed his whole energies in deceiving me; I shall consider that the heavens, the earth, colors, figures, sound, and all other external things are nought but the illusions and dreams of which this genius has availed himself in order to lay traps for my credulity; I shall consider myself as having no hands, no eyes, no flesh, no blood, nor any senses, yet falsely believing myself to possess all these things; I shall remain obstinately attached to this idea, and if by this means it is not in my power to arrive at the knowledge of any truth, I may at least do what is in my power [i.e., suspend my judgment], and with firm purpose avoid giving credence to any false thing, or being imposed upon by this arch deceiver, however powerful and deceptive he may be.[5]

QUICK REVIEW
To find indubitable foundational truths, Descartes tried to doubt all his beliefs by realizing that everything might be a dream or an illusion of a powerful god; any beliefs that could not be doubted would be basic indubitable truths. One was "I think, therefore I am."

5 René Descartes, "Meditation One," in *Meditations on First Philosophy*, vol. 1, *The Philosophical Works of Descartes*, trans. and ed. Elizabeth S. Haldane and G. R. T. Ross (Cambridge, England: Cambridge University Press, 1911).

Thus, Descartes took doubt to its outer limits. Our sense perceptions, he held, may be illusions or the products of our own dreams or hallucinations. Our ideas may be nothing more than the products of an evil, all-powerful devil that puts these ideas in our minds. In this way, Descartes came to doubt everything of which he could not be certain. He then asked this question: Is there anything that survives an attempt to cast doubt on absolutely everything? Is there any truth that is so certain that it cannot be doubted? Ultimately, he discovered what he felt was an indubitable truth: "I think, therefore I am."

> Doubtless, then, I exist, since I am deceived; and, let him deceive me as he may, he can never bring it about that I am nothing, so long as I shall be conscious that I am something. So that it must, in fine, be maintained, all things being maturely and carefully considered, that this proposition, I am, I exist, is necessarily true each time it is expressed by me, or conceived in my mind.[6]

Descartes reasoned that even if he was being deceived about everything else, he could not be deceived about the fact that he was thinking he was being deceived. That is, even if everything he thought about was an illusion, he could not doubt that he was thinking about that illusion. And if he was thinking, then he must exist. Thus, the doubting self is a self whose existence cannot be doubted, a self that not only doubts but also affirms, wills, and imagines—in short, we can be certain the thinking self exists.

Descartes, then, was absolutely certain of the truth of the proposition "I think, therefore I am." But then he asked himself: what was it about this proposition that made him so certain of its truth?

> After this I considered generally what in a proposition is requisite in order to be true and certain; for since I had just discovered one which I knew to be such, I thought that I ought also to know in what this certainty consisted. And having remarked that there was nothing at all in the statement, "I think, therefore I am" which assures me of having thereby made a true assertion, excepting that I see very clearly that to think it is necessary to be, I came to the conclusion that I might assume, as a general rule, that the things which we conceive very clearly and distinctively are all true.[7]

So Descartes concludes that what makes him certain about the idea that "I think, therefore I am" is the clarity and distinctness with which he apprehends this idea. From this conclusion he draws a crucial lesson: Clarity and distinctness are the marks of certitude. What exactly does Descartes mean by clarity and distinctness? Descartes apparently believes that we have a clear idea of something when we know exactly what it is—that is, when we know its essential properties or essential nature—and we have a distinct idea of something when we can readily distinguish it from other things.

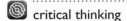

critical thinking

Descartes says that because all the sensory qualities of the wax gradually change, it follows that his knowledge that the wax remains the same cannot be based on his senses. Does this really follow?

But what is the source of our clear and distinct ideas? Where do those clear and distinct ideas come from? This is an important question, for in answering it, Descartes lays a rationalistic basis for knowledge. In one of the most epistemologically important of all his writings, his *Second Meditation*, Descartes attempts to

---

6 René Descartes, "Meditation Two," in *Meditations on First Philosophy*, vol. 1, *The Philosophical Works of Descartes*, vol. 1, trans. and ed. Elizabeth S. Haldane and G. R. T. Ross (Cambridge, England: Cambridge University Press, 1911).

7 René Descartes, *Discourse on the Method of Rightly Conducting the Reason, and Seeking Truth in the Sciences*, in *The Philosophical Works of Descartes*, vol. 1, trans. and ed. Elizabeth S. Haldane and G. R. T. Ross (Cambridge, England: Cambridge University Press, 1911), 101.

explain how thinking and reasoning without the aid of the senses can be the source of real knowledge about the world. In the selection that follows, note how he abstracts from the sense qualities of a piece of wax to demonstrate why the mind—and not the senses—is the ultimate criterion of knowledge. In this way, he establishes a rationalistic foundation for knowledge:

> Let us begin by considering the commonest matters, those which we believe to be the most distinctly comprehended, to wit, the bodies which we touch and see; not indeed bodies in general, for these general ideas are usually a little more confused, but let us consider one body in particular. Let us take, for example, this piece of wax: it has been taken quite freshly from the hive, and it has not yet lost the sweetness of the honey which it contains; it still retains somewhat of the odor of the flowers from which it has been culled; its color, its figure, its size are apparent; it is hard, cold, easily handled, and if you strike it with the finger, it will emit a sound. Finally all the things that are requisite to cause us distinctly to recognize a body, are met with in it. But notice that while I speak and bring it near the fire what remained of the taste is exhaled, the smell evaporates, the color alters, the figure is destroyed, the size increases, it becomes liquid, it heats, scarcely can one handle it, and when one strikes it, no sound is emitted. Does the same wax remain after this change? We must confess that it remains; none would judge otherwise. What then did I know so distinctly in this piece of wax? It could certainly be nothing of all that the senses brought to my notice, since all those things that fall under taste, smell, sight, touch, and hearing, we find have changed, and yet the same wax remains.
>
> . . . We must then grant that . . . it is my mind alone which perceives . . . this piece of wax. . . . But what is this piece of wax which cannot be understood except by the mind? It is certainly the same that I see, touch, imagine, and finally it is the same which I have always believed it to be from the beginning. But what must particularly be observed is this: it is perceived neither by an act of vision, nor of touch, nor of imagination . . . but only by an intuition of the mind.[8]

QUICK REVIEW
Using the example of a piece of wax that the mind knows is the same physical body when it melts but that to the senses looks completely different, Descartes concludes that reason, without the aid of the senses, is what knows the body of the wax.

© Oleg Prikhodko/iStockphotoe.com

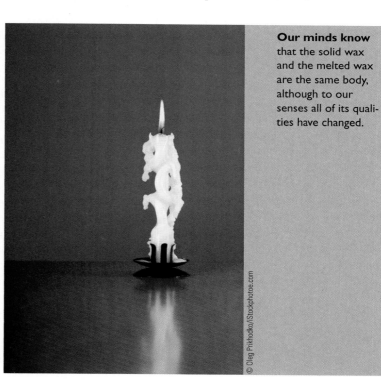

Our minds know that the solid wax and the melted wax are the same body, although to our senses all of its qualities have changed.

Descartes points out here that our minds know that as it melts, the wax remains the same bodily thing although to our senses all of its qualities have changed. Thus, our knowledge of what the wax itself is—an enduring physical body—does not derive from the senses or the imagination. If that knowledge were derived from the senses, we would have to say that when the wax melts, it is no longer what it was because to our senses it changes completely. Consequently, our knowledge that the melted wax is the same body as the unmelted wax is

8 Ibid., 190–191.

something that we know with the mind and not with the senses. Thus, Descartes concludes, our knowledge of what a thing essentially is is grasped by an "intuition" of the mind—that is, by a direct insight into the essential nature of the thing. In the case of the wax, we know the solid wax and the melted wax are the same because the mind grasps its essential nature as a physical body, and so knows that it remains essentially the same physical body even when all its qualities change.

Descartes' view that reason is the ultimate source of our most basic knowledge, our knowledge even of the nature of the physical bodies we perceive with our senses, is an example of extreme rationalism. Not all rationalists are as thoroughgoing as Descartes. Some rationalists hold that although some of our basic knowledge derives completely from reason, some of it also depends on the senses. The extreme rationalist, like Descartes, holds that all our basic or "foundational" knowledge derives solely from reason, without the aid of the senses. Descartes does believe, of course, that we acquire some ideas through our senses. He notes, for example: "But if I hear a noise, if I see the sun, or if I feel its heat, I have all along judged that these sensations proceeded from certain objects existing out of myself."[9] Our knowledge of sounds, of what the sun looks like and what its heat feels like, are examples of the simple kind of knowledge of the world "outside" us that, Descartes suggests, is acquired through the senses. But our knowledge of the essential nature of the body that gives off sounds or that glows like the sun or that emits heat, is acquired by the mind alone.

The extreme nature of Descartes' rationalism is especially evident in the way he approaches our knowledge of God and the world. Descartes argues that an imperfect creature like himself could not make up the idea of a perfect God. He concludes that the source of such an idea must be something perfect—God. He then infers that this perfect being, God, must exist.

QUICK REVIEW
Descartes argues that he could not have produced the idea of a perfect being, God, and neither could he have acquired it through the senses; only God could have put it into his mind, so God must exist. Because God is good, He does not deceive, so we can rely on the powers of knowing He has given us.

Notice that in these kinds of reasonings, Descartes never appeals to the testimony of his senses. His claims appeal to the mind alone; he believes that the mind is the source of those ideas that pass the test of clarity and distinctness. Similarly, he argues for the existence of the world and other selves by reasoning entirely with the clear and distinct ideas within his mind. Could a perfect God, he asks, deceive me into perceiving my own body, the outer world, and other individuals, as I obviously do? Could He deceive me into thinking they exist when in fact they do not? Remember that Descartes knew only that he himself existed as a thinking thing. True, he did perceive his own body and the outer world, but consistent with his method of doubt, he reasoned that these might be illusions, the devilish tricks of some mad genius. But he has now proved that a perfect being exists. Is such trickery and deception inherent in the idea he has of a perfect being—an idea that he did not acquire through his senses? He concludes that the essential nature of a perfect being rules out deception. Therefore, he reasons, the world and other selves do indeed exist, for otherwise God would be deceiving us. But notice that we know they exist not because our senses tell us they exist but because the mind has reasoned to their existence on the basis of its clear and distinct ideas.

Innate Ideas

But another question remains: How do these clear and distinct ideas get into our minds? Where do they come from if not the senses? Descartes and other rationalists used the notion of innate ideas to answer this question. **Innate ideas** are ideas

9 Ibid.

that are present in the mind from birth: We are born with them. The rationalist, Plato, for example, believed that we are born with certain ideas fully formed in our minds—for example, the concepts of geometry. But, at birth, these ideas are hidden away in the depths of the mind or memory, so the young infant is not consciously aware of them. As the person grows up, these ideas can slowly emerge into the person's awareness.

What kind of ideas might be innate? Most rationalists believe that at least the basic principles of logic and math are innate. These include the basic axioms of geometry, such as the proposition that the shortest distance between two points is a straight line. They also include the basic laws of arithmetic, such as the proposition that if equal numbers are added to equal numbers, the results are equal. Moreover, some rationalists believe that the basic rules of science are also innate. This includes, for example, the rule that every event has to have a cause. It also includes the rule that nothing comes from nothing. Some rationalists believe that not only are *propositions* like these innate but that the individual *concepts* are also innate. These concepts include the concepts of "point," "line," "straight," "equality," "event," and "cause."

Why would anyone think that such propositions and concepts are innate? This question is at the heart of a problem that we still struggle with today: Where else could our knowledge of these propositions and concepts have come from? Many philosophers agree with Descartes that we cannot come to know these propositions and concepts by observing the world around us. In other words, we cannot know these by looking at things outside the mind. The things we see around us never quite live up to these propositions and concepts in our mind. For example, in geometry, mathematicians think of a line as having no thickness and a point as having no size. But the lines we see in the world around us are always more or less thick. And points are always of one size or another. In arithmetic, as we conceptualize it in our minds, *equal* means perfectly identical. Yet in the world around us, two objects are never perfectly identical to each other. Or consider the proposition that *every event has a cause.* In the world around us and over a lifetime, we may observe perhaps a few hundred thousand or even a few million events. Yet we certainly do not observe *every event.* How then is it that our minds know, without observing all events, that *every* event must have a cause?

QUICK REVIEW
Rationalists such as Plato, Descartes, Leibniz, and the Indian Jain philosophers believe that the ideas and truths that the mind knows without relying on its senses are innate—in other words, we were born with these ideas in our minds, or they developed from what we were born with. We could not have acquired them by observation because our experience of the world is too limited and its objects are too imperfect.

Apparently, there are certain propositions and concepts that are in our mind, yet it seems we do not come to know these by observing things in the world around us. Where, then, does our knowledge of these come from? We are born with this knowledge, say rationalist philosophers. The rationalist philosopher Plato, in particular, often discussed this issue in his dialogues. His demonstration of how we become aware of the innate ideas we have is clearer than the explanations of Descartes or other rationalists, so we will focus on his arguments. In his dialogue, *Meno,* Plato provides what is probably the best example of a person—a slave boy in this case—becoming aware of the innate ideas he had in his mind but did not consciously know he had.

Plato's **Meno.** In *Meno,* Plato tells us how Socrates once made a slave boy "remember" his knowledge of geometry by showing him some imperfect figures drawn on the ground. Socrates shows the slave boy a square that is supposed to be two feet by two feet, or four square feet in size (see Figure 5.1a). Socrates asks the boy how he would draw a second square that is exactly twice the size of the first square. At first, the boy says that if you double the length of each side of the first square, you will get a second square that is exactly twice the size of the first square. But when Socrates draws a second square that is approximately four feet by four feet (Figure 5.1b), the boy quickly realizes that his first answer is wrong. If you double the length of each

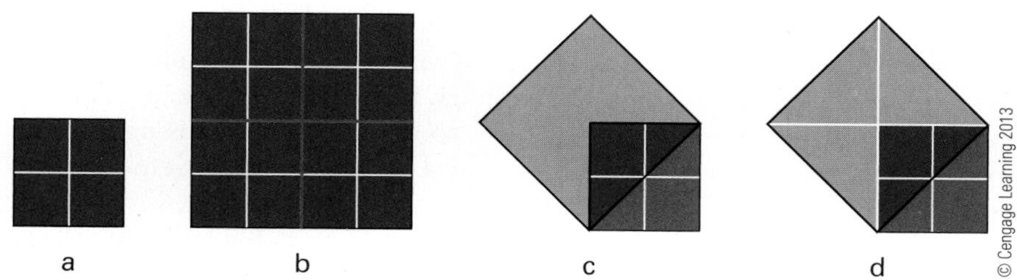

Figure 5.1 Socrates used similar diagrams to prove his theory of innate ideas.

side of a square, you get a new square that is exactly four times as big as the first square. Yet the boy knows this without making exact measurements of the squares that Socrates draws on the ground. And even if the boy had measured the squares, they would probably not have turned out to be exactly the right sizes. So, where did the boy's knowledge come from?

Socrates then repeats his original question: How do you draw a second square that is exactly twice the size of the first square? The boy hesitates. Socrates draws a diagonal line from one corner to the other in the first square (Figure 5.1c). Then, he draws a second, larger square, using this diagonal line as the side of the larger square. Socrates asks the boy how big this second square is. The boy is unsure. So Socrates draws some diagonals in the larger square, dividing it into four small triangles (Figure 5.1d). Then, Socrates invites the boy to count the triangles in the first square and the triangles in the second square. Immediately, it flashes on the boy: The second square drawn on the diagonal has to be exactly twice the size of the first square! The boy "knows" this, even though, again, he does not measure Socrates' very imperfect figures. Plus, if he had measured the squares that Socrates drew on the ground, it would certainly have turned out that the second square was not exactly twice the size of the first square. So, again, where did the boy's knowledge come from? It could not have come from just looking at how big the second square was compared to the first because, again, the squares Socrates draws on the ground are rough and inexact, and so the big square is not exactly twice as big as the small one. In a discussion with Meno, the master of the slave, Socrates answers the question about where the boy's knowledge came from:

QUICK REVIEW
In *Meno*, Plato argues that a slave boy's knowledge of the Pythagorean theorem could not have come from observing the imperfect figures drawn on the ground, but must have come into his mind before he was born.

SOCRATES: What do you say of your slave, Meno? Weren't all of his answers given out of his own head?

MENO: Yes, his answers were all his own.

SOCRATES: And yet, you just told us that you never taught him geometry?

MENO: That's true.

SOCRATES: But he had these opinions somewhere inside him, didn't he?

MENO: Yes.

SOCRATES: So the person who does not know something may still have true opinions about the subject buried within himself without actually being aware of them?

MENO: He may.

SOCRATES: And just now these opinions were stirred up in the boy, as if in a dream. But if we asked him many more of these same kinds of questions, in many different forms, wouldn't he eventually come to know the subject as well as anyone else?

MENO: I think so.

SOCRATES: Without anyone telling him the answers, he can recover his knowledge from within himself, if he is only asked questions?

MENO: Yes.

SOCRATES: And this spontaneous recovery of the knowledge that is in him is a form of remembering what is already in him?

MENO: True.

SOCRATES: And this knowledge which he now remembers, he must have acquired at some earlier time?

MENO: Yes. . . .

SOCRATES: Has anyone ever taught him these things? You should know, Meno, since he was raised in your house?

MENO: No, no one ever taught him this.

SOCRATES: Then, if he did not acquire these truths in this life, isn't it clear that he acquired and learned them during some other period?

MENO: Apparently.

SOCRATES: Before he was born with a human form?

MENO: Yes. . . .

SOCRATES: And if the truth about reality is always in our soul, the soul must be immortal. So we must take courage and try hard to discover—that is, to remember—the knowledge within us that we are not yet aware of.[10]

In this fascinating dialogue, Plato tries to show that there is only one way we could have come to have our knowledge of geometry. We could not have acquired our knowledge of geometry by observing things after we were born or by being told these things. We must have had this knowledge in some form in our minds at birth. But how did it get into our minds? Plato answers: We must have acquired this knowledge before we were born! Before we were born, Plato believes, our souls must have lived in a perfect universe where we actually observed perfectly shaped lines, squares, and triangles, along with other perfect ideas. When we are born into this imperfect world, we carry those perfect ideas within us, buried in the depths of memory.

Most rationalist philosophers reject Plato's claim that before we were born we existed in another perfect universe. But many rationalists, including Descartes, accept Plato's more basic insight: We do not acquire the basic truths of math and science by observing the world around us but are born with them. In the following passage, Descartes indicates his agreement with Plato's fundamental insight:

> [W]e come to know them [innate ideas] by the power of our own native intelligence, without any sensory experience. All geometrical truths are of this sort—not just the most obvious ones, but all the others, however abstruse they may appear. Hence, according to Plato, Socrates asks a slave boy about the elements of geometry and thereby makes the boy able to dig out certain truths from his own mind which he had not previously recognized were there, thus attempting to establish the doctrine of reminiscence. Our knowledge of God is of this sort.[11]

10 Plato, *Meno*, 85c–86a. This translation © 1998 by Manuel Velasquez.

11 René Descartes, letter of 1643, in John Cottingham, Robert Stoothoff, and Dugald Murdoch (eds.), *The Philosophical Writings of Descartes*, vol. 3 (Cambridge: Cambridge University Press, 1984), 222–223.

PHILOSOPHY AND LIFE

Innate Ideas?

Two recent scientific studies suggest that people have innate ideas that are not learned through sense experience but are present from birth. One study by Perin, Berger, and Markram, examined how neurons are organized in the brains of newborns. Neurons are brain cells that process, transmit, and preserve thoughts and information. Scientists believe that neurons represent or "encode" information or thoughts by forming circuits that connect them with each other. According to the authors, "*neuronal circuitry is often considered a clean slate that can be... arbitrarily molded by experience.*" In other words, scientists believed that at birth the brain contained no encoded information, and that whatever information brain neurons encoded after birth came from sense experiences. However, the study discovered that many neurons are already connected in small networks from birth. The study concluded that "*experience cannot freely mold*" all the neurons of the brain, because from birth the brain contains "*neuronal groups that . . . emerged during embryonic development independent of experience.*" In short, these small networks of neurons seem to represent innate concepts that are present in the brain from birth and independent of sense experience.

The second study, by Hespos and vanMarle, reviewed earlier research on the concepts babies seem to have. The study states:

> We review how object and substance knowledge interfaces with number knowledge systems [in infants]. The evidence supports the view that certain core principles about these domains are present as early as we can test for them and the nature of the underlying representation is best characterized as primitive initial concepts that are elaborated and refined through learning and experience. . . .
> Infants have detailed knowledge about how objects behave and interact from the first weeks of life.

According to the authors, experiments with babies as young as two months suggest they possess such "initial concepts." How do scientists know what babies are thinking? Scientists rely on the expressions on babies' faces and on other responses babies make when they see physical objects being manipulated by the scientists. For example, when babies are shown a ball rolling behind a small screen and coming out on the other side, they show very little reaction and very soon look away from the scene. Apparently such a scene conforms with their knowledge of how physical objects behave. But when they are shown a ball rolling behind a small screen and not coming out the other side, babies seem surprised, they stare at the screen for a long time, and then perhaps look behind the screen for the missing ball. Such experiments have shown that babies know that physical objects continue to exist even when they are not seen, and know that physical objects don't just blink out of existence. Other similar experiments have shown that babies know what a physical object is, know that physical objects continue to exist even when one is not looking at them, know that two physical objects cannot occupy the same space at the same time, and know that physical objects cannot pass through each other. Babies also know that liquid substances do not behave like physical objects, that liquids can separate, and that objects (like a straw) can pass through them. Finally, babies seem to have some knowledge of small numbers—for example, they know the difference between one cookie, two cookies, and three cookies (they prefer the larger quantity!).

QUESTIONS

1. Do these studies show that babies have the kind of innate ideas that Descartes, Plato, and other rationalists had in mind?
2. Do you see any similarities between the claims Descartes makes about his wax example and the findings of these studies?

Sources: Rodrigo Perin, Thomas K. Berger, and Henry Markram, "A Synaptic Organizing Principle for Cortical Neuronal Groups," *Proceedings of the National Academy of the Sciences*, March, 2011; Susan J. Hespos and Kristy vanMarle, "Physics for Infants: Characterizing the Origins of Knowledge about Objects, Substances, and Number," *Wiley Interdisciplinary Reviews: Cognitive Science*, vol. 3 (January/February 2012), no. 1, pp. 19–27.

Descartes thought that it was clear that some of the foundational ideas on which the rest of our knowledge is based are contained fully formed in our reason from the time we are born, but we are not aware of them until later. As he put it: [W]hen we say that an idea is innate in us, we do not mean that it is always there before us.

This would mean that no idea was innate. We simply mean that we have within ourselves the faculty of summoning up the idea." When we summon up an innate idea, we become aware of it as if we were recalling a memory: "on first discovering [innate ideas] it seems that I am not so much learning something new as remembering what I knew before; or it seems like noticing for the first time things which were long present within me although I had never turned my mental gaze on them before." Descartes believed, for example, that human beings are born with innate ideas of the three fundamental kinds of things in the universe: God, minds, and material bodies. Although it takes time for us to become consciously aware of these ideas, Descartes thought that we know how to use these ideas even before we think directly about what their nature is. His example of the wax shows this. Everyone—even a child—knows that a physical body is a thing that continues to exist even as all its qualities change, and so, as he notes, everyone knows that the solid wax and the melted wax are the same physical body. We each know from childhood what a body is, at least well enough to know that when wax melts it is still the same body of wax. The idea of a body, then, is innate and fully formed and operating in our mind even before we have consciously thought about what a body is. Not everyone agreed with this view of innate ideas, however.

Leibniz: Innate Ideas Are "Tendencies." Another rationalist, Gottfried W. Leibniz (1646–1716), disagreed with Descartes' view that the mind has fully formed innate ideas within itself. Leibniz agreed that we do not acquire our knowledge of the most basic truths about the world by observing the world around us. He also agreed that those truths must somehow be innate in us, i.e., in some sense we are born with them. But Leibniz was not willing to say that we are born with fully formed truths or concepts in our minds. Innate ideas, Leibniz claimed, are in us only as "tendencies" or "dispositions":

> If there were veins in a block of marble which marked out the shape of Hercules rather than other shapes, then that block would be more determined to that shape and Hercules would be innate in it, in a way, even though labor would be required to expose the veins and to polish them into clarity, removing everything that prevents their being seen. This is how ideas and truths are innate in us—as inclinations, dispositions, tendencies, or natural potentials, and not as actualities.[12]

At birth, the mind does not come equipped with fully formed innate ideas. Rather, people's minds have within them an inborn capacity or tendency to form those ideas, and as people mature, their experiences gradually shape these tendencies and turn them into fully formed ideas.

Despite these differences, rationalists have generally agreed with Plato, Descartes, and Leibniz that we have innate ideas. Nevertheless, the theory of innate ideas is difficult for other philosophers to accept. How can we have knowledge inside our minds, they ask, if we are not aware of it? To say that we "know" something is to say that we at least believe it. But how can we believe something without being aware of it? To many philosophers, it seems pointless to say that we have knowledge if we are not aware of it. But if we do not accept the theory of innate ideas, the question remains: How do we acquire our knowledge of so many basic truths that seem to lie beyond what our observations of the world around us can provide?

---

12 Gottfried W. Leibniz, "New Essays on the Human Understanding," in *Leibniz Selections*, ed. Philip P. Wiener (New York: Charles Scribner's Sons, 1951), 373.

Jainism. Western philosophers are not the only ones who have argued in support of a rationalist theory of innate ideas. Some of the philosophers of India have held similar views. Take Jainism, for example, an important philosophy of India that originated several centuries before Christ and that today is still embraced by some six million people. (The great twentieth-century philosopher Mohandas K. Gandhi was a Jain philosopher.) Philosophers of the school of Jainism hold that even before our senses perceive an object, we already have the knowledge of that object in our minds.[13] When we see an object, our perception of the object merely serves to uncover the innate knowledge of that object that we already had within us. The philosophers of Jainism hold that every human being carries within his or her mind a complete knowledge of everything in the universe. What explains our unconscious but complete knowledge of the universe? According to the philosophers of Jainism, the mind is not limited by time or space but is present everywhere. Because our mind is everywhere, it must know everything. However, throughout most of our lives we are unaware of the unlimited knowledge within us because our past unethical actions and decisions (perhaps in former lives!) create a veil of impurity that covers over the potentially unlimited knowledge within us, hiding it from us. Nevertheless, when we get rid of the baggage of our past wrongdoing, and when we are free from our bondage to material things, we will be liberated and will become fully conscious of our Godlike knowledge. A key to our future liberation is the practice of *ahimsa*, the avoidance of all aggression, injury, or harm to other living things. Until then, we must be satisfied with recovering the innate knowledge that is within us piece by piece through the use of our intellect and our senses.

Let us end this discussion of rationalism by considering briefly what Descartes' view of clear and distinct ideas might suggest about the controversy over recovered memories discussed earlier. Some people with recovered memories have made the point that "the clarity of the new memories is striking, photographic." Descartes probably would object to applying his theories to memories of sense experiences, but he did hold that clarity and distinctness of ideas were indicators of true knowledge. The clarity, the detailed sharpness, and the convincing qualities of many recovered memories would seem to imply that they are "clear and distinct," and so can be accepted as true knowledge. That is, the inherent qualities of the recollected memories by themselves—their clarity, their distinctness, and their certitude—validate them as sources of self-evident knowledge about the past. Indeed, that is exactly what many lawyers have argued: The clarity and distinctness of recovered memories prove that they must be true. For example, one attorney is quoted as saying this: "I find it highly unlikely that someone who can remember what pattern was on the wallpaper and that a duck was quacking outside the bedroom window where she was molested by her father when she was four years old is making it up. Why in the hell would your mind do this?"

QUICK REVIEW
If Descartes' criteria of "clearness and distinctness" as indicators of valid knowledge are applied to recovered memories (something Descartes would probably not allow), they would suggest that such memories are valid.

Juries hearing courtroom cases of childhood sexual abuse based on sharply detailed recovered memories have also agreed that the clarity and distinctness of recovered memories make them self-evidently true. A follower of Descartes might even argue that because God is not a deceiver, He would not put such clear and distinct memories in our minds unless they were true. But readers should ask themselves an important question: Are we justified in claiming that memories

13 Bibhu Padhi and Minakshi Padhi, *Indian Philosophy and Religion: A Reader's Guide* (Jefferson, NC: McFarland, 1990), 67.

need no external validation and that they are self-evidently true when they are clear and distinct? Does the clarity and distinctness of a memory—or of any other idea—really guarantee its truth, as Descartes claimed? On the other hand, if the inherent clarity and distinctness of recovered memories are not sufficient for us to count them as self-evident sources of knowledge of the past, then how are they to be validated?

PHILOSOPHY AT THE MOVIES

Watch *Proof* (2005) which tells the story of Catherine and her father, Robert, who died a couple of days earlier. Robert was a brilliant mathematician until he became mentally ill, forcing Catherine to cut short her own studies in mathematics, and return home to take care of him. Catherine gives her boyfriend a notebook in which someone has written the proof of a revolutionary mathematical theory. Although Catherine claims she wrote the proof herself, her boyfriend and her sister suspect her father wrote the proof. Explain what rationalism would say is the source of our knowledge of a mathematical proof like the one in the notebook.

5.3 Can the Senses Account for All Our Knowledge?

Both in the East and in the West, a view of epistemology emerged that contrasts sharply with rationalist views of knowledge and that is now called "empiricism." Empiricism is the view that all knowledge about the world comes from or is based on the senses. Reacting sharply to rationalistic claims, empiricists claim that the human mind contains nothing except what experience has put there. Thus, all ideas originate in sense experience. Consequently, empiricism teaches that true knowledge is **a posteriori**. That is, it depends on experience; it is knowledge stated in empirically verifiable or falsifiable statements.

Empiricism obviously makes a lot of sense where our ordinary knowledge of the world is concerned. It is through observation with our senses that we acquire the knowledge that the sky is blue, that trees are green, that lemons taste sour, and that the seasons change in a regular cycle through winter, spring, summer, and fall. Sense observations also underlie almost all the knowledge of the natural sciences, such as the astronomer's knowledge that Halley's comet returns to earth every 75 years; the chemist's knowledge that when oxygen and hydrogen burn, they produce water; the physicist's knowledge that at the surface of the earth objects fall at the accelerating rate of 32 feet per second per second; and the biologist's knowledge that monkeys form social hierarchies. In all these cases, our knowledge comes from, and is based on, sense experience.

It is not surprising, then, that Eastern as well as Western philosophers have embraced empiricism. For example, the Charvaka philosophers of India, mentioned earlier in Section 3.2, were empiricists insofar as they held that the only valid source of knowledge is sense perception. Other Indian philosophers, such as the philosophers of the Nyaya (which means "Logic") school, can also be classified as empiricists. Although the Nyaya philosophers agreed that there are other valid sources of knowledge besides sense perception, they claimed that all other sources of knowledge ultimately depend on sense perception. In reasoning or "inference," for example, we must ultimately reason from knowledge that we acquired from perception, whereas knowledge acquired from the testimony of others must ultimately depend on what someone witnessed through sense perception.[14]

QUICK REVIEW
Western empiricists such as Locke, Berkeley, and Hume, and Indian Charvaka and Nyaya philosophers hold that all our knowledge comes through sense observations.

In the West, empiricism has also had a long history. Elements of empiricism can be found in the writings of Aristotle (384–322 BCE), Saint Thomas Aquinas (1225–1274), Sir Francis Bacon (1561–1626), and Thomas Hobbes (1588–1679). In modern times, however, the most noteworthy attack on rationalism was the war waged by three Western philosophers termed the *British empiricists:* John Locke (1632–1704), George Berkeley (1685–1753), and David Hume (1711–1776).

Locke and Empiricism

To read more of Locke's *Essay Concerning Human Understanding*, go to CourseMate for this text and browse by chapter or philosopher.

The English philosopher John Locke (1632–1704) was the first to launch a systematic attack on the rationalist belief that reason alone could provide us with knowledge. The rationalists, Locke believed, went astray when they claimed that "there are in the understanding certain innate principles . . . which the soul receives in its very first being, and brings into the world with it." According to Locke, the only real argument the rationalists could produce for their belief in innate ideas was the one from "universal consent"—that because people everywhere have certain ideas in their minds, such ideas must be innate. The fundamental problem with this argument, Locke claimed, is that there are no ideas that all human beings are aware of:

> But . . . this argument of universal consent, which is made use of to prove innate principles, seems to me a demonstration that there are none such: because there are none to which all mankind give a universal assent. . . . For, first, it is evident that all children and idiots have not the least apprehension or thought of them. And the want of that is enough to destroy that universal assent which must needs be the necessary concomitant of all innate truths.[15]

John Locke: "For since the mind, in all its thoughts and reasonings, hath no other immediate objects but its own ideas, it is evident that our knowledge is only conversant about them."

© Lebrecht Music and Arts Photo Library/Alamy

Locke, instead, compared the mind to a blank slate—in Latin, a "tabula rasa"—on which experience makes its mark. In *An Essay Concerning Human Understanding*, he states the nature of his proposed doctrine clearly:

> Let us then suppose the mind to be, as we say, white paper, void of all characters, without any ideas:—How comes it to be furnished? Whence comes it by that vast store which the busy and boundless fancy of man has painted on it with almost endless variety? Whence has it all the *materials* of reason and knowledge? To this I answer, in one word, from *experience*. In that all our knowledge is founded. . . . Our observation employed either, about external sensible objects, or about the internal operations of our minds . . . is that which supplies our

14 Stephen H. Phillips, "Epistemology, Indian Schools of," in *Encyclopedia of Philosophy* (New York: Macmillan, 1967), vol. 3, 390.
15 John Locke, *An Essay Concerning Human Understanding*, ed. A. C. Fraser (Oxford: Clarendon, 1894), I, ii, 4–5.

> understandings with all the *materials* of thinking. These two are the fountains of knowledge, from whence all the ideas we have, or can naturally have, do spring . . . First, our senses, conversant about particular sensible objects, do convey into the mind several distinct perceptions of things, according to those various ways wherein those objects do affect them. And thus we come by those [simple] *ideas* we have of yellow, white, heat, cold, soft, hard, bitter, sweet, and all those which we call sensible qualities . . . Secondly, the other fountain from which experience furnisheth the understanding with ideas is the perception of the operations of our own mind within us . . . And such are [the simple ideas of] perception, thinking, doubting, believing, reasoning, knowing, willing, and all the different actings of our own minds.[16]

QUICK REVIEW
Locke argued that there were no ideas that all humans share, so no "innate" ideas that all people have when they come into the world. Instead, at birth the mind is a tabula rasa, or blank slate, that only experience can fill.

The obvious objection to Locke's claim that all our ideas come either from our sense perceptions or from perceptions of our mental operations, is that we obviously have ideas that we do not get through sense perception nor from perceptions of our mental operations. For example, the idea of gratitude is not something we see walking around outside of us, nor is it one of the "actings of our own minds." What is the source of such ideas? Locke claimed that we ourselves construct such ideas, using as building blocks the "simple" ideas we get from our senses or from our awareness of our mental activities:

> The mind has a power to consider several [simple ideas] united together as one idea . . . as itself has joined them together. Ideas thus made up of several simple ones put together, I call *complex*;—such as are beauty, gratitude, a man, an army, the universe. . . . In this faculty of repeating and joining together its ideas, the mind has great power in varying and multiplying the objects of its thoughts, infinitely beyond what sensation or reflection furnished it with: but all this still confined to those simple ideas which it received from those two sources, and which are the ultimate materials of all its compositions.[17]

It's tempting to be lulled by the apparent simplicity and common sense of Locke's assertions about knowledge. But automatic acceptance misses important philosophical implications. Consider the fact that we humans make all sorts of claims, from apparently ordinary ones such as "It's raining," "It's the hottest day of the year," and "The lemon is sour" to more complex ones such as "$E = mc^2$." Most people would say, and for at least the simplest of these statements even a rationalist like Descartes would agree, that these claims are based on sense perception. If you ask people, for example, how they know it's raining, they might tell you to go outside and *see* for yourself. If you ask them how they know that today is the hottest day of the year, they might tell you they *looked* out the window and then *listened* to the weather report. If asked how they know that a lemon is sour and sugar is sweet, they might tell you to *taste* them yourself. The question of knowledge, it seems, is bound up with what we perceive. Through perception we feel confident that we *know* how things are.

But should we be so confident? Can't there be a difference between things as they "really" are and our perception of them? Are things always necessarily what they appear to be to our senses? Suppose you're in a hospital recovering from an operation and still somewhat groggy from the anesthesia, when you see your long-dead grandfather walk into your room. You pinch yourself, blink, shake your head, turn away, and look back, but he's still standing there. Eventually he leaves. But you're left wondering: Was he really there, as your senses insisted he was?

16 Ibid., II, i, 2–5.
17 Ibid., II, xii, 1–2.

QUICK REVIEW
A problem that empiricists like Locke face is that if we know only what our sense experiences show us, then we have no way of knowing whether our sense experiences "match" the world beyond our sense experiences, or even whether there is a world beyond our sense experiences.

Obviously, things in reality can be different from what they appear to be to our senses, and this difference can undermine our claim to know things on the basis of our senses. This is a fundamental epistemological problem that arises with all sense-based knowledge claims. Two responses can be made to this problem: Either (1) claim that no qualitative distinction exists between what I seem to experience, and what things are like in reality (for example, between my experience of my grandfather in my room and what is really in my room), or (2) agree that what I experience must be distinguished from the reality itself (for example, my experience of my grandfather must be distinguished from what is really in my room). In the first instance, (1), we face serious and perhaps insurmountable difficulties in claiming that any reality exists outside of our experience because we are claiming that reality is indistinguishable from our experience. In other words, there's no difference between your experience of your grandfather and what is actually in your room, no difference between your experience and reality. Although this would guarantee our claims to know reality on the basis of our sense experience, it would mean that the universe is made up of nothing more than my own sense experiences. As you will see, some empiricist philosophers take this position. In the second instance, (2), we face equally serious difficulties in trying to determine precisely how to know whether our sense perceptions square with reality. If we must distinguish our experiences of things from the way things actually are, then how do we know that our experiences ever in fact correspond with the objective reality of things?

In proposing his theory of knowledge, empiricist Locke took option (2). He asserted not only that knowledge originates in sense experience but also that physical objects exist outside us that cause our perceptions and that are independent of our perceptions of them. In effect, he distinguished between our *perceptions* of objects, and the *objects* that cause us to have those perceptions: "I can no more doubt, whilst I write this, that I see white and black, and that something really exists that causes that sensation in me, than that I write or move my hand."[18] But although Locke distinguished between external objects and the ideas they cause in us, he held that we directly perceive only our ideas and not the external objects that cause them: "In fine, then, when our senses do actually convey into our understandings any idea, we cannot but be satisfied that there doth something at that time really exist without [outside] us, which doth affect our senses, and by them give notice of itself to our apprehensive faculties, and actually produce that idea which we then perceive."[19] Thus, for Locke our knowledge of things is more accurately termed our knowledge of our *ideas* of things. And so the key problem arises: How can we be sure that the ideas we have are accurate representations of external objects? And even more disconcerting: How can we be sure that there even are any external objects?

QUICK REVIEW
Locke claimed that primary or measurable qualities such as weight, size, and shape are really "in" the objects we perceive, whereas secondary qualities such as colors, tastes, and sounds are not "in" the objects we perceive but are sensations in us that objects cause us to have. Because our experiences of primary qualities are "copies" of the primary qualities that are really in objects, these experiences are reliable indicators of the world "outside" us.

Primary and Secondary Qualities. Locke argued that we can be sure that at least some of our ideas are accurate representations of things in the external world. According to Locke, every physical object has certain inherent qualities that are in the object itself whether or not anyone perceives them. These he called **primary qualities**. Generally, primary qualities can be measured—for example, size, shape, and motion—and these measurable qualities "give us an idea of the thing as it is in itself."[20] Locke also held that there are qualities that are not within an object itself

18 Ibid., IV, xi, 2.
19 Ibid., IV, xi, 9.
20 Ibid.

PHILOSOPHY AND LIFE

Science and the Attempt to Observe Reality

Can we ever observe the world as it is, independently of ourselves? Or do our very attempts to observe the world always *change* the world? Psychologists and sociologists often face this problem, because the very fact that people are being observed leads them to behave differently from how they would behave if they were not being observed. The more accurately you try to determine how angry you feel, for example, the less you experience the anger you are trying to observe.

Or consider the results of a famous series of experiments called the Hawthorne studies, which tried to discover what kinds of job conditions would improve the productivity of workers. Workers were observed under various different working conditions (including noise, darkness, bright light, music, silence). The Hawthorne researchers discovered, much to their surprise, that the productivity of the workers they studied always improved no matter what the conditions. It was only much later that the researchers realized that it was the fact that the workers were being *observed* and were being rewarded with so much *attention* that led them to be more productive. Making objective observations—that is, observations that are not contaminated by the observer's activities and choices—is very difficult when observing the psychological or social world.

But surely the *physical* world can be observed objectively—that is, without it being changed by our observations. Or can it? Consider the problem of trying to measure precisely the temperature of a volume of warm water: If we insert a thermometer into the water, the temperature of the thermometer will change the original temperature of the water.

But it is when we reach the basic constituents of all matter—subatomic particles—that our attempts to observe the physical world most radically alter that world. For to observe that world, we must shoot some kind of radiation (light rays or gamma rays) at it and observe the reflected radiation. But the energy of the radiation always disturbs the subatomic particles, leaving us uncertain about what was there before the observation. In fact, modern physics explicitly holds that on principle it is impossible to observe subatomic particles without disturbing them so much that we cannot be sure where they are or how fast they are moving. Here is how a physics textbook explains the impossibility of observing the subatomic world in a way that would eliminate our uncertainty about that world:

> In Newtonian mechanics, still applicable to the macroscopic world of matter, both the position and velocity of a body are easily calculable; e.g., both the position and the velocity of the earth in its orbit can be known precisely at any instant. Inside the atom this is not possible. We have already learned that electrons orbiting within atoms can absorb light energy in units proportional to the frequency of the light and that in doing so they shift energy levels. Now suppose that we could "see" an electron. You need light to see it, but when you turn on the light to see it, the electron absorbs some of the light energy and instantly moves to another energy level with a different velocity. This is implied in Heisenberg's uncertainty principle: *It is impossible to obtain accurate values for the position and momentum of an electron simultaneously.* In other words, observation causes a reaction on the thing observed. . . . This principle of uncertainty . . . sets fundamental limits upon our ability to describe nature.

QUESTIONS

1. What implications do the Hawthorne experiments and the uncertainty principle have for epistemology?
2. Do the Hawthorne experiments and the uncertainty principle demonstrate that we can never hope to know the world as it really is?

Sources: Augustine Brannigan and William Zwerman, "The Real 'Hawthorne Effect,'" *Society* 38.2 (Jan/Feb 2001): 55–60; Verne H. Booth, *Elements of Physical Science: The Nature of Matter and Energy* (London: Macmillan, 1970), 327–328.

although it may seem to us that they are. For example, when we perceive a tree, we perceive its color, smell, texture, and maybe even its taste. In the fall, we perceive the tree with one color, in the spring another—and it may be one color at dawn and another at noon. Without its leaves, the tree may be odorless; with them, it may be fragrant. What exactly are these qualities—colors, smells, textures, tastes? What we term *color* and *smell*, and so on, are merely powers in the tree that cause these sensations in us. The color and smell are not qualities in the tree itself, but merely ideas it causes in us:

> Qualities thus considered in bodies are, First, such as are utterly inseparable from the body, in what state soever it be; and such as in all the alterations and changes it suffers, all the force can be used upon it, it constantly keeps; and such as sense constantly finds in every particle of matter which has bulk enough to be perceived; and the mind finds inseparable from every particle of matter. . . . Take a grain of wheat, divide it into two parts; each part has still solidity, extension, figure, and mobility: divide it again, and it retains still the same qualities; and so divide it on, till the parts become insensible; they must retain still each of them all those qualities. . . . These I call original or primary qualities of body, which . . . produce simple ideas in us, viz. solidity, extension, figure, motion or rest, and number. . . . Secondly . . . [there are] qualities which in truth are nothing in the objects themselves but power to produce various sensations in us . . . as colours, sounds, tastes, & c. These I call secondary qualities. The ideas of primary qualities of bodies are resemblances of them, and their patterns do really exist in the bodies themselves, but the ideas produced in us by these secondary qualities have no resemblance of them at all. There is nothing like our ideas [of secondary qualities] existing in the bodies themselves. . . . The particular bulk, number, figure, and motion of the parts of fire or snow are really in them,- whether any one's senses perceive them or no: and therefore they may be called real qualities, because they really exist in those bodies. But light, heat, whiteness, or coldness, are no more really in them than sickness or pain is in manna. Take away the sensation of them; let not the eyes see light or colours, nor the ears hear sounds; let the palate not taste, nor the nose smell, and all colours, tastes, odours, and sounds . . . vanish and cease.[21]

Locke claims that the tree has in itself no green color; it has only the power to produce in our senses a "sensation" that we call green. This claim, he thinks, is proved by the fact that a sensation will "vanish and cease" as soon as our senses stop observing. Primary qualities, however, are in bodies whether we are observing them or not; for when we perceive a body it always has primary qualities, and our minds cannot think of a body without primary qualities. Primary qualities, Locke concludes, "really exist in the bodies themselves" and so their ideas in us are "resemblances of them."

So according to Locke we know how things are because our ideas of primary qualities actually resemble the primary qualities of objects in the external world. For example, if we experience the tree as being a certain height, we can trust that idea to represent how the tree really is; if we experience it to have a certain shape, we can trust that idea to represent how the tree really is. Thus, Locke believed, we can come to have true knowledge of the things around us by having sense experiences of their primary qualities, since these sense experiences represent the qualities external entities actually have.

critical thinking

Locke claims that primary qualities must be real, although secondary qualities are not. Do you think Locke provides an adequate argument for this claim?

Critical Realists. During the early part of the twentieth century, a group of philosophers composed a book titled *Essays in Critical Realism.* Their view showed a marked Lockean flavor. Like Locke, the critical realists did not believe that the perception of entities is so direct as to be indistinguishable from the things themselves. It is not the outer object that is present in the consciousness, they argued, but **sense data**. Sense data are the images or sensory impressions—the

21 Ibid., II, viii, 9, 10, 15.

immediate contents of sensory experience—that, according to the critical realists, indicate the presence and nature of perceived objects. Only by inference can we go beyond sense data to the object itself.

Critical realists have accepted much of what Locke claimed. They believe that sense data provide accurate contact with the primary qualities of entities, so these data reveal what the real qualities of objects are and thus what the external world is like. Critical realists believe that three factors are involved in perception: (1) a perceiver, knower, or conscious mind; (2) the entity or object, consisting of primary qualities; and (3) the sense data, which serve as a bridge between the perceiver and the object.

Problems with Locke. But the nagging questions we noted earlier still remain, for Locke as well as for critical realists: First, how do we know that our perceptions—or "sense data"—truly or accurately represent the external world? Locke claims that we know our ideas of primary qualities accurately represent the qualities of external objects. But the fact is that according to Locke we have no direct knowledge of any external objects so we have no direct knowledge of their actual primary qualities. All the information we have about external objects is what our perceptions provide and apart from these perceptions we know nothing about external objects. So there is no way that we can check whether our perceptions are giving us accurate information about external objects, whether that information is about their primary qualities or their secondary qualities.

But there is a more troubling issue. How do we even know that there are external objects? Locke tried to answer this question with the assertion that *something* outside us had to cause them so that we know at least that something is out there. The ideas produced in us are obviously not the external objects themselves. Nevertheless, Locke claims, we know that *something out there must have caused these ideas* to arise in us. The production of ideas in us, whether of primary or secondary qualities, claimed Locke, is evidence that there are things outside us that are producing these ideas in us:

> When our senses do actually convey into our understandings any idea, we cannot but be satisfied that there doth something *at that time* really exist without [outside] us, which doth affect our senses, and by them give notice of itself to our apprehensive faculties, and actually produce that idea which we then perceive; and we cannot so far distrust their testimony, as to doubt that such *collections* of simple ideas as we have observed by our senses to be united together, do really exist together.[22]

QUICK REVIEW
Critics of Locke say we have no way of knowing whether our experiences are accurate copies of objects outside us, or even whether objects exist outside us.

But how can Locke be sure of any of this? If all we know are the ideas in us, how can Locke, or anyone else, know that there are things outside us that are causing these ideas? How can we know that, as he says, "there doth something *at that time* really exist without us, which doth affect our senses"?

In Locke's own time other empiricists objected that he could not account for the accuracy and origin of our ideas. The foremost challenge was presented by the Irish bishop George Berkeley, who we met in Chapter 3. There we were interested in Berkeley's idealism—that is, his metaphysical view of what reality is. Here, we will be interested in his views on knowledge (i.e., what we can *know* about reality). The two are, as we will see, related.

22 Ibid., 1–2.

 critical thinking

Berkeley assumes that because ideas exist, the minds that hold those ideas must also exist. Does this assumption hold up if we accept his view that we should not assume that something exists if it is not perceived?

 To read more of Berkeley's works, go to CourseMate for this text and browse by chapter or philosopher.

QUICK REVIEW
Berkeley argued that Locke's primary qualities are as mind-dependent as Locke had claimed secondary qualities are.

QUICK REVIEW
Berkeley argued that Locke was wrong to claim that the ideas of primary qualities are accurate copies of the qualities of external material bodies. Since an idea can only be like another idea, our ideas of primary qualities must be copies of other ideas (i.e., primary qualities must be ideas). Since ideas can exist only in the mind, primary qualities can exist only in the mind and so are not qualities of external material bodies.

Berkeley and Subjectivism

George Berkeley agreed with Locke that all our ideas originate in sensory experience. Although he also accepted Locke's argument that secondary qualities are **subjective**, Berkeley insisted that Locke's primary qualities were also subjective (i.e., they are mind-dependent and so can exist only in the mind). In *A Treatise Concerning the Principles of Human Knowledge*, Berkeley says the following:

> They who assert that figure, motion, and the rest of the primary or original qualities do exist without mind in unthinking [material] substances, do at the same time acknowledge that colors, sounds, heat, cold and such like secondary qualities, do not; which they tell us are sensations, existing in the mind alone. . . . Now if it be certain that those original [primary] qualities are inseparably united with [the] other sensible [secondary] qualities, and not, even in thought, capable of being abstracted [separated] from them, it plainly follows they exist only in the mind [just like the secondary qualities]. But I desire anyone to reflect, and try whether he can, by any abstraction of thought conceive the extension and motion of a body without all other sensible [secondary] qualities. For my own part, I see evidently that it is not in my power to frame an idea of a body extended and moving but I must . . . give it some color or sensible [secondary] quality, which is acknowledged to exist only in the mind. In short, extension, figure and motion, abstracted from all other [secondary] qualities, are inconceivable. Where therefore the other sensible [secondary] qualities are, there must these [primary qualities] be also, to wit, in the mind and nowhere else. I shall farther add, that, after the same manner as modern philosophers prove certain sensible qualities to have no existence in Matter, or without the mind, the same thing may be likewise proved of all other sensible qualities whatsoever. Thus, for instance, it is said that heat and cold are affections only of the mind, and not at all patterns of real beings, existing in the corporeal substances which excite them, for that the same body which appears cold to one hand seems warm to another. Now, why may we not as well argue that figure and extension are not patterns or resemblances of qualities existing in Matter, because to the same eye at different stations, or eyes of a different texture at the same station, they appear various, and cannot therefore be the images of anything settled and determinate without the mind? . . . In short, let any one consider those arguments which are thought manifestly to prove that colors and taste exist only in the mind, and he shall find they may with equal force be brought to prove the same thing of extension, figure, and motion.[23]

In other words, if heat or cold is a secondary quality and exists only in the mind, as Locke insists, then primary qualities like figure and extension also exist only in the mind, since figure and extension are inseparable from the secondary qualities. Berkeley also points out that bodies do not retain their primary qualities unchanged any more than they retain their secondary qualities. For example, the shape of a coin appears round from one angle and flat from another. Why? Because, says Berkeley, all qualities, including primary qualities, are dependent on us, so as we change our perspective, so do the primary qualities of the object. Primary qualities are as mind-dependent as secondary qualities.

But Berkeley attacked more than Locke's claim that primary qualities exist in external objects. Berkeley also attacked Locke's fundamental assumption that our ideas of primary qualities can accurately represent the primary qualities of external

23 George Berkeley, *A Treatise Concerning the Principles of Human Knowledge*, vol. 1, *The Works of George Berkeley*, ed. George Sampson (London: George Bell & Sons, 1897), 183–184.

objects, i.e., that primary qualities give us knowledge about external objects. Berkeley argued that on principle, our ideas cannot represent any external reality:

> [But] what do we perceive besides our own ideas or sensations? And is it not plainly repugnant that any one of these, or any combination of them, should exist unperceived? . . . The sensible qualities are color, figure, motion, smell, taste, etc., i.e. the ideas perceived by sense. Now, for an idea to exist in an unperceiving [material] thing is a manifest contradiction, for to have an idea is . . . [the same] as to perceive; that therefore wherein color, figure, and the like qualities exist must perceive them [i.e., such qualities must exist in a mind] . . . But, say you, though the ideas themselves do not exist without the mind, yet there may be things like them, whereof they are copies or resemblances, which things exist without the mind in an unthinking [material] substance. I answer, an idea can be like nothing but an idea; a color or figure can be like nothing but another color or figure. If we look but never so little into our thoughts, we shall find it impossible for us to conceive a likeness except only between our ideas. Again, I ask whether those supposed originals or external things, of which our ideas are the pictures or representations, be themselves perceivable or no? If they are, then they are ideas and we have gained our point [for what is perceived has to be an idea]; but if you say they are not, I appeal to any one whether it be sense to assert a color is like something which is invisible; [or whether] hard or soft, [can be] like something which is intangible; and so of the rest.

Berkeley is making two points here. First, ideas obviously can only exist in a mind. But any qualities we perceive—colors, shapes, smells, solidity—are ideas. So all qualities, including primary qualities, can only exist in a mind. Secondly, an idea can only be similar to another idea. Ideas, then, can be accurate copies only of other ideas. So if our ideas of primary qualities are accurate copies of primary qualities, those primary qualities must be ideas. And since ideas can only exist in a mind, primary qualities must exist in the mind. Our ideas, then, cannot represent the primary qualities of external objects outside the mind. The only thing our ideas can accurately represent are other ideas—and such ideas, like all ideas, must exist in the mind.

In a final blow to Locke's philosophy, Berkeley struck at the key weakness in Locke's view: His assertion that we know that there are external objects because they must cause our sensations:

QUICK REVIEW
Berkeley argued Locke was wrong to claim that we know there are external objects because they must cause our sensations. We have no access to such objects, Berkeley argued, and just as dreams are not caused by external objects, our perceptions need not be caused by external objects.

> But, though it were possible that solid, figured, movable substances may exist without the mind, corresponding to the ideas we have of bodies, yet how is it possible for us to know this? Either we must know it by sense or by reason. As for our senses, by them we have the knowledge only of our sensations [and] ideas, . . . but they do not inform us that things exist without the mind . . . like to those which are perceived. . . . [So] if we have any knowledge at all of external things, it must be by reason, inferring their existence from what is immediately perceived by sense. But . . . it is granted on all hands (and what happens in dreams . . . puts it beyond dispute) that it is possible we might be affected with all the ideas we have now, though there were no bodies existing without resembling them.[24]

Locke's assumption that our sensations had to be caused by external objects, was unjustified, Berkeley claimed. Just as our dreams do not need to be caused by external objects, so too the sensations we have need not be caused by anything at

24 Ibid., 185.

all. And since we perceive only the sensations in our minds and know nothing beyond our sensations, we cannot use our senses to check whether there are external objects that cause our sensations.

QUICK REVIEW
Both primary and secondary qualities, Berkeley argued, are sensations in us and so are mind-dependent. Besides minds and their sensations and ideas, nothing exists.

As we noted in the last chapter, Berkeley drew from these considerations about what we can know, the metaphysical conclusion that the reality we perceive consists of ideas in our minds. Thus, whereas Locke, as we saw, took the second of the two responses to the objection that our experiences can differ from the way things actually are, Berkeley took the first response. In other words, Locke acknowledged that there is a difference between our experiences of things and things themselves, and as we saw, that opened the door to the objection that we can never know whether our experience is an accurate representation of external objects. Berkeley, on the other hand, kept the door to that objection firmly shut by claiming that there is no difference between our experience and the things we experience. The things we experience are identical to the ideas we have in the mind. There are no objects external to the mind.

Berkeley's thinking could have become **solipsism**, the position that only I exist and that everything and everyone else is just an idea in my subjective consciousness, so that what is real is whatever seems real to me in my own private world of ideas. To avoid such excesses, Berkeley relied on the view that there is an outside source that maintains and is responsible for our ideas about the world around us: God. Things in our world continue to exist for us and others even when I do not perceive them, because God continues to perceive them and makes them available to me when I look around. God always has the world—a world composed of ideas, of course—"in mind," and what is real is the world in God's mind, not just what seems real to me. Thus God guarantees the objectivity of our knowledge by guaranteeing a stable world that we all perceive in the same way and that is the ultimate criterion of reality and of true knowledge of reality.

QUICK REVIEW
The claim that there is no world beyond my sensations could lead to solipsism, the view that nothing else exists besides my own mind and its contents. Berkeley avoided solipsism by saying that God exists and that He produces the sensations in my mind and maintains them even when I do not perceive them.

But given Berkeley's claims, the existence of God creates a major problem for him: How can he know that God exists? If we cannot know that any external material objects exist, how can he know that some external nonmaterial being like God exists? In one of his dialogues between Hylas (substitute "Locke") and Philonus (substitute "Berkeley"), Berkeley anticipates just such an objection:

HYLAS: Answer me, Philonus. Are all our ideas perfectly inert beings? Or have they any agency included in them?

PHILONUS: They are altogether passive and inert.

HYLAS: And is not God an agent, a being purely active?

PHILONUS: I acknowledge it.

HYLAS: No idea therefore can be like unto, or represent, the nature of God.

PHILONUS: It cannot.

HYLAS: Since therefore you have no idea of the mind of God, how can you conceive it possible that things should exist in His mind? . . . You admit . . . that there is a spiritual Substance, although you have no idea of it; while you deny there can be such a thing as material Substance, because you have no notion or idea of it. Is this fair dealing? To act consistently, you must either admit Matter or reject Spirit.[25]

25 George Berkeley, *Three Dialogues Between Hylas and Philonus*, vol. 1, *The Works of George Berkeley*, ed. George Sampson (London: George Bell & Sons, 1897), 364–365.

"Admit Matter or reject Spirit" was something Berkeley seemed unwilling to do. Berkeley was a Christian minister, an Anglican bishop, in fact. So his attack on the idea of an external material reality was motivated by his desire to rid the world of materialism because he thought that materialism was the ultimate source of atheism and the greatest obstacle to religion. If he could convince the world that there is no material reality—that everything is spiritual, either idea or mind—then perhaps the world would no longer be misled by materialism and would turn to God. That desire prompted the ingenious efforts that resulted in what he called his philosophy of "immaterialism," a philosophy that relied on the theory that all we know are ideas in our mind, and so we have no knowledge of external material objects and so cannot claim they exist. But as "Hylas" suggests in the earlier passage, if he carried his "immaterialism" to its logical conclusion, then he would have to admit that his views concerning knowledge left him no reason to think God exists. Berkeley was unwilling to take that step, and so he claimed that the orderliness of some of his ideas gave him knowledge of a God who produces that order. But the view that we know only what is in our minds had logically led him to conclude that we have no knowledge of any "external material objects" so we cannot claim they exist; that same view should, logically, have led him to conclude that since we know only the ideas in our mind, we have no knowledge of any external independent "God," and so we cannot claim God exists.

QUICK REVIEW
Critics of Berkeley say that he has no more grounds for claiming that God exists outside our minds than he has for claiming that material objects exist outside the mind. Because he rejects material objects, he should reject God or accept both.

In short, Berkeley seems to have used the theory of knowledge we now call empiricism—the view that our only source of knowledge are the sense experiences we have—to disprove what he disbelieved to begin with, but then he recoiled from empiricism when it threatened his deepest convictions. Nevertheless, Berkeley remains a critical link in understanding the dialectical development of empiricism, which the Scottish philosopher David Hume, unlike Berkeley, was willing to extend to its logical limits.

Hume and Skepticism

To read more of Hume's works, go to CourseMate for this text and browse by chapter or philosopher.

It's fair to say that David Hume pushed Locke's and Berkeley's empiricism to a thorough skepticism—that is, to a denial of the possibility that we can have certain knowledge about much of what we all take for granted. How Hume came to his skeptical conclusions is a long and complex affair, which we can only sketch here. (For a fuller discussion of Hume, see the Historical Showcase at the end of this chapter.)

Hume asserts that all the contents of the mind can be reduced to those given by the senses and experience. He calls these *perceptions.* In Hume's view, perceptions take two forms, what he terms *impressions* and *ideas.* The distinction between them and how they relate to knowing are vital to understanding Humean thought. In *An Enquiry Concerning Human Understanding,* Hume explains what he means by ideas and impressions:

> Here, therefore, we may divide all the perceptions of the mind into two classes or species, which are distinguished by their different degrees of force and vivacity. The less forcible and lively are commonly denominated *Thoughts* or *Ideas.* The other species want a name in our language, and in most others; I suppose, because it was not requisite for any, but philosophical purposes, to rank them under a general term or appellation. Let us therefore use a little freedom, and call them *Impressions*; employing that word in a sense somewhat different from the usual. By the term *impression,* then, I mean all our more lively perceptions,

> when we hear, or see, or feel, or love, or hate, or desire, or will. And impressions are distinguished from ideas, which are the less lively perceptions of which we are conscious, when we reflect on any of those sensations or movements above mentioned.[26]

QUICK REVIEW
Hume accepted Berkeley's view that all we experience are our own sensations and ideas, which he called "impressions." Because all our knowledge is derived from sense impressions, he argued that if an idea is not derived from a sense impression, it is meaningless or nonexistent.

Thus, those impressions we get directly from the senses are quite vivid—for example, those of a color we see or an emotion we feel. However, their vividness declines when we subsequently reflect upon them or have ideas about them. The pain you feel when you hammer your thumb is an impression; the memory of what you felt is an idea. Every idea we have in our heads, Hume claimed, has to come from some earlier sense impression. What about ideas we have of things we've never perceived with our senses, such as a golden mountain or a pink elephant? Hume answers that in such cases our imagination combines impressions that were earlier acquired from our senses: "When we think of a golden mountain, we only join two consistent ideas, *gold* and *mountain*, with which we were formerly acquainted." Therefore, the senses are the source of all our knowledge:

> It seems a proposition, which will not admit of much dispute, that all our ideas are nothing but copies of our impressions, or, in other words, that it is impossible for us to think of anything, which we have not antecedently felt, either by our external or internal senses.

From this insight, Hume drew the portentous conclusion that there can be no genuine knowledge without corresponding sense impressions. This is a crucial point for Hume. He claims that all of our knowledge must be derived from impressions that come either from our outer senses (sight, hearing, touch, taste, smell) or from our inner senses (our inner feelings, such as anger, sorrow, pain). Consequently, we cannot have genuine knowledge of a thing unless we can point to the impression from which the idea of that thing is derived. As he puts the point:

> When we entertain . . . any suspicion that a philosophical term is employed without any meaning or idea (as is but too frequent), we need but enquire, from what impression is that supposed idea derived? And if it be impossible to assign any, this will serve to confirm our suspicion [that the term has no meaning].[27]

QUICK REVIEW
Because the idea of causal connection is not derived from any sense impression, it does not exist in the real world; causality is nothing more than the habitual expectation that events in the future will be followed by the same kind of events that followed them in the past. This habitual expectation is formed by repeatedly seeing the same sequence of events.

Causality as Habit. Hume used this principle—that we can have knowledge only if we can point to a sense impression from which it is derived—to prove that many of our common "ideas" are meaningless. One particular idea that he argues is meaningless is our common idea of **causality**—our idea that when one object causes another object to do something, there is some kind of real connection between them, some kind of "power" or force by which the cause really exerts its causality on its effect. Hume asks us to look carefully at any case of one object causing another object to do something. Take, for example, a rapidly moving billiard ball that strikes a second billiard ball so that the second ball moves rapidly away. No matter how hard we look, he says, all we will see is one ball moving quickly, then touching the second ball, and then the second ball moving quickly. We see nothing more: We see no connection between the objects; we see no power or force going from one to

26 David Hume, *An Enquiry Concerning Human Understanding*, ed. L. A. Selby-Bigge (Oxford: Clarendon, 1894), 18.
27 Ibid., sec. 2, para. 17.

the other. We see one event followed by another event but see no causality anywhere between them:

> To be fully acquainted, therefore, with the idea of [causal] power or necessary [causal] connection, let us examine its impression; and in order to find the impression with greater certainty, let us search for it in all the sources, from which it may possibly be derived. . . . When we look about us towards external objects, and consider the operation of causes, we are never able, in a single instance, to discover any power or necessary connection; any quality, which binds the effect to the cause, and renders the one an infallible consequence of the other. We only find, that the one does actually, in fact, follow the other. The impulse of one billiard-ball is attended with motion in the second. This is the whole that appears to the outward senses. . . . Consequently, there is not, in any single, particular instance of cause and effect, anything which can suggest the idea of power or necessary connection. . . . And as we can have no idea of any thing which never appeared to our outward sense or inward sentiment, the necessary conclusion seems to be that we have no idea of [any causal] connection or [causal] power at all, and that these words are absolutely without any meaning when employed either in philosophical reasonings or common life.[28]

Because we have no impression of causality, there is no such thing as causality outside of us, no real connection between cause and effect. Events simply succeed each other. What, then, is the source of our feeling that when one object strikes another there is some force or power that "makes" or "forces" the second to move? Habit. Hume argues that when we repeatedly see an event of one kind followed by an event of another kind, the mind becomes habituated to the sequence and comes to expect or believe that events of the first kind will always be followed by events of the second kind. For example, if over and over we see that when one moving object touches another, the second object starts moving, the mind becomes habituated to the sequence. So, when it again sees one moving object touch another, it has a feeling of expectancy that the second object will now start to move. There is nothing more to causality than this habituated feeling or expectation in us that events of the first kind will be followed by events of the second kind. This feeling in us is created by repeated past experience of seeing events of the first kind always followed by events of the second kind. The idea that there is really any causal power going from one event to the other is "meaningless."

QUICK REVIEW
Because past experience is the only basis for thinking the future will be like the past, and we can rely on past experience only if the future will be like the past, there is no noncircular way of showing that we are justified in expecting that the future will be like the past.

Not only is causality nothing more than a feeling of expectation in our minds, even this expectation is unjustified. Hume points out that we have no good reason to expect that future events will follow each other like the past events we experienced. It is true that in the past when one moving object touched another, the second started to move. But why should we expect the future to be like the past? The only reason why we think that the future will be like the past is because in the past, the future has always been like the past. But this, Hume points out, is circular reasoning! Just because in our *past* the future resembled the past, this *past experience* cannot show that the *future* will continue to resemble the past. To think otherwise is to use the past as the basis for predicting the future, when we don't know whether we can rely on the past to predict the future. So, without circular reasoning we have no way of justifying our expectation that the future will be like the past. Not only is causality nothing more than an expectation in our mind, but this expectation itself is unjustified.

---

28 Ibid., sec. 7, part 1, para. 50.

thinking critically • Inductive Generalizations

The problem regarding causal reasoning that Hume is pointing to is actually a special instance of a more general problem called the "Problem of Induction." To understand the general problem, it helps to have a good understanding first of what an "inductive generalization" is.

QUICK REVIEW
Inductive generalizations are probable arguments whose premises indicate that something is true of a limited sample, and whose conclusion claims that the same is true of the whole population.

An inductive generalization is a probable argument that moves from premises about what is true in *some* cases to a conclusion about what probably will be true in *all* similar cases. The limited group of cases in the premises is called the "sample," and the entire group of cases in the conclusion is called the "population." Here's a simple one-premise example:

(1) The 1,500 Toyotas that readers of *Consumer Reports* have owned were very reliable.
(2) So probably all Toyotas will be very reliable.

Here the *sample* consists of the 1,500 Toyotas owned by readers of *Consumer Reports*, and the *population* consists of all Toyotas.

The premises of an inductive generalization may contain explicit statistics about the sample. The argument will then apply the statistics about the sample in the premises to the whole population in the conclusion. For example:

(1) 90 percent of the 1,500 Toyotas that readers of *Consumer Reports* have owned were very reliable.
(2) So probably 90 percent of all Toyotas will be very reliable.

Notice that while the first example here contains no explicit statistics, it *assumes* that we are talking about 100 percent of the sample and 100 percent of the population:

(1) [100 percent of] The 1,500 Toyotas that readers of *Consumer Reports* have owned were very reliable.
(2) So probably [100 percent of] all Toyotas will be very reliable.

QUICK REVIEW
The strength of an inductive generalization depends on the size of the sample (the larger the sample, the stronger the argument), and on how representative it is (to what extent the characteristics of the sample match the relevant characteristics of the whole population).

Like all probable arguments, an inductive generalization is a strong argument if its premises make the conclusion very probable, and weak if they do not. So how do you figure out the strength of an inductive generalization? The strength of an inductive generalization depends on two factors: *how large* the sample is, and *how representative* the sample is:

(a) All other things being equal, the larger the sample is, the stronger the argument will be. (However, if the members of the population are extremely similar to each other—like the virtually identical bolts made by a factory machine—a very small sample can provide a strong argument.)

(b) The more representative the sample is, the stronger the argument. A sample is representative to the extent that its characteristics match the relevant characteristics of the whole population. (For example, if one third of the population has relevant characteristic X, then one third of the sample should have characteristic X.) A relevant characteristic is one that could affect the feature that is being generalized.

QUICK REVIEW
The form of an inductive generalization is: (1) N percent of the A's in a group are F; (2) The group of A's is a large and representative sample of A's; therefore (3) probably N percent of all A's are F.

An inductive generalization always assumes (or explicitly indicates) that its sample is appropriately large and representative. We can summarize all this by saying that if all the premises and assumptions of an inductive generalization are made explicit, it will have the following form:

(1) N percent of the A's in a group are F.
(2) The group of A's is a large and representative sample of A's.
(3) So probably N percent of all A's are F.

Here N is a numerical percent (which is often omitted), A's are the members of the population and the sample, and F is the feature or features being generalized.

We obviously make inductive generalizations all the time. But our everyday generalizations usually don't mention percentages and don't provide much information about how large or representative our sample is, and often they don't even mention that the conclusion is only probable. We might say, for example, "The three Toyota Corollas I've owned turned out to be pretty reliable, so I think all Toyota Corollas are going to be reliable," or "All five of my Chinese friends are smart and study a lot, so I think all Chinese must be like that." If we assume that one Toyota Corolla is pretty much identical to another in all the relevant characteristics, then our generalization about Toyotas might be a strong one, although a sample of three is very small. But Chinese, like any other group of people, differ from each other in numerous ways that are relevant to how smart and studious a person is. So generalizing from a sample of five relies on a sample that is neither large enough nor representative. When we argue from a sample that's too small, we make a "hasty generalization," and if our sample is not representative, we say it is "biased." The generalization involving my Chinese friends commits the fallacy of being a hasty generalization, and it uses a biased sample.

Now that you understand how inductive generalizations work (and how to evaluate the strength of an inductive generalization), we can return to the "problem of induction." The problem of induction is this: How do we know that what we found to be true of a sample in the past will be true of all similar items in the future? What justifies this move from some past observations to all future observations? Notice that the problem of induction has two parts: (1) what justifies an inference from *some* to *all*, and (2) what justifies an inference from *past* to *future*? Both parts of the problem of induction question the fact that the conclusions of inductive generalizations move beyond the evidence provided by its premises.

Hume asked what justifies our attempts to generalize from the *causes* we observed in the past, to a conclusion about all similar *causes* in the future. But as our discussion of inductive generalization should make clear, causes are just one of an infinite range of things we can generalize about. So the problem to which Hume drew our attention is not just about causes. It is a problem that afflicts all inductive generalizations.

QUICK REVIEW
Hume's criticism of causal reasoning applies to all inductive generalizations and is now called "The Problem of Induction" which asks: What justification do we have for inferring that what was true of a sample in the past will be true of a whole population in the future? Arguing that since inductive generalization has been successful in the past it will be successful in the future is itself an inductive generalization and so assumes that inductive generalization is justified, which is what must be proved.

The problem of induction can't be solved by providing standards for good inductive generalizations. As our earlier discussion of inductive generalization shows, we have such standards. For example, in an inductive generalization, the sample must be large and representative. But the problem of induction generalization remains: How do we know that what was true of a large and representative sample of things in the past will be true of all similar things tomorrow?

You might think that one way to argue that we can rely on inductive generalization is by pointing to how successful it is: It's justified because it works! Inductive generalization successfully shows us what we have to do to boil water, to bake a cake, to fix a car, to win a game, to cure a headache, to go to the moon, to send a rocket to Mars. Since it's been so successful, it must be reliable. But there's a problem here: The argument assumes what it is supposed to prove. The argument is saying that because inductive generalization has been so successful in the past, we know it will be successful in the future. But this assumes that what has been true in the past will be true in the future; yet this assumption is what has to be proved.

Or you might want to argue that we can rely on inductive generalization because we know that nature is uniform and that the world works in accordance with regular patterns. So we know that a pattern we observed in nature yesterday is the one we will see in nature in the future. But this argument again assumes what it is supposed to prove. It says that since nature has been uniform in the past, it will be uniform in the future. So it assumes that what has been true in the past will be true in the future, which again is the assumption that must be proved.

You might even be tempted to say that we should just stop making inductive generalizations if we don't know whether they can be justified. But we can't stop. You can prove this to yourself by trying to go through a single waking day—even a single hour—without doing or believing something that is based on an inductive generalization. You won't succeed. All your experience lies in the past, and you have to rely on that past experience as you plan and move into your future. So you are forced to continuously generalize from what you've experienced in the past to what you will experience in your future. Inductive generalization is inescapable. It is also too useful to give up. Inductive generalization amplifies and expands our knowledge in a remarkable way. It takes the relatively few things we've experienced in the relatively few places we've seen in the past and extends what we've experienced out to an entire world. In fact, if you are an astronomer or cosmologist, inductive generalization lets you take what you and others have discovered on the relatively small patch of this planet that we inhabit, and extend it out not just to a whole planet, but to the entire universe. In view of all that we would have to give up, how can we possibly stop using inductive generalizations?

Is there an answer, then, to the problem of induction? To this day, no one has come up with an answer that has persuaded everyone. Nevertheless, when we discuss Immanuel Kant in the next section, we will see an answer that has persuaded at least some philosophers.

Can We Know an External World Exists? Hume's views suggested another disturbing possibility: Perhaps the external world does not exist at all. True, we assume there is an external, regular, and predictable world outside us. But how can we know for sure that there is a world beyond our sense impressions when all we know are our own impressions? We have no way of peering beyond these impressions, no way of going beyond these impressions to see whether they are connected to an external world. Because we can know only what our sense impressions convey to us, and because our sense impressions provide no basis for saying there is anything beyond them, we cannot say an external world exists:

> **QUICK REVIEW**
> Because we have no access to an external world beyond our sense impressions, we have no justification for believing that any external world exists beyond our impressions and ideas.

> Almost before the use of reason, we always suppose an external universe, which depends not on our perception, but would exist, though we and every sensible creature were absent or annihilated. . . . [But] by what argument can it be proved, that the perceptions of the mind must be caused by external objects, entirely different from them, though resembling them (if that be possible) . . . ? It is a question of fact, whether the perceptions of the senses be produced by external objects, resembling them: how shall this question be determined? By experience surely; as all other questions of a like nature. But here experience is, and must be entirely silent. The mind has never anything present to it but the perceptions, and cannot possibly reach any experience of their connection with objects. The supposition of such a connection is, therefore, without any foundation in reasoning. . . . The mind has never anything present to it but [its] perceptions, and cannot possibly reach [beyond them to] any experience of their connection with [external] objects. The supposition of such a connection is, therefore, without any foundation in reasoning.[29]

29 Ibid., sec. 12, part 1, paras. 118 and 119.

Hume concedes that we always act *as if* a real external world of things exists. The apparent constancy in things leads us to believe that they have an independent existence external to us. But the assumption that our impressions are connected with independent external things lacks any justification. There is no way for the mind to reach beyond its impressions to an external world.

This discussion may resemble Berkeley's doctrine that to be is to be perceived. But recall that Berkeley has a God who sustains things in a continued existence when no person is perceiving them. Hume, who is perhaps more consistent, does not rely on any such theological prop. Indeed, how could he? After all, we prove that God exists by showing that the things around us had to be caused by God. But Hume has shown that causality is just a figment in our minds: There is no real causality in the things around us. So, we cannot say that the things around us really are caused by anything. Causality is just in the mind. Hume applies the doctrine of empiricism as rigorously as he can, regardless of its implications.

Hume's theory ends in skepticism—that is, Hume concludes that we can never know whether or not any of our ideas about the external world are accurate, or even whether there is an external world. We cannot know whether anything really causes anything else to happen. We cannot know whether there is a God. Perhaps all this was inevitable. Descartes had earlier pointed out that our sensations or ideas may or may not correspond to the world outside the mind. These sensations or ideas may be generated by illusions, by our own dreams or hallucinations, or even by an evil, all-powerful being that causes these sensations or ideas to form in our minds. This possibility—that the sensations or ideas within us might not represent the real world outside—led Descartes to doubt everything. But he was able to banish his doubts by reasoning that God would not lead us to think a world outside existed unless such a world really did exist.

Hume also accepted Descartes' basic premise: It is possible that the ideas in our minds may not correspond to a reality outside the mind. But unlike Descartes, Locke, or Berkeley, Hume did not rely on God to save him from skepticism. With cold logic, Hume argued that even our ideas about God may not correspond to reality. Indeed, Hume claimed, we are acquainted only with the impressions and ideas in our minds and have no access to any other reality. We have no way of knowing that the impressions and ideas in our minds represent any reality outside the mind.

Many contemporary philosophers are inclined to agree with Hume. For example, Barry Stroud argues that we have to accept Descartes' claim that because we might be dreaming, the sensations and thoughts in our minds might not correspond to any reality outside the mind. But once we accept the possibility that the sensations and thoughts within us might not represent a real world outside or independent of the mind, Humean skepticism is inevitable. We have no way of checking to see what the real world might be like except by using the sensations and thoughts within us. Real knowledge of the world is forever lost to us:

> If we are in the predicament Descartes finds himself in at the end of his *First Meditation* we cannot tell by means of the senses whether we are dreaming or not; all the sensory experiences we are having are compatible with our merely dreaming of a world around us while that world is in fact very different from the way we take it to be. Our knowledge is in that way confined to our sensory experiences. There seems to be no way of going beyond them to know that the world around us really is this way rather than that. . . .
>
> What *can* we know in such a predicament? We can perhaps know what sensory experiences we are having, or how things seem to us to be. At least that much of our knowledge will not be threatened by the kind of attack Descartes makes on our knowledge of the world beyond our experiences. What we can know turns

QUICK REVIEW
Contemporary philosophers such as Barry Stroud agree with Hume's view that we have no way of knowing whether there is any external world beyond our sensory experiences.

out to be a great deal less than we thought we knew before engaging in that assessment of our knowledge. Our position is much more restricted, much poorer, than we had originally supposed. We are confined at best to what Descartes calls "ideas" of things around us, representations of things or states of affairs which, for all we can know, might or might not have something corresponding to them in reality. We are in a sense imprisoned within those representations, at least with respect to our knowledge. Any attempt to go beyond them to try and tell whether the world really is as they represent it to be can yield only more representations, more deliverances of sense experience which themselves are compatible with reality's being very different from the way we take it to be on the basis of our sensory experiences. . . .

critical thinking

Stroud claims that all our sensory experiences are compatible with our merely dreaming. Is this true?

We would be in the position of someone waking up to find himself locked in a room full of television sets and trying to find out what is going on in the world outside. For all he can know, whatever is producing the patterns he can see on the screens in front of him might be something other than well-functioning cameras directed on to the passing show outside the room. The victim might switch on more of the sets in the room to try to get more information, and he might find that some of the sets show events exactly similar or coherently related to those already visible on the screens he can see. But all those pictures will be no help to him without some independent information, some knowledge that does not come to him from the pictures themselves, about how the pictures he does see before him are connected with what is going on outside the room. The problem of the external world is the problem of finding out, or knowing how we could find out, about the world around us if we were in that sort of predicament. It is perhaps enough simply to put the problem this way to convince us that it can never be given a satisfactory solution.[30]

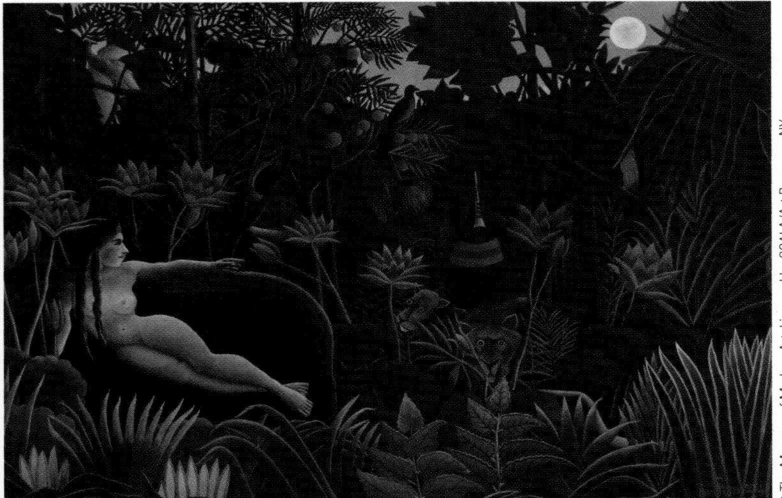

© The Museum of Modern Art, Licensed by SCALA/Art Resource, NY

***The Dream,* Henri** Rousseau. "All the sensory experiences we are having are compatible with our merely dreaming of a world around us while that world is in fact very different from the way we take it to be."

We began this chapter with a discussion of the controversy over the theory of recovered memories. Does empiricism shed any light on that controversy? Clearly, the empiricist would deny the rationalist view that when recovered memories are clear and distinct, they must be true. An empiricist such as Locke would instead say that ideas provide true knowledge only when they are based on sense experience. Hume would agree, holding that ideas should never be accepted as true unless they can be shown to have been "derived" from some "sense impression." Recovered memories, then, should not be accepted unless they can be corroborated with some kind of independent sense experience. A skeptic in the spirit of Hume might go further and hold that, just as we must remain skeptical about our ordinary perceptions, so too must we remain skeptical about the truth of recovered memories. "The mind," Hume suggested, "is a kind of theater, where several perceptions successively make their appearance, pass, re-pass, glide away, and mingle in an infinite variety of postures and situations." When memories are "recovered" in therapy, the Humean

30 Barry Stroud, *The Significance of Philosophical Skepticism* (Oxford: Clarendon, 1984), 31–33.

skeptic might suggest, they simply become one more element in this jumble of ideas in the mind. It is no more possible to know whether one of them is true than it is to establish that any of our other ideas correspond to an independent reality.

But not all philosophers have accepted Hume's skepticism. In fact, it was precisely to resolve this skepticism that in the eighteenth century Immanuel Kant turned his attention to questions about the nature of knowledge. His investigations eventually resulted in a unique blend of empiricism and rationalism called *transcendental idealism.* This new approach to knowledge, Kant claimed, is the only way of resolving the skepticism of the rationalists and empiricists.

QUESTIONS

1. Do you agree with Locke's view that we can have no ideas without first having sensory experiences?
2. Does Berkeley's idealism deny an objective reality?
3. What evidence would you give to prove that while you were sleeping, a physical reality outside you persisted?
4. Explain why Hume concludes that there's no rational justification for saying that anything has a continued and independent existence outside us.
5. Describe what you consider to be the fundamental epistemological difference between Hume and Berkeley.
6. Justify the assertion that Hume pushed Locke's empiricism to its logical conclusion.
7. Do you see any way of showing that Barry Stroud is wrong when he says that we are like "someone waking up to find himself locked in a room full of television sets and trying to find out what is going on in the world outside"? Do you think there is any way of finding out what is "going on in the world outside" your mind?

PHILOSOPHY AT THE MOVIES

Watch *Contact* (1997) in which Dr. Ellie Arroway, a scientist who conducts research for SETI (Search for Extra Terrestrial Intelligence) by scanning outer space with a radio telescope, one day discovers a radio signal from distant intelligent beings that provides plans for a machine to journey to their part of the universe, a journey Ellie wants to undertake. Is Ellie an empiricist at the beginning of this movie? At the end? How do Ellie's views on knowledge affect the beliefs she is willing to accept? Does the movie suggest any reasons why Ellie's views on knowledge may be wrong?

5.4 Kant: Does the Knowing Mind Shape the World?

The question that concerned the German philosopher Immanuel Kant (1724–1804) was how to deal with Hume's wholesale skepticism. He sensed that philosophy had reached a pivotal point. The rationalists had claimed that the mind, by itself, is a source of knowledge. The empiricists replied that the senses are the only valid sources of knowledge, and Hume went on to argue that the senses provide no evidence for the causal laws of science. Kant thought he could show that although all our knowledge of the world begins with our senses as the empiricists claimed, the mind by itself (as rationalists insisted) can provide us with knowledge of the laws of science. In showing this, Kant fashioned a new view of knowledge that claims that both reason and the senses contribute to our knowledge of the world.

QUICK REVIEW
Kant tried to show that, as empiricists claimed, our knowledge begins with the senses, but as rationalists claimed, the mind is a source of knowledge of universal laws.

Kant's new view, now called **transcendental idealism**, holds that the world that appears to be around us is a world that our mind constructs by arranging the sensations that come from the senses into whatever structures or patterns the mind itself provides. In other words, the senses are the source of the sensations—the colors, sounds, smells—that the mind arranges into the world we experience, while the way those sensations are arranged—their structure—comes from the mind. Because the mind arranges everything we perceive according to its own rational rules or laws, the mind can know these laws that govern everything we perceive. Although these ideas of Kant are difficult to comprehend, their originality and depth well repay the effort it takes to understand them.

Hume's Challenge

In *The Critique of Pure Reason*, his most important work, Kant accepted Hume's view that experience is the only basis for real knowledge. Nevertheless, he added, reason or the mind also contributes something to our knowledge:

> [W]e have no knowledge antecedent to experience, and with experience all our knowledge begins. But though all our knowledge begins with experience, it does not follow that it all arises out of experience. For it may well be that even our empirical knowledge is made up of what we receive through [sense] impressions and of what our own faculty of knowledge . . . supplies from itself.[31]

QUICK REVIEW
Kant argued that when the mind organizes its sense impressions into the world we know, it inserts rational structures into this world and these structures are universal laws that the mind can know because the mind put these structures into the world.

Kant pointed out that although our senses reveal the tastes, smells, sounds, and shapes of objects, as Hume had said, they don't reveal relationships among objects, such as causal relationships. So, the mind has to be the source of our knowledge of how objects are related to each other. To understand what Kant meant, it is important to see where Kant agreed with Hume and where he disagreed.

The Basic Issue

To read more of Kant's works, go to CourseMate for this text and browse by chapter or philosopher.

Kant believed that Hume's arguments had almost destroyed science. Hume had argued that the universal laws of science, particularly cause-and-effect laws, go beyond the evidence of our senses. Scientists observe a few times that certain causes are followed by certain effects. They see several times, for example, that when one moving object hits another similar object, the two bounce away from each other with equal velocities. Scientists infer a universal law from these observations: *Every* action will *always* cause an equal and opposite reaction, which is Newton's third law of motion. But how do scientists know that the phenomenon they see a few times will happen *every* time in the future? Hume asserted that scientists cannot know this, so they have no evidence for jumping from what they observe *sometimes* in the *past* to conclusions about what will happen *every time* in the *future*. The universal laws of science, then, go beyond the evidence provided by our sense observations and so are ultimately unjustified.

QUICK REVIEW
Hume argued that when scientists observe that *sometimes* in the *past* one event caused another and conclude that this will happen *every* time in the *future*, they cannot really know this conclusion is true.

When Kant read Hume's arguments, he woke up to the fact that our unthinking acceptance of the laws of science may have no firm foundation:

> I openly confess that my recollection of David Hume was the very thing which many years ago first awoke me from my dogmatic slumber and gave my

31 Immanuel Kant, *Critique of Pure Reason*, 2nd ed., trans. Norman Kemp Smith (London: Macmillan, 1929; original work published 1781), 1–2.

investigations in the field of speculative philosophy a quite new direction. But I was far from following him in the conclusions at which he arrived.[32]

Kant agreed with Hume that in some fields of knowledge we reach conclusions that go beyond the evidence our senses provide. The most important for us here are two fields of knowledge:

1. *Mathematics*, such as geometry which contains universal laws like "The shortest distance between any two points is always a straight line"; and arithmetic, which gives us universal statements such as "The sum of 3 and 7 always equals 10."
2. *Natural science*, where we find universal statements such as "Every event must have a cause," and "Every action causes an equal and opposite reaction."

QUICK REVIEW
Kant wanted to show that, despite Hume, we have real knowledge of statements that are synthetic (give us information about the world) and a priori (universal statements that go beyond what our senses can perceive) in mathematics and natural science.

Kant used special terminology to describe such statements or laws. These statements, Kant said, are *synthetic a priori* statements. Synthetic statements are statements that give us information about the world around us. For example, the statement of science that "Every event must have a cause" tells us how things will always happen in the universe around us. Kant contrasted synthetic statements with *analytic* statements that do not give us information about the world because they are true or false by definition. For example, "All triangles have three sides" is analytic because, by definition, a triangle is a three-sided figure. *A priori* statements, on the other hand, are universal and necessary statements that tell us what *must* be true of *every* member of some group. For example, geometry tells us that the shortest distance between *any* two points *must* be a straight line. As Kant (and Hume) pointed out, *a priori* statements go beyond what we can observe because normally we can't observe *all* the members of a group and our senses can't tell us what *must* be, but only what *is*. We establish that *a priori* statements are true by using the reasoning processes of the mind, such as the mental reasoning processes we use in geometry. Kant contrasted *a priori* statements with what he calls *a posteriori* statements such as "Some swans are black," which we can establish only by observation.

Space, Time, and Mathematics

Kant set out to show that despite Hume's skeptical attacks, we can—at least in mathematics and science—have real knowledge of statements that give us information about the world (i.e., synthetic statements) and that we can establish by mental reasoning alone (i.e., *a priori* statements). Kant wanted to show, then, that synthetic *a priori* statements in mathematics and science are justified regardless of Hume's objections.

To show this, Kant began by accepting Hume's view of the senses. All our knowledge of the world begins with the countless sensations that stream past our senses: colors, shapes, sounds, tastes, feels, smells. Hume wrote, "The mind is a kind of theater where several perceptions successively make their appearance, pass, repass, glide away, and mingle in an infinite variety of postures and situations."[33] Kant agreed. But Kant noticed something both empiricists and rationalists had missed. It is true that sensations stream through our senses. Yet we do not experience a mere display of sensations streaming through us. When you look around the room you do not merely see numerous patches of color streaming past your vision. Instead, you see *objects*, such as your desk, some books, a sheet of paper, and the walls of the

32 Immanuel Kant, *Prolegomena to Any Future Metaphysics*, trans. Lewis White Beck (New York: Bobbs-Merrill, 1950), 8.

33 David Hume, *A Treatise of Human Nature*, ed. L. A. Selby-Bigge (Oxford: Clarendon, 1894), 252–253.

QUICK REVIEW
Kant agreed with Hume that our senses bring us a chaotic multitude of ever-changing sensations (colors, smells, sounds, etc.). But Kant argued that the mind organizes these constantly changing sensations by arranging them into objects that we experience as located in space and time. He argued that we cannot get our ideas of space and time from experience because experience presupposes space and time.

room. The world we experience is not a mere jumble of numerous sensations but an organized world of stable objects.

The same is true of your other senses. Each sense presents a stream of changing sensations. But you experience these sensations as belonging to solid objects outside you. If you listen and observe right now, for example, you do not just sense ringing, booming, rustling sound sensations in your ears. Instead, you hear noises that seem to come from some particular place in the room. The rustling noises are from the papers on your desk. The booming sound you attribute to a truck driving past. The ringing you attribute to the telephone. Each sensation of sound, sight, touch, and smell seems to be the sound, sight, touch, or smell of an object located somewhere in the space around you.

How can this be? How is it that the stream of ever-changing sensations we receive through our senses is transformed into the objects that we perceive? Sensations cannot arrange themselves on their own, Kant claimed, so it must be our mind that organizes them into the objects that seem to be in the world that surrounds us. This remarkable insight of Kant—that the mind organizes its sensations into the

PHILOSOPHY AND LIFE

Knowledge and Gestalt Psychology

Some patterns of visual stimulation are more meaningful to us than others. Consider the following pattern. How would you describe it?

____
____

____
____

____
____

Probably you'd say that you see three sets of two horizontal lines each rather than six separate lines. This is so because you perceive items close to each other as a whole. Now consider this pattern:

O X O
O X O
O X O

Because we perceive items that resemble each other as units, you'd probably describe what you see as two vertical rows of circles and one of *X*s rather than three horizontal rows of circles and *X*s.

Why is one pattern of visual stimulation meaningful while another is not? One answer lies in past experience: Patterns that outline shapes are meaningful if they match shapes that you have experienced and remembered. But meaningfulness also seems to be imposed by the organization of the visual system.

Some years ago, a group of German psychologists, Kurt Koffka and Wolfgang Köhler among them, studied the basic principles of organization in perception. They insisted that a perception of form is an innate property of the visual system. This group of psychologists became known as Gestaltists, from the German word *gestalt*, meaning "form."

Gestaltists focus on subjective experience and the exploration of consciousness. They see the most significant aspect of experience as its wholeness or interrelatedness. Thus, Gestaltists believe that any attempt to analyze behavior by studying its parts is futile because such an approach loses the basic characteristic of experiences: their organization, pattern, and wholeness. For Gestaltists, no stimulus has constant significance or meaning. It all depends on the patterns surrounding events. For example, a 5'10" basketball player looks small when seen as part of a professional basketball team, but of normal size as part of a random group of individuals.

As part of their focus on subjective experience and the exploration of consciousness, Gestalt psychologists formulated a number of descriptive principles of perceptual organization. Two are illustrated previously in the two simple patterns: the principles of similarity and proximity.

QUESTIONS

1. Do Gestaltists owe anything to the theories of knowledge that preceded their investigations?
2. What connections do you see between Gestalt psychology and the views of Kant?

objects we see in the world around us—is the key to his theory of knowledge: The world we know is a world the mind constructs from its sensations.

In particular, Kant went on to argue, the mind organizes its sensations into objects by making them seem as if they are located in the space "outside" of us. The mind makes space appear to us as something that surrounds us outside, and in this space it positions the objects it puts together out of its sensations. Space, then, is just a structure of the mind that the mind uses to organize its sensations.

The argument Kant gave for this view of space was that we could not think of objects as outside of us unless we already knew what space is because *outside* refers to space. So, space must first be in the mind, even before we start to use it to think of objects as things outside of us in space. Space is not something we get to know from what is outside us. It is a part of our mind even before we perceive things as outside us:

> Space is not a . . . concept [we] derived from outer experiences. For in order that certain sensations be referred to something outside me (that is, to something in another region of space from that in which I find myself), . . . the representation of space [already] must be presupposed.[34]

Moreover, Kant claimed, time, like space, is also a structure in the mind. The mind makes it seem to us as if we and the objects around us exist in time. But time is just another mental structure that the mind uses to organize the many sensations it receives. Just as the mind organizes its sensations into objects that it positions in space, it also positions these objects at specific points in time. Kant argued for this view by pointing out that "Time is not a . . . concept . . . derived from any experience" because before we can experience things happening "before" or "after" or "simultaneous with" other things, "the representation of time [must be] presupposed."[35] Time must be part of our minds even before we can perceive things as existing in time.

In effect, Kant was saying that space and time don't really exist in the real world outside of us. Space and time are structures within our minds. Our minds use these structures to organize and order the sensations that stream into us.

QUICK REVIEW
Space and time, Kant claimed, are structures in the mind that we use to organize our many sensations. Geometry consists of the laws of space and arithmetic consists of the laws of time. So, by reasoning about the structures of space and time within us, we can have real knowledge of the synthetic *a priori* laws of mathematics—that is, of the universal laws of geometry and arithmetic.

Kant's view, that space and time are structures in the mind, gave him a way to prove that the universal laws of mathematics really do apply to every object in the universe we perceive. We get the laws of mathematics, Kant asserts, by reasoning about the structures of space and time that we carry around within our own minds. Geometry, for example, gives us the laws of space, such as the law that the shortest distance between any two points *in space* is a straight line. And arithmetic gives us the laws of numbers that, Kant says, are the result of adding units successively *in time*; so arithmetic gives us the laws of time. We can establish the laws of geometry and arithmetic entirely within our minds, then, because the structures of space and time are already in the mind, and by just reasoning about these, we can establish the laws of geometry and arithmetic.

Kant called attention to how our minds put every object we perceive into these structures of space and time. In fact, we cannot perceive anything that is not positioned in space and time. So, every object we perceive, or can ever perceive, has to obey the laws of space and time, which are the laws of geometry and arithmetic. We can be certain, then, that the synthetic *a priori* laws of mathematics that the mind establishes without using the senses must apply to every object in the universe we

34 Immanuel Kant, *Critique of Pure Reason*, B38.
35 Ibid., B46.

perceive. In other words, even though the synthetic *a priori* laws of mathematics go beyond the evidence of our senses, we know that they are true and must apply to all the objects in the universe we see around us.

Causality and the Unity of the Mind

But if Kant really was to answer Hume's skepticism, he had to prove that we also have good reason to believe that the synthetic *a priori* causal laws of science that the mind establishes must hold everywhere in the universe we see. Kant proves this in a way that is similar to the way he proves that we are justified in believing the synthetic *a priori* statements of mathematics are true everywhere. That is, Kant argued that when the mind organizes its sensations into objects that change, the mind puts these changes—that is, these events—into causal relationships with each other. So, we can be certain that every event (change in an object) that we perceive is caused by some prior event (change in an object).

Kant begins his argument for these claims by pointing out that when I look at the world around myself, I perceive objects that change in time but that remain the same object. We receive a stream of sensations, and these are organized into objects that change. While I'm cooking an egg for breakfast, for example, a white oval patch of color may appear in my vision, I feel a cool hardness and hear a cracking sound, and then see a transparent flowing patch of white with a yellow blob at the center that swirls and is replaced by a bubbly yellow patch of color that then streams into a pan. I am not just aware of these color and sound sensations, however; instead, I perceive an object that changes over time: an egg being broken, and then the same egg being scrambled, and last the same scrambled egg being poured into a frying pan. I perceive an object, an egg, that undergoes changes as time passes, yet it remains the same object.

QUICK REVIEW
Kant said we perceive objects that change over time. To perceive such an object, the mind must collect and remember sensations, and be aware these belong to the same object. But to collect, remember, and be aware of sensations in this way means that the mind is a unified awareness that endures through time. And because the mind is a unified awareness, it can know the many sensations it receives only if it connects them all into a unified world of interrelated objects.

Kant pointed out that to transform sensations into objects that change like this, the mind has to do three things to its sensations. First, it has to "run through" or receive the many different sensations as they stream by. Second, it has to remember each sensation after it vanishes and is replaced by a new sensation. Third, the mind has to be conscious that the earlier sensations and the later ones are all sensations of the same object. At breakfast, for example, my mind apprehends the sensations of white color, of cracking sounds, of a transparent flowing patch with a yellow blob of color at the center, and so on. The mind has to remember each of these sensations as it appears, and then vanishes. The mind must be conscious that all these different sensations belong to the same object so that I end up seeing the same egg when I break it, when I mix it, and when I pour it into a pan.

> In order to change the multiplicity [of sensations] into a single object, it is necessary first to run through and collect the multiplicity [of sensations]. . . . [Second,] if I were always to drop out of thought the earlier sensations . . . , and did not reproduce them [in my memory] while advancing to the next ones, then a complete perception [of an enduring object] would never form. . . . [Third,] if we were not conscious that what we are thinking of now is the same as what we thought a moment before, all reproduction in the series of perceptions would be in vain. Each perception would . . . be a new one.[36]

Now the mind can do all this, Kant pointed out, only if the mind itself also endures through time. For my mind to collect, remember, and be conscious of the sensations that come to me at different times, my mind has to be present

36 Ibid., A99–A103.

through each of these times. In short, the process of producing an object that remains the same object as it changes over time (like my breakfast egg) requires that my mind also remains the same mind during that process. This means, according to Kant, that the mind is a single unified awareness that remains the same unified awareness as time passes. As you will see next, this idea that the mind is a single unified awareness is the key step in Kant's argument. In fact, Kant made up a special term for this unified awareness: the "transcendental unity of apperception."

Kant claims that because the mind is a unified awareness it requires unity in what it knows. That is, if the mind is to know the world, it *must* see the world as a unified whole. In fact, he pointed out, because the mind is a single awareness, it can know several sensations only if they are all brought together into its single awareness. And to be contained in one unified awareness, sensations *must* be joined together into one connected unified whole:

> Sensations would be nothing to us, and would not concern us in the least, if they were not received into our [unified] consciousness. Knowledge is impossible in any other way. . . . For perceptions could not be perceptions of anything for me unless they . . . could at least be connected together into [my] one consciousness. This principle stands firm *a priori*, and may be called the "transcendental principle of unity" for all the multiplicity of our perceptions and sensations.[37]

Kant's point is that the mind connects and unifies its sensations into a unified world of interrelated objects because *it must.* My mind *must* connect my various sensations together because they must all be brought into my unified awareness.

It may help to summarize Kant's argument up to this point. Kant says (1) we perceive objects that change in time yet remain the same object; (2) to perceive such an object the mind must collect and remember the sensations it receives at different times, and be conscious the sensations all belong to the same object; (3) to collect, remember, and be thus conscious of sensations at different times, the mind has to remain the same unified awareness during those times; (4) because the mind is a unified awareness, it can be aware of several sensations only if they are joined together into a single unified whole; (5) so, if the mind is to be aware of its many sensations, it must connect them together into a single unified whole—that is, a single unified world of interconnected objects.

QUICK REVIEW
One of 12 relationships that the mind uses when it connects its many sensations into a single unified world of interrelated objects is the relationship of cause and effect. The mind must connect its sensations with causal relationships so it can see changes in these objects as independent of itself. So, the unified independent world of changing objects we see around us must be governed by cause-and-effect relationships.

What connections does the mind make among the changing objects it puts together from its sensations? Kant says that the changing objects the mind connects into the unified world we perceive outside ourselves are connected to each other by twelve kinds of relationships or "categories." The most important of these for our purposes is the relationship of cause and effect, which Hume had tried to undermine. How does Kant show that the changing objects that must be connected into a unified world must be connected by cause and effect?

Kant noted that the objects we perceive outside ourselves change independently of us. In other words, the changes of objects I see in the world are not changes I produce, but changes that occur independently of myself. Kant argued that the mind has to impose cause-and-effect relationships on the changes that we perceive if they are to appear to be changes that occur *independently* of ourselves. If the changes of objects in the world were not *caused* by other objects in the world, he pointed out, I would not be able to tell the difference between changes of objects in the world and changes I produce. For example, when I see a color moving across my vision, how

37 Ibid., A116.

can I tell whether the color is moving because I am moving or because a colored object in the world is itself moving? I know that an object in the world outside me is itself moving or changing only when I see the change as caused by some other object outside me, and not, say, by me moving my head. That is, I know events are happening in the world and not in me when I know that the events were forced to happen by other events in the world. So, causal relationships are one of the relationships that my mind has to impose on events in the world if I am going to see those events as happening independently of me. But, in fact, I do see a world of objects that change independently of me. Thus, the mind must impose cause-and-effect relationships on all the events we see.

To understand what Kant is saying, suppose you are watching someone play pool on a green pool table. You see a green billiard ball strike a red billiard ball, which then rolls rapidly on the green felt toward a blue ball, and then you see the red ball strike the blue one, which in turn quickly rolls away. Looking at these events in terms of Kant's theory, we might say that what you saw began with certain sensations. Your mind had sensations of a round patch of green color moving and touching a round patch of red, which then moved across a field of green color until it touched a round patch of blue, which then moved quickly away. Your mind organized these sensations into objects in space so that you saw a green billiard ball hitting a red billiard ball that rolled across the green pool table until it hit and knocked a blue ball away. You know this scene is not just a vision you are producing in your own imagination; it is something happening in the actual world apart from you. How do you know this? Because you know that the events you see are not being produced by yourself but are *caused* by moving billiard balls that bring about these changes independently of you. And these events do not occur arbitrarily because you know that what happened *had* to happen because when *any* hard moving ball hits a second similar hard ball, the second *must* be moved. That is, you know these events occur independently of yourself because they are governed by a causal law that is universal and necessary.

Let's pause to summarize once again. Kant argued (1) that the mind is a unified awareness. (2) So, if it is to be aware of its many sensations, it must connect these sensations together into a single unified world of connected objects. (3) One of the ways the mind connects its sensations into a single unified world of interrelated objects is by making all changes causally related to other changes in that world. That is, every event we perceive must be caused by some other event. (4) These causal relationships are connections the mind *must* make so that it can bring a unified and *independent* world into its awareness. (5) The world we are aware of, then, has to be a unified world in which all independent events or changes must have a cause.

All of this proves that Hume was wrong about the causal laws of science. Hume had pointed out that we do not actually see causal relationships, so he concluded that we cannot know there are real causal relationships in the world. Kant partly agreed. True, we do not see causality because it is a relationship between objects and is not a visible object. But we still know that causality is operating in the world. We know it's there because the mind puts it there. The mind puts it there so that it can perceive a unified world that is independent of itself. All events that we will ever be able to perceive as part of this external independent world, then, must be caused by other events in that same world.

QUICK REVIEW
Contrary to what Hume said, scientists can know that every event they perceive must have a cause. They can know this because the mind must put causality into the world it perceives so it can bring this unified independent world of objects into its unified mind.

The implications of Kant's views are astounding. First, if Kant is right, the world we see around us is a world that our own mind constructs. Sensations stream into us, and the mind organizes these into the interrelated objects that make up the world we perceive. Second, if Kant is right, then cause and effect are, and always will be, part of the world as we perceive it. Hume, then, was wrong when he claimed that we have no reason to think that events are really connected together by the universal and necessary causal laws of science. On the contrary, events in the world *we* perceive will always have to be connected by cause and effect. Third, if Kant is right, then the things we see around us might not be the way things are in themselves. What we see around us is a world our minds have put together out of a multitude of sensations. But perhaps the world as it really is in itself is not like the world we humans experience. For all we know, the world we experience is utterly unlike the world as it is in itself.

Expressing a view called **phenomenalism**, Kant called the world that our minds construct, and that appears to be around us, the "phenomenal" world. The world as it might be in itself, apart from our mind, he called the "noumenal" world. Clearly, we can never know what the noumenal world is really like. All we can ever know is the phenomenal world that we perceive after the mind has fabricated it out of our sensations.

QUICK REVIEW
We perceive only the world as it has been constructed by the mind out of its sensations (the phenomena), and we do not perceive the world as it is in itself (the noumena).

So, Kant agreed with the empiricists' claim that the senses provide the sensations we need to know anything about the world around us. But the rationalists are also right when they claim that our minds can know the universal laws that order the world. For example, we can know that in the world that we see, every event will have a cause. We can come to know these laws by simply reasoning inside our minds because these laws are inside our minds to begin with. Yet they are also in the world as *we* perceive it because the mind puts them there when it constructs the unified world of interconnected independently changing objects.

Notice that Kant also resolved a key problem with which both the rationalists and the empiricists had struggled: How can we know that our ideas accurately represent the world outside of us? Descartes raised doubts about whether our ideas about the world were accurate. For all we know, what we perceive "in" our minds might not really be what is "out there" in the world. Hume concluded that we can never know whether our ideas accurately represent the world "outside" or even whether there is such a world. But Kant responded to Hume's skepticism with an answer that was simple but revolutionary. We know our ideas can represent the world accurately because the mind itself constructs the world. Thus, skepticism is banished.

 critical thinking

Kant assumes that if the world as we experience it is constructed by the mind, then the ideas in our minds must correspond to that world. Is this assumption correct?

Kant wrote that his revolutionary claim that the world must conform to the mind was a kind of "Copernican" revolution in knowledge.[38] Copernicus revolutionized astronomy by rejecting the view that the sun revolves around the earth and replacing it with the view that the earth revolves around the sun. In a similar way, Kant replaced the view that the mind must conform to the world (i.e., our mind must make its knowledge match what the world is like) with the view that the world must conform to the mind (i.e., what the world is like depends on what our mind makes it be). Only this revolutionary view, Kant held, has the power to free us from skepticism.

The theory that Kant proposed truly revolutionized philosophy. Many philosophers, of course, rejected Kant's ideas. In particular, many rejected his core idea that the mind constructs the world that it knows. But many other philosophers who followed Kant adopted his central idea and developed it in new and excitingly different directions. Perhaps the most important of these were the so-called Romantic philosophers.

Romantic Philosophers

The Romantics were thinkers, poets, artists, and philosophers who were fascinated by the strange and exotic, particularly in cultures and in nature. They tended to

38 Ibid., Bxvi.

elevate feeling and emotion above impersonal and cold reason. For example, the Romantic poet William Wordsworth, inviting his sister to go with him for a walk in the woods in his poem "To My Sister," wrote the following:

> *One moment now may give us more*
> *Than years of toiling reason:*
> *Our minds shall drink at every pore*
> *The spirit of the season. . . .*
> *And bring no book: for this one day*
> *We'll give to idleness.*

Many Romantics agreed with Kant that we shape and create the world we see around us. But they did not believe that the categories the mind uses to organize the world are universal and based on reason. That is, they did not believe that these categories are the same everywhere. Neither did they believe that impersonal reason is the source of those categories. Instead, many argued, a person's history, culture, and language shape the categories she uses to organize her world. And people from different cultures use different categories to construct their worlds.

QUICK REVIEW
Romantic philosophers such as Humboldt agreed that the mind constructs reality, but they held that it does so not according to rational structures but according to its history, culture, and language.

The Romantic philosopher Wilhelm von Humboldt, for example, was also a linguist who had studied the various languages of different cultures. He argued that the language of each culture contains the basic categories and structures that the people of that culture use to understand and organize their experience. We construct the world that we see according to the categories of the language that our culture happens to use. The world that we see around us, then, mirrors the language that our culture and our history happen to give us. If Humboldt is correct, then the members of different cultures live in different worlds. The world in which a person lives, and the way that the universe looks to the person, depend on the language the person speaks.

Humboldt's theories were accepted by many anthropologists and other social scientists. Perhaps the most well known are the Americans Edward Sapir and Benjamin Lee Whorf, who together developed the Sapir-Whorf hypothesis. The Sapir-Whorf hypothesis says that the structure of a language determines how a speaker of that language thinks. Sapir expressed this hypothesis as follows:

> Human beings do not live in the objective world alone . . . but are very much at the mercy of the particular language which has become the medium of expression for their society. . . . The fact of the matter is that the "real world" is to a large extent unconsciously built up of the language habits of the group. . . . We see and hear and otherwise experience very largely as we do because the language habits of our community predispose certain choices of interpretation.[39]

Whorf spent many years studying the Native American Hopi language. He wrote that in the Hopi language, words referring to units of time (such as *day* or *year*) differ from other words because they do not have plural forms. And they cannot be counted separately (using *one, two, three,* etc.), but only in terms of their place in a single series (*first, second, third,* etc.). Whorf concluded that the Hopi think of time as cyclic recurrences of the same units of time. Each day for the Hopi is a recurrence of the day before, rather than a completely new day. Because they perceive time in this way, Whorf argued, the Hopi repeat the same ceremonial acts each time period. And because it is always the same day again, they feel that the power of these acts

39 Quoted in William O. Bright, "Languages of the Americas," *Encyclopaedia Britannica CD,* 1998.

keeps building up. The power of the ceremony of yesterday is present today because today is yesterday repeating itself. Thus, the language of the Hopi makes them see and feel time as a cyclic recurrence. By contrast, our language makes us look at time as progressing continuously into a new time that has never occurred before and, once past, will never recur again. Kant saw reason as constructing reality, but the new Kantians believe that *language* constructs our reality.

Sikyati Hand with Bee, 1973 (acrylic & feather on canvas), Kabotie, Michael (1942–2009)/Fred Jones Jr. Museum of Art, University of Oklahoma, USA/Richard H. and Adeline J. Fleischaker Collection, 1996/ The Bridgeman Art Library

The language of the Hopi makes them see and feel time as a cyclic recurrence.

Constructivist Theories and Recovered Memories

Theories like Kant's are sometimes called *constructivist* theories because they hold that reality as we know it is constructed by us. We put together the world as we know it, and for each of us there is no reality apart from the reality we build.

A number of psychologists have developed constructivist theories of the human individual, including George Kelly, Ernst von Glaserfeld, and Humberto R. Maturana. Constructivist psychologists hold that human beings construct the world they know on the basis of the meanings and expectations they have acquired through their life experiences. So-called radical constructivists hold, as Kant did, that we are acquainted only with the world we construct and that we cannot affirm any reality beyond this world. In his book, *Radical Constructivism: A Way of Knowing and Learning*, psychologist von Glaserfeld writes: "Constructivism, thus, does not say there is no world and no other people, it merely holds that insofar as we know them, both the world and others are models that we ourselves construct."[40]

Several sociologists have also developed constructivist theories, including Kenneth Gergen, Peter Berger, and Thomas Luckmann. Berger and Luckmann, for example, in their classic book *The Social Construction of Reality*, argue that the members of a society, through their interactions, construct their common "reality," which consists of the categories, meanings, and institutions that become reinforced in their repeated interactions with each other.

The idea that we construct what we know as the "real world" clearly has profound implications but is easily misunderstood. For example, consider the phenomenon of recovered memories of childhood sexual abuse discussed earlier. What might a Kantian approach to such recovered memories say? Are such memories valid sources of knowledge? Think about this before we leave Kant and his followers.

The person in therapy who recovers her repressed memories gradually constructs a detailed picture of a past reality that is very different from the reality that she had previously remembered. In the spirit of Kant, we might want to say that the past world that is constructed from these memories must be as fully real as the world that we currently see around us. After all, the world that we see around us is also constructed by the mind and so is no more "privileged" and no more "real"

40 Ernst von Glaserfeld, *Radical Constructivism: A Way of Knowing and Learning* (London: The Falmer Press, 1995), 137.

than the world that our mind might gradually piece together out of its recovered memories. So, for the person who comes to believe in a past world in which she was sexually abused, that awful world is every bit as real, and must be taken as seriously, as the present world that her mind similarly constructs. A theory in the spirit of Kant might suggest that recollected memories must provide accurate knowledge of past reality because this past reality is constructed from the memories themselves. Perhaps some of Kant's "romantic" followers might accept this conclusion, especially those who think that each of us constructs his or her own world.

QUICK REVIEW
Kant would agree that recovered memories are valid sources of knowledge only if they are causally connected to the world we perceive around us.

However, Kant would object that this conclusion overlooks an important part of his theory. In his theory, we can know only one real world: the world in which objects are causally related to each other. In the world we see around us, for example, bullets can cause death, and fire can cause painful burns. So, bullets and fires are part of the real world. Other "worlds" that our minds might construct—like the worlds of our dreams—are not real because they are not causally related to the world around us. For example, a bullet that I shoot in a dream cannot cause someone's death in the real world, and a fire that I dream cannot cause someone in the real world a painful burn. If recollected memories provide true knowledge of reality, then, the events they depict must be more than mental constructs. Real events must, then, be causally related to the actual world around us.

This aspect of Kant's theory can shed light on whether recovered memories are valid sources of knowledge. His theory implies that recollected memories can be taken as a true basis of knowledge only if the events they depict have had some causal effects on the world around us. People who suspect they may be survivors of childhood sexual abuse need to determine whether the world remembered by the alleged victims of sexual abuse is more than a mental construct. Kant would say that they need to find independent causal effects of the abuse in the real world that indicate the abuse was actually part of the real world, such as recordings or bodily injuries.

Still, not everyone has agreed with Kant's theory. Some people continue to insist that our sense experience must conform to an independent world of things if it is to give us real knowledge. We want to know if the world that we construct from our sense experience is an accurate picture of the world that is really there, independent of our sense experience. But Kant would say that we can never know what reality is like apart from our mental construct of it. Thus, Kant's theory that we construct the world we see around us seems to drive us to a deep skepticism about our ability to know the world as it really is.

QUICK REVIEW
Kant's theory leaves us with a kind of skepticism about whether we can know reality as it really exists independently of the workings of our mind.

One problem with Kant's position is that in his view, the senses are our link to reality, so the question arises again whether there is a difference between reality and what we experience. If experience is the only true basis of knowledge, then it is reasonable to question the reliability of the senses as sources of that knowledge. After all, the mind can't organize our sensory experiences until it receives them. Of course, Kant claims that what the senses give us does not correspond to how things are to begin with—it is already informed by the categories. Thus, we never perceive things as they actually are. If things as such are unknowable, then we appear to be faced with thorough skepticism. We could also wonder about the mental categories themselves—whether Kant has provided a complete list and description, and whether they're the same for everyone or, as some constructivists claim, different for different people.

Despite these apparent drawbacks, Kant's views, and the views of his followers, are a serious attempt to analyze the nature of knowledge. Kant not only shows the limitations of knowledge but also validates knowledge within its proper field. More specifically, Kant is noteworthy for his portrayal of the active nature of the mind.

This conception of our mind's role as a creator of the world we perceive constitutes a new way of considering the nature of the self and the world we know.

QUESTIONS

1. Kant claims that true knowledge has its basis in experience. At the same time, he states that true *a priori* knowledge is possible. Is this a contradiction?
2. Kant concludes that we can obtain only knowledge of appearances (phenomena) and never of the way things actually are (noumena). Does this make him a skeptic? If not, what distinguishes his view from skepticism?
3. Many authors have noted that Kant's theory of the unity of consciousness changed the dispute between rationalists and empiricists. What do you think that these authors mean by this?

PHILOSOPHY AT THE MOVIES

Watch *Criminal* (2004) in which Richard, a seasoned con man, teams up with Rodrigo, a young man just beginning to con people, and the two decide to try to sell a counterfeit antique bank note to a rich collector named Hannigan who is staying in the hotel run by Richard's sister, Valerie. How do the cons of Richard and Rodrigo early in the film depend on the way their victims construct their world? How do your expectations lead you to construct what you see in the film in a way that lets the filmmaker lead you to the conclusions he wants? Does the fact that the expectations of the film's victims and your own expectations about the film lead you and the victims to construct the world in a certain way support or undermine the theories of Kant and/or his followers?

Movies with similar themes: *Matchstick Men* (2003), *Ocean's Eleven* (2001), *Ocean's Twelve* (2004), *Ocean's Thirteen* (2007).

5.5 Does Science Give Us Knowledge?

We have examined three approaches to knowledge: the rationalist view, that some of our knowledge of reality derives from reason without the aid of the senses; the empiricist view, that our knowledge of reality must derive from our sense experience; and the transcendentalist view, that the fundamental structures of reality (such as the causal relationship by which all events are causally connected to prior events) can be discovered by reason, whereas the particular contents of reality (such as the nature of particular events and causes) must be derived from our sense experience.

But what can we learn from these approaches to knowledge? Do they have any practical contribution to make to our lives? One contribution these approaches to knowledge can make, is that they can help us separate real knowledge from its counterfeits. We are surrounded by claims about astrology, ESP, psychic predictions, the prophecies of Nostradamus, the healing powers of crystals and pyramids, UFOs, paranormal phenomena, parapsychology, clairvoyance, psychokinesis, reincarnation, and so on and so on. How can we tell which, if any, of these claims we should take seriously? In one way or another, they all claim to be "scientific." But are they? To see how the approaches to knowledge that we've studied can help us separate real scientific knowledge from views that claim to be scientific but are not, we will turn now to look at the nature of scientific knowledge. Our aim is to determine how true scientific knowledge differs from pseudoscience (i.e., from bogus science). We will discuss several views of science, and as we do so we will see that the three approaches to knowledge each make important contributions to our understanding of what scientific knowledge is and how it differs from pseudoscience.

For many people today, science is the most reliable source of knowledge. Many of us hold that scientific claims about the world are as close to the truth as we can get. People use the term *scientific* to suggest reliability, validity, and certainty. Thus, when we want to say that a certain belief is unreliable or dubious, we say it is "unscientific." On the other hand, we describe a claim as "scientific" when we want to distinguish it from claims that are fraudulent or based on superstition, mere intuition, or prejudice. The methods of the sciences, many of us hold, are the best methods we have for getting genuine knowledge of reality. But what are these methods, and what justifies our reliance on them?

Perhaps the most obvious characteristic of science is its reliance on sense observation. In fact, for many people a theory is scientific to the extent that it is based on sense observations. Empiricists, in particular, claim that science is justified because it is based on sense observations. But what, exactly, does this mean? Clearly, when we just observe, say, a falling rock we don't immediately "see" that it is falling at an accelerating rate of 32 feet per second per second, much less do we "see" this law of falling bodies. How, then, are scientific laws and theories supposed to be related to our sense observations?

Inductive Reasoning and Simplicity

One of the earliest and most influential views of the relationship between scientific theories and sensory observations is *inductionism.* This view holds that science is based on inductive reasoning—that is, reasoning that moves from many particular observations to claims about the general laws that govern what we observe. Inductive reasoning was first suggested as the core of the scientific method by Francis Bacon (1561–1626), a philosopher who has been called the father of empiricism. Unlike most of his contemporaries, Bacon refused to unquestioningly accept the views of the ancient Greek philosophers. Bacon insisted that instead of relying on ideas from the past, scientists should investigate nature by careful sense observation and experimentation. They should collect as many facts as possible about the subject they are studying, perhaps using experiments to generate additional facts. Once all the facts are collected, they should carefully sift through the facts, looking for common patterns, until they derive general laws about those facts, or, as he put it: moving "from . . . sense and particulars up to the most general propositions."

QUICK REVIEW
Inductionism holds that scientific knowledge is based on sense observation: making particular observations, generalizing to general laws, and confirming the laws through additional observations.

Two centuries after Bacon, another philosopher, the empiricist John Stuart Mill (1806–1873), tried to improve on Bacon by laying out what he called *canons,* or methods of **induction**. These were rules for determining which generalizations were supported by the many particular facts and observations the scientist collected. In the spirit of Bacon, Mill claimed that scientific method is characterized by three features:

1. *The accumulation of particular observations.* Scientific method begins with the collection of as many observed facts as possible about the subject we are investigating.
2. *Generalization from the particular observations.* Scientific method then proceeds by inferring general laws from the accumulated particular facts.
3. *Repeated confirmation.* Scientific method continues to accumulate more particular facts to see whether the generalization continues to hold true. The more particular instances of a "law" we find, the more confirmation the law has and the higher its probability.

Thus, for the inductionist empiricist, real science is distinguished from unscientific opinions, superstitions, and bias by its reliance on generalization from particular sensory observations and by repeated confirmation. The pseudosciences, according to the inductionist, are not solidly based on sense observations, generalization, and repeated confirmation.

Scientists who have used this empiricist process of compiling observations, generalizing from the observations, and repeatedly confirming the generalization are not hard to find. During the seventeenth century, Galileo Galilei (1564–1642) became interested in studying the motions of falling objects. Most scientists of his time were content to accept the commonsense opinion of Aristotle, who had declared that objects fall faster the heavier they are. But Galileo decided to find out for himself. He devised a number of experiments in which he repeatedly measured how fast metal balls of different weights fell when dropped about a hundred feet. Much to his surprise, he found that every ball fell at the same rate, no matter how heavy it was. Moreover, Galileo also found that as each ball fell, it moved faster and faster. Pressing his study, Galileo built long, smooth inclined planes and rolled balls down them. For years he worked, carefully releasing the balls and timing them. After a large number of observations, he formulated the important generalization that all objects fall to the earth at the same constantly accelerating rate of 32 feet per second per second. Aristotle was wrong. Countless scientists after Galileo have confirmed his law of falling bodies, making it a highly probable law.

In a similar way, Gregor Mendel (1822–1884) formulated the basic laws of heredity by growing and repeatedly cross-breeding peas and observing the numbers of offspring with certain colors and shapes in each generation. From these observations, he generalized his laws, which say, for example, that in the second generation the ratio of a dominant genetic trait to a recessive trait is 3:1. Mendel's laws have been repeatedly confirmed by biologists and are now accepted as some of the fundamental laws of biology.

QUICK REVIEW
But generalizations always go beyond finite observations, and many generalizations can fit any finite set of observations. So, sense observations by themselves cannot select the correct general laws. Also, great scientific theories are not mere generalizations. Reason must play a role in science.

But inductionism carries several problems. One major problem we already saw when we were discussing Hume and the Problem of Induction: Every generalization has to go *beyond* the observations on which it is based. For example, Galileo observed relatively few metal balls falling relatively short distances before concluding that *every* object *always* falls to the earth at a constantly accelerating speed. Because a generalization always goes beyond the observational evidence, the evidence cannot really prove the generalization. Another problem is that a large (potentially infinite) number of different generalizations or "laws" will fit any set of observations and all those different generalizations are equally "confirmed" by the observations of the scientist. For example, Galileo observed several falling metal balls as they dropped a hundred feet and found that each time they were moving at an accelerating rate. From these observations, he could have concluded (1) that objects fall at an accelerating rate until they drop one hundred feet and then they fall at a uniform rate, or (2) that objects fall at an accelerating rate until they reach a certain speed and then they begin to slow down, or (3) that objects fall at an accelerating rate at those points at which Galileo measured their fall, but sometimes they fall at a uniform rate in between those points. When so many generalizations are compatible with the observations, why should we accept one generalization rather than another?

Some inductionists have pointed to the criterion of *simplicity* as a way of deciding among competing generalizations. The scientist generally chooses the simplest generalization compatible with sensory observations. None of the generalizations suggested in the last paragraph is as simple as Galileo's.

But simplicity seems to be a rationalist criterion, not an empiricist criterion: It tells us that the world must follow simpler rather than more complex laws. And this

PHILOSOPHY AND LIFE

Society and Truth

In *The Art of Awareness*, J. Samuel Bois reports the following experiment:

> A psychologist employed seven assistants and one genuine subject in an experiment where they were asked to judge how long was a straight line that they were shown on a screen. The seven assistants, who were the first to speak and report what they saw, had been instructed to report unanimously an evidently incorrect length. The eighth member of the group, the only naive subject in the lot, did not know that his companions had received such an instruction, and he was under the impression that what they reported was really what they saw. In one-third of the experiments, he reported the same incorrect length as they did. The pressure of the environment had influenced his own semantic reaction and had distorted his vision. When one of the assistants, under the secret direction of the experimenter, started reporting the correct length, it relieved that pressure of the environment, and the perception of the uninformed subject improved accordingly.

QUESTION

1. To what extent does our sense knowledge depend on what we think we *should* be seeing?

Source: J. Samuel Bois, *The Art of Awareness* (Dubuque, IA: William C. Brown, 1973).

criterion does not seem to be established by sense observation but by reason. Thus, the inductionist method seems forced to incorporate an element of rationalism into its procedures.

But even if the inductionist can deal with this problem, there is a more serious reason why inductionism is not an adequate theory of the relation between scientific knowledge and sense observations. The problem is that almost none of the great scientific theories are mere generalizations from a few facts. For example, as we saw in Chapter 2, Darwin's theory of evolution claims that species evolve as a result of inherited variations and natural selection. Darwin did not establish his theory by observing a few species evolve in this way and then generalizing to the conclusion that all species evolve like this. In fact, Darwin never observed the evolution of any species because the evolution of a single species would take many lifetimes. So contrary to the theory that science is based on induction, Darwin's Theory was not a generalization based on a few sense observations.

In fact, although simple low-level scientific laws are sometimes established by induction, the greatest and most fundamental *theories* of science were not established by induction alone. Galileo's law of falling bodies is an example of a relatively simple and low-level law that, we can argue, was established by induction. But this law describes the behavior of a very limited range of objects: those that fall to the surface of the earth. On the other hand, Isaac Newton (1642–1727) developed a broad and comprehensive theory incorporating three laws of motion and a law of universal gravitation. Newton's theory explains the motions of the moon, the planets in the solar system, and the motions of distant stars and galaxies, as well as the way objects fall to the surface of the earth. Yet Newton did not establish his theory by merely generalizing from some sensory observations. Instead, he seems to have familiarized himself with the previous findings of numerous scientists and then he creatively fashioned a comprehensive theory that drew all of their findings together and that went beyond them in a way that no one had suspected was possible. Clearly, scientific method consists of more than mere inductive generalizations. But what is this "more"?

The Hypothetical Method and Falsifiability

Because induction cannot account for broad scientific theories, many thinkers have turned in a different direction. What distinguishes scientific knowledge, they have claimed, is the use of the *hypothetical method.* William Whewell (1794–1866), an opponent of John Stuart Mill, pointed out that advances in scientific knowledge do not depend only on generalizations based on several observations. Instead, Whewell contended, the greatest scientific advances occur when scientists make a creative guess or **hypothesis** about what causes or explains a particular phenomenon, and then *test* this hypothesis by sense observations and experimentation:

> The conceptions by which facts are bound together are suggested by the sagacity of discoverers. This sagacity cannot be taught. It commonly succeeds by guessing; and this success seems to consist in framing several tentative hypotheses and selecting the right one. But a supply of appropriate hypotheses cannot be constructed by rule, nor without inventive talent.[41]

Darwin's theory of evolution seems to be a good example of what Whewell had in mind. Darwin's theory began as a hypothesis intended to explain a large number of observations: the discovery that fossils buried in ancient layers of rock were different from but apparently related to surviving species; the observation that living species occurred in groups that seemed related to one another as though they had common ancestors; the discovery that some butterfly species had gradually changed color over time in ways that made them more likely to escape being eaten by birds; the discovery that certain species had become extinct apparently as a result of competition with other species; and so on. All of these observations could be explained, he held, by the hypothesis that species change over time by a process of natural selection, in which species that are best adapted to their environment survive and reproduce. So Darwin's theory of evolution was not a mere generalization from observations. It was, instead, a creative idea advanced to explain a large number of facts. Darwin showed that all the previously unconnected varieties of animals and plants, both fossilized and living, could be put into a sequence that showed evolution happened over immense periods of time, and his theory explained how this evolution had taken place. After Darwin, countless biologists used Darwin's theory to guide their investigations, to structure their experiments, and to decide which observations were worth making.

At the very heart of the scientific method, then, is an element, a contribution, made by reason. Reason—the ability to synthesize, to relate, and to creatively formulate new conceptual structures—seems to be the source of the hypotheses that scientists come up with and use to guide their research. This is an important point because it implies that reason makes an essential contribution to science. Moreover, it is a point that the transcendental idealist Kant made when he wrote that reason is the source of the basic "questions" or hypotheses that the scientist uses to explore the world of nature. As he points out, even Galileo was guided by a hypothesis when he decided to test his law of falling bodies by rolling metal balls down long, smooth inclined planes:

> When Galileo caused balls, the weights of which he had himself previously determined, to roll down an inclined plane; when Torricelli made the air carry a weight which he had calculated beforehand to be equal to that of a definite volume of

41 William Whewell, *History and Philosophy of the Inductive Sciences* (1840), quoted in Stewart Richards, *Philosophy and Sociology of Science* (New York: Schocken, 1984), 529.

> water; or in more recent times when Stahl changed metals into oxides, and oxides back into metal, by withdrawing something and then restoring it, a light broke upon all students of nature. They learned that reason has insight only into that which it produces after a plan of its own, and that it must not allow itself to be kept, as it were, in nature's leading-strings, but must itself show the way with principles of judgment based upon fixed laws, constraining nature to give answers to questions of reason's own determining. Accidental observations, made in obedience to no previously thought-out plan, can never be made to yield a necessary law, which alone reason is concerned to discover. Reason, holding in one hand its principles, according to which alone concordant appearances can be admitted as equivalent to laws, and in the other hand the experiment which it has devised in conformity with these principles, must approach nature in order to be taught by it. It must not, however, do so in the character of a pupil who listens to everything that the teacher chooses to say, but of an appointed judge who compels the witnesses to answer questions which he has himself formulated.[42]

In formulating a hypothesis, the scientist turns away from the senses, and relies on reason to help her create new relationships, new structures, and new connections and to organize these into a theory that orders, systematizes, and explains whatever observations other scientists have made. In formulating hypotheses, Kant might have said, the scientist also relies on other "laws of reason," such as the criterion of simplicity. Then, the scientist returns to sensory observations by asking whether the theory accurately predicts new observations, whether it suggests fresh research and new experiments, or whether it points the way toward other corroborating observations. Thus, while sense observations are essential to scientific method, nevertheless, the creative use of reason is equally essential to the hypothetical methods used by science.

QUICK REVIEW
Whewell's "hypothetical method" view of science says reason formulates generalizations and broad theories that are tested by sense observations and experiments. Popper added that they must be capable of being falsified by observable events.

The most influential proponent of the hypothetical method in the twentieth century was an empiricist, the philosopher Karl Popper (1902–1994). Popper agreed that scientific theories are not mere generalizations from experience, and he accepted the view that science progresses by formulating hypotheses that can explain many different phenomena and that guide later research. But what really distinguishes the claims of science from unscientific claims, Popper claimed, is that scientific claims or hypotheses must be capable of being *falsified* through empirical observations.

Many unscientific theories are said by their supporters to be confirmed by observation and experience. For example, astrologers point to observed events that are consistent with some of their predictions and say that these verify their theories. Similarly, people who believe in biorhythms or extrasensory perception selectively point to observed facts that tend to confirm their theories. But any theory, Popper pointed out, can be shown to be consistent with some observed facts. Science does not proceed by trying to find facts that confirm a theory. Instead, the mark of science is that it tries to *disprove* or *falsify* proposed theories. A real scientific theory is not just one that is confirmed by some observations that suggest it is true, but one that survives repeated attempts to prove it is false. Popper wrote, "there is no more rational procedure than the method of trial and error—of conjecture and refutation; of boldly proposing theories; of trying our best to show that these are erroneous; and of accepting them tentatively if our critical efforts are unsuccessful."[43]

Popper's view that a scientific theory must be *capable of being falsified by observable events* does not mean that scientific statements are those that are actually shown to

42 Kant, *Critique of Pure Reason*, 20.
43 Karl Popper, *Conjectures and Refutations* (1963), quoted in Richards, *Philosophy and Sociology of Science*, 52.

be false. Rather, a statement is scientific when some observable events or discoveries exist that *could* show the statement to be false. Science advances when the scientist formulates a hypothesis that implies that some observable event will occur and then tries to falsify the hypothesis by experiments and observations to see whether the predicted observable event occurs as his or her hypothesis says it will. If a theory stands up to many attempts to falsify it, then we are justified in believing it. The more times we try to prove it false, and fail, the more reliable the theory is. For example, astronomers had noticed that the orbit of the planet Uranus was irregular; Newton's theory of motion predicted that the disturbance was caused by the gravitational attraction of an unknown planet in a certain orbit near Uranus. When astronomers searched that part of the sky, they eventually discovered the planet Neptune. Thus, Newton's theory made the kind of prediction that could prove it was false. Instead, the prediction turned out to be true, thereby confirming the theory. Newton's theory also predicts the trajectories of cannon balls and the motions of everything from trains to molecules. All these predictions could have disproved his theory if they turned out to be wrong. Instead, the predictions turned out true, thereby providing even more confirmation for his theory.

In a similar way, Darwin's theory of evolution predicted that under Cambrian rock formations (thought to be 500 million to 600 million years old), in older pre-Cambrian rock, scientists should be able to find fossils of organisms simpler than those in the younger Cambrian rock. The theory of evolution (in part) hypothesizes that organisms developed gradually from simple to increasingly complex forms. If evolution is a sound theory, then older pre-Cambrian formations should contain simpler fossil forms than those in the Cambrian layers of rocks. That is exactly what biologists found in 1947 in pre-Cambrian rocks in Australia. So the prediction of the theory of evolution was not wrong, and the theory was not falsified; it was instead confirmed.

It is important to see that the hypothetical method and the falsifiability criterion that Popper suggests imply that scientific knowledge is never more than probable; it is always open to revision based on new evidence or a new interpretation of existing evidence. A scientific hypothesis may predict certain events, and these events may occur as the hypothesis suggests. But it is always possible that other predictions of the hypothesis, not yet tested, may turn out to be wrong. A scientific hypothesis, like a generalization, always goes beyond the limited facts or observations that it was formulated to explain. For this reason, it is always open to refutation; it is always merely probable, never certain.

Paradigms and Revolutions in Science

Popper's view, however, ignores the extent to which scientists are human beings. As humans they work together, they are trained in universities to accept certain laboratory and research methods, and they are deeply convinced that the basic theories of their subject are correct. As a result, scientists tend to continue accepting a basic theory even if they run into observations that falsify the theory. In fact, despite Popper's claim that scientists are continuously trying to disprove their theories, scientists may stubbornly cling to a theory for decades after the appearance of experimental results that are inconsistent with the theory.

The American philosopher and historian of science Thomas Kuhn (1922–1996) tried to take this phenomenon into account by arguing that we should think of scientific knowledge as the product of communities of scientists who accept and work with that knowledge. Examples of these communities might include the community of biologists who accept and use Darwin's theory, the community of

QUICK REVIEW
Kuhn argued that science is a social activity in which a community of scientists accepts a "paradigm" consisting of theories and methods of discovery and proof, which are periodically overturned by scientific revolutions that establish new paradigms.

physicists and astronomers who accept and use Newton's and Einstein's theories, and the community of chemists who accept and use molecular theory. A person who decides to become a scientist receives a long "indoctrination" into the theories and research methods of their scientific community. This research tradition or *paradigm* of science includes a way of thinking and doing research; the student-scientist is taught the basic theories of the field and the correct methods for applying and extending those basic theories. Examples of paradigms are the theory of the atom in chemistry, the Copernican theory that the earth and planets revolve around the sun in astronomy, and the theory of evolution in biology. In each of these cases, the community of scientists working in the field—of chemistry, astronomy, or biology—accept the basic theory, and use it to guide their research. According to Kuhn:

> These remarks should begin to clarify what I take a paradigm to be. It is, in the first place, a fundamental scientific achievement and one which includes both a theory and some exemplary applications to the results of experiment and observation. More important, it is an open-ended achievement, one which leaves all sorts of research still to be done. And, finally, it is an accepted achievement in the sense that it is received by a group whose members no longer try to rival it or to create alternates for it. Instead, they attempt to extend and exploit it in a variety of ways.[44]

Moreover, Kuhn argued, science does not always grow gradually, as the inductionists and the falsificationists say it does. Instead, science leaps forward through major *revolutions*. Most of the time, scientists hold onto their theories even if a few observations show up that do not fit their theory. Such observations are called "anomalies." So long as there are relatively few anomalies scientists hold on to their theories. But when too many observations accumulate that do not square with a theory, a "crisis" results. Some scientists, particularly younger ones, start to rethink the theory. They develop new theories that take the anomalies into account. Then a revolution may occur in the scientific community. Some scientists (usually the older established ones) continue to hold on to the old theory while other (usually young) scientists turn to the new theory. New research programs and methods are developed for this new theory, and when young people enter the field, they start to get indoctrinated into the new theory. Eventually the new theory becomes the new paradigm for that field of science:

QUICK REVIEW
During scientific revolutions, older scientists try to hold on to the old theories and resist the new paradigm. Kuhn suggests that the new paradigm is not necessarily truer than the old.

> Scientific revolutions are here taken to be those noncumulative developmental episodes in which an older paradigm is replaced in whole or in part by an incompatible new one. . . . Why should a change of paradigm be called a revolution? . . . Political revolutions are inaugurated by a growing sense, often restricted to a segment of the political community, that existing institutions have ceased adequately to meet the problems posed by an environment that they have in part created. In much the same way, scientific revolutions are inaugurated by a growing sense, again often restricted to a narrow subdivision of the scientific community, that an existing paradigm has ceased to function adequately in the exploration of an aspect of nature to which that paradigm itself had previously led the way. In both political and scientific development, the sense of malfunction that can lead to crisis is prerequisite to revolution.[45]

44 Thomas Kuhn, "The Function of Dogma in Scientific Research," in *Scientific Knowledge: Basic Issues in the Philosophy of Science*, ed. Janet A. Kourany (Belmont, CA: Wadsworth, 1987), 259.
45 Thomas Kuhn, "The Nature and Necessity of Scientific Revolutions," *in Scientific Knowledge*, 311.

The history of science is filled with examples of such scientific revolutions, Kuhn said. Examples include the change from the medieval theory that the sun revolves around the earth to the revolutionary theory of Copernicus that the earth revolves around the sun; the change from Newton's theory that time and space are absolute and unchanging to the revolutionary new theory of Einstein that time and space are relative; and the change from the theory that animal and plant species do not change to Darwin's revolutionary new theory of evolution. The new paradigms, Kuhn insisted, give us new ways of seeing the world, new ways of thinking, and new goals and methods for investigating nature.

Although Kuhn's insights into the way that science progresses are extremely valuable, they leave an important question unanswered: What is the difference between real science and claims that are unscientific? Kuhn's view seems to provide us with no way of answering this question other than to say that a theory is scientific if the community of scientists accepts it. As he wrote in one of his early works, "What better criterion could there be [of scientific knowledge] than the decision of the scientific group?"[46] Kuhn's view tells us, then, that true scientific knowledge must be consistent with the knowledge prevailing among the community of scientists. Yet any group of people might claim to be a "community of scientists." For example, the International Flat Earth Research Society (http://theflatearthsociety.org) claims to be a group of scientists who aim "to establish as a fact that this earth is flat and plane and that it does not spin and whirl 1000 miles an hour and to expose modern astronomical science as a fraud, myth, a false religion." How can we distinguish real science from bogus science when we don't know how to distinguish a community of real scientists from a community of bogus scientists?

In his later writings, Thomas Kuhn responded to this important question:

> What, I ask to begin with, are the characteristics of a good scientific theory? . . . First, a theory should be accurate: Within its domain, that is, consequences deducible from a theory should be in demonstrated agreement with the results of existing experiments and observations. Second, a theory should be consistent, not only internally or with itself, but also with other currently accepted theories applicable to related aspects of nature. Third, it should have broad scope: In particular, a theory's consequences should extend far beyond the particular observations, laws, or subtheories it was initially designed to explain. Fourth, and closely related, it should be simple, bringing order to phenomena that in its absence would be individually isolated and, as a set, confused. Fifth—a somewhat less standard item, but one of special importance to actual scientific decisions—a theory should be fruitful of new research findings: it should, that is, disclose new phenomena or previously unnoted relationships among those already known.[47]

QUICK REVIEW
Kuhn suggested a good scientific theory was accurate, consistent with other accepted theories, broad, simple, and fruitful.

Many of the criteria that Kuhn suggests here are closely related to the rationalist tradition. For example, the criterion of consistency is not established by sense observation: It is based on reason, on the idea that rationality demands consistency. The same can be said about his criterion that a good scientific theory must bring "order" into our sensory observations. This, as we suggested, is a function of reason: to develop a theory that, as Kant indicated, can connect and relate what the senses provide and that can provide the basis for further investigations of nature.

critical thinking

Kuhn assumes that the five criteria he lists will separate a good scientific theory from all bogus science. Is this assumption correct?

Looking over the various views of how science acquires its knowledge, we can now see that scientific method incorporates elements from the views of the

46 Thomas Kuhn, *The Structure of Scientific Revolutions* (London: Oxford University Press, 1973).
47 Thomas Kuhn, *The Essential Tension: Selected Studies in Scientific Tradition and Change* (Chicago: University of Chicago Press, 1977), 321.

empiricists, the rationalists, and the transcendental idealists. As inductionism insists, scientific knowledge ultimately depends on sense observations, a source of knowledge that empiricists emphasize. The use of the hypothetical method in science, especially its appeal to simplicity and consistency, reminds us of the rationalist elements that scientific method incorporates. And the creative use of reason to formulate hypotheses that can guide science's research into nature and that can bring order into our sensory observations, brings into the scientific method an element emphasized by the transcendental idealists.

But as we noted at the beginning of this discussion of how science acquires its knowledge of nature, one of the things we hope to draw from this discussion is an understanding of how science differs from pseudoscience. We turn now to that issue.

thinking critically • Distinguishing Science from Pseudoscience

Let's try now to summarize what we've seen and reach some conclusions about what distinguishes science from pseudoscience.

First, our discussion of inductionism suggests that particularly in the establishment of low-level laws, science relies on the inductive method of observation, generalization, and repeated confirmation by new observations. When rival generalizations are in all other respects equal, scientists tend to accept the simplest one, the one that accounts for the facts most economically. But more important than simplicity is the number and variety of new observations that confirm a generalization. Pseudosciences, on the other hand, do not rely on the inductive method to establish any of their claims.

Second, the discussion of the hypothetical method suggests that especially in the establishment of general theories—but also in the establishment of some low-level laws-scientific knowledge requires the creative formulation of hypotheses that can guide research and be tested by observation. Not all creative guesses or hypotheses are on an equal level. A scientific hypothesis must not only be testable by observation. It must also make predictions that can be observed, and it must be capable of guiding new research and suggesting new experiments that can test the hypothesis. Pseudoscientific theories, like astrology, do not provide the basis for this kind of research and experiments.

© Michael Knight/iStockphoto.com

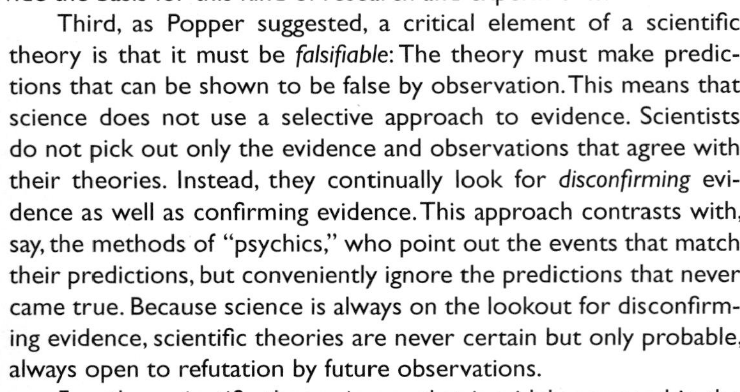

Third, as Popper suggested, a critical element of a scientific theory is that it must be *falsifiable*: The theory must make predictions that can be shown to be false by observation. This means that science does not use a selective approach to evidence. Scientists do not pick out only the evidence and observations that agree with their theories. Instead, they continually look for *disconfirming* evidence as well as confirming evidence. This approach contrasts with, say, the methods of "psychics," who point out the events that match their predictions, but conveniently ignore the predictions that never came true. Because science is always on the lookout for disconfirming evidence, scientific theories are never certain but only probable, always open to refutation by future observations.

Fourth, a scientific theory is one that is widely accepted in the community of scientists; they use the theory to guide their research but may abandon it in a scientific revolution when confronted with too many anomalies for which the theory can no longer account. This means that the evidence on which scientific theories are based must be made available to other people. Experiments or observations that confirm a theory must be capable of being replicated or repeated by others in the community of scientists. This approach contrasts with the methods of, say, UFO researchers, who rely on "sightings" by individuals that cannot be duplicated or repeated by others. Moreover, when confronted with sufficient "anomolies" that cannot be explained by their theory, scientists will eventually abandon a theory, whereas pseudoscientific groups will not. For example, astrologers have tenaciously clung to their theories for centuries, no matter how much evidence has accumulated against them.

Fifth, as Kuhn suggests, a scientific theory must meet five criteria: It must be in accurate agreement with observations; it must be consistent with other prevailing scientific theories; it must have broad consequences that extend beyond the phenomena it was originally designed to explain and that organize and relate phenomena that were previously thought to be disconnected; it must be as simple as possible and simpler than the phenomenon to be explained, and it must be fruitful by suggesting fresh research and new experiments. Pseudoscientific theories generally do not meet these five criteria.

Clearly, these features of science are not shared by the many pseudoscientific claims that we read in newspapers and magazines and find on the Internet. They distinguish genuine science from, say, biorhythm theory, theories of extrasensory perception, parapsychology, astrology, pyramid power, and UFOs. These nonscientific theories are not in agreement with what many other people have observed, they are not consistent with science, they are used as ad hoc explanations of past events but cannot explain or predict future events, they do not look for evidence that can disprove or falsify the theories, they do not help us organize and understand phenomena that were previously felt to be disconnected, and they certainly do not lead to new research programs or fresh scientific experiments. Instead, they are simply grab-bag theories: Their supporters grab at any new findings that seem to agree with their theory, and they stuff these findings into their bag of "evidence."

QUICK REVIEW
The scientific method seems to be distinguished from pseudoscience by the following: (1) it is based on sense observation and rationality; (2) it relies on the inductive method for its low-level laws; (3) it proceeds by formulating hypotheses that can guide research, (4) that are falsifiable, (5) and that are widely accepted in the community of scientists; and (6) its theories are accurate, consistent with other accepted theories, broad, simple, and fruitful.

Is the Theory of Recovered Memories Science or Pseudoscience?

We discussed earlier the controversy over the theory of repressed memory and of recovered memory therapy. Proponents of this theory, as we saw, claim that the theory is scientifically valid. But how does the theory fare when measured against the features that distinguish a real scientific theory from pseudoscience? On several counts, the theory of repressed memory and of recovered memory therapy measures up quite favorably. For example, the theory is widely accepted in the community of scientists composed of psychologists, particularly those belonging to the psychoanalytic school. Furthermore, the theory is in accurate agreement with observations made in clinical practice, it is consistent with certain other psychological theories, it has implications that extend beyond the phenomenon of recovered memories, it is very successful at organizing and relating psychological phenomena that were previously thought to be disconnected, and it is fruitful in suggesting fresh research and experiments. Yet in other respects the theory seems to fail as a genuine scientific theory. In particular, one of the disturbing aspects of recovered memory theory is that it may not be falsifiable. In fact, efforts of critics to disprove the theory have typically been met with the response that the critics are "in denial," and patients in therapy are encouraged to believe that "the existence of profound disbelief is an indication that memories are real."

The scientific validity of the theory of repressed memory and of recovered memory therapy, then, is a complex and troubling issue. It is an issue that demonstrates the importance of having clear views on the valid sources of knowledge and of scientific truth. And it is an issue that readers might profitably continue to pursue on their own, using the concepts and understandings they have developed in the course of this chapter.

QUICK REVIEW
Although the theory of recovered memories meets some of these criteria, it fails to meet others and so seems in some respects to be based on pseudoscience.

QUESTIONS

1. Pick some theory that you believe is pseudoscientific and some theory that is widely accepted as a legitimate part of science. Use the characteristics of science enumerated in this section to explain why the first theory is not scientific and the second is. Are these characteristics adequate for distinguishing between science and pseudoscience?
2. Evaluate these statements: (a) Science gives us an exact and certain knowledge of reality; (b) the primary goal of science is the accumulation of facts or data.
3. Some people argue that because scientists rely on hypotheses and accepted theories to guide their research, they approach reality with preconceptions that inevitably distort what they observe. Is this true? Would it be possible to investigate nature without preconceptions? Explain your answers.
4. What characteristics of science are present in the way that you ordinarily try to find out something about the people and the world around you? Which characteristics are absent? Does this make your knowledge more or less reliable than that of the scientist?
5. Based on the characteristics of science outlined in the chapter, can science answer the question of whether God exists?

PHILOSOPHY AT THE MOVIES

Watch *Kinsey* (2004), which portrays the life of famous sex researcher Alfred Kinsey who revolutionized the study of human sexual behavior as well as society's approach to sexuality. Which of the various theories of science and scientific knowledge are confirmed or disconfirmed by Kinsey's approach to research and by the discoveries he made?

Movie with a related theme: *A Beautiful Mind* (2001).

Chapter Summary

The issues of who we are and how we are to live are tied to the question of knowledge. Historically, philosophers have asked this question: If there are different kinds of knowledge of reality, how can they be obtained? The most common view is that there are two main sources of such knowledge: reason—favored by the rationalists—and sense observation—favored by empiricists. Among the outstanding rationalists is René Descartes, who attempted to demonstrate the validity of *a priori* knowledge—that is, knowledge independent of sensory perception.

In vigorous reaction to Descartes and the rationalists are the British empiricists: Locke, Berkeley, and Hume. They insist that all knowledge of reality is *a posteriori*—that is, it follows from experience. One crucial problem that empiricists face arises from their distinction between an objective reality and our experience of it. If these are differentiated, how do we know that our experiences correspond with how things are? Locke's answer is that our experiences represent the outside world. Berkeley says that all we ever know are our own ideas; only conscious minds and their perceptions exist. For Hume, reality is not truly knowable.

Immanuel Kant proposed his theory of transcendental idealism to demonstrate that knowledge of reality is possible. Whereas Kant argues that true knowledge of reality has its basis in sensory experience, he also claims that the mind has innate capacities to order that sensory experience and thus arrive at knowledge.

We have seen that modern science incorporates elements of all these traditions. Scientific "knowledge" is based on induction and simplicity, on the hypothetical method and creativity, on falsifiability and predictive power, on wide acceptance by the community of scientists, as well as on accuracy, consistency, explanatory power, the ability to relate what was previously disconnected, and fruitfulness. Pseudoscientific theories such as astrology do not possess these features.

The main points of this chapter, then, are the following:

5.1 Why Is Knowledge a Problem?

- To understand and resolve controversies like the controversy over recovered memories, it is necessary to have an understanding of what knowledge is.
- There are two common views regarding the sources of knowledge: rationalism and empiricism.
- Memory does not provide us with new knowledge, but preserves knowledge that we acquire from other sources.

5.2 Is Reason the Source of Our Knowledge?

- René Descartes was a rationalist concerned with discovering something that he could hold as true beyond any doubt. He concluded that reason provides our knowledge of the essential nature of reality, that the existence of God guarantees that we are not deceived, and that some of our knowledge is innate. All of this, he claimed, could be established by reason alone.
- With the example of a slave boy who reveals his knowledge of geometry, Plato argued that we have an innate knowledge of geometry that we acquired in a previous existence.

5.3 Can the Senses Account for All Our Knowledge?

- Empiricism states that all knowledge comes from or is based on sensory perception and is *a posteriori.*
- John Locke held that we have knowledge of the primary qualities of things, such as their size, shape, and weight, and that such primary qualities really exist in external objects. Secondary qualities such as colors, smells, and sounds, are sensations in us caused by the powers of external objects; these qualities do not really exist in external objects. We know the external world through the primary qualities we perceive by our senses, and we know there are external objects because they must cause our sensations.
- According to George Berkeley's subjectivist theory of knowledge, we know only our own ideas. He argues that Locke's primary qualities are as mind-dependent as secondary qualities, and that we have no knowledge of external material objects.
- David Hume pushed Locke's and Berkeley's empiricism to its logical conclusion, arguing that all knowledge depends on our sense impressions and that we cannot claim something exists unless we perceive it through some sense impression. Since we have no sense impressions of the self, an external world, or of causal relations, we cannot say these are real. Moreover, we have no justification for claiming that our past experiences of causes provide us knowledge of future causes.

- The Problem of Induction is the problem of showing that we are justified in claiming that since some things were observed to have certain features in the past, all of those types of things will have those same features in the future.

- **Inductive generalizations are probable arguments whose premises indicate that something is true of a limited sample, and whose conclusion claims that the same is true of the whole population. Their strength depends on how large and how representative the sample is.**

5.4 Kant: Does the Knowing Mind Shape the World?

- Immanuel Kant's transcendental idealism, an alternative to empiricism and rationalism, distinguishes between things as we experience them (phenomena) and things as they are in themselves (noumena); we know phenomena but have no knowledge of noumena. The mind, claimed Kant, organizes our sensations and posits relationships among them by arranging these sensations into the world we perceive. Through an awareness of these relationships, we acquire knowledge that is synthetic and a priori, such as our knowledge of causal relationships. The mind organizes its many sensations into a unified world because it is a unified awareness and so must unify its many sensations to bring them into its unified awareness. The mind unifies its many sensations by connecting them with causal relationships and other kinds of relationships.

5.5 Does Science Give Us Knowledge?

- Inductionism is the view that all science is based on the process of sensory observation, generalization, and repeated confirmation. This process is often used to establish scientific laws, and simplicity is one criterion for choosing among competing generalizations.

- The hypothetical method view says that science is also based on the creative formulation of hypotheses whose predictions are then tested and used to guide research. Karl Popper argued that falsifiability is a criterion of scientific theories.

- Thomas Kuhn argued that scientific theories are those that are widely accepted by a community of scientists. They are the basis of paradigms that guide research but that are abandoned in a scientific revolution, when too many anomalies appear that cannot be accounted for by the paradigm.

- Scientific theories must be accurate, consistent with other widely accepted theories, capable of explaining phenomena other than those they were developed to explain, capable of organizing phenomena that were previously thought to be unrelated, and fruitful insofar as they generate new research and new discoveries.

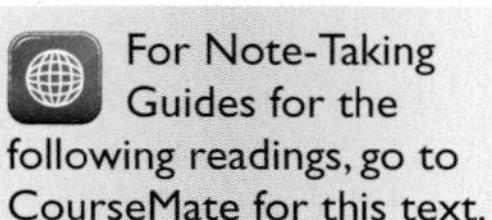
For Note-Taking Guides for the following readings, go to CourseMate for this text.

5.6 Readings

The first reading that follows is the intriguing story "An Occurrence at Owl Creek Bridge," by Ambrose Bierce. As a Southern planter is being hanged by Union soldiers during the Civil War, he falls free and, escaping, travels the many miles to his wife and the home he desperately wants to see again, only to lose them in a final moment in which the illusory nature of his hoped-for world is revealed. Bierce's story forces us to ask whether we can know that we are not deceiving ourselves about the world we see around us.

In the next article, contemporary philosopher Peter Unger argues that in fact we can never know for sure whether our beliefs about the world are true or whether they are deceptions introduced into our mind by some "exotic" means or by our ordinary impulses. Unger begins by considering what he calls the "exotic and bizarre case of a deceiving scientist" who artificially implants false beliefs in our minds, and then he goes on to consider more "ordinary" cases of being deceived by our natural impulses. He concludes that we can never really know anything about the external world. Unger suggests that if we are to be rational and undogmatic, we should stop using the words "I know."

In the last article, Thomas Nagel, also a contemporary philosopher, raises the possibility that all of our knowledge about the world around us might be a giant illusion. He then examines an argument by which people have sometimes tried to prove that such skepticism is meaningless. However, Nagel concludes that this argument against skepticism fails. Yet, he suggests, we have no choice but to live as if our ordinary beliefs about the world around us are true.

AMBROSE BIERCE

An Occurrence at Owl Creek Bridge

A man stood upon a railroad bridge in northern Alabama, looking down into the swift water twenty feet below. The man's hands were behind his back, the wrists bound with a cord. A rope closely encircled his neck. It was attached to a stout cross-timber above his head and the slack fell to the level of his knees. Some loose boards laid upon the sleepers supporting the metals of the railway supplied a footing for him and his executioners—two private soldiers of the Federal army, directed by a sergeant who in civil life may have been a deputy sheriff. At a short remove upon the same temporary platform was an officer in the uniform of his rank, armed. He was a captain. A sentinel at each end of the bridge stood with his rifle in the position known as "support," that is to say, vertical in front of the left shoulder, the hammer resting on the forearm thrown straight across the chest—a formal and unnatural position, enforcing an erect carriage of the body. It did not appear to be the duty of these two men to know what was occurring at the center of the bridge; they merely blockaded the two ends of the foot planking that traversed it.

Beyond one of the sentinels nobody was in sight; the railroad ran straight away into a forest for a hundred yards, then, curving, was lost to view. Doubtless there was an outpost farther along. The other bank of the stream was open ground—a gentle acclivity topped with a stockade of vertical tree trunks, loopholed for rifles, with a single embrasure through which protruded the muzzle of a brass cannon commanding the bridge. Midway of the slope between the bridge and fort were the spectators—a single company of infantry in line, at "parade rest," the butts of the rifles on the ground, the barrels inclining slightly backward against the right shoulder, the hands crossed upon the stock. A lieutenant stood at the right of the line, the point of his sword upon the ground, his left hand resting upon his right. Excepting the group of four at the center of the bridge, not a man moved. The company faced the bridge, staring stonily, motionless. The sentinels, facing the banks of the stream, might have been statues to adorn the bridge. The captain stood with folded arms, silent, observing the work of his subordinates, but making no sign. Death is a dignitary who when he comes announced is to be received with formal manifestations of respect, even by those most familiar with him. In the code of military etiquette silence and fixity are forms of deference.

The man who was engaged in being hanged was apparently about thirty-five years of age. He was a civilian, if one might judge from his habit,* which

*Clothing.—Ed.

was that of a planter. His features were good—a straight nose, firm mouth, broad forehead, from which his long, dark hair was combed straight back, falling behind his ears to the collar of his well-fitting frock coat. He wore a mustache and pointed beard, but no whiskers; his eyes were large and dark gray, and had a kindly expression which one would hardly have expected in one whose neck was in the hemp. Evidently this was no vulgar assassin. The liberal military code makes provision for hanging many kinds of persons, and gentlemen are not excluded.

The preparations being complete, the two private soldiers stepped aside and each drew away the plank upon which he had been standing. The sergeant turned to the captain, saluted and placed himself immediately behind that officer, who in turn moved apart one pace. These movements left the condemned man and the sergeant standing on the two ends of the same plank, which spanned three of the crossties of the bridge. The end upon which the civilian stood almost, but not quite, reached a fourth. This plank had been held in place by the weight of the captain; it was now held by that of the sergeant. At a signal from the former the latter would step aside, the plank would tilt and the condemned man go down between two ties. The arrangement commended itself to his judgment as simple and effective. His face had not been covered nor his eyes bandaged. He looked a moment at his "unsteadfast footing," then let his gaze wander to the swirling water of the stream racing madly beneath his feet. A piece of dancing driftwood caught his attention and his eyes followed it down the current. How slowly it appeared to move! What a sluggish stream!

He closed his eyes in order to fix his last thoughts upon his wife and children. The water, touched to gold by the early sun, the brooding mists under the banks at some distance down the stream, the fort, the soldiers, the piece of drift—all had distracted him. And now he became conscious of a new disturbance. Striking through the thought of his dear ones was a sound which he could neither ignore nor understand, a sharp, distinct, metallic percussion like the stroke of a blacksmith's hammer upon the anvil; it had the same ringing quality. He wondered what it was, and whether immeasurably distant or near by—it seemed both. Its recurrence was regular, but as slow as the tolling of a death knell. He awaited each stroke with impatience and—he knew not why—apprehension. The intervals of silence grew progressively longer, the delays became maddening. With their greater infrequency the sounds increased in strength and sharpness. They hurt his ear like the thrust of a knife; he feared he would shriek. What he heard was the ticking of his watch.

He unclosed his eyes and saw again the water below him. "If I could free my hands," he thought, "I might throw off the noose and spring into the stream. By diving I could evade the bullets and, swimming vigorously, reach the bank, take to the woods and get away home. My home, thank God, is as yet outside their lines; my wife and little ones are still beyond the invader's farthest advance." As these thoughts, which have here been set down in words, were flashed into the doomed man's brain rather than evolved from it the captain nodded to the sergeant. The sergeant stepped aside.

II

Peyton Farquhar was a well-to-do planter, of an old and highly respected Alabama family. Being a slave owner and like other slave owners a politician he was naturally an original secessionist and ardently devoted to the Southern cause. Circumstances of an imperious nature, which it is unnecessary to relate here, had prevented him from taking service with the gallant army that had fought the disastrous campaigns ending with the fall of Corinth, and he chafed under the inglorious restraint, longing for the release of his energies, the larger life of the soldier, the opportunity for distinction. That opportunity, he felt, would come, as it comes to all in war time. Meanwhile he did what he could. No service was too humble for him to perform in aid of the South, no adventure too perilous for him to undertake if consistent with the character of a civilian who was at heart a soldier, and who in good faith and without too much qualification assented to at least a part of the frankly villainous dictum that all is fair in love and war.

One evening while Farquhar and his wife were sitting on a rustic bench near the entrance to his grounds, a gray-clad soldier rode up to the gate and asked for a drink of water. Mrs. Farquhar was only too happy to serve him with her own white hands. While she was fetching the water her husband approached the dusty horseman and inquired eagerly for news from the front.

"The Yanks are repairing the railroads," said the man, "and are getting ready for another advance. They have reached the Owl Creek bridge, put it in order and built a stockade on the north bank. The commandant has issued an order, which is posted everywhere, declaring that any civilian caught interfering with the railroad, its bridges, tunnels or trains will be summarily hanged. I saw the order."

"How far is it to the Owl Creek bridge?" Farquhar asked.

"About thirty miles."

"Is there no force on this side the creek?"

"Only a picket post half a mile out, on the railroad, and a single sentinel at this end of the bridge."

"Suppose a man—a civilian and student of hanging—should elude the picket post and perhaps get the better of the sentinel," said Farquhar, smiling, "what could he accomplish?"

The soldier reflected. "I was there a month ago," he replied. "I observed that the flood of last winter had lodged a great quantity of driftwood against the wooden pier at this end of the bridge. It is now dry and would burn like tow."

The lady had now brought the water, which the soldier drank. He thanked her ceremoniously, bowed to her husband and rode away. An hour later, after nightfall, he repassed the plantation, going northward in the direction from which he had come. He was a Federal scout.

III

As Peyton Farquhar fell straight downward through the bridge he lost consciousness and was as one already dead. From this state he was awakened—ages later, it seemed to him—by the pain of a sharp pressure upon his throat, followed by a sense of suffocation. Keen, poignant agonies seemed to shoot from his neck downward through every fiber of his body and limbs. These pains appeared to flash along well-defined lines of ramification and to beat with an inconceivably rapid periodicity. They seemed like streams of pulsating fire heating him to an intolerable temperature. As to his head, he was conscious of nothing but a feeling of fullness—of congestion. These sensations were unaccompanied by thought. The intellectual part of his nature was already effaced; he had power only to feel, and feeling was torment. He was conscious of motion. Encompassed in a luminous cloud, of which he was now merely the fiery heart, without material substance, he swung through unthinkable arcs of oscillation, like a vast pendulum. Then all at once, with terrible suddenness, the light about him shot upward with the noise of a loud splash; a frightful roaring was in his ears, and all was cold and dark. The power of thought was restored; he knew that the rope had broken and he had fallen into the stream. There was no additional strangulation; the noose about his neck was already suffocating him and kept the water from his lungs. To die of hanging at the bottom of a river!—the idea seemed to him ludicrous. He opened his eyes in the darkness and saw above him a gleam of light, but how distant, how inaccessible! He was still sinking, for the light became fainter and fainter until it was a mere glimmer. Then it began to grow and brighten, and he knew that he was rising toward the surface—knew it with reluctance, for he was now very comfortable. "To be hanged and drowned," he thought, "that is not so bad; but I do not wish to be shot. No; I will not be shot; that is not fair."

He was not conscious of an effort, but a sharp pain in his wrist apprised him that he was trying to free his hands. He gave the struggle his attention, as an idler might observe the feat of a juggler, without interest in the outcome. What splendid effort!—what magnificent, what superhuman strength! Ah, that was a fine endeavor! Bravo! The cord fell away; his arms parted and floated upward, the hands dimly seen on each side in the growing light. He watched them with a new interest as first one and then the other pounced upon the noose at his neck. They tore it away and thrust it fiercely aside, its undulations resembling those of a water snake. "Put it back, put it back!" He thought he shouted these words to his hands, for the undoing of the noose had been succeeded by the direst pang that he had yet experienced. His neck ached horribly; his brain was on fire; his heart, which had been fluttering faintly, gave a great leap, trying to force itself out at his mouth. His whole body was racked and wrenched with an insupportable anguish! But his disobedient hands gave no heed to the command. They beat the water vigorously with quick, downward strokes, forcing him to the surface. He felt his head emerge; his eyes were blinded by the sunlight; his chest expanded convulsively, and with a supreme and crowning agony his lungs engulfed a great draught of air, which instantly he expelled in a shriek!

He was now in full possession of his physical senses. They were, indeed, preternaturally keen and alert. Something in the awful disturbance of his organic system had so exalted and refined them that they made record of things never before perceived. He felt the ripples upon his face and heard their separate sounds as they struck. He looked at the forest on the bank of the stream, saw the individual trees, the leaves and the veining of each leaf—saw the very insects upon them: the locusts, the brilliant-bodied flies, the grey spiders stretching their webs from twig to twig. He noted the prismatic colors in all the dewdrops upon a million blades of grass. The humming of the gnats that danced above the eddies of the stream, the beating of the dragon flies' wings, the strokes of the waterspiders' legs, like oars which had lifted their boat—all these made audible music. A fish slid along beneath his eyes and he heard the rush of its body parting the water.

He had come to the surface facing down the stream; in a moment the visible world seemed to wheel slowly round, himself the pivotal point, and he saw the bridge, the fort, the soldiers upon the bridge, the captain, the sergeant, the two privates, his executioners. They were in silhouette against the blue sky. They shouted and gesticulated, pointing at him. The captain had drawn his pistol, but did not fire; the others were unarmed. Their movements were grotesque and horrible, their forms gigantic.

Suddenly he heard a sharp report and something struck the water smartly within a few inches of his head, spattering his face with spray. He heard a second report, and saw one of the sentinels with his rifle at his shoulder, a light cloud of blue smoke rising from the muzzle. The man in the water saw the eye of the man on the bridge gazing into his own through the sights of the rifle. He observed that it was a gray eye and remembered having read that gray eyes were keenest, and that all famous marksmen had them. Nevertheless, this one had missed.

A counter-swirl had caught Farquhar and turned him half round; he was again looking into the forest on the bank opposite the fort. The sound of a clear, high voice in a monotonous singsong now rang out behind him and came across the water with a distinctness that pierced and subdued all other sounds, even the beating of the ripples in his ears. Although no soldier, he had frequented camps enough to know the dread significance of that deliberate, drawling, aspirated chant; the lieutenant on shore was taking a part in the morning's work. How coldly and pitilessly—with what an even, calm intonation, presaging, and enforcing tranquillity in the men—with what accurately measured intervals fell those cruel words:

"Attention, company! . . . Shoulder arms! . . . Ready! . . . Aim! . . . Fire!"

Farquhar dived—dived as deeply as he could. The water roared in his ears like the voice of Niagara, yet he heard the dulled thunder of the volley and, rising again toward the surface, met shining bits of metal, singularly flattened, oscillating slowly downward. Some of them touched him on the face and hands, then fell away, continuing their descent. One lodged between his collar and neck; it was uncomfortably warm and he snatched it out.

As he rose to the surface, gasping for breath, he saw that he had been a long time under water; he was perceptibly farther down stream—nearer to safety. The soldiers had almost finished reloading; the metal ramrods flashed all at once in the sunshine as they were drawn from the barrels, turned in the air, and thrust into their sockets. The two sentinels fired again, independently and ineffectually.

The hunted man saw all this over his shoulder; he was now swimming vigorously with the current. His brain was as energetic as his arms and legs; he thought with the rapidity of lightning.

"The officer," he reasoned, "will not make that martinet's error a second time. It is as easy to dodge a volley as a single shot. He has probably already given the command to fire at will. God help me, I cannot dodge them all!"

An appalling splash within two yards of him was followed by a loud, rushing sound, *diminuendo,* which seemed to travel back through the air to the fort and died in an explosion which stirred the very river to its deeps! A rising sheet of water curved over him, fell down upon him, blinded him, strangled him! The cannon had taken a hand in the game. As he shook his head free from the commotion of the smitten water he heard the deflected shot humming through the air ahead, and in an instant it was cracking and smashing the branches in the forest beyond.

"They will not do that again," he thought; "the next time they will use a charge of grape. I must keep my eye upon the gun; the smoke will apprise me—the report arrives too late; it lags behind the missile. That is a good gun."

Suddenly he felt himself whirled round and round—spinning like a top. The water, the banks, the forests, the now distant bridge, fort and men—all were commingled and blurred. Objects were represented by their colors only; circular horizontal streaks of color—that was all he saw. He had been caught in a vortex and was being whirled on with a velocity of advance and gyration that made him giddy and sick. In a few moments he was flung upon the gravel at the foot of the left bank of the stream—the southern bank—and behind a projecting point which concealed him from his enemies. The sudden arrest of his motion, the abrasion of one of his hands on the gravel, restored him, and he wept with delight. He dug his fingers into the sand, threw it over himself in handfuls and audibly blessed it. It looked like diamonds, rubies, emeralds; he could think of nothing beautiful which it did not resemble. The trees upon the bank were giant garden plants; he noted a definite order in their arrangement, inhaled the fragrance of their blooms. A strange, roseate light shone through the spaces among their trunks and the wind made in their branches the music of Æolian harps. He had no wish to perfect his escape—was content to remain in that enchanting spot until retaken.

A whiz and rattle of grapeshot among the branches high above his head roused him from his dream. The baffled cannoneer had fired him a random farewell. He sprang to his feet, rushed up the sloping bank, and plunged into the forest.

All that day he traveled, laying his course by the rounding sun. The forest seemed interminable; nowhere did he discover a break in it, not even a woodman's road. He had not known that he lived in so wild a region. There was something uncanny in the revelation.

By nightfall he was fatigued, footsore, famishing. The thought of his wife and children urged him on. At last he found a road which led him in what he knew to be the right direction. It was as wide and straight as a city street, yet it seemed untraveled. No fields bordered it, no dwelling anywhere. Not so much as the barking of a dog suggested human habitation. The black bodies of the trees formed a straight wall on both sides, terminating on the horizon in a point, like a diagram in a lesson in perspective. Overhead, as he looked up through this rift in the wood, shone great golden stars looking unfamiliar and grouped in strange constellations. He was sure they were arranged in some order which had a secret and malign significance. The wood on either side was full of singular noises, among which—once, twice, and again—he distinctly heard whispers in an unknown tongue.

His neck was in pain and lifting his hand to it found it horribly swollen. He knew that it had a circle of black where the rope had bruised it. His eyes felt congested; he could no longer close them. His tongue was swollen with thirst; he relieved its fever by thrusting it forward from between his teeth into the cold air. How softly the turf had carpeted the untraveled avenue—he could no longer feel the roadway beneath his feet!

Doubtless, despite his suffering, he had fallen asleep while walking, for now he sees another scene—perhaps he has merely recovered from a delirium. He stands at the gate of his own home. All is as he left it, and all bright and beautiful in the morning sunshine. He must have traveled the entire night. As he pushes open the gate and passes up the wide white walk, he sees a flutter of female garments; his wife, looking fresh and cool and sweet, steps down from the veranda to meet him. At the bottom of the steps she stands waiting, with a smile of ineffable joy, an attitude of matchless grace and dignity. Ah, how beautiful she is! He springs forward with extended arms. As he is about to clasp her he feels a stunning blow upon the back of the neck; a blinding white light blazes all about him with a sound like the shock of a cannon—then all is darkness and silence!

Peyton Farquhar was dead; his body, with a broken neck, swung gently from side to side beneath the timbers of the Owl Creek Bridge.

PETER UNGER

A Defense of Skepticism

A Classical Form of Skeptical Argument

There are certain arguments for skepticism which conform to a familiar . . . pattern or form. These arguments rely, at least for their psychological power, on vivid descriptions of exotic *contrast cases.* The following is one such rough argument, this one in support of skepticism regarding any alleged *knowledge of an external world.* The exotic contrast case here concerns an evil scientist, and is described to be in line with the most up to date developments of science, or science fiction. We begin by arbitrarily choosing something concerning an external world which might conceivably, we suppose, be *known,* in one way or another, e.g., that there are rocks or, as we will understand it, that there is at least one rock.

Now, first, *if* someone, anyone *knows* that there are rocks, then the person *can know* the following quite exotic thing: There is *no* evil scientist deceiving him into *falsely* believing that there are rocks. This scientist uses electrodes to induce experiences and thus carries out his deceptions, concerning the existence of rocks or anything else. He first drills holes painlessly in the variously colored skulls, or shells, of his subjects and then implants his electrodes into the appropriate parts of their brains, or protoplasm, or systems. He sends patterns of electrical impulses into them through the electrodes, which are themselves connected by wires to a laboratory console on which he plays, punching various keys and buttons in accordance with his ideas of how the whole thing works and with his deceptive designs. The scientist's delight is intense, and it is caused not so much by his exercising his scientific and intellectual gifts as by the thought that he is deceiving various subjects about all sorts of things. Part of that delight is caused, on this supposition, by his thought that he is deceiving a certain person, perhaps yourself, into falsely believing that there are rocks. He is, then, an evil scientist, and he lives in a world which is entirely bereft of rocks.

Now, as we have agreed, (1) *if you know* that there are rocks, then you *can know* that there is no such scientist doing this to you [i.e., deceiving you to falsely believe that there are rocks]. But (2) no one *can* ever *know* that this exotic situation does *not obtain*; no one *can* ever *know* that there is *no* evil scientist who is, by means of electrodes, deceiving him into falsely believing there to be rocks. That is our second premise, and it is also very difficult to deny. So, thirdly, as a consequence of these two premises, we have our skeptical conclusion: (3) You never *know* that there are rocks. But of course we have chosen our person, and the matter of there being rocks, quite arbitrarily, and this argument, it surely seems, may be generalized to cover any external matter at all. From this, we may conclude, finally, that (4) nobody ever *knows* anything about the external world.

[A philosopher's] attempt to reverse our argument will proceed like this: (1) According to your argument, nobody ever *knows* that there are rocks. (2) But I *do* know that there are rocks. This is something concerning the external world, and I do know it. Hence, (3) somebody *does know* something about the external world. . . . And so, while I might not have known *before* that there is no such scientist, at least (4) I *now* do know that there is no evil scientist who is deceiving me into falsely believing that there are rocks. So far has the skeptical argument failed to challenge my knowledge successfully that it seems actually to have occasioned an increase in what I know about things.

While the robust character of this reply has a definite appeal, it also seems quite daring. Indeed, the more one thinks on it, the more it seems to be somewhat foolhardy and even dogmatic. One cannot help but think that for all this philosopher really can *know,* he might have all his experience artificially induced by electrodes, these being operated by a terribly evil scientist who, having an idea of what his "protege" is saying to himself, chuckles accordingly. . . .

[Suppose you were this philosopher.] Now, we may suppose that electrodes are removed, that your experiences are now brought about through your perception of actual surroundings, and you are, so to speak, forced to encounter your deceptive tormentor. Wouldn't you be made to feel quite *foolish,* even *embarrassed,* by your claims to *know*? Indeed, you would seem to be exposed quite clearly as having been, not only wrong, but rather irrational and even dogmatic. . . .

It seems much better, perhaps perfectly all right, if you are instead only *confident* that there is no such scientist. It seems perfectly all right for you to *believe* there to be no evil scientist doing this. If you say, not only that you believe it, but that you have some *reason* to believe this thing, what you say *may* seem somewhat suspect, at least on reasoned reflection, but it doesn't have any obvious tint of dogmatism or irrationality to it. . . .

Ordinary Cases

Largely because it is so exotic and bizarre, the case of a deceiving scientist lets one feel acutely the apparent irrationality in thinking oneself to know. But the exotic cases have no monopoly on generating feelings of irrationality.

[For example,] you may think you *know* that a certain city is the capital of a certain state, and you may feel quite content in this thought while watching another looking the matter up in the library. You will feel quite foolish, however, if the person announces the result to be *another* city, and if subsequent experience seems to show that announcement to be right. This will occur, I suggest, even if you are just an anonymous, disinterested bystander who happens to hear the question posed and the answer later announced. This is true even if the reference was a newspaper, *The Times,* and the capital was changed only yesterday. But these feelings will be very much less apparent, or will not occur at all, if you only feel very confident, at the outset, that the city is thus-and-such, which later is not announced. You might of course feel that you shouldn't be quite so confident of such things, or that you should watch out in the future. But you probably *wouldn't* feel, I suggest, that you were *irrational* to be confident of that thing at that time. Much less would you feel that you were *dogmatic* in so being. . . .

It is hard for us to think that there is any important similarity between such common cases as these and the case of someone thinking himself to *know* that *there are rocks.* Exotic contrast cases, like the case of the evil scientist, help one to appreciate that these cases are really essentially the same. By means of contrast cases, we encourage thinking of all sorts of new sequences of experience, sequences which people would never begin to imagine in the normal course of affairs. How would you react to such developments as *these,* no matter *how* exotic or unlikely? It appears that the proper reaction is to feel as irrational about claiming knowledge of rocks as you felt before, where, e.g., one was apparently caught in thought by the library reference to the state's capital. Who would have thought so, before thinking of contrast cases? Those cases help you see, I suggest, that in *either* case, no matter whether you are in fact right in the matter or whether wrong, thinking that you *know* manifests an attitude of dogmatism. Bizarre experiential sequences help show that there is no essential difference between any two external matters; the apparently most certain ones, like that of rocks, and the ones where thinking about *knowing* appears, even without the most exotic skeptical aids, *not* the way to think.

Reprinted from *Ignorance* by Peter Unger. Copyright © Oxford University Press, 1975.

THOMAS NAGEL

How Do We Know Anything?

Ordinarily you have no doubts about the existence of the floor under your feet, or the tree outside the window, or your own teeth. In fact most of the time you don't even think about the mental states that make you aware of those things: you seem to be aware of them directly. But how do you know they really exist? Would things seem any different to you if in fact all these things existed *only* in your mind—if everything you took to be the real world outside was just a giant dream or hallucination, from which you will never wake up? . . .

How can you know that isn't what's going on? If all your experience were a dream with *nothing* outside, then any evidence you tried to use to prove to yourself that there was an outside world would just be part of the dream. If you knocked on the table or pinched yourself, you would hear the knock and feel the pinch, but that would be just one more thing going on inside your mind like everything else. It's no use: If you want to find out whether what's inside your mind is any guide to what's outside your mind, you can't depend on how things *seem*—from inside your mind—to give you the answer.

But what else is there to depend on? All your evidence about anything has to come through your mind—whether in the form of perception, the testimony of books and other people, or memory—and it is entirely consistent with everything you're aware of that *nothing at all* exists except the inside of your mind. . . .

Some would argue that radical skepticism of the kind I have been talking about is meaningless, because the idea of an external reality that *no one* could ever discover is meaningless. The argument is that a dream, for instance, has to be something from which you *can* wake up to discover that you have been asleep; a hallucination has to be something which others (or you later) *can* see is not really there. Impressions and appearances that do not correspond to reality must be contrasted with others that *do* correspond to reality, or else the contrast between appearance and reality is meaningless.

According to this view, the idea of a dream from which you can never wake up is not the idea of a dream at all: it is the idea of *reality*—the real world in which you live. Our idea of the things that exist is just our idea of what we can observe. (This view is sometimes called verificationism.) Sometimes our observations are mistaken, but that means they can be corrected by other observations—as when you wake up from a dream or discover that what you thought was a snake was just a shadow on the grass. But without some possibility of a correct view of how things are (either yours or someone else's), the thought that your impressions of the world are not true is meaningless.

If this is right, then the skeptic is kidding himself if he thinks he can imagine that the only thing that exists is his own mind. He is kidding himself, because it couldn't be true that the physical world doesn't really exist, unless somebody could *observe* that it doesn't exist. And what the skeptic is trying to imagine is precisely that there is no one to observe that or anything else—except of course the skeptic himself, and all he can observe is the inside of his own mind. So solipsism is meaningless. It tries to subtract the external world from the totality of my impressions; but it fails, because if the external world is subtracted, they stop being mere impressions, and become instead perceptions of reality.

Is this argument against solipsism and skepticism any good? Not unless reality can be defined as what we can observe. But are we really unable to understand the idea of a real world, or a fact about reality, that can't be observed by anyone, human or otherwise?

The skeptic will claim that if there is an external world, the things in it are observable because they exist, and not the other way around: that existence isn't the same thing as observability. And although we get the idea of dreams and hallucinations from cases where we think we *can* observe the contrast between our experiences and reality, it certainly seems as if the same idea can be extended to cases where the reality is not observable.

If that is right, it seems to follow that it is not meaningless to think that the world might consist of nothing but the inside of your mind, though neither you nor anyone else could find out that this was true. And if this is not meaningless, but is a possibility you must consider, there seems no way to prove that it is false, without arguing in a circle. So there may be no way out of the cage of your own mind. This is sometimes called the egocentric predicament.

And yet, after all this has been said, I have to admit it is practically impossible to believe seriously that all the things in the world around you might not really exist. Our acceptance of the external world is instinctive and powerful: we cannot just get rid of it by philosophical arguments. Not only do we go on acting *as if* other people and things exist: we *believe* that they do, even after we've gone through the arguments which appear to show we have no grounds for this belief. (We may have grounds, within the overall system of our beliefs about the world, for more particular beliefs about the existence of particular things: like a mouse in the breadbox, for example. But that is different. It assumes the existence of the external world.)

If a belief in the world outside our minds comes so naturally to us, perhaps we don't need grounds for it. We can just let it be and hope that we're right. And that in fact is what most people do after giving up the attempt to prove it: even if they can't give reasons against skepticism, they can't live with it either. But this means that we hold on to most of our ordinary beliefs about the world in face of the fact that (a) they might be completely false, and (b) we have no basis for ruling out that possibility.

We are left then with three questions:

1. Is it a meaningful possibility that the inside of your mind is the only thing that exists—or that even if there is a world outside your mind, it is totally unlike what you believe it to be?
2. If these things are possible, do you have any way of proving to yourself that they are not actually true?
3. If you can't prove that anything exists outside your own mind, is it all right to go on believing in the external world anyway?

From *What Does It All Mean? A Very Short Introduction to Philosophy* by Thomas Nagel. © 1987 by Thomas Nagel. Reprinted by permission of Oxford University Press, Inc.

5.7 HISTORICAL SHOWCASE

Hume

This showcase features a British philosopher who profoundly influenced our views on human knowledge: David Hume. Hume raised profound questions about what we can know, what humans are, and whether God exists.

The man who most deeply influenced our modern perspectives on knowledge is the eighteenth-century philosopher David Hume. To a large extent, the philosophers who followed Hume either enthusiastically embraced his empiricist views or desperately sought to refute his claims. In either case, they were reacting to the radical empiricism he formulated. Everyone who comes after Hume must take his arguments into account.

This chapter showcases Hume because of his pervasive influence on our views of knowledge. In addition, by considering Hume's work, you can appreciate how our views of knowledge can affect our views of human nature, God, and the sciences. Hume's empiricist views on knowledge led him to raise crucial questions in all of these areas.

David Hume, the "ultimate skeptic," was born in 1711 into a comfortable family who lived on a small country estate called Ninewells in Edinburgh, Scotland. Hume's father died when David was two. His mother, who took over the task of rearing him, said of the boy: "Davey is a well-meanin' critter, but uncommon weakminded." Nevertheless, a few weeks before his twelfth birthday, Hume entered Edinburgh University, where his family hoped he would be able to earn a degree in law. But university life was unpleasant for Hume, and two years later he dropped out without finishing his degree, having convinced his family that he could as easily study law at home. As Hume later wrote, "My studious disposition, my sobriety, and my industry gave my family a notion that the law was a proper profession for me. But I found an insurmountable aversion to everything but the pursuits of philosophy and general learning, and while they fancied I was poring over [the legal texts of] Voet and Vinnius, Cicero and Vergil were the authors which I was secretly devouring."[1] As a teenager, Hume sat around the house reading, all the while complaining he was being forced to struggle with various physical and mental ailments.

© Scottish National Portrait Gallery, Edinburgh, Scotland/The Bridgeman Art Library

David Hume: "Here, therefore, is a proposition which might banish all metaphysical reasonings: When we entertain any suspicion that a philosophical term is employed without any meaning, we inquire, from what impression is that supposed idea derived? And if it be impossible to assign any, this will confirm our suspicion."

Then, in his late teens, Hume convinced himself that he had found a truly new philosophy. As he put it, "There seemed to be opened up to me a new Scene of Thought, which transported me beyond measure and made me, with an ardour natural to young men, throw up every other pleasure or business to apply entirely to it." David then spent much of his day trying to think out and express to others the "new" thoughts he believed that he had discovered.

Although living at home, Hume apparently managed to get around. At the age of twenty-two he was accused by a young woman named Anne Gal-braith of fathering her child, who had been conceived out of wedlock. Hume was sent away to work in the office of a Bristol merchant, but before the year was out he had quit the job he so detested and was sent to live in France on a tiny allowance. There, he spent the next three years living in "rigid frugality" while writing a book, *A Treatise of Human Nature*, in which he tried to express his new philosophy. The book was published in 1737, and by 1739 David was once again living at home in Ninewells, confident that he would soon be famous. To his bitter disappointment, when the book appeared, no one cared: "It fell dead-born from the press, without reaching such distinction as even to excite a murmur from the zealots."[2]

In 1745, Hume tried to get a position teaching ethics at Edinburgh University but was turned down. Instead, he took the job of tutor to a young marquise, who unfortunately turned out to be insane.

1 David Hume, *The Essays Moral, Political and Literary* (Oxford: Oxford University Press, 1963), 608.
2 Ibid.

The next several years Hume spent alternately working as a secretary for a general and living at home. He wrote continuously during this period, producing, among other things, a much shorter and simplified version of his *Treatise* titled *An Enquiry Concerning Human Understanding* and numerous essays on politics, literature, history, and economics. In 1752, Hume secured a position as librarian at Edinburgh University but was fired when the curators objected that his selection of books, such as *The History of Love-Making Among the French,* was obscene.

But by 1763 Hume's writings had made him famous, and that year, when he traveled to France as secretary for the British ambassador, he found himself at the center of the intellectual life of Parisian high society. There, he met and had an intense love affair with the Countess de Boufflers. Three years later, having grown homesick, Hume left the countess and returned to England. After working for three years as undersecretary of state, Hume retired in 1769 to Edinburgh, where he lived "very opulent" and, finally, very famous, until his death in 1776.

Like Berkeley before him, Hume based his philosophy on the observation that all of our genuine knowledge (or "thoughts") about the world around us derives from the sensations provided by our senses. To explain this, Hume divided the contents of our minds into two groups, our sensations (which he called *impressions*) and our thoughts. All our thoughts, he held, are "copies" of our sensations and are derived from them. Even complex thoughts about things that do not exist, such as the thought of a golden mountain, are formed by putting together memories of simple sensations we once experienced: the sensation of gold and the sensation of mountain. Hume concluded that because genuine knowledge depends on prior sensory experience, assertions that are not based on sensory experience cannot be genuine knowledge:

> Everyone will readily allow that there is a considerable difference between the perceptions of the mind when a man feels the pain of excessive heat or the pleasure of moderate warmth, and when he afterwards recalls to his memory this sensation or anticipates it by his imagination. . . .
>
> Here, therefore, we may divide all the perceptions of the mind into two classes or species, which are distinguished by their different degrees of force and vivacity. The less forcible and lively are commonly denominated *Thoughts* or *Ideas*. . . . Let us . . . use a little freedom and call [the other class] *Impressions*. . . . By the term *impression,* then, I mean all our more lively perceptions, when we hear, or see, or feel, or love, or hate, or desire, or will. . . .
>
> Nothing, at first view, may seem more unbounded than the thought of man. . . . What never was seen or heard of, may yet be conceived. . . .
>
> But though our thought seems to possess this unbounded liberty, . . . all this creative power of the mind amounts to no more than the faculty of compounding, transposing, augmenting, or diminishing the materials afforded us by the senses and experience. When we think of a golden mountain, we only join two consistent ideas, *gold* and *mountain,* with which we were formerly acquainted. . . . In short, all the materials of thinking are derived either from our outward or our inward sentiments. . . . Or, to express myself in philosophical language, all our ideas or more feeble perceptions are copies of our impressions or more lively ones.
>
> To prove this, the two following arguments will, I hope, be sufficient. First: When we analyze our thoughts or ideas, however compounded or sublime, we always find that they resolve themselves into such simple ideas as were copied from a precedent feeling or sentiment. Even . . . the idea of GOD as meaning an infinitely intelligent, wise, and good Being, arises from reflecting on the operations of our own mind, and augmenting, without limit, those qualities. . . .
>
> Second: If it happens, from a defect of the organ, that a man is not susceptible of [some] sensation, we always find that he is as little susceptible of the correspondent ideas. A blind man can form no notion of colors, [nor] a deaf man of sounds.
>
> Here, therefore, is a proposition which . . . might . . . banish all that jargon which had so long taken possession of metaphysical reasonings. . . . When we entertain any suspicion that a philosophical term is employed without any meaning or idea (as is but too frequent), we need but inquire, *from what impression is that supposed idea derived?* And if it be impossible to assign any, this will serve to confirm our suspicion.[3]

Hume's "proposition"—that meaningful concepts must be "derived" from "impressions"—was a crucial step in his attempt to undermine our claims

3 David Hume, *An Enquiry Concerning Human Understanding,* ed. L. A. Selby-Bigge (Oxford: Clarendon, 1894), 17–20.

to knowledge. If a concept is not based on the sensations or "impressions" of our sense experience, he held, then it must be meaningless. Hume applied this idea ruthlessly. He argued that claims about the existence of an external world are meaningless. All we are acquainted with are the sensations we have. We have no grounds, then, for saying that an external world also exists that somehow causes us to have those sensations:

> By what argument can it be proved, that the perceptions of the mind must be caused by external objects, . . . and could not arise either from the energy of the mind itself, . . . or from some other cause still more unknown to us?
>
> It is a question of fact, whether the perceptions of the senses be produced by external objects resembling them: how shall this question be determined? By experience surely, as all other questions of a like nature. But here experience is, and must be entirely silent. The mind has never anything present to it but the perceptions, and cannot possibly reach any experience of their connection with objects. The supposition of such a connection is, therefore, without any foundation in reasoning.[4]

Not only are we unable to know whether there is an outer world; we are also unable to claim that there is any *inner self.* The very idea of a personal *me,* of the inner person called "I," has no foundation, Hume claims:

> There are some philosophers who imagine we are every moment intimately conscious of what we call our SELF; that we feel its existence and its continuance in existence; and are certain, beyond the evidence of a demonstration, both of its perfect identity and simplicity. . . .
>
> Unluckily all these positive assertions are contrary to that very experience which is pleaded for them, nor have we any idea of *self.* . . . For from what impression could this idea be derived? . . . If any impression gives rise to the idea of self, that impression must continue invariably the same, through the whole course of our lives; since self is supposed to exist after that manner. But there is no impression constant and invariable. Pain and pleasure, grief and joy, passions and sensations succeed each other, and never all exist at the same time. It cannot, therefore, be from any of these impressions, or from any other, that the idea of self is derived; and consequently there is no such idea. . . .
>
> For my part, when I enter most intimately into what I call *myself* I always stumble on some particular perception or other, of heat or cold, light or shade, love or hatred, pain or pleasure. I never can catch *myself* at any time without a perception, and never can observe anything but the perception. . . .
>
> [S]etting aside some metaphysicians . . . , I may venture to affirm of the rest of mankind, that they are nothing but a bundle or collection of different perceptions, which succeed each other with an inconceivable rapidity, and are in a perpetual flux and movement. . . . The mind is a kind of theater, where several perceptions successively make their appearance, pass, repass, glide away, and mingle in an infinite variety of postures and situations.[5]

We cannot know whether there is any outer world beyond our sensations because all we are acquainted with are our sensations. Neither can we know whether there is an inner self because, again, all we experience is a constant flow of sensations, and we never perceive, among these sensations, an object called an inner self. All we can say, Hume claims, is that we are "a bundle or collection of different perceptions." Beyond the existence of *these* perceptions, we can know nothing.

What, then, is left for us to know? Perhaps a great deal. For we are at least acquainted with the perceptions our senses display before us. And from these perceptions we can reason to others. For example, if I perceive a flame, then I know that there will be heat; if I hear a voice, then I know that a person must be present. This kind of knowledge is based on our knowledge of cause and effect. I have learned that flames *cause* heat, so I reason from the flame to the heat; I have found that voices are the *effects* of people, so I reason from the voice to the person. In fact, all the natural sciences consist of laws based on our knowledge of cause and effect. On the basis of a few experiments, for example, the science of physics asserts that if an object is dropped, gravity will cause it to fall at 32 feet per second. Clearly, then, from the present things we perceive, our knowledge of causes enables us to know what the future will be like. And all the natural sciences—physics, chemistry, biology—are based on this kind of causal knowledge.

4 Ibid., 152–153.

5 David Hume, *A Treatise of Human Nature,* ed. L. A. Selby-Bigge (Oxford: Clarendon, 1896), 251–253.

But Hume, in a devastating attack on knowledge, argues that none of our knowledge of cause and effect has a rational basis. And if our causal knowledge is not rationally justified, then all the natural sciences are similarly unjustified. Hume begins by pointing out that all our knowledge of causal laws rests on our experience of the world:

> All reasoning concerning matter of fact seems to be founded on the relation of *Cause and Effect*. . . . A man, finding a watch or any other machine in a desert island, would conclude that there had once been men in that island. All our reasonings concerning fact are of the same nature. . . . The hearing of an articulate voice and rational discourse in the dark assures us of the presence of some person. Why? Because these are the effects of the human [being]. . . .
>
> If we would satisfy ourselves, therefore, concerning the nature of that evidence which assures us of matters of fact, we must inquire how we arrive at the knowledge of cause and effect.
>
> I shall venture to affirm, as a general proposition which admits of no exception, that the knowledge of this relation . . . arises entirely from experience, when we find that any particular objects are constantly conjoined with each other.[6]

All causal knowledge, Hume is saying, is based on our experience that in the past, events of one kind have been "constantly conjoined" with events of another kind. In the past, for example, I may have seen that when one billiard ball hits another, the second ball always rolls away. Thus, the event of one billiard ball striking another has been "constantly conjoined" in my past experience with the event of the second ball rolling away. All the causal laws of the natural sciences and all the causal knowledge of our everyday lives, then, are based on our past experience of such "constant conjunctions." But this scientific and everyday reliance on past experience, Hume points out, raises a problem. How do we know that past experience is a reliable guide to the future?

> We always presume when we see like sensible qualities, . . . that effects similar to those which we have experienced will follow from them. . . . The bread which I formerly ate nourished me. . . . But does it follow that other bread must also nourish me at another time? The consequence seems nowise necessary. . . . These two propositions are far from being the same: *I have found that such an object has always been attended with such an effect,* and *I foresee, that other objects which are, in appearance similar, will be attended with similar effects.* The connection between these two propositions is not intuitive.[7]

In this passage, Hume suggests that all causal reasoning is based on the *assumption* that the future will be like the past. When I see a flame and reason that it will be hot, it is because *in the past* when I perceived flame I also perceived heat. But, Hume asks, how do we know that the future will be like the past? Clearly, there is no way of *proving* that the future will be like the past:

> That there are no demonstrative arguments in the case seems evident, since it implies no contradiction that the course of nature may change, and that an object, seemingly like those which we have experienced, may be attended with different or contrary effects. May I not clearly and distinctly conceive that a body falling from the clouds, and which in all other respects resembles snow, has yet the taste of salt or feeling of fire? Is there any more intelligible proposition than to affirm that all the trees will flourish in December and January and decay in May and June? Now whatever is intelligible and can be distinctly conceived, implies no contradiction and can never be proved false by any demonstrative argument.[8]

So, we cannot *prove* with "demonstrative arguments" that the future will be like the past. Perhaps, then, we know that the future will be like the past because of *past experience*? No, Hume replies, we cannot use past experience to show that the future will be like the past. For if we don't know that the future will be like the past, then we don't know that *past* experience is a reliable guide. To argue that past experience proves we can rely on past experience is to argue in a circle:

> For all inferences from experience suppose, as their foundation, that the future will resemble the past, and that similar powers will be conjoined with similar sensible qualities. If there be any suspicion that the course of nature may change, and that the past may be no rule for the future, all experience becomes useless, and can give rise to no inference or conclusion. It is impossible, therefore, that any arguments

6 Hume, *An Enquiry Concerning Human Understanding,* 26–27.

7 Ibid., 33–34.

8 Ibid., 35.

> from experience can prove this resemblance of the past to the future, since all these arguments are founded on the supposition of that resemblance. Let the course of things be allowed hitherto ever so regular, that alone, without some new argument or inference proves not that for the future it will continue so. Their secret nature and consequently all their effects and influence, may change, without any change in their sensible qualities. This happens sometimes, and with regard to some objects: why may it not happen always, and with regard to all objects? What logic, what process of argument, secures you against this supposition?[9]

Hume's conclusion is devastating: We have no way of *knowing* that causal claims are justified. All the causal laws of the sciences and our everyday causal reasonings are based on an assumption that we cannot prove or rationally justify: the assumption that the future will be like the past. But if we cannot rationally show that the future will be like the past, then why do we continually move past our experience to conclusions about the future? Because, Hume claims, we are creatures of nonrational habit:

> Suppose [a person] has lived so long in the world as to have observed similar objects or events to be constantly conjoined together. What is the consequence of this experience? He immediately infers the existence of one object from the appearance of the other. . . . There is some . . . principle which determines him to form such a conclusion.
>
> This principle is CUSTOM or HABIT. For wherever the repetition of any particular act or operation produces a propensity to renew the same act or operation, without being impelled by any reasoning or process of the understanding, we always say that this propensity is the effect of *custom*. . . .
>
> Custom, then, is the great guide of human life. It is that principle alone which renders our experience useful to us, and makes us expect, for the future, a similar train of events with those which have appeared in the past.[10]

All claims about causal connections, then, are based on our experience that, in the past, events of a certain kind have been "constantly conjoined" with events of another kind. And habit moves us from this past experience to the conclusion that, in the future, all similar events will be similarly conjoined. In other words, from our past experience of the constant conjunction of events, we conclude by habit that one kind of event "causes" a second kind. But we cannot provide any rational justification for this habit of moving from the past to the future. All the causal laws of the sciences and all the causal "knowledge" of everyday life are based on nonrational "habit."

We cannot know whether an external world exists; we cannot say that the self exists; we cannot rationally justify the causal laws of any of the natural sciences or the causal reasonings of our everyday life. Can skepticism extend further? Yes. Hume went on to attack the foundations of religious belief: the claim that God exists.

Hume believed that the best arguments for God's existence were causal arguments: those that hold that God must exist because the design of the universe requires an all-powerful intelligent Creator. But all causal reasonings depend on past experience, Hume points out, and we have no past experience of other gods creating universes. Although our past experience of human beings and their products leads us to say that things such as watches require intelligent human creators, we have no past experience of other universes and gods that could lead us to say that universes require intelligent gods to create them:

> In works of *human* art and contrivance, it is allowable to advance from the effect to the cause, and returning back from the cause, to form new inferences concerning the effect. . . . But what is the foundation of this method of reasoning? Plainly this: that man is a being whom we know by experience. . . . When, therefore, we find that any work has proceeded from the skill and industry of man, as we are otherwise acquainted with the nature of the animal, we can draw a hundred inferences concerning what may be expected from him; and these inferences will all be founded in experience and observation.
>
> The case is not the same with our reasonings from the works of nature. The Deity is known to us only by his productions, and is a single being in the universe, not comprehended under any species or genus, from whose experienced attributes or qualities we can, by analogy, infer any attribute or quality in him. . . .
>
> I much doubt whether it be possible for a cause to be known only by its effect . . . [when it has] no parallel and no similarity with any other

9 Ibid., 37–38.
10 Ibid., 42–44.

> cause or object that has ever fallen under our observation. It is only when two species of objects are found to be constantly conjoined, that we can infer the one from the other; and were an effect presented, which was entirely singular, and could not be comprehended under any known *species,* I do not see that we could form any conjecture or inference at all concerning its cause. If experience and observation and analogy be, indeed, the only guides which we can reasonably follow in inferences of this nature, both the effect and cause must bear a similarity and resemblance to other effects and causes which we know, and which we have found in many instances to be conjoined with each other. I leave to your own reflection to pursue the consequences of this principle.[11]

The consequence of this principle, of course, is that we cannot argue from the existence of an orderly universe to the existence of an intelligent God. Hume's skepticism, then, leaves our edifice of knowledge in shambles. The external world, the self, the causal laws of the natural sciences, our everyday causal reasoning, and our religious claims are all called into question. Can knowledge be saved? Many people think that Hume's arguments definitively destroyed all hope that it might be. But in Germany, a very ordinary man, Immanuel Kant, was spurred by Hume's skepticism into constructing what many people look on as the most breathtakingly creative response that could be made to Hume. Whether that response succeeded, you must decide after reading the showcase on Kant in the next chapter.

11 Ibid., 143–144, 148.

QUESTIONS

1. How would you explain Hume's distinction between "impressions" and "ideas"? How can Hume say that all ideas are "copies" of impressions? Does Hume bring up any ideas that he thinks are *not* copies of impressions?
2. Hume says that philosophical terms must be tested by asking "from what impression is that supposed idea derived?" Do you think this is a good test? Are there any terms or "supposed ideas" that you would have to reject if you applied this test to your own ideas? If you applied this test to Hume's own philosophical terms, do you think they would all pass his test? Why?
3. How are Hume's ideas about the self similar to the Buddhist view of the self examined in Chapter 2? Do you think Hume's view of the self is a correct analysis of *your* self? Why?
4. How would you summarize Hume's criticism of the assumption that the future will resemble the past? Can you detect any weaknesses in his criticism? Explain in your own words what Hume means when he writes, "It is impossible, therefore, that any arguments from experience can prove this resemblance of the past to the future, since all these arguments are founded on the supposition of that resemblance."
5. Hume asserts that all ideas are copies of impressions. Is this a generalization from his own experience? If so, then how do you think Hume would respond to this criticism: "Because Hume has shown that past experience cannot provide real knowledge of the future, he cannot claim to know that all ideas must be, now and in the future, copies of impressions"?
6. Do you see any way of showing that Hume must be mistaken in his claim that the causal laws of the sciences rest on nothing more than "habit"?

CHAPTER

6 Truth

No one is so wrong as the man who knows all the answers.
THOMAS MERTON

OUTLINE AND LEARNING OBJECTIVES

6.1 Knowledge, Truth, and Justification

Objectives | When finished you will be able to:

- Explain why knowledge has been defined as a justified true belief, and why this definition has been questioned.
- Explain what justification is and how foundationalism and coherentism approach justification.

6.2 What Is Truth?

Objectives | When finished you will be able to:

- Explain and evaluate the correspondence, coherence, and pragmatic views of truth.
- Explain why these views matter.

6.3 Does Science Give Us Truth?

Objectives | When finished you will be able to:

- Describe some of the main strengths and weaknesses of the instrumental, realist, and conceptual relativist views of science.
- Explain how these views of science are related to the pragmatic, correspondence, and coherence theories of truth.

6.4 Can Interpretations Be True?

Objectives | When finished you will be able to:

- Explain why truth matters when interpreting texts.
- Relate the correspondence, pragmatic, and coherence views of truth to Aquinas', Wittgenstein's, and Gadamer's views of true interpretations.

Chapter Summary

© Jasmine/iStockphoto.com

6.5 Readings: Akutagawa, "In a Grove"

Tomlinson, "After Truth: Post-Modernism and the Rhetoric of Science"

Searle, "Reality and Truth"

6.6 Historical Showcase: Kant

6.1 Knowledge, Truth, and Justification

Suppose you have a girlfriend. You've been dating her for a long time. Although you love her passionately, you're unsure that she still loves you. You're not sure about her love because she doesn't seem as interested in your company as she used to be. Sometimes she seems bored with you and more interested in others. Yet when you ask her, she says, "Yes, I still love you very much." Is she telling you the truth? The very thought that she might not be telling the truth makes you miserable. You ask her outright whether she's telling you the truth. She's offended that you should doubt her. "Of course I'm telling you the truth!" she says. "Of course I still love you!" Perhaps for several days you decide that you'll take her words as true. After all, when you suspect her words are false, you feel awful. Because it makes you feel better and because you're *pragmatic*, you decide to accept that her words are true. At least this way you feel the way you want to feel.

But then you start to feel bad again and think that this kind of truth isn't what you need. Getting at the truth about your lover, you think, is more than just accepting whatever succeeds in making you feel good. So, you start thinking about a different kind of truth. You think that maybe the truth about her love lies in what her actions indicate. Her protestations of love just don't fit with what you believe her actions show; in other words, her statements don't *cohere* with your beliefs about what her actions mean. You tell her that you don't think she's telling you the truth when she says she loves you because her actions show that her love has gone. She replies that you're mistaken. You're putting meanings on her actions that aren't there. Her actions don't mean she is bored with you, she says. It's just that she feels relaxed around you now and feels she can be herself without always needing to put up a happy front with you. Now you're extremely perplexed. You were ready to think that her words were true only if they fit with your beliefs about what her actions meant. Yet you aren't sure now whether these beliefs of yours about what her actions mean are themselves true.

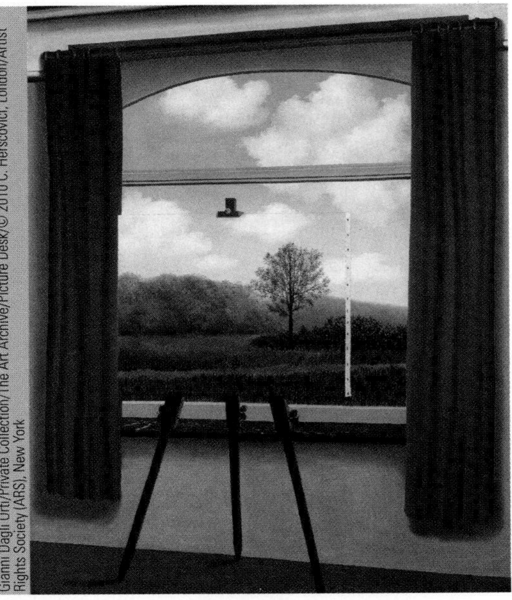

Even though we distinguish between truth and falsity hundreds of times a day, we may have difficulty expressing that distinction. What is truth? *La condition humaine* (the human condition), 1933. Artist: René Magritte, 1898–1967, Belgian. Location: private collection.

Gianni Dagli Orti/Private Collection/The Art Archive/Picture Desk/© 2010 C. Herscovici, London/Artist Rights Society (ARS), New York

Then you become convinced that the truth you most want is the truth about what really lies in her heart. You want the facts. What matters isn't what makes you feel good inside yourself or what fits with the other beliefs inside your head. What you want is the truth about what's out there in the real world; you want the truth about what's really going on there inside her heart. What you want to know is whether what she says *corresponds* with what in fact her real feelings are. So, though you dread the answer, you ask her, "What do you really feel in your heart toward me?" Her response leaves you even more perplexed: "I'm not sure I know. I think the feelings I have for you are feelings of love. But I don't think I understand myself, or love, well enough to be sure. I think I have a lot of feelings toward you in my heart, but I'm often confused about my feelings and don't quite know what they are or what they mean. That's all I can tell you."

Now you're completely at a loss. You thought you could get at the truth if you could just get outside yourself and find out what was really there inside her heart. Yet what is in her heart is as amorphous as a cloud. You wonder now what truth itself is or even if there's such a thing as truth. Is truth just what makes us have the good feelings we want to have? Is it what fits with our system of beliefs and meanings? Is truth about what corresponds with the facts in the real world outside of us? What do we mean, then, when we say that a belief or statement is true?

QUICK REVIEW
In different situations in real life we seem to believe *truth* means different things and is established in different ways: Truth may be (1) what gets us what we want, (2) what fits with our other beliefs and meanings, and (3) what corresponds with what is "out there" in the real world.

The history of philosophy records several ways of looking at truth that are similar to the three kinds of truth you've just been considering. The pragmatic theory says, roughly, that our beliefs are true when they work (i.e., when they get us what we want). The coherence theory says that a belief is true when it fits with our other beliefs and meanings. The correspondence theory says that a belief is true when it corresponds with what is "out there" in the real world. Each of these makes a unique contribution to understanding the nature of truth. As our short discussion already suggests, it's important to be clear about what truth means, particularly when we're searching for the truth about ourselves and our relationships with others. Shortly, we'll look at the three theories starting with the correspondence theory, and then turning to the coherence view, and finally ending with the pragmatic theory. Later, when we look at truth in science and in the interpretation of people's words and actions, we will see that these three theories again play an important role in understanding truth in these areas.

Before we turn to look at what truth is, however, we're going to try to get an understanding of some important "epistemic" concepts (concepts related to knowledge). In particular, we're going to see how the important concepts of knowledge, justification, belief, and truth are related to each other.

Knowledge as Justified True Belief

What do you mean when you say you *know* something? For instance, "I know my girlfriend loves me." Just what do you mean when you say that? Stating the question more formally, if we let p represent any proposition, what are you asserting when you claim: "I know that p"?

For one thing, you must *believe* that p is the case. If you *know* that your girlfriend loves you, then you have to at least *believe* she does. Think about it. Imagine what your friends would think if you said, "I know that my girlfriend loves me, but I don't believe she does." They'd think you were weird, and rightly so. After all, if you're claiming to know something, how can you not believe it? Of course, we sometimes seem to dissociate belief from knowledge, as in "I know the president has been assassinated, but I just don't believe it!" However, this is a rhetorical utterance. We *do* believe it; otherwise, we wouldn't be shocked. Intellectually we believe it, but emotionally we're incredulous. To assert that you know p, then, is to assert at least that you believe p. Thus, "I know p" implies "I believe p."

Knowledge also implies having evidence or justification for what you believe. When you say, "I know that my girlfriend loves me," you imply not only that you believe it but also that you have some evidence or reasons to believe it. So, "I know *p*" implies "I have evidence or justification for *p*." Suppose that someone claimed to know that the stock market will plunge next week. You'd likely ask, "How do you know that?" If the person responds, "I just believe it for no reason," you wouldn't take the claim seriously. Belief indicates merely an attitude toward something; it may, however, not be justified, and then could not count as knowledge. A belief is justified when you have adequate evidence or reasons for the belief. If someone claims to know that the stock market will plunge next week, he is implying that he believes it and that his belief is justified, that is, he has adequate evidence or sufficient reasons for his belief.

So, can we say that knowledge is a justified belief? Not quite. Suppose you believe your girlfriend loves you, and your justification for that belief is that she has told you she loves you several times. But a week later you discover she has been having an affair with your best friend and although she stopped loving you several months ago, she has not wanted to hurt you and so has been lying about her feelings toward you. Can you continue to say that last week you knew she loved you? No. If your belief that she loved you was false, then you cannot say that you *knew* she loved you. You would have to say that you *thought* she loved you, but you didn't really *know*. Knowledge is more than having a justified belief. Real knowledge requires that what you say you know has to be true. Knowledge is a justified belief that's *true*. You may believe your girlfriend loves you, and your belief may be justified. Still, to *know* she loves you, you need more than justified belief: Your belief must also be true.

QUICK REVIEW
The traditional view of knowledge says that it is justified true belief.

We have now reached a useful and traditional characterization of knowledge. Knowledge is (1) a belief that is (2) justified and (3) true. To understand knowledge fully, then, we must understand justification and truth, two of the central topics of this chapter. Before we examine these topics, however, let us ask how adequate this traditional characterization of knowledge is. Is knowledge nothing more than a justified true belief? Is having a justified true belief sufficient for having knowledge, or does knowledge involve something more?

Unfortunately, it turns out that the notion of justified true belief does not fully capture what knowledge is. Knowledge is more than a justified true belief. But figuring out what more it involves is very difficult. To understand this difficulty, consider the following example of a person who has a justified true belief but does not have knowledge. Incidentally, this kind of example is called a *Gettier example*, after the philosopher Edmund Gettier, who first drew our attention to these examples and to the difficulties that they raise for our concept of knowledge.

QUICK REVIEW
Gettier showed that knowledge is more than justified true belief by giving examples in which someone's belief is true and is justified, but the true belief is based on a falsehood. Philosophers are still unsure what more knowledge involves.

Suppose that John is a very careful person who before today has never made a mistake. Today he plans to buy some low-fat milk at the store. By mistake, however, he incorrectly tells his friend Sam that he intends to buy whole milk. Later, when John goes to the store (still planning to buy low-fat milk), he accidentally picks up a container of whole milk. Not realizing his mistake, he pays for the milk and leaves the store with it. Now suppose that someone asks Sam whether he knows what kind of milk John bought at the store. Sam, of course, replies that he knows that John bought whole milk. Notice that Sam is indeed justified in thinking that John bought whole milk because he knows that John tells the truth and has never before made a mistake. Sam also believes that John bought whole milk. And, by accident, it is true that John bought whole milk. So, Sam has a justified true belief. Nevertheless, we would all agree that Sam doesn't really know that John bought whole milk. Because Sam's belief was based on a falsehood (the statement that John made when he told Sam that he intended to buy whole milk) that turned out to be true entirely by accident, we are reluctant to say that his belief is genuine knowledge, even though it is a justified true belief.

This example shows that knowledge is more than a justified true belief. But what more is needed to have genuine knowledge? Unfortunately, we cannot say. Many philosophers have spent a lot of time and effort trying to uncover what this "more" is. Yet no one has come up with a solution that has persuaded everyone. Nevertheless, we do know that knowledge requires at least a justified true belief, so these notions merit discussion.[1]

Justification

critical thinking

Gettier examples assume that people are justified in believing things when they rely on their past experience. Is this assumption correct?

Lots of things can be justified or unjustified including our decisions and actions, desires and emotions, punishments and laws, as well as beliefs, propositions, and statements. Here we will be concerned mainly with the justification of beliefs, propositions, and statements.

Justification and truth are not the same (although as we'll see, some philosophers have argued that they are the same). For example, ancient people were justified in believing that the earth was flat yet it was not true that it was flat. Nevertheless justification and truth are related: the reasons that justify a belief should make it probable that the belief is true. For example, if I've read many thousands of sentences in the *Encyclopaedia Britannica* and all of them have been true, then very probably the next one I read in the *Encyclopaedia* will also be true. Because of this high probability, I am *justified* in believing that the next sentence I read will be true. But justification does not *guarantee* truth. Even when there is a high probability a belief is true, it can often still be false.

Justification is a significant part of our lives.[2] It's important to know, for example, whether your beliefs about yourself or your friends are justified or whether your beliefs about God or morality or society are justified. Your self-image, your views about the people you know, and your relationships with lovers, friends, and family are all directly affected by what you feel you are justified in believing about them. The issue of justification, then, is more than a philosophical abstraction. In every part of your personal life, what you feel you are justified in believing influences how you relate and respond to the world, how you live your life, and how you deal with the people around you. Given the important role that justification plays in our lives, it is not surprising that "justified" is a value-laden concept.[3] Some philosophers, for example, argue that if a belief is *not* justified, you have an *obligation* to *not* believe it and you do *wrong* if you choose to believe it. Such conclusions imply that people—such as Kierkegaard—who say they believe in God because they make a "leap of faith" when their belief is not fully justified, are acting wrongly!

QUICK REVIEW

The justification of a belief depends on the kind of belief it is and whether it is an *a priori* belief that is based on reason and not observation, or an empirical belief that is based on observation, or a scientific belief justified by inductive generalization or by inference to the best explanation.

So, when are we justified in believing something? Something—a decision, action, feeling, law, etc.—is justified when there are good reasons for it. A belief, then, is justified when we have good reasons to accept it. Different kinds of beliefs, of course, will demand different kinds of justifications or reasons. Factual or empirical beliefs as we saw in the last chapter, are ultimately justified by reasons that are at least partly based on sense-observations, while *a priori* beliefs such as mathematical beliefs will usually be justified by mental reasoning that may have little to do with

1 Gettier's essay and several attempts to deal with this issue can be found in Paul K. Moser and Arnold vander Nat, eds., *Human Knowledge: Classical and Contemporary Approaches*, 3rd ed. (New York: Oxford University Press, 2002).

2 For discussions of justification, see Matthias Steup, ed., *Knowledge, Truth and Duty: Essays on Epistemic Justification, Responsibility, and Virtue* (New York: Oxford University Press, 2000).

3 John Locke, *An Essay Concerning Human Understanding*, ed. A. C. Fraser (New York: Dover, 1959), IV, xvii, 24; for another view see Richard J. Hall and Charles R. Johnson, "The Epistemic Duty to Seek More Evidence," *American Philosophical Quarterly*, April 1998.

sense observations. Scientific beliefs may be justified by inductive generalizations based on many repeated observations, or, like Darwin's theory of evolution, may be justified by an inference to the best explanation. In spite of the many different kinds of justifications, we will focus our attention on the kinds of justification demanded by two fundamental categories of beliefs: basic and nonbasic beliefs. Regardless of their subject matter, all beliefs are either basic or nonbasic.

QUICK REVIEW
A basic belief is justified but not by other beliefs; a nonbasic belief is justified by other beliefs, for example, by being inferred from other beliefs.

Basic and Nonbasic Beliefs. A basic belief is one that we immediately know is true without having to infer it from other beliefs—in other words, a basic belief is one that does not need to be justified by other beliefs. Some examples of basic beliefs that various philosophers have suggested are "I'm feeling a pain," "I seem to see something red," and "A is A." We know directly that beliefs like these are true, these philosophers claim, so they do not have to be justified by appealing to other beliefs. On the other hand, nonbasic beliefs are those we believe because we infer them from other beliefs we have. For example, I know that it's raining outside because I hear a pitter-patter sound and I believe that when I hear that sound it means it's raining. The belief that it's raining outside is a nonbasic belief because I infer it from my belief that when I hear a pitter-patter sound this means it's raining. Nonbasic beliefs, then, are beliefs that are justified by other beliefs.

Many, perhaps most, beliefs of ours are nonbasic beliefs because they are justified by other beliefs. My belief that Columbus discovered America, for example, is justified by the fact that I read about it in a history book and I believe that what the history book says is true. Even simple beliefs, like my belief that I see a robin on the grass, are based on other beliefs, some about birds generally, others about robins in particular (such as their color and plumage), and these beliefs in turn rest on other beliefs about the reliability of the people who taught me these things, and my beliefs about their reliability in turn are justified by other beliefs about the likelihood that they are truthful, and so on.

Even simple beliefs, like my belief that I see a robin, are based on other beliefs.

© laurien/iStockphoto.com

Foundationalism. This distinction between basic and nonbasic beliefs raises the troubling question of whether our nonbasic beliefs can ultimately be justified. How do we know that all our nonbasic beliefs rest on a solid foundation—that is, that we are ultimately justified in holding them? Several philosophers have argued that if our nonbasic beliefs are justified, then they ultimately have to depend on our basic beliefs. Philosophers who hold this apparently commonsense view are called foundationalists because they hold that all nonbasic beliefs—in fact, all our knowledge—rests on a foundation of basic beliefs. They argue that if all beliefs had to be justified by other beliefs, then ultimately we would have no real justification for any of our beliefs.

Suppose, for example, that belief A had to be justified by some other belief, B, and that belief B had to be justified by some other belief, C, and that belief C had to be justified by some other belief, D, and D had to be justified by some other belief, E, and so on without end. We would never reach a belief that needed no further justification because any belief we came to would still need to be justified by some other belief, so by itself it would be unjustified. All our beliefs, then, would ultimately depend on unjustified beliefs. The only way to avoid this conclusion, foundationalists argue, is to admit that at some point we must reach beliefs that are justified but that don't need to be justified by other beliefs; these would have to be basic beliefs.

Until recently, almost all philosophers have been foundationalists of one kind or another, including Plato, Aristotle, Thomas Aquinas, René Descartes, John Locke, George Bishop Berkeley, David Hume, Immanuel Kant, Bertrand Russell, Rudolf Carnap, Moritz Schlick, A. J. Ayer, Clarence I. Lewis, and the contemporary philosophers Alvin Goldman, Roderick M. Chisholm, Paul Moser, and Laurence BonJour.[4] Here is how Locke put his foundationalist view:

> Our Observation employ'd either about *external, sensible Objects; or about the internal Operations of our Minds, perceived and reflected on by our selves, is that which supplies our Understandings with all the materials of thinking.* These two are the Fountains of Knowledge, from whence all the *Ideas* we have, or can naturally have, do spring.[5]

All our knowledge, and so all our beliefs, Locke is saying, are ultimately justified by beliefs based on our observation of the external world and of our interior mind.

But not all foundationalists have held that our beliefs are ultimately justified by sense observation. As you recall from the previous chapter, the rationalist René Descartes, claimed that the most basic belief is expressed by the proposition "I think, therefore I am." Descartes argued that this basic belief is justified because it is an indubitable belief that we clearly and distinctly know is true and that this basic belief could be used to justify all nonbasic beliefs such as the belief that I am a thinking being and that God exists.

QUICK REVIEW
Foundationalists argue that our nonbasic beliefs are justified by basic beliefs, otherwise our beliefs would ultimately depend on unjustified beliefs. For many foundationalists, basic beliefs consist of beliefs about what we seem to perceive directly or what appears to us.

In the twentieth century, the German empiricist philosopher Rudolf Carnap (1891–1970) suggested that basic beliefs were those that could be expressed by what he called "protocol sentences" that report our most elementary sense experiences, like seeing "red here now." Carnap argued that you know when you are having a sensation of red and you can't be mistaken. So these simple beliefs are infallible and provide a solid basis on which our other beliefs can be justified. Other empiricists have argued that basic beliefs are those that describe what we seem to be experiencing, such as "I seem to see red," "I seem to hear a high-pitched sound," or "I seem to feel pain." We can't be wrong about such basic beliefs, so they provide a firm foundation on which we can justify all our other nonbasic beliefs.

Although a lot of philosophers have been foundationalists, several others have pointed out that there are some deep problems with foundationalism. In particular, the very idea of basic beliefs is problematic—that is, the claim that there are beliefs that we get through some kind of direct experience without relying on any other beliefs may be mistaken. The American philosopher Wilfrid Sellars (1912–1989), for example, was among the first to argue that *all* our beliefs depend on other beliefs, so none can be basic beliefs.[6]

QUICK REVIEW
Wilfrid Sellars argued that all our beliefs must be justified by other beliefs, so there are no basic beliefs that serve as the foundations of all our other beliefs.

To see what Sellars means, take an example of a simple belief that Carnap and other philosophers said was the kind that could serve as the foundation of all our other beliefs: I am seeing "red here now." Although this "belief" looks like it is as basic as a belief can be, it nevertheless depends on other beliefs. For the belief, like all beliefs, uses concepts, and concepts depend on beliefs. The concepts of "red," of "here," and of "now" are each based on beliefs our culture has given us about what colors are, what location in space is, and what time is. So, even this apparently simple belief depends on other beliefs. Sellars said that the idea that there are

4 See Roderick Chisholm, *Theory of Knowledge,* (Englewood Cliffs: Prentice-Hall, 1989); Alvin Goldman, *Epistemology and Cognition,* (Cambridge, MA: Harvard University Press, 1986); Laurence BonJour, "Toward a Defense of Empirical Foundationalism," in M. DePaul (ed), *Resurrecting Old-Fashioned Foundationalism,* (Lanham, MA: Rowman and Littlefield, 2000).

5 Locke, *Essay Concerning Human Understanding,* II, i, 2.

6 Wilfrid Sellars, *Science, Perception and Reality,* (London: Routledge, 1963).

propositions that are given to us through some kind of direct experience and that are not justified by other propositions is a "myth"; it is, he claimed, "The Myth of the Given." The beliefs we have about our most elementary experiences, Sellars argued, must depend on other beliefs that we get from our culture, language, and history.

But if our nonbasic beliefs are not justified by basic beliefs, then how are they justified? If every belief has to be justified by some other belief, which has to be justified by some other belief, and so on, then we can never come to a belief that is justified by itself (like "I see red here now"). We would, instead, always end up with a belief that has to be justified by some other belief that by itself is unjustified. If there are no basic beliefs, then must all of our beliefs ultimately rest on unjustified beliefs?

Coherentism. Philosophers like Sellars, who say there are no basic beliefs, reply to this last question by arguing that although there are no basic beliefs, our beliefs don't have to rest on unjustified beliefs. Instead, our beliefs can justify each other in a kind of circle. Suppose that belief A is justified by belief B, and belief B is justified by belief C, and belief C is justified by belief D, then belief D might be justified by belief A. Another way of putting this is that our beliefs form an interconnected system or "web" of beliefs in which our beliefs mutually support or justify each other.

QUICK REVIEW
Coherentists argue that our nonbasic beliefs are not justified by basic beliefs. Instead, beliefs are justified if they fit into a coherent system of consistent and mutually supportive beliefs that we accept, and they are unjustified if they cannot fit into this system or "web" of belief.

To understand what a web of beliefs might be like, consider this example: I believe that when I use my eyes I see the world as it really is; and this belief is justified by my belief that the many times I've used my eyes they showed me the world as it really was; and this belief is justified by my belief that when I checked by asking other people they confirmed that my eyes showed me the world as it really was; and this belief is justified because I believe that I really saw other people confirming what my eyes showed me; and all these beliefs are justified because I believe that when I use my eyes I see the world as it really is—which is where we started. So, in this somewhat simplistic example, justification is circular. But what matters is that all the beliefs in the circle "hang together" and support each other: They form a whole consistent picture of how our vision works, how we check with others to confirm our vision, and how the world is as our vision shows us it is.

Philosophers have described this kind of mutual support our beliefs can give each other by saying that our beliefs "cohere" with each other to form a "web" of consistent and mutually reinforcing beliefs. Later in this chapter, when we look at theories of truth, you will see the idea of coherence again. Here, what's important is to see that many philosophers have turned to the idea of a coherent system of beliefs to explain how our beliefs can be justified without appealing to basic beliefs. In their view, a new belief is justified for you if it fits the coherent system of beliefs that you already accept and carry around in your head; if a new belief does not fit into your system of beliefs—if it contradicts the beliefs you already accept—then it is not justified for you to accept the new belief. This does not mean that your system of coherent beliefs can never be changed by new beliefs. Sometimes you might repeatedly observe something and these repeated observations keep producing a new belief in you that contradicts what you've always believed. For example, suppose you're Galileo and you repeatedly observe things through your new telescope that keep suggesting to you that the earth revolves around the sun. Yet you've always believed that the sun revolves around the earth. You could keep rejecting the new belief and stick to your old system of beliefs. Or you might decide to adjust your belief system by letting go of the old beliefs about the sun that don't fit the new belief, and thus accept the new belief into your belief system.

But there's a problem with coherentism. Isn't it possible that all our beliefs could mutually support each other when all of them were in fact false? Suppose our beliefs were like the beliefs of the characters in a fictional novel, so that they all formed a consistent, mutually supportive web of beliefs about a world that does not exist; a world, perhaps, in which trees have thoughts, animals are inhabited by good or evil spirits, most people are aliens disguised as humans, events are controlled by unseen deities, and the "findings" of science are elaborate hoaxes. In short, suppose our beliefs were the consistent beliefs of an insane person. Then our beliefs would be false although they "cohered" with each other. What's worse, if coherence with the beliefs we already have is the only way of justifying our beliefs, then it seems we could never escape this world of insanity with its web of perfectly coherent but false beliefs.

So, who is right? Are your beliefs justified by their dependence on a foundation of indubitable basic beliefs you directly know like the foundationalists say? Or do your beliefs ultimately depend on each other and nothing more, like the coherentists say? Do you ultimately justify your beliefs by relying on either sense experiences or *a priori* propositions that need no justification? Or do you justify all your beliefs by fitting them into your more or less coherent belief system and rejecting those that do not fit?

QUESTIONS

Which of the following can be justified beliefs? Why?

1. This dog before me is an English shepherd.
2. I have a heart.
3. All things have qualities.
4. Hubert Humphrey once lived.
5. Three times 2 is 6.
6. The sun will rise tomorrow.
7. A robin is a bird.
8. There's intelligent life in outer space.
9. If the battery in my car is dead, my car won't start.
10. If I release this pen and it's unsupported, it will fall.

PHILOSOPHY AT THE MOVIES

Watch *The Truman Show* (1998), in which Truman Burbank, not realizing that all his life he has lived in a television studio staged to look like a small town with "friends" who are really actors, and also not realizing that all his activities have been continuously televised to people around the world, finally tries to escape when it dawns on him that nothing around him is what it seems to be. Is Christof right when he says to Truman: "There's no more truth out there than there is in the world I created for you"? What does truth mean for Christof? Is Truman justified in believing that the town around him is real? Should having beliefs that are justified matter to Truman so long as he's happy? Why? Is it better to be happy and deceived or to struggle but know the truth? Why?

6.2 What Is Truth?

In June 2004, a Belgian jury found Marc Dutroux guilty of murder. He had kidnapped, imprisoned, and repeatedly raped six girls—all children—and murdered four of them: two 8-year-olds who starved to death in a dungeon in his basement and two others whom he buried alive. The Dutroux case had dragged on for almost ten years amid numerous charges that government officials were protecting Dutroux. Dutroux, who made videos of himself raping the children, claimed he was part of a network of pedophiles that included government officials in Belgium and around Europe for whom he procured children. A young woman, Regina Louf, subsequently came forward and said that as a child she had been sexually abused and tortured by the pedophile network to which Dutroux belonged. She identified several members of the network including Belgian and European police officers, bankers, doctors, businessmen, judges, politicians, and members of the nobility. Then, several other women came forward with similar stories. Faced with an outraged public, the government appointed the Dutroux Inquiry Commission to get to the truth about the Dutroux case.[7]

The meetings of the Commission were televised and often heated. During a Commission meeting, two witnesses, a policeman named Lesage and a judge named Doutrewe, were questioned about an important file on Dutroux. Under oath, the policeman testified that he had sent the file to the judge who must have received it. The judge, also under oath, asserted vehemently that the file was not sent to him and so he never received it. The next day Professor Yves Winkin, a well-known professor of anthropology, was interviewed by *Le Soir*, a Belgian newspaper:

> *Le Soir*: The confrontation [between Officer Lesage and Judge Doutrewe] was stimulated by an almost ultimate search for truth. Does truth exist?
>
> *Winkin*: I think that all the work of the Commission is based on a sort of presupposition that there exists, not *a* truth, but *the* truth—which if one presses hard enough, will finally come out. However, anthropologically, there are only partial truths, shared by a larger or smaller number of people: a group, a family, a firm. There is no transcendent truth. Therefore, I don't think that judge Doutrewe or officer Lesage are hiding anything: both are telling their truth. Truth is always linked to an organization, depending upon the elements that are perceived as important. It is not surprising that these two people, representing two very different professional universes, should each set forth a different truth.[8]

Winkin's statement about the Dutroux Commission has significant implications about the nature of truth. First, it implies that what is true in relation to one person need not be true in relation to another person. Truth is relative: Whether a statement is true depends on who makes the statement. Second, it claims that there is no such thing as *the* truth about whether there were government officials who were pedophiles protecting Dutroux. That is, in Winkin's view there's no such thing as the real "objective" truth about whether there's a ring of powerful people in Europe who kidnap, abuse, and torture children, and whether they protected Dutroux from prosecution. If your group "shares" the belief that there is ring of pedophiles operating throughout Europe, then it's true that there is; but if your group doesn't share these beliefs,

7 The information in this paragraph is based on the following sources: BBC News, "Belgian Sex Ring 'Ignored,' " January 22, 2002, http://news.bbc.co.uk/2/hi/europe/1774436.stm (accessed June 10, 2009); BBC News, "Regina Louf's Testimony," May 2, 2002, http://news.bbc.co.uk/1/hi/programmes/correspondent_europe/1962244.stm (accessed June 10, 2009); BBC News, "Belgium's X-Files—An Olenka Frenkiel Investigation," May 2, 2002, http://news.bbc.co.uk/2/hi/programmes/correspondent/1944428.stm (accessed June 10, 2009); Rachael Bell, "Marc Dutroux," Tru TV Tru Crime Library, http://www.trutv.com/library/crime/serial_killers/predators/dutroux/evil_1.html (accessed June 10, 2009); Institute for the Study of Globalization and Covert Politics, "Beyond the Dutroux Affair," http://www.isgp.eu/dutroux/Belgian_X_dossiers_of_the_Dutroux_affair.htm#girl (accessed June 10, 2009).

8 Quoted in Alan Sokal and Jean Bricmont, *Fashionable Nonsense* (New York: Picador USA, 1998).

then it isn't true that such a ring exists and we should not look for it. Third, in Winkin's view we can't even say that it's either true or false that Lesage sent the file to Judge Doutrewe. If you're Lesage, then because you just *believe* you sent the file, it's really *true* that you sent it. And if you're Doutrewe, then you don't *believe* Lesage sent the file, so it's really *true* that he didn't. Both beliefs are really true even though they contradict each other.

David Martin/AFP/Getty Images

Accused pedophile Marc Dutroux pretends to have a heart attack in front of the courthouse upon his arrival to appear before the Council Chamber in 2002.

Winkin's view of truth is one that many philosophers also hold. Some theories of truth would at least partially support Winkin's views, including, as you will see, some versions of the pragmatic and the coherence theories of truth. But there is at least one theory that firmly rejects Winkin's views, and that is the correspondence theory of truth.

Correspondence Theory

Undoubtedly the most popular theory of truth is the **correspondence theory**, which says that truth is an agreement or correspondence between a proposition and some fact in the real world. Thus, "Water boils at 212 degrees Fahrenheit at sea level" is a true proposition because it corresponds with the fact that in the real world, water does boil at 212 degrees Fahrenheit at sea level. The correspondence theory assumes, then, that there is a real world whose existence does not depend on our beliefs, thoughts, or perceptions—that is, it assumes that a real world exists and has always existed whether or not we have been around to believe it, to think about it, or to perceive it. This independent world or reality contains facts. A belief, statement, or proposition is true when what it states corresponds with a fact in this real independent world.

QUICK REVIEW
The correspondence theory says that a proposition is true when it agrees with or corresponds to a fact.

The correspondence theory has had a long history. Aristotle stated a simplified form of the theory when he said in his *Metaphysics* that "to say of what is that it is, and of what is not that it is not, is true." Presumably, he meant that if what a statement says corresponds with what is in reality, then it is true. Aquinas provided a somewhat fuller but still succinct version of the theory when he wrote the following in his treatise *On Truth*: "A judgment is said to be true when it conforms to the external reality." Closer to our own time, a number of philosophers have proposed versions of the correspondence theory, including Descartes, Spinoza, Locke, Leibniz, Hume, and Kant.

Russell's Correspondence Theory.

Bertrand Russell, a modern philosopher, is a classic example of a correspondence theorist. Russell maintains that there is a realm of facts whose existence does not depend on us. A belief is true when it corresponds with a fact—that is, when it corresponds to some fact in the real world. Thus, the belief that Paris is in France is true because that belief corresponds to the fact that Paris is in France. In *The Problems of Philosophy*, Russell expresses his position:

> [I]t is to be observed that the truth or falsehood of a belief always depends upon something which lies outside the belief itself. If I believe that Charles I died on the scaffold, I believe truly, not because of any intrinsic quality of my belief, which can be discovered by merely examining the belief, but because of an historical event which happened two and a half centuries ago. If I believe that Charles I died in his bed, I believe falsely: no degree of vividness in my belief, or of care in arriving at it, prevents it from being false, again because of what happened long ago, and not because of any intrinsic property of my belief. Hence, although truth and falsehood are properties of beliefs, they are properties dependent upon the relations of the beliefs to other things, not upon any internal quality of the beliefs.
>
> . . . the above requisite leads us to adopt the view—which has on the whole been commonest among philosophers—that truth consists in some form of correspondence between belief and fact.[9]

QUICK REVIEW
Russell explains correspondence by saying that a sentence corresponds to a fact when the relations among the words or constituents of the sentence mirror the relations among the terms or parts of a fact.

In the preceding passage, Russell claims that the truth or falsity of a belief does not depend on the nature of the belief itself, but on something "outside the belief." In particular, truth is a relationship between a belief and things in the world outside the belief. In other words, truth is a "correspondence between belief and fact."

critical thinking

Russell assumes that if the truth or falsehood of a belief depends on something outside the belief itself, it follows that truth and falsity must depend on facts. Does this really follow?

Russell goes on to try to explain what he means by "correspondence"—that is, what it means to say that a belief "corresponds" to a fact. Russell calls the constituents or parts of a belief its "objects" or "object-terms." For example, in the belief that Booth shot Lincoln, the objects are *Booth*, *shot*, and *Lincoln*. Russell claims that when we believe something, we relate things—that is, we arrange them in a certain order or relationship. In a statement of the belief, this order is indicated by word arrangement. For example, the belief that Booth shot Lincoln is different from the belief that Lincoln shot Booth. Although their object-terms are the same, their order or relationship is different. What makes one true and the other false? The arrangement of the object terms in the true belief corresponds to the way things are arranged in a fact. If the relationship among the terms in the *belief* or *statement* is the same as the relationship of the corresponding objects in a *fact*, then the belief or statement is true:

> Thus a belief is *true* when it corresponds with a certain associated complex [fact], and *false* when it does not. Assuming, for the sake of definiteness, that the objects of the belief are two terms and a relation, the terms being put in a certain order by the "sense" of the believing, then if the two terms in that order are united by the relation into a complex [fact], the belief is true; if not, it is false. This constitutes the definition of truth and falsehood that we were in search of. Judging or believing is a certain complex unity of which a mind is a constituent; if the remaining constituents, taken in the order which they have in the belief, form a complex unity [i.e., a fact], then the belief is true; if not, it is false. . . . We may restate our theory as follows: If we take such a belief as 'Othello believes that Desdemona loves Cassio', we will call Desdemona and Cassio the *object-terms*, and loving the *object-relation*. If there is a complex unity 'Desdemona's love for Cassio', consisting of the object-terms related by the object-relation in the same order as they have in the belief, then this complex unity is called the *fact corresponding to the belief*. Thus a belief is true when there is a corresponding fact, and is false when there is no corresponding fact.[10]

---

9 Bertrand Russell, *The Problems of Philosophy* (London: Oxford University Press, 1912), 283–284.
10 Ibid., 285.

For Russell, then, a belief is true when and only when it relates its object-terms in the same way that the corresponding objects are related in a real fact. Take, for example, my belief that Joe loves Mary. This belief is true if the way that my belief relates Joe, love, and Mary is the same way that Joe, love, and Mary are related in the real world—that is, if in the real world it is a fact that Joe loves Mary.

But notice how puzzling this is. For example, what are the "objects" in a belief? Beliefs aren't physical things made up of "objects," so it is not clear exactly what the "objects" of a belief are. Moreover, when Russell gives examples of the "objects" of a belief, his examples are the words that make up a sentence, like "Desdemona" and "loves" and "Cassio." So let's assume that the "objects" of a belief are more or less equivalent to the words of the sentence that expresses the belief. Then Russell seems to be saying that a belief or a sentence that expresses the belief is true when the words of the sentence are related to each other in the same way that the parts of a fact are related to each other. But this is even more puzzling: How can the *people,* Desdemona and Cassio, be related to each other in the same way that *words* are related to each other? Words are related by their physical positions on paper, but people are not. So how can the relationship between words or "object-terms" be the same as the relationship between the real objects that make up a fact? Russell apparently thinks that beliefs or sentences are like pictures. A picture is an accurate representation of a scene when the parts of the picture are related to each other in the same way that the parts of the scene are related to each other. In a similar way, Russell seems to think, a belief is true when its parts are related to each other in the same way that the parts of the corresponding fact are related to each other. But the whole trouble with this approach is that beliefs and sentences are not pictures of things; they are not even remotely like pictures.[11]

But a correspondence theory of truth doesn't need Russell's complicated views about beliefs, facts, objects, and their relationships. All that a correspondence theory of truth requires is the simple idea that whether beliefs (or statements or propositions) are true depends on the way things are in reality. Not surprisingly there are other correspondence theories of truth that are simpler than Russell's. For example, the American philosopher Roderick Chisholm gives us this short formula as a summary of his theory of truth:

> T is a sentence token that is true in $L =_{\text{def}} T$ is a sentence token and there is a state of affairs h such that (1) T expresses h in L and (2) h obtains.[12]

In this formula, a "sentence token" is just a particular sentence; L means a language; h refers to some state of affairs; and $=_{\text{def}}$ is equivalent to "by definition means that." So in ordinary words, Chisholm's summary says: That a particular sentence of some language is true, by definition means that (1) the sentence expresses a state of affairs and (2) that state of affairs obtains. Or, in short, a sentence is true if and only if it expresses a state of affairs that obtains in reality.

There are, then, different versions of the correspondence theory of truth. Some focus on beliefs, others on statements, others on propositions. Some say that "facts" make beliefs true, others that "states of affairs" make them true, and others that "conditions" in the real world make them true. Some say that beliefs must "mirror"

---

11 On the relationship between Russell and the Picture Theory of language, see Edna Daitz, "The Picture Theory of Meaning," *Mind,* New Series, vol. 62, no. 246 (Apr., 1953), pp. 184–201, and V. Hope, "The Picture Theory of Meaning in the Tractatus as a Development of Moore's and Russell's Theories of Judgment," *Philosophy,* vol. 44, no. 168 (Apr., 1969), pp. 140–148.

12 Roderick M. Chisholm, *Theory of Knowledge,* 2nd ed. (Englewood Cliffs, NJ: Prentice Hall, 1977), 138.

or "picture" the real world, others that they must correctly "describe" the real world, and others that they must "express" what obtains in the real world. But what they all have in common is the basic claim that truth depends on reality.

Because it seems so natural and reasonable, many—perhaps most—philosophers in the West and the East have accepted some version of the correspondence theory of truth. In the West, some of its more prominent early adherents, as indicated earlier, have included Aristotle and Aquinas. In the East, almost all the great schools of India have implicitly or explicitly assumed the correspondence theory. For example, the members of the great Nyaya-Vaisesika or "Logic" school of Indian philosophy explicitly claim that a belief or an "awareness" is true when it reflects or corresponds to a fact that is independent of our consciousness. Our knowledge of facts, they go on to argue, can come from perception, reasoning, analogy, or the testimony of others. Today, a number of prominent contemporary philosophers have defended the correspondence theory of truth, including David M. Armstrong, Donald Davidson, John Searle, and many others.

QUICK REVIEW
Critics say that the correspondence theory wrongly assumes we can determine whether our beliefs correspond to an external reality; but our only access to an external world is through our senses and we cannot know whether our senses give us an accurate picture of an external reality because we cannot get beyond our senses to check this out.

QUICK REVIEW
Other critics say we cannot define the fact to which a true statement is supposed to correspond without using the true statement itself. Searle replies that this is because the word *fact* is supposed to indicate the conditions in reality that make a specific proposition true. This is a significant use of *fact*, but it means that a fact can be defined only in relation to the proposition it makes true.

Challenges to the Correspondence Theory. Although the correspondence theory seems altogether reasonable, many philosophers have raised significant objections to it. One key problem that critics have pointed out is that the correspondence theory assumes that we're able to determine whether our beliefs correspond to or match a reality that is external to ourselves. Many philosophers have questioned this assumption. Our only access to an external world, they have argued, is through the information our senses provide. But we have no way of knowing whether that information is accurate because we cannot get beyond our senses to check out the external world. We have no direct access to an "external world." In effect, critics are asking, "Because we know only our experiences, how can we ever get outside them to verify what reality actually is?" The correspondence theory of truth seems to assume that we know not only our experiences of things but also facts about an external world—that is, how the world beyond our experiences actually is. But, critics ask, can we ever really know such an external world? And if the correspondence theory says truth depends on an external world we can't know, then doesn't the correspondence theory put truth forever out of our reach?

Then there's the question of just what a *fact* is. Critics claim that *fact* as used by correspondence theorists is nothing more than "true proposition," as in "It's a fact that I'm six feet tall." To show this, critics ask this question: To which fact is a true proposition supposed to "correspond"? For example, to which fact does the proposition "The cat is on the mat" correspond? The obvious answer is that "the cat is on the mat" is supposed to correspond to the fact that the cat is on the mat. But then identifying the fact to which a true proposition corresponds requires using the true proposition itself. Moreover, the correspondence theory is saying nothing more than "a true proposition is one that corresponds to what the proposition says." So, using *fact* in this way results in circularity: A proposition is true if it corresponds to what a true proposition says.

Some correspondence theorists respond to these accusations by claiming that *fact* means the same as "actual state of affairs." Consequently, they argue, the correspondence theory says that a true proposition is one that corresponds to an actual state of affairs. But then, critics ask, exactly to which actual state of affairs does a true proposition correspond? And it seems that the only answer is the state of affairs that the true proposition describes! In other words, it doesn't matter if the correspondence theorist defines truth in terms of facts or states of affairs since in either case he runs into the same problem: Both facts and states of affairs seem to be nothing more than what true propositions state. So, the correspondence theory is pointless since in effect it says nothing more than "a true proposition is one that corresponds to what the true proposition says." What is gained by this?

Recently, philosopher John Searle, who agrees that true propositions are those that correspond to facts, tried to answer those critics who object that since facts can be identified only by using a true proposition, the correspondence theory is pointless.[13] He admits that there is no way to say what fact a proposition expresses other than by using the proposition itself, but this does not mean that the correspondence theory has no point. Searle argues that the word *fact* was developed precisely so that we could talk about and refer to what it is about the real world that makes a given proposition true. That is, we use the word *fact* to indicate those conditions in the real world that make a specific proposition true. So, of course, there is no way to specify a fact without using the proposition that is made true by that fact: A specific fact is nothing more than a specific proposition's truth conditions. The fact and the proposition have to go together. But this doesn't mean that the word *fact* doesn't tell us something significant. Its importance is that it tells us that what makes a proposition true is some specific set of conditions in the real world. In other words, the importance of the word *fact* is that it lets us say that it is something about the real independent world that makes the proposition true. Propositions, then, are not made true by something in our minds. We use the word *fact* so that we can assert that propositions are made true by specific conditions in the real world, independent of the mind.

It is not clear whether Searle's defense of facts works, and some critics say it doesn't. But even if Searle is right, critics claim that there are other problems with the correspondence theory. The correspondence theory uses the word *corresponds*, yet *corresponds* is a word that is as unclear and confusing as the word *fact*. Just what does it mean to say that a true belief "corresponds" to a fact or a state of affairs? It doesn't correspond in the way that a color sample on a color chart corresponds with a color of paint on a wall. With color samples, there's a resemblance between the sample and the wall paint. Yet there's no resemblance between a belief and a fact or state of affairs, and none between a sentence and a fact or state of affairs. A belief does not seem to correspond to a fact in the way that a picture mirrors the scene it portrays, which apparently is what Russell's theory proposes. Does a statement correspond to a fact in the way that titles of books on library cards correspond to the books themselves? Is there a similar sort of one-to-one correspondence between statements and facts? Just as for each book there's a card, and for each card a book, so also for each statement there's a fact and for each fact a statement? If so, what have we gained? It seems at least as clear to say that a true proposition describes an actual state of affairs and thus dispose of the inherently misleading term *correspondence*.

Finally, there is the problem of negative statements. To what fact or state of affairs does the negative statement "No unicorns exist" correspond? Does it correspond to some sort of negative fact? But what is a negative fact or negative state of affairs? And what about hypothetical statements like "If it rains, then the ground gets wet"? Are there supposed to be "hypothetical facts" to which hypothetical statements correspond? But what on earth would a hypothetical fact look like?

QUICK REVIEW
Critics also say we cannot explain what *correspondence* means and cannot explain to what "facts" true negative statements and true hypothetical statements correspond.

Tarski's Definition of Truth. The traditional correspondence theories encounter several problems, then, particularly the problem of explaining what the words "facts" and "correspondence" are supposed to mean. For that reason, the philosopher

13 John R. Searle, *The Construction of Social Reality* (New York: Free Press, 1995).

***La Trahison des** Images*, René Magritte. Translation: "This is not a pipe." Just how does a true proposition correspond to a fact or a state of affairs? There's no resemblance between a proposition and a state of affairs. Does a statement correspond to fact in the way that titles of books on library cards correspond to the books themselves? That is, is there some sort of one-to-one correspondence? If so, what is gained?

Banque d'Images, ADAGP/Art Resource, NY/© 2010 C. Herscovici, London/Artist Rights Society (ARS), New York

and logician Alfred Tarski developed an interesting and important version of the correspondence theory that does not refer to "facts" or "correspondence." Truth, Tarski suggests, is a property of sentences. A sentence is true when things are as it says things are. Take, for example, the Latin sentence "*Nix est alba*," which says that snow is white. So, the Latin sentence "*Nix est alba*" is true if and only if snow is white. We can write this on three lines:

1. The Latin sentence "*Nix est alba*" is true in Latin
2. if and only if
3. snow is white.

Notice that line 1 is about the truth, specifically about the truth of a specific sentence in a certain language. But line 3 is not about truth but about specific conditions in the real world. So, together the three lines tell us that what makes this specific sentence true in a certain language is these specific conditions in the real world. We almost have Tarski's version of the correspondence theory. To get his version of the correspondence theory, we just need to generalize from this example. Suppose we let the letter *L* stand for any language and the letter *S* stand for any sentence in that language. And suppose we let *p* stand for a statement of the conditions that make that sentence true. Then, we can say this:

> For any language *L*, any sentence S in language *L*, and any statement *p* that states the conditions that make *S* true in language *L*: The sentence *S* in language *L* is true if and only if *p*.

And that is Tarski's version of the correspondence theory. Notice that it tells us what it means to say that a sentence in a language is "true," and it says that a sentence in a language is true when *conditions in the real world* are as it says they are. It captures the two main features of a correspondence theory: (1) It tells us what truth is, and (2) it tells us that truth depends on conditions in the real world. But it nowhere uses the term *fact* or *corresponds*! To many people, Tarski's theory is brilliant.

Yet you may object that Tarski's definition of truth is circular. After all, doesn't he say that *p* has to "state the conditions that make *S* true"? Isn't he using the concept of truth to define *p* and then saying that the "truth" of a sentence is defined by *p*? The answer is yes and no. Tarski does use the notion of truth in our *English* language to define what *p* is. But then he uses *p* to define what truth is in *any language other than English.* If we were more careful, we would have written Tarski's theory of truth like this:

> For any (non-English) language *L,* any sentence S in language *L,* and any (English) statement *p* that states the conditions that make *S* true in language *L*: The sentence S in language *L* is true if and only if *p*.

QUICK REVIEW
Tarski's version of the correspondence theory gets around these problems. It says that for any (non-English) language *L*, any sentence *S* in *L*, and any (English) statement *p* of the conditions that make the sentence *S* true, the sentence *S* in *L* is true if and only if *p*. Critics point out that this doesn't tell us what truth is in the language we ourselves use.

Tarski's theory tells us in one language (English) what truth means in another language. Tarski argued that this is the best we can hope for. We can say what truth is in one language (such as Latin), but only if we use another language (such as English) to do that, and we have to make use of the notion of truth in that other language (English). We might say that his definition of truth takes us pretty far: It lets us define truth in every language except one—the one we use to state the definition.

Tarski's version of the correspondence theory is extremely important, and many philosophers think it's the best definition of truth we have. Still, some argue that because his theory does not tell us what truth is in the main language we use to define his theory (such as English), we are left not knowing what truth is supposed to mean in the most important language of all: the one we use! Other critics argue that his theory is not really a correspondence theory of truth, but just a theory about what the "truth conditions" of a sentence in a language are. Tarski, when he first developed the theory, said that it was a version of the correspondence theory but later changed his mind and claimed it wasn't. You will have to decide that issue for yourself. For now we have to turn to a group of philosophers who reject the correspondence theory of truth altogether.

Coherence Theory

According to the **coherence theory** of truth, a belief is true if it "coheres" with other beliefs that we regard as true. The essential test is not correspondence between a belief and a fact in the real world, but coherence between a belief and other beliefs in one's mind. The coherence theory of truth insists that, properly speaking, truth is a property of a related group of consistent beliefs. A particular belief is true if it is, or can be, integrated within the framework of all the other beliefs that we already accept as true. Earlier, we discussed the coherence theory of *justification.* The coherence theory of *truth* has some similarities to the coherence theory of *justification.* In fact, some defenders of the

Yale University Library

Brand Blanshard: "A judgment of fact can be verified only by the sort of apprehension that can present us with a fact, and this must be a further judgment. And an agreement between judgments is best described not as a correspondence, but as coherence."

PHILOSOPHY AND LIFE

Truth and Paradox

The concept of truth was intensively studied by logicians during the twentieth century. In fact, the vigorous attempts that logicians and mathematicians made to clarify the notion of truth led to some of the greatest and most far-reaching mathematical discoveries of the century. Much of this work was inspired by the realization that the very notion of truth seems to give rise to troublesome paradoxes and contradictions.

One of the earliest examples of the troublesome contradictions that the notion of truth can create is attributed to the ancient Greek philosopher Eubulides, who wrote, "A man says that he is not telling the truth. Is what he says true or false?" If what the man says is true, then the man is not telling the truth, so what he says must be false! But if what the man says is false, then it is false that he is not telling the truth, so what he says must be true! Thus, assuming what the man says is true leads us to a contradiction, and assuming what the man says is not true also leads us to a contradiction. In either case, the very notion of truth seems to generate a contradiction.

The same kinds of contradictions are generated by much simpler statements, such as "This statement is not true" or

The sentence in the box on this page is false.

But why should it matter that the very concept of truth generates contradictions? Because, unfortunately, once a single contradiction is allowed, it is easy to prove with rigorous logic that any *statement whatsoever* is true. That is, anything can be proved once you accept a contradiction. This is fairly easy to show.

Let the letter *Q* stand for any statement you want, such as "Unicorns exist." Now suppose that you accept as true the statement "God is good." Call this statement *P*. And suppose you also accept as true the contradictory statement "God is not good." Call this statement *not-P*. Now consider the following statement:

1. *Either P is true or Q is true.*

You must accept that statement 1 is true because you previously accepted that *P* is true. However, because you also accepted *not-P*, this means that *P* is not true. That is, you must also accept statement 2:

2. *P is not true.*

Now you have accepted statements 1 and 2. But from statements 1 and 2, of course, it logically follows that

3. *Q is true.*

And so you must accept that *Q* is true—that is, that unicorns exist! By accepting the contradiction that *P* is true and that *not-P* is also true, we can logically prove that unicorns exist. In fact, anything at all can be proved with rigorous logic once a contradiction is accepted.

The terrible consequences that would follow should the concept of truth involve contradictions were what led twentieth-century logicians and mathematicians to invest considerable energy in trying to come up with ways to avoid contradictions. Unfortunately, this work has not yet come to any firm conclusions. The possibility that our notion of truth may be contradictory still lurks.

QUESTIONS

1. Can you conceive of some ways of avoiding the contradictions that truth seems to involve? Does Tarski's correspondence theory of truth suggest a way of avoiding these contradictions?
2. Can you conceive of some ways of avoiding the argument that once a contradiction is accepted, anything can be proved?

coherence theory of truth have argued that a coherence theory of justification *is* a coherence theory of truth. Once we show that a belief is *justified*, they argue, we have shown that it is *true*.

QUICK REVIEW
The coherence theory says that truth is a property of a related group of consistent and accepted beliefs, and a particular belief is true if it coheres with the group of accepted beliefs.

Geometry is a good example of the coherence theory in operation. Geometry constructs an entire system of "truths," or theorems, by building on a few basic statements, or "axioms." In science, likewise, theories generally gain respectability when they are coherent with the body of accepted judgments. Brand Blanshard (1892–1987), a twentieth-century coherence theorist, in fact argued in favor of the coherence theory by pointing out that even the correspondence theory has to verify a statement by using other statements, beliefs, or judgments. So, to discover a true proposition, even the correspondence theorist has to rely on its coherence with other statements, beliefs, or judgments. Blanshard illustrates this point:

> Suppose we say, "the table in the next room is round"; how should we test this judgment? In the case in question, what verifies the statement of fact is the perceptual judgment that I make when I open the door and look. But then what verifies the perceptual judgment itself. . . .To which the reply is, as before, that a judgment of fact can be verified only by the sort of apprehension that can present us with a fact, and that this must be a further judgment. And an agreement between judgments is best described not as a correspondence, but as coherence.[14]

What Blanshard is getting at here is that to know whether a table is round, I must take a look and then form a belief that what I am looking at is a round table. But how do I know that I can rely on the beliefs formed by using my eyes? Only because there are other beliefs I have, such as that my eyes have been reliable in the past, that when there is the kind of light I saw in the room I generally do not make mistakes, that when I see an oval shape like I saw from the angle at which I was looking at the table, it usually means that the table is really round, and so forth. So in the end, to figure out whether the table is round, I have to rely on the fact that my judgment of its roundness "coheres" or is consistent with a bunch of other beliefs I have.

QUICK REVIEW
Blanshard argues that we can verify a statement only by using other statements, so there is no way of determining the truth of a statement other than by seeing whether it coheres with other accepted statements. So coherence theory is right.

 critical thinking
Does the coherence theory assume that our knowledge of reality is exactly like our knowledge of mathematics? Is this assumption correct?

Blanshard gives a fuller illustration of the meaning of coherence in his book *The Nature of Thought.* There he compares the way an organized group of coherent beliefs fits together to the way that several different groups of things fit together, such as a mere heap of junk, a more organized pile of stones, the even more organized parts that make up a machine, and the yet even more organized parts of an organism's body:

QUICK REVIEW
According to Blanshard, an ideally coherent system of beliefs would be one in which any single belief could be deduced from the others, in which no belief was arbitrary, and in which each belief was related in some way to every other belief.

> At the bottom would be a junk heap, where we could know every item but one and still be without any clue as to what that remaining item was. Above this would come a stone-pile, for here you could at least infer that what you would find next would be a stone. A machine would be higher again, since from the remaining parts one could deduce not only the general character of a missing part, but also its special form and function. This is a high degree of coherence, but it is very far short of the highest. You could remove the engine from a motorcar while leaving the other parts intact, and replace it with any one of thousands of other engines, but the thought of such an interchange among human heads or hearts shows at once that the interdependence in a machine is far below that of the body. Do we find then in organic bodies the highest conceivable coherence? Clearly not. Though a human hand, as Aristotle said, would hardly be a hand when detached from the body, still it would be something definite enough; and we can conceive systems in which even this something would be gone. Abstract a number from the number series and it would be a mere unrecognizable *x*; similarly, the very thought of a straight line involves the thought of the Euclidean space in which it falls. It is perhaps in such systems as Euclidean geometry that we get the most perfect examples of coherence that have been constructed. If any proposition were lacking, it could be supplied from the rest; if any were altered, the repercussions would be felt through the length and breadth of the system. Yet even such a system as this falls short of the ideal system. Its postulates are unproved; they are independent of each other, in the sense that none of them could be derived from any other or even from all the others together; its clear necessity is bought by an abstractness so extreme as to have left out nearly everything that belongs to the character of

14 Brand Blanshard, The Nature of Thought (New York: Macmillan, 1941), 464–465.

PHILOSOPHY AND LIFE

Historical Facts

Julius Caesar crossing the Rubicon to begin a civil war against Pompey, 49 BCE.

What is a historical fact? Take, for example, what passes for a simple historical fact: "In the year 49 BCE, Caesar crossed the Rubicon." This is a familiar fact, and one of some importance. Yet, as the most distinguished American historian Carl L. Becker pointed out more than a half century ago, this simple fact has strings tied to it. It depends on numerous other facts so that it has no meaning apart from the web of circumstances that produced it. This web of circumstances, of course, was the chain of events arising out of the relation of Caesar to Pompey, the Roman Senate, and the Roman Republic. As Becker states,

> Caesar had been ordered by the Roman Senate to resign his command of the army in Gaul. He decided to disobey the Roman Senate. Instead of resigning his command, he marched on Rome, gained the mastery of the Republic, and, at last, we are told, bestrode the narrow world like a colossus. Well, the Rubicon happened to be the boundary between Gaul and Italy, so that by the act of crossing the Rubicon with his army Caesar's treason became an accomplished fact and the subsequent great events followed in due course. Apart from these great events and complicated relations, the crossing of the Rubicon means nothing, is not an historical fact properly speaking at all. . . . [It is] a symbol standing for a long series of events which have to do with the most intangible and immaterial realities, viz.: the relation between Caesar and the millions of people of the Roman world.

Clearly, for Becker "the simple historical fact" is only a symbol, an affirmation about an event. And because it's hardly worthwhile to term a symbol cold or hard, indeed dangerous to call it true or false, one might best speak of historical facts as being more or less appropriate.

QUESTIONS

1. Could Becker's analysis be applied to this statement: "The Japanese bombed Pearl Harbor on December 7, 1941"?
2. Would it be accurate to say that historians deal not with an event but with statements that affirm the fact that the event occurred? If so, what's the difference?

Source: Carl L. Becker, "What Are Historical Facts?" Quoted in *Coming Age of Philosophy*, ed. Roger Eastman (San Francisco: Canfield, 1973), 451–452.

actual things. A completely satisfactory system would have none of these defects. No proposition would be arbitrary, every proposition would be entailed by the others jointly and even singly, no proposition would stand outside the system. The integration would be so complete that no part could be seen for what it was without seeing its relation to the whole, and the whole itself could be understood only through the contribution of every part.[15]

15 Brand Blanshard, *The Nature of Thought* (New York: Macmillan, 1941), 464–465. Reprinted by permission of George Allen & Unwin Ltd.

Blanshard is describing the kind of ideal group of coherent beliefs toward which we should strive. He claims that in a fully coherent system of beliefs, all the beliefs are in harmony with all the other beliefs in the system, and each belief supports (provides evidence for) the other beliefs. Moreover, any one belief could be deduced from the other beliefs, and the whole set of beliefs would be highly ordered, like the theorems that can be deduced from the axioms of geometry. Blanshard, of course, is not the only philosopher to have accepted the coherence theory of truth. In the West, the great rationalist philosophers Leibniz, Spinoza, and Hegel all accepted the coherence theory, as did several modern empiricists, such as Otto Neurath and C. G. Hempel, and many other twentieth-century philosophers, including H. H. Joachim and F. H. Bradley. Some contemporary coherentists include Dummett and Putnam.

Several Eastern philosophers have also embraced the coherence view of truth. In the previous chapter, we saw that the great seventh-century Indian philosopher Shankara held that a judgment about reality should be "sublated" when it does not fit in with other, fuller judgments about reality. This is a form of the coherence theory. Several members of the Yogacara school of Buddhist philosophy also accepted a form of coherentism. For example, the Indian philosopher Dharmakirti (circa 600–660) said that any belief or "awareness" based on sense perception should be rejected if it does not cohere or agree with the fuller system of beliefs we have. In his view, coherence with other beliefs or "awarenesses" is both the nature of truth and the way we determine whether a belief or an awareness is true.

Still, is the systemic coherence of beliefs with one another by itself a guarantee of truth? Recall that until the sixteenth century, almost everyone believed that the earth was the center of the solar system. Why did everyone believe this? Because it made sense and accorded with commonsensical observation. It fit in with the widespread experience of things and with religious belief. Moreover, in the second century CE the astronomer Ptolemy had elaborated and developed these observations into a complicated but consistent theory. His theory, which said that the sun revolves around the earth, could even be used to predict astronomical events successfully. In fact, the major difference between Ptolemy's theory and the theory of Copernicus which replaced it was that Copernicus' was simpler. (With the refinements that Kepler, Galileo, and Newton later proposed, its predictions were also much more accurate.) Yet both theories were consistent. The point is that coherence does not seem to distinguish between consistent truth and consistent error. A judgment may be true if it is consistent with other judgments, but what if the other judgments are false? If first judgments are not true, they can produce a system of consistent error.

QUICK REVIEW
Critics point out that in the past, societies accepted statements that we now know were false, such as "The sun revolves around the earth."

Another objection is that, contrary to what Blanshard argues, a coherence theory in the last analysis seems to rely on correspondence. After all, if a judgment is coherent, it must cohere with another judgment. But what of the very first judgments we make? With what do they cohere? If they are first, they cannot cohere with anything. Their truth, then, can be verified only by determining whether they report an actual fact. But this is the correspondence theory.

QUICK REVIEW
Critics ask how the original group of statements came to be accepted when there was not yet any group of statements for them to "cohere" with.

But the correspondence and coherence theories do not exhaust all the options. There is a third major theory of truth, called the pragmatic theory of truth.

Pragmatic Theory

Because of the evident weaknesses in the correspondence and coherence theories, philosophers have suggested another possibility, the pragmatic theory of truth. The pragmatic theory of truth says that a belief is true if it works and is useful—for example, by letting us make accurate predictions.

QUICK REVIEW
The pragmatic theory of truth holds that there are no absolute and unchanging truths; a statement is true if it is useful to believe—that is, if it aids us individually or collectively in the struggle for survival, if it passes the tests of science, or if it meets the needs and interests of our human nature.

The pragmatic theory of truth is quite different from both the correspondence theory and the coherence theory. The pragmatist may claim that it is possible we know only our experiences, so truth cannot be what corresponds with reality. The pragmatist may also view the coherence theory as too impractical. Instead, the pragmatist wants to introduce usefulness as the measure of truth and insists that we can define truth only in relation to consequences. A statement is true if people can use that statement to achieve results that satisfy their interests. There is, then, no absolute or unchanging truth. To verify a belief as truth, we should see whether accepting the belief meets the needs and interests of our human nature over a long period of time, or whether after a prolonged period it passes the tests of science, or whether it aids us individually or collectively in the biological struggle for survival. In a nutshell, the pragmatic view of truth holds that a belief is true if it is useful to believe.

Many Eastern philosophers have accepted this pragmatic view of truth. In India, for example, the philosopher Vatsyayana (circa 350 BCE), who wrote the oldest commentary on the *Nyayasutra,* stated in the opening passage of his commentary that the truth of a belief or an "awareness" is known by its fruits: A false awareness is one that leads us to engage in the wrong actions and that prevents us from getting what we want, while the true awareness is the one that has successful results.

Pragmatism. In the West, the pragmatic theory of truth has become a cornerstone of pragmatism, the essentially American philosophy mentioned in Chapter 3. Recall that pragmatism developed during the nineteenth and twentieth centuries, especially through the writings of Charles S. Peirce (1839–1914), William James (1842–1910), and John Dewey (1859–1952). The pragmatists were tired of older European outlooks, especially those that viewed humans primarily in rationalistic terms. They saw humans as needing to use the practical consequences of beliefs to decide truth and validity. Especially objectionable to pragmatists is the traditional idea of truth as something fixed and inert. Pragmatists see truth as dynamic and changing, subjective and relative. Like the correspondence and coherence theories, the pragmatic theory of truth has many versions. But the classic version was put forth by William James in *Pragmatism: A New Name for Some Old Ways of Thinking.* In it, he clearly distinguishes the pragmatic theory from other theories of truth:

> Truth, as any dictionary will tell you, is a property of certain of our ideas. It means their "agreement," as falsity means their disagreement, with "reality." Pragmatists and intellectualists both accept this definition as a matter of course. They begin to quarrel only after the question is raised as to what may precisely be meant by the term "agreement," and what by the term "reality," when reality is taken as something for our ideas to agree with.
>
> In answering these questions the pragmatists are more analytic and painstaking, the intellectualists more offhand and unreflective. The popular notion is that a true idea must copy its reality. Like other popular views, this one follows the analogy of the most usual experience. Our true ideas of sensible things do indeed copy them. Shut your eyes and think of yonder clock on the wall, and you get just such a true picture or copy of its dial. But your idea of its "works" (unless you are a clockmaker) is much less of a copy, yet it passes muster, for it in no way clashes with the reality. Even though it should shrink to the mere word "works," that word still serves you truly; and when you speak of the "time-keeping function" of the clock, or of its spring's "elasticity," it is hard to see exactly what your ideas can copy.
>
> You perceive that there is a problem here. Where our ideas cannot copy definitely their object, what does agreement with that object mean? Some idealists seem to say that they are true whenever they are what God means that we ought to think about that object. Others hold the copy-view all through, and speak as if our

ideas possessed truth just in proportion as they approach to being copies of the Absolute's eternal way of thinking.

These views, you see, invite pragmatistic discussion. But the great assumption of the intellectualists is that truth means essentially an inert static relation. When you've got your true idea of anything, there's an end of the matter. You're in possession; you *know*; you have fulfilled your thinking destiny. You are where you ought to be mentally; you have obeyed your categorical imperative; and nothing more need follow on that climax of your rational destiny. Epistemologically you are in stable equilibrium.

Pragmatism, on the other hand, asks its usual question. "Grant an idea or belief to be true," it says, "what concrete difference will its being true make in any one's actual life? How will the truth be realized? What experiences will be different from those which would obtain if the belief were false? What, in short, is the truth's cash-value in experiential terms?"

The moment pragmatism asks this question, it sees the answer: *True ideas are those that we can assimilate, validate, corroborate and verify. False ideas are those that we cannot.* That is the practical difference it makes to us to have true ideas; that, therefore, is the meaning of truth, for it is all that truth is known as.

This thesis is what I have to defend. The truth of an idea is not a stagnant property inherent in it. Truth *happens* to an idea. It *becomes* true, is *made* true by events. Its verity *is* in fact an event, a process: the process namely of its verifying itself, its *verification*. Its validity is the process of its validation.

But what do the words *verification* and *validation* themselves pragmatically mean? They again signify certain practical consequences of the verified and validated idea. It is hard to find any one phrase that characterizes these consequences better than the ordinary agreement-formula—just such consequences being what we have in mind whenever we say that our ideas "agree" with reality. They lead us, namely, through the acts and other ideas which they instigate, into or up to, or towards, other parts of experience with which we feel all the while—such feeling being among our potentialities—that the original ideas remain in agreement. The connections and transitions come to us from point to point as being progressive, harmonious, satisfactory. This function of agreeable leading is what we mean by an idea's verification.[16]

QUICK REVIEW
James argued that the truth of an idea depends on the practical difference it makes: "True ideas are those that we can assimilate, validate, corroborate and verify." An idea is validated or verified if as a consequence of believing the idea we find we are led to experiences that are "progressive, harmonious, satisfactory."

According to James, we do not base truth on a comparison of a statement with some objective external reality. Neither is truth based on coherence with other beliefs. In James' view, the essential problem with those outlooks is that their adherents have failed to ask the right questions. They shouldn't ask how judgments correspond or relate to reality, but *what difference they make*. For James, the truth of an idea or judgment depends on what he calls "the practical difference it makes" in our lives. And by making a practical difference he means that believing the idea or judgment will lead to progressive, harmonious, and satisfactory consequences. Ideas and judgments have to be tested, investigated, and used by a community for a long period of time and then accepted as true if they seem to continue to lead to useful consequences. For example, believing in most scientific theories has enabled us to make great technological progress, believing in the ideas of democracy has made our lives with one another and our societies more harmonious, and believing in the many daily judgments that we are led to make by using our senses or in the many bits of practical knowledge that we use to live and make our way through our world has made our daily lives more satisfactory than they would otherwise be. So, we accept all these beliefs. And accepting them for these reasons makes them true.

critical thinking

Does James assume that truth is a kind of event? That it can change with time? Is this plausible? Does James assume that a proposition is neither true nor false until it is verified? Does his view imply that if we cannot prove something is true, then it is false?

16 William James, *Pragmatism: A New Name for Some Old Ways of Thinking* (New York: Longmans, Green, 1907), 198–199.

Modern Pragmatism. Pragmatism continues to be one of the most vigorous living philosophies. In fact, many contemporary philosophers believe that pragmatism is the most vital and promising of all approaches to truth. Nevertheless, contemporary pragmatists approach truth differently from William James. Whereas James gave a definition of *truth*, modern pragmatists tend to argue that we should forget about trying to define this elusive idea. Instead, we should get on with the more important activity of living in open-minded, democratic communities. Richard Rorty, one of the foremost living philosophers and a staunch advocate of pragmatism, writes the following:

> We pragmatists . . . are making the purely *negative* point that we would be better off without the traditional distinctions between knowledge and opinion, construed as the distinction between truth as correspondence to reality and truth as a commendatory term for well-justified belief. Our opponents call this negative claim "relativistic" because they cannot imagine that anybody would seriously deny that truth has an intrinsic nature. So when we say that there is nothing to be said about truth save that each of us will commend as true those beliefs which he or she finds good to believe, the realist is inclined to interpret this as one more positive theory about the nature of truth: a theory according to which truth is simply the contemporary opinion of a chosen individual or group. Such a theory would, of course, be self-refuting. But we pragmatists do not have a theory of truth, much less a relativistic one.[17]

QUICK REVIEW
The contemporary pragmatist Rorty claims we do not need theories of truth; the most we can say is that we "commend" as true whatever passes our community's "procedures of justification." Because there are many communities, there are many different but equally valid truths.

Nevertheless, Rorty holds that what can be said about the notion of truth is that truth is whatever has passed society's "procedures of justification." He proposes "the ethnocentric view that there is nothing to be said about either truth or rationality apart from descriptions of the familiar procedures of justification which a given society, ours, uses in one or another area of inquiries."[18] Thus, the modern pragmatist, like William James, wants to get rid of the traditional idea that truth is correspondence with an external reality. Instead, the modern pragmatist wants us to recognize that when people say something is true, they are merely trying to "commend" it as good to believe. We commend a statement as true when it passes the tests that our community uses to distinguish what is true from what is false. Different communities, of course, may have different procedures or criteria for separating true from false. Scientists use one set of procedures for deciding what they will accept as true, whereas poets, lawyers, literary critics, and movie producers use others. But no group's procedures lead to more truth about reality than any other group's. No single truth about an independent reality exists. There are only the many truths that emerge from the many different procedures that different communities use because they have found that these procedures produce worthwhile or useful results.

QUICK REVIEW
This kind of pragmatic theory seems to imply that when our community all thought that the earth was flat, it really was true that it was flat. But this seems wrong.

Criticisms of Pragmatism. Pragmatism has been the subject of intense criticism. The main criticism has been that it seems to base truth on the fallible judgments of human communities. What's true may be justified for a certain community to believe, but what's justified for them to believe isn't necessarily true. Pragmatism seems to reduce epistemology to psychology.

To understand this basic criticism of pragmatism, consider a simple fact: What we were justified in believing yesterday may turn out to be false today. For example, five hundred years ago we were justified in believing the earth was flat. Today, we

17 Richard Rorty, "Science as Solidarity," in *Dismantling Truth*, ed. Hilary Lawson and Lisa Appignanesi (New York: St. Martin's, 1989), 11.

18 Ibid., 11.

know it is round. Pragmatism does not seem to be able to account for this simple fact. Pragmatism says that truth is whatever a community is justified in believing after it has used its "procedures of justification." It would seem that the pragmatist would have to say that the earth really was flat five hundred years ago because we were justified in believing it was flat then. Because we are justified in believing it is round today, it is really round now! This seems clearly absurd. As we saw early in this chapter, there is a difference between truth and justification, but pragmatism makes them identical.

Some pragmatists have tried to deal with this objection. Truth, they say, is what an ideal community would be justified in believing if it continued its investigations indefinitely, examined all the evidence, made no mistakes, and was perfectly open to all points of view. Thus, some pragmatists introduce the notion of an ideal community working in ideal circumstances to explain how truth can be justification even though we can be justified in believing something that is not true. A belief that we are justified in believing but that is untrue is simply a belief that an ideal community working in ideal circumstances would not be justified in believing.

QUICK REVIEW
To get around the previous criticism, some pragmatists say that truth is what an ideal community would accept if it continued its investigations into the idea's usefulness indefinitely. But this is like one of the metaphysical ideas that pragmatists say they reject.

However, this response seems to replace one metaphysical hang-up with another. Pragmatists have said that the idea that truth requires an external reality to which true beliefs must "correspond" is so much metaphysical garbage. But to say that we have instead to believe in some kind of imaginary "ideal community" to understand the difference between truth and falsity seems also to be metaphysical garbage.

Moreover, what view should pragmatists have about their own views about truth? Shouldn't they say that their theory is true if it is more useful than other theories? But in what sense is the pragmatic theory more useful than the more traditional philosophies? Any judgment about usefulness seems to involve a large dose of subjectivity. Couldn't traditional philosophers claim that their views of truth are better in terms of their own preferences? It seems that they can. In fact, can we ask whether it is true that one view is more useful than another in a sense in which *true* does not mean "useful"?

Does Truth Matter?

These debates over the nature of truth may at first seem dry and irrelevant. What does it matter whether the correct view of truth is the correspondence theory, the coherence theory, or the pragmatic theory? After all, whatever truth is, it seems that we will continue to believe the same truths and live the same lives. But, in fact, the parties to these debates are fighting over matters that directly affect each of us. It affects, for example, our views on the case with which we began our discussion of truth: the case of Marc Dutroux who was accused of having sex with, and then killing, several children and who was said to have been part of a ring of pedophiles that included powerful men throughout Europe who protected him. As you saw, some thinkers claimed that there is no objective truth about these matters and that the truth depends on the beliefs your group happens to "share." Where do the three theories of truth stand on these issues?

Consider, first, that both the coherence and the pragmatic views are opposed to the correspondence view of truth. This is only natural because the correspondence view holds that truth is objective. That is, it holds that truth depends on what the real world is like, not on what a particular person or group accepts. Both the coherence and pragmatic views, on the other hand, reject the idea that truth is objective. Instead, they hold that the truth of a claim depends on what the group that makes the claim accepts. The coherence theory says that a claim is true if it coheres with the other beliefs that a group accepts. The pragmatic theory says that a claim is true if it passes the procedures of justification that a group uses. Both theories agree that if a group accepts a claim (because it coheres with their other beliefs or because it passes their procedures of justification), then the claim is true for that group. Moreover, any conflicting claims accepted by other groups are equally true (if they meet the same criteria). One group's accepted claims are as true as the accepted claims of any other group. Ultimately, then, to reject the correspondence view of truth is to reject objectivity and to choose a relativism that sees each group's accepted claims as equally valid.

We must be careful, though, in how we use the word *relativism.* Rorty and other pragmatists say that, in a sense, they are not relativists about truth. They are not relativists, Rorty claims, if by *relativism* we mean that every belief is as good as any other and truth is whatever a group believes. Such relativism, Rorty has said, is just a "bogeyman" intended to "frighten children." However, he concedes, pragmatists agree that they are relativists about truth if by *relativism* we mean that truth is whatever a group *accepts because it passes that group's procedures of justification.* Pragmatists are relativists, then, in this more restricted sense.

QUICK REVIEW
The correspondence theory of truth says truth depends on an objective reality, but the coherence and pragmatic theories say truth depends on what a group accepts. Such relativist theories imply that beliefs accepted by any group are true and as valid as any other beliefs, no matter how racist, superstitious, nonhistorical, or biased.

But why does it matter that pragmatism and coherence are relativist views of truth? Consider some consequences of rejecting objectivity. If we reject objectivity, then we must agree that every group's accepted claims are equally true (as long as the group's claims are accepted because they pass their procedures of justification). We must agree that if members of a racist group accept the claim that they are superior to other races, their claim is as true as our claim that no race is superior to another. We must agree that if males as a group accept the claim that they are superior to women, then their claim is as true as women's claim that males are not superior to females. It means that if one group accepts the claim that the Holocaust never happened, then that claim is as true as historians' claim that Nazi Germans slaughtered six million Jews during World War II. And, of course, it means that if one group accepts the claim that having sex with children—as Marc Dutroux did—is good, their claim is as valid as another group's claim that having sex with children is evil.

In short, if truth is what a group accepts or finds justified, then whatever one group accepts is as true as what an opposing group accepts. One group's biases, prejudices, or superstitions become as legitimate as the objections that other groups may raise to these biases, prejudices, or superstitions. If no objective truth exists, then the consequence, it seems, is that any claim accepted by a group becomes truth.

QUICK REVIEW
Defenders of relativist theories argue that their views on truth are more tolerant, democratic, and inclusive than an objective theory such as correspondence. Although the theories to some extent can be seen as complementary theories about truth in different realms, our lives can force us to choose one or the other.

For many who hold a relativist theory of truth, these consequences are not necessarily bad. For example, some pragmatists hold that toleration is a critically important value that only relativism can preserve. Toleration is the virtue of acknowledging that we do not have a monopoly on truth and that the claims of others may be as valid as the claims we accept. Toleration is the virtue that relativism prizes. Thus, defenders of relativism claim that relativism is inclusive and democratic, whereas objective views of truth are exclusive and undemocratic. Objective views of truth are exclusive and undemocratic because they imply that the views of some groups are wrong and so they exclude such views.

So, you see that the choice among the theories of truth is not an abstract irrelevant exercise. A lot hangs on which theory you ultimately accept. If you opt for objectivity, you will move toward the correspondence view that truth depends on facts about the world independent of what any group happens to accept. Accepting objectivity may lead you to say that some views (like the views of a racist or a pedophile) are wrong no matter how many people accept them. On the other hand, if you opt for relativism, you will move toward the coherence or pragmatic view that truth depends on what this or that group accepts. Accepting relativism may lead you toward a more tolerant, inclusive, and democratic recognition that the views of others are equally valid. Both paths are attractive; both paths have dangerous pitfalls.

Reconciling the Theories of Truth

Is there any way to reconcile the three theories? Can we say, for example, that each of the theories tells us only part of what truth is and that you need all the theories to get a full picture of truth? To a certain extent, this is possible, and some philosophers have proposed as much.[19] One way to do this is to view the unique contribution that each theory makes to the realm of truth. Unquestionably, the correspondence theory fits the empirical physical realm. Suppose I say it's true that New York is three thousand miles from Los Angeles, it's true that a fire needs oxygen, or it's true that it's raining. Then I am probably taking *truth* to mean "correspondence." If the statements correspond to the facts, then I accept them as true.

On the other hand, coherence provides a useful way of understanding logical, necessary, or systemic truth. Thus, if I want to know whether it's true that a chair cannot be a nonchair, that 56 divided by 7 is 8, or that all bachelors are unmarried, then I need only see whether these statements fit in with other statements that I accept as true.

Finally, the pragmatic test seems to reveal the meaning of truth as applied to the many value judgments that we make. Thus, "Lying is wrong," "God exists," "Pleasure is an intrinsic good," and other such statements form an important part of our lives. So do value judgments in the arts, politics, education, and other walks of life. Frequently, the best—and sometimes the only—way to verify such judgments is by applying the tests of workability. Do these beliefs lead to satisfying lives? The pragmatic theory thus helps us understand what truth can mean in the realm of values.

We can see the theories of truth as complementary. Rather than viewing them as incompatible, we can use them to understand the truth of the various kinds of statements that we utter. Still, this strategy of approaching the theories of truth as complementary can take us only a certain distance, for the question still remains: How are we to evaluate the claims that others accept when we disagree with these claims and when they have an impact on the way we live? Shall we be tolerant pragmatists and say that racists or sexists are entitled to their views? What if their racism or sexism is directed against us? Or what shall we say about the adult who believes in sex with children? Shall we be tolerant relativists and say that this belief is as valid as ours? Or shall we opt for an objective view of the truth and say that this view is false and that we must not allow the person to act on it?

In short, our lives together seem to force us to choose between the objectivity and exclusivity of the correspondence theory and the relativism and tolerance of the coherence or pragmatic theories. In the end, it seems, we must opt for one or the other of these theories and the significant consequences each implies for our lives.

Deflating Truth

But perhaps we don't have to opt for one or the other. Recently, several philosophers have suggested a way of dealing with truth that doesn't force us to accept any of the theories. They say, in fact, that we should reject all of the theories because

---

19 This view is now called "Alethic Pluralism"; see C. Wright, *Truth and Objectivity*, (Cambridge, MA: Harvard University Press, 1992), and M. P. Lynch, *Truth as One and Many*, (Oxford: Clarendon Press, 2009).

truth really doesn't refer to anything important at all. The three theories, they suggest, are like pretentious windbags who try to inflate the concept of truth into an important and serious concept. But this kind of "truth-talk," they say, must be deflated. In reality, when we say that a statement is true, we do not add anything at all to what we say. So, truth is really an empty concept.

We can understand the point that "deflationists" are making if we consider a simple point they make: When we say that a statement "is true," we are saying nothing more or less than what the statement itself says. For example, when I say:

1. "Snow is white" is true.

I am saying exactly what I say when I just say:

2. Snow is white.

According to the deflationists, statement 1 gives us exactly the same information that statement 2 gives us; hence 1 and 2 are really equivalent. But if 1 and 2 are equivalent, then "is true" adds nothing to the statement "Snow is white" that is not already conveyed by my simple statement "Snow is white"! Truth adds nothing to our statements!

QUICK REVIEW
Deflationists argue that because "is true" adds nothing to a statement, it has no substantive meaning; hence, they reject all three theories of truth.

If the deflationists are right, then the three theories of truth are really off track. The three theories assume that truth is a substantive concept—that it adds something to our statements—and all three theories go off on a hunt for the property that "truth" refers to. But if the deflationists are correct, then truth is not really a property: It refers to nothing at all, and the three theories are looking for something that doesn't exist. Why, then, do we even have the concept of truth? According to deflationists, we have the concept of truth because sometimes we need to talk about large (or unlimited) groups of statements and it's impractical to list all the statements. For example, when I want to say that you are trustworthy, I might say, "Every statement you make is true," or "Everything you say is true." Even in these cases, though, deflationists insist that saying a group of statements "is true" doesn't add any new information to the statements themselves.

Are the deflationists correct? Many philosophers—perhaps most—are vehemently opposed to the deflationary view of truth. How, they ask, can deflationists say that truth refers to nothing at all when truth is so important and central to our lives? But many others embrace the deflationist view as a refreshing way of escaping the conundrums into which theories of truth seem to lead us. You, the reader, have to decide who is right.

QUESTIONS

1. Is describing truth as a correspondence between a statement and how things actually are an example of begging the question? In what sense does such a definition not answer the question "What is truth?" but endorse a version of that question?

2. Take some theory, perhaps in psychology, anthropology, economics, or history, and put it to the coherence test. Does it pass? Can you find an opposing theory that passes as well? What might you conclude about the coherence theory of truth?

3. In what sense do claims of extrasensory perception not fit in with what we claim to know? In what sense do they?

4. Demonstrate how the coherence theory of truth ultimately seems to rely on the correspondence theory. How would proponents of the coherence theory object to this claim?

5. Consider the fact that you are studying to enter some profession. Demonstrate how this intention is working as a truth in your life and serving as the cornerstone for a structure of other truths.
6. Take some political event from the recent past, such as the collapse of the communist nations or our own attempts to deal with tax reform. Show how the coherence theory of truth operated to formulate policy and direct activity. Do you think these examples are a vindication of the coherence theory of truth? An indictment? Both? Neither?
7. Cite a belief that you consider true primarily on pragmatic grounds.
8. In opposition to the pragmatists and their theory of truth, critics charge, "But don't you see that you're encouraging us to see things as we would have them and not as they are?" Do you agree with this criticism?
9. Can you think of any belief that, although true, does not work? Some belief that, although it could work, is not true?
10. What statements about yourself do you accept on pragmatic grounds? On the grounds of coherence? On the grounds of correspondence with reality?

PHILOSOPHY AT THE MOVIES

Watch *The Usual Suspects* (1995) in which Verbal, an eyewitness to a waterfront explosion, explains to the police how he and four other men got together in jail after they were arrested on suspicion of stealing a truck, and how they ended up at the scene of the explosion. What is true and what is false in this movie? On what view of truth do you base your answer? Does the film depend on one theory of truth more than another? Explain.

© Photos 12/Alamy

6.3 Does Science Give Us Truth?

In the previous chapter, we discussed the scientific method as a source of knowledge. We noted that it incorporates elements of empiricism, rationalism, and transcendental idealism, but we did not answer this question: Does science give us the truth? Now that we have looked closely at the question "What is truth?" let's return to the issue of whether there is truth in science. Does our discussion of the correspondence, coherence, and pragmatic theories of truth help us understand scientific truth?

Many people hold that science clearly gives us the truth about the world. After all, science has enabled us to cure hundreds of deadly diseases, to put people into space and on the moon, to send our voices and moving pictures over thousands of miles in an instant, to make computers that can carry out a million calculations in a fraction of a second. Radio, television, rockets, telescopes, the hydrogen bomb, computers, electricity, vaccines, antibiotics, heart transplants, telephones, tape recorders, cars, airplanes, submarines, microwaves, satellites, and weather forecasting all testify to what people can create by relying on the truth of science. The success of these endeavors, many believe, is clear proof that science gives us the truth. Yet does it?

To focus our inquiry, we're going to have to look at some scientific theories. As we go along, we'll look at two theories: the standard theory of matter and Copernicus' theory of the solar system. We will see that it's hard to know in what sense, if any, they are true.

Since the beginning of the twentieth century, scientists have accepted the atomic theory of matter. This theory says that the objects around us are made of atoms.

Each atom consists of a small central nucleus made up of protons and neutrons and a surrounding cloud of electrons. For many years, scientists held the theory that these three kinds of particles—protons, neutrons, and electrons—are the basic building blocks from which all things are made. But experiments eventually led scientists to a new theory: The protons and neutrons are themselves made of even smaller, more basic particles. The experiments that led scientists to change their theories were done in gigantic tubes called *particle accelerators* or *colliders*, some over a mile long. From one end of one of these tubes, a device shoots particles (electrons and atoms) toward the other end. At the other end, these particles smash into other particles at terrific speeds. Many of these collisions can be detected in "cloud chambers" or "bubble chambers" in which the speeding particles and collisions make tiny tracks or lines that can actually be seen and photographed (see Figure 6.1). Other collisions are detected using Geiger counters and other sensitive instruments that can record the collisions. In these collisions, electrons sometimes bounce off of the particles at the other end, like tiny billiard balls hitting one another. In other collisions, protons and neutrons seem to break apart into smaller things when hit by the speeding electrons.

As a result of these experiments with colliders, scientists now accept what is called the standard theory of matter. This theory says that all the ordinary material objects in the universe—from toads and trees to stars and galaxies—are made up of four kinds of tiny basic particles: two kinds of quarks, which make up the protons and neutrons in the nuclei of atoms; electrons, which surround the nuclei; and neutrinos, which can move very fast, have virtually no mass, and are shot out of nuclear reactions. These four kinds of particles are held together and acted upon by four forces: a strong nuclear force, which holds quarks together in the atomic nucleus; a weak nuclear force, which sets off certain kinds of radioactive decay; electromagnetism, which builds atoms into molecules and molecules into the objects we see; and gravity, which holds together the planets, stars, and whole galaxies. Each of these

© Omikron/Photo Researchers, Inc.

Figure 6.1—Photograph of the tracks made in a bubble chamber when a tiny subatomic particle—a proton—collided with another particle in the area at the center right and broke up into at least nine particles. The tracks left by these nine particles branch away from the point of collision and streak toward the bottom of the image. The various spirals scattered around the bubble chamber are other tracks left by electrons whose trajectories were curved by strong magnets.

four forces is associated with a particle: Photons carry the electromagnetic force, gluons carry the strong nuclear force, bosons carry the weak force, and gravitons carry gravity. Is this standard theory of matter true? And what does it mean to say that it is—or is not—"true"?

The Instrumentalist View

If you asked them, most scientists would say that the standard theory of matter is true. Yet is it? Well, ask yourself this: What does it mean to say that quarks, neutrinos, and electrons exist? No one has ever seen or heard or touched one of these particles, and no one ever will. They are unobservable "theoretical entities." That is, they are entities mentioned in theories, but we cannot directly observe them. So in what sense is it true that these theoretical entities exist?

Perhaps you might want to say that it is "true" that unobservable theoretical entities like electrons exist in this sense: The standard theory of matter, which says that electrons exist, predicts that when bits of matter hit each other at very high speeds, the dials on appropriate detectors will move and little tracks will appear in cloud chambers. Now, in fact, when scientists shoot bits of matter together at extremely high speeds in "particle colliders," the dials move and the tracks appear exactly as the theory predicts. The accuracy of these predictions, you might think, proves that the theory is true. So, it is "true" that electrons exist insofar as accepting the theories in which electrons play a role allows us to make successful predictions.

QUICK REVIEW
The standard theory of matter is a scientific theory that holds that everything is composed of four kinds of particles held together and acted upon by four forces; the Copernican theory says that the earth and the planets revolve around the sun. The question is in what sense these theories are "true."

Still, do successful predictions really prove that a theory is true and that its theoretical entities exist? Couldn't the theory just be a formula that works but that isn't literally true? Granted, the theory lets scientists predict what they will see when they shoot bits of matter together. But this successful prediction does not necessarily mean that the theory is literally true. Neither does successful prediction mean that it is literally true that these theoretical entities exist.

In fact, many scientists and philosophers interpret the standard theory as saying something like this: "If we *assume* that matter is partly made of little electrons, we can predict that the dials on detectors will move when matter collides. But this does not mean it is literally true that little electrons exist. It only means that with this assumption we can make accurate predictions." In short, photons, gluons, gravitons, and bosons are only imaginary things mentioned in formulas or theories that let us accurately predict what will happen when we do certain experiments. Scientific theories that talk about such unobservable theoretical entities are not true in the same literal sense that, say, it is true that the moon exists. Instead, such theories are *assumed* to be true even though we know that they are *not really* true; and they are assumed to be true because that assumption allows us to use the theories to predict what will happen.

This view of scientific theories and of theoretical entities is the instrumentalist view. You have probably noticed that this view has some similarities to the pragmatic theory of truth. In fact, the instrumentalist view of scientific theories incorporates some fundamental aspects of the pragmatic theory of truth. The **instrumentalist view**, like the pragmatic theory, emphasizes the importance of knowing whether a scientific theory "works," and that knowing whether a theory works determines whether the theory is acceptable. However, unlike the pragmatic view of truth, the instrumentalist view of scientific theories does not claim that scientific theories are literally true when they work. By saying that a theory "works," the instrumentalist means that it lets us accurately predict what will happen when we do certain things, but he does not believe that the unobservable theoretical entities of the scientific theory are literally real. They are invented or fictitious entities that serve as useful but imaginary constructs. They are useful because if we act *as if* they exist, we can make accurate scientific predictions.

QUICK REVIEW
The instrumentalist view of scientific theories is based on the pragmatic view of truth and says a theory is acceptable if it lets us make accurate predictions about experiments and observations. Theories are invented, not discovered. It is not literally true that the unobservable entities of the theory exist, but acting as if they do lets us make successful predictions.

The instrumentalist view has a long history. For example, in the sixteenth century, the astronomer Copernicus proposed that the earth and the planets revolve around the sun. As noted earlier in this chapter, everyone then believed that the earth stood still and the sun and planets revolved around it. This was the theory of the astronomer Ptolemy. People believed that God, who created the universe, put humans and their earth at the center of the universe. Theologians claimed that the Bible itself declares that the sun revolved around the earth while the earth stood still. And church authorities were willing to persecute anyone who opposed these views. So, in the preface to Copernicus' book, a friend of his wrote that Copernicus was not trying to describe the real universe. Instead, Copernicus' proposal was just an imaginary model meant to "save the appearances." That is, it gave scientists a way of accurately calculating and predicting where the sun and the planets would appear in the sky. Readers, he wrote, should not take Copernicus' proposal as a description of the real structure of the universe. In reality, the sun revolves around the earth. Copernicus' proposal that the earth and planets revolve around the sun was just a useful but fictitious device for calculating the positions of the planets. In short, Copernicus' theory that the earth revolves around the sun should be interpreted instrumentally.

Most scientists at the time agreed. In reality, they said, the earth stood still at the center of the universe while the sun and planets spun around it as Ptolemy said. Copernicus' assumption that the sun stood still while the earth and planets spun around it was false. But this false assumption, they felt, gave them a better way of calculating where the planets will be on any given day in the future. Here is how a book on astronomy written in 1594 put it: "Copernicus affirmeth that the earth turneth about and that the sun standeth still in the midst of the heavens, by help of which false supposition he hath made truer demonstrations of the motions and revolutions of the celestial spheres, than ever were made before."[20]

QUICK REVIEW
When first published, Copernicus' theory was interpreted as only instrumentally true. Galileo was punished for saying it was a literally true description of the solar system.

However, scientists found more and more problems with the old view of Ptolemy that the earth stands still while the sun and planets rotate around it. Eventually, more and more scientists began to think that Copernicus' proposal was a description of the way the universe really is. This got some of these scientists into trouble with the church. The most famous was Galileo. In 1632, he published *A Dialogue Concerning the Two Great World Systems*, in which he argued that Copernicus' view was an accurate description of the way the universe really was. For his efforts, Galileo was put on trial by the church's Inquisition, which condemned Galileo for "vehement suspicion of heresy" and sentenced him to house arrest for life. Eventually, Galileo had to retract his views. Nevertheless, the future would vindicate him and his rejection of the instrumentalist interpretation of Copernicus' new theory. How then did Galileo interpret Copernicus? He interpreted him as a "realist" would.

The Realist View

An alternative to the instrumentalist view is the **realist view** of scientific truth, which is a version of the correspondence theory of truth. According to the realist view, scientific theories are literally true or false. The entities that a scientific theory talks about—such as the electrons, quarks, neutrinos, gluons, bosons, gravitons, and

20 Quoted in Michael R. Gardner, "Realism and Instrumentalism in Pre-Newtonian Astronomy," in *Scientific Knowledge*, ed. Janet A. Kourany (Belmont, CA: Wadsworth, 1987), 370.

photons of the standard theory of matter—really exist in the world "out there." A theory—such as Copernicus', which says that the earth and planets revolve around the sun—is meant to describe the way the universe really is.

According to the realist, the world around us contains entities with definite properties. These entities have relationships to one another that are independent of us. That is, the world is made up of entities in a definite structure. The aim of science, according to the realist, is to explain this world by discovering exactly what this structure is. In other words, the aim of science is to develop theories that tell us what entities exist, what their properties are, and how they are related to each other. A scientific theory is true if the entities and properties it talks about really exist in the world and if these really have the relationships the theory says they have. That is, the realist says a scientific theory is true when the entities and properties it refers to and the relationships it describes *correspond* to real entities that exist in the world and their real relationships and properties. According to the realist, if the standard theory of matter is true, then electrons, gluons, and quarks are real; they really have the properties the theory says they have; and they are related in the way the theory says they are. If Copernicus' theory of the universe is true, then the planets, earth, and sun are really related to one another as his theory says they are.

QUICK REVIEW
The realist view of science is based on the correspondence theory of truth and says a theory is true if the entities, properties, and relationships that it describes *correspond* to real entities, properties, and relationships in the world. Theories are discovered, not invented. The aim of science is to provide accurate descriptions of the universe. Theories allow accurate predictions because they are true; they are not true because they allow accurate predictions.

Realists and instrumentalists have very different views about the aim of science. According to the instrumentalist, the aim of science is to make accurate predictions so that we can satisfy our human needs. For the realist, the aim of science is to provide true explanations of the world by telling us exactly what the structure of the world is. Notice also that the realist and the instrumentalist differ on how science proceeds. According to the instrumentalist, the scientist *invents* or makes up useful scientific truth. But according to the realist, the scientist *discovers* scientific truth. The realist believes that the truth is already there, waiting to be uncovered by the scientist. The instrumentalist believes that truth does not exist until the scientist invents it and shows that it gives us the right predictions.

Realists argue that scientific theories give us accurate predictions simply because they correspond to the way the world is. Theories are not true because they make accurate predictions, as the instrumentalist holds; rather, they make accurate predictions because they correspond to reality. Moreover, says the realist, most scientists will not say that they are trying to make up imaginary entities that can help them predict the future. Instead, they will say that they are trying to discover what reality is really like: They are trying to figure out what entities really exist and how those entities are really related.

The Conceptual Relativist View

QUICK REVIEW
The conceptual relativist view of scientific theories is based on Kuhn and the coherence theory of truth. It says that communities of scientists accept research methods, programs, theories, and values that form a "conceptual framework" that is true by definition. New findings or beliefs are true if they fit in with the community's conceptual framework.

A third view of scientific truth, the **conceptual relativist view**, shares many characteristics of the coherence theory of truth. Conceptual relativism owes much to the philosophy of Thomas Kuhn, whom we discussed in the preceding chapter. Many people whom Kuhn has influenced have come to the conclusion that a true scientific theory is nothing more than a theory that a community of scientists accepts. A community of working scientists, they claim, has its own unique way of seeing the world. The scientists who are members of the community have their own way of conducting research, their own research programs, their own way of interpreting what happens in their experiments, their own theories and beliefs about nature, and their own values about what counts in scientific research. These research methods, programs, theories, and values are a "conceptual framework," or system of beliefs about the world.

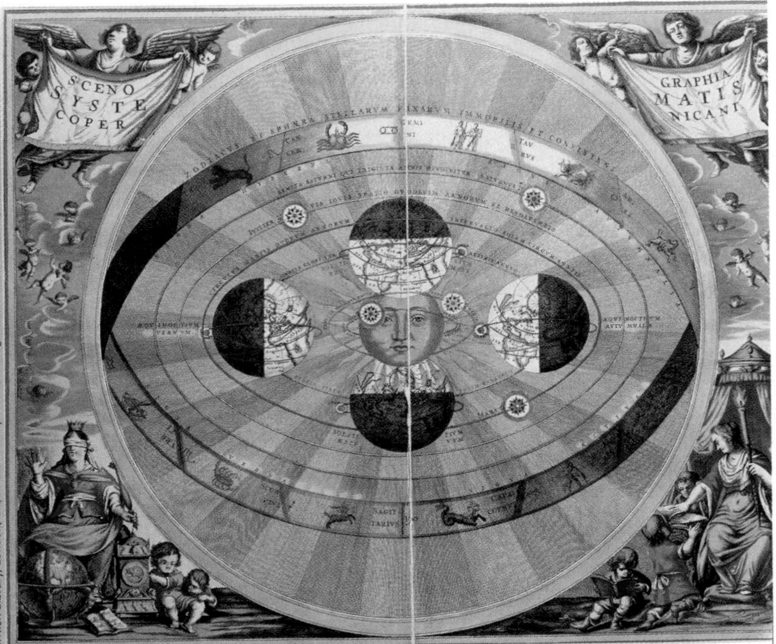

A seventeenth-century rendering of Copernicus' model for the earth and planets revolving around the sun. Scenographia: Systematis Copernicani Astrological Chart, c.1543, devised by Nicolaus Copernicus (1473–1543) from *The Celestial Atlas, or the Harmony of the Universe* (*Atlas coelestis seu harmonia macrocosmica*), c.1660. Andreas Cellarius (seventeenth century).

British Library, London, UK/British Library Board, All Rights Reserved/The Bridgeman Art Library

For example, astronomers before Copernicus believed in an old theory that they found in books by Aristotle and Ptolemy. This theory said that the sun and planets revolve around the earth. They combined this theory with religious beliefs and values that said God put the earth at the center of the universe. And they looked at the sky with the naked eye to confirm these theories. These theories, methods, values, and beliefs made up the conceptual framework of astronomers before Copernicus. After Copernicus, scientists began to believe that they should not rely on what they found in old books and texts. Neither should they look to the church to decide scientific matters. They began to believe that, instead, they should rely on their own observations. They began to look at the sky by using the newly discovered telescope. They came to believe in Copernicus' theory that the earth and planets revolve around the sun. These new beliefs, methods, theories, and values made up a new conceptual framework.

According to the conceptual relativist, the beliefs that make up the conceptual framework of a group of scientists are true by definition. New scientific findings or new scientific theories are true if they fit in with the accepted conceptual framework of the group. For the conceptual relativist, then, what is true in science is what coheres with the scientific theories, beliefs, values, and research methods of a community of scientists. A particular research finding is true or false only in relation to a particular conceptual framework. The conceptual relativist believes that the standard theory of matter is true, for example, if it fits in with the beliefs, the methods, the values, and the other theories of contemporary scientists. Copernicus' theory is true if it fits in with the beliefs, methods, and other theories of contemporary astronomers.

One reason that conceptual relativists hold these views about scientific theories, they say, is that both the realist and instrumentalist views are radically flawed. Both the realist and the instrumentalist mistakenly believe that they can somehow know or observe the real world independently of their theories. Instrumentalists believe that they can independently check the world to see whether a theory's predictions are accurate. Realists believe that they can independently check the world to see whether a theory corresponds with reality. Yet these independent checks are not possible, say the conceptual relativists. Our observations and perceptions of the world are always colored and influenced by our beliefs and theories about what we *should* be seeing. Observations are always "theory laden," say conceptual relativists. Consequently, our theories about reality influence what we think we are seeing when we observe reality.

For example, suppose that a scientist who believes in the standard theory of matter sees a little white trail in a cloud chamber. He will see the little trail as the track left behind by an electron as it moved through the chamber. He will see it this way because that is what the standard theory leads him to think he is seeing. On the other hand, suppose you or I looked at the same vapor trail without knowing anything about the standard theory of matter. Then, all we would see would be little wispy lines that appeared and then vanished inside a glass bottle. In fact, our theories and beliefs influence even our ordinary perceptions. As you read this page, for example, you do not just see black scratches on white paper, which is all that an illiterate person might see. Instead, you see words that have meaning and sense. You see meaningful words instead of black scratches because of the beliefs and theories you have about what books and writing are. These beliefs and theories affect what you see when you look at this page.

QUICK REVIEW
Conceptual relativists say all observations are "theory laden." In other words, they are influenced by our values, beliefs, and theories—our conceptual frameworks—about what we should be seeing. So, theories cannot be verified by somehow observing the real world independently of our theories as instrumentalists and realists assume; we can see only if our theories fit in with the beliefs and theories we already accept.

Theories, then, can never be checked against some independently observed reality because our theories have already influenced what we observe before we observe it. Consequently, we are forced to check our theories by seeing how they fit in with all our other accepted theories and beliefs, including the theory-laden observations we make of reality. We can never escape this web of belief and theory. Because theories can be checked only against other theories, we say a scientific theory is true when it fits in with our other accepted theories and beliefs.

An important implication of Kuhn's view that theories can never be checked to see how well they describe reality is that we cannot say that one theory explains or describes reality more accurately than another. As Kuhn points out, science periodically undergoes "conceptual revolutions." For example, when Copernicus' new theory replaced the old theory that the sun revolves around the earth, this was a "conceptual revolution." Kuhn suggested that when a new theory replaces an old one in such a revolution, there may be no rational reason for saying that the new theory is better than the old one. Many conceptual relativists who have followed Kuhn have agreed with this suggestion. They have concluded that there are no grounds for saying that one conceptual framework is better than another. That is, we cannot say that one conceptual framework corresponds to, or explains, reality more accurately than another or that one gives us better predictions. Truth is nothing more than coherence with an accepted conceptual framework. When scientists abandon one framework and replace it with another, we often must attribute the change to nonrational causes and events rather than to scientists' belief that the new framework describes or explains the world more accurately than the old.

QUICK REVIEW
Periodically, communities of scientists exchange one conceptual framework for another in a "conceptual revolution." But the new framework is not more true than the old; it does not more accurately describe an independent real world or necessarily make more accurate predictions. It just better achieves whatever values are prized in the community's conceptual framework.

Conceptual relativists, then, do not accept the realist view that true scientific theories are supposed to explain or describe what the external universe is like: true scientific theories do not "correspond" to a real world "out there." Neither do they necessarily accept the instrumentalist view that scientific theories are true to the extent that they can be used to predict the future. Conceptual relativists believe that a scientific theory is true if it coheres or fits in with the accepted beliefs and values—the conceptual framework—of a community of working scientists. Thus, conceptual relativism is similar to the coherence theory of truth.

We saw earlier that we can interpret truth in at least three ways: as correspondence, as coherence, and as pragmatic. We have seen now that we can also interpret truth in science in three ways: according to the realist view, the instrumentalist view, and the relativist view. These three ways of understanding truth in science are similar to the three views of truth we examined earlier in this chapter. Which of these is correct? No one can answer that question for you. Scientists and philosophers themselves are divided on this question. In fact, the question itself is a paradox. For in asking which of these three views of truth is correct, aren't you asking which of them is true? Yet doesn't each view interpret the meaning of truth in a different way? Truth in science, it has turned out, is much more complicated than it first appeared to be.

QUESTIONS

1. Some realists claim that through the progress of science, certain so-called unobservable theoretical entities such as the atom have become observable. For example, they point to "pictures" that scientists have taken of single atoms. This proves, they say, that they were right all along when they held that the theoretical entities of true theories really exist. How would an instrumentalist or a conceptual relativist answer this claim?
2. Can you think of any statements of science that you think we accept as true because they clearly correspond to reality? Can you think of any statements of science that you think we accept as true merely because they provide accurate predictions? Can you think of any statements of science that we probably accept as true merely because they cohere with other parts of science?
3. Is it possible that the three views of scientific truth—realist, instrumentalist, and conceptual relativist—are actually complementary rather than incompatible? Explain.
4. Does it really matter whether one or the other of these views of scientific truth is correct? What difference would it make in the way you see yourself if one of these views—say, the conceptual relativist view—turned out to be correct? What difference would it make in the way you see the world around you—the planets, the stars, the plant and animal species?
5. Psychology is the scientific study of human beings. If the instrumentalist view of scientific theory turned out to be correct, how would it change what you have learned about human beings from psychology? If the conceptual relativist view of scientific theory turned out to be correct, how would it change what you have learned from psychology?

PHILOSOPHY AT THE MOVIES

Watch *Living Proof* (2008; originally a TV movie), which tells the true story of Dr. Denny Slamon, a UCLA physician and researcher conducting research on the drug Herceptin because he believes it will stop the growth of certain breast cancer tumors by binding to a protein molecule that regulates the replication of tumor cells, a process that is not directly observable. What view of scientific truth does this movie seem to accept? What view of scientific truth do the various characters in this movie seem to hold?

6.4 Can Interpretations Be True?

Science is not the only area of our lives where truth is important but difficult to pin down. Truth is also crucial to us when we try to interpret books, poems, movies, scripture, and people's words and actions. When someone speaks to you, you need to interpret that person's *words*: What did she mean by that? When you see someone doing something, you interpret her *actions*: Why did she do that, and what is the meaning of what she did? When you read a poem or look at a movie, you need to interpret it: What is the poem or movie trying to say? When you go to church or read the Bible, you try to interpret the words of passages in scripture. When a lawyer or a judge looks at a statute or even the Constitution, she must interpret it to determine its meaning.

But when is an interpretation true? Suppose you chance upon this passage in the Bible: "You shall not lie with a male as with a woman; it is an abomination" (Leviticus 18:22). What does it mean? Obviously, you say, it is pointing out that homosexual activities are immoral. Yet many biblical scholars say that this "obvious" interpretation is mistaken. Homosexual relations between males, they say, were part of the ritual practices of some of the religions that opposed Judaism when this text was written. What the text is really saying, then, is to avoid the ritual practices of foreign religions. So which interpretation is true? The "obvious" one that first occurred to you or the one that some biblical scholars have proposed?

Or instead take a poem, such as William Blake's famous "The Tyger":

Tyger! Tyger! Burning bright
In the forests of the night,
What immortal hand or eye
Could frame thy fearful symmetry?

In what distant deeps or skies
Burnt the fire of thine eyes?
On what wings dare he aspire?
What the hand dare seize the fire?

And what shoulder, and what art,
Could twist the sinews of thy heart?
And when thy heart began to beat,
What dread hand? And what dread feet?

What the hammer? What the chain?
In what furnace was thy brain?
What the anvil? What dread grasp
Dare its deadly terrors clasp?

When the stars threw down their spears,
And watered heaven with their tears,
Did he smile his work to see?
Did he who made the Lamb make thee?

Tyger! Tyger! Burning bright
In the forests of the night,
What immortal hand or eye
Could frame thy fearful symmetry?

design network/iStockphoto.com

Tyger! Tyger!

What does this poem mean? Some literary experts have argued that the Tyger is here a symbol of the evil self who "sustains its own life at the expense of its fellow-creatures."[21] The "forests of the night," they claim, symbolize for Blake the "fallen world"—that is, the material world where evil reigns. The Lamb is a symbol for Jesus Christ. The answer to the question Blake asks at the end is no: The God who made the Lamb did not make the evil in the heart of the evil predator. Yet other critics

21 Kathleen Raine, "Who Made the Tyger," *Encounter*, June 1954, 50.

argue for an opposite interpretation: "There can be no doubt that *The Tyger* is a poem that celebrates the holiness of tigerness."[22] They claim that the word "*forests* suggests tall straight forms, a world that for all its terror has the orderliness of the tiger's stripes." Blake, they say, transforms the ferocity of the tiger into the symbol of goodness. Still a third group of critics have claimed that the tiger in Blake's poem is *both* good and evil, and a fourth group that it is "beyond good and evil." Yet others conclude that the poem "is a maze of questions in which the reader is forced to wander confusedly."[23] What, then, is the true interpretation of the poem? Does it have a true interpretation?

Or take a legal text. The United States Constitution states in Amendment Fourteen, which Congress ratified in 1868, that "No State shall make or enforce any law which shall . . . deny to any person . . . the equal protection of the law." What is the true interpretation of this text? Some legal scholars say it clearly means that a state cannot support a preferential treatment program. A preferential treatment program gives preference to women or minorities over white males when applying for jobs or colleges. Such programs, they argue, do not treat white males as equal to women or minorities and thus "clearly" violate the meaning of the Constitution's Fourteenth Amendment. Other legal scholars have argued that women and minorities have been disadvantaged in the past. Preferential programs are needed now to make them more equal to white males. So, these scholars say, the true meaning of Amendment Fourteen clearly allows preferential treatment programs.[24] Who is right? What is the true interpretation of the Constitution? Some might want to reply that the Supreme Court decides its true interpretation. But this only pushes the problem back a step. How should the judges of the Supreme Court decide which is the true interpretation?

QUICK REVIEW
When we interpret books, poems, legal texts, scriptures, and people's words and actions, we must make sure that our interpretations are true. But what is a true interpretation? *Hermeneutics* is the study of interpretations.

Hermeneutics is the study of the interpretation of words and actions. The word comes from the name of the ancient Greek god Hermes, who carried messages from the gods up in heaven to mortals down on earth. The messages were transmitted through "oracles," humans with the ability to hear and report these messages. But often the messages of the gods were unclear, ambiguous, or had multiple meanings. So recipients of the messages relied on professional interpreters to explain them. Hermeneutics developed from these attempts to interpret the words of the gods. But it was not the Greek gods that gave interpreters their hardest problems. Hermeneutics became an even larger concern for those who believed in the Judaic and Christian God.

Symbolic Interpretation and Intention

For both Christianity and Judaism, the Bible contains the words of God because God inspired the writers to write these words. But like the words of the Greek oracles, the words of the Bible can be unclear, ambiguous, or can be interpreted in many different ways. How can a believer know what he or she must do if the Bible can be interpreted in many ways? Which interpretation should he or she live by?

During the Middle Ages, philosophers and theologians developed ever-new interpretations of passages in the Bible. Many believed that besides its literal meaning, a Bible passage could have deeper symbolic meanings. For example, the thirteenth-century philosopher–theologian Thomas Aquinas (1224–1274)

22 E. D. Hirsch, *Innocence and Experience* (New Haven, CT: Yale University Press, 1964), 247–248.
23 L. J. Swingle, "Answers to Blake's 'Tyger': A Matter of Reason or of Choice," *Concerning Poetry* 2 (1970), 67.
24 See Howard N. Meyer, *The Amendment that Refused to Die: Equality and Justice Deferred: The History of the Fourteenth Amendment* (Madison Books: 2000).

held that a text could have many "spiritual" interpretations. And, he claimed, they could all be true:

> The first and basic meaning of a [biblical] text is the historical or literal meaning conveyed by the words themselves. But the things and events described by the literal meaning can also have a meaning. This is the spiritual meaning of the [biblical] text. . . . Now there are three kinds of spiritual meaning. First, things and events in the Old Testament can symbolize things and events in the New Testament. This is called the allegorical sense [of the Bible]. Second, the actions of Jesus Christ described or symbolized [in the Bible] express how we ought to live. This is the moral meaning [of the Bible]. Third, the things described in the Bible can symbolize what eternal glory [after death] will be like. This is the anagogical sense. So a word in the Bible can have several meanings.[25]

QUICK REVIEW
Aquinas claimed that a scriptural text could have several true interpretations, including the literal interpretation and at least three kinds of symbolic interpretations; these interpretations were all intended by God, who inspired the Bible. But how can one know whether an interpretation is true or false when so many are possible, and how are we to know exactly which one God intended?

In some ways, Aquinas' willingness to accept many true interpretations made the problem of interpretation worse. How can a believer know which interpretation of the Bible is true if there can be many interpretations? Aquinas' solution was simple: The Church decides which interpretations of the Bible are true and which are false. In particular, the Church decides which symbolic interpretations are true.

But doesn't this solution create even more problems? First, how is the Church itself supposed to decide which interpretations are true? How is it to choose among the many literal and symbolic interpretations that human creativity can devise? Setting the Church up as an authority just pushes the problem back one step. The difficulty of trying to sift through many symbolic interpretations to find the true ones suggests a deeper problem with symbolic interpretations. Aren't symbolic interpretations really examples of seeing what you want to see? Aren't symbolic interpretations arbitrary? Symbolic interpretations seem to read into a text whatever meaning the reader would like to see.

Two hundred years after Aquinas, the Protestant reformer Martin Luther rejected the whole idea of symbolic interpretations. There was, he said, only one true meaning of scripture, and that is the literal meaning. The nineteenth-century philosopher Friedrich Schleiermacher (1768–1834) agreed, but provided a rationale for this view. A text is a product of the history and culture of the person who wrote it, he argued. To interpret the text, we have to know the historical situation of the author. We have to figure out, in short, what the author was thinking and intending when he wrote whatever he wrote: "The language and the history of the time the writer was living in is the context within which individual texts have to be interpreted."

QUICK REVIEW
Luther and Schleiermacher rejected symbolic interpretations and said only the literal interpretation of a Bible text could be true, and this meant knowing the author's historical context so that one could figure out what he intended the text to mean. The true interpretation of a text is what the author intended.

Schleiermacher is not the only one who argued that there is one true and literal interpretation of a text. The philosopher Wilhelm Dilthey (1833–1911) also argued that the true interpretation of a text is the meaning that the original human author intended. To find this original meaning, he claimed, we need to put ourselves in the place and time of the historical author and try to understand what he intended by the words he wrote. To understand the actions or words of any person, we must "relive" the life of the other person. This applies, he said, not only to interpreting words but also to interpreting anything that humans produce, including art, poetry, speeches, laws, and even human history.

QUICK REVIEW
Dilthey agreed that the only true interpretation of a text is the meaning that its human author intended, and finding this requires putting ourselves in the place and time of the historical author to "relive" his life.

Schleiermacher and Dilthey, like Aquinas, obviously embraced the correspondence theory of truth. A true interpretation is one that corresponds to what the original author of a poem, law, scripture passage, or work of art intended. Aquinas took the true interpretation to be the one that God intended because God was in a

25 Thomas Aquinas, *Summa Theologica*, I, Q. 1, a. 10, trans. and abridged by Manuel Velasquez.

sense the ultimate author of scripture. But Schleiermacher and Dilthey insisted we must look for what the historical human authors intended.

QUICK REVIEW
Aquinas, Luther, Schleiermacher, and Dilthey all accepted the correspondence theory of truth: A true interpretation is one that corresponds to what the author (God for Aquinas, the human author for the others) intended.

Many scholars accept the ideas of Schleiermacher and Dilthey. Literary critics have carefully studied what life was like at the time a poet such as Blake wrote to figure out what he intended the words of his poem to mean. Legal scholars have argued that to interpret a law—such as the Fourteenth Amendment of the Constitution—we need to get back to what those who originally passed the law intended it to mean. And theologians have studied life in ancient Palestine to try to determine what the authors of the Bible meant by the words they used.

But there's another way to think about interpretation. Ask yourself this: Why is interpretation even needed? Why are there many possible ways of interpreting texts? Isn't the real problem the ambiguity of language? If the language and words that we use to express our meaning were perfectly clear and unambiguous, then would there even be a problem of interpretation? What if we could develop a language that was completely clear and unambiguous? Wouldn't this eliminate the possibility of different interpretations? Wouldn't an unambiguous language eliminate the need for hermeneutics?

Wittgenstein and the Ideal Clear Language

QUICK REVIEW
Wittgenstein argued that a problem with interpreting language is that it is unclear; what is needed is an ideal language that is unambiguous. He set about describing such a language.

The idea of an unambiguous language that people could interpret in only one way was first suggested by the seventeenth-century rationalist philosopher Gottfried Leibniz (1646–1716). Leibniz argued that we should strive to develop a perfect language in which we could express our ideas with complete clarity. In this perfect language, Leibniz claimed, "there will be no equivocations or amphibolies, and everything which will be said intelligibly in that language will be said with propriety."[26] Even disagreements over interpretations could be settled "by calculating" the true meaning in this perfect language.

Leibniz never completed his ideal language. But in the early part of the twentieth century, the Austrian philosopher Ludwig Wittgenstein (1889–1951) published a seventy-five-page book titled *Tractatus-Logico-Philosophicus.* His book changed the course of philosophy. Wittgenstein claimed to provide the basics of the kind of ideal language that Leibniz had only dreamed about. In his book, Wittgenstein described an ideal language that, he claimed, could express all legitimate meanings unambiguously.

QUICK REVIEW
Wittgenstein said the world consists of complex facts made up of atomic facts and that an ideal language consists of complex propositions made up of elementary propositions. Elementary propositions represent atomic facts. A proposition is true when the structure of its elementary parts corresponds to the structure of the atomic facts that make up the complex fact it represents.

Reality, he argued, consists of facts, both complex facts and simple facts. The simplest facts are "atomic facts," and complex facts are built out of these atomic facts. The propositions of an ideal language, he said, will provide "pictures" of these facts. A proposition will correctly picture a fact—and so will be true—when it has the same kind of "structure" as the fact. That is, if a true proposition expresses a fact, that proposition must have words that correspond to the parts of the fact, and the structure of the words must correspond to the structure of the parts of the facts. (Wittgenstein's views on truth are very similar to those of Russell who was his teacher, friend, and collaborator.) Wittgenstein, who wrote in an oracular fashion himself, expressed these points as follows:

> The world is the totality of facts, not of things. . . .
> The object is the fixed, the existent. . . .
> In the atomic fact the objects are combined in a definite way.

26 Gottfried Leibniz, "Preface to the General Science," in *Leibniz Selections,* ed. Philip P. Wiener (New York: Scribner's, 1951), 16.

> The way in which objects hang together in the atomic fact is the structure of the atomic fact. . . .
>
> We make to ourselves pictures of facts. . . .
>
> The elements of the picture stand, in the picture, for the objects.
>
> The picture consists in the fact that its elements are combined with one another in a definite way.
>
> That the elements of the picture are combined with one another in a definite way, represents that the things are so combined with one another.
>
> This connection of the elements of the picture is called its structure.[27]

In an ideal language, Wittgenstein argues, the simplest atomic facts will be expressed by simple elementary propositions. Just as complex facts are made up of atomic facts, in an ideal language complex propositions will be made up of elementary propositions. With this ideal language, Wittgenstein claimed, all facts can be expressed in a clear and unambiguous way. In fact, wrote Wittgenstein, "Everything that can be thought of at all can be thought of clearly; everything that can be said can be said clearly."[28]

QUICK REVIEW
In this ideal language, all facts can be expressed unambiguously. If something cannot be expressed in this ideal language, it is illegitimate to try to say it at all.

Wittgenstein's theory of language was, in effect, a hermeneutic. Wittgenstein held that the only legitimate meanings were those that could be expressed in his ideal language of facts. If a meaning could not be expressed or "spoken" in his ideal language, it was not legitimate. As he put it, "Whereof one cannot speak, thereof one must be silent."[29] The only true interpretations are those that can be spoken in an ideal language that refers only to facts.

QUICK REVIEW
Wittgenstein's theory was based on the correspondence theory of truth and said that a proposition is true when its structure accurately "pictures" the structure of the fact it represents.

Clearly, Wittgenstein had embraced a correspondence theory of truth. Propositions are true when they correspond to the facts. Meanings are legitimate only when they can be expressed in propositions that correspond to facts.

But as Wittgenstein got older, he abandoned his search for an ideal language of facts. He also left behind his allegiance to the correspondence theory of truth. And he again changed the course of philosophy.

The older Wittgenstein came to believe that his whole earlier approach to language had been wrong. It was a mistake, Wittgenstein argued in his later life, to think that language can serve a single purpose and express a single meaning. His idea that a language can provide an unambiguous picture of reality was based on this mistake. We must instead acknowledge that we use language for many different purposes and in many different human activities or "games." The meaning of language or a text cannot be isolated from our human activities. The meaning of a language or a text does not depend on the "facts" it pictures. Instead, the meanings of language depend on how people use language in the many different activities of life:

QUICK REVIEW
The older Wittgenstein argued that the meaning of a text does not depend on the "facts" it pictures, but on the meaning people give it as they use it in the many activities or "games" of life. Language can have many meanings if it is used in many different games.

> But how many kinds of sentences are there? You say assertion, question, and command?—There are *countless* kinds, countless different kinds of use of what we call "symbols," "words," "sentences." And this multiplicity is not something fixed, given once for all; but new types of language, new language-games, as we may say, come into existence, and others become obsolete and get forgotten. . . . Here the term "language game" is meant to bring into prominence the fact that the *speaking* of language is part of any activity, or of a form of life.[30]

---

27 Ludwig Wittgenstein, *Tractatus-Logico-Philosophicus*, 1.1 and 2.026–2.1512, quoted in *The Great Treasury of Western Thought*, ed. Mortimer J. Adler and Charles Van Doren (New York: R. R. Bowker, 1977), 403, 1267.

28 Ibid., 4.116.

29 Ibid., 6.57.

30 Ludwig Wittgenstein, *Philosophical Investigations*, 3rd ed., trans. G. E. M. Anscombe (New York: Macmillan, 1953), 11e.

These later views of Wittgenstein are vitally important for hermeneutics. Wittgenstein himself did not directly discuss hermeneutics. Nevertheless, his views have clear implications for us. First, if he is right, then the dream of a clear language is just that: a dream. Second, and more important, the meaning of words is not a fixed thing. So, the true interpretation of a text is also not fixed. The meaning of a text arises from the meaning that people give it as they use it in their life activities. Meaning is use. The true interpretation of a text is the interpretation that people give it as they use it.

QUICK REVIEW
The true interpretation of a text is the interpretation that people give it in the game of life in which it is used. This view is based on a pragmatic theory of truth because it says that an interpretation of a text is true if it is an interpretation that people find useful in one of their life activities.

Clearly, in these later views Wittgenstein no longer holds the correspondence theory of truth. His view of truth is now much more pragmatic. For example, an interpretation of a scripture is true for a group of people if it is an interpretation that has a use in their forms of life. The same can be said for poetry and art. A true interpretation of a poem may be one that can enrich and give significance to the life of the reader. And the true interpretation of a law, such as the Fourteenth Amendment of the U.S. Constitution, depends on the needs and concerns of those who must use the law to order their society.

While Wittgenstein was developing his new views on meaning in England, European philosophers were also developing new views on meaning. Wittgenstein had developed his new views by rejecting his own older view that language can have only one meaning. European philosophers developed their new views by rejecting the view that there is one true interpretation of a text. For example, Dilthey and Schleiermacher had said that the one true interpretation of a text is the meaning that the original author intended. But many European philosophers now objected that we can't ever really know the intentions of the original author, especially if the author lived centuries ago in a different culture. The most important of these new European philosophers is the German philosopher Hans-Georg Gadamer (1900–2002).

Gadamer and Prejudice

QUICK REVIEW
Gadamer argued that when interpreting someone's words, one must rely on and be influenced by one's personal experience and the inescapable values and beliefs of one's culture. So, people in different times and cultures will interpret the words differently. A text has no single true interpretation, but there are many true interpretations depending on who is reading it and when and where it is being read.

Gadamer pointed out that when a person tries to interpret someone's words, she must rely on the resources provided by her own personal experience and culture. Our culture consists of the values and beliefs of our time and our society. The culture that we absorb as we grow up is a "prejudice" that influences how we interpret someone else's words. For example, suppose that because of the way I was raised in my culture, I believe in angels and devils. Then, when I read a Bible story about how Jesus cast devils out of a man, I may interpret the story as literally true. But suppose I grew up in a culture that does not believe in devils. Then, when I read this story, I may interpret it as a story that just symbolizes the ability of Jesus to overcome evil. My prior cultural beliefs prejudice how I interpret the story. There is no way to rid ourselves completely of these prejudices, says Gadamer. We have to interpret the words and actions of people in terms of our own historical culture. We can try to understand and correct our prejudices. But we can never completely escape them.

Because each person interprets the meaning of a text on the basis of her own personal experience and culture, people living in different times and cultures must interpret texts differently. None of these interpretations is more true than the others. As Gadamer puts it, "A text is understood only if it is understood in a different way every time."[31] A text, then, does not have a single true interpretation. Instead, the true meaning of a text depends on who is reading it and when and where they

31 Hans-Georg Gadamer, *Truth and Method*, trans. and ed. Garrett Barden and John Cumming (New York: Seabury, 1975), 275.

are reading it. A text can have as many true interpretations as there are people who read it in different cultures:

> An inevitable difference between the interpreter and the author [is] created by the historical distance between them. Every age has to understand a transmitted text in its own way, for the text is part of the whole of the tradition in which the age takes an objective interest and in which it seeks to understand itself. The real meaning of a text, as it speaks to the interpreter, does not depend on the contingencies of the author and whom he originally wrote for. It certainly is not identical with them for it is always partly determined also by the historical situation of the interpreter and hence by the totality of the objective course of history.[32]

However, Gadamer did not think that we can just dream up any interpretations we want and pin them on texts. Instead, says Gadamer, interpreting a text is like talking to a person. We speak, and then the other person speaks; then, with a better understanding of the person, we speak again. Then, the other person also speaks again, and the process continues. In the same way, Gadamer insists, we have to carry on a dialogue with the text. First, we interpret the text in terms of the prejudices and concerns of our culture. Then, we try to understand what new things the text itself is trying to express and what it might have meant in its culture. When we do this, our own cultural prejudices change and get closer to the meaning of the text. Then, we use our newly informed cultural prejudices to come up with a better interpretation of the text. We try again to understand the text itself and its meaning in its own culture. Again our cultural prejudices change, coming closer to the meaning of the text. As we continue this dialogue, we keep developing better and more true interpretations of the text. Still, we never completely get rid of our prejudices. Our interpretations are always a combination of our own cultural prejudices and what the text was trying to say in its own culture.

> QUICK REVIEW
> Interpreting a text requires trying to understand both what it meant in its own culture and what it means to a person with one's experience and culture.

Gadamer, then, seems to hold to a coherence view of truth. The true interpretation is the one that best coheres with both the prejudices of our own culture and what we believe the text meant in its own culture. Truth emerges from the union of these two cultural "horizons." But there are many true interpretations, for different interpretations will fit in with the prejudices of people living in different cultures and times.

> QUICK REVIEW
> The true interpretation is the one that best coheres with both our own experience and our culture and what we believe the text means in its own culture. This is based on a coherence theory of truth.

If Gadamer is correct, then a poem like Blake's "The Tyger" has no single true interpretation. Moreover, whatever its true meaning, it is *not* necessarily the meaning that Blake intended. Instead, it means whatever you, the reader, interpret it to mean in terms of your own cultural values and beliefs and what the poem seems to be trying to say. Similarly, a law, such as the Constitution's Fourteenth Amendment, has no single true interpretation. It means whatever we, today, interpret it to mean in terms both of the current cultural values of U.S. society and what the amendment seems to have meant in the past. And a scripture text has no single true meaning. It means whatever the believers of each age interpret it to mean in light of their own cultural concerns and what the scripture seems to have meant when it was written.

> QUICK REVIEW
> Hirsch criticizes Gadamer by distinguishing the "meaning" of a text from its "significance." The meaning is what the original author intended and does not change; the significance can change from person to person and from culture to culture.

Is Gadamer right? Is there no single true interpretation of our words and actions? Many people believe so. But not everyone. Some thinkers, such as E. D. Hirsch, argue that Gadamer and his followers have confused the "meaning" of a text with its "significance."[33] The meaning of a text is what the author intended to convey literally with the words that he used. The significance of a text is the implications the text

32 Ibid., 274–275.
33 E. D. Hirsch, *Validity in Interpretation* (New Haven, CT: Yale University Press, 1967).

has for our actions and lives. Although the significance of a text can change from one person or culture to another, Hirsch claims, its meaning remains the same. To find this fixed true meaning of a text, he argues, we have to do what Dilthey suggested: We have to discover what the author intended. A true interpretation is the one that corresponds with the author's intention.

We are left with a choice that in the end comes down to deciding among the theories of truth. Aquinas, Schleiermacher, and Dilthey tell us that the true interpretation is the one that corresponds with the intentions of the author, whether that author is a person or God. Wittgenstein suggests that any interpretation is true if it is one that gives pragmatic significance to our forms of life. And Gadamer tells us that a true interpretation is one that coheres with the prejudices of our culture and what we believe a text meant in its own culture.

QUESTIONS

1. Discuss the meaning or point of a movie, novel, or poem with your friends. Which theory of interpretation do you see them using? Which theory do most of them seem to use? What is the theory of truth that they seem to be using?
2. Which theory of interpretation do you think is most appropriate for interpreting poetry or other works of literature? For interpreting a passage in a scripture or holy book? For interpreting a law? Why?
3. Can each of the various theories of interpretation explained earlier be used to interpret the *actions* of people? Explain why or why not.
4. Can the various theories of interpretation be used to interpret the meaning of a dream? Why or why not? Can dreams be true or false? Why or why not?
5. Notice that when you interpret a text, you have to proceed by interpreting one word or phrase or sentence at a time. Yet the meaning of the word, phrase, or sentence cannot become clear until you have interpreted the whole text. At the same time, you cannot understand the meaning of the whole text until you understand the meaning of each part. So, you cannot understand the meaning of each part until you have understood the whole, and you cannot understand the whole until you have understood the parts. Does this circularity mean that it is really impossible to interpret a text? Explain why or why not.

PHILOSOPHY AT THE MOVIES

Watch *The People vs. Larry Flynt* (1996), which tells the story of Larry Flynt, publisher of the pornographic magazine *Hustler*, and his attempts to defend himself against being charged with illegally making and selling pornography. In this film, what views are apparent on what the true interpretation of the Constitution is?

Chapter Summary

We opened this chapter by noting that knowledge is at least warranted true belief. We discussed the various modes of warrantability as they apply to various kinds of statements. We then discussed three theories of truth: the correspondence, coherence, and pragmatic theories. And we explored three related views of truth in science. The main points of this chapter are:

6.1 Knowledge, Truth, and Justification

- Knowledge is at least justified true belief, but Gettier examples show that something more is required for genuine knowledge.

- *Justification* is another name for the reasons or evidence that make a belief probable.
- Basic beliefs are beliefs that need no justification, while nonbasic beliefs are beliefs that must be justified to be acceptable.
- Foundationalism holds that all nonbasic beliefs are ultimately justified by basic beliefs; coherentism holds that there are no basic beliefs and that all beliefs are justified by other beliefs, i.e., by the extent to which they are supported by and consistent with the accepted "web of belief."

6.2 What Is Truth?

- The three traditional theories of truth are the correspondence, coherence, and pragmatic theories.
- The correspondence theory of truth claims that the truth of a statement depends on its relation to facts. A statement is true if and only if it corresponds to some fact. Objection: If we know only our sensory experiences, how can we ever get outside them to verify what reality actually is? What does correspondence mean? Precisely what is a fact?
- The coherence theory of truth claims that the truth of a statement depends on its relation to other statements. A statement is true if and only if it coheres or fits in with the system of beliefs that we already accept. Objection: Coherence is no guarantee of truth. A system of mutually supporting and consistent but false beliefs can produce a coherent system of consistent error.
- The pragmatic theory claims that truth depends on what works. A statement is true if and only if it effectively solves a practical problem and thereby experientially satisfies us. The pragmatist sees the human as needing to use the practical consequences of beliefs to determine their truth and validity. Objection: There's no necessary connection between truth and workability. Truth is rendered a psychological, not an epistemological, concern, and it can become relative.
- It is important to understand which theory of truth is most acceptable to us since some theories imply that truth is relative and if truth is relative then whatever a group of people accepts will be true no matter how evil their beliefs may be.

6.3 Does Science Give Us Truth?

- There are three views of truth in science: the instrumentalist, realist, and conceptual relativist views. The instrumentalist view has similarities to the pragmatic theory, the realist view to the correspondence theory, and the conceptual relativist view to the coherence theory.

6.4 Can Interpretations Be True?

- Truth is important for hermeneutics, which is the attempt to interpret people's words and actions. For Aquinas, scripture has many true symbolic interpretations, but the true interpretation is the one that corresponds to what the author intended and the ultimate author of scripture is God. For Schleiermacher and Dilthey, the only true interpretation is the one that corresponds to what the historical author intended. Wittgenstein abandoned his early ideal of a clear language of facts in which all texts would have a clear meaning, and proposed, pragmatically, that the meaning of words depends on how they are successfully used in a "form of life," so texts can have as many true interpretations as there are forms of life in which it is used. For Gadamer, an interpretation emerges from uniting our cultural "prejudices" with what the text was trying to say in its own culture, so there are as many true interpretations of a text as there are cultural contexts with which an interpretation can cohere.

In the final analysis, no single theory—correspondence, coherence, or pragmatic—may provide a complete solution to the problem of truth. Each has shortcomings and strengths. Equally important, each theory can play a part in the way we understand truth in the search for and discovery of self.

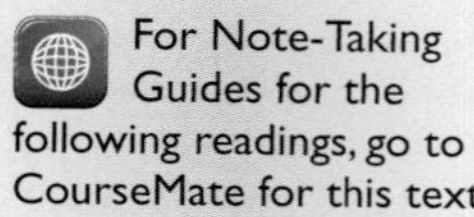
For Note-Taking Guides for the following readings, go to CourseMate for this text.

6.5 Readings

Is all truth relative? Is the truth held by one person or group as valid as the truth of any other person or group, even when those truths are incompatible? The short story by Japanese author Ryunosuke Akutagawa suggests that there may be as many truths as there are persons who are witnesses to the truth. Philosopher Hugh Tomlinson believes there are and he argues in the second reading that the traditional realist view of truth, which holds that there is one reality and one truth corresponding to that reality, must give way to the new postmodern view that there are many truths and many realities. John Searle, however, in the third reading argues that the view that there is one "way that things are" is a presupposition of all theories and so not all claims are equally true. So is everyone's truth equally valid as Tomlinson argues, or must we agree with Searle's argument that there is only one true account of reality?

RYUNOSUKE AKUTAGAWA

In a Grove

THE TESTIMONY OF A WOODCUTTER QUESTIONED BY A HIGH POLICE COMMISSIONER

Yes, sir. Certainly, it was I who found the body. This morning, as usual, I went to cut my daily quota of cedars, when I found the body in a grove in a hollow in the mountains. The exact location? About 150 meters off the Yamashina stage road. It's an out-of- the-way grove of bamboo and cedars.

The body was lying flat on its back dressed in a bluish silk kimono and a wrinkled head-dress of the Kyoto style. A single sword-stroke had pierced the breast. The fallen bamboo-blades around it were stained with bloody blossoms. No, the blood was no longer running. The wound had dried up, I believe. And also, a gadfly was stuck fast there, hardly noticing my footsteps.

You ask me if I saw a sword or any such thing?

No, nothing, sir. I found only a rope at the root of a cedar near by. And . . . well, in addition to a rope, I found a comb. That was all. Apparently he must have made a battle of it before he was murdered, because the grass and fallen bamboo-blades had been trampled down all around.

"A horse was near by?"

No, sir. It's hard enough for a man to enter, let alone a horse.

THE TESTIMONY OF A TRAVELING BUDDHIST PRIEST QUESTIONED BY A HIGH POLICE COMMISSIONER

The time? Certainly, it was about noon yesterday, sir. The unfortunate man was on the road from Sekiyama to Yamashina. He was walking toward Sekiyama with a woman accompanying him on horseback, who I have since learned was his wife. A scarf hanging from her head hid her face from view. All I saw was the color of her clothes, a lilac colored suit. Her horse was a sorrel with a fine mane. The lady's height? Oh, about four feet five inches. Since I am a Buddhist priest, I took little notice about her details. Well, the man was armed with a sword as well as a bow and arrows. And I remember that he carried some twenty odd arrows in his quiver.

Little did I expect that he would meet such a fate. Truly human life is as evanescent as the morning dew or a flash of lightning. My words are inadequate to express my sympathy for him.

THE TESTIMONY OF A POLICEMAN QUESTIONED BY A HIGH POLICE COMMISSIONER

The man that I arrested? He is a notorious brigand called Tajomaru. When I arrested him, he had fallen off his horse. He was groaning on the bridge at Awataguchi. The time? It was in the early hours of last night. For the record, I might say that the other day I tried to arrest him, but unfortunately he escaped. He was wearing a dark blue silk kimono and a large plain sword. And, as you see, he got a bow and arrows somewhere. You say that this bow and these arrows look like the ones owned by the dead man? Then Tajomaru must be the murderer . . .

THE TESTIMONY OF AN OLD WOMAN QUESTIONED BY A HIGH POLICE COMMISSIONER

Yes, sir, the corpse is the man who married my daughter. He does not come from Kyoto. He was a samurai in the town of Kokufu in the province of Wakasa. His name was Kanazawa no Takehiko, and his age was twenty-six. He was of a gentle disposition, so I am sure he did nothing to provoke the anger of others.

My daughter? Her name is Masago, and her age is nineteen. She is a spirited, fun-loving girl, but I am sure she has never known any man except Takehiko. She has a small, oval, dark-complected face with a mole at the corner of her left eye.

Yesterday Takehiko left for Wakasa with my daughter. What bad luck it is that things should have come to such a sad end! What has become of my daughter? I am resigned to giving up my son-in-law as lost, but the fate of my daughter worries me sick. For heaven's sake leave no stone unturned to find her. I hate that robber Tajomaru, or whatever his name is. Not only my son-in-law, but my daughter . . . (Her later words were drowned in tears.)

TAJOMARU'S CONFESSION

I killed him, but not her. Where's she gone? I can't tell. Oh, wait a minute. No torture can make me confess what I don't know. Now things have come to such a head, I won't keep anything from you.

Yesterday a little past noon I met that couple. Just then a puff of wind blew, and raised her hanging scarf, so that I caught a glimpse of her face. Instantly it was again covered from my view. That may have been one reason; she looked like a Bodhisattva. At that moment I made up my mind to capture her even if I had to kill her man.

Why? To me killing isn't a matter of such great consequence as you might think. When a woman is captured, her man has to be killed anyway. In killing, I use the sword I wear at my side. Am I the only one who kills people? You, you don't use your swords. You kill people with your power, with your money. Sometimes you kill them on the pretext of working for their good. It's true they don't bleed. They are in the best of health, but all the same you've killed them. It's hard to say who is a greater sinner, you or me. (An ironical smile.)

But it would be good if I could capture a woman without killing her man. So, I made up my mind to capture her, and do my best not to kill him. But it's out of the question on the Yamashina stage road. So I managed to lure the couple into the mountains.

It was quite easy. I became their traveling companion, and I told them there was an old mound in the mountain over there, and that I had dug it open and found many mirrors and swords. I went on to tell them I'd buried the things in a grove behind the mountain, and that I'd like to sell them at a low price to anyone who would care to have them. Then . . . you see, isn't greed terrible? He was beginning to be moved by my talk before he knew it. In less than half an hour they were driving their horse toward the mountain with me.

When he came in front of the grove, I told them that the treasures were buried in it, and I asked them to come and see. The man had no objection—he was blinded by greed. The woman said she would wait on horseback. It was natural for her to say so, at the sight of a thick grove. To tell you the truth, my plan worked just as I wished, so I went into the grove with him, leaving her behind alone.

The grove is only bamboo for some distance. About fifty yards ahead there's a rather open clump of cedars. It was a convenient spot for my purpose. Pushing my way through the grove, I told him a plausible lie that the treasures were buried under the cedars. When I told him this, he pushed his laborious way toward the slender cedar visible through the grove. After a while the bamboo thinned out, and we came to where a number of cedars grew in a row. As soon as we got there, I seized him from behind. Because he was a trained, sword-bearing warrior, he was quite strong, but he was taken by surprise, so there was no help for him. I soon tied him up to the root of a cedar. Where did I get a rope? Thank heaven, being a robber, I had a rope with me, since I might have to scale a wall at any moment. Of course it was easy to stop him from calling out by gagging his mouth with fallen bamboo leaves.

When I disposed of him, I went to his woman and asked her to come and see him, because he seemed to have been suddenly taken sick. It's needless to say that this plan also worked well. The woman, her sedge hat off, came into the depths of the grove, where I led her by the hand. The instant she caught sight of her husband, she drew a small sword. I've never seen a woman of such violent temper. If I'd been off guard, I'd have got a thrust in my side. I dodged, but she kept on slashing at me. She might have wounded me deeply or killed me. But I'm Tajomaru. I managed to strike down her small sword without drawing my own. The most spirited woman is defenseless without a weapon. At least I could satisfy my desire for her without taking her husband's life.

Yes, . . . without taking his life. I had no wish to kill him. I was about to run away from the grove, leaving the woman behind in tears, when she frantically clung to my arm. In broken fragments of words, she asked that either her husband or I die. She said it was more trying than death to have her shame known to two men. She gasped out that she wanted to be the wife of whichever survived. Then a furious desire to kill him seized me. (Gloomy excitement.)

Telling you in this way, no doubt I seem a crueler man than you. But that's because you didn't see her face. Especially her burning eyes at that moment. As I saw her eye to eye, I wanted to make her my wife even if I were to be struck by lightning. I wanted to make her my wife . . . this single desire filled my mind. This was not only lust, as you might think. At that time if I'd had no other desire than lust, I'd surely not have minded knocking her down and running away. Then I wouldn't have stained my sword with his blood. But the moment I gazed at her face in the dark grove, I decided not to leave there without killing him.

But I didn't like to resort to unfair means to kill him. I untied him and told him to cross swords with me. (The rope that was found at the root of the cedar is the rope I dropped at the time.) Furious with anger, he drew his thick sword. And quick as thought, he sprang at me ferociously, without speaking a word. I needn't tell you how our fight turned out. The twenty-third stroke . . . please remember this. I'm impressed with this fact still. Nobody under the sun has ever clashed swords with me twenty strokes. (A cheerful smile.)

When he fell, I turned toward her, lowering my blood-stained sword. But to my great astonishment she was gone. I wondered to where she had run away. I looked for her in the clump of cedars. I listened, but heard only a groaning sound from the throat of the dying man.

As soon as we started to cross swords, she may have run away through the grove to call for help. When I thought of that, I decided it was a matter of life and death to me. So, robbing him of his sword, and bow and arrows, I ran out to the mountain road. There I found her horse still grazing quietly. It would be a mere waste of words to tell you the latter details, but before I entered town I had already parted with the sword. That's all my confession. I know that my head will be hung in chains anyway, so put me down for the maximum penalty. (A defiant attitude.)

THE CONFESSION OF A WOMAN WHO HAS COME TO THE SHIMIZU TEMPLE

That man in the blue silk kimono, after forcing me to yield to him, laughed mockingly as he looked at my bound husband. How horrified my husband must have been! But no matter how hard he struggled in agony, the rope cut into him all the more tightly. In spite of myself I ran stumblingly toward his side. Or rather I tried to run toward him, but the man instantly knocked me down. Just at the moment I saw an indescribable light in my husband's eyes. Something beyond expression . . . his eyes make me shudder even now. That instantaneous look of my husband, who couldn't speak a word, told me all his heart. The flash in his eyes was neither anger nor sorrow . . . only a cold light, a look of loathing. More struck by the look in his eyes than by the blow of the thief, I called out in spite of myself and fell unconscious.

In the course of time I came to, and found that the man in blue silk was gone. I saw only my husband still bound to the root of the cedar. I raised myself from the bamboo-blades with difficulty, and looked into his face; but the expression in his eyes was just the same as before.

Beneath the cold contempt in his eyes, there was hatred. Shame, grief, and anger . . . I don't know how to express my heart at that time. Reeling to my feet, I went up to my husband.

"Takejiro," I said to him, "since things have come to this pass, I cannot live with you. I'm determined to die, . . . but you must die, too. You saw my shame. I can't leave you alive as you are." This was all I could say. Still he went on gazing at me with loathing and contempt. My heart breaking, I looked for his sword. It must have been taken by the robber. Neither his sword nor his bow and arrows were to be seen in the grove. But fortunately my small sword was lying at my feet. Raising it over head, once more I said, "Now give me your life, I'll follow you right away." When he heard these words, he moved his lips with difficulty. Since his mouth was stuffed with leaves, of course his voice could not be heard at all.

But at a glance I understood his words. Despising me, his look said only, "Kill me." Neither conscious nor unconscious, I stabbed the small sword through the lilac-colored kimono into his breast.

Again at this time I must have fainted. By the time I managed to look up, he had already breathed his last—still in bonds. A streak of sinking sunlight streamed through the clump of cedars and bamboos, and shone on his pale face. Gulping down my sobs, I untied the rope from his dead body. And . . . and what has become of me since I have no more strength to tell you. Anyway I hadn't the strength to die. I stabbed my own throat with the small sword, I threw myself into a pond at the foot of the mountain, and I tried to kill myself in many ways. Unable to end my life, I am still living in dishonor. (A lonely smile.) Worthless as I am, I must have been forsaken even by the most merciful Kwannon. I killed my own husband. I was violated by the robber. Whatever can I do? Whatever can I . . . I . . . (Gradually, violent sobbing.)

THE STORY OF THE MURDERED MAN, AS TOLD THROUGH A MEDIUM

After violating my wife, the robber, sitting there, began to speak comforting words to her. Of course I couldn't speak. My whole body was tied fast to the root of a cedar. But meanwhile I winked at her many times, as much as to say "Don't believe the robber." I wanted to convey some such meaning to her. But my wife, sitting dejectedly on the bamboo leaves, was looking hard at her lap. To all appearances, she was listening to his words. I was agonized by jealousy. In the meantime the robber went on with his clever talk, from one subject to another. The robber finally made his bold, brazen proposal. "Once your virtue is stained, you won't get along well with your husband, so won't you be my wife instead? It's my love for you that made me be violent toward you."

While the criminal talked, my wife raised her face as if in a trance. She had never looked so beautiful as at that moment. What did my beautiful wife say in answer to him while I was sitting bound there? I am lost in space, but I have never thought of her answer without burning with anger and jealousy. Truly she said, . . . "Then take me away with you wherever you go." This is not the whole of her sin. If that were all, I would not be tormented so much in the dark.

When she was going out of the grove as if in a dream, her hand in the robber's, she suddenly turned pale, and pointed at me tied to the root of the cedar, and said "Kill him! I cannot marry you as long as he lives." "Kill him!" she cried many times, as if she had gone crazy. Even now these words threaten to blow me headlong into the bottomless abyss of darkness. Has such a hateful thing come out of a human mouth ever before? Have such cursed words ever struck a human ear, even once? Even once such a . . . (A sudden cry of scorn.) At these words the robber himself turned pale. "Kill him," she cried, clinging to his arms. Looking hard at her, he answered neither yes nor no . . . but hardly had I thought about his answer before she had been knocked down into the bamboo leaves. (Again a cry of scorn.) Quietly folding his arms, he looked at me and said, "What will you do with her? Kill her or save her? You have only to nod. Kill her?" For these words alone I would like to pardon his crime.

While I hesitated, she shrieked and ran into the depths of the grove. The robber instantly snatched at her, but he failed even to grasp her sleeve.

After she ran away, he took up my sword, and my bow and arrows. With a single stroke he cut one of my bonds. I remember his mumbling, "My fate is next." Then he disappeared from the grove. All was silent after that. No, I heard someone crying. Untying the rest of my bonds, I listened carefully, and I noticed that it was my own crying. (Long silence.)

I raised my exhausted body from the root of the cedar. In front of me there was shining the small sword which my wife had dropped. I took it up and stabbed it into my breast. A bloody lump rose to my mouth, but I didn't feel any pain. When my breast grew cold, everything was as silent as the dead in their graves. What profound silence! Not a single bird-note was heard in the sky over this grave in the hollow of the mountains. Only a lonely light lingered on the cedars and mountains. By and by the light gradually grew fainter, till the cedars and bamboo were lost to view. Lying there, I was enveloped in deep silence.

Then someone crept up to me. I tried to see who it was. But darkness had already been gathering round me. Someone . . . that someone drew the small sword softly out of my breast in its invisible hand. At the same time once more blood flowed into my mouth. And once and for all I sank down into the darkness of space.

"In a Grove", from *Rashomon and Other Stories* by Ryunosuke Akutagawa, translated by Takashi Kojima. Copyright 1952 by Liveright Publishing Corporation. Used by permission of Liveright Publishing Corporation.

HUGH TOMLINSON

After Truth: Post-Modernism and the Rhetoric of Science

Common-Sense Realism

The modern notion of truth draws much of its plausibility from a set of metaphysical views which form an "externalist" perspective on the world, what Putnam has called a "God's Eye point of view".[1] This perspective is now deeply embedded in our "common-sense" attitude to the world. The "common-sense realist" sees the world as being objectively ordered independently of all human activity. Science seeks to provide theories which "mirror" this objective ordering, theories which are, in a word, "true".

The basic "given" of common-sense realism is unobjectionable: the world is relatively independent of our dealings with it. But this is elevated into an ontological thesis that there is a single, objectively structured reality independent of human thoughts and actions. According to the realist:

> the world consists of some fixed totality of mind-independent objects. There is exactly one true and complete description of "the way the world is". Truth involves some sort of correspondence between words or thought-signs and external things and sets of things.[2]

This correspondence view of truth provides an apparently straightforward and easily applicable picture of the relation between words and world. It is a picture which fits with the way which we use simple sentences about ordinary material objects. We look to the world, to the "thing referred to", in order to decide whether such sentences are appropriate or not: to decide whether "there is food in the fridge", I can look in the fridge. . . .

According to the realist picture "truth" is given by a particular relationship between words and world: a sentence is true when it corresponds to the world. This involves two aspects: the items to be related and the relationship itself. From his own perspective, the realist must be in a position to give a coherent account of both.

The items to be related seem obvious and straightforward: words and objects. The common-sense realist thinks of the world as consisting, paradigmatically, of unproblematically identifiable physical objects with simple properties. From a "God's Eye point of view" the world "really is" divided up into objects, independently of human description and ordering.

This view of objects runs counter to the whole thrust of modern philosophy since Kant. It is ultimately dependent on the idea of the world as "God's project", divided up according to divine categories. It was Kant's fundamental insight that "we are giving the orders", that both concepts and experience are necessary components of knowledge. We can only have experience of a world which is already structured by our concepts; it is "our world". What counts as a particular object depends on the classificatory concepts which we use. We cannot "leap outside" these concepts and directly compare them with "unconceptualized objects". . . .

It seems that all that words can ever be related to are objects which depend on the words used. Truth is, then, not "objective" and unique, but "subjective" in the sense that it depends on the particular language used. There are as many truths as there are languages and the notion of truth can no longer provide a final and objective justification for science.

Relativism and Post-Modernism

This account of realism can be summarized by saying that, on close examination, it collapses into relativism. This collapse has two phases. First, the insight that the world is "our world", that what counts as a fact depends on our theories, means that there is no "reality" for theories to correspond to. . . .

Secondly, if there are a number of incommensurable theories there are as many worlds as there are theories. In Feyerabend's words, "we . . . cannot assume that two incommensurable theories deal with one and the same objective state of affairs. . . . Hence, unless we want to assume that they deal with nothing at all we must admit that they deal with different worlds."[3] This view is commonly called relativism. . . .

The post-modernist story is a simple one: realism, in any of its forms, cannot be made coherent in its own terms. We have, as Putnam says, reached "the demise of a theory that lasted for over two thousand years. That it persisted so long and in so many forms in spite of the internal contradictions and obscurities which were present from the beginning testifies to the naturalness and strength of the desire for a God's Eye View."[4]

References

1. See Hilary Putnam, *Reason, Truth and History* (Cambridge: Cambridge University Press, 1981), 50ff.
2. Ibid., 49.
3. P. Feyerabend, *Science in a Free Society* (London: Verso, 1978), 70.
4. Putnam, *Reason, Truth and History*, 74.

Reprinted from *Dismantling Truth: Reality in the Post-Modern World*, ed. Hilary Lawson and Lisa Appignanesi (New York: St. Martin's, 1989). Copyright © Hilary Lawson and Lisa Appignanesi. Reprinted with permission of St. Martin's Press, Inc.

JOHN SEARLE

Reality and Truth

Among the . . . positions that form our cognitive Background, perhaps the most fundamental is a certain set of presuppositions about reality and truth. Typically when we act, think, or talk, we take for granted a certain way that our actions, thoughts, and talk relate to things outside us. . . . [W]e take the following for granted: there exists a real world that is totally independent of human beings and of what they think or say about it, and statements about objects and states of affairs in that world are true or false depending on whether things in the world really are the way we say they are. These two Background presuppositions have long histories and various famous names. The first, that there is a real world existing independently of us, I like to call "external realism.". . . The second view, that a statement is true if things in the world are the way the statement says they are, and false otherwise, is called "the correspondence theory of truth." This theory comes in a lot of different versions, but the basic idea is that statements are true if they correspond to, or describe, or fit, how things really are in the world, and false if they do not. . . .

[E]xternal realism underlies . . . the correspondence theory of truth. Thinkers who wish to deny the correspondence theory of truth . . . typically find it embarrassing to have to concede external realism . . .

I do not believe it makes any sense to ask for a justification of the view that there is a way that things are in the world independently of our representations, because any attempt at justification presupposes what it attempts to justify. Any attempt to find out about the real world at all presupposes that there is a way that things are. That is why it is wrong to represent external realism [the claim that there exists a real world that is totally independent of all our representations, thoughts, language, and so on] as the view that there are material objects in space and time, or that mountains and molecules, and so on, exist. Suppose there were no mountains and molecules, and no material objects in space and time. Then those would be facts about how the world is, and thus would presuppose external realism. That is, the negation of this or that claim about the real world presupposes that there is a way that things are, independently of our claims . . . [E]xternal realism is not a theory. It is not an opinion I hold that there is a world out there. It is, rather, the framework that is necessary for it to be even possible to hold opinions or theories about such things as planetary movements. When you debate the merits of a theory such as the heliocentric theory of the solar system, you have to take it for granted that there is a way that things really are. Otherwise, the debate can't get started. Its very terms are unintelligible. But that assumption, that there is a way that things are independent of our representations of how they are, is external realism. External realism is not a claim about the existence of this or that object, but rather a presupposition of the way we understand such claims. . . . This does not mean that realism is an unprovable theory; rather, it means that realism is not a theory at all, but the framework within which it is possible to have theories.

From John Searle, *Mind, Language and Society,* (New York: Basic Books, 1998) excerpts from pp, 12, 13, 31, 32. Copyright © 1999 John R Searle. Reprinted by permission of Basic Books, a member of the Perseus Books Group.

6.6 HISTORICAL SHOWCASE

Kant

In the previous chapter, we saw how Hume's empiricism led philosophy into the dead end of skepticism. If Hume's radical empiricism is accepted, then we can never hope to learn the truth about ourselves, God, or the universe.

In this chapter, we showcase a philosopher who claimed to have found a way around Hume's skepticism and who, in doing so, revolutionized our views about knowledge and truth. This is the eighteenth-century philosopher Immanuel Kant.

Immanuel Kant is regarded by many as the greatest of all philosophers, especially in the field of epistemology. His unique contribution was to argue that the world of our experience is a world that our own mind constructs. Our mind can indeed know the truth about the world around us, he argued, because that world is constructed by the mind itself.

© Private Collection/The Bridgeman Art Library International

Immanuel Kant: "There can be no doubt that all our knowledge begins with experience. But though all our knowledge begins with experience, it does not follow that it all arises out of experience. For it may well be that even our empirical knowledge is made up of what we receive through impressions and of what our own faculty of knowledge supplies from itself."

We showcase Kant in this chapter because of the radical and profound contributions he made to our conceptions of knowledge and truth. But reading Kant also allows us to see how his revolutionary views about knowledge influenced his views on morality and God. Kant is a good example of how our epistemological views affect our positions on other philosophical issues.

Although he revolutionized philosophy, Kant lived a very ordinary life. He spent all of his eighty years (1724–1804) in the small town in which he was born: Königsberg (now Kaliningrad, Russia). There he grew up, and there he went to college, supporting himself in part by his winnings from playing pool with other students. Kant remained in Königsberg after graduating, eventually becoming a teacher at the local university. As a teacher, Kant came to schedule his activities so precisely that neighbors used to set their clocks when he passed their houses on his daily afternoon walk. Although Kant remained a bachelor all of his life, he had a number of close women friends and had a reputation for being a funny, witty, and entertaining host at the dinner parties he frequently had.

The Problem of Synthetic *a priori* Knowledge

Although Kant never left his birthplace, his books put him in touch with all the intellectual currents of the eighteenth century. He was well acquainted with the tremendous new discoveries in the natural sciences and was especially impressed with Newton's discoveries in physics. But when Kant came across the writings of Hume, these discoveries seemed threatened. For Hume argued that our so-called scientific knowledge is not rationally justified. In particular, he pointed out that the cause-and-effect laws of science go beyond the evidence scientists have for them. Scientists observe a *few times* that certain events have been conjoined *in the past,* and they conclude that those kinds of events *must always* cause each other *in the future.* But how do scientists know that events must always be causally connected in the future as in the past?

Kant realized that Hume's objection was devastating. If Hume was correct, then all our scientific knowledge was unjustified. Moreover, Kant soon discovered that other areas of knowledge also contained judgments that went beyond the evidence of our senses:

> I openly confess that my recollection of David Hume was the very thing which many years ago first interrupted my dogmatic slumber and gave my investigations in the field of speculative philosophy a quite new direction. I was far from following him in the conclusions at which he arrived. . . .
>
> I therefore first tried to see whether Hume's objection could not be put into a general form. I soon found that the concept of the connection of cause and effect was by no means the only concept by which the understanding thinks the connection of things *a priori* [that is, independently of experience].[1]

Kant found three areas of knowledge in which our statements about the world go beyond the evidence provided by our sensory experience:

1. In the sciences of geometry and arithmetic. For example:
   "The shortest distance between two points must always be a straight line."
   "The square of the hypotenuse of a right-angle triangle must always equal the sum of the squares of the other two sides."
   "The sum of 798 and 857 must always equal 1655."
2. In the natural sciences. For example:
   "All events must always have a cause."
3. In philosophical metaphysics. For example:
   "There must exist a God that causes the universe."

1 Immanuel Kant, *Prolegomena to Any Future Metaphysics,* trans. Lewis White Beck (New York: Bobbs-Merrill, 1950), 8.

Kant termed these *synthetic* statements to indicate that each gives us genuine information about the world around us. For example, geometry tells us that the world will always obey the law that the square of the hypotenuse of right triangles equals the sum of the squares of the other two sides, and the natural sciences tell us that all events must have a cause. By contrast, Kant used the term *analytic* to refer to statements that merely give us information about the meanings of words, such as "Bachelors are unmarried males."

Kant also called the statements in the list *a priori,* pointing out two features of such statements: First, as Hume said, these statements go beyond what we can establish through our sensory experience. For example, we could never check *all* right triangles, yet geometry says the square of their hypotenuses *always* equals the sum of the squares of the other two sides. Second, we establish that these statements *must* be true by relying on our thought processes. The laws of geometry, for example, are established in the mind. *A priori* statements, then, are necessary and universal: They state something that we know by mental processes *must* be true and that *always* holds. By contrast, Kant used the term *a posteriori* to refer to statements that can be established by sensory observations, such as "This room is empty" and "The sky above is blue." *A posteriori* statements are neither necessary nor universal.

But how can we know *a priori* propositions about the world without going outside of our minds? For example, how do we know that the outer world must always obey the laws of geometry when we can establish these laws completely within the mind? How do we know that every event must always have a cause when we have not examined every event? Is Hume correct in saying that such synthetic *a priori* statements are unjustified?

> Now the proper problem of pure reason is contained in the question: How are *a priori* synthetic judgments possible? . . .
>
> Among philosophers, David Hume came nearest to envisaging this problem, but still he was very far from conceiving it with sufficient definiteness and universality. He occupied himself exclusively with the synthetic proposition regarding the connection of an effect with its cause, and he believed himself to have shown that such an *a priori* proposition is entirely impossible. . . . If he had envisaged our problem in all its universality, . . . he would then have recognized that, according to his own argument,

> pure mathematics, which certainly contains *a priori* synthetic propositions, would also not be possible. . . .
>
> In the solution of our above problem, then, we are at the same time deciding as to the possibility of the employment of pure reason in establishing and developing all those sciences which contain *a priori* knowledge of objects, and have therefore to answer the questions: How is pure mathematics possible? How is pure science of nature possible? . . . How is metaphysics . . . possible?[2]

To save our knowledge from Hume's skepticism, Kant had to show that we are justified in making statements that give us real information about the world but are established completely within the mind. To solve that problem, Kant embarked on what he called "a critique of pure reason"—an investigation of what our minds can know apart from the senses.

Space, Time, and Mathematics

Kant began his investigation by granting Hume's view of our senses. Hume pointed out that all our knowledge of the world begins with sensations within us: colors, shapes, sounds, tastes, feels, smells. The senses, Hume said, provide us with a continual stream of endlessly changing:

> perceptions which succeed each other with an inconceivable rapidity and are in a perpetual flux and movement. . . . The mind is a kind of theater, where several perceptions successively make their appearance, pass, re-pass, glide away, and mingle in an infinite variety of postures and situations.[3]

But Kant noticed something Hume had missed. It is true that all we receive from the senses are the sensations within us. Yet we do not *experience* a mere display of sensations within us. When I open my eyes, I do not experience changing sensations of light and colors playing in my vision. Instead, I see *objects* that appear to be *outside* of me. For example, when I look down, I see not a squarish blob of whiteness but the white page of a book a few inches away. Somehow, the sensations (colors and shapes) that continually play in my vision appear to me as objects outside of me.

The same is true of my other senses. They, too, provide only a stream of sensations within me. But I experience them as belonging to particular objects outside of me. For example, I do not merely sense ringing, booming, rustling sound sensations in my hearing. Instead, I hear noises that seem to come from some particular place in the room: perhaps a rustling noise from the pages of my book or a voice from a particular person in front of me. Each sensation of sound, feel, and smell appears to be the sound, feel, and smell of objects outside me.

Kant argued that somehow our mind takes these many separate sensations and *organizes* them into objects that appear to be outside ourselves, in space. It is as if my mind carries within it a three-dimensional representation of space, and every sensation is given a position in this mental image of space.

In fact, Kant argues, we could not experience objects as being outside of us without this three-dimensional representation of space in our minds. Even to perceive objects as outside of ourselves, we *already* have to know what outside is—that is, we have to know what space is. Moreover, although we can imagine an empty space without objects, we cannot imagine an object that is not in space. This also proves, according to Kant, that our mental representation of space has to be in our minds prior to our experience of objects:

> Space is not an empirical concept which has been derived from outer experiences. For in order that certain sensations be referred to something outside me (that is, to something in another region of space from that in which I find myself), and, similarly, in order that I may be able to represent them as outside and alongside one another, and . . . as in different places, the representation of space also must be presupposed. The representation of space cannot, therefore, be . . . obtained from the relations of outer . . . [experience]. On the contrary, this outer experience is itself possible at all only through that representation.
>
> Space is a necessary *a priori* representation which underlies all outer perceptions. We can never represent to ourselves the absence of space, though we can quite well think of it as empty of objects. It must therefore be regarded as the condition of the possibility of . . . [sensory experiences], and not as . . . [something] dependent on them.[4]

2 Immanuel Kant, *Critique of Pure Reason*, trans. Norman Kemp Smith (New York: St. Martin's, 1929; original work published 1781), B19, B22.

3 David Hume, *A Treatise of Human Nature*, ed. L. A. Selby-Bigge (Oxford: Clarendon, 1896), 252–253.

4 Kant, *Critique*, B38, B39. (Note that the word *intuition* has been replaced here and elsewhere in the translations that follow with the much more familiar term *perception*.)

Space, then, is merely a mental representation that helps us organize our sensations so that they appear to us to be objects outside of us. There is nothing more to space than this mental image. Space does not exist independently of us outside our mind:

> Space does not represent any property of things in themselves, nor does it represent them in their relation to one another. That is to say, space does not represent any determination that attaches to objects themselves and which remains even when abstraction has been made of all the subjective conditions of perception.
>
> It is therefore solely from the human standpoint that we can speak of space, of extended objects, etc. . . . This predicate can be ascribed to things only insofar as they appear to us, that is, only to objects of sensibility [of the senses].[5]

Kant's view—that space does not exist outside the mind—may seem strange. But his view provides the key to one of his major questions: How do we know that the laws of geometry must hold true for all objects in the world even though these laws are established within the mind? Kant's solution is simple and brilliant.

First, he argues, the laws of geometry are nothing more than the laws of the mental image of space that is in our minds. That is why we can establish the laws of geometry by simply examining our inner image of space without having to examine the outer world.

Second, Kant points out, the mind puts every object we experience into this mental representation of space. All our sensations are organized by the mind into objects within its representation of space so that they appear to us as if they exist in space outside. Every object we experience will have to appear within this mental image and therefore must obey its laws. Because the laws of geometry are the laws of our mental representation, every object we experience will have to obey the laws of geometry.

Thus, Kant provides a solution to the problem that had puzzled philosophers for centuries: How do we know without going outside our minds that all objects obey the laws of geometry? The only solution, Kant held, is that we establish the laws of geometry completely *a priori* by simply looking within our own minds' three-dimensional image of space. We know all the objects we perceive will obey these laws because the mind places all objects within this mental image so that for us they are in space.

5 Ibid., B42–B43.

Using similar arguments, Kant showed that all our experience must obey the laws of arithmetic. The laws of arithmetic, he said, are the laws of time: They are laws about how units follow one after another, just like numbers follow one after another.

But where do we get our image of time? Just as we organize sensations by inserting them in space, we also organize them by inserting them in time. So, time is also one of the structures of the mind. Time is like a long filing system we use to organize our sensations by placing each one at a certain point in the system. Because the image of time is within us, we can know its laws just by examining it. And because the mind makes everything we experience appear to be in time, everything must obey the laws of time. And these laws are the laws of arithmetic.

So the synthetic *a priori* statements of geometry and arithmetic are justified. Although these statements give us information about the structure of the world, we do not have to examine every object in the world to know these statements hold true of everything we will ever perceive. The synthetic *a priori* statements of geometry and arithmetic can be established by simply examining our inner images of time and space. Space and time are merely structures within the mind in which we position the objects our mind makes out of the sensations it receives so that to our minds these objects exist in space and time.

Our Unified Mind Must Organize Sensations into Changing Objects

But Kant also had to show that the synthetic a priori statements of the natural sciences were justified. In particular, he had to show that the causal laws of science were justified. How did he do this? Kant's solution to this problem is remarkably similar to his solution to the problem of geometry and mathematics. Kant points out that the mind organizes its sensations so that they appear to us as objects that change through time. How does the mind do this? The mind organizes its sensations into such independent objects by using twelve rules or "categories." The most important of these rules or categories turns out to be the basic law underlying the natural sciences: that all perceived events must have a cause. So, just as we know that every object we experience will be organized in space and time, we can also be sure that every event we experience will be causally related to other events. How exactly did Kant prove this? Kant's argument is difficult, but with a bit of work it can be understood.

Kant first points out that our sensations appear to us to be of independent objects that last through time and that change. For example, during the time I look at a book, I believe that I continue seeing the same book. My sensations appear to me to be of an object that lasts through time. And as I turn its pages, the same book appears to me to be changing.

To make my sensations appear to be changing objects, Kant says, the mind has to bring its sensations together in three ways. First, the mind has to receive or "apprehend" the many separate sensations provided by the senses. For example, each separate moment I look at the changing white book, my senses produce new and different sensations of white color. To keep perceiving the book, then, I have to keep receiving all of these separate sensations. Second, the mind has to remember the past sensations. For example, in perceiving the book, I have to keep in mind the past sensations of white as I receive new sensations. If I continually forgot the past sensations, it would be as though a new book were continually appearing before me each moment. Third, the mind has to connect or relate the later sensations to the earlier ones. That is, the mind has to recognize that the earlier sensations and the later ones are sensations of the same object. For example, I must recognize that my later, slightly different sensations of the book are sensations of the same book I saw earlier. Otherwise, the earlier and later sensations would appear to me as many separate images of different books floating in my memory. This recognition or connection of earlier and later sensations is what finally makes me believe that I am seeing the same book but that it is changing through time:

> Each perception [of an object] is made up of a multiplicity [of sensations]. . . . In order to change this multiplicity [of separate sensations] into a single thing [an object], it is necessary first to run through and collect the multiplicity [of sensations]. This act I call the "synthesis of apprehension." . . .
>
> But if I were always to drop out of thought the earlier sensation. . . ., and did not reproduce them [in my memory] while advancing to the next ones, then a complete perception [of an object] would never form. . . . The synthesis of apprehension is therefore inseparably connected with [what I will call] the "synthesis of reproduction."
>
> [Moreover,] if we were not conscious that what we are thinking of now is the same as what we thought a moment before, all reproduction in the series of perceptions would be in vain. Each perception would . . . be a new one. . . . The multiplicity could never form a whole, because it would not have that unity that [my] consciousness alone can give it [by recognizing that what I perceive now is the same as what I perceived earlier].[6]

But the mind's ability to collect sensations into unified objects that change through time would not be possible unless the mind itself also lasted through time. For example, suppose that I am looking at a book and receiving new sensations of white color each passing moment. If the later sensations are to be connected to the earlier ones, the *same* mind has to receive the earlier and the later ones. This means my mind has to last through time: It has to last through the earlier and later sensations. Thus, the process of receiving, remembering, and connecting sensations into objects that last through time requires a mind that also lasts through time. The unification of sensations into objects requires a "unified" mind that connects sensations:

> [But] there can be in us no kind of knowledge, no connection or unifying of one bit of knowledge with another, unless there is a unified consciousness which precedes all the data of perception. . . . This pure original unchanging consciousness I call "transcendental apperception."[7]

The mind, then, is a single consciousness that remains the same through time, contrary to Hume's claim that the mind is only a bundle of disconnected sensations. In fact, Kant argues, the mind *must* connect its sensations because it must bring all these separate sensations into itself:

> If we want to discover the internal foundation of this unifying of perception . . ., we must begin with pure [transcendental] apperception. Sensations would be nothing to us, and would not concern us in the least, if they were not received into our [unified] consciousness. . . . Knowledge is impossible in any other way. We are conscious *a priori* of our own enduring identity with regard to all perceptions we know. Our enduring identity is a necessary condition for

6 Immanuel Kant, *Kritik Reinen Vernunft* [*Critique of Pure Reason*] (Leipzig, Germany: Johann Friedrich Hartknoch, 1981), A99–A103. This translation is by Manuel Velasquez.

7 Ibid., A107.

> us to have these perceptions. For perceptions could not be perceptions of anything for me unless they . . . could at least be connected together into [my] one consciousness. This principle stands firm *a priori,* and may be called the "transcendental principle of the unity" of all the multiplicity of our perceptions (and therefore also of sensation).[8]

What Kant is saying here is that our mind connects and unifies its sensations because it *has to.* It has to connect them together because the many sensations my senses produce must all enter one mind: my own single mind. But to enter into my one mind, they have to be brought together into one.

As Kant says, this point—that the mind *has to* unify its sensations—is crucial. If the mind has to unify its sensations into objects, then we know that the connections the mind imposes on objects are necessary.

What kinds of connections does the mind make between objects? Kant argues that there are twelve kinds of connections or "categories" that the mind must impose on its sensations. Only the most important of these, the relation of cause and effect, concerns us here.

Causality Is in the World As We Experience It

Kant tries to show that the mind *must* impose causal relationships on its sensations if they are to appear as objects that change independently of us. Kant begins his argument by pointing out that changes we perceive can follow one another in an order that I can determine or in an order that is fixed. But changes whose order I determine are not changes in independent objects outside of me; they are merely changes in me. For example, if I look first at the roof of a house and then at the windows, the order of my perceptions is determined by my own will. I can change the order by simply looking first at the windows and then at the roof. So, these changes in my perceptions are merely changes in *me.* They are not independent changes in the *objects* outside of me. On the other hand, changes whose order is fixed or "necessary" are changes that I see as changes in independent objects outside of me. For example, if I see a boat being carried down a river by the current, I will first perceive the boat upriver, and then I will perceive the boat downstream. The order of these perceptions cannot be determined by my own will: I cannot change the order. So, I know that the changes in my perceptions of the boat are changes in the *objects* outside of me, not merely changes in *me.* And I know this only because the order of these changes is fixed by necessary causal laws and not by me. If our sensations are to appear as objects that change independently of ourselves, they must be related by causal laws:

> The Principle of the succession of time, according to the Law of Causality: All changes take place according to the law of connection between cause and effect.
>
> Proof: The apprehension of the multiplicity of phenomena is always successive. The perceptions of the parts [of objects] follow one upon another. . . . Thus, for instance, the apprehension of the multiplicity in the phenomenal appearance of a house that stands before me is successive. . . . Every apprehension of an event is [similarly] . . . a perception following on another perception. But as this applies to all synthesis of apprehension, as in the phenomenal appearance of a house, that apprehension would not be different from any other.
>
> But I observe that if in a phenomenon which contains an event I call the antecedent state of perception *A,* and the subsequent *B, B* can only follow *A* in my apprehension, while the perception *A* can never follow *B,* but can only precede it. I see, for instance, a ship gliding down a stream. My perception of its place below follows my perception of its place higher up in the course of the stream, and it is impossible in the apprehension of this phenomenon that the ship should be perceived first below and then higher up. We see, therefore, that the order in the succession of perceptions in our apprehension is here determined, and our apprehension regulated by that order. In the former example of a house my perceptions could begin with the apprehension of the roof and end in the basement, or begin below and end above; they could apprehend the manifold of the empirical perception from right to left or from left to right. There was therefore no determined order in the succession of these perceptions. . . . [But] in the apprehension of an event there is always a rule which makes the order of successive perceptions necessary. . . . Thus only can I be justified in saying, not only of my apprehension, but of the phenomenon itself, that there exists in

8 Ibid., A 116.

> it a succession, which is the same as to say that I cannot arrange the apprehension otherwise than in that very order. . . .
>
> If therefore experience teaches us that something happens, we must always presuppose that something precedes on which it follows by rule. Otherwise I could not say of the object that it followed, because its following in my apprehension only, without being determined by rule in reference to what precedes, would not justify us in admitting an objective following. It is therefore always with reference to a rule by which phenomena as they follow, that is as they happen, are determined by an antecedent state, that I can give an objective character to my subjective synthesis (of apprehension); nay, it is under this supposition only that an experience of anything that happens becomes possible.[9]

Thus, Kant proved that all events in the world we experience have to be causally connected. Let us review the steps of his argument. First, Kant showed that the mind connects ("synthesizes") its sensations into objects that last through time. It does this through apprehension, reproduction, and recognition. Second, this connecting of sensations into objects shows that our mind is unified. Third, because the mind is unified, it *must* connect its sensations together. Fourth, one of the connections the mind must impose on its sensations is the connection of cause and effect, for our sensations would not seem to us to be sensations of independently changing objects unless they were causally connected to one another.

Hume, then, was wrong. Hume said that the laws of the sciences are not well founded, in particular the laws of causality: We have no evidence that events must always be causally connected to one another. However, Kant proved that all events we experience in the world outside of us *must* be connected by causal laws. For that world is a world that the mind puts together out of its sensations by bringing these sensations together into a single mind. To bring sensations together so that they seem to be sensations of independently changing objects, the mind must connect them by causal relations. The mind, that is, *must* use the category of cause and effect to connect our sensations so that they appear to us as the independently changing world of trees, oceans, mountains, and stars that we see around us. Only by recognizing that we construct the world in our mind in this way, Kant says, can we escape Hume's skepticism about the causal laws of science.

Kant called the world as it appears in our minds the phenomenal world and distinguished it from the noumenal world. The noumenal world is the collection of things as they exist in themselves apart from our perception of them in our mind. Clearly, we can never know what the noumenal world is like: All we can know is the phenomenal world of things as they appear to us after they have been organized by the mind.

What about Hume's skepticism about God? Reluctantly, Kant agreed that we cannot *prove* that there is a God. The cosmological proofs for God, Kant pointed out, say that God must exist because God had to "cause" the universe. But the only causality in the universe is the causality our own minds put there; the concept of a cause is merely a category of the mind, nothing more. So, we cannot appeal to causality to prove that God exists. Other metaphysical arguments for the existence of God, Kant held, make similar illegitimate use of concepts that are merely categories of the mind. None of these metaphysical arguments are valid proofs of the existence of God.

But Kant's views on God do not end here. Kant attempted to show that the existence of God should be accepted on the basis of our moral commitments. To understand this aspect of Kant, we must examine his views on morality.

Two Versions of the Categorical Imperative of Morality

Kant argued that a person is moral to the extent that he or she follows a principle he called the **categorical imperative**: "I ought never to act unless I can will my maxim to serve as a universal law." For Kant, a "maxim" is the reason a person has for doing something. And a maxim "serves as a universal law" if every person consistently acts on that reason. So, the categorical imperative is the moral principle that whenever I do something, my reasons for doing it must be reasons that I would (and could) be willing to have everyone act on. For example, suppose that I wonder whether I should help the needy, and my reason for being reluctant to help them is simply that I do not want to take the trouble. According

9 Immanuel Kant, *Critique of Pure Reason*, trans. Friedrich Max Müller (New York: Macmillan, 1896), 774, 155–160.

to Kant, I must ask myself this: Would I be willing to have everyone refrain from helping others when they did not want to take the trouble? Clearly, I would *not be* willing to have everyone do this because I myself might need the help of others in some situations. Therefore, it would be wrong for me to refrain from helping those in need. Kant claims that sometimes it is absolutely *impossible* for everyone to act on the immoral reasons we are tempted to act on. In such cases, it is absolutely immoral to act on those reasons:

> The ordinary reason of humanity in its practical judgments agrees perfectly with this, and always has in view the principle here suggested. For example, suppose that I ask myself: Would it be morally permissible for me to make a promise I do not intend to keep when I am in trouble? . . . The shortest and most unerring way for me to discover whether a lying promise is consistent with duty is to ask myself: Could I will to have my maxim (that is, the principle, "I will get out of my difficulties with false promises") serve as a universal law, for myself as well as for others; and would I be able to say to myself, "Everyone may make a false promise when he finds himself in a difficulty that he cannot escape in any other way"? As soon as I ask myself these questions, I become aware that although I might desire to lie, I could not will to have lying become a universal law. For if lying promises became the rule, there would soon be no promises at all. There would be no promises because people would stop believing each other when they said that they intended to keep their promises; and if one person over hastily accepted the lying promise of another, that person would soon learn to do the same thing to others. So as soon as my maxim became a universal law, it would destroy itself.
>
> I do not, therefore, need any great genius to see what I have to do so that my will can be morally good. Even if I have very little experience of the world, even if I cannot prepare for all contingencies ahead of time, all I have to ask myself is this: Could you will to have your maxim serve as a universal law? If not, then you should not act on that maxim.[10]

How does Kant argue for the categorical imperative? For Kant, moral right and wrong depend on the interior motives on which the person acts. Kant argues that to the degree that a person is interiorly motivated merely by self-interest or by the pleasure he gets from an action, the action "has no moral worth." A person's behavior has moral worth only to the extent that the person is motivated by "duty"—that is, by the belief that all human beings ought to act this way. Consequently, an action has moral worth only to the extent that the person is motivated by reasons that he or she feels everyone else can and ought to act on.

Kant claimed that the categorical imperative could be expressed in a second way: "Act in such a way that you always treat humanity, whether in your own person or in the person of any other, never simply as a means, but always at the same time as an end." Never treat people *only* as means but always also as ends. By this, Kant means that we should never treat people only as tools to be manipulated or forced into serving our interests. Instead, we should always treat people as ends—that is, as free rational persons who must be given the opportunity to decide for themselves whether they will go along with our plans:

> A man who is thinking of making a lying promise will realize that he would be using others merely as means because he would not be letting them participate in the goal of the actions in which he involves them. For the people I would thus be using for my own purposes would not have consented to be treated in this way and to that extent they would not have participated in the goals to be attained by the action. Such violations of the principle that our humanity must be respected as an end in itself are even clearer if we take examples of attacks on the freedom and property of others. It is obvious that the person who violates such rights is using people merely as means without considering that as rational beings they should be esteemed also as ends; that is, as beings who must be able to participate in the goals of the actions in which they are involved with him.[11]

According to Kant, this second way of expressing the categorical imperative is really equivalent to the first. The first version says that what is morally right for me must be morally right for others, or that

10 Immanuel Kant, *Grundlegung zur Metaphysik der Sitten* [*Groundwork of the Metaphysics of Morals*], in *Immanuel Kant Werkausgabe*, vol. 7, ed. Wilhelm Weischedel (Frankfurt, Germany: Insel Verlag Wiesbaden, 1956), 28–30. This translation copyright © 1987 by Manuel Velasquez.

11 Ibid., 62.

everyone must be treated the same. The second version says that just as I give myself the opportunity to decide what I will do, I must also give others the same opportunity or, again, that everyone must be treated the same. However, unlike the first version, the second version emphasizes that morality requires us to respect the freedom of all rational persons.

The Moral Argument for God's Existence

Kant points out that if the categorical imperative defines morality, then morality and happiness do not necessarily coincide. For the morally good person is the one who follows the categorical imperative even when this is not in her self-interest and even when she takes no pleasure in doing so. Consequently, morally good people often suffer and fail to get what is in their self-interest. On the other hand, evil people who consistently pursue their self-interest and pleasure, even by taking advantage of others, often prosper. In this world, good people who deserve happiness often do not receive it, whereas evil people who do not deserve it do receive it.

This mismatch between morality and happiness is wrong, Kant holds, and all of us believe that it ought not to be this way. In fact, we feel an obligation to seek a world where the good prosper and the evil do not, and our sense of obligation requires us to believe that such a world is possible. Kant calls such a perfect world a *summum bonum*, the supremely good state of affairs. But, he says, only a good God could bring such a perfect world into existence (perhaps in another life). So, if we believe such a world is possible (and we have an obligation to believe it is), we must assume that God exists. Thus, although we cannot prove that God exists, morality forces us to assume so:

> We ought to endeavor to promote the *summum bonum*, which, therefore must be possible. Accordingly, the existence of a cause of all nature, distinct from nature itself, and containing the principle of this connection, namely the exact harmony of happiness with morality, is also *postulated*. . . . The *summum bonum* is possible in the world only on the supposition of a Supreme Being having a causality corresponding to moral character. Now a being that is capable of acting on the conception of laws is an *intelligence* (a rational being), and the causality of such a being according to this conception of laws is his will; therefore the supreme cause of nature, which must be presupposed as a condition of the *summum bonum*, is a being which is the cause of nature by *intelligence* and *will*, consequently its author, that is God. . . . Now it was seen to be a duty for us to promote the *summum bonum*. Consequently it is not merely allowable, but it is a necessity connected with duty as a requisite, that we should presuppose the possibility of this *summum bonum*. And as this is possible only on condition of the existence of God, it inseparably connects the supposition of this with duty; that is, it is morally necessary to assume the existence of God.[12]

Thus, Kant shifted the argument for God's existence away from metaphysics, where every other philosopher had placed it. Other philosophers had assumed that God's existence had to be proved by relying on metaphysical concepts such as the concept of causality, and such arguments had been ruthlessly demolished by the skepticism of Hume. Kant tried to show that these arguments had to fail because metaphysical concepts are merely categories in our minds; they can tell us nothing about things as they are in themselves. Instead, Kant claimed, we must believe in God on the basis of our moral commitments: Morality forces us to hold that God exists. For morality tells us that good people must be rewarded and evil ones punished, and only a God could bring about such a *summum bonum*. By thus placing belief in God in the realm of morality, Kant hoped, belief would be secure from the attacks of Humean skepticism.

Despite his very ordinary life, then, Kant's philosophy was truly revolutionary. Kant taught us to believe that the world conforms to the categories of the mind, whereas we had always assumed that the mind must conform its categories to the world. He taught us that morality requires us to respect the freedom of others whether or not this pleases us and, consequently, that being moral and being happy may not coincide in this life. And he taught us to believe in God on the basis of morality instead of on the basis of metaphysical arguments. These were truly new ways of looking at the universe, new ways of thinking about ourselves and the world in which we live. It is hard to imagine a more revolutionary view of our situation.

---

12 Immanuel Kant, *Critique of Practical Reason*, trans. T. K. Abbott (London: Longmans Green, 1927), 220–222.

QUESTIONS

1. In your own words, explain Kant's problem: "How are *a priori* synthetic judgments possible?"
2. Summarize in your own words how Kant tries to show that *a priori* synthetic judgments in geometry and arithmetic are possible.
3. In your own words, why does Kant say that our mind *must* connect its sensations together into objects? Why does Kant say that the mind must connect its sensations into objects that are causally connected? In your view, does Kant really answer Hume?
4. Some people have said that Kant cannot be called a rationalist or an empiricist. Why do you think they say this? Do you see any rationalist elements in Kant? Do you see any empiricist elements?
5. Is Kant's first version of the categorical imperative the same as the **Golden Rule** (Do unto others as you would have them do unto you.)?
6. In your view, what would Kant's categorical imperative imply about the morality of suicide? About the morality of the death penalty? Explain.
7. Do you believe that Kant's argument for accepting the existence of God is correct? Why?

CHAPTER

7 Ethics

Ethics is not a doctrine about how to make ourselves happy but about how we are to be worthy of happiness.
IMMANUEL KANT

OUTLINE AND LEARNING OBJECTIVES

7.1 What Is Ethics?

OBJECTIVE | When finished, you'll be able to:

- Explain what it means to say that ethics is the study of morality.

7.2 Is Ethics Relative?

OBJECTIVE | When finished, you'll be able to:

- Describe and critically evaluate the theory of ethical relativism.

7.3 Do Consequences Make an Action Right?

OBJECTIVE | When finished, you'll be able to:

- Explain, evaluate, and use the theories of ethical egoism, act utilitarianism, and rule utilitarianism.

7.4 Do Rules Define Morality?

OBJECTIVE | When finished, you'll be able to:

- Explain, evaluate, and apply scriptural divine command theories, natural law theory, Kantian ethics, and Buddhist ethics.

7.5 Is Ethics Based on Character?

OBJECTIVES | When finished, you'll be able to:

- Explain, evaluate, and use virtue ethics.
- Explain and critically evaluate the ethic of caring as a feminist ethic.

7.6 Can Ethics Resolve Moral Quandaries?

OBJECTIVE | When finished, you'll be able to:

- Apply ethical theories to the moral issues of abortion and euthanasia.
- Engage in moral reasoning that uses ethical theory and avoids fallacious moral thinking.

Chapter Summary

© iStockphoto.com

7.7 Readings: Fyodor Dostoyevsky, "The Heavenly Christmas Tree"
Peter Singer, "Famine, Affluence, and Morality"

7.8 Historical Showcase: Nietzsche and Wollstonecraft

7.1 What Is Ethics?

Our moral decisions are an inescapable part of who we are. Listen to the voices of these young men and women:

> All the other times when I did care about [birth control], when I was so afraid, I didn't get any satisfaction out of it at all, even during the whole intercourse. It seemed so one-way. Here I'm so wrapped up in being scared and he's getting the good end of it. He's not really worrying about what's going to happen to you. He's only worrying about himself. This time I think what I really thought was if you don't think about it, maybe you'll get something out of it. So I guessed it wouldn't be a hassle, I wouldn't worry about it. And I did get a lot more out of it, not worrying about it. I had thought about getting birth control pills with my boyfriend before, but that worked to where it was a one-way street for his benefit, not for mine. It would be mine because I wouldn't get pregnant, but safe for him, too, because I wouldn't put him on the spot. So I get sick of being used. I'm tired of this same old crap; forget it. I'm not getting pills for his benefit. So I never got them and I never thought I would have to 'cause I wasn't looking for anyone since I was tired of being used. Sex was a one-way street. He gets all the feelings, girls have all the hassles. She gets more emotional and falls head over heels while he could give a damn. I'm sick of it, so I thought, Hang it all [and got pregnant].[1]
>
> I was 26 and she was 22. . . . For her it was the second [abortion]. . . . She was 16 the previous time, and the guy had blamed her and was cruel about it. Having to go through it again traumatized her. I didn't know what to do. It numbed me out. My feelings for her and about her were pretty twisted. . . . She broke up eventually with me in a cut-and-dried, cold fashion, which I think was the result of the abortion. . . . To this day, I feel loss. I have a lack of understanding as to why it's so hard for me to accept how I feel, the pain or hurt or whatever it is. I want to derail it, but I think about it when I'm alone or when somebody brings it up. I don't really allow the feeling, even now, as I talk about it. I'm knotting in the stomach, uptight. . . . I feel guilty. Morally, in this day and age, it's not the end of the world. I don't see it as taking life away. I feel guilty in the sense that it's an unpleasant situation. You did start something, but I don't feel it's killing. If I did, I'd go nuts, I suppose.[2]
>
> [After this abortion,] I'd like to get married and have a baby, but I doubt I ever will. I look too much for love and adoration, and I get them mixed up with sex. I guess I do it to get people to validate me. . . . [After the abortions,] I never think about the babies at all. . . . I remember a conversation I had with a friend who'd just had an abortion. It's just an embryo, I told her, preferring to use the clinical definition. It's not a being, just a bunch of splitting cells. My friend said, "It's murder. How can you deny it's a life? It's murder, but it's justifiable homicide." . . . I agree with her, of course, but I just won't admit it. . . . Truth is hard to take, and I just don't know if I'm ready for it.[3]

These remarks remind us of the personal and moral questions we all must face: questions about the morality of sexual relationships, about the ethics of using

1 Quoted in Kristin Luker, *Taking Chances: Abortion and the Decision Not to Contracept* (Berkeley: University of California Press, 1975), 127–128.
2 Quoted in Arthur B. Shostak and Gary McLouth, *Men and Abortion* (New York: Praeger, 1984), 86.
3 Quoted in Linda Bird Franke, *The Ambivalence of Abortion* (New York: Random House, 1978), 63.

people, about taking responsibility for the consequences of our actions, about the morality of abortion. They also remind us of the public decisions we must make as a society: whether to allow women to have abortions, whether to force unwed fathers to support their children, whether to provide sexual education in grade schools, whether to provide welfare to unwed mothers. We can answer these questions only on the basis of our moral values. Much of what we are and do, in fact, is determined by our moral values because our values shape our thoughts, feelings, actions, and perceptions.

QUICK REVIEW
We daily face moral questions that should be answered by values we have chosen for ourselves.

Our values are, to a large extent, absorbed from the society around us: from family and friends; from television, radio, and the Internet; from books and magazines, from Church and school. As children we adopt the values of our culture without thinking, much like how we learn to speak our native language, or learn the rules of good manners, or the customs of our social groups. Yet given the large and pervasive influence our values have on who we are, what we believe, and what we do, this unreflective embrace of values is not necessarily a good thing. To unthinkingly adopt the values proposed by those around you is to live your life according to the values they have chosen for you and not according to those you have chosen for yourself. The fundamental question is this: Will you live the life that other people want you to live and do what other people want you to do, or will you move through your life on a road you have mapped out for yourself? Will you live someone else's life, or will you live by values you have chosen for yourself?

To examine your values, to shape and rethink them in the light of your own experience and your own reasoning, is the philosophical task of ethics, the subject of this chapter.

Ethics is the study of morality. It is a branch of philosophy that tries to determine what things in life are morally good and which actions are morally right. So ethics deals with morality, but it is not the same as morality. **Morality** consists of the standards that an individual or a group has about what is right and wrong or good and evil. Your moral standards include, for example, your beliefs about whether it's wrong to lie to your friends or wrong to tell one friend what another told you in confidence, about whether it's moral to cheat on your girlfriend or your boyfriend, about the morality of forcing sex on an unwilling partner, about racism and sexism, about whether its wrong to cheat on a test, and whether suicide, abortion, or euthanasia are wrong. Generally speaking, moral standards deal with matters to which we attach great importance because they involve serious harm or injury to others or to oneself. The moral standards most of us have against lying, theft, rape, enslavement, murder, child abuse, assault, slander, fraud, suicide, greed, gluttony, the use of addictive drugs, and lawbreaking all plainly deal with matters that we feel are important because they involve the infliction of serious harm to others or to oneself.

As we suggested earlier, ethics "studies" these kinds of moral standards. A person engages in ethics when a person examines his or her moral standards or the moral standards of society and asks whether these standards are reasonable or unreasonable, whether they are supported by good reasons or poor ones or no reasons at all. A person starts to do ethics when she takes the moral standards that she has absorbed from her family, her church, her society—and critically evaluates those standards: Do the standards really make sense? What are the reasons for or against these standards? Why should I continue to believe in them? What can be said in their favor, and what can be said against them? Are they reasonable or stupid? You may have once asked yourself, for example, whether you should tell your friend the truth about her boyfriend or lie to her. Telling the truth would just hurt her feelings and make her upset with you. So is it sometimes permissible to lie? Are some things—such as people's feelings—more important than telling the truth?

Why is honesty between friends important, anyway? What makes lying wrong? Is lying wrong because lying injures people? Then, is lying right when telling the truth will hurt people more? What makes something right and wrong, and why are these so important?

QUICK REVIEW
Ethics is the study of morality; it involves reflecting on one's moral standards or the moral standards of a group or a society, and asking whether they are reasonable.

When a person asks these kinds of questions about her moral standards or about the moral standards of her society, she has started to do ethics. Ethics, then, is the study of moral standards that aims at developing standards that we believe are reasonable, standards that we have thought about ourselves and that we have decided for ourselves are justified. It is, in short, the attempt to ensure that the standards we live by are truly our own standards, chosen because we ourselves believe they are reasonable, and not just those that others have chosen for us and that we have unthinkingly accepted.

We begin our study of ethics by looking at an important challenge to ethics. This is the theory philosophers call ethical relativism, which holds that moral right and wrong depend on the society or culture to which you belong. As you will see, this theory implies that we cannot say that one group's moral beliefs are any better or worse than another's. But as you will also see, the theory of ethical relativism carries with it a number of serious problems.

QUESTIONS

1. What values or personal qualities are important to you?
2. Do you feel that you have chosen your own moral values, or have your moral values been imposed on you by your parents, school, peers, and society? To the extent that your moral values are imposed on you, can you do anything about changing them? What?
3. Explain the difference between ethics and morality.

PHILOSOPHY AT THE MOVIES

Watch *The Woodsman* (2004), which recounts the story of Walter, a convicted sex offender just released from prison, who, trying to start a new life with Vickie who's aware of his history, finds he can escape neither himself nor his past. What values do you think should guide Vickie as she tries to decide how to relate to Walter? Should Walter be allowed to start a new life as he wants to do? Why or why not?

7.2 Is Ethics Relative?

Ethics is not the only way to study morality. Sociology, anthropology, psychology, and other social sciences also study morality. But the social sciences study morality through a descriptive or factual investigation of moral behavior and beliefs. These social sciences are concerned with how people *in fact* behave or what people *in fact* believe about moral right and wrong. Ethics, on the other hand, asks how people *ought* to behave or what people *ought* to believe about moral right and wrong. For example, anthropologists tell us that the Inuit (Eskimos) used to abandon their elderly on the ice and allow them to die of starvation and exposure. They also inform us that in certain tribes in Nigeria, when twins are born one of the infants is killed.[4] Anthropology, as such, does not try to determine whether it was right or wrong for the Inuit

4 Helen L. Ball and Catherine M. Hill, "Twin Infanticide," *Current Anthropology*, vol. 37, no. 5 (December 1996), 856–863.

to abandon their elderly or for African tribes to kill a twin at birth. Ethics, on the other hand, tries to answer the question of whether it is *morally right* for the Inuit, in their circumstances, to abandon their elderly, or whether killing twins is *right* for African tribes, in their circumstances. The social sciences ask what people actually do or actually believe about moral right and wrong, whereas ethics asks what people ought to do or ought to believe about moral right and wrong.

Although ethics and the social sciences study morality in very different ways, both have addressed one important issue: moral diversity. Many anthropologists have emphasized how different the moralities of different societies are. For example, many societies think that slavery is unjust, whereas others have felt slavery is permissible; some societies believe that infanticide is wrong, but other societies practice it frequently; some see female circumcision as a moral obligation while others condemn the practice, referring to it as "female genital mutilation." In fact, societies differ about the morality of abortion, polygamy, patricide, slavery, suicide, nepotism, sexual and ethnic discrimination, genocide, homosexuality, euthanasia, pornography, pedophilia, and the torture of animals. This diversity of moral standards has led many anthropologists to embrace a view called *descriptive relativism.* Descriptive relativism holds that different societies or cultures have different moralities and that what the people of one society or culture believe is morally wrong, people of other cultures believe is morally right. Although certain questions still surround the issue (for example: What are the boundaries of a "culture"), descriptive relativism is generally accepted as true. Some philosophers and anthropologists, however, have gone a step beyond descriptive relativism and embraced *ethical relativism.*

QUICK REVIEW
Descriptive relativism affirms that societies differ in their moral standards.

Ethical relativism (also referred to as "moral relativism") is the view that moral right and wrong depends on a person's society or culture. That is, ethical relativism is the view that claims about moral right and wrong are really claims about what is morally right or wrong according to a specific society or culture. The ethical relativist holds that each society has its own morality that its members internalize, and a form of behavior is morally right for a person if and only if the morality of that person's society approves of that kind of behavior.

QUICK REVIEW
Ethical relativism is the view that what is morally right or wrong depends on one's culture or society and that there is no single correct set of moral standards that everyone should follow everywhere and always.

Ethical relativism differs from descriptive relativism. As we noted, descriptive relativism holds that what people *believe* is morally right and wrong differs from one society to another. Ethical relativism, however, holds that what *actually is* morally right and wrong differs from one society to another. According to the moral relativist, the only moral standards each of us can use to judge right and wrong are the moral standards of our culture and the standards of our culture determine what is morally right and wrong for each of us. Moreover, because the only moral standards people can use to evaluate right and wrong are those of their own culture, there is no way people can stand apart from their culture and objectively determine that the standards of one culture are morally right and those of another are morally wrong. The standards of one culture are neither more nor less justified than those of another, and there is no single set of "correct" moral standards that everyone everywhere should follow.

QUICK REVIEW
Moral or ethical relativism argues that because societies differ in the moral standards they accept, there is no single correct set of moral standards everyone should adopt; instead, people should follow the standards that their own society accepts.

The main argument in support of ethical relativism appeals to descriptive relativism and goes something like this: If there were a single set of "correct" moral standards of right and wrong by which everyone should live, then the moral standards people use to determine right and wrong would not differ from one society to another. But the moral standards people use to determine right and wrong clearly differ from one society to another (as descriptive relativism holds). So there is no single set of correct moral standards of right and wrong by which everyone should live. The only moral standards there are, then, are those that each person absorbs from their society's culture, and these are the standards by which each must live. Here is how the anthropologist Melville J. Herskovits summarized the argument for ethical relativism (which he referred to as "cultural relativism") after explaining that European and African cultures had different moral standards:

> Differences of this sort, and the many others that have been revealed by the cross-cultural approach, have led us to a concept technically called "cultural relativism." This concept holds that there is no absolutely valid moral system, any more than there is an absolutely valid mode of perceiving the natural world. The traditions of a people dictate what for them is right and wrong, how they are to interpret what they see and feel and hear, and they live according to these imperatives . . . How does the individual come to know the values of his society? These are learned through a process that I have been forced, for want of a better word, to call enculturation. In its essence, this is . . . socialized learning, to which all human beings are exposed. Most of the enculturative process is effortless; we learn our cultural lessons so well that our knowledge is internalized and comes to have a strong emotional as well as cognitive content.[5]

Notice two points that Herskovits makes. First, he claims that no moral system can be said to be "absolutely valid," i.e., there are no moral standards that all people ought to live by; there are only the standards of each person's own culture. Second, he claims that what is right or wrong for a person is whatever that person's culture or "traditions" say is right or wrong. And third, he claims that the moral standards a person accepts are acquired through a process of "enculturation." The implication of this third point is that our moral standards have no more of a rational basis than those of any other culture: they are merely the traditions that happen to have been handed down to us by our ancestors.

Yet the theory of ethical relativism has been subjected to intense criticism. Consider, first, that ethical relativism claims that something is morally right for a person if the moral system of that person's culture says it is morally right. But this claim seems to be wrong. Suppose that it is a fact that all members of my culture hold that abortion is morally right. Then, apparently, abortion would have to be morally right for me, regardless of what I might think. Or suppose that everyone else in my culture believes that slavery is right. Then it would be wrong for me to think that slavery is unjust. Indeed, if my society's beliefs determine what the correct morality is for me, then it seems that I can never criticize my own society's beliefs. Since, according to ethical relativism, the moral norms of my society define what is right or wrong for me, the theory would not only give me no way to criticize the moral norms of my society, it would also require that I conform to those norms. For the ethical relativist, morality must be, as Herskovits says, "conformity to the code of the group."

Another problem with ethical relativism that critics often raise, is a problem with the argument that is supposed to prove it. The ethical relativist argues that the many cultural disagreements about moral matters show that no morality is valid for all societies. But Philosopher James Rachels points out a problem with this argument:

> The fact that different societies have different moral codes proves nothing. There is also disagreement from society to society about scientific matters: in some cultures people believe that the earth is flat, and that evil spirits cause disease. We do not on that account conclude that there is no truth in geography or in medicine. Instead, we conclude that in some cultures people are better informed than in

---

5 Melville J. Herskovits, *Cultural Relativism: Perspectives in Cultural Pluralism,* Frances Herskovits, ed., (New York: Random House, 1972).

> others. Similarly, disagreement in ethics might signal nothing more than that some people are less enlightened than others. At the very least, the fact of disagreement does not, by itself, entail that truth does not exist. Why should we assume that, if ethical truth exists, everyone must know it?[6]

Yet another objection to ethical relativism is that if ethical relativism is true, then moral disagreements would be impossible. This is a strange result because the relativist argues that ethical relativism is true *because people and societies disagree* about moral issues. But consider this: The relativist holds that claims about moral right and wrong are really claims about what is morally right or wrong according to one's culture. So suppose you and I are arguing about abortion because you say abortion is wrong, and I say abortion is not wrong. Then, according to the ethical relativist, all you are saying is that abortion is wrong according to the standards of *your* culture, and all I am saying is that abortion is not wrong according to the standards of *my* culture. But then we don't disagree! You are just talking about your culture's standards, and I am talking about my culture's standards, so there is no real disagreement because we are talking about two different things. Moreover, just as individuals cannot disagree with each other about their moral judgments, according to the ethical relativist, societies too cannot have moral disagreements with each other. For when the members of one society say something is right, they are, according to the relativist, just talking about what their culture accepts, and anyone who "disagrees" will really be talking about what their culture accepts. We cannot argue about what is really or "absolutely" morally right or wrong, we can only talk about what this or that culture believes is morally right or wrong.

There are other problems with ethical relativism. Is it really true that there are no moral standards that all societies recognize? Think about it. If a society is going to survive, don't its members have to accept some moral standards about how they should behave toward one another? Won't a society collapse if its members don't recognize the moral standard to refrain from arbitrarily murdering their neighbors? Won't the language of a society collapse if its members don't recognize the moral standard of telling the truth? Won't a society's ability to make contracts and agreements collapse if its members don't recognize the obligation to keep one's promises? Although societies may differ in many of their moral beliefs, aren't there certain basic moral standards that all societies have to accept just to survive?

QUICK REVIEW
Problems with ethical relativism include these: (1) Since ethical relativism claims that the moral standards of one's society determine what is right and wrong, it implies that those standards cannot be questioned. (2) From the fact that societies differ in the moral standards they accept, it does not follow that there is no correct group of moral standards. (3) If claims of right and wrong are claims about one's own society, then claims of right and wrong cannot disagree with each other. (4) There are some moral values that all societies must accept if they are to survive.

Moreover, even when two societies seem to have very different moral standards, at a deeper, more fundamental level, the two societies may share the same moral values. Take "twin infanticide," the practice of killing one of the two babies when twins are born which, as we noted earlier, was common in certain Nigerian tribes but condemned by most Western societies. Western societies condemn infanticide of any kind because they value human life. Does this mean that societies that practice twin infanticide do not value human life? Not necessarily. Anthropologists have found that societies that permit twin infanticide exist in harsh and demanding physical environments where food is scarce and malnourishment is widespread. In such circumstances, "The feeling is that the mother cannot successfully nurse both twins and that if she tried both would die. Through infanticide, at least one twin has a chance."[7] It is not just the twin's lives that are at risk: "In attempting to nurse and carry two infants, the mother's health might also suffer, with consequences for other children in the family."[8] So societies that permit twin infanticide apparently do so because they, too, value human life. Nevertheless, to secure the value of human life in their harsh environments, such societies must resort to the extreme measure

6 James Rachels, "Can Ethics Provide Answers?" *Hastings Center Report* 10, no. 3 (June 1980): 34.
7 Ball and Hill, "Twin Infanticide," op. cit., 858.

of twin infanticide. Nigerian tribes, then, may share the same fundamental moral values we have. But their different circumstances or their different beliefs about the world may lead them to accept as moral certain practices that would be immoral in our more affluent circumstances.

In spite of the many objections to ethical relativism, we should not reject the theory altogether. A fundamental point the theory is trying to make is that we should be tolerant of the moral beliefs of others. In particular, we should not assume that our own moral beliefs are the correct ones or even the best ones. The moral beliefs embedded in a culture different from our own have been fashioned over many centuries in response to the particular circumstances of that culture. Societies that face extreme hardships must adapt to those hardships with moralities that may look very different from ours. Yet their moralities may be trying to achieve the same basic human values for which we strive. In fact, some societies may have hit upon moral outlooks that are much better responses to the world than our own. We should, then, be tolerant and respectful of those different moral outlooks.

Yet having respect and tolerance does not mean that we cannot criticize and evaluate the moral beliefs of other cultures and of our own culture. A relativist like Herskovits claims that we "internalize" our moral standards by just absorbing them from our culture without reasoning about them. To a large extent this is true. Yet it is always possible for us to think about the standards we have "internalized" and to rationally evaluate them. For example, we can ask whether our own moral beliefs or those of our own groups—family, friends, society—are reasonable, whether they are consistent, whether they look toward the true well-being of our society, whether they conform to the facts of human nature, whether they respect the dignity of persons, and whether they help produce admirable moral characters. We can also ask these same questions of the moral beliefs of other cultures. Asking questions like these may lead us to conclude that our own moral beliefs are defective and that the moral beliefs of other societies are more reasonable than ours are. By reasoning in this way, we are attempting to figure out what is "really" or "absolutely" right or wrong. Ethical relativism, which says that your culture must determine your moral beliefs, would not allow you to reach this conclusion.

We can't explore ethical relativism any further. Whether or not we agree with ethical relativism, each of us must still decide what we ought to do and how we ought to live. Such decisions require that we have some reasonable moral standard on which to base our decisions. So, whether or not you accept ethical relativism, the question remains: What are reasonable beliefs to hold about how I ought to live?

QUESTIONS

1. Explain the difference between cultural relativism and ethical relativism. Do you think that the fact that people disagree about moral right and wrong shows that ethical relativism is true? Explain.

2. During World War II, the Nazis in Germany believed that exterminating Jews and homosexuals was morally justifiable. Would an ethical relativist say that it was morally right to invade Nazi Germany to prevent the Germans from exterminating Jews and homosexuals? Explain.

3. Listen to some of your friends discussing or arguing about some moral issue—that is, some issue that involves right and wrong or good and evil. On the basis of how they argue about the issue, would you say that they are relativists or absolutists? Next, ask them directly whether they are relativists or absolutists. Do any of your friends seem

8 Ibid.

to be absolutists when they argue about a moral issue, yet say that they are relativists? Explain what you think is going on in such cases.

PHILOSOPHY AT THE MOVIES

Watch *Nowhere in Africa (Nirgendwo in Afrika)* (2001) in which Walter, a Jew living in Germany during the Nazi era, travels to Africa as World War II is about to break out. When he has his family join him there, he discovers that, while his daughter Regina quickly adjusts to their new home, his wife, Jettel, dislikes Africa and their life there. List the many ethical issues this movie raises. Was it wrong for Jettel to agree to the British soldier's request? Was it wrong for Walter to insist the family return to Germany? Does this film depict cultural relativism? Ethical relativism? Does the film imply or reject the idea that people of different cultures ultimately have the same values?

Movie with a related theme: *Enemy Mine* (1985).

7.3 Do Consequences Make an Action Right?

Consider this true story:

> Matthew Donnelly was a physicist who had worked with X-rays for thirty years. Perhaps as a result of too much exposure, he contracted cancer and lost part of his jaw, his upper lip, his nose, and his left hand, as well as two fingers from his right hand. He was also left blind. Mr. Donnelly's physicians told him that he had about a year left to live, but he decided that he did not want to go on living in such a state. He was in constant pain—one writer said that "at its worst, he could be seen lying in bed with teeth clenched and beads of perspiration standing out on his forehead." Knowing that he was going to die anyway, and wanting to escape his misery, Mr. Donnelly begged his three brothers to kill him. Two refused, but one did not. The youngest brother, 36-year-old Harold Donnelly, carried a .30-caliber pistol into the hospital and shot Matthew to death.[9]

When questioned, Harold Donnelly said that he did not feel that killing his brother was immoral. It was much better for his brother to die than to suffer the terrible consequences of continuing to live. The consequences justified the killing.

Traditionally, many ethicists have contended that we should decide moral right and wrong by looking at the consequences of our actions. If the consequences are good, the act is right. If the consequences are bad, the act is wrong. Thus, a **consequentialist theory** measures the morality of an action by how good or bad its consequences are. In particular, consequentialists consider the amount of non-moral good and the amount of non-moral bad that an action produces. The morally right action is the one that produces more good (or less bad) non-moral consequences compared to any other action that could be performed in its place. Notice that consequentialist theories say we evaluate the morality of an action by examining only its *non-moral* consequences. Consequentialist theories consider only the non-moral consequences of actions, because it would be circular to explain an immoral action as one that has immoral consequences. To avoid this kind of circularity, consequentialists insist that when evaluating the morality of an action, we should consider only the non-moral consequences of the action. To evaluate whether it was moral or immoral for Harold to shoot his brother Matthew, for example, a consequentialist might look at the *pain* that Matthew no longer had to suffer once Harold killed him, the *sorrow* that Harold will probably feel when Matthew was dead, the

9 James Rachels, *The Elements of Moral Philosophy* (New York: Random House, 1986), 82.

suffering Harold would undergo if he has to go to prison, the *distress* Harold might feel knowing he killed his own brother, the *satisfactions* Harold and his family would feel knowing that Matthew was no longer suffering, and so on. But the consequentialist would not consider whether Harold's action caused an injustice, or whether it was selfish, or whether it would lead to future immoral actions.

QUICK REVIEW
Consequentialist ethical theories hold that a morally right action is one that produces more non-moral good or less non-moral bad consequences than any other action.

A consequentialist theory determines what is right on the basis of what is good. But we need to distinguish two kinds of goods: instrumental goods and intrinsic goods. Instrumental goods are good because they get us other good things. Intrinsic goods are good in themselves; they are desirable for themselves and not because of what else they might get us. For example, having a wisdom tooth removed is not a pleasant experience, but it is instrumentally good because it is a means to the good of having healthy teeth; on the other hand, the pleasures of skiing are intrinsically good because they are desirable for themselves and not for some further good they can get us. (Some things, of course, are both instrumentally good and intrinsically good.) Similarly, an intrinsically evil or bad thing is undesirable for itself, while an instrumentally evil or bad thing is undesirable because it will produce some other evil.

According to consequentialists, the rightness or wrongness of our actions depend on how much intrinsic good they produce and how much intrinsic evil they diminish. So what things are intrinsically good? Consequentialists have not agreed on an answer to that question. Nevertheless, a good number have adopted **hedonism**, the view that only pleasure or happiness is intrinsically good and that only pain or unhappiness is intrinsically evil. All other things, hedonists claim, are good to the extent that they bring us pleasure or diminish pain. For example, the ancient Greek philosopher Epicurus (341–270 BCE) argued that pleasure is the chief goal of life. But we must weigh our pleasures carefully to ensure that they do not later cause us greater pain:

To read more of Epicurus' principal doctrines, go to CourseMate for this text and browse by chapter or philosopher.

QUICK REVIEW
Hedonist egoists such as Epicurus claim that good consequences are those that produce pleasure, whereas bad consequences are those that produce pain.

> The purpose of all our actions is to be free from pain and fear, and, when we have attained this, the tempest of the soul will be laid to rest, since a living creature does not need to search for something that is lacking, nor to look for anything else by which the good of the soul and of the body will be fulfilled. . . . We speak of pleasure as the starting point and the goal of a happy life because it is our primary kindred good and because every act of choice and aversion originates with it, and because we come back to it when we judge every good by using the feeling of pleasure as our criterion. . . . And since pleasure is our first and kindred good, we should not choose every pleasure whatsoever, but pass over pleasures when they will later produce greater pains. And we should consider a pain superior to other pleasures when submission to the pain brings us as a consequence a greater pleasure. Although all pleasure is good because it is a kindred good, not all pleasure should be chosen, just as all pain is evil and yet not all pain is to be shunned. It is by measuring one against another, and by looking at their conveniences and inconveniences, that all these matters must be judged. . . When we say, then, that pleasure is the purpose of life, we do not mean the pleasures of the prodigal or the pleasures of sensuality. . . . I mean, instead, the pleasure that consists in freedom from bodily pain and mental agitation. The pleasant life is not the product of one drinking party after another or of having sex with men or women, or of eating the delicacies of a luxurious meal. On the contrary, it is the result of sober thinking—namely, investigation of the reasons for every act of choice and aversion, and elimination of those false ideas about the gods and death which are the chief source of mental disturbances.[10]

10 Epicurus, "Letter to Menoeceus," in *The Philosophy of Epicurus*, ed. George K. Strodach (Evanston, IL: Northwestern University Press, 1963), 175.

Many consequentialists claim that other things besides pleasure are intrinsically good. Some consequentialists have claimed that knowledge, or power, or beauty are intrinsic goods. Some associated the good with self-realization, the full development of people's capacities and abilities. Some Christian consequentialists have identified the good with love, and have argued that actions are right to the extent that they increase the amount of love in the world. Other philosophers have been "pluralists," holding that there are many kinds of intrinsic goods. The point is that consequentialists are not necessarily hedonists.

An obvious question arises here: In examining the consequences of an action, are we supposed to consider the consequences an action has only for the person performing the action? Or are we supposed to consider the consequences the action will have on everyone? If you evaluate the consequences just for Harold in the preceding illustration, for example, your judgment will be different than if you evaluate the consequences for Harold, for his brother Matthew, for Matthew's family, for the doctors and nurses in the hospital, etc. In deciding what to do, then, should we evaluate consequences only for the agent, or should we consider the effects on everyone who is affected by the agent's action? The answers to these questions form the basis for two kinds of consequentialist theories: egoism and utilitarianism.

QUICK REVIEW
Some consequentialists hold that intrinsic goods include not just pleasure but also knowledge, power, beauty, self-realization, or love.

Ethical Egoism

Some ethicists claim that in deciding the morality of an action, we should consider only the good and bad consequences for the agent, i.e., for the person who performs the action. These ethicists are called *egoists*. **Ethical egoism** contends that we act morally when we act in a way that best promotes our own long-term interests. Ethical egoism recognizes that our actions have consequences that can be good or bad for us. So, ethical egoism says that an action is morally right when it produces more good and fewer bad consequences for ourselves than any other action we could perform in its place. Here is how American libertarian author Harry Browne argued for ethical egoism:

> The Unselfishness Trap is the belief that you must put the happiness of others ahead of your own. Unselfishness is a very popular ideal, one that's been honored throughout recorded history. . . . So perhaps we should look more closely at the subject to see if the ideal is sound . . .
>
> Each person always acts in ways he believes will make him feel good or will remove discomfort from his life. . . . One man devotes his life to helping the poor. Another one lies and steals. . . . One woman devotes herself to her husband and children. Another one seeks a career as a singer.
>
> In every case, the ultimate motivation has been the same. Each person is doing what he believes will assure his happiness. . . . For the thief and the humanitarian each have the same motive—to do what he believes will make him feel good. In fact, we can't avoid a very significant conclusion: Everyone is selfish. Selfishness isn't really an issue, because everyone selfishly seeks his own happiness.[11]

QUICK REVIEW
Ethical egoism claims that a morally right action is one that produces more good and fewer bad consequences for oneself than any other action.

Brown is saying that the belief that you should put the happiness of others ahead of your own happiness is false. He is claiming, in other words, that you should put your own happiness ahead of the happiness of others. Why should you always put your own happiness ahead of the happiness of others? Because, Browne argues, everyone else always puts their own happiness ahead of the happiness of others.

---

11 Harry Brown, *How I Found Freedom in an Unfree World* (Macmillan Publishing Co., 1973); copyright owned by Pamela Wolfe Browne at http://www.trendsaction.com, email PLWBrowne@HarryBrowne.org.

Browne's argument relies on a view about people that is called "psychological egoism"—a view we discussed in Chapter 2—which holds that people always act out of self-interest. Notice that *ethical* egoism holds that people *ought* to act out of self-interest, while *psychological* egoism holds that people *always* act out of self-interest (whether they ought to or not). In the preceding passage, Browne is arguing that since psychological egoism is true—since everyone always acts out of self-interest—it follows that you (and everyone else) ought to always act out of self-interest. Browne does not tell us why he thinks psychological egoism logically implies ethical egoism; the two, after all, are different. Browne may think that since everyone else always acts out of self-interest, in fairness you too should act out of self-interest. Or he might think that morality requires you to do only what you are able to do; since you are only able to act out of self-interest, morality must require you to act out of self-interest. But notice that it is odd to say that everyone *ought* to be selfish if everyone already *is* selfish. If everyone is going to act selfishly anyway, why would you have to tell them that they ought to do so?

Problems of Ethical Egoism. Many philosophers believe that arguments like Browne's are mistaken because the theory of psychological egoism is mistaken. One argument for psychological egoism—for claiming that people always act out of self-interest—is that when people do something, it is always the case that they wanted to do it. Since people always do what they want to do, the psychological egoist argues, their actions are always motivated by selfishness. But American philosopher James Rachels criticizes this argument in the following passage:

> It is the *object* of a want that determines whether it is selfish or not. The mere fact that I am acting on *my wants* does not mean that I am acting selfishly; that depends on *what* it is that I want. If I want only *my own good*, and care nothing for others, then I am selfish; but if I also want *other people to be well-off and happy*, and if I act on that want, then my action is not selfish.[12]

QUICK REVIEW
Problems with ethical egoism include: It is unclear what is morally right when people's interests conflict; ethical egoism is not impartial because it favors one's own interests, so it is not consistent with a moral point of view.

Critics also claim that ethical egoism runs into problems when people's interests conflict. Suppose we are competing against each other, say in a race, so that it is in your interests to win the race, and it is in my interests to win the race. The philosopher Kurt Baier (1917–2010) argued that in situations like these ethical egoism leads to contradictions and so has to be false. If we are competing in a race, then it is in my interests to win, so (according to ethical egoism) I ought to win. However, claims Baier, it is wrong to prevent someone from doing what he ought to do, so it is wrong for you to prevent me from winning. Yet it is also in your interests to win the race, so it is also wrong for you to not prevent me from winning. But then ethical egoism has led us into a contradiction: that it is wrong for you to prevent me from winning and also wrong for you to not prevent me from winning.

Some ethicists think that the most serious weakness of ethical egoism is that it is inconsistent with "the moral point of view." Any theory of ethics, these critics argue, must evaluate people's actions from the moral point of view. By the "moral point of view," they mean the point of view of someone who is impartial, i.e., who is not biased in favor of one individual or group over another. Kurt Baier, for example, described the moral point of view as the point of view "of an independent, unbiased, impartial, objective, dispassionate, disinterested observer."[13] Ethical egoism,

12 Rachels, op. cit., 58.

13 Kurt Baier, *The Moral Point of View* (Ithaca, NY: Cornell University Press, 1958), 201.

Baier and others have argued, is clearly not consistent with the moral point of view because it claims that you should be partial to your own interests.

QUICK REVIEW
Utilitarianism claims that a morally right action is one that produces more good and fewer bad consequences for everyone than any other action. For traditional utilitarians good consequences consist of pleasure or happiness, bad consequences consist of pain or unhappiness.

Utilitarianism

In contrast to ethical egoism, utilitarianism asserts that the standard of morality is the promotion of good for everyone and not just for oneself. In brief, utilitarianism claims that a morally right action is one that produces more good or fewer bad consequences for everyone than any other action that could be performed in its place. Again, as with all consequentialist positions, good and evil mean nonmoral good and evil.

Jeremy Bentham (1748–1832) and John Stuart Mill (1806–1873) are considered the classic proponents of utilitarianism. The utilitarianism they developed claimed that only pleasure or happiness has intrinsic value, while pain or unhappiness are intrinsically evil. Their utilitarianism was, in short, based on a hedonistic philosophy. In the words of John Stuart Mill, author of the short but influential work, *Utilitarianism*:

> The creed which accepts as the foundation of morals, Utility, or the Greatest Happiness Principle, holds that actions are right in proportion as they tend to promote happiness, wrong as they tend to produce the reverse of happiness. By happiness is intended pleasure, and the absence of pain; by unhappiness, pain, and the privation of pleasure. . . . [T]he happiness which forms the utilitarian standard of what is right in conduct, is not the agent's own happiness, but that of all concerned.[14]

© UCL Art Collections, University College London, UK/The Bridgeman Art Library

Jeremy Bentham: "Nature has placed mankind under the governance of two sovereign masters, *pain* and *pleasure*. They govern us in all we do, in all we say, in all we think. The principle of utility recognizes this subjection."

As we noted earlier, utilitarian consequentialists can claim that other things besides happiness or pleasure are intrinsically good and should be considered when determining moral right and wrong. Nevertheless, traditional utilitarians—such as Mill and Bentham—claim that pleasure and the absence of pain are the fundamental goods on which morality depends. Because we will here focus primarily on traditional utilitarianism we will assume that *good* refers to pleasure or happiness.

To read more from Bentham's *Introduction to the Principles of Morals and Legislation*, go to CourseMate for this text and browse by chapter or philosopher.

Like Mill's *Utilitarianism*, Bentham's *Introduction to the Principles of Morals and Legislation* is a classic explanation of the utilitarian theory of ethics. Bentham's treatise unequivocally asserts that pleasure and pain are the fundamental criteria of moral right and wrong; notice, however, that although he begins by appealing to

14 John Stuart Mill, *Utilitarianism*, (1871), excerpts from chapter 2.

psychological egoism, he ends by claiming that the principle of utility requires us to act in the interests of "the community":

QUICK REVIEW
Bentham claims pain and pleasure govern us in all we do; his principle of utility says that morally right actions are those that increase the happiness or pleasures of the community, and that the pleasures and pains our actions produce for everyone should be measured so that we can choose the one that produces the greatest quantity of pleasure or the least quantity of pain for everyone affected by the action.

> Nature has placed mankind under the governance of two sovereign masters, *pain* and *pleasure*. It is for them alone to point out what we ought to do, as well as to determine what we shall do. On the one hand the standard of right and wrong, on the other the chain of causes and effects, are fastened to their throne. They govern us in all we do, in all we say, in all we think: every effort we can make to throw off our subjection, will serve but to demonstrate and confirm it. In words a man may pretend to abjure their empire: but in reality he will remain subject to it all the while. The *principle of utility* recognizes this subjection. . . .
>
> By the principle of utility is meant that principle which approves or disapproves of every action whatsoever, according to the tendency which it appears to have to augment or diminish the happiness of the party whose interest is in question: or, what is the same thing in other words, to promote or to oppose that happiness. . . .
>
> By utility is meant that property in any object, whereby it tends to produce benefit, advantage, pleasure, good, or happiness (all this in the present comes to the same thing), or (what comes again to the same thing) to prevent the happening of mischief, pain, evil, or unhappiness to the party whose interest is considered; if that party be the community in general, then the happiness of the community. . .
>
> An action then may be said to be conformable to the principle of utility or, for shortness sake, to utility (meaning with respect to the community at large), when the tendency it has to augment the happiness of the community is greater than any it has to diminish it. . . . Of an action that is conformable to the principle of utility one may always say . . . that it . . . ought to be done, or . . . that it is right it should be done . . . [or] that it is a right action.
>
> These [following] are the circumstances which are to be considered in estimating a pleasure or a pain . . . [When] the value of a pleasure or a pain is considered, it will be greater or less, according to seven circumstances: to wit . . .
>
> 1. Its *intensity*.
> 2. Its *duration*.
> 3. Its *certainty* or *uncertainty*.
> 4. Its *propinquity* or *remoteness*.
> 5. Its *fecundity* [the chance it has of being followed by sensations of the *same* kind: that is, pleasures, if it be a pleasure; pains, if it be a pain].
> 6. Its *purity* [the chance it has of not being followed by sensations of the *opposite* kind: that is, pains, if it be a pleasure; pleasures, if it be a pain].
>   And one other; to wit:
> 7. Its *extent*; that is, the number of persons to whom it *extends*; or (in other words) who are affected by it.
>
> To take an exact account then of the general tendency of any act by which the interests of a community are affected, proceed as follows. Begin with any one person of those whose interests seem most immediately to be affected by it: and take an account: Of the value of each . . . *pleasure* which appears to be produced by it . . . [and] the value of each *pain* which appears to be produced by it. . . .
>
> Sum up all the values of all the *pleasures* on the one side, and those of all the *pains* on the other. The balance, if it be on the side of pleasure, will give the *good* tendency of the act . . . with respect to the interests of *that individual* person; if on the side of pain, the *bad* tendency of [the act].
>
> [Then] take an account of the *number* of persons whose interests appear to be concerned; and repeat the above process with respect to each [person]. *Sum up* the numbers expressive of the degrees of *good* tendency which the act has with respect to each individual . . . to whom the tendency of it is *good* upon the whole . . . ; do this again with respect to each individual . . . to whom the tendency of it is *bad* upon the whole. Take the *balance* which if on the side of *pleasure*, will give the

critical thinking

Is there any problem with Bentham's attempt to combine his claim that pleasure and pain "govern us in all we do" with his claim that the principle of utility requires us to "augment the happiness of the community"?

critical thinking

Bentham assumes that pleasure and happiness have a size and can be measured. Is this assumption plausible?

> general *good tendency* of the act, with respect to the total number or community of individuals concerned; if [the balance is] on the side of pain, [it will indicate] the general *evil tendency* [of the act] with respect to the same community.[15]

Notice how clearly Bentham makes the point that his utilitarian theory requires that we *measure* the *quantity* (or "value") of pleasures and pains an action causes to *everyone* whom the action touches. For according to his theory, the morally right action, from among those available to us in any situation, is the one that will produce the greatest *quantity* of pleasure for everyone or (when all available actions produce more pain than pleasure) the least *quantity* of pain for everyone. In the preceding passage, Bentham suggests that pleasures and pains can be measured by how intense they are, how long they last, how certain they are to occur, how soon they will occur, how likely they are to produce additional pleasures or pains, and how many people will feel the pleasures or pains. Bentham also claims that to determine the total *quantity* of pleasure and pain an action produces, we must first *add* up all of the pleasures it produces, and then *add* up all its pains, and finally *subtract* the *total quantity* of pains from the *total quantity* of pleasures. We must do this for each action that is available to us at the moment, and then choose the action that will produce the greatest quantity of pleasure; but when all the available actions produce more pain than pleasure, we must choose the action that will produce the lowest quantity of pain.

QUICK REVIEW
In Bentham's utilitarianism, good consequences consist of happiness or pleasure, and bad consequences consist of unhappiness or pain; the quantity of pleasure produced by an action is measured by its intensity, duration, certainty, likelihood to produce more pleasure, and so on.

 critical thinking

Bentham and Mill assume that pleasure and happiness are necessarily good. Is this assumption correct? Is pleasure or happiness good for a person when acquired through evil means?

The view that pleasures and pains can be measured and then added and subtracted from each other has been repeatedly criticized. What yardstick can we use to measure pleasures and pains? Moreover, suppose one kind of pleasure (e.g., the pleasure of drinking a beer) is as intense, as long, as certain, etc., as another kind of pleasure (e.g., the pleasure of listening to a Beethoven symphony); must we conclude they are equally valuable? And how can we compare the pleasures and pains you feel, with those I feel? What if I insist that my pleasures and pains are much more intense than yours, while you insist yours are more intense? How can we possibly know who is right?

Perhaps not surprisingly, Mill thought Bentham was too focused on the quantitative aspects of pleasure and pain, and so he suggested that the *quality* of pains and pleasures is as important or perhaps even more important. In particular, Mill argued that the "pleasures of the intellect, of the feelings and imagination, and of the moral sentiments" which only humans can experience have "a much higher value . . . than those [pleasures] of mere sensation" which other animals can also experience:

> It is quite compatible with the principle of utility to recognize the fact, that some kinds of pleasure are more desirable and more valuable than others. It would be absurd that . . . the estimation of pleasures should be supposed to depend on quantity alone. If I am asked, what I mean by difference of quality in pleasures, or what makes one pleasure more valuable than another . . . there is but one possible answer. Of two pleasures, if there be one to which all or almost all who have experience of both give a decided preference, irrespective of any feeling of moral obligation to prefer it, that is the more desirable pleasure. If one of the two is, by those who are competently acquainted with both, placed so far above the other that they prefer it, even though knowing it to be attended with a greater amount of discontent, and would not resign it for any quantity of the other pleasure which their nature is capable of, we are justified in ascribing to the preferred enjoyment

QUICK REVIEW
Mill claimed the quality of pleasures and pains is as important as their quantity when determining what one ought to do, and that the value of two kinds of pleasures depends on the preferences of those who have experienced both; he argues that people prefer the higher over the lower pleasures because they would rather be "a human being dissatisfied than a pig satisfied."

15 Jeremy Bentham, *Introduction to the Principles of Morals and Legislation*, (1823), excerpts from chapters 1 and 4.

> a superiority in quality, so far outweighing quantity as to render it, in comparison, of small account. Now it is an unquestionable fact that those who are equally acquainted with and equally capable of appreciating and enjoying both [higher and lower pleasures], do give a most marked preference to the manner of existence which employs their higher faculties. Few human creatures would consent to be changed into any of the lower animals, for a promise of the fullest allowance of a beast's pleasures; no intelligent human being would consent to be a fool, no instructed person would be an ignoramus, no person of feeling and conscience would be selfish and base, even though they should be persuaded that the fool, the dunce, or the rascal is better satisfied with his lot than they are with theirs. They would not resign what they possess more than he for the most complete satisfaction of all the desires which they have in common with him. . . . It is better to be a human being dissatisfied than a pig satisfied; better to be Socrates dissatisfied than a fool satisfied. And if the fool, or the pig, are of a different opinion, it is because they only know their own side of the question. The other party to the comparison knows both sides.[16]

In this famous passage, Mill claims that one kind of pleasure is more valuable than a second kind if most people prefer the first over the second after they have experienced both. This point is important, for it suggests that the value we give to a particular kind of pleasure should be determined by the value most experienced people would give it. Moreover, he claims, most people would generally prefer the higher pleasures to the lower pleasures, so the higher pleasures are more valuable than the lower ones. You may object that Mill is wrong because you feel most people prefer the "lower" pleasures of sex, food, and drink, over the "higher" pleasures of, say, listening to a Beethoven symphony. But to prove his point, Mill proposes a "thought experiment." Imagine that somehow you were forced to choose between (1) being an animal whose "lower" pleasures were all fully satisfied but who could experience none of the "higher" pleasures, or (2) being a human being who could experience the "higher" pleasures but who was otherwise "dissatisfied." Would you choose (1) or (2)? Mill thinks that virtually everyone would prefer (2), so he concludes that everyone prefers the higher pleasures over the lower ones. (Think about Mill's thought experiment. Do you agree? Why?)

If we accept Mill's view, then when assessing pleasures and pains we must first determine which are "higher" and which are "lower" and give the "higher" pleasures and pains greater values than the "lower" ones. We can then go on to add up the values of all the pleasures produced by each available action and subtract the values of its pains, and, finally, choose the action that will produce the greatest amount of pleasure or happiness (or the least amount of pain or unhappiness).

In developing their utilitarian views, Bentham seems to have had in mind a particular kind of utilitarian theory, termed **act utilitarianism**, while Mill seems to have advocated a different kind called **rule utilitarianism**.

Act Utilitarianism. Act utilitarianism contends that in any situation, the morally right action is the one that will produce the greatest amount of pleasure or the least amount of pain for everyone. In other words, before you act, ask yourself this: What will be the consequences of my action not only for myself but also for everyone else affected by my action? If its consequences are good (that is, if the action will produce more happiness or pleasure than any other action I could perform in its place), then the action is right; if they are bad (that is, if the action will produce

16 Mill, *Utilitarianism*, excerpts from chapter 2.

more unhappiness or pain than the alternatives), then the action is wrong. In effect, for act utilitarians, the end justifies the means. This can raise problems.

Suppose, for example, that you are a judge living in a small town in South Africa many years ago. The police bring a black man before you and charge him with raping a white woman the night before. The woman, who is the only witness, has positively identified him although the rape took place in the dark of night. The rape has incensed the townspeople, and a mob of vigilantes has formed. The mob declares that if you do not agree to sentence the black man to death, they will raid the small black settlement outside the town and kill several dozen black women in revenge. You know that they will carry out this threat and that you have no way of stopping them. A few hours ago, though, by sheer improbable coincidence you happened to be alone at the bedside of a dying friend who—just before dying—confessed that he had committed the rape. It would be useless to bring this utterly improbable story to the mob; they would simply accuse you of trying to get the black man off the hook by making up an unlikely story. What should you do?

QUICK REVIEW
Act utilitarianism claims that the morally right action is the particular act that itself produces more pleasure and less pain for everyone. Act utilitarianism seems to sometimes require injustices and rights violations.

The implications of act utilitarianism are clear: You should sentence the black man to death although you know that he is innocent. By sentencing him to death, you would be sacrificing one innocent life to save several other innocent people; if you declare him innocent, you would be saving one life but condemning several others to death. Utilitarianism here seems to require us to condemn an innocent man to death, which seems terribly unjust and a violation of the innocent man's rights.

Rule Utilitarianism. Some utilitarians have argued that we get into such dilemmas when we apply the "greatest happiness" principle to a *particular act* rather than to the *general rule* that the act is following. What we should be concerned with is following the *rules* that have the best consequences, not with carrying out the *act* that has the best consequences. Mill took this approach when he wrote that "the standard of morality" consists of "the rules and precepts for human conduct, by the observance of which an existence [exempt as far as possible from pain, and as rich as possible in enjoyments] might be . . . secured to all mankind."[17] This approach, called rule utilitarianism, means that we should act so that the *rules* (or standards) governing our actions are those that will produce the greatest happiness for the most people.

For example, courts and judges should operate with the rule "We should never punish people for something they didn't do." Clearly, if everyone followed this rule, it would have good consequences for society: People would know that the legal system would never arbitrarily punish them, and they would not suffer the fear and anxiety of never knowing how the courts would deal with them. And clearly, the opposite alternative—the rule that we can sometimes punish people for things they didn't do—would produce much worse consequences if we all started to follow it because it would create fear, anxiety, and uncertainty. Consequently, say rule utilitarians, the South African judge should stick to the rule that would have the best consequences for everyone over the long term if everyone followed it. He should not condemn the innocent man although condemning this particular man in this particular instance might produce more collective happiness. In short, we should try to find and follow those rules that will have the best consequences for everyone over the long term, instead of trying to do what will have the best consequences at one particular time.

QUICK REVIEW
Rule utilitarianism claims that the morally right action is the one that follows those rules that will produce more pleasure and less pain if followed by everyone. Rule utilitarianism is supposed to not have the wrong implications that act utilitarianism does. Mill was a rule utilitarian.

But is it that simple? Consider, first, the problem of trying to figure out the consequences of promoting one rule over another. What research can establish with

17 Ibid.

certainty that one rule will have better social consequences than another? Given our general ignorance of how societies function, it seems impossible to give definitive answers to this question.

QUICK REVIEW
Critics claim that moral rules will produce more pleasure and less pain if they allow for exceptions, but once moral rules allow exceptions, they have the same wrong implications that act utilitarianism has.

Second, rules that allow for exceptions seem to promise more happiness than rules that don't, but such rules are problematic. We have suggested, for example, that we should follow the rule "We should never punish people for something they didn't do." But wouldn't society be better off in the long run if we promoted instead the rule "We should never punish people for something they didn't do, *except in those instances where punishing them will leave everyone else better off?*" This rule will ensure that we do not *usually* punish innocent people, but it will allow for those exceptions that increase happiness, so this rule should produce more happiness than the first rule. Nevertheless, notice that following this second rule will again cause the judge to execute the innocent black man. Thus, rules that allow for exceptions produce the most happiness, but such rules allow the same injustices and rights violations that act utilitarianism does. It is not clear, then, that rule utilitarianism is really an improvement over act utilitarianism.

Some Implications of Utilitarianism

Despite these difficulties, many people believe that utilitarianism provides a powerful analysis of ethics. To get a better understanding of utilitarianism and its strengths and weaknesses, let us consider what it implies for a moral issue raised at the beginning of this chapter: our sexual behavior.

Sex is central to human life and raises a bewildering variety of moral questions. Are some forms of sexual activity—for example, incest, homosexuality, and adultery—morally deficient, or are there no limits on what is morally permissible in sex? For act utilitarianism, the answer to these questions is straightforward: Any action is morally permissible—in fact, morally obligatory—if it produces a greater balance of pleasure over pain than any other available action. This seems to imply that virtually any sexual activity can be morally permissible—including incest, adultery, and homosexuality—in some circumstances. All sexual activities would be permissible in some circumstances because they are all intensely pleasurable and at least sometimes their pleasures outweigh their harms. Many act utilitarians have reached exactly that conclusion. For example, in *Having Love Affairs*, philosopher Richard Taylor offers an act utilitarian justification of adultery. He argues that extramarital affairs based on love often produce more good than harm for a married person, so they are then morally justified:

QUICK REVIEW
Taylor and other act utilitarians argue that because all sexual activity—including incest, adultery, and homosexuality—usually produces more pleasure and less pain than any other action, all sexual activity can be morally right. To many, this view seems overly permissive.

> The joys of illicit and passionate love, which include but go far beyond the mere joys of sex, are incomparably good. And it is undeniable that those who never experience love affairs, and who perhaps even boast of their faultless monogamy year in and year out, have really missed something.[18]

Taylor goes on to argue that if revealing the affair to one's spouse will injure the spouse and the marriage relationship, then one should conceal the affair. Lying is justified, on act utilitarian grounds, if the net benefits of lying to one's spouse about an affair are greater than those of telling the truth. Other philosophers have used similar arguments to justify gay and lesbian sexual acts. Some have even argued that if the partners are consenting adults who take suitable contraceptive precautions,

18 Richard Taylor, *Having Love Affairs* (Buffalo, NY: Prometheus, 1982), 12.

incest is morally permissible. This approach to sex would seem to rule out only those sexual acts that clearly involve harmful violence or great risks of harm. For example, this approach rules out violent rape or casual sex that risks contracting AIDS or some other venereal disease.

But is this approach to sex too permissive? Are some sexual acts, such as incest, intrinsically wrong? Isn't it immoral for the adulterer to break his marriage promises and then lie about it to his spouse? Perhaps even utilitarians would find Taylor's analysis too facile. Utilitarianism urges us to look beyond the immediate pleasure an action produces for oneself. It says we should also consider the beneficial and harmful consequences that our actions will produce for others now and in the future. When seen in this light, act utilitarianism might condemn many sexual activities—such as incest, adultery, and homosexuality—because of their harmful effects both on the individual involved and, more generally, on society.

In fact, a rule utilitarian approach to the ethics of sexuality focuses on such broader social effects explicitly. It asks whether the long-term social consequences of moral rules that permit a certain type of sexual activity will benefit or harm society. The Ramsey Colloquium developed such an argument against various forms of sex. The Ramsey Colloquium is a group of Christian and Jewish scholars who have argued that moral doctrines that permit adultery, divorce, and homosexuality will prove harmful to society:

> It is important to recognize the linkages among the component parts of the sexual revolution. [W]idespread adultery, easy divorce, . . . and the gay and lesbian movement have not by accident appeared at the same historical moment. They have in common a declared desire for liberation from constraint—especially constraint associated with an allegedly oppressive culture and religious tradition. They also have in common the presupposition that the body is little more than an instrument for the fulfillment of desire, and that the fulfillment of desire is the essence of the self. Finally, they all rest on a doctrine of the autonomous self. We believe it is a false doctrine that leads neither to individual flourishing nor to social well-being.
>
> Marriage and the family—husband, wife and children, joined by public recognition and legal bond—are the most effective institutions for the rearing of children, for the directing of sexual passion and for human flourishing in community. . . . Gay and lesbian "domestic partnerships" should not be socially recognized as the moral equivalent of marriage. Marriage and the family are institutions necessary for our continued social well-being. In an individualistic society that tends to liberation from all constraint, they are fragile institutions in need of careful and continuous support.[19]

QUICK REVIEW
Rule utilitarians such as the Ramsey Colloquium argue that moral rules that prohibit adultery, divorce, and homosexuality will produce more pleasure and less pain than other rules, so it is wrong to engage in adultery, divorce, and homosexuality. Critics argue that it is not clear that such rules will have the consequences the Ramsey Colloquium claims they will.

The members of the Ramsey Colloquium argue that moral rules tolerant of homosexuality, adultery, and divorce have harmful consequences on family structures and society's well-being. They imply that it is wrong to accept and follow such permissive moral rules. But is this rule utilitarian view about the morality of sexual activities correct? Is it clear to you that the acceptance of the moral permissibility of adultery, divorce, and homosexuality will have the harmful effects that critics allege? Some have argued that the reasons for the decline of the family are many and complex, and that it is simplistic to blame this decline on permissive sexual attitudes. The problem with these rule utilitarian arguments, as with almost any utilitarian approach to ethics, is that they place such heavy burdens of information gathering on us. How are we to know exactly what the significant future consequences of our moral rules or our individual actions will be?

19 The Ramsey Colloquium, "Morality and Homosexuality," in *Today's Moral Issues*, ed. Daniel Bonevac (Mountain View, CA: Mayfield, 1996), 272–274.

Despite the questions it raises, utilitarianism identifies an important aspect of morality. It is true that future consequences are difficult to predict. Yet no one can deny that morally upright behavior, including sexual behavior, should attend to the consequences of what we do. We cannot deny that we should try to minimize the future harms that our sexual behaviors might inflict on ourselves and others. The problem, as we have seen, is that consequences are not all that matter in ethics. Therefore, we must turn to different approaches to ethics that can help us discern the other important elements of the moral life.

QUESTIONS

1. Some people argue that everyone is ultimately an ethical egoist. What do they mean by this? Do you agree? Would this prove that egoism is the basis for all ethics?
2. What are the connotations of the word *egoism*? Are these connotations compatible with what you now know about ethical egoism?
3. You and five friends are exploring some caves when a cave-in traps you all in a large chamber. The only way out is a small hole just big enough for a thin person to crawl through. Tom, who is very thick around the waist, is the first to crawl into the hole and gets stuck. For two days you all try to pull or push him out but only wedge him in tighter. The air is becoming hard to breath because oxygen is running out. One of you has a small dynamite charge that you can use to blow his body out of the hole, although this will kill him. You all must decide whether to kill him to save the five of you who are all thin people, or leave him in the hole where he will probably survive once help comes but you five will surely die in the next few hours.

PHILOSOPHY AT THE MOVIES

© Archives du 7eme Art/Photos 12/Alamy

Watch *Extreme Measures* (1996) in which Guy Luthan, a young doctor working in a hospital, comes upon an agitated patient wandering the streets who suffers convulsions and then dies. When Luthan tries to find out where the patient came from, he is accused of a crime and fired by the hospital. This makes him more determined to uncover the patient's background, until he stumbles upon a secret medical project that promises great benefits for humanity.

Movie with related theme: *Abandon Ship!* (sometimes titled *Seven Waves Away*; 1957).

7.4 Do Rules Define Morality?

A **nonconsequentialist theory** maintains that the morality of an action depends on factors other than consequences. The two main types of nonconsequentialist theories are those that propose a single rule to govern human conduct and those that propose multiple rules. Two significant single-rule nonconsequentialist theories are the divine command theory and Immanuel Kant's categorical imperative theory. Buddhist ethics represents a kind of multiple-rule theory.

Divine Command Theory

The **divine command theory** is a nonconsequentialist normative theory that says we should always do the will of God. Whatever the situation, if we do what God commands, then we do the right thing; if we disobey God's commands, then, no matter what the consequences, we do wrong. There are two main types of divine command theories: those that hold that God's commands are found in sacred scriptures and those that hold that God's commands are found in human nature.

Scriptural Divine Command Theories. A divine command theory does not state that we should obey God's laws because in so doing we will promote our own or the general good. Perhaps we will accomplish these ends, but the sole justification for obeying God's law is that God wills it. The theory also does not defend the morality of an action by promising some supernatural reward to the faithful. True, perhaps God will reward the faithful, and perhaps behaving righteously is in one's best long-term interests. But divine command theorists wouldn't justify moral actions on such egoistic grounds.

For divine command theorists, morality is independent of what any individual thinks or likes and what any society happens to sanction. God establishes moral laws; they are eternally true and are universally binding on all people, regardless of whether everyone obeys them. Such God-established laws are generally interpreted in a religious tradition and are often expressed in that religion's sacred scriptures. The Ten Commandments found in the Jewish scriptures are a good example:

critical thinking

Does a divine command theory assume that if God commands something, then we should do it even if it will not achieve any good for ourselves or others? Is this assumption plausible?

> And God spoke all these words, saying, I am the Lord your God . . . you shall have no other gods before me. . . . Remember the Sabbath day, to keep it holy. . . . Honor your father and your mother. . . . You shall not kill. You shall not commit adultery. You shall not steal. You shall not bear false witness against your neighbor. You shall not covet your neighbor's house. You shall not covet your neighbor's wife, or his manservant, or his maidservant, or his ox, or his mule, or anything that is your neighbor's.[20]

But contrast this Judaic view of God's commands with what many Christians today accept as the more significant expression of God's will in the Christian scriptures, the words of Jesus:

> And Jesus lifted up his eyes on his disciples, and said: . . . I say to you that hear, Love your enemies, do good to those who hate you, bless those who curse you, pray for those who abuse you. To him who strikes you on the cheek, offer the other also; and from him who takes away your cloak do not withhold your coat as well. Give to everyone who begs from you; and of him who takes away your goods, do not ask them back again. And as you wish that men should do to you, do so to them.[21]

Finally, contrast these expressions of God's commands in the Christian scriptures with what many adherents of the Islamic faith accept as the expression of God's will in the Koran, the scriptures of Islam:

> Thy Lord has decreed you shall not serve any but Him, and to be good to your parents. . . . And give the kinsman his right, and the needy, and the traveller; and never squander. . . . And keep not thy hand chained to thy neck, nor outspread it widespread altogether. . . . And slay not your children for fear of poverty. . . . And approach not fornication. . . . And do not approach the property of the orphan save in the fairest manner. . . . And fulfil the covenant. And fill up the measure when you measure, and weigh with the straight balance. . . . And pursue not what thou has not knowledge of. . . . And walk not in the earth exultantly. All of that—the wickedness of it is hateful in the sight of thy Lord.[22]

These laws, claim their adherents, apply to everybody everywhere, and their value does not depend on what produces human satisfaction, either individually

20 Exodus 20:2–17.
21 Luke 6:27–31.
22 Sura 17:22–39.

or collectively. The justification of such moral laws is divine authority expressed through humans and their institutions and scriptures.

QUICK REVIEW
Divine command theory is a nonconsequentialist theory that says the morally right action is the one that God commands, for example, in scripture. Critics argue that there are too many conflicting scriptures and that we cannot know which one reports the true commands of God; also, if something is right because God commands it, then even cruelty could be morally right.

However, even a cursory look at scriptural divine command theory reveals some inherent weaknesses. First, and as the preceding samples make excruciatingly clear, different sacred scriptures exist. Which one expresses what God commands? It is true that there is some overlap in what each says. For example, both Judaism and Islam say that God commands us to respect our parents. But they differ in many respects about the specifics of what God commands. How are we to know which of these scriptures is right? Which one should we follow? Beyond that, how do we know that any of these writings represent the inspired word of God? Some assert that the scriptures say so. But isn't it circular reasoning to say that because a book says it's true, it must be true? And what of the fact that all these scriptures assert that they are the true, inspired word of God? Beyond that, can we be sure that God even exists? What help are these scriptural commands to the unbeliever, the agnostic, and the atheist? If morality is following what some religions say are God's commands, does it follow that the unbeliever can have no morality? And if God does exist, can we be sure that God expressed His law in one source and not in another?

There is also a deeper, more fundamental problem, one that we saw when we discussed Plato's *Euthyphro* in Chapter 1. The problem is this: Are actions right because God commands them, or does God command them because they are right? If God commands certain actions *because* they are right, then morality does not depend on God but on a power superior to God that determines what actions are right. This consequence is not acceptable to most believers. On the other hand, if actions are right *because* God commands them, then anything that God commands must be right. Should God command cruelty, then cruelty would be right—a consequence that is also difficult to accept. So whether God commands actions because they are right, or they are right because God commands them, we reach a consequence that is unacceptable.

There is another kind of ethics that also appeals to God's command but that, paradoxically, does not require belief in God. This is natural law ethics.

Natural Law Ethics. Natural law ethics holds that humans should live according to nature. The Stoics, followers of the school of thought originally founded by Zeno around 300 BCE, held a natural law ethic. For example, they believed that there is a kind of universal natural order in the world put there by God that the human mind can discover. To the extent that humans live according to this universal order, particularly as it is exhibited in their own human nature, they will flourish and be happy.

To read more from Epictetus' Discourses, go to CourseMate for this text and browse by chapter or philosopher.

The ancient Stoic philosopher Epictetus (circa 50–130), for example, wrote the following:

> The business of the wise and good man is to live conforming to nature: and as it is the nature of every soul to assent to the truth, to dissent from the false, and to remain in suspense as to that which is uncertain; so it is its nature to be moved toward the desire of the good, and to aversion from the evil; and with respect to that which is neither good nor bad it feels indifferent. . . . When the good appears, it immediately attracts to itself; the evil repels from itself.[23]

Here, Epictetus is saying that if we look at human nature, we will see that it has certain natural tendencies. We have a natural tendency to believe what we discover is

23 Epictetus, *Discourses*, III, 3.

PHILOSOPHY AND LIFE

Embryonic Stem Cell Research

Human embryonic stem cells are cells taken from several-day-old embryos and are capable of turning into virtually any type of human cell, from blood cells to muscle, skin, brain, stomach, heart, pancreatic, or liver cells. Stem cells are perfect for replacing the diseased or injured tissues of patients with spinal cord injuries, heart disease, diabetes, osteoarthritis, and rheumatoid arthritis, and those of burn and stroke victims. Scientists believe that if stem cells from aborted embryos are implanted into the brains of patients suffering from Alzheimer's (which causes memory loss) or Parkinson's disease (which causes tremors, rigidity, and eventually complete paralysis), the embryo's cells could take over the functions the patient's own brain cells can no longer perform, and the patient could recover fully or partially. Researchers believe that stem cells from aborted embryos can be transplanted into the pancreatic tissues of diabetics, into the brain tissues of patients with Huntington's disease, into the spines of patients with multiple sclerosis, into the livers of patients with Hurler's syndrome, or into the tissues of patients suffering from more than 155 genetic disorders and could produce full or partial cures of these crippling illnesses. Some researchers have suggested that injecting stem cells into muscle or skin can enhance these tissues, raising the possibility that athletes could take embryonic stem cell injections to improve their performance or that embryonic cells could be used for cosmetic purposes.

Opponents of abortion have argued that to use, or conduct research on, stem cells is morally wrong because acquiring embryonic stem cells involves aborting or destroying the embryo, which they believe is a human being. In 1995, Congress imposed a ban prohibiting spending federal funds on "research in which a human embryo or embryos are destroyed, discarded, or knowingly subjected to risk of injury or death." After his election, President George W. Bush was lobbied by patient groups, scientific organizations, and the biotechnology industry to lift this ban. Anti-abortion groups urged him not to do so. On August 9, 2001, Bush announced that he would allow federal funding for such research but only on stem cells already in existence, not on any stem cells acquired through future destruction of embryos. Bush's decision left both supporters and opponents of stem cell research unhappy. But on March 9, 2009, newly elected President Barack Obama reversed the Bush policy. Declaring that the previous administration had "forced what I believe is a false choice between sound science and moral values," Obama lifted the ban on using federal funds for stem cell research regardless of the source of the stem cells. Although many scientists celebrated the new policy, opponents of abortion saw it as a defeat for morality on a basic question of human life.

QUESTIONS

1. In your view, is it moral to transplant or conduct research on the cells of aborted embryos? Would it be moral to abort an embryo intentionally to provide researchers with stem cells? Would it be moral to use stem cells to improve athletic performance or for cosmetic purposes?
2. In your judgment, is a ban on the use of federal funds for embryonic stem cell research immoral? Was Bush's 2001 decision immoral? Was Obama's 2009 decision moral?

Source: American Association for the Advancement of Science, "AAAS Policy Brief: Stem Cell Research," http://www.aaas.org/spp/cstc/briefs/stemcells (accessed March 3, 2004); Claudia Kalb, "A New Stem Cell Era," *Newsweek*, online edition, March 9, 2009, http://www.newsweek.com/id/188454 (accessed May 28, 2009).

true, to reject what is false, and to suspend belief about matters we are unsure of. In the same way, we have a natural tendency to desire what we judge is good for us and a natural tendency to feel repelled by what we judge is bad for us. We also have a natural tendency to feel indifferent about what is neither beneficial nor harmful to us. The morally good person, he suggests, is the person who lives according to these basic natural tendencies. The morally evil person is the one who violates these basic tendencies, perhaps by gratifying his cravings for things that his judgment says are bad for him. Moral rightness, then, is conduct that conforms to these natural tendencies.

QUICK REVIEW
Natural law ethics says that human nature has certain natural tendencies and that morally right actions are those that follow these natural tendencies. Because God created these tendencies, following them is doing what God intended us to do.

What does this have to do with God and God's commands? The key idea is that God made human nature. So, if one lives according to what human nature requires, one is living according to what God intended when He made humans. If you live according to your nature, Epictetus says, then you can be "conscious that you are obeying God." In short, the requirements of human nature are the commands of God. Humans can discover those commands by looking at their own nature, and in following these commands they are morally good.

Natural law ethics (including the key idea that to follow human nature is to obey God's will), then, began with the ancient Greeks. Nevertheless, the classical proponent of the idea that reason can discover God's commands by reflecting on human nature is the Christian philosopher/theologian Thomas Aquinas. Aquinas held that because God created the universe, the laws that govern it are laws that God imposed on it. In particular, God imposed on human beings certain "natural laws" through the natural inclinations that He built into human nature when He created humans. The most important of these inclinations are our reasoning abilities:

> Now rational creatures [such as humans] are also subject to God's provident direction, but in a way that makes them more like God than all other creatures. For God directs rational creatures by instilling in them certain natural inclinations and [reasoning] abilities that enable them to direct themselves as well as other creatures. Thus human beings also are subject to God's eternal law and they too derive from that law certain natural inclinations to seek their proper ends and proper activities. These inclinations of our nature constitute what we call the "natural law" and they are the effects of God's eternal law imprinted in our nature.[24]

According to Aquinas, morality arises when our reason becomes aware of the "natural inclinations" that God built into human nature. In particular, Aquinas holds, our reason tells us that we have a moral obligation to pursue those goods toward which we are naturally inclined and to refrain from destroying them:

> A thing is good if it is an end that we have a natural inclination to desire; it is evil if it is destructive of what our nature is inclined to desire. Consequently, those kinds of things that our nature is inclined to desire are perceived by our reason as good for our human nature. And our reason will conclude that those kinds of things ought to be pursued in our actions. But if our reason sees a certain type of thing as destructive of what human nature is inclined to desire, it will conclude that that type of thing ought to be avoided.
>
> We can therefore list the basic [moral] precepts of the natural law by listing the kinds of things that we naturally desire. First, like every other nature, human nature is inclined to desire its own survival. Consequently it is a natural [moral] law that we ought to preserve human life and avoid whatever is destructive of life. Secondly, like other animals, human nature is inclined to desire those things that nature teaches all animals to desire by instinct. For example, all animals have an instinctive desire to come together in a union of male and female, and an instinctive desire to care for their young. [So it is morally right to pursue these things.] Thirdly, human nature is inclined to desire those goods that satisfy our intellects. This aspect of our nature is proper to human beings. Thus, human nature is inclined to desire knowledge (for example, to know the truth about God) and an orderly society. Consequently, it is a natural [moral] law that we ought to dispel ignorance and avoid harming those among whom we live.[25]

critical thinking

Does natural law ethics assume that what happens naturally ought to happen? Is this assumption true?

Thus, by reflecting on our natural human inclinations, we can discover the specific goods that God commands humans to promote: human life, family, knowledge,

---

24 Saint Thomas Aquinas, *Summa Theologica*, I–II, Q. 91, a. 2. This translation copyright © 1978 by Manuel Velasquez.

25 Ibid., I–II, Q. 94, a. 2.

and an orderly society. Actions are morally right when they aim at securing these goods, and they are morally wrong when they aim at destroying these goods.

Some examples might clarify what Aquinas means and might also clarify some important features of natural law ethics. Consider the issue of suicide. Aquinas held that suicide was immoral. But he did not condemn suicide merely because the Christian scriptures say that it is wrong to take one's life. Instead, Aquinas argued that human nature has a built-in inclination to desire life. For example, consider how each of us instinctively wants to stay alive and instinctively avoids life-threatening situations. Because we are naturally inclined to desire life, Aquinas held, our reason knows immediately that life is a fundamental human good that we should not destroy. And because God is the source of this inclination, the requirement that we should not destroy life is His command. Suicide, then, is wrong because it destroys what our reason knows is a fundamental human good and by destroying this good, suicide violates the command of God. Or consider the issue of social injustice, which Aquinas also considered immoral. We are naturally inclined to desire an orderly society, he claimed, because our human nature has a built in inclination to socialize with others in communities that are peaceful, law-abiding, and orderly. But social injustices, he argued, undermine or destroy the social order. Consequently, it is wrong to engage in activities that lead to social injustice. It would be wrong, for example, to support laws or policies that discriminate against minorities or that allow some to starve while others live in luxury. Other kinds of activities, like theft, fraud, assault, and deception, also undermine or destroy social order and so are also immoral.

But what are we to do when there are conflicts among the goods toward which we are inclined? That is, what are we to do when we can secure one good only by destroying another? What should I do, for example, when I can save my life only by destroying another life? Is killing in self-defense wrong? To deal with such conflicts, Aquinas proposed what is now called the "principle of double effect." Aquinas suggested that actions sometimes produce two or more effects. Killing in self-defense results in saving my life and in the destruction of the life of my attacker. When actions have such double effects, Aquinas argued, what matters is one's intention. If one's intention is aimed at saving one's own life and if the evil one inflicts is absolutely necessary to save one's life and is proportional to (i.e., equal to or less than) the value of a human life, it is permissible to "allow" the destruction of life as an unavoidable side effect of preserving one's own life. But it would be wrong for one to deliberately intend or want the death of the other person.

QUICK REVIEW
Aquinas' "principle of double effect" says that when an action has both a good and a bad effect—it produces one good but destroys another—it is morally permissible to perform the action and "allow" the bad effect so long as one's intention is aimed at the good effect and not the bad, and so long as the evil is necessary, and proportional to, the good one achieves.

Today, there are many philosophers who have adapted Aquinas' natural law theory. For example, the British philosopher John Finnis (1940–) presented a sophisticated natural law theory in his book *Natural Law and Natural Rights.*[26] But Finnis argues that we need to revise Aquinas' four fundamental goods and expand them to include seven basic forms of good:

> Now besides life, knowledge, play, aesthetic experience, friendship, practical reasonableness, and religion, there are countless objectives and forms of good. But I suggest that these other objectives and forms of good will be found, on analysis, to be ways or combinations of ways, of pursuing (not always sensibly) and realizing (not always successfully) one of these seven basic forms of good, or some combination of them.[27]

Clearly, natural law theory does not raise all of the problems that scriptural divine command theories raise. For example, natural law theory does not have to

26 John Finnis, *Natural Law and Natural Rights* (Oxford: Oxford University Press, 1980), 90.
27 John Finnis, "Natural Law and Unnatural Acts," *Heythrop Journal* 11, no. 4 (October 1970): 380.

deal with the problem that many different scriptures exist, each claiming to tell us what God commands. In fact, one of the most important advantages of natural law theory is that one does not even have to believe in God to accept the theory. For the theory claims that morality is based on living according to our human nature, and this claim does not require belief in God. All people, whether they believe in God or not, can discover what morality requires by reflecting on their own human nature. Those who believe in God, of course, will take the additional step of concluding that because God made human nature, it embodies what God intends for humans. But the unbeliever can reject this additional step and still agree that our human nature is the best guide to moral right and wrong.

Neither does natural law theory have to deal with the problem that God might command something that is bad for us. For in natural law theory, whatever is good for our nature is what God commands. And what God commands when He makes our nature will be what is good for us.

QUICK REVIEW
Critics of natural law ethics say that it is not clear why we are morally obligated to follow our natural inclinations, it is not clear exactly what goods we are naturally inclined toward, and it is not clear that one can keep from intending a foreseen evil as the principle of double effect says one must.

Nevertheless, natural law theory has had its critics. For example, critics have asked why we should be morally obligated to pursue the goods that our natural inclinations seek. Why are our *inclinations* the measure of what is naturally good for us? Isn't it at least logically possible that we might be naturally inclined to things that are not necessarily good for us? Children often have desires for things that are bad for them. Isn't it possible for adults to similarly have inclinations toward what is evil? In addition, doesn't natural law have some damaging ambiguities? For example, natural law doesn't seem sure exactly what the fundamental goods are supposed to be. Aquinas argued that there were four, whereas modern natural law philosopher Finnis has opted for a rather different group of seven. How are we to decide not just how many there are, but exactly what they are supposed to be?

Finally, consider the problem of conflicts between fundamental goods—situations in which pursuing one good requires destroying another. Clearly, such conflicts are common in human life. Aquinas uses the principle of double effect to deal with such conflicts. He claims that we must only intend to preserve the one good and not intend to destroy the other good. But, in such cases, can we really limit our intention to the pursuit of the good? When I am forced to kill a person in self-defense, for example, don't I really intend to destroy the life of that person? When I foresee that one of my actions will have many effects, don't I necessarily intend those effects to happen? But if the principle of double effect doesn't work, then won't the problem of conflicts between fundamental goods end up destroying natural law theory?

Implications of Divine Command Ethics

Although divine command ethics has several limitations, many philosophers believe that, if used carefully, it can give us significant insights into the morality of important aspects of human life. One of the topics that divine command theorists have addressed at some length, in fact, is the topic we earlier discussed in relation to utilitarian theory: sexual activity. What light can natural law theory shed on the morality of sex?

For natural law theory, the injunction that we should "live according to nature," when applied to sexual activity, implies that we must take seriously the basic good toward which sexual activity is naturally oriented. Some natural law ethicists have argued that it is clear that sex is naturally oriented toward the good of procreation which is part of the basic good of family. Consequently, it is immoral to engage in any sexual activity that does not remain open to this good. John Finnis argues as follows:

> [T]he choice to exclude the possibility of procreation while engaging in intercourse is always, and in an obvious and unambiguous way . . . a choice directly and immediately against a basic value. . . . And if a question is raised about solitary

> sexual acts or sexual intercourse outside the vagina (whether homo- or heterosexual), the [natural law] response . . . turns on the fact that all sexual activity . . . [must retain] . . . a sufficient openness and respect towards [this basic procreative value]. . . . [S]ome sexual acts are (as types of choice) always wrong because [they are] an inadequate response, or direct closure, to [this] basic procreative value.[28]

In this natural law approach, a sexual activity is immoral and "unnatural" if it cannot result in pregnancy or if we take steps to block the possibility of a pregnancy. This would include all homosexual activities, as well as oral sex, anal sex, masturbation, bestiality, sex with dead bodies, sex with inanimate objects, and sadomasochistic sex.

For many people, the moral condemnation of such forms of sex is exactly right. They believe that natural law theory (at least as Finnis interprets it) correctly identifies the fundamental purpose of sex—reproduction—and correctly evaluates sexual activities in terms of this fundamental purpose. Moreover, many people feel that, unlike utilitarianism, this approach correctly shows that there are certain forms of sexual activity that are intrinsically immoral whatever the consequences. Consider, in fact, that many people (rightly or wrongly) describe as "unnatural" precisely those forms of sex that the natural law condemns: sex with animals, sex with the dead, sadomasochistic sex, and so on.

But can't sex serve many purposes other than procreation, such as pleasure, intimacy, play, and communication? Why should reproduction be singled out as the only morally relevant purpose of sex? Suppose that in some sense, say a biological or functional sense, the purpose of our sexual organs is reproduction. Still, why should this biological fact make it immoral to use them for other purposes? In an evolutionary or biological sense, the purpose of teeth is to chew food and the purpose of eyes is to see. But is there anything immoral about using one's teeth to pry the top off a beer bottle or to use one's eyes to flirt? Although evolution has adapted our sexual organs for the function of procreation, these organs also have other functions, including that of providing pleasure. What is wrong with using them solely for the latter purpose?

However, there are other, more liberal natural law approaches to sex. For example, Donald Levy provides a different approach to sexual matters. He rejects the view that sexual activities are necessarily wrong when they cannot issue in reproduction. Instead, he argues, sexual activities are unnatural and immoral when they deny a basic good without necessity and do so for the sake of sexual pleasure. This understanding of natural law, Levy suggests, does not imply that, say, homosexuality is unnatural:

> QUICK REVIEW
> Finnis, a natural law ethicist, claims that sexual acts that "exclude the possibility of procreation" are "unnatural" and so morally wrong; other natural law ethicists, such as Levy, argue that sexual acts are not necessarily wrong when they exclude procreation, but only when they destroy a basic human good.

> [W]hat I count as the basic human goods can be rather completely listed: life, health, control of one's bodily and psychic functions, the capacity for knowledge and love. . . . I suggest that an unnatural act is one that denies a person (oneself or another) one or more of these basic human goods without necessity, that is, without having to do so in order to prevent losing some other basic human good. . . . Denying oneself or another a basic human good without some other basic human good being expected or intended to be made possible thereby is always wrong. . . .
>
> The perverted is a subclass of the unnatural. When a person denies himself or another one of the basic human goods (or the capacity for it) and no other basic human good is seen as resulting thereby, and when pleasure is the motive of the denial, the act is perverted. When the pleasure is sexual, the perversion is sexual.
>
> The child molester is a case of sexual perversion. . . . [T]he young girl sexually initiated by an older person can easily be traumatized; that there is no way of undoing the harmful effects with the ease and certainty with which they were induced establishes the correctness of classifying the case as one of sexual perversion. . . .
>
> That perversion degrades is a necessary truth . . . as I have defined perversion. . . . Although the definition of [perversion] does not, by itself, produce criteria strong

28 John Finnis, "Natural Law and Unnatural Acts," *Heythrop Journal* 11, no. 4 (October 1970): 380.

> enough to allow us to be decisive in the important case of homosexuality, the definition [does] seem to require rape to be included among the sexual perversions . . . [because] rape does degrade.[29]

Levy is suggesting here that we do not have to interpret natural law as saying that the morality of a sexual act depends on whether the act can result in procreation. Instead, he suggests, natural law should be seen as saying that a sexual act is morally wrong only if it *destroys* a concrete instance of a basic human good. For example, child molestation is wrong because it destroys the psychic functioning of the child (which is an aspect of the child's human life). Rape is wrong because it destroys the psychic functioning of the adult victim. It is difficult to say, on the other hand, that homosexuality is destructive of a basic human good, and so that it is unnatural or morally wrong. Levy's natural law approach, with its more tolerant view of homosexuality and, perhaps, of other forms of sex, seems more aligned with contemporary views of sexual morality.

Yet perhaps we should not so quickly dismiss the more conservative natural law views of philosophers like Finnis. It is true that the natural law view of Finnis has significant problems. Still, his view alerts us to an aspect of sex that is morally important, namely, the relationship of sexual intercourse to reproduction. For many people, the fact that sexual intercourse can result in pregnancy raises important moral issues for anyone considering sex.

Philosophers have not been indifferent to the objections brought against natural law theory and other divine command theories. In the eighteenth century, Immanuel Kant attempted to present a nonconsequentialist theory based not on devine authority but on human reason alone.

QUESTIONS

1. If you were to make a list of the fundamental human goods toward which we are "naturally inclined," what would you include in the list? What would you exclude? What criteria would you use to decide what belongs on the list and what does not?
2. Aquinas interprets the injunction that we should "live according to nature" to mean that we should respect the fundamental goods toward which reason sees we are naturally inclined. Suggest other ways of understanding the injunction that we should "live according to nature" that are different from the way that Aquinas interprets the injunction. What are the implications of your interpretation of "live according to nature" for the morality of sex?
3. Although natural law theory is usually not classified as a consequentialist theory, many people have argued that it has consequentialist elements. In what ways is natural law theory consequentialist? In what ways is it not consequentialist?

© Pictorial Press Ltd./Alamy

PHILOSOPHY AT THE MOVIES

Watch *Breaking the Waves* (1996) in which Bess, a sweet, simple girl who speaks to God, marries Jan, a big man who works on an oil rig and who, when paralyzed from the neck down in a work accident, asks Bess to sleep with another man, a request that Bess sees as a sacrifice God wants and that she believes will save Jan. Does this film hold that actions are right because God commands them or that God

29 Donald Levy, "Perversion and the Unnatural as Moral Categories," *Ethics* 90, no. 2 (January 1980): 191–202. Reprinted by permission of The University of Chicago Press.

commands certain actions because they are right? Do the bells at the end indicate that God was truly speaking to Bess? Is it morally right for Bess to do what she believes God commands her to do? Does this movie suggest any problems with divine command ethics, or does it support divine command ethics?

Kant's Categorical Imperative

Of all philosophers, the eighteenth-century German philosopher Immanuel Kant has had the greatest influence on contemporary ethics. Kant was a deeply religious man. Yet he rejected divine command theories of ethics as well as utilitarian theories. Kant held that a person has the ability to decide for herself what she will do and her reasons for doing it. Kant called this ability to choose for oneself "autonomy of the will," and he argued that a legitimate theory of ethics must recognize our autonomy. He contrasted this with heteronomy. *Heteronomy* is allowing someone or something else to determine what we do. The trouble with divine command theories is that they say that the Church or the Bible or human nature should determine what we will do. Utilitarian theories are worse. Utilitarian theories say that our desires for pleasure should determine our actions. So, both divine command theories and utilitarian theories are heteronomous and fail to recognize human autonomy. A proper theory of ethics, Kant held, should respect our freedom to choose what we will do, subject only to the constraint that what is morally permissible for us to do should also be permissible for everyone else. Kant argues for these views by analyzing the notions of "a good will," moral "duty," and what he calls "maxims" which are the reasons we have for doing what we do.

QUICK REVIEW
Kant claimed that autonomy—the freedom to choose for oneself what one will do and the reasons on which one will act—is the heart of ethics. To let something or someone else decide what one will do is "heteronomy" and is wrong because moral action should depend on one's own will—one's own decision-making ability.

The "Good Will." The "will," for Kant, is our ability to choose what we will do and the reasons on which we will act. As such, the will is at the core of who a person is and why the person behaves as he or she does. So if we want to determine what a morally good person is and what the morally good person does, we must begin by asking what a morally good will is. That is precisely where Kant begins one of his greatest works, the *Foundations of the Metaphysics of Morals.* In the passage that follows, which is taken from the first pages of this work, Kant argues that only a good will—that is, a good person—is "good without qualification" so we ought to strive to have a good will (i.e., to be a good person).

> It is impossible to think of anything in the universe—or even beyond it—that is good without qualification, except a good will. Intellectual talents such as intelligence, cleverness, and good judgment are undoubtedly good and desirable in many respects; so also are character traits such as courage, determination, and perseverance. But these gifts of nature can become quite evil and harmful when they are at the service of a will that is not good. It is the same with gifts of fortune such as power, wealth, honor, and even health and that general well-being and contentment we call happiness. These will produce pride and conceit unless the person has a good will, which can correct the influence these have on the mind and ensure that it is adapted to its proper end. Moreover, an impartial rational spectator would not feel any pleasure at seeing a person without a good will enjoying continuous happiness. Thus it seems that having a good will is a necessary condition for even deserving happiness.[30]

QUICK REVIEW
The will is a person's ability to make decisions on the basis of reasons; Kant argues that nothing is good without qualification except a good will; and a good will is one that chooses what is morally right because it is right and not because it is enjoyable or in one's self-interest.

30 Immanuel Kant, *Grundlegung zur Metaphysik der Sitten* [*Groundwork of the Metaphysics of Morals*], in *Immanuel Kant Werkausgabe,* vol. 7, ed. Wilhelm Weischedel (Frankfurt, Germany: Insel Verlag Wiesbaden, 1956), 18. This translation copyright © 1987 by Manuel Velasquez.

QUICK REVIEW
Kant argued the following: (1) A person with a good will does what is right because he believes it is morally right to do it. (2) To believe it is morally right to do something, is to believe it is what all human beings ought to do. (3) Therefore, a person with a good will—a good person—is one who does what is right because he believes it is what all human beings ought to do.

Kant believed that since a good will is good without qualification, we should strive to have a good will. But what is a "good will"? Kant claims that a good will (a good person) is *not* one that does its moral duty because doing so is in its self-interest, nor because it wants the pleasure or enjoyment it gets from doing its duty. Instead, a good will carries out its moral duty simply because it believes it is its moral duty. In other words, a morally good person does what is right because he believes it is the morally right thing to do. Kant argues for this claim by asking us to consider examples of people who do what is morally right, but some do it for the sake of self-interest, some for the enjoyment it gives them, and some do it because they believe it is their moral duty.

> We must next develop the idea of a will that is esteemed as good in itself . . . To do this, we will look at the notion of doing one's moral duty, which is related to the notion of a good will . . .
>
> We begin by considering how we sometimes do what we have a moral duty to do, but we do it not *because* we believe it is our duty, but for some other reason . . . For example, a shop-keeper has a moral duty not to overcharge his immature customers. But not over-charging is in his self-interest . . . because by charging everyone the same, even a child will be willing to buy from him. The shop-keeper does his moral duty. But he does not do it *because* he believes it is his duty nor *because* he enjoys treating his customers well . . . He does it out of self-interest [and we can see his action has no moral value].
>
> Secondly, consider that we each have a duty to continue living, and almost everyone also enjoys living. But for that reason, the anxious care most people take to continue living, [we can see,] has no intrinsic [moral] value. . . . People continue living, which is their moral duty, but they don't do so *because* they believe it is their moral duty. On the other hand, imagine a person who has suffered so much adversity and . . . sorrow that he no longer enjoys living and wishes he were dead. Yet he continues living . . . because he believes that is his moral duty. [It is clear that] such a person's reason for living does have moral value.
>
> Thirdly, think about how we each have a moral duty to help others when we can. Now some people have such sympathetic natures that . . . they enjoy . . . making others happy. I claim that when one helps others *only* for the sake of the enjoyment one gets from doing so, . . . one's action has no true moral value. Such actions have no more moral value than anything else one might do *solely* for the enjoyment one will get from doing it, such as seeking to be honored. . . . On the other hand, imagine someone whose mind is clouded by a sorrow that has extinguished all feelings toward others, yet who has the power to help those in distress. Suppose he tears himself out of his dead insensibility and helps them not because it is enjoyable for him, but because he believes he has a moral duty to help them. [Clearly] his action will then have genuine moral value . . .
>
> So we are left . . . with this proposition: our actions have true moral value when . . . [they are done] not because we enjoy doing them, [nor because they are in our self-interest], but because we believe we have a moral duty to do them.[31]

Duty and the First Version of the Categorical Imperative. The person with a morally good will, then, is the person who does what is right because he believes it is his moral duty to do it. But what does it mean to say that something is one's moral duty? Kant answers this question by pointing out that if I believe a certain kind of conduct is a moral duty, I "respect" or look up to that kind of conduct as something required by a moral law that everyone ought to follow. As he puts it: "Duty is the necessity of acting from respect for a law" and "a law is an objective principle valid for

31 Ibid., 24–25.

every rational being and a principle on which everyone ought to act."[32] So a person has a morally good will when the person does what is right because he believes it is what everyone in a situation like his ought to do. Kant concludes that being morally good requires that one behave only as one believes that everyone ought to behave.

Kant summarizes this conclusion in what he calls the principle "of the categorical imperative": "*I ought never to act except in such a way that I can will that my maxim should become a universal law.*"[33] A maxim is the reason a person in a certain situation has for doing what he does, and that maxim would "become a universal law" if every person in a similar situation chose to do the same thing for the same reason. So Kant's categorical imperative says that it is morally right for a person to do something for a certain reason if and only if the person could be willing to have everyone in a similar situation do the same thing for the same reason. Kant claims that this principle is the fundamental principle of morality.

In the following passage, Kant gives four examples to illustrate what the categorical imperative requires in practice. Notice that in the first two examples Kant asks whether the maxim on which a person wants to act *could be* a law that everyone in the world followed, while in the last two examples he asks whether the person *would be willing* to live in a world in which that maxim was a law everyone followed.

QUICK REVIEW
Kant concludes that it is morally right for me to do something for a certain reason only if I could be willing to have everyone in a similar situation do the same thing for that same reason. In other words, it is morally wrong for me to do something unless it is something that everyone could do and that I am willing to have everyone do.

 critical thinking

Does Kant assume that a person could never will to universalize evil or harm? Is this assumption correct?

> We will now enumerate a few duties [that follow from the categorical imperative]. We will adopt the usual practice of classifying duties into perfect and imperfect duties and subclassifying each of these into duties to ourselves and duties to others.
>
> 1. *Perfect duty to oneself.* Imagine a man who has been reduced to despair by a series of misfortunes. Suppose he feels tired of living, but is still able to ask himself whether it would be contrary to duty to take his own life. So he asks whether the maxim of his action could become a universal law of nature. His maxim is this: "Out of self-love I will adopt the principle that I will end my life once it contains more evils than satisfactions." Our man can then ask himself whether this principle, which is based on the feeling of self-love, can become a universal law of nature that everyone follows. He will see at once that a system of nature that contained a law that destroyed life by means of the very feeling whose function it is to sustain life would contradict itself. Therefore, such a law could not be part of a system of nature. Consequently, his maxim cannot become a universal law of nature so it violates the basic principle of morality.
> 2. *Perfect duty to others.* Imagine another person who finds himself forced to borrow some money. He knows that he will not be able to repay it, but he also knows that nobody will lend him anything unless he [falsely] promises to repay it. So he is tempted to make such a [false] promise. But he asks himself: Would such a promise be consistent with moral duty? If he were to make such a promise the maxim of his action would be this: "When I need money, I will borrow it and promise to repay it even if I know that I will never do so." Now I personally might be able to live according to this principle of self-interest. But the question is: Is it right? So I ask myself: What if my maxim were to become a universal law that everyone followed? Then I see at once that it could never even become a universal law of nature since it would contradict itself. For suppose it became a general rule that everyone is to make promises even when they never intend to keep them. Then promising itself could not continue, nor could we gain those benefits we hoped to gain by promising. For people would no longer believe anyone's promises, but would mock all "promises" as empty deceptions. [Since my maxim cannot become a universal law, it is morally wrong for me to act on it.]

32 Ibid., 28 and 50.
33 Ibid., 29.

QUICK REVIEW
Kant argues that committing suicide, making false promises, failing to develop one's talents, and failing to help those in need are all morally wrong because they are all actions that not everyone could do, or actions that I would not be willing to have everyone do even toward me.

3. *Imperfect duty to oneself.* Imagine a third man who has a useful natural ability that he could develop through practice and exercise. However, he is comfortably situated and would rather indulge in pleasure than make the effort needed to develop and improve himself. But he asks himself whether his maxim of neglecting his natural gifts as he is tempted to do is consistent with his duty. He sees then that a system of nature could conceivably exist with such a universal law, even if everyone (like the South Sea islanders) were to let his talents rust and devoted his life to idleness, amusement, and sex—in a word, to pleasure. But although his maxim *could* be conceived as a universal law of nature, he would not be willing to have it be a universal law of nature; that is, he would not be willing to have such a law implanted in us like a natural instinct. For our natural abilities enable us to achieve whatever goals we might have, so every rational person who has any goals whatever necessarily wants to have his abilities develop.
4. *Imperfect duty to others.* Imagine a fourth man who is prosperous, while he sees that others have to put up with great wretchedness. Suppose he could help them but he asks himself: What concern is it of mine? Let everyone have whatever happiness God or his own efforts can give him. For my part I will not steal from people or envy their fortune. But I do not want to add to their well-being or help them when they are in need! Undoubtedly, if such a way of thinking became universal, the human race could continue to exist; it might even be better off than if everyone were to talk about sympathy and good will and occasionally practiced it, but generally continued to cheat whenever they could and betrayed and violated the rights of others. However, although that maxim *could* be a universal law of nature, one would not be willing to have it be a universal law of nature for then one's will would be inconsistent with itself. For we know that many situations will arise in which one will need the love and help of others. So if one's maxim were a law of nature, one would find oneself in a world deprived of the help he knows he will need.[34]

Kant's **categorical imperative**, then, is the principle that it is morally right for me to do something for a certain reason only if I could be willing to have everyone in a similar situation do what I do for that same reason. Kant's examples show that the categorical imperative really has two aspects: it says that I should never do something for a certain reason unless (1) it *is possible* for everyone to do the same thing for the same reason, and (2) I *am willing* to have everyone do the same thing for the same reason, even toward me. Notice that these two moral requirements correspond roughly to two very common ways in which we identify wrongful actions. First, when someone is considering doing something wrong, we sometimes ask them: "What if everyone did that?" When we ask "What if everyone did that?" we are asking people to consider part (1) of Kant's categorical imperative. Second, when someone is considering doing something wrong, we also sometimes ask them, "How would you like it if everyone did that to you?" When we ask this, we are asking people to consider part (2) of Kant's categorical imperative.

In the preceding passage, Kant provided four examples of how the categorical imperative should be applied. Some additional examples may make his views clearer. Take the first aspect of Kant's categorical imperative: that I should never do something for a certain reason *unless everyone can do the same thing for that same reason.* Consider this example: Is it wrong for you to cheat on an exam because you want to? Kant would say this: Ask yourself whether it is possible for everyone to cheat on an exam because they want to; can cheating for such a reason be universal? Clearly, if everyone always cheated on exams when they wanted to, the

34 Ibid., 28, 51–55.

very practice of giving exams would break down. For what teacher would give an exam knowing that everyone who wants to is going to cheat on it? Because it is not possible for everyone to cheat on exams whenever they want, it is wrong for you to cheat on this exam merely because you want to. Or consider a game, such as poker or football or checkers. Is it wrong for you to secretly cheat during a game because you want to win? Ask yourself whether it is possible for everyone to always cheat at games because they want to win. Obviously, if everyone always cheated at games when they wanted to win, all game activities would soon break down and cease. Since it is not possible for everyone to cheat at games whenever they want, it is wrong for you to cheat at a game whenever you want. Or consider lying. Is it wrong for you to lie because you want to hide what you are really thinking? If everyone lied whenever they wanted to hide their thoughts, then no one's utterances could be trusted, so language would soon break down and no one would be able to make even lying statements. Because everyone cannot lie to hide their thoughts, it is wrong for you to do so. In short, the first aspect of Kant's categorical imperative says that it is wrong to make an exception of yourself: If everyone cannot do something for the reason you are doing it, then it is wrong for you to do it.

Kant's categorical imperative has a second aspect: it also implies that there are some actions that are wrong, not because it is impossible for everyone to do them, but because we are *not willing* to have everyone do them, even toward us. For example, consider racism. Is it wrong to discriminate against someone because you do not like their race? Ask yourself whether you would be willing to have everyone discriminate against others when they didn't like their race, even doing this to you. Clearly, it is possible for a society to exist in which everyone discriminates like this. But would you be willing to live in such a world? Probably not, for if everyone discriminates against people whose race they don't like, then you will likely be discriminated against on some occasions and this you probably are not willing to have people do. So, discriminating against others because you do not like their race is wrong for you.

A Second Version of the Categorical Imperative: Treating People as Ends.

Although Kant claimed that there is only one categorical imperative, he also felt that we could express it in more than one way. The first version of the categorical imperative says, in effect, that what is morally right (or wrong) for one person must be morally right (or wrong) for everyone. This implies that everyone is of equal value. In Kant's words, everyone has the same "absolute value," an idea he also expressed by saying that everyone is an "end in himself." Because everyone is of equal value, no one should be used to serve the interests of another without their consent, but must always be treated as having an "absolute value." Kant summarized these ideas by restating his categorical imperative in these words: *Act so that you always treat people as ends in themselves, and never merely use them as means.* In the following passage, he explains this second version of the categorical imperative and illustrates it with four examples:

> Now I say that man and generally any rational being exists as an end in himself. In all his actions, whether they concern himself or other rational beings, we must always regard a man as an end and not merely as a means to be arbitrarily used by this or that will. . . . Accordingly [a second version of] the categorical imperative can be formulated as follows: *So act as to treat humanity, whether in your own person or in that of any other, always as an end and never merely as a means.* We will now inquire whether this version can be applied in practice. We will again consider our previous four examples:
>
> 1. *Strict duty to oneself.* A person who is thinking of committing suicide should ask himself whether his action is consistent with the idea that humanity is an end in itself. If he kills himself to escape his suffering, he is using a person

QUICK REVIEW
Kant gives a second version of the categorical imperative:
(1) Every human being is an end in himself—a person whose capacity to choose for himself must be respected—so (2) we should not use people *only* as means to achieve our own goals but should always at the same time treat them as ends in themselves—as persons whose capacity to choose for themselves must be respected.

(himself) merely as a means to maintain a tolerable existence. But a person is not a thing. That is to say, a person [including oneself] cannot be used merely as a means, but must always be respected as an end in himself. I cannot, therefore, dispose of my own person by mutilating, despoiling, or killing myself. . . .

2. *Strict duty to others.* A man who is thinking of making a lying promise will realize that he would be using others merely as means because he would not be letting them participate in the goal of the actions in which he involves them. For the people I would thus be using for my own purposes would not have consented to be treated in this way and to that extent they would not have participated in the goals to be attained by my action. . . .
3. *Meritorious duty to oneself.* We should not only refrain from violating our own humanity as an end in itself, but we should also try to make our actions harmonize with the fact that our humanity is such an end. Now humanity has certain abilities that we can perfect to a greater or lesser extent. . . . When we neglect to develop these abilities we are not doing something that is destructive of humanity as an end in itself. But such neglect clearly does not advance humanity as an end in itself.
4. *Meritorious duty to others.* All men by nature want to be happy. Now humanity probably could survive even if people never helped each other achieve their happiness, but merely refrained from deliberately harming one another. But this would only be a negative way of making our actions harmonize with the idea that humanity is an end in itself. The positive way of harmonizing with this idea would be for everyone to help others achieve their goals so far as he can. The goals of every person who is an end in himself should also be my goals if my actions are really to be in full harmony with the idea that the person's humanity is an end in itself.[35]

QUICK REVIEW
To treat people as ends in themselves is to treat them as they freely and knowingly consent to be treated, but to treat them *only* as means is to use them to achieve one's goals without letting them decide whether they want this or not. So, Kant's second version of the categorical imperative says that I should treat people only as they freely and knowingly consent to be treated, not merely use them as means to my own goals.

QUICK REVIEW
The second version of Kant's categorical imperative rules out deception, force, coercion, and manipulation, but it allows us to use people as means to our goals so long as they freely and knowingly consent to it.

Kant's second version of the categorical imperative implies that we should not use people as objects, as things we merely use to achieve our goals. Instead, he claims, we should always at the same time allow them to choose whether or not they will join us in our actions. As he puts it in the preceding passage, a person must let others "participate in the goal of the actions in which he involves them."

Again, some additional examples may clarify what Kant has in mind in this second version of the categorical imperative. For Kant, to respect a person as an *end* is to respect her capacity to freely and knowingly choose for herself what she will do. To treat a person as a means is to use the person to achieve my personal goals. In effect, this second version of the categorical imperative says that we should treat people only as they freely and knowingly consent to be treated, and not merely use them as a means to our own goals. Kant would say that it is wrong to force or to manipulate a person into doing something because in manipulating or forcing a person I am failing to treat the person as she has freely and knowingly consented to be treated. Is it wrong to lie or to steal from a person? Lying or stealing involves doing something to a person without her free and knowing consent and so these are both wrong. What about helping those in great need? Kant would say that when people are in great need (such as the very poor), their ability to choose for themselves is compromised. Because we have a duty to promote people's capacity to choose for themselves, we should help those whose poverty prevents them from exercising their capacity to choose for themselves.

Notice that Kant is not saying that it is wrong to use people for our own ends. He is saying only that it is wrong to use people for our own ends *when we have not given them a choice in the matter.* For example, consider ordering a taxi driver to take

35 Ibid., 68.

you to the airport. Clearly, you are "using" the driver as a "means" to get to the airport. Does this make it immoral? Kant would doubtless say that it is not wrong. For when the taxi driver accepted the job of driving a taxi, he was consenting to take people to the destination they ordered him to. So, when you now order him to take you to the airport, you treat him as a means, but at the same time you are treating him as he *previously* consented to be treated. So you do not merely treat him as a means, but also as an end in himself. Notice also that Kant is not saying that it is wrong to do things to people that at the moment they do not want you to do. Take, for example, a teacher who flunks a student or a judge who puts a lawbreaker in jail. Clearly, neither the student nor the lawbreaker wants to be treated this way. So, is it immoral to do this to them? Kant would probably again say that in reality each is being treated as he *previously* consented to be treated. The student consented to be graded by the teacher when he signed up for the course knowing what it required. The lawbreaker consented to be treated according to the laws of this country when he chose to live or remain in it knowing what its laws required.

Finally, notice that, like the first version, this second version of the categorical imperative also corresponds to some common ways we have of indicating that an action was wrong. Consider, for example, how often you have heard a friend of yours say something like: "He just used me!" or "She was just using me!" or "He just treated me like an object!" Such expressions are direct descendants of Kant's second version of the categorical imperative: do not use people merely as means. Or consider how people often say that there is nothing wrong with sex between "consenting adults" or say that before treating a patient or experimenting on a person, one should get the person's "informed consent." Such expressions are directly related to Kant's claim that people must be treated as ends, i.e., as they have consented to be treated.

Conflicts. Nevertheless, Kant's theory has a few problems. First, duties frequently conflict, and Kant's theory does not seem to give us an obvious way of resolving such conflicts. If, as Kant argues, it is always wrong to tell a lie and always wrong to break a promise, then which do I choose when these duties conflict? Second, the acts that the categorical imperative says are *always* wrong do not always seem wrong. For example, Kant says that it is wrong to lie, no matter what good might come of telling the lie. Yet is it wrong to lie to save your life? To save someone from serious pain or injury? There seems to be no compelling reason why certain actions should be prohibited without exception.

QUICK REVIEW
Critics say Kant's theory cannot deal with conflicts among duties; critics also claim that his theory implies that certain acts (such as lying) are always wrong no matter what the circumstances might be, and this implication seems mistaken.

Some Implications of Kantian Ethics. Many people today believe that Kantian ethics provides rich insights into the moral life. To see more clearly the kind of understanding of morality that Kant's ethics provides, let us consider the topic we discussed earlier: sexual behavior. The philosopher Thomas Mappes has pointed out that the idea that it is wrong to just "use another person" or treat her like "an object" derives from Kant's principle that it is morally wrong to use a person "merely as a means." But what, exactly, do these Kantian ideas imply about ethics in sex? Mappes explains what it is to use a person sexually:

> The morally significant sense of "using another person" is best understood by reference to the notion of voluntary informed consent. . . . Using another person (in the morally significant sense) can arise in at least two important ways: via coercion, which is antithetical to voluntary consent, and via deception, which undermines the informed character of voluntary consent. . . . It seems clear, then, that A may sexually use B in at least two distinctive ways, (1) via coercion and (2) via deception.

> There are a host of clear cases in which a [fully competent adult] person "uses" another precisely because the former employs deception. . . . Consider this example. One person, A, has decided, as a matter of personal prudence based on past experience, not to become sexually involved outside the confines of a loving relationship. Another person B, strongly desires a sexual relationship with A but does not love A. B, aware of A's unwillingness to engage in sex without love, professes love for A, thereby hoping to win A's consent to a sexual relationship. B's ploy is successful; A consents. When the smoke clears and A becomes aware of B's deception it would be both appropriate and natural for A to complain, "I've been used."
>
> Forcible rape is the most conspicuous, and most brutal way of sexually using another person via coercion. . . . A man who rapes a woman by the employment of sheer physical force, by simply overpowering her, employs occurrent coercion. . . . When the victim of rape is treated as if she were a physical object, there we have one of the most vivid examples of the immoral using of another person.
>
> Frequently, forcible rape involves not occurrent coercion but dispositional coercion. In dispositional coercion, the relevant factor is not physical force but the threat of harm. . . . For example, a man threatens to kill or beat a woman if she resists his sexual demands. She "consents," that is, she submits to his demands. . . . [But] it is coerced.
>
> Although the threat of immediate and serious bodily harm stands out as the most brutal way of coercing consent to sexual interaction, we must not neglect the employment of other kinds of threats to this same end. . . . Consider . . . the following case: Mr. Supervisor makes a series of increasingly less subtle sexual overtures to Ms. Employee. These advances are consistently and firmly rejected by Ms. Employee. Eventually, Mr. Supervisor makes it clear that the granting of "sexual favors" is a condition of her continued employment. . . . [This] case [also] . . . involve[s an] attempt to sexually use another person.[36]

QUICK REVIEW
Using Kant's theory, Mappes argues that it is wrong to sexually use a person through coercion or deception, which is why rape and sexual harassment of employees are wrong.

Kant's theory is clearly very useful for helping us see what our moral obligations are. In fact, in some respects, it sheds more light on common dilemmas in sexual matters than do other approaches to the morality of sex. For Kant's theory identifies the central importance of showing respect for the dignity of our sexual partners and the key significance of consent in morally legitimate sexual interactions.

QUICK REVIEW
Critics say that Kant's theory implies that any kind of sexual activity between informed and consenting persons is morally right, and this seems too permissive; other critics argue that free, rational consent may not be possible where sex is concerned.

However, some people have criticized this Kantian approach to sex because, like utilitarianism, it is too permissive. Utilitarianism approves of any sexual activity if its pleasures and advantages are sufficiently great. Yet the Kantian approach seems to approve of virtually any consensual sexual activity. This seems to allow all sexual activity between informed and voluntarily consenting adults, including incest, homosexuality, and even adultery if one's spouse consents to the adultery. For many people, this is clearly a morally objectionable result.

Moreover, many have questioned whether the Kantian approach to sex makes idealistic assumptions about how real our consent can be. In the throes of sexual desire, in the sexual heat of the moment, are people really able to give their voluntary informed consent? Isn't the sometimes overwhelming power of sex incompatible with free, rational consent? Feminists have suggested that sexual roles are designed to ensure male dominance over women and to mask from women their own real sexual desires and needs. In the context of such false consciousness, isn't the Kantian faith in informed consent unreal? For example, does the prostitute genuinely consent to her situation? Some feminists have even questioned whether any woman truly consents to sex.

---

36 Thomas A. Mappes, "Sexual Morality and the Concept of Using Another Person," in *Social Ethics: Morality and Social Policy*, ed. Thomas A. Mappes and Jane S. Zembaty (New York: McGraw-Hill, 1992).

QUESTIONS

1. Would it be possible or desirable to universalize the following maxims?
   a. "Never work unless you absolutely must."
   b. "Always do your own thing unless it hurts somebody else."
   c. "Give nothing and expect nothing in return."
   d. "Sell all you have and give to the poor."
   e. "Let your conscience be your guide."
   f. "Always stick by your friends."
   g. "Never discriminate against someone on the basis of race, religion, color, or sex."
   h. "Never punish a child physically."
   i. "Without prior approval, never take something that doesn't belong to you."

PHILOSOPHY AT THE MOVIES

Watch *Liar, Liar* (1997) in which Fletcher Reed, a successful lawyer and habitual liar who regularly breaks his promises to spend time with his son, Max, misses Max's birthday party. When Max makes a birthday wish that for a full day his father be unable to lie, Fletcher finds that no matter how much he struggles, he cannot lie—which makes it particularly difficult to defend his client in court. Kant claims that the categorical imperative implies that it is always wrong to lie; utilitarianism claims that it is permissible to lie if lying has better consequences than any other alternative. What is the view of this movie?

Buddhist Ethics

Buddhist ethics cannot be considered a divine command theory because Buddhism does not believe in a God that issues commands. Yet Buddhism provides important insight into the moral life, and for centuries it has influenced the moral behavior of millions. Because many people in the West today are turning to it for enlightenment, here we briefly consider its implications for ethics.

We can begin with two generalizations about Buddhism's emphasis on ethical behavior. First, volitional (voluntary) actions are considered supremely important because, according to the moral law of causation (karma), they determine our destiny. What we have voluntarily done will determine what we will become. Classical Buddhism understood this in terms of the doctrine of successive rebirths—what you are in this life is determined by what you did in your past lives. But some contemporary Buddhists have interpreted the doctrine of karma in terms of a single human life—what you are today is determined by the choices you made earlier in your present life. In either case, our volitional actions are all important in determining who and what we now are as well as who and what we will become. A second generalization we can make about Buddhism, is that its ethics is considered a form of wisdom and not a set of obligations:

> QUICK REVIEW
> Buddhism considers volitional actions as supremely important because they contribute to a person's karma, which then determines a person's future; Buddhism also considers morality and wisdom to be closely related.

> Morality is washed all round with wisdom, and wisdom is washed all round with morality. Wherever there is morality, there is wisdom and wherever there is wisdom there is morality. From the observing of the moralities comes wisdom and from observing of wisdom comes morality. Morality and wisdom together reveal the height of the world. It is just as if one should wash one hand with the other or one foot with the other; exactly so is morality washed round with wisdom and wisdom with morality.[37]

37 *Dighanikaya*, vol. 1, ed. T. W. Rhys Davies and J. E. Carpenter (Pali Text Society, 1947), 124.

Buddha: "Morality is washed all round with wisdom, and wisdom is washed all round with morality. . . . It is just as if one should wash one hand with the other or one foot with the other; exactly so is morality washed round with wisdom and wisdom with morality."

© Bernice Williams/iStockphoto.com

The point is important. Unlike Western ethics, Buddhist ethics does not conceive of ethics as a set of obligations, rights, or duties, nor as a set of imperatives, nor even as a set of standards for evaluating our actions or assigning blame. Ethics is, instead, the accumulated wisdom we have about those areas of our lives with which we must be concerned if we are to deal with what Buddhism considers the fundamental problem of human life: suffering.

To understand the central role of suffering in Buddhist ethics, we must return to the Four Noble Truths, which we very briefly described in Chapter 4 but which we must now examine more closely by looking at their implications for ethics:

> And this is the Noble Truth of Sorrow. Birth is sorrow, age is sorrow, disease is sorrow, death is sorrow; contact with the unpleasant is sorrow, separation from the pleasant is sorrow, every wish unfulfilled is sorrow—in short, all the five components of individuality are sorrow.
>
> And this is the Noble Truth of the Arising of Sorrow. It arises from craving, which leads to rebirth, which brings delight and passion, and seeks pleasure now here, now there—the craving for sensual pleasure, the craving for continued life, the craving for power.
>
> And this is the Noble Truth of the Stopping of Sorrow. It is the complete stopping of that craving, so that no passion remains, leaving it, being emancipated from it, being released from it, giving no place to it.
>
> And this is the Noble Truth of the Way which leads to the Stopping of Sorrow. It is the Noble Eightfold Path—[having] Right Understanding, Right Resolve, Right Speech, Right Conduct, Right Livelihood, Right Effort, Right Mindfulness, and Right Concentration.[38]

QUICK REVIEW
The Four Noble Truths of Buddhism are as follows: (1) Whatever is tied to our individuality, such as birth, age, disease, death, and pain, brings suffering. (2) We suffer because we crave things: pleasure, life, power. (3) Only putting an end to craving will end our suffering. (4) Craving can be ended only by following the Noble Eightfold Path of right understanding, right thought, right speech, right conduct, right livelihood, right effort, right mindfulness, and right concentration.

Buddhism sees itself as the solution to a human problem, and the first noble truth explains that problem: suffering. Suffering pervades our world and our existence: It is a universal human experience. We feel pain, both the physical pains of diseases and injuries, and the mental anguish that accompanies the loss of those we loved, as well as the frustration of living in a world where nothing remains the same and nothing lasts. Our bodies age, our strength and skills decline, we suffer diseases and the deaths of loved ones, pleasures are short-lived, the intensity of the love and passion we felt for a lover subsides and ends. The five "components of individuality," which consist of our physical bodies, our feelings, our perceptions, our mental activities, and our consciousness, are all subject to suffering.

---

38 William Theodore de Bary, *Sources of Indian Tradition*, vol. 1, from *Samyutta Nikaya* (New York: Columbia University Press, 1958), 99.

But we cannot alleviate suffering unless we know what its causes are. The second Noble Truth is an explanation of the fundamental causes of our suffering. The fundamental cause of suffering, the Buddha claimed, is our craving for things, a craving that is continually frustrated because nothing is permanent. We crave pleasure but all pleasures are short-lived; we crave continued life yet we must die; and we crave power, yet all power is fleeting. Craving manifests itself in three vices: attachment to some things, aversion to other things, and confusions about the true nature of the world. These are vices because they are at the root of suffering.

The Third Noble Truth makes the point that since craving is the fundamental cause of suffering, we can eliminate suffering by eliminating craving. Specifically, we must eliminate our attachments, our aversions, and our confusions. Three confusions are crucial: the confused belief that things in the world are permanent, the confused belief that we are individual selves, and the confused belief that human existence is not all suffering.

The Fourth Noble Truth, explains the way that craving can be eliminated. Craving, the root of suffering, can be eliminated by following the Eightfold Path, namely by cultivating (1) correct understanding, (2) correct resolve, (3) correct speech, (4) correct conduct, (5) correct livelihood, (6) correct effort, (7) correct mindfulness, and (8) correct concentration.

To have *correct understanding* one must not only understand, accept, and live according to the four noble truths, but must become genuinely convinced of the three basic ideas: nothing is permanent, there is no self, and all life is suffering. Failure to accept the three basic ideas leads us to continually seek permanence in what is impermanent, to seek personal happiness through activities that increase the sufferings of others or oneself, to assume we have a self that we must care for when we have none, and to see what is repugnant as attractive. The most fundamental failure of understanding, however, is the belief that one is an enduring individual self, for from that flows all our selfishness and our clinging to things. *Correct resolve* refers to having both the determination and the detachment needed to follow and remain on the eightfold path. To have *correct speech* is to refrain from saying what is false or useless, and to use speech only to benefit others and not to add to their suffering. The precept on correct speech prohibits lying, slandering, gossiping, cursing, and creating dissension, and enjoins honesty, friendliness, sincerity, and clarity. *Correct conduct* is behavior that does not harm oneself or others, i.e., behavior that does not cause suffering. Specifically, it prohibits injuring others, destroying or stealing their property, murder, fornication, engaging in personal habits that abuse one's body, that allow one's body to deteriorate, or that pollute the body and its organs in any way. Having a *correct livelihood* means making one's living in occupations that do not increase the sufferings of others—humans or animals. This precept is usually interpreted as ruling out occupations like weapons manufacturing, butchering or hunting animals, and making or selling alcoholic drinks; it also rules out occupations that create attachments or cravings, such as marketing that arouses consumer desires for things. *Correct effort* refers to keeping one's mind focused on what matters—the eightfold path through which the causes of suffering are eliminated—and not allowing oneself to get sidetracked by unhealthy thoughts and desires. The word "effort" implies an act of the will and indicates the importance of using one's will to stay on the eightfold path. *Correct mindfulness* is being completely aware of what is happening in one's mind and body: one's physical body, one's sensations, one's mind, and one's thoughts. Exercises such as concentrating on one's breathing or the practice of paying full attention to what one is doing at the moment, can help one achieve correct mindfulness and move toward insight and enlightenment. Finally, *correct concentration* consists of achieving a meditative state of pure consciousness in which there is "neither perception nor non-perception" nor thoughts, nor ideas, nor any other contents in one's mind. This is a state toward which one can progress in four stages: first, ridding ourselves of all negative desires and thoughts and allowing only positive feelings; second, eliminating intellectualization; third, eliminating all feelings including positive ones; and, fourth, eliminating all sensations so that only pure undistracted awareness remains.[39]

It's important, however, not to view these precepts as a set of absolute rules, for Buddhism, as we saw, stresses the elimination of suffering, not the fulfillment of obligations. In other words, blind obedience to the precepts is not encouraged because they are merely means to an end: the elimination of suffering.

QUICK REVIEW
The ideal according to some Buddhist texts is to not indulge in sexual pleasures but to work toward the goal of eliminating suffering; several texts condemn homosexuality, adultery, and prostitution insofar as these are obstacles to this key goal.

What are the implications of Buddhism for sexual ethics? Although Buddhism suggests that there are various grades of pleasure, some of which are sexual pleasures, it takes the view that a life of pure pleasure will, by its inner nature, end up in boredom and interfere with the healthy functioning of familial and social life. More importantly, it can stimulate the kind of craving that is at the root of suffering, and it can distract us from following the eightfold path. The ideal, according to some Buddhist texts, is lived by those who reach a state in which "they do not indulge their sexual pleasures." Other Buddhist texts, such as the commentary on the five precepts in the *Visuddhimagga* by the Buddhist monk Buddhaghosa (circa 400), suggest that the "sexual misconduct" condemned by the Buddha includes "intercourse with men and then also with . . . women who have been betrothed, women bought with money, kept women. . . ." Thus, these Buddhist views would condemn homosexuality, adultery, prostitution, and having a mistress. Yet the focus of Buddhism is not on the wrongness of these or any other specific activities but on the elimination of suffering. Because the pursuit of sexual pleasure leads us away from this key goal, it is to be set aside.

QUESTIONS

1. Apply each of Buddhism's five precepts to appropriate aspects of your life. What changes would you need to make?
2. What weaknesses, if any, do you detect in Buddhist ethics?
3. What social changes might implementation of Buddhist ethics bring about? For example, how would it alter advertising or marketing generally? What impact would it have on television?

© KPA Honorar & Belege/United Archives Gmb/Alamy

PHILOSOPHY AT THE MOVIES

Watch *Little Buddha* (1993) in which a group of Tibetan Buddhist monks determines that a boy living in Seattle named Jesse Conrad is the reincarnation of a great deceased Buddhist teacher named Lama Dorje. They travel to Seattle to find him and then ask his parents if they can take the boy back to Tibet for testing to determine whether he is in fact the reincarnation of Lama Dorje. What roles do the Noble Eightfold Path and the five precepts play in this movie? What role does the idea of karma play in this movie? What other key Buddhist beliefs does this movie demonstrate?

39 Michael C. Brannigan, *Striking a Balance: A Primer in Traditional Asian Values*, (Plymouth, United Kingdom: Lexington Books, 2010), 51–61.

7.5 Is Ethics Based on Character?

The ethical theories that we've discussed so far (with the exception of Buddhist ethics) focus on principles or rules that define the actions we are morally obligated or have a moral duty to perform. For example, utilitarianism is based on Mill's principle that "actions are right in proportion as they tend to promote happiness, wrong as they tend to produce the reverse of happiness." Kant based his ethics on the principle that one should "act so as to treat humanity . . . always as an end and never merely as a means." Modern ethics has been concerned mostly with studying such universal rules or principles, which tell us which actions are morally right or how people ought to act.

Many philosophers now feel dissatisfied with this approach to ethics. One major problem, they say, is that this approach results in disagreements that cannot be resolved. Utilitarians disagree with Kantians, and both disagree with followers of natural law ethics. Contemporary philosopher Alasdair MacIntyre writes:

> The most striking feature of contemporary moral utterance is that so much of it is used to express disagreements; and the most striking feature of the debates in which these disagreements are expressed is their interminable character. I do not mean by this just that such debates go on and on—although they do—but also that they apparently can find no terminus. There seems to be no rational way of securing moral agreement in our culture.[40]

MacIntyre and others argue that with its preoccupation with conflicting rules and principles, modern ethics seems to have forgotten a part of morality that earlier ages recognized: moral virtue or character. The moral life, these philosophers suggest, is not just a matter of acting on moral rules. Instead, morality is about becoming a good person and cultivating morally desirable character traits such as honesty, courage, compassion, and generosity. Instead of trying to discover universal rules about which we will inevitably disagree, ethics should try to identify the character traits or "virtues" of the morally good person and explain how we can develop and acquire these traits. Ethics should not emphasize *doing* but *being*; it should look not only at how we are obligated to *act*, but also at the kind of person we ought to *be*.

QUICK REVIEW
MacIntyre argues that ethics should not be concerned with rules about what one should do, but with the virtues that make us morally good persons.

Virtue ethics, as this approach to ethics is called, is not new. It is, in fact, an approach that the ancient Greek philosopher Aristotle made the cornerstone of his moral philosophy. There is no better way of understanding virtue ethics than by examining his views, including his views on friendship and love. We then turn to examine a controversial issue: whether the virtues of women should differ from those of men.

Aristotle's Theory of Virtue

In his great work *Nicomachean Ethics*, Aristotle wrote that human beings can be happy only if they fulfill their basic human purpose or "function." That is, humans can be happy only if they act as humans are specifically meant to act. Because only humans can reason, Aristotle concluded that humans are meant to act with reason. That is, we humans will be happy only if we have the ability to act with reason in the various circumstances of our life. Because the ability to do

To read more from Aristotle's *Nichomachean Ethics*, go to CourseMate for this text and browse by chapter or philosopher.

40 Alasdair MacIntyre, *After Virtue* (Notre Dame, IN: University of Notre Dame Press, 1984), 3.

something well is a virtue, Aristotle concludes that humans will achieve happiness only by developing their virtues:

> If in all our activities there is some end we seek for its own sake, and if everything else is a means to this same end, it obviously will be our highest and best end. Clearly there must be some such end since everything cannot be a means to something else since then there would be nothing for which we ultimately do anything and everything would be pointless. . . .
>
> Now happiness seems more than anything else to answer to this description. For happiness is something we always choose for its own sake and never as a means to something else. But fame, pleasure, . . . and so on, are chosen partly for themselves but partly also as a means to happiness, since we believe that they will bring us happiness. Only happiness, then, is never chosen for the sake of these things or as a means to any other thing. . . .
>
> So it appears that happiness is the ultimate end and completely sufficient by itself. It is the end we seek in all that we do.
>
> The reader may think that in saying that happiness is our ultimate end we are merely stating a platitude. So we must be more precise about what happiness involves.
>
> Perhaps the best approach is to ask what the specific purpose or function of man is. For the good and the excellence of all things that have a purpose—such as musicians, sculptors, or craftsmen—depend on their purpose. So if man has a purpose, his good will be related to this purpose.
>
> Our biological activities we share in common even with plants, so these activities cannot be the purpose or function of man since we are looking for something specific to man. The activities of our senses we also plainly share with other things: horses, cattle, and other animals. So there remain only the activities that belong to the rational part of man. . . . So the specific purpose or function of man involves the activities of that part of his soul that belongs to reason, or that at least is obedient to reason. . . .
>
> Now the function of a thing is the basis [of its goodness], but its good is something added to this function. For example, the function of a musician is to play music, and the good musician is one who not only plays music but who in addition does it well. So, the good for man would have to be something added to this function of carrying on the activities of reason; it would be carrying on the activities of reason but doing so well. But a thing carries out its proper functions well when it has the proper virtues. So the [ultimate] good for man is carrying out those activities of his soul [which involve reason] and doing so with the proper virtue or excellence.[41]

QUICK REVIEW
Aristotle's ethic of virtue says humans will achieve happiness—their ultimate end—only by fulfilling their specific purpose, which is to exercise their reason, and to do so in an excellent or virtuous way.

But what does it mean to have the virtue of using our reason well in our lives? Aristotle points out that where our desires, emotions, and actions are involved, both going to excess and falling short are vices. We act well when we seek the midpoint between excess and deficiency; acting well, in short, is being moderate in what we desire, feel, and do. We acquire the virtues of living reasonably, then, when we acquire the various abilities needed to control our desires, emotions, and actions so that they neither go to excess nor fall short. Having such virtues is the key to happiness because these virtues enable us to act as humans were meant to act:

> Consider that the expert in any field is the one who avoids what is excessive as well as what is deficient. Instead he seeks to hit the mean and chooses it. . . . Acting well in any field is achieved by looking to the mean and bringing one's actions into line with this standard of moderation. For example, people say of a good work of

41 Aristotle, *Nicomachean Ethics*, bk. 1, chs. 2, 7. This translation copyright © 1992 by Manuel Velasquez.

> art that nothing could be taken from it or added to it, implying that excellence is destroyed through excess or deficiency but achieved by observing the mean. The good artist, in fact, keeps his eyes fixed on the mean in everything he does. . . .
>
> Virtue, therefore, must also aim at the mean. For human virtue deals with our feelings and actions, and in these we can go to excess or fall short or we can hit the mean. For example, it is possible to feel fear, confidence, desire, anger, pity, pleasure, . . . and so on, either too much or too little—both of which extremes are bad. But to feel these at the right times, and on the right occasions, and toward the right persons, and with the right object, and in the right fashion, is the mean between the extremes and is the best state, and is the mark of virtue. In the same way, our actions can also be excessive or can fall short or can hit the mean.
>
> Virtue, then, deals with those feelings and actions in which it is wrong to go too far and wrong to fall short but in which hitting the mean is praiseworthy and good. . . . It is a habit or acquired ability to choose . . . what is moderate or what hits the mean as determined by reason.
>
> But it is not enough to speak in generalities. We must also apply this to particular virtues and vices. Consider, then, the following examples.
>
> Take the feelings of fear and confidence. To be able to hit the mean [by having just enough fear and just enough confidence] is to have the virtue of courage. . . . But he who exceeds in confidence has the vice of recklessness, while he who has too much fear and not enough confidence has the vice of cowardliness.
>
> The mean where pleasure . . . is concerned is achieved by the virtue of temperance. But to go to excess is to have the vice of self-indulgence, while to fall short is to have the vice of being austere. . . .
>
> Or take the action of giving or receiving money. Here the mean is the virtue of generosity. . . . But the man who gives to excess and is deficient in receiving has the vice of prodigality, while the man who is deficient in giving and excessive in taking has the vice of stinginess. . . .
>
> Or take one's feelings about the opinion of others. Here the mean is the virtue of proper self-respect, while the excess is the view of vanity, and the deficiency is the vice of small-mindedness. . . .
>
> The feeling of anger can also be excessive, deficient, or moderate. The man who occupies the middle state is said to have the virtue of being even-tempered, while the one who exceeds in anger has the vice of being bad-tempered, while the one who is deficient in anger has the vice of being apathetic.[42]

QUICK REVIEW
Excellence in any field is achieved by hitting the mean and not by excess or deficiency. So being virtuous in our actions and feelings is achieved by hitting the mean as determined by reason and avoiding excess or deficiency in our actions and feelings.

For Aristotle, then, a virtue is the ability to be reasonable in our actions, desires, and emotions, and to be reasonable is to act with moderation. For example, courage is the ability to deal with fear in a moderate way and not in an excessive or deficient manner; temperance is the ability to respond to pleasures in a moderate way and not give in to them in an excessive manner. We are not born with such abilities, he points out, but acquire them by training in our communities. In particular, we acquire them in youth by being trained repeatedly to respond to situations in a reasonable manner. As Aristotle puts it, we become virtuous by being trained to act virtuously in the appropriate situations until it becomes a habit. At first, acting virtuously is difficult, but when we have acquired the virtue, it becomes easy and pleasant:

> As is the case with any skill, we acquire the virtues by first doing virtuous acts. We acquire a skill by practicing the activities involved in the skill. For example, we become builders by building, and we learn to play the harp by playing the harp. In the same way, we become just by doing just acts, temperate by doing temperate acts, and courageous by doing acts of courage. . . .

---

42 Ibid., bk. 2, chs. 6, 7.

QUICK REVIEW
Virtue is acquired by repeatedly being made to act virtuously until it becomes a habit; vices are acquired by repeatedly acting viciously until it becomes a habit. When a virtue is acquired, one is able to do virtuous acts and to feel pleasure in virtuous acts.

> Both the moral virtues and the corresponding vices are developed or destroyed by similar kinds of actions, as is the case with all skills. It is by playing the harp that both good and bad harp players are produced [good players by repeatedly playing well, poor players by repeatedly playing poorly]. And the same is true of builders and all the rest: by building well they develop into good builders, and by building badly into bad builders. In fact, if this were not so they would not need a teacher and everyone would be born either good or bad at their trade. The same holds for the virtues. By what we do in our interactions with others we will develop into just persons or into unjust ones; and by the way we respond to danger, training ourselves to respond with fear or with confidence, we will become either cowardly or courageous. The same can be said of our appetites and feelings of anger: By responding in one way or another to these we will become either temperate and even-tempered or self-indulgent and ill-tempered. In short, acts of one kind produce character traits of the same kind. This is why we should make sure that our actions are of the proper kind: for our character will correspond to how we act. It makes no small difference, then, whether a person is trained in one way or another from his youth; it makes a very great difference, in fact, all the difference.
>
> Not only are character traits developed and destroyed in the same way, they also manifest themselves in similar ways. This is something we can actually see with strength. Strength is produced by taking plenty of nourishment and doing plenty of exercise, and it is the man with strength, in turn, that is best able to do these things. It is the same with the virtues. By abstaining from pleasures we develop temperance, and it is the man with temperance that is best able to abstain from them. The same holds for courage: by habituating ourselves to disregard danger and to face it, we become courageous, and it is when we have become courageous that we are best able to face danger.
>
> A test of the presence of a certain character trait is the pleasure or pain that accompanies our actions. The person who abstains from bodily pleasures and feels pleased at this, is temperate, while the person who feels pain at having to abstain is self-indulgent. And the person who stands his ground against fearful things and takes pleasure in this or at least is not pained, is courageous, while the man for whom this is painful is a coward.[43]

To understand how virtue theory can help us assess moral behavior, let's consider the issue that we discussed earlier when examining other approaches to morality: sexual behavior. As Aristotle notes, our moral character is shaped through the actions we choose, and our character in turn influences the actions we choose. Through our actions, we shape the kind of person we gradually become, and the kind of person we are is, in turn, expressed through our actions. To assess the moral rightness or wrongness of moral behavior, then, we must look at the kind of character that the behavior produces, and the kind of character that such behavior expresses. If the behavior tends to produce a virtuous character and is the expression of a virtuous character, then it is morally right; if it produces a vicious character or is the expression of a vicious character, then it is morally wrong. Now consider how philosopher Janet Smith uses this approach to evaluate the moral quality of adultery:

> The very importance of the attempt to live an ethical life lies in the fact that in acting the individual forms herself or himself either for the better or for the worse. One of the foremost questions to be asked by the moral agent in the decision to do an action is: What kind of person will I become if I do this act?

43 Ibid., bk. 2, chs. 1, 2, 3.

> Let us now consider how the choice to commit adultery might reveal and affect one's moral character. . . .
>
> If it is true . . . that adulterers can be said to have undesirable moral characteristics and/or that they are forming undesirable moral characters through their choice to commit adultery, this would be taken as an indication . . . that adultery is a morally bad action. . . .
>
> For an analysis in accord with an ethics of virtue, answers to the following questions would be useful: What sort of people generally commit adultery? Are they, for instance, honest, temperate, kind, etc.? . . .Why do adulterers choose to have sex with people other than their spouses? Are their reasons selfish or unselfish ones? Do they seem to speak of their reasons for their choice honestly or do they seem to be rationalizing? What sort of lives have they been leading prior to the action that they choose; are they the sorts of lives that exhibit the characteristics we admire?
>
> Most may agree that some true generalizations could be made about adulterers that would lead us to think that in general adultery is not compatible with the moral virtues that we admire. The reaction of the American public to the extramarital affairs of [clergyman] Jim Bakker and [politician] Gary Hart reveal well the widespread view that lying predictably accompanies the act of adultery and that adulterers are not to be trusted. Certainly, if someone told us that he or she wanted to be an honest, trustworthy, stable and kind individual with good family relationships, and wanted to know if an adulterous affair would conflict with this goal, we would have little hesitation in advising against adultery.[44]

QUICK REVIEW
According to the virtue theory of Smith, one can evaluate the moral quality of sexual behaviors by asking whether those behaviors develop virtues or vices.

At least in the hands of Janet Smith, virtue ethics implies a conservative view of adultery. According to Smith, adultery seems to be connected with several vices. She suggests that adultery seems to be something done by people who are dishonest, intemperate, disloyal, and selfish. Adultery, then, is an act in which these vices are expressed. Moreover, she suggests, adultery seems to encourage the development of these same vices. Adultery puts people into positions where they have strong incentives to lie to their spouses, to be self-indulgent, and to be disloyal to their spouses. Thus, adultery seems to further the development of these vices. Because adultery is an expression of vice and because it tends to develop these vices further, an ethic of virtue would condemn adultery.

However, it is important to keep in mind that Smith's argument merely shows that adultery is usually associated with vices. It is possible that in some cases adultery might not be associated with lying, for example. A virtue approach such as Smith's cannot show that any action is always wrong. It can show only that certain actions, such as adultery, are usually or generally wrong.

Love and Friendship

QUICK REVIEW
Aristotle, who claimed that friendship is a virtue and is one of life's necessities, argued that two people are friends when each wishes good for the other, both are aware of this, and each does so because he believes the other is good, pleasurable, or useful.

We have so far ignored an aspect of our moral lives that many people associate with virtue and that many philosophers, particularly Aristotle, believe is an essential component of living morally: the ability to love and befriend others. Aristotle, for example, argued that friendship, which he believed was based on love, is a kind of virtue that is essential to human life. Because love and friendship are so central to a virtuous life, and because they are topics that Aristotle felt were crucial parts of his theory of virtue, we briefly examine them here.

Aristotle argued that although a kind of "friendship" can be based on pleasure or utility, true friendship is based on two people's mutual recognition of the

---

44 Janet Smith, "Moral Character and Abortion," in *Doing and Being,* ed. Janet Graf Haber (New York: Macmillan, 1993), 442–456.

goodness of the other. Such friends, he claims, are "other selves." Aristotle's discussion of friendship is as important and insightful for us today as when it was written:

> After discussing virtue, it is only natural to turn to a discussion of friendship, since friendship is a virtue or implies virtue, and is one of life's necessities. For without friends no one would choose to live, even if he had all other goods. . . .
>
> We can identify the main kinds of friendship in terms of what someone can be loved for. . . . People can be loved for any of three reasons: because they are good, because they give us pleasure, or because they are useful to us. . . . There are, then, these three reasons for friendship. We say of a friend that we ought to wish him to have what is good. But . . . there is friendship only when this wish is reciprocated. And we should also add "when it is recognized." For . . . how could we say two people are friends if they do not know their mutual feelings? To be friends, then, they must mutually recognize that each wishes good for the other, and each must wish good to the other for one of three reasons [because the other is good, or is pleasurable, or is useful]. . . .
>
> Now those who love each other for their usefulness do not love each other for themselves but because of what one gets from the other. The same is true of those who love for the sake of the pleasure they get from each other. . . . In either case, it is not the other person himself who is loved; instead what is loved is the pleasure or utility that one gets from the other. So these friendships are not real friendships [in the full sense]. . . .
>
> For the most part the friendships of young people seem to be based on pleasure; for young people often . . . seek mainly what gives them pleasure. . . . This is why they quickly become friends and quickly cease to be so; their friendships change when the one in whom they took pleasure changes, and pleasures change quickly. . . . This is why they fall in love and then out of love so quickly. . . . Still, people who love because of the pleasure they give each other want to spend their days and lives together; for this is how they can attain what they seek in their friendship.
>
> Friendship in the full sense is the friendship of people who are good, and who are similar in virtue; for these want what is good for each other because of the good they see in each other, and they are each good themselves. Now those who wish good to their friend for their friend's own sake are real friends; for they are friends because of who they are, and not because of what one provides the other. Their friendship, therefore, lasts as long as they are good, and the goodness of a person is an enduring thing. Such friends . . . are generally also useful to each other and find pleasure in each other. . . . [However,] such friendships are rare because good people are rare . . . and they require time and familiarity. . . . Nor can they . . . be real friends until they have come to appreciate the good that is lovable in each, and each has come to trust the other. . . . These, then, are friends without qualification; the others are counted as friends only in a qualified sense due to their resemblance to these true friends.
>
> Friendship seems to originate in a man's relationship to himself. For the defining characteristics of friendship seem to be present in a man's relationship to himself. For (1) a friend is one who wishes good to his friend and who does what is good or seems good for his friend; (2) a friend wishes his friend to exist and live for his friend's own sake . . .; (3) Some say a friend is one with whom one spends time; (4) others say a friend is one who has the same tastes; (5) and that he is someone who grieves and rejoices with his friend. . . . Now each of these is found in the good man's relation to himself . . . For (1) he wishes for himself what is good or seems good and he does what is good . . . for himself . . . ; and (2) he wishes that he himself will continue to exist and live. . . . And (3) he . . . enjoys spending time with himself since the memories of his past and his hopes for the future are good, and therefore pleasant. . . .(5) He grieves and rejoices . . . with himself; and (4) whatever he finds painful or pleasant to himself at one time, is painful or pleasant to himself at other times. . . . So since each of these characteristics are found in the good man's

QUICK REVIEW
When people are friends because they find each other pleasurable or useful, neither loves his friend for himself but for what he gets from him, so they are not real friends in the full sense. When people wish good for each other because of the good each sees in the other, they are real friends in the full sense because each loves the other for what he is, not for what he provides; such friendships require time, familiarity, and trust.

> relationship to himself, he is related to his friend as to himself, his friend is another self . . . and friendship is like one's love for oneself.[45]

For Aristotle, love is central to friendship. In fact, he distinguishes the three types of friendship according to the three kinds of ways we can love a person. Yet Aristotle says very little about love itself. That notion obviously demands attention.

Modern philosophers who have studied love generally distinguish three types of love: *philia*, *eros*, and *agape*. *Philia* (a Greek word that gave us the name "Philadelphia," City of Brotherly Love) is the kind of brotherly love that is involved in friendship as Aristotle discussed it. It is the kind of deep mutual liking that friends or family members can have for one another. *Eros*, on the other hand, is the kind of intensely passionate attraction that one may feel toward a person or even toward a thing, such as music or beauty or something else toward which one feels intensely passionate and attracted. Finally, *agape* refers to the kind of love that, in Christianity at least, God has toward people and that a person can have toward God and, by extension, that a Christian should have toward all human beings. Unlike *eros*, *agape* is not a passionate and intense attraction. And unlike *philia*, *agape* is not a response to something good, pleasurable, or useful in the beloved. Instead, *agape* is gratuitous: It is freely given. The Christian God loves (and the Christian should love) each person even when there is nothing in the person that is good, pleasurable, or useful. In fact, God does not love people because they are good; instead, God's love *makes* people good: *Agape* is creative insofar as it creates goodness in the one who is loved.

QUICK REVIEW
The three traditional kinds of love are *philia* (brotherly love), *eros* (an intensely passionate love), and *agape* (the love that God or a Christian has for every person even if there is nothing good, pleasurable, or useful about that person).

But what is love itself? We can, of course, love many things: power, money, travel, animals, foods, art, people, and so on. Here we focus on love of one person for another person. When we have this kind of love—and maybe all kinds of love are like this—we have a strong, positive attitude toward the person's goodness or value. We see the person herself as good or valuable and respond with positive regard. But we have many kinds of strong, positive responses toward the good in people, including liking, respecting, and admiring. What more is love besides a strong, positive attitude toward a person's goodness?

One of the oldest answers to this question is based on Aristotle's suggestion that "a friend is one who wishes good to his friend and who does what is good or seems good for his friend . . . and wishes to spend time with his friend." That is, when I love you, I want you to flourish and to do well for your own sake (not for my sake), and I try to do what is good for you for your own sake (again, not for my sake). I want to be with you; I grieve when you grieve and rejoice when you rejoice. The philosopher Gabrielle Taylor tries to summarize these ideas:

QUICK REVIEW
The relationship view says love consists of a positive response to something good in a person and thus wishing for and doing what is good for her, wanting to be with her, wanting her to flourish and do well for her own sake, and empathizing with her.

> If x loves y, then x wants to benefit and be with y, etc., and he has these wants because he believes y has some determinate characteristics in virtue of which he thinks it worthwhile to benefit and be with y.[46]

To love a person, in this view, is to respond positively to something good or worthwhile in that person and, because of this, to want to promote that person's well-being, to be with that person, and empathize with that person. On this view, then, love is a kind of relationship in which a person sees good in another and responds by doing good to that person, trying to be with that person, and so on.

---

45 Aristotle, *Nichomachean Ethics*, excerpts from bk. 9, chs. 1, 2, 3, and 4, and bk. 10, ch. 4. This translation © 2006 by Manuel Velasquez.

46 Gabrielle Taylor, "Love," *Proceedings of the Aristotelian Society* 76 (1976): 157.

QUICK REVIEW
The emotion view says love is an emotion that arises when one sees the beloved as attractive and valuable; this complex emotion is a pleasure one feels when the person does well and pain when the person does not; it is a heightened awareness of the person; it is an attraction toward and cherishing of the person; it is a desire to be with the person.

QUICK REVIEW
The union view of love says it is a kind of union between two persons; one version sees this union as identifying with the other's interests and concerns; another version says it is a "fusion of two souls" that forms a new shared identity that is a new entity, a "we."

QUICK REVIEW
The creative view of love says love is not a response to the goodness already present in another person but that it creates goodness in the other person so that the loved one becomes better; love sees the potential good in another and brings it out of her.

However, critics of this "relationship view" of love say that it leaves out an essential aspect of love: Love is first and primarily an emotion, not a relationship. That is, love is an emotion that arises in you as a response to seeing your loved one as attractive and valuable in herself. The emotion of love is, in part, the pleasure that you feel at the thought of this unique person's existence and well-being, and a pain at the thought of her nonexistence or failure to do or be well. The emotion of love also includes feeling a heightened awareness and perception of the person, an attraction toward and cherishing of the person, and a desire to be with the person. From this complex emotion, this view holds, arises the sort of response that the relationship view emphasizes: doing good to the other, trying to be with the other, and so on. However, these responses are consequences of the emotion of love, not its essence.

Yet another group of philosophers argues that this "emotion view" of love still leaves out a central feature of love: to love is to form a bond, a close union with another person. What kind of union is involved in love? Aristotle said that a friend is "another self." So, one way of understanding the union of lovers is as a kind of identification with the other's interests and concerns. The interests and concerns of the person I love become my interests and concerns. But another way of understanding the union of lovers is to see it as the creation of a totally new entity, a new "we." The "we" that lovers form, philosopher Robert Solomon says, is a kind of new shared identity, a "fusion of two souls" in which each lover defines who he or she is in terms of the shared relationship. "A theory of love," he writes, "is primarily a theory of the . . . shared self, a self mutually defined and possessed by two people."[47] However, opponents say that this view of the union of love goes too far because although lovers do become close, they do not fuse together into some new entity. Moreover, when love verges on becoming this tight of a union, the lovers lose their own identity and freedom so that love becomes a loss of self and a kind of slavery instead of being liberating and an enhancement of who one is.

A fourth theory of love criticizes the view that love is a response to the goodness of the loved one. This "creative" theory of love says that all love is like *agape*: It *creates* goodness in the one who is loved; it makes the loved one better. Does this refer to the fact that "love is blind," that lovers sometimes see in loved ones those qualities they want to see and fail to see their unpleasant qualities? This can't be the right understanding of the creative power of love, for this is really the creation of an irrational delusion. Instead, the true creative power of love shows itself in the way that a lover sees the potential good in another and brings it out of her. If I love you, for example, I expect and believe that you will be a good person, and seeing this, you live up to my expectation. I may also believe, and encourage you to believe, that you will succeed in what you do, and seeing this, you actually do succeed.

Obviously, there are many different views on the nature of love. But perhaps they are not all wrong. It is possible, in fact, to see each of the many different views as shedding light on one of love's many different aspects. From this perspective, love is a complex reality that consists of many different aspects, each of which is emphasized by one or more of the theories. Love, then, can be seen as a relationship in which one responds to the goodness seen in another by wanting and doing what is good for her for her own sake, it is an emotion that feels pleasure in the beloved and that feels a heightened awareness and attraction for the beloved, it is a kind of union—a "we"—that is formed together with the beloved, and it is creative of

47 Robert Solomon, *About Love: Reinventing Romance for Our Times* (New York: Simon & Schuster, 1988), 24.

goodness in the beloved. Can love be all of these things? Can it be more? You must decide the answer to these questions by looking closely at your own experience of love and of the friendships that love has created in your own life.

Male and Female Ethics?

Whereas Aristotle (and most of his followers today) believed that love is an important part of a life of virtue, he did not put love at the center of morality, and neither did he claim that friendship and love are the most important of the virtues. Recently, however, several philosophers who have explored the differences between the way that men and women think about ethics have argued that something akin to love should lie at the center of an adequate theory of ethics. We end this exploration of virtue ethics by looking at a feminist approach to virtue ethics that makes caring and concern for others part of the very foundations of ethics.

Philosophers (usually male ones) have in the past claimed that men and women have different ethics. Often they accompany their claim with the suggestion that the ethics of women is somehow inferior to that of men. Understandably and justifiably, these claims and suggestions have angered women.

Recently, however, several female philosophers have also begun to suggest that men and women have different moralities. Nevertheless, they have argued, the moralities of women are equal to or superior to those of men. In particular, they have suggested, men tend to focus on issues that an ethics of principles emphasizes, whereas women tend to focus on issues that an ethics of virtue emphasizes.

Carol Gilligan: "Moral development for a woman is marked by progress toward more adequate ways of caring for herself and others."

© Frazer Harrison / Getty Images

Carol Gilligan. The psychologist Carol Gilligan was one of the first women to suggest that men and women approach ethics differently. She is also one of the first to suggest that the ethics of women is not inferior to that of men. In her important book *In a Different Voice: Women's Conception of Self and Morality* (1982), Gilligan argued against the views of Lawrence Kohlberg, a psychologist whose work seems to imply that women, on average, are less morally developed than men are.

Kohlberg argued that just as people's physical abilities develop through stages—a child must crawl before he or she walks or runs—people's moral abilities also develop through stages. He called the three main stages of moral development the preconventional, conventional, and postconventional levels. Parents and authority figures tell children at the first or preconventional level what is right and what is wrong. Children obey to avoid punishment. Consequently, at the preconventional level of moral development, morality focuses on the self. It is a matter of following authority and avoiding punishment. As the child matures into adolescence, he or she develops attachments and loyalties to groups: family, friends, church, and nation. Consequently, at the conventional level, morality is based on being accepted by those in one's groups and on following their conventional moral standards and rules. If the

QUICK REVIEW
Kohlberg argued that moral development moves through three levels: a preconventional level, focused on the self; a conventional level, focused on being accepted by a group and accepting the group's conventional morality; and a postconventional level, focused on moral principles. The postconventional level of moral principles is the most advanced form of morality. Most women seemed to Kohlberg to remain at the less advanced conventional level.

QUICK REVIEW
Gilligan argued that Kohlberg's levels are those through which men's morality develops, but women's morality develops through a different sequence of levels based on caring for oneself and for others. Because women are always focused on caring relationships, they seem to always be stuck in Kohlberg's second level, but in reality they are developing through different levels of caring.

QUICK REVIEW
Gilligan claims that moral development in women moves through (1) a level in which they are overly devoted to caring for themselves, (2) a level in which they are overly devoted to caring for others, and (3) a level in which they balance caring for others and for themselves.

adolescent continues to mature morally, he or she will begin to examine and question the conventional moral standards absorbed earlier in life. The adolescent may start to evaluate these standards in terms of whether they serve everyone's welfare, whether they are just, and whether they respect everyone's moral rights. For the person at this most mature or postconventional level of moral development, morality is based on universal moral principles of human welfare, justice, and rights.

However, not everyone develops fully through all the levels. Some people remain at the preconventional level all their lives, others make it to the conventional level and then go no further, and only a minority of people seem to make it all the way to the most advanced, postconventional level of moral development. Significantly, more men than women seem to make it to Kohlberg's postconventional level. Women seem to remain often at the conventional level, where attachments and loyalties to family, friends, and others are important. This implies, according to Kohlberg's theory, that by and large women are less morally developed than men are.

Enter Carol Gilligan. Gilligan pointed out a significant flaw in Kohlberg's work: He had developed his stages of moral development by studying mostly men. Consequently, Gilligan argued, his theory really describes how men's morality develops and not how women's morality develops. If women do not advance to Kohlberg's third level of male development, it is because they advance instead to a third level of female development that Kohlberg's theory ignores. Based on her own studies of women, Gilligan argued that women's morality is mostly a matter of caring and being responsible for others with whom they are involved in personal and loving relationships. Women end up getting shoved into Kohlberg's conventional level of morality because that is the only level that takes relationships and personal attachments into account. But women develop by showing increasing maturity in the way they deal with relationships.

Gilligan argued that moral development for a woman is marked by progress toward more adequate ways of caring for herself and for others. Women move through three levels of development: (1) a stage in which they are overly devoted to caring for themselves, (2) a stage in which they are overly devoted to caring for others, and (3) a stage in which they achieve a balance between caring for self and caring for others.

Gilligan claimed that at the earliest or preconventional level of moral development, the female child sees morality as a matter of taking care of herself. As the girl moves to a second or conventional level of moral development, she comes to accept the conventional standards and norms of her friends and family. These typically emphasize that, as a woman, she should devote herself to loving and caring for others even if this means neglecting her own needs. The woman at the conventional level sees morality in terms of her responsibility for maintaining the relationships within which she is enmeshed and on which others depend. If she continues to develop, she will enter a third, postconventional level of moral development. During this third stage, she will begin to question the conventional standards she had earlier accepted. She will become critical of those standards that require her to sacrifice her own needs to take care of others. She will come to see herself as a self-in-relation-to-others and will see that caring for others is deeply related to and depends upon her caring for herself. At this level, she sees morality in terms of maintaining relationships through caring for herself-in-relation-to-others.

According to Gilligan, this female perspective on morality is very different from the way men typically look at morality. When faced with moral decisions, women focus on the relationships of the people involved and see morality as a matter of taking care of the people in these loving relationships. When men face moral decisions, they focus on the individuals involved and see morality as a matter of following the moral rules or principles that apply to these individuals. Women focus on personal relationships; men focus on impartial rules and principles. In short, women tend to exhibit the personal virtues of caring and being in relationships, but men tend to exhibit the more impersonal focus on moral rules, principles, and obligations.

QUICK REVIEW
Gilligan concludes that for women, morality is focused on caring for others and maintaining personal relationships, whereas for men, morality consists of following impersonal rules and principles.

But though women tend to approach ethics differently from men, Gilligan has argued, a woman's approach to ethics is not inferior. Caring and responsibility for sustaining relationships are virtues that society greatly needs. Society, she suggests, tends to disconnect people and to promote competition, **individualism**, separation, and independence. A male emphasis on impersonal rules and principles further encourages these tendencies. Moreover, these tendencies have broken down our communities and our networks of relationships. We need the virtues of caring and responsibility for others to ensure that society does not become a collection of isolated individuals who guard their individual rights and justice but who are lonely, unattached, unloving, and uncaring.

Nel Noddings. Philosopher Nel Noddings has gone further than Gilligan in developing a female ethic based on the virtue of caring. In her book *Caring: A Feminine Approach to Ethics and Moral Education*, Noddings holds that the "feminine" virtue of caring is more fundamental than the "masculine" focus on principles:

> One might say that ethics has been discussed largely in the language of the father: in principles and propositions, in terms such as justification, fairness, justice. The mother's voice has been silent. Human caring and the memory of caring and being cared for, which I shall argue form the foundation of ethical response, have not received attention except as outcomes of ethical behavior.[48]

Noddings argues that ethics is about specific individuals in actual encounters with other specific individuals; ethics is not about abstract principles of justice and rights. The ethical person is the person who cares for another specific individual during an actual encounter with that unique person and who manifests her concern for that specific individual in concrete, loving deeds. In such relationships, the caring person does not consult abstract principles or universal rules that somehow fit all humanity, and neither does she reason about morality as if it were a geometry problem. Instead, she consults her immediate "feelings, needs, impressions, and . . . sense of personal ideal" and responds to the unique individual with whom she is dealing.

QUICK REVIEW
Noddings argues that a feminine ethic based on the virtue of caring for specific individuals in personal relationships is superior to a male ethic based on abstract principles of justice and rights.

Noddings claims that as a person grows and acquires a "growing store of memories of both caring and being cared for," she acquires the capacity to care for others as well as for herself. Gradually, the growing person forms a picture of her ideal self as a caring person. She finds the freedom to choose whether to live up to this ideal picture of herself. Ethical behavior arises when one feels caring for another person and freely chooses to act on this feeling, motivated by the desire to live up to the ideal of being a caring person: "The source of ethical behavior is, then, in twin sentiments—one that feels directly for the other and one that feels for and with the best self, who may accept and sustain the initial feeling rather than reject it."[49]

QUICK REVIEW
According to Noddings, ethical behavior consists of feeling caring toward others and choosing to act on this feeling, motivated by the desire to live up to the ideal of being a caring person.

48 Nel Noddings, *Caring: A Feminine Approach to Ethics and Moral Education* (Berkeley: University of California Press, 1984), 1.

49 Ibid., 80.

QUICK REVIEW
Gilligan and Noddings now agree that both men and women can approach morality either from a caring perspective or from universal moral principles, but women tend to deal with moral issues in terms of the caring relationships involved, whereas men tend to deal with them from a principle-based perspective.

Carol Gilligan and Nel Noddings have recently tempered their views. Both now agree that men as well as women are capable of approaching morality from the perspective of caring. Both also agree that women as well as men may approach morality in terms of universal moral principles. However, women see things in terms of the virtue of caring more instinctively than do men, who in turn are more likely to appeal to moral rules and principles.[50]

QUICK REVIEW
Critics claim that an ethic of care merely reinforces sexist stereotypes of women that drive women into the "caring" professions and forces women to care for others whatever the costs because that is what they are good at. Other critics say that an ethic of care cannot deal with moral issues that involve people with whom we have no personal relationship.

Criticisms. But a crucial question is this: Is it good that women focus on the moral virtue of caring whereas men focus on impersonal moral rules and principles? Some philosophers have argued that it is not. Our culture has traditionally said that women are "by nature" good at caring for others and has consequently relegated that job to women as mothers, wives, lovers, nurses, and schoolteachers. Thus, Gilligan and Noddings are indirectly encouraging this traditional view of women while giving men more justification for avoiding the caring tasks that could enrich their lives and personalities. For example, the lives of fathers could be enriched by their spending more time nurturing and caring for their children. But Gilligan and Noddings imply that this is not a task for men, but for women.

Other philosophers have criticized the very idea of an ethics based on caring for specific individuals with whom we have personal relationships. Such an ethics seems too narrow to encompass all our moral concerns. Clearly, we are personally related to only a few people. Through modern technology, however, our actions affect many more people than those with whom we can have personal relationships. For example, the environmental pollution that we produce with our machines and products can harm people far distant from us in time and space. Yet we will never know most of these people and never have a personal relationship with them. If ethics is only a matter of caring for those with whom we have concrete personal relationships, then ethics will have nothing to say about the wrongness of harming unknown others through environmental pollution.

The jury is still out in the case of the feminist ethic of care. This approach to ethics is still relatively young and requires more exploration and discussion. We have discussed it here, however, to see what a feminist theory of virtue might look like, a theory that places personal relationships, love, and caring at the very foundations of ethics.

Conclusions

Clearly, the virtue approach to ethics, such as Aristotle's or Noddings', differs greatly from the principles approach that Mill, Kant, and others employ. The virtue approach, in fact, reminds us of several things that the rules approach neglects. First, as we have already noted, the virtue approach emphasizes the character traits of the morally good person and the development of these traits, whereas the principles approach neglects character and focuses instead on one's duties and obligations. Yet character is undoubtedly a fundamental moral concern. Isn't each of us vitally concerned about the sort of person we are becoming? Doesn't each of us care about the sort of character we display? Isn't our character at the core of who we are, as well as at the center of how we relate to others?

Second, the virtue approach reminds us of the importance of community and early training, which the principles approach ignores. As Aristotle says, a person's

---

50 See Carol Gilligan, "Moral Orientation and Moral Development," in *Women and Moral Theory*, ed. Eva Feder Kittay and Diana T. Meyers (Totowa, NJ: Rowman & Littlefield, 1987), 19–33; see also the articles in *Mapping the Moral Domain*, ed. Carol Gilligan, Victoria Ward, and Jill McLean (Cambridge, MA: Center for the Study of Gender, Education, and Human Development, 1988).

character traits are generally developed by "training" and learning within communities (such as the family, the church, the school, as well as other private and public associations like gangs, corporations, and prisons) that shape our character by the values they prize and the traits they encourage or discourage. Thus, the idea of community is critically important to virtue ethics.

Third, this approach to ethics reminds us of the importance of our ideals about what people should be like and the virtues that the ideal person displays, especially as exemplified by the examples of our heroes and idols. The lives of morally exemplary people can illustrate virtue more clearly than anything else and can also inspire us to imitate them. The examples of Jesus, Saint Theresa of Avila, Socrates, Joan of Arc, the Buddha, Mother Teresa, Gandhi, Florence Nightingale, Martin Luther King, Jr., Rosa Parks, Malcolm X, Harriet Truman, César Chávez, and others have inspired millions to cultivate the virtues they exhibited in their lives.

Fourth, the virtue approach encourages us to look closely at aspects of our moral lives that are almost ignored by a principles approach, such as friendship and love. Focusing on rights, obligations, moral rules, and moral principles tends to make us blind to the important roles that love and friendship play in our ethical lives. Moreover, the virtue approach, by focusing on the way in which character traits develop and evolve through a person's life, helps us to understand how traits such as caring and concern can be developmentally related to a person's progress through the various stages of life and can form the basis for an important approach to the ethical life, an approach that may be particularly attractive to women.

QUICK REVIEW
The virtue approach to ethics emphasizes people's character, stresses that our communities shape our character, reminds us of the importance of moral exemplars, and calls our attention to important aspects of the moral life, such as love, friendship, caring, and concern.

Because virtue theory provides such powerful insights into our moral lives, many philosophers today see it as better than an ethic of rules and principles, such as utilitarianism and Kantian ethics. For example, Alasdair MacIntyre has urged the adoption of virtue theory as the best way to understand our moral lives:

> If human life is understood as a progress through harms and dangers, moral and physical, which someone may encounter and overcome in better and worse ways and with a greater or lesser measure of success, the virtues will find their place as those qualities the possession and exercise of which generally tend to success in this enterprise and the vices likewise as qualities which likewise tend to failure. Each human life will then embody a story whose shape and form will depend upon what is counted as a harm and danger and upon how success and failure, progress and its opposite, are understood and evaluated.[51]

But the virtue approach is not without its difficulties. The main problem that critics have raised about virtue ethics is that it does not help answer the kinds of moral questions that people most frequently ask. People seem to turn to ethics when they face situations in which they must decide what to do and the morality of the alternatives is unclear. For example, an unmarried woman finds herself pregnant and asks herself, "Should I have an abortion?" Or a woman whose injured husband has been diagnosed as "brain dead" is asked in the hospital whether she wants to have his life-support system disconnected. In such situations, people ask themselves, "What should I *do*?" instead of "What should I *be*?" But virtue ethics does not directly address the question of what one should *do*. Neither the woman considering an abortion nor the woman considering disconnecting her husband's life support is helped by being told that the good person has the qualities of honesty, courage, compassion, and generosity. They don't want to know what kind of

QUICK REVIEW
Critics of virtue theory argue that it offers no guidance when people want to know what they should do, not what kind of person they should be.

51 Alasdair MacIntyre, *After Virtue*, 135.

character they should develop but what they should do right now. Theirs is a question about the morality of actions, not the morality of character. In situations such as these, an ethics of principle seems much more helpful than an ethics of virtue. An ethics of principle provides rules that can help us see which actions are moral and which are not.

QUESTIONS

1. What are the virtues or character traits that you believe are most important for the morally good person to have in today's world? Why are these important? How would you go about cultivating this kind of a character?
2. Make a list of the virtues or character traits that you believe most people would characterize as feminine and a list of those that you believe most people would characterize as masculine. In your view, is there anything sexist about these lists? Explain. Why do people see men and women in this way?

PHILOSOPHY AT THE MOVIES

Watch *Iris* (2001), the true story of British writer and philosopher Iris Murdoch and her relationship with her husband, John Bayley. The movie traces her life from the time when she and John first meet and fall in love as young teachers to the period forty years later when Alzheimer's disease gradually robs her of her memory and leaves her completely dependent on John's care. Make a list of Iris Murdoch's and John Bayley's virtues and vices as portrayed in the movie. On which of these virtues does the movie place the highest value? Which do you think are most valuable? Are there any traits of Iris Murdoch that the movie portrays as virtues but that most people would portray as vices, or traits portrayed as vices that most would consider virtues?

7.6 Can Ethics Resolve Moral Quandaries?

Having completed our overview of major ethical theories, we should now ask this question: How should we use these theories in our own moral lives? Unfortunately, the answer to this question is not simple. As we have seen, all the theories have shortcomings. Nevertheless, each of the theories identifies aspects of our behavior that we should take into account when we make moral decisions: the pleasures and pains our actions will cause, the basic goods our nature prompts us to pursue, the obligations we believe all humans should live up to, treating people as ends and not as mere means; and the virtues and vices our actions both express and develop. Thus, each theory focuses our attention on morally important aspects of the moral life that the other theories tend to ignore. When we make a decision, then, if we want to make sure we take all the morally relevant features of our situation into account, we should look at our actions in the light of all the theories and not just of one of them.

QUICK REVIEW
No single ethical theory can elucidate all aspects of all moral decisions, yet each identifies some of the ethical considerations involved in moral decisions; by using all the theories, we come to see all or most of the considerations we need to take into account when making moral decisions.

This, of course, complicates things because the theories may conflict with one another. Our lives sometimes place us in situations in which utilitarian theory may tell us to do one thing, while Kantian theory or virtue tells us to do something else. Such conflicts are unavoidable in a world like ours, where all situations are multifaceted. In the real world, the situations we confront do not have a single or a few simple features but present us with many different complex characteristics and qualities, multiple relationships, and complicated histories. Each theory will pick out a subset of these features and use them to decide what to do, while another will focus on different features, and so may lead us to a different conclusion. This is a point that the American philosopher John Dewey makes:

> In view of the part played by the actual conflict of . . . [moral theories] in moral situations and the genuine uncertainty which results as to what should be done, I am inclined to think that one cause for the inefficacy of moral philosophies has been that in their zeal for a unitary view they have oversimplified the moral life. The outcome is a gap between the tangled realities of practice and the abstract forms of theory. A moral philosophy which should frankly recognize the impossibility of reducing all the elements in moral situations to a single commensurable principle, which should recognize that each human being has to make the best adjustment he can among . . . [theories] which are genuinely disparate, would throw light upon the actual predicaments of conduct and help individuals in making a juster estimate of the force of each competing [theory].[52]

As Dewey suggests, we have to recognize that in real life our moral decisions will often involve uncertainty because we must rely on moral principles that can lead us in conflicting directions.

This does not mean that these different approaches to ethics are useless. By considering each of the theories in turn, and asking what each of them would say about a moral issue, we can come to a full and informed understanding of all the factors that we should take into consideration when making moral decisions. But in the end, as Dewey notes, "each human being has to make the best adjustment he can" among these various theories. This means that we have to weigh and think about the various different factors identified by the theories, decide which features of the situation are most important or carry most weight, and then make our decision. The fundamental worth of studying and understanding ethical thought is not to find a theory that will automatically make our decisions for us. Instead, the aim is to find conceptual tools and theoretical frameworks that are reasonable and that help us see what is morally important in human life. Ethics is the search for reasonable ethical values and moral principles that will help us make our own informed decisions in complex moral situations. Thus, while the study of ethical theories makes us aware of the many moral options available to us, the ultimate decisions are ours to make.

To illustrate the complexity of moral decisions and how a grasp of the normative theories can help to elucidate their various morally significant aspects, let us examine two important life and death moral issues that many of us are destined to face (or perhaps have already faced). These are the issues of euthanasia and abortion.

Abortion

Abortion is a moral issue that raises questions about life and death, about what a person is and when one becomes a person, about the meaning of life, about the rights of women, and about the duties of men.

Abortion is the deliberate ending of a pregnancy before live birth. In 1973, the U.S. Supreme Court ruled in the case of *Roe v. Wade* that the Constitution guarantees each citizen a fundamental "right to privacy" and "that the right of personal privacy includes the abortion decision, but this right is qualified and must be considered

---

52 John Dewey, "Three Independent Factors in Morals" [1930] in John Dewey, *The Later Works, 1925–1953*, vol. 5, ed. Jo Ann Boydston (Carbondale: Southern Illinois University Press, 1981–1989).

against important state interests in regulation." In particular, the Supreme Court ruled, government may not make laws restricting abortions performed during the first six months of pregnancy. However, during the last three months of pregnancy, government "in promoting its interest in the potentiality of human life, may, if it chooses, regulate, and even proscribe, abortion except where it is necessary, in appropriate medical judgment, for the preservation of the life or health of the mother."

Although the Supreme Court settled the *legal* issue, the *moral* issue still remains: When, if ever, is it moral for a person to choose to have an abortion? The issue of abortion frequently raises conflicting feelings in the person faced with the situation. Consider the real case of this mother of three (anonymously named "Jane Doe") and the contradictory emotions and moral judgments that tear at her:

QUICK REVIEW
Although the Supreme Court in 1973 ruled that state laws had to allow abortions in the first six months of pregnancy, the morality of abortion remains undecided. Many, including those who have had abortions, often have contradictory feelings about the ethics of having an abortion.

> We were sitting in a bar on Lexington Avenue when I told my husband I was pregnant. . . . [T]he news was greeted with shocked silence. . . . My husband talked about his plans for a career change in the next year, to stem the staleness that fourteen years with the same investment banking firm had brought him. A new baby would preclude that option. The timing wasn't right for me either. I had just taken on a full-time job. A new baby would put me right back in the nursery. . . . It was time for us, we tried to rationalize. There just wasn't room in our lives now for another baby. We both agreed. And agreed. And agreed.
>
> How could it be that I, who am so neurotic about life that I step over bugs rather than on them . . . could so arbitrarily decide that this life shouldn't be? "It's not a life," my husband had argued, more to convince himself than me. "It's a bunch of cells smaller than my fingernail." But any woman who has had children knows that certain feeling in her taut, swollen breasts, and the slight but constant ache in her uterus that signals the arrival of a life.
>
> When my name was called [at the abortion clinic], my body felt so heavy the nurse had to help me into the examining room. I waited for my husband to burst through the door and yell "stop," but of course he didn't.
>
> "You're going to feel a burning sensation now," [the doctor] said, injecting Novocaine into the neck of the womb. The pain was swift and severe, and I twisted to get away from him. He was hurting my baby, I reasoned. . . . "Stop," I cried. "Please stop." He shook his head, busy with his equipment. "It's too late to stop now," he said. "It'll just take a few more seconds."
>
> What good sports we women are. And how obedient. Physically the pain passed even before the hum of the machine signaled that the vacuuming of my uterus was completed, my baby sucked up like ashes after a cocktail party.[53]

QUICK REVIEW
Some argue that the fetus is not a person with a right to life because it lacks certain mental traits, but critics respond that infants, retarded adults, and future generations also lack these traits yet have a right to life.

Clearly, Jane Doe's decision to have an abortion was an agonizing one, filled with contradictory feelings and distressing uncertainties. We must certainly sympathize with her anguish and the anxious doubts she had about what she was doing even as she did it. But let us also ask the question that lay behind her anguish: Was this abortion morally justified?

Many people who say abortion is not wrong argue that the fetus is not a "person." Because only persons have a moral right to life, they conclude, the fetus does not have a moral right to life. For example, philosopher Mary Anne Warren asks us to imagine that an alien encountered new creatures on some planet. How would the alien know whether such creatures were mere animals that could be killed and eaten or were, instead, persons with a moral right to life? She argues that a creature is a person only if it exhibits five traits:

---

53 From "Jane Doe, 'There Just Wasn't Room in Our Lives for Another Baby,'" *The New York Times*, May 14, 1976. Copyright © 1976 by the New York Times Co. Reprinted by permission of the author.

> I suggest that the traits which are most central to the concept of personhood, or humanity in the moral sense, are, very roughly, the following:
>
> 1. Consciousness (of objects and events external and/or internal to the being), and in particular the capacity to feel pain;
> 2. Reasoning (the *developed* capacity to solve new and relatively complex problems);
> 3. Self-motivated activity (activity which is relatively independent of either genetic or direct external control);
> 4. The capacity to communicate, by whatever means, messages of an indefinite variety of types, that is, not just with an indefinite number of possible contents, but on indefinitely many possible topics;
> 5. The presence of self-concepts, and self-awareness, either individual or racial, or both.
>
> We needn't suppose that an entity must have *all* of these attributes to be properly considered a person. . . . All we need to claim, to demonstrate that a fetus is not a person, is that any being which satisfies *none* of (1)-(5) is certainly not a person.[54]

Because fetuses do not possess any of these traits, she concludes, "a fetus is a human being which is not yet a person, and which therefore cannot coherently be said to have full moral rights." This view is similar to the suggestion of Jane Doe's husband that the fetus is "just a bunch of cells." But critics have objected to this type of argument by pointing out that infants, retarded adults, the mentally ill, and future generations do not have all the required traits, and some have none of them. Yet infants, retarded adults, and future generations, they claim, clearly have a moral right to life. So the criteria she suggests must be mistaken. Yet neither is it clear that we can prove that fetuses *are* persons. Like Jane Doe, we are left with the troubling uncertainties that the fetus may be a human "life" and "a baby," yet perhaps it might not be. Many philosophers have concluded that the issue of abortion can't be decided by arguments about whether a fetus is or is not a person.

A Kantian Approach. Although the arguments over the "personhood" of the fetus have been inconclusive, there are other ways of approaching the morality of abortion. For example, philosopher Richard Hare argues that if we adopt a Kantian approach to morality, as summarized by the Golden Rule, we will conclude that abortion is generally immoral:

> [T]he Christian "Golden Rule" [and] the Kantian Categorical Imperative [provide the same type of argument]. . . . [But] I shall use that form of the argument which rests on the Golden Rule that we should do to others as we wish them to do to us. It is a logical extension of this form of argument to say that we should do to others what *we are glad was* done to us. Two (surely readily admissible) changes are involved here. The first is a mere difference in the two tenses which cannot be morally relevant. Instead of saying that we should do to others as we wish them (in the future) to do to us, we say that we should do to others as we wish that they had done to us (in the past). The second is a change from the hypothetical to the actual; instead of saying that we should do to others as we wish that they had done to us, we say that we should do to others as we are glad that they did to us. I cannot see that this could make any difference to the spirit of the injunction. . . .
>
> The application of this injunction to the problem of abortion is obvious. If we are glad that nobody terminated the pregnancy that resulted in our birth, then we

QUICK REVIEW
Hare claims that because we should do to others what we are glad was done to us, we should not abort a fetus that would have a life like ours if we are glad we were not aborted.

54 Mary Anne Warren, "On the Moral and Legal Status of Abortion," *The Monist*, vol. 57 (1973), no. 4: 100.

are enjoined not, *ceteris paribus*, to terminate any pregnancy which will result in the birth of a person having a life like ours.[55]

This kind of Kantian approach reaches what we can call a "conservative" position on abortion. It allows aborting a mentally defective fetus that would not have a life like ours. But it would condemn having an abortion for the sake of one's career.

QUICK REVIEW
Utilitarians argue that abortion is justified when it has better consequences than the alternatives.

A Utilitarian Approach. However, many utilitarians propose a very different approach to abortion. Utilitarians who have supported the moral rightness of abortion have argued that any action that, on balance, has better consequences than the alternatives is morally permissible. Because abortion sometimes has better consequences than any other alterative—such as avoiding financial burdens, avoiding disgrace, or bearing a defective infant—it is sometimes morally justified. However, utilitarians are quick to point out that we should take into account all the consequences of our actions, including the effects on our future behavior. For example, philosopher Jane English argues that once the fetus comes to look like a person, killing it will lessen the respect we have for persons in general. At that point, then, it would be wrong to abort the fetus:

QUICK REVIEW
English, a utilitarian, claims that it is wrong to abort a fetus in the late months of pregnancy—when it looks like a person—because doing so lessens the respect we have for persons in general.

> Even if a fetus is not a person, abortion is not always permissible, because of the resemblance of a fetus to a person [and the bad consequences that killing such person-like creatures would have on our behaviors toward persons]. . . . [So] it would be wrong for a woman who is seven months pregnant to have an abortion just to avoid having to postpone a trip to Europe. In the early months of pregnancy when the fetus hardly resembles a baby at all, then, abortion is permissible whenever it is in the interests of the pregnant woman or her family. The reasons would only need to outweigh the pain and inconvenience of the abortion itself. In the middle months when the fetus comes to resemble a person, abortion would be justifiable only when the continuation of the pregnancy of the birth of the child would cause harm—physical, psychological, economic or social—to the woman. In the later months of pregnancy, even on our current assumption that a fetus is not a person, abortion seems to be wrong except to save a woman from significant injury or death.[56]

The utilitarian argument of Jane English comes to the conclusion that the Supreme Court was right to prohibit abortions only in the last three months of pregnancy. Moreover, her utilitarian argument would perhaps imply that the abortion decision of Jane Doe was justified. Or would it? Can we be certain that the consequences of an abortion are better than the consequences of having allowed the fetus to be born? Can we know that the future life of a fetus will produce less happiness than the happiness produced by aborting it?

The Value of a Future Life Approach. Another approach to abortion—one that has some similarities with natural law theory—has been proposed by philosopher Don Marquis. He begins by arguing that killing an adult human being is wrong because it deprives one of a fundamental good: one's own future life with all its

55 R. M. Hare, "Abortion and the Golden Rule," *Philosophy & Public Affairs* 4, no. 3 (Spring 1975): 207.
56 Jane English, "Abortion and the Concept of a Person," in *The Ethics of Abortion*, ed. R. M. Baird and S. E. Rosenbaum (Buffalo, NY: Prometheus, 1989), 83–92.

experiences, activities, projects, and enjoyments. Since it is wrong to deprive an adult of this good, it must be equally wrong to deprive a fetus of that same good:

> [W]e can start from the following unproblematic assumption concerning our own case: it is wrong to kill us. Why is it wrong? . . . The loss of one's life deprives one of all the experiences, activities, projects, and enjoyments that would otherwise have constituted one's future. . . . Therefore, when I die, I am deprived of all of the value of my future. Inflicting this loss on me is ultimately what makes killing me wrong. . . . The claim that the primary wrong-making feature of a killing is the loss to the victim of the value of its future has obvious consequences for the ethics of abortion. The future of a standard fetus includes a set of experiences, projects, activities, and such which are identical with the futures of adult human beings and are identical with the futures of young children. Since the reason that is sufficient to explain why it is wrong to kill human beings after the time of birth is a reason that also applies to fetuses, it follows that abortion is prima facie seriously morally wrong.[57]

Marquis' argument is an argument by analogy. Critics have argued that his analogy is mistaken. Adult humans can be said to have a future that is "theirs" because they have planned that future themselves and have some control over that future. Fetuses, obviously, cannot think and so there is no future that they have planned for themselves or that they can control. So, critics claim, fetuses do not have a future that is "theirs" as adults do, so killing them takes nothing from them that was "theirs." Marquis' argument has been widely debated. But you will have to judge for yourself whether it is acceptable.

Virtue Theory's Approach. One last perspective on abortion that we can examine is the approach of virtue theory. As we have seen, virtue theory can evaluate the morality of behavior by examining the kind of moral character that such behavior produces. If behavior produces virtue, then it is morally desirable; if it produces vices, then it is morally wanting. Notice how Janet Smith takes precisely this approach:

> The one characteristic that is nearly universal among women deciding to have abortions is that they are engaged in relationships that are not conducive to raising a child. . . . The relationships of women who have abortions seem characterized by instability, poor communication, and lack of true mutuality. Those involved in such relationships seem to be characterized by irresponsibility and confusion about what they really want—which results in them being dishonest both with themselves and with their partners. . . . Studies show that the women having abortions . . . display carelessness and indifference in their use of contraception. . . . These women seem not to have much self-knowledge, nor do they seem to be self-determining—they seem to be "letting things happen" that, were they reflective and responsible individuals, they might not accept as actions for themselves. . . . They . . . characterize abortion and indeed their own decision as taking a human life. If, then, it is a virtue to act in accord with one's principles, many of the women having abortions seem not to have this virtue and are acting in a way that will not advance their possession of it.
>
> An ethics of virtue assesses actions by the type of character that produces and chooses these actions. Abortion, in the eyes of this interpreter, does not fare well as a moral action, according to this analysis.[58]

QUICK REVIEW
Using virtue theory, Smith argues that abortion is wrong because it produces and is produced by a moral character characterized by the vices of irresponsibility, dishonesty, carelessness, indifference, and lack of principles.

57 Don Marquis, "Why Abortion is Immoral," *The Journal of Philosophy*, vol. 86, no. 4 (April 1989), 183–202. Excerpts (176 words) from pages 189, 190, and 192.

58 Janet Smith, "Moral Character and Abortion," in *Doing and Being*, ed. Joram G. Haber (New York: Macmillan, 1993), 442–454.

From the perspective of an ethics of virtue as Smith understands virtue ethics, abortion does not appear to be a morally upright option. According to Smith, abortion is wrong because it seems to produce a moral character characterized by carelessness, irresponsibility, dishonesty, and lack of principles. Were any of these traits evident in the characters of Jane Doe and her husband? If so, then this would tend to confirm Smith's argument. But it is important to keep in mind, as Smith herself tells us, that her argument shows only that certain vices are *usually* associated with abortion. It is always an open possibility that for some people, the traits generally associated with abortion will not for them accompany the decision to have an abortion.

Comparing Approaches. The various theories of ethics we have examined provide us with insight into different aspects of the morality of abortion. None of the theories by itself is adequate, for each is limited to a particular perspective on the ethics of abortion. Utilitarianism alerts us to the importance of reflecting on the good and bad consequences of choosing to have or to reject an abortion, both for ourselves and for society. Kant reminds us that it is important to ask what the significance of a fetus's future life is and whether we ourselves would value having such a life. The natural law focus on the value of a future life reminds us of the loss that abortion may involve. Virtue ethics reminds us of the importance of personal responsibility and integrity in choosing for or against abortion. Taken together, then, these theories reveal several morally critical considerations that a person should keep in mind when evaluating abortion.

However, these theories do not decide the issue for you. They tell you only what you should consider when making up your own mind about the morality of abortion. In the end, it is you who must reflect upon and weigh the importance of each of the considerations to which moral theories point, and it is you who must decide which of these considerations seems the most reasonable and seems to carry the most weight.

Euthanasia

QUICK REVIEW
In passive euthanasia, a person is allowed to die from a disease without treatment that could prolong her life; in active euthanasia, something is done or given to the person that causes her death.

Literally, *euthanasia* means "good death." However, the term today refers to any action that knowingly results in the death of a person suffering from a painful and incurable disease, as long as the action is intended to be merciful. Often, we distinguish between active and passive euthanasia. The distinction (which some philosophers question) is based on the difference between killing someone and allowing someone to die. In passive euthanasia, death is caused by the patient's disease, which is allowed to run its natural course without any treatment that might prolong the patient's life. In active euthanasia, the immediate cause of death is not the patient's disease but something that is done or given to the patient to cause his or her death, such as a lethal drug. To focus our discussion, consider this case:

> On Sunday, June 21, 1992, Jennifer Cowart, age thirty-two, and her brother George Kowalski, age twenty-eight, traveled to Pensacola Beach, Florida, for a day of relaxation. At the end of the day, Jennifer and George were heading back to their vehicle when Jennifer noticed a go-kart track. The two entered the track, bought tickets, and began riding. Within one minute, Jennifer's go-kart bumped into one of the side guardrails, flipped on its side, and burst into flames. Jennifer was seat-belted in the go-kart and could not get out. George tried to run into the fire to save his sister, but the flames were too intense. Bystanders attempted to use a fire extinguisher, but it did little to lessen the inferno. Jennifer was trapped in the burning go-kart for two minutes when her seat belt finally burned through and she fell to the ground. George grabbed his sister and pulled her away from the fire. Jennifer was alive. She was lying on the asphalt alert, oriented, and coherent.

> She had suffered 3rd and 4th degree burns covering ninety-five percent of her body. She was suffering the worst pain imaginable. At the scene, Jennifer begged the rescue personnel to "let me die." Instead, Jennifer was flown to a burn center in Mobile, Alabama, where she remained for one year until she . . . died. Medical personnel described Jennifer as suffering from the most agonizing physical pain they had ever witnessed. They said there was no way to effectively alleviate Jennifer's pain without permanently sedating her, which would have resulted in death. Thus, this was not done. Jennifer was so badly burned that her two children (age nine and five) were not permitted to see her for the entire one-year period she was hospitalized. Jennifer was aware that she had lost her ears, nose, fingers, toes, and that she had very limited use of her legs and arms. She knew she would forever have problems with her kidneys, liver, lungs, and all other body organs. She knew that she was so badly disfigured that if she ever got out of the hospital and went to any public place that people would be frightened of her. . . . I could not stop asking the question: "Who gave the medical profession the authority to keep Jennifer alive under these conditions?" She had been begging to die, and her chance of survival was less than ten percent. Yet, the medical providers made the decision to perform heroic efforts to save her.[59]

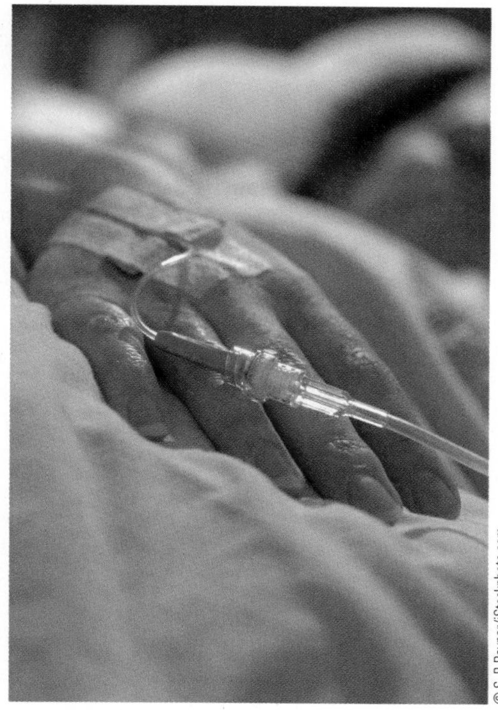
© S. P. Rayner/iStockphoto.com

Clearly, the author of this true story is not asking whether the doctors had the legal authority to keep Jennifer alive. The author is asking, instead, whether the doctors had a moral right to keep her alive. He is suggesting that perhaps the doctors should have allowed her to die without any form of treatment aimed at prolonging her life, or perhaps that they should have attempted "permanently sedating her, which would have resulted in death." If her doctors had allowed her to die without administering any life-prolonging treatment, they would have been engaged in a form of "passive euthanasia"; on the other hand, administering sedative drugs that would result in her death would have been a form of "active euthanasia."

Natural Law: Pro and Con. Whatever the legality of euthanasia might be, the moral question still remains: Is active euthanasia morally permissible? The conservative position on this question has been set out by many natural law ethicists, such as J. Gay-Williams:

> Every human being has a natural inclination to continue living. Our reflexes and responses fit us to fight attackers, flee wild animals, and dodge out of the way of trucks. In our daily lives we exercise the caution and care necessary to protect

59 Martin Levin, "Physician-Assisted Suicide: Legality and Morality," accessed August 31, 2012, at http://www.levinlaw.com/news/2002/5/8/physician-assisted-suicide-legality-and-morality. Reprinted with the permission of the author.

> ourselves. Our bodies are similarly structured for survival. . . . Euthanasia does violence to this natural goal of survival. It is literally acting against nature because all the processes of nature are bent towards the end of bodily survival. . . .
>
> By reason alone, then, we can recognize that euthanasia sets us against our own nature. Furthermore, in doing so, euthanasia does violence to our dignity. Our dignity comes from seeking our ends. When one of our goals is survival, and actions are taken that eliminate that goal, then our natural dignity suffers. Unlike animals, we are conscious through reason of our nature and our ends. Euthanasia involves acting as if this dual nature—inclination towards survival and awareness of this as an end—did not exist. Thus, euthanasia denies our basic human character and requires that we regard ourselves or others as something less than fully human.[60]

QUICK REVIEW
Gay-Williams uses natural law ethics to argue that because we have a natural inclination toward life and because our dignity comes from seeking that toward which we have a natural inclination, it is wrong to destroy life through euthanasia.

The natural law position, then, argues that life is a fundamental human good whose inviolable value we can uncover by reflecting on our natural inclinations. Because active euthanasia destroys this fundamental human good, it is immoral.

Therefore, it would be wrong for a doctor to follow Alsop's suggestion and put Jack to death.

But we have seen that natural law reasoning has some shortcomings. In particular, natural law does not make clear why we have a moral obligation to follow our natural inclinations. Perhaps a natural law ethicist could respond that we are obligated to follow our natural inclinations because these embody God's commands. Yet what light can such a divine command approach to euthanasia provide for the nonbeliever?

Utilitarianism: Pro and Con. Utilitarianism provides a different approach to euthanasia. Philosopher James Rachels expresses the utilitarian argument in favor of active euthanasia as follows:

> Terminal patients sometimes suffer pain so horrible that it can hardly be comprehended by those who have not actually experienced it. . . . The argument from mercy says: euthanasia is justified because it provides an end to that. . . .
>
> I want now to present a . . . version of the argument from mercy, which is inspired by utilitarianism. I believe that the following argument is sound and proves that active euthanasia can be justified:
>
> 1. If an action promotes the best interests of everyone concerned, and violates no one's rights, then that action is morally acceptable.
> 2. In at least some cases, active euthanasia promotes the best interests of everyone concerned and violates no one's rights.
> 3. Therefore, in at least some cases active euthanasia is morally acceptable.
>
> How can it be wrong to do an action that is merciful, that benefits everyone concerned, and that violates no one's rights?[61]

QUICK REVIEW
Rachels uses utilitarianism to argue that when euthanasia benefits everyone concerned by putting an end to a person's pain and suffering and violates no one's rights, it is morally justified.

It is important to notice that Rachels qualifies his argument with the proviso that "no one's rights" should be violated by an act of euthanasia. In particular, Rachels wants to rule out the possibility of involuntary euthanasia—that is, euthanasia in which the patient does not consent to being put to death. A patient has the right to refuse to be put to death, Rachels holds, and active euthanasia is not justified when it violates this right.

---

60 J. Gay-Williams, "The Wrongfulness of Euthanasia," in *Intervention and Reflection: Basic Issues in Medical Ethics*, ed. Ronald Munson (Belmont, CA: Wadsworth, 1979).

61 James Rachels, "More Impertinent Distinctions and a Defense of Active Euthanasia," in *Biomedical Ethics*, ed. Thomas A. Mappes and Jane S. Zembaty (New York: McGraw-Hill, 1981), 355–359.

Obviously, Rachels disagrees with the natural law position on euthanasia. In Rachels' view, it would have been morally legitimate for a doctor to have put Jennifer to death. Yet, does the utilitarian argument ignore the broader consequences of euthanasia? In most cases, won't the death of a person inflict great grief, emotional pain, distress, and even economic deprivation on those who are left behind? Moreover, once we allow physicians to put to death those who request it, will physicians gradually lose their commitment to saving life? Will society move down a slippery slope toward allowing doctors to put to death anyone whose life society deems no longer valuable (as may have happened during the Nazi era in Germany)?

A Kantian Approach. Rachels holds that his conclusion is supported not only by utilitarianism but also by a Kantian approach to euthanasia. One problem with utilitarianism, as we have seen, is that utilitarianism assumes that only consequences matter when evaluating an action, and consequences are difficult to predict. A Kantian approach does not rely on consequences:

> Kant argued that we should act only on rules that we are willing to have applied universally; that is, we should behave as we would be willing to have everyone behave. . . . If we would not be willing for the rule to be followed universally, then we should not follow it ourselves. Thus, if we are not willing for others to apply the rule to us, we ought not apply it to them.
>
> The application of all this to the question of euthanasia is fairly obvious. Each of us is going to die someday, although most of us do not know when or how. But suppose you were told that you would die in one of two ways, and you were asked to choose between them. First, you could die quietly, and without pain, from a fatal injection. Or second, you could choose to die of an affliction so painful that for several days before death you would be reduced to howling like a dog, with your family standing by helplessly, trying to comfort you, but going through its own psychological hell. It is hard to believe that any sane person, when confronted by these possibilities would choose to have a rule applied that would force upon him or her the second option. And if we would not want such a rule, which excludes euthanasia, applied to us, then we should not apply such a rule to others.[62]

QUICK REVIEW
Rachels also uses Kantian ethics to argue that because we would not be willing to live by a rule that forced us to suffer pain when we had a terminal illness instead of being put painlessly to death, it is wrong to apply such a rule to others.

This Kantian approach implies that it would have been morally permissible to put Jennifer Cowart to death. Although Rachels does not mention it in the preceding passage, he believes the Kantian approach requires that doctors get Jennifer's informed consent. Yet does such a Kantian approach assume a kind of ideal situation that cannot be obtained in a hospital situation? How realistic is it to expect a person suffering the extremities of a painful terminal illness—drugged, depressed, and perhaps subject to the subtle manipulations of an exhausted family—to be able to make choices that are free and rational?

Comparing Views. The moral theories of natural law, utilitarianism, and Kantian ethics, then, do not agree on the subject of euthanasia. But this does not mean that the three approaches are useless. On the contrary, each approach again calls our attention to one or more of the factors that we must take into account to evaluate the morality of active euthanasia. Natural law reminds us that human life is a basic good with intrinsic value. It informs us that we should not take life without serious cause and without due consideration. The utilitarian argument of Rachels suggests that in some cases the evil of pain may override the value of the basic good of life. And Rachels' proviso reminds us of the key importance of securing a person's voluntary

QUICK REVIEW
Each theory sheds a different light on considerations to keep in mind when deciding whether euthanasia is morally justified.

62 Ibid.

consent before administering euthanasia. Finally, the Kantian argument reminds us of our fundamental interdependence: What we may want others to do for us when we are in need, we should now consider doing for those presently in need.

 thinking critically • Moral Reasoning

We said earlier that ethical theories do not automatically tell us what we should do in a specific situation or about a specific issue such as abortion. For one thing, the theories can provide conflicting advice. Moreover, each theory considers only one or a few of the morally important aspects of a situation, so each theory by itself provides an incomplete assessment of the situation. For these reasons, using the theories to help us make our moral decisions requires considering what each theory says, and trying to use the insights of all the theories.

QUICK REVIEW
Conscientious moral reasoning involves: (1) recognizing that a situation raises ethical issues, (2) getting the relevant facts about the situation, (3) identifying the options for responding to the situation, (4) evaluating the ethics of each option using the ethical theories, (5) making a decision by weighing what the theories suggest.

But how do we go about doing this? What kind of reasoning or thinking is involved in making a conscientious moral decision? We can, of course, be sloppy in the way we make our moral decisions, for example, by making our decisions solely on the basis of our emotions. But how would we make a moral decision if we were conscientiously trying to do our best by making the best use of our reasoning and thinking abilities? We can summarize the process of reasoning that can lead up to a conscientious moral decision in five steps:

1. Recognizing that a situation raises an ethical issue.
2. Getting the relevant facts about the situation.
3. Identifying the options for responding to the situation.
4. Evaluating the ethics of each of the options.
5. Making a decision.

To understand these five steps, let us discuss them one by one.

1. *Recognizing that a situation raises an ethical issue.* Before we can even start to think about the ethical issues a situation raises, we need to recognize that such issues are present. We noted earlier that moral standards are those that deal with matters that involve harming or injuring others or oneself. Situations that raise ethical issues, then, will be those that involve serious harm or injury to others or to oneself. Such situations would include, for example, lying that has serious consequences for others or using street drugs to which we ourselves can become addicted. But not all injuries raise ethical issues (a painful medical operation, for example, might not raise any ethical issues). In addition a situation that raises an ethical issue is one in which the harm that is inflicted is the kind that potentially could violate our moral standards. This does not mean that we *know* the harm or injury violates our moral standards. It only means that we *suspect it could* violate our moral standards. The suspicion or feeling that harm that is being inflicted, or could be inflicted, may violate our moral standards signals that we face a situation that raises ethical issues and so requires closer ethical scrutiny.
2. *Getting the relevant facts about the situation.* In order to clarify whether an ethical issue is actually present in a situation we face, and to determine what the issue is, we must inform ourselves about the situation. We need to answer questions like these: What exactly is the harm that is involved and how certain are we that it will occur? Who is harmed and how many are harmed? Is there something special about those who are harmed (for example, have they committed a crime)? Who is inflicting the harm, is their action intentional, and what is their relationship to those whom they are harming (for example are there any promises, commitments, obligations or family relationships between them)? How significant is the harm

and how imminent is it? Are any benefits produced by the harm and if so, what are those benefits, how large are they, and who receives them? Are there any other morally relevant features of the situation; that is are there any other facts that can influence or make a difference to the moral assessments we make about the situation?

3. *Identifying the options for responding to the situation.* When we are clear about the nature of the situation, we can turn to asking what others or we *could* do about the situation. This does not mean trying to figure out what others or we *should do* about the situation. Instead, it means identifying the many different things we *could do* to respond to, or deal with, the situation. What are the various courses of action that we could take to deal with the situation? What does each of these courses of action involve; that is, what are the probable consequences of each course of action?
4. *Evaluating the ethics of each of the options.* This is the point at which the ethical theories we have studied can and should enter into our moral reasoning. We ask how each of the courses of action available to us measures up to the moral principles advanced by the theories of ethics we have studied, in light of all the relevant facts. In particular, and given the facts we have, we ask:
   a. The utilitarian question: Which course of action will produce the most benefits and do the least harm?
   b. The Kantian questions: Which course of action treats everyone involved as ends and not merely as means, and which course of action would I be willing to have everyone adopt in any similar situation?
   c. The natural law question: Which course of action best respects the basic human goods of life, family, knowledge and an orderly society?
   d. The virtue questions: Which course of action expresses a morally virtuous character or will tend to develop a morally virtuous character? Which course of action expresses a morally vicious character or will tend to develop such a character?
5. *Making a decision.* After considering what each of these theories says about each of the options available to us, we must choose that course of action that we believe is best supported by the theories. Sometimes, of course, the theories will conflict. In such cases, we must do our best to figure out which theory seems most relevant or germane to the kind of ethical issue that is involved, or which theory we believe should be given the greatest weight in the particular situation.

We should note that one of the most common mistakes people make in their moral reasoning, is being inconsistent: failing to reach the same conclusions about cases that are the same in all relevant respects. When we are dealing with non-moral matters, we generally recognize that if two things are the same in all relevant respects, then a judgment we make about one, should also apply to the other. For example, if two apples are exactly alike in ripeness, sweetness, texture, size, shape, color, and everything else related to evaluating their commercial grade, then if one is judged to be "Grade A," the other should also be judged to be "Grade A." More generally: consistency requires that two things should be treated the same when they are the same in all the relevant respects, i.e., in all the respects that are relevant to the treatment in question.

QUICK REVIEW
Consistency in moral reasoning requires making the same moral judgments about ourselves that we make about others who are in circumstances that are the same as ours in all the relevant respects. To avoid the consistency requirement we engage in fallacious ways of thinking.

Unfortunately, when we are reasoning about moral matters, we often fail to live up to the consistency requirement. We may reason, for example, to the conclusion that other people are behaving immorally when they lie about their experience on their job resumes. Yet when we (or a friend or family member) "exaggerate" our experience on our own job resume, we may tell ourselves that it is morally permissible for us to engage in that kind of "white lie." When we do this, we violate the consistency requirement unless there are relevant differences between our situation and the situation of those we condemned for falsifying their job resume. All reasoning should be consistent, and consistency in moral reasoning means at least that we must be willing to accept the consequences of making the same moral judgments about ourselves that we make about others who are in circumstances that are the same as ours in all the relevant respects. (Two sets of circumstances are the same in all the relevant respects when all those factors that have a bearing on the judgment that an action is right or wrong in one set of circumstances, are also present in the other.)

We tend to violate the consistency requirement in our moral reasoning because we do not want to admit, even to ourselves, that we are guilty of the same wrongs that we attribute to others. In fact, we engage in a number of fallacious mental tricks to avoid reasoning to the conclusion that what we are doing or intend to do is immoral. We *use euphemisms* to convince ourselves that our situation does not raise ethical issues. Businessmen, for example, refer to firing people as "downsizing"; government officials refer to torture as "enhanced interrogation techniques"; politicians refer to lies as "misstatements" or "less than precise words." We *rationalize* the harms we inflict by telling ourselves that we do it in pursuit of a worthy cause. The president of a company, for example, may fraudulently deceive his stockholders by telling himself that he is doing it for the sake of his employees. We *diminish the magnitude of the harm* we do by comparing it to other larger evils. I may think, for example, that the office supplies I steal at work are inconsequential compared to what I have seen others do or compared to the wrongs I think the company has inflicted on me. We *dehumanize those we harm* so we can avoid seeing that we are injuring human beings like ourselves. For example, we may think of the employees we fire as "human resources"; during the U.S. war in Vietnam soldiers referred to enemy soldiers as "gooks"; Hitler referred to the Jewish population as "the Jewish problem," and referred to murdering them as "the final solution." And we *attribute to others the responsibility* for harmful actions we have carried out. We may injure someone and think, "He (the victim) forced me to do it," or "He (the victim) had it coming to him," or "My boss made me do it" or "I was just following orders."

These are but a few of the fallacious mental tricks that we use to inconsistently avoid accepting the judgment of a piece of moral reasoning that concludes that we are guilty of the same wrongs that we attribute to others. We should strive to avoid them, just like we try to avoid other fallacious ways of thinking.

QUESTIONS

1. Consider a situation that confronted you with a moral dilemma. Discuss what each of these theories of obligation would have required you to do: natural law, utilitarianism, Kant's categorical imperative, virtue ethics, Buddhist ethics. Does each of these theories provide clear guidance about what you should do? Explain.

2. Try living a day according to the utilitarian principle. What problems do you find yourself facing as you go through your day attempting to apply utilitarianism? Try the same with the other approaches to ethics that we have discussed.

3. Some philosophers hold that utilitarianism imposes extremely heavy obligations on us. Others hold that Kant's categorical imperative imposes even heavier obligations. Which of these two approaches do you think would be easier to follow? Why?

4. Write down the fundamental moral principles that you feel you should live up to. Why are these principles appropriate? How would you show someone that you are not mistaken in adopting them?

PHILOSOPHY AT THE MOVIES

Watch *The Sea Inside (Mar Adentro)* (2004), the true story of Ramon Sampedro, a Spanish quadriplegic who for decades fights government officials to allow him to end his life, while friends like the woman Rosa try to convince him that his life is worth living. Do you believe that Ramon Sampedro is justified in asking for euthanasia? Why or why not? Were officials justified in preventing him from practicing euthanasia on himself? Explain your answers in terms of the moral theories described in this chapter.

Chapter Summary

Whether or not we choose to acknowledge them as such, the moral values we hold and the obligations we feel constitute expressions of who we are, how we see things, and how we wish to be seen by others. In choosing a moral lifestyle, we're really defining who we are. Nevertheless, if our morality is to be an expression of the self we have truly chosen to be, we must carefully reflect on our values and decide for ourselves whether or not they are reasonable. We must weigh their merits and liabilities in the light of our own lives, circumstances, and understanding of human nature. Such reflection places heavy emphasis on self-growth, especially on increasing our knowledge and awareness of self and the world.

The main points of the chapter are:

7.1 What Is Ethics?

- Ethics is the study of those values that relate to our moral conduct, including questions of good and evil, right and wrong, and moral responsibility.

7.2 Is Ethics Relative?

- The descriptive study of ethics, which raises the issue of ethical relativism, studies ethics from a factual point of view. Ethics is the search for principles of moral behavior that are reasonable.

7.3 Do Consequences Make an Action Right?

- Consequentialist theories claim that the morality of an action depends only on its consequences.
- Egoism is the consequentialist position that states the following: Always act in such a way that your actions promote your best long-term interests.
- Act utilitarianism is the consequentialist position that states this: Always act so that your actions produce the greatest happiness for everyone.
- Rule utilitarianism is the consequentialist position that states the following: Always follow those rules that tend to produce the greatest happiness for everyone.

7.4 Do Rules Define Morality?

- Nonconsequentialist theories claim that the morality of an action depends on factors other than consequences.
- Divine command theory is a nonconsequentialist theory that enjoins us to follow the law of God. There are scriptural and natural law versions of divine command theory.

- Kant's categorical imperative is a nonconsequentialist position that states this: Always act in such a way that your reasons for acting are reasons you could will to have everyone act on in similar circumstances, and always treat persons as ends and not merely as means.
- Buddhism emphasizes volition and ties morality to wisdom. Its moral code is expressed in precepts that invite followers to refrain from certain actions and to develop certain virtues.

7.5 Is Ethics Based on Character?

- Virtue ethics identifies the character traits of the morally good person; it emphasizes the kind of person we should become instead of principles of action. Some virtue theories argue that male and female virtues differ.

7.6 Can Ethics Resolve Moral Quandaries?

- Application of the normative theories to issues such as abortion and euthanasia suggests that each theory provides important and distinctive insights into factors that should be taken into account when making moral decisions.
- **Conscientious moral reasoning involves: (1) recognizing that a situation raises ethical issues, (2) getting the relevant facts, (3) identifying our options, (4) evaluating the ethics of each option, and (5) making a decision. It also fulfills the consistency requirement and avoids fallacious mental tricks by which we seek to escape the consistency requirement.**

7.7 Readings

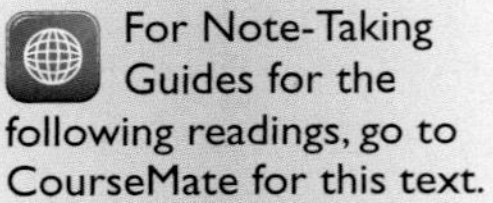
For Note-Taking Guides for the following readings, go to CourseMate for this text.

The following readings focus on a pressing moral issue that we have not yet discussed in this chapter: What moral obligations, if any, does each of us have toward the poor? The first selection, "The Heavenly Christmas Tree" is a classic short story by Fyodor Dostoyevsky that raises this question. In his story, Dostoyevsky asks us to consider a situation that, he suggests, "must have happened somewhere at some time." His story describes the plight of an impoverished boy wandering the streets of a large city on Christmas Eve. In the second reading, Australian philosopher Peter Singer, an avowed utilitarian, argues that we have an obligation to help the starving people of the world even if this means doing without luxuries. Singer claims that if we can prevent something bad from happening without sacrificing anything that is of comparable value, then we are obligated to prevent it. Because starvation is bad, we are obligated to prevent it, and because luxuries—such as more clothes or a better music system—are not of comparable value to preventing starvation, we are obligated to spend our money on preventing starvation rather than on such luxuries.

FYODOR DOSTOYEVSKY

The Heavenly Christmas Tree

I am a novelist, and I suppose I have made up this story. I write "I suppose," though I know for a fact that I have made it up, but yet I keep fancying that it must have happened somewhere at some time, that it must have happened on Christmas Eve in some great town in a time of terrible frost.

I have a vision of a boy, a little boy, six years old or even younger. This boy woke up that morning in a cold damp cellar. He was dressed in a sort of little dressing gown and was shivering with cold. There was a cloud of white steam from his breath, and sitting on a box in the corner, he blew the steam out of his mouth and amused himself in his dullness watching it float away. But he was terribly hungry. Several times that morning he went up to the plank bed where his sick mother was lying on a mattress as thin as a pancake, with some sort of bundle under her head for a pillow. How had she come here? She must have come with her boy from some other town and suddenly fallen ill. The landlady who let the "corners" had been taken two days before to the police station, the lodgers were out and about as the holiday was so near, and the only one left had been lying for the last twenty-four hours dead drunk, not having waited for Christmas. In another corner of the room a wretched old woman of eighty, who had once been a children's nurse but was now left to die friendless, was moaning and groaning with rheumatism, scolding and grumbling at the boy so that he was afraid to go near her corner. He had got a drink of water in the outer room, but could not find a crust anywhere, and had been on the point of waking his mother a dozen times.

He felt frightened at last in the darkness: it had long been dusk, but no light was kindled. Touching his mother's face, he was surprised that she did not move at all, and that she was as cold as the wall. "It is very cold here," he thought. He stood a little, unconsciously letting his hands rest on the dead woman's shoulders, then he breathed on his fingers to warm them, and then quietly fumbling for his cap on the bed, he went out of the cellar. He would have gone earlier, but was afraid of the big dog, which had been howling all day at the neighbor's door at the top of the stairs. But the dog was not there now, and he went out into the street.

Mercy on us, what a town! He had never seen anything like it before. In the town from which he had come, it was always such black darkness at night. There was one lamp for the whole street, the little, low-pitched, wooden houses were closed up with shutters, there was no one to be seen in the street after dusk, all the people shut themselves up in their houses, and there was nothing but the howling of packs of dogs, hundreds and thousands of them barking and howling all night. But there it was so warm and he was given food, while here—oh, dear, if he only had something to eat! And what a noise and rattle here, what light and what people, horses and carriages, and what a frost! The frozen steam hung in clouds over the horses, over their warmly breathing mouths; their hoofs clanged against the stones through the powdery snow, and every one pushed so, and—oh, dear, how he longed for some morsel to eat, and how wretched he suddenly felt. A policeman walked by and turned away to avoid seeing the boy.

Here was another street—oh, what a wide one, here he would be run over for certain; how everyone was shouting, racing and driving along, and the light, the light! And what was this? A huge glass window, and through the window a tree reaching up to the ceiling; it was a fir tree, and on it were ever so many lights, gold papers and apples and little dolls and horses; and there were children clean and dressed in their best running about the room, laughing and playing and eating and drinking something. And then a little girl began dancing with one of the boys, what a pretty little girl! And he could hear the music through the window. The boy looked and wondered and laughed, though his toes were aching with the cold and his fingers were red and stiff so that it hurt him to move them. And all at once the boy remembered how his toes and fingers hurt him, and began crying, and ran on; and again through another window-pane he saw another Christmas tree, and on a table cakes of all sorts—almond cakes, red cakes and yellow cakes, and three grand young ladies were sitting there, and they gave the cakes to any one who went up to them, and the door kept opening, lots of gentlemen and ladies went in from the street. The boy crept up, suddenly opened the door and went in. Oh, how they shouted at him and waved him back! One lady went up to him hurriedly and slipped a coin into his hand, and with her own hands opened the door into the street for him! How frightened he was. And the coin rolled away and clinked upon the steps; he could not bend his red fingers to hold it tight.

The boy ran away and went on, where he did not know. He was ready to cry again but he was afraid, and ran on and on and blew his fingers. And he was miserable because he felt suddenly so lonely and terrified, and all at once, mercy on us! What was this again? People were standing in a crowd admiring. Behind a glass window there were three little dolls, dressed in red and green dresses, and exactly, exactly as though they were alive. One was a little old man sitting and playing a big violin, the two others were standing close by and playing little violins and nodding in time, and looking at one another, and their lips moved, they were speaking, actually speaking, only one couldn't hear through the glass. And at first the boy thought they were alive, and when he grasped that they were dolls he laughed. He had never seen such dolls before, and had no idea there were such dolls! And he wanted to cry, but he felt amused, amused by the dolls. All at once he fancied that some one caught at his smock behind: a wicked big boy was standing beside him and suddenly hit him on the head, snatched off his cap and tripped him up. The boy fell down on the ground, at once there was a shout, he was numb with fright, he jumped up and ran away. He ran, and not knowing where he was going, ran in at the gate of some one's courtyard, and sat down behind a stack of wood: "They won't find me here, besides it's dark!"

He sat huddled up and was breathless from fright, and all at once, quite suddenly, he felt so happy: his hands and feet suddenly left off aching and grew so warm, as warm as though he were on a stove; then he shivered all over, then he gave a start, why, he must have been asleep. How nice to have a sleep here! "I'll sit here a little and go and look at the dolls again," said the boy, and smiled thinking of them. "Just as though they were alive! . . ." And suddenly he heard his mother singing over him. "Mammy, I am asleep; how nice it is to sleep here!"

"Come to my Christmas tree, little one," a soft voice suddenly whispered over his head.

He thought that this was still his mother, but no, it was not she. Who it was calling him, he could not see, but some one bent over and embraced him in the darkness; and he stretched out his hands to him, and . . . and all at once—oh, what a bright light! Oh, what a Christmas tree! And yet it was not a fir tree, he had never seen a tree like that! Where was he now? Everything was bright and shining, and all round him were dolls; but no, they were not dolls, they were little boys and girls, only so bright and shining. They all came flying round him, they all kissed him, took him and carried him along with them, and he was flying himself, and he saw that his mother was looking at him and laughing joyfully. "Mammy, Mammy; oh, how nice it is here, Mammy!" And again he kissed the children and wanted to tell them at once of those dolls in the shop window. "Who are you, boys? Who are you, girls?" he asked, laughing and admiring them.

"This is Christ's Christmas tree," they answered. '"Christ always has a Christmas tree on this day, for the little children who have no tree of their own. . . ." And he found out that all these little boys and girls were children just like himself; that some had been frozen in the baskets in which they had as babies been laid on the doorsteps of well-to-do Petersburg people, others had been boarded out with Finnish women by the Foundling and had been suffocated, others had died at their starved mother's breasts in the Samara famine, others had died in the third-class railway carriages from the foul air; and yet they were all here, they were all like angels about Christ, and He was in the midst of them and held out His hands to them and blessed them and their sinful mothers. . . . And the mothers of these children stood on one side weeping; each one knew her boy or girl, and the children flew up to them and kissed them and wiped away their tears with their little hands, and begged them not to weep because they were so happy.

And down below in the morning the porter found the little dead body of the frozen child on the wood stack; they sought out his mother too. . . . She had died before him. They met before the Lord God in heaven.

Why have I made up such a story, so out of keeping with an ordinary diary, and a writer's above all? And I promised two stories dealing with real events! But that is just it, I keep fancying that all this may have happened really—that is, what took place in the cellar and on the wood stack; but as for Christ's Christmas tree, I cannot tell you whether that could have happened or not.

Fyodor Dostoyevsky, *Short Stories* (New York: Books, Inc., 1900).

PETER SINGER

Famine, Affluence, and Morality

. . . I begin with the assumption that suffering and death from lack of food, shelter, and medical care is bad. I think most people will agree about this, although one may reach the same view by different routes. I shall not argue for this view. People can hold all sorts of eccentric positions, and perhaps from some of them it would not follow that death by starvation is in itself bad. It is difficult, perhaps impossible, to refute such positions, and so for brevity I will henceforth take this assumption as accepted. Those who disagree need read no further.

My next point is this: if it is in our power to prevent something bad from happening, without thereby sacrificing anything of comparable moral importance, we ought, morally, to do it. By "without sacrificing anything of comparable moral importance" I mean without causing anything else comparably bad to happen, or doing something that is wrong in itself, or failing to promote some moral good, comparable in significance to the bad thing we can prevent. This principle seems almost as uncontroversial as the last one. It requires us only to prevent what is bad, and not to promote what is good, and it requires this of us only when we can do it without sacrificing anything that is, from the moral point of view, comparably important. I could even, as far as the application of my argument to the Bengal emergency* is concerned, qualify the point so as to make it: if it is in our power to prevent something very bad from happening, without thereby sacrificing anything morally significant, we ought, morally, to do it. An application of this principle would be as follows: if I am walking past a shallow pond and see a child drowning in it, I ought to wade in and pull the child out. This will mean getting my clothes muddy, but this is insignificant, while the death of the child would presumably be a very bad thing.

The uncontroversial appearance of the principle just stated is deceptive. If it were acted upon, even in its qualified form, our lives, our society, and our world would be fundamentally changed. For the principle takes, firstly, no account of proximity or distance. It makes no moral difference whether the person I can help is a neighbor's child ten yards from me or a Bengali whose name I shall never know, ten thousand miles away. Secondly, the principle makes no distinction between cases in which I am the only person who could possibly do anything and cases in which I am just one among millions in the same position.

I do not think I need to say much in defense of the refusal to take proximity and distance into account. The fact that a person is physically near to us, so that we have personal contact with him, may make it more likely that we *shall* assist him, but this does not show that we *ought* to help him rather than another who happens to be further away. If we accept any principle of impartiality, universalizability, equality, or whatever, we cannot discriminate against someone merely because he is far away from us (or we are far away from him). Admittedly, it is possible that we are in a better position to judge what needs to be done to help a person near to us than one far away, and perhaps also to provide the assistance we judge to be necessary. If this were the case, it would be a reason for helping those near to us first. This may once have been a justification for being more concerned with the poor in one's own town than with famine victims in India. Unfortunately for those who like to keep their moral responsibilities limited, instant communication and swift transportation have changed the situation. From the moral point of view, the development of the world into a "global village" has made an important, though still unrecognized, difference to our moral situation. Expert observers and supervisors, sent out by famine relief organizations or permanently stationed in famine-prone areas, can direct our aid to a refugee in Bengal almost as effectively as we could get it to someone in our own block. There would seem, therefore, to be no possible justification for discriminating on geographical grounds.

There may be a greater need to defend the second implication of my principle—that the fact that there are millions of other people in the same position, in respect to the Bengali refugees, as I am, does not make the situation significantly different from a situation in which I am the only person who can prevent something very bad from occurring. Again, of course, I admit that there is a psychological difference between the cases; one feels less guilty about doing nothing if one can point to others, similarly placed, who have also done nothing. Yet this can make no real difference to our moral obligations. Should I consider that I am less obliged to pull the drowning child out of the pond if on looking around I see other people, no further away than I am, who have also noticed the child but are doing nothing? One has only to ask this question to see the absurdity of the view that numbers lessen obligation. It is a view that is an ideal excuse for inactivity: unfortunately most of the major evils—poverty, overpopulation, pollution—are problems in which everyone is almost equally involved.

If my argument so far has been sound, neither our distance from a preventable evil nor the number

* Bengal is an Indian state that at the time of this writing was undergoing famine, its citizens migrating as refugees to other countries.—Ed.

of other people who, in respect to that evil, are in the same situation as we are, lessens our obligation to mitigate or prevent that evil. I shall therefore take as established the principle I asserted earlier. As I have already said, I need to assert it only in its qualified form: if it is in our power to prevent something very bad from happening, without thereby sacrificing anything else morally significant, we ought, morally, to do it.

The outcome of this argument is that our traditional moral categories are upset. The traditional distinction between duty and charity cannot be drawn, or at least, not in the place we normally draw it. Giving money to the Bengal Relief Fund is regarded as an act of charity in our society. The bodies which collect money are known as "charities." These organizations see themselves in this way—if you send them a check, you will be thanked for your "generosity." Because giving money is regarded as an act of charity, it is not thought that there is anything wrong with not giving. The charitable man may be praised, but the man who is not charitable is not condemned. People do not feel in any way ashamed or guilty about spending money on new clothes or a new car instead of giving it to famine relief. (Indeed, the alternative does not occur to them.) This way of looking at the matter cannot be justified. When we buy new clothes not to keep ourselves warm but to look "well-dressed" we are not providing for any important need. We would not be sacrificing anything significant if we were to continue to wear our old clothes, and give the money to famine relief. By doing so, we would be preventing another person from starving. It follows from what I have said earlier that we ought to give money away, rather than spend it on clothes which we do not need to keep us warm. To do so is not charitable, or generous. Nor is it the kind of act which philosophers and theologians have called "supererogatory"—an act which it would be good to do, but not wrong not to do. On the contrary, we ought to give the money away, and it is wrong not to do so. . . .

From *Philosophy and Public Affairs*, vol. 1, no. 3 (Spring 1972): 231–235, 238–240, 242–243. Copyright © 1972 by Princeton University Press. Excerpts reprinted by permission of Princeton University Press.

7.8 HISTORICAL SHOWCASE

Nietzsche and Wollstonecraft

Many people are skeptical about the claims of morality, holding that morality is a sham of some kind. In this showcase, therefore, we discuss the views of a nineteenth-century philosopher who was completely skeptical about morality: Friedrich Nietzsche.

We then discuss the views of Mary Wollstonecraft. Wollstonecraft accepted a view of morality very much like Kant's view that morality is based on reason. Her confidence in ethics and reason is the basis of her view that women are, and should be treated as, the equals of men. Far from being skeptical of morality, she saw it as the foundation of sexual equality and built on it the first clearly articulated feminist philosophy.

By considering and contrasting the views of these philosophers, you may find it easier to make up your own mind about the future and reality of moral principles.

NIETZSCHE

The most powerful attack ever launched against morality was made by Friedrich Nietzsche. Nietzsche was born in 1844 in Roeken, Germany. His father having died when Nietzsche was four, he was raised in a household consisting of his mother, sister, grandmother, and two aunts. In 1864, Nietzsche went off to college, studying first at the University of Bonn and then transferring to the University of Leipzig. There, perhaps experiencing the first effects of his freedom, Nietzsche soon contracted syphilis, which at that time was incurable. The disease had little immediate effect on his scholarly skills, however, and he soon managed to impress his professors, particularly the widely respected Friedrich Ritschel. When Nietzsche graduated from Leipzig, Ritschel gave him an enthusiastic recommendation, and in 1869 Nietzsche quickly secured a position as a professor at the University of Basel. Unfortunately, his health soon began to deteriorate because of his disease, and in 1878 poor health forced Nietzsche to resign his position. Most of the rest of his life was spent in terrible loneliness. Several times he proposed marriage to different women but was firmly rejected by each. In 1889, Nietzsche abruptly went mad. He spent much of the next eleven years in a madhouse or under the care of his doting sister. He died on August 25, 1900.

© Lebrecht Music and Arts Photo Library/Alamy

Friedrich Nietzsche: "God is dead! God remains dead! And we have killed him! How shall we console ourselves, the most murderous of all murderers? Shall we not ourselves have to become Gods?" Friedrich Nietzsche, portrait. German philosopher.

"God Is Dead"

In the major writings he produced before he went mad, Nietzsche proposed the insightful view that the traditional values and ethical systems of the West were collapsing even as he wrote. The major source of their collapse, he felt, was the loss of belief in God. "God is dead," he declared, having been killed by our own modern philosophies and beliefs. Because we no longer believe in God, it is difficult for us to believe in the traditional values and ethical views that Christians and others have defended by appealing to God. The death of God has left us floating directionless in a cold, empty space. Nietzsche announced the death of God by using the highly poetic image of a madman:

> *The Madman.*—Have you ever heard of the madman who on a bright morning lighted a lantern and ran to the market-place calling out unceasingly: "I seek God! I seek God!"—As there were many people standing about who did not believe in God, he caused a great deal of amusement. Why! is he lost? said one. Has he strayed away like a child? said another. Or does he keep himself hidden? Is he afraid of us? Has he taken a seavoyage? Has he emigrated?—the people cried out laughingly, all in a hubbub. The insane man jumped into their midst and transfixed them with his glances. "Where is God gone?" he called out, "I mean to tell you! *We have killed him,*—you and I! We are all his murderers! But how have we done it? How were we able to drink up the sea? Who gave us the sponge to wipe away the whole horizon? What did we do when we loosened this earth from its sun? Whither does it now move? Whither do we move? Away from all suns? Do we not dash on unceasingly? Backwards, sideways, forwards, in all directions? Is there still an above and below? Do we not stray, as through infinite nothingness? Does not empty space breathe upon us? Has it not become colder? Does not night come on continually, darker and darker? Shall we not have to light lanterns in the morning? Do we not hear the noise of the gravediggers who are burying God? Do we not smell the divine putrefaction?— for even Gods putrefy! God is will wipe the blood from us? With what water could we cleanse ourselves? What lustrums, what sacred games shall we have to devise? Is not the magnitude of this deed too great for us? Shall we not ourselves have to become Gods, merely to seem worthy of it? There never was a greater event,—and on account of it, all who are born after us belong to a higher history than any history hitherto!"— Here the madman was silent and looked again at his hearers; they also were silent and looked at him in surprise. At last he threw his lantern on the ground, so that it broke in pieces and was extinguished. "I come too early," he then said, "I am not yet at the right time. This prodigious event is still on its way, and is traveling,—it has not yet reached men's ears. Lightning and thunder need time, the light of the stars needs time, deeds need time, even after they are done, to be seen and heard. This deed is as yet further from them than the furthest star,—*and yet they have done it*!"—It is further stated that the madman made his way into different churches on the same day, and there intoned his *Requiem aeternam deo.*[1]

But the death of God, for Nietzsche, was not necessarily a bad thing. For belief in God had encouraged the illusion that there are

1 Friedrich Nietzsche, *The Joyful Wisdom*, trans. Thomas Common, in *The Complete Works of Friedrich Nietzsche*, vol. 10, ed. Oscar Levy (New York: Macmillan, 1944), 167–169.

universal and absolute truths that everyone must accept. In fact, Nietzsche maintained, there is no absolute truth. Instead, all our beliefs are nothing more than so many interpretations or "perspectives," ways we have of looking at the world. There is an indefinite number of possible interpretations of the world, all of them equally true and equally false. But some of these are more useful than others because some have the advantage of enabling us to live and gain power over the world. Such "useful" beliefs, although as false as any others, are the ones we count as part of the "truth." As Nietzsche put it, "*Truth is that sort of error* without which a particular type of living being could not live. The value for *life* is ultimately decisive."[2]

Will to Power

Although Nietzsche did not believe that there is one "true" interpretation of the universe, he did think that some interpretations or ways of understanding the universe are better than others. Every event in the universe, Nietzsche maintained, can be interpreted as being produced by a force he called the "will to power." It was a useful hypothesis, he felt, to interpret events in the universe in terms of something with which we are familiar—the activity of our own wills:

> We must risk the hypothesis that everywhere we recognize "effects" there is an effect of will upon will; that all mechanical happenings, insofar as they are activated by some energy, are willpower, will-effects.—Assuming, finally, that we succeeded in explaining our entire instinctual life as the development and ramification of one basic form of will (of the will to power, as I hold); assuming that one could trace back all the organic functions to this will to power, including the solution of the problems of generation and nutrition (they are one problem)—if this were done, we should be justified in defining *all* effective energy unequivocally as *will to power*.[3]

If everything in the universe is interpreted as a result of a will to power, then all human actions must also be seen as outcomes of the will to power. The primary drives of human beings are not the pursuit of pleasure and the avoidance of pain (as Mill had argued). Instead, human beings are primarily motivated by the desire to increase their power over things and over people. As Nietzsche put it, "Life itself is essential assimilation, injury, violation of the foreign and the weaker, suppression, hardness, the forcing of one's own forms upon something else, ingestion and—at least in its mildest form—exploitation."[4] In fact, Nietzsche felt, our theories and beliefs about the world should also be seen as instruments of the will to power. Interpretations of the world are instruments we use to extend our power over the world and over one another.

Just as there are no absolute truths about the world, so also there are no absolute truths about morality. Any morality, Nietzsche claimed, is also merely an interpretation of the world: "There are no moral phenomena, only moralistic interpretations of phenomena," and "There are no moral facts." Like any other kind of interpretation, a morality cannot be said to be absolutely true or false; it can only be a more-or-less useful instrument for the will to power. Moralities, then, are interpretations used as instruments to exert power over others or over the natural world. For example, Nietzsche argues that Kant, like every other moralist, proposed his moral theory to impose his own values:

> Apart from the value of such assertions as "there is a categorical imperative in us," one can always ask: What does such an assertion indicate about him who makes it? There are systems of morals which are meant to justify their author in the eyes of other people; other systems of morals are meant to tranquilize him, and make him self-satisfied; with other systems he wants to crucify and humble himself; with others he wishes to take revenge; with others to conceal himself; with others to glorify himself and gain superiority and distinction;—this system of morals helps its author to forget, that system makes him, or something of him, forgotten; many a moralist would like to exercise power and creative arbitrariness over mankind; many another, perhaps, Kant especially, gives us to understand by his morals that "what is estimable in me, is that I know how to obey—and with you it *shall* not be otherwise than with me!"[5]

---

2 Quoted in Frederick Copleston, *A History of Philosophy,* vol. 7 (Garden City, NY: Doubleday, 1963), 183.

3 Friedrich Nietzsche, *Beyond Good and Evil,* trans. M. Cowan (Chicago: Henry Regnery, 1955), 43.

4 Ibid., 201.

5 Friedrich Nietzsche, *Beyond Good and Evil,* trans. Helen Zimmern, in *The Complete Works of Friedrich Nietzsche,* vol. 2, ed. Oscar Levy (New York: Macmillan, 1944), 106.

Mill's argument for utilitarianism, Nietzsche argues, was also an attempt to impose on others his personal preferences. In Mill's case, these were preferences he shared with his fellow British citizens. Utilitarian arguments are merely an attempt to impose on the world the values of the English:

> Observe, for example, the indefatigable, inevitable English utilitarians. . . . In the end, they all want *English* morality to be recognized as authoritative, inasmuch as mankind, or the "general utility," or "the happiness of the greatest number,"— no! the happiness of *England* will be best served thereby. They would like, by all means, to convince themselves that the striving after *English* happiness, I mean after *comfort* and *fashion* (and in the highest instance, a seat in Parliament), is at the same time the true path of virtue; in fact, that insofar as there has been virtue in the world hitherto, it has just consisted in such striving.[6]

The ethical systems proposed by the major moral philosophers, then, are nothing more than manifestations of the will to power. The same is true of the popular moralities the masses follow. In his survey of the history of moralities, Nietzsche wrote, he had discovered two basic kinds of popular moralities. One kind was the "slave moralities" that weak people—especially the Christians—had devised as instruments to acquire power over the strong. The other kind was the "master moralities" that had been devised by the strong to assert their power over the weak.

A master morality will normally develop in those individuals who are the strongest, those who are born with the power to dominate others. This type of morality values strength, intelligence, courage, revenge, and power seeking. In this morality a person is good to the extent that he or she has the strength to overpower others. This type of morality extols the individual.

On the other hand, a slave morality is fashioned by weak groups of people. A slave morality values whatever is useful or beneficial to the weak, such as sympathy, kindness, pity, patience, humility, and helping those in need. In a slave morality, the good person is the one who helps the weak, whereas the dominating individual is seen as evil. Slave moralities are the moralities of the herd because they extol the group and not the individual:

> In a tour through the many finer and coarser moralities which have hitherto prevailed or still prevail on the earth, I found certain traits recurring regularly together and connected with one another, until finally two primary types revealed themselves to me, and a radical distinction was brought to light. There is master-morality and slave-morality;—I would at once add, however, that in all higher and mixed civilizations, there are also attempts at the reconciliation of the two moralities; but one finds still oftener the confusion and mutual misunderstanding of them, indeed, sometimes their close juxtaposition—even in the same man, within one soul. The distinctions of moral values have either originated in a ruling caste, pleasantly conscious of being different from the ruled—or among the ruled class, the slaves and dependents of all sorts. In the first case, when it is the rulers who determine the conception "good," it is the exalted, proud disposition which is regarded as the distinguishing feature, and that which determines the order of rank. The noble type of man separates from himself the beings in whom the opposite of this exalted, proud disposition displays itself: he despises them. Let it at once be noted that in this first kind of morality the antithesis "good" and "bad" means practically the same as "noble" and "despicable";—the antithesis "good" and "evil" is of a different origin. The cowardly, the timid, the insignificant, and those thinking merely of narrow utility are despised; moreover, also, the distrustful, with their constrained glances, the self-abasing, the dog-like kind of men who let themselves be abused, the mendicant flatterers, and above all the liars;—it is a fundamental belief of all aristocrats that the common people are untruthful. "We truthful ones"—the nobility in ancient Greece called themselves. It is obvious that everywhere the designations of moral value were at first applied to *men*, and were only derivatively and at a later period applied to *actions*; it is a gross mistake, therefore, when historians of morals start with questions like, "Why have sympathetic actions been praised?" The noble type of man regards himself as a determiner of values; he does not require to be approved of; he passes the judgment: "What is injurious to me is injurious in itself"; he knows that it is he himself only who confers honor on things; he is a creator of values. He honors whatever he recognizes in himself; such morality is self-glorification. In the foreground there is the feeling of plenitude, of power, which seeks to overflow, the happiness of high tension, the consciousness of a wealth

---

6 Ibid., 174.

which would fain give and bestow:—the noble man also helps the unfortunate, but not—or scarcely—out of pity, but rather from an impulse generated by the super-abundance of power. The noble man honors in himself the powerful one, him also who has power over himself, who knows how to speak and how to keep silence, who takes pleasure in subjecting himself to severity and hardness, and has reverence for all that is severe and hard. "Wotan placed a hard heart in my breast," says an old Scandinavian Saga: it is thus rightly expressed from the soul of a proud Viking. Such a type of man is even proud of *not* being made for sympathy; the hero of the Saga therefore adds warningly: "He who has not a hard heart when young, will never have one." The noble and brave who think thus are the furthest removed from the morality which sees precisely in sympathy, or in acting for the good of others, or in *désintéressement,* the characteristic of the moral; faith in oneself, pride in oneself, a radical enmity and irony towards "selflessness," belong as definitely to the noble morality, as do a careless scorn and precaution in presence of sympathy and the "warm heart."—It is the powerful who *know* how to honor, it is their art, their domain for invention. The profound reverence for age and for tradition—all law rests on this double reverence,—the belief and prejudice in favor of ancestors and unfavorable to newcomers, is typical in the morality of the powerful; and if, reversely, men of "modern ideas" believe almost instinctively in "progress" and the "future," and are more and more lacking in respect for old age, the ignoble origin of these "ideas" has complacently betrayed itself thereby. A morality of the ruling class, however, is more especially foreign and irritating to present-day taste in the sternness of its principle that one has duties only to one's equals; that one may act towards beings of a lower rank, toward all that is foreign, just as seems good to one, or "as the heart desires," and in any case "beyond good and evil": it is here that sympathy and similar sentiments can have a place. The ability and obligation to exercise prolonged gratitude and prolonged revenge—both only within the circle of equals,—artfulness in retaliation, *raffnement* of the idea in friendship, a certain necessity to have enemies (as outlets for the emotions of envy, quarrelsomeness, arrogance—in fact, in order to be a good *friend*): all these are typical characteristics of the noble morality, which, as has been pointed out, is not the morality of "modern ideas," and is therefore at present difficult to realize, and also to unearth and disclose.—It is otherwise with the second type of morality, *slave-morality.* Supposing that the abused, the oppressed, the suffering, the unemancipated, the weary, and those uncertain of themselves, should moralize, what will be the common element in their moral estimates? Probably a pessimistic suspicion with regard to the entire situation of man will find expression, perhaps a condemnation of man, together with his situation. The slave has an unfavorable eye for the virtues of the powerful; he has a skepticism and distrust, a *refinement* of distrust of everything "good" that is there honored—he would fain persuade himself that the very happiness there is not genuine. On the other hand, *those* qualities which serve to alleviate the existence of sufferers are brought into prominence and flooded with light; it is here that sympathy, the kind, helping hand, the warm heart, patience, diligence, humility, and friendliness attain to honor; for here these are the most useful qualities, and almost the only means of supporting the burden of existence. Slave-morality is essentially the morality of utility. Here is the seat of the origin of the famous antithesis "good" and "evil":—power and dangerousness are assumed to reside in the evil, a certain dreadfulness, subtlety, and strength, which do not admit of being despised. According to slave-morality, therefore, the "evil" man arouses fear: according to master-morality, it is precisely the "good" man who arouses fear and seeks to arouse it, while the bad man is regarded as the despicable being. The contrast attains its maximum when, in accordance with the logical consequences of slave-morality, a shade of depreciation—it may be slight and well-intentioned—at last attaches itself even to the "good" man of this morality; because, according to the servile mode of thought, the good man must in any case be the *safe* man: he is good-natured, easily deceived, perhaps a little stupid, *un bonhomme.* Everywhere that slave-morality gains the ascendancy, language shows a tendency to approximate the significations of the words "good" and "stupid."—A last fundamental difference: the desire *for freedom,* the instinct for happiness and the refinements of the feeling of liberty belong as necessarily to slave-morals and morality, as artifice and enthusiasm in reverence and devotion are the regular symptoms of an aristocratic mode of thinking and estimating.—Hence we can understand without further detail why love as a *passion*—it is our European specialty—must absolutely be of noble origin; as is well known, its invention is due to

> the Provençal poet-cavaliers, those brilliant ingenious men of the "gai saber" [happy science], to whom Europe owes so much, and almost owes itself.[7]

Although Nietzsche clearly favored the "master moralities" and argued that we should rid ourselves of our "slave moralities," he did not feel that one morality was more "true" than another. Because there is no longer any God, there are no longer any objective moralities. Moralities are our own inventions:

> What then, alone, can our teaching be?—That no one gives man his qualities, either God, society, his parents, his ancestors, nor himself (this nonsensical idea, which is at last refuted here, was taught as "intelligible freedom" by Kant, and perhaps even as early as Plato himself). No one is responsible for the fact that he exists at all, that he is constituted as he is, and that he happens to be in certain circumstances and in a particular environment. The fatality of his being cannot be divorced from the fatality of all that which has been and will be. This is not the result of an individual attention, of a will, of an aim, there is no attempt at attaining to any "ideal man," or "ideal happiness" or "ideal morality" with him—it is absurd to wish him to be careering towards some sort of purpose. *We* invented the concept "purpose"; in reality purpose is altogether lacking. One is necessary, one is a piece of fate, one belongs to the whole, one is in the whole—there is nothing that could judge, measure, compare, and condemn our existence, for that would mean judging, measuring, comparing and condemning the whole. *But there is nothing outside the whole!* The fact that no one shall any longer be made responsible, that the nature of existence may not be traced to a *causa prima*, that the world is an entity neither as a sensorium nor as a spirit—*this alone is the great deliverance*—thus alone is the innocence of becoming restored. . . . The concept "God" has been the greatest objection to existence hitherto. . . . We deny God, we deny responsibility in God: thus alone do we save the world.[8]

The significance of Nietzsche's attack on morality cannot be overstated. If Nietzsche is correct, then moral principles are nothing more than subtle or not-so-subtle tools that the weak use to secure their power over the strong. Morality is a sham. The moral principles proposed by Christians, utilitarians, or Kantians are nothing more than their attempt to impose their will on others. When I say, for example, that everyone should be charitable or that everyone should seek to maximize the happiness of everyone else, I am really trying to get you to be charitable to me or to maximize my happiness. Moral principles are thus nothing more than an expression of the will to power.

Thus, just as Hume's views had threatened epistemology, so Nietzsche's views threatened to destroy morality.

To read more of Nietzsche's works, go to CourseMate for this text and browse by chapter or philosopher.

WOLLSTONECRAFT

Mary Wollstonecraft is recognized today as the first major feminist philosopher. A hard-working, independent, and enterprising woman, Wollstonecraft

© Tate, London/Art Resource, NY

Mary Wollstonecraft: "I see not the shadow of a reason to conclude that [the] virtues [of men and women] should differ in respect to their nature. In fact, how can they, if virtue has only one eternal standard?" John Opie (1761–1807); Mary Wollstonecraft (Mrs. William Godwin), c. 1790–1791.

7 Ibid., 227–232.

8 Friedrich Nietzsche, *The Twilight of the Idols*, trans. A. M. Lucovici, in *The Complete Works of Friedrich Nietzsche*, vol. 16, 43.

went against the conventions of the day. In an age when women were supposed to stay at home, Wollstonecraft left home to support herself at the age of nineteen and managed to achieve what was then unthinkable: She became an internationally known philosopher.

The second of seven children, Mary Wollstonecraft was born on April 27, 1759. Her father, a gentleman farmer who managed to dissipate the small fortune he inherited from his own father, was subject to uncontrollable fits of rage, frustration, and drunkenness. As a nine-year-old, Wollstonecraft felt she had to watch "whole nights at their chamber door" to protect her mother from her father's violence.

At the age of nineteen, seeking independence in defiance of her parents' wishes, Wollstonecraft left home to work for two years as a live-in companion to a wealthy and tyrannical widow who continually reminded her of her lower status.

Wollstonecraft was forced to return home in 1781 to care for her sick mother. Subjected once again to a violent family life, Wollstonecraft became embittered and depressed. The death of her mother in 1782 let Wollstonecraft leave home again, and she moved in with the family of her close friend Fanny Blood. Although Fanny's family was impoverished, Wollstonecraft there found peace and tranquility.

In 1784, Wollstonecraft, her two sisters, and Fanny opened a school in Newington Green, a town near London. Although the school prospered at first, it eventually ran up a huge debt and had to be closed. Needing money, Wollstonecraft turned to writing and in 1786 published *Thoughts on the Education of Daughters*. The book attracted little attention. Later that year, Wollstonecraft took the job of governess to the three daughters of Lord and Lady Kingsborough. Wollstonecraft hated her aristocratic employers, who constantly reminded her that she was of a lower social class. In a letter to her sister, she described Lady Kingsborough as a "haughty and disagreeable" woman whose "proud condescension added to my embarrassment."[9] After only ten months, Lady Kingsborough fired her.

Wollstonecraft moved to London in 1787, where she took a job as an editor and writer for a journal. Here at last she prospered. Working at the journal was intellectually exciting, and the work allowed her to devote herself to her own writing, which now succeeded beyond her dreams. During the next few years she published numerous works, including two controversial works that made her internationally famous: *A Vindication of the Rights of Men* and *A Vindication of the Rights of Women*.

Wollstonecraft fashioned a philosophy based on a fundamental moral principle that she first set out in *A Vindication of the Rights of Men*, a work devoted to refuting the elitist philosophy of Edmund Burke. Burke held that people are fundamentally unequal and that the privileges of the upper class should be preserved. Mindful of her own unhappy experiences with upper-class women, Wollstonecraft rejected Burke's view as foolish. She argued that all human beings possess reason and that reason is the source of the equal moral rights that all human beings have. As Wollstonecraft put the matter in *A Vindication of the Rights of Men*, where she imagines herself talking to Burke:

> The birthright of man, to give you, sir, a short definition of this disputed right, is such a degree of liberty, civil and religious, as is compatible with the liberty of every other individual with whom he is united in a social compact, and the continued existence of that compact. . . .
>
> It is necessary emphatically to repeat, that there are rights which men inherit at their birth, as rational creatures, who were raised above the brute creation by their improvable faculties; and that, in receiving these, not from their forefathers, but, from God, prescription can never undermine natural rights.[10]

According to Wollstonecraft, reason is the source of morality because it is reason that allows us to restrain our animal passions. This ability to rise above our animal nature is what sets us off from the animal world and is the source of the respect to which all humans who acquire virtue have an equal right:

> In what respect are we superior to the brute creation, if intellect is not allowed to be the guide of passion? Brutes hope and fear, love and hate; but without a capacity to improve, a power of turning these passions to good or evil, they neither acquire virtue nor wisdom—Why? Because the Creator has not given them reason.

9 *The Collected Letters of Mary Wollstonecraft*, ed. Ralph M. Wardle (Ithaca, NY: Cornell University Press, 1979), 164.

10 From Mary Wollstonecraft, *A Vindication of the Rights of Men* (1790), in *A Wollstonecraft Anthology*, ed. Janet M. Todd (Bloomington: Indiana University Press, 1977), 65, 67.

> Children are born ignorant, consequently innocent; the passions are neither good nor evil dispositions, till they receive a direction. . . . If virtue is to be acquired by experience, or taught by example, reason, perfected by reflection, must be the director of the whole host of passions . . .—She must hold the rudder, or let the wind blow which way it list, the vessel will never advance smoothly to its destined port. . . . Who will venture to assert that virtue would not be promoted by the more extensive cultivation of reason?[11]

Expressing a view that she would never abandon, Wollstonecraft claimed that to the extent that women fail to develop their reason and fail therefore to rise above animal feeling and passion, they will not merit the respect that is due to a developed human being. When women fail to acquire the same "manly" virtues that males cultivate—fortitude, humanity, justice, wisdom, and truth—they give up their equality with men. Burke, she points out, claimed that women should not attempt to acquire the virtues of males but should attempt instead to make themselves pleasing to men by cultivating the virtues of littleness, weakness, and beauty. But in convincing women to pursue this path, Wollstonecraft argues, Burke has robbed them of the very thing—a developed reason—that would give them a right to moral respect:

> You may have convinced them that littleness and weakness are the very essence of beauty; and that the Supreme Being, in giving women beauty in the most supereminent degree, seemed to command them, by the powerful voice of nature, not to cultivate the moral virtues that might chance to excite respect, and interfere with the pleasing sensations they were created to inspire. Thus confining truth, fortitude, and humanity within the rigid pale of manly morals, they might justly argue that to be loved—woman's high end and great distinction—they should learn to list, to totter in their walk, and nickname God's creatures. Never, they might repeat after you, was any man, much less a woman, rendered amiable by the force of these exalted qualities, fortitude, justice, wisdom, and truth; and thus forewarned of the sacrifice they must make to these austere, unnatural virtues, they would be authorized to turn all their attention to their persons, systematically neglecting morals to secure beauty.[12]

11 Ibid., 73–74.
12 Ibid., 76–77.

This idea, that women are rendered inferior to men by society's insistence that they not develop their reason and by their own acquiescence in that insistence, forms the basis of Wollstonecraft's greatest work, *A Vindication of the Rights of Women*. Here, Wollstonecraft argues that society in general and men in particular keep women in an undeveloped and morally inferior state. Tragically, women themselves acquiesce in the inferior role assigned to them by men:

> The conduct and manners of women, in fact, evidently prove that their minds are not in a healthy state; for, like the flowers which are planted in too rich a soil, strength and usefulness are sacrificed to beauty; and the flaunting leaves, after having pleased a fastidious eye, fade, disregarded on the stalk, long before the season when they ought to have arrived at maturity.—One cause of this barren blooming I attribute to a false system of education, gathered from the books written on this subject by men who, considering females rather as women than human creatures, have been more anxious to make them alluring mistresses than affectionate wives and rational mothers; and the understanding of the sex has been so bubbled by this specious homage, that the civilized women of the present century, with a few exceptions, are only anxious to inspire love, when they ought to cherish a nobler ambition, and by their abilities and virtues exact respect.[13]

It is particularly through an inferior education that women are kept in a state of immaturity and dependency, she argues. They are trained to think that they must devote themselves to pleasing men and to becoming dependent on them. Women must resist these enticements:

> The education of women has, of late, been more attended to than formerly; yet they are still reckoned a frivolous sex, and ridiculed or pitied by the writers who endeavour by satire or instruction to improve them. It is acknowledged that they spend many of the first years of their lives in acquiring a smattering of accomplishments; meanwhile strength of body and mind are sacrificed to libertine notions of beauty, to the desire of establishing themselves,—the only way women can rise in the world,—by marriage. And this desire making mere animals of them, when they marry they act as such children may

13 Ibid., 85.

> be expected to act:—they dress, they paint, and nickname God's creatures. . . .
>
> In the present state of society, a little learning is required to support the character of a gentleman; and boys are obliged to submit to a few years of discipline. But in the education of women, the cultivation of the understanding is always subordinate to the acquirement of some corporeal accomplishment; even while enervated by confinement and false notions of modesty, the body is prevented from attaining that grace and beauty which relaxed half-formed limbs never exhibit. Besides, in youth their faculties are not brought forward by emulation; and having no serious scientific study, if they have natural sagacity it is turned too soon on life and manners. They dwell on effects and modifications, without tracing them back to causes; and complicated rules to adjust behavior are a weak substitute for simple principles.[14]

The popular view that women must be educated differently from men is based on the theory that the moral virtues of women are very different from those of men. Wollstonecraft argues strenuously against this popular view. Morality, she claims, is not based on gender: It is a mistake to believe that there is one morality for men and a different one for women. Women and men must be educated as equals, she argues, because both are equally endowed with reason and because a single standard of morality applies equally to men and to women. The claim that male morality is different from female morality, she argues, is what allows men to maintain a "tyranny" over women:

> To account for and excuse the tyranny of man, many ingenious arguments have been brought forward to prove that the two sexes, in the acquirement of virtue, ought to aim at attaining a very different character: or, to speak explicitly, women are not allowed to have sufficient strength of mind to acquire what really deserves the name of virtue. Yet it should seem, allowing them to have souls, that there is but one way appointed by Providence to lead mankind to either virtue or happiness. . . .
>
> I see not the shadow of a reason to conclude that their virtues should differ in respect to their nature. In fact, how can they, if virtue has only one eternal standard? I must therefore, if I reason consequentially, as strenuously maintain that they have the same simple direction, as that there is a God. . . .
>
> Women, I allow, may have different duties to fulfill; but they are human duties, and the principles that should regulate the discharge of them, I sturdily maintain, must be the same.[15]

Wollstonecraft did not deceive herself about the difficulties of overcoming the inequalities between men and women. From childhood, an unrelenting social conditioning teaches women that their place in society is to remain dependent on men and to not develop their reason as equals to men. But Wollstonecraft is confident that women will flourish as the equals of men when they are freed from the deadening influence of this conditioning:

> Novels, music, poetry, and gallantry, all tend to make women the creatures of sensation. . . . This overstretched sensibility naturally relaxes the other powers of the mind, and prevents intellect from attaining that sovereignty which it ought to attain to render a rational creature useful to others, and content with its own station: for the exercise of the understanding, as life advances, is the only method pointed out by nature to calm the passions. . . . Yet to their senses are women made slaves, because it is by their sensibility that they obtain present power. . . .
>
> Asserting the rights which women in common with men ought to contend for, I have not attempted to extenuate their faults, but to prove them to be the natural consequence of their education and station in society. If so it is reasonable to suppose that they will change their character, and correct their vices and follies, when they are allowed to be free in a physical, moral, and civil sense.[16]

Now free of debt and a famous intellectual, Wollstonecraft traveled to France, which was then in the throes of a revolution. There, while the exhilarating madness of the French Revolution unfolded around her, Wollstonecraft met Gilbert Imlay, a dashing and liberal-thinking young American adventurer and war speculator. She fell passionately in love with him and in 1793 found herself pregnant with his child. On May 14, 1794, she gave birth to a girl, whom she named Fanny, after her friend. Imlay now withdrew his affection, and after several separations, he left her for good and went to England. In early 1795,

14 Ibid., 86, 89.

15 Ibid., 87, 90, 95.

16 Ibid., 98, 114.

Locke and Natural Moral Laws

In contrast with Hobbes' pessimism, John Locke viewed humans as essentially moral beings who ought to obey natural moral rules. Where Hobbes saw warfare as the human's natural state, Locke saw our natural state as at least partly regulated by natural moral laws. As a result, Locke viewed humans as free and equal by nature, regardless of the existence of any government.

Government, he argued, doesn't decree mutual respect for the freedom and liberties of all—nature does. Humans are by nature free, rational, and social creatures. They establish governments because three things are missing in the state of nature: (1) a firm, clearly understood interpretation of the natural but unwritten moral laws; (2) unbiased judges to resolve disputes; and (3) a power capable of enforcing justice when one is wronged. So, individuals enter into a social contract to maintain their natural rights. In one portion of his brilliant and most influential political writing, *Essay Concerning the True and Original Extent and End of Civil Government,* Locke explains the end or purpose of political society and government:

> 123. If man in the state of Nature be so free as has been said, if he be absolute lord of his own person and possessions, equal to the greatest and subject to nobody, why will he part with his freedom, this empire, and subject himself to the dominion and control of any other power? To which is it obvious to answer, that though in the state of Nature he hath a right, yet the enjoyment of it is very uncertain and constantly exposed to the invasion of others; for all being kings as much as he, every man his equal, and the greater part no strict observers of equity and justice, the enjoyment of the property he has in this state is very unsafe, very insecure. This makes him willing to quit this condition which, however free, is full of fears and continual dangers; and it is not without reason that he seeks out and is willing to join in society with others who are already united, or have a mind to unite for the mutual preservation of their lives, liberties and estates, which I call by the general name—property.
>
> 124. The great and chief end, therefore, of men uniting into commonwealths, and putting themselves under government, is the preservation of their property; to which in the state of Nature there are many things wanting.
>
> First, there wants an established, settled, known law, received and allowed by common consent to be the standard of right and wrong, and the common measure to decide all controversies between them. For though the law of Nature be plain and intelligible to all rational creatures, yet men, being biased by their interest, as well as ignorant for want of study of it, are not apt to allow of it as a law binding to them in the application of it to their particular cases.
>
> 125. Secondly, in the state of Nature there wants a known and indifferent judge, with authority to determine all differences according to the established law. For every one in that state being both judge and executioner of the law of Nature, men being partial to themselves, passion and revenge is very apt to carry them too far, and with too much heat in their own cases, as well as negligence and unconcernedness, make them too remiss in other men's.
>
> 126. Thirdly, in the state of Nature there often wants power to back and support the sentence when right, and to give it due execution. They who sat by any injustice offended will seldom fail where they are able by force to make good their injustice. Such resistance many times makes the punishment dangerous, and frequently destructive to those who attempt it.
>
> 127. Thus mankind, notwithstanding all the privileges of the state of Nature, being but in an ill condition while they remain in it are quickly driven into society. Hence it comes to pass, that we seldom find any number of men live any time together in this state. The inconveniences that they are therein exposed to by the

To read more from Locke's *Essay Concerning Civil Government*, go to CourseMate for this text and browse by chapter or philosopher.

> irregular and uncertain exercise of the power every man has of punishing the transgressions of others, make them take sanctuary under the established laws of government, and therein seek the preservation of their property. It is this makes them so willingly give up every one his single power of punishing to be exercised by such alone as shall be appointed to it amongst them, and by such rules as the community, or those authorized by them to that purpose, shall agree on. And in this we have the original right and rise of both the legislative and executive power as well as of the governments and societies themselves.[5]

critical thinking

Does social contract theory assume that political rights pertain only to those who can enter a social contract with others? Is this assumption correct? Does the assumption leave out any significant creatures?

In short, individuals make an agreement or contract to create a political entity—the state or government—capable of preserving their inherent rights of "life, liberty, and estate." This social contract is based on the consent of the majority, and all agree to abide by the decisions of the majority. The state's authority is limited by the terms of the contract, which is continually reviewed by the citizenry. So, unlike Hobbes' absolutistic state, Locke's state is specific and limited. Most important, one of the fundamental moral rights in Locke's political state is the right to resist and to challenge authority. Hobbes believed that resistance to authority is never justified, but Locke regarded such a right as essential.

Although the contrast between Hobbes and Locke is sharp, they do agree that rationality enables humans to perceive the necessity of entering a social contract to create the state. More important, they both agree on the source of the state's authority: the consent of the governed. Locke, like Hobbes, felt that the power the state exerts is justified because it is a power that we have consented to accept. Our ancestors, Locke believed, consented to the original establishment of government. And each of us today consents again to that same government when we voluntarily choose to continue to live under that government.

Yet Locke, much more than Hobbes, also emphasized freedom. It was Locke's firm belief that government should leave people free to live and pursue whatever form of life they choose. In fact, it is the duty and purpose of government to protect the individual's freedom to pursue happiness as each sees fit.

It is difficult to exaggerate the tremendous influence that Locke's views had on political events of his time. Locke's views were adopted by several nations during what is sometimes called the "century of revolutions." In 1776, for example, the American colonies sounded a Lockean chord in these lines from the Declaration of Independence:

> We hold these truths to be self-evident. That all men are created equal. That they are endowed by their Creator with certain unalienable rights. That among these are life, liberty and the pursuit of happiness. That to secure these rights, governments are instituted among men, deriving their just powers from the consent of the governed. That whenever any Form of Government becomes destructive of these ends, it is the Right of the People to alter or to abolish it, and to institute a new Government, laying its foundation on such principles and organizing its powers in such form, as to them shall seem most likely to effect their safety and Happiness.

The similarities to Locke's position are not accidental, for the Declaration of Independence was written by Thomas Jefferson, who was an avid reader of, and disciple of, Locke.

---

5 John Locke, *Essay Concerning the True and Original Extent and End of Civil Government*, vol. 4 (1690) (Oxford: Clarendon, 1894), 4.

© Capitol Collection, Washington, DC, USA/The Bridgeman Art Library

***Signing the Declaration** of Independence*, John Trumbull. Both the Declaration and Locke's contract agree that when a government infringes on the individual rights of life, liberty, and the pursuit of happiness (or "estates," for Locke), the people have a right to dismiss it.

Rousseau and the General Will

Contract theory, especially as Locke developed it, led directly to the social philosophy of Jean Jacques Rousseau (1712–1778). Some philosophers consider Rousseau the foremost philosopher of the social contract theory. However, Rousseau did not appeal to a self-evident natural moral law as Locke had. He argued that if people are to act morally, they must live under laws that they freely accept. Rousseau's emphasis, then, was on personal moral autonomy, the capacity and right of individuals to live under laws that they choose for themselves. Thus, for Rousseau the fundamental requirement of a morally acceptable government is that the governed have freely subscribed to a common body of law.

Rousseau began his most important political work, *Of the Social Contract*, with the sensational words "Man was born free, but he is everywhere in chains." The key question, for Rousseau, is how we all came to be bound by the "chains" of the all-powerful authority of the state and how we can be free while living enchained by an all-powerful state. Rousseau answers this question by arguing that each person is by nature free and autonomous, but if there is no government there is no peace, and everyone's property is at risk. How can a person remain free when a powerful government is needed to maintain the peace and protect one's property? Rousseau argues that a person can remain free and autonomous so long as he obeys only those rules and powers that he himself chooses. The power of the state, then, can be consistent with human freedom if the state and its authority are something that the individual freely chooses for himself. And this is what the individual in fact does when he joins together with others in a pact in which everyone mutually and freely agrees to give up his natural rights and come under the "supreme direction of the general will" in exchange for the rights and security of a citizen in the state. Because each citizen is an integral part of this larger body—the general will—what the general will decides and does is really what each citizen is deciding and doing. Thus, in obeying the state, the individual is truly obeying himself and is therefore free: The power of the state is a morally justified power. In the following passage, taken from his most important work, *Of the Social Contract*, Rousseau describes the contract or pact that unites all citizens together into a "general will":

> The clauses of this contract are so determined by the nature of the act that the slightest modification would render them vain and ineffectual; so that, although

QUICK REVIEW
Rousseau argued that without government, people's property and security are at risk. But government is justified only if it is consistent with human freedom and autonomy. Government is justified if it is the outcome of a pact in which every citizen agrees to unite under a "general will," for in obeying the general will, the citizen is obeying himself and so is free and autonomous.

> they have never perhaps been formally enunciated, they are everywhere the same, everywhere tacitly admitted and recognized, until, the social pact being violated, each man regains his original rights and recovers his natural liberty while losing the conventional liberty for which he renounced it.
>
> These clauses, rightly understood, are reducible to one only, viz, the total alienation to the whole community of each associate with all his rights; for, in the first place, since each gives himself up entirely, the conditions are equal for all; and, the conditions being equal for all, no one has any interest in making them burdensome to others.
>
> Further, the alienation being made without reserve, the union is as perfect as it can be, and an individual associate can no longer claim anything; for, if any rights were left to individuals, since there would be no common superior who could judge between them and the public, each, being on some point his own judge, would soon claim to be so on all; the state of nature would still subsist, and the association would necessarily become tyrannical or useless.
>
> In short, each giving himself to all, gives himself to nobody; and as there is not one associate over whom we do not acquire the same rights which we concede to him over ourselves, we gain the equivalent of all that we lose, and more power to preserve what we have.
>
> If, then, we set aside what is not of the essence of the social contract, we shall find that it is reducible to the following terms: "Each of us puts in common his person and his whole power under the supreme direction of the general will; and in return we receive every member as an indivisible part of the whole."
>
> Forthwith, instead of the individual personalities of all the contracting parties, this act of association produces a moral and collective body, which is composed of as many members as the assembly has voices, and which receives from this same act its unity, its common self (*moi*), its life, and its will. This public person, which is thus formed by the union of the individual members, formerly took the name of city, and now takes that of republic or body politic, which is called by its members state when it is passive, sovereign when it is active, power when it is compared to similar bodies. With regard to the associates, they take collectively the name of people, and are called individually citizens.[6]

To read more from Rousseau's *Social Contract*, go to CourseMate for this text and browse by chapter or philosopher.

Rousseau's reference to the "general will" deserves some elaboration because the concept of the general will is a cornerstone of his social contract. The general will should be contrasted with the "will of all," or unanimity of feeling. A group of wills is general when each member of the group aims at the common good, which is what Rousseau has in mind. True, the general will and the will of all might result in the same course, for each group member may see his or her own best interests being served. But Rousseau felt that agreement is more likely when everyone tries to determine whether a proposed action is best for the good of all, for the general good, rather than just for self.

Rousseau argues further that the general will, unlike the will of all, represents a true consensus—it's what everyone wants. Even when the minority must conform to the will of the majority, there is no coercion or violation of personal freedom because everyone, even the minority members, seeks the general good. In other words, all parties agree on the end; they differ only in what they believe the means should be. Ultimately, they all get what they want: promotion of the common good.

Rousseau argued that in the state, governed as it was by the general will, the individual was truly free because in obeying the general will he, in effect, obeyed himself. True, it may seem to this or that individual that he is "forced" to obey the

---

6 Jean Jacques Rousseau, *Of the Social Contract, in Ideal Empires and Republics*, ed. Oliver H. G. Leigh (London: M. Walter Dunne, 1901), 13–14.

laws of the state. But, said Rousseau, this merely shows that "man must be forced to be free." When "forced" by the state to obey the general will, the individual becomes truly free even though he may not think so. As you may have guessed, many of Rousseau's contemporaries claimed that his argument here was deeply mistaken: Being "forced to obey" the general will is not necessarily a form of freedom, particularly when the general will of a society becomes tyrannical or otherwise imposes its values and preferences on the individual.

Contemporary Social Contract: Rawls

The social contract theory of Hobbes, Locke, and Rousseau was severely criticized in the eighteenth century by that most skeptical of all skeptics, David Hume. Hume struck a simple but devastating blow to social contract theory. He pointed out that there never was a social contract. Governments, he argued, are established by conquest or are handed on by the right of succession. If we go back in history, he pointed out, we will find no signs of people coming together to choose their governments. Social contract is, in short, a complete fiction:

> [Some] philosophers . . . assert . . . that government in its earliest infancy arose from consent, or rather the voluntary acquiescence of the people. . . . They affirm that all men are born equal and owe allegiance to no prince or government, unless bound by the obligation and sanction of a promise. . . .
>
> But would these reasoners look abroad into the world, they would meet with nothing that, in the least, corresponds to their ideas. . . . On the contrary, we find everywhere princes who claim their subjects as their property and assert their independent right of sovereignty, from conquest or succession. We find also, everywhere, subjects, who acknowledge this right in their prince. . . . Were you to preach, in most parts of the world, that political connections are founded altogether on voluntary consent or a mutual promise, the magistrate would soon imprison you, as seditious, for loosening the ties of obedience; if your friends did not before shut you up as delirious, for advancing such absurdities. . . . Almost all the governments which exist at present, or of which there remains any record in history, have been founded originally either on usurpation or conquest or both, without any pretense of a fair consent or voluntary subjection of the people.[7]

So devastating was Hume's attack that most philosophers gave up on social contract theory. For more than a century, the theory fell out of favor, and philosophers almost completely ignored it.

Toward the end of the twentieth century, however, social contract theory once more resurfaced. Harvard philosopher John Rawls (1921–2002) reshaped social contract theory into a powerful new way of thinking about the nature of government and society.

Rawls agreed with Hume that the social contract is a historical fiction. People never have, and never do, come together and decide to start a government. However, Rawls argued, this does not matter. The key idea in social contract theory is that it gives us a way of thinking about what the nature and purpose of government should be. Social contract theory says that to figure out what kind of government we should have, we should imagine that we are starting our society and our government from scratch. What kind of government and society would we choose for ourselves if we were in this starting or "original" position?

---

7 David Hume, "Of the Original Contract," in *Essays, Literary, Moral, and Political* (New York: Ward, Lock & Tyler, n.d., c. 1870), 272–273.

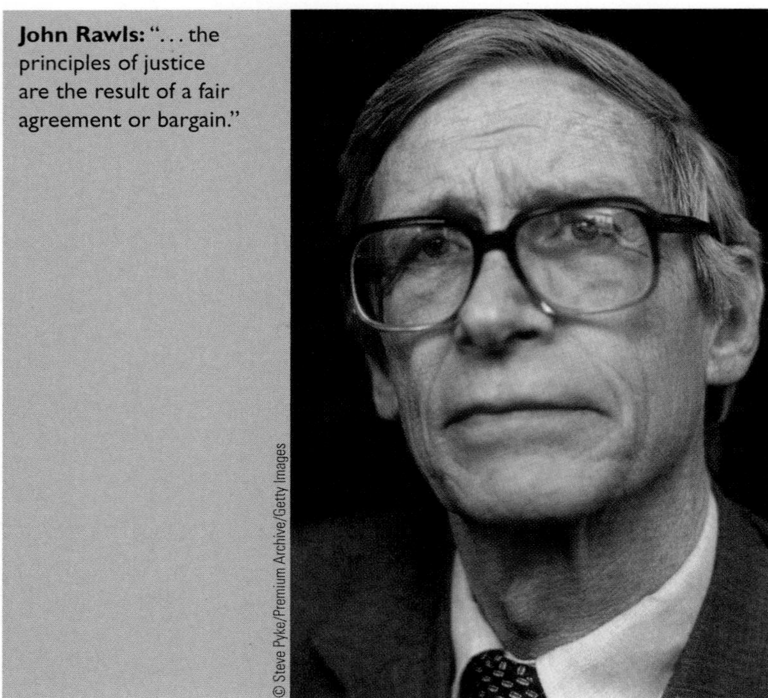
John Rawls: "... the principles of justice are the result of a fair agreement or bargain."

© Steve Pyke/Premium Archive/Getty Images

Rawls proposed that if we are to determine what a just government is and, more generally, what the just principles for a society are, we must set aside everything that leads us to favor ourselves over others. A just government is one that is equally fair to everyone and shows favoritism to none. But how will we set aside the things that unjustly lead us to favor ourselves over others? Rawls suggested an ingenious answer. Imagine, he proposed, that we were about to start a new society and a new government. Suppose that by some miracle none of us knows anything about what he or she will be like in that new society. For example, we don't know whether we will be male or female, black or white, rich or poor, young or old, smart or dumb, talented or untalented, needy or self-sufficient, religious or atheist. Then, we would be forced to choose a government and society that are fair to everyone no matter what they happen to be like. If I do not know, for example, whether I will be black or white in this new society, then I will insist on a government that favors neither blacks nor whites. I will want a government that does not discriminate. Or suppose that I do not know whether in our new society I will be rich or poor, atheist or religious, talented or untalented. Then, I will insist on a government that favors neither the rich nor the poor, neither the atheist nor the religious person, and neither the talented nor the untalented:

QUICK REVIEW
Rawls agrees with Hume that the social contract is a historical fiction but said that it helps us see what a just government is. Rawls argues that a just government is one we would choose to live under if we chose without knowing whether we would be rich or poor, black or white, and so forth. For under such a "veil of ignorance," we would choose a form of government that was fair to everyone by providing everyone with equal political rights and economic opportunities.

> Thus we are to imagine that those who engage in social cooperation choose together, in one joint act, the principles which are to assign basic rights and duties and to determine the division of social benefits. Men are to decide in advance how they are to regulate their claims against one another and what is to be the foundation charter of their society. . . .
>
> In justice as fairness the original position of equality corresponds to the state of nature in the traditional theory of the social contract. This original position is not, of course, thought of as an actual historical state of affairs, much less as a primitive condition of culture. It is understood as a purely hypothetical situation characterized so as to lead to a certain conception of justice. Among the essential features of this situation is that no one knows his place in society, his class position or social status, nor does anyone know his fortune in the distribution of natural assets and abilities, his intelligence, strength and the like. . . . Since all are similarly situated and no one is able to design principles to favor his particular condition, the principles of justice [for society and government] are the result of a fair agreement or bargain.[8]

Notice what social contract has become for Rawls. It is no longer a description of how we formed the governments that we *actually* have. Instead, it is now just an imaginary device that is supposed to tell us what kind of government we *ought to* have.

8 John Rawls, *A Theory of Justice* (Cambridge, MA: Harvard University Press, 1972), 11, 12, 13.

Nevertheless, the social contract for Rawls still helps explain what justifies the power and authority of government. For Rawls, the power of our government is justified if our government is the kind of government that we would choose in the original position. The authority of our government is justified not because we *actually consented* to live under our government in the state of nature. This was the view of Hobbes, Locke, and Rousseau, which Hume devastated with his criticisms. Instead, says Rawls, the authority of government is justified because we *would consent* to live under that type of government if we were in the original position.

What kind of government would we choose in the original position? Later in this chapter we examine the principles of justice that Rawls says we would want government to live by if we were in the original position. It will suffice here to say that a just government, according to Rawls, is one that does not favor one way of life over another. It does not favor one religion over another. It does not favor one ethnic group over another. It does not favor one culture over another. Instead, it leaves every person free to pursue the form of life that suits her best because of her personal preferences and desires. The just government is one that provides equal political rights and equal economic opportunities for everyone without showing favoritism to any. And the just government is one that provides a suitable minimum standard of living for the least advantaged members of society.

With Rawls, we have come to the most recent major version of social contract theory. Rawls' theory has had as great an impact on thinkers today as the theories of Hobbes, Locke, and Rousseau had in their day. Yet the theory, particularly in the version of Rawls, has been subjected to intense criticisms. We turn now to look at two major critiques of social contract theory: the communitarian critique and the feminist critique.

The Communitarian Critique

Communitarianism is the view that the actual community in which we live should be at the center of our analysis of society and government. Communitarians emphasize the social nature of human beings. They argue that our very identity—who we are—depends on our relationships to others in our communities. We are embedded in our community and its cultural practices. So, we cannot hope to understand ourselves or our government apart from our community and its cultural traditions. Although not all would identify themselves as such, several contemporary philosophers are usually identified as communitarians, including Charles Taylor, Alasdair MacIntyre, and Michael J. Sandel. Among the classical philosophers who are sometimes identified as early communitarian thinkers are Aristotle and Hegel.

The key problem with social contract theory, argue communitarians, is that it neglects people's social nature by focusing on the individual. In making this general criticism, communitarians bring a number of more specific complaints against social contract theory.

First, some communitarians have argued, the social contract theory assumes that government or the state is an artificial construct. But the state, communitarian philosophers have argued, is natural. For example, Aristotle argued long ago that government or the state is a natural outgrowth of our natural tendency to associate with other human beings. Just as the family and the tribe are outgrowths of our natural tendencies to live with one another, so is the state:

> We get the clearest view of a thing, whether it be the state or anything else, when we see how it originates and develops. At the origins, then, we have the union of male

> and female, who cannot live without each other. Men and women come together so that the race may continue. Their union is not something that they decide on their own. They come together in a family because, in common with other animals and plants, humans have a natural desire to reproduce themselves. . . . From this relationship between men and women . . . comes the first association, which is the family. . . . When several families develop together, and their association aims at more than the supply of their daily needs, we have the first society, which is the village. . . . When several villages have joined together in a single complete community, large enough to be self-sufficing, the state has come into existence. Thus, the state originates in the bare needs of life. But it continues in existence for the sake of providing its members the good life. Since the earlier forms of society are natural, so is the state. For the state is their purpose and completion, and the nature of a thing is revealed in its completion. The nature of anything, in fact, is revealed when it is fully developed, whether we are speaking of a man, a horse, or a family. . . .
>
> In addition, we should note that the state is by nature prior to the family and to the individual, since the whole is prior to the part. For example, the whole body is prior to the foot and the hand, for if the whole body were to be destroyed, the foot and hand would die. . . . We know that the state is a creation of nature and that it is prior to the individual by the fact that the individual apart from the state is not self-sufficient. The individual is like a part that is dependent on the whole. If there were a being who could not live in society or who did not need to live in society because he was self-sufficient, then he would have to either be animal or a god. He could not be a real part of the state. A social instinct is implanted in all people by their nature.[9]

Notice that Aristotle says that the state is "prior to the individual." By this he means, first, that humans cannot develop fully unless they live in the state. In particular, Aristotle argued, our political abilities and social virtues emerge and develop only in the state. The state is nature's way of bringing these capacities out in us. Second, Aristotle also wants to say that the state is more important than an individual citizen. Just as the whole human body is more important than one of its parts, so the whole association of humans that we call the state is more important than one of its members.

QUICK REVIEW
Communitarians argue that social contract theory mistakenly ignores Aristotle's and Hegel's claim that government is not an artificial construct but is a natural outgrowth of our social nature; it is necessary for full human development and is the source of the culture and tradition that make us who we are.

The idea that the state is a natural outgrowth of our human nature was echoed in the nineteenth century by the German philosopher Georg Wilhelm Friedrich Hegel (1770–1831). Like Aristotle, Hegel believed that the state is the completion of all earlier human associations and more important than the individual. He also agreed with Aristotle's claim that humans can develop fully only within the state. In particular, argued Hegel, humans can develop their freedom only within the state. Moreover, the individual will develop fully only if he embraces the cultural practices of the state of which he is a member:

> The State . . . is that form of reality in which the individual has and enjoys his freedom. But he can do so only if he recognizes, believes in, and wills that which is common to the Whole. And this must not be understood . . . [to mean that the state] is a means provided for his benefit. Nor [is the state a means by which] each individual . . . limits his own freedom so that [every individual] can secure a small space of liberty for himself. Rather, we affirm, that Law, Morality, Government, and they alone, are the positive reality and completion of Freedom. . . .
>
> It must further be understood that all the worth which the human being possesses—all spiritual reality, he possesses only through the State. . . . Thus only is

9 Aristotle, *Politics*, bk. I, ch. ii, translated by Manuel Velasquez.

> he fully conscious; thus only is he a partaker of morality—of a just and moral social and political life. . . .
>
> Summing up what has been said of the State, we find that . . . its vital principle, what actuates the individuals who compose it—is Morality. The State, its laws, its arrangements, constitute the rights of its members; its natural features, its mountains, air, and waters, are their country, their fatherland, their outward material property; the history of this State are their deeds; what their ancestors have produced, belongs to them and lives in their memory. All is their possession, just as they are possessed by it; for it constitutes their existence, their being.
>
> . . . It is this matured totality which thus constitutes one Being, the spirit of one people. To it the individual members belong; each one is the Son of his Nation, and at the same time . . . the Son of his Age. None remains behind it, still less [does anyone] advance beyond it. This spiritual Being, the Spirit of his time, is his; he is a representative of it; it is that in which he originated, and in which he lives.[10]

For Hegel, freedom is more than just not interfering with the lives of others. People are free to the extent that they can do more: The more abilities they have, the freer they are. Because the state is the arena in which people can most fully develop their abilities, only in the state can the range of activities open to people be expanded and widened to their fullest extent. Therefore, only in the state can people be truly free.

Already it should be clear that the communitarian views of Aristotle and Hegel directly contradict several of the assumptions of social contract theory. First, they contradict the assumption that the state is an artificial construct. Social contract theory assumes that there is no state until people come together and deliberately think it up and create it; the state does not just naturally grow and develop. However, Aristotle and Hegel reject this assumption. The state, they argue, is a natural outgrowth of our human tendencies to live together. Social contract theory is thus mistaken in its fundamental assumption that the state is an artificial construct that humans must deliberately put together.

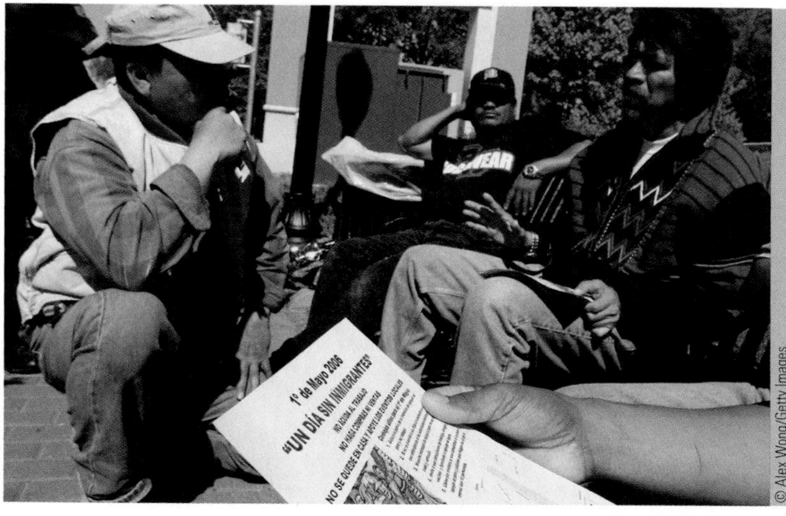

© Alex Wong/Getty Images

Arnoldo Borja (right), a community organizer of Virginia Justice Center, organizes Latino day laborers so they can claim their political and civil rights as Americans. Hegel wrote: "all the worth which the human being possesses, he possesses only through the State. Thus only is he fully conscious and a partaker of a just social and political life." When marginalized groups claim their political and civil rights, they participate in the life of the state and experience the worth, consciousness, and justice that only participation in the state can provide.

---

10 Georg Wilhelm Friedrich Hegel, *The Philosophy of History*, trans. J. Sibree (New York: Dover, 1956), 38, 39, 52.

Second, Aristotle and Hegel contradict the assumption that before the state exists, there are fully formed people who can come together to create a state. Hobbes, Locke, Rousseau, and even Rawls assume this. But Aristotle and Hegel point out that it is not possible for people to develop fully before the state exists. If there were no state, humans could not know what one is, nor would they know how to go about organizing themselves into a state. And only in the state does the individual develop the freedom required to enter an agreement. In short, before there is a state, there can be no fully formed human individuals capable of coming together to form one through some sort of agreement.

Third, and perhaps most important, communitarians agree with Hegel that the state and its cultural practices are the source of the identity of all individuals. That is, in the state we acquire the cultures and traditions that we use to define ourselves. Think, for example, of how a person growing up in the United States comes to think of himself or herself as an "American." An American thinks of himself or herself as being part of a long history that begins with the pilgrims and the thirteen colonies. An American thinks of himself or herself as part of a history that includes George Washington, Abraham Lincoln, Teddy Roosevelt, John Kennedy, and Barack Obama. An American thinks of himself or herself as part of a nation that includes its mountains and national parks, its rebellions and wars, its music and literature. In short, our very sense of who we are depends on the cultural traditions of the state to which we belong.

Yet, as we saw, the social contract view, particularly as developed by Rawls, believes that the state must support no particular culture but leave people free to choose their own cultural preferences. Michael J. Sandel, one of the foremost communitarian thinkers alive today, has written the following about social contract theory, particularly Rawls' version:

> Its central idea is that government should be neutral toward the moral and religious views its citizens espouse. Since people disagree about the best way to live, government should not affirm in law any particular vision of the good life. Instead, it should provide a framework of rights that respects persons as free and independent selves, capable of choosing their own values and ends.[11]

QUICK REVIEW
Communitarian views, contrary to social contract theory, imply that (1) the state is not an artificial construct (2) because without the state, humans could not develop, for there would be no one to enter a social contract in "the state of nature," (3) and because our culture and traditions make us who we are, the state should support the cultural traditions of its people, including their religion, morality, and cultural values.

Sandel argues that it is a mistake to think that government should be neutral toward the different moral, religious, and cultural views found in a community. As Hegel argued, if an individual is to develop fully, she must live in a state that supports and nourishes a strong set of cultural traditions. Different states will support different cultural traditions, of course. For example, the state and government of Mexico support a culture and a tradition that are very different from those that the state and government of the United States support. But each state and its government must favor and support some set of cultural traditions. The government of each state must educate its people so that they learn about these cultural traditions and come to accept their values. For us in the United States, says Sandel, the government must support a cultural tradition that has always valued participation in the political process:

> Participating in politics . . . means deliberating with fellow citizens about the common good and helping to shape the destiny of the political community. But to deliberate well about the common good requires more than the capacity to choose

11 Michael J. Sandel, *Democracy's Discontent* (Cambridge, MA: Belknap Press of Harvard University Press, 1996), 4.

> one's ends and to respect others' rights to do the same. It requires a knowledge of public affairs and also a sense of belonging, a concern for the whole, a moral bond with the community whose fate is at stake. To share in self-rule requires that citizens possess, or come to acquire, [these] qualities of character, or civic virtues. But this means that [we] cannot be neutral toward the values and ends . . . citizens espouse. [We require] . . . a formative politics, a politics that cultivates in citizens the qualities of character self-government requires.[12]

Communitarians argue, then, that government must not stay away from morality and cultural values. Instead, it must strive to teach citizens the morality and cultural values that are part of their traditions.

But are the communitarians right? Consider, first, the idea that the state is natural and not an artificial construct. Is this really true? Doesn't it take a great deal of human ingenuity and effort to maintain a state? Doesn't this suggest that the state is something that human beings construct? Or take the criticism that because people need a state to develop fully, they cannot form a government in the state of nature. It is true that there are some abilities that can develop only within the political institutions of the state. But are these abilities really needed for a stateless group of people to come together and agree to form a rudimentary government?

Consider, finally, what is perhaps the most important objection of communitarians. This is the objection that government should support the cultural traditions of its people. Ask yourself this: Should all cultural traditions be supported and transmitted? Before the Civil War, many whites living in the South argued that they had developed a distinct culture and way of life on their large plantations. Slavery was a part of this Southern culture. So, slavery as a cultural tradition should not be destroyed, they argued. In a similar way, many people have argued that the view that women should stay home, take care of children, and be subservient to their husbands is part of a distinct culture and way of life that should not be destroyed. Are all these cultural traditions equally valuable? If they are not, then are communitarians wrong to claim that government should support whatever traditional cultural values a nation has?

It is not clear, then, that communitarianism has made its case against the social contract tradition. However, there is a second important position that has also attacked the idea of the social contract.

Social Contract and Women

A significant and glaring set of problems can be raised with regard to the tradition of contract theory that Hobbes, Locke, and Rousseau represent. At the heart of contract theory is the idea that authority over adults depends on their consent. Rulers have no authority to rule unless their subjects agree or consent to that rule. For Hobbes, Locke, and Rousseau, consent alone can justify or legitimize the authority of the state. This fundamental idea is underlined in our own Declaration of Independence when it states that governments derive their just powers "from the consent of the governed." A social contract is necessary to establish the state because the contract is the means through which citizens consent to be ruled by a government.

The Traditional View. But this fundamental idea raises an important question that many women have asked: What justifies the authority that males have traditionally exercised over females, particularly in the family? For example, Hobbes writes that

12 Ibid., 5–6.

a family consists of "a man and his children; or of a man and his servants; or of a man, and his children, and servants together: wherein the Father or Master is the Sovereign."[13] Locke similarly tells us that in the family, "the Rule . . . naturally falls to the Man's share, as abler and stronger [than the Woman]."[14] And Rousseau writes that in the family, "when a woman complains of the unjust inequality which man has imposed on her, she is wrong; this inequality is not a human institution, or at least it is not the work of prejudice but of reason."[15]

Hobbes, Locke, and Rousseau are merely describing the traditional view of the family, in which the man rules and the woman is ruled. But they write as if this rule of the male over the female were perfectly justified. How is this possible in view of their fundamental point that authority over adults is justified only if they consent? Do adult women, half of the human race, somehow "consent" to let men, the other half, rule over them in families? Clearly, this is not the case: Women do not enter a social contract giving men the right to rule over them. Then, doesn't it follow that it is unjustified for men to exercise authority over adult women as they have done in the traditional family?

The fact that Hobbes, Locke, and Rousseau do not apply to women the idea that ruling requires consent should alert us to another glaring problem that their theories raise. The "free" and "equal" people who enter into the social contract and who subsequently become citizens of the state are all and only men. Women are left out. Hobbes explicitly states that "commonwealths have been erected by the Fathers, not by the Mothers of families."[16] Locke, as we have seen, assumes that men are the "natural" heads of families, and it is these male heads of families who enter the social contract. And Rousseau tells us that before humanity entered the social contract, families had already been established, headed by men who subsequently formed the social contract.

QUICK REVIEW
Feminists argue that social contract theory wrongly assumes that family structures are justified because often in families males rule over females without their consent, and social contract theory wrongly assumes that the "public" sphere of the state should not interfere with the "private" sphere of the family.

Thus, social contract theory, at least as developed by Hobbes, Locke, and Rousseau, explicitly indicates that the state is created by an agreement that *males* make with one another. Because people acquire political rights only by entering such an agreement, it would seem logical to conclude that only males have political rights in the state. Hobbes, Locke, and Rousseau were males interested in writing about how males come to be governed by a state, and they simply ignored the situation of the female half of the human race. Consequently, these philosophers failed to apply their principle that adults must be ruled by consent to the situation of women in families.

Public and Private Spheres. Why did they fail to apply their fundamental principles to the family? These failures are perhaps related to a basic assumption we all unconsciously make: that "private" or "personal" matters, such as family matters, have nothing to do with the "public" matters of politics—what happens to women within the family is a private matter unrelated to the politics that rules our public lives. Recently, however, a number of female philosophers have pointed out that this unconscious separation of the "public" from the "private" is the source of many of the political and economic inequalities to which women are subjected. For example, political philosopher Carole Pateman writes that "the dichotomy between the public and the private . . . is, ultimately, what the feminist movement is

13 Hobbes, *Leviathan*, ed. A. D. Lindsay (New York: J. M. Dent, 1950), 172.
14 Locke, *Two Treatises of Government*, ed. Peter Laslett (London: Cambridge University Press, 1963), 210.
15 Rousseau, *Emile*, quoted in Susan Moller Okin, *Women in Western Political Thought* (Princeton, NJ: Princeton University Press, 1979), 11.
16 Hobbes, *Leviathan*, 168.

about."[17] We must examine this claim, which has important implications for how we think about the state and which may help us see why Hobbes, Locke, and Rousseau so easily ignored half of the human race and were so willing to accept the glaringly unjustified and unequal position of women in the family.

Courtesy of The Advertising Archives

Traditionally, women have shouldered the major part of the unpaid work in the "private" life of the family: cooking for everyone, cleaning up the house, doing the laundry, and caring for the children. Some feminists argue this frees men to engage in the more powerful "public" life of economic and political activities, while women are relegated to a relatively powerless and unequal role.

Private life, for us, includes life within the family and the domestic and personal activities that take place within a home, such as sex; raising children; expressing intimacy, love, and affection; and doing domestic chores. Public life, on the other hand, includes the economic and political activities that take place outside the family and the home, such as paid work, buying and selling goods, voting, running for political office, and participating in legal processes. It is taken almost for granted today that the public should not interfere with the private. "A man's home is his castle," we say, implying that the world should not interfere with what goes on in the home.

QUICK REVIEW
Feminists also argue that social contract theory divides the "public" life of politics and economics, in which men predominate, from the "private" life of the family, where women are confined to labor so that men can participate in public life. This unjustly relegates women to powerless roles, gives men political and economic power, and insulates family relations from public criticism.

But this separation of the private and the public, several female philosophers have pointed out, has kept women in an inherently unequal position. Traditionally, women have taken on the major burden of domestic work: cooking for everyone in the family, cleaning up the house, doing the laundry, and caring for the children. This gives men the time and freedom to leave the home and enter public life. Thus, the labor performed by women within the private sphere gives men the freedom to participate in the public sphere, while keeping women occupied and confined in the private.

Confining women to the private and men to the public sphere is not necessarily unfair. However, in our society, real economic and political power is available only in the public world. Men are paid for the work they perform in the public world whereas women are not paid for the work they perform in the private home, so men acquire the economic power that wealth brings and women are left economically powerless. Women may try to work for pay outside the home, but they are always disadvantaged, feminists claim, because they are still expected to do most of the housework and child care. Moreover, because women take over these domestic tasks, men are also free to run for public office and engage in those political and legal processes that are the source of political power. Women remain preoccupied at home with domestic tasks that carry no political power. Some women may become active in public affairs, but this is always difficult because domestic tasks continue to encroach on their time and because their private lives have not prepared them for engaging in the public world of politics.

In short, then, we separate the public from the private and relegate women to laboring in the private sphere, thereby freeing men to take over the public world. But because the public world is the source of economic and political power, men come to hold most of the power in our society, and women either remain wholly powerless or are greatly disadvantaged by the burdens that the private sphere puts on them.

---

17 Carole Pateman, "Feminist Critiques of the Public/Private Dichotomy," in *Private and Public in Social Life*, ed. Stanley Benn and Gerald Gaus (London: Croom Helm, 1983), 82.

Thus, the separation of the private world from the public world is the fundamental means by which women are forced into political and economic powerlessness. Moreover, because private domestic matters are assumed to have nothing to do with politics, political philosophers have ignored the private sphere of the family, even though the structure of the family (where women must labor) is the key that enables men to assume political and economic power. The contemporary political philosopher Susan Okin elaborates on these points in her book *Justice, Gender, and the Family*:

> Thus feminists have turned their attention to the politics of what had previously been regarded—and . . . still is seen by most political theorists—as paradigmatically nonpolitical. That the personal sphere of sexuality, of housework, of child care and family life is political became the underpinning of most feminist thought. Feminists of different political leanings and in a variety of academic disciplines have revealed and analyzed the multiple interconnections between women's domestic roles and their inequality and segregation in the workplace, and between their socialization in gendered families and the psychological aspects of their oppression. We have strongly and persistently challenged the long-standing underlying assumption of almost all political theories: that the sphere of family and personal life is so separate and distinct from the rest of social life that such theories can justifiably assume but ignore it.
>
> The interconnections between the domestic and the nondomestic aspects of our lives are deep and pervasive. Given the power structures of both, women's lives are far more detrimentally affected by these interconnections than are men's. Consider two recent front-page stories that appeared on subsequent days in the *New York Times.* The first was about a tiny elite among women: those who work as lawyers for the country's top law firms. If these women have children with whom they want to spend any time, they find themselves off the partnership track and instead, with no prospects of advancement, on the "mommy track." "Nine-to-five" is considered part-time work in the ethos of such firms, and one mother reports that, in spite of her twelve-hour workdays and frequent work on weekends, she has "no chance" of making partner. The article fails to mention that these women's children have fathers, or that most of the men who work for the same prestigious law firms also have children, except to report that male lawyers who take parental leave are seen as "wimp-like." The sexual division of labor in the family, even in these cases where the women are extremely well qualified, successful, and potentially influential, is simply assumed.
>
> The next day's *Times* reported on a case of major significance for abortion rights. . . . The all-male panel of judges ruled 7 to 3 that the state may require a woman under eighteen years who wishes to obtain an abortion to notify both her parents—even in cases of divorce, separation, or desertion—or to get special approval from a state judge. The significance of this article is amplified when it is juxtaposed with the previous one. For it shows us how it is that those who rise to the top in the highly politically influential profession of law are among those who have had the least experience of all in raising children. There is a high incidence of recruitment of judges from those who have risen to partnership in the most prestigious law firms. . . . Here we find a systematically built-in absence of mothers (and presumably of "wimp-like" participating fathers, too) from high-level political decisions concerning some of the most vulnerable persons in society—women, disproportionately poor and black, who become pregnant in their teens, and their future children. It is not hard to see here the ties between the supposedly distinct public and domestic spheres.
>
> This is but one example of what feminists mean by saying that "the personal is political," sometimes adding the corollary "the political is personal." Contemporary feminism poses a significant challenge to the long-standing and still-surviving assumption of political theories that the sphere of family and personal life is sharply distinct from the rest of social and political life, that the state can and

QUICK REVIEW
Okin argues that the public or nondomestic world where economic and political power is centered, and the private domestic world of the family where women are unequal and psychologically oppressed, have deep and pervasive interconnections that affect women detrimentally.

should restrain itself from intrusion in the domestic sphere, and that political theories can therefore legitimately ignore it.[18]

The problems that feminist thinkers have identified in political theory seem to call the whole social contract tradition into question. This tradition, and much of Western political theory, seems to be built on the assumption that our private lives and our public affairs are and should be separate. But by ignoring the private domain, the assumption ignores the most fundamental source of political and economic inequalities: the family.

Perhaps, however, it is better to see this discussion as a call to reform our ways of thinking about the family and its relationship to politics. Instead of rejecting social contract theory, perhaps we should extend its political ideals of consent, equality, and freedom into the world of the family. These political ideals, fashioned and bequeathed to us by Hobbes, Locke, and Rousseau, need not be seen as corrupt. In fact, we may say that the reason traditional social contract theory falls short is not because of the political ideals on which it is based but because it does not extend the political ideals of consent, equality, and freedom far enough. Our task, then, is to see how the ideals of equality, freedom, and consent can be applied to family life. Is this possible? That is a question each of us, as we have moved out of the families in which we were raised and into new families of our own, must answer for ourselves.

QUESTIONS

1. What is the fundamental difference between Hobbes' and Locke's contract theory concepts? Between these and Rousseau's theory? Between these and Rawls' theory?
2. The contract theory contends that we should obey the state because we have contractually promised to do so. How, if at all, have you contracted to obey the state?
3. The Declaration of Independence contends that "whenever any Form of Government becomes destructive" of individual life, liberty, and the pursuit of happiness, "it is the Right of the People to alter or to abolish it." Under what circumstances, if any, would you personally exercise this right? Specifically, what conditions would have to prevail for you to act to alter or abolish your form of government?
4. Think of ways that your identity depends on cultural traditions. Do you think that it is the purpose of government to protect these cultural traditions? Suppose that a large, established group of people in the United States has cultural traditions brought here from another nation. Should the U.S. government protect those traditions? Why or why not?
5. Do you think that it is possible or desirable to "extend the political ideals of consent, equality, and freedom" into the family? Explain.
6. Feminists argue that social contract theory does not include women. Are there any other beings that the theory excludes? Is this situation good, bad, or neutral?

PHILOSOPHY AT THE MOVIES

Watch *The Lord of the Flies* (1990), in which a group of schoolboys marooned on an island organize themselves into a rudimentary society, but then divide into two competing camps that descend into violence. With whose view of the state of nature and the origin of government does this film most agree: the view of Hobbes, Locke, or Rousseau? How are the men who rescue the boys similar to the boys?

18 Susan Okin, *Justice, Gender, and the Family* (New York: Basic Books, 1989), 125–127.

8.3 What Is Justice?

Whether we believe that government rests on individual consent or on community values, we want government to be just. But what is justice? It's common to think of justice in retributive terms—that is, in terms of crime and the punishments that government inflicts on criminals. But we can think of justice in other terms. In fact, in a larger sense, justice deals with distribution, not merely retribution. Questions arise daily, for example, about the way that wealth and income are distributed among us. On any given day about 40 to 45 million Americans live in poverty, and about 30 to 35 million of those do not know where their next meal will come from. On the other hand, the average CEO of one of the Fortune 500 companies makes about $12 million per year, or about 343 times what an average American worker makes. Are such large inequalities just? Is it just that some should be spending their money on yachts while others are starving? Figures like these raise numerous questions: Should we try to make people's incomes more equal? Should we try to channel more of our resources to those in need? If individuals belong to groups that have been unfairly discriminated against, should these persons receive special consideration and treatment? Who should have access to medical care? Only those who can afford it? Everyone who needs it? Those who are likely to benefit most?

QUICK REVIEW
Justice includes both retributive justice, which looks at how fair punishments are, and distributive justice, which looks at how fairly society distributes benefits and burdens.

Issues of distribution needn't be confined to wealth and goods, however. Equally important is the distribution of privilege and power. Education raises such issues. Who should have access to government-supported public education? Everyone? Everyone but immigrants? Only those who can afford to pay? Only those who show promise of benefiting society? Other questions of privilege and power can also be asked. Who shall be permitted to vote? To drive? To drink? Should everyone be treated the same under the law, or should certain individuals—for example, juveniles—receive special consideration?

All of these issues raise questions of distributive justice. *Distributive justice* is concerned with the fair and proper distribution of public benefits and burdens among the members of a community. Burdens include work and the costs that must be paid to develop society's productive capacities. The benefits include, of course, all the goods that people want and that society produces. Although distributive justice operates in all organizations, it applies chiefly to how government distributes benefits and burdens among its members.

Clearly, the subject of distributive justice touches many areas, from jobs to income, from taxes to medical services. Embedded in any answer to the question of how jobs should be assigned, economic goods should be distributed, income and taxes determined, and medical resources allocated will be a principle of distributive justice—that is, some assumption about the proper way of distributing what is available when there isn't enough for all. For example, it's commonly argued that jobs should be distributed on the basis of talent and ability. Again, it is sometimes said that large corporations should be given tax breaks so they can reinvest their savings, thus increasing jobs and productivity, which in turn will benefit the whole of society. President Barack Obama has claimed that medical services should be provided on the basis of need. And during the 2009 recession, the government gave away about $1 trillion taxpayer dollars to several banks, an insurance company, and some auto manufacturers, saying that these companies "needed" these funds to continue operating and that if they were to fail, the whole of society could fall into a disastrous economic depression. Each of these assertions implies some standard that should be considered in the distribution of certain resources: merit, social benefit, and need. Whether these or other principles should be taken into account is a basic concern of distributive justice.

PHILOSOPHY AND LIFE

The Purpose of Business

Business is the single most important and all-pervasive social institution of modern societies. Everything we eat, drink, wear, read, drive, or use as entertainment is manufactured, packaged, and sold by a business; the money we spend ultimately comes from business. Even politics is overwhelmed by the influence of business.

Yet we rarely ask what its purpose is. Is the purpose of business to make profits? Or does business have a social responsibility to improve our society? In 1970, the Nobel Prize–winning economist Milton Friedman set out what became a classical but controversial view of the responsibilities of a business and its executives:

> In a free-enterprise, private-property system, a corporate executive is an employee of the owners of the business. He has direct responsibility to his employers [the stockholders]. That responsibility is to conduct the business in accordance with their desires, which generally will be to make as much money as possible while conforming to the basic rules of the society, both those embodied in law and those embodied in ethical custom. . . . There is one and only one social responsibility of business—to use its resources and engage in activities designed to increase its profits so long as it stays within the rules of the game, which is to say, engages in open and free competition without deception or fraud.

Forty years later, John Mackey, founder and CEO of Whole Foods, joined the hundreds of people who have responded to Friedman:

> I strongly disagree [with Friedman]. At Whole Foods, we measure our success by how much value we can create [not just for stockholders, but] for all six of our most important stakeholders: customers, employees, investors, vendors, communities, and the environment. Many thinking people will readily accept my arguments that caring about customers and employees is good business. . . . [Moreover,] a certain amount of corporate philanthropy is [also] good business. . . . As we mature, most people grow beyond . . . egocentrism and begin to care about others—their families, friends, communities, and countries. Our capacity to love can expand even further, to loving people from different races, religions, and countries—potentially to unlimited love for all people and even for other sentient creatures. This is our potential as human beings, to take joy in the flourishing of people everywhere. Whole Foods gives money to our communities because we care about them and feel a responsibility to help them flourish as well as possible.

Milton Friedman penned a response to John Mackey, in which he defended the principles he laid out forty years earlier:

> Whole Foods Market behaves in accordance with the principles I spelled out in my 1970 article. . . . Had it devoted any significant fraction of its resources to exercising a [real] social responsibility unrelated to the bottom line, it would be out of business by now or would have been taken over. Mackey [says] . . . "successful businesses put the customer first" [and] "Corporate philanthropy is simply good business."[As] I wrote in 1970: "It may well be in the long run [business] interests of a corporation . . . to devote resources to providing amenities to the community. . . . [T]his is one way for a corporation to generate goodwill . . . [so such] expenditures . . . are entirely . . . in its own self-interest."

QUESTIONS

1. Do you agree that in a "free-enterprise, private-property" society, a business's only duty is to "increase its profits"? Do businesses have a duty to refrain from actions that are legal but that harm employees, customers, or the environment?
2. Do you agree with Mackey's view that "love for all people" should motivate a business to "care" for and contribute to the "flourishing" of customers, employees, investors, vendors, communities, and the environment?
3. What does Friedman mean when he writes that Whole Foods "behaves in accordance with the principles I spelled out in my 1970 article"? Do you agree?

Source: Milton Friedman, "The Social Responsibility of Business Is to Increase Its Profits," *The New York Times Magazine*, September 13, 1970; M. Friedman and John Mackey, "Rethinking the Social Responsibility of Business," *Reasononline*, October 2005, http://www.reason.com/news/show/32239.html (accessed May 25, 2009).

One way of approaching questions of distributive justice is to start with what is sometimes called "formal justice." Aristotle and other philosophers have argued that formal justice is the root meaning of *justice*. Formal justice is the requirement that we should treat similar people similarly. For example, if Jack and Jill, carry the same amount of water for us, then we should pay them the same. We should not pay Jack more merely because he is a man. Neither should we pay Jill more merely because her skin is white and Jack's is not. Formal justice, then, is a kind of consistency. Formal justice says that we should treat two cases the same when they are the same. But this raises a key question: When should we consider people to be "the same"? In many respects, Jack and Jill are not the same. We just indicated that Jack is not white but Jill is, and Jack is a man whereas Jill is a woman. But these differences are not relevant when deciding how much they each should be paid for the work they did. On the other hand, if Jill carries a bucket of water for us that is twice as big as Jack's, then this is relevant to how much each should get. The amount of work that people do is a relevant difference when deciding what they should be paid for their work. The principle of formal justice, then, can be stated as follows:

> Formal justice obtains when individuals who are similar in all respects relevant to the kind of treatment in question are given similar benefits and burdens, and individuals who are dissimilar in a relevant respect are treated dissimilarly.

QUICK REVIEW
The principle of formal justice says people should be treated the same when they are similar in relevant respects and differently when they differ in relevant respects. Material principles of justice indicate what kinds of differences are "relevant."

This formal principle of justice tells us something about what justice and injustice are. For example, if we agree that sex and race are not relevant differences when considering people for jobs, then the principle tells us that racial and sexual discrimination in hiring is unjust. On the other hand, if we agree that experience, skill, education, and ability are relevant when choosing people for a certain job, then it is morally just to favor those who have more experience, skills, education, and ability.

Yet the formal principle of justice does not settle all the issues. In fact, it does not settle the most pressing controversies that swirl around the issue of justice. For example, is need relevant when deciding whether it is just for government to provide welfare to people? Or take affirmative action programs, which show preference to women and minorities who have been disadvantaged in the past. Are these programs based on "relevant differences"? Are they just? What kinds of differences among people are relevant, and what kinds are not? The formal principle of justice leaves this fundamental question unanswered.

Over the centuries, society has suggested many kinds of "relevant differences" among people. These are called "material" or "substantive" principles of justice. For example, a simple principle that we all think is just is "first come, first served." When we are waiting to buy tickets at a movie theater or concert, for example, we stand in a line where the first to arrive is served first, and latecomers are served last. We think it is unjust when a latecomer crowds in line ahead of us. The reason, of course, is because when waiting to receive a service or good, we believe that a relevant difference among us is who took the trouble to get there first.

But there are other, broader views of what justice means when we are talking about society. Thus, the person who invokes talent and ability as the proper principle of job distribution probably views justice in terms of merit. Likewise, the person who argues for special tax advantages for large corporations is viewing justice in terms of social utility. And those who think that medical resources should be equally available to all view justice chiefly in terms of equality: Everyone should be treated equally in the sense that all should get the same medical care. In fact, merit, social utility, and equality have served as focal points for various theories of justice down through the years and continue to exert profound influence on our current views of justice and the proper relationship between the individual and society.

Justice as Merit

Plato proposed one of the first substantive theories of justice, one associated with giving individuals what is their due. In Plato's theory, justice in the state is exactly what it is in the individual: a harmony between the various parts for the good of the whole. Social justice, then, requires cooperation among the members of a society so that society will function best. As a result, the interests of the individual must be subordinated to the larger interests and good of society.

Such a notion had significant implications for the overwhelming majority of the Greek population, who were poor and powerless. The submissive role that these people played, especially the slaves, was vital to the overall success of the society. Yet their interests and rights were kept to a minimum. Indeed, they expected reward only insofar as their actions benefited their superiors. Such an attitude could be fostered only in a rigidly structured society, whose sharply drawn class divisions left no confusion about one's place, role, or expectations in life. This is precisely the kind of society that Plato has in mind in *The Republic*: a system in which every individual has his or her place, and justice means that each person acts and is treated accordingly. In Plato's view, then, justice becomes associated with merit, in the sense that individuals are treated and given a station in life according to their talents and accomplishments. People's natural talents, Plato held, make them fit for certain social roles or statuses, and what people get depends on their role or status. In the following passage from *The Republic*, Plato indicates his position quite clearly:

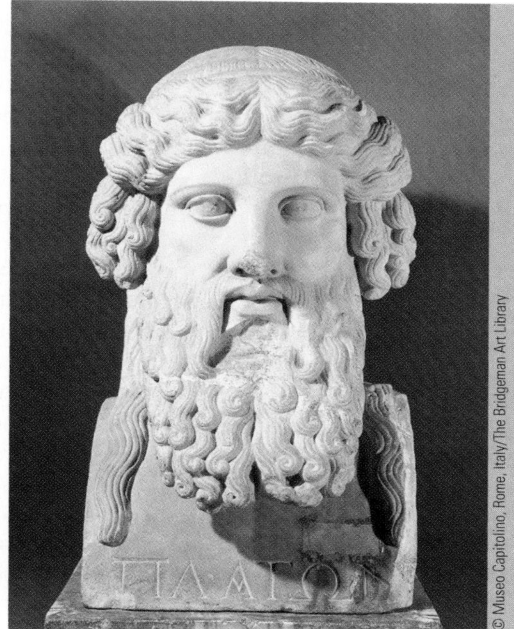

© Museo Capitolino, Rome, Italy/The Bridgeman Art Library

Plato: "When one who is by nature a worker attempts to enter the warrior class, or one of the soldiers tries to enter the class of guardians, this meddling brings the city to ruin. That then is injustice. But the doing of one's own job by each class is justice and makes the city just."

> Is the exclusive aim of judges in delivering judgment that no citizen should have what belongs to another or be deprived of what is his own?
>
> That is their aim.
>
> That is what we call justice?
>
> Yes.
>
> In some way then possession of one's own and the performance of one's own task could be agreed to be justice.
>
> That is so.
>
> Consider then whether you agree with me in this: if a carpenter attempts to do the work of a cobbler, or a cobbler that of a carpenter, and they exchange their tools and the esteem that goes with the job, or the same man tries to do both, and all the other exchanges are made, do you think that this does any great harm to the city?
>
> No.
>
> But I think that when one who is by nature a worker or some other kind of moneymaker is puffed up by wealth, or the mob, or by his own strength, or some

other such thing, and attempts to enter the warrior class, or one of the soldiers tries to enter the group of counselors and guardians, though he is unworthy of it, and these exchange their tools and the public esteem, or when the same man tries to perform all these jobs together, then I think you will agree that these exchanges and this meddling bring the city to ruin.

They certainly do.

The meddling and exchange between the three established orders [of workers, warriors, and guardian rulers] does very great harm to the city and would most correctly be called wickedness.

Very definitely.

And you would call the greatest wickedness worked against one's own city injustice?

Of course.

That then is injustice. And let us repeat that the doing of one's own job by the moneymaking, warrior, and guardian groups, when each group is performing its own task in the city, is the opposite: it is justice and makes the city just.

I agree with you that this is so.[19]

critical thinking

Does Plato assume that it is just to sacrifice the happiness and the freedom of the individual for the sake of the larger society? Is this assumption correct?

To read more from Plato's *The Republic*, go to CourseMate for this text and browse by chapter or philosopher.

Apparent in this selection and throughout *The Republic* is Plato's insistence not only on class distinctions but also on the natural *inequality* of individuals. For Plato, however, class distinctions are not based on birth or on one's aristocratic or other family origins. Instead, Plato argued that people, whatever their family background, have different natural talents and abilities. These natural talents and abilities—not their family backgrounds—make them fit for different social roles. At the top of society are those whose talents and accomplishments make them fit to rule. Below them are those whose natural courage and aggressiveness make them fit to enter the military class. Next come those whose skills fit them to be free workers and artisans. At the bottom, almost unmentioned by Plato, are the slaves. Those with higher social status merit more than those below them, so justice requires that they get more.

Aristotle also shared the assumption that individuals are unequal and that justice is giving to unequal individuals their unequal due. Indeed, in his *Politics*, Aristotle defended slavery because he believed that those who were slaves were naturally suited for that role and would be wretched and ineffectual were they made free.

> That some should rule and others be ruled is not only necessary, but advantageous; for from the hour of their birth some are marked out to be ruled, others to rule. . . . It is clear that the rule of the mind over the body, and of reason over the passions, is natural and advantageous; whereas the equality of the two or the rule of the inferior is always hurtful . . . Where, then, there is such a difference between people as that between mind and body . . . the lower sort are by nature slaves, and it is better for them as for all inferiors that they should be under the rule of a master.[20]

QUICK REVIEW
Justice as merit holds that benefits and burdens should be distributed unequally according to people's ability, effort, achievement, or social status. Plato argued that people have different talents and abilities, so society will function best if each person plays the role for which he or she is best suited. Critics claim that such inequality is unjust.

Both Aristotle and Plato believed that the abilities and achievements of different people entitled them to different statuses in society. Justice means that each should act and be treated according to his or her abilities, achievements, and social status. We can summarize this notion of justice in a more general way with this statement:

> A just society is one that distributes benefits and burdens according to merit as measured by a person's talent, ability, effort, achievement, intelligence, or social status.

19 Plato, *The Republic*, trans. G. M. A. Grube (Indianapolis: Hackett, 1974). Reprinted by permission.
20 Aristotle, *Politics*, bk. 1, ch. 5. Translated by Manuel Velasquez.

Notice that the principle of merit tries to put some teeth into the principle of formal justice. The principle of formal justice says that people should be treated the same except when there are relevant differences between them. In effect, Plato and Aristotle hold that the main "relevant difference" among people is *merit*—what people deserve in light of their talents and achievements. This view plays an important role in many of our perceptions of justice. We feel that among athletes it is just that the highest honors should be awarded on the basis of achievement. The gold medal should go to the one who runs or swims the fastest, the one who lifts the most, or the one who throws the discus the farthest. Many college scholarships are awarded on merit: on the grades a person achieved in high school and on standardized tests. We feel it is just when jobs are awarded according to merit as indicated by a candidate's abilities and accomplishments.

On the other hand, Plato and Aristotle might question the justice of some contemporary practices. For example, it seems safe to say that both would object to heterogeneous grouping in public schools (that is, the practice of placing students of diverse abilities in the same class, as opposed to homogeneous grouping, in which only students of like ability are placed in the same class). They would object to the view that "all men are created equal" and that everyone should have equal political rights. They would certainly object to the view that everyone has an equal right to hold political office.

Many people today find Plato's and Aristotle's theories of justice objectionable because of their assumption that individuals have or should have an unequal status. But isn't the presupposition of equality as much an assumption as the presupposition of inequality and, as such, doesn't equality require a defense as much as inequality? Can the view that people are or should be "equal" be defended?

Justice as Equality

We can readily identify with the idea of equality. After all, we have been reared in a society built on the premise that "all men are created equal." *Equal* here, of course, means "the same." Accordingly, in the United States it is widely believed that everyone is entitled to a period of roughly the same kind of education, that the sexes and races should be treated the same, that individuals should be treated the same before the law, that everyone should have the same job opportunities and the same access to medical care, that everyone should have the same right to practice religion, speak freely, travel, and so on. Similarly, we reject slavery on principle because it violates our belief that everyone is equal. We even object to snobbery, presumably because we believe that one person is not necessarily better than another because of wealth, family, intelligence, or some other source of unequal status. The point is that we needn't look far to see evidence that, at least in theory, our society is erected on a commitment to egalitarianism.

Yet what, exactly, does this commitment to equality mean? One way of trying to capture the meaning of *equality* is by taking the term quite strictly. Strict equality means exactly equal shares. We can summarize the view that justice is, strictly, giving to each an equal share, in the following statement:

> In a just society, every person will be given exactly equal shares of that society's benefits and burdens.

This view is known as *strict egalitarianism*. Notice that the strict egalitarian view takes a definite position on formal justice. The strict egalitarian claims that there are *no* relevant differences among people when it comes to justice. Justice demands strict equality regardless of the differences among people.

QUICK REVIEW
Justice as strict equality holds that everyone should have equal shares of society's benefits and burdens. Egalitarians say there are no relevant differences among people, so all should be treated equally. Critics reply that people's needs are relevant when distributing benefits, and their abilities when distributing burdens.

Equality has been an ideal for Americans since the nation was founded. The Declaration of Independence states, for example, that "all men are created equal." Nevertheless, promoting strict equality leads to difficult theoretical and operational problems. To get an idea of these problems, consider the practice of heterogeneous grouping in the classroom. Consistent with the belief that everyone is equal, we try to ensure that everyone has roughly the same educational opportunities, at least in the formative years. Accordingly, thirty students of widely differing abilities and capacities may be placed in the same class at the same time with the same instructor. Faced with such essential diversity, teachers often end up aiming their teaching at the nonexistent "average" class member. As likely as not, the instructional level will be too high for the slowest class members and too low for the swiftest. As a result, the slowest don't learn, and the swiftest get bored; both "turn off." Is this just?

Again, modern medical technology has made the wondrous dream of organ transplants an astonishing reality. Corneas, hearts, kidneys, bone marrow, and even livers and lungs can be transplanted with more or less success. But there's a rub: Demand exceeds supply. Who should get available organs when there aren't enough to go around? By a strict egalitarian calculation, everyone who needs a heart should have an equal chance of getting it. But suppose that two people are in need of the only available heart. One of them is an internationally renowned neurosurgeon in her forties whose survival promises to benefit countless persons. The other is a sixty-five-year-old derelict who for three decades has wantonly abused his body and whose survival promises little benefit for anyone, except possibly himself. Is it just to treat these individuals as equals in determining who will receive the heart? Or is it more just that they be treated as unequals?

The problem, of course, is that people are not equal, and their inequalities seem to demand an unequal sharing in society's resources. Human beings have different needs, different abilities, different desires, and different virtues. They put forward different efforts and have different skills and different physical abilities. In fact, humans seem to be unequal in all respects. Don't we have to take these differences into account when we distribute benefits among people? Suppose that every worker were given exactly the same wage. Then, better workers would have no incentive to work hard because hard work would get them exactly the same as loafing. Suppose that every needy person is given the same basket of goods. Then some will get more than they need, and others will get less than they need. On the other hand, if people are given exactly the same burdens, then some will get more than they can bear, whereas others will not get enough. Take the burdens of work. If everyone has to do exactly the same amount of work, then people who are unskilled or handicapped will have to do as much as people who are strong and skilled. This does not seem to be the best way to arrange work burdens. People's differences, then, seem to demand that they receive different shares of society's benefits and burdens.

QUICK REVIEW
Justice as moderate egalitarianism holds that political rights and economic opportunities should be distributed equally but that all other economic benefits and burdens should be distributed according to the relevant differences among people. Critics respond that even political rights—for example, of criminals—should not be equal and that equality of opportunity is not possible.

Some egalitarians respond to these criticisms by proposing a more moderate form of egalitarianism. They distinguish two kinds of equality: political equality and economic equality. People have political equality when they have an equal right to participate in our political processes. Certainly, moderate egalitarians argue, we would all agree that people should have equal political rights. Such equal rights include an equal right to vote, an equal right to run for political offices, equal civil rights, and equal rights to due process. Strict egalitarianism should be the rule in the political arena. But what about the economic arena? Here, say moderate egalitarians, we again have to make a distinction. Economic equality can mean either equality of income and wealth, or equality of economic opportunity. The objections that critics of strict egalitarianism make, they say, are problems that result if we try to make everyone's income and wealth equal. But differences among people have to be recognized when distributing income and wealth. On the other hand, moderate egalitarians continue, there is nothing wrong with equality of economic opportunity. Everyone should have an equal opportunity to get those jobs and positions that carry higher levels of income and wealth. Society might secure equality of economic opportunity by giving everyone the same chance at an education and by eliminating all racial and sexual discrimination in jobs and other positions. So, moderate egalitarians conclude, strict equality is justified in the political arena, and it is also justified in the economic arena if we are talking about equality of opportunity. But other economic benefits and burdens should be distributed according to relevant differences among people. This moderate form of egalitarianism can be summarized as follows:

> A just society is one in which political rights and economic opportunities are distributed equally, whereas other economic benefits and burdens are distributed unequally according to the relevant differences among people.

But is even such a modified egalitarianism correct? Aren't there some differences among people that lead us to say that even political rights should not be equal? Consider the criminal. Is it wrong to say that the convicted criminal should not have the same political rights that other citizens have? Or take the person who cannot read or the person who has an IQ less than 50. Should such people have the same right to vote as all others? Consider equality of opportunity. Can we really hope to achieve equality of opportunity? Won't differences among people always sabotage our attempts to achieve equality of opportunity? Suppose that we give everyone the same education. Some students will be more motivated, be smarter, and have fewer distractions than others. Such students will graduate with better qualifications than others. So, not everyone will have the same opportunities when they graduate, even if everyone gets the same education. People's inequalities, then, seem to undercut the egalitarian's attempts to achieve both political equality and equality of opportunity.

For Plato and Aristotle, the natural differences among people posed no great problem because they associated justice with unequal merit. But for modern theorists, the tension between recognizing people's differences and pursuing equality poses an urgent problem. Indeed, it is one that philosophers have engaged for several centuries and one that has given rise to the theory of justice associated with social utility.

Justice as Social Utility

One view of justice that occurs to many people today is this: Justice is what promotes the general welfare—that is, the well-being or happiness of citizens. The ultimate criterion of justice, then, is utility: society is just when it promotes the utility or happiness of all or at least the majority of its members.

As we saw in the last chapter, John Stuart Mill was one of the modern founders of utilitarianism, the view that we should aim at securing the happiness of society's members. Mill argued that society should always try to minimize social harms and maximize social benefits. In *Utilitarianism*, Mill discusses the concept of justice, and concedes that the notion of equality is often part of both our conception and practice of social justice. But he does not believe that equality constitutes the essence of justice for a society. Although the notion of justice seems

John Stuart Mill: "Justice remains the appropriate name for certain social utilities which are vastly more important, and therefore more absolute and imperative, than any others are as a class." *John Stuart Mill (1806–1873),* 1973 (oil on canvas), George Frederick Watts (1817–1904).

© Trustees of the Watts Gallery, Compton, Surrey, UK/The Bridgeman Art Library

to vary among different persons, says Mill, individuals ultimately interpret justice in terms of utility. Thus, for example, while people may claim that justice is equality, they will readily abandon the pursuit of equality when they feel that society's utility is better served through some practice that requires inequality. Then they are likely to say, for example, that a famous surgeon and a skid-row bum should not be treated as equals in determining who will get an available heart. Because preserving the life of the surgeon promises more social benefit, the surgeon should get the organ. More generally, Mill claims, we tend to see justice as an "absolute obligation" only because the requirements of justice provide more social utility than any other kind of moral rules. So, we can summarize Mill's views on justice in the following statement:

> The just society is the one that distributes benefits and burdens in whatever way will produce the greatest social benefits or (when only net harms result) inflict the lowest social harms.

In Mill's view, utility or "expediency" is the fundamental criterion in determining what is just and unjust. By expediency, Mill means what is advantageous to society. Whatever the institution, policy, or program, its justice depends ultimately on its expediency—the extent to which it will be advantageous to society. Is reverse discrimination just? It may be, if it serves the public interest better than any other alternative proposed to ensure comparable opportunities. Does a fee-for-service medical system best serve society's interests? Individual answers may vary, but each of them, Mill would probably say, will be based on an opinion about the expediency of the practice. What is expedient will be just; what is not expedient will not be just. In the following passage from *Utilitarianism,* he makes these points:

QUICK REVIEW
Justice as social utility holds that benefits and burdens should be distributed so as to maximize social benefits and minimize social harms. Critics argue that social utility wrongly implies that injustices such as slavery are sometimes just, and that it is just to sacrifice the welfare of individuals or small groups for the sake of the general welfare.

> While I dispute the pretensions of any theory which sets up an imaginary standard of justice not grounded on utility, I account the justice which is grounded on utility to be the chief part, and incomparably the most sacred and binding part, of all morality. Justice is a name for certain classes of moral rules, which concern the essentials of human well-being more nearly, and are therefore of more absolute obligation, than any other rules for the guidance of life. . . .
>
> Justice, [therefore,] is a name for certain moral requirements which, regarded collectively, stand higher in the scale of social utility. . . .
>
> It has always been evident that all cases of justice are also cases of expediency; the difference is in [a] peculiar sentiment which attaches to the former, as contradistinguished from the latter. . . . [T]his characteristic sentiment . . . is simply the natural feeling of resentment. . . .
>
> Justice [, therefore,] remains the appropriate name for certain social utilities which are vastly more important, and therefore more absolute and imperative, than any others are as a class; and which, therefore, ought to be, as well

> as naturally are, guarded by a sentiment [that is] . . . distinguished from the milder feeling which attaches to the mere idea of promoting human pleasure or convenience.[21]

Because Mill's utilitarian theory of justice is a logical extension of his ethical theories, it is understandable that it should invite some of the same objections. First, even if what we consider expedient or advantageous we also consider just, should we do so? For example, some people have argued that slavery can be advantageous for a society under some conditions. In fact, some have argued that in primitive societies, slavery gave some people the leisure needed to develop theories and technologies that in the long run made those societies better off than they would have been if everyone had been forced to spend all their time laboring. If these arguments are correct, then the utilitarian would have to agree that slavery in such situations is just. But to many people this seems wrong: Slavery is unjust to the slave no matter how much it benefits the slave owner.

To read more from Mill's *Utilitarianism*, go to CourseMate for this text and browse by chapter or philosopher.

A second, related problem with social utility arises from the inevitable clash of individual and public interests. Surely, in some cases the general utility can be served only at the expense of an individual or perhaps a small group. Take, for example, the volatile issue of nuclear waste disposal sites. Nuclear power plants can provide a sizable fraction of the electrical power that citizens use and from which many draw significant benefits. These plants can also produce large amounts of radioactive wastes, which have to be stored somewhere. But many people fear that radioactive storage sites pose some level of risks to individuals living near them. Is it just for the government to insist that these individuals must bear even a small risk for the good of society? Of course, one could respond that the utility of a specific act by itself cannot give an adequate concept of justice, that what is needed is a theory of general practice along the lines of rule utilitarianism. But as we have seen (in Chapter 7), rule utilitarianism still allows the possibility of a practice that systematically increases the general utility at the expense of some individual or group. Is this just?

Justice Based on Need and Ability

Socialism is one of the major political philosophies of the modern world. Many countries base their social institutions on socialism, including those nations that are still "communist." Although there are many different versions of socialism, we can say, generally, that socialism holds that the wealth society produces belongs to everyone in society and so should be shared by everyone in society. Modern socialists often advocate government ownership of all factories and business enterprises. They also support government programs that distribute to everyone in society a share of the income and wealth produced by these enterprises.

There are many kinds of socialism, so it is probably not accurate to speak of *the* socialist view of justice. Still, philosophers traditionally take the dictum that Karl Marx proposed as the socialist view on distributive justice. As Marx wrote in his short work *Critique of the Gotha Program*, "From each according to his ability, to each according to his need."[22] This socialist principle can be summarized as follows:

> In a just society work burdens should be distributed according to people's abilities, and benefits should be distributed according to people's needs.

---

21 John Stuart Mill, *Utilitarianism* (New York: Bobbs-Merrill, 1957), 68–69. Reprinted by permission.

22 Karl Marx, *Critique of the Gotha Program* (London: Lawrence and Wishart, 1938), 14, 107. This slogan was earlier stated by Louis Blanc in *L'Organization du Travail* (Paris, 1850) and later by Nikolai Lenin in his short pamphlet "Marxism on the State."

Marx's slogan is another interpretation of what *relevant difference* means in the principle of formal justice. For Marx, the key differences that are relevant when distributing things justly are people's abilities and needs. Justice requires that jobs and tasks should be assigned to people according to the skills and abilities that they have. Those with few or no abilities, of course, should have light or easy tasks, whereas those who are extremely able and talented should have heavier and more complex jobs. On the other hand, the goods that society produces—food, clothing, housing, medical care, luxuries—should be distributed according to people's needs. The greater a person's need for a specific kind of good, the more he or she should receive of that good; the less a person's need for a certain good, the less of that good he or she should receive.

We use the principle of distribution according to need and ability in many areas of our lives. In athletics, for example, the members of a team will distribute burdens according to each team member's abilities. And team members tend to stand together and help one another according to each one's need. In business, managers sometimes use this principle when they assign tasks to workers, giving the hard and complex tasks to those with commensurate abilities. And when workers seem to have special needs, many managers will try to accommodate them by giving them extra resources. In society at large, we believe that people's needs should be one of the criteria that government uses to distribute benefits. For example, this is the key idea behind government welfare programs, aid to the needy, and loans to people in disaster areas. We also believe that income taxes should be levied according to people's ability to pay: The more people earn, we think, the more income taxes they should pay.

But the group in which use of the socialist principle is most prominent is the family. Able family members willingly work to support and help the family, whereas those who are in need are willingly supported by the family's resources. In fact, the principle of need and ability has been argued for because of the notion that societies should be communities in which benefits and burdens are distributed on the model of the family.

QUICK REVIEW
Socialist justice holds that burdens should be distributed by ability and benefits by need. Marx argued that people develop their potential by working according to their ability, and distributing benefits by need promotes human happiness. Critics reply that this view gives no incentive to work; it may work in families but not in societies; it requires coercion.

However, Karl Marx offers a different argument. Marx argues that people should realize their human potential through productive work that exercises their particular abilities. This means that work should be distributed according to people's abilities. Second, he argues, the benefits produced through work should be used to promote human happiness and well-being. This implies that goods should be used first to meet people's basic needs and then their other, nonbasic needs.

But many people have objected to the socialist principle. First, they have argued, under the socialist principle there would be no relation between how hard a person works and the compensation that person receives. Compensation, after all, would be based on need, not effort. So, workers would have no incentive to work hard. Second, critics have asked, how practical is it to try to model a whole society on the family? People are self-interested and competitive. Outside the family they are not motivated by the willingness to share and help that is a natural response to life in the family. Finally, critics claim, the socialist principle can't succeed unless government forces people to live by its dictates. Under the socialist principle, people can't freely choose the job they want but must take the job that fits their abilities. So, government has to step in to decide what job best fits people's abilities and to make them take that job. Second, under socialism, people can't freely choose the goods they want but instead must take the goods that fit their basic needs. This means that government, again, has to step in and decide what goods best meet a person's needs. Therefore, to match jobs with abilities and goods with needs requires coercion or the use of force by government.

Justice Based on Liberty

Like socialism, liberalism is one of the major political philosophies of the modern age. Liberalism is the view that liberty is the most important value that society and government can promote. In particular, liberals support freedom of conscience, freedom of speech, freedom of association, and freedom of occupation. Liberals also support equal political rights and civil liberties. During the twentieth century, liberalism divided into two camps: classical liberalism and welfare liberalism. Classical liberals favor a limited government that stays out of the free market and does not try to distribute economic goods. Welfare liberals favor a government that makes up for the harmful effects of the free market, particularly by providing economic help to the least advantaged.

We have seen that socialism has a view on justice. Liberalism also has strong views on justice. However, because liberalism is now made up of two conflicting camps, we can expect that liberalism will have two contrasting views on justice. Let's begin with the views on justice that welfare liberals support. To get a clearer idea of these views, we look at a philosopher whom we have already met: John Rawls.

Justice in Welfare Liberalism. As we have seen, Rawls argues that the principles of justice that should govern society are those that would be chosen by people who do not know whether in their society they will be rich or poor, talented or untalented, black or white, male or female, and so forth. Principles that would be chosen behind such a "veil of ignorance," he claims, would be fair to everyone because without such knowledge, one would not choose principles that advantage the rich or the poor, the talented or the untalented, black or white, male or female, and so on. Principles that are perceived as unfair to some group, Rawls claims, will not be acceptable if one does not know whether one is going to be a member of that group. Moreover, Rawls argues, the principles on which a stable society is based must be principles that are fair to everyone. If the principles that govern a society are perceived by some group as being unfair to themselves, then society will not be stable but subject to unrest. For this reason, also, the principles that are chosen to govern society must be fair to everyone.

What principles of justice will be fair to everyone? Rawls proposes three principles: the principle of equal liberty, the principle of equal opportunity, and the difference principle.

The *principle of equal liberty* is meant to govern primarily society's political institutions (its constitution, government, courts, legislative system, and laws). The principle of equal liberty states that "each person participating in a [political] practice or affected by it has an equal right to the most extensive liberty compatible with a like liberty for all."[23] Basically, the principle of equal liberty means that each person must have as many political rights and freedoms as possible, as long as everyone else can have the same ("equal") political rights and freedoms. For example, everyone must have at least the same voting rights, the same legal rights, the same right to trial by jury, the same freedom of speech, the same freedom of conscience, the same freedom of the press, and so on. In the political sphere, then, everyone must be equal, and everyone must be granted the maximum degree of freedom compatible with everyone else having the same degree of freedom. Because the principle of equal liberty requires equality, Rawls argues, it is fair to everyone. Moreover, society's political institutions will be stable as long as they are based on this fair principle.

---

23 John Rawls, "Justice as Fairness," in *Philosophy, Politics, and Society*, ed. Peter Laslett and W. G. Runciman (New York: Barnes & Noble, 1962), 133.

PHILOSOPHY AND LIFE

Welfare

About 12.5 percent of our population, or 37 million Americans, lived in poverty in 2007, and 15.3 percent or 46 million Americans had no health insurance; about 1 out of every 5 children was poor. Also in 2009, unemployment was at 8.9 percent, which meant that 13.7 million adult citizens were unemployed and looking for jobs. According to the U.S. Department of Health and Human Services, at least 760,000 Americans are homeless on any given night, and over a five-year period about 3 percent of Americans (about 8 million people) become homeless for one or more nights and are forced to sleep on the streets, in cars, or anywhere else they can find a place to lie down. Numerous cities have sprouted "tent cities" on their outskirts where homeless and jobless individuals and families live in flimsy camping tents. News reports have described the plight of the homeless:

> Jim Gibson, a 50-year-old contractor had a job and an apartment. Today he [lives in a tent and] struggles to stay clean and fed. The widower and grandfather says he is "trying to survive and look for work. The only work I've found is holding an advertising sign on a street corner."
>
> 53-year-old Dave Cutch . . . was a welder in Colorado. "So the company I'm working for, I get laid off," Cutch says. . . . Months went by without work. Cutch lost his house, his car was stolen, his savings ran out. "Trying to get back on my feet, you know," Cutch says. "Daily I still go out looking for a job. But the thing I'm running into is when I put the application in they ask me, 'Where do you live at?' And I go, 'Actually, I don't have a place to live. I'm homeless.' That's it. They don't hire me."
>
> 9-year-old Brehanna didn't understand. Her family was being evicted. . . . Her father, Joe Ledesma, a homebuilder for 20 years, was without a job and couldn't find another. . . . Joe Ledesma [now] spends most days searching for jobs. [His wife,] Heidi Ledesma, who at 42 is disabled because of severe arthritis in her ankles, shuffles her feet and limps. . . . She cooks for her family—not in a home, but in the crowded kitchen of a . . . homeless center. "I never thought this would happen to us," she says. "Not in a million years."

QUESTION

1. Should the government tax employed citizens to provide welfare for individuals and families like those discussed here who are jobless and homeless? Why?

Sources: *Los Angeles Times*, March 20, 2009; Richard Gonzalez, "Sacramento Tent City Reflects Economy's Troubles," NPR News, March 16, 2009, http://www.npr.org/templates/story/story.php?storyId=101900138 (accessed May 25, 2009); Mary Hudetz, "Homebuilder Copes with Homelessness," *The Daily Reporter*, May 8, 2009, http://dailyreporter.com/blog/2009/05/08/homebuilder-copes-with-homelessness, (accessed September 8, 2009).

The *principle of equal opportunity* is supposed to govern a society's economic institutions. The principle states that desirable jobs and positions should be open to anyone who is qualified by his or her abilities. This means that job qualifications should be related to the requirements of the job and should not discriminate by race or sex. It also means that society should provide people with the training and education needed to qualify for desirable jobs, for example, by providing a system of free public schools and free or virtually free universities and training schools.

critical thinking

Rawls assumes that economic incentives are needed to get people to contribute to society. Is this assumption correct?

Rawls' *difference principle* is also primarily intended to govern a society's economic institutions. Unlike the political arena, where everyone must be equal, the economic arena must allow for some inequalities. Rawls holds that inequalities are necessary in the economic arena to serve as incentives for greater productivity. If greater economic rewards (income and wealth) are given to those who work harder and who have greater abilities, they will be motivated to be more productive, and all society can benefit from this greater productivity.

But inequalities obviously raise the possibility of unfairness and therefore of instability. Those who are disadvantaged (those who cannot work or who have few talents and abilities) can be disfavored by principles that allow inequalities. Consequently, Rawls proposes that inequalities should be allowed only if the plight of the disadvantaged is relieved (through welfare programs, for example) by the extra productivity that unequal work incentives can produce. The difference principle that he proposes to govern the inequalities in our social and economic institutions is as follows: "Social and economic inequalities are to be arranged so that they are . . . to the greatest benefit of the least advantaged."[24]

Rawls calls this the difference principle because it focuses on the differences among people. Rawls' principles of justice, which we can take as the principles of justice of welfare liberalism, can be summarized as follows[25]:

> The distribution of benefits and burdens in a society is just if
>
> 1. each person has the most political liberty compatible with equal liberty for all, and
> 2. economic inequalities are arranged so that
>   a. everyone has an equal opportunity to qualify for all positions, and
>   b. inequalities produce benefits for the least advantaged persons.

QUICK REVIEW
Justice in the welfare liberalism of Rawls requires equal liberty in society's political institutions, equal opportunity for desirable jobs and positions, and the difference principle, which says economic inequalities are just only if they produce benefits for the least advantaged. Rawls says these principles are fair to everyone and so would be chosen "behind a veil of ignorance" and would promote social stability.

The second principle is fair, Rawls argues, because it is based on reciprocity, on "tit-for-tat." The principle benefits those who have talents and abilities because they have an equal opportunity to compete for the more favored jobs and positions. Their efforts thus add to the productivity of society. But the disadvantaged also benefit because the goods produced by the efforts of the talented benefit the disadvantaged through welfare programs. Thus, the advantaged "repay" the disadvantaged for the inequalities from which they benefit. This reciprocity makes the principle fair to everyone.

Although many people support the ideals of fairness that Rawls' principles embody, not everyone does so. In particular, classical liberals criticize Rawls.

Justice in Classical Liberalism. One of Rawls' strongest classical liberal critics was his Harvard colleague Robert Nozick (1938–2002). Nozick agreed that in the political arena, people should be equal and should have as much liberty as is possible. In his book *Anarchy, State, and Utopia,* however, Nozick points out that Rawls advocates a "patterned" theory of justice in economic affairs. A patterned theory is one that says goods should be distributed among the members of a society according to a certain pattern or formula. If goods are not yet distributed according to his formula, then goods must be taken from some citizens and given to others until the required distribution is achieved. Rawls' theory requires that goods be distributed according to his two principles.

Nozick objects that any patterned theory will always require the unjust use of force and coercion. People's free choices, he says, will always change any pattern that society tries to establish. Then, government will unjustly have to force some individuals to give their goods to others until the required distribution is achieved again.

Nozick provides an ingenious example to illustrate his claim. He asks us to imagine a society in which all money is already distributed according to a patterned concept of justice (like egalitarianism or like Rawls' principles). We will call this

---

24 John Rawls, *A Theory of Justice* (Cambridge, MA: Harvard University Press, 1972), 255.
25 Ibid., 298–303.

"just" distribution D1. In D1, each person holds the money that each should justly hold, no more and no less. Now suppose that a basketball star—Wilt Chamberlain—agrees to play basketball if he can get 25 cents per ticket each game. Millions of fans freely choose to give him 25 cents to watch him play each game. As a result of these many free choices, at the end of the season Wilt Chamberlain has $250,000 more than anyone else does. So at the end of the season, goods are no longer distributed according to the "just" distribution D1. We can call this new distribution D2 and we can see that in D2 money is no longer distributed according to the concept of justice with which we began, since now Wilt Chamberlain has $250,000 more than he should have:

> Suppose a distribution favored by one of these [patterned] conceptions is realized. Let us suppose it is your favorite one and let us call this distribution D1: perhaps everyone has an equal share, perhaps shares vary in accordance with some dimension you treasure. Now suppose that Wilt Chamberlain is greatly in demand by basketball teams, being a great gate attraction . . . He signs the following sort of contract with a team: In each home game, twenty-five cents from the price of each ticket of admission goes to him. . . . The season starts, and people cheerfully attend his team's games; they buy their tickets, each time dropping a separate twenty-five cents of their admission price into a special box with Chamberlain's name on it. They are excited about seeing him play; it is worth the total admission price to them. Let us suppose that in one season one million persons attend his home games, and Wilt Chamberlain winds up with $250,000, a much larger sum than the average income . . . Is he entitled to this income? Is this new distribution, D2, unjust? . . . If Dl was a just distribution, and people voluntarily moved from it to D2, transferring parts of their shares that they were given under Dl (what was it for if not to do something with?), isn't D2 also just?[26]

Nozick claims that this new distribution, D2, is just. Yet it would be unjust according to the "patterned" concept of justice with which we began. Therefore, the patterned principles will require that some of Chamberlain's money should be taken away from him and given to others until the distribution is once again just according to the patterned principles. Thus, patterned principles continually require that goods be taken from some and given to others to reestablish the distribution that people's free choices continually change. However, Nozick argues that if a distribution is changed by people's free choices, then there can be nothing wrong with it. The fans knew their money was going to the basketball star, so they can have no complaint. And the goods of those who did not see the game are unaffected. Thus, there was really nothing wrong with the distribution that resulted from these free choices.

What kind of justice does Nozick propose? In keeping with his ideas about the importance of free choice, Nozick argues that justice is respecting people's free choices. Any distribution of economic benefits and burdens is just, says Nozick, if it is the result of individuals freely choosing to exchange with each other the goods that each person already owns. In summary, Nozick holds the following principle, which we may take as the principle of justice of classical liberalism:

> Benefits and burdens are distributed justly when society allows every individual the freedom to do what he chooses to do for himself or for others, the freedom to keep what he makes for himself or what others choose to give him, and the freedom to keep what he has or give it to whomever he chooses.[27]

---

26 Robert Nozick, *Anarchy, State and Utopia* (New York: Basic Books, 1974), 161–162.
27 Ibid., 160.

Nozick thus raises several objections to Rawls' principles. One is that Rawls is using the better-off people in society as means to ensure the welfare of the worst-off. Nozick regards this as fundamentally unjust because it uses people as means. As a corollary, he claims Rawls is not impartial, for he is seeing things only through the eyes of the least advantaged. Finally, he objects to Rawls' apparent contention that when individuals have more than what his two principles allow, they are not entitled to keep what they own. A person's entitlement to what he or she owns is very much a part of Nozick's thinking, and his work was largely devoted to spelling out this concept.

But perhaps in applying Rawls' difference principle to a specific transaction, Nozick has warped it, or at least overburdened it. After all, Rawls' principle is addressing the backdrop against which public policies and decisions about redressing inequalities are to be made. It is not speaking directly to specific, small-scale instances of the sort that Nozick cites. More important, Rawls does not argue that all property should be shared. He says only that society must help the most disadvantaged members. This does not at all mean that everyone has a right to an equal share. In other words, Rawls' concept of justice does not equate fair distribution with equal distribution. Individuals have a just claim to whatever they have acquired, as long as the acquisition was itself fair.

QUICK REVIEW
Justice in the classical liberalism of Nozick holds that equality and maximum liberty are just in the political arena but that economic goods should be distributed as people freely choose to distribute what they make or are given; principles, such as Rawls', that distribute goods according to a pattern require unjust coercion when people's free choices upset that pattern, and this approach will use people as means and take from them what they are entitled to. Rawls might reply that his principles do not apply to the kind of individual choices Nozick is talking about, but only to the broad laws and institutions of society.

In the following paragraph from "A Kantian Conception of Equality," Rawls makes these very points concerning his difference principle:

> In explaining this principle, several matters should be kept in mind. First of all, it applies in the first instance to the main public principles and policies that regulate social and economic equalities. It is used to adjust the system of entitlements and rewards, and the standards and precepts that this system employs. Thus the difference principle holds, for example, for income and property taxation, for fiscal and economic policy; it does not apply to particular transactions or distributions, nor, in general, to small scale and local decisions, but rather to the background against which these take place. No observable pattern is required of actual distributions, nor even any measure of the degree of equality. . . . What is enjoined is that the inequalities make a functional contribution to those least favored. Finally, the aim is not to eliminate the various contingencies, for some such contingencies [that is, social primary goods such as (1) rights, liberties, and opportunities; (2) income and wealth; (3) the social bases of self-respect] seem inevitable. Thus even if an equal distribution of natural assets seemed more in keeping with the equality of free persons, the question of redistributing these assets (were this conceivable) does not arise, since it is incompatible with the integrity of the person. Nor need we make any specific assumptions about how great these variations are: we only suppose that, as realized in later life, they are influenced by all three contingencies. The question, then, is by what criterion a democratic society is to organize cooperation and arrange the system of entitlements that encourages and rewards productive efforts. We have a right to our natural abilities and a right to whatever we become entitled to by taking part in a fair social process. The problem is to characterize this process.[28]

In the last analysis, Rawls' welfare liberalism is most significant and controversial because it has connected justice with aiding the least advantaged. Although most, if not all, of us today would agree that government should secure equal political rights, many would not have government provide material goods and social services to the disadvantaged. Indeed, in the last fifteen years there has been a concerted

---

28 John Rawls, "A Kantian Conception of Equality," *Cambridge Review* (February 1974), 97.

effort to roll back welfare programs. In claiming that justice requires a social order that respects the right of individuals to material goods and social services, Rawls puts considerable distance between himself and contemporary classical liberalism.

Justice poses a profound problem to social and political philosophers. We have surveyed philosophers over a span of more than two millennia, but no single theory of justice has received their universal endorsement. Indeed, our own society seems ambivalent, at various times giving priority to merit, social utility, equality, need, ability, and freedom. The challenge continues to be what it has always been: to effect a proper balance—whatever and wherever that may be—among these public and private values.

QUESTIONS

1. Is it just to be taxed to fund something that you do not morally subscribe to?
2. Can you think of a situation in which it is more just to treat people differently than to treat them equally?
3. Is the law requiring young people to remain in school until a certain age just? Is the one that requires parents or guardians to enroll their children or charges in a school just?
4. Think of situations in your personal life where you subscribe to some of the various types of justice discussed in the preceding section. What kinds of situations are appropriate for each type of justice?
5. Rawls argues for a view of justice from the position of the most disadvantaged in society. Would it be unrealistic to argue a case for a view from the position of the most advantaged in society? How might you do this?
6. Applying Rawls' difference principle to our society, which groups do you think would receive preferential economic treatment? Why?
7. What evidence indicates that Rawls' theory is already operating in our society?

Archives du 7eme Art/Photos 12/Alamy

PHILOSOPHY AT THE MOVIES

Watch *Slumdog Millionaire* (2008) in which Jamal, an eighteen-year-old who grew up in the slums of Mumbai, becomes a contestant on the Indian television game show *Who Wants to Be a Millionaire* and is suspected of cheating when he is able to answer the questions, although his answers are based on his experiences as he grew up struggling to survive as an orphan on the streets. What events, situations, or conditions portrayed in this film seem to you to be unjust? On which view(s) of justice are your views based?

8.4 Limits on the State

We have seen how different thinkers—such as Hobbes, Locke, and Rousseau— have tried to show that the state is morally justified in exercising its legal authority over us, even when we do not like what it is doing to us. Some of these thinkers—such as Thomas Hobbes—thought that once they had shown that the authority of the state is justified, then it followed that the state's power over its citizens is absolute or unlimited. In Hobbes' view, the ruler can do whatever it wants, and the citizen is obligated to obey. But most political and social philosophers have rejected Hobbes' view and have held, instead, that there are important moral limits on what the state may do and how it may exercise its authority. We have discussed, in fact, several philosophers who argue that there is at least one important limit on the state: The state must be just. Although these philosophers have very distinct views on what justice is, they all agree that a state must promote justice.

But are there any other limits on the authority of the state? For example, if the laws that the state enacts are unjust, do citizens still have an obligation to continue to obey the state? And are there any limits to the state's authority other than the requirement that the state and its laws must be just? For example, do people's human rights place any limits on what the state may do to its citizens or on the kinds of laws the state may enforce? And if so, exactly what rights must the state recognize? And what about the state's relations to other states? Is the state justified, for example, in using force and violence against other states, or are there limits to the use of international force?

These are the kinds of questions that we examine in this section. We begin by considering why the theory of civil disobedience claims that citizens are not morally required to obey the authority of the state when its laws are unjust. We then examine how the right to freedom and other human rights impose further limits on the authority of the state. Last, we discuss whether there are any moral limits on the use of violence between states—the organized state violence that we refer to as "war"—and what can be said about the kind of violence that we now term *terrorism.*

Unjust Laws and Civil Disobedience

According to the dictionary, *law* means a general rule or body of general rules that is enforced by government and that regulates the behavior of citizens. Clearly, the laws that governments enact are not always just. The laws of the United States, for example, once supported slavery, and until the twentieth century, U.S. law not only permitted, but actually enforced racial and sexual discrimination.

Many people claim that when laws are unjust or immoral we are under no obligation to obey them because unjust laws are, in fact, not genuine laws. On April 12, 2012, for example, the Catholic bishops of the United States issued a statement objecting to a new federal law that required all employers, including Catholic employers, to provide employees with health insurance that would give employees access to birth control products including those that could induce abortions. Believing that abortion is a sinful form of homicide, the bishops felt that the new law forced Catholics to facilitate abortions and thereby violated their conscience and was unjust:

> It is a sobering thing to contemplate our government enacting an unjust law. An unjust law cannot be obeyed. . . . If we face today the prospect of unjust laws, then Catholics in America, in solidarity with our fellow citizens, must have the courage not to obey them. No American desires this. No Catholic welcomes it. But if it should fall upon us, we must discharge it as a duty of citizenship and an obligation of faith. . . . An unjust law is "no law at all."[29]

The view on which the bishops based their statement is an old one, with roots going back to the ancient Greeks. The great Greek playwright, Sophocles, for example, wrote in his play Antigone, "no king's law can override the unwritten and immutable laws of God . . . which are eternal." Taking a similar stance, the Christian philosopher and theologian Saint Augustine later wrote in his work, *On Free Choice of the Will,* "It seems to me that an unjust law is no law at all."

29 Cheryl Wetzstein, "Bishops Plea Against Obeying 'Unjust Laws,'" *Washington Times,* April 12, 2012.

Several centuries later, Saint Thomas Aquinas, who was profoundly influenced by Augustine, agreed with the claim that "an unjust law is no law at all." A human law, Aquinas held, is a true law only when it does not violate the moral law or force its citizens to violate the moral law. Morality, as Aquinas conceived it and as we saw in the last chapter, is not an arbitrary set of rules for behavior; rather, the basis of moral obligation is built into our very nature in the form of various inclinations toward the basic goods in which we find our happiness, such as the inclination that leads us to value life, the inclination that leads us to value having and raising children, and the inclination that leads us to value truth. The rules of conduct corresponding to these inherent human features Aquinas called **natural law**. Accordingly, to say that a law violates the moral law is to say that it violates the natural law that directs us toward those goods in which we find our happiness.

Aquinas reasoned that since law governs human actions, and since human actions aim at achieving happiness, law must aim at achieving the happiness of those whom it governs—that is, it must aim at the happiness of the community, or, as he sometimes put it, at the common good of all. Law, moreover, must be a product of reason, since we use our reason to figure out what we must do to achieve our aims. And since the purpose of law is to direct a community toward its own happiness, law must be made by the whole community and everyone must know what it is. Aquinas concludes in a famous definition:

> From the four preceding considerations, we arrive at a definition of law: Law is nothing other than a directive that reason formulates, that aims at the common good, that is made by the whole community or by a ruler who is charged with caring for the whole community, and that is made known to everyone in the community.[30]

The key element in this definition, of course, is the idea that a true law must aim at the common good of the whole community. The common good of the community is achieved when each person is enabled to achieve the basic goods toward which our nature inclines us—that is, when each person is able to live according to the natural or moral law. A true law, Aquinas concluded, must be consistent with the natural or moral law, and if a law violates the natural or moral law, it is not a genuine law.

Aquinas' view on the relation between morality and the law has been a point of great controversy. He is claiming that morality is part of the essential nature—the essence—of law: A rule issued by a government is not a law unless it is morally just. Although many philosophers have agreed with Aquinas, many others have strongly objected to this way of linking law and morality. The British legal philosopher John Austin (1790–1859), for example, argued that a law is nothing more than a command issued by the ruler, backed by threats of punishment and maintained by a habit of obedience. Consequently, once a law has been issued by a ruler who has the power to punish and whom citizens habitually obey, it is a valid law whether or not it is moral, and whether we like it or not:

> The existence of law is one thing; its merit or demerit is another. Whether it be or be not is one enquiry; whether it be or be not conformable to an assumed [moral] standard, is a different enquiry. A law, which actually exists, is a law, though we happen to dislike it, or though it vary from the text, by which we regulate our approbation and disapprobation.[31]

---

30 Saint Thomas Aquinas, *Summa Theologica*, I-IIae, q.90, a.4; translated by the author.

31 J. Austin, The Province of Jurisprudence Determined, W. Rumble (ed.), (Cambridge: Cambridge University Press, 1995) (first published, 1832), 157.

Opponents of Aquinas' view such as Austin are generally called *positivists.* Positivists hold that so long as a piece of legislation has been passed by a legitimate authority, it is a law that we are obligated to obey regardless of its morality. A law is a law and must be obeyed.

Notice that Aquinas' theory of law provides something that a positivist theory cannot provide, something that has been particularly relevant to many oppressed minorities. Aquinas' theory of law implies that citizens have the right to disobey laws that are unjust or immoral. This conclusion follows from his idea that a true law must accord with the natural law of morality:

> QUICK REVIEW
> Aquinas claimed that a true human law is one that does not violate the moral law and must be obeyed. But if a government enacts an unjust law that violates the moral law, it is not a true law and so does not have to be obeyed. Critics argue that a true law is any rule that government enacts, including unjust laws; such true laws must be obeyed.

> As Saint Augustine says, "that which is not just seems to be no law at all." Consequently, an ordinance is a valid law only to the extent that it is just. Now we say that something is just when it conforms to the [moral] principles of our reason and the basic moral principles of our reason are the natural law. So an ordinance enacted by humans is a valid law only to the extent that it conforms to the natural law. If an ordinance contradicts the natural law then it is not a valid law but a corruption of law. . . .
>
> The ordinances human beings enact may be just or unjust. If they are just then we have a moral obligation to obey them since they ultimately derive from [the natural law which in turn is based on] the eternal law of God. . . .
>
> However, an ordinance may be unjust for one of two reasons. First, it may be contrary to the rights of humans; and second, it may be contrary to the rights of God.
>
> A "law" can be contrary to the rights of humans in any of three ways. First, the "law" might not be aimed at achieving the common good. This would be the case, for example, if a ruler passed legislation that imposed heavy taxes that merely fed the ruler's greed and had no communal benefits. Second, the "law" might not have been enacted by a legitimate authority. This would be the case, for example, if someone tried to enforce a law without having been delegated the legal authority to do so. Third, the "law" might distribute burdens unjustly. This would be the case, for example, if a law were aimed at achieving the common good, but the burdens involved in achieving that good were distributed unjustly among the citizens. Ordinances that are contrary to the rights of humans in any of these three ways are not valid laws but acts of violence. . . . We have no moral obligation to obey such ordinances except perhaps to avoid giving bad example or to prevent social disorder. . . .
>
> Finally, a law can also be unjust when it is contrary to the rights of God. This would be the case, for example, if a tyrant were to pass a law requiring the worship of idols or any act that is against divine law. It is utterly wrong to obey such laws.[32]

Laws are just and must be obeyed, then, only when (1) they serve the common good of the whole community, (2) they do not exceed the authorized power of the lawmaker, (3) they do not unjustly discriminate against some and unfairly advantage others, and (4) they do not require citizens to violate their religious beliefs. If a law fails on any of these counts, it is no law at all and so citizens have no obligation to obey it. Often this point is expressed by saying that human laws must conform to the "higher law" of morality, and when they do not, we must remain "true to our conscience" by obeying the higher law.

Although positivists have criticized the natural law view of what a true law is, many political leaders have embraced the view of Aquinas, particularly those who, suffering under unjust or discriminatory laws, have advocated disobeying such laws in favor of the "higher law" of conscience. In his famous "Letter from Birmingham

32 Aquinas, *Summa,* I–IIae, q.95, a.2, and q.96, a.4. Translated by the author.

Jail," civil rights leader Martin Luther King Jr. relied in part on this point to defend his civil disobedience of segregation laws:

QUICK REVIEW
King agreed with Aquinas and concluded that because discriminatory laws are unjust, they are not true laws and one is not obligated to obey them; such civil disobedience must be carried out openly, respectfully, nonviolently, and with a willingness to accept the penalty.

> One may well ask, "How can you advocate breaking some laws and obeying others?" The answer is found in the fact that there are two types of laws: There are just and unjust laws. I would agree with Saint Augustine that "An unjust law is no law at all." Now what is the difference between the two? How does one determine when a law is just or unjust? A just law is a man-made code that squares with the moral law or the law of God. An unjust law is a code that is out of harmony with the moral law. To put it in the terms of Saint Thomas Aquinas, an unjust law is a human law that is not rooted in eternal and natural law. Any law that uplifts human personality is just. Any law that degrades human personality is unjust. All segregation statutes are unjust because segregation distorts the soul and damages the personality. It gives the segregator a false sense of superiority, and the segregated a false sense of inferiority. . . .
>
> I hope you can see the distinction I am trying to point out. In no sense do I advocate evading or defying the law as the rabid segregationist would do. This would lead to anarchy. One who breaks an unjust law must do it *openly, lovingly*, . . . and with a willingness to accept the penalty. I submit that an individual who breaks a law that conscience tells him is unjust, and willingly accepts the penalty by staying in jail to arouse the conscience of the community over its injustice, is in reality expressing the very highest respect for law.[33]

King drew on the logical consequences of Aquinas' natural law view: If regulations are true laws only when they are moral and just, then people have no obligation to obey an unjust or immoral law. As King suggests in the preceding passage, he advocated nonviolent disobedience as a response to unjust laws such as laws that discriminate on the basis of race. Civil disobedience of the kind advocated by King is the act of disobeying an unjust law openly, peacefully, and with a willingness to pay the penalty to bring about a change in the law.

Of course, the very idea that an unjust law need not be obeyed makes many people uncomfortable. Who is to decide when a law is unjust? Clearly, each individual must decide this for himself or herself. But doesn't this doctrine lead to an anarchic and chaotic situation in which each person individually decides which rules are true laws and which are not?

QUICK REVIEW
Gandhi argued that one has a right to disobey unjust laws and advocated nonviolent "passive" resistance to unjust laws because using violence to overthrow unjust laws will lead to more violence.

In spite of these problems, for many minorities who have suffered discrimination under oppressive and unjust regimes, this right to disobey unjust laws has been critical. The great statesman of India, Mohandas K. Gandhi, who had a profound influence on King, held that oppressed people have a moral right to disobey unjust laws; he preached this view in his campaign against the British which eventually forced the British to give India its independence. Gandhi did not, however, endorse the natural law theory of Aquinas. Instead, Gandhi based his views on a foundation of Hindu spirituality that emphasized the power of truth and love, which he sometimes referred to as "soul force," or passive resistance. Like King, Gandhi advocated nonviolent resistance to unjust laws, holding that using violence as a means to overthrow unjust laws would simply result in more violence:

> Passive resistance is a method of securing rights by personal suffering; it is the reverse of resistance by arms. When I refuse to do a thing that is repugnant to my conscience, I use soul-force. For instance, the government of the day has passed a law which is applicable to me. I do not like it. If by using violence I force the

33 Martin Luther King Jr., "Letter from Birmingham Jail," in *Civil Disobedience: Theory and Practice*, ed. Hugo Adam Bedau (New York: Pegasus, 1969), 77–78.

> Government to repeal the law, I am employing what may be termed body-force. If I do not obey the law but accept the penalty for its breach, I use soul-force. It involves sacrifice of self. . . . It is a superstition and ungodly thing to believe that an act of a majority binds a minority. Many examples can be given in which acts of majorities will be found to have been wrong and those of minorities to have been right. . . . So long as the superstition that men should obey unjust laws exists, so long will their slavery exist. And a passive resister alone can remove such a superstition. To use brute-force, to use gunpowder, is contrary to passive resistance, for it means that we want our opponent to do by force that which we desire but he does not. And, if such a use of force is justifiable, surely he is entitled to do likewise by us. And so we should never come to an agreement.[34]

It is clear, then, that our views about law are extremely important and that these views will have significant implications for the position that we take on obedience to the law and obedience to the higher law of conscience. If morality is part of the essence of law, then unjust regulations are not real laws and need not be obeyed; nonviolent—or perhaps even violent—resistance to such "laws" is morally justified in the name of a higher law.

Freedom

If we valued only efficiency in government, then any evaluation of the rightful limits of governmental authority would be relatively simple. We would need only to determine whether or not governmental instructions as exercised through law best served the public interest. Evaluated strictly on social utility, it is entirely possible that the most authoritarian government might prove the most efficient.

Yet clearly our society is concerned with more than efficiency, with more than a well-oiled governmental machine. We are also concerned with justice and individual freedoms, issues that are not always compatible with efficiency. Contract theory regards both justice and individual liberty as of paramount importance. But contract theory is not clear about how justice and other kinds of moral considerations should be balanced against important individual liberties.

The liberties that concern us here are political and social freedoms, including freedom of thought, freedom of association, and the important freedom of being able to live as one wants without interference from others. History records many heroic battles fought to secure these freedoms. Freedom finds what may be its classic defense in John Stuart Mill's essay *On Liberty*, in which the British social and political philosopher presents a powerful case for liberty.

Mill's central concern in this essay is the freedom of the individual. He is specifically concerned with the extent to which government and society must be prohibited from interfering with an individual's life. In essence, Mill argues that society in general, and government in particular, must leave the individual free to live his life as he chooses so long as he is harming no one. This concern for freedom grew out of Mill's fear of what he called the "tyranny of the majority," the tendency of government—and society in general—to persecute and suppress any forms of life or ways of thinking that it dislikes, and to force individuals to conform to what the majority wants:

> The will of the people . . . practically means the will of the most numerous or the most active part of the people—the majority, or those who succeed in making

34 Mohandas K. Gandhi, *Hind Swaraj or Indian Home Rule* (1909), reprinted in *Social and Political Philosophy*, ed. John Somerville and Ronald E. Santoni (Garden City, NY: Doubleday, 1963), 510.

> themselves accepted as the majority; the people, consequently, may desire to oppress a part of their number, and precautions are as much needed against this as against any other abuse of power. . . . [I]n political speculations "the tyranny of the majority" is now generally included among the evils against which society requires to be on its guard.
>
> Like other tyrannies, the tyranny of the majority was at first, and is still vulgarly, held in dread, chiefly as operating through the acts of the public authorities. But . . . when society is itself the tyrant . . . its means of tyrannizing are not restricted to the acts which it may do by the hands of its political functionaries. Society can and does execute its own mandates. . . . Protection, therefore, against the tyranny of the magistrate is not enough; there needs protection also against the tyranny of the prevailing opinion and feeling, against the tendency of society to impose, by other means than civil penalties, its own ideas and practices as rules of conduct on those who dissent from them; to fetter the development and, if possible, prevent the formation of any individuality not in harmony with its ways, and compel all characters to fashion themselves upon the model of its own.[35]

Against this tendency of society to impose a "tyranny" over the individual, Mill proposed a fundamental principle that is now sometimes called the "harm principle," which imposes a significant limit on the power of government:

> The object of this essay is to assert one very simple principle, as entitled to govern absolutely the dealings of society with the individual in the way of compulsion and control, whether the means used be physical force in the form of legal penalties or the moral coercion of public opinion. That principle is that the sole end for which mankind are warranted, individually or collectively, in interfering with the liberty of action of any of their number is self-protection. That the only purpose for which power can be rightfully exercised over any member of a civilized community, against his will, is to prevent harm to others. . . . It is perhaps hardly necessary to say that this doctrine is meant to apply only to human beings in the maturity of their faculties. We are not speaking of children or of young persons below the age which the law may fix as that of manhood or womanhood. . . .
>
> But there is a sphere of action in which society, as distinguished from the individual, has, if any, only an indirect interest. . . . This, then, is the appropriate region of human liberty. It comprises, first, the inward domain of consciousness demanding liberty of conscience in its most comprehensive sense, liberty of thought and feeling, absolute freedom of opinion and sentiment on all subjects. . . . Secondly, the principle requires liberty of tastes and pursuits, of framing the plan of our life to suit our own character; of doing what we like . . . without impediment from our fellow-creatures, so long as what we do does not harm them, even though they should think our conduct foolish, perverse, or wrong. Thirdly, . . . the liberty, within the same limits, of combination among individuals; freedom to unite for any purpose not involving harm to others: the persons combining being supposed to be of full age and not forced or deceived.[36]

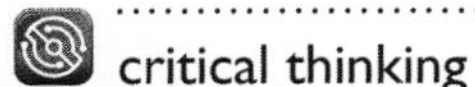

Does Mill assume that if each part of society (each person) prospers, then the whole of society will prosper? Is this assumption correct?

Mill supported his view by arguing that this principle would promote the greatest utility or happiness for everyone in our society. People must be left free not because they have a right to be free but because society will be better off if everyone is left free to think, live, and associate as they want:

> I forgo any advantage which could be derived to my argument from the idea of abstract right as a thing independent of utility. I regard utility as the ultimate appeal on all ethical questions; but it must be utility in the largest sense, grounded on the

35 John Stuart Mill, *On Liberty* (London: J. M. Dent, 1910), ch. 1.
36 Ibid., ch. 2, paras. 13, 15, and 16.

> permanent interests of man as a progressive being. Those interests, I contend, authorize the subjection of individual spontaneity to external control only in respect to those actions of each which concern the interests of other people.[37]

To show that "utility in the largest sense" requires liberty, Mill first argues that society will benefit if all people are allowed to hold and debate whatever beliefs they want. For if the government tries to force people to believe what it wants them to believe, it may force them to believe what is false. Only free and open debate can establish the truth and make our beliefs vital and clear:

> [T]he peculiar evil of silencing the expression of an opinion is, that it is robbing the human race; posterity as well as the existing generation; those who dissent from the opinion, still more than those who hold it. If the opinion is right, they are deprived of the opportunity of exchanging error for truth; if wrong, they lose, what is almost as great a benefit, the clearer perception and livelier impression of truth, produced by its collision with error.[38]

Not only will society benefit when people are allowed to believe, say, and debate what they choose, but it will also benefit when people are allowed to live as they choose:

> As it is useful that while mankind are imperfect there should be different opinions, so is it that there should be different experiments of living; that free scope should be given to varieties of character, short of injury to others; and that the worth of different modes of life should be proved practically, when any one thinks fit to try them. . . .
>
> He who lets the world, or his own portion of it, choose his plan of life for him, has no need of any other faculty than the ape-like one of imitation. He who chooses his plan for himself, employs all his faculties. He must use observation to see, reasoning and judgment to foresee, activity to gather materials for decision, discrimination to decide, and when he has decided, firmness and self-control to hold to his deliberate decision. . . . It is possible that he might be guided in some good path, and kept out of harm's way, without any of these things. But what will be his comparative worth as a human being?
>
> But neither one person nor any number of persons, is warranted in saying to another human creature of ripe years, that he shall not do with his life for his own benefit what he chooses to do with it. He is the person most interested in his own well-being: the interest which any other person, except in cases of strong personal attachment, can have in it, is trifling, compared with that which he himself has; the interest which society has in him individually (except as to his conduct to others) is fractional, and altogether indirect: while, with respect to his own feelings and circumstances, the most ordinary man or woman has means of knowledge immeasurably surpassing those that can be possessed by any one else.[39]

QUICK REVIEW
Fearing the "tyranny of the majority," Mill says that "the only purpose for which power can be rightfully exercised over any member of a civilized community, against his will, is to prevent harm to others." He argues that this promotes social utility because free thinking and debate help achieve the truth, and letting people live as they want helps prove the worth of different forms of life, lets people do what is in their best interests, and develops their abilities. So, government must leave people free to think, live, and associate, as they want.

Thus, society in general and government in particular must grant each individual the freedom to believe what she wishes, the freedom to live as she wishes, and the freedom to associate with whomever she wishes, so long as she harms no one in the process. It is wrong for society or government to interfere in the life of an adult, even if it does so for the adult's own good.

To read more from Mill's *On Liberty*, go to CourseMate for this text and browse by chapter or philosopher.

37 Ibid., ch. 1, para. 14.
38 Ibid., ch. 2, para. 64.
39 Ibid., ch. 3.

Although Mill appears to have drawn an important line of demarcation between society and individual, the distinction in some ways seems fuzzy. Mill says that society is justified in interfering in people's lives when they do something that "harms" others. But what constitutes "harm to others"? Suppose hearing you defend communism or pederasty or homosexuality or atheism offends me and makes me feel mental anguish. Can society step in and make you stop? If not, then what, exactly, does "harm to others" mean?

Furthermore, Mill argues that because the individual and not society is the best judge of what advances self-interest, society must leave the individual free to decide what is in his own best interests in all pursuits that do not affect others. But it seems that we do not always know our best interests. Suppose that a man who enjoys heroin "shoots up" every day and says this is in his best interests. Or suppose that a motorcyclist insists it is in his best interests to ride without a helmet or a driver insists that it is in her best interests to ride without a seat belt. These matters might be part of "doing what we like . . . so long as what we do does not harm [others] even though they should think our conduct foolish, perverse, or wrong." So, according to Mill, they should be left free from our interference. Yet most of us would agree that these people's behavior is clearly not in their best interests. Couldn't one argue that in cases like these it is all right to interfere with their behaviors by outlawing heroin, passing laws that require motorcycle helmets, and enforcing laws that require seat belts?

Part of the problem is that Mill's concept of freedom guarantees an absolute freedom from outside interference in any adult activity that does not affect others. But this ignores our responsibility toward each other. Perhaps in some cases we are justified in helping others by keeping them from doing things that clearly are not in their best interests. Or is Mill right?

Human Rights

Because of the shortcomings of relying solely on freedom as a basis for determining the limits of the law, many people have felt that the law should also be judged by the respect that it shows for human rights. All people, they believe, have certain basic rights, and the law should show respect for such rights. In fact, some people have held that when a law fails to respect human rights, the law is evil and need not be obeyed.

Although the notion of a right is difficult to pin down, it has played a crucial role in our history. For example, the Declaration of Independence asserts that "all men are endowed by their Creator with certain unalienable rights . . . among these are life, liberty, and the pursuit of happiness." Several years later, the U.S. Constitution was amended to include the Bill of Rights, which was intended primarily to guarantee individuals freedom from the intrusions of government including freedom of religion, freedom of speech, freedom of the press, freedom of assembly, freedom from unreasonable search and seizure, and the rights to due process and to trial by jury. In 1948, the United Nations published the Universal Declaration of Human Rights, stating that all human beings have "the right to own property, . . . the right to work, . . . the right to a just and favorable remuneration, . . . [and] the right to rest and leisure." And, more recently, we have witnessed an explosion of appeals to rights—gay rights, prisoners' rights, women's rights, animal rights, smokers' rights, fetal rights, and employee rights.

Just what is a right? The philosopher H. J. McCloskey has defined a **right** as a justified entitlement or claim on others.[40] For example, if I have a right to privacy,

40 H. J. McCloskey, "Rights—Some Conceptual Issues," *Australasian Journal of Philosophy* 54 (1976): 99–115.

then I have a justified claim to be left alone by others. And if I have a right to an education, then I have a justified claim to be provided with an education by society.

The flip side of a right is a **duty**, which is an obligation imposed on individuals. That is, if someone has a right to something, then others have certain duties or obligations toward that person. If you have a right to privacy, then everyone else has a duty to leave you alone; if you have a right to an education, then society has a duty to provide you with an education. Rights are always correlated with duties.

There are two main kinds of rights, depending on the kind of justification or basis that they are given: legal rights and moral rights. *Legal rights* depend on the laws of a nation or country. For example, the laws of the United States give all citizens a legal right to equal treatment under the law. However, the laws of South Africa, throughout the 1980s and into the 1990s, failed to give black people the legal right to equal treatment.

Moral rights, or, as they are sometimes called, *human rights,* are rights that all people have simply because they are human beings; these rights are justified or supported by moral principles that impose the same obligations on all human beings. For example, although the laws of South Africa once said that black people did not have the legal right to equal treatment, most people throughout the world agreed that the South African legal system was morally wrong and that black people everywhere, including South Africa, have a moral right to equal treatment because the moral principle of respect for human dignity requires equality of treatment.

QUICK REVIEW
Rights impose duties on others; negative rights impose duties on others to leave people free to engage in certain activities; positive rights impose duties on others to provide the right-holder with certain goods. Moral or human rights are rights that all humans have.

Thus, moral or human rights are in a sense much more significant than legal rights because we judge and evaluate legal rights in terms of people's moral rights. That is, when a country's laws violate people's moral rights, we say that the law is wrong and must be changed. The Civil War, a bloody, costly, and tragic confrontation, was fought in part because the slavery laws of the South were seen to violate the moral rights of black Americans. The civil rights movement of the sixties was a bitter struggle to change discriminatory laws that violated the moral rights of minorities and women. And we have seen bloody clashes in South Africa, Latin America, and parts of Asia over the injustice of laws that are seen to violate the moral rights of various groups. Thus, when the law violates people's moral rights, the law must be changed.

Some philosophers divide human rights into two groups: negative rights and positive rights. *Negative rights* are rights that protect freedoms of various kinds. The right to privacy, the right not to be killed, the right to travel, and the right to do what one wants with one's property are all negative rights because they all protect some form of human freedom or liberty. Negative rights impose a negative duty on other people: the duty not to interfere with a person's activities in a certain area. For example, the right of free association imposes on others the duty not to prevent people from associating with whom they please. Negative rights are in fact the "freedoms-from" that Mill emphasizes in *On Liberty.* Negative rights impose minimal duties on others because they merely require that others not act.

Positive rights are rights that guarantee people certain goods: the right to an education; the right to adequate medical care, food, and housing; the right to a fair trial; the right to a job; and the right to a clean environment. Thus, positive rights impose on people a positive duty: the duty to actively help a person to have or to do something. If the poor have a right to adequate medical care, for example, then we as a society have a duty to ensure that they are provided with such care. Consequently, respecting a positive right requires more than merely not acting; positive rights impose on us the duty to act positively on behalf of others.

Without understanding the distinction between negative and positive rights, it is hard to understand many of the intense social controversies that confront our society. Many people today believe that the law should enforce only negative rights.

The Third of May, Francisco Goya. To what extent ought the state and its primary instrument, government, exercise authority and power over the individual? Location: Museo del Prado, Madrid, Spain.

© SCALA/Art Resource, NY

They believe that the purpose of government is to guarantee only the freedoms-from that Mill advocated. Such people hold that government should not be involved in welfare programs, farm subsidies, or any other redistributive programs; ideally, government should only protect citizens from one another and from foreign invasion. But, as we have seen, many other Americans believe that government should do more than enforce these negative rights: It should also guarantee people's positive rights through programs that provide the needy with a minimum level of well-being.

Both positive rights and negative rights have been defended on the basis of a variety of philosophies. But perhaps the most influential defense of human rights has been the approach advocated by the philosopher Immanuel Kant. He maintained that every human being has a worth or a dignity that must be respected. The individual's worth, Kant held, gives each person a value that is "beyond all price." Because of this intrinsic value or dignity, each person is an "end in himself"—that is, a being for whose sake we should all act. Consequently, Kant claimed, we each have a duty to respect every other person's freedom, as well as to help others achieve their happiness. This is the meaning of words of his that we have already seen:

QUICK REVIEW
Kant argued that because every person as an "end in himself" has an intrinsic value or dignity that everyone else must respect, each person has a duty to respect other people's freedom and to help others achieve their happiness. So, everyone has negative and positive rights.

> Violations of the principle that our humanity must be respected as an end in itself are even clearer if we take examples of attacks on the freedom and property of others. It is obvious that the person who violates such rights is using people merely as means without considering that as rational beings they should be esteemed also as ends; that is, as beings who must be able to participate in the goals of the actions in which they are involved with him. . . .
>
> Humanity probably could survive even if people never helped each other achieve their happiness, but merely refrained from deliberately harming one another. But this would only be a negative way of making our actions harmonize with the idea that humanity is an end in itself. The positive way of harmonizing with this idea would be for everyone to help others achieve their goals as far as he can.[41]

41 Immanuel Kant, *Grundlegung zur Metaphysik der Sitten* [*Groundwork of the Metaphysics of Morals*], in *Immanuel Kant Werkausgabe,* vol. 7, ed. Wilhelm Weischedel (Frankfurt, Germany: Insel Verlag Wiesbaden, 1956). This translation copyright © 1987 by Manuel Velasquez.

Because of their fundamental human dignity, then, all persons have positive as well as negative human rights. For this reason, Kant held that government may legitimately levy taxes to care for the welfare, education, and development of persons "who are not able to support themselves."[42]

Some philosophers who agree that everyone has a basic dignity interpret the notion of human dignity differently from Kant. For example, Robert Nozick has argued that human dignity implies only that people should be free from having others interfere with their lives. In short, the only rights that humans have are negative rights to be left alone. Therefore, government should guarantee only people's negative rights and not their positive ones.

However, many contemporary philosophers agree with Kant's conclusions, even if they do not always accept his views about dignity. For example, philosopher Thomas Donaldson holds that people have both negative and positive human rights, even though he does not believe that these are necessarily based on human dignity. Instead, Donaldson holds that human rights are rights that should fulfill three conditions: They must protect something of very great importance to human beings, they must be subject to substantial and recurrent threats, and the obligations they impose on others must be fair and affordable. Donaldson has suggested the following list of basic human rights:

1. The right to freedom of physical movement.
2. The right to ownership of property.
3. The right to freedom from torture.
4. The right to a fair trial.
5. The right to nondiscriminatory treatment (freedom from discrimination on the basis of such characteristics as race or sex).
6. The right to physical security.
7. The right to freedom of speech and association.
8. The right to a minimal education.
9. The right to political participation.
10. The right to subsistence.[43]

QUICK REVIEW
Donaldson claims that moral rights must protect things of great importance that are subject to substantial and recurrent threat and must impose fair and affordable obligations. He claims that all governments must respect such rights and that wealthier nations should help the poorer ones provide such rights.

According to Donaldson, each of these human rights protects something of great importance to human life, each is subject to recurrent threats from governments and others around the world at the present time, and each imposes fair and affordable burdens on governments or others. Consequently, all governments of all nations should be required to live up to them. In addition, Donaldson holds, the governments of the wealthier nations should help the poorer nations provide these rights for their people.

A currently divisive issue in the United States, as we have seen, is how much the government should interfere to guarantee positive rights. Some contend that there is already too much interference, that the executive, legislative, and particularly the judicial branches of government are poking their collective noses into areas where they do not belong. In short, there are too many bad laws. Others claim that governmental interference is needed, that society has grown too unwieldy for individuals to fight their own battles for freedom. In short, there are too few good laws. Although these positions differ in their solutions, they are concerned with the

42 Immanuel Kant, *The Metaphysical Elements of Justice*, trans. W. Hastie (New York: Bobbs-Merrill, 1965), 93.
43 Thomas Donaldson, *The Ethics of International Business* (New York: Oxford University Press, 1989), 81.

problem that has occupied us in this chapter: how best to strike a balance between public and private interest. In other words, they are concerned with the problem of justice.

War and Terrorism

We have discussed some of the moral limits on what the state may do to its citizens. But are there any limits on what the state may do to other states or to the citizens of other states? For example, is it ever wrong for nations to use violence or force upon each other? Are there any moral limits on what warring nations can do to each other? Is it ever wrong for the citizens of one nation to use violence upon the citizens of another? If the members of one group feel threatened by the members of another group, can they legitimately use violence against them?

Several violent incidents during the past two decades have made these questions particularly pressing for Americans. In 1989, when General Noriega took over the government of Panama and said that the United States was no longer welcome in Panama, the U.S. military invaded Panama and replaced Noriega with Panamanian officials who were friendly to the United States. In 1990, Iraq invaded Kuwait. The Kuwaiti government appealed to the United Nations for help, and with the blessings of the United Nations, the U.S. military subsequently landed in Kuwait, defeated Iraq, and invaded deep into Iraqi territory. On September 11, 2001, a band of terrorists flew two jets into the World Trade Center's Twin Towers in New York City, destroying the buildings and killing about 3,000 Americans. In response, the United States invaded Afghanistan and overthrew its government, the Taliban regime, which was alleged to be harboring Osama Bin Laden, the accused leader of the terrorist band that destroyed the Twin Towers. The following year, the United States invaded Iraq and overthrew the government of Saddam Hussein on the grounds that his regime was harboring weapons of mass destruction and so posed a threat to the security of the United States. Also during the past two decades, numerous terrorist groups have attacked and killed civilians—in airplanes, on subways, on trains, in buildings, and on city streets—to protest what the terrorists perceive as injustices. Suicide bombers in Iraq killed hundreds of American soldiers and Iraqi citizens.

Thoughtful presidents, generals, and citizens have pondered the question of whether such acts of violence and war are ethically justified. Our political leaders, then, are anxious to justify their military actions as "ethical and just." But what, exactly, are the moral principles that govern the use of force? Are there really any moral limits on how wars should be waged? And what is the moral status of terrorism and of counterterrorism? Three main positions have been developed in the West in response to these questions: political realism, pacifism, and just war theory.

Political Realism. Political realism, sometimes called "realpolitik," is the view that there are no moral limits on what one nation may do to another in pursuit of its own interests. The classic proponent of this position is Thomas Hobbes, who wrote that nations exist in a "state of nature" so long as there is no international government (what he calls a "common power") that can force them to behave justly with each other. In this state of nature, Hobbes held, "the nature of man" is such that people continually quarrel and so are in a continual state of war. In this state of war, where no international body exists to force nations to obey any rules, there can be no binding moral obligations to constrain nations. Instead, the only constraint on one nation's behavior is the force or power of other nations:

> In the nature of man, we find three principal causes of quarrel. First, competition; secondly, diffidence; thirdly, glory. The first maketh men invade for gain; the second for safety; and the third, for reputation. The first use violence to make themselves masters of other men's persons, wives, children, and cattle; the second, to defend them; the third, for trifles, as a word, a smile, a different opinion, and any other sign of undervalue, either direct in their persons or by reflection in their kindred, their friends, their nation, their profession, or their name.
>
> Hereby it is manifest that during the time men live without a common power to keep them all in awe, they are in that condition which is called war; and such a war as is of every man against every man. For war consisteth not in battle only, or in the act of fighting, but in a tract of time, wherein the will to contend by battle is sufficiently known. . . .
>
> But though there had never been any time wherein particular men were in a condition of war one against another, yet in all times kings and persons of sovereign authority, because of their independency, are in continual jealousies, and in the state and posture of gladiators, having their weapons pointing, and their eyes fixed on one another; that is, their forts, garrisons, and guns upon the frontiers of their kingdoms, and continual spies upon their neighbors, which is a posture of war. . . .
>
> To this war . . . , this also is consequent: that nothing can be unjust. The notions of right and wrong, justice and injustice, have there no place. Where there is no common power, there is no law; where no law, no injustice. Force and fraud are in war the two cardinal virtues. Justice and injustice are none of the faculties neither of the body nor mind. If they were, they might be in a man that were alone in the world, as well as his senses and passions. They are qualities that relate to men in society, not in solitude. It is consequent also to the same condition that there be no property, no dominion, no mine and thine distinct; but only that to be every man's that he can get, and for so long as he can keep it.[44]

If political realism is accepted, then morality has no place in international relations. There is nothing wrong with any violent act that a nation might undertake in pursuit of its own "national interests." Right and wrong, just and unjust—these are terms that can apply to individual human beings living in a society where government can enforce law and order, but they cannot be applied to the relations between nations. Consequently, the use of violence between nations can never be condemned as morally wrong or unjust, but only as imprudent or not in the nation's best interests. Wars, then, can never be said to be wrong or immoral, but only stupid or against the national interest. In a similar vein, the realist might argue that even terrorism cannot be criticized as wrong or immoral when it is undertaken against the citizens of foreign nations. In the view of the realist, terrorism may be stupid or useless, but it is not immoral.

QUICK REVIEW
Political "realists" such as Hobbes argue that because nations exist in a state of nature without a "common power" to enforce justice, they are in a "state of war" in which concepts of morality or justice do not apply. So, violence between nations is neither right nor wrong but only for or against a nation's best interests. Critics argue that because acts of war are acts of human individuals, we can and do apply moral concepts to acts of war; moreover, there are international bodies that can enforce justice.

Political realism has had many defenders over the years. Many contemporary politicians and statesmen and stateswomen continue to embrace the view today. But is the view acceptable? Critics of realism argue that there is no reason to accept the political realist's claim that we cannot apply moral terms to the relations between nations. In fact, critics say, we apply moral terms to international violence all the time, and there seems nothing wrong with doing so. We apply moral terms to the relations between nations when we say, for example, that it is unjust

44 Thomas Hobbes, *Leviathan*, pt. 1, ch. 13.

for a powerful nation to wage war on a weak nation merely to take over its land and resources, or when we say that it is wrong for one nation to violate the human rights of the citizens of another nation. For example, observers have said that it was unjust for Iraq to invade Kuwait and take over its land and oil fields in 1990, and many historians have said that it was wrong for the German Nazis to invade France and export its Jewish citizens to be killed in their concentration camps during World War II. Examples like these show that the political realist is wrong in claiming that we cannot apply moral terms to the relations between nations, including their wars. Moreover, what reason can the realist give for thinking that morality does not apply to any given area of human life? Because acts of war are the actions of human beings, and because all human actions can be judged by the standards of morality, it follows that war and terrorism can be judged "moral" or "immoral." The realist is therefore mistaken in thinking that morality does not apply to war.

There are other objections to political realism. The political realist assumes that there is no international body that can force nations to abide by any rules. But this, critics say, seems wrong. The critics of realism point out that today several nations have come together in groups capable of forcing one another to abide by international laws. These groups include the United Nations, the World Trade Organization, the NATO states, the European Union, the OECD, and other regional groups of nations. These groups provide the "common power" that Hobbes said is necessary if relations between nations are to be judged by the standards of morality. Thus, there seems to be nothing to prevent even Hobbes from agreeing that morality applies to wars fought between modern nations.

Some defenders of realism have responded to this criticism by providing a different kind of defense of realism. Some have argued that the primary moral obligation of a ruler or a statesman is to advance the interests of the state. This moral obligation, realists may claim, is an obligation that overrides any other moral obligations the ruler may have. Why does the ruler have this obligation? The realist may give this argument in defense of realism: The purpose of government is to advance the interests of its citizens. Rulers and statesmen act on behalf of government; they are "agents" of government who, in agreeing to accept government office, agree to further the purpose of government. Therefore, rulers and statesmen accept an obligation to do whatever they need to do to advance the interests of the nation even in its relations with other nations.

However, critics of realism have responded that this argument in defense of realism admits a key point that undermines realism: It admits that morality applies to government and its actions. If morality applies to the actions of officials who decide what the nation will do in its relations with other nations, then morality applies to the decisions they make about war or other acts of international violence. This second argument for realism, then, tries to show that morality does not apply to international relations, but it does this by assuming that morality *does* apply to international relations. It seems, then, that the only consistent argument for realism is the kind of argument that Hobbes gave. But that kind of realism, we have seen, is open to serious objections.

Pacifism. Unlike the realist, the pacifist asserts that morality applies to the relations between nations and, in particular, to violence among nations and so to war. There are two forms of pacifism: absolute pacifism and conditional pacifism. The absolute pacifist holds that war is always wrong, whereas the conditional pacifist holds that although war—especially modern war—is generally wrong, there may be some rare situations in which war might be justified.

Pacifists are not cowards. Many pacifists have refused to fight in the face of extreme pressures and violence directed against them. Others have accepted imprisonment and even execution rather than compromise their pacifist principles. And many have proclaimed themselves "conscientious objectors" rather than join their nation's war effort. Most democratic nations, including the United States, have laws that allow pacifists and others opposed to war to register as conscientious objectors rather than be drafted, provided that they are willing to substitute some nonviolent form of public service.

Why do absolute pacifists hold that war is always wrong? Some absolute pacifists have held this view on religious grounds. Many Christians have held, for example, that the teachings of Jesus—"Love your enemies" and "When a man strikes you on one cheek, offer him your other cheek"—directly prohibit the use of violence, even in self-defense. During Christianity's first three centuries, most Christians accepted the view of Origen, who argued that Christians could not "go forth as soldiers" because "the Lord has abolished the sword." Many Buddhists are also pacifists because of their religion. The Buddha, the founder of Buddhism, demanded that his followers completely abstain from any violence: "Avoid killing, or harming any living thing," and "In times of war give yourself to the mind of compassion, helping living beings abandon the will to fight." Buddhists have often accepted death rather than fight in a war.

However, other absolute pacifists view war as immoral not on religious grounds but on utilitarian grounds. They argue that war is always wrong because of the terrible evils that it always inflicts, including death, intense human suffering, economic losses, widespread destruction of human goods and achievements, and the infliction of moral and spiritual degradation both on those who wage the war and on those who are victimized by the war. It is unjustified, such pacifists hold, to embark on a course of action that will produce such large evils unless doing so will produce some correspondingly large benefit. But the evils necessarily connected with war are so large that there is no benefit that can outweigh the evils that war produces. Therefore, war is always morally unjustified.

Other pacifists defend the view that war is always wrong by appealing to a deontological argument. Some pacifists, for example, adopt Kant's theory and argue that because of the dignity or sanctity of the human person, every human being has a right not to be killed and a right not to have violence used against him or her. Because war necessarily involves violence and killing, war is absolutely immoral.

But is the pacifist right? It is true, critics agree, that as the utilitarian argument for pacifism asserts, war involves great evils. But aren't there some human goods whose value is so large that we are justified in using war to protect those goods? Consider how, during the last century, Adolf Hitler and the German Nazi party invaded several nations and systematically tortured and exterminated millions of innocent people merely because they were Jews. Even though World War II was a great evil, was it not justified as a means of defeating Hitler and preventing him from inflicting even greater evils? Or consider the American Revolution, which was fought to achieve liberty from the tyranny of Great Britain. Wasn't the good that came from independence more than worth the evil that the American Revolution involved?

Other critics of absolute pacifism have pointed out that pacifism implies that it would be wrong to use violence even to defend oneself against the attack of an unjust attacker or to defend another innocent victim who was being unjustly attacked by a violent agent. But this implication of pacifism is mistaken, critics claim, because there is obviously nothing wrong with defending oneself against an unjust attack, and neither is it wrong to help the innocent victim of an unjust attack. Because pacifism has such obviously false implications, it must itself be false.

QUICK REVIEW
Absolute pacifists hold that war is always immoral either on religious grounds or because the evils of war always outweigh the good war might produce, or because the violence of war violates human dignity. Critics argue there are some goods that outweigh the evils of war, that it is not wrong to defend oneself or others against unjust attack, and that pacifism is inconsistent because if people have a right not to be subjected to violence, then they have a right to be defended from violence even with violence.

Critics of the absolute version of pacifism have argued that the deontological argument for pacifism is based on inconsistent views. Philosopher Jan Narveson, for example, argues that if, as the deontological pacifist claims, it is always wrong to inflict violence on people, then it follows that people have a right not to have violence inflicted on them. But if people have a right not to have violence inflicted on them, then they must have a right to be defended when others are inflicting violence on them. But if people have a right to be defended when others are inflicting violence on them, then they have a right to use violence in defense of their rights. So, the absolute pacifist's claim that violence is always wrong leads to the contradictory conclusion that it is right to use violence to defend oneself against violence! Narveson concludes that the absolute pacifist is mistaken: It is not always wrong to use violence on people. Instead, whereas it is usually wrong to use violence on people, the use of violence is morally justified when defending oneself and others from violence.[45]

QUICK REVIEW
Conditional pacifists hold that although there might be some good that could justify some low levels of violence, modern wars inflict so much violence that their violence outweighs any possible good that could be achieved. Critics point out that the view of the conditional pacifist implies that the costs of war have to be weighed against its benefits.

Some pacifists have turned away from absolute pacifism and, instead, have adopted a kind of "conditional" pacifism. The conditional pacifist agrees with the critics that in some extreme and extremely rare situations, war might be justified. However, the conditional pacifist continues, the kinds of wars that now confront us are always wrong. It is possible, of course, to imagine an ideal war between ideally decent enemies, in which the benefits of fighting the war might outweigh its horrible costs. But such an idealistic situation is unrealistic: It does not happen in the real world in which we now live. Modern wars are fought with weapons that necessarily inflict widespread injuries and suffering on numerous innocent parties: civilians, children, the aged. When used at Hiroshima and Nagasaki, nuclear weapons inflicted tens of thousands of deaths in a single instant; so-called obliteration bombing raids against the Germans during World War II killed tens of thousands at a time; "conventional" bombs used in the Korean War, the Vietnam War, and the Gulf War also indiscriminately killed and maimed soldiers and civilians alike by the thousands. Moreover, once war is declared, nations are willing to do virtually anything to avert defeat, and governments often unleash horrific destruction on the "enemy." So terrible are the evils inflicted by modern wars that they would always outweigh any imaginable good that might be achieved through war.

However, critics argue that the conditional pacifist admits a key point that undermines the pacifist position: The conditional pacifist admits that to properly evaluate the justice of a war, one needs to weigh its costs against its benefits. Once this is admitted, critics claim, then the conditional pacifist has opened the door to the view that despite the qualms of the conditional pacifist, it may be that some wars—even modern wars—are morally justified. And if war is sometimes justified, then we must ask this question: Under what conditions is war justified? Just war theory tries to answer that question.

Just War Theory. Just war theory rejects the realist claim that morality should not be applied to war. It also rejects the pacifist claim that war is so evil that it is always immoral. Instead, just war theory holds that although war is evil because killing is wrong, it is sometimes morally justified for a state to engage in war because the state has an obligation to defend its citizens, protect the innocent, and enforce justice. Just war theory then sets out several principles to determine when war is morally justified.

45 Jan Narveson, "Pacifism: A Philosophical Analysis," *Ethics* 75, no. 4 (July 1965): 259–271.

Many thinkers have contributed to the development of just war theory, including Saint Augustine, Saint Thomas Aquinas, Francisco de Vitoria (1548–1617), Hugo Grotius (1583–1645), Samuel Pufendorf (1632–1704), and Christian Wolff (1679–1754). In modern times, the Harvard philosopher Michael Walzer has argued in his book *Just and Unjust Wars* that just war theory is the most appropriate theory for determining the ethics of war. Today, many government officials agree with Walzer, and when embarking on a military campaign, they make at least a show of demonstrating that their campaign is ethically acceptable because it follows the principles of just war theory—even if they do not always use the term "just war theory." On May 1, 2012, for example, the U.S. government revealed that its military had been killing individual al-Qaida leaders in Pakistan using remotely piloted aircraft so precisely targeted that they could kill an individual with little collateral damage and without harming innocent civilians. When John Brennan, White House counterterrorism advisor, made this revelation, he delivered a lengthy speech in which he hastened to argue "these targeted strikes against al-Qaida terrorists are indeed ethical and just" because they adhere to the ethical "principles of the law of war that govern the use of force." The "principles of the law of war" that he appealed to in his speech were the principles of "just war theory," including, he stated, "the principle of necessity," "the principle of distinction [between innocent civilians and military targets," "the principle of proportionality," and "the principle of humanity [that limits unnecessary suffering]."

Saint Augustine was among the first to claim that although war is evil, it is "just" if it is fought under certain conditions. However, it was Saint Thomas Aquinas who first clearly and systematically stated the criteria that a just war would have to meet. Addressing the question of whether war was ever justified, Aquinas wrote the following:

> In order for a war to be just, three things are necessary. First, the decision to wage the war must be made by a ruler who has the authority to do so. For a private individual has no right to declare war, since he can seek for redress of his rights from the tribunal of his superior. Moreover a private individual lacks the authority to call together the people, which has to be done in wartime. And as the care of the common good is committed to those who are in authority, it is their business to watch over the common good of the city, kingdom or province subject to them. And just as it is lawful for them to use the sword when they punish evil-doers in defending the common good against internal disturbances, . . . so too, it is their business to have recourse to the sword of war to defend the common good against external enemies. . . . Secondly, a just cause is required, namely that those who are attacked, should be attacked because they deserve it on account of some fault. Which is why Augustine says: "A just war is wont to be described as one that avenges wrongs, when a nation or state has to be punished, for refusing to make amends for the wrongs inflicted by its subjects, or to restore what it has seized unjustly." Thirdly, it is necessary that the belligerents should have a rightful intention, so that they intend the advancement of good, or the avoidance of evil. Hence Augustine says: "True religion looks upon as peaceful those wars that are waged not for motives of aggrandizement, or cruelty, but with the object of securing peace, of punishing evil-doers, and of uplifting the good." For it may happen that a war is declared by a legitimate authority, and for a just cause, and yet it may be unlawful because of a wicked intention. Hence Augustine says: "The passion for inflicting harm, the cruel thirst for vengeance, an unpacific and relentless spirit, the fever of revolt, the lust of power, and such like things, all these are rightly condemned in war."[46]

---

46 Thomas Aquinas, *Summa Theologica*, I–II, q.40, a.1.

Clearly, it is Aquinas' view that although war is not a good thing, it is morally justified under certain conditions. The three conditions he gives can be summarized as follows:

1. *Legitimate authority.* The war must be legally declared by a public authority who is legitimately authorized to commit a people to war; the war must not be declared by a private individual or group that has not been entrusted with the care of the common good or by someone without the legal authority to declare war.
2. *Just cause.* The war must be pursued for a morally just cause or purpose, such as self-defense or to take back what was unjustly seized; it is wrong to engage in a war against a nation that has done nothing to deserve it.
3. *Right intention.* Those who are engaged in fighting the war must have a rightful intention; that is, they must intend only to achieve the just end and must not be motivated, for example, by a desire to inflict injury out of sheer cruelty or revenge.

QUICK REVIEW
The just war theory of Aquinas says that war is morally justified if it is (1) declared by a legitimate authority, (2) fought for a just cause, and (3) fought with a right intention—the intention to achieve the just end and not to inflict needless injuries. Others have added that a just war (4) must be fought as a last resort, (5) when there is a real and certain danger, and (6) a reasonable probability of success, and (7) the end is proportional to the probable harm. These are *jus ad bellum* (justice when approaching war) conditions.

In the centuries that followed, many thinkers who were sympathetic to Aquinas' just war theory nevertheless pointed out several shortcomings. For example, if a country could avoid a war through diplomacy or if a country had no hope of winning a war, then it should not go to war even if the war met Aquinas' three conditions. To fix Aquinas' theory, thinkers supplemented his three conditions with several others. Here are the four most important added conditions:

4. *Last resort.* The war must be fought only as a last resort; it is wrong to engage in a war if there are other means of achieving one's ends.
5. *Real and certain danger.* War can be declared only when there is a certain and imminent danger of an attack or invasion by a foreign power; it is wrong to launch a preemptive strike on a country merely because a government is afraid that the country might become belligerent sometime in the future.
6. *Reasonable probability of success.* There must be a reasonable probability of achieving the end for which the war is fought; it is wrong to commit a nation to a war that is hopeless or futile.
7. *Proportional end.* The war must be aimed at achieving a goal whose value is proportional to the injuries that the war will probably inflict; it is wrong to enter a war that will produce more harm than good.

These seven conditions today are referred to as the *jus ad bellum* conditions of the just war theory. *Jus ad bellum* is a Latin phrase that means "justice [when] approaching war," so these are the seven conditions that must be present when a nation enters or declares war.

But proponents of just war theory have also discussed how nations must conduct themselves during a war. These additional conditions are referred to as the *jus in bello* conditions of the just war theory. *Jus in bello* is Latin for "justice [when] in war," so it refers to the kinds of methods or means that must be used in a just war. The two *jus in bello* conditions that proponents of the just war theory have developed are these:

8. *Proportional means.* It is wrong during war to use methods of warfare that inflict harms that are not proportional to the end to be achieved; it is wrong to use weapons or methods that will inflict more suffering or deaths than are truly necessary to achieve one's ends.

9. *Noncombatant immunity*. Whereas it is permissible during war to target or kill military combatants (soldiers and others actively engaged in fighting a war), it is wrong to intentionally target or kill innocent noncombatants (children, the aged, and any other civilians not actively engaged in fighting a war); it is also wrong to use methods or weapons that cannot discriminate between noncombatants and combatants.

QUICK REVIEW
The two main *jus in bello* (justice when in war) conditions of just war theory are (1) the means used must be proportional to the end, and (2) combatants must not intentionally target noncombatants and must be able to discriminate between combatants and noncombatants.

The principles of just war theory are not based on any single philosophy. The various thinkers who have contributed to the development of just war theory have proposed many different kinds of arguments for the seven *jus ad bellum* and the two *jus in bello* conditions. Aquinas, for example, defends the claim that war must be declared by a legitimate authority (principle 1) by appealing to the idea that only a legitimate government has the right to take life in defense of the state, to gather the people into an army, and to use violence to correct wrongs; private individuals do not have such a right and so cannot wage war against others. He argues that war must be fought for a just cause (principle 2) by claiming that it is wrong even for the state to take life unless it is done to defend the state and its people or to correct a wrongful injury against the state or its people. And he defends the view that war must be fought with a good intention (principle 3) because in his view, an agent's intention determines the morality of the agent's action. The principles that war should be fought only as a last resort (principle 4) and only when there is a certain and imminent danger of attack (principle 5) have been defended by thinkers who have argued that the killing, destruction, and sufferings of war are such great evils that war should be entered only when there is absolutely no other way for a nation to avoid certain attack. The principles that it is wrong to commit a nation to a war that is hopeless (principle 6), that a war must aim at achieving a good that is greater than the harms it will produce (principle 7), and that methods of war must not inflict more injuries than are necessary to achieve one's ends (principle 8) have all been defended on the basis of utilitarianism, which states that we have a moral duty to maximize good and minimize harm. The principle that it is legitimate to target combatants or soldiers but wrong to intentionally kill innocent noncombatants (principle 9) has been defended by appealing to natural law ethics, which says that it is always wrong to directly destroy an innocent human life. It has also been defended on the basis of Immanuel Kant's categorical imperative, which states that persons should be treated as ends—that is, as they have consented to be treated. Kantians have argued that by entering the military and going to war, soldiers have consented to engage in mortal combat and so can be killed, whereas civilians, who are not actively engaged in fighting, have not so consented.

The theory of just war is not just a view of Western thinkers. Some Eastern philosophers have expounded versions of just war theory. Sikhism, for example, produced several thinkers who developed the concept of "Dharam Yudh," meaning "war in defense of righteousness." Like Western philosophers, Sikhs also hold that although war is evil, it is sometimes a justified evil. The theory of Dharam Yudh holds that war is justified only if (1) it is fought as a last resort, (2) it is not undertaken for revenge, (3) its armies are disciplined and do not include paid mercenaries, (4) the nation uses only the minimum force needed to achieve success, (5) civilians are not harmed, and (6) there is no looting or theft of property or territory.

QUICK REVIEW
The various conditions of just war theory are defended on the basis of several philosophies. Eastern philosophies such as Sikhism have also developed similar theories of just war.

Notice that there is a substantial overlap between the theory of Dharam Yudh and just war theory.

QUICK REVIEW
Pacifist critics of just war argue that the theory has encouraged war; others argue that it is vague about what constitutes a "legitimate authority," a "just cause," a "last resort," a "reasonable probability of success," "proportionality," and a "noncombatant." Others claim that modern weapons cannot discriminate between combatants and noncombatants, so the theory is irrelevant in modern warfare.

Just war theory is subject to a number of criticisms. Pacifists have argued that historically, the theory has been used only as an excuse for going to war and has not been used to avoid war. Consequently, the pacifist claims, just war theory has encouraged war instead of having served to limit war.

Other critics have argued that just war theory is too vague. It is not clear, for example, what the theory means when it states that war must be declared by the legitimate authority. Does this mean that when citizens rebel against an unjust and oppressive government, their rebellion is always unjust? It is also not clear what the theory means by a "just cause." A just cause certainly includes defending oneself against an actively invading force or helping a weak nation defend itself against an invading force. But does just cause include attacking a nation whose government is violating the human rights of its own citizens (as Muammar Gaddafi's Libyan regime was doing when attacked by U.S. and other United Nations forces in 2011) or attacking a nation to prevent it from launching a future attack (like the U.S. did when it invaded Iraq in 2003 to prevent it from developing "weapons of mass destruction")? And consider the principle of "last resort." Does this principle mean that a nation has to wait until after it has tried every form of persuasion and diplomacy before resorting to war? If so, then doesn't this waiting simply give the enemy more time to kill people and to gather its forces so as to inflict greater harm on the waiting nation? Or consider the principle of "reasonable probability of success." Does this mean that small and weak nations must always refrain from defending themselves against large and powerful nations that are bound to win any war against them? Neither is it clear what "proportionality" means: How is one supposed to measure the value of the goods that war will produce (such as a democratic government) against the loss of life that it will inevitably inflict? Because the principles of just war theory are not clear, critics continue, it is easily subject to misuse by cynics who want to use it to justify wars that are not really justified. Moreover, even those who are sincerely interested in using the theory to determine the justice of a conflict will find themselves hampered by the theory's lack of clarity.

Critics have also argued that modern weapons of war have made just war theory irrelevant. Modern methods of warfare, such as the use of chemical, biological, and nuclear weapons and of large conventional bombs, as well as modern methods of bombing such as so-called saturation bombing, have made it difficult or impossible to distinguish between combatants and noncombatants in modern war. Consequently, today it is not possible to use the principle of discrimination unless one is prepared to condemn all wars that use modern methods of warfare.

Despite its critics, however, just war theory today remains the most widely accepted theory for determining when war is morally justified. Its defenders say that although the theory is sometimes unclear, it is still clear enough to be useful in judging many wars. Moreover, many of its principles—such as principle 9, on noncombatant immunity—have been incorporated into international laws that define and punish war crimes, such as the so-called Geneva Protocol and the Geneva Convention. In fact, many international and military courts have been convened over the years to prosecute soldiers and deposed leaders for failing to respect noncombatant immunity and so committing war crimes.

Terrorism. So far, we have been discussing the ethics and morality of war and methods of warfare. Does this discussion shed any light on terrorism or the use of violence to fight it? Terrorism has been defined in many different ways. Some definitions focus on the idea that acts of terrorism are acts of violence designed to create terror among the members of a society, others focus on the idea that terrorism is violence in pursuit of a political goal such as a more just government,

PHILOSOPHY AND LIFE

Society and the Bomb

The decision to drop the atomic bomb that killed tens of thousands of the civilian inhabitants of the city of Hiroshima on August 6, 1945, was made while the United States was at war with Japan. Henry L. Stimson, the American Secretary of War at the time, later explained that he advised President Truman to drop the bomb on the basis of utilitarian reasoning:

> I felt that to extract a genuine surrender from the [Japanese] Emperor and his military advisers, they must be administered a tremendous shock which would carry convincing proof of our power to destroy the Empire. Such an effective shock would save many times the number of lives, both American and Japanese, that it would cost. . . . Our enemy, Japan, . . . had the strength to cost us a million more [lives]. . . . Additional large losses might be expected among our allies and . . . enemy casualties would be much larger than our own. . . . My chief purpose was to end the war in victory with the least possible cost in lives. . . . The face of war is the face of death; death is an inevitable part of every order that a wartime leader gives. The decision to use the atomic bomb was a decision that brought death to over a hundred thousand Japanese. . . . But this deliberate, premeditated destruction was our least abhorrent choice.

Objecting to this kind of utilitarian justification for killing the inhabitants of cities with nuclear weapons, philosopher-theologian John C. Ford wrote the following:

> [Is] it permissible, in order to win a just war, to wipe out such an area with death or grave injury, resulting indiscriminately, to the majority of its ten million inhabitants? In my opinion the answer must be in the negative. . . . [It] is never permitted to kill directly noncombatants in wartime. Why? Because they are innocent. That is, they are innocent of the violent and destructive action of war, or of any close participation in the violent and destructive action of war.

QUESTIONS

1. Is killing the innocent always wrong, no matter what the consequences?
2. Would you side with Stimson or Ford about the morality of dropping the bomb?
3. Do you agree that in some circumstances the use of nuclear weapons is morally permissible?

Source: Henry L. Stimson, "The Decision to Use the Atomic Bomb," *Harpers* (February 1947), 101–102, 106–107; John C. Ford, "The Hydrogen Bombing of Cities," *Theology Digest* (Winter 1957).

and still others focus on the idea that terrorism is violence that is intentionally directed against noncombatants. After reviewing all of these various definitions, political philosopher C. A. J. Coady comes to the following conclusion:

> If we define terrorism as the tactic of intentionally targeting noncombatants with lethal or severe violence for political purposes, we will capture a great deal of what is being discussed with such passion and we can raise crucial moral and political questions about it with some clarity. We might narrow the definition in certain respects by incorporating a reference to the idea that the attacks or threats are meant to produce political results via the creation of fear, and we could widen it by including noncombatant property as a target where it is significantly related to life and security.[47]

QUICK REVIEW
Coady defines terrorism as intentionally targeting noncombatants with lethal or severe violence to achieve political purposes, perhaps through the creation of fear and perhaps including the targeting of property that is related to life or security.

Defined in this way, what can we say about the ethics of terrorism and of using violence to fight terrorism? As we have mentioned, political realism would not

47 C. A. J. Coady, "Terrorism," *Encyclopedia of Ethics*, ed. L. C. Becker (New York: Garland, 1992), 1241–1244.

QUICK REVIEW
Political realism would not condemn terrorism as immoral, and it would claim that it is not wrong to use any amount of violence to protect a nation's citizens from terrorists.

condemn terrorism as immoral because, according to the realist, the terms *morality* and *immorality* do not apply to states and the actions that states take against their enemies while pursuing the nation's interests. Moreover, the political realist would hold that a nation should do everything it can to protect its citizens from terrorists and to defend its interests, so the realist would hold that all the violence and power of the state may legitimately be used to crush dangerous terrorist movements wherever they may exist, even if doing so requires using substantial force and violence. Any method, even the use of torture, would be legitimate if, in the circumstances, it is the most effective way to protect the nation's interests. The reason the political realist would hold that it is not immoral for the state to use any form of violence in pursuit of the terrorist is that, again, the realist believes that morality does not apply to the actions that states take against their enemies. The realist would hold, of course, that a nation must be careful and prudent in its use of violence lest it create enemies that later harm its interests. But so long as its own long- and short-range interests are adequately protected, the state may use as much violence as it wants to protect itself from terrorism.

QUICK REVIEW
Pacifism would condemn terrorism as immoral but would not approve using violence in pursuit of terrorists.

The pacifist, on the other hand, would obviously condemn terrorism as immoral because terrorism is a form of violence. However, the absolute pacifist would not approve of using violence in pursuit of the terrorist because the absolute pacifist is opposed to all use of violence including, of course, torture. Instead, the pacifist would recommend using persuasion, diplomacy, and other nonviolent methods to deal with terrorism.

QUICK REVIEW
Just war theory would condemn terrorism because it is usually violence that is not authorized by a legitimate authority; it is usually not for a just cause and is motivated by revenge; it has no clear goal, and there is little hope that the violence will achieve its goal; and, most important, it targets and kills innocent noncombatants. Just war theory would approve the use of violence against terrorists only if it adheres to the nine principles of just war.

Just war theory is also clear about the ethics of terrorism, although its view is more complicated than the view of the realist or the pacifist. First, the acts of terrorists are virtually never officially authorized by a legitimate government, so they fail principle 1 of the just war theory (although some forms of terrorism are "state sponsored" and so may be authorized by a legitimate government). Second, they are sometimes undertaken for a cause that is not just and are motivated by revenge, so terrorism violates principles 2 and 3. Third, most acts of terrorism are undertaken without a very clear and specific goal and with little hope that the violence will achieve its goal, so terrorism violates principles 6 and 7. But the issue that just war critics of terrorism single out as the terrorist's most significant moral violation is that the terrorist targets innocent civilians who are noncombatants, so the terrorist violates principle 9. Terrorism, just war proponents conclude, is nothing more than rationalized murder inflicted in pursuit of a hopeless goal, so it is morally unjustified.

QUICK REVIEW
Defenders of terrorist tactics argue that some forms of terrorism can meet the conditions of just war theory and so can be morally justified, particularly when all citizens of a target nation actively support an unjust government that is oppressing the terrorists, so these citizens can be treated as combatants by the terrorists.

However, although the just war theorist would condemn terrorism, he or she would not necessarily approve of all forms of violence—such as torturing captured terrorists to elicit information from them—in pursuit of the goal of eliminating terrorist threats. The just war theorist would hold that when using violence to eliminate terrorism, the state must continue to adhere to the nine principles of just war. This means that the state must not use more violence than necessary to achieve its ends; the threat of terrorism must be real and imminent; the violence used against terrorism must have a reasonable chance of success; the harms inflicted must be proportional to the good to be achieved; innocent citizens must not be intentionally killed or harmed.

But do the precepts of the just war theory indicate clearly that the use of some forms of violence, such as torture, are morally permissible or impermissible in the fight against terrorism? Some critics argue that these precepts indicate clearly that the use of torture is wrong; in particular, they argue, they show it was wrong for the U.S. government to use the kind of torture methods that documents indicate our government has used on captured terrorist suspects to force them to

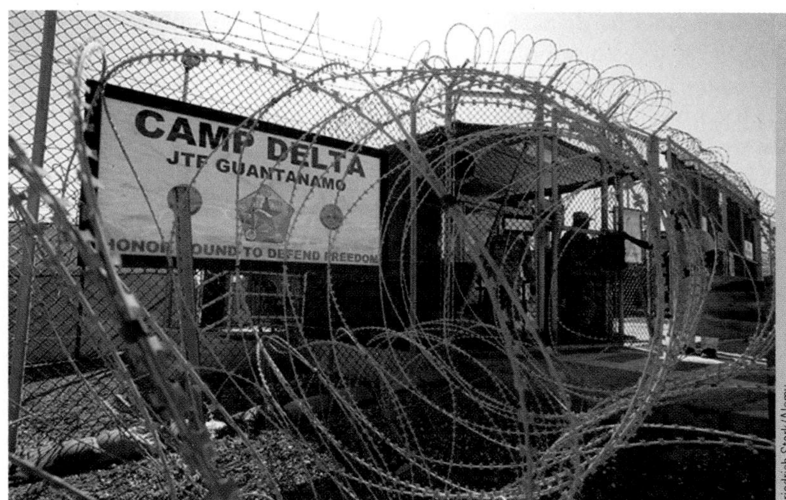

Friedrich Stark/Alamy

Entrance to the detention camp Delta on U.S. Naval station Guantanamo Bay, Cuba. President George W. Bush signed an executive order stating that the U.S. military could indefinitely imprison at Guantanamo any non-citizen accused of being involved in international terrorism; there prisoners were subjected to sleep deprivation, "waterboarding," beatings, and other acts of violence later characterized as "torture."

divulge whatever information they had. These considerations were especially relevant when the Bush administration admitted in October 2008 that it gave the CIA permission to use "waterboarding," sleep deprivation, beatings, and other forms of "torture" on prisoners it thought were terrorists. In some cases, those accused of terrorism turned out to be innocent. To use such forms of torture, the critics argue, is to use more violence than is needed to elicit information from prisoners because more benign techniques are as, or more, effective than torture; moreover, torture has little chance of success because victims make up false stories to get the torture to stop and so the results of torture are unreliable; and the pain inflicted is too often out of proportion to the value of the information that can be gained. So, just war theory condemns torture. On the other hand, defenders of the use of torture claim that just war theory does not necessarily condemn torture. They claim that in many cases only torture can force captives to divulge valuable information they may have; moreover, although victims might make up some false stories, these can often be checked by interviewing others; and in some cases, the harm inflicted on a prisoner is small in comparison to the value of the information that torture might disclose. Although just war theory provides a solid basis for condemning terrorism, then, it seems to provide an ambiguous basis for justifying or condemning the use of some forms of violence—torture, in particular—in fighting terrorism.

Some thinkers have responded to the condemnation of terrorism by arguing that terrorism is not necessarily as evil as just war theory would make it out to be. It is possible to imagine a country whose citizens are subjected to great injustices by the government of another nation and where the only means of ending those injustices is through terrorist attacks on the citizens of the oppressive government. If terrorism is the only or the least costly means of ending such injustices, and if ending the injustices is of sufficiently great value, then utilitarian ethics would imply that terrorism is morally justified.

Some defenders of terrorism also argue that when the government of one nation oppresses the citizens of another nation, the citizens of the oppressive nation are not necessarily "innocent." When the citizens of a nation support an oppressive government or benefit from its oppressive acts, they say, those citizens share some of the responsibility for the oppressive acts of government. The terrorist might argue that those citizens then lose their innocence and become legitimate targets of terrorist violence. In such cases, the terrorist concludes, killing citizens who happen to be in a store or restaurant that is bombed does not violate the principle of noncombatant immunity because those citizens are not innocent noncombatants.

Is terrorism, then, sometimes justified, or is it always wrong? This is a question that you, the reader, will have to answer for yourself. In this short discussion of a very large issue, we have tried to review some of the key perspectives that can be brought to bear on the moral status of terrorism in the hope that this review will help you think through the issue on your own.

QUESTIONS

1. What laws, if any, do you regard as unjust? Why?
2. Does the state have the right to make laws concerning homosexuality, pornography, and marijuana?
3. To what extent do you feel that your own ability to live as you believe is limited by laws?
4. Do you think that every American has the right to a college education?
5. Do you think that every American has the right to medical care?
6. Do you believe that all people have the right to determine the political system under which they live? If you do, does one state have a moral obligation to assist another that is fighting to exercise that right? Is there any point at which that obligation ends?
7. Use the theories of political realism, pacifism, and just war to discuss and evaluate the morality of a recent U.S. military action.

PHILOSOPHY AT THE MOVIES

Watch *The Fog of War* (2003), a documentary that interviews Robert McNamara, who during World War II helped plan the bombing of German and Japanese cities that killed thousands of their inhabitants in massive firestorms, helped plan the flights that dropped two atomic bombs on Japan, and who, as secretary of defense under two presidents, was chiefly responsible for directing the failed war in Vietnam. Which view of war does this film seem to support: political realism, pacifism, or just war theory? Which view does McNamara seem to support?

Chapter Summary

This chapter opens by keying on a recurring issue in any determination of the proper relation between individual and society: the problem of justice. Since the time of the Greeks, philosophers have proposed theories associating justice with merit, social utility, and fairness (equality). A related issue is how the state justifies its claims to power and authority. Although there are a number of theories of the legitimacy of the state, contract theory is the view on which our own society's conception of power and governance is based. Even if the power of the state can be justified by contract theory, though, the question remains: What, if any, are the limits to the power of the state? Whatever their leaning, contract theorists believe that the state and government have the right and duty to exercise control through law, which has traditionally demarcated individual and society. Laws guarantee freedom from interference, but in a broader sense they also guarantee positive rights.

The main points of the chapter are:

8.1 What Is Social and Political Philosophy?

- Social philosophy is the philosophical study of society and its problems and the application of moral principles to these problems, including the problems of human rights, justice, and freedom.
- Political philosophy is the subdivision of social philosophy that focuses on the proper role of the state or government in society.

8.2 What Justifies the State?

- Many today accept a contractual justification for the power and authority of the state—that is, the state acquires its legitimacy through the consent of the governed.
- Contract theory has its roots in the thought of Thomas Hobbes, John Locke, and Jean Jacques Rousseau.
- Contract theory was revived in the twentieth century by John Rawls, who argues that the social contract is an imaginary device for determining what a just society and government would be like.
- Contract theory has been criticized by communitarians, who argue that it ignores the social nature of human beings, and by feminists, who argue that it assumes a nonconsensual division between the private realm of the family, to which women are relegated, and the public realm of politics and economics, in which men participate.

8.3 What Is Justice?

- Distributive justice refers to the fairness with which a community distributes benefits and burdens among its members; the principle of formal justice says that equals should be treated equally.
- The classical Greek view of justice, as expressed by Plato and Aristotle, associates justice with merit.
- Egalitarians argue either for strict equality or for equality of political rights and economic opportunities.
- The socialist principle of justice is summarized in Karl Marx's slogan: "From each according to his ability, to each according to his need."
- Whereas welfare liberals such as John Rawls argue that justice requires economic aid for the disadvantaged, classical liberals such as Robert Nozick argue that people's free choices should be respected in all economic matters.
- Several British philosophers of the eighteenth and nineteenth centuries, among them John Stuart Mill, associate justice with social utility, which raises the problem of balancing individual rights and interests with the common good.

8.4 Limits on the State

- Thomas Aquinas argued that the laws of the state must be consistent with natural law and that citizens have no obligation to obey a human law when it violates natural law and so is unjust.

- The laws of the state must be consistent with the right to freedom. The right to freedom, such as is enumerated in the Bill of Rights, provides guarantees against state interference.
- Human rights are classified into negative and positive rights. Although everyone agrees that the laws of the state must be changed when they conflict with human rights, some hold that the state need only enforce people's negative rights, whereas others hold that governments must also provide for people's positive rights.
- Political realism, pacifism, and just war theory are three views on the morality of war. Political realism says that morality does not apply to war, whereas pacifism says that war is immoral. Just war theory says that war is evil but is morally justified if it meets both the *jus ad bellum* conditions (legitimate authority, just cause, right intention, last resort, real and certain danger, reasonable probability of success, proportional end) and the *jus in bello* conditions (proportional means and noncombatant immunity). Just war theory also condemns terrorism.

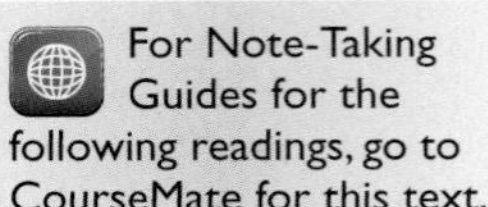

For Note-Taking Guides for the following readings, go to CourseMate for this text.

8.5 Readings

Is war morally justified? The first reading is taken from E. M. Remarque's famous novel on World War I, a realistic and terrifying polemic against war. In the reading, Paul Baumer, a young German soldier fighting in the trenches, gets lost as he crawls along the ground trying to find his own company during a bombardment. He takes shelter in a muddy shell hole while machine gun bullets fly just above his head. In the second reading, philosopher Bertrand Russell argues that although some wars may have been morally justified in the past, wars today cannot be morally justified. He argues that the great evils that modern wars unleash, far outweigh the goods for which modern wars are fought. These readings, should prompt you to ask whether our own government's use of war and violence to achieve its ends is morally justified.

ERICH MARIA REMARQUE

From *All Quiet on the Western Front*

Excerpt from: Erich Maria Remarque, *All Quiet on the Western Front*, trans. A. W. Wheen (Boston: Little, Brown and Company, 1958), chap. 9, pp. 217, 219, and 223–229. [Copyright 1929, 1930 by Little Brown and Company; Renewed 1957, 1958 by Erich Maria Remarque.]

A shell crashes. Almost immediately two others. And then it begins in earnest. A bombardment. Machine-guns rattle. Now there is nothing for it but to stay lying low. Apparently an attack is coming. Everywhere the rockets shoot up. Unceasing.

I lie huddled in a large shell-hole, my legs in the water up to the belly. . . .

[Then] I have this one shattering thought: What will you do if someone jumps into your shell-hole? Swiftly I pull out my little dagger, grasp it fast and bury it in my hand once again under the mud. If anyone jumps in here I will go for him; it hammers in my forehead; at once, stab him clean through the throat, so that he cannot call out; that's the only way; he will be just as frightened as I am, when in terror we fall upon one another, then I must be first.

The rattle of machine-guns becomes an unbroken chain. Just as I am about to turn round a little, something heavy stumbles, and with a crash a body falls over me into the shell-hole, slips down and lies across me.

I do not think at all, I make no decision—I strike madly home, and feel only how the body suddenly convulses, then becomes limp, and collapses. When I recover myself, my hand is sticky and wet.

The man gurgles. It sounds to me as though he bellows, every gasping breath is like a cry, a thunder—but it is only my heart pounding. I want to stop his mouth, stuff it with earth, stab him again, he must be quiet, he is betraying me; now at last I regain control of myself, but have suddenly become so feeble that I cannot any more lift my hand against him.

So I crawl away to the farthest corner and stay there, my eyes glued on him, my hand grasping the knife—ready, if he stirs, to spring at him again. But he won't do so any more; I can hear that in his gurgling. . . .

These hours . . . The gurgling starts again—but how slowly a man dies! For this I know—he cannot be saved. Indeed I have tried to tell myself that he will be, but at noon this pretence breaks down and melts before his groans. If only I had not lost my revolver crawling about, I would shoot him. Stab him I cannot.

By noon I am groping on the outer limits of reason. Hunger devours me, I could almost weep for something to eat, I cannot struggle against it. Again and again I fetch water for the dying man and drink some myself.

This is the first man I have killed with my hands, whom I can see close at hand, whose death is my doing. . . .

But every gasp lays my heart bare. This dying man has time with him, he has an invisible dagger with which he stabs me: Time and my thoughts.

I would give much if he would but stay alive. It is hard to lie here and to have to see and hear him.

In the afternoon, about three, he is dead.

I breathe freely again. But only for a short time. Soon the silence is more unbearable than the groans. I wish the gurgling were there again, gasping, hoarse, now whistling softly and again hoarse and loud.

It is mad, what I do. But I must do something. I prop the dead man up again so that he lies comfortably although he feels nothing any more. I close his eyes. They are brown, his hair is black and a bit curly at the sides.

The mouth is full and soft beneath his moustache; the nose is slightly arched, the skin brownish; it is now not so pale as it was before, when he was still alive. For a moment the face seems almost healthy;—then it collapses suddenly into the strange face of the dead that I have so often seen, strange faces, all alike.

No doubt his wife still thinks of him; she does not know what has happened. He looks as if he would often have written to her; —she will still be getting mail from him—Tomorrow, in a week's time—perhaps even a stray letter a month hence. She will read it, and in it he will be speaking to her.

My state is getting worse; I can no longer control my thoughts. What would his wife look like? Like the little brunette on the other side of the canal? Does she belong to me now? Perhaps by this act she becomes mine. I wish Kantorek were sitting here beside me. If my mother could see me—The dead man might have had thirty more years of life if only I had impressed the way back to our trench more sharply on my memory. If only he had run two yards farther to the left, he might now be sitting in the trench over there and writing a fresh letter to his wife.

But I will get no further that way; for that is the fate of all of us: if Kemmerich's leg had been six inches to the right; if Hay Westhus had bent his back three inches further forward—

The silence spreads. I talk and must talk. So I speak to him and say to him: Comrade, I did not want to kill you. If you jumped in here again, I would not do it, if you would be sensible too. But you were only an idea to me before, an abstraction that lived in my mind and called forth its appropriate response. It was that abstraction I stabbed. But now, for the first time, I see you are a man like me. I thought of your hand-grenades, of your bayonet, of your rifle; now I see your wife and your face and our fellowship. Forgive me, comrade. We always see it too late. Why do they never tell us that you are just poor devils like us, that your mothers are just as anxious as ours, and that we have the same fear of death, and the same dying and the same agony—Forgive me, comrade; how could you be my enemy? If we threw away these rifles and this uniform you could be my brother just like Kat and Albert. Take twenty years of my life, comrade, and stand up—take more, for I do not know what I can even attempt to do with it now.

It is quiet; the front is still except for the crackle of rifle-fire. The bullets rain over; they are not fired haphazardly, but shrewdly aimed from all sides. I cannot get out.

"I will write to your wife," I say hastily to the dead man, I will write to her, she must hear it from me, I will tell her everything I have told you, she shall not suffer, I will help her, and your parents too, and your child—

His tunic is half open. The pocketbook is easy to find. But I hesitate to open it. In it is the book with his name. So long as I do not know his name perhaps I may still forget him, time will obliterate it, this picture. But his name, it is a nail that will be hammered into me and never come out again. It has the power to recall this forever; it will always come back and stand before me.

Irresolutely I take the wallet in my hand. It slips out of my hand and falls open. Some pictures and letters drop out. I gather them up and want to put them back again, but the strain I am under, the uncertainty, the hunger, the danger, these hours with the dead man have confused me, I want to hasten the relief, to intensify and to end the torture, as one strikes an unendurably painful hand against the trunk of a tree, regardless of everything.

There are portraits of a woman and a little girl, small amateur photographs taken against an ivy-clad wall. Along with them are letters. I take them out and try to read them. Most of it I do not understand, it is so hard to decipher and I know scarcely any French. But each word I translate pierces me like a shot in the chest;—like a stab in the chest.

My brain is taxed beyond endurance. But I realize this much, that I will never dare to write to these people as I intended. Impossible. I look at the portraits once more; they are clearly not rich people. I might send them money anonymously if I earn anything later on. I seize upon that, it is at least something to hold on to. This dead man is bound up with my life, therefore I must do everything, promise everything, in order to save myself; I swear blindly that I mean to live only for his sake and his family, with wet lips I try to placate him—and deep down in me lies the hope that I may buy myself off in this way and perhaps even yet get out of this; it is a little stratagem: if only I am allowed to escape, then I will see to it. So I open the book and read slowly: —Gerard Duval, printer.

With the dead man's pencil I write the address on an envelope, then swiftly thrust everything back into his tunic.

I have killed the printer, Gerard Duval. I must be a printer, I think confusedly, be a printer, a printer—

BERTRAND RUSSELL

The Ethics of War

From Bertrand Russell, "The Ethics of War," in *Justice in Wartime* (Chicago: The Open Court Publishing Co., 1916), pp. 20–39.

I.

It is necessary, in regard to any war, to consider, . . . the evils inseparable from war and [that are] equally certain whichever side may ultimately prove victorious. So long as these are not fully realized, it is impossible to judge justly whether a war is or is not likely to be beneficial to the human race. Although the theme is trite, it is necessary therefore briefly to remind ourselves what the evils of war really are.

To begin with the most obvious evil: large numbers of young men, the most courageous and the most physically fit in their respective nations, are killed, bringing great sorrow to their friends, loss to the community, and gain only to themselves. Many others are maimed for life, some go mad, and others become nervous wrecks, mere useless and helpless derelicts. Of those who survive many will be brutalized and morally degraded by the fierce business of killing, which, however much it may be the soldier's duty, must shock and often destroy the more humane instincts. As every truthful record of war shows, fear and hate let loose the wild beast in a not inconsiderable proportion of combatants, leading to strange cruelties, which must be faced, but not dwelt upon if sanity is to be preserved.

Of the evils of war to the non-combatant . . . it is not necessary to enlarge. . . . Even assuming the utmost humanity compatible with the conduct of military operations, it cannot be doubted that, if the troops of the Allies penetrate into the industrial regions of Germany, the German population will have to suffer a great part of the misfortunes which Germany has inflicted upon [its opponents]. . . .

The evils which war produces outside the area of military operations are perhaps even more serious, for though less intense they are far more widespread. Passing by the anxiety and sorrow of those whose sons or husbands or brothers are at the front, the extent and consequences of the economic injury inflicted by war are much greater than is usually realized. It is common to speak of economic evils as merely material, and of desire for economic progress as grovelling and uninspired. . . . But with regard to the poorer classes of society, economic progress is the first condition of many spiritual goods and even often of life itself. An overcrowded family, living in a slum in conditions of filth and immorality, where half the children die from ignorance of hygiene and bad sanitation, and the remainder grow up stunted and ignorant–such a family can hardly make progress mentally or spiritually, except through an improvement in its economic condition. And without going to the very bottom of the social scale, economic progress is essential to the possibility of good education, of a tolerable existence for women, and of that breadth and freedom of outlook upon which any solid and national advance must be based. . . . It cannot be doubted that the desire on the part of the rich to distract men's minds from the claims of social justice has been more or less unconsciously one of the motives leading to war in modern Europe. Everywhere the well-to-do and the political parties which represent their interests have been the chief agents in stirring up international hatred and in persuading the working man that his real enemy is the foreigner. Thus war, and the fear of war, has a double effect in retarding social progress: it diminishes the resources available for improving the condition of the wage-earning classes, and it distracts men's minds from the need and possibility of general improvement by persuading them that the way to better themselves is to injure their comrades in some other country. . . .

II.

Are there any wars which achieve so much for the good of mankind as to outweigh all the evils we have been considering? I think there have been such wars in the past, . . . For the purposes of classification we may roughly distinguish four kinds of wars, though of course in any given case a war is not likely to be quite clearly of any one of the four kinds. With this proviso we may distinguish: (1) Wars of Colonization; (2) Wars of Principle; (3) Wars of Self-defence; (4) Wars of Prestige. Of these four kinds I should say that the first and second are fairly often justified; the third seldom, except against an adversary of inferior civilization, and the fourth, which is the sort to which the present war [World War I] belongs, never. Let us consider these four kinds of war in succession.

By a war of colonization I mean a war whose purpose is to drive out the whole population of some territory and replace it by an invading population of a different race. Ancient wars were very largely of this kind, of which we have a good example in the Book of Joshua. In modern times the conflicts of Europeans with American-Indians, Maories, and other aborigines in temperate regions, have been of this kind. . . . In order that such wars may be justified, it is necessary that there should be a very great and undeniable difference between the civilization of the colonizers and that of the dispossessed natives. It is necessary also that the climate should be one in which the invading race can flourish. When these conditions are satisfied the conquest becomes justified, though the actual fighting against the dispossessed inhabitants ought, of course, to be avoided as far as is compatible with colonizing. Many humane people will object in theory to the justification of this form of robbery, but I do not think that any practical or effective objection is likely to be made.

Such wars, however, belong now to the past. . . . What are nowadays called colonial wars do not aim at the complete occupation of a country by a conquering race; they aim only at securing certain governmental and trading advantages. They belong, in fact, rather with what I call wars of prestige, than with wars of colonization in the old sense . . .

III.

The second type of war which may sometimes be justified is what may be called the war of principle. To this kind belong the wars of Protestant and Catholic, and the English and American civil wars. In such cases, each side, or at least one side, is honestly convinced that the progress of mankind depends upon the adoption of certain beliefs–beliefs which, through blindness or natural depravity, mankind will not regard as reasonable, except when presented at the point of the bayonet. Such wars may be justified: for example, a nation practising religious toleration may be justified in resisting a persecuting nation holding a different creed. . . . But wars of principle are much less often justified than is believed. . . . It is very rarely that a principle of genuine value to mankind can only be propagated by military force: as a rule, it is the bad part of men's principles, not the good part, which makes it necessary to fight for their defence. And for this reason the bad part rather than the good rises to prominence during the progress of a war of principle. A nation undertaking a war in defence of religious toleration would be almost certain to persecute those of its citizens who did not believe in religious toleration. A war on behalf of democracy, if it is long and fierce, is sure to end in the exclusion from all share of power of those who do not support the war. . . . This common doom of opposite ideals is the usual, though not the invariable, penalty of supporting ideals by force. While it may therefore be conceded that such wars are not invariably to be condemned, we must nevertheless scrutinize very skeptically the claim of any particular war to be justified on the ground of the victory which it brings to some important principle. . . .

Men do right to desire strongly the victory of ideals which they believe to be important, but it is almost always a sign of yielding to undue impatience when men believe that what is valuable in their ideals can be furthered by the substitution of force for peaceful persuasion. To advocate democracy by war [for example] is only to repeat, on a vaster scale and with far more tragic results, the error of those who have sought it hitherto by the assassin's knife and the bomb of the anarchist.

IV.

The next kind of war to be considered is the war of self-defence. This kind of war is almost universally admitted to be justifiable. The justification of wars of self-defence is very convenient, since so far as I know there has never yet been a war which was not one of self-defence. Every strategist assures us that the true defence is offence; every great nation believes that its own overwhelming strength is the only possible guarantee of the world's peace and can only be secured by the defeat of other nations. . . . The claim of each side to be fighting in self-defence appears to the other side mere wanton hypocrisy, because in each case the other side believes that self-defence is only to be achieved by conquest. So long as the principle of self-defence is recognized as affording always a sufficient justification for war, this tragic conflict of irresistible claims remains unavoidable.

In certain cases, where there is a clash of differing civilizations, a war of self-defence may be justified on the same grounds as a war of principle. I think, however, that, even as a matter of practical politics, the principle of non-resistance contains an immense measure of wisdom if only men would have the courage to carry it out. The evils suffered during a hostile invasion are suffered because resistance is offered . . . What one civilized nation can achieve against another by means of conquest is very much less than is commonly supposed. It is said, both here and in Germany, that each side is fighting for its existence; but when this phrase is scrutinized, it is found to cover a great deal of confusion of thought induced by unreasoning panic. We cannot destroy Germany even by a complete military victory, nor conversely, could Germany destroy England even if our Navy were sunk and London occupied by the Prussians. English civilization, the English language, English manufactures would still exist, and as a matter of practical politics it would be totally impossible for Germany to establish a tyranny in this country. If the Germans, instead of being resisted by force of arms, had been passively permitted to establish themselves wherever they pleased, the halo of glory and courage surrounding the brutality of military success would have been absent, and public opinion in Germany itself would have rendered any oppression impossible. . . .

In a word, it is the means of repelling hostile aggression which make hostile aggression disastrous. . . . As between civilized nations, therefore, non-resistance would seem . . . the course of practical wisdom. Only pride and fear stand in the way of its adoption.

V.

The last kind of war we have to consider is what I have called the war of prestige. Prestige is seldom more than one element in the causes of a war, but it is often a very important element. . . . Men desire the sense of triumph, and fear the sense of humiliation which they would have in yielding to the demands of another nation. Rather than forego the triumph, rather than endure the humiliation, they are willing to inflict upon the world all those disasters which it is now suffering and all that exhaustion and impoverishment which it must long continue to suffer. The willingness to inflict and endure such evils is almost universally praised; it is called high-spirited, worthy of a great nation, showing fidelity to ancestral traditions. The slightest sign of reasonableness is attributed to fear, and received with shame on the one side and with derision on the other. In private life exactly the same state of opinion existed so long as duelling was practised, and exists still in those countries in which this custom still survives. It is now recognized, at any rate in the Anglo-Saxon world, that the so called honor which made duelling appear inevitable was a folly and a delusion. It is perhaps not too much to hope that the day may come when the honor of nations, like that of individuals, will be longer measured by their willingness to inflict slaughter.

8.6 HISTORICAL SHOWCASE

Marx and Rawls

Two social philosophies tend to dominate much of our contemporary debate over the appropriate nature of our society: Marxism and liberalism. These two philosophies, in fact, tend to dominate much of the thinking of modern societies. The democratic and capitalist nations mainly adhere to the tenets of liberalism, whereas the socialist and communist nations continue to see themselves (even as they undergo tremendous changes) as adherents to the tenets of Marxism.

Therefore, it is appropriate for us to showcase in this chapter on society two thinkers—Karl Marx and John Rawls—who present and argue for the principles underlying these two dominant social philosophies. The writings of Marx are the origins of those social philosophies that call themselves Marxist, and John Rawls is considered by many to have articulated the central principles of modern liberalism.

MARX

Karl Marx, a seminal social philosopher of the modern age, is widely misunderstood. Marx was born in 1818 in Trier in the Rhineland to Jewish parents who, faced with anti-Semitism, turned Lutheran. After completing his studies at the gymnasium in Trier, Marx attended the universities of Bonn and Berlin.

When Marx entered the University of Berlin in 1836, the dominant intellectual influence throughout Germany and at the university was the philosophy of Georg Hegel (1770–1831). Central to Hegel's thought was the idea that reality is not fixed and static, but changing and dynamic. Life is constantly passing from one stage of being to another; the world is a place of constant change. But Hegel did not believe the change itself is arbitrary. On the contrary, he thought it proceeds according to a well-defined pattern or method, termed a **dialectic**.

The idea of the dialectic is that reality is full of contradictions. As reality unfolds, the contradictions are resolved and something new emerges. The procedure of the dialectical method can be represented as follows:

Thesis. Assertion of position or affirmation.
Antithesis. Assertion of opposite position or negation.
Synthesis. Union of the two opposites.

The Hegelian dialectic presumably expresses the process of development that Hegel believed pervades everything. By this account, there is only one reality: Idea. The only thing that is real is the rational; the Idea is thought itself thinking itself out. The process of thought thinking itself out is the dialectic.

In thinking itself out, thought arrives at the main antithesis to itself: inert matter. At this point Idea objectifies itself in matter: It becomes Nature or, for Hegel, the creation of the world. Life is the first sign of synthesis. Thought reappears in matter, organizing plants and displaying conscious instinct in animals. Ultimately, thought arrives at self-consciousness in human beings. The dialectic continues through human history.

To understand a society or culture, therefore, it is crucial to recognize the dialectical process that is

© Chinese School, (20th century)/Private Collection/Archives Charmet/The Bridgeman Art Library

Karl Marx: "What constitutes the alienation of labor? First, that the work is *external* to the worker, that it is not part of his nature; and that, consequently, he does not fulfill himself in his work but denies himself, has a feeling of misery rather than well-being, does not develop freely his mental and physical energies but is physically exhausted and mentally debased." Portrait of Karl Marx (1818–1893), c. 1970 (chromolitho). Artist: Chinese School (twentieth century).

operating. Each period in the history of a culture or society has a character of its own. This character can be viewed as a stage in the development from what preceded it to what follows it. This development proceeds by mental or spiritual laws. In effect, a culture has a personality of its own. Indeed, by Hegel's reckoning, the whole world or all of reality can be identified with a single character or personality—with what Hegel variously called *the Absolute, world self,* or *God* (taken in a pantheistic sense). All of human history, then, can be viewed as the progressive realization of this Absolute Spirit that is the synthesis of the thesis, Idea thinking itself out, with the antithesis, Idea spread out into Nature.

While at the University of Berlin, Marx read Hegel's complete works. He was drawn to a revolutionary aspect of Hegel's philosophy, namely, that history moves through a dialectical process of development. Marx also joined the Berlin Club of Young Hegelians but soon became convinced that philosophy alone was inadequate to change the world. What was needed was social and political action.

After completing his doctoral dissertation in 1841, Marx turned to socialistic journalism, taking an editorial position in 1842 at the *Rheinische Zeitung* (*Rhineland Gazette*). In this position, Marx became familiar with the social problems of the day and deepened the social orientation of his thought. Soon he became editor in chief of the newspaper and took it in a radical direction, conducting a campaign against Christian religion and the Christian state. As a result, the newspaper was shut down by the state censor in March 1843.

The suppression of the *Rheinische Zeitung* marked a new period in Marx's intellectual development, during which he began to formulate his materialistic concept of history and eventually became a communist. Also during this time, which he spent in Paris, Marx turned to a critical examination of Hegelian thought and in 1843 published an article on the subject: "Introduction to the Critique of Hegel's Philosophy." The article portrayed religion as an illusion resulting from the fact that the world is alienated and estranged from its real nature. Total revolution, Marx argued, is necessary to emancipate society from this condition.

Marx's critique of Hegel was significantly influenced by the work of Ludwig Feuerbach (1804–1872). In his *Essence of Christianity* (1841), Feuerbach had tried to show that Hegel's idealism was wrongheaded in that it had succeeded in eliminating physical reality. By contrast, Feuerbach held that philosophy is the science of reality, which consists of physical nature. Part of the illusion Feuerbach saw in Hegel was Hegel's belief in Absolute Spirit or God progressively realizing itself in history. In fact, according to Feuerbach, the ideas of religion are produced by human beings as a reflection of their own needs. Because individuals are dissatisfied or "alienated" in their practical lives, they need to believe in illusions such as those fostered in Hegelian philosophy. Thus, metaphysics is no more than an "esoteric psychology"; it is the expression of feelings within ourselves rather than truths about the universe. In particular, religion is the expression of alienation. Individuals can be freed from the illusions of religion only by realizing their purely human destiny in this world.

Feuerbach's influence on Marx was so great that Marx grew convinced that dialectical philosophy would avoid idealism by starting from human reality rather than from an ideal Absolute Spirit. Also, it could avoid mechanistic materialism by taking the concrete nature of the human being as its initial principle.

Although his reading of Feuerbach altered Marx's view of Hegel, Marx did preserve Hegel's notions of historical development and of alienation. These he wove into his own materialist concept of history. Like Hegel, Marx saw historical development operating in everything, but this development was material in character, not spiritual. The key to all history lay not in the individual's idea but in the economic conditions of his or her life. Again, while adopting Hegel's notion of alienation, Marx did not see it as metaphysical or religious in nature, but social and economic.

Marx's view of alienation can be found in his "Economic and Philosophic Manuscripts" (1844). His materialistic concepts of history can be found in various works of the same period: *The Holy Family* (1845), *The German Ideology* (1846), and *The Poverty of Philosophy* (1847). Until recently, Marx was best known as the author of *Das Kapital* (1867) and the *Communist Manifesto* (1848), which he wrote with friend and collaborator Friedrich Engels. Today, largely as a result of the publication of his early writings, the philosophical aspect of Marx's work has caught scholars' attention. Indeed, it is now thought that Marx's later writings cannot be fully understood and interpreted without reference to his earlier works, especially "Economic and Philosophic Manuscripts" and *The German Ideology.*

View of History

Distinctive in Marx's understanding of the world as a whole is his interpretation of history. Marx was firmly convinced that he had discovered a scientific method for studying the history of human societies, that eventually there would be a single science that combined the science of mankind with natural science. Accordingly, he held that there are universal laws behind historical change. Just as we can predict natural events such as eclipses, we can predict the future large-scale course of history from a knowledge of these laws. Just as physicists aim to uncover the natural laws of the universe, so Marx believed that he was laying bare the economic laws of modern society, the material laws of capitalist production. These laws, presumably, are working with iron necessity toward inevitable results.

Like Hegel, Marx held that each period in each culture has its own character and personality. Therefore, the only true universal laws in history are those concerned with the process by which one stage gives rise to the next. He viewed this developmental process as roughly divided into the Asiatic, the ancient, the feudal, and the "bourgeois" (capitalist) phases. When conditions are right, said Marx, each stage must give way to the next. Ultimately, capitalism will give way to communism. Writing with Engels in the *Communist Manifesto*, Marx puts it this way:

> *The history of all hitherto existing society is the history of class struggles.*
>
> Freeman and slave, patrician and plebian, lord and serf, guild-master and journeyman, in a word, oppressor and oppressed, stood in constant opposition to one another, carried on an uninterrupted, now hidden, now open fight, a fight that each time ended, either in a revolutionary re-constitution of society at large, or in the common ruin of the contending classes.
>
> In the earlier epochs of history, we find almost everywhere a complicated arrangement of society into various orders, a manifold gradation of social rank. In ancient Rome we have patricians, knights, plebians, slaves; in the middle ages, feudal lords, vassals, guild-masters, journeymen, apprentices, serfs; in almost all of these classes, again, subordinate gradations.
>
> The modern bourgeois society that has sprouted from the ruins of feudal society, has not done away with class antagonisms. It has but established new classes, new conditions of oppression, new forms of struggle in place of the old ones.
>
> Our epoch, the epoch of the bourgeoisie, possesses, however, this distinctive feature; it has simplified the class antagonisms. Society as a whole is more and more splitting up into two great hostile camps, into two great classes directly facing each other: Bourgeoisie and Proletariat.[1]

Marx believed that the universal laws operating in history are economic in nature. Moreover, he saw a causal connection between the economic structure and everything in society such that the mode of production of material life determines the general character of the social, political, and spiritual processes of life. In a word, the economic structure is the real basis by which everything else about society is determined.

Based on this view of history, Marx predicted that capitalism will become increasingly unstable economically. The class struggle between the *bourgeoisie* (ownership class) and *proletariat* (working class) will increase, with the proletariat getting both poorer and larger in number. The upshot will be a social revolution: The workers will seize power and eventually institute the new communist phase of history.

View of Human Nature

Related to Marx's view of history is his view of human nature, which we alluded to in Chapter 2. Apart from some obvious biological factors, such as the need to eat, Marx denies the existence of any essential human nature—that is, something that is true of every individual at all times everywhere. However, he does allow that humans are social beings, that to speak of human nature is really to speak about the totality of social relations. Accordingly, whatever any of us does is a social act, which presupposes the existence of other people standing in certain relations to us. In short, everything is socially learned.

The social influence is especially apparent in every activity of production. Producing what we need to survive physically is a social activity: It always requires that we interact and cooperate with others. Given Marx's account, it follows that the kind of individuals we are and the kinds of things we do are determined by the kind of society in which we live. In other words, for Marx it isn't the consciousness of individuals that defines their beings, but their social

1 Karl Marx and Friedrich Engels, *Communist Manifesto*, trans. Samuel Moore (Chicago: Regnery, 1969).

being that determines their consciousness. In commenting incisively on this point, professor of philosophy Leslie Stevenson writes the following:

> In modern terms, we can summarize this crucial point by saying that sociology is not reducible to psychology, i.e., it is not the case that everything about men can be explained in terms of facts about individuals; the kind of society they live in must be considered too. This methodological point is one of Marx's most distinctive contributions, and one of the most widely accepted. For this reason alone, he must be recognized as one of the founding fathers of sociology. And the method can of course be accepted whether or not one agrees with the particular conclusions Marx came to about economics and politics.[2]

Professor Stevenson goes on to point out that despite Marx's denial of individual human nature, Marx is prepared to offer at least one generalization about human nature. It is that humans are active, productive beings who distinguish themselves from other animals by the central, overriding fact that they produce their own means of subsistence. Indeed, according to Marx, it is not only natural for humans to work for their livings but right as well. Thus, by Marx's account, the life of productive activity is the right one for humans.

Granted that it is proper for humans to work for their livings, what may be said about the product of that work? Like Locke before him and numerous other thinkers after him (including Rawls and Nozick), Marx thought that individuals have a legitimate claim to the product of their own labor. But Marx rejects the notion that they are entitled to own property that they have not personally produced. Neither is property ownership permissible when it enriches the already affluent at the expense of other people, thereby forcing these people to work without benefit of the products of their labor. But this, according to Marx, is precisely what capitalism encourages: the exploitation of the large working class (proletariat) at the hands of the affluent few who own the means of production (bourgeoisie). Again, here are Marx and Engels writing on this subject in the *Communist Manifesto*:

> The bourgeoisie, wherever it has got the upper hand, has put an end to all feudal, patriarchal, idyllic relations. It has pitilessly torn asunder the motley feudal ties that bound man to his "natural superiors," and has left remaining no other nexus between man and man than naked self-interest, callous "cash payment." It has drowned the most heavenly ecstasies of religious fervor, of chivalrous enthusiasm, of Philistine sentimentalism, in the icy water of egotistical calculation. It has resolved personal worth into exchange value, and in place of the numberless indefeasible chartered freedoms, has set up that single, unconscionable freedom—Free Trade. In one word, for exploitation, veiled by religious and political illusions, it has substituted naked, shameless, direct, brutal exploitation.
>
> The bourgeoisie has stripped of its halo every occupation hitherto honored and looked up to with reverent awe. It has converted the physician, the lawyer, the priest, the poet, the name of science, into its paid wage-laborers.
>
> The bourgeoisie has torn away from the family its sentimental veil, and has reduced the family relation to a mere money relation.
>
> The bourgeoisie has disclosed how it came to pass that the brutal display of vigor in the Middle Ages, which Reactionists so much admire, found its fitting complement in the most slothful indolence. It has been the first to show what man's activity can bring about. It has accomplished wonders far surpassing Egyptian pyramids, Roman aqueducts, and Gothic cathedrals; it has conducted expeditions that put in the shade all former Exoduses of nations and crusades.
>
> The bourgeoisie cannot exist without constantly revolutionizing the instruments of production, and thereby the relations of production, and with them the whole relations of society. Conservation of the old modes of production in unaltered form, was, on the contrary, the first condition of existence for all earlier industrial classes. Constant revolutionizing of production, uninterrupted disturbance of all social conditions, everlasting uncertainty and agitation distinguish the bourgeois epoch from all earlier ones. All fixed, fast-frozen relations, with their train of ancient and venerable prejudices and opinions, are swept away, all new-formed ones become antiquated before they can ossify. All that is solid melts into air, all that is holy is profaned, and man is at last compelled to face, with sober senses, his real conditions of life, and his relations with his kind.
>
> The need of a constantly expanding market for its products chases the bourgeoisie over the whole surface of the globe. It must nestle everywhere, settle everywhere, establish connections everywhere.

---

2 Leslie Stevenson, *Seven Theories of Human Nature* (London: Oxford University Press, 1974), 54.

The bourgeoisie has through its exploitation of the world-market given a cosmopolitan character to production and consumption in every country. To the great chagrin of Reactionists, it has drawn from under the feet of industry the national ground on which it stood. All old-fashioned national industries have been destroyed and are daily being destroyed. They are dislodged by new industries, whose introduction becomes a life and death question for all civilized nations, by industries that no longer work up indigenous raw material, but raw material drawn from the remotest zones; industries whose products are consumed, not only at home, but in every quarter of the globe. In place of the old wants, satisfied by the productions of the country, we find new wants, requiring for their satisfaction the products of distant lands and climes. In place of the old local and national seclusion and self-sufficiency, we have intercourse in every direction, universal interdependence of nations. And as in material, so also in intellectual production. The intellectual creations of individual nations become common property. National one-sidedness and narrow-mindedness become more and more impossible, and from the numerous national and local literatures there arises a world-literature.

The bourgeoisie, by the rapid improvement of all instruments of production, by the immensely facilitated means of communication, draws all, even the most barbarian, nations into civilization. The cheap prices of its commodities are the heavy artillery with which it batters down all Chinese walls, with which it forces the barbarians' intensely obstinate hatred of foreigners to capitulate. It compels all nations, on pain of extinction, to adopt the bourgeois mode of production; it compels them to introduce what it calls civilization into their midst, i.e., to become bourgeois themselves. In a word, it creates a world after its own image.

The bourgeoisie has subjected the country to the rule of the towns. It has created enormous cities, has greatly increased the urban population as compared with the rural, and has thus rescued a considerable part of the population from the idiocy of rural life. Just as it has made the country dependent on the towns, so it has made barbarian and semi-barbarian countries dependent on the civilized ones, nations of peasants on nations of bourgeois, the East on the West.

The bourgeoisie keeps more and more doing away with the scattered state of the population, of the means of production, and of property. It has agglomerated population, centralized means of production, and has concentrated property in a few hands. The necessary consequence of this was political centralization. Independent, or but loosely connected provinces, with separate interests, laws, governments and systems of taxation, became lumped together in one nation, with one government, one code of laws, one national class-interest, one frontier and one customs-tariff.

The bourgeoisie, during its rule of scarce one hundred years, has created more massive and more colossal productive forces than have all preceding generations together. Subjection of Nature's forces to man, machinery, application of chemistry to industry and agriculture, steam-navigation, railways, electric telegraphs, clearing of whole continents for cultivation, canalization of rivers, whole populations conjured out of the ground—what earlier century had even a presentiment that such productive forces slumbered in the lap of social labor?[3]

According to Marx, the result of bourgeoisie exploitation is alienation, a key concept in his political and social philosophy.

Concept of Alienation

Marx borrowed his notion of alienation from Hegel and also from Feuerbach. For Hegel, alienation has its roots in a distinction between a subject and supposedly alien object. For Marx, the human can be considered the subject, and nature—that is, the human-created world—can be viewed as object. Humans are alienated from nature, from the world and the social relations they create. What is the cause of this alienation? Marx is rather fuzzy about this. At one point he traces its roots to the ownership of private property. Elsewhere he says that private property is not the cause but the effect of alienation. Whether private property is a cause or effect of alienation, one thing is evident: Marx associates alienation with economics, with the ownership of private property. Specifically, alienation consists of individuals not fulfilling themselves in work. Rather, because work is imposed on them as a means of satisfying the needs of others, they feel exploited and debased. What about workers who are paid handsomely for their efforts? Nevertheless, says Marx, they remain estranged. Insofar as the fruits of their labor are enjoyed by someone else, the work ultimately proves meaningless to them.

3 Marx and Engels, *Communist Manifesto.*

In the following selection from his "Economic and Philosophic Manuscripts," Marx summarizes his notion of alienation as the separation of individuals from the objects they create, which in turn results in separation from other people and ultimately from oneself:

> We shall begin from a *contemporary* economic fact. The worker becomes poorer the more wealth he produces and the more his production increases in power and extent. The worker becomes an ever cheaper commodity the more goods he creates. The *devaluation* of the human world increases in direct relation with the *increase in value* of the world of things. Labor does not only create goods; it also produces itself and the worker as a *commodity*, and indeed in the same proportion as it produces goods. . . .
>
> All these consequences follow from the fact that the worker is related to the *product of his labor as* to an *alien* object. For it is clear on this presupposition that the more the worker expends himself in work the more powerful becomes the world of objects which he creates in face of himself, the poorer he becomes in his inner life, and the less he belongs to himself. It is just the same as in religion. The more of himself man attributes to God the less he has left in himself. The worker puts his life into the object, and his life then belongs no longer to himself but to the object. The greater his activity, therefore, the less he possesses. What is embodied in the product of his labor is no longer his own. The greater this product is, therefore, the more he is diminished. The *alienation* of the worker in his product means not only that his labor becomes an object, assumes an *external* existence, but that it exists independently, *outside himself*, and alien to him, and that it stands opposed to him as an autonomous power. The life which he has given to the object sets itself against him as an alien and hostile force. . . .
>
> The worker becomes a slave of the object; first, in that he receives an *object of work*, i.e., receives *work*, and secondly, in that he receives *means of subsistence*. Thus the object enables him to exist, first as a *worker*, and secondly, as a *physical subject*. The culmination of this enslavement is that he can only maintain himself as a *physical subject* so far as he is a *worker*, and that it is only as a *physical subject* that he is a worker. . . .
>
> What constitutes the alienation of labor? First, that the work is *external* to the worker, that it is not part of his nature; and that, consequently, he does not fulfill himself in his work but denies himself, has a feeling of misery rather than well-being, does not develop freely his mental and physical energies but is physically exhausted and mentally debased. The worker, therefore, feels himself at home only during his leisure time, whereas at work he feels homeless. His work is not voluntary but imposed, *forced labor*. It is not the satisfaction of a need, but only a *means* for satisfying other needs. Its alien character is clearly shown by the fact that as soon as there is no physical or other compulsion it is avoided like the plague. External labor, labor in which man alienates himself, is a labor of self-sacrifice, of mortification. Finally, the external character of work for the worker is shown by the fact that it is not his own work but work for someone else, that in work he does not belong to himself but to another person. . . .
>
> We arrive at the result that man (the worker) feels himself to be freely active only in his animal functions—eating, drinking and procreating, or at most also in his dwelling and in personal adornment—while in his human functions he is reduced to an animal. The animal becomes human and the human becomes animal.
>
> Eating, drinking and procreating are of course also genuine human functions. But abstractly considered, apart from the environment of human activities, and turned into final and sole ends, they are animal functions.
>
> We have now considered the act of alienation of practical human activity, labor, from two aspects: (1) the relationship of the worker to the *product of labor* as an alien object which dominates him. This relationship is at the same time the relationship to the sensuous external world, to natural objects, as an alien and hostile world; (2) the relationship of labor to the *act of production* within *labor*. This is the relationship of the worker to his own activity as something alien and not belonging to him, activity as suffering (passivity), strength as powerlessness, creation as emasculation, the *personal* physical and mental energy of the worker, his personal life (for what is life but activity?), as an activity which is directed against himself; independent of him and not belonging to him. This is *self-alienation* as against the above-mentioned alienation of the *thing*.[4]

4 Karl Marx, "The Economic and Philosophic Manuscripts of 1844," in *Karl Marx: Early Writings*, trans T. B. Bottomore. Copyright © T. B. Bottomore, 1963. Used with permission of McGraw-Hill Book Co.

Marx goes on to infer yet a third aspect of estranged labor from the preceding two: the estrangement of the individual from the species itself. But this needn't concern us here.

In Marx's view, when workers are alienated, they cannot be free. They may have the political and social freedoms of speech, religion, and governance that classical liberals delineate. But freedom from government interference and persecution does not necessarily guarantee freedom from economic exploitation. And it is for this kind of freedom, freedom from alienation, that Marx and Engels feel such passion.

Sense of Freedom

How can humans be free of alienation? To begin with, they must recognize that the key to freedom and the lack of it lies in economics. Therefore, humans must return to a "natural" state in which they and their labor are one. This natural state is similar to Rousseau's in the sense that it recognizes the corrupting influence of society and calls for a conception of the state that will allow humans to be unselfish and nondestructive. But don't misunderstand. Marx is not advocating the end of work. On the contrary, he holds that work is humanizing, ennobling. Thus, he is urging people to liberate themselves from alienated work. Without this kind of freedom, which is basically a freedom from material need, other freedoms are a sham.

Basically, Marx prescribes a fairer distribution of wealth as a means for combating alienation and ensuring freedom. For Marx, justice requires that the means of production be owned by everyone. In unvarnished terms, in part this means no ownership of property except for those products a person makes directly. It also means an end to the worker/owner distinction, thereby making everyone a laborer who shares in the benefits of his or her labor. Specifically, Marx calls for nationalization of land, factories, transport, and banks as a way of attaining freedom from alienation. But insofar as Marx presumably believes that (1) the state is the basis of all social ills, and (2) nationalization evidently will exacerbate this by concentrating power in the hands of the state, it isn't at all clear how such institutional changes could affect freedom. This observation has led Leslie Stevenson to suggest that we understand Marx as saying,

> at least in his early phase, that alienation consists in the lack of community. In other words, since the State is not a real community, individuals cannot see their work as contributing to a group of which they are members. It would follow that freedom from alienation would be won by decentralizing, not nationalizing, the State in genuine communities or "communes." These entities would be characterized by the abolition of money, specialization, and private property.[5]

Indeed, it may be this community element of Marx's vision that explains why Marx continues to win and hold followers. After all, it is difficult to disagree with such ideas as a decentralized society in which individuals cooperate in communities for the common good, technology is harnessed and directed for the interest of all, and the relationship between society and nature is harmonized. At the same time, Marx gives no good reason for assuming that the communist society will achieve any of these ideals. In fact, if the history of Russia in the past century is any indication, quite the opposite seems the case.

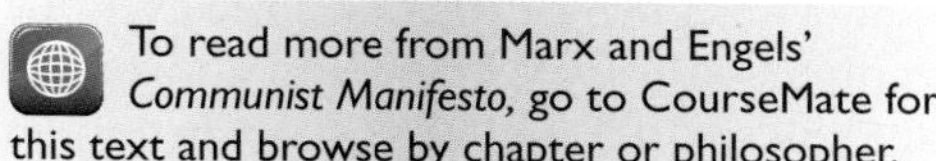

To read more from Marx and Engels' *Communist Manifesto,* go to CourseMate for this text and browse by chapter or philosopher.

RAWLS

A substantial part of the world's population today lives in societies that still claim to be based on the socialist views proposed by Marx. Most of the rest of the world lives in societies that by and large follow a philosophy termed *liberalism*. Liberalism has its roots in the individualism of John Locke and John Stuart Mill. At the heart of early liberalism was the view that the best society is one in which individuals are left free to pursue their own interests and fulfillment as each chooses. As Mill argued, the only restraints to which adult individuals should be subject are those necessary to keep one individual from harming others.

Contemporary liberalism has retained this fundamental commitment to individual liberty but has added to it an awareness of the extent to which economic realities can indirectly limit an individual's liberty. For example, the choices of a poor person are much restricted by that person's poverty, whereas wealth and property endow the rich with choices and power not available to the poor. Therefore,

5 Stevenson, *Seven Theories of Human Nature*, 58.

contemporary liberalism has tended to incorporate the view that individuals can be constrained to provide economic support for the poor through welfare programs. Contemporary liberalism has also tended to accept the view that individuals should be given some protection against the economic power of the wealthy through laws that protect the worker. Undoubtedly, these contemporary modifications of liberalism have been greatly influenced by Marx. To a large extent, in fact, contemporary liberalism is the response that capitalist societies have made to Marx.

Perhaps the best representative of contemporary liberalism is John Rawls (1921–2002), a philosopher who taught at Harvard University. In his now-classic work *A Theory of Justice*, Rawls presents a brilliant and often passionate argument in support of contemporary liberalism. Many philosophers hold, in fact, that the modern world is faced with a fundamental choice between two kinds of societies: the kind of socialist society advocated by Marx and the kind of liberal society advocated by Rawls.

Rawls was born in 1921 and received his doctorate in philosophy from Princeton University in 1950. From 1953 to 1959 he taught at Cornell University and then moved to the Massachusetts Institute of Technology. In 1962, he began teaching philosophy at Harvard University.

For Rawls, the most important question to ask about a society is this one: Is it just? The laws and institutions of a society must embody justice, or they must be reformed:

> Justice is the first virtue of social institutions, as truth is of systems of thought. A theory however elegant and economical must be rejected or revised if it is untrue; likewise laws and institutions no matter how efficient and well-arranged must be reformed or abolished if they are unjust. Each person possesses an inviolability founded on justice that even the welfare of society as a whole cannot override. For this reason justice denies that the loss of freedom for some is made right by a greater good shared by others. It does not allow that the sacrifices imposed on a few are outweighed by the larger sum of advantages enjoyed by many. Therefore in a just society the liberties of equal citizenship are taken as settled; the rights secured by justice are not subject to political bargaining or to the calculus of social interests. The only thing that permits us to acquiesce in an erroneous theory is the lack of a better one; analogously, an injustice is tolerable only when it is necessary to avoid an even greater injustice. Being first virtues of human activities, truth and justice are uncompromising.[6]

If we are to analyze the justice of society, Rawls claims, we must look not at the particular actions of individuals but at society's basic political, economic, and social *institutions.* Like Marx, Rawls acknowledges that social relationships have a deep and profound effect on the individual's sense of fulfillment. A society's institutions are what primarily determine what we can do and what our lives as individuals will be like. From the very beginning they favor some of us and hamper others:

> Many different kinds of things are said to be just and unjust: not only laws, institutions, and social systems, but also particular actions of many kinds, including decisions, judgments, and imputations. We also call the attitudes and dispositions of persons, and persons themselves, just and unjust. Our topic, however, is that of social justice. For us the primary subject of justice is the basic structure of society, or more exactly, the way in which the major social institutions distribute fundamental rights and duties and determine the division of advantages from social cooperation. By major institutions I understand the political constitution and the principal economic and social arrangements. Thus the legal protection of freedom of thought and liberty of conscience, competitive markets, private property in the means of production, and the monogamous family are examples of major social institutions. Taken together as one scheme, the major institutions define men's rights and duties and influence their life-prospects, what they can expect to be and how well they can hope to do. The basic structure is the primary subject of justice because its effects are so profound and present from the start. The intuitive notion here is that this structure contains various social positions and that men born into different positions have different expectations of life determined, in part, by the political system as well as by economic and social circumstances. In this way the institutions of society favor certain starting places over others. These are especially deep inequalities. Not only are they persuasive, but they affect men's initial chances in life; yet they cannot possibly be justified by an appeal to the notions of merit

6 Reprinted by permission of the publisher from *A Theory of Justice* by John Rawls, pp. 3–4, Cambridge, Mass.: The Belknap Press of Harvard University Press, Copyright © 1971, 1999 by the President and Fellows of Harvard College.

> or desert. It is these inequalities, presumably inevitable in the basic structure of any society, to which the principles of social justice must in the first instance apply. These principles, then, regulate the choice of a political constitution and the main elements of the economic and social system. The justice of a social scheme depends essentially on how fundamental rights and duties are assigned and on the economic opportunities and social conditions in the various sectors of society.[7]

But what principles and rules should govern our social institutions? What guidelines and formulas should we follow when designing our institutions if those institutions are to be just? Rawls argues that to discover what just institutions should be like, we should engage in a kind of imaginary experiment. Imagine, he says, that before people formed a society, they could all gather together in a large meeting. And suppose that at this imaginary first meeting (or "original position"), no one knew what place each person would have in their future society. No one knew whether he or she would turn out to be rich or poor, owner or worker, ruler or ruled. In fact, suppose that no one knew even whether he or she would turn out to be male or female, intelligent or stupid, healthy or sick, strong or weak, black or white. In other words, suppose that everyone at this original meeting is "behind a veil of ignorance," where no one knows what each will be like in the future society.

Suppose, then, that the people at this original meeting had to choose the basic rules or principles that would govern their future society. Clearly, Rawls says, the parties in such an original position would have to be perfectly fair to everyone because no one would know who he or she might turn out to be. In such a situation, a person would not choose principles that favor whites over blacks because in their future society that person might turn out to be black. Neither would a person choose principles that favor the rich over the poor because the person might turn out to be poor. In short, the veil of ignorance would force everyone to choose principles that would be perfectly just to everyone:

> Thus we are to imagine that those who engage in social cooperation choose together, in one joint act, the principles which are to assign basic rights and duties and to determine the division of social benefits. Men are to decide in advance how they are to regulate their claims against one another and what is to be the foundation charter of their society. Just as each person must decide by rational reflection what constitutes his good, that is, the system of ends which it is rational for him to pursue, so a group of persons must decide once and for all what is to count among them as just and unjust. The choice which rational men would make in this hypothetical situation of equal liberty, assuming for the present that this choice problem has a solution, determines the principles of justice.
>
> In justice as fairness the original position of equality corresponds to the state of nature in the traditional theory of the social contract. This original position is not, of course, thought of as an actual historical state of affairs, much less as a primitive condition of culture. It is understood as a purely hypothetical situation characterized so as to lead to a certain conception of justice. Among the essential features of this situation is that no one knows his place in society, his class position or social status, nor does any one know his fortune in the distribution of natural assets and abilities, his intelligence, strength, and the like. I shall even assume that the parties do not know their conceptions of the good or their special psychological propensities. The principles of justice are chosen behind a veil of ignorance. This ensures that no one is advantaged or disadvantaged in the choice of principles by the outcome of natural chance or the contingency of social circumstances. Since all are similarly situated and no one is able to design principles to favor his particular condition, the principles of justice are the result of a fair agreement or bargain. For given the circumstances of the original position, the symmetry of everyone's relations to each other, this initial situation is fair between individuals as moral persons, that is, as rational beings with their own ends and capable, I shall assume, of a sense of justice. The original position is, one might say, the appropriate initial status quo, and thus the fundamental agreements reached in it are fair. This explains the propriety of the name "justice as fairness": it conveys the idea that the principles of justice are agreed to in an initial situation that is fair. The name does not mean that the concepts of justice and fairness are the same, any more than the phrase "poetry as metaphor" means that the concept of poetry and metaphor are the same.[8]

7 Ibid., 7.

8 Ibid., 11–13.

Rawls then argues that the imaginary parties to this original position would not choose utilitarian principles. Utilitarian principles, Rawls claims, sometimes require some people to suffer losses for the sake of maximizing society's utility. Clearly, a person in the original position would not agree to this because that person might turn out to be one of the people forced to suffer losses. Instead, Rawls claims, the parties would settle on these two principles of justice: first, that everyone in society must have equal political rights and duties, and second, that the only justifiable economic inequalities are those required to make everyone better off by serving as incentives:

> In working out the conception of justice as fairness one main task clearly is to determine which principles of justice would be chosen in the original position. To do this we must describe this situation in some detail and formulate with care the problem of choice which it presents. These matters I shall take up in the immediately succeeding chapters. It may be observed, however, that once the principles of justice are thought of as arising from an original agreement in a situation of equality, it is an open question whether the principle of utility would be acknowledged. Offhand it hardly seems likely that persons who view themselves as equals, entitled to press their claims upon one another, would agree to a principle which may require lesser life prospects for some simply for the sake of a greater sum of advantages enjoyed by others. Since each desires to protect his interests, his capacity to advance his conception of the good, no one has a reason to acquiesce in an enduring loss for himself in order to bring about a greater net balance of satisfaction. In the absence of strong and lasting benevolent impulses, a rational man would not accept a basic structure merely because it maximized the algebraic sum of advantages irrespective of its permanent effects on his own basic rights and interests. Thus it seems that the principle of utility is incompatible with the conception of social cooperation among equals for mutual advantage. It appears to be inconsistent with the idea of reciprocity implicit in the notion of a well-ordered society. Or, at any rate, so I shall argue.
>
> I shall maintain instead that the persons in the initial situation would choose two rather different principles: the first requires equality in the assignment of basic rights and duties, while the second holds that social and economic inequalities, for example inequalities of wealth and authority, are just only if they result in compensating benefits for everyone, and in particular for the least advantaged members of society. These principles rule out justifying institutions on the grounds that the hardships of some are offset by a greater good in the aggregate. It may be expedient but it is not just that some should have less in order that others may prosper. But there is no injustice in the greater benefits earned by a few provided that the situation of persons not so fortunate is thereby improved. The intuitive idea is that since everyone's well-being depends upon a scheme of cooperation without which no one could have a satisfactory life, the division of advantages should be such as to draw forth the willing cooperation of everyone taking part in it, including those less well situated. Yet this can be expected only if reasonable terms are proposed. The two principles mentioned seem to be a fair agreement on the basis of which those better endowed, or more fortunate in their social position, neither of which we can be said to deserve, could expect the willing cooperation of others when some workable scheme is a necessary condition of the welfare of all. Once we decide to look for a conception of justice that nullifies the accidents of natural endowment and the contingencies of social circumstance as counters in quest for political and economic advantage, we are led to these principles. They express the result of leaving aside those aspects of the social world that seem arbitrary from a moral point of view.[9]

Rawls later elaborates his principles. The two principles of justice that would be chosen, he writes, can be formulated as follows:

> First: each person is to have an equal right to the most extensive basic liberty compatible with a similar liberty for others. Second: social and economic inequalities are to be arranged so that they are both (a) to the greatest benefit of the least advantaged and (b) attached to offices and positions open to all under conditions of fair equality of opportunity.[10]

According to Rawls, the parties to the original position would choose the first principle, which requires equal political freedoms for everyone, because each person would want to at least be equal to everyone else in the political sphere. However, he claims, the parties would agree to allow social

9 Ibid., 14–15.
10 Ibid., 60, 83.

and *economic* inequalities if such "inequalities set up various incentives which succeed in eliciting more productive efforts" from people. For example, allowing higher wages for some people can spur them on to produce more goods, and this added productivity will work to everyone's benefit. But the parties to the original position will each want to have an equal chance at these more lucrative positions. Consequently, they will insist that these positions be "open to all under conditions of fair equality of opportunity." Moreover, the parties to the original position will want to protect themselves in case they turn out to be among the "least advantaged." So they will agree that the benefits produced by allowing inequalities should be used to protect the least advantaged.

Rawls' two principles, then, are the principles that he thought anyone—ourselves included—would choose if he or she were behind the veil of ignorance. And because the original position requires us to be absolutely fair and just, these two principles are themselves just and express what justice requires of us.

And what does justice require of us, according to Rawls? Certainly not the kind of socialist state advocated by Marx, in which individuals are not free to own and exchange private property; in which all land, factories, transport, and banks are nationalized and controlled by the state; and in which free markets are prohibited. Neither does justice require an absolute equality. Instead, Rawls argues, justice requires freedom and merely *political* equality. In particular, justice requires freedom from the interference of the state, and it allows (although it does not *require*) private property and free markets. Justice also allows *economic* inequalities, whereas it requires that the state must provide adequate welfare programs for the poor and the disadvantaged.

In short, justice requires and allows more or less what Western social, economic, and political institutions require and allow. This is perhaps not surprising because Rawls' philosophy is intended to defend Western liberal ideals. It is, perhaps, the most powerful alternative to contemporary Marxism and the most powerful contemporary defense of liberalism.

QUESTIONS

1. In your own words, explain what the bourgeoisie is and how it developed. Does the bourgeoisie exist today? Explain.
2. To what extent does Marx's concept of alienation apply to modern workers? To what extent does it apply to modern college students? How would Marx analyze the contemporary trend toward careerism among today's college students (that is, the trend to see a college education as preparation for a job or a career instead of as a humanizing and liberating activity)?
3. Explain in your own words what Rawls' "original position" is and why it is supposed to show us the meaning of justice. Do you agree that using the original position is an adequate way of determining what justice requires? Why? Do you think that Rawls' two principles of justice are adequate? Why?
4. How do Rawls' views about society differ from Marx's? What assumptions do you think Marx and Rawls make that lead each of them to such different conclusions?
5. What do you think Rawls would have said about the justice or injustice of making pornography illegal? About making drugs such as marijuana and cocaine illegal? About nationalizing businesses? About the international problem of poverty?

9 Postscript: The Meaning of Life

There is both pleasure and pain in tragedy and comedy, not only on the stage, but on the greater stage of human life.
PLATO

OUTLINE AND LEARNING OBJECTIVES

9.1 **Does Life Have Meaning?**

OBJECTIVE | When finished, you'll be able to:

- Interpret the question whether life has meaning and explain why it is important.
- Explain why some argue that the question itself is meaningless.

9.2 **The Theistic Response to Meaning**

OBJECTIVE | When finished, you'll be able to:

- Describe how some have found the meaning of life in a divine reality, and critically evaluate this view.

9.3 **Meaning and Human Progress**

OBJECTIVE | When finished, you'll be able to:

- Describe how some have found the meaning of life in human progress, and critically evaluate this view.

9.4 **The Nihilist Rejection of Meaning**

OBJECTIVE | When finished, you'll be able to:

- Describe the nihilist response to the question of whether life has meaning and explain how nihilists have argued for their response; critically evaluate the nihilist view.

9.5 **Meaning as a Self-Chosen Commitment**

OBJECTIVE | When finished, you'll be able to:

- Explain the idea of subjective meaning as something created by the individual and why some have held this view; critically evaluate this view.

Chapter Summary

© LeNico/iStockphoto.com

We have completed our overview of the central questions of philosophy: What am I? Is there a God? What is real? What can I know? What is truth? What ought I to do? What is a just society? We close now with a look at a question that is usually omitted from introductory courses in philosophy: Does life have any meaning? It is omitted because it is a difficult question and discussing it requires understanding some of the views that students are not exposed to until after taking an introductory philosophy course. Yet for many people this is an urgent question, one that brings them to philosophy in the first place and that demands an answer. It is fitting that we conclude our philosophical journey with this question, both because the question is so important and because, having examined the central issues of philosophy, we are now better prepared to inquire into the question of life's meaning. Since our discussion draws upon several philosophical views from earlier chapters, it also serves to bring these perspectives together. For these reasons, we call this closing chapter a "postscript."

9.1 Does Life Have Meaning?

Perhaps the most important question in philosophy is the question "Does life have meaning?" The philosopher and novelist Albert Camus, in fact, argued that it is the only important philosophical question:

> There is but one truly serious philosophical problem, and that is suicide. Judging whether life is or is not worth living amounts to answering the fundamental question of philosophy. All the rest—whether or not the world has three dimensions, whether the mind has nine or twelve categories—comes afterwards. These are games; one must first answer [the fundamental question]. . . .
>
> If I ask myself how to judge that this question is more urgent than that, I reply that one judges by the actions it entails. I have never seen anyone die for the ontological argument. Galileo, who held a scientific truth of great importance, abjured it with the greatest ease as soon as it endangered his life. In a certain sense, he did right. That truth was not worth the stake. Whether the earth or the sun revolves around the other is a matter of profound indifference. To tell the truth, it is a futile question. On the other hand, I see many people die because they judge that life is not worth living. I see others paradoxically getting killed for the ideas or illusions that give them a reason for living (what is called a reason for living is also an excellent reason for dying). I therefore conclude that the meaning of life is the most urgent of questions.[1]

QUICK REVIEW
Camus claimed that the most urgent and "the one truly serious question in philosophy" is the question whether life has meaning and thus worth living, because people are willing to die for this question.

People often ask about the meaning of life when death enters their lives: either the death of someone they love or their own imminent death. Death brings everything we are or ever hoped to be to a complete end. What's the point of all our striving, then? The shortness of human life, the insignificance of human life in the face of the great immensity and eternity of the universe, the apparent unconcern and uncaring impersonal coldness of the universe—all these factors can lead people to question whether human life in general, and their life in particular, have any meaning.

But for many people, the question of whether life has any meaning arises even when death is not near. Many people seem to reach a point in their lives when

1 Albert Camus, "An Absurd Reasoning," from *The Myth of Sisyphus and Other Essays*, trans. Justin O'Brien (New York: Knopf, 1955).

nothing seems of any value, when the things they have spent their lives chasing begin to seem pointless, and they feel like Shakespeare's Macbeth when he realized that all his killing, striving, and achievement had left him with nothing but despair:

> *Life's but a walking shadow, a poor player*
> *That struts and frets his hour upon the stage*
> *And then is heard no more. It is a tale*
> *Told by an idiot, full of sound and fury,*
> *Signifying nothing.*

The despair that gripped Macbeth is the despair that comes when a person becomes convinced that life is pointless and has no meaning. Perhaps no one has written of such despair more poignantly than the great Russian novelist Leo Tolstoy:

> In my writings I had advocated what to me was the only truth, that it was necessary to live in such a way as to derive the greatest comfort for oneself and one's family.
>
> Thus I proceeded to live. But five years ago something very strange began to happen with me: I was overcome by minutes at first of perplexity and then of an arrest of life, as though I did not know how to live or what to do, and I lost myself and was dejected. But that passed, and I continued to live as before. Then those minutes of perplexity were repeated oftener and oftener, and always in one and the same form. These arrests of life found their expression in ever the same questions: "Why? Well, and then?"
>
> At first I thought that those were simply aimless, inappropriate questions. . . . But the questions began to repeat themselves oftener and oftener, answers were demanded more and more persistently, and like dots that fall in the same spot, these questions, without any answers, thickened into one black blotch. . . .
>
> I felt that what I was standing on had given way, that I had no foundation to stand on, that that which I lived by no longer existed, and that I had nothing to live by. . . .
>
> All this happened to me when I was surrounded on every side by what is considered to be complete happiness. I had a good, loving, and beloved wife, good children, and a large estate, which grew and increased without any labor on my part. I was respected by my neighbors and friends, more than ever before, was praised by strangers, and, without any self-deception, could consider my name famous. . . . And while in such condition I arrived at the conclusion that I could not live. . . .
>
> This mental condition expressed itself to me in this form: my life is a stupid, mean trick played on me by somebody. . . . Involuntarily I imagined that there, somewhere, there was somebody who was now having fun as he looked down upon me and saw me, who had lived for thirty or forty years, learning, developing, growing in body and mind, now that I had become strengthened in mind and had reached that summit of life from which it lay all before me, standing as a complete fool on that summit and seeing clearly that there was nothing in life and never would be. And that was fun to him. . . .
>
> I could not ascribe any sensible meaning to a single act or to my whole life. I was only surprised that I had not understood this from the start. All this had long ago been known to everybody. Sooner or later there would come diseases and death (they had come already) to my dear ones and to me, and there would be nothing left but stench and worms. All my affairs, no matter what they might be, would sooner or later be forgotten, and I myself should not exist. So why should I worry about all these things? How could a man fail to see this and live,—that was surprising! A person could live only so long as he was drunk; but the moment he sobered up, he could not help seeing that all that was only a deception, and a stupid deception at that! . . .
>
> "My family?" I said to myself. "But my family, my wife and children, they are also human beings. They are in precisely the same condition that I am in: they must either live in the lie or see the terrible truth. Why should they live? Why should

QUICK REVIEW
Tolstoy, an accomplished and wealthy writer with a loving family, came to feel that life had no meaning, as if someone had played a mean trick on him; he felt that life was meaningless for his family and everyone.

> I love them, why guard, raise, and watch them? Is it for the same despair which is in me, or for dullness of perception? Since I love them, I cannot conceal the truth from them,—every step in understanding will lead them up to this truth. And the truth is death."
>
> "Art and Poetry?" For a long time, under the influence of the success of human praise, I tried to persuade myself that that was a thing which could be done, even though death should come and destroy everything, my deeds, as well as my memory of them; but soon I came to see that this, too was a deception. It was clear to me that art was an adornment of life, a decoy of life. But life had lost all its attractiveness for me. How, then, could I entrap others? So long as I did not live my own life, and a strange life bore me on its waves; so long as I believed that life had some sense, although I was not able to express it,—the reflections of life of every description in poetry and in the arts afforded me pleasure, and I was delighted to look at life through this little mirror of art; but when I began to look for the meaning of life, when I experienced the necessity of living myself, that little mirror became either useless, superfluous, and ridiculous, or painful to me. I could no longer console myself with what I saw in the mirror, namely, that my situation was stupid and desperate. It was all right for me to rejoice so long as I believed in the depth of my soul that life had some sense; then the play of lights—of the comical, the tragical, the touching, the beautiful, the terrible in life—afforded me amusement. But when I knew that life was meaningless and terrible, the play in the little mirror could no longer amuse me. . . .[2]

QUICK REVIEW
With no meaning to express in his art, Tolstoy stopped writing and became depressed.

Tolstoy felt that life for him—one of the world's most accomplished and acclaimed writers—no longer had meaning. Previously, his family and his writing had sustained him. In his love for his family he had found "the only truth," and in poetry and art he had found "reflections of life" that had sustained him. But now that he realized he no longer knew the meaning of life—perhaps had never known it—neither his art nor his family sustained him. Finding no meaning to express in his art, he stopped writing and fell into a deep depression.

We return to Tolstoy shortly when we examine how he eventually answered the question of the meaning of life. Here we need to note only that Tolstoy's need to find meaning in life is a need that all of us have. Events force almost all of us to ask eventually whether the things we have devoted our lives to achieving have any real meaning. This is the question that first brings many people to philosophy, and it is the question that we now discuss.

What Does the Question Mean?

QUICK REVIEW
Ayer, Carnap, and the other logical positivists claim that the question is meaningless because it is not a factual question that can be resolved through sense perception. Critics reply that many important questions can't be answered through sense perception.

But what, exactly, does this question mean? There are some philosophers who have claimed that the question itself has no meaning: It is literally meaningless. This is the position of the logical positivists, whose empiricist views we saw earlier when we discussed reality. A. J. Ayer and Rudolf Carnap, for example, argue that aside from tautologies, the only meaningful questions are factual questions whose answers can be found through sense observation. Questions about the meaning of life, they claim, cannot be resolved by sense perception and so have no meaning.

But most people today believe that the logical positivists are mistaken. In particular, people reject the idea that questions are meaningless if they cannot be resolved through sense perception. Many of our most pressing social, religious, and

2 Leo Tolstoy, *My Confession*, trans. Leo Wiener (London: J. M. Dent & Sons, 1905), reprinted in E. D. Klemke, ed., *The Meaning of Life* (New York: Oxford University Press, 1981), 9–13.

moral questions seem to make perfectly good sense yet cannot be resolved through our senses. Moreover, many modern philosophers have shown—as we will see—that the question of the meaning of life can be given a perfectly understandable sense.

But if the question is not meaningless, what, then, does it mean? One way of understanding the question "What is the meaning of life?" is to take it as asking whether my life has a larger or more important purpose than merely living. In other words, is my individual life related to something bigger or more important that gives my life value?

This seems to be the way that Leo Tolstoy understood the question when despite being respected and loved, he fell into a deep depression caused by his feeling that life is meaningless. Tolstoy came out of his profound funk when he reached the conclusion that if life is to have meaning, it has to be related to something larger and more important than himself.

QUICK REVIEW
Tolstoy and others take the question to be asking whether life has a larger or more important purpose than merely living.

9.2 The Theistic Response to Meaning

One way, perhaps the most common way, that people answer the question of whether life has meaning is in terms of their relationship to God. This is an ancient response to the question. For example, we saw earlier in Chapter 2 that Thomas Aquinas argues that everything has a purpose, including human beings:

> Now here on earth, the simplest elements exist for the sake of compound minerals; these latter exist for the sake of living bodies, among which plants exist for animals, and animals for humans. . . . Now humans naturally desire, as their ultimate purpose, to know the first cause of all things. But the first cause of all things is God. So the ultimate purpose of human beings is to know God.[3]

Aquinas' view can be called the theistic response to the question of meaning. The theistic response claims that human life has meaning because humans are part of a larger plan or order devised by God. Within that plan, all things in the universe have purpose and value. The purpose of human beings, in particular, is to know God and be perfectly united with Him. Life on earth, while brief, is valuable insofar as it is a preparation for that future union with God. Human life, then, is not a tiny, insignificant, and meaningless "hour upon the stage" that ends with nothing. Human life has a meaning insofar as it has a purpose that relates me to a larger more significant whole, a whole within which I have a place.

QUICK REVIEW
Aquinas' theistic response to the question is that the meaning of human life is related to the purpose that humans have in a larger plan or cosmic order devised by God, and this purpose is to know and be united with God. Tolstoy accepted this as a reason for living.

This theistic response is the one that led Tolstoy out of his depression. As Tolstoy wrote,

> Rational knowledge brought me to the recognition that life was meaningless—my life stopped, and I wanted to destroy myself. When I looked around at people, at all humanity, I saw that people lived and asserted that they knew the meaning of life. I looked back at myself: I lived so long as I knew the meaning of life. As to other people, so even to me, did faith give the meaning of life and the possibility of living. . . . What, then, was faith? I understood . . . that faith was the knowledge of the meaning of human life, in consequence of which man did not destroy himself, but lived. . . . If a man lives he believes in something. If he did not believe that he ought to live for some purpose, he would not live.

3 Thomas Aquinas, *Summa Contra Gentiles*, bk. III, ch. 22, paras. 7, 8, ch. 25, para. 11, translated by Manuel Velasquez.

> Then I began to cultivate the acquaintance of the believers from among the poor, the simple and unlettered folk, of pilgrims, monks, dissenters, peasants. . . . I began to examine closely the lives and beliefs of these people, and the more I examined them, the more did I become convinced that they had the real faith, that their faith was necessary for them, and that it alone gave them a meaning and possibility of life. . . .
>
> I began to love these people. . . . Thus I lived for about two years, and within me took place a transformation. . . . What happened with me was that the life of our circle—of the rich and the learned—not only disgusted me, but even lost all its meaning. All our acts, reflections, sciences, arts—all that appeared to me in a new light. I saw that all that was mere pampering of the appetites, and that no meaning could be found in it; but the life of all the working masses, of all humanity, which created life, presented itself to me in its real significance. I saw that that was life itself and that the meaning given to this life was truth, and I accepted it.[4]

QUICK REVIEW
Each religion offers its own view of the cosmic whole in terms of which human life has meaning, but all theistic views give meaning to life by relating the individual to a divine reality that is larger and more important than the individual is.

There is, of course, not just one theistic response. Each of the world's religions provides its own interpretation of the larger cosmic whole of which humans are but a part and in terms of which human life has meaning. Some, like Islam, infuse life with meaning in a way that is much like the theist response of Christianity. Other religions, like Hinduism and Buddhism, relate human life to a view of the universe that is very different from the universe of Christianity. Hinduism asserts the doctrine of rebirth and karma and holds out the goal of absorption into Brahman after ascending the stages of consciousness. Buddhism also asserts the doctrine of rebirth and the experience of liberation from the great wheel of rebirth through the eightfold way whose goal is enlightenment. But despite their profound differences, all religions give meaning to life by relating the individual to a divine reality that is larger and more important than the individual is.

The theist response to the search for meaning satisfies many believers, but it also raises difficult questions. First, the response obviously can depend on accepting the belief that God exists. However, we saw when we discussed the many proofs for the existence of God in Chapter 4 that it is very difficult to prove to ourselves that there is a god. The theist response, then, says little to the nonbeliever.

Second, some, like the American philosopher Kurt Baier, have argued that there is something "morally repugnant" about the theist response.[5] The theist view claims that humans have meaning because they have a purpose that is assigned them by God. But to see humans in this way is to see them as objects or things. Consider that tools and utensils have purposes. For example, the purpose of a knife is to cut; the purpose of a hammer is to nail. To say that humans have a purpose is to see humans as tools that are being used by God. But it is morally wrong to use humans as tools. As we saw when we discussed Kant's views on ethics, humans should be treated as ends and never used as means.

QUICK REVIEW
Critics argue that the theistic response is irrelevant to the nonbeliever. Baier claims that to say humans have a purpose assigned to them by God reduces humans to tools that God is using. Nielsen says from the fact that someone else (e.g., God) has a purpose for me, it does not follow that my life has meaning because values are not established by facts.

Third, some critics, such as the philosopher Kai Nielsen, have claimed that the theist response makes an illogical jump.[6] The theistic response says that because God has a purpose for my life, my life has meaning. But the second part of this statement does not follow from the first. For example, suppose that when you were born, your father had a purpose for you: He wanted you to carry on the family name and take over the family business. Clearly, from the fact that your father had a purpose for you, it does not follow that your life must have meaning. In a similar way, critics claim that from the fact that God or some being out in the universe somewhere has

---

4 Leo Tolstoy, *My Confession*, 23–24.

5 Kurt Baier, "The Meaning of Life," in *The Meaning of Life*, ed. Steven Sanders and David R. Cheney (Englewood Cliffs, NJ: Prentice Hall, 1980), 56.

6 Kai Nielsen, "Linguistic Philosophy and 'The Meaning of Life,'" in *The Meaning of Life*, ed. Sanders and Cheney, 129–154.

© Louvre, Paris, France/The Bridgeman Art Library International

Liberty Leading the People, by Eugène Delacroix (1830). Hegel claims that if the individual person becomes a part of the progressive movement of history toward ever greater freedom, his or her life will have meaning. Apart from this forward sweep of history, the individual cannot find meaning.

a purpose for you, it does not follow that your life must have a meaning. If some being on a star somewhere, or even God, decides to assign you a purpose, it does not follow that this purpose gives meaning to your life. A life with meaning seems to be a life with value, and facts about other beings—even facts about God—cannot give value to your life.

9.3 Meaning and Human Progress

Many philosophers have accepted the view that the individual life has meaning only when it is related to something bigger or more important than the individual's life. But, instead of suggesting that God is the "bigger" whole that gives life meaning, they have proposed that there are other, larger realities that can infuse the individual's life with meaning. In particular, some philosophers have suggested that contributing to human progress can give meaning to human life.

Georg Hegel, for example, argued that history shows progress. "The History of the world," Hegel wrote, "is none other than the progress of the consciousness of freedom."[7] As history develops, Hegel claims, people see more clearly that humans are essentially free, and more people actually become free. In the ancient "Oriental" empires of China, India, and Egypt, Hegel claims, only one person—the emperor—was recognized as completely free. Everyone else was treated despotically. These empires were succeeded by the Greek and Roman empires, in which all citizens were recognized as free. But many people in these empires were slaves and had no freedom. The Greek and Roman empires, then, recognized that only *some* are free. These empires were eventually succeeded by the nations of the modern world. In the modern nations, which Hegel calls the "German nations," slavery is abolished and all people are finally recognized as free:

> The Orientals have not attained the knowledge that Spirit—Man as such—is free; and because they do not know this, they are not free. They only know that one is

7 Georg Wilhelm Friedrich Hegel, *The Philosophy of History*, trans. J. Sibree (New York: Dover, 1956), 19.

> free. But on this very account, the freedom of that one is only caprice; ferocity—brutal recklessness of passion, or a mildness and tameness of the desires, which is itself only an accident of Nature—mere caprice like the former—that one is therefore only a Despot; not a free man.
>
> The consciousness of Freedom first arose among the Greeks, and therefore they were free; but they and the Romans likewise, knew only that some are free—not man as such. Even Plato and Aristotle did not know this. The Greeks, therefore, had slaves; and their whole life and the maintenance of their splendid liberty, was implicated with the institution of slavery: a fact, moreover, which made that liberty on the one hand only an accidental, transient and limited growth; on the other hand, constituted it a rigorous thraldom of our common nature—of the human.
>
> The German nations, under the influence of Christianity, were the first to attain the consciousness that man, as man, is free: that it is the freedom of Spirit, which constitutes its essence.[8]

QUICK REVIEW
Hegel argues that the larger reality that gives an individual life meaning is the historical progress of the world toward an ever greater consciousness of freedom. The individual's life has meaning to the extent that he or she takes part in this progressive movement of history by participating in the spirit of the age, the way in which freedom is evolving in his time.

The progress that we see in history, Hegel holds, is not continuous. Here history moves forward, there it pauses, and there it may briefly regress. But in its overall sweep, history keeps moving toward a better and more perfect world:

> The mutations which history presents have been long characterized in general, as an advance to something better, more perfect. . . . This peculiarity in the world of mind has indicated in the case of man . . . a real capacity for change, and that for the better—an impulse of perfectibility. . . .
>
> Universal history—as already demonstrated—shows the development of the consciousness of Freedom on the part of Spirit, and of the consequent realization of that Freedom. This development implies a gradation—a series of increasingly adequate expressions or manifestations of Freedom.[9]

Hegel claims that if the individual person becomes a part of this progressive movement of history, his or her life will have meaning. In fact, as we saw in Chapter 2, Hegel argues that apart from this forward sweep of history, the individual cannot find meaning. All meaning for the individual lies in entering and participating in the spirit of the age, the particular way in which freedom is evolving during the individual's lifetime.

QUICK REVIEW
Marx also argues that the meaning of life is found by participating in the progressive movement of history, but for him history was progressing economically toward a classless society, and meaning lay in joining in the struggle to overthrow old capitalist structures and thereby help achieve the classless society.

Other philosophers have also proposed that we can see progress in history and that by taking part in this progress the individual finds meaning in life. Karl Marx, who adopted many of Hegel's ideas about how history moves from an Asiatic, through an ancient, and on to a modern society, also felt that history was progressing toward a better and more perfect world. However, progress for Marx is economic progress: "In broad outline, the Asiatic, ancient, feudal and modern bourgeois modes of production may be designated as epochs marking progress in the economic development of society."[10] For Marx, the more perfect future world would be a world without economic classes—the classless society: "In place of the old bourgeois society, with its classes and class antagonisms, we shall have an association in which the free development of each is the condition for the free development of all."[11] Such a society would be a just society in which, as we saw in Chapter 8, benefits and burdens are distributed according to need and ability. To find meaning

8 Ibid., 18.

9 Ibid., 54, 63.

10 Karl Marx, *Toward a Critique of Political Economy*, 13: 10, trans. A. Wood, quoted in *A Dictionary of Philosophical Quotations*, ed. A. J. Ayer and Jande O'Grady (Oxford, England: Blackwell, 1992), 291.

11 Karl Marx and Friedrich Engels, *Manifesto of the Communist Party*, 6: 505, quoted in *Dictionary of Philosophical Quotations*, 288.

in life, the individual must join in the struggle to overthrow the old capitalist structures, which will give way to the new, classless society.

Others have proposed different ways to contribute to human progress. Some have suggested that as scientific knowledge progresses, life acquires meaning for the scientist through the contributions that he or she makes to this progress. Others suggest that society can evolve and become better, and that by contributing to making ours a better or more just society a person's life can have meaning. Still others believe that human life can be made better in many different ways, and so for them life has meaning when they contribute to any of these ways of making human life better.

But do these ideas of progress make sense today? Does history really reveal any kind of progress toward a goal? Doesn't history, on the contrary, exhibit decline, not progress? Take, for example, the state of the environment. Isn't the environment dirtier, uglier, more polluted, more crowded, and more degraded today than ever before? Or look at the state of the world. Haven't the grim experiences of two world wars in the past century and two smaller wars in the first decade of the present century, been enough to put an end to the traditional idea of progress and to optimistic feelings about the future? The title of a widely read book by historian Oswald Spengler that was written after the First World War seems to be a perfect description of our situation: *Decline of the West.* Critics argue that personal meaning and value cannot be based on this kind of history.

QUICK REVIEW
Others propose different views of human progress but agree that by advancing human progress, individual life gains meaning. But critics argue that there is little evidence that humanity is "progressing." Critics also question whether the proposed "goals" of human progress are worth seeking.

Moreover, if there is human progress in history, then it must have a goal, and this goal must be valuable. But why should we accept the idea that greater freedom or a "classless society" or any other goal is worth seeking? Why should such goals matter to me? Even if such goals are valuable, how can we be sure that history is moving to achieve them? If humans have free will (which we discussed earlier), then doesn't this mean that there is no way of knowing ahead of time that humans will choose to move toward some specific goal?

The American philosopher Francis Fukuyama has recently added a startling complication to these ideas. Fukuyama has argued that history is no longer progressing toward any goal. History has already reached the goals that Hegel said history was moving toward. Fukuyama summarizes his views as follows:

> I argued that a remarkable consensus concerning the legitimacy of liberal democracy as a system of government had emerged throughout the world over the past few years, as it conquered rival ideologies like hereditary monarchy, fascism, and most recently communism. More than that, however, I argued that liberal democracy may constitute the "end point of mankind's ideological evolution" and the "final form of human government," and as such constituted the "end of history." That is, while earlier forms of government were characterized by grave defects and irrationalities that led to their eventual collapse, liberal democracy was arguably free from such fundamental internal contradictions. This was not to say that today's stable democracies, like the United States, France, or Switzerland, were not without injustice or serious social problems. But these problems were ones of incomplete implementation of the twin principles of liberty and equality on which modern democracy is founded, rather than of flaws in the principles themselves. While some present-day countries might fail to achieve stable liberal democracy, and others might lapse back into other, more primitive forms of rule like theocracy or military dictatorship, the ideal of liberal democracy could not be improved upon.[12]

QUICK REVIEW
Fukuyama argues that history is no longer progressing toward any goal because in achieving liberal democracies it has already achieved its goal.

History, then, has attained all its goals. So, there can be no more progress: We have reached the end of historical progress.

---

12 Francis Fukuyama, *The End of History and the Last Man* (New York: Avon, 1992), xi.

Fukuyama's view forces us to think again about the social issues that we discussed in Chapter 8. There we discussed whether a liberal society is the best there is or whether it can be improved upon. If it is true that a government based on liberalism is the best there can be, and if all the world has accepted this view, then Fukuyama is right. We've reached our goal, and there can be no more human progress. It is foolish, then, to think that our lives can have meaning by contributing to human progress.

Yet many people today believe that humanity is in some sense still progressing. They believe that our lives can have meaning by contributing toward this progress and by "making this a better world." For example, the historian Charles Van Doren has argued that although there is little evidence for progress in economic, political, moral, or artistic matters, there is nonetheless clear progress in human knowledge. We might not be becoming better people, but at least we know more now than we ever did in our earlier history.

9.4 The Nihilist Rejection of Meaning

Yet for many people the ideas of being part of God's plan or of contributing to human progress no longer make sense. Unable to find meaning in God or human progress, many philosophers have argued that life has no meaning. The philosopher Arthur Schopenhauer argued, for example, that everything passes away and "that which in the next moment exists no more, and vanishes utterly, like a dream, can never be worth a serious effort." Schopenhauer concluded that "All good things are vanity, the world in all its ends [is] bankrupt, and life [is] a business which does not cover its expenses":

> A quick test of the assertion that enjoyment outweighs pain in this world, or that they are at any rate balanced, would be to compare the feelings of an animal engaged in eating another with those of the animal being eaten. . . .
>
> History shows us the life of nations and finds nothing to narrate but wars and tumults; the peaceful years appear only as occasional brief pauses and interludes. In just the same way the life of the individual is a constant struggle, and not merely a metaphorical one against want or boredom, but also an actual struggle against other people. He discovers adversaries everywhere, lives in continual conflict and dies with sword in hand. . . .
>
> That human life must be some kind of mistake is sufficiently proved by the simple observation that man is a compound of needs which are hard to satisfy; that their satisfaction achieves nothing but a painless condition in which he is only given over to boredom; and that boredom is a direct proof that existence is in itself valueless, for boredom is nothing other than the sensation of the emptiness of existence.[13]

QUICK REVIEW
Nihilists argue that life has no meaning. Schopenhauer claims that life has more pain than enjoyment and that the boredom we feel when all our needs are satisfied proves "the emptiness of existence." Taylor argues that the transitory nature of all our achievements shows that living has no meaning.

The contemporary American philosopher Richard Taylor also argues for the view that human life has no meaning:

> We toil after goals, most of them—indeed every single one of them—of transitory significance and, having gained one of them, we immediately set forth for the next, as if that one had never been, with this next one being essentially more of the same. Look at a busy street any day, and observe the throng going hither and thither. To what? Some office or shop, where the same things will be done today

13 Arthur Schopenhauer, *Essays and Aphorisms*, trans. R. J. Hollindale (London: Penguin Books, 1970), 41–50.

© Smithsonian American Art Museum, Washington, DC/Art Resource, NY

The Waiting Room, by George Tooker (1959). Richard Taylor argues that if we look at a busy street and observe the throng doing the same things today that they did yesterday and will repeat tomorrow, we can see that life is a meaningless repetition of pointless activities.

> as were done yesterday, and are done now so they may be repeated tomorrow . . . most such effort is directed only to the establishment and perpetuation of home and family; that is, to the begetting of others who will follow in our steps to do more of the same. . . . Our achievements, even though they are often beautiful, are mostly bubbles; and those that do last, like the sand-swept pyramids, soon become mere curiosities. . . . Nations are built upon the bones of their founders and pioneers, but only to decay and crumble before long, their rubble then becoming the foundation for others directed to exactly the same fate.[14]

The views of both Schopenhauer and Taylor are based on the *nihilist* view that there is now no larger whole or plan to which we can contribute. Both God and the idea of progress no longer make sense. Moreover, human life and all that humans produce are too insignificant and fleeting to be a source of meaning. Human life is just an endless repetition of the same meaningless events that came before. What is left?

9.5 Meaning as a Self-Chosen Commitment

Some philosophers, such as R. M. Hare, have argued that the nihilist response is mistaken.[15] The key mistake of the nihilist is to fail to see that a person's life can have meaning if the person chooses goals that give direction to the person's life and the person believes that these goals matter, that they are valuable and worth pursuing. Family, country, religion, friends—all these can become my personal goals, and if these matter to me, then by choosing to pursue them, I can give my life meaning and value.

QUICK REVIEW
Hare argues that a person gives her life a meaning by choosing goals that matter to her and that give direction to her life. Meaning that arises out of such personal choices is "subjective" meaning.

Many philosophers have argued that life can have such a "subjective" meaning through the goals or purposes that we freely undertake to pursue. One of the

14 Richard Taylor, "The Meaning of Life," in *The Meaning of Life*, ed. Klemke, 146.
15 See R. M. Hare, "Nothing Matters," in *The Meaning of Life*, ed. Klemke, 241–247.

earliest was Kierkegaard, for whom, as we saw in Chapter 4, the starting point in life is choosing something for which one is willing to live or die:

> What I really lack is to be clear in my mind what I am to do, not what I am to know, except insofar as a certain understanding must precede every action. The thing is to understand myself, to see what God really wishes me to do; the thing is to find a truth which is true for me, to find the idea for which I can live and die.[16]

Kierkegaard described three lifestyles, which he called *aesthetic*, *ethical*, and *religious*. Which of these lifestyles was best for oneself, he felt, is never clear. Yet the key to living authentically is to make a decisive choice among them. And, in so choosing, one creates the meaning of one's life:

> Every human being . . . has a natural need to formulate a life-view, a conception of the meaning of life and of its purpose. The person who lives aesthetically also does that, and the popular expression heard in all ages . . . [to describe this stage of life is]: One must enjoy life. . . . We encounter [some aesthetic] life-views that teach that we are to enjoy life . . . [through something] outside the individual. This is the case with every life-view in which wealth, honors, noble birth, etc., are made life's task and its content. . . . [Other] life-views teach that we are to enjoy life . . . [through something] within the individual himself . . . ordinarily defined as talent. It [may be] a talent for practical affairs, a talent for business, a talent for mathematics, a talent for writing, a talent for art, a talent for philosophy. Satisfaction in life, enjoyment, is sought in the unfolding of this talent. . . .
>
> In contrast to an aesthetic life-view . . . we often hear about another life-view that places the meaning of life in living for the performance of one's moral duties. This is supposed to signify an ethical view of life. . . . [But it is] a mistake to [see duty as something that is imposed] from outside the individual. . . . The truly ethical person . . . does not have duty outside himself but within himself. . . . When a person has felt the intensity of duty with all his energy, then he is ethically matured, and then duty will break forth within him. . . .
>
> The story of Abraham [in the Bible] contains . . . a teleological suspension of the ethical. . . . [Abraham faithfully obeyed God's command to sacrifice the life of his only beloved son although human sacrifice violated his moral duty; at the last moment, God stayed Abraham's hand.] Abraham represents faith. . . . He acts by virtue of the absurd. . . . By his act he transgressed the ethical altogether and had a higher telos outside it, in relation to which he suspended it. . . . Why then does Abraham do it? For God's sake and—the two are wholly identical—for his own sake. He does it for God's sake because God demands this proof of his faith; he does it for his own sake so that he can prove it.[17]

QUICK REVIEW
Kierkegaard argues that one gives one's life subjective meaning by choosing something for which one is willing to live or die, in particular by committing oneself to an aesthetic, ethical, or religious life.

Notice that for Kierkegaard, the meaning of life is subjective. It is by our personal or subjective choice of an aesthetic, ethical, or religious life that we determine the meaning of life for us. For example, we can choose to pursue wealth or honor, or enjoyment of our talents. Then pleasure becomes the meaning of life. Such a life is limited, and the individual may eventually feel that it is not a true existence. Then, he must decide whether to stay at the aesthetic stage, whose attractions he knows, or, by an act of will, to commit himself to the ethical stage.

---

16 Søren Kierkegaard, *The Journals of Kierkegaard*, trans. and ed. A. Dru (London: Collins, 1958), 44.

17 Søren Kierkegaard, *Either/Or*, vol. II, trans. Howard V. Hong and Edna H. Hong, reprinted in Denise Peterfreund White, ed., *Great Traditions in Ethics*, 8th ed. (Belmont, CA: Wadsworth, 1996), 228–230, 232.

The commitment to the ethical stage of life involves embracing internally the rational universal moral obligation to restrain one's desire for pleasure. Moral integrity and honesty become the meaning of life. At first, one confidently assumes that one can live up to the moral law. But eventually the individual comes to see that he cannot do all that morality requires, and he experiences guilt or sin. The individual realizes that he can remain at the ethical level and keep trying to do what is right and continually fail, or he can admit that he is estranged from God, whom he needs, and choose to move to the next stage.

But the move to the religious stage is filled with uncertainty because it is a commitment not to a rational principle, but to a subjective relationship with a person, God, who cannot be rationally understood. The move to the religious stage requires a "leap of faith" like Abraham's decision to trust God, a leap that is made alone, without any guarantee of being right, a leap made in "fear and trembling." But we must choose, and what we choose becomes the meaning of life for us.

Many years later, the French philosopher Jean-Paul Sartre took up several of these existential themes. Sartre was an atheist. Nevertheless, he agreed with Kierkegaard that the meaning of life is the result of a choice. Neither God nor the idea of progress can provide us with purpose and meaning unless we choose to commit ourselves to these. Then, it is our choice itself that makes them meaningful and a source of value.

We met Sartre earlier when we were discussing human nature in Chapter 2 and when we discussed existentialism in Chapter 3. Recall that Sartre holds that there are no fixed values to give meaning to our lives. Until we choose, life has no fixed purpose, no set values to pursue, and no objective meaning. But by choosing a cause, a religion, a life goal, I create the meaning of my life. Here is how Sartre puts this idea:

> If God does not exist, we find no values or commands to turn to which legitimize our conduct. So, in the bright realm of values, we have no excuse behind us, nor justification before us. We are alone, with no excuses. . . .
>
> To say that we invent values means nothing else but this: life has no meaning a priori. Before you come alive, life is nothing; it's up to you to give it a meaning, and value is nothing else but the meaning that you choose.[18]

But in the end, doesn't Sartre leave us without a compass as we struggle to find meaning in our lives? If Sartre is right, then before we choose, one thing has no more value than another thing. If Sartre is right, then we should be able to find meaning in our lives by choosing anything at all. But this is clearly not true. A person cannot think that her life has meaning if she decides to devote it to making tiny little piles of sand on the beach. If we are to believe that our life has meaning, we have to devote ourselves to goals or causes that we think (even before we choose) have value and are worth devoting ourselves to.

Sartre and Kierkegaard, then, may be right when they claim that nothing can give my life meaning unless I choose it and make it my own. But Sartre, at least, seems wrong to claim that before I choose, nothing has value. On the contrary, what I choose to devote my life to must be something that I determine ahead of time is valuable and worth pursuing. If it is not valuable independent of my choice, it cannot give my life meaning.

So does life have meaning? For many people, life does have meaning because they believe that they have a part to play in a larger valuable whole that gives their life value, purpose, and a goal. For them, meaning might come from seeing themselves as part of a larger divine plan, or from seeing themselves as contributing

QUICK REVIEW
Sartre, an atheist, claims that only subjective meaning is possible and that we give subjective meaning to our lives by choosing to commit ourselves to something and thereby giving it value; nothing has value before it is chosen. Critics argue that one must believe something is valuable before one can choose to devote oneself to it.

QUICK REVIEW
The idea of subjective meaning suggests that because meaning can be created through our choices, life can have meaning through our commitment to any of a wide variety of worthy human concerns, such as family, art, loving relationships, raising children, healing, helping, moral integrity, and religious faith.

18 Jean-Paul Sartre, *Existentialism and Human Emotions* (New York: Philosophical Library, 1957), 23, 49.

to human progress. But for many, these sources of meaning are no longer useful. Some reject God; some reject the idea of human progress; still others reject both. The result is that many accept nihilism: They conclude that life has no meaning.

But Kierkegaard and Sartre reveal another possibility: the possibility of creating meaning through honest and authentic choices. In a way, even those who look to God or human progress for meaning must choose to commit themselves to such a choice. But if meaning can be created through subjective choice, then the range of meaning is wider than God and human progress. Life can have meaning through a commitment to any of a variety of human concerns. For one person, meaning may come through a commitment to family or to loving relationships, for another through a commitment to art, to political life, or to healing or helping others; for another, meaning may come through a commitment to living honestly and with moral integrity, and for yet another through a commitment to religious faith.

However, the key question is the one that Sartre forces us to face: Can anything—whatever it might be—we choose make life meaningful for us? If so, then meaning is easy: We can find meaning by committing ourselves to the pursuit of money, the pursuit of pleasure, self-development, or even making little piles of sand on the ocean shore. Or, as Kierkegaard suggests, can life can have meaning only if we commit ourselves to a cause or an ideal that, ahead of time, we know is worth pursuing? Is finding meaning the difficult pursuit of moving through ever more authentic stages of life, finding at each stage that what I have committed myself to is not worthy enough and that I need more, finding at each stage that meaning requires a commitment to what I know ahead of time matters, and matters more than my current pursuits?

QUESTIONS

1. What meaning, if any, do you believe life has? Explain why you believe that life has the meaning (or lack of meaning) that you describe.
2. Do you agree with Hegel that human history exhibits progress? Does human history exhibit the kind of progress that Hegel said it did? Do you, or people you know, find meaning in contributing to human progress in some way? Explain your answers.
3. If you sat down to write the story of your life, do you think that your life's story would exhibit progress? Why? Would it exhibit meaning? Why?
4. Does it matter whether or not life has meaning? If life has no meaning but you are having a lot of fun, should you look closely at the question of whether life has meaning? If you are happy and unbothered, is it better to ignore the question, or is there some reason to look at the question closely anyway? Explain your answer.
5. What are some of the implications of Fukuyama's view that history has ended?
6. Explain what you think the meaning of your life is. If you think life has no meaning, then explain why you think this.

Photos 12/Alamy

PHILOSOPHY AT THE MOVIES

Watch *About Schmidt* (2002) in which Warren Schmidt, after retiring from his job as an actuary and having his wife die, feels useless and alienated, and travels in a Winnebago to visit his daughter to try to convince her not to marry a waterbed salesman. What is the meaning of life for Warren's friend Ray? Does the film seem to agree with Ray? Does Warren believe or come to believe that his life has a meaning? Explain. What does it mean when at the end of the movie Warren cries over the picture that Ndugu drew? Is he crying because he sees that life has meaning after all or because he sees that life has no meaning?

Chapter Summary

We have now come to the end of our philosophical journey. If you must leave a philosophy course having learned only one thing, the prized possession might be to travel with a philosophical attitude. Having a philosophical attitude means having one's eyes open as one journeys through the many decisions that will give shape and meaning to our lives.

A philosophical attitude is not achieved with a single philosophy course, although it may begin with one. Rather, the philosophical attitude needs lifelong nurturing to flourish and strengthen. And it requires something else—courage—the courage to continue on the journey once begun.

The main points of this chapter are:

9.1 Does Life Have Meaning?

- For many people, the question of whether life has any meaning arises even when death is not near.
- Logical positivists claim the question is meaningless.

9.2 The Theistic Response to Meaning

- The theistic response to the question of the meaning of life holds that the meaning of life is to be explained in terms of the individual's relationship to a larger divine plan.

9.3 Meaning and Human Progress

- Hegel and Marx define the meaning of life in terms of contributing toward human progress. For Hegel, history progresses toward a fuller expansion of freedom; for Marx, history progresses toward a classless society. Fukuyama argues that the end of history has passed, so there is no longer any human progress.

9.4 The Nihilist Rejection of Meaning

- The nihilist response to the meaning of life is the claim that life has no meaning, a view that Arthur Schopenhauer embraced.

9.5 Meaning as a Self-Chosen Commitment

- The existentialists Søren Kierkegaard and Jean-Paul Sartre argue that the meaning of life is created by what one chooses; for Sartre things have no value apart from our choices, while for Kierkegaard God has value even apart from our choices.

Glossary

All terms highlighted in the text are defined in this glossary. Some of these terms carry nuances that are unmentioned here. Every attempt has been made to be concise without being misleading.

A

a posteriori pertaining to knowledge that is empirically verifiable; based on inductive reasoning from what is experienced

a priori pertaining to knowledge whose possession is logically prior to experience; reasoning based on such knowledge

act utilitarianism in normative ethics, the position that an action is moral if it produces the greatest happiness for the most people

agnosticism a claim of ignorance particularly of religious matters; the claim that God's existence can be neither proved nor disproved

analogy a comparison of two things in an argument which is intended to demonstrate that since the two share one aspect, they must share another as well

anthropomorphism the attributing of human qualities to nonhuman entities, especially to God

antirealism the doctrine that the objects of our senses do not exist independently of our perceptions, beliefs, concepts, and language

argument a group of statements consisting of premises and conclusions of such a type that the premises are intended to prove or demonstrate the conclusion

argument from design *see* design argument

atheism denial of theism; the view that God or a god does not exist

atman the Hindu idea of the true self; the ego or soul; pure consciousness

autonomy the freedom of being able to decide for oneself by using one's own rationality

avidya in Buddhism, the cause of all suffering and frustration; ignorance or unawareness that leads to clinging

axiom a proposition regarded as self-evident or true

B

behaviorism a school of psychology that restricts the study of human nature to what can be observed rather than to states of consciousness

Brahman the Hindu concept of an impersonal Supreme Being; the source and goal of everything; the ultimate reality

C

categorical imperative Immanuel Kant's ethical formula: Act as if your maxim (general rule by which you act) could be willed to become a universal law; the principle that what is morally right for one person in one set of circumstances is also morally right for anyone else in similar circumstances

categorical syllogism the most important kind of categorical argument. The categorical syllogism contains exactly *two premises* and *a conclusion.* In addition, a categorical syllogism contains only *three terms*

causality, causation events connected together as cause and effect; the relationship between two events in which one brings about or produces the other

cause whatever is responsible for or leads to a change, motion, or condition; an event that brings about another event

coherence theory a theory contending that truth is a property of a related group of consistent statements

communitarianism view that the actual community in which we live should be at the center of our analysis of society and government

compatibilism view that rejects the idea that determinism rules out freedom and responsibility and that argues instead that causal determinism is compatible with freedom

conceptual relativist view the view that a true scientific theory is nothing more than a theory that coheres with the conceptual framework accepted by a community of scientists

consequentialist theory in ethics, the position that the morality of an action is determined by its nonmoral consequences

contract theory in social philosophy, the doctrine that individuals give up certain liberties and rights to the state, which in turn guarantees such rights as life, liberty, and the pursuit of happiness

correspondence theory a theory contending that truth is an agreement between a proposition and a fact

cosmological argument argument for the existence of God that claims that there must be an ultimate causal explanation for why the universe as a totality exists

critical thinking the kind of thinking we do when we base our beliefs and actions on unbiased and valid reasoning that uses well-founded evidence, that avoids false generalizations and unrecognized assumptions, and that considers opposing viewpoints

D

deduction the process of reasoning to logically certain conclusions

deductive argument an argument in which the premises are intended to show that the conclusion must necessarily be true so long as the premises are true

deductive reasoning *see* deduction

defining characteristic a characteristic in whose absence a thing would not be what it is

design argument an argument for the existence of God that claims that the order and purpose manifest in the working of things in the universe require a God

determinism the theory that everything that occurs happens in accordance with some regular pattern or law; the view that human actions are completely determined by prior events

dharma in Buddhism, one's duty as set forth by the Buddha; the principles whereby self-frustration is ended; the Eightfold Path prescribed by the Buddha

divine command theory a nonconsequential normative theory that says we should always do what God commands; the view that actions are morally right if and only if God commands or permits them, and morally wrong if and only if God forbids them

dualism a theory that holds that reality is composed of two distinct kinds of substances, neither of which can be reduced to the other, such as: spirit/matter or mind/body

duty in ethics, an obligation; what one is morally required to do; what a morally upright individual must do

E

egoism ethical theory that contends that we act morally when we act in a way that promotes our own interests

empiricism the position that knowledge has its origins in and derives all of its content from experience

essence that which makes an entity what it is; that defining characteristic in whose absence a thing would not be itself

ethical egoism in ethics, the view that we act morally when we act in a way that promotes our own interests

ethical relativism a view that denies the existence of any universally applicable moral standard; a view that claims that the truth or validity of a moral standard is not absolute but depends on the standards held or accepted by a social group

ethics the branch of philosophy that tries to determine the good and right thing to do

existence actuality

existentialism a twentieth-century philosophy that denies any essential human nature and holds that each of us creates our own essence through our free actions

F

free will the capacity or power to act without one's actions being causally determined by events or conditions outside one's control

functionalism explanation of mental activities and states as terms that mediate or relate perceptual inputs and behavioral outputs

G

Golden Rule the ethical rule that holds: Do unto others as you would have them do unto you

H

hedonism the view that only pleasure is intrinsically worthwhile

human nature what constitutes something as a human being; what makes us different from anything else; the collection of qualities that make us human

hypothesis in general, an assumption, statement, or theory of explanation, the truth of which is under investigation

I

idealism in metaphysics, the position that reality is ultimately nonmatter; the view that reality consists of mind and its contents

identity theory the theory that mental states are really physical brain states

indeterminism the view that some individual choices are not causally determined by preceding events over which the individual has no control

individualism the social theory that emphasizes the importance and primacy of the individual, of his or her rights, and of his or her independence of action

induction the process of reasoning to probable explanations or judgments

inductive reasoning *see* induction

inference to the best explanation an argument that assumes that the theory that best explains a large set of facts is probably true

infinite regress an infinite series of causally or logically related terms that has no first or initiating term

innate ideas ideas that, according to some philosophers such as Plato, can never be found in experience but that are inborn

instrumentalist view in epistemology, the view that scientific theories can be true only in the sense that they enable us to accurately predict what will happen and that any unobservable entities postulated by the theory do not literally exist

intuition a source of knowledge that does not rely on the senses or reason but on direct awareness of something

J

judgment asserting or denying something in the form of a proposition

K

karma the Hindu law of sowing and reaping; the law that, according to Hinduism, determines that the form and circumstances we assume in each reincarnated state depend upon our actions in prior incarnations

L

libertarianism in metaphysics, the view that determinism is false and that people are free to choose to act other than they do; in social philosophy, the view that the right to freedom from restraint takes priority over all other rights

logical positivism the philosophical school of thought, associated with Carnap and Ayer, that claims that only analytic and empirically verifiable statements are meaningful and that because metaphysical and ethical statements are neither, the latter are meaningless

M

materialism the metaphysical position that reality is ultimately composed of matter

maya in Buddhism, the world of illusion

mechanism the view that all natural processes can be explained in terms of mechanical laws that govern matter and its motions

metaphysics the branch of philosophy that studies the nature of reality

monism the view that reality is reducible to one kind of thing or one explanatory principle

monotheism the view that there is a single God

morality the standards that an individual or a group has about what is right and wrong or good and evil

N

natural law a pattern of necessary and universal regularity; a universal moral imperative derived from the nature of things; a moral standard inferred from the nature of human beings that indicates how everyone ought to behave

nihilism the view that nothing exists, that nothing has value; the social view that conditions are so bad that they should be destroyed and replaced by something better

nirvana in Buddhism, enlightenment that comes when the limited clinging self is extinguished

nonconsequentialist theory in ethics, a theory that holds that the morality of an action is determined by more than just its consequences

O

objective possessing a public nature that is independent of us and our judgments about it

objective idealism the position that ideas exist in an objective state; associated originally with Plato

omniscient all-knowing

ontological argument an argument for the existence of God based on the nature of God's being

P

perception the processes of seeing, hearing, smelling, touching, and tasting; an observation made through these processes

phenomenalism the belief, associated with Kant, that we can know only appearances (phenomena) and never what is ultimately real (noumena), that the mind has the ability to sort out sense data and provide relationships that hold among them

phenomenology the philosophical school founded by Edmund Husserl that contends that being is the underlying reality, that what is ultimately real is our consciousness, which itself is being

philosophy the love of wisdom; the activity of critically and carefully examining the reasons behind our most fundamental assumptions

political philosophy that part of social philosophy that looks at the nature and proper role of the state or government in society

positivism the view that only analytic and empirically verifiable propositions are meaningful; the view that all nonanalytic knowledge must be derived from or based on what can be empirically experienced or perceived

postmodernism late-twentieth-century movement that rejects the view that there is only one reality and that through rational inquiry we are progressing toward an ever fuller unified scientific understanding of that one reality

pragmatism the philosophical school of thought, associated with Dewey, James, and Peirce, that tries to mediate between idealism and materialism by rejecting all absolute first principles, tests truth through workability, and views the universe as pluralistic

pre-Socratics the Greek philosophers before Socrates

primary qualities according to Locke, those qualities that inhere in an object, including size, shape, weight, and so on

psychological egoism the view that human beings are so constituted that they must always act out of self-interest

R

rationalism the position that reason alone, without the aid of sensory information, is capable of arriving at the knowledge of some undeniable truths

realism the doctrine that the objects of our senses exist independently of their being experienced

realist view the view that scientific theories are literally true or false and that the unobservable entities postulated in a scientific theory really exist if the theory is true

reason the capacity for thinking logically and making inferences; the process of following relationships from thought to thought and of ultimately drawing conclusions

reductionism the view that one kind of thing is constituted by or reducible to another kind of thing; in particular the view that processes such as thought and life are nothing more than physical or chemical processes

relativism the view that the truth or falsity of a class of propositions depends upon the beliefs held by a social group; the view that all human judgments are conditioned by factors such as culture and personal experience

religious belief the doctrines of a religion about the universe and one's relation to the supernatural

right a justified entitlement or claim on others

rule utilitarianism the normative ethical position that we should act so that the rule governing our actions is the one that would produce the greatest happiness for the most people if everyone were to follow it

S

samsara in Buddhism, the cycle of birth and life

scientific method a form of investigation based on collecting, analyzing, and interpreting sense data to determine the most probable explanation

self the ego or "I" that exists in a physical body and that is conscious and rational

sense data images or sensory impressions

skepticism in epistemology, the view that no knowledge of reality is possible

social philosophy the philosophical study of society including the study of the application of moral principles to the problems of society, and the study of the nature of freedom, equality, justice, political obligation, and the state

solipsism an extreme form of subjective idealism, contending that only I exist and that everything else is a product of my subjective consciousness

soul an immaterial entity that is identified with a consciousness, mind, or personality

sound argument an argument that is both valid and has true premises

subjective that which refers to, or depends on, the knower; that which exists in the consciousness but not apart from it

subjective idealism in epistemology, the position that all we ever know are our own ideas

T

tautology a statement whose predicate repeats its subject in whole or in part

teleology the view that natural organisms have a purpose or are designed to achieve an end; a view that maintains that purposes inhere in nature and affirms that the universe either was consciously designed for, or is operating under some partly conscious, partly unconscious, purpose

theism the belief in a personal God who intervenes in the lives of the creation

theology the rational study of God, including religious doctrines

transcendental idealism in epistemology, the view that the *form* of our knowledge of reality derives from reason but its *content* comes from our senses

V

valid in logic, having a conclusion that follows from the premises by logical necessity

value *(as a verb)* to impose worth on something; to believe that something has worth

value *(as a noun)* an object or quality that is believed to have worth or be desirable; that which is worthy of pursuit; that which is, or ought to be, regarded highly or held dear

virtue ethics in ethics, a moral theory that holds that the moral life should be concerned with cultivating a virtuous character rather than following rules of action

Index

Abortion, 456–457, 459, 477, 509–514
"After Trust: Post-Modernism and the Rhetoric of Science" (Tomlinson), 442–443
Agape, 501, 502
Agnosticism, 267–271
Ahimsa, 16–17
Akutagawa, Ryunosuke, 438–442
Albert the Great, 297–298
Alienation, 606, 611–613
All Quiet on the Western Front (Remarque), 600–602
Alpert, Judie, 316
Alsop, Steward, 514–515
Alston, William P., 294–296
Analects, The (Confucius), 138–141
Analogical knowledge of God, 299–301
Analogy, argument by, 253–254
Analytic propositions, 172, 445
Anarchy, State, and Utopia (Nozick), 571
An Essay Concerning Human Understanding (Locke), 101
Anselm, Saint, 242–246, *244*
Antirealism, 179–186
Apology (Plato), 27–29
A posteriori knowledge, 333, 445
A priori knowledge, 320, 353, 355–356, 397, 444–446
Aquinas, Thomas; empiricism, 334; on ethics, 479; on existence of God, 246–251; historical showcase, 297–302; on human nature, 63, 478–479; on meaning of life, 621; on social contract, 541; on truth, 399, 403, 430–431; on unjust laws and civil disobedience, 576–577; on war, 591–592
Arguments: by analogy, 253–254; categorical syllogism, 175–178; deductive, 53; evaluating, 24; inductive, 53; sound, 53
Aristotle: empiricism, 334; on ethics, 506; feminist challenge to, 79; on four causes, 134; on government, 541, 550–553; historical showcase, 133–138; influence on Aquinas, 246, 297; on justice, 560, 562–563; on love and friendship, 499–503; on reason, 60; on self, 110; on social contract, 541; on truth, 399, 403; on virtue ethics, 495–499
Armstrong, David M., 91, 406
Art of Awareness, The (Bois), 366
Art: Plato on, 127
Assumptions, 7, 8–9
Atheism, 234–235, 260–267, 282–283
Atman, 46–47, 287
Atomistic self, 107–109
Augustine, Saint: on evil, 264; feminist challenge to, 79; on good *vs.* evil, 62–63; on knowledge, 321; on reality, 155; on social contract, 541; on spirits, 148; on time, 213–215; on unjust laws and civil disobedience, 575, 577; on war, 591
Austin, John, 576–577
Autonomy, 4, 483–491. *See also* Freedom
Ayer, Alfred J., 171–172, 175–178, 399, 620

Bacon, Sir Francis, 334, 364
Baier, Kurt, 466–467, 622
Baker, Lynn, 94
Basic belief, defined, 398–400
Bazerman, Max, 59
Becker, Carl L., 412
Before the Beginning (Ellis), 258
Behaviorism, 90–91
Behe, Michael J., 70
Being. *See* Reality
Being and Nothingness (Sartre), 75, 198, 201
Being and Time (Heidegger), 193–194
"Being More Real" (Nozick), 225–226
Belief. *See also* God, existence of; Knowledge: behaviorism on, 91; correspondence theory and, 403–409; Hinduism, 287; justification and, 397–401; knowledge and, 395–397; religious, 240–241, 272–279
Bentham, Jeremy, 467–469
Berger, Peter, 361
Bergson, Henri, 70, 218–219
Berkeley, George: empiricism, 334; historical showcase, 231–235; on reality, 155–158; subjectivism, 340–343
Beyond God the Father (Daly), 283–284
Bhagavad-Gita, 286–287
Bible: interpretation of, 430–432; sacred Scripture, 240, 474–483, 516
Bierce, Ambrose, 377–381
Big Bang, 248–249
Blake, William, 429
Blanshard, Brand, 410–413
Bois, J. Samuel, 366
BonJour, Laurence, 321, 399
Bosanquet, Bernard, 158
Bracketing, experience, 190–192, 200
Bradley, Francis Herbert, 158, 413
Brahman, 42–43, 286–287, 321
Brennan, John, 591
Brothers Karamazov, The (Dostoevsky), 292–294
Browne, Harry, 17, 465–466
Buber, Martin, 199
Buddha, 35–36, 287–288
Buddhaghosa, 494
Buddhism: defining religion, 239; on existence of God, 268–269; Heidegger and, 194; idealism, 158; on meaning of life, 622; on pacifism, 589; on self, 103–104; on truth, 413
Burke, Edmund, 532

Camus, Albert, 199, 618
Caring: A Feminine Approach to Ethics and Moral Education (Noddings), 505–506
Care, ethic of, 503–508
Carnap, Rudolf, 174, 620; on truth, 399
Carruthers, Peter, 321
Categorical imperative of morality, 450–452, 483–491, 511, 517
Categorical syllogism arguments, 175–178
Causality: Aristotle on, 133–134; Descarte on, 327; as habit, 344–348; Hume on, 388–390; Kant on, 356–359, 445, 449–450; karma, 491–494
Chalmers, David J., 95
Charvaka philosophers, 148–149, 333
Chisholm, Roderick M., 399, 405
Chomsky, Noam, 321

Christianity. *See also* Aquinas, Thomas; Augustine, Saint: *agape*, 501; on euthanasia, 516; on evil, 264–267; on human nature, 62–65, 478–479; on meaning of life, 622; on pacifism, 589; on reality, 155; religion, significance of, 238–239; unjust laws and civil disobedience, 575–576
Cialdini, Robert, 59
City of God (Augustine), 155
Civil disobedience, 32, 575–579
Civilization and Its Discontents (Freud), 51
Civil rights movement, 583
Civil War, 583
Claims: supporting with reasons and arguments, 15–16; vague and ambiguous, 12–13
Clark, Robert E. D., 252
Clifford, W. K., 274
Coady, C. A. J., 595
Coherence theory of truth, 400–401, 409–413
Collins, Francis, 250
Communism, 567–568
Communist Manifesto (Marx), 606, 607, 608–609
Communitarianism, 549–553
Compatibilism, 209–211
Computer view of human nature, 92–93
Conceptual relativism, 425–428
Confessions (Augustine), 79
Confucius, 138–141
Conscious Mind, The (Chalmers), 95
Consciousness: Berkeley on, 155–158, 342; computer model, 94; dualism on, 95; Husserl on, 188, 189–192; identity theory, 88–89; materialist view, 151–153; mind-body problem, overview, 82–83; religious experiences, 276; Sartre on, 197
Consequentialism, 463–474
Contract theory: communitarianism, 549–553; freedom and, 579–582; Hobbes on, 541–542; Locke on, 543–544; Rawls on, 547–549; Rousseau on, 545–547; women and, 553–557
Conway, Anne, 306–310, 321
Corey, Michael A., 252
Correspondence theory, 403–409, 419
Cosmological argument for God, 246–251
Critical realism, 338–339
Critical thinking; argument's premises, evaluating an, 85–87; arguments by analogy, 253–254; arguments, conditional and disjunctive, 160–163; arguments, evaluating, 24; assumptions, 8–9; best explanations, inference to the, 71–74; categorical syllogism arguments, 175–178; claims, supporting with reasons and arguments, 15–16; claims, vague and ambiguous, 12–13; deductive arguments, validity, and soundness, 52–54; explanation, inference to the best, 71–74; fallacies, formal and informal, 268–270; inductive generalizations, 346–347; moral reasoning, 518–520; premises, conclusions, and assumptions, 31–34; reasoning, 10; science vs. pseudoscience, 372–373; values, sltudy of, 16–18
Critique of Pure Reason, The (Kant), 352
Critique of the Gotha Program (Marx), 567
Crito (Plato), 29–34

Daly, Mary, 283–285
Darrow, Clarence, 202–203
Darwin, Charles, natural selection, 65–74, 366; theory of evolution, 255, 367, 369
Dasein, 193–194
Das Kapital (Marx), 606
Davidson, Donald, 406
Davies, Paul, 252, 257–258
Davis, Stephen T., 276–277
De Anima (Aristotle), 134–135
de Beauvoir, Simone, 199
Declaration of Independence, 544, 582
Decline of the West (Spengler), 625
Deductive argument, 53, 148–149
Deflationist theory of truth, 419–420
"Defense of Skepticism" (Unger), 381–383
de La Mettrie, Julien Offroy, 150
de LaPlace, Pierre Simon, 205
Dembski, William A., 70–71, 256–257
Democritus, 149
Deontological argument, 589
Descartes, René, on doubt and reason, 321–326; on enduring self, 100; on existence of God, 245; historical showcase, 302–306; on human nature, 71, 83–87; on knowledge, 321; on self, 108; on truth, 399
Descent of Man (Darwin), 66–67
Design argument, existence of God, 251–259
Determinism, 13, 204–206
DeWeese, Garrett I., 122–123
Dewey, John, 166–167, 168, 414, 509
Dharma, 288
Dharmakirti, 413
d'Holbach, Paul Henri, 13–14
Dialogue Concerning the Two Great World Systems, A (Galileo), 424
Dialogues (Plato), 20–35
Dialogues Concerning Natural Religion (Hume), 261–262
Difference principle, 570
Dilthey, Wilhelm, 431, 434
Diotima, 98
Discourse on Method (Descarte), 303
Discrimination, 560
Distributive justice, 558
Divine command theory, 474–483
"Divine Watchmaker" (Paley), 251–253
Dostoevsky, Fyodor, 292–294, 522–524
Doubt, Descartes on, 321–326
Draper, Paul, 263
Dualism, 83–87, 95–96, 122–125, 164–165
Dummett, 413
Dutroux, Marc, 401–403, 417, 418

Eastern philosophy: Buddha, 35–36; differences from Western, 288–289; empiricism and, 333–334; existence of God, 286–289; on freedom, 14–15; Heidegger and, 194; idealism and, 158–160; on knowledge and, 320–321; on materialism, 148–149; on self, 102–105; on truth, 413, 414; Upanishads, 46–47; The Vedas, 45–46; on war, 593
Eddington, Sir Arthur, 157
Egalitarianism, 563–565
Egoism, 17–18, 51, 465–467. *See also* Self
Eliminative materialism, 94–95
Ellis, Albert, 37

Ellis, George, 258–259
Emotions. *See also* Happiness: Hobbes on, 150; James on, 273; logical positivism, 173–174; love, 501; Plato on, 58–60, 131–132; religion and, 240, 275
Empirical statements, 171–172
Empiricism: correspondence theory, 419; defined, 318; justification, 397; meaning of life, 620; science and knowledge, 363–374; senses accounting for knowledge, 333–351
End of the Party, The (Greene), 118–121
Engels, Friedrich, 606
English, Jane, 512
Enquiry Concerning Human Understanding, An (Hume), 343–344, 386
Epicetus, 476–478
Epicurus, 464
Equality, as justice, 563–565
Eros, 501
Essay Concerning Human Understanding, An (Locke), 334, 399
Essay Concerning the True and Original Extent and End of Civil Government (Locke), 543–544
Essays in Critical Realism (Drake and Santayana), 338–339
Essence, 83
Essence of Christianity (Feuerbach), 606
Ethical egoism, 465–467
Ethical relativism, 459–462
Ethics: Aristotle on, 495–499; Buddhism, 491–494; consequentialist theory, 463–474; definition of, 456–458; divine command theory, 474–483; Dostoyevsky on, 522–524; future life approach, 512–513; gender differences, 503–506; Kant on, 483–491; love and friendship, 499–503; moral development, 503–505; moral quandaries, 508–509; moral reasoning, 518–520; nonconsequentialist theory, 474–494; relativism, 458–463; Singer on, 524–526; social philosophy and, 539; study of, 16–18; virtue, overview, 495
"Ethics of Belief, The" (Clifford), 274
"Ethics of War, The" (Russell), 602–604
Euthanasia, 463, 514–518
Euthyphro (Plato), 20–24
Evil, 62–63, 260–271, 287, 589–594
Evolution, 65–74, 366, 367, 369, 371
Examined Life, The (Nozick), 146
Existence, 13–16, 158, 348–351. *See also* God, existence of; Reality
Existentialism, 74–77, 186–187, 194–201, 281–283
"Existentialism and Human Emotions" (Sartre), 197
Existentialism and Humanism (Sartre), 76

Fallacies, formal and informal, 268–270
Falsifiability, 367–369, 372–373
"Famine, Affluence, and Morality" (Singer), 524–526
Feminist philosophy, 9; epistemology, 11; ethics and gender, 503–506; on human nature, 77–81; male bias, 38–39; on sexual behavior, 490; social contract and, 553–557; Wollstonecraft, Mary, 531–535
Feuerbach, Ludwig, 606
Feyerabend, Paul, 181
Finnis, John, 479, 480–481
Ford, John C., 595
Forms, Plato, 127–133
Foundationalism, 398–400
Foundations of the Metaphysics of Morals (Kant), 483–484
Four Noble Truths, 268–269, 492–493
Frankl, Victor, 14
Freedom: Buddhist philosophy, 35–36; to choose, 196; determinism, 13; evil and, 265; existentialist view, 74, 196–199; goal of philosophy, 4, 7; God and free will, 266; Hegel on, 550–551; liberalism and, 572; Locke on, 543–544; Marx on, 611; overview, 579–582; Rousseau on, 545–547
Freud, Sigmund, 50–51, 205, 268
Friedman, Milton, 559
Friendship and ethics, 499–503
Fukuyama, Francis, 625
Functionalism on human nature, 91–94
Future of an Illusion, The (Freud), 268

Gadamer, Hans-Georg, 434–436
Galileo, 322, 365, 367–368, 413, 424
Gandhi, Mahatma, 16–17, 332, 578–579
Gautama, Siddhartha, 287–288
Gay-Williams, J., 515–516
Gergen, Kenneth, 361
German Ideology, The (Marx), 606
Gestalt psychology, 354
Gettier, Edmund, 396
Gilligan, Carol, 503–505, 506
God. *See also* Religion: Aquinas on, 298–299; atheism, agnosticism and evil, 260–271; authority of, 541; Berkeley on, 157, 234–235, 342; Buddhism, 287–288; Conway on, 306–310; cosmological argument, 246–251; Descarte on, 302, 323; design argument, 251–259; divine command theory, 474–483; dualism, view of, 85; Eastern and Western differences, 288–289; existence of, 13–16; experience of, 275–278; feminist theology, 283–285; Hinduism, 286–287; Hume on, 349, 389–390; Idealism and, 164; Judeo-Christian tradition, 62–65; Kant on, 452; law and morality, 575–579; meaning of life, 622; natural law theory, 479–480; Nietzsche on, 527–528; ontological argument, 242–246; overview, 241–242; radical theology, 279–283; religion, significance of, 238–241; religious belief and experience, 272–279; Sartre on, 197–201; time and, 214
Gödel, Kurt, 246
Godwin, William, 535
Goodman, Nelson, 181–182
Good *vs.* evil, 62–63, 467–474, 476–478
Gould, Stephen Jay, 70
Government: communitarianism, 549–553; freedom and, 579–582; Hobbes on, 230, 541–542; human rights, 582–586; justice, as social utility, 565–567; justice, defined, 558–561; justice, equality as, 563–565; justice, liberty and, 569–574; justice, merit as, 561–563; justice, need and ability, 567–568; justification of state, 540–541; law and morality, 29–34; limits on, 574–575; Locke on, 543–544; political philosophy defined, 538–540; Rawls on, 547–549; Rousseau on, 545–547; unjust laws and civil disobedience, 575–579; war and terrorism, 586–598; women and social contract, 553–557

Great Learning, The (Confucius), 141
Greene, Graham, 118–121
Grimshaw, Jean, 183–184
Grotius, Hugo, 591
Groundwork of the Metaphysics of Morals (Kant), 483–486

Hall, Richard, 397
Hanson, N. R., 152
Happiness: Aristotle on, 135–138, 495–499; Kant on, 270–271, 452, 584–585; Mill on, 580–581; Plato on, 131–132; utilitarianism, 471
Hare, R. M., 511–512, 627–630
Harm principle, 580
Hartshorne, Charles, 245
Having Love Affairs (Taylor), 472
"Heavenly Christmas Tree, The," (Dostoyevsky), 522–524
Hedonism, 465–467
Hegel, Georg W., on government, 550–553; influence on Marx, 605; on knowledge, 321; on meaning of life, 623–626; on relational self, 110–112; on truth, 413
Heidegger, Martin, 192–194
Heisenberg, Werner, 152, 337
Hempel, C. G., 413
Heraclitus, 44
Hermeneutics, 430, 433
Herskovits, Melville J., 460
Hesiod, 44
Hick, John, 238, 250–251, 265–267
Hinduism: on meaning of life, 622; philosophy, 14–15, 286–287
Hirsch, E. D., 435–436
Historical Showcase: Aquinas, Thomas, 297–302; Aristotle, 133–138; Berkeley, George, 231–235; Confucius, 138–141; Conway, Anne, 306–310; Descartes, René, 302–306; Hobbes, Thomas, 227–231; Hume, David, 385–390; Kant, Immanuel, 444–453; Marx, Karl, 605–611; Nietzsche, Friedrich, 526–531; Plato, 126–133; Rawls, John, 611–615; Wollstonecraft, Mary, 531–535
Hobbes, Thomas: on contract theory, 541–542, empiricism, 334; on freedom, 209; historical showcase, 227–231; on human nature, 51, 87–88, 586–588; materialism, 150; women and social contract, 553–554
Holy Family, The (Marx), 606
Hospers, John, 205–206
How Do We Know Anything" (Nagel), 383–384
Hubbard, Ruth, 181
Hubble, Edwin, 249
Human nature: behaviorist view, 90–91; computer view, 92–93; Darwinian challenge, 65–74; dualist view of, 83–87, 95–96; eliminative materialism, 94–95; enduring self, 96–106; existentialist view, 74–77; feminist view of, 77–81; functionalist view, 91–94; Hobbes on, 586–588; identity theory, 88–90; importance of understanding, 54–56; Judeo-Christian view, 62–65; Marx on, 607–609; materialist view, 87–88; mind-body problem, overview, 82–83; natural law ethics, 476–480; overview, 50–54; Sartre on, 197; self-sufficiency, 106–115; traditional rationalistic view, 57–62
Human progress, 623–626
Human rights, 582–586
Hume, David, causality, 358; empiricism, 334; on existence of God, 248, 254–255, 258, 261–263; on government, 547; historical showcase, 385–390; Kant rebuttal to, 352–363; on self, 104–105; skepticism and, 343–351; on truth, 399
Husserl, Edmund, 187–192, 199–200
Huxley, Thomas, 267
Hypothetical method, 367–369

Idealism: Berkeley on, 155–158, 162, 231–235; ethics and, 507; objections to, 163–165; objective, 160–163; reality as nonmatter, 154–165; subjective, 155–156; Vasubandhu on, 158–160
Idea of the Holy, The (Otto), 276
Ideas, 167–168, 232–233, 340–341, 343–344. *See also* Knowledge
Identity theory, 88–90
Imlay, Gilbert, 534–535
Immaterialism, 166
Immortality, 13–16, 128–131
"In a Grove" (Akutagawa), 438–442
Indeterminism, 211
Inductionism, 364–366
Inductive argument, 53
"Inductive Argument from Evil and the Human Cognitive Condition, The" (Alston), 294–296
Inductive generalizations, 346–348
Inductive reasoning, 148–149, 364–366. *See also* Reason
Inequality, 561–563, 564–565, 607, 615
Innate ideas, 326–333
Instrumentalist view of science, 423–424
Intelligent design, 251–259
Intelligent Design: The Bridge Between Science and Theology (Dembski), 256–257
Interpretation, truth and, 428–436
"Introduction to the Critique of Hegel's Philosophy" (Marx), 606
Introduction to the Principles of Morals and Legislation (Bentham), 467–469
Islam, 239, 475, 622

James, William, on belief in God, 272–275; on human nature, 114; on reality, 166, 168–169; on religious experience, 276; on truth, 414–415
Jefferson, Thomas, 544
Jesus Christ, 62. *See also* Christianity
Joachim, H. H., 413
Johnson, Charles, 397
Judaism: defining religion, 239; on euthanasia, 517; extermination of Jews, 588, 589; human nature, 62–65; religion, significance of, 238–239
Jus ad bellum, 592–593
Just and Unjust Wars (Walzer), 591
Justice: civil disobedience, 32; defined, 558–561; equality as, 563–565; ethics and, 16; just war theory, 590–594; liberty and, 569–574; merit as, 561–563; need and ability, 567–568; Plato on, 24–27; Rawls on, 549, 612–614; as social utility, 565–567
Justice, Gender and the Family (Okin), 556–557
Justification, 394–401, 410–413
Just war theory, 590–594

Kant, Immanuel: on ethics, categorical imperative, 483–491, 511–512; on euthanasia, 517; on existence of God, 244–245,

270–271; on freedom, 210–211; historical showcase, 444–453; on human rights, 584–585; on knowledge, 353, 444–446; pacifism and, 589; on reason, 367–368; on self, 109; on time, 216–218; transcendental idealism, 351–363; on truth, 399; on war, 593
"Kantian Conception of Equality, A" (Rawls), 573
Karma, 14–15, 35, 287, 288, 491–494
Kelly, George, 361
Kepler, 413
Kierkegaard, Søren, 194–197, *279*, 279–281, 628–629
King, Martin Luther Jr., 577–578
Knowledge: Aristotle on, 135; Berkeley on, 156, 232; of God, 242, 299–301; Hume on, 385, 386–390; Kant, transcendental idealism, 351–363, 444–446; materialists on, 148–149; Nagel on, 383–384; problem of, 314–319; reason and, 319–333; science and, 363–374; senses and, 333–351; study of, 11–13; trust and, 394–401
Koffka, Kurt, 354
Kohlberg, Lawrence, 503–505
Köhler, Wolfgang, 354
Koran, 475
Koskovich, Thomas, 203
Kuhn, Thomas, 369–372, 425–428

Language: antirealism, 181–186; human nature and, 71; interpretation and truth, 428–436; knowledge and, 11–13; logical positivism, 171–179; trust and, 405, 407–409, 433–434; world view and, 360
Language, Truth, and Logic (Ayer), 171–172
Law, 29–34, 575–579; Aquinas on, 301–302; unjust, 575–579. *See also* Government
Leibniz, Gottfried, 245; Ann Conway and, 310; on human nature, 84; innate ideas, 327, 331; on knowledge, 321; on truth, 413, 432–434
Leslie, John, 158
"Letter from Birmingham Jail" (King), 577–578
Leviathan (Hobbes), 227–231, 541–542
Levy, Donald, 481–482
Lewis, Clarence I., 399
Lewis, C. S., 271
Liberalism, 569–574, 611–615
Libertarianism, 206–209
Liberty, 569–574
Lloyd, Genevieve, 38–39, 80–81
Locke, John: empiricism, 334–339; on enduring self, 101–102; natural moral laws, 543–544; on truth, 397, 399
Loeb, Richard, 202
Loftus, Elizabeth, 316
Logical positivism, 171–179, 620–621
Lokyata, 148
Love, 62–65, 300–301, 499–503
Luckmann, Thomas, 361
Luther, Martin, 431

MacIntyre, Alasdair, 495, 507, 549
Mackey, John, 559
Mackie, J. L., 263
Mahabharata, 286–287
Malcolm, Norman, 89, 246
Malebrance, Nicholas, 84–85
Maloney, Russell, 223–224
Man a Machine (de La Mettrie), 150
"Many worlds" theory, 258
Mappes, Thomas, 489–490
Marquis, Don, 512–513
Marx, Karl; *Critique of the Gotha Program*, 567–568; the meaning of life, 624–625; social philosophy, 605–611
Materialism: atheism as, 260; Berkeley on, 343; eliminative materialism, 94–95; on freedom, 204–205; Hobbes, overview of, 227–231; on human nature, 87–88; objections to, 150–153; on reality, 148–154; theories of, 421–424
Maturana, Humberto R., 361
Mavrodes, George, 70, 255
Maxwell, James, 320
McCloskey, H. J., 582–583
McTaggart, J. M. E., 158, 215–216
Meaning: human progress and, 623–626; interpretation and, 428–436; of life, overview, 618–621; of life, theistic response, 621–623; logical positivism, 171–179; nihilism, 626–627; self-chosen commitment, 627–630; truth and, 433–434
Meditations (Descarte), 100
Meditations on First Philosophy (Descartes), 324
Memory: Augustine on, 214; as enduring self, 101–102; knowledge and, 314–319; recovered, 314–319, 332–333, 350–351, 361–363, 373
Mendel, Gregor, 365
Mercer, Mark, 51–54
Merit, as justice, 561–563
Merleau-Ponty, Maurice, 187, 217
Metaphysics, 13–16; antirealism, 179–186; existentialism, 192, 194–201; freedom, reality of, 202–212; overview of, 146–147; phenomenology, 187–194, 199–201; pragmatism, 166–171
Metaphysics (Aristotle), 403
Mill, John Stuart; hypothetical method and falsifiability, 367; inductive reasoning and simplicity, 364; Liberty, 579–582; utilitarianism, 467, 469–470, 565–567
Mind, 353–356, 447–449
Mind-body problem: behaviorist view, 90–91; computer view, 92–93; dualist view of, 83–87, 95–96; eliminative materialism, 94–95; functionalist view, 91–94; identity theory, 88–90; materialist view, 87–88; overview, 82–83; Searle on, 123–125
"Mind-Body Problem, The" (Searle), 123–125
Mind of God, The (Davies), 257–258
Mirage, 321
Monotheism, 11–12, 241
Morality, 16–18; Aquinas on, 302; Aristotle on, 495–499; Buddhism on, 491–494; consequentialist theory, 463–474; development of, 503–505; divine command theory, 474–483; ethics, definition of, 456–458; freedom and, 209–211; gender differences, 503–506; James on, 274; just was theory, 590–594; Kant on, 270–271, 450–452, 483–491; love and friendship, 499–503; materialism and, 149; moral quandaries, 508–509; Nietzsche on, 528; non-consequentialist theory, 474–494; Plato on, 128; political realism, 587; relativism, 458–463; Singer on, 524–526; terrorism and, 595–596; virtue, overview, 495; Wollstonecraft on, 533

Moral reasoning, 518–520
Moreland, J. P., 122–123
Morris, Desmond, 55
Moser, Paul, 399
Moulton, Janice, 38
Movie themes: enduring self, 106; ethics, 458, 463, 474, 482–483, 491, 494, 508, 521; God, belief in, 259, 271, 279, 289–290; human nature, 56, 82, 96, 115; knowledge, 319, 333, 363, 374; materialism, 154; meaning of life, 630; philosophy generally, 11, 19, 35, 40; reality, 147, 165, 171, 179, 186, 202, 212, 220; religion, 241; senses, 351; social, political philosophy, 540, 557, 574; truth, 401, 421, 428, 436; war, 598
Movies, Philosophy at the: *Abandon Ship!* (1957), 474; *About Schmidt* (2002), 630; *A. I. Artificial Intelligence* (2001), 154; *Apostle, The* (1997), 279; *Artificial Intelligence: A. I.* (2001), 96; *Beautiful Mind, A* (2001), 374; *Bend It Like Beckham* (2002), 115; *Bicentennial Man* (1999), 96, 154; *Blade Runner* (1982), 96, 154; *Bourne Identity, The* (2002), 106; *Borat* (2006), 115; *Breaking the Waves* (1996), 482–483; *Buddy Boy* (1999), 147; *Clockwork Orange, A* (1971), 40; *Contact* (1997), 179, 351; *Control* (2004), 82; *Crash* (2005), 540; *Criminal* (2004), 363; *Crucible, The* (1996), 319; *Enemy Mine* (1985), 463; *Eternal Sunshine of the Spotless Mind* (2004), 106; *Euthyphro* (Plato), 20–24; *Examined Life, The* (Nozick), 146; *eXistenZ* (1999), 165; *Exorcism of Emily Rose, The* (2005), 259; *Extreme Measures* (1996), 474; *50 First Dates* (2004), 106; *Fog of War, The* (2003), 598; *Gattaca* (1997), 212; *He Said, She Said* (1991), 186; *Hilary and Jackie* (1998), 171; *Hunger*, 35; *I, Robot* (2004), 96, 154; *Into the Wild* (2007), 35; *Iris* (2001), 508; *Kinsey* (2004), 374; *Leaving Las Vegas* (1995), 202; *Liar, Liar* (1997), 491; *Little Buddha* (1993), 494; *Living Proof* (2008), 428; *Long Walk Home, The* (1990), 115; *Lord of the Flies, The* (1990), 557; *Machinist, The* (2004), 147; *Matchstick Men* (2003), 363; *Matrix* (1999), 165; *Matrix, The* (1999), 11; *Matrix Reloaded* (2003), 165; *Matrix Revolutions* (2003), 165; *Memento* (2000), 106; *Mulholland Drive* (2001), 147; *My Big Fat Greek Wedding* (2002), 115; *My Dinner with Andre* (1981), 19; *Nowhere in Africa (Nirgendwo in Afrika)* (2001), 463; *Ocean's Eleven* (2001), 363; *Ocean's Thirteen* (2007), 363; *Ocean's Twelve* (2004), 363; *Pleasantville* (1998), 40; *Proof* (2005), 333; *Revolutionary Road* (2008), 40; *River's Edge* (1986), 56; *Schindler's List* (1993), 56; *Sea Inside, The (Mar Adentro)* (2004), 521; *Seven Pounds* (2008), 56; *Seven Waves Away* (1957), 474; *Shadowlands* (1993), 271; *Sixth Sense, The* (1999), 147; *Slumdog Millionaire* (2008), 574; *Spring, Summer, Winter, Fall and Spring* (2003), 289–290; *Terminator II: Judgment Day* (1991), 220; *Terminator III: Rise of the Machines* (2003), 220; *Thirteenth Floor, The* (1999), 165; *Total Recall* (1990), 106, 165; *Truman Show, The* (1998), 401; *Usual Suspects, The* (1995), 421; *Vanilla Sky* (2001), 165; *Water* (2005), 241; *Woodsman, The* (2004), 458
Mysticism, 275–278
Myth of the Cave, 4–6

Nagel, Ernest, 260–271
Nagel, Thomas, 383–384
Narveson, Jan, 590
Natural evil, 265
Natural law, 302, 476–480; 508–509, 515–516, 543–544, 576–577
Natural Law and Natural Rights (Finnis), 479
Natural selection, 65–74, 255
Nature, state of, 543–544
Nature of Thought, The (Blanshard), 411
Need, justice and, 567–568
Neurath, Otto, 413
New Introductory Lectures in Psychoanalysis (Freud), 268
New Pathways in Science (Eddington), 157
Newton, Sir Isaac: laws of motion and universal gravitation, 247, 366, 369; and determinism, 205; time and space theory, 371; on truth, 413
Nicomachean Ethics (Aristotle), 135–137, 495–499
Nielsen, Kai, 622
Nietzsche, Friedrich, 199, 526–531
Nihilism, 200–201, 626–627
Nirvana, 288
Noble Eightfold Path, 287–288, 492, 493–494
Noddings, Nel, 505–506
Nonbasic belief, defined, 398–400
Nonviolent resistance, 16–17, 32, 578
No-self view, 102–105
Nozick, Robert, 225–226, 571–573, 585
Numinous experience, 276–278
Nyaya, 333
Nyaya-Vaisesika, 406

Objective idealism, 155, 157, 160–163
"Occurrence at Owl Creek Bridge, An" (Bierce), 377–381
Of the Social Contract (Rousseau), 545–547
Okin, Susan, 556–557
One World: The Interaction of Science and Theology (Polkinghome), 258
On Free Choice of the Will (Augustine), 575
On Liberty (Mill), 281–579
Ontological argument for God, 242–246
On Truth (Aquinas), 403
Otto, Rudolf, 276

Pacifism, 588–590, 594, 596
Paley, William, 252–253
Paradigms, science, 369–372
Parmenides, 44–45
Parmenides (Plato), 128
Passional nature, 273
Pateman, Carole, 554–555
Patriarchy, 283–285. *See also* Feminist philosophy
Peirce, Charles S., 166, 168, 414
Penzias, Arno, 249
Perception. *See also* Senses: Berkeley on, 155–158; Descarte on, 325–326; empiricism, 318, 333–351, 363–374, 397, 419, 620; Hume on, 343–344; Kant on, 352–363, 445–446; knowledge and, 319–333
Perception of Reality (James), 168–169
Pericitone, 7–8

Personal identity, problem of, 98–99
Phaedo (Plato), 61, 77–78, 128–130
Phaedrus (Plato), 132
Phenomenology, 187–194, 199–201, 359
Phenomenology of Perception (Merleau-Ponty), 187
Philo, 79–80
Philosophical Fragments and Concluding Unscientific Postscript (Kierkegaard), 279–281
Philosophy: in action, 19–35; epistemology, 11–13; ethics, 16–18; male bias, 38–39; metaphysics, 13–16; overview, 4–10; value of, 35–40
Philosophy and Life: business, purpose of, 559; civil disobedience, 32; decisions, 208; embryonic stem cell research, 477; the experience machine, 146; Gestalt psychology, 354; God and free will, 266; historical facts, 412; human nature, 59; innate ideas, 330; knowledge, 157, 354; neutrinos, 153; nuclear weapons, 595; parallel universes, 173; philosophical issues, 15; Rational Emotive Behavior Therapy, 37; religion and science, 250; science and reality, 337; selflessness, 55; society and truth, 366; truth and paradox, 410; welfare and, 570
Philosophy of Religion (Hick), 265
Physics (Aristotle), 134
Pinker, Steven, 211
Plantinga, Alvin, 246
Plato; *Dialogues*, 20–35; on obeying the state, 29–34; on enduring self, 98; historical showcase, 126–133; on holiness, 20–24; on human nature, 57–58, 130–131; on innate ideas, 327–331; on justice, 24–27, 561–563; on knowledge, 321, 327–331; Myth of the Cave, 4–6; philosopher king, 132; on reality, 155; on self, 57–58, 77–78; on social contract, 541; on soul, 61
Pleasure, 287, 464–465, 470
Political authority: communitarianism, 549–553; Confucius on, 140; freedom and, 579–582; Hobbes on, 541–542; human rights, 582–586; justice, as social utility, 565–567; justice, defined, 558–561; justice, equality as, 563–565; justice, liberty and, 569–574; justice, merit as, 561–563; justice, need and ability, 567–568; justification of state, 540–541; limits on, 574–575; Locke on, 543–544; Rawls on, 547–549; Rousseau on, 545–547; unjust laws and civil disobedience, 575–579; war and terrorism, 586–598; women and social contract, 553–557
Political philosophy, defined, 538–540
Political realism, 586–588, 595–596
Politics (Aristotle), 562
Polkinghorne, J. C., 258
Popper, Karl, 368–369
Positivists, 577
Postmodernism, 183, 443
Poverty of Philosophy, The (Marx), 606
Pragmatism, 166–171, 413–417, 418–419, 423
Pragmatism (James), 168
Pre-Socratic thinkers, 19, 43–45
Principia Mathematica Philosophia Naturalis (Newton), 205
Principles of the Most Ancient and Modern Philosophy, The (Conway), 307
Problems of Philosophy. The (Russell), 404
Proslogion (Anselm), 243
Pseudoscience, 365, 372–373
Psychological egoism, 51
Pufendorf, Samuel, 591
Punishment, 202–212
Putnam, Hilary, 73, 181–182, 413

Quantum physics, 258
Quantum theory, 209

Rachels, James, 17–18, 460–461, 466, 516–517
Radhakrishnan, Sarvepalli, 14–15
Radical Constructivism: A Way of Knowing and Learning (von Glaserfeld), 361
Radical theology, 279–283
Rational Emotive Behavior Therapy, 37
Rationalism, 317, 319–333, 371–372
Rationalistic view, human nature, 57–62, 77–78
Rawls, John, 547–549, 552, 569–574, 611–615
Realism, 424–425, 442–443, 586–588, 595–596
Realists, critical, 338–339
Reality: antirealism, 179–186; constructivist theory, 361–363; Descarte on, 306; existentialism, 187, 194–201; freedom, 202–212; Hegel on, 605; Heidegger on, 192–194; Hinduism, 286–287; idealism, 154–165; importance of understanding, 144–146; logical positivism, 171–179; materialism, 148–154; phenomenology, 187–194, 199–201; pragmatism, 166–171; questions of, 146–147; Sartre on, 197; study of, 13–16; time, 212–219; truth and, 406, 414–415; Wittgenstein and, 432–433
"Reality and Truth" (Searle), 443–444
Realpolitik, 586–588
Reason: Aquinas on, 298; Christian theology and, 242; Descarte on, 303–304, 321–326; existence of God, 242–246; feminist challenge to, 77–81; Hobbes on, 542; knowledge and, 317–318, 319–333, 364–366; Locke on, 543; materialists on, 148–149; rationalistic view, 57–62; scientific method, 367–368; Wollstonecraft on, 532–533
Reasoning: defined, 10; inductive generalizations, 346–348
Reconstruction in Philosophy (Dewey), 166–167
Recovered memories, 314–319, 332–333, 350–351, 361–363, 373
Reductionism, 87–88
Reid, Thomas, 102
Relativism, 188, 402–403, 417–419, 458–463
Religion: atheism, agnosticism and evil, 260–271; belief and experience, 240–241, 272–279; Buddhism, 287–288; cosmological argument, for God, 246–251; design argument, existence of God, 251–259; divine command theory, ethics, 474–483; Eastern and Western differences, 288–289; existence of God, overview, 241–242; feminist theology, 283–285; Feuerbach on, 606; on meaning of life, 621–622; ontological argument for God, 242–246; personal experience of divine, 275–278; radical theology, 279–283; and science, 241–242, 250; significance of, 238–241

Religious experience, defined, 240–241
Remarque, Erich Maria, 600–602
Republic, The (Plato): human nature, 57–58; justice, 24–27, 561–562; Myth of the Cave, 4–6; perfection, 127; philosopher king, 132; on soul, 130–131
Responsibility, 74, 202–212
Rights, 582–586
"Road, The" (Hick), 238
Rolston, Holmes, 258
Romantic philosophers, 359–361
Rorty, Richard, 181, 416, 418
Rousseau, Jean Jacques, 545–547
Rowe, William L., 263
Royce, Josiah, 157
Russell, Bertrand, 260, 399, 403–406, 432, 602–604
Ryle, Gilbert, 90

Samsara, 288
Sandel, Michael, 549, 552–553
Sapir, Edward, 360
Sapir-Whorf hypothesis, 360
Sartre, Jean-Paul, 74–77, 197–201, 206–209, 629–630
Schleiermacher, Friedrich, 431, 434
Schlick, Moritz, 399
Schopenhauer, Arthur, 249, 626
Science: design argument, 251–259; embryonic stem cell research, 477; Kant on, 353; knowledge and, 319–320, 363–374; paradigms and revolutions, 369–372; reality and, 337; religion and, 241–242, 250; truth and, 421–428; universal laws of, 352
Science and Religion (Rolston), 258
Scientific method, 149–150, 364–366
Scripture, sacred, 240, 474–483, 516. *See also* Bible; Religion
Searle, John: on human nature, 93–94, 123–125; on reality, 184–186; on reality and truth, 443–444; on truth, 406, 407
Second Meditation (Descartes), 324–325
Second Sex, The (de Beauvoir), 199
Self: dualist view of, 83–87, 122–123; egoism, 17, 51, 465–467; enduring self, 96–106; existentialist view, 74–77; Hinduism on, 287; Hume on, 387; Kierkegaard on, 195–197; knowledge and, 321; views of, 55
Self-interest, 50–52, 452
Self-sufficiency, 106–115
Sellars, Wilfrid, 399
Senses, 104; Berkeley on, 231–235; Descarte on, 325–326; empiricism, 318, 333–351, 363–374, 397, 419, 620; Hobbes on, 150, 228; Hume on, 386–390; Kant on, 216–218, 351–363, 445–446; knowledge and, 317–318, 319–351; materialists on, 148–149; scientific hypothesis and, 368; truth and, 397–398
Sexism, 183–184
Sexual behavior: Buddhism on, 494; divine command ethics, 480–482; Kant on, 489–490; as moral issue, 456–457; utilitarianism, 472–474; virtue ethics, 498–499
Shakespeare, William, 154, 239, 619
Shankara, 321, 413
Siddhartha, 103, 287–288
Simon, William E., 538
Singer, Peter, 524–526
Sinnot, Edmund W., 251–252
Skepticism, 234–235, 321–326, 343–351, 381–383
Smart, J. J. C., 88, 216
Smart, Ninian, 240
Smith, Janet, 498–499, 513–514
Social Construction of Reality, The (Berger and Luckmann), 361
Social contract theory: communitarianism, 549–553; freedom and, 579–582; Hobbes on, 541–542; Locke on, 543–544; Rawls on, 547–549; Rousseau on, 545–547; women and, 553–557
Socialism, 567–568
Social philosophy: communitarianism, 549–553; defined, 538–540; freedom and, 579–582; Hobbes on, 541–542; human rights, 582–586; justice, as social utility, 565–567; justice, defined, 558–561; justice, equality as, 563–565; justice, liberty and, 569–574; justice, merit as, 561–563; justice, need and ability, 567–568; justification of state, 540–541; limits on state, 574–575; Locke on, 543–544; Rawls on, 547–549; Rousseau on, 545–547; unjust laws and civil disobedience, 575–579; war and terrorism, 586–598; women and social contract, 553–557
Socrates, 19–35, 61, 77–78; trial, 27–29
Solipsism, 342
Solomon, Robert, 502
"Song of Myself" (Whitman), 107
Sophocles, 575
Soul. *See also* Self: Aristotle on, 134–135; Augustine on, 148; dualist view, 122–123; as enduring self, 100; good *vs.* evil, 62–63; immortality of, 13–16; materialists on, 149; Plato on, 61, 128–131
Sound argument, 53
Spender, Dale, 181, 182–183
Spengler, Oswald, 625
Spinoza, Baruch, 245, 321, 413
Sprague, Elmer, 163
Standard theory of matter, 421–424
Stanley, Liz, 181
State. *See* Government
State of nature, 543–544, 586–588. *See also* Social Philosophy
Stenstad, Gail, 11–12
Stevenson, Leslie, 608
Story of a Good Brahman (Voltaire), 42–43
Stroud, Barry, 349
Sublation, 321
Suicide, 479, 618
Summa Contra Gentiles (Aquinas), 246, 298
Summa Theologica (Aquinas), 246, 247, 298, 299, 430–431
Suzuki, D. T., 194
Swinburne, Alvin, 252
Swinburne, Richard, 264–265, 277–278
Symposium, The (Plato), 98
Synthetic a priori knowledge, 444–446
Synthetic statements, 172, 353, 356

Tarski, Alfred, 407–409
Tautologies, 171–172, 283
Taylor, Charles, 109–112, 549
Taylor, Gabrielle, 501
Taylor, Richard, 472, 626–627
Tegmark, Max, 173
Teilhard de Chardin, Pierre, 70
Tempest, The (Shakespeare), 154
Ten Commandments, 475
Teresa, Saint, 275–276
Terrorism, 586, 594–598
Thales, 43–44
Theism, 241, 264–267
Theology: Aquinas on, 298; defined, 241; on meaning of life, 621–622; radical theology, 279–283

Theory of Justice, A (Rawls), 612–614
Theravada, 103
The Vedas, 45–46
Thought on the Education of Daughters (Wollstonecraft), 532
Three Dialogues Between Hyklas and Philonus (Berkeley), 342
Tillich, Paul, 199, 281–283
Time, 212–219, 307, 353–356, 446–447
"Toast to Captain Jerk" (Maloney), 223–224
Tolstoy, Leo, 619–620, 621–622
Tomlinson, Hugh, 442–443
Torture, 596–597
Transcendental idealism, 318, 351–363
Treatise Concerning the Principles of Human Knowledge (Berkeley), 231, 232, 340
Treatise of Human Nature, A (Hume), 104–105, 385
Truth: Akutagawa on, 438–442; correspondence theory, 403–409; deflating, 419–420; Descartes on, 303–304; epistemology, 11–13; importance of, 417–419; interpretation and, 428–436; Kierkegaard on, 279; knowledge and, 317, 394–401; Newton on, 413; Nietzsche on, 527–528; overview, 401–403; pragmatic theory, 413–417; reconciling theories of, 419–420; science and, 421–428; Searle on, 443–444; society and, 366; Tomlinson on, 442–443
Turing, Alan, 92–93
Turing Test, 92
Twenty Verses and Their Commentary (Vasubandhu), 158
Tyranny of the majority, 579–580
Uncertainty, principle of, 337
Unger, Peter, 381–383
Universal Declaration of Human Rights, 582
Upanishads, 46–47
Utilitarianism: act, 470–471; ethics and, 467–474; on euthanasia, 516–517; moral quandaries and, 508–509, 512; Nietzsche on, 529; rule, 471–472
Utilitarianism (Mill), 467, 565–567

Valid argument, 54–56
Vagueness and ambiguity, 12–13
Values: Aristotle on, 495–499; Buddhism, 491–494; consequentialist theory, 463–474; divine command theory, 474–483; ethics, definition of, 456–458; gender differences, 503–506; Kant, categorical imperative, 483–491; love and friendship, 499–503; moral development, 503–505; moral quandaries and, 508–509; nonconsequentialist theory, 474–494; relativism, 458–463; Singer on, 524–526; study of, 16–18; virtue, overview, 495
Van Doren, Charles, 626
Varieties of Religious Experience (James), 276
Vasubandhu, 158–160
Vijnanavada, 158
Vindication of the Rights of Men (Wollstonecraft), 532
Vindication of the Rights of Women (Wollstonecraft), 532, 533
Violence: just war theory, 590–594; overview, 586; pacifism and, 588–590; political realism, 586–588; terrorism and, 594–598; unjust law and, 578–579
Virtue: Aristotle on, 135–138, 495–499; conclusions about, 506–508; Confucius, 139–140; gender differences, 503–506; love and friendship, 499–503; moral quandaries, 508, 513–514; Plato on, 131; study of, 16–18
Voltaire, 42–43
von Glaserfeld, Ernst, 361
von Humboldt, Wilhelm, 360

Walzer, Michael, 591
War: just war theory, 590–594; overview, 586; pacifism, 588–590; political realism, 586–588
Warren, Mary Anne, 510
Web of belief, 400. *See also* Belief
Welfare liberalism, 569–574
Whewell, William, 367
Whitehead, Alfred North, 126
Whitman, Walt, 107
Whorf, Benjamin Lee, 360
"Will to Believe, The" (James), 272–275
Wilson, Robert, 249
Winkin, Yves, 402–403
Wise, Sue, 181
Wittgenstein, Ludwig, 432–434
Wolff, Christian, 591
Wollstonecraft, Mary, 526, 531–535
Woodhouse, Mark, 15
Wordsworth, William, 360

Yogacarin, 158, 413
Young, Pamela Dickey, 285–286

Zen buddhism. *See* Buddhism
Zeno, 44–45, 476